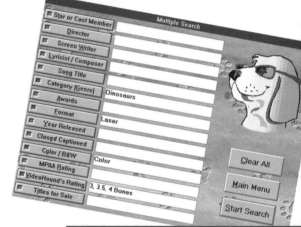

Praise for the VideoHound Family

VideoHound's GOLDEN MOVIE RETRIEVER

"A personal favorite in its newest edition: *VideoHound's Golden Movie Retriever 1994*. *VideoHound* is pure fun. This is one you can curl up with and read, just for fun."
— *San Diego Union-Tribune*

"An indispensable reference. This is simply the best book available."
— *Roanoke Times & World News*

"Worth its weight in rental fees. This may be the best $17.95 you ever spent. It really works."
—*Staten Island Advance*

"*VideoHound's Golden Movie Retriever* is by far the best reference work. The volume's capsule reviews are reliably on target. Offers more for the money. For serious video tracking, the hound is the sound choice."
—*Houston Chronicle*

"*Hound* takes the lead in a blaze of supplemental lists."
—*The New York Times*

"Indispensable."
—*New York Newsday*

"If one can't find a video film in this book, it probably isn't worth finding. An invaluable source book for any video enthusiast."
—*The Ottawa Citizen*

"An immensely valuable book. The pure mass of nicely organized information on these 1500 pages is boggling. A fun and essential volume, and a bargain at $17.95."
—*Boomer*

"The best descriptive reference book I've seen about what's on video."
—*Providence Journal-Bulletin*

"The VideoHound can help you sniff out the location of even the hardest-to-find videos with his highly useful distributors' guide. One of the most information-packed compendiums on the market."
—*A&E Monthly / The New York Times Syndicate*

VideoHound MULTIMEDIA

"The consumer version of an industrial-strength video database, it's scope is impressive. If you are a voracious consumer of video arcana with a taste for camp, *VideoHound* is a full-course meal. What makes the CD-ROM unique is the cross-referencing of videos in more than 1,000 categories."
—*USA Today*

"Cross-references titles by a number of useful categories. The minds behind this package know and love movies."
—*Entertainment Weekly*

"Talk about astounding. A must have for movie buffs."
—*Rapport Magazine*

More Praise for the VideoHound Family

VideoHound MULTIMEDIA

"**VideoHound** does the hypertext thing best.... offers far more raw information than does the competition."
—*Chicago Tribune*

"Look no further—**VideoHound** provides movie watchers with an easily searchable film database that can answer just about all your cinematic questions. Should be in every video store — and every "home theater" as well."
—*Multimedia World*

"Move over *Cinemania*, there's a new dog in town. Of all the CD-ROM movie guides, **VideoHound Multimedia** is the best for finding useful info about movies. The ultimate search engine for video junkies. A must-have for true video-hounds."
—*CD-ROM Today*

"In addition to the 3,500 portraits of actors, actresses, and directors, a picture of the video box is displayed for about 10,000 movies. It is a unique and lovely feature, as it helps a lot in spotting the box on the shelves. Printouts of individual titles and videographies are superb. Customers in Blockbuster have to resort to rubbernecking in the store, while we leisurely consult the **VideoHound** printouts we make before heading out.
—*Information Today*

VideoHound's POCKET MOVIE GUIDE

"Humorously irreverent descriptions of more than 1,000 of the most popular videos. A good source for finding out about films you might not have originally considered renting . . . and it's always amusing."
—*The Providence Journal-Bulletin*

"The pocket guide, which carries on the tradition of shrewd irreverence that Hound fans have come to know and love, is a good size to take along on trips to the video store."
—*The Henderson (KY) Gleaner*

"Easy to skim through. Well worth a look."
—*Roanoke Times & World-News*

"Put it in the glove compartment of your car for those times when you get to the video store and draw a blank."
—*Houston Chronicle*

"Ever wander around a video store aimlessly trying to figure out what to rent? You might want to pick up a copy of **VideoHound's Pocket Movie Guide**."
—*Staten Island Advance*

VideoHound's
FAMILY
VIDEO
RETRIEVER

VideoHound's
FAMILY
VIDEO
RETRIEVER

VISIBLE
INK
PRESS

DETROIT • WASHINGTON, D.C. • LONDON

VideoHound's
**FAMILY
VIDEO
RETRIEVER**

Copyright © 1995 by Visible Ink Press

Published by Visible Ink Press™, a division of
Gale Research Inc., 835 Penobscot Building,
Detroit, MI 48226-4094

Visible Ink Press and *VideoHound* are trademarks of
Gale Research Inc.

ISBN 0-8103-7866-3

Printed in the United States of America
All rights reserved

10 9 8 7 6 5 4 3 2 1

CREDITS

Contents

Foreword

BY BRIAN HENSON

My first professional collaboration with my father, Jim Henson, occurred when I was five years old and he cast me in "The Counting Film - Number Three" for *Sesame Street*. I sat at a table and distinctively said "three peas," as the numbers 1, 2 and 3 appeared next to the peas on my plate. It was a virtuoso performance and one that undoubtedly stands out as a high point in the annals of vegetable counting. For me, it served as a wonderful introduction to the simple edict that my father applied to all his work — that good family entertainment should be both fun and enlightening. As he once wrote, "I believe that we can use television and film to be an influence for good; that we can help shape the thoughts of children and adults in a positive way." Over the years, I have tried to never lose sight of that fundamental rule.

Today, the influence that television programs and home videos have over children is greater than ever as kids spend more and more time in front of the TV set. As such, it is vital that parents make informed choices with regards to what their children are watching. The good news is that there is a huge amount of family entertainment currently available to choose from. Conversely, the bad news is that identifying "good" family entertainment can be a challenge. The overwhelming amount of films and specials out there makes it impossible for parents to preview everything their kids want to see.

Given that, it is my pleasure to write this foreword for the *VideoHound's Family Video Retriever.* The guide provides a comprehensive listing of 4,000 movies and special features, reviewing each title in terms of content, age-group recommendations and even adult interest. This information allows parents to judge each entry as to whether or not it is appropriate for their youngsters.

In addition to providing a means of vetting their children's entertainment, *VideoHound's Family Video Retriever* can also assist parents in identifying videos that cover specific topics of interest. If a child is particularly excited by dinosaurs, then the guide can help determine which movies might spark his or her imagination. If a kid is a Teenage Mutant Ninja Turtle fanatic, the guide provides a listing of the different film versions that deal with the Turtles' exploits. And perhaps, by flipping through the *VideoHound's Family Video Retriever,* parents will remember some favorite movie from their own childhood that they want to share with their children.

But the real fun is picking videos together as a family and then watching them together as a family. Seeing "The Wizard of Oz" or "The Thief of Baghdad" again through the eyes of a child is a wonderful experience, and one that can help pave the way to healthy family dialogues on a full range of topics. Movies open youngsters up to new worlds and new ideas, and can help familiarize them with a wide variety of life's experiences. All in all, they provide a great adventure for parents to share with their children.

Kermit the Frog

Introduction

Watching a video with the kids can be one of life's simple pleasures. Friday or Saturday night at the movies is a time to enjoy a laugh or a tear together. If your household is anything like VideoHound's, your children share in the decision-making on what is watched. If little Jenny or Jimmy really, really want to see a certain video, the parental unit will likely be easy prey for their well-developed persuasive techniques. And if your children really really love a certain video, chances are you'll get numerous opportunities to experience the thrill of watching it over and over again.

Nobody really knows how kids can watch the same video three or four times a day. But upon becoming attached to a video, a child will enjoy it as if for the first time even after extended repeat viewings. Intimate knowledge of coming events, dialogue, etc. does not at all diminish little Mary's enjoyment of the video, because secretly, she believes that video watching is interactive, with her participation causing the story to change. (As a mere pup, VideoHound believed that under the right circumstances, the Wicked Witch in "The Wizard of Oz" might eventually triumph over poor Dorothy, which troubled him greatly but eventually led to his so-called career in film criticism.) In fact, child/video bonding may become so intense that child and cassette (or disc in technologically advanced households) become inseparable, creating some symbiotic relationship perplexing to the adult mind.

Filmmakers, however, are not puzzled. They're blessed with the knowledge that children are likely to watch the same tape over and over again. Donny, Jr.'s favorite video is likely to enjoy repeated rentals or an outright purchase. Add this to the preference of many families to enjoy their video recreation together, and you have a huge market that Hollywood is only belatedly discovering, leading to a recent glut of "family" fare on the video shelf.

So with young Matthew's notable ability to obsess on a particular video and your kids' exposure to round-the-clock marketing directed at their wee solar plexuses, Tommy or Jane may develop a yen to see a video that you're not sure is appropriate for their age and interests, or for your age and interests. Is it too violent, too sexy, too vulgar? Is it written for a three-year-old with no redeeming value for a thirty-year-old or vice versa? How do you find video fare that satisfies the family's various cinematic desires?

Consult *VideoHound's Family Video Retriever.* Designed to help you make quality viewing decisions, *VideoHound's Family Video Retriever* reviews and indexes 4,000 films and kidvid features, providing you with the most comprehensive guide to family video entertainment. *Video Hound* reviews the good, the bad, and the ugly, steering you away from low-caliber efforts and towards high-quality viewing experiences.

Within *VideoHound,* family means a household, usually with one or more small appliances, comprising one or more adults and children, the one or more kids ranging in age from toddlers to high school seniors, the one or more adults hoping to score something from the video shop that all can enjoy. We've tried to create a *VideoHound* that meets the expectations of these families in all their shapes and sizes.

Complicating matters is the kids themselves: small, large, and in-between, they're all over the map in terms of maturity, intellect, and interests. One thing they do share is a kind of video sophistication. With the infusion of cable television and home video, children are exposed to much more in the way of violence, sexual situations, and language (just watching MTV alone puts the young person on a different video plateau). Your job, moonlighting as professional media controller, boldly going into ever murkier technological realms, has never been tougher. We've attempted to provide enough information so that you can make an informed decision on whether the video is right for *your* family.

In addition to all the usual video guide stuff, *VideoHound's Family Video Retriever* tells you the appropriate viewing age range for the video and provides a content advisory when necessary. Plus *VideoHound* provides critical reviews with lots of facts and trivia, cast listings, the titles of the numbers in each musical, the unique "bone" rating system, information on where to find the video, and five indexes to serve as pointers. We even throw in the occasional photograph to give it the proper graphic mix. You'll find *G*, *PG*, and *PG-13* movies, as well as a selection of *R* movies with strong teen interest. For young families, we review the wonderful worlds of Sesame Street and Barney, providing the best listing of available kidvid. We've also included a host of unrated movies, produced prior to the imposition of the MPAA system in 1968. Many of these are rightly regarded as classics, but perhaps you've never considered gems like "To Kill A Mockingbird" or "Singin' in the Rain" as family treats. Rediscovery can be a ton of fun. In the right hands (yours), *VideoHound* should prove to be a powerful friend of the family.

For your part, have fun with this book. Some people tend to regard family videos like medicine - something you don't want to take, but must, and then only with an expert's prescription. If anything, we want to prove that the VCR or laserdisc player can be a source of delight for both child viewers and grownups to enjoy - sometimes even at the same time.

CARING FOR YOUR PET

VideoHound's Family Video Retriever begins with the special! bonus!! section of several articles on family video producers today, surveying the state of Disney, Canada's family movie-making genius, a short history of the Muppets, the toy-kidvid connection, Japanese animation, and of course, lots of other stuff too numerous to mention.

The main section follows, arranged in alphabetical order (the result of an inspired moment). If you don't know precisely where to look for the information you need, *VideoHound* provides five indexes to help you find it.

Many movies are released under variant titles; the Alternate Title Index keeps track of them and refers you back to the proper listing. The MPAA Index lists the movies under their appropriate MPAA designation (G, PG, PG-13, and R) as well as a concise listing of the unrated movies covered.

The Cast & Director Index is next, listing the work of 10,000 actors and directors. Keep in mind that the list is inclusive for those movies listed within the *Family Video Retriever.* If you know a cast name but not the movie title, this index will quickly enable you to find the right video.

The Category Index follows, listing movies under some 300 topics, ranging from broad categories like *Amazing Adventures* (action-adventure), *Laugh Riots* (comedy) and *Cowboys & Indians* (westerns) to more particular categories such as *Family Ties, Jungle Stories, Scary Beasties, Silly Detectives,* and *Growing Pains.* Series listings include *Mickey Mouse & Friends, Charlie Brown & the Peanuts Gang, Andy Hardy, Tom & Jerry,* and, of course, *The Magnificent Muppets.*

Finally, *VideoHound* concludes with a guide providing the names and addresses of the distributors of the videos listed. Some videos can be darn hard to find; this guide will provide you with a solid lead for tracking the wayward video. At the end of each review are three-letter codes for the distributor(s) (to a maximum of three distributors) of the title; the address and phone number are provided in the Distributor Guide.

ACKNOWLEDGMENTS

VideoHound and pack thank Brian Henson, Susan Berry and Lynn Callé at Jim Henson Productions for their help. We appreciate the patience and skills of Don Dillaman, Evi Seoud, Mike Boyd and Marco Di Vita. The Kobal Collection is much appreciated for their fast and efficient turnaround. Mary Krzewinksi exhibited her usual care and creativity on the design, and for that we're grateful. Thank you Don Wellman for delivering the right kind of copy. We promise never to forget that Chris Tomassini delayed her vacation to help us finish. Thank you Terry Colon for the artwork. And a special thank you to Beth Fhaner for hanging in there.

An Example of One of the 4,000 Reviews Located Elsewhere

① Aladdin ② 🦴🦴🦴🦴

③ Disney naturally took the crown for the most financially successful cartoon of all time. Boy meets princess, loses her, finds her, wins her from evil vizier and nasty parrot. Superb animation triumphs over mostly average songs and storyline by capitalizing on Williams' talent for ad-libbing with lightning speed as Aladdin's irrepressible big blue genie, though one wonders if his celebrity spoofs (Arsenio Hall, for example) will endure for as long as the imagery in "Pinocchio" or "Beauty and the Beast." For all ages: adults will enjoy the 1,001 Williams impersonations while kids will get a kick out of the genie, the romantic storyline, and the songs. Be forewarned: very small children may be frightened by some of the scarier sequences. **④** ♪♫ A Whole New World; Prince Ali; Friend Like Me; One Jump Ahead; Arabian Nights. **⑤ Hound Advisory**: Genie roughhousing.

⑥ 1992 **⑦** **⑧** *(G/Family)* **⑨** 90m **⑩** C **⑪** D: Ron Clements, John Musker; **⑫** W: Ron Clements, John Musker, Ted Elliot, Terry Rossio; **⑬** M: Alan Menken, Howard Ashman, Tim Rice; **⑭** V: Robin Williams, Scott Weinger, Linda Larkin, Jonathan Freeman, Frank Welker, Gilbert Gottfried, Douglas Seale, Brad Kane, Lea Salonga **⑮ Award Nominations:** Academy Awards 92: Best Song ("Friend like Me"), Best Sound, Best Sound Effects Editing; **⑯ Awards:** Academy Awards 92: Best Original Score, Best Song ("A Whole New World"); Golden Globe Awards '93: Best Song ("A Whole New World"), Best Score; MTV Movie Awards '93: Best Comedic Performance (Williams). **⑰** VHS, Beta, LV, CDV **⑱** $24.95 **⑲** DIS, BTTV, WTA

❶ Title—The book is arranged alphabetically by title on a word by word basis, including articles, prepositions, and conjunctions (the ampersand (&) is alphabetized as "and"). Leading articles (*A, An, The*) are ignored in English-language titles. The equivalent foreign articles are not ignored, however: *The Addams Family* appears under "A" while *Les Miserables* appears under "L." **Other points to keep in mind:**

- Acronyms appear alphabetically as if regular words. For example, *D.A.R.Y.L.* is alphabetized as *Daryl*.

- Common abbreviations in titles file as if they are spelled out. For instance, *Mrs. Doubtfire* follows *Miss Firecracker*.

- Proper names in titles are alphabetized beginning with the individual's first name; for example, *Ollie Hopnoodle's Haven of Bliss* is under "O."

- Titles with numbers (*13 Ghosts*) are alphabetized as if the number was spelled out under the appropriate letter, in this case, "Thirteen." When numeric titles gather in close proximity to each other (*2000 Year Old Man, 2001: A Space Odyssey, 2010: The Year We Make Contact*), the titles will be arranged in a low (*2000*) to high (*2010*) sequence.

- In the event that more than one version of a title exists (for instance, *20,000 Leagues Under the Sea* has four versions listed while *A Christmas Carol* has three), the order will be chronological ranging from the earliest version to the most recent version.

❷ Critical Rating—*VideoHound* rates movies on a sliding scale from one to four bones, with the truly bad earning a Woof! Movies are rated within their genres (and occasionally large sub-genres), with comedies being rated against comedies, action-adventure against action-adventure, disaster flicks against other disasters, and so on. Kidvid, short subjects, recycled cartoons, or TV episodes generally are not rated. The scale:

WOOF! Stinky, often in a memorable way. Director often uses pseudonym. Actors wear disguises. Credits list "Bubba" as caterer/security/costume designer. Filmed in a vacant warehouse.

🐾—Quality control efforts lacking. Crew checks may have bounced. Director recently escaped from prison and had to work fast. Actors mystified by lack of script. Lighting guy had a few loose bulbs.

🐾🐾—Perhaps worth a look-see if enormous amounts of time on hands is a problem.

🐾🐾—Toying with respectability, though has myriad weak spots that may create the need for a mid-film snooze.

🐾🐾🐾—Average film with average entertainment value for the average viewer. By law of averages, someone should like these. Beauty may be in eye of average beholder.

🐾🐾🐾—Better quality goods with fewer lows and more frequent highs. Storyline is good, cast knows how to act, and lighting technicians enjoy their work.

🐾🐾🐾🐾—A delicacy, to be tasted like the finest morsel of day-old food left in the bowl. Among the best the movie-world has to offer.

🐾🐾🐾🐾—Must be a masterpiece or a classic or a work of art or at the very least, a real good movie. Writer, director, actors, photographer, and yes, the lighting technicians all conspire to create cinematic gem.

---

❸ **Description/review**—all the facts and some of the trivia that are fit to print. Contains information on colorized versions, sequels, remakes, and sources of adaptations.

❹ **Songs**—a list of episodic singing and dancing occurring during musicals.

❺ **Hound Advisory**—an indication of content areas to which the viewer may be sensitive. Generally, if a film has content that may be inappropriate for some ages, *VideoHound* will indicate via these core phrases, paired occasionally with additional comments.

Mature themes—a range of topics, from existential despair to death to political corruption to relationship woes that younger viewers may find puzzling, upsetting, or boring.

Salty language—occasional or very rare swear words, generally of the mild sort, and excluding the big bad "f" word.

Profanity—real swearing, from moderate to marathon quantities.

Obscenity—very much like profanity, but spelled differently.

Alcohol talk—liquor or drunkenness is not shown but is mentioned in the dialogue, sometimes in a negative context, but more often as something glamorous and exciting.

Alcohol Use—drinking and/or drunkenness is shown onscreen, negatively or positively.

Drug talk—similar to alcohol talk, though the topic is narcotics, ranging from marijuana to crack to heroin. Caffeine and tobacco are excepted.

Drug use—drug use is explored onscreen, in either a negative or positive manner.

Sex talk—sex isn't shown, but is discussed frankly.

Sex—Explicit or discreet sex is shown onscreen.

Brief nudity—male or female nudity, but only for an instant.

Nudity—male or female nudity for more than

an instant.

Roughhousing—mild fisticuffs or other forms of generally bloodless, non-explicit violence, usually without gunplay.

Violence—common mayhem, from kung-fu to gunfights, sometimes fatal but handled in an unrealistic, sanitary, "entertaining," cartoon-like manner much beloved by filmmakers.

Brutality—violence in which a vivid and explicit sense of physical pain, trauma and damage is conveyed, usually for serious dramatic purposes but occasionally just for the heck of it.

Carnage—gore galore, usually for comic or horror effect. Not often found in family fare, unless family is of the Addams variety.

❻Year released—year of original release, either theatrically, on television, or direct to video.

❼MPAA Rating—G, PG, PG-13, and R (no NC-17 movies are listed). The MPAA rating will not be present within the kidvid reviews.

❽Age Range—Approximate age ranges that video may be appropriate for, as follows:

> Preschool (ages 2-4)
> Primary (ages 5-10)
> Jr. High (ages 11-13)
> Sr. High (ages 14-17)
> Adult (ages 18 and over)
> Family (suitable for all ages)

❾Length—running time.

❿Black and white (B) or **color** (C)

⓫Director (W/D: indicates writer/director)

⓬Writers—Guys and gals who wrote or helped write the script.

⓭Composers/Lyricists—They wrote or arranged or, occasionally, selected the music.

⓮Cast—"C" or "V"; V indicates voiceovers. Also notes cameos.

⓯Award Nominations—nominations from major award-giving bodies that did not result in actual awards.

⓰Awards—including Academy Awards, Golden Globe, Cannes Film Festival, Canadian Genie, British Academy of Film and Television Arts, Australia Film Institute, French Cesar, Independent Spirit, and the MTV awards.

⓱Format—Beta, VHS, CDV (CD-I and other compact disc formats) and/or LV (laserdisc)

⓲Price—recorded at highest retail level at press time.

⓳Distributor code(s)—up to three distributor codes are listed. Check the Distributor Guide in the back of *VideoHound* for full contact information.

Category List

Adapted from a
  Cartoon
Adapted from the
  Radio
Adapted from TV
Africa
AIDS
Airborne
Aliens - Nasty
Aliens - Nice
Amazing Adventures
Amazing Animals
Amnesia
Amusement Parks
Andy Hardy
Angels
Apartheid
Asia
At the Movies
Australia
Baby Talk
Babysitters
Ballet
Ballooning
Baseball
Basketball
Beach Blanket Bingo
Bedtime Stories
Bereavement
Best Friends
The Big Sting
Bigfoot
Biking
Biopics
Birds
Blindness
Books
Books to Film
Books to Film: J.M.
  Barrie
Books to Film:
  Frances Hodgson
  Burnett
Books to Film:
  Rudyard Kipling
Books to Film: Astrid
  Lindgren
Books to Film: Jack

London
Books to Film: L.M.
  Montgomery
Books to Film: Mark
  Twain
Bowling
Boxing
Boy Meets Girl
Buses
Business Gone
  Berserk
Canada
Cartoon Classics
Cartoon Tunes
Cartoonmercials
Cats
Cave People
Charlie Brown & the
  Peanuts
Chases
Child Abuse
Childhood Visions
China
Christmas Holidays
Circuses & Carnivals
Civil Rights
Civil War
Classics
Clowning Around
Cold Spots
College Capers
Comedy with an
  Edge
Coming to America
Computers
Cool Cars
Courtroom Capers
Cowboys & Indians
Crime Doesn't Pay
Dads
Deafness
Demons & Wizards
Detectives
Dinos
Disaster Strikes
Disney Animated
  Movies
Disney Family

Movies
Divorce
Dr. Seuss
Doctors & Nurses
Documentaries
Down Under
Drama
Eco-Vengeance!
Ecotoons
Elementary School
  Escapades
Explorers
Fairy tales
Family Ties
Fantasy
Fast Cars
Film Noir
Film Stars
Firemen
Folk Tales
Football
France
Funny Adventures
Gangs
Garfield
Genies
Ghosts, Ghouls, &
  Goblins
Giants
Gifted Children
Go Fish
Godzilla & Friends
Going Native
Golf
Gory Stories
Gotta Dance!
Gotta Sing!
Grand Hotel
Great Britain
Great Death Scenes
Great Depression
Great Escapes
Growing Older
Growing Pains
Gymnastics
Hallmark Hall of
  Fame
Heaven Sent

Heists
High School Hijinks
High Seas Adventure
Historical
  Happenings
Hockey
Holidays
Home Alone
Homeless
Horses
Hospitals
Hunting
In Concert
Inventors
Ireland
Islands in the Sea
Italy
It's the Mob
It's True
James Bond
Japan
Judaism
Jungle Stories
Kidnapped!
A Kid's Best Friend
Kindness of
  Strangers
King of Beasts
Korean War
Labor Unions
Lassie
Laugh Riots
Lawyers
Life in the 'Burbs
Live Action
Lost Worlds
Macho Men
Mad Scientists
Magic
Magic Carpet
Marriage
Martial Arts
The Meaning of Life
Medieval Romps
Mental Retardation
Mickey Mouse &
  Friends
Miners

Missing Persons
Misspelled Titles
Mistaken Identity
Modern Cowboys
Moms
Monsters, General
Mountains
The Muppets
Music
Musician Biopics
Mysteries
Nashville Narratives
Nasty Nazis
Native America
Newsroom Note
Nifty '50s
Nuclear War
Nuns & Priests
The Olympics
On the Farm
On the Run
Only the Lonely
Oooh...That's Scary!
Opera
Orphans
Our Gang
Over the Airwaves
Overlooked Gems
Parades
Parenthood
Period Piece
Physical Problems
Poetry
Policemen
Postwar
POW/MIA
Presidential Pics
Price of Fame
Puppets
Race Against Time
Rags to Riches
Raiders of the Lost
  Ark
Rebel With a Cause
Rebel Without a
  Cause
Red Scare
Repressed Men

Rescue Missions
Revolutionary War
The Right Choice
Robots
Rodeos
Royalty
Running
Savants
Scary Beasties
Scary Bugs
Scary Plants
Sci Fi
Scientists
Scotland
Scuba Diving
Serial Adventures
Sesame Street
Shutterbugs

Silence is Golden
Silly Detectives
Silly Spoofs
Sing-Alongs
Sixties Sagas
Skateboarding
Skating
Skiing
Slavery
Soccer
Southern Belles
Southern Sagas
Special F/X
   Extravaganzas
Sports Comedies
Sports Dramas
Spy Stories
Star Wars

Stepparents
Storytelling
Struggling Musicians
Stupid Crime
Submarines
Subways
Summer Camp
Super Heroes
Supernatural Tales
Surfing
Survival
Swashbucklers
Table Manners
Tall Tales & Legends
   Series
Teacher, Teacher
Team Efforts
Tearjerkers

Technological
   Nightmares
Teen Tribulations
That's Showbiz
Three Stooges
Time Travel
Tom & Jerry
Toys
Trading Places
Trains
Treasure Hunt
Trees
TV Movies
TV Series
TV Tales
Twins
UFOs
Vacations

Vampires
Viva Las Vegas!
Volcanos
Voodoo
Waitresses
War, General
Wedding Bells
Werewolves
Winnie the Pooh
Witches' Brew
WonderWorks
World War I
World War II
Wrestling
Wrong Side of the
   Tracks

The Movie Ratings System

What the Heck (!$%*!) is It Anyway?

The present movie ratings system celebrated its 25th anniversary in November, 1993. It's hard to believe that only the present generation grew up with that well-known Hollywood alphabet of G, PG, R, plus late-comers PG-13 and NC-17 (and the outmoded M, GP and X).

Sometimes it's even harder to believe that the ratings system has lasted. The video revolution has filled our living rooms with thousands of previously unreleased, foreign and otherwise unrated titles (like virtually all made-for-TV movies and shows). Yet exactly because of that fact, parents still look to those magic letters for guidance. A 1993 survey showed public trust in the ratings rising steadily since its inception in 1968, to reach a high of 75% in 1990. Obviously the present rating codes fill a vital need.

The Motion Picture Association of America explains their own MPAA rating system thus: "It provides advance cautionary warning to parents so that parents can make their own decisions about the movies their children attend."

The MPAA rating (a voluntary service from the film industry by the way, not a government creation) isn't supposed to be a tool of censorship. Nor is it supposed to label a movie as intrinsically `good' or `bad.' It's also not supposed to take the place of a parent or baby sitter.

Yet at times it's done all three. The fact is that the Classification and Ratings Administrations (CARA), the actual folks who have endured screenings and assign ratings to over 11,400 features, are a committee of ordinary mortals. They hand down no stone tablets from Mount Sinai; their opinions and judgments are sometimes inconsistent, petty, hypocritical - and all the while lambasted by filmmakers, critics and citizens for being both too harsh and too lenient.

Film critic Stephen Farber sat on the ratings board for a brief period in the early 1970s, and out of that frustrating experience he penned a revealing memoir, "The Movie Rating Game." In particular, Farber found movies that responsibly tackled urgent subjects for young people, especially sexual morality and drug use, got slapped with R (and even X) ratings, preventing most underaged viewers from seeing them. At the same time, bloody violence was often tolerated. One board member even endorsed screen savagery, on the grounds that watching it gave kids an outlet for their (sexual?) aggression.

In the years since Farber's book some other disturbing trends have emerged that seem to twist the MPAA code meanings. Take the fate of the G category, which technically means 'General Audiences.' In theory it applies retroactively to every Hollywood feature before 1968 - be it "Lassie" or "From Here to Eternity," and film studios after '68 would sometimes appeal to CARA to get a PG judgment lowered to G.

These days, however, G is often interpreted as either cartoons or children's entertainment of the mildest sort, with little appeal beyond preschool. In other words, box-office poison unless your name is "Aladdin."

As a result modern family films have thrown in stronger elements, like violence and swearing, to court CARA's more 'respectable' PG. Rumor has it that even "Star Wars" dodged an undesired G this way. But G and PG were intended as two very different classes, and parents may be surprised by more than one PG video largely unsuitable for youngsters.

In short, the MPAA rating codes have to be taken with the proverbial grain of salt. Yet it's the only widespread rating system we have, and CARA in all fairness is one of those agencies whose failures stand out like bonfires and whose good work goes quietly unnoticed.

We can sympathize because in this book we tried our own 'content advisories' to make up for the MPAA's occasional oversights or shortcomings. It hasn't been easy. When a video does carry a CARA-imposed rating, we mention that as well - and sometimes whether we agreed or not.

THE MOTION PICTURE CLASSIFICATIONS AND RATINGS

G: GENERAL AUDIENCES. All ages admitted.
PG: PARENTAL GUIDANCE SUGGESTED. Some material may not be suitable for children.
PG-13:   PARENTS STRONGLY CAUTIONED. Some material may be inappropriate for children under 13.
R: RESTRICTED. Under 17 requires accompanying parent or adult guardian.
NC-17:   NO CHILDREN UNDER 17. (age may vary in certain areas)

Discontinued Rating Codes, still listed on some tapes...

M: SUGGESTED FOR MATURE AUDIENCES - ADULTS AND MATURE YOUNG PEOPLE
GP: (Later modification of the M rating, later altered to PG)
X: PERSONS UNDER 17 NOT ADMITTED.

Bonus Section of Relevant Readings

Whither Disney?:
The Six Faces of Uncle Walt

In the Golden Age of Hollywood, studios were like brand name labels. In the public mind, each stood for something. Warner Brothers did great gangster pictures and searing social dramas. MGM meant lavish, all-star musicals, swashbucklers and costumed escapism. If it was a wild western, it had to be a Republic Picture, and Universal unveiled classic movie monsters ("Dracula" "Frankenstein" "The Invisible Man") plus respectful literary and stage adaptations.

That's all gone now; the surviving movie factories put out basically anything that sells tickets. Stars and directors move freely from one place to another, and diversity is the safest way to go. Only one of the great studios still has a name that triggers instant recognition; Disney. Then and now, the Disney name is synonymous with quality children's films and family entertainment, in the timeless tradition of "Snow White and the Seven Dwarfs" and "The Absent-Minded Professor" up through "Who Framed Roger Rabbit?" and "The Lion King."

You may not recognize titles like "Nikki, Wild Dog of the North" or "So Dear to My Heart." But once you learn that they're Disney productions you can trust what you're getting for your videocassette purchase or rental.

But when is Disney not Disney? In the 1980s, the Magic Kingdom staked out new realms in the territory of mass-audience motion pictures - more mature, even raw subjects far removed from Cinderella's Palace. For this purpose the corporation created two associated entities, Touchstone and Hollywood Pictures, with their own home video labels. They also acquired Miramax, an established distributor of fine foreign and independent films like "The Crying Game." And, after negotiations that make most peace treaties look like handshakes, Disney brought the Jim Henson Muppet catalogue into the fold with its very own label. And then there's Buena Vista Home Video, a regular catch-all of family titles.

Does Disney's traditional family touch reach in some form over all their video output? Even Disney spokespeople deny it, citing an adult-oriented Hollywood Pictures thriller "Guilty as Sin" and the Touchstone drama "What's Love Got to Do with It?"

Walt Disney: The Man Behind the Mouse

But the fact is that Disney Studios have shown a polished profession-alism in everything they produce. Intentionally or not, a bit of the Disney spirit seems to creep into other works distributed by the company. Disney-less pics, like Touchstone's "Sister Act," Hollywood's "Captain Ron," or even the independently made Miramax release "Into the West" could, with minor adjustments, conceivably have met the high standards of Uncle Walt himself.

Let's allow the Disney video division themselves the last word. According to a recent fact sheet, here is how they define their own branch-es.

WALT DISNEY HOME VIDEO - The videocassettes released under the Walt Disney Home Video label include all Disney animated films and live-action features. These are usually G-rated and, less frequently, PG. The videos are traditionally marketed to mom, families and children. Recent releases include "Aladdin," the number-one selling video of all time, "The Mighty Ducks," and "The Adventures of Huck Finn."

BUENA VISTA HOME VIDEO - Acquisitions, newly produced video products with non-Disney characters, music video and variety pro-grams are released under the Buena Vista Home Video label. Buena Vista's video lines range from Eric Hill's "Spot" stories, to longstanding animated character franchises like "Alvin and the Chipmunks." Buena Vista's music and variety titles include "Elvis: The Great Performances" and most recently "Johnny Carson: His Favorite Moments From the Tonight Show."

JIM HENSON VIDEO - Videocassettes released under the Jim Henson Video label include classic, award-winning and new-to-video Muppet programming. Recent releases include "The Muppet Christmas Carol," a top seller in 1993. The label is also releasing its first direct-to-video programs: Muppet Classic Fairytales, including "Rumpelstiltskin," "Elves and the Shoemaker" and "King Midas."

TOUCHSTONE AND HOLLYWOOD PICTURES HOME VIDEO -Touchstone and Hollywood Pictures videocassettes are PG, PG-13 and R-rated films with more broad-based audience appeal and top Hollywood talent. Recent Touchstone Home Video releases include the hits "What's Love Got to Do With It?" and "Alive." Hollywood Pictures Home Video releases include "The Joy Luck Club" and "Tombstone."

MIRAMAX HOME ENTERTAINMENT - The studio's Miramax Home Entertainment arm includes critically and often multi-award winning productions that are usually independently produced. Recent releases include the critically acclaimed Golden Globe winner and Academy Award nominee "Farewell My Concubine," the magical adventure "Into the West" and the hit comedies "Strictly Ballroom" and "The Snapper."

`Toons Without Pity

Sex, nudity, drugs, murder, carnage are all coming to screens big and small, near you. Nothing new about that, right? But we're talking about cartoons.

Yes, cartoons. No longer can it be taken for granted that anything animated is 100% family-approved, G-rated, kindergarten-grade fun. While a "Lion King" or "American Tail" still fits that bill, more 'sophisticated' - meaning explicit - animation has arrived at the local video store.

It began in this country with the '60s underground comix, adult-oriented comic books that tackled taboo subjects. Successful comics have a habit of turning into cartoons, and when artist R. Crumb's satirical "Fritz the Cat," a free-thinking feline who experimented with sex, drugs and radical politics, came to movie theaters in 1972 it won the distinction of being the first cartoon to be rated X by the MPAA.

Of course, no law says that cartoons must be eternally cuddly and childish. Animation, like any other creative endeavor, is free expression, and incurs all the hazards that such freedom of expression implies. Indeed "Fritz the Cat" animator Ralph Bakshi (a respected vet of the TerryToon studios who helped revive "Mighty Mouse" for a Saturday-morning TV show in the '80s) has never tried to peddle his harder-edged, profane efforts like "American Pop" and "Cool World" as all-ages entertainment. Parents who idly pick them up on videocassette to amuse the young ones really should've read their labels and MPAA ratings first.

Bakshi's roughest stuff pales, however, in comparison to features now finally emerging from Japan, the world capital of adult animation. Japanimation - or "anime" - is best-known to American audiences through export versions of TV 'toons like "Speed Racer" or "Astro Boy." The Japanese still craft wonderful children's entertainment, such as the recent "My Neighbor Totoro."

But that's kids' stuff; another branch of anime has evolved into a full-fledged adult art form. Movies like the violence-filled futuristic spectacle "Akira" (said to be the most expensive 'toon epic ever devised), the hit-man super thriller "The Professional: Golgo 13" and the blood-soaked barbarian adventure "Fist of the North Star" were never intended for the tiny tots.

Such adult anime remains a cult item on videocassette in the US, nowhere near as common as "All Dogs Go to Heaven." And when it does show up unexpurgated on the rental shelves, the distributors don't mince words. "A cornucopia of sex and violence" declares Streamline Picture's unrated box for "The Professional - Golgo 13." "Contains scenes of violence and sexuality. Recommended for mature audiences." They aren't joking.

So be an informed consumer. Read those labels, perhaps ask for advice. Don't be scared off by unfamiliar titles either, because there is great stuff out there; the point is, don't assume that just because it's a cartoon, it's no harsher than a wascally wabbit with a stick of Acme dynamite.

Mondo Muppet

Not every Muppet you meet is a green felt frog or a glamour pig. The technology that helped Kermit ride a bicycle in "The Great Muppet Caper" and put Big Bird on skates for "A Sesame Street Christmas" helped found Jim Henson's Creature Shop. These days, the Shop is more than just a home for the Cookie Monster and Fozzie. It's a special-effects lab that puts Muppet magic into a general range of all-ages entertainment.

It was 1955 when college-undergrad Jim Henson first contributed puppet segments to a Washington D.C. local program that became known as "Sam and Friends." Muppets and video were made for each other, literally. It's said that Henson designed the soft-faced, malleable Muppets to suit the harsh closeups of the TV cameras. His cloth creations (and, for the record, Kermit isn't made of green felt but a special, heavy-duty synthetic material) seemed expressive and alive onscreen. Traditional wooden marionettes, intended to be seen at a distance, looked stiff and inanimate on the tube. Within a few years Henson won both a local Emmy and nationwide exposure with a guest appearance on "The Tonight Show." By the late 1960s he was invited to bring his characters to a new kids' show on public television - "Sesame Street."

The success of "Sesame Street" and the similar "Electric Company" brought the Muppets a whole generation of young fans. But you could also find Muppetry exploring new and innovative directions. Jim Henson's Oscar-nominated short subject "Timepiece" consisted of nonstop camera tricks and transformations, including an exotic dancer who becomes both a plucked chicken and a gyrating skeleton. Some of the most complex Muppets of the era were a ribald tribe of prehistoric beasts who appeared on early segments of "Saturday Night Live," shortly before Miss Piggy and friends got a weekly half-hour all to themselves - "The Muppet Show" - in September, 1976. It became an international hit with young and old, and the first "Muppet Movie" followed in 1979.

That same year Jim Henson's Creature Shop opened for business in London, where "The Muppet Show" was taped. In 1982 the Creature Shop was showcased by "The Dark Crystal," a fantasy feature with no humans whatsoever, just a never-before-seen assembly of screen creatures utilizing

Rowlf the Dog

Muppet techniques. The box-office winner proved, even more so than the earlier Kermit/Piggy musical comedies, that a feature motion picture could be 100% pure Muppet.

Soon the Creature Shop was inventing new creations for other filmmakers, in such productions as "The Empire Strikes Back," "Labyrinth," "Dreamchild," "Return to Oz," the musical "Little Shop of Horrors" "The Bear," "The Polar Bear King," "The NeverEnding Story III," the TV comedy "Dinosaurs" and the "Teenage Mutant Ninja Turtles" series.

Originally 'Muppet' meant a combination of marionette and puppet, but now the term has expanded to include animatronics, in which realistic, living motion is simulated in mechanical models, using computerized electronics, radio-control, hydraulics, rods -basically anything that gets the job done. The common factor is Jim Henson's Creature Shop, now with branches in New York and Los Angeles, continuing the legacy that started with a (more or less) green felt frog.

Toy Ploy

Entertainment tie-ins, souvenirs and promotional knick-knacks have been around for ages, from the first Mickey Mouse watch to the latest Flintstones meals at McDonalds. But in the 1980s such marketing ran amok in the world of TV cartoon shows, many of which turned into mere half-hour ads for toy products, aimed straight at kid viewers.

Now most of those animated sales ploys have been released on cassette, and parents should decide if a commercial in sheep's clothing is worth the rental dollars, not to mention the time.

On one hand, existing toys like G.I. Joe, Barbie, Mr. Potato Head and even Rubik's Cube were transformed into generally dismal 'toons. Even more pernicious were cartoons conceived in tandem with brand-new lines of gaudy playthings. Their mission: to convince your children that they must have the toys. It works too, as child fantasy and commercial appetites merge in the marketplace. Entertainment value or otherwise redeeming qualities are optional extras. The good news is that many of the animated infomercials are well past their trend cycle. The bad news is they have been replaced by numerous animated adventurers with must-have toy tie-ins. You may resist, but you'll certainly not come away unscarred.

The classic example of merchandising via screen adventures: "He-Man and the Masters of the Universe" (later joined by "She-Ra, Princess of Power"), a cartoon series hatched in 1981, right alongside a vast assortment of He-Man action figures and accessories from Mattel. Saturation of Saturday-morning airwaves helped sell $500 million worth of He-Man merchandise in 1984 alone, according to Business Week. The same article enshrined "Transformers," another 'toon-toy combo, as "the most successful toy introduction ever." Thanks partly to their boob-tube incarnations, the transforming robot action figures made $100 million for Hasbro in their first year.

What inspired the plaything plague? Deregulation. In the 1980s the Reagan-era FCC eased rules governing the quality of children's television. Left completely to the mercies of the marketplace, kid TV became exactly that: marketplaces for junky toys. And during commercial breaks in the toy-inspired cartoons, youngsters would get...more commercials for the toys.

Advocacy groups like Action for Children's Television and the National Association for Better Broadcasting were outraged by this trend, and were trying to pass legislation against it in 1987 when the fever broke. Later amalgamations of toys/cartoons failed to catch on either way, and attempts at so-called interactive shows like "Captain Power and the Soldiers of the Future" (which supposedly allowed viewers to play along via a special video signal transmitted to their $40 toy rayguns), didn't last. Of course, the Mighty Morphin Power Rangers are the hottest kidvid and toy combo, proving that video, TV and the movies are still a potent marketing force.

If nothing else, the mass of such mindless titles now permanently preserved on tape testify to what untrammelled greed can do to children's entertainment. Meanwhile, we've compiled this far-from-complete accounting of toy TV shows and the manufacturers that share the guilt:

AMERICAN GREETINGS - Care Bears, Strawberry Shortcake, My Pet Monster

COLECO - Teddy Ruxpin, Wrinkles, Cabbage Patch Kids

FISHER-PRICE - Puffalumps

HALLMARK - Rainbow Brite, Pretty Piggies

HASBRO - My Little Pony, Glo Friends, G.I. Joe, Visionaries, Bucky O'Hare, Transformers, Mr. Potato Head, Colorforms

KENNER - Robotman, Silverhawks

MATTEL - He-Man and the Masters of the Universe/She-Ra, Lady Lovelylocks, Barbie, Captain Power and the Soldiers of the Future

TONKA - Maple Town, Pound Puppies, Spiral Zone, Gobots

The Tale of Shelley Duvall

The big-budget 1980 live-action version of the classic cartoon "Popeye," starring Robin Williams, may have been a disappointment at the box office, but in one way it made history. During on-location shooting on the island of Malta, leading lady Shelley Duvall brought with her a set of children's tales for reading during the off hours. "I opened up to 'The Frog Prince' one day," she later recalled, "and thought, 'Wouldn't Robin make a great frog?'"

Williams agreed, and suggested British comic actor/director Eric Idle for the project as well. Their collaboration became the genesis of "Faerie Tale Theatre," an anthology of classic fairy tales Duvall produced between 1982 and 1985 for Showtime Cable, later widely released on Playhouse Video cassettes. The show's rare combination of storybook whimsy, childhood delight and occasional modern satire made it a hit.

Duvall, a college student planning to be a research scientist, was recruited into acting by Robert Altman, who would in fact later cast her as Olive Oyl in "Popeye." For years the thin, toothy Texan played various dramatic, somewhat neurotic roles, like the frail-seeming wife of a maniac in the horror blockbuster "The Shining." But since the age of 17 Shelley Duvall had been collecting antique storybooks and fairy tale lore. Now she became Hollywood's resident Mother Goose.

Following the example of Robin Williams, stars flocked to appear in Duvall's tales. Mick Jagger, Susan Sarandon, Billy Crystal, Joan Collins, Christopher Reeve, Jim Belushi, Lee Remick, Matthew Broderick, Liza Minelli, Jeff Bridges, Frank Zappa and many more - including Duvall - logged guest roles in stories by Jacob and Wilhelm Grimm, Hans Christian Andersen and Mother Goose. Moreover, major filmmakers like Tim Burton, Francis Ford Coppola and Tony Bill signed on to direct segments.

Duvall followed up with an all-American frontier anthology "Shelley Duvall's Tall Tales and Legends," very close in spirit to FTT, and continued the amphibian fixation with two modern twists on the old Frog Prince tale, "Frog" and "Frogs!" for the PBS family anthology "WonderWorks."

Her 90-minute musical special "Mother Goose Rock 'n' Rhyme," done for the Disney Channel, cast her as Bo Peep, opposite such performers as

Paul Simon, Little Richard and Cyndi Lauper. It's on video, as is a later Showtime series "Shelley Duvall's Bedtime Stories," in which another galaxy of movie and TV stars like John Candy, Bette Midler, Michael J. Fox, Sissy Spacek and Christian Slater narrate animated editions of modern children's books. Recently she's launched record albums, music-videos and a new Showtime Cable series, "Mrs. Piggle-Wiggle," starring Jean Stapleton - plus yet another celestial array of guest stars.

Shelly Duvall has been called the most important individual on the children's entertainment scene since Jim Henson. Her advice on dealing with young viewers: "You have to be honest. They can see everything...I think they're a lot smarter than people give them credit for."

Serials - A User's Guide

Home video offers a chance for modern viewers to relive a vanished form of kids' entertainment - the weekly movie serials, which had their finest years from 1935 to 1945. But you don't just push `play' and keep watching; first you'll need some background and instructions.

In fact, movie serials - or chapter plays,' as they were called at the time - had been in production since early in the silent era, with the famous "Perils of Pauline," and lasted until 1956's obscure "Blazing the Overland Trail," when the serial and its stock characters, like Commando Cody, Flash Gordon, the Green Hornet, Batman and Superman, gave way to broadcast TV programs. But with few exceptions (like the campy 1960s "Batman" or the BBC's "Dr. Who") no prime-time programs have really duplicated the unpretentious fun of the movie-house serial.

Using characters and stories often inspired by popular comics or radio adventures, serials would typically last for around a dozen action-packed chapters, each 12 to 20 minutes in length. The first episode would be the longest, typically setting up the premise of a hero (or heroes), a mystery villain - not unmasked until the very last chapter - and something for them to fight over, like a secret formula, a lost treasure or a superweapon.

Though a few serials, notably "The Green Hornet," has chapters that are largely complete mini-adventures in themselves, the classic serial segment ends with those notorious cliffhangers. You'll see, for instance, the car carrying the unconscious hero go off a bridge and explode. All is lost! At least until the start of the next chapter, which replays the same sequence - but with the vital missing scene in which the hero awakens up and jumps free of the doomed auto in time. And the story would continue. This was the simple but irresistible trick that kept youngsters hooked week after week, waiting for the next serial installment to reach their local matinee.

That's the important point to remember when watching serials today: these films were not made to be watched all the way through in one sitting. With running times stretching toward four hours or more, even the greatest serials can grow tedious if played in marathon form. Instead, watch one, maybe two episodes at a time. Take breaks. Go for popcorn.

We know of one viewer who makes a game out of it, challenging kid viewers to write down their guesses about how Spy Smasher or whoever escapes the latest peril, then proceeding to the next chapter to see if they got it right.

For that reason, make sure that when you rent a serial you've got custody for two days or more. But note that few video emporiums stock serials in quantity (which necessarily must come out on tape in multivolume sets). So you might have to seek out specialty stores, libraries, or mail-order distributors who carry the vintage chapter plays.

It's worth it. Yesterday's serials inspired today's Indiana Jones and James Bond epics, and will continue to transfix viewers of all ages with a taste for adventure and a willingness to "join us again for the next exciting chapter of...!"

Canada's Best-Kept Secret

Rock Demers has been called 'the Walt Disney of the North,' his name synonymous with the finest family-oriented feature. His movies are widely awaited the world over - except in the United States, where he's still a well-kept secret, and tantalizingly few of his "Tales for All" features are generally available on tape.

The Quebec-based producer is proof that nice movies can finish first. Demers, who originally studied to be a teacher, is a lifelong movie fan, founding several film societies and serving as director of the Montreal International Film Festival in the 1960s. Through this work he established ties with some of the new and exciting moviemakers in Europe and elsewhere, so that when he turned to film distribution and production the pieces were all in place.

Demers first began by distributing quality children's films from around the world to the Canadian Broadcasting Corporation, then to French network television. He also set up a regional bureau to promote film production in Quebec. In 1980 he put it all together with Les Productions La Fete, his own company specializing in family entertainment, each feature bearing the sub-label "Contes pour Tous (Tales for All)."

Plans originally called for nine Tales for All, but audience reaction was so strong that Les Productions La Fete has just completed the 15th. Written and directed by many of Demers' international associates from the film festival days, the stories have taken place in Poland, Romania, Argentina, Australia and, of course, Canada. Plots range from fantasy to family drama to rambunctious comedy, but Demers sets some basic ground rules:

— Stories must appeal to all ages.
— Lead parts must be played by children 10 to 12 years old. For that reason, Demers seldom uses the same young actors twice ("Children of this age change so fast").
— Boys and girls are equally adept at activities; there are no stereotyped gender roles.
— Scripts should avoid simplistic concepts of characters who are either all shining virtue or entirely evil. "I've never met anyone who is all good or all bad."

Rock Demers of Productions La Fete

And most (but not every one) are shot in French. English-language release versions are also prepared, expertly dubbed.

The first Tale for All was 1984's "The Dog Who Stopped the War (La Guerre des Tuques)," a critical and popular success that swept international awards and turned into the highest-grossing Canadian film of the year. The second, "The Peanut Butter Solution (Operation Beurre de Pinottes)," also outperformed expectations. The third, "Bach and Broccoli (Bach et Bottine)," was a sensation.

The Tales for All have a wonderful sense of fun and a refreshing knack for showing how believable kids really might behave, whether facing a conflict with a troubled adult ("Bach and Broccoli") or a magic spell that shrinks you down to a postage stamp (the delightful "Tommy Tricker and the Stamp Traveller").

Despite their success on the international scene and at film festivals, only a few of the early Tales for All were generally released by the major video distributors. Les Productions la Fete now markets their movies themselves. They can be reached at 225 rue Roy est, Bureau 203, Montreal, Quebec, Canada H2W 1M5. A quick rundown of the Tales for All:

1. "The Dog Who Stopped the War" (1984)
2. "The Peanut Butter Solution" (1985)
3. "Bach and Broccoli" (1986)

4. "The Young Magician" (1987)
5. "The Great Land of Small" (1987)
6. "Tadpole and the Whale" (1988)
7. "Tommy Tricker and the Stamp Traveller" (1988)
8. "Summer of the Colt" (1989)
9. "Bye Bye Red Riding Hood" (1989)
10. "The Case of the Witch Who Wasn't" (1990)
11. "Vincent and Me" (1990)
12. "Reach for the Sky" (1991)
13. "The Clean Machine" (1992)
14. "The Flying Sneaker" (1992)
15. "The Return of Tommy Tricker"

Les Productions la Fete is also the source for an early Demers production "The Christmas Martian" (1972), ranked among the first of the many great family features to come out of Canada.

Videohound's
Family Video Retriever

Videohound's Family Video Retriever

Abbott and Costello Cartoon Festival

Compilation of episodes from a syndicated Hanna-Barbera TV cartoon, putting animated editions of the comedy team in assorted wide-ranging adventures. Abbott provided his own voice, while Irwin imitated Costello, who had passed away years earlier. Best to stick with real live versions, whose movies and live-action comedy show of the '50s are available on videocassette (and uncannily manage to make it to the front of every reference book).
1966 (*Family*) 60m/C **V:** Bud Abbott, Mel Blanc, Don Messick. **VHS, Beta $19.95** *VCI*

Abbott and Costello Meet Captain Kidd 🦴🦴

With pirates led by Captain Kidd on their trail, Abbott and Costello follow a treasure map. Bland A&C swashbuckler spoof might hold children's attention, but the usually reliable Laughton seems distinctly disinterested as Kidd. One of the comedy duo's few color films.
1952 (*Family*) 70m/C Bud Abbott, Lou Costello, Charles Laughton, Hillary Brooke, Fran Warren, Bill Shirley, Leif Erickson; **D:** Charles Lamont. **VHS, Beta, LV $29.95** *NOS, VCI*

Abbott and Costello Meet Dr. Jekyll and Mr. Hyde 🦴🦴

Abbott and Costello take on evil Dr. Jekyll, who has transformed himself into the wolfmanish Mr. Hyde and is terrorizing London. An attempt at recapturing the success of "Abbott and Costello Meet Frankenstein" that falls short.
1952 (*Family*) 77m/B Bud Abbott, Lou Costello, Boris Karloff, Craig Stevens, Helen Westcott, Reginald Denny; **D:** Charles Lamont. **VHS, Beta $14.95** *MCA*

Abbott and Costello Meet Frankenstein 🦴🦴🦴

Big-budget A&C classic is one of their best efforts and was, until "Ghostbusters," the nimblest big screen mix of horror and comedy (well, that's if you don't count "Young Frankenstein"). Two unsuspecting baggage clerks deliver a crate containing the not quite dead remains of Dracula and Dr. Frankenstein's monster to a wax museum. The fiends are revived, wreaking havoc with the clerks. Chaney - the wolfman - makes a special appearance to warn the boys that trouble looms, and Price has a unique 'cameo' at the end. Last and most kid-friendly film to use the Universal creatures pioneered in the 1930s. **Hound Advisory:** Monster rough-housing.
1948 (*Family*) 83m/B Bud Abbott, Lou Costello, Lon Chaney Jr., Bela Lugosi, Glenn Strange, Lenore Aubert, Jane Randolph; **D:** Charles T. Barton; **V:** Vincent Price. **VHS, Beta, LV $14.95** *MCA*

Abel's Island

Wealthy mouse is carried away to an uninhabited isle by a storm, where he 'eeks' out a simple, castaway existence and learns to appreciate the basic things in life. Fine version of William Steig's book, animated by Michael Sporn.
1988 (*Family*) 28m/C **D:** Michael Sporn; **V:** Tim Curry, Lionel Jeffries. **VHS, Beta $14.95** *KUI, RAN, LME*

Above the Rim 🦴🦴🦴

Vulgar, violent hoopster drama about a fiercely competitive inner-city playground game. Kyle-Lee Watson (Martin), a self-involved high school star raised by a saintly single mom (Pinkins), is torn between the lure of the streets and his college recruiting chances. His odds aren't made any easier by homeboy hustler Birdie (Shakur), who wants to improve his chances of making money on the local games by making sure Watson plays for his team. Energetic b-ball sequences, strong performances lose impact amid formulaic melodrama and the usual courtside obscenities. Debut for director Pollack. **Hound Advisory:** Violence and profanity.
1994 (R/*Sr. High-Adult*) 97m/C Duane Martin, Tupac Shakur, Leon, Marlon Wayans, Tonya Pinkins, Bernie Mac; **D:** Jeff Pollack; **W:** Jeff Pollack, Barry Michael Cooper; **M:** Marcus Miller. **VHS, LV** *COL*

The Absent-Minded Professor 🐾🐾🐾⍼

Classic Disney fantasy of the era. Professor Brainard forgets his wedding day to invent an anti-gravity substance called flubber (flying rubber, get it?), causing inanimate objects and people to become airborne. Will his fiancee understand? Will the villain Wynn succeed in stealing the stuff? Great sequence of the losing school basketball team taking advantage of flubber during a game. Newly colorized version also available on cassette. The movie which helped popularize flubber-like products such as Silly Putty and Whammo Superballs (the early sixties were a very flubberized era). Followed by "Son of Flubber."

1961 (*Family*) 97m/C Fred MacMurray, Nancy Olson, Keenan Wynn, Tommy Kirk, Leon Ames, Ed Wynn; *D:* Robert Stevenson. **VHS, Beta, LV $19.99** *DIS, BTV*

Ace Ventura: Pet Detective 🐾🐾⍼

Shamelessly silly detective satire casts human cartoon Carrey, he of the rubber limbs and spasmodic facial muscles, as Ace, the guy who'll find missing pets, big or small. When the Miami Dolphins' mascot Snowflake is kidnapped, he abandons his search for an albino pigeon to save the lost dolphin just in time for the Super Bowl. Brain candy running full throttle with juvenile humor, some charm, and the hyper-energetic Carrey, not to mention Young as the police chief with a secret. With the look of a small budget and trashed by the critics, box office smash laughed all the way to the bank, along with Carrey, who catapulted into nearly instant superstardom after seven seasons as the geeky white guy on "In Living Color." Alrighty indeed. **Hound Advisory:** Scatological humor, salty language, roughhousing.

1993 (PG-13/*Jr. High-Adult*) 87m/C Jim Carrey, Dan Marino, Courteney Cox, Sean Young, Tone Loc; *D:* Tom Shadyac; *W:* Jim Carrey, Tom Shadyac, Jack Bernstein; *M:* Ira Newborn. **VHS, LV, 8mm $24.96** *WAR*

Across the Great Divide 🐾🐾⍼

Two orphans must cross the rugged snow-covered Rocky Mountains in 1876 in order to claim their inheritance - a 400-acre plot of land in Salem, Oregon. Pleasant and scenic nature adventure from those reliable folks who brought you the "Wilderness Family" series.

1976 (G/*Family*) 102m/C Robert F. Logan, George Flower, Heather Rattray, Mark Hall; *D:* Stewart Raffill; *W:* Stewart Raffill; *M:* Angelo Badalamenti. **VHS, Beta $9.98** *MED, VTR*

Across the Tracks 🐾🐾

Two brothers, one a rebel, the other a straight-A jock, are at odds when the black sheep is pressured into selling drugs. In an attempt to save his brother from a life of crime, the saintly one convinces him to join the school track team, and the two face off in a big meet. Fairly realistic teen drama about a 'good' kid who's not so perfect and a 'bad' kid who's really not such a bad guy. Strong story elements make this tape available in both R and PG-13 versions. **Hound Advisory:** Drunkenness and drug use, violence, profanity, and inferences of irresponsible sex.

1989 (PG-13/*Sr. High-Adult*) 101m/C Rick Schroder, Brad Pitt, Carrie Snodgress; *D:* Sandy Tung; *W:* Sandy Tung; *M:* Joel Goldsmith. **VHS $19.95** *ACA*

Adam's Rib 🐾🐾🐾🐾

Classic war between the sexes cast Tracy and Hepburn as married attorneys on opposite sides of the courtroom in the trial of blonde bombshell Holliday, charged with attempted murder of the lover of her philandering husband. The battle in the courtroom soon takes its toll at home as the couple is increasingly unable to leave their work at the office. Sharp, snappy dialogue by Gordon and Kanin with superb direction by Cukor. Perhaps the best of the nine movies pairing Tracy and Hepburn. Also available colorized.

1950 (*Family*) 101m/B Spencer Tracy, Katharine Hepburn, Judy Holliday, Tom Ewell, David Wayne, Jean Hagen, Hope Emerson, Polly Moran, Marvin Kaplan, Paula Raymond, Tommy Noonan; *D:* George Cukor; *W:* Garson Kanin, Ruth Gordon; *M:* Miklos Rozsa. **VHS, Beta, LV $19.95** *MGM, VYG, HMV*

The Addams Family 🐾🐾⍼

The TV ghouls gets a high-octane Hollywood treatment (much closer to the original Charles Addams comics than the popular sitcom actually was) that's funny in fits and starts, but no big deal except the budget. Weirdo claiming to be long-lost Uncle Fester shows up at the Addams' home to swindle the family out of their immense fortune. Never mind the thin plot, it's all a series of twists to highlight the morbid clan's eccentricities. Ultimately disappointing but the ensemble cast, sets, and special effects are terrific, and some critics noted ironically that the Addamses were the least dysfunctional family on the big screen in quite some time. Box office hit that inspired a satisfactory sequel. **Hound Advisory:** Supernatural roughhousing, salty language. Grim jokes about electric chairs, torture and so forth are completely offset by the Addams' unflagging cheeriness.

1991 (PG-13/*Jr. High-Adult*) 102m/C Anjelica Huston, Raul Julia, Christopher Lloyd, Dan Hedaya, Elizabeth Wilson, Judith Malina, Carel Struycken, Dana Ivey, Paul Benedict, Christina Ricci, Jimmy Workman, Christopher Hart, John Franklin; *Cameos:* Marc Shaiman; *D:* Barry Sonnenfeld; *W:* Larry Thompson, Caroline Thompson; *M:* Marc Shaiman. **VHS, Beta, LV $14.95** *PAR*

Addams Family Values 🐾🐾🐾

The creepy Addams' are back, but this time they leave the dark confines of the mansion to meet the "real" world. New baby Pubert inspires homicidal jealousy in sibs Wednesday and Pugsley, causing Gomez and Morticia to hire a gold-digging, serial-killing nanny with designs on Fester. A step above its predecessor, chock full of black humor, subplots, and one-liners. Cusack fits right in with a salaciously over the top performance and Ricci nearly steals the show again as the deadpan Wednesday. **Hound Advisory:** Profanity, sex talk, roughhousing.

1993 (PG-13/*Jr. High-Adult*) 93m/C Anjelica Huston, Raul Julia, Christopher Lloyd, Joan Cusack, Carol Kane, Christina Ricci, Jimmy Workman, Kaitlyn Hooper, Kristen Hooper, Carel Struycken, David Krumholtz, Christopher Hart, Dana Ivey, Peter MacNicol, Christine Baranski, Mercedes McNab; *D:* Barry Sonnenfeld; *W:* Paul Rudnick; *M:* Marc Shaiman. **VHS, Beta** *PAR*

Flubber takes flight in "The Absent Minded Professor" (1961)

Adios Amigo 🦴🦴

Offbeat, nearly all-black western comedy has ad-libbing Pryor hustling as a perennially inept con man. Excessive violence and vulgarity are avoided in an attempt to provide good clean family fare; too bad the results aren't more rewarding.
1975 (PG/*Jr. High-Adult***)** 87m/C Fred Williamson, Richard Pryor, Thalmus Rasulala, James Brown, Robert Philip, Mike Henry; **D:** Fred Williamson; **W:** Fred Williamson. **VHS, LV $9.95** *SIM, VMK*

Adventures in Babysitting 🦴🦴

During a babysitting job, suburban teen Chris gets a distress call to pick up her runaway friend and has to drag three little kids with her downtown. Flat tire on the freeway starts a chain of perilous encounters with gangsters, prostitutes, African Americans (horrors!), and the unsuspecting parents of the supposedly at-home kids. One of those new, 'sophisticated' Disney comedies (made under their Touchstone banner) featuring a slight, borderline distasteful plot hinging mainly on Shue's enormous charm. Naturally, she delivers the anti-drug message at the start of the tape. **Hound Advisory:** Roughhousing, alcohol use, profanity beyond the call of duty. Sex talk (no action) includes running gags about a Playboy-type magazine whose centerfold model happens to resemble Chris.
1987 (PG-13/*Jr. High-Adult***)** 102m/C Elisabeth Shue, Keith Coogan, Maia Brewton, Anthony Rapp, Calvin Levels, Vincent D'Onofrio, Penelope Ann Miller, George Newbern, John Ford Noonan, Lolita David, Albert Collins; **D:** Chris Columbus; **W:** David Simkins; **M:** Michael Kamen. **VHS, Beta, LV, 8mm $89.95** *TOU*

Adventures in Dinosaur City 🦴

Low-budget kiddie movie made it to videocassette before "Jurassic Park" arrived in theaters but loses in nearly every other respect. Invention transports adolescents to a fantasy realm paralleling their favorite TV cartoon - about crime-fighting dinosaurs in the prehistoric era - and the kids assist a heroic T.Rex and his partners against their paper-mache foes. Certainly designed to be less scary than the Spielberg spectacle, but entertainment value verges on extinction.
1992 (PG/*Primary-Adult***)** 88m/C Omri Katz, Shawn Hoffman, Tiffanie Poston, Pete Koch, Megan Hughes, Tony Doyle, Mimi Maynard; **D:** Brett Thompson; **W:** Willie Baronet, Lisa Morton; **M:** Fredric Teetsel. **VHS, LV $89.98** *REP*

Adventures in Dinosaurland

Animated story of a little dinosaur who takes kids back to the stone age.
1983 (*Family***)** 44m/C **VHS $14.95** *FHE*

Adventures in Odyssey: The Knight Travellers

Nicely-animated cartoon in which young Dylan comes to the aid of a kindly inventor whose time-travelling "imagination station," designed for moral instruction, has been stolen and misused by the evil Fred Faustus.
1991 (*Family***)** 30m/C **VHS** *WTA*

Adventures in Spying 🦴🦴

Brian McNichols is on his summer vacation when he discovers a notorious drug lord lives in his neighborhood. There's a $50,000 reward for the villain's apprehension, so Brian and friends try to get the man's picture for the police. Action-packed and geared towards the junior high set, but relies too heavily on coincidence and other plot connivances to compete with espionage flicks aimed at an older market.
1992 (PG-13/*Jr. High-Adult***)** 92m/C Jill Schoelen, Bernie Coulson, Seymour Cassel, G. Gordon Liddy, Michael Emil; **D:** Hil Covington; **W:** Hil Covington; **M:** James Stemple. **VHS $89.95** *NLC*

The Adventures of a Gnome Named Gnorm 🦴

Subterranean hobbit-like dwarf digs his way to "Upworld" (the original title), modern Los Angeles. Immediately Gnorm the gnome witnesses a murder and a young LAPD detective pals around with him to find out who did it. You'll barely care; clumsy hybrid of cop and fantasy cliches doesn't satisfy either way. Gaps on the audio are remains of profanity removed in an evident attempt to peddle this as a "family" film. Snout-faced Gnorm (only semi-convincingly designed by director and f/x ace Winston) may hold kids' interest for a short while. **Hound Advisory:** Violence, sex talk (even smarmier coming from a gnome).
1993 (PG/*Primary-Adult***)** 86m/C **VHS $94.99** *PGV*

The Adventures of a Two-Minute Werewolf

When a teenage boy watches a scary horror movie, he turns into a werewolf, for a while. A comic alternative to "Teen Wolf," based on the book by Gene DeWeese; originally aired as an ABC Weekend Special.
1991 (*Family***)** 60m/C Lainie Kazan, Melba Moore, Barrie Youngfellow. **VHS $12.98** *SVI, AIM*

The Adventures of an American Rabbit 🦴🦴

Feature cartoon adventure of unassuming young Rob Rabbit who finds himself receiving the Legacy from a bunny wizard. Before he knows it, Rob has become the superpowered, patriotic protector of animals the world over. All you need to know is that American Rabbit was fully animated — in Japan.
1986 (*Family***)** 85m/C **VHS $14.98** *BAR*

The Adventures of Babar

The charming elephant leaves the jungle to see the outside world in this adaptation of Jean and Laurent de Brunhoff storybooks. Not a cartoon like one would expect; this French adaptation features live actors in elaborate pachyderm costumes.
1985 (*Family***)** 60m/C **VHS, Beta** *VCD*

The Adventures of Baron Munchausen 🦴🦴🦴◁

The director of "Time Bandits" reached a high point with this imaginative, chaotic, and under-appreciated marvel based on the tall tales of the Baron, an adventurous aristocrat of European folklore. Interrupting a stage play based on his exploits, the elderly Munchausen recounts mighty battles, perilous bets, meetings with the King of the Moon (Williams), the god Vulcan and his wife Venus, and other odd, fascinating, and funny characters. Wonderful special f/x and visually stunning sets occasionally dwarf the actors but add up to a sumptuous, epic treat in the "Wizard of Oz" tradition. **Hound Advisory:** Surrealistic roughhousing. Some nightmare imagery (including a bony, flying Angel of Death) may be too much for tiny tots. Storyline demands a fair amount of concentration to follow.
1989 (PG/*Jr. High-Adult*) 126m/C John Neville, Eric Idle, Sarah Polley, Valentina Cortese, Oliver Reed, Uma Thurman, Sting, Jonathan Pryce, Bill Paterson, Peter Jeffrey, Alison Steadman, Charles McKeown, Dennis Winston, Jack Purvis; *Cameos:* Robin Williams; *D:* Terry Gilliam; *W:* Terry Gilliam; *M:* Michael Kamen. **VHS, Beta, LV, 8mm $19.95** *COL, CRC*

Adventures of Black Beauty

Some of the chapters in Anna Sewell's famous "autobiography of a horse" are presented in a new, animated edition.
1988 (*Primary-Jr. High*) 58m/C **VHS $96.00** *RHU*

The Adventures of Buckaroo Banzai Across the Eighth Dimension 🦴🦴🦴

A man of many talents, Buckaroo Banzai (Weller) travels through the eighth dimension in a jet-propelled Ford Fiesta to battle Planet 10 aliens led by the evil Lithgow. Buckaroo incorporates his vast knowledge of medicine, science, music, racing, and foreign relations to his advantage. Offbeat and often humorous cult sci-fi trip.
1984 (PG/*Family*) 100m/C Peter Weller, Ellen Barkin, Jeff Goldblum, Christopher Lloyd, John Lithgow, Lewis Smith, Rosalind Cash, Robert Ito, Pepe Serna, Vincent Schiavelli, Dan Hedaya, Yakov Smirnoff, Jamie Lee Curtis; *D:* W.D. Richter; *M:* Michael Boddicker. **VHS, Beta, LV $9.99** *VES, LIV*

The Adventures of Bullwhip Griffin 🦴🦴◁

Rowdy, family comedy-adventure set during the California Gold Rush. Proper English butler accompanies his mistress from Boston to San Francisco to find her gold-panning brother. Series of unlikely events soon make the servant into Bullwhip Griffin, the most feared hero in the west. Amusing Disney effort, based on Sid Fleischman's book "By the Great Horn Spoon." **Hound Advisory:** Roughhousing.
1966 (*Family*) 110m/C Roddy McDowall, Suzanne Pleshette, Karl Malden, Harry Guardino; *D:* James Neilson. **VHS, Beta $69.95** *DIS*

Adventures of Buster the Bear

Joe the Otter doesn't want to share the fish in the stream with Buster, until Grandfather Bullfrog shows him that sharing makes life fun. From the Thornton W. Burgess characters in his "Fables of the Green Forest."

1978 (*Preschool-Primary*) 52m/C **VHS, Beta** *FHE*

Adventures of Captain Future

Captain Future turned out not to have much of one in the TV cartoon universe. The short-lived character and his crew use a time machine to go back a million years to save the planet Prometheus, where they encounter Martians and strange prehistoric creatures. Two volumes, available separately.
1980 (*Primary*) 54m/C **VHS, Beta** *FHE*

The Adventures of Captain Marvel 🦴🦴◁

Well-remembered cliff-hanging serial featuring a comic-strip titan who, for a while, was more popular than Superman. Exploring ancient ruins, mild-mannered archaeologist Billy Batson meets a mystic who gives him the awesome powers to say "Shazam!" and transform into the caped, flying Captain Marvel. The superhero battles against a masked villain out to steal a deadly weapon of antiquity. On tape in two cassettes. Live-action Saturday-morning TV show of the '70s, "Shazam!" is also available.
1941 (*Family*) 240m/B Tom Tyler, Frank "Junior" Coghlan, Louise Currie; *D:* William Witney. **VHS, LV $29.98** *VCN, REP, MLB*

The Adventures of Charlie and Cubby

Charlie the Crocodile and his friend Cubby teach kids the value of sharing in this offbeat claymation series originating from the former Soviet Union.
1987 (*Preschool-Primary*) 60m/C **VHS** *NO*

The Adventures of Curious George

Includes two animated episodes based on the series by Margaret and H.A. Ray. In "Curious George," the Man in the Yellow Hat captures George in Africa and brings him home where the monkey tries to learn a new lifestyle. "Curious George Goes to the Hospital" has George eating a puzzle piece, getting a tummyache, and seeking help at the hospital.
1993 (*Preschool-Primary*) 30m/C **VHS $9.95**

The Adventures of Frank and Jesse James

Republic Pictures, home of some of the slickest Saturday-matinee serials, made this cowboy saga portraying the outlaw James brothers of the west as good guys, trying to compensate for crimes committed in their names by hitting paydirt in a silver mine. Followup to "Jesse James Rides Again." A double cassette, with 13 action-packed chapters.
1948 (*Family*) 180m/B Steve Darrell, Clayton Moore, Noel Neill, Stanley Andrews; *D:* Yakima Canutt. **VHS $29.98** *REP, MOV*

The Adventures of Frontier Fremont 🦴🦴

A rough and tumble story of a man who leaves the city, grows a beard, and makes the wilderness his home (and the animals his friends). Mountain life, that's the life for me. Almost indistinguishable from Haggerty's "Grizzly Adams," with the usual redeeming panoramic shots of majestic mountains. 1975 *(Family)* 95m/C Dan Haggerty, Denver Pyle; *D:* Richard Friedenberg. **VHS, Beta $41.00** *VCI*

The Adventures of Huck Finn 🦴🦴⌐

Decent Disney attempt at Mark Twain's complex classic. Mischievous Huck and runaway slave Jim travel down the muddy Mississippi, getting into all sorts of close scrapes and adventures in the pre-Civil War era. The Disney touch dominates: racial slurs are eliminated, Twain's rich dialogue paraphrased (a mistake) and Tom Sawyer written out. Gorgeous photography. **Hound Advisory:** Violence, alcohol use.
1993 *(PG/Jr. High-Adult)* 108m/C Elijah Wood, Courtney B. Vance, Robbie Coltrane, Jason Robards Jr., Ron Perlman, Dana Ivey, Anne Heche, James Gammon, Paxton Whitehead, Tom Aldredge, Curtis Armstrong, Mary Louise Wilson, Frances Conroy; *D:* Stephen Sommers; *W:* Stephen Sommers; *M:* Bill Conti. **VHS, Beta, LV $39.99** *DIS, BTV*

The Adventures of Huckleberry Finn 🦴🦴

Twain's classic about the original American punk rebel Huck Finn, running away down the Mississippi in a raft and saving a fugitive slave, gets the same bland treatment MGM gave their later "Our Gang" shorts. Rooney is ideally cast, if overaged, as the incorrigible but good-hearted hero, and the script is sometimes funny, but far from Twain - Tom Sawyer doesn't even appear.
1939 *(Family)* 89m/B Mickey Rooney, Lynne Carver, Rex Ingram, William Frawley, Walter Connolly; *D:* Richard Thorpe. **VHS, Beta $19.98** *MGM, HMV*

The Adventures of Huckleberry Finn 🦴🦴⌐

Lively adaptation of the Twain saga in which Huck and runaway slave Jim raft down the Mississippi in search of freedom and adventure. Miscasting of Hodges as Huck hampers the proceedings, but Randall shines as the treacherous King. Strong supporting cast includes silent-era star Buster Keaton as a lion-tamer and real-life boxing champ Moore as Jim.
1960 *(Family)* 107m/C Tony Randall, Eddie Hodges, Archie Moore, Patty McCormack, Neville Brand, Mickey Shaughnessy, Judy Canova, Andy Devine, Sherry Jackson, Buster Keaton, Finlay Currie, Josephine Hutchinson, Parley Baer, John Carradine, Royal Dano, Sterling Holloway, Harry Dean Stanton; *D:* Michael Curtiz. **VHS, Beta $19.98** *MGM, FCT*

The Adventures of Huckleberry Finn 🦴🦴

Classic adventure by Mark Twain of an orphan boy and a runaway slave done again as a TV movie and starring alumni of the sitcom "F-Troop." Lacks the production values of earlier versions.
1978 *(Family)* 100m/C Forrest Tucker, Larry Storch, Kurt Ida, Mike Mazurki, Brock Peters; *D:* Jack B. Hively. **VHS, Beta** *NO*

The Adventures of Huckleberry Finn 🦴🦴🦴⌐

Made for PBS-TV and closer than any other version in capturing the mighty Mark Twain novel - and it's still just two-thirds of the original story, following Huck's escape from abusive Pap and his journey down the Mississippi with the runaway slave Jim, whom Huck rescues (sort of) with the dubious help of visiting Tom Sawyer. Also here: Huck's view of a bloody feud between two 'grand' plantation families, a grim episode left out of many adaptations. This one doesn't avoid the racism, injustice and rampant religious hypocrisy that Samuel Clemens attacked. As Huck, Day just doesn't look scruffy and ill-bred enough for the role. Strangely, Oakes, who's Tom Sawyer, does! On tape in a two-volume set; a 121-minute condensed version is also available on one cassette. **Hound Advisory:** Violence, alcohol use, mature themes.
1985 *(Family)* 240m/C Sada Thompson, Lillian Gish, Richard Kiley, Jim Dale, Barnard Hughes, Patrick Day, Frederic Forrest, Geraldine Page, Butterfly McQueen, Samm-Art Williams; *D:* Peter Hunt. **VHS, Beta $19.95** *MCA*

Adventures of Little Koala: Laura and the Mystery Egg

Roobear and pals as they embark on an Easter adventure. 19?? *(Family)* ?m/C **VHS** *FHE*

Adventures of Little Lulu and Tubby

"Good Luck Guard" has Lulu trying to join Tubby's club for boys. In "The Endurance Test," Lulu gets back at Tubby when they go on an all-day hike, without any food for Tubby. Animated version of the vintage Nancy-and-Sluggo-esque comic strip. Additional volumes available.
1978 *(Family)* 50m/C **VHS, Beta $29.95** *FHE*

The Adventures of Mark Twain 🦴🦴🦴⌐

Clay-animation wizard Will Vinton hit it big with the California Raisins commercials that caught the public fancy, but too few have seen his studio's splendid first feature, a whimsical but thoughtful pastiche of Mark Twain's lesser-known writings like "Tom Sawyer Abroad" and "Captain Stormalong's Trip to Heaven." The aged Sam Clemens himself is shown piloting a balloon to rendezvous with Halley's Comet (a true obsession of the author), and he explains the World According to Twain to stowaways Huck Finn, Tom Sawyer and Becky Thatcher. There's no way to imagine this fantastic storyline outside of the animation medium, and Vinton's visuals just get better and better as they go along. Recommended for young and old alike. **Hound Advisory:** Mature themes lurk around the edges, just as in Twain's own work. Note the chilling portrayal of Satan as an angel devoid of conscience in "The Mysterious Stranger" adaptation.
1985 *(G/Family)* 86m/C *D:* Will Vinton; *W:* Susan Shadburne; *V:* James Whitmore, Chris Ritchie, Gary Krug, Michele Mariana. **VHS, Beta, LV** *BAR*

Huck and Jim exchange fish stories in "The Adventures of Huck Finn"

Adventures of Mighty Mouse, Vol. 1

Animated cartoons featuring the super mouse, vintage animator Paul Terry's most popular Terrytoon star, a takeoff on the newly minted Superman character. Mighty Mouse made his debut in 1942, and these shorts hail from that era. Additional volumes available.
194? (*Family*) 30m/C **VHS, Beta** *FOX*

The Adventures of Milo & Otis 🐾🐾🐾

Milo is a trouble-prone tabby kitten, and Otis is his best pal, a pug-nosed pup. They romp on a farm until Milo is accidentally swept off in a box on a river. Otis follows, and after many adventures both come home with families of their own. Delightful live-action children's adventure in which no humans appear isn't strong on plot but compensates with comedian Moore's priceless narration (he also does all the character voices). Edited from a 1986 Japanese production, "Koneko Monogatari," that was record-breaking success in its homeland, but universal in appeal. Also known as "Milo & Otis."
1989 (*G/Family*) 89m/C **D:** Masanori Hata; **W:** Mark Saltzman; **M:** Michael Boddicker. **VHS, Beta, LV** $19.95 *COL, RDG, HMV*

The Adventures of Oliver Twist

Animated version of Dickens' masterpiece about the wildly changing fortunes of an impoverished orphan cast out on the streets of London.
1993 (*Primary*) 91m/C **VHS** $14.99 *SVI*

The Adventures of Peter Cottontail

Animated series featuring the mischievous rabbit created by Thornton W. Burgess, and his continuing exploits throughout 26 two-episode tapes.
1986 (*Primary*) 30m/C **VHS, Beta** *AIM*

The Adventures of Peter Cottontail and His Friends of the Green Forest

Series of 26 videotapes with two stories on each chronicling the adventures of Peter Cottontail and other Thornton W. Burgess characters.
1988 (*Preschool-Primary*) 60m/C **VHS, Beta** $50.00 *AIM*

Adventures of Pinocchio

Group of tales about the puppet who wants to become a real boy.
1988 (*Primary-Jr. High*) 63m/C **VHS** *NO*

The Adventures of Pinocchio 🐾🐾

Animated adaption of the children's classic by Collodi about the wooden puppet whose one wish is to become a real boy; not to be confused with the glorious Walt Disney version.
198? (*Family*) 90m/C **VHS** $19.95 *STE*

The Adventures of Raggedy Ann & Andy: Pirate Adventure

Raggedy Ann and Andy recover leprechaun's stolen pot of gold in this excerpt from the TV cartoon. Additional volumes available.
1994 (*Preschool*) 30m/C **VHS** $9.98 *FOX*

Adventures of Red Ryder 🐾🐾

The thrills of the rugged west are presented in this 12-episode serial. Based on the then-famous comic strip character.
1940 (*Family*) 240m/B Donald (Don "Red") Barry, Noah Beery Sr.; **D:** William Witney. **VHS, Beta** $80.00 *VCN, MLB*

Adventures of Reddy the Fox

While Granny Fox is away, Reddy the Fox gets into all kinds of trouble, until, much to his relief, Granny returns to set everything right. Based on Thornton W. Burgess' "Fables of the Green Forest."
1978 (*Preschool-Primary*) 52m/C **VHS, Beta** *FHE*

The Adventures of Robin Hood 🐾🐾🐾

Rollicking Technicolor tale of the legendary outlaw, regarded as the Mother of All Swashbucklers. The justice-minded rebel of Sherwood Forest battles the Normans, outwits evil Prince John, duels Sir Guy of Gisbourne, and gallantly romances the initially scornful Maid Marian. Grand castle sets and lush forest photography display ample evidence of the huge (in 1938) budget of $2 million plus. Flynn's youthful enthusiasm as the Saxon hero is contagious, and he performed most of his own stunts. Also available in letter-box format. **Hound Advisory:** Violence.
1938 (*Family*) 102m/C Errol Flynn, Olivia de Havilland, Basil Rathbone, Alan Hale, Una O'Connor, Claude Rains, Patric Knowles, Eugene Pallette, Herbert Mundin, Melville Cooper, Ian Hunter, Montagu Love; **D:** Michael Curtiz; **W:** Norman Reilly, Seton I. Miller; **M:** Erich Wolfgang Korngold. **Award Nominations:** Academy Awards '38: Best Picture; **Awards:** Academy Awards '38: Best Film Editing, Best Interior Decoration, Best Original Score. **VHS, Beta, LV** $19.98 *MGM, FOX, CRC*

The Adventures of Rocky & Bullwinkle: Birth of Bullwinkle

Jay Ward's classic TV 1959 cartoon "Rocky and His Friends" proved that a 'kiddie' show could have a fun dose of sophisticated satire for grownups too. The antics of Bullwinkle Moose and Rocky the Flying Squirrel (plus supporting performers like Dudley Do-Right, Aesop and Son, Mr. Peabody and Sherman) are on tape courtesy of Disney. Note that "Birth of Bullwinkle" in no way means this is an original episode; it's a reference to the classical painting parody on the box, a gag continued in ensuing volumes: "Blue Moose," "Canadian Gothic," "La Grande Moose," "Mona Moose," "Norman Moosewell," "Vincent Van Moose," and "Whistler's Moose."
1991 (*Family*) 38m/C **V:** June Foray, William Conrad, Bill Scott. **VHS, Beta, LV** $12.99 *BVV, FCT, WTA*

The Adventures of Sherlock Holmes' Smarter Brother 🦴🦴🦴

The unknown brother of the famous Sherlock Holmes takes on some of his brother's more disposable excess cases and makes some hilarious moves. Moments of engaging farce borrowed from the Mel Brooks school of parody (and parts of the Brooks ensemble as well).
1978 (PG/*Jr. High-Adult*) 91m/C Gene Wilder, Madeline Kahn, Marty Feldman, Dom DeLuise, Leo McKern, Roy Kinnear, John Le Mesurier, Douglas Wilmer, Thorley Walters; *D:* Gene Wilder; *W:* Gene Wilder. VHS, Beta *FOX*

The Adventures of Sinbad the Sailor 🦴🦴

Sinbad receives a map to a treasure island where fabulous stores of jewels are hidden, and, in his search, falls in love with the King's daughter in this animated adventure.
1973 (*Preschool-Primary*) 88m/C VHS, Beta $59.98 *LIV, FHE, WTA*

The Adventures of Sinbad the Sailor

Animated version of the classic Sinbad stories.
1985 (*Preschool-Primary*) 47m/C VHS, Beta *NO*

Adventures of Smilin' Jack

WWII flying ace Smilin' Jack Martin comes to life in this action-packed serial. Character from the Zack Moseley comic strip about air force fighting over China.
1943 (*Family*) 90m/B Tom Brown, Sidney Toler; *D:* Ray Taylor. VHS, Beta $26.95 *SNC, NOS, VAN*

The Adventures of SuperTed

Four animated adventures from Britain featuring the teddy bear transformed by a friendly alien into a flying, intergalactic super bear.
1990 (*Family*) ?m/C VHS, Beta $29.95 *TTC*

The Adventures of Teddy Ruxpin

Teddy Ruxpin and his friend Grubby the Octopede set out on a search for a fabulous treasure, but are captured by the grime-encrusted Mudblups. Commercialism-encrusted cartoon intended to promote the talking Teddy Ruxpin toys.
1986 (*Preschool*) 44m/C VHS, Beta $14.98 *LIV*

The Adventures of the Ding-A-Ling Brothers

These zany brothers win the World Champion Soccer Cup and travel across pirate-filled seas.
1987 (*Preschool-Primary*) 60m/C VHS *NO*

Adventures of the Flying Cadets 🦴🦷

Early aerial war adventure serial in 13 chapters.
1944 (*Family*) 169m/B Johnny Downs, Regis Toomey; *D:* Ray Taylor, Lewis D. Collins. VHS, Beta $39.95 *VYY, VCN, NOS*

The Adventures of the Little Koala and Friends

Excerpt from the cable-TV cartoon stars Roobear, a koala cub, caught up in a mystery Down Under with messages about conservation and animal protection implicit.
1987 (*Family*) 47m/C VHS $14.95 *FHE*

The Adventures of the Little Prince

The Antoine de Saint-Exupery character returns in TV cartoon form to help earthbound characters solve their problems. See individual titles under "The Little Prince."
1983 (*Family*) 25m/C VHS, Beta $14.98 *INJ, VES, WTA*

Adventures of the Little Prince

Episodes of an animated TV series based on the novel by Antoine de Saint Exupery, about a young boy from an asteroid who travels to other worlds in search of love and happiness. See also "The Little Prince: Back to Earth."
1987 (*Preschool-Primary*) 90m/C VHS $14.98 *INJ*

The Adventures of the Wilderness Family 🦴🦴

Modern-day family, the Robinsons (as in Swiss Family, hint, hint) are fed up with the city and retreat to the mountains of Colorado, build a log cabin and adopt a pioneer lifestyle. First and best-known of several back-to-nature pics that migrated through regional theaters in the mid-70s.
1976 (G/*Family*) 100m/C Robert F. Logan, Susan Damante Shaw; *D:* Stewart Raffill; *W:* Stewart Raffill. VHS, Beta, LV $9.98 *MED, VTR*

The Adventures of Tin Tin

Animated retelling of the travails of Tin Tin, valiant boy reporter — Herge's Belgian comic-book character phenomenally popular with European fans as he trots the globe from one adventure to the next. These cartoons preserve Herge's straightforward art and narratives, and titles include "The Black Island," "The Crab With the Golden Claw," "Objective: Moon Espionage," "Red Rackham's Treasure," "The Secret of the Unicorn," and "The Shooting Star."
1987 (*Family*) 60m/C VHS *NO*

The Adventures of Tom Sawyer 🦴🦴

Tom Sawyer, mischievous Missouri boy, gets into all kinds of trouble in this white-washed, made-for-TV adaptation of the Mark Twain classic. Everyone (except for Tyler as the homeless Huck Finn) seems remarkably well-groomed; even Injun Joe wears his Sunday best. **Hound Advisory:** Violence, alcohol use.
1973 (*Family*) 76m/C Jane Wyatt, Buddy Ebsen, Vic Morrow, John McGiver, Josh Albee, Jeff Tyler. VHS, Beta $39.95 *MCA*

Adventures of Tom Sawyer

Troll Video's animated retelling of the Mark Twain classic.
1988 (*Primary-Jr. High*) 73m/C VHS *NO*

The Adventures of Ultraman

Revised version of the Japanese series "Ultraman," a futuristic hero from a distant planet who is able to get quite large when necessary and battle Godzilla lookalikes. **1981** *(Family)* 90m/C **VHS, Beta $24.95** *FHE*

The Adventures of Walt Disney's Alice

Three early Disney shorts featuring Lewis Carroll's cast of characters: "Alice's Egg Plant," "Alice's Orphan," and "Alice the Toreador." Silent. **1925** *(Family)* 35m/B **VHS, Beta $29.95** *JEF*

Aesop and His Friends

Collection of Aesop's most beloved fables: "The Fox and the Crow," "The Lion and the Mouse," "The Grasshopper and the Ant," "The City Mouse and the Country Mouse," plus "The Snowman's Dilemma" and "The Owl and the Pussycat" as told by Cyril Ritchard. **1982** *(Preschool-Jr. High)* 50m/C **VHS, Beta** *MAS*

Aesop's Fables

Cool Cos presents this cartoon special with morals, ideal for teaching kids what's right and wrong. From the same producers as Cosby's "Fat Albert" series. **1988** *(Preschool-Primary)* 30m/C Bill Cosby. **VHS $14.95** *SVE, WAR*

Aesop's Fables: The Boy Who Cried Wolf/The Wolf and the Lamb

Two stories from the legendary talespinner noted for his use of animals to convey messages. **19??** *(Preschool-Primary)* ?m/C **VHS**

Aesop's Fables, Vol. 1: The Hen with the Golden Egg

Nine cartoon fables are retold in this collection, including "The Lion in Love," "The Dog and His Image," and "The Crow and the Fox." Plus 6 more. Additional volumes available. **1987** *(Family)* 50m/C **VHS, Beta $29.98** *VES, LIV, WTA*

Africa Screams 𝄞𝄞◁

Abbott and Costello go on an African safari in possession of a secret map. Unheralded independent A&C film is actually quite good in the stupid vein, with lots of jungle slapstick, generally good production values and a supporting cast of familiar comedy faces. **1949** *(Family)* 79m/B Lou Costello, Bud Abbott, Shemp Howard, Hillary Brooke, Joe Besser, Clyde Beatty; **D:** Charles T. Barton. **VHS, Beta, LV $9.95** *KAR, MRV, CNG*

Africa Texas Style 𝄞𝄞

East African rancher hires an American rodeo star and his faithful Navajo sidekick to help run his wild game ranch. Decent family adventure from "Flipper" creator Ivan Tors, which served as the pilot for the TV series "Cowboy in Africa." Features lots of wildlife footage (actually shot at Africa U.S.A. outside Los Angeles). **1967** *(Family)* 109m/C Hugh O'Brian, John Mills, Nigel Green, Tom Nardini; **Cameos:** Hayley Mills; **D:** Andrew Marton; **M:** Malcolm Arnold. **VHS $19.98** *REP*

African Journey

A moving, cross-cultural drama of friendship. A young black American goes to Africa for the summer to be with his divorced father who is working in the diamond mines. There he meets a young black African like himself; they overcome cultural clashes and learn respect for one another. Beautiful scenery, filmed in Africa. Part of the "Wonderworks" series. **1989** *(Family)* 174m/C Jason Blicker, Pedzisai Sithole. **VHS $79.95** *PME, HMV, BTV*

The African Queen 𝄞𝄞𝄞𝄞

After bible-thumping spinster Hepburn's missionary brother is killed in WWI Africa, hard-drinking, dissolute steamer captain Bogart offers her safe passage. Not satisfied with sanctuary, she persuades him to destroy a German gunboat blocking the British advance. The two spend most of their time battling aquatic obstacles and each other, rather than the Germans. Time alone on a African river turns mistrust and aversion to love, a transition effectively counterpointed by the continuing suspense of their daring mission. Classic war of the sexes script adapted from C.S. Forester's novel makes wonderful use of natural dialogue and humor. Shot on location in Africa. **1951** *(Family)* 105m/C Humphrey Bogart, Katharine Hepburn, Robert Morley, Theodore Bikel, Peter Bull, Walter Gotell; **D:** John Huston; **W:** John Huston, James Agee. **Award Nominations:** Academy Awards '51: Best Actress (Hepburn), Best Director (Huston), Best Screenplay; **Awards:** Academy Awards '51: Best Actor (Bogart). **VHS, Beta, LV $59.98** *FOX, FCT, TLF*

Against A Crooked Sky 𝄞𝄞

During the frontier days a 15-year-old boy sets out with an elderly trapper to rescue his sister, captured by Apaches. Family oriented western with an element of danger but otherwise standard ingredients. **Hound Advisory:** Violence, including the killing of a heroic dog. **1975** *(G/Family)* 89m/C Richard Boone, Stewart Peterson, Clint Ritchie, Geoffrey Land, Jewel Blanch; **D:** Earl Bellamy. **VHS, Beta $14.98** *LIV, VES*

The Age of Innocence 𝄞𝄞𝄞

Magnificently lavish adaptation of Edith Wharton's novel of passion thwarted by convention is visually stunning, but don't expect action since these people kill with a word or gesture. Lead performances are strong though perhaps miscast, with Ryder an exception. Outwardly docile and conventional, she nevertheless holds on to her husband with steely manipulation. Woodward's narration of Wharton's observations helps sort out what goes on behind the proper facades. Although slow, see this one for the beautiful period authenticity, thanks to Scorsese, who obviously labored over the small details. He shows up as a photographer; his parents appear in a scene on a train.

1993 (PG/*Jr. High-Adult*) 138m/C Daniel Day-Lewis, Michelle Pfeiffer, Winona Ryder, Richard E. Grant, Alec McCowen, Miriam Margolyes, Sian Phillips, Geraldine Chaplin, Stuart Wilson, Mary Beth Hurt, Michael Gough, Alexis Smith, Jonathan Pryce, Robert Sean Leonard; *Cameos:* Martin Scorsese; *D:* Martin Scorsese; *W:* Jay Cocks, Martin Scorsese; *M:* Elmer Bernstein. **Award Nominations:** Academy Awards '93: Best Adapted Screenplay, Best Art Direction/Set Decoration, Best Supporting Actress (Ryder); Directors Guild of America Awards '93: Best Director (Scorsese); Golden Globe Awards '94: Best Actress—Drama (Pfeiffer), Best Director (Scorsese), Best Film—Drama; **Awards:** Academy Awards '93: Best Costume Design; British Academy Awards '94: Best Supporting Actress (Margolyes); Golden Globe Awards '94: Best Supporting Actress (Ryder); National Board of Review Awards '93: Best Director (Scorsese), Best Supporting Actress (Ryder). VHS, LV, 8mm *COL*

Ah, Wilderness! 🐾🐾🐾◁

Well-done comedy based on the Eugene O'Neill play about a teenage boy (Linden) in small-town America, learning to be a man in the course of one summer. His father is of little help on the topic, so a rascally uncle pushes the youth to experiment with booze and girls. A minor classic, with Rooney in a supporting role as an underaged brat; in the mediocre 1948 musical remake "Summer Holiday" (also on video) he played the lead. **Hound Advisory:** Alcohol use.
1935 (*Jr. High-Adult*) 101m/B Wallace Beery, Lionel Barrymore, Aline MacMahon, Eric Linden, Cecilia Parker, Spring Byington, Mickey Rooney, Charley Grapewin, Frank Albertson; *D:* Clarence Brown. VHS $19.98 *MGM, BTV*

The Air Up There 🐾🐾

Jimmy Dolan (Bacon) is an assistant college basketball coach who's a little down-on-his-luck. Figuring he needs a career boost, he heads to the African village of Winabi to recruit talented (and tall) Saleh (Maina) to play b-ball at his college. But Saleh is next in line to be the tribe's king and doesn't want to leave. Stupid American in foreign country learning from the natives story is lighthearted, but relies heavily on formula - and borders on the stereotypical, though climatic game is a lot of fun. **Hound Advisory:** Salty language and roughhousing.
1994 (PG/*Jr. High-Adult*) 108m/C Kevin Bacon, Charles Gitona Maina, Sean McCann, Dennis Patrick; *D:* Paul Michael Glaser; *W:* Max Apple; *M:* David Newman. VHS, LV *HPH*

Airborne 🐾◁

It's dueling in-lines as cool California dude Mitchell gets transplanted to Cincinnati for a school year, and has to prove himself when those midwestern school bullies come after him. Skating race allows Mitchell to show the Ohioans a thing or two about rollerblades. Wee wheel epic appealing largely to ball-bearing brained.
1993 (PG/*Jr. High-Adult*) 91m/C Shane McDermott, Seth Green, Brittney Powell, Edie McClurg, Pat O'Brien; *D:* Rob Bowman; *W:* Bill Apablasa; *M:* Stewart Copeland. VHS, Beta, LV *WAR*

Airheads 🐾🐾◁

"Wayne's World" meets "Dog Day Afternoon." Silly farce has three metal heads (Buscemi, Fraser, Sadler) holding a radio station hostage in order to get their demo tape played. Events snowball and they receive instant fame. Cast and crew rich with subversive comedic talents, including Sandler and Farley from "Saturday Night Live." Metal-heavy soundtrack authenticity supplied by White Zombie and The Galactic Cowboys. **Hound Advisory:** Profanity and roughhousing.
1994 (PG-13/*Jr. High-Adult*) 91m/C Brendan Fraser, Steve Buscemi, Adam Sandler, Chris Farley, Michael McKean, Judd Nelson, Joe Mantegna, Michael Richards, Ernie Hudson, Amy Locane, Nina Siemaszko, John Melendez; *D:* Michael Lehmann; *W:* Rich Wilkes; *M:* Carter Burwell. VHS *NYR*

Airplane! 🐾🐾🐾🐾

Classic lampoon of disaster flicks is stupid but funny and launched a bevy of wanna-be spoofs. But it's still the best. Former pilot who's lost both his girl (she's the attendant) and his nerve takes over the controls of a jet when the crew is hit with food poisoning. The passengers become increasingly crazed and ground support more surreal as our hero struggles to land the plane. Clever, fast-paced, and very funny parody mangles every Hollywood cliche within reach. The gags are so furiously paced that when one bombs it's hardly noticeable. Launched Nielsen's second career as a comic actor. And it ain't over till it's over: don't miss the amusing final credits. Followed by lower flying "Airplane 2: The Sequel."
1980 (PG/*Family*) 88m/C Robert Hays, Julie Hagerty, Lloyd Bridges, Peter Graves, Robert Stack, Leslie Nielsen, Stephen Stucker, Ethel Merman; *Cameos:* Kareem Abdul-Jabbar, Barbara Billingsley; *D:* Jerry Zucker, Jim Abrahams, David Zucker; *W:* Jerry Zucker, Jim Abrahams, David Zucker; *M:* Elmer Bernstein. VHS, Beta, LV, 8mm $14.95 *PAR*

Airplane 2: The Sequel 🐾🐾

Not a Zucker, Abrahams and Zucker effort, and sorely missing their slapstick and script finesse. The first passenger space shuttle has taken off for the moon and there's a mad bomber on board. Given the number of stars mugging, it's more of a loveboat in space than a fitting sequel to "Airplane." Nonetheless, some funny laughs and gags.
1982 (PG/*Jr. High-Adult*) 84m/C Robert Hays, Julie Hagerty, Lloyd Bridges, Raymond Burr, Peter Graves, Sonny Bono, William Shatner, Chad Everett, Stephen Stucker, Rip Torn, Ken Finkleman, Sandahl Bergman; *D:* Ken Finkleman; *M:* Elmer Bernstein. VHS, Beta, LV $14.95 *PAR*

Airport 🐾🐾🐾

Old-fashioned disaster thriller built around an all-star cast, fairly moronic script, and an unavoidable accident during the flight of a passenger airliner. A box-office hit that paved the way for many lesser disaster flicks (including its many sequels) detailing the reactions of the passengers and crew as they cope with impending doom. Considered to be the best of the "Airport" series; adapted from the Arthur Hailey novel.
1970 (G/*Family*) 137m/C Dean Martin, Burt Lancaster, Jean Seberg, Jacqueline Bisset, George Kennedy, Helen Hayes, Van Heflin, Maureen Stapleton, Barry Nelson, Lloyd Nolan; *D:* George Seaton; *W:* George Seaton. **Award Nominations:** Academy Awards '70: Best Adapted Screenplay, Best Art Direction/Set Decoration, Best Cinematography, Best Costume Design, Best Film Editing, Best Picture, Best Sound, Best Supporting Actress (Stapleton), Best Original Score; **Awards:** Academy Awards '70: Best Supporting Actress (Hayes); Golden Globe Awards '71: Best Supporting Actress (Stapleton). VHS, Beta, LV $14.98 *MCA, BTV*

Airport '75 🐾🐾

After a mid-air collision, a jumbo 747 is left pilotless. Airline attendant Black must fly da plane. She does her cross-eyed best in this absurd sequel to "Airport" built around a lesser "all-star cast." Safe on the ground, Heston tries to talk the airline hostess/pilot into landing, while the impatient Kennedy continues to grouse as leader of the foam-ready ground crew. A slick, insincere attempt to find box office magic again (which unfortunately worked, leading to two more sequels). **1975** (PG/*Jr. High-Adult*) 107m/C Charlton Heston, Karen Black, George Kennedy, Gloria Swanson, Helen Reddy, Sid Caesar, Efrem Zimbalist Jr., Susan Clark, Dana Andrews, Linda Blair, Myrna Loy; *D:* Jack Smight. **VHS, Beta** **$59.95** *GKK*

Airport '77 🎜🎜

Billionaire Stewart fills his converted passenger jet with priceless art and sets off to Palm Beach for a museum opening, joined by an uninvited gang of hijackers. Twist to this in-flight disaster is that the bad time in the air occurs underwater, a novel (and some might say, desperate) twist to the old panic in the plane we're all gonna die formula. With a cast of familiar faces, some of them stars and some of them just familiar faces, this is yet another sequel to "Airport" and another box-office success, leading to the last of the tired series in 1979. **Hound Advisory:** Violence. **1977** (PG/*Jr. High-Adult*) 114m/C Jack Lemmon, James Stewart, Lee Grant, Brenda Vaccaro, Joseph Cotten, Olivia de Havilland, Darren McGavin, Christopher Lee, George Kennedy, Kathleen Quinlan; *D:* Jack Smight. **VHS, Beta, LV** **$14.98** *MCA*

Aladdin 🎜

Spencer, a massive guy who usually plays roughneck cow-pokes in spaghetti westerns, does the genie bit for a little boy in this silly Italian comedy that modernizes the Aladdin fable - but not the primitive f/x. **1986** (PG/*Jr. High-Adult*) 97m/C Bud Spencer, Luca Venantini, Janet Agren, Julian Voloshin, Umberto Raho; *D:* Bruno Corbucci. **VHS, Beta $9.95** *MED*

Aladdin 🎜🎜🎜🎜◁

Disney naturally took the crown for the most financially successful cartoon of all time. Boy meets princess, loses her, finds her, wins her from evil vizier and nasty parrot. Superb animation triumphs over mostly average songs and storyline by capitalizing on Robin Williams' talent for ad-libbing with lightning speed as Aladdin's irrepressible big blue genie, though one wonders if his celebrity spoofs (Arsenio Hall, for example), will endure for as long as the imagery in "Pinocchio" or "Beauty and the Beast." Adults will enjoy the 1,001 impersonations while kids will get a kick out of the adventure. 🎜A Whole New World; Prince Ali; Friend Like Me; One Jump Ahead; Arabian Nights. **1992** (G/*Family*) 90m/C *D:* Ron Clements, John Musker; *W:* Ron Clements, John Musker, Ted Elliot, Terry Rossio; *M:* Alan Menken, Howard Ashman, Tim Rice; *V:* Robin Williams, Scott Weinger, Linda Larkin, Jonathan Freeman, Frank Welker, Gilbert Gottfried, Douglas Seale, Brad Kane, Lea Salonga. **Award Nominations:** Academy Awards '92: Best Song ("Friend Like Me"), Best Sound, Best Sound Effects Editing; **Awards:** Academy Awards '92: Best Song ("A Whole New World"), Best Original Score; Golden Globe Awards '93: Best Song ("A Whole New World"), Best Score; MTV Movie Awards '93: Best Comedic Performance (Williams). **VHS, Beta $24.99** *DIS, BTV, WTA*

Aladdin and His Magic Lamp 🎜🎜

Russian-produced animated saga of the young man and his magic lamp, showcasing spectacular special effects and lavish, colorful production. **1968** (*Family*) 90m/C **VHS, Beta $39.95** *VGD*

Aladdin and His Magic Lamp

Another version of the classic tale brought to life via animation, before the conclusive Disney edition. **1969** (*Family*) 72m/C *D:* Jean Image. **VHS $59.95** *WTA, RHI*

Aladdin and His Magic Lamp

Young Aladdin discovers a magic lamp which grants him everything he wishes for. Animated production not to be confused with the Disney classic version. **1988** (*Family*) 70m/C **VHS, Beta $39.95** *PSM*

Aladdin and the Magic Lamp

The genie and Aladdin set out to become way-cool dudes in this modern animated version. **1990** (*Preschool-Primary*) 25m/C **VHS $9.99** *VTR*

Aladdin and the Wonderful Lamp

Japanese-animated version of the classic tale wherein Aladdin must summon his magical genie to defeat the wicked wizard and own the most valuable treasures in the land. **1982** (*Family*) 65m/C **VHS, Beta** *MED*

Alakazam the Great! 🎜◁

American version of the Japanese cartoon feature "Saiyu-ki" wasn't all that great once it had been dubbed in English. Plot deals with a boastful monkey sent on a dangerous quest which teaches him humility. **1961** (*Preschool*) 84m/C *D:* Lee Kresel; *V:* Frankie Avalon, Dodie Stevens, Jonathan Winters, Arnold Stang, Sterling Holloway. **VHS $14.95** *CNG*

Alan & Naomi 🎜🎜◁

In 1944, 14-year-old Brooklyn kid Alan Silverman is asked to befriend a child refugee of the war raging across Europe. Naomi witnessed the Nazis killing her father and has retreated into a world of her own. Reluctantly, the boy builds a nurturing friendship with the fragile girl that becomes a growing experience for him as well. Fine performances elevate an earnest but somewhat cliched coming-of-age tale. Based on the novel by Myron Levoy. **Hound Advisory:** Roughhousing, mature themes. **1992** (PG/*Jr. High-Adult*) 95m/C Lukas Haas, Vanessa Zaoui, Michael Gross, Amy Aquino, Kevin Connolly, Zohra Lampert; *D:* Sterling Van Wagenen; *W:* Jordan Horowitz; *M:* Dick Hyman. **VHS, LV $89.95** *COL*

Ali Baba and the Forty Thieves 🎜🎜◁

Ali Baba, small son of the Caliph of Baghdad, escapes the massacre of his family by Mongol invaders and finds refuge with Merry-Men bandits. Once grown to manhood, Ali leads the Forty Thieves to try and recapture his kingdom. Colorful, swashbuckling hit that helped save Universal Pictures from bankruptcy, though for modern audiences it's a bit short on magic (the 'open Sesame' cave is all that passes for f/x), long on palace romance. Universal spinoffs and imitations followed, also available on video, including 1952's "Son of Ali Baba" and others which reused extensive footage from this flick.

Gameshow Genie mystifies Disney's "Aladdin" (1992)

1943 (*Jr. High-Adult*) 87m/C Jon Hall, Turhan Bey, Maria Montez, Andy Devine, Kurt Katch, Frank Puglia, Fortuna Bonanova, Moroni Olsen, Scotty Beckett; *D:* Arthur Lubin; *W:* Edmund Hartmann. **VHS $14.98** *MCA, FCT*

Ali Baba and the Forty Thieves

The thieves and Ali Baba are set loose in this animation based on Arabian folklore.
1991 (*Family*) 25m/C **VHS $14.95** *VTR, WKV, MCA*

Ali Baba's Revenge

Efforts of Al Huck, his rodent sidekick, and a goofy genie combine to overthrow the tyrannical king of Alibaba. The Alibaban peasants (all cats) revolt behind Huck's leadership in response to unfair taxes.
1984 (*Preschool-Jr. High*) 53m/C *D:* H. Shidar; *V:* Jim Backus. **VHS, Beta** *MPI*

Alice in Wonderland 🎵🎵⏴

French-produced version of the Lewis Carroll classic which combines the usage of Lou Bunin's puppets and live action to tell the story, with actors portraying both Carroll and Queen Victoria. Released independently to cash in on the success of the Disney version, this takes a more adult approach to the story and is worth viewing on its own merits. Uncle Walt was

not enchanted, though, and sought legal action. History does not record whether he uttered "Off with their heads!"
1950 (*Family*) 83m/C Carol Marsh, Stephen Murray, Pamela Brown, Felix Aylmer, Ernest Milton; *D:* Dallas Bower. **VHS, Beta $39.95** *MON, WTA*

Alice in Wonderland 🎵🎵🎵

Classic Disney dream version of Lewis Carroll's famous children's story about a girl who falls down a rabbit hole into a magical world populated by strange creatures. Beautifully animated with some startling images, but served with a strange dispassion, warmed by a fine batch of songs, including "I'm Late," "A Very Merry Un-Birthday," and the title song. Wynn's vocals perfectly suit the Mad Hatter. 🎵Alice in Wonderland; I'm Late; A Very Merry Un-Birthday.
1951 (*G/Family*) 75m/C *D:* Clyde Geronomi; *V:* Kathryn Beaumont, Ed Wynn, Sterling Holloway, Jerry Colonna, Hamilton Luske, Wilfred Jackson. **VHS, Beta, LV $24.99** *DIS, FCT, KUI*

Alice in Wonderland 🎵🎵

All-star updated adaptation of the Lewis Carroll classic, made for network TV. This time instead of Alice tumbling down a rabbit hole she falls through her television set (natch). But her adventures still include the White Rabbit, Mad Hatter, March Hare, Cheshire Cat, and the King and Queen of

Hearts, many of whom insist on singing some unenthralling songs. Followed by "Alice Through the Looking Glass."
1985 *(Family)* 90m/C Red Buttons, Anthony Newley, Ringo Starr, Telly Savalas, Robert Morley, Sammy Davis Jr., Steve Allen, Steve Lawrence, Eydie Gorme; *D:* Harry Harris. **VHS $19.98** *FCT*

Alice in Wonderland in Paris

Five short films, the first of which sets the stage for the following four. Alice travels to France to meet her heroine Madeline and adventure ensues.
19?? *(Family)* 52m/C *D:* Gene Dietch. **VHS $9.95** *WTA*

Alice's Adventures in Wonderland

British adaptation of Lewis Carroll's timeless fantasy of the little girl who falls into a rabbit hole and, in this case, meets an all-star ensemble decked out in gaudy makeup and costumes, singing forgettable songs. The curious may check it out just for that amazing cast.
1972 *(Family)* 96m/C Fiona Fullerton, Michael Crawford, Ralph Richardson, Flora Robson, Peter Sellers, Robert Helpmann, Dudley Moore, Michael Jayston, Spike Milligan, Michael Hordern; *D:* William Sterling; *W:* William Sterling; *M:* John Barry. **VHS, Beta** *VES*

Alive 🦴🦴◁

Recounts the true-life survival story of a group of Uruguayan rugby players in 1972. After their plane crashes in the remote, snowy Andes (in a spectacular sequence) they're forced to turn to cannibalism during a 10-week struggle to stay alive. Marshall doesn't focus on the gruesome idea, choosing instead to focus on all aspects of their desperate quest for survival. The special effects are stunning, but other parts of the film are never fully realized, including the final scene. Based on the nonfiction book by Piers Paul Read. **Hound Advisory:** Profanity; cannibalism.
1993 (R/ *Sr. High-Adult)* 127m/C Ethan Hawke, Vincent Spano, Josh Hamilton, Bruce Ramsay, John Haymes Newton, David Kriegel, Kevin Breznahan, Sam Behrens, Illeana Douglas, Jack Noseworthy, Christian Meoli, Jake Carpenter; *Cameos:* John Malkovich; *D:* Frank Marshall; *W:* John Patrick Shanley; *M:* James Newton Howard. **VHS, Beta, LV $19.99** *TOU*

All Dogs Go to Heaven 🦴🦴

Beautifully animated musical mess from Bluth shows the perils of having 10 - count 'em - credited writers. Dog crook Charlie is killed by his canine boss and goes to Heaven, but he's bored and heads back to Earth, where he becomes top dog in the rackets via an orphan girl who can predict horse races. But he turns into a good guy at the end in a plot that's all over the place; there's an alligator who befriends Charlie for no more reason than to be a convenient rescuer later on, and if the story takes place in 1939 Louisiana, why do the bad guys have a ray gun? Ad-heavy cassette also sags with a public service announcement for the Boys & Girls Clubs of America and a fabric softener commercial. **Hound Advisory:** Alcohol use.
1989 (G/ *Preschool)* 85m/C *D:* Don Bluth; *W:* Don Bluth, David A. Weiss; *M:* Ralph Burns; *V:* Burt Reynolds, Judith Barsi, Dom DeLuise, Vic Tayback, Charles Nelson Reilly, Melba Moore, Candy Devine, Loni Anderson. **VHS, Beta, LV, 8mm $14.95** *MGM, RDG, WTA*

All I Want for Christmas 🦴🦴

Paramount bet there was a market for low-budget G-rated fare with this holiday quickie, only to get eggnog on their faces from the low audience turnout. Blame the squishy, low intensity script about a little girl wanting to reunite her estranged parents, so she and her brother play various tricks to bring the ex-spouses together. Heavy xmas-in-New York ambiance, and charming performers, but be aware that comic actor Nielsen, star of the ad campaign, barely has two minutes onscreen as a department store Santa.
1991 *(G/Family)* 92m/C Thora Birch, Leslie Nielsen, Lauren Bacall, Jamey Sheridan, Harley Jane Kozak, Ethan Randall, Kevin Nealon, Andrea Martin; *D:* Robert Lieberman; *W:* Richard Kramer, Thom Eberhardt, Gail Parent; *M:* Neal Israel, Bruce Broughton. **VHS, LV $19.95** *PAR*

All New Adventures of Tom Sawyer: Mischief on the Mississippi

The continuing adventures of Mark Twain's Tom Sawyer, Huck Finn, and Becky Thatcher in cartoon form. Additional volumes available.
1980 *(Family)* 95m/C **VHS $26.99** *JFK*

All the President's Men 🦴🦴🦴◁

True story of the Watergate break-in that led to the political scandal of the decade, based on the best-selling book by Washington Post reporters Bob Woodward and Carl Bernstein. Intriguing, terse thriller is a nail-biter even though the ending is no secret. Expertly paced by Pakula with standout performances by Hoffman and Redford as the reporters who slowly uncover and connect the seemingly isolated facts that ultimately lead to criminal indictments of the Nixon Administration. Deep Throat Holbrook and Robards as executive editor Ben Bradlee lend authenticity to the endeavor, a realistical portrayal of the stop and go of journalistic investigations.
1976 (PG/ *Family)* 135m/C Robert Redford, Dustin Hoffman, Jason Robards Jr., Martin Balsam, Jane Alexander, Hal Holbrook, F. Murray Abraham, Stephen Collins, Lindsay Crouse; *D:* Alan J. Pakula; *W:* William Goldman; *M:* David Shire. **Award Nominations:** Academy Awards '76: Best Director (Pakula), Best Film Editing, Best Picture, Best Supporting Actress (Alexander); **Awards:** Academy Awards '76: Best Adapted Screenplay, Best Art Direction/Set Decoration, Best Sound, Best Supporting Actor (Robards); New York Film Critics Awards '76: Best Director (Pakula), Best Film, Best Supporting Actor (Robards). **VHS, Beta, LV $19.98** *WAR, BTV*

All the Right Moves 🦴🦴◁

Stefan is a high school football hero hoping for a college athletic scholarship so he can vacate the Pennsylvania mill town where he grew up. But his rebellious attitude and feuds with the ambitious coach (who wants a change of scenery himself) jeopardize Stef's career plans. Familiar material, yet strong performances and a sympathetic teen hero - who knows that football isn't the only thing in life - push this serious-minded restless youth drama into field goal range. **Hound Advisory:** That R rating is deserved, for profanity and for one scene in which Stef and his girlfriend, who'd been trying to save herself for marriage, finally have sex. Nudity, profanity, alcohol use.

"Alice in Wonderland" encounters flowers with an attitude

1983 (**R**/*Sr. High-Adult*) 90m/C Tom Cruise, Lea Thompson, Craig T. Nelson, Christopher Penn; **D:** Michael Chapman; **W:** Michael Kane. **VHS, Beta, LV** **$14.98** *FOX, FXV*

All This and Tex Avery Too!

Animation great Tex Avery and his wild sense of humor changed the style and boundaries of cartoons forever. This two-hour compilation contains 14 'toons done by Avery, featuring some of the best-known creations from the Bugs Bunny/Warner Brothers stable; a must for aficionados.
1992 (*Primary-Jr. High*) 120m/C **D:** Tex Avery. **LV $34.98** *MGM*

Allan Quartermain and the Lost City of Gold 🎞️🎞️📹

While trying to find his brother, Quartermain discovers a lost African civilization, in this weak adaptation of an H. Rider Haggard adventure. An ostensible sequel to the equally shallow "King Solomon's Mines."
1986 (**PG**/*Jr. High-Adult*) 100m/C Richard Chamberlain, Sharon Stone, James Earl Jones; **D:** Gary Nelson; **W:** Gene Quintano, Lee Reynolds. **VHS, Beta** **$9.99** *FHE, MED, VTR*

Allegro Non Troppo 🎞️🎞️🎞️

Energetic and bold collection of animated skits mixed with live-action and set to classical music. No, not Disney's "Fantasia," but a worthy Italian imitator. Watch for the evolution of life set to Ravel's "Bolero," or the memories of an abandoned housecat set to "Valse Triste" of Sibelius. Some animation fans believe this even surpasses Walt's efforts, though the appeal is to a slightly older crowd, and non-cartoon segments lack sparkle. Animator Bruno Bozetto's individual segments are also available separately on short cassettes.
1976 (**PG**/*Family*) 75m/C Maurizio Nichetti; **D:** Bruno Bozzetto. **VHS, LV** **$29.95** *BMG, IME, INJ*

Alligator 🎞️🎞️🎞️

Dumped down a toilet 12 long years ago, lonely alligator Ramon resides in the city sewers, quietly eating and sleeping. In addition to feasting on the occasional stray human, Ramon devours the animal remains of a chemical plant's experiment involving growth hormones and eventually begins to swell at an enormous rate. Nothing seems to satisfy Ramon's ever-widening appetite: not all the people or all the buildings in the whole town, but he keeps trying, much to the regret of the guilt-ridden cop and lovely scientist who get to know each other while trying to nab the gator. Mediocre special effects are only a distraction in this witty eco-monster take. **Hound Advisory:** Violence.
1980 (**R**/*Jr. High-Adult*) 94m/C Robert Forster, Lewis Teague, Jack Carter, Henry Silva, Robin Riker, Dean Jagger; **D:** Lewis Teague; **W:** John Sayles, Frank Ray Perilli. **VHS, Beta $14.98** *LIV*

Alligator Pie

Flight of fancy from the imagination of a six-year old boy involved with one adventure after another along with a bevy of make-believe friends. Originally a CBC Children's Television teleplay; based on the book by Dennis Lee.

1992 (*Preschool-Primary*) 48m/C **VHS $149.00**

Almos' a Man 🎞️🎞️📹

Black teenager feels he needs a gun to assert himself, but the first shot he fires causes a tragedy that changes his life. Another "Boyz N the Hood" L.A. rap opera? No, a wrenching adaptation of a Richard Wright short story set on a farm in the 1930s. Ambiguous ending provokes much thought even as it exasperates. From the PBS-TV "American Short Story" series, intro'd by Henry Fonda. **Hound Advisory:** Violence.
1978 (**G**/*Sr. High-College*) 51m/C Madge Sinclair, Robert Dogui, LeVar Burton. **VHS, Beta $24.95** *MON, MTI, KAR*

Almost an Angel 🎞️📹

Another in a recent spat of angels and ghosts assigned back to earth by the head office. Life-long criminal (Hogan) commits heroic act before final exit and finds himself a probationary angel returned to earth to gain permanent angel status. He befriends a wheelchair-bound man, falls in love with the guy's sister, and helps her out at a center for potential juvenile delinquents. Melodramatic and hokey in many places, driven by Hogan's crocodilian charisma. **Hound Advisory:** Salty language.
1990 (**PG**/*Jr. High-Adult*) 98m/C Paul Hogan, Linda Kozlowski, Elias Koteas, Doreen Lang, Charlton Heston; **D:** John Cornell; **W:** Paul Hogan. **VHS, LV** **$14.95** *PAR*

Almost Angels 🎞️🎞️

Two boys romp in Austria as members of the Vienna Boys Choir. Lesser sentimental Disney effort that stars the actual members of the Choir; not much of a draw for today's Nintendo-jaded young viewers, and not to be confused with the better known convent-school comedy "The Trouble With Angels" and its sequel.
1962 (*Family*) 85m/C Vincent Winter, Peter Weck, Hans Holt; **D:** Steve Previn. **VHS, Beta $69.95** *DIS*

Aloha, Bobby and Rose 🎞️🎞️📹

A mechanic and his girlfriend in L.A. become accidentally involved in an attempted robbery and murder and go on the run for Mexico, of course. Semi-satisfying drama in the surf, with fine location photography.
1974 (**PG**/*Sr. High-Adult*) 90m/C Paul LeMat, Dianne Hull, Robert Carradine, Tim McIntire, Edward James Olmos, Leigh French; **D:** Floyd Mutrux. **VHS, Beta** **$49.95** *MED*

Aloha Summer 🎞️🎞️

Six surfing teenagers of various ethnic backgrounds learn of love and life in 1959 Hawaii while riding the big wave of impending adulthood, with a splash of kung fu thrown in for good measure. Sensitive but somewhat bland. **Hound Advisory:** Roughhousing, nudity, sex.
1988 (**PG**/*Jr. High-Adult*) 97m/C Chris Makepeace, Lorie Griffin, Don Michael Paul, Sho Kosugi, Yuji Okumoto, Tia Carrere; **D:** Tommy Lee Wallace. **VHS, Beta, LV $19.98** *WAR, LHV*

Alvin & the Chipmunks: A Chipmunk Christmas

The classic Chipmunk Christmas tale has Alvin giving away his beloved harmonica to a little boy. Unfortunately, Dave has booked the trio for a Christmas concert at Carnegie Hall and expects Alvin to perform a harmonica solo. The Chipmunks perform "Christmas Don't Be Late" and more traditional Christmas carols.
1981 *(Family)* 25m/C **VHS, Beta** $12.99 *BVV, WTA*

Alvin & the Chipmunks: Alvin's Christmas Carol

Dicken's "A Christmas Carol" is given the Chipmunk spin when Alvin is a Scroogelike little chipmunk visited by three ghosts, Dave, Simon, and Theodore.
19?? *(Family)* 30m/C **VHS** $12.99 *BVV, WTA*

Alvin & the Chipmunks: Batmunk

The famous television cartoon Chipmunks spoof "Batman" features Simon as Batmunk, the Caped Crimefighter, and Alvin as the villainous Jokester, whose criminal cohorts have been stealing all the toys in the city. Additional volumes available.
199? *(Family)* 25m/C **VHS, Beta** $12.99 *BVV, WTA*

Always 🐾🐾◁

Hotshot fire-fighting pilot Dreyfuss flies low over one too many burning bushes and meets a fiery end. In the afterlife, he discovers from ethereal presence Hepburn that his spirit is destined to become a guardian angel to greenhorn fire-fighting flyboy Johnson who steals his girl's heart. Warm remake of "A Guy Named Joe," one of Spielberg's favorite movies, displays a certain self-conscious awareness of its source that occasionally becomes tiresome in spite of all those forest fires. Though both seem fresh from an over-acting seminar, Dreyfuss and Hunter eventually ignite some sparks, but Goodman steals the flaming scenery as the good bud. Old-fashioned tree-burning romance includes actual footage of the 1988 Yellowstone fire. **Hound Advisory:** Tame sexual situations; brief profanity.
1989 *(PG/Jr. High-Adult)* 123m/C Holly Hunter, Richard Dreyfuss, John Goodman, Audrey Hepburn, Brad Johnson, Marg Helgenberger, Keith David, Roberts Blossom; *D:* Steven Spielberg; *W:* Jerry Belson; *M:* John Williams. **VHS, Beta, LV** $19.95 *MCA, FCT*

Amadeus 🐾🐾🐾◁

Entertaining adaptation by Shaffer of his play about the intense rivalry between 18th century composers Antonio Salieri and Wolfgang Amadeus Mozart. Abraham's Salieri is a man who desires greatness but is tortured by envy and sorrow. His worst attacks of angst occur when he comes into contact with Hulce's Mozart, an immature, boorish genius who, despite his gifts, remains unaffected and delighted by the beauty he creates while irking the hell out of everyone around him. Terrific period piece filmed on location in Prague; excellent musical score, beautiful sets, nifty billowy costumes,

and realistic American accents for the 18th century Europeans. ♫Concert No. 27 for Pianoforte and Orchestra in B Flat Major; Ave Verum Corpus; A Quintet For Strings in E Flat; A Concerto for Clarinet and Orchestra in A Major; Number 39 in E Flat Major; Number 40 in G Minor; Number 41 in C Major. **Hound Advisory:** Mature themes; mild violence.
1984 *(PG/Jr. High-Adult)* 158m/C F. Murray Abraham, Tom Hulce, Elizabeth Berridge, Simon Callow, Roy Dotrice, Christine Ebersole, Jeffrey Jones, Kenny L. Baker, Cynthia Nixon, Vincent Schiavelli; *D:* Milos Forman; *W:* Peter Shaffer. **Award Nominations:** Academy Awards '84: Best Actor (Hulce), Best Cinematography, Best Film Editing; **Awards:** Academy Awards '84: Best Actor (Abraham), Best Adapted Screenplay, Best Art Direction/Set Decoration, Best Costume Design, Best Director (Forman), Best Makeup, Best Picture, Best Sound; Cesar Awards '85: Best Foreign Film; Directors Guild of America Awards '84: Best Director (Forman); Golden Globe Awards '85: Best Actor—Drama (Abraham), Best Director (Forman), Best Film—Drama, Best Screenplay. **VHS, Beta, LV** $14.98 *REP, GLV, BTV*

Amahl and the Night Visitors

Dramatization of Gian Carlo Menotti's English-language Christmas opera that was written specifically for TV in 1951. Amahl is a poor, crippled boy in ancient Jerusalem whose widowed mother has unexpected guests - the Three Kings on their way to visit to the newborn Christ. Beautifully filmed on location in Israel, and a rare example of opera that's accessible to younger viewers. For some others, see "The Maestro's Company" and "The Tales of Hoffmann."
1978 *(Jr. High-Adult)* 120m/C Teresa Stratas, Giorgio Tozzi, Willard White, Robert Sapolsky. **VHS, Beta** $19.95 *HMV, MVD, KAR*

Amazing Adventures of Joe 90

Another of Britain's 'Super Marionation' spectaculars from Gerry and Sylvia Anderson, who perfected a painstaking but undeniably popular method of doing live-action sci-fi epics using miniature sets, expert special f/x, and casts made up entirely of puppets. In this sample, Joe is a 9-year-old secret agent who is the equal of any adult when it comes to an appetite for adventure. These tapes include three outings; for other puppet productions by Andersons, see "Thunderbirds" and "Stingray."
1968 *(Preschool-Primary)* 90m/C **VHS, Beta** *FHE*

The Amazing Dobermans 🐾🐾

Family-oriented pooch performance piece featuring longtime song-and-dance favorite Astaire in one of his odder roles as a reformed con man whose five trained dobermans help an undercover agent in foiling a gambling and extortion racket. The last in a series that includes "The Daring Dobermans" and "The Doberman Gang."
1976 *(G/Family)* 96m/C Fred Astaire, Barbara Eden, James Franciscus, Jack Carter, Billy Barty; *D:* Byron Ross Chudnow; *M:* Alan Silvestri. **VHS, Beta** $9.95 *MED*

Amazing Grace & Chuck 🐾🐾

Upon visiting a missile site in Montana, 12-year-old Little Leaguer Chuck begins a passive protest against nuclear weapons by refusing to play until nations forge a peace agreement. Hearing the news, pro-basketball star Amazing Grace Smith (Denver Nugget English) also quits his team. Soon athletes everywhere join the movement, US and Soviet

leaders take notice. Hey, it could happen ... right? Gentle, somewhat outdated political fantasy with good intentions but lacking coherence and plausibility. **Hound Advisory:** Salty language.
1987 **(PG**/*Preschool)* 115m/C Jamie Lee Curtis, Gregory Peck, William L. Petersen, Joshua Zuehlke, Alex English; ***D:*** Mike Newell; ***M:*** Elmer Bernstein. **VHS, Beta, LV** $19.99 *HBO*

Amazing Mr. Blunden ❙❙

"Back to the Future" British-style, as two children in 1918 are beseeched by phantom kids from a century earlier to journey back via time-travel potion to stop a murder plot by wicked 1818 in-laws. Fine Dickensian atmosphere at times (actors personally wish the viewer a hearty "Goodbye!" at the end), but slow-moving. Lousy f/x make one appreciate the first-rate production values in even the dreariest Disney fantasies. Adapted from Antonia Barber's novel, "The Ghosts." **Hound Advisory:** Alcohol use, salty language, roughhousing.
1972 **(G**/*Family)* 100m/C Laurence Naismith, Lynne Frederick, Garry Miller, Marc Granger, Rosalyn London, Diana Dors; ***D:*** Lionel Jeffries; ***M:*** Elmer Bernstein. **VHS, Beta** $19.95 *MED*

The Amazing Spider-Man

Collection of Spider-Man's most exciting adventures from Saturday-morning cartoons.
1982 *(Family)* 100m/C **VHS, Beta** $24.98 *MCA*

American Anthem ❙

Young gymnast must choose between family responsibilities or the parallel bars. Olympic gymnast Gaylord makes his movie debut but doesn't get the gold. Good fare for young tumblers, but that's about it. Followed by two of the films' music videos and tape-ads featuring Max Headroom.
1986 **(PG-13**/*Jr. High-Adult)* 100m/C Mitch Gaylord, Janet Jones, Michelle Phillips, Michael Pataki; ***D:*** Albert Magnoli; ***M:*** Alan Silvestri. **VHS, Beta, LV** $19.98 *LHV, WAR*

American Boyfriends ❙❙

Lackluster sequel to "My American Cousin," nevertheless of interest to viewers following the emotional travails of restless rural Canadian girl Sandy, now a teenager. Voyaging south to Oregon for the wedding of her bad-boy cousin Butch (on whom she had a crush in the original), Sandy and a friend spar with first romance. **Hound Advisory:** Salty language, mature themes.
1989 **(PG-13**/*Jr. High-Adult)* 90m/C Margaret Langrick, John Wildman, Jason Blicker, Lisa Repo Martell; ***D:*** Sandy Wilson; ***W:*** Sandy Wilson. **VHS, Beta, LV** $79.95 *LIV*

An American Christmas Carol ❙❙

Charles Dickens' classic story retold with limited charm and tacked-on history lessons in a made-for-television effort starring the Fonz. This time a miserly Depression-era industrialist (young Winkler, in heavy age makeup) learns the true meaning of Christmas through the usual trio of ghosts.
1979 *(Family)* 98m/C Henry Winkler, David Wayne, Dorian Harewood; ***D:*** Eric Till; ***M:*** Hagood Hardy. **VHS, Beta** $12.98 *VES, LIV*

American Dreamer ❙❙

Housewife wins a trip to Paris as a prize from a mystery writing contest. Silly from a blow on the head, she begins living the fictional life of her favorite literary adventure. Sporadic comedy with a good cast wandering about courtesy of a clumsy screenplay. **Hound Advisory:** Violence and sex.
1984 **(PG**/*Sr. High-Adult)* 105m/C JoBeth Williams, Tom Conti, Giancarlo Giannini, Coral Browne, James Staley; ***D:*** Rick Rosenthal; ***M:*** Lewis Furey. **VHS, Beta** $19.98 *FOX*

American Flyers ❙❙❙☙

Two competitive brothers train for a grueling three-day bicycle race in Colorado while tangling with personal drama, including fears that one of them may have inherited dad's health problems and is sure to drop dead during the home stretch. Written by bike movie specialist Steve Tesich (who scripted the far superior "Breaking Away") with a lot of the usual cliches - the last bike ride, battling siblings, eventual understanding -gracefully overridden by fine photography. Interesting performances, especially Chong as a patient girlfriend. **Hound Advisory:** Mature themes, salty language.
1985 **(PG-13**/*Jr. High-Adult)* 113m/C Kevin Costner, David Marshall Grant, Rae Dawn Chong, Alexandra Paul, John Amos, Janice Rule, Robert Townsend, Jennifer Grey, Luca Bercovici; ***D:*** John Badham; ***W:*** Steve Tesich; ***M:*** Lee Ritenour, Greg Mathieson. **VHS, Beta, LV** $19.98 *WAR*

American Folk Heroes and Tall Tales

Collection of animated versions of various folk tales. Included are "The Legend of Sleepy Hollow," "John Henry," "Johnny Appleseed," "Paul Bunyan," "Pecos Bill," and "Rip Van Winkle."
1988 *(Primary-Jr. High)* 53m/C **VHS** $132.00

American Graffiti ❙❙❙❙

Teens of every era can relate to George Lucas' take on the more innocent early '60s. It's all one hectic but typical summer night; California high school friends have just graduated, unsure what the next big step is. They spend the hours cruising, dating, listening to rock'n'roll radio (legendary D.J. Wolfman Jack's appearance is magic) and meeting at the drive-in. Honest, humane, and consistently brilliant, with a cast of mostly unknowns who went on to stardom. Partial inspiration for TV's "Happy Days" was followed by less successful, "More American Graffiti." **Hound Advisory:** Alcohol use.
1973 **(PG**/*Family)* 112m/C Richard Dreyfuss, Ron Howard, Cindy Williams, MacKenzie Phillips, Paul LeMat, Charles Martin Smith, Suzanne Somers, Candy Clark, Harrison Ford, Bo Hopkins, Joe Spano, Kathleen Quinlan, Wolfman Jack; ***D:*** George Lucas; ***W:*** George Lucas, Gloria Katz, Willard Huyck. **Award Nominations:** Academy Awards '73: Best Director (Lucas), Best Film Editing, Best Picture, Best Story & Screenplay, Best Supporting Actress (Clark); **Awards:** Golden Globe Awards '74: Best Film—Musical/Comedy. **VHS, Beta, LV** $14.95 *MCA, FCT*

American Heart ❙❙❙☙

Jack (Bridges) is a suspicious ex-con, newly released from prison, with few prospects and little hope. He also has a teenaged son, Nick (Furlong), he barely remembers but who desperately wants to have his father back in his life. Jack is

reluctantly persuaded to let Nick stay with him in his cheap hotel where Nick befriends fellow resident, Molly, a teenage hooker, and other castoff street kids. Superb performances by both male leads - Furlong, both yearning and frustrated as he pursues his dream of having a family, and Bridges as the tough parolee, unwilling to open his heart. Hardboiled, poignant, and powerful. **Hound Advisory:** Profanity; brutality; brief nudity; alcohol use; drug use; mature themes.
1992 (R/ *Sr. High-Adult*) 114m/C Jeff Bridges, Edward Furlong, Lucinda Jenney, Tracey Kapisky, Don Harvey, Margaret Welsh; **D:** Martin Bell; **W:** Peter Silverman; **M:** James Newton Howard. **Award Nominations:** Independent Spirit Awards '94: Best Cinematography, Best First Feature, Best Supporting Actor (Furlong), Best Supporting Actress (Jenney); **Awards:** Independent Spirit Awards '94: Best Actor (Bridges). **VHS, LV $92.98** *LIV, BTV*

An American in Paris 🎬🎬🎬🎬

Lavish, imaginative musical features a sweeping score, and knockout choreography by Kelly. Ex-G.I. Kelly stays on in Paris after the war to study painting, supported in his efforts by rich American Foch, who hopes to acquire a little extra attention. But Kelly loves the lovely Caron, unfortunately engaged to an older gent. Highlight is an astonishing 17-minute ballet which holds the record for longest movie dance number -and one of the more expensive, pegged at over half a million for a month of filming. For his efforts, the dance king won a special Oscar citation. While it sure looks like Paris, most of it was filmed in MGM studios. ♫S'Wonderful; I Got Rhythm; Embraceable You; Love Is Here To Stay; Tra-La-La; I'll Build a Stairway to Paradise; Nice Work If You Can Get It; By Strauss; Concerto in F (3rd Movement).
1951 (*Family*) 113m/C Gene Kelly, Leslie Caron, Oscar Levant, Nina Foch, Georges Guetary; **D:** Vincente Minnelli; **W:** Alan Jay Lerner; **M:** George Gershwin, Ira Gershwin. **Award Nominations:** Academy Awards '51: Best Director (Minnelli), Best Film Editing; **Awards:** Academy Awards '51: Best Art Direction/Set Decoration (Color), Best Color Cinematography, Best Costume Design (Color), Best Picture, Best Story & Screenplay, Best Score; Golden Globe Awards '52: Best Film—Musical/Comedy; National Board of Review Awards '51: 10 Best Films of the Year. **VHS, Beta, LV, 8mm $14.95** *MGM, TLF, BTV*

An American Summer 🎬🎬

Chicago kid Tom is stuck with his spacey aunt in California during the summer of '78. At first this convivial coming-of-age tale looks like a exercise in nostalgia, then you note a familiar fence-painting gag, a rascal named Fin, an abandoned mine ... It's really an unpretentious adaptation of Mark Twain's "Adventures of Tom Sawyer," twisted to fit modern times. Clever gimmick, but no improvement over the original. **Hound Advisory:** While Tom and Huck smoked forbidden tobacco, their counterparts here do marijuana with glass-eyed satisfaction. The Injun Joe character, meanwhile, is a killer pusher. Profanity.
1990 (*Family*) 100m/C Brian Austin Green, Joanna Kerns, Michael Landes. **VHS** *NO*

An American Tail 🎬🎬🎬

While emigrating to America in the 1880s, young Russian mouse Fievel gets separated from his family and learns to live by his wits in old New York's nooks and crannies. The bad guys are of course cats, who exploit the newcomer mice as cheap labor. Obviously producer Steven Spielberg had a high-

minded history lesson planned with the sentimental, metaphorical plot, but the kids will keep watching for the excellent animation (by the Don Bluth Studios, a collection of expatriate Disney artists) and lively character voices. Aggressive marketing tried to create Fievel Fever, but the kid's no Mickey (though he did earn a sequel). Soundtrack includes the platinum selling song "Somewhere Out There."
1986 (G/*Family*) 81m/C **D:** Don Bluth; **M:** James Horner; **V:** Dom DeLuise, Madeline Kahn, Phillip Glasser, Christopher Plummer, Nehemiah Persoff, Will Ryan, John Finnegan, Cathianne Blore. **VHS, Beta, LV $24.98** *MCA, WTA, APD*

An American Tail: Fievel Goes West 🎬🎬🎬

Fievel and the Mousekewitz family head west to seek their fortune, and the boy hero learns his hero Marshall Wylie Burp, a once-mighty lawdog, has almost given up fighting bad guys. The second Fievel epic got treated like vermin by critics, but it's actually a bit better than the first "American Tail," with superior animation and clever genre spoofs that older viewers will enjoy (like a great cover version of "Rawhide.") The first cartoon feature made entirely by Steven Spielberg's Amblimation studio. Laser edition is letterboxed and features chapter stops.
1991 (G/*Family*) 75m/C **D:** Phil Nibbelink, Simon Wells; **W:** Flint Dille; **M:** James Horner; **V:** John Cleese, Dom DeLuise, Phillip Glasser, Amy Irving, Jon Lovitz, Cathy Cavadini, Nehemiah Persoff, Erica Yohn, James Stewart. **VHS, Beta, LV $24.98** *MCA, WTA*

Amos and Andrew 🎬🎬

Occasionally embarrassing attempt at comedy stops short of endorsing the stereotypes it tries to parody. Prizewinning African-American author Andrew Sterling (Jackson) is seen moving into a house on an island previously reserved for uptight white folks, and the neighbors call the cops, assuming he's a thief. Chief of police Coleman eagerly gets into the act, then exploits drifter Amos (Cage) in a cover-up attempt when he realizes his mistake. Amos and Andrew are soon housemates under siege by the police, resulting in chaos, comedy, and a mighty poor lesson in race relations. **Hound Advisory:** Violence and profanity.
1993 (PG-13/*Jr. High-Adult*) 96m/C Nicolas Cage, Samuel L. Jackson, Michael Lerner, Margaret Colin, Giancarlo Esposito, Dabney Coleman, Bob Balaban, Aimee Graham, Brad Dourif, Chelcie Ross, Jodi Long; **D:** E. Max Frye; **W:** E. Max Frye; **M:** Richard Gibbs. **VHS, LV $19.95** *COL, IME, NLC*

Amy 🎬🎬🎬

Superior Disney drama that was originally intended for television but was judged special enough for theaters. In the early 1900s, young housewife Amy, following the death of her deaf son, finds a sense of purpose in life that makes her leave behind a domineering husband to teach at a school for the deaf and blind. Eventually she organizes a football game between the handicapped kids and the other children in the neighborhood. Not as sentimental as one might dread.
1981 (G/*Family*) 100m/C Jenny Agutter, Barry Newman, Kathleen Nolan, Margaret O'Brien, Nanette Fabray, Chris Robinson, Lou Fant; **D:** Vincent McEveety. **VHS, Beta $69.95** *DIS*

Anansi

Anansi is a spider who manages to outwit a prideful snake but then gets caught up in his own lies. Adaptation of a Jamaican folktale which features the reggae music of UB40. One of a terrific video storybook series "Rabbit Ears: We All Have Tales," with celebrities reciting folk legends and fairytales from different nations and cultures to wonderful (non-animated) illustrations. Other productions include "The Boy Who Drew Cats," "Br'er Rabbit and the Wonderful Tar Baby," "The Fool and the Flying Ship," "The Emperor's New Clothes," "Finn McCoul," "King Midas and the Golden Touch," "Koi and the Kola Nuts," "The Legend of Sleepy Hollow," "Paul Bunyan," "Pecos Bill," "Puss in Boots," "Stormalong," "Thumbelina," "The Ugly Duckling," and many others; see individual listings for descriptions.
1991 *(Family)* 30m/C **M:** UB40. **VHS $9.95** *FCT, MLT*

Anchors Aweigh ♫♫♫

Snappy big-budget (for then) musical about two horny sailors, one a girl-happy dancer and the other a shy singer. While on leave in Hollywood they return a lost urchin to his sister. The four of them try to infiltrate a movie studio to win an audition for the girl from maestro Iturbi. Kelly's famous dance with Jerry the cartoon Mouse (of "Tom and Jerry" fame) is the second instance of combining live action and animation. The young and handsome Sinatra's easy crooning and Grayson's near operatic soprano are blessed with music and lyrics by Styne and Cahn. Lots of fun, with conductor-pianist Iturbi contributing. ♫We Hate to Leave; I Fall in Love Too Easily; The Charm of You; The Worry Song; Jalousie; All of a Sudden My Heart Sings; I Begged Her; What Makes the Sun Set?; Waltz Serenade.
1945 *(Family)* 139m/C Frank Sinatra, Gene Kelly, Kathryn Grayson, Jose Iturbi, Sharon McManus, Dean Stockwell, Carlos Ramirez, Pamela Britton; **D:** George Sidney; **M:** Jules Styne, Sammy Cahn. **Award Nominations:** Academy Awards '45: Best Actor (Kelly), Best Color Cinematography, Best Picture, Best Song ("I Fall in Love Too Easily"); **Awards:** Academy Awards '45: Best Score. **VHS, Beta, LV $19.98** *MGM*

And Baby Makes Six ♫♫◁

TV drama about an unexpected pregnancy that creates new challenges for a couple with three grown children. Dewhurst is excellent as usual. Followed by "Baby Comes Home."
1979 *(Jr. High-Adult)* 100m/C Colleen Dewhurst, Warren Oates, Maggie Cooper, Mildred Dunnock, Timothy Hutton, Allyn Ann McLerie; **D:** Waris Hussein; **W:** Shelley List. **VHS, 8mm** *NO*

And Now for Something Completely Different ♫♫♫

A compilation of skits from BBC-television's "Monty Python's Flying Circus" featuring Monty Python's own weird, hilarious brand of humor. Sketches include "The Upper Class Twit of the Year Race," "Hell's Grannies" and "The Townswomen's Guild Reconstruction of Pearl Harbour." A great introduction to Python for the uninitiated, or a chance for the converted to see their favorite sketches again.

1972 (PG/ *Sr. High-Adult)* 89m/C John Cleese, Michael Palin, Eric Idle, Graham Chapman, Terry Gilliam, Terry Jones; **D:** Ian McNaughton; **W:** John Cleese, Michael Palin, Graham Chapman, Terry Gilliam, Terry Jones. **VHS, Beta, LV $19.95** *COL, TVC*

And Now Miguel ♫♫

Plodding tale of a young boy who wants to take over as head shepherd of his family's flock and must prove himself on the grazing trail. Filmed in New Mexico, it's scenic but a bit of a drag in spite of child actor Cardi's competent performance. Based on the novel by Joseph Krumgold.
1966 *(Jr. High-Adult)* 95m/C Pat Cardi, Michael Ansara, Guy Stockwell, Clu Gulager, Joe De Santis, Pilar Del Rey, Buck Taylor; **D:** James B. Clark. **VHS $24.95** *NOS*

And the Children Shall Lead

News of Martin Luther King's civil rights movement comes to a small town in Mississippi in 1964, dividing two once-peaceful families. One is affluent and white, the other are the kinfolk of their longtime black cook. The point is made that hope for racial equality lies with the attitudes of their children -well, some of their children, anyway. This drama done for the "WonderWorks" TV series is special in that it never simplifies the issues of racism, nor disrespects its characters, even the most bigoted ones.
1985 *(Family)* 60m/C Danny Glover, LeVar Burton, Pam Potillo, Denise Nicholas, Andrew Prine; **D:** Michael Pressman. **VHS $29.95** *PME, PTB, HMV*

And You Thought Your Parents Were Weird! ♫♫

Whiz kids invent an R2D2-style robot that gets possessed by the spirit of their deceased dad. The cutie gadget provides fatherly guidance and companionship for mom. When it turns out his demise wasn't an accident, machine and sons set out to foil the evildoers. Silly family fantasy, in slightly questionable taste but harmless.
1991 (PG/ *Jr. High-Adult)* 92m/C Marcia Strassman, Joshua Miller, Edan Gross, John Quade, Sam Behrens, Susan Gibney, Gustav Vintas, Eric Walker; **D:** Tony Cookson; **W:** Tony Cookson; **M:** Randall Miller; **V:** Alan Thicke, Richard Libertini. **VHS $92.95** *VMK*

Andre ♫♫◁

Feel-good human-animal interaction from the man from snowy river. True story of a seal with an inclination to swim hundreds of miles every summer to visit the family in Maine that saved his life. Sort of a "Free Willy" in reverse with an appealing smaller sea mammal who does clever tricks while consorting with likewise appealing small human Majorino, portraying a shy little girl who blossoms with the arrival of Andre. Created a brief moment of controversy when it was revealed that Andre was actually a sea lion, not a seal as depicted in the original story. **Hound Advisory:** Salty language.
1994 (G/ *Family)* 94m/C Keith Carradine, Tina Majorino, Chelsea Field, Keith Szarabajka, Shane Meier; **D:** George Miller; **W:** Dana Baratta. **VHS** *NYR*

Androcles and the Lion ♫♫◁

Stagebound Hollywood production of the George Bernard Shaw play that uses the famous Aesop's fable as a jumping-off

Fievel celebrates the holidays in "An American Tail"

point for a satire of imperial Rome, where a tailor saves Christians from a hungry lion he had previously befriended. Sharp dialogue, geared more for adult sensibilities than kids, but still a semi-satisfying experience.
1952 (*Jr. High-Adult*) 105m/B Jean Simmons, Alan Young, Victor Mature, Robert Newton, Maurice Evans; *D:* Chester Erskine. **VHS, Beta $19.95** *COL, SUE*

The Andromeda Strain 🎬🎬◁

A satellite falls back to earth carrying a deadly bacteria that must be identified in time to save the population from extermination. The tension inherent in the bestselling Michael Crichton novel is talked down by a boring cast. Also available in letter-box format.
1971 (*G/Family*) 131m/C Arthur Hill, David Wayne, James Olson, Kate Reid, Paula Kelly; *D:* Robert Wise. **VHS, Beta, LV $59.95** *MCA*

Andy and the Airwave Rangers 🎬🎬

Sci-fi thriller scaled down for kid viewers. Anna discovers she has telepathic powers. Her mother reveals the schoolgirl's actually a clone, psychically in tune with her widely scattered identical 'sisters.' Based on the young-adult novel by Mildred Ames. **Hound Advisory:** Violence.
1989 (*Family*) 75m/C Dianne Kay, Vince Edwards, Bo Svenson, Richard Thomas, Erik Estrada; *D:* Deborah Brock. **VHS, LV $79.95** *COL*

Andy Hardy Gets Spring Fever 🎬🎬

Andy falls for a beautiful acting teacher, and then goes into a funk when he finds she's engaged. Judge Hardy and the gang help heal the big wound in his heart. A lesser entry (and the seventh) from the popular series.
1939 (*Family*) 88m/B Mickey Rooney, Lewis Stone, Ann Rutherford, Fay Holden, Cecilia Parker, Sara Haden, Helen Gilbert; *D:* Woodbridge S. Van Dyke. **VHS, Beta $19.95** *MGM*

Andy Hardy Meets Debutante 🎬🎬◁

Garland's second entry in series, wherein Andy meets and falls foolishly for glamorous debutante Lewis with Betsy's help while family is on visit to New York. Judy/Betsy sings "I'm Nobody's Baby" and "Singing in Rain." Also available with "Love Finds Andy Hardy" on laser disc.
1940 (*Family*) 86m/B Mickey Rooney, Judy Garland, Lewis Stone, Ann Rutherford, Fay Holden, Sara Haden, Cecilia Parker, Diana Lewis, Tom Neal; *D:* George B. Seitz. **VHS, Beta, LV $19.95** *MGM*

Andy Hardy's Double Life 🎬🎬◁

In this entertaining installment from the Andy Hardy series, Andy proposes marriage to two girls at the same time and gets in quite a pickle when they both accept. Williams makes an early screen splash.
1942 (*Family*) 91m/B Mickey Rooney, Lewis Stone, Ann Rutherford, Fay Holden, Sara Haden, Cecilia Parker, Esther Williams, William Lundigan, Susan Peters, Robert (Bobby) Blake; *D:* George B. Seitz. **VHS, Beta $19.95** *MGM, MLB*

Andy Hardy's Private Secretary 🎬🎬

After Andy fails his high school finals, he gets help from a sympathetic faculty member. As the secretary, Grayson makes a good first impression in one of her early screen

appearances. The Hardy series was often used as a training ground for new MGM talent.
1941 (*Family*) 101m/B Mickey Rooney, Kathryn Grayson, Lewis Stone, Fay Holden, Ian Hunter, Gene Reynolds, Sara Haden; *D:* George B. Seitz. **VHS, Beta $19.95** *MGM*

Angelo My Love 🎬🎬🎬

Compassionate docudrama about New York's modern gypsy community. Follows the adventures of 12-year-old Angelo Evans, the streetwise son of a fortune teller, who, with a fresh view, explores the ups and downs of his family's life. Duvall financed the effort and cast non-professional actors in this charming tale of reality and fairy-tale. **Hound Advisory:** Profanity.
1983 (*R/Sr. High-Adult*) 91m/C Angelo Evans, Michael Evans, Steve "Patalay" Tsiginoff, Cathy Kitchen, Millie Tsiginoff; *D:* Robert Duvall; *M:* Michael Kamen. **VHS, Beta, LV $59.95** *COL*

Angels in the Outfield 🎬🎬◁

Remake of the 1951 fantasy about a lowly baseball team who, along with some heavenly help animated by Disney, find themselves on a winning streak. The new lineup includes Glover as manager of the hapless California Angels, Danza as a washed-up pitcher, and Lloyd as captain of the celestial spirits. Gordon-Levitt plays the foster child who believes he'll get his family back together if the Angels win the pennant. Familiar ground still yields good, heartfelt family fare. Oakland A's third baseman Carney Lansford served as technical advisor, molding actors into fair semblance of baseball team. Excellent special effects from Magic Lantern. **Hound Advisory:** Salty language.
1994 (*PG/Family*) 102m/C Danny Glover, Tony Danza, Christopher Lloyd, Brenda Fricker, Ben Johnson, Joseph Gordon-Levitt, Jay O. Sanders; *D:* William Dear; *W:* Holly Goldberg Sloan. **VHS**

Animal Behavior 🎬◁

Speech researcher and a music professor have a rocky campus romance, brought together in part by a lab chimp with a sign-language vocabulary, kept apart by dumb mixups. The monkey (and a subplot about an autistic child) may get kids slightly interested, but adults will find this flaccid farce an unrewarding experiment. **Hound Advisory:** Profanity, sex talk.
1989 (*PG/Jr. High-Adult*) 79m/C Karen Allen, Armand Assante, Holly Hunter, Josh Mostel, Richard Libertini; *D:* Jenny Bowen; *W:* Susan Rice; *M:* Cliff Eidelman. **VHS, Beta, LV $89.99** *HBO*

Animal Crackers 🎬🎬🎬

Kid viewers haven't embraced the Marx Brothers comedy team as enthusiastically as they have the Stooges. But give movie Marxism a chance, especially with this freeform hilarity loosely plotted around the theft of a painting at a wealthy estate where Capt. Rufus T. Spaulding (Groucho) is a houseguest and Zeppo, Chico and Harpo are party crashers. Only a boring romantic/musical subplot without the Brothers (a common Hollywood time-filler in those days) prevents this from being nonstop laughs. The one that gave the world the line "One morning I shot an elephant in my pajamas..."

"Andre" models the latest in tropical fashions (1994)

1930 (G/*Family*) 98m/B Groucho Marx, Chico Marx, Harpo Marx, Zeppo Marx, Lillian Roth, Margaret Dumont, Louis Sorin, Hal Thompson, Richard Greig; *D:* Victor Neerman; *W:* Morrie Ryskind. **VHS, Beta, LV** $14.98 *MCA, FCT*

Animal Farm 🦴🦴🦴

British feature cartoon (a rarity all in itself) based on the George Orwell allegorical satire of Communism. Barnyard animals successfully overthrow their masters. Now what to do? Napoleon the power-crazed pig knows, and using propaganda and mob psychology, he takes control and turns the farm into a totalitarian dictatorship even worse than before. A bit talky for kiddie viewers, but it puts across Orwell's important ideas with some success.
1955 (*Family*) 73m/C *D:* John Halas, Joy Batchelor; *V:* Maurice Denham, Gordon Heath. **VHS, Beta, LV, 8mm** $24.95 *VYY, KUI, VTR*

Animals Are Beautiful People

After Jamie Uys became known worldwide for "The Gods Must Be Crazy," home video revived this earlier theatrical documentary feature, a hit in his native South Africa. Uys brings his trademark wit and thoughtful sentiment to footage of baboons, elephants, cheetahs and other wildlife of the veldt.
1984 (*Family*) 92m/C *D:* Jamie Uys. **VHS, Beta** $14.95 *WAR*

Animalympics: Winter Games

Made-for-TV cartoon companion to the feature "Animalympics" with the characters of the ZOO Network covering the first Animal Winter Games.
1982 (*Primary-Jr. High*) 30m/C *V:* Gilda Radner, Billy Crystal, Harry Shearer, Michael Fremer. **VHS** $14.95 *LIV, WTA, FHE*

Anne of Avonlea 🦴🦴🦴🦴

Equally excellent mini-series sequel to "Anne of Green Gables" in which the heroine grows up and discovers romance. The same cast returns and Sullivan continues his tradition of lavish filming on Prince Edward Island and beautiful costumes. Based on the characters from L.M. Montgomery's classic novels "Anne of Avonlea," "Anne of the Island," and "Anne of Windy Poplars." The Canadian Broadcasting Corporation, PBS, and Disney worked together on this WonderWorks production. On two tapes.
1987 (*Family*) 224m/C Megan Follows, Colleen Dewhurst, Wendy Hiller, Frank Converse, Patricia Hamilton, Schuyler Grant, Jonathan Crombie, Rosemary Dunsmore; *D:* Kevin Sullivan; *W:* Kevin Sullivan; *M:* Hagood Hardy. **VHS, Beta, LV** $29.95 *KUI, BVV, DIS*

Anne of Green Gables 🦴🦴🦴

Lonely Canadian couple adopt orphan girl Anne, who keeps them on their toes with her lively imagination and wins a permanent place in their hearts. Warm but loose adaptation of Lucy Maud Montgomery's popular novel is entertaining, though no match for the 1985 remake. Lead actress was previously known as Dawn O'Day but identified with the fictional heroine so closely she assumed Anne's name in real life.
1934 (*Family*) 79m/B Anne Shirley, Tom Brown, O.P. Heggie; *D:* George Nichols; *M:* Max Steiner. **VHS, Beta** $19.98 *RKO, TTC*

Anne of Green Gables 🦴🦴🦴🦴

Splendid production of the famous Lucy Maud Montgomery classic about a young orphan girl growing to young adulthood with the help of a crusty old brother and sister. With beautiful Prince Edward Island as a backdrop and splendid period costumes, the characters come to life under Sullivan's direction. One of the few instances where an adaptation lives up to (if not exceeds) the quality of the original novel. A WonderWorks presentation that was made with the cooperation of the Disney channel, the Canadian Broadcasting Corporation, and PBS. Followed by "Anne of Avonlea." On two tapes.
1985 (*Family*) 197m/C Megan Follows, Colleen Dewhurst, Richard Farnsworth, Patricia Hamilton, Schuyler Grant, Jonathan Crombie, Marilyn Lightstone, Charmion King, Rosemary Radcliffe, Jackie Burroughs; *D:* Kevin Sullivan; *W:* Kevin Sullivan, Joe Weisenfeld; *M:* Hagood Hardy. **VHS, Beta, LV** $29.95 *KUI, BVV, IGP*

Annie 🦴🦴🦴

Stagy big-budget adaptation of the comic-strip-derived Broadway musical has an ideal cast, ideal music, less-than-ideal script that tends to sag under the weight of colossal production values (did they really need the roller-skating elephants?). Entertaining nonetheless, with Burnett a standout as orphanage superintendant Miss Hannigan, scheming to part Little Orphan Annie from her adoptive millionaire Daddy Warbucks. ♫Tomorrow; It's the Hard Knock Life; Maybe; I Think I'm Gonna Like It Here; Little Girls; We Got Annie; Let's Go to the Movies; You're Never Fully Dressed Without a Smile; Easy Street.
Hound Advisory: Alcohol use.
1982 (PG/*Family*) 128m/C Aileen Quinn, Carol Burnett, Albert Finney, Bernadette Peters, Ann Reinking, Tim Curry; *D:* John Huston; *M:* Ralph Burns. **VHS, Beta, LV, 8mm** $14.95 *COL, FCT, MLT*

Annie Hall 🦴🦴🦴🦴

Acclaimed coming-of-cinematic-age film for Allen is based in part on his own life. His love affair with Hall/Keaton is chronicled as an episodic, wistful comedy commenting on family, love, loneliness, communicating, maturity, driving, city life, careers, and various other topics. Abounds with classic scenes, including future star Goldblum and his mantra at a cocktail party; Allen and the lobster pot; and Allen, Keaton, a bathroom, a tennis racket, and a spider. The film operates on many levels, as does Keaton's wardrobe, which started a major fashion trend. Don't blink or you'll miss several future stars in bit parts. Expertly shot by Gordon Willis. **Hound Advisory:** Profanity, sex talk.
1977 (PG/*Sr. High-Adult*) 94m/C Woody Allen, Diane Keaton, Tony Roberts, Paul Simon, Shelley Duvall, Carol Kane, Colleen Dewhurst, Christopher Walken, Janet Margolin, John Glover, Jeff Goldblum, Sigourney Weaver, Marshall McLuhan, Beverly D'Angelo, Shelley Hack; *D:* Woody Allen; *W:* Woody Allen, Marshall Brickman. **Award Nominations:** Academy Awards '77: Best Actor (Allen); **Awards:** Academy Awards '77: Best Actress (Keaton), Best Director (Allen), Best Original Screenplay, Best Picture; British Academy Awards '77: Best Actress (Keaton), Best Director (Allen), Best Film; Directors Guild of America Awards '77: Best Director (Allen); Golden Globe Awards '78: Best Actress—Musical/Comedy (Keaton); National Board of Review Awards '77: 10 Best Films of the Year, Best Actress (Keaton); National Society of Film Critics Awards '77: Best Actress (Keaton), Best Film. **VHS, Beta, LV** $14.95 *MGM, FOX, VYG*

Annie Oakley

This biography of the acclaimed shooting star covers her career from age 15 to retirement, including some actual silent footage of Miss Oakley filmed by Thomas Edison in 1923. Made for television. From the "Tall Tales & Legends" series by Shelly Duvall.
1985 (*Family*) 52m/C Jamie Lee Curtis, Cliff DeYoung, Brian Dennehy; **D:** Michael Lindsay-Hogg. **VHS, Beta $19.98** *FOX*

Another Stakeout 🎬🎬

Sequel six years after the original finds Dreyfuss and Estevez partnered again for another stakeout, this time to keep an eye on Moriarty, a reluctant witness against the Mob. The two spying and squabbling detectives find themselves in an upscale neighborhood where blending in proves difficult. O'Donnell is a breath of fresh air as a wisecracking assistant district attorney tagging along on the stakeout, much to the boys' distress. Stowe briefly reprises her role as Dreyfuss' girlfriend. Writer Kouf reportedly had difficulty penning the script, obviously settling for the tried and true. **Hound Advisory:** Profanity and violence.
1993 (**PG-13**/*Sr. High-Adult*) 109m/C Richard Dreyfuss, Emilio Estevez, Rosie O'Donnell, Cathy Moriarty, Madeleine Stowe, John Rubinstein, Marcia Strassman, Dennis Farina, Miguel Ferrer; **D:** John Badham; **W:** Jim Kouf. **VHS, LV $96.83** *TOU*

The Ant and the Aardvark

Collection of theatrical short cartoons by the animators of the "Pink Panther" series, featuring a endless struggle for supremacy between the title ant-agonists.
1969 (*Preschool-Jr. High*) 32m/C **VHS, Beta $14.95** *MGM, WTA*

Antarctica 🎬🎬

Unique adventure, based on a true incident of a Japanese 1957 Polar expedition forced by storms to evacuate and abandon their loyal team of sled dogs to certain death. Much later humans returned to find some huskies still surviving. Movie speculates what happened in between, as the canines battle against starvation, icequakes, killer whales, the unknown - and not always winning. Whenever a dog dies its freeze-frame 'obit' is posted for maximum impact, and young pooch-lovers may be upset. A Far East box-office sensation, worth discovering on cassette, although the US video version (dubbed in English) is technically uneven. Fine musical score by Vangelis. **Hound Advisory:** Animal violence.
1984 (*Family*) 112m/C Ken Takakura, Masako Natsume, Keiko Oginome; **D:** Koreyoshi Kurahara; **M:** Vangelis. **VHS, Beta $59.98** *FOX*

Any Which Way You Can 🎬🎬

Those with an interest in rowdy orangutan adventures will appreciate sequel to "Every Which Way But Loose." Bad brawler Philo Beddoe and his buddy Clyde, the orangutan, return for another of life's little lessons. This time Philo is tempted to take part in a big bout for a large cash prize. Clyde steals scenes, brightening up the no-brainer story.
1980 (**PG**/*Jr. High-Adult*) 116m/C Clint Eastwood, Sondra Locke, Ruth Gordon, Harry Guardino; **D:** Buddy Van Horn. **VHS, Beta, LV $19.98** *WAR*

The Apple Dumpling Gang 🎬🎬

Three frisky, too-cute children in the Wild West find a giant gold nugget and stage a bank robbery to protect their interests, but things don't go quite as planned. Unmistakably mid-70s Disney (not much of a compliment), marking the first of several collaborations between Knotts and Conway as a kiddie-comedy team. **Hound Advisory:** Roughhousing.
1975 (**G**/*Family*) 100m/C Bill Bixby, Susan Clark, Don Knotts, Tim Conway, David Wayne, Slim Pickens, Harry Morgan; **D:** Norman Tokar; **M:** Buddy Baker. **VHS, Beta $19.99** *DIS*

The Apple Dumpling Gang Rides Again 🎬🎬

Would-be outlaws Amos and Theodore continue terrorizing the West in their bungling attempt to go straight. Fans of Conway or Knotts may appreciate this sequel to Disney's "The Apple Dumpling Gang"; others will decide this VCR's not big enough for the two of them.
1979 (**G**/*Family*) 88m/C Tim Conway, Don Knotts, Tim Matheson, Kenneth Mars, Harry Morgan, Jack Elam; **D:** Vincent McEveety; **M:** Buddy Baker. **VHS, Beta $69.95** *DIS*

The Apprenticeship of Duddy Kravitz 🎬🎬🎬🎬

Jewish teenager in Montreal circa 1948 is driven by an insatiable need to be the "somebody" everyone has always told him he will be. Series of get-rich-quick schemes backfire in different ways, and he becomes most successful at driving people off, even as he attains his superficial goals. Young Dreyfuss, then on the verge of stardom, is at his best. Made in Canada with thoughtful detail, and great performances. Script by Mordecai Richler, from his novel. **Hound Advisory:** Mature themes, sex talk, alcohol use.
1974 (**PG**/*Jr. High-Adult*) 121m/C Richard Dreyfuss, Randy Quaid, Denholm Elliott, Jack Warden, Micheline Lanctot, Joe Silver; **D:** Ted Kotcheff; **W:** Mordecai Richler, Lionel Chetwynd. **Award Nominations:** Academy Awards '74: Best Adapted Screenplay; **Awards:** Berlin International Film Festival '74: Golden Berlin Bear. **VHS, Beta $14.95** *PAR*

Arachnophobia 🎬🎬🎬

First theatrical release from Disney's Hollywood Pictures division is a seriocomic version of a nature-on-the-rampage horror story. Lethal South American spiders wind up breeding in a California community somewhere off the beaten track. There they wreak havoc on two-legged antagonists, including utterly arachnophobic town doctor Daniels and gung-ho insect exterminator Goodman. Script's a bit yawn-inspiring but effective shocks and gore-venom effects make this a cautious choice for youngsters. **Hound Advisory:** Violence, profanity.
1990 (**PG-13**/*Jr. High-Adult*) 109m/C Jeff Daniels, John Goodman, Harley Jane Kozak, Julian Sands, Roy Brocksmith, Stuart Pankin, Brian McNamara, Mark L. Taylor, Henry Jones, Peter Jason, James Handy; **D:** Frank Marshall; **W:** Wesley Strick, Don Jakoby; **M:** Trevor Jones. **VHS, Beta, LV $14.99** *HPH*

Archie, Vol. 1

Nearly 10 years of Saturday-morning cartoons (and the Hound defies you to tell the difference between a 1968

episode and a 1978 one!) have provided the home-video market with oodles of reruns based on the durable Bob Montana comic strip. Three separate cartoons feature the escapades of Archie, Jughead, Veronica, Betty, Reggie, Mr. Weatherbee, and the rest of the gang from Riverdale High. Additional volumes available.
1978 *(Primary-Jr. High)* 60m/C **VHS, Beta** *NO*

Arena 𝄚𝄚

Remember old boxing melodramas about good-natured palookas, slimy opponents, gangsters and dames? This puts those cliches in a garish sci-fi setting, with handsome Steve Armstrong battling ETs and the astro-mob to be the first human pugilistic champ in decades. A really cute idea (from the screenwriters of "The Rocketeer"), but it conks out at the halfway point. Worth a look for buffs.
1988 (PG-13/ *Sr. High-Adult)* 97m/C Paul Satterfield, Claudia Christian, Hamilton Camp, Marc Alaimo, Armin Shimerman, Shari Shattuck, Jack Carter; *D:* Peter Manoogian; *W:* Danny Bilson, Paul DeMeo; *M:* Richard Band. **VHS, LV** **$14.95** *COL*

Ariel's Undersea Adventure, Vol. 1: Whale of a Tale

Compilation of episodes from the Disney TV cartoon series spun off from the modern classic "The Little Mermaid," featuring Ariel and her friends in two further undersea adventures. "A Whale of a Tale" has Ariel adopting a lost baby whale. In "Urchin," Ariel makes friends with a mer-boy who has been swimming with gangsters and their friendship is put to the test. Additional volumes available.
1992 *(Family)* 44m/C **VHS, LV** **$12.99** *DIS*

Army of Darkness 𝄚𝄚𝄚

Campbell returns for a third "Evil Dead" round as the square-jawed, none too bright hero, Ash, in this comic book extravaganza. He finds himself hurled back to the 14th-century through the powers of an evil book. There he romances a babe, fights an army of skeletons, and generally causes all those Dark Age knights a lot of grief, as he tries to get back to his own time. Raimi's technical exuberance is apparent and, as usual, the horror is graphic but still tongue-in-cheek. **Hound Advisory:** Graphic gore and violence all delivered with a smile.
1992 (R/ *Sr. High-Adult)* 77m/C Bruce Campbell, Embeth Davidtz, Marcus Gilbert, Ian Abercrombie, Richard Grove, Michael Earl Reid, Tim Quill, Patricia Tallman, Theodore Raimi, Ivan Raimi; *Cameos:* Bridget Fonda; *D:* Sam Raimi; *W:* Ivan Raimi, Sam Raimi; *M:* Danny Elfman, Joseph Lo Duca. **VHS, Beta, LV** **$19.98** *MCA, FCT*

Arnold of the Ducks

Animated adventure, sort of a Tarzan-of-the-Apes spoof, about a lost baby rescued by ducks and raised as one of their own. Part of the CBS Storybreak series done for network TV and hosted by Captain Kangaroo himself, Bob Keeshan.
1985 *(Family)* 25m/C **VHS** **$14.98** *WTA, KUI, FOX*

Around the World in 80 Days 𝄚𝄚𝄚

Niven is Jules Verne's unflappable Victorian Phileas Fogg, who wagers that he can circumnavigate the Earth in four-score days. With his faithful manservant Passepartout they set off on a spectacular race against the clock. Perpetual favorite provides ample entertainment, although the small screen definitely diminishes its impact. More than 40 cameo appearances by many of Hollywood's biggest names occasionally slow the action.
1956 (G/ *Family)* 178m/C David Niven, Shirley MacLaine, Cantinflas, Robert Newton, Charles Boyer, Joe E. Brown, Martine Carol, John Carradine, Charles Coburn, Ronald Colman; *Cameos:* Melville Cooper, Noel Coward, Andy Devine, Reginald Denny, Fernandel, Marlene Dietrich, Hermione Gingold, Cedric Hardwicke, Trevor Howard, Glynis Johns, Buster Keaton, Evelyn Keyes, Peter Lorre, Mike Mazurki, Victor McLaglen, John Mills, Robert Morley, Jack Oakie, George Raft, Cesar Romero, Gilbert Roland, Red Skelton, Frank Sinatra, Ava Gardner; *D:* Michael Anderson Sr.; *W:* James Poe, John Farrow, S.J. Perelman; *M:* Victor Young. **Award Nominations:** Academy Awards '56: Best Art Direction/Set Decoration (Color), Best Costume Design (Color), Best Director (Anderson); **Awards:** Academy Awards '56: Best Adapted Screenplay, Best Color Cinematography, Best Film Editing, Best Picture, Best Original Score; Golden Globe Awards '57: Best Actor—Musical/Comedy (Cantinflas), Best Film—Drama; National Board of Review Awards '56: 10 Best Films of the Year; New York Film Critics Awards '56: Best Film. **VHS, Beta, LV** **$29.98** *WAR, BTV, HMV*

Around the World in 80 Days

The Jules Verne classic is brought to life via animation.
1991 *(Family)* 47m/C **VHS** **$9.99** *STE*

Arthur 𝄚𝄚𝄚

Spoiled, alcoholic billionaire Moore stands to lose everything he owns when he falls in love with a waitress. He must choose between wealth and a planned marriage, or poverty and love. Surprisingly funny, with an Oscar for Gielgud as Moore's valet, and great performance from Minnelli. Arguably the best role Moore's ever had, and he makes the most of it, taking the one-joke premise to a nomination for Oscar actor. **Hound Advisory:** Profanity; alcohol use.
1981 (PG/ *Jr. High-Adult)* 97m/C Dudley Moore, Liza Minnelli, John Gielgud, Geraldine Fitzgerald, Stephen Elliott, Jill Eikenberry, Lou Jacobi; *D:* Steve Gordon; *M:* Burt Bacharach. **Award Nominations:** Academy Awards '81: Best Actor (Moore), Best Original Screenplay; **Awards:** Academy Awards '81: Best Song ("Arthur's Theme"), Best Supporting Actor (Gielgud). **VHS, Beta, LV, 8mm** **$19.98** *WAR, FCT, BTV*

Arthur 2: On the Rocks 𝄚𝄚

When Arthur finally marries his sweetheart, it may not be "happily ever after" because the father of the girl he didn't marry is out for revenge. When Arthur discovers that he is suddenly penniless, a bit of laughter is the cure for the blues and also serves well when the liquor runs out. A disappointing sequel with few laughs. **Hound Advisory:** Mild profanity.
1988 (PG/ *Adult)* 113m/C Dudley Moore, Liza Minnelli, John Gielgud, Geraldine Fitzgerald, Stephen Elliott, Ted Ross, Barney Martin, Jack Gilford; *D:* Bud Yorkin; *M:* Burt Bacharach. **VHS, Beta, LV, 8mm** **$14.95** *WAR, FCT*

Aspen Extreme 𝄚

Former Aspen ski instructor writes and directs a movie on (what else?) ski instructors in (where?) Aspen. Long on ski shots and short on plot, this movie never leaves the bunny hill. Two Detroiters leave Motown for Snowtown to pursue a life on the slopes. T.J (Gross) soon has his hands full with two beautiful women (Polo and Hughes) who encourage his dream of becoming a writer. His friend Dexter (Berg), however, acquires a few bad habits, and the whole movie just goes downhill from there. **Hound Advisory:** Profanity; suggested sex; alcohol use.

1993 (PG-13/*Jr. High-Adult*) 128m/C Paul Gross, Peter Berg, Finola Hughes, Teri Polo, Martin Kemp, Nicolette Scorsese, William Russ; *D:* Patrick Hasburgh; *W:* Patrick Hasburgh; *M:* Michael Convertino. VHS, Beta, LV $94.95 HPH, BVV

Asterix: Asterix the Gaul

Asterix the Gaul and his sidekick, Obelix, take on an inept legion of Roman warriors when they try to invade Asterix's Gallic territory. Additional volumes available.

1967 (*Family*) 67m/C VHS, Beta, LV $49.95 DIS, APD, WTA

At the Circus 🎬🎬🎵

The Marx Brothers invade the circus to save it from bankruptcy and cause their usual comic insanity, though they've done it better before. Beginning of the end for the boys, a step down in quality from their classic work, though frequently darn funny. ♫Lydia the Tattooed Lady; Step Up and Take a Bow; Two Blind Loves; Blue Moon.

1939 (*Family*) 87m/B Groucho Marx, Chico Marx, Harpo Marx, Margaret Dumont, Kenny L. Baker, Florence Rice, Eve Arden, Nat Pendleton, Fritz Feld; *D:* Edward Buzzell. VHS, Beta, LV $19.95 MGM

At the Earth's Core 🎬🎬

A Victorian scientist invents a giant burrowing machine, which he and his crew use to dig deeply into the Earth. To their surprise, they discover a lost world of subhuman creatures and prehistoric monsters. Based on Edgar Rice Burrough's novels. **Hound Advisory:** Violence.

1976 (PG/*Jr. High-Adult*) 90m/C Doug McClure, Peter Cushing, Caroline Munro; *D:* Kevin Connor. VHS, Beta WAR, OM

Atom Man vs. Superman

Serial followup to "The Adventures of Superman" (on video as "Superman: The Serial"), shows Clark Kent changing into the Man of Steel to take on arch-villain Lex Luthor, in a storyline more faithful than most to the vintage comic books. In 15 chapters. **Hound Advisory:** Roughhousing.

1950 (*Family*) 251m/B Kirk Alyn, Lyle Talbot, Noel Neill, Tommy "Butch" Bond, Pierre Watkin; *D:* Spencer Gordon Bennet. VHS, Beta $29.98 WAR, MLB

Attack of the Killer Tomatoes WOOF!

Candidate for worst film ever made, deliberate category. Horror spoof that defined "low budget" stars several thousand ordinary tomatoes that suddenly turn savage and begin attacking people. No sci-fi cliche remains untouched in this dumb parody. A few musical numbers are performed in lieu of an actual plot. Followed by "Return of the Killer Tomatoes."

1977 (PG/*Jr. High-Adult*) 87m/C *D:* John DeBello. VHS, Beta $19.95 MED

Attic In the Blue

Animated story about an ancient whaler who goes on a dangerous mission to find his lost love, accompanied only by his octopus-like companion.

1992 (*Family*) 27m/C VHS $39.95 FCT, WTA, PIC

Au Revoir Les Enfants 🎬🎬🎬🎬

During the Nazi occupation of France, the headmaster of a Catholic boarding school hides three Jewish boys among the students by altering their names and identities. One gentile boy, Julien, forms a friendship with one of the fugitives that ends tragically in a Gestapo raid. Compelling and emotional coming-of-age tale, based on an incident from director Malle's own history. Mature theme makes it more suitable for older kids. Both French-language subtitled and English-dubbed versions are available. **Hound Advisory:** Mature themes, profanity, sex talk, roughhousing, alcohol use.

1987 (PG/*Jr. High-Adult*) 104m/C Gaspard Manesse, Raphael Fejto, Francine Racette, Stanislas Carre de Malberg, Philippe Morier-Genoud, Francois Berleand, Peter Fitz, Francois Negret, Irene Jacob; *D:* Louis Malle; *W:* Louis Malle; *M:* Franz Schubert, Camille Saint-Saens. **Award Nominations:** Academy Awards '87: Best Foreign Language Film, Best Original Screenplay; **Awards:** British Academy Awards '88: Best Director (Malle); Cesar Awards '88: Best Director (Malle), Best Film; Los Angeles Film Critics Association Awards '87: Best Foreign Film; Venice Film Festival '87: Best Film. VHS, Beta, LV $19.98 INJ, ORI, FCT

Audrey Rose 🎬🎬

Ivy's parents are terrified when their daughter has dreadful dreams. A mystery man steps in and declares that his deceased little Audrey Rose has been reincarnated in their child. Result is a New-Age courtroom custody drama, not the horror flick the advertising claims; interesting in that aspect, as adults argue over what's best for the girl(s). Adapted by Frank DeFelitta from his novel. **Hound Advisory:** Mature themes.

1977 (PG/*Sr. High-Adult*) 113m/C Marsha Mason, Anthony Hopkins, John Beck, John Hillerman; *D:* Robert Wise; *W:* Frank De Felitta. VHS, Beta $14.95 MGM

The Aurora Encounter 🎬🎬

Small spaceman lands his flying jalopy in Texas around 1900, befriending Earth kids but panicking authorities (one villain played by the original George "Spanky" McFarland!). Warmhearted but ragged cheapie claims a basis in fact, but inspiration was "E.T." all the way. Potentially disturbing note: alien is portrayed by a little boy with a very real genetic disorder that gave him a gnomelike appearance. **Hound Advisory:** Violence - though resurrection follows, natch.

1985 (PG/*Jr. High-Adult*) 90m/C Jack Elam, Peter Brown, Carol Bagdasarian, Dottie West, George "Spanky" McFarland; *D:* Jim McCullough. VHS, Beta $14.95 NWV, STE, HHE

Author! Author! 🎬🎬🎵

Sweet, likable comedy about a playwright who is about to taste success with his first big hit. Suddenly his wife walks out, leaving him to care for her four children and his own son. He soon learns to juggle being father and writer without compromising either one.

1982 (PG/*Jr. High-Adult*) 100m/C Al Pacino, Tuesday Weld, Dyan Cannon, Alan King, Andre Gregory; *D:* Arthur Hiller; *W:* Israel Horovitz; *M:* Dave Grusin. **VHS, Beta $14.98** *FOX*

Avalanche 🎬⏪

Disasterama as vacationers at a new winter ski resort find themselves at the mercy of a monster avalanche leaving a so-called path of terror and destruction in its wake. Talented cast is buried by weak material, producing a snow-bound adventure yawn.
1978 (PG/*Jr. High-Adult*) 91m/C Rock Hudson, Mia Farrow, Robert Forster, Rick Moses; *D:* Corey Allen. **VHS, Beta $9.98** *SUE*

Avalon 🎬🎬🎬

Powerful but quiet portrait of the break-up of the family unit as seen from the perspective of an immigrant clan settled in Baltimore at the close of WWII. Initially, the family is unified in their goals, thoughts, and social lives. Gradually, all of this disintegrates; members move to the suburbs and television replaces conversation at holiday gatherings. Based on Levinson's experiences within his own family of Russian Jewish origins. **Hound Advisory:** Profanity, violence, mature themes.
1990 (PG/*Sr. High-Adult*) 126m/C Armin Mueller-Stahl, Aidan Quinn, Elizabeth Perkins, Joan Plowright, Lou Jacobi, Leo Fuchs, Eve Gordon, Kevin Pollak, Israel Rubinek, Elijah Wood, Grant Gelt, Bernard Hiller; *D:* Barry Levinson; *W:* Barry Levinson; *M:* Randy Newman. **VHS, Beta, LV, 8mm $19.95** *COL, FCT*

Babar and Father Christmas

Canadian cartoon depiction of Babar-ism, this time in a holiday mode as Father Christmas (a sort of Euro-Santa) pays a visit to Babar's African kingdom.
1986 (*Preschool-Primary*) 30m/B **VHS, Beta $9.98** *MED, VTR, APD*

Babar Comes to America

Babar, Celeste, and Artur head to Hollywood to make a movie but get sidetracked several times along the way.
1984 (*Preschool-Primary*) 23m/C **VHS $14.95** *FCT*

Babar: Monkey Business

Babar the little elephant finds himself up to his trunk in fun thanks to a mischievous simian.
1991 (*Family*) 30m/C **VHS, Beta $12.95** *FHE, WTA*

Babar Returns

Excerpts from the Babar TV cartoon series from Canada's Nelvana Productions. Here the pachyderm potentate tells his daughter Flora the story of how he was crowned king of the elephant herd.
1989 (*Family*) 49m/C **VHS, Beta $14.95** *FHE, FCT, WTA*

Babar the Elephant Comes to America

Further cartoon adventures of de Brunhoffs' famous character depicts Babar setting out for Hollywood by balloon and seeing much of the USA in the process. Done by the Bill Melendez team responsible for prime time "Peanuts" cartoon specials.
1985 (*Family*) 25m/C **VHS, Beta $14.98** *LIV, INJ, WTA*

Babar the Little Elephant

Actor Ustinov narrates Jean de Brunhoff's story of the wise elephant's younger days, in one of the Babar tales animated by the "Peanuts" team.
1987 (*Preschool-Primary*) 25m/C **VHS, Beta $14.98** *VES, LIV, WTA*

Babar: The Movie 🎬🎬

Babar, crowned king of the elephants while merely a boy (kid? cub? calf? that's it, calf), must devise a plan to outwit an angry hoard of rhinos attacking the village of his lady love Celeste. Canada's Nelvana animation studios did this adaption of the classic characters of Jean and Laurent de Brunhoff, but storybook-style visuals feel largely TV grade.
1988 (G/*Family*) 75m/C *D:* Alan Bunce; *W:* Gavin Magrath, Gordon Pinsent, Sarah Polley, Chris Wiggins, Elizabeth Hanna. **VHS, Beta, LV, 8mm $24.95** *FHE, IME, WTA*

Babar's First Step

In this recent Babar tale, the elephant king tells his grandchildren the painful story of his mother's death and his own acceptance of loss. Could be upsetting to youngsters, but is also possibly an excellent vehicle for inviting children to talk about the death of a loved one.
1990 (*Family*) 49m/C **VHS $14.95** *FHE, WTA*

Babar's Triumph

Babar gathers together all his animal friends to discuss ways in which they can save their jungle.
1989 (*Family*) 51m/C **VHS $14.95** *FHE, WTA*

The Babe 🎬🎬🎬⏪

Follows the life of legendary baseball player Babe Ruth, portrayed as a sloppy drunkard whose appetites for food, drink, and sex were as large as he was. Alvarado and McGillis do well as the Babe's first and second wives, but this is Goodman's show from start to finish. Though a lackluster script laced with soap opera fails to complete the game, Goodman's amazing turn as the party-animal Bambino is reason enough to watch. That last at-bat is inspiring. **Hound Advisory:** Alcohol use; sexual situations; bullying; salty language.
1992 (PG/*Jr. High-Adult*) 115m/C John Goodman, Kelly McGillis, Trini Alvarado, Bruce Boxleitner, Peter Donat, J.C. Quinn, Richard Tyson, James Cromwell, Joe Ragno, Bernard Kates, Michael McGrady, Stephen Caffrey; *D:* Arthur Hiller; *W:* John Fusco; *M:* Elmer Bernstein. **VHS, LV $19.98** *MCA*

Babes in Arms 🎬🎬

Hey, let's put on a show! The children of several vaudeville performers team up to put on a show to raise money for their financially impoverished parents. Judy and Mickey work, worry, and kick up their heels. Loosely adapted from the Rodgers and Hart Broadway musical of the same name though featuring few of the songs. ♫Babes in Arms; I Cried for

Elephants gather in "Babar: The Movie"

You; Good Morning; You Are My Lucky Star; Broadway Rhythm; Where or When; Daddy Was a Minstrel Man; I'm Just Wild About Harry; God's Country.

1939 *(Family)* 91m/B Judy Garland, Mickey Rooney, Charles Winninger, Guy Kibbee, June Preisser; **D:** Busby Berkeley; **M:** Richard Rodgers, Lorenz Hart. **VHS, Beta, LV $19.98** *MGM*

Babes in Toyland

Lavish Disney production of Victor Herbert's timeless operetta, with Toyland being menaced by the evil Barnaby and his Bogeymen. Yes, Annette had a life after Mickey Mouse and before the peanut butter commercials. Somewhat charming, although the roles of the lovers seem a stretch for both Funicello and Kirk. But the flick does sport an amusing turn by Wynn.

1961 *(Family)* 105m/C Annette Funicello, Ray Bolger, Tommy Sands, Ed Wynn, Tommy Kirk; **D:** Jack Donohue. **VHS, Beta $14.99** *DIS*

Babes in Toyland

Young girl must save Toyland from the clutches of the evil Barnaby and his monster minions. Bland TV remake (with new songs by Bricusse) of the classic doesn't approach the original, even with the way-out cast. The good news; video

release was trimmed down from the original broadcast version, a 150 minute ordeal.

1986 *(Family)* 96m/C Drew Barrymore, Noriyuki "Pat" Morita, Richard Mulligan, Eileen Brennan, Keanu Reeves, Jill Schoelen, Googy Gress; **D:** Clive Donner; **M:** Leslie Bricusse. **VHS, LV $9.98** *ORI*

Babes on Broadway

Hey, let's put on another show! Mickey and Judy put on a show to raise money for a settlement house. Nearly the best of the Garland-Rooney series, with imaginative numbers staged by Berkeley. ♫Babes on Broadway; Anything Can Happen in New York; How About You?; Hoe Down; Chin Up! Cheerio! Carry On!; Mama Yo Quiero; F.D.R. Jones; Waiting for the Robert E. Lee.

1941 *(Family)* 118m/B Mickey Rooney, Judy Garland, Fay Bainter, Richard Quine, Virginia Weidler, Ray Macdonald, Busby Berkeley; **D:** Busby Berkeley. **VHS, Beta, LV $19.98** *MGM*

Baby Boom

When a hard-charging female executive becomes the reluctant guardian of a baby girl - a gift from a long-lost relative - she adjusts with difficulty to motherhood and life outside the rat race. Fairly harmless collection of cliches helped by Keaton's witty, nervous performance as the New York business lady vastly transformed by tot. To best appreciate flick, see it with a bevy of five- and six-year-olds (a good age

for applauding the havoc that a baby creates). **Hound Advisory:** Sex talk, salty language.
1987 (PG/Sr. High-Adult) 103m/C Diane Keaton, Sam Shepard, Harold Ramis, Sam Wanamaker, James Spader, Pat Hingle, Mary Gross, Victoria Jackson, Paxton Whitehead, Annie Golden, Dori Brenner, Robin Bartlett, Christopher Noth, Britt Leach; **D:** Charles Shyer; **W:** Charles Shyer, Nancy Meyers; **M:** Bill Conti. **VHS, Beta, LV $14.95** *MGM, FCT, FOX*

Baby on Board 🎵🎵

Kane plays the wife of a Mafia bookkeeper who is accidentally killed in a gangland murder. Out for revenge, she tracks her husband's killer to JFK airport with her four-year old daughter in tow. Just as she pulls the loaded gun from her purse and takes aim, a pickpocket snatches her purse, accidentally firing the gun. Now she's on the run and she jumps into the first cab she can find, driven by Reinhold. New York City is turned upside down as mother, daughter, and cabbie try to elude the mob in this predictable comedy. **Hound Advisory:** Violence.
1992 (PG/Jr. High-Adult) 90m/C Carol Kane, Judge Reinhold, Geza Kovacs, Errol Slue, Alex Stapley, Holly Stapley; **D:** Francis Schaeffer. **VHS, Beta, LV $89.95** *PSM*

Baby. . .Secret of the Lost Legend 🎵🎵

Writer and his paleontologist wife, following reports of dinosaurs still lurking in the African jungle, risk their lives to reunite a hatchling brontosaurus with its giant mother. The Volkswagen-sized baby is (obviously a puppet) cute but hardly convincing by "Jurassic Park" standards; neither is the script of this Disney adventure. **Hound Advisory:** Dinosaur violence (baby's dad gets the Bambi's-mother treatment so beloved at Disney), topless native women, sex between the married protagonists.
1985 (PG/Family) 95m/C William Katt, Sean Young, Patrick McGoohan, Julian Fellowes; **D:** B.W.L. Norton. **VHS, Beta, LV $79.95** *TOU*

The Baby-Sitter's Club

The phenomenally popular series of juvenile paperbacks by Ann M. Martin have been brought faithfully and frothfully to video in a series of half-hour cassettes, in which the organized group of neighborhood baby-sitters (six adolescent girls and one guest boy) learn various life lessons on and off the job. Tapes include: "The Baby-Sitters and the Boy Sitters," "Claudia and the Mystery of the Secret Passage," "Dawn and the Dream Boy," "Dawn and the Haunted House," "Dawn Saves the Trees," "Jessi and the Mystery of the Stolen Secrets," "Mary Anne and the Brunettes," "The Baby-Sitters Club Special Christmas," "Stacey Takes a Stand," "Stacey's Big Break," and "The Baby-Sitters Remember."
1990 (Primary-Sr. High) 30m/C **VHS $12.95** *GKK*

Baby, Take a Bow 🎵🎵

Temple's first starring role. As a cheerful Pollyanna-type she helps her father, falsely accused of theft, by finding the true thief. She's cute as a dimple, she is.
1934 (Family) 76m/B Shirley Temple, James Dunn, Claire Trevor, Alan Dinehart; **D:** Harry Lachman. **VHS, Beta $19.98** *FOX*

Baby's Day Out 🎵🎵

Poor man's "Home Alone" refits tired Hughes formula using little tiny baby for original spin. Adorable Baby Bink crawls his way onto the city streets, much to his frantic mother's dismay, and unwittingly outsmarts his would-be kidnappers. As in HA I and II, the bad guys fall victim to all sorts of cataclysmic Looney Tunes violence. Small kids will get a kick out of this one. Particular problem for the moviemakers was that the nine-month old Worton twins were past the year mark by the end of the shoot, a world of difference in infantdom. Blue screens and out-of-sequence shooting were used to overcome the developmental gap. **Hound Advisory:** Violence; salty language.
1994 (PG/Family) 98m/C Adam Worton, Jacob Worton, Joe Mantegna, Lara Flynn Boyle, Joe Pantoliano, Fred Dalton Thompson, John Neville, Brian Haley, Matthew Glave; **D:** Patrick Read Johnson; **W:** John Hughes; **M:** Bruce Broughton. **VHS** *NYR*

Bach & Broccoli 🎵🎵🎵🎵

Rather than go to a foster home, Fanny tries to charm her bachelor uncle, a self-centered musician, into adopting her and her skunk Broccoli. But the man turns out to have a deep personal reason for his discomfort around her that has nothing to do with the odiferous pet. Sentimental comedy-drama with expert poignancy and the rare virtue of equal respect for both its young and grownup characters. Third in Canadian producer Rock Demers' "Tales for All" series of quality family films.
1987 (Preschool-Primary) 96m/C Mahee Paiement; **D:** Andre Melancon. **VHS, Beta $14.98** *FHE, LIV, FCT*

The Bachelor and the Bobby-Soxer 🎵🎵🎵

Playboy Grant is brought before Judge Loy for disturbing the peace and sentenced to court her teen-age sister Temple. Cruel and unusual punishment? Maybe, but the wise Judge hopes that the dates will help Temple over her crush on handsome Grant. Instead, Loy and Grant fall for each other.
1947 (Family) 95m/B Cary Grant, Myrna Loy, Shirley Temple, Rudy Vallee, Harry Davenport, Ray Collins, Veda Ann Borg; **D:** Irving Reis; **W:** Sidney Sheldon. **VHS, Beta, LV $14.98** *CCB, MED, RKO*

Back Home 🎵🎵🎵

Disney TV period drama about an English girl sent to America for her own safety during the darkest days of WWII. After the Allied victory she returns to Great Britain and boarding school, and must adjust to a family and society now foreign to her.
1990 (Family) 103m/C Hayley Carr, Hayley Mills, Jean Anderson, Rupert Frazer, Brenda Bruce, Adam Stevenson, George Clark; **D:** Piers Haggard. **VHS** *DIS*

Back to Hannibal: The Further Adventures of Tom Sawyer and Huckleberry Finn 🎵🎵🎵

Disney TV-movie reunites Twain's characters as adults (15 years after events in "The Adventures of Huckleberry

Finn"). Huck is a tabloid reporter, while Tom is a Chicago lawyer; both are brought together to save their freed-slave friend Jim, falsely accused of murder in the killing of Becky Thatcher's husband. Indisputably intriguing premise, but merely mediocre treatment. Contrived script even brings back those con-artists, the King and the Duke, for an unnecessary encore. **Hound Advisory:** Roughhousing, alcohol talk.

1990 (*Family*) 92m/C Raphael Sbarge, Mitchell Anderson, Megan Follows, William Windom, Ned Beatty, Paul Winfield; **D:** Paul Krasny; **M:** Lee Holdridge. **VHS $19.99** DIS

Back to School 🎬🎬◁

Under-educated, obnoxious millionaire Dangerfield enrolls in college to help his wimpy son, Gordon, achieve campus stardom. His motto seems to be "if you can't buy it, it can't be had." At first, his antics embarrass his shy son, but soon everyone is clamoring to be seen with the pair as Gordon develops his own self-confidence. Typical rude and silly Dangerfield enterprise proves a consistent chucklefest. **Hound Advisory:** Vulgar humor.

1986 (PG-13/*Sr. High-Adult*) 96m/C Rodney Dangerfield, Keith Gordon, Robert Downey Jr., Sally Kellerman, Burt Young, Paxton Whitehead, Adrienne Barbeau, M. Emmet Walsh, Severn Darden, Ned Beatty, Sam Kinison, Kurt Vonnegut Jr., Robert Picardo, Terry Farrell, Edie McClurg, Jason Hervey; **D:** Alan Metter; **W:** Will Aldis, Steven Kampmann, Harold Ramis, Peter Torokvei, Steven Kampmann; **M:** Danny Elfman. **VHS, Beta, LV $19.98** HBO

Back to the Beach 🎬◁

Frankie and Annette return to the beach as self-parodying, middle-aged parents with rebellious kids, and the usual run of sun-bleached, lover's tiff comedy ensues. Plenty of songs and guest appearances from television past. Tries to bring back that surf, sun, and sand feel of the original "Beach Party" movies, but instead seems nostalgia wound around a mid-life crisis. ♫Absolute Perfection; California Sun; Catch a Ride; Jamaica Sky; Papa-Oom-Mow-Mow; Sign of Love; Sun, Sun, Sun, Sun, Sun; Surfin' Bird; Wooly Bully. **Hound Advisory:** Salty language.

1987 (PG/*Jr. High-Adult*) 92m/C Frankie Avalon, Annette Funicello, Connie Stevens, Jerry Mathers, Bob Denver, Barbara Billingsley, Tony Dow, Paul (Pee Wee Herman) Reubens, Edd Byrnes, Dick Dale, Don Adams, Lori Loughlin; **D:** Lyndall Hobbs; **M:** Stephen Dorff. **VHS, Beta, LV $19.95** PAR

Back to the Future 🎬🎬🎬

When the neighborhood mad scientist constructs a time machine from a sportscar, his youthful companion Marty McFly accidentally transports himself to 1955 - and immediately fouls up history by preventing his own future parents from meeting. Marty must do all he can to bring the mismatched mates together again, elude the local bully, and get back...to the future. Crammed with rich details and a comic pace almost too frenzied, this Spielberg production was a megahit that made a superstar out of Fox, perfectly cast as the resourceful '80s boy who introduces rock 'n roll to the uncomprehending '50s high schoolers. Followed by two sequels and a cartoon TV series, all available on video. **Hound Advisory:** Profanity, roughhousing.

1985 (PG/*Family-Family*) 116m/C Michael J. Fox, Christopher Lloyd, Lea Thompson, Crispin Glover, Wendie Jo Sperber, Marc McClure, Thomas F. Wilson, James Tolkan, Casey Siemaszko, Billy Zane, George DiCenzo, Courtney Gains, Claudia Wells, Jason Hervey, Harry Waters Jr., Maia Brewton, J.J. Cohen; *Cameos:* Huey Lewis; **D:** Robert Zemeckis; **W:** Robert Zemeckis, Bob Gale; **M:** Alan Silvestri. **Award Nominations:** Academy Awards '85: Best Original Screenplay, Best Song ("The Power of Love"), Best Sound; **Awards:** People's Choice Awards '86: Best Film. **VHS, Beta, LV $19.95** MCA, FCT, TLF

Back to the Future, Part 2 🎬🎬🎬◁

The Doc and Marty McFly are time-hopping again after they find the present radically changed because of their earlier trips to future and past. Three generations of McFlys are visited by the pair while they try to set things straight. Fast, furious, and funny, but not quite as memorable as the first BTTF (which you need to watch immediately before this in order to comprehend storyline). Leads to a cliffhanger ending, setting the stage for Part III. **Hound Advisory:** Profanity, sex talk, roughhousing.

1989 (PG/*Jr. High-Adult*) 107m/C Michael J. Fox, Christopher Lloyd, Lea Thompson, Thomas F. Wilson, Harry Waters Jr., Charles Fleischer, Joe Flaherty, Elisabeth Shue, James Tolkan, Casey Siemaszko, Jeffrey Weissman, Flea, Billy Zane, J.J. Cohen, Darlene Vogel, Jason Scott Lee, Crispin Glover, Ricky Dean Logan; **D:** Robert Zemeckis; **W:** Robert Zemeckis, Bob Gale; **M:** Alan Silvestri. **VHS, Beta, LV $19.95** MCA

Back to the Future, Part 3 🎬🎬

Marty learns Doc Brown met an early death in a gunfight after being flung to 1885 in Part II. The boy time-warps back to the Wild West era of his hometown to save his friend, meets his own ancestors, the future villain's ancestors, and so on. Filmed simultaneously with Part II, but you wouldn't know it; pace is slower, more romantic and wheezier than the lickety-spit action of earlier two chapters. It's like slowing from 85 mph to 20 in a school zone. Gets an extra half-bone for completing all the storylines tidily. Complete trilogy is available as a boxed set. **Hound Advisory:** Roughhousing, alcohol use, profanity.

1990 (PG/*Jr. High-Adult*) 118m/C Michael J. Fox, Christopher Lloyd, Mary Steenburgen, Thomas F. Wilson, Lea Thompson, Elisabeth Shue, Matt Clark, Richard Dysart, Pat Buttram, Harry Carey Jr., Dub Taylor, James Tolkan, Marc McClure, Wendie Jo Sperber, J.J. Cohen, Ricky Dean Logan, Jeffrey Weissman; **D:** Robert Zemeckis; **W:** Bob Gale, Robert Zemeckis; **M:** Alan Silvestri. **VHS, Beta, LV $19.95** MCA

Backbeat 🎬🎬🎬

Explores the Beatles' early days between '60 and '62, when they were playing Hamburg's underground music scene. Storyline driven by the triangle of John Lennon, his best friend and original bass player, Stu Sutcliff, more painter than musician, and the woman Stu left the band for, Astrid Kirchherr, the photographer who came up with the band's signature look. Hart's dead-on as Lennon, playing him a second time (check out "The Hours and Times"). Energetic, enjoyable debut for director Softley is best when the music takes center stage. Produced by Don Was, the soundtrack captures the Fab Four's early bar band sound with a "supergroup" comprised of alternative rockers from current hot bands. **Hound Advisory:** Profanity; nudity; sex; drug use.

1994 (R / *Sr. High-Adult*) 100m/C Stephen Dorff, Sheryl Lee, Ian Hart, Gary Bakewell, Chris O'Neill, Scot Williams, Kai Wiesinger, Jennifer Ehle; *D:* Iain Softley; *W:* Michael Thomas, Stephen Ward, Iain Softley; *M:* Don Was. **VHS, LV $94.99** *PGV*

Bad Company 🦴🦴🦴◁

Thoughtful study of two very different teens in the old west, both Civil War draft dodgers, who roam the vast, often bleak frontier and turn to a fruitless life of crime. Cast and script are perfect in a realistic, unglamorized portrait of young men of the 'wild west.' A movie that really hasn't gotten the attention it deserves. Try it rather than the later R-rated "Young Guns" series. **Hound Advisory:** Violence; mature themes.
1972 (PG / *Jr. High-Adult*) 94m/C Jeff Bridges, Barry Brown, Jim Davis, John Savage; *D:* Robert Benton; *W:* David Newman. **VHS, Beta, LV $14.95** *PAR*

Bad Medicine WOOF!

A youth who doesn't want to be a doctor is accepted by a highly questionable Latin American school of medicine. Remember that it was for medical students like these that the U.S. liberated Grenada. **Hound Advisory:** Profanity, sex, adult situations.
1985 (PG-13 / *Jr. High-Adult*) 97m/C Steve Guttenberg, Alan Arkin, Julie Hagerty, Bill Macy, Curtis Armstrong, Julie Kavner, Joe Grifasi, Robert Romanus, Taylor Negron, Gilbert Gottfried; *D:* Harvey Miller. **VHS, Beta $79.98** *FOX*

The Bad News Bears 🦴🦴🦴◁

Misfit Little League team gets whipped into shape by a cranky, sloppy, beer-drinking coach who scandalizes winning-is-everything parents by recruiting a tomboy girl pitcher. O'Neal and Matthau score home runs with their cantankerous, sometimes touching relationship, and the supporting juvenile cast displays great teamwork as they pull together for the big game. Mega-hit spawned two sequels, a TV series and many imitators. This was the first mainstream movie to showcase kids with realistic sandlot mouths, so be forewarned - the kids display a certain anti-authority attitude and let choice remarks fly, pioneering the era of rebellious toilet-talking tykes on the silver screen. By later standards these samples of 1976 profanity ("hell" and "damn") are mild indeed. On the positive values side, there's the usual, though skillfully subtle, lesson on sportsmanship and cooperation. At any rate, it's darn funny and kinda touching. **Hound Advisory:** Continuous beer drinking; ballpark language, morally complex kids and adults.
1976 (PG / *Family*) 102m/C Walter Matthau, Tatum O'Neal, Vic Morrow, Joyce Van Patten, Jackie Earle Haley; *D:* Michael Ritchie. **VHS, Beta, LV, 8mm $14.95** *PAR*

The Bad News Bears Go to Japan 🦴

Second sequel to the classic in which the famed Little Leaguers volunteer to represent the USA on the field against an undefeated team of Japanese tykes. But the Bears need money for the Tokyo trip, and in steps publicity hungry talent agent Curtis. Dull comedy/travelogue, without much time devoted to baseball, or even to the kids themselves. See the original. **Hound Advisory:** Alcohol use. The foul language of earlier Bears adventures is nearly absent.
1978 (PG / *Jr. High-Adult*) 102m/C Tony Curtis, Jackie Earle Haley, Tomisaburo Wakayama, George Wyner; *D:* John Berry. **VHS, Beta, LV $19.95** *PAR*

The Bad News Bears in Breaking Training 🦴◁

Minor-league sequel with the Bears, lacking the social commentary of the first film, coming across as just another ragtag kiddie sports franchise - the Mighty Ducks without ice. With a chance to take on a Houston team, the kids devise a way to get to Texas and play at the famed Astrodome. Followed halfheartedly by "The Bad News Bears Go to Japan" (1978). **Hound Advisory:** Baseballish Bear language.
1977 (PG / *Family*) 105m/C William Devane, Clifton James, Jackie Earle Haley, Jimmy Baio; *D:* Michael Pressman; *W:* Paul Brickman. **VHS, Beta, LV $14.95** *PAR*

The Bad Seed 🦴🦴◁

Mother makes tortuous discovery all parents hope to avoid: her cherubic eight-year-old daughter harbors an innate desire to kill. Based on Maxwell Anderson's powerful Broadway stage play (with many in the cast reprising their roles), it's stiff but anxiety inspiring. Remade for television in 1985.
1956 (*Jr. High-Adult*) 129m/B Patty McCormack, Nancy Kelly, Eileen Heckart, Henry Jones, Evelyn Varden, Paul Fix; *D:* Mervyn LeRoy; *M:* Alex North. **Award Nominations:** Academy Awards '56: Best Actress (Kelly), Best Black and White Cinematography, Best Supporting Actress (Heckart, McCormack); **Awards:** Golden Globe Awards '57: Best Supporting Actress (Heckart). **VHS, Beta $59.95** *WAR*

Bagdad Cafe 🦴🦴🦴

A large German woman, played by Sagebrecht, finds herself stranded in the Mojave desert after her husband dumps her on the side of the highway. She encounters a rundown cafe where she becomes involved with the off-beat residents. A hilarious story in which the strange people and the absurdity of their situations are treated kindly and not made to seem ridiculous. Spawned a short-lived TV series with Whoopi Goldberg.
1988 (PG / *Jr. High-Adult*) 91m/C Marianne Sagebrecht, CCH Pounder, Jack Palance, Christine Kaufmann, Monica Calhoun, Darron Flagg; *D:* Percy Adlon; *W:* Percy Adlon; *M:* Bob Telson. **Award Nominations:** Academy Awards '88: Best Song ("Calling You"); **Awards:** Cesar Awards '89: Best Foreign Film. **VHS, Beta $14.98** *FCT, VTR*

The Ballad of Paul Bunyan

TV special uses animation to retell the legend of the legendary lumberjack, from his discovery as a baby in an extra-large floating crib to the day he dug Niagara Falls as part of a logging competition. Also on tape in a double-feature cassette with another Rankin/Bass rendering of an American legend, "Johnny Appleseed."
1972 (*Family*) 30m/C *D:* Arthur Rankin Jr., Jules Bass. **VHS $6.95** *STE, PSM*

Ballet Shoes 🦴🦴◁

Cheerful all-ages entertainment set in Victorian London, where three adopted sisters in a struggling, eccentric family look to a career on the stage, and their guardian Sylvia goes

Bambi and Flower go nose to nose

to extremes to ensure that girls can afford to remain in the dance academy. BBC-TV production based on the book by Noel Streatfeild.

19?? (*Family*) 120m/C **VHS $29.95** *BFS, HMV*

Bambi 𝄞𝄞𝄞𝄞

True Disney classic, detailing the often harsh education of a newborn deer and his friends in the forest. Proves that Disney animation was - and still is - the best to be found. Thumper still steals the show and the music is delightful, including "Let's Sing a Gay Little Spring Song," "Love is a Song," "Little April Shower," "The Thumper Song," and "Twitterpated." Stands as a genuine perennial from generation to generation. Based very loosely on the book by Felix Salten. **Hound Advisory:** Bambi's mama dies, a tragedy that still evokes discussion today when compared to death scenes in such movies as "The Lion King."

1942 (G/*Family*) 69m/C **D:** David Hand; **W:** Larry Morey; **M:** Frank Churchill, Edward Plumb; **V:** Bobby Stewart, Peter Behn, Stan Alexander, Cammie King, Donnie Dunagan, Hardie Albright, John Sutherland, Tim Davis, Sam Edwards, Sterling Holloway, Anne Gillis, Perce Pearce. **VHS, Beta, LV $26.99** *DIS, APD, RDG*

Bananas 𝄞𝄞𝄞

Intermittently hilarious pre-"Annie Hall" Allen fare is full of the director's signature angst-ridden philosophical comedy. A frustrated product tester from New York runs off to South America, where he volunteers his support to the revolutionary force of a shaky Latin-American dictatorship and winds up the leader. Don't miss cameos by Stallone and Garfield. Witty score contributes much.

1971 (PG/*Jr. High-Adult*) 82m/C Woody Allen, Louise Lasser, Carlos Montalban, Howard Cosell, Charlotte Rae, Conrad Bain; *Cameos:* Sylvester Stallone, Allen (Gooritz) Garfield; **D:** Woody Allen; **W:** Woody Allen; **M:** Marvin Hamlisch. **VHS, Beta, LV $14.95** *MGM, FCT, FOX*

The Band Wagon 𝄞𝄞𝄞𝄞

Theater set is cleverly satirized as Hollywood song-and-dance man with sagging career finds trouble when he is persuaded to star in a Broadway musical. Faust-obsessed director (Buchanan) falls prey to arthouse demons and the female lead (Charisse) doesn't seem to think much of the dancing partnership. Engaging, witty look behind the scenes has great numbers written by Howard Dietz and Arthur Schwartz and wonderful dancing. ♫That's Entertainment; Dancing in the Dark; By Myself; A Shine On Your Shoes; Something to Remember You By;

High and Low; I Love Louisa; New Sun in the Sky; I Guess I'll Have to Change My Plan.
1953 (*Family*) 112m/C Fred Astaire, Cyd Charisse, Oscar Levant, Nanette Fabray, Jack Buchanan, Bobby Watson; *D:* Vincente Minnelli; *M:* Arthur Schwartz, Jason James Richter. **VHS, Beta, LV $19.98** *MGM, FCT*

Bandolero! 🎬🎬◁

In Texas, Stewart and Martin are two fugitive brothers who escape the gallows, take Welch as a hostage, and run into trouble with their Mexican counterparts. Straight-ahead western is an enjoyable romp with fine performances.
1968 (PG/*Family*) 106m/C James Stewart, Raquel Welch, Dean Martin, George Kennedy, Will Geer, Harry Carey Jr., Andrew Prine; *D:* Andrew V. McLaglen; *M:* Jerry Goldsmith. **VHS, Beta $19.98** *FOX*

Bang Bang Kid 🎬🎬

A western spoof about a klutzy gunfighter defending a town from outlaws.
1967 (G/*Primary*) 78m/C Tom Bosley, Guy Madison, Sandra Milo; *D:* Stanley Prager. **VHS, Beta** *NO*

Bang the Drum Slowly 🎬🎬🎬

Touching story of a journeyman major league catcher who discovers that he is dying of Hodgkins disease and wants to play just one more season. Weakening ball player De Niro is supported by star pitcher Moriarty through thick and thin. Well-made locker room tearjerker (hey, there's no crying in baseball!) is based on a novel by Mark Harris and had been adapted earlier for television with Paul Newman and Albert Salmi. **Hound Advisory:** Mature themes.
1973 (PG/*Jr. High-Adult*) 97m/C Robert De Niro, Michael Moriarty, Vincent Gardenia, Phil Foster, Ann Wedgeworth, Heather MacRae, Selma Diamond, Danny Aiello; *D:* John Hancock. **Award Nominations:** Academy Awards '73: Best Supporting Actor (Gardenia); **Awards:** National Board of Review Awards '73: 10 Best Films of the Year; New York Film Critics Awards '73: Best Supporting Actor (De Niro). **VHS, Beta, LV $14.95** *PAR, FCT*

Barbarosa 🎬🎬🎬

Offbeat western about an aging, legendary outlaw constantly on the lam who reluctantly befriends a naive farmboy and teaches him survival skills. Nelson and Busey are a great team, solidly directed. Lovely Rio Grande scenery. **Hound Advisory:** Violence.
1982 (PG/*Family*) 90m/C Willie Nelson, Gilbert Roland, Gary Busey, Isela Vega; *D:* Fred Schepisi; *M:* Bruce Smeaton. **VHS, Beta, LV $19.95** *FOX*

The Barefoot Executive 🎬🎬

Mailroom boy who works for a national television network discovers that his girlfriend's pet chimpanzee has a knack for picking hit TV shows. He uses the critter to rise through the corporate ranks, a story based on the real-life climb of many present day execs. Bland Disney family comedy could have used the primate's help in its joke selection.
1971 (G/*Family-Family*) 92m/C Kurt Russell, John Ritter, Harry Morgan, Wally Cox, Heather North; *D:* Robert Butler. **VHS, Beta** *DIS, OM*

Barnaby and Me 🎬🎬

Let's see, you and da kids are looking for something different in the engaging animal category. You've seen dogs, cats, seals, dolphins, chimpanzees, maybe a kangaroo or two, but never an adorable koala bear? Have we got a movie for you. The Six Flags amusement park empire tried to enter the family film biz by producing this seldom-seen made for TV marsupial adventure from Down Under. An international con man being pursued by the mob complicates his life by falling for a lovely young woman whose daughter has a pet koala named Barnaby.
1977 (*Family*) 90m/C Sid Caesar, Juliet Mills, Sally Boyden; *D:* Norman Panama. **VHS, Beta $14.95** *ACA*

Barney & Friends: Barney Rhymes with Mother Goose

Big purple dinosaur is back with a dozen classic songs and rhymes, including "Polly Put the Kettle On" and "Little Jack Horner."
1993 (*Preschool*) 30m/C **VHS $14.95** *LGV*

Barney & Friends: Barney's Best Manners

Big purple dinosaur and his pals have a picnic with games and songs to teach manners, including "Please and Thank-You," "Snackin' on Healthy Food," "Does Your Chewing Gum Lose Its Flavor," and for fun "Three Little Fishies."
1993 (*Preschool-Primary*) 30m/C **VHS $14.95** *LGV*

Barney & the Backyard Gang

Video series featuring the mind-numbingly popular Barney the Purple Dinosaur; he smiles, he sings, he's so nice he makes Big Bird look like Boris Badenov. Here Barney transforms a swimming pool into a flying saucer, and his gang of wee pals are taken on a wondrous adventure involving everything from pirates to mermaids. Additional volumes available.
1990 (*Family*) 30m/C Sandy Duncan. **VHS** *NO*

Barney in Concert

Barney the purple Tyrannosaurus Rex mimics Ed Sullivan by putting together his own variety show in front of both parents and children. Songs include "Pop Goes the Weasel," "We Are Barney and the Backyard Gang," and "Hurry, Hurry, Drive the Firetruck." The multiracial audience also gets to hear a rap chant by the Backyard Gang, and the Hebrew alphabet, sung by preschoolers from a Dallas, Texas Hebrew school.
1991 (*Preschool*) 55m/C **VHS** *NO*

Barney's Christmas Surprise

This Barney is not the purple dinosaur but a lovable English sheepdog with a mouse friend named Roger. Six animated short stories are told of Barney's adventures with Christmas, skiing, and dieting.
1992 (*Preschool-Primary*) 30m/C **VHS $14.99** *GKK*

Baron Munchausen 🎬🎬🎬

Not to be confused with the Terry Gilliam's "Munchausen," this costly epic about the adventurous aristocrat of Teutonic

VIDEOHOUND'S FAMILY VIDEO RETRIEVER

lore was done for the 25th anniversary of Germany's UFA film studios. Contemplative, sometimes ponderous plot finds a modern descendent of Baron Munchausen retelling tall tales of his immortal ancestor in uncanny detail. Can he possibly be ... ? Paced and nuanced for adults rather than kids, and showcasing the biggest stars of the era - which happened to be that of the Third Reich, the reason this seldom screened outside of wartime Germany. Now available for reappraisal thanks to video, in subtitled or English-dubbed editions. **Hound Advisory:** Brief nudity in a sultan's harem. Fantasy violence, and a tearjerking death scene.

1943 (*Sr. High-Adult*) 120m/C Hans Albers, Kaethe Kaack, Hermann Speelmanns, Leo Slezak; *D:* Josef von Baky. **VHS, Beta $59.95** *INJ, VCD, GLV*

Batman 🦇🦇🦇

Blockbuster fantasy epic that brought a dark, adult perspective to the comic book. Keaton plays the mild-mannered Bruce Wayne with enough nervous tics (he sleeps hanging upside down) to suggest a damaged personality when he steps into his Caped Crusader costume to fight the crime that long ago took his parents' lives. Nicholson steals the show as the disfigured, genuinely sadistic Joker whose connection to Batman turns out to be very personal. Some said this was too violent for kids, but marketing made it a moot point, with Batman toys and souvenirs gleefully peddled to youngsters, and the same problem arose with the sequel "Batman Returns." Best for older kids only, though nearly all age ranges have thus far taken a peek. **Hound Advisory:** Frequent violence isn't realistic but often crosses the line into gruesome, especially the Joker's fondness for deadly chemicals. Profanity, sex.

1989 (PG-13/*Jr. High-Adult*) 126m/C Michael Keaton, Jack Nicholson, Kim Basinger, Robert Wuhl, Tracy Walter, Billy Dee Williams, Pat Hingle, Michael Gough, Jack Palance, Jerry Hall; *D:* Tim Burton; *W:* Sam Hamm, Warren Skaaren; *M:* Danny Elfman, Prince. **VHS, Beta, LV, 8mm $19.98** *FOX, WAR*

Batman: Mask of the Phantasm 🦇🦇

Feature-length theatrical release based on the '90s TV cartoon series that rendered Batman in 'toon form with some of the flair (and none of the mean spirit) of the Tim Burton movies. Major complaint was the bigscreen animation was identical to the small screen's, but on home video that matters not. Story illuminates Bruce Wayne's past more than the live-action epics, as Batman gets blamed for the murders of Gotham City gangsters, and there's a predictable connection to his long-lost first love. Interesting stuff for Batfans, but tale concludes like a comic book - full of infuriating, 'stay-tuned' loose ends. Yes, that is "Star Wars" Jedi Hamill doing the voice of the evil Joker. **Hound Advisory:** Violence.

1993 (PG/*Jr. High-Adult*) 77m/C *D:* Eric Radomski, Bruce W. Timm; *W:* Michael Reeves, Alan Burnett, Paul Dini, Martin Pako; *M:* Shirley Walker; *V:* Kevin Conroy, Dana Delany, Mark Hamill, Stacy Keach, Hart Bochner, Abe Vigoda, Efrem Zimbalist Jr., Dick Miller. **VHS $19.96** *WAR*

Batman Returns 🦇🦇🦇

More of the same from director Burton, with Batman/Bruce Wayne in a supporting role overshadowed by provocative villains. There's the cruelly misshapen Penguin, whose own father (former Pee Wee Herman Rubens, of all people) tried to kill him at birth; now he has a nightmare plot against Gotham City's children. And there's the exotic, dangerous Catwoman - a wickedly sexy character with more than a passing interest in Batman. Plotting takes a distant second to special effects, grotesque sets, thunderous music. Despite a big budget, grandiose sequel is of the love it or leave it variety, and insanely dark elements really make one wonder what age group it was intended for. A certain fast food chain caught flak for pushing "Batman Returns" merchandise onto kids. **Hound Advisory:** Mature themes, violence, profanity, sex talk.

1992 (PG-13/*Jr. High-Adult*) 126m/C Michael Keaton, Danny DeVito, Michelle Pfeiffer, Christopher Walken, Michael Gough, Michael Murphy, Cristi Conaway, Pat Hingle, Vincent Schiavelli, Jan Hooks, Paul (Pee Wee Herman) Reubens, Andrew Bryniarski; *D:* Tim Burton; *W:* Daniel Waters; *M:* Danny Elfman. **VHS $19.98** *WAR*

*batteries not included 🦇🦇🦇

As a real estate developer schemes to demolish a city tenement, the few remaining residents are aided by flying china. Turns out the levitating dishes are aliens with a talent for home improvement. Steven Spielberg produced this sci-fi reworking of the old elves-and-the-shoemaker fairy tale, with the usual superb special f/x, awed stares, and utter schmaltz. Of the human actors, only crusty Cronyn doesn't get carried away by the cutes. **Hound Advisory:** Violence, sex talk - there's a pretty embarrassing scene in which the two main space creatures get intimate, extraterrestrial-style.

1987 (PG/*Family*) 107m/C Hume Cronyn, Jessica Tandy, Frank McRae, Michael Carmine, Elizabeth Pena, Dennis Boutsikaris; *D:* Matthew Robbins; *W:* Matthew Robbins, Brad Bird, Brent Maddock, S.S. Wilson; *M:* James Horner. **VHS, Beta, LV $19.95** *MCA*

Battle Beyond the Stars 🦇🦇🦇

The planet Akir must be defended against alien raiders, so Thomas recruits a team of spacegoing mercenaries. Sci-fi takeoff on the Japanese adventure "The Seven Samurai" is one of the better "Star Wars" ripoffs, thanks to the pen of John Sayles. Producer Roger Corman later used excerpts of it in more kid- oriented features "Space Raiders" and "Andy and the Airwave Rangers." **Hound Advisory:** Space violence.

1980 (PG/*Primary-Adult*) 105m/C Richard Thomas, Robert Vaughn, George Peppard, Sybil Danning, Sam Jaffe, John Saxon, Darlanne Fluegel; *D:* Jimmy T. Murakami; *W:* John Sayles; *M:* James Horner. **VHS, Beta, LV $19.98** *VES, LIV*

Battle for Moon Station Dallos

Confusing but well-drawn Japanese cartoon feature about a guerilla war for independence waged by slave-like 'colonists' on the moon. Dallos is a mysterious lunar city the freedom fighters actually worship as a god. Inconclusive ending leaves room for lots of sequels. Notable as an example of 'adult' japanimation (deadly serious, with no silly robot or talking animal sidekicks) that's safe for kids; it avoids the sex, graphic carnage, profanity and nudity that have made the genre notorious. Also reportedly the first Japanese animated feature

made for their domestic direct-to-video market, rather than the theater or TV. **Hound Advisory:** Violence.
1986 *(Family)* 84m/C **D:** Mamoru Oshii. **VHS, Beta $14.99** *JFK, WTA*

Battle for the Planet of the Apes 🐾🐾

Final chapter is the least interesting in the five-movie simian saga. Tribe of human atomic bomb mutations are out to make life miserable for the peaceful ape tribe. The story is told primarily in flashback with the opening and closing sequences taking place in the year 2670 A.D. **Hound Advisory:** Violence.
1973 *(G/Family)* 96m/C Roddy McDowall, Lew Ayres, John Huston, Paul Williams, Claude Akins, Severn Darden, Natalie Trundy; **D:** J. Lee Thompson. **VHS, Beta $19.98** *FOX*

Battle of Britain 🐾🐾🐾◁

A powerful retelling of the most dramatic aerial combat battle of WWII, showing how the understaffed Royal Air Force held off the might of the German Luftwaffe.
1969 *(G/Family)* 132m/C Michael Caine, Laurence Olivier, Trevor Howard, Kenneth More, Christopher Plummer, Robert Shaw, Susannah York, Ralph Richardson, Curt Jurgens, Michael Redgrave, Nigel Patrick, Edward Fox; **D:** Guy Hamilton. **VHS, Beta, LV $19.98** *MGM, FOX*

Battle of the Bullies WOOF!

Canadian TV special about an unsalvageable nerd who plots a high-tech revenge upon a slew of high school bullies.
1985 *(Family)* 45m/C Manny Jacobs, Christopher Barnes, Sarah Inglis. **VHS, Beta $19.95** *NWV*

Battlestar Galactica 🐾🐾

Pilot episode (later released to theaters) of the glitzy family-hour sci-fi TV series. Crew of the last great starship must survive the human-exterminating, robot Cylons while questing for the legendary lost home, Earth. Grand f/x by the original "Star Wars" team, but George Lucas was not amused by the obvious imitation. TV episodes and feature-length cassette compilations are also available, but the costly saga was cancelled before telling the ultimate fate of mankind. Sorry. **Hound Advisory:** Space violence.
1978 *(PG/Family)* 125m/C Lorne Greene, Dirk Benedict, Karen Jensen, Jane Seymour, Patrick Macnee, Terry Carter, John Colicos, Richard A. Colla, Laurette Spang, Richard Hatch; **D:** Richard A. Colla. **VHS, Beta, LV $14.98** *MCA, MOV*

Battling with Buffalo Bill

12 episodes of the vintage serial concerning the exploits of the legendary Indian fighter.
1931 *(Family)* 180m/B Tom Tyler, Rex Bell, Franklin Farnum. **VHS, Beta $29.95** *VCN*

The Bay Boy 🐾🐾◁

Set in the 1930s in Nova Scotia, this period piece captures the coming-of-age of a rural teenage boy. Young Sutherland's adolescent angst becomes a more difficult struggle when he witnesses a murder, and is tormented by the secret.

1985 *(R/Sr. High-Adult)* 107m/C Liv Ullmann, Kiefer Sutherland, Peter Donat, Matthieu Carriere, Joe MacPherson, Isabelle Mejias, Alan Scarfe, Chris Wiggins, Leah K. Pinsent; **D:** Daniel Petrie; **M:** Claude Bolling. **VHS, Beta, LV $79.98** *ORI*

B.C.: A Special Christmas

TV cartoon short based on the sarcastic newspaper comic strip by Johnny Hart, about a gang of sophisticated cave-dwellers and their assorted follies. In this holiday-themed special, two of the tribe members (voices provided by the comedy team of Bob & Ray) scheme to get rich through inventing Santa Claus, only to be thwarted when the real thing shows up.
1971 *(Family)* 25m/C **V:** Bob Elliott, Ray Goulding. **VHS, Beta, LV $14.95** *COL, SUE, NLC*

B.C.: The First Thanksgiving

Another cartoon version of the fave Johnny Hart comic strip (though with a different animation team than the earlier "A Special Christmas"). The caveman B.C. and his friends discover fire, meaning hot soup for Thanksgiving. The tribe goes in search of a turkey for flavoring, but the bird has other ideas.
1972 *(Family)* 25m/C **V:** Don Messick, Daws Butler, Bob Holt. **VHS, Beta, LV $14.98** *SUE, NLC, WTA*

Be My Valentine, Charlie Brown/Is This Goodbye, Charlie Brown?

Two Peanuts specials: In "Be My Valentine, Charlie Brown," Charlie waits by his mailbox hoping for a valentine. Linus and Lucy are moving because of their father's job transfer to another city in "Is This Goodbye, Charlie Brown?"
1983 *(Family)* 50m/C **VHS, Beta** *SHV*

Beach Blanket Bingo 🐾🐾🐾

Fifth entry in the "Beach Party" series (after "Pajama Party") is by far the best and has achieved near-cult status. Both Funicello and Avalon are back, but this time a very young Evans catches Avalon's eye. Throw in a mermaid, some moon-doggies, skydiving, sizzling beach parties, and plenty of nostalgic golly-gee-whiz fun and you have the classic '60s beach movie. Totally implausible, but that's half the fun when the sun-worshipping teens become involved in a kidnapping and occasionally break into song. Followed by "How to Stuff a Wild Bikini." ♫Beach Blanket Bingo; The Cycle Set; Fly Boy; The Good Times; I Am My Ideal; I Think You Think; It Only Hurts When I Cry; New Love; You'll Never Change Him.
1965 *(Family)* 96m/C Frankie Avalon, Annette Funicello, Linda Evans, Don Rickles, Buster Keaton, Paul Lynde, Harvey Lembeck, Deborah Walley, John Ashley, Jody McCrea, Marta Kristen, Timothy Carey, Earl Wilson, Bobbi Shaw; **D:** William Asher; **W:** Sher Townsend, Leo Townsend; **M:** Les Baxter. **VHS, Beta, LV** *NO*

Beach Party 🐾🐾

Started the "Beach Party" series with the classic Funicello/Avalon combo. Scientist Cummings studying the mating habits of teenagers intrudes on a group of surfers, beach bums, and bikers, to his lasting regret. Typical beach party

bingo, with sand, swimsuits, singing, dancing, and bare minimum in way of a plot. Followed by "Muscle Beach Party." ♫Beach Party; Don't Stop Now; Promise Me Anything; Secret Surfin' Spot; Surfin' and a-Swingin'; Treat Him Nicely.
1963 (*Family*) 101m/C Frankie Avalon, Annette Funicello, Harvey Lembeck, Robert Cummings, Dorothy Malone, Morey Amsterdam, Jody McCrea, John Ashley, Candy Johnson, Dolores Wells, Yvette Vickers, Eva Six; **D:** William Asher; **W:** Lou Rusoff; **M:** Les Baxter. **VHS, Beta** *NO*

The Bear 🦴🦴🦴

Breathtaking moments in this innovative, somewhat slow nature drama about an orphan bear cub tagging after a grown male grizzly and dealing with hunters. The humans have almost no personality; a near-wordless narrative unfolds essentially from the cub's-eye-view, right down to some curious dream sequences. Jim Henson designed remote-controlled bears for more difficult scenes, and the differences are undetectable from animal thespians Bart and Douce (a cub as lovable as any "E.T." special effect). French-made, in English, and a huge money maker in Europe. Based on an even better novel by James Oliver Curwood. **Hound Advisory:** Sex between consenting bears. Bambious death of parental bear; also violence and, believe it or not, accidental drug use, as the cub eats an amanita mushroom and trips out. At least he doesn't make a habit of it.
1989 (*PG/Jr. High-Adult*) 92m/C Jack Wallace, Tcheky Karyo, Andre Lacombe; **D:** Jean-Jacques Annaud; **W:** Gerard Brach, Michael Kane; **M:** Bill Conti. **VHS, Beta, LV $14.95** *COL, RDG, HMV*

The Bears & I 🦴🦴

Young Vietnam vet helps Indians regain their land rights while raising three orphan bear cubs. Beautiful photography in this Disney sanitization of the nonfiction book by Robert Franklin Leslie.
1974 (*G/Adult-Family*) 89m/C Patrick Wayne, Chief Dan George, Andrew Duggan, Michael Ansara; **D:** Bernard McEveety; **M:** Buddy Baker. **VHS $69.95** *DIS*

Beastmaster 🦴🦴

Dumb but watchable barbarian adventure, with cutesy-critter appeal and lacking the explicit brutality of "Conan" and others of its ilk. Beastmaster Singer is a young warrior with the power to communicate with animals. Accompanied by a small posse of furry and feathered friends and slave girl Roberts, he battles evil cult tyrant Torn. An unrecognizable adaption (by director Coscarelli and co-producer Paul Pepperman) of Andre Norton's sci-fi novel of the same title. **Hound Advisory:** Barbarian violence, nudity, sex.
1982 (*PG/Jr. High-Adult*) 119m/C Marc Singer, Tanya Roberts, Rip Torn, John Amos, Josh Milrad, Billy Jacoby; **D:** Don A. Coscarelli. **VHS, Beta, LV $19.98** *MGM*

Beastmaster 2: Through the Portal of Time 🦴◁

This time the laughs are intentional as the Beastmaster follows an evil monarch through a dimensional gate to modern-day L.A., where the shopping is better for both trendy clothes and weapons. Fun for genre fans, with a

behind-the-scenes featurette on the tape. **Hound Advisory:** Violence.
1991 (*PG-13/Jr. High-Adult*) 107m/C Marc Singer, Kari Wuhrer, Sarah Douglas, Wings Hauser, James Avery, Robert Fieldsteel, Arthur Malet, Robert Z'Dar, Michael Berryman; **D:** Sylvio Tabet; **M:** Robert Folk. **VHS, LV $14.98** *REP*

Beat Street 🦴🦴

Intended as a quick cash-in on the break dancing trend, this essentially plotless musical features kids trying to break into local show biz with their rapping and dancing skills. Features the music of Afrika Bambaata and the Soul Sonic Force, Grand Master Melle Mel and the Furious Five, and others. ♫Beat Street Breakdown; Baptize the Beat; Stranger in a Strange Land; Beat Street Strut; Us Girls; This Could be the Night; Breakers Revenge; Tu Carino (Carmen's Theme); Frantic Situation. **Hound Advisory:** Profanity and violence.
1984 (*PG/Family*) 106m/C Rae Dawn Chong, Leon Grant, Saundra Santiago, Guy Davis, Jon Chardiet, Duane Jones, Kadeem Hardison; **D:** Stan Lathan. **VHS, Beta, LV $79.98** *VES, LIV*

Beauty and the Beast 🦴🦴🦴🦴

Classic live-action French version of the famous story. Belle, completely devoted to her father, yields to fate when the old man picks a rose from an accursed Beast's garden and must surrender a daughter or die. But as she dwells in the Beast's bizarre castle Belle feels the monster's pain and loneliness. Meanwhile, her old suitor (Marais, also playing the Beast) schemes to steal the Beast's treasures. Not always comprehensible, especially at the end, and this compliant Belle seems weak-willed compared with Disney's spunky heroine. But for dreamlike, visual poetry you won't find a better tale-spinner than Cocteau. The Beast's estate, full of helpful, disembodied arms (a la Thing in "The Addams Family") and baleful, staring statues won't soon be forgotten, especially by nightmare-prone toddlers. In French with English subtitles.
1946 (*Family*) 90m/B Jean Marais, Josette Day, Marcel Andre, Mila Parely, Nane Germon, Michel Auclair, Georges Auric; **D:** Jean Cocteau. **VHS, Beta, LV $19.95** *INJ, SUE, MLB*

Beauty and the Beast

Non-Disney animated version of the Brothers Grimm fairy tale classic which first aired on the Nickelodeon cable-TV channel.
1988 (*Family*) 47m/C **VHS $9.99** *FHE*

Beauty and the Beast 🦴🦴🦴🦴

Wonderful Disney musical combines superb animation, splendid characters, and lively songs in the legendary story about beautiful, willful Belle who becomes the unwilling guest of the fearsome and disagreeable Beast. Supporting cast includes the castle servants, a delightful bunch of singing household objects. Notable as the first animated feature to be nominated for the Best Picture Oscar. Awarding-winning title song as well as other Menken/Ashman tunes were good enough that this was soon transmuted into a smash Broadway stage musical. The deluxe video version features a work-in-progress rough film cut, a compact disc of the soundtrack, a

lithograph depicting a scene from the film, and an illustrated book. ♫Beauty and the Beast; Belle; Something There; Be Our Guest.
1991 (G/*Family*) 84m/C **D:** Kirk Wise, Gary Trousdale; **M:** Alan Menken, Howard Ashman; **V:** Paige O'Hara, Robby Benson, Rex Everhart, Richard White, Jesse Corti, Angela Lansbury, Jerry Orbach, David Ogden Stiers, Bradley Michael Pierce, Jo Anne Worley, Kimmy Robertson. **Award Nominations:** Academy Awards '91: Best Picture, Best Song ("Belle", "Be Our Guest"), Best Sound; **Awards:** Academy Awards '91: Best Song ("Beauty and the Beast"), Best Score; Golden Globe Awards '92: Best Film—Musical/Comedy. **VHS, LV $24.99** *DIS, OM*

Bebe's Kids 🐾🐾🗨

The first black-oriented cartoon feature is based on characters created in routines by the late comedian Robin Harris. He's personified as an ineffectual ladies' man who takes a lovely woman out on their first date, but there's a surprise - five kids, her own and four little terrors she's baby-sitting. Their trip to a restrictive amusement park takes some funny shots at both black and white culture and Disneyland. Not entirely successful, but a notable 'toon change of pace with rapper Tone Loc's vocals (for a tough-talking diapered infant) stealing the show, just as he did in "Ferngully." The video includes the seven-minute animated short "Itsy Bitsy Spider," that accompanied the feature in most theaters. **Hound Advisory:** Alcohol use, but the PG-13 rating seems highly unfair.
1992 (PG-13/*Family*) 74m/C **D:** Bruce Smith; **W:** Reginald Hudlin; **M:** John Barnes; **V:** Faizon Love, Vanessa Bell Calloway, Wayne Collins, Jonell Green, Marques Houston, Tone Loc, Nell Carter, Myra J. **VHS, Beta, LV $14.95** *PAR, WTA*

Bedknobs and Broomsticks 🐾🐾🗨

During WWII, three London kids are evacuated to the country home of prim Miss Eglantine Price, who turns out to be studying witchcraft by mail order. Her shaky command of magic takes them on a variety of adventures, some animated, and obviously intended to recall "Mary Poppins," though this overlong Disney romp isn't quite in that classic league until a wild ending pitting Nazi invaders against marching suits of clothes. Based on stories by Mary Norton.
1971 (G/*Family*) 117m/C Angela Lansbury, Roddy McDowall, David Tomlinson, Bruce Forsyth, Sam Jaffe; **D:** Robert Stevenson. **Award Nominations:** Academy Awards '71: Best Art Direction/Set Decoration, Best Costume Design, Best Song ("The Age of Not Believing"), Best Original Score; **Awards:** Academy Awards '71: Best Visual Effects. **VHS, Beta, LV $24.99** *DIS, WTA*

Bedrock Wedlock

Compilation of Hanna-Barbera cartoon episodes, led by a notable "Flintstones" flashback episode in which a young Fred's wedding plans to Wilma nearly go awry. Also included are segments with characters like Wally Gator, Yogi Bear, Loopy D'Loop and more.
1989 (*Family*) 80m/C **V:** Mel Blanc, Jean VanDerPyl, Alan Reed. **VHS, Beta $29.95** *TTC, WTA*

Bedrockin' and Rappin'

Join your favorite Hanna-Barbera cartoon characters, including the Flintstones, Scooby-Doo and Top Cat, for an exciting, unique rap session.
1991 (*Family*) 30m/C **VHS, Beta $9.95** *TTC, WTA*

The Bees WOOF!

Sting of a poor movie is painful. A strain of bees have ransacked South America and are threatening the rest of the world. The buzz is that no one is safe. Cheap rip-off of "The Swarm," which is saying something.
1978 (PG/*Jr. High-Adult*) 93m/C John Saxon, John Carradine, Angel Tompkins, Claudio Brook, Alicia Encinas; **D:** Alfredo Zacharias. **VHS, Beta $29.98** *WAR*

Beethoven 🐾🐾

Anxious St. Bernard pup escapes dognappers and wanders to the home of the Newtons, who adopt him over dad's objections. Beethoven grows into a huge, slobbering dog, a favorite - even a substitute parent - to the kids, but a headache for persnickety Mr. Newton, until a rematch with those dognappers (longtime Disney good guy Jones is ironically cast as the murderous ringleader). A hit, though it's most a case of teaching a new dog some very old tricks. Every dumb gag and pathos detail can be sniffed out long in advance, and the ending fails to make a case for film realism. Written by "Home Alone" creator John Hughes, under a pseudonym. **Hound Advisory:** Roughhousing.
1992 (PG/*Family*) 89m/C Charles Grodin, Bonnie Hunt, Dean Jones, Oliver Platt, Stanley Tucci, Nicholle Tom, Christopher Castile, Sarah Rose Karr, David Duchovny, Patricia Heaton, Laurel Cronin; **D:** Brian Levant; **W:** John Hughes, Amy Holden Jones. **VHS, LV $19.98** *MCA, FCT*

Beethoven's 2nd 🐾🐾🗨

Sequel has awwww factor going for it as new daddy Beethoven slobbers over four adorable and appealing St. Bernard pups and his new love Missy. Same basic evil subplot as the first, with wicked kidnappers replacing evil vet. During the upheaval, the Newtons take care of the little yapping troublemakers, providing the backdrop for endless puppy mischief and exasperation on Grodin's part. Silly subplots and too many human moments tend to drag, but the kids will find the laughs (albeit stupid ones). **Hound Advisory:** Roughhousing; alcohol use.
1993 (PG/*Family*) 87m/C Charles Grodin, Bonnie Hunt, Nicholle Tom, Christopher Castile, Sarah Rose Karr, Debi Mazar, Christopher Penn, Ashley Hamilton; **D:** Rod Daniel; **W:** Len Blum; **M:** Randy Edelman. **VHS, LV $24.98** *MCA*

Beetle Bailey: Military Madness

The long-running Mort Walker comic strip about the antics of sad-sack slacker Bailey and his bunkmates at Camp Swampy were animated for an early '60s TV cartoon show. Four additional half-hour collections are available: "Pranks in the Ranks," "Pride of Camp Swampy," "Sarge's Last Stand," and "You're in the Army Now."
1963 (*Family*) 30m/C **V:** Howard Morris. **VHS $9.99** *BFV*

Beetlejuice 🐾🐾🐾

Recently deceased young couple become novice ghosts faced with scaring an obnoxious new family out of their old home. They hire a weirdo pro poltergeist for the job, but the afterlife becomes more complicated when the maniacal Beetlejuice becomes distracted by Router, the gloomy teen

"Beethoven" and family pose (1992)

daughter befriended by the ghostly marrieds. Gaudy, funny, surreal and somewhat incoherent comedy of spooks, with inventive makeup f/x, music, and set designs. Followed by a cartoon TV series for kids. **Hound Advisory:** Salty language, supernatural violence - rapid aging, shrinking heads, that sort of stuff, not exactly realism.
1988 *(PG/Adult)* 92m/C Michael Keaton, Geena Davis, Alec Baldwin, Sylvia Sidney, Catherine O'Hara, Winona Ryder, Jeffrey Jones, Dick Cavett; *D:* Tim Burton; *W:* Michael McDowell, Warren Skaaren; *M:* Danny Elfman. **VHS, Beta, LV, 8mm $19.98** *WAR, FCT, TLF*

Being There 🎜🎜🎜◁

A feeble-minded gardener, whose entire knowledge of life comes from watching television, is sent out into the real world when his employer dies. Equipped with his prize possession, his remote control unit, the gardener unwittingly enters the world of politics and is welcomed as a mysterious sage. Sellers is wonderful in this satiric treat adapted by Jerzy Kosinski from his novel.
1979 *(PG/Jr. High-Adult)* 130m/C Peter Sellers, Shirley MacLaine, Melvyn Douglas, Jack Warden, Richard Dysart, Richard Basehart; *D:* Hal Ashby. **Award Nominations:** Academy Awards '79: Best Actor (Sellers); Cannes Film Festival '80: Best Film; **Awards:** Academy Awards '79: Best Supporting Actor (Douglas); Golden Globe Awards '80: Best Actor—Musical/Comedy (Sellers), Best Supporting Actor (Douglas); National Board of Review Awards '79: 10 Best Films of the Year, Best Actor (Sellers). **VHS, Beta, LV $19.98** *FOX, FCT, WAR*

The Bellboy 🎜🎜◁

MDA Telethons aren't the only connection between Lewis and children; the comedian's frenetic screen persona resembles a nine-year-old kid running wild, and there's quite a similarity between early Jerry and the later Pee Wee Herman. Young viewers should especially enjoy Jerry's slapstick antics here. Plotless but clever outing is set at Miami's grand Fountainbleau Hotel, with the star/writer/director in a nearly wordless role as a goofball bellhop whose every errand turns into disaster.
1960 *(Family)* 72m/B Jerry Lewis, Alex Gerry, Bob Clayton, Sonny Sands; *Cameos:* Milton Berle, Walter Winchell; *D:* Jerry Lewis; *W:* Jerry Lewis. **VHS, Beta, LV $59.95** *LIV*

The Belle of New York 🎜🎜

A turn-of-the-century bachelor falls in love with a Salvation Army missionary in this standard musical. 🎜Naughty But Nice; Baby Doll; Oops; I Wanna Be a Dancin' Man; Seeing's Believing; Bachelor's Dinner Song; When I'm Out With the Belle of New York; Let a Little Love Come In.
1952 *(Family)* 82m/C Fred Astaire, Vera-Ellen, Marjorie Main, Keenan Wynn, Alice Pearce, Gale Robbins, Clinton Sundberg; *D:* Charles Walters. **VHS, Beta $19.98** *MGM, FHE*

The Belles of St. Trinian's 🎜🎜🎜

Classic British comedy based on a popular comic strip by Ronald Searle about a girls' school and its rampaging inmates. The little hellions are mainly the background here; star is master character actor Sim in a gender-bending dual role as both the head mistress and her petty-crook twin brother, who scheme to save the school from financial ruin. The dreadful St. Trinian's tykes had more prominent parts in later sequels: "Blue Murder at St. Trinian's," "The Pure Hell of St.

Trinian's," and "The Great St. Trinian's Train Robbery."
Hound Advisory: Alcohol talk.
1953 *(Family)* 86m/B Alastair Sim, Joyce Grenfell, Hermione Baddeley, George Cole, Eric Pohlmann, Renee Houston, Beryl Reid; *D:* Frank Launder; *M:* Malcolm Arnold. **VHS, Beta $39.95** *HMV*

The Bells of St. Mary's 🎜🎜🎜◁

Easy-going priest finds himself in a subtle battle of wits with the Mother Superior over how the children of St. Mary's school should be raised. It's the sequel to "Going My Way." Songs include the title tune and "Aren't You Glad You're You?" Also available in a colorized version.
1945 *(Family)* 126m/B Bing Crosby, Ingrid Bergman, Henry Travers; *D:* Leo McCarey. **Award Nominations:** Academy Awards '44: Best Actress (Bergman); Academy Awards '45: Best Actor (Crosby), Best Director (McCarey), Best Film Editing, Best Picture, Best Song ("Aren't You Glad You're You"), Best Original Score; **Awards:** Academy Awards '45: Best Sound; Golden Globe Awards '46: Best Actress—Drama (Bergman); New York Film Critics Awards '45: Best Actress (Bergman). **VHS, Beta, LV $39.98** *REP, IGP*

The Belstone Fox 🎜🎜

Plodding British animal drama from the same producer as "Born Free." Not a complete success but an interesting comparison with Disney's superficially similar (and sunnier) "The Fox and the Hound." A fox cub is raised by a hunter for the sole purpose of being someday chased down and killed for sport in one of England's traditional country pastimes. Will a hunting dog who has befriended the fox carry out the foul deed? Might be a bit disturbing for young children. Based on the novel "Ballad of the Belstone Fox" by David Rook.
1973 *(Family)* 103m/C Eric Porter, Rachel Roberts, Jeremy Kemp; *D:* James Hill. **VHS, Beta** *SUE*

Ben and Me

Classic Disney cartoon short in which Amos the mouse befriends Benjamin Franklin and takes his own look at events leading up to the American Revolution. Also available with "Bongo" on laserdisc.
1954 *(Primary-Jr. High)* 25m/C *D:* Hamilton Luske; *V:* Sterling Holloway. **VHS, Beta $12.99** *MTI, DSN, WTA*

Beneath the Planet of the Apes 🎜🎜◁

In the first sequel to the sci-fi classic, another Earth astronaut passes through the warp. He follows the same paths as Taylor, through Ape City and to the ruins of bomb-blasted New York's subway system, where warhead-worshipping human mutants are found living. Strain of sequelling shows instantly, though the next in the series, "Escape from the Planet of the Apes." improves matters. **Hound Advisory:** Violence.
1970 *(G/Family)* 108m/C Charlton Heston, James Franciscus, Kim Hunter, Maurice Evans, James Gregory, Natalie Trundy, Jeff Corey, Linda Harrison, Victor Buono; *D:* Ted Post. **VHS, Beta, LV $19.98** *FOX, FUS*

The Beniker Gang 🎜🎜◁

Five orphans are sprung from the big house and become an extended family. They're supported by the eldest who writes a syndicated advice column. Sincere drama will likely interest the kids.

1983 (G/*Family-Family*) 87m/C Andrew McCarthy, Jennie Dundas, Danny Pintauro, Charlie Fields; *D:* Ken Kwapis. **VHS, Beta $59.95** *WAR*

Benji 🐾🐾🐾

Surprise hit that came out of nowhere (no Hollywood company wanted to release it) and became a minor classic. Successfully tells its simple tale from a dog's point-of-view, as a resourceful neighborhood stray mutt saves two children from kidnappers and finds romance with a pampered pooch named Tiffany. Benji is still one of the most sympathetic and winning animal actors ever. And yes, that is Aunt Bea from TV's "Andy Griffith Show" as the lady whose cat Benji routinely chases. Followup: "For the Love of Benji."

1974 (G/*Family*) 87m/C Benji, Peter Breck, Christopher Connelly, Patsy Garrett, Deborah Walley, Cynthia Smith; *D:* Joe Camp. **Award Nominations:** Academy Awards '74: Best Song ("Benji's Theme (I Feel Love)"); **Awards:** Golden Globe Awards '75: Best Song ("I Feel Love"). **VHS, Beta $19.99** *VES, FCT, APD*

Benji at Work

Behind-the-scenes documentary look at how the lovable dog learns how to act, done in connection with the feature "Oh Heavenly Dog."

1993 (*Preschool-Primary*) 30m/C Chevy Chase, Jane Seymour. **VHS** *NO*

Benji the Hunted 🐾🐾🐾

Humans are virtually absent in this Benji adventure, released through Disney, but the critters make up for it as the heroic canine discovers some adorable orphaned cougar cubs, and battles terrain and predators to bring the kitties to safety. Not as fast-paced as others in the series, but solidly entertaining. Unusual touch: Benji isn't just a stray mutt here, he's playing himself, the superstar dog lost in the Oregon woods during a location shoot. Frank Inn, Benji's Santa-lookalike owner, also appears.

1987 (G/*Family*) 89m/C Benji, Red Steagall, Frank Inn; *D:* Joe Camp. **VHS, Beta, LV $19.99** *DIS*

Benji's Very Own Christmas Story 🐾🐾

Canine thespian Benji and his friends go on a magic trip and meet Kris Kringle and learn how Christmas is celebrated around the world. Also included: "The Phenomenon of Benji," a documentary about Benji's odyssey from the animal shelter to international stardom.

1983 (*Family*) 60m/C **VHS, Beta $14.99** *BFV*

Benny & Joon 🐾🐾🐾

Depending on your tolerance for cute eccentrics and whimsy, this will either charm you with sweetness or send you into sugar shock. Masterson is Joon, a mentally disturbed young woman who paints and has a habit of setting fires. She lives with overprotective brother Benny (Quinn). Sam (Depp) is the outsider who charms Joon, a dyslexic loner who imperso-nates his heroes Charlie Chaplin and Buster Keaton with eerie

accuracy. Depp is particularly fine with the physical demands of his role, but the film's easy dismissal of Joon's mental illness is a serious flaw. The laserdisc version is letterboxed. **Hound Advisory:** Mature themes; sex talk.

1993 (PG/*Jr. High-Adult*) 98m/C Johnny Depp, Mary Stuart Masterson, Aidan Quinn, Julianne Moore, Oliver Platt, CCH Pounder, Dan Hedaya, Joe Grifasi, William H. Macy, Eileen Ryan; *D:* Jeremiah S. Chechik; *W:* Barry Berman; *M:* Rachel Portman. **VHS, Beta, LV $19.98** *MGM*

The Berenstain Bears' Christmas

The distinctive cartoon bear clan from the creative team of Stan and Jan Berenstain act out little morality plays within their rollicking animated adventures. In this holiday offering, Papa Bear decides that this year he will find his perfect Christmas tree, but during his bumbling trek through the wintery woods he realizes how important a simple spruce is to the critters who dwell in it. The cassette also includes "Inside Outside Upside Down" and "The Bike Lesson."

1990 (*Family*) 30m/C **VHS, Beta $9.95** *RAN, WTA, VEC*

Berenstain Bears' Comic Valentine

Brother Bear receives a mysterious Valentine from Miss Honey Bear, a secret admirer; but can he keep his mind on the upcoming holiday hockey match against the Beartown Bullies?

1982 (*Family*) 25m/C **VHS, Beta** *SUE*

Berenstain Bears' Easter Surprise

Boss Bunny, who usually controls the seasons, has quit; Poppa Bear's vainglorious effort to construct an Easter egg machine is a failure; and Brother Bear anxiously awaits his "Extra Special" Easter Surprise.

1981 (*Family*) 25m/C **VHS, Beta** *SUE*

Berenstain Bears Meet Big Paw

Brother and Sister Bear meet up with the legendary monster Big Paw and find out he is not such a bad beast after all. Additional volumes available.

1980 (*Family*) 25m/C **VHS, Beta, LV $9.98** *SUE, WTA*

Bernard and the Genie 🐾🐾🐾

Fired from his job, jilted by his girlfriend at Christmas, Bernard's troubles seemed to be solved - or are they just beginning? - when he rubs a magic lamp and becomes the surprised master of a funky genie. Holiday TV comedy from Britain is aimed at young and old alike, meaning a curious mix of childish elements (including a genuine Teenage Mutant Ninja Turtle cameo) and bawdy stuff. Great cast; Henry, the lamp occupant, is a comic superstar in England, as is Atkinson. **Hound Advisory:** Sex talk, roughhousing.

1991 (G/*Family*) 70m/C Alan Cumming, Lenny Henry, Rowan Atkinson; *D:* Paul Weiland. **VHS $19.98** *FOX, BTV*

The Best Christmas Pageant Ever

Troublemaking kids participate in the school Christmas pageant, guaranteeing a manger scene that nobody will soon

forget. Lukewarm holiday heartwarmer, made for TV, based on the book by Barbara Robinson.
1986 (*Primary-Adult*) 60m/C Dennis Weaver, Karen Grassle. **VHS $19.95** *RHV*

The Best of Betty Boop, Vol. 1

Sweet Betty Boop sashays through 11 of her classic cartoon adventures in this collection of original shorts. Mastered from the original negatives.
1939 (*Family*) 90m/C *V:* Mae Questel. **VHS $14.98** *REP, WTA*

The Best of Betty Boop, Vol. 2

Another collection of original cartoons starring the "Boop-Oop-a-Doop" girl, assisted by Bimbo and Koko the Clown. These black-and-white cartoons have be recolored for this release.
1939 (*Family*) 85m/C *V:* Mae Questel. **VHS, Beta $14.98** *REP, WTA*

Best of Bugs Bunny & Friends

Collection of classics from great cartoon stars Bugs Bunny, Daffy Duck, Tweetie Pie, and Porky Pig. Includes "Duck Soup to Nuts," "A Feud There Was," and "Tweetie Pie."
1940 (*Family*) 53m/C *D:* Friz Freleng, Chuck Jones, Robert McKimson. **VHS, Beta** *MGM*

The Best of Gumby

Special 30th Anniversary celebration of Art Clokey's 1957 television solo show for the Gumbster, following his debut the previous year on "Howdy Doody." Contains seven all-time favorite episodes of Gumby at his best. See also "Gumby" and "The World According to Gumby."
1987 (*Family*) 45m/C **VHS, Beta $14.95** *FHE, WTA*

The Best of Terrytoons

Created by Paul Terry in 1929, the Terrytoons were one of the longest continuous cartoon series in history. Remember, this was in the days before Saturday-morning TV, yet Terry used techniques of modern, assembly-line animation that would later be standard practice with Hanna-Barbera, Filmation, and other kidvid mainstays. This one-hour compilation gathers the more famous of the many, many Terrytoon characters, including Mighty Mouse, Deputy Dawg, Gandy Goose, Dinky Duck, Terry Bears and Little Roquefort. Terrytoon collections from the silent era include "Cat's Meow...Kitty Kartoons by Paul Terry" and "The Cats and Mice of Paul Terry."
1983 (*Family*) 60m/C **VHS, Beta** *NO*

The Best of Times 🦴🦴

Slim story of two grown men who attempt to redress the failures of the past by reenacting a football game they lost in high school due to a single flubbed pass. With this cast, it should have been better. **Hound Advisory:** Profanity, suggested sex.
1986 (*PG/Jr. High-Adult*) 105m/C Robin Williams, Kurt Russell, M. Emmet Walsh, Pamela Reed, Holly Palance, Donald Moffatt, Margaret Whitton, Kirk Cameron; *D:* Roger Spottiswoode; *W:* Ron Shelton. **VHS, Beta, LV, 8mm $14.98** *SUE, NLC*

Bethie's Really Silly Clubhouse

Children's entertainer Bethie opens her clubhouse to a group of youngsters who want to learn about animals. Lots of jokes and silly songs.
1994 (*Preschool-Primary*) 30m/C **VHS**

Better Off Dead 🦴🦴🦴⬠

Compulsive teenager's girlfriend leaves him and he decides to end it all. After several abortive suicide attempts, he decides instead to out-ski her obnoxious new boyfriend. Uneven but funny, thanks largely to Cusack's charm and Armstrong's support. Not as tasteless as it might sound at first, with some genuine heart. **Hound Advisory:** Salty language, mature themes.
1985 (*PG/College-Adult*) 97m/C John Cusack, Curtis Armstrong, Diane Franklin, Kim Darby, David Ogden Stiers, Dan Schneider, Amanda Wyss, Taylor Negron, Vincent Schiavelli, Demian Slade, Scooter Stevens; *D:* Steve Holland; *W:* Steve Holland; *M:* Rupert Hine. **VHS, Beta, LV $79.98** *FOX*

Betty Boop

The Fleischer Brothers' classic cartoon flapper character is probably best known to modern audiences for her cameo (as a has-been!) in "Who Framed Roger Rabbit?" Betty in her prime can be found on tape in several collections, including three volumes of "Betty Boop Festival" (sadly, no longer distributed).
193? (*Family*) 30m/C *V:* Mae Questel, Mel Blanc. **VHS, LV** *CNG*

Betty Boop Special Collector's Edition: Volume 1

Betty Boop returns in this collection of vintage cartoons, presented in glorious, original B&W, with appearances by jazz greats Cab Calloway and Don Redman. Vol. 2 features an additional 90 minutes of Boop-oop-a-doop, plus more with Calloway and his orchestra.
1935 (*Family*) 90m/B *D:* Dave Fleischer, Max Fleischer; *V:* Louis Armstrong, Mae Questel. **VHS, LV $19.98** *REP, WTA*

The Beverly Hillbillies 🦴🦴🦴⬠

Big-screen transfer of the long-running TV show may appeal to fans. Ozark mountaineer Jed Clampett discovers oil, becomes an instant billionaire, and packs his backwoods clan off to the good life in California. Minimal plot finds dim-bulb nephew Jethro and daughter Elly May looking for a bride for Jed. Not that any of it matters. Everyone does fine by their impersonations, particularly Varney as the good-hearted Jed and Leachman as stubborn Granny. Ebsen, the original Jed, reprises another of his TV roles, detective Barnaby Jones. And yes, the familiar strains of the "Ballad of Jed Clampett" by Jerry Scoggins starts this one off, too. **Hound Advisory:** Salty language.
1993 (*PG/Jr. High-Adult*) 93m/C Jim Varney, Erika Eleniak, Diedrich Bader, Cloris Leachman, Dabney Coleman, Lily Tomlin, Lea Thompson, Rob Schneider, Linda Carlson, Penny Fuller, Kevin Connolly; *Cameos:* Buddy Ebsen, Zsa Zsa Gabor, Dolly Parton; *D:* Penelope Spheeris; *W:* Larry Konner, Mark Rosenthal, Jim Fisher, Jim Staahl; *M:* Lalo Schifrin. **VHS** *FXV*

Beverly Hills Brats 🐾

Lonely Hollywood kid hires a bumbling burglar to kidnap him, in order to gain his parents' attention. Then both of them are snatched by real crooks. How did a great cast like this get involved in such a dimwitted farce? **Hound Advisory:** The neglectful father is a cosmetic surgeon, prompting gags and photos of female body parts. Profanity, sex talk.
1989 (PG-13/*Jr. High-Adult*) 90m/C Martin Sheen, Burt Young, Peter Billingsley, Terry Moore; **D:** Dimitri Sotirakis; **M:** Barry Goldberg. **VHS, Beta, LV $89.95** *LIV, IME, VTR*

Beverly Hills Cop 🐾🐾🐾

When a close friend of smooth-talking Detroit cop Axle Foley is brutally murdered in L.A., he traces the murderer to the posh streets of Beverly Hills. There he must stay on his toes to keep one step ahead of the killer and two steps ahead of the law. Better than average Murphy vehicle is followed by two lesser sequels. **Hound Advisory:** Profanity and violence.
1984 (R/*Family*) 105m/C Eddie Murphy, Judge Reinhold, John Ashton, Lisa Eilbacher, Ronny Cox, Steven Berkoff, James Russo, Jonathan Banks, Stephen Elliott, Bronson Pinchot, Paul Reiser, Damon Wayans, Rick Overton; **D:** Martin Brest; **W:** Danilo Bach, Dan Petrie Jr.; **M:** Harold Faltermeyer. **Award Nominations:** Academy Awards '84: Best Original Screenplay; **Awards:** People's Choice Awards '85: Best Film. **VHS, Beta, LV, 8mm $14.95** *PAR*

Beverly Hills Cop 2 🐾🐾

The highly successful sequel to the highly successful original repeats formula with essentially the same plot, dealing this time with Foley infiltrating a band of international munitions smugglers. Spawned a hit soundtrack and yet another sequel in a successful attempt to run a good thing straight into the ground. **Hound Advisory:** Violence; profanity; brief nudity.
1987 (R/*Sr. High-Adult*) 103m/C Eddie Murphy, Judge Reinhold, Juergen Prochnow, Ronny Cox, John Ashton, Brigitte Nielsen, Allen (Gooritz) Garfield, Paul Reiser, Dean Stockwell; **D:** Tony Scott; **W:** Larry Ferguson, Warren Skaaren; **M:** Harold Faltermeyer. **VHS, Beta, LV, 8mm $14.95** *PAR*

Beverly Hills Cop 3 🐾🐾

Yes, Detroit cop Axel Foley (Murphy) just happens to find another case that takes him back to his friends on the Beverly Hills PD. This time he uncovers a criminal network fronting WonderWorld, an amusement park with a squeaky-clean image. Fast-paced action, lots of gunplay, and Eddie wisecracks his way through the slow spots. Reinhold returns as the still impossibly naive Rosewood, with Bronson briefly reprising his role as Serge of the undeterminable accent. Critically panned box office disappointment relies too heavily on formula and is another disappointing followup. **Hound Advisory:** Violence and profanity.
1994 (R/*Sr. High-Adult*) 109m/C Eddie Murphy, Judge Reinhold, Hector Elizondo, Timothy Carhart, Stephen McHattie, Theresa Randle, John Saxon, Alan Young, Bronson Pinchot; **Cameos:** Al Green, Gil Hill; **D:** John Landis; **W:** Steven E. de Souza; **M:** Nile Rodgers. **VHS** *PAR*

Beverly Hills Teens

Compilation of episodes from a syndicated TV cartoon series about obscenely wealthy California kids and their zany adventures. Additional volumes available.
1989 (*Primary*) 120m/C **VHS, Beta $39.95** *JFK, WTA*

Big 🐾🐾🐾

Charming modern fable of an impatient 12-year-old boy who makes a wish to be 'big.' When he awakens the next morning he's got the body of a 30-year-old man. Thrown out by his terrified mom, the hero must learn to live as a grownup. His talent for evaluating toys gets him a job in a big corporation, a luxury apartment - even an office romance. Hanks is totally believable as a guileless man-child, while Perkins scores in the perilous role of the yuppie cynic attracted to him. Marshall directs with humanity, and the whole thing clicks from the beginning. Toy store scene with the giant piano keyboard is a classic. **Hound Advisory:** Yes, the hero has a love affair with the high-powered businesslady, an episode handled with taste and conscience. Alcohol use, salty language.
1988 (PG/*Family*) 98m/C Tom Hanks, Elizabeth Perkins, John Heard, Robert Loggia, Jared Rushton, David Moscow, Jon Lovitz, Mercedes Ruehl; **D:** Penny Marshall; **W:** Gary Ross; **M:** Howard Shore. **Award Nominations:** Academy Awards '88: Best Actor (Hanks), Best Original Screenplay; **Awards:** Golden Globe Awards '89: Best Actor—Musical/Comedy (Hanks); People's Choice Awards '89: Best Film—Musical/Comedy. **VHS, Beta, LV $19.98** *FOX, HMV*

Big Bird in China

"Sesame Street" mainstay Big Bird is guided through China by a six-year-old in search of the legendary phoenix. Along the way, they visit Chinese schools, children, watch a T'ai Ch'i demonstration, and learn Chinese words, traditions, and culture.
1987 (*Family*) 75m/C Big Bird. **VHS $24.95** *KUI, RAN*

Big Bird in Japan

Big Bird and his pal Barkley the Dog lose their way while visiting Tokyo. As they wander about, they meet all sorts of interesting people, including a young girl who could be the legendary Bamboo Princess. Includes four new songs.
1991 (*Family*) 60m/C **VHS, Beta $14.95** *RAN*

The Big Bus 🐾🐾

The wild adventures of the world's first nuclear-powered bus as it makes its maiden voyage from New York to Denver. Clumsy disaster-movie parody.
1976 (PG/*Jr. High-Adult*) 88m/C Joseph Bologna, Stockard Channing, Ned Beatty, Ruth Gordon, Larry Hagman, John Beck, Jose Ferrer, Lynn Redgrave, Sally Kellerman, Stuart Margolin, Richard Mulligan, Howard Hesseman, Richard B. Shull; **D:** James Frawley; **M:** David Shire. **VHS, Beta $49.95** *PAR*

Big Business 🐾🐾

Strained high-concept comedy about two sets of identical twins, each played by Tomlin and Midler, mismatched at birth by a near-sighted country nurse. One set is raised in the city amid wealth and splendor while the other grows up in a less auspicious rural setting. Fate conspires to bring the twins together, as the city duo tries to buy out the factory where the country twins work. From there on, it's a one-joke series of zany consequences and episodes of mistaken identity. Nice cast, some fairly funny moments, great technical effects, semi-lame script suffers from case of the repeats. **Hound Advisory:** Salty language.

1988 (PG/*Jr. High-Adult*) 98m/C Bette Midler, Lily Tomlin, Fred Ward, Edward Herrmann, Michele Placido, Barry Primus, Michael Gross, Mary Gross, Daniel Gerroll, Roy Brocksmith; *D:* Jim Abrahams. **VHS, Beta, LV, 8mm $89.95** *TOU*

Big Girls Don't Cry. . .They Get Even 𝄃

Teenage Laura flees her oft-broken home because of her odious stepfamily. She joins her one nice relation at his wilderness retreat, but the whole much-remarried clan arrives to look for her. At last the bimbo mistress, lusty ex-husbands, spoiled ex-wives, and bratty half-siblings learn to get along. Icky, ineffective "family comedy" gives the bad-sitcom treatment to divorce and adultery, yet pretends to have insights. **Hound Advisory:** Sex talk, salty language, mature themes.
1992 (PG/*Jr. High-Adult*) 98m/C Hillary Wolf, Griffin Dunne, Margaret Whitton, David Strathairn, Ben Savage, Adrienne Shelly, Patricia Kalember; *D:* Joan Micklin Silver. **VHS, LV** *COL, NLC*

Big Jake 𝄃𝄃

Aging Texas cattle man who has outlived his time swings into action when outlaws kidnap his grandson and wound his son. He returns to his estranged family to help them in the search for Little Jake. O'Hara is once again paired up with Wayne and the chemistry is still there. **Hound Advisory:** Violence.
1971 (PG/*Family*) 90m/C John Wayne, Richard Boone, Maureen O'Hara, Patrick Wayne, Chris Mitchum, Bobby Vinton; *D:* George Sherman; *M:* Elmer Bernstein. **VHS, Beta, LV $19.98** *FOX*

Big Mo 𝄃𝄃

True story of the friendship that developed between Cincinnati Royals basketball stars Maurice Stokes and Jack Twyman after a strange paralysis hit Stokes.
1973 (G/*Family*) 110m/C Bernie Casey, Bo Svenson, Stephanie Edwards, Janet MacLachlan; *D:* Daniel Mann. **VHS, Beta $69.95** *VES*

Big Red 𝄃𝄃𝄃

Solid Disney adaptation of the favorite Jim Kjelgaard novel, filmed on location against the spectacular beauty of French Canada's Quebec Province. Orphan boy is hired by a grumpy adult to care for a champion Irish setter. The kid saves the dog, who later repays the favor during an attack by a mountain lion.
1962 (*Primary-Jr. High*) 89m/C Walter Pidgeon, Gilles Payant; *D:* Norman Tokar. **VHS, Beta $69.95** *DIS*

Big Shots 𝄃𝄃

Two 12-year-old kids, one naive and white, the other black and streetwise, search the seamy side of town for a stolen watch. Intermittently fun, but with detours into violence and crime that take a great deal of delight out of what should have been a childish romp. **Hound Advisory:** Violence, profanity.
1987 (PG-13/*Jr. High-Adult*) 91m/C Ricky Busker, Darius McCrary, Robert Joy, Paul Winfield, Robert Prosky, Jerzy Skolimowski; *D:* Robert Mandel; *W:* Joe Eszterhas; *M:* Bruce Broughton. **VHS, Beta, LV $19.98** *LHV, WAR*

The Big Store 𝄃𝄃𝄃

Marx Brothers vehicle has some big laughs, but lacks the rapid-fire hilarity that made them famous, as Groucho, Chico and Harpo work as department-store detectives and foil a kidnapping and takeover attempt. Unfortunately, they don't foil the some pointless musical numbers dropped in to kill time, though one of them gives Harpo an especially charming pantomime at the harp, accompanying two non-identical mirror images of himself. Tape includes the short subject "A Night at the Movies," with humorist Robert Benchley showing what could go wrong for a filmgoer in days before VCRs. **Hound Advisory:** Roughhousing.
1941 (*Family*) 96m/B Groucho Marx, Harpo Marx, Chico Marx, Tony Martin, Margaret Dumont, Virginia Grey, Virginia O'Brien; *D:* Charles Riesner. **VHS, Beta $19.95** *MGM, CCB*

Big Top Pee Wee 𝄃𝄃𝄃

Herman's second feature following the success of "Pee Wee's Big Adventure" hasn't got the manic hilarity of its predecessor. Slightly out-of-character Herman owns a farm, has a girlfriend (!) and is the only resident of his community with the properly childlike nature to welcome a traveling circus into town. Eventually Pee Wee joins the show for a dreamlike finale that adds a quality of magic mostly lacking in the rest of the picture. **Hound Advisory:** Yes it's true, Pee Wee has sex, but it's handled in a discreet, offscreen manner.
1988 (PG/*Jr. High-Adult*) 86m/C Paul (Pee Wee Herman) Reubens, Kris Kristofferson, Susan Tyrrell, Penelope Ann Miller; *D:* Randal Kleiser; *W:* Paul (Pee Wee Herman) Reubens; *M:* Danny Elfman. **VHS, Beta, LV, 8mm $14.95** *PAR*

Big Trouble in Little China 𝄃𝄃𝄃

Trucker plunges beneath the streets of San Francisco's Chinatown to battle an army of spirits. An uproarious comic-book-film parody with plenty of action and a keen sense of sophomoric sarcasm. **Hound Advisory:** Violence.
1986 (PG-13/*Jr. High-Adult*) 99m/C Kurt Russell, Suzee Pai, Dennis Dun, Kim Cattrall, James Hong, Victor Wong, Kate Burton; *D:* John Carpenter; *W:* Gary Goldman, W.D. Richter; *M:* John Carpenter, Alan Howarth. **VHS, Beta, LV $14.98** *FXV, FOX*

Bigfoot and Wildboy

Two volumes of live-action adventures from a Sid & Marty Krofft Saturday-morning show of the '70s, in which Sasquatch teams up with a Tarzan-type kid to fight assorted fiends.
1977 (*Family*) 72m/C Ray Young, Joseph Butcher, Yvonne Regalado, Monica Ramirez. **VHS, Beta $9.95** *NLC, SUE*

Bikini Beach 𝄃𝄃𝄃

Surfing teenagers of the "Beach Party" series follow up "Muscle Beach Party" with a third fling at the beach and welcome a visitor, British recording star "Potato Bug" (Avalon in a campy dual role). But, golly gee, wealthy Wynn wants to turn their sandy, surfin' shores into a retirement community. What to do? Sing a few songs, dance in your bathing suits, and have fun. Classic early '60s nostalgia is

"Big" Tom Hanks (right) and Robert Loggia tickle the ivories

better than the first two efforts; followed by "Pajama Party." ♫Because You're You; Love's a Secret Weapon; Bikini Drag. **1964** (*Family*) 100m/C Annette Funicello, Frankie Avalon, Martha Hyer, Harvey Lembeck, Don Rickles, Stevie Wonder, John Ashley, Keenan Wynn, Jody McCrea, Candy Johnson, Danielle Aubry, Meredith MacRae, Dolores Wells, Donna Loren, Timothy Carey; **D:** William Asher; **W:** William Asher, Leo Townsend, Robert Dillon; **M:** Les Baxter. **VHS, Beta $9.98** *SUE*

Bill 🎵🎵🎵

Made-for-TV movie based on a true story about a mentally retarded man who sets out to live independently after 44 years in an institution. Rooney gives an affecting performance as Bill and Quaid is strong as the filmmaker who befriends him. Awarded Emmys for Rooney's performance and the well written script. Followed by "Bill: On His Own." **1981** (*Preschool*) 97m/C Mickey Rooney, Dennis Quaid, Largo Woodruff, Harry Goz; **D:** Anthony Page. **VHS, Beta $59.95** *LIV*

Bill and Coo 🎵🎵

Award-winning novelty short feature was celebrated in its day, but once you get the gimmick that's it; a melodramatic love story with a villain and hero - using an all bird cast. **1947** (*Family*) 61m/C **D:** Dean Riesner. **VHS, Beta, 8mm $19.95** *VYY, MRV, NOS*

Bill & Ted's Bogus Journey 🎵🎵

Big-budget sequel to B & T's first movie has better f/x but a lesser quota of laughs for all that effort. Slain - bloodlessly - by lookalike robot duplicates from the future, the airhead heroes pass through Heaven (a Mt. Olympus-style kingdom) and Hell (a military academy). Finally, they trick the Grim Reaper into bringing them back for a second duel with their heinous terminators. Episodes of a Bill & Ted cartoon series are also available on tape. **1991** (*PG/Jr. High-Adult*) 98m/C Keanu Reeves, Alex Winter, William Sadler, Joss Ackland, Pam Grier, George Carlin, Amy Stock-Poynton, Hal Landon Jr., Annette Azcuy, Sarah Trigger, Chelcie Ross, Taj Mahal, Roy Brocksmith, William Shatner; **D:** Pete Hewitt; **W:** Chris Matheson, Edward Solomon; **M:** David Newman. **VHS $14.98** *ORI*

Bill & Ted's Excellent Adventure 🎵🎵🎵

Utopian future of the Earth rests on whether two '80s boys pass their high-school history final. Time-travelling trouble-shooter Rufus comes to the rescue in his cosmic phone booth, and Bill and Ted share a field trip through time as they goof up the lives of important world figures. Fun, brainless comedy earns its bones because the slang-speaking heroes are the most innocuous teen twits in recent movies. They may look

like Beavis & Butthead and adore heavy-metal music, but there's no malice in these dudes and considerable humor as they set Lincoln, Napoleon, and Joan of Arc loose in a Southern California shopping mall. **Hound Advisory:** Salty language; don't look to these guys as role models.
1989 (PG/*Jr. High-Adult*) 105m/C Keanu Reeves, Alex Winter, George Carlin, Bernie Casey, Dan Shor, Robert Barron, Amy Stock-Poynton, Ted Steedman, Ted Steedman, Rod Loomis, Al Leong, Tony Camilieri; **D:** Stephen Herek; **W:** Chris Matheson, Edward Solomon; **M:** David Newman. **VHS, Beta, LV, 8mm $14.95** *COL, SUE, NLC*

Bill Cosby, Himself 🦴🦴◁

An alternative to the popular (but foul-mouthed) comedy concerts starring Richard Pryor or Eddie Murphy or Robert Townsend, cool Cos offers this record of his congenial standup act. Cosby shares his funny observations on marriage, drugs, alcohol, dentists, child-bearing and child-rearing. Performance was recorded at Toronto's Hamilton Place Performing Arts Center; the video includes some of Cosby's own home movies. Also available: "Bill Cosby: 49." **Hound Advisory:** Sex talk, drug talk, salty language.
1981 (PG/*Family*) 104m/C Bill Cosby; **D:** Bill Cosby. **VHS, Beta, LV $19.98** *FOX*

Bill: On His Own 🦴🦴🦴

Rooney is again exceptional in this sequel to the Emmy-winning TV movie "Bill." After 44 years in an institution, a mentally retarded man copes more and more successfully with the outside world. Fine supporting cast and direction control the melodramatic potential.
1983 (*Jr. High-Adult*) 100m/C Mickey Rooney, Helen Hunt, Teresa Wright, Dennis Quaid, Largo Woodruff, Paul Leiber, Harry Goz; **D:** Anthony Page. **VHS $59.95** *LIV*

Billie 🦴◁

Duke stars as a tomboy athlete who puts the boys' track team to shame. Some amusing but very predictable situations, plus a few songs from Miss Duke. Based on Ronald Alexander's play "Time Out for Ginger."
1965 (*Family*) 86m/C Patty Duke, Jim Backus, Jane Greer, Warren Berlinger, Billy DeWolfe, Charles Lane, Dick Sargent, Susan Seaforth Hayes, Ted Bessell, Richard Deacon; **D:** Don Weis; **W:** Ronald Alexander. **VHS, Beta, LV $19.98** *MGM*

The Billion Dollar Hobo 🦴◁

Vernon, unsuspecting heir of a multimillion dollar fortune must duplicate his benefactor's experience as a hobo during the Depression in order to collect his inheritance. Slow-moving stuff, scripted in part by Conway, targeted at the young.
1978 (G/*Family*) 96m/C Tim Conway, Will Geer, Eric Weston, Sydney Lassick; **D:** Stuart E. McGowan. **VHS, Beta $59.98** *FOX*

A Billion for Boris 🦴🦴◁

TV fixed by Boris' kid brother carries news broadcasts from the future, so the boy hero plans to make money for his widowed mom by betting on the next day's horse races. The mother-son relationship is fresh and interesting, more so than the familiar stuff about precognition, gambling and kidnap-

pers. Based on a book by "Freaky Friday" author Mary Rodgers. **Hound Advisory:** Salty language.
1990 (*Jr. High-Adult*) 89m/C Lee Grant, Tim Kazurinsky; **W:** Mary Rogers. **VHS, Beta $79.95** *IMP*

Billy Bunny's Animal Song

Muppet characters Billy Bunny, Cecil, Percival, Edgar Bear, the Termite, and the Porcupine share eight songs with onscreen lyrics to which children can sing and dance. Hosted by Kermit the Frog.
1993 (*Family*) 30m/C **VHS, Beta $12.99** *JHV, BVV, BTV*

Billy Galvin 🦴🦴◁

Independently made drama with heart, if not many surprises. Billy wants to be just like his father, a blue-collar ironworker. But bullheaded dad wants his kids to do better in life, not just the same grind, and the stubborn pair square off over the boy's future. **Hound Advisory:** Profanity.
1986 (PG/*Jr. High-Adult*) 95m/C Karl Malden, Lenny Von Dohlen, Joyce Van Patten, Toni Kalem, Keith Szarabajka, Alan North, Paul Guilfoyle, Barton Heyman; **D:** John Gray; **W:** John Gray; **M:** Joel Rosenbaum. **VHS, Beta $79.95** *LIV, VES*

Billy Jack 🦴🦴

On an Arizona Indian reservation, a half-breed ex-Green Beret with pugnacious martial arts skills (Laughlin) stands between a rural town and a school for runaways. Laughlin stars with his real-life wife Taylor. Features the then-hit song "One Tin Soldier," sung by Coven. The movie and its marketing by Laughlin inspired a "Billy Jack" cult phenomenon. A Spanish-dubbed version of this film is also available. Followed by a sequel in 1974, "Trail of Billy Jack," which bombed.
1971 (PG/*Sr. High-Adult*) 112m/C Tom Laughlin, Delores Taylor, Clark Howat; **D:** Tom Laughlin; **W:** Tom Laughlin. **VHS, Beta, LV $14.95** *WAR*

Billy Possum

Three animated episodes from the creator of Peter Cottontail, Thornton W. Burgess, here with other characters from his "Fables of the Green Forest." Segments include "Uncle Billy Regrets," "Whose Footprint Is That?" and "Lost in the Green Forest."
1979 (*Preschool*) 60m/C **VHS, Beta $29.95** *WTA, FHE*

Bingo 🦴🦴◁

Much-needed spoof of hero-dog movies. The resourceful Bingo is left behind when his adopted family moves from Denver to Green Bay. During his incredible journey to rejoin them, the superintelligent mutt skateboards, solves math problems, performs CPR, and even has the villains cheering for him in the absurd finale. Some very funny moments as time goes by.
1991 (PG/*Jr. High-Adult*) 90m/C Cindy Williams, David Rasche, Robert J. Steinmiller Jr., David French, Kurt Fuller, Joe Guzaldo, Glenn Shadix; **D:** Matthew Robbins; **W:** Jim Strain; **M:** Richard Gibbs. **VHS, LV $19.95** *COL*

Bingo Long Traveling All-Stars & Motor Kings 🦴🦴🦴

Set in 1939, this follows the comedic adventures of a lively group of black ball players who have defected from the old Negro National League. The All-Stars travel the country challenging local white teams and disarming racial tension with humor. Warm and winning, with an undercurrent of seriousness. **Hound Advisory:** Salty barnstorming ballpark language, violence, sex talk.

1976 (PG/*Family***)** 111m/C Billy Dee Williams, James Earl Jones, Richard Pryor, Stan Shaw; **D:** John Badham; **W:** Matthew Robbins; **M:** William Goldstein. **VHS, Beta $49.95** *MCA, FCT*

The Birch Interval 🦴🦴🦴

It's 1947, and 11-year-old Jesse is sent to live with Amish kinfolk in their isolated Pennsylvania community. Even in the bucolic setting the girl senses adult passions and prejudices in her secretly troubled family. Heartfelt little movie from the creators of "Sounder," with a respectful but never patronizing or simplistic portrayal of the Amish way of life. Based on the novel by Joanna Crawford. **Hound Advisory:** Mature themes.

1978 (PG/*Jr. High-Adult***)** 104m/C Eddie Albert, Rip Torn, Ann Wedgeworth; **D:** Delbert Mann; **W:** Joanna Crawford. **VHS, Beta $9.95** *MED*

The Birds 🦴🦴🦴🦴

Hitchcock attempted to top the success of "Psycho" with this terrifying tale of Man versus Nature, in which Nature alights, one by one, on the trees of Bodega Bay to stage a bloody act of revenge upon the civilized world. Only Hitchcock can twist the harmless into the horrific while avoiding the ridiculous; this is perhaps his most brutal film, and one of the cinema's purest, horrifying portraits of apocalypse. Based on a short story by Daphne Du Maurier; screenplay by novelist Evan Hunter (aka Ed McBain). **Hound Advisory:** Violence.

1963 (*Adult***)** 120m/C Rod Taylor, Tippi Hedren, Jessica Tandy, Veronica Cartwright, Suzanne Pleshette; **D:** Alfred Hitchcock. **VHS, Beta, LV $19.95** *MCA*

The Black Arrow 🦴🦴

Exiled bowman returns to England to avenge the injustices of a villainous nobleman. Disney's made-for-cable version of the Robert Louis Stevenson medieval romp lacks the panache of their (shorter) 1948 adaptation.

1984 (*Family***)** 93m/C Oliver Reed, Benedict Taylor, Georgia Slowe, Stephan Chase, Donald Pleasence; **D:** John Hough. **VHS, Beta $69.95** *DIS*

Black Beauty 🦴🦴

Very loose adaptation of Anna Sewell's horse's point-of-view novel. Young girl develops a kindred relationship with an extraordinary colt, then has to go in search of the animal when they're separated.

1946 (*Family***)** 74m/B Mona Freeman, Richard Denning, Evelyn Ankers; **D:** Max Nosseck. **VHS, Beta $9.99** *CCB, MED, VTR*

Black Beauty 🦴🦴🦴◁

Anna Sewell's oft-filmed 'Autobiography of a Horse' gets a respectable treatment, following the title mare from one owner until she's finally reunited with her favorite master. Perhaps the biggest surprise is offscreen; movie came from a British outfit otherwise specializing in low-grade horror and exploitation pictures.

1971 (G/*Family***)** 105m/C Mark Lester, Walter Slezak; **D:** James Hill. **VHS, Beta, LV $14.95** *PAR, FCT*

Black Beauty

Animated version of the classic children's tale that follows a magnificent horse from one owner to another.

1978 (*Family***)** 49m/C **VHS $12.98** *WTA*

Black Beauty 🦴🦴🦴

Remake of the classic Anna Sewell children's novel about an oft-sold horse whose life has its shares of ups and downs. Timeless tale still brings children and adults to tears. Six-year-old quarterhorse named Justin gives a nuanced portrayal as the Black Beauty, recalling Olivier in "Hamlet." Directorial debut of "Secret Garden" screenwriter Thompson. **Hound Advisory:** Roughhousing.

1994 (G/*Family***)** 85m/C Andrew Knott, Sean Bean, David Thewlis, Jim Carter, Alun Armstrong, Eleanor Bron, Peter Cook, Peter Davison, John McEnery, Nicholas Jones; **D:** Caroline Thompson; **W:** Caroline Thompson. **VHS, LV** *WAR*

The Black Hole 🦴🦴

Disney's answer to "Star Wars" was this high-tech space adventure about a mad genius planning to pilot his starship right into a black hole. Except for the top quality special effects, it's creaky vehicle much in love with its own gadgetry, like two cutesy robots (one with a western drawl) who are plenty annoying but still the best-drawn characters. Dig that wild religious ending. **Hound Advisory:** Ray gun battles had some parents questioning the violence and overall darkness, but it's strictly video game stuff.

1979 (G/*Family***)** 97m/C Maximilian Schell, Anthony Perkins, Ernest Borgnine, Yvette Mimieux, Joseph Bottoms, Robert Forster; **D:** Gary Nelson; **M:** John Barry. **VHS, Beta, LV** *DIS, OM*

Black Magic 🦴🦴

Insomniac Alex, haunted by the nightly appearances of his dead cousin Ross, goes to Ross' hometown to see if he can find a way to make the apparition disappear. On the way, he runs into his cousin's ex-girlfriend Lilian and falls in love. Problem is, Lilian's a witch, maybe. Lightweight made for cable TV fare.

1992 (PG-13/*Jr. High-Adult***)** 94m/C Rachel Ward, Judge Reinhold, Brion James, Anthony LaPaglia; **D:** Daniel Taplitz; **W:** Daniel Taplitz. **VHS, LV $89.98** *MCA*

The Black Planet 🦴🦴

Offbeat Australian cartoon feature, an environmentalist satire of the Cold War. Scientists discover a mystery 'Black Planet' orbiting nearby, and a Kennedy-like president finances a space program to explore it. But a senator and a general

wanted that money for war; they conspire to sabotage the rocket, while an ecologist and a feminist repeatedly bumble into the way. Not as strident or overbearing as it sounds, though simplistic animation and jokes limit this to smaller viewers. **Hound Advisory:** Alcohol use.
1982 (*Family*) 78m/C **D:** Paul Williams. **VHS, Beta $39.98** *SUE*

The Black Stallion 🐾🐾🐾🐾

Young Alec Ramsey and a majestic Arabian stallion are the only survivors of a shipwreck, and the two develop a deep affection for each other while stranded on a desert island in an exceptionally beautiful (almost wordless) first half. Rescued, they return to Alec's suburban home in the U.S., and the Black (as he's called) seems to be an unmanageable misfit until he fulfills his destiny at the racetrack. Superb, visionary entertainment for adults and kids, based on the book by Walter Farley. The PG rating is ridiculous.
1979 (PG/Family*) 120m/C Kelly Reno, Mickey Rooney, Teri Garr, Clarence Muse; **D:** Carroll Ballard; **W:** Bill Wittliff, Melissa Mathison, Jeanne Rosenberg; **M:** Carmine Coppola. **Award Nominations:** Academy Awards '79: Best Film Editing, Best Supporting Actor (Rooney); **Awards:** Academy Awards '79: Best Sound Effects Editing. **VHS, Beta, LV $19.98** *MGM, FOX, TLF*

The Black Stallion Returns 🐾🐾🐾

Sequel to "The Black Stallion" follows the adventures of young Alec as he travels to the Sahara to search for his beautiful horse, which was stolen by an Arab chieftain who claims rightful ownership (Arabs in general are portrayed as fearsome but sympathetic). Expect a typical boy's adventure, nothing near the mystical quality of the first "Black Stallion" and the kids won't be disappointed - though some of the dialogue really hurts. **Hound Advisory:** Salty language, roughhousing.
1983 (PG/Family*) 103m/C Kelly Reno, Teri Garr, Vincent Spano; **D:** Robert Dalva; **M:** Georges Delerue. **VHS, Beta, LV $19.98** *FOX*

The Black Tulip

Alexandre Dumas' classic tale is told here as a man grows the world's first black tulip, only to have it stolen.
1991 (*Preschool-Primary*) 50m/C **VHS $12.95** *SVI*

The Black Widow

Fortune-teller plots to steal scientific secrets and take over the world, in this Republic serial in thirteen episodes. Forman plays the villainess, known as Sombra the Spider Woman (pic's alternate title), sort of a takeoff on her role as the Spider Lady in the original "Superman" chapter play.
1947 (*Family*) 164m/B Bruce Edwards, Carol Forman, Anthony Warde; **D:** Spencer Gordon Bennet. **VHS $19.98** *VCN, REP, MLB*

Blackbeard's Ghost 🐾🐾

Mediocre Disney comedy in which the famed 18th-century pirate's spirit is summoned to wreak ghostly mischief in order to prevent an old family home from being turned into a casino.
1967 (*Family*) 107m/C Peter Ustinov, Dean Jones, Suzanne Pleshette, Elsa Lanchester, Richard Deacon; **D:** Robert Stevenson. **VHS, Beta, LV $14.99** *DIS*

Blackstar

Saturday-morning-cartoon recycling of the adventures of John Blackstar, an astronaut who passes through a black hole and finds Sagar, a perilous new world of friends and foes awaiting. This empty-headed stuff came from the producers of the similar "He-Man and the Masters of the Universe" show, but fortunately proved not at all as popular. Additional volumes available.
1981 (*Preschool-Jr. High*) 60m/C **VHS, Beta $29.95** *FHE*

Blacula 🐾🐾

The African Prince Mamuwalde stalks the streets of Los Angeles trying to satisfy his insatiable desire for blood. Mildly successful melding of blaxploitation and horror that spawned a sequel, "Scream, Blacula, Scream." **Hound Advisory:** Violence.
1972 (PG/Sr. High-Adult*) 92m/C William Marshall, Thalmus Rasulala, Denise Nicholas, Vonetta McGee; **D:** William Crain. **VHS, Beta, LV $9.98** *ORI*

Blake of Scotland Yard

Byrd, also the screen's early Dick Tracy, plays a former Scotland Yard inspector who battles against The Scorpion, a mystery villain with a death ray. A serial in 15 episodes, also available under the same title in a condensed 70-minute edition.
1936 (*Family*) 70m/B Ralph Byrd, Herbert Rawlinson, Joan Barclay, Lloyd Hughes; **D:** Robert F. Hill. **VHS, Beta $24.95** *VYY, DVT, VCN*

Blame It on the Night 🐾🐾

Rock star inherits his illegitimate military-cadet son after the boy's mother dies. Taking the kid on the road during a concert tour, with all the pressures and temptations of the rock 'n' roll lifestyle, turns into a growing experience for them both, but not enough of one. Mick Jagger helped write the story for this maudlin, tune-filled drama. **Hound Advisory:** Mature themes, drug use, sex.
1984 (PG-13/Jr. High-Adult*) 85m/C Nick Mancuso, Byron Thames, Leslie Ackerman, Billy Preston, Merry Clayton; **D:** Gene Taft. **VHS, Beta $79.98** *FOX*

Blank Check 🐾🐾

11-year-old Preston, bullied at school and scorned by his big brothers, figures out that money means power and respect. When he gets a blank check from a mobster who ran over his bike, the savvy lad cashes it for a million bucks, and goes on a spending orgy under an assumed name. Nice setup, but when the mobster and his goons come snooping around Preston's new toy-crammed castle, this Disney romp devolves into a blatant "Home Alone" ripoff. Preston should have set aside a couple grand to buy more inspiration. **Hound Advisory:** Roughhousing.
1993 (PG/Jr. High-Adult*) 93m/C Brian Bonsall, Miguel Ferrer, Michael Lerner, Tone Loc, Rick Ducommun, Karen Duffy; **D:** Rupert Wainwright; **W:** Colby Carr, Blake Snyder; **M:** Nicholas Pike. **VHS, LV** *DIS*

Black Beauty (1994)

Blankman 🦴🦴

Self-appointed superhero Wayans makes up in creativity what he lacks in superpowers, fighting crime in his underwear and a cape made from his grandmother's bathrobe. Life is simple, until an ambitious TV reporter (Givens) finds out about him. Silly one-joke premise is carried as far as it will go. Fans of Wayans will appreciate, as will those in the mood for some stupid fun. **Hound Advisory:** Violence and profanity.
1994 (PG-13/*Jr. High-Adult*) 92m/C Damon Wayans, Robin Givens, David Alan Grier, Jason Alexander, Jon Polito; **D:** Mike Binder; **W:** Damon Wayans, J.F. Lawton. VHS *NYR*

Bless the Beasts and Children 🦴🦴🦴

Six misfit adolescent boys dumped by their parents at an Arizona dude ranch for the summer do some growing up when they determine to save a majestic herd of buffalo from authorized slaughter. Message-laden drama still manages to work. Based on the novel by Glendon Swarthout. **Hound Advisory:** Violence, salty language, mature themes.
1971 (PG/*Sr. High-Adult*) 109m/C Billy Mumy, Barry Robins, Miles Chapin, Darel Glaser, Bob Kramer, Ken Swofford, Jesse White; **D:** Stanley Kramer. VHS, Beta $14.95 *COL*

Blood Brothers

Single episode from the network mountain man drama "The Life and Times of Grizzly Adams," in which the hero recounts his first encounter with his Indian blood brother Nakuma. Beautiful scenery.
1977 (*Adult*) 50m/C Dan Haggerty, Denver Pyle, Don Shanks. VHS, Beta $14.98 *MCG*

The Blue Bird 🦴🦴🦴

When Miss Shirley missed a chance to star in "The Wizard of Oz," the 20th Century Fox studios holding her contract came up with this misfire fantasy, based on Maurice Maeterlinck's story, as an "Oz" competitor. The child star plays a peasant girl who vainly seeks the fabled Blue Bird of Happiness in various fantasy lands inhabited by numerous Hollywood guest stars. Strangely (perhaps appropriately) joyless and stiff, it became Temple's first major box-office disappointment. Long ignored and worth a look on tape as a real curio.
1940 (*Family*) 98m/C Shirley Temple, Gale Sondergaard, John Russell, Eddie Collins, Nigel Bruce, Jessie Ralph, Spring Byington, Sybil Jason; **D:** Walter Lang. VHS, Beta $19.98 *FOX, MLB*

Blue Chips 🦴🦴🦴

Nolte does Indiana coach Bobby Knight in this saga of Western U basketball coach Pete Bell, suffering through his first losing season. What follows is a tug of war between rich alumni who want to win at any cost and his ethics as he recruits for a new season. Larger than life hoopster O'Neal's film debut. McDonnell and Woodard are merely afterthoughts, but look for cameos from many real life gamesters, including Knight, Dick Vitale, and Larry Bird. Average script is bolstered by exciting game footage, shot during real games for authenticity. **Hound Advisory:** Profanity.

1994 (PG-13/*Jr. High-Adult*) 108m/C Nick Nolte, Shaquille O'Neal, Mary McDonnell, Ed O'Neill, J.T. Walsh, Alfre Woodard; *Cameos:* Larry Bird, Bobby Knight, Rick Pitino; **D:** William Friedkin; **W:** Ron Shelton; **M:** Nile Rodgers, Jeff Beck, Jed Leiber. VHS, Beta *PAR*

Blue Fin 🦴🦴

Young boy and his semi-estranged fisherman father learn lessons of love and courage when their tuna boat is disabled and both have to work together to save the ship. Set in the waters off Australia.
1978 (PG/*Family*) 93m/C Hardy Kruger, Greg Rowe; **D:** Carl Schultz. VHS, Beta $59.98 *SUE*

Blue Fire Lady 🦴🦴

Girl's love of horses meets opposition from her father, so she sets out on her own, getting a job at a seedy racetrack and turning an unmanageable mare into a champion through her tender care. Okay equine fare from Australia, hindered by a muddy, low-budget look. **Hound Advisory:** Alcohol use.
1978 (*Family*) 96m/C Cathryn Harrison, Mark Holden, Peter Cummins. VHS, Beta $19.95 *MED*

Blue Murder at St. Trinian's 🦴🦴🦴

Second in a series of madcap British comedies (after "Belles of St. Trinian's") about a ferocious pack of English schoolgirls, first rendered in the cartoon drawings of Ronald Searle. This time they take a field trip to Europe and make life miserable for a jewel thief. Fantasy scene in ancient Rome shows the girls thrown to the lions — and terrifying the lions.
1956 (*Jr. High-Adult*) 86m/B Joyce Grenfell, Terry-Thomas, George Cole, Alastair Sim, Lionel Jeffries, Thorley Walters; **D:** Frank Launder; **M:** Malcolm Arnold. VHS $24.95 *VYY, VDM, FUS*

Blue Skies Again 🦴🦴

Spunky young woman determined to play major league baseball locks horns with the chauvinistic owner and the gruff manager of her favorite team. **Hound Advisory:** Salty language, sex talk.
1983 (PG/*Jr. High-Adult*) 91m/C Robyn Barto, Harry Hamlin, Mimi Rogers, Kenneth McMillan, Dana Elcar, Andy Garcia; **D:** Richard Michaels. VHS, Beta $69.95 *WAR*

The Blue Yonder 🦴🦴

Disney TV feature about an 11-year-old boy who travels back in time to meet his grandfather, an early pilot who disappeared flying solo across the Atlantic, just before Charles Lindberg. Should little Jonathan try to warn his ancestor or let history go unaltered? The answer isn't too satisfying, and the low-intensity yarn will interest mainly aviation buffs.
1986 (*Family*) 89m/C Art Carney, Peter Coyote, Huckleberry Fox; **D:** Mark Rosman. VHS, Beta $69.95 *DIS*

Blues Busters 🦴🦴

Late entry in the "Bowery Boys/East Side Kids" series of short-feature comedies that began in the 1930s with a crew of young urban wise guys and their antics, a fave with kids of the era. In this one, eternal doofus Sach (Hall) emerges from a tonsillectomy with a velvety singing voice. Slip (Gorcey), the boys' leader and eternal purveyor of get-rich-quick

schemes, tries to use Sach's new crooning abilities to turn their neighborhood soda shop into a nightclub.
1950 *(Family)* 68m/B Leo Gorcey, Huntz Hall, Adele Jergens, Gabriel Dell, Craig Stevens, Phyllis Coates, Bernard Gorcey, David Gorcey; **D:** William Beaudine. **VHS $14.98** *WAR*

Bluetoes the Christmas Elf

Yuletide cartoon about Bluetoes, an elf who's just too clumsy to help Santa on Christmas eve. Yet fate gives the little fella the break he deserves.
1988 *(Family)* 27m/C **VHS $14.95** *FHE, WTA, FCT*

The Bluffers: Fantasy-Filled Adventure Begins

Episodes from the cartoon series about woodland creatures living in fantasy kingdom of Bluffoonia, whose forests must be continually protected against exploitation. Four episodes per tape.
1984 *(Preschool-Primary)* 90m/C **VHS, Beta $29.95** *JFK, WTA*

The Bluffers: Mystery of Clandestino's Castle

The further adventures of the motley forest-dwelling animals, as they foil their evil king's designs on the environment.
1984 *(Preschool-Primary)* 90m/C **VHS, Beta $29.95** *JFK, WTA*

BMX Bandits 𝄞𝄞

Three adventurous Aussie teens put their BMX skills to the test when they witness a crime and are pursued by the criminals.
1983 *(Family)* 92m/C Nicole Kidman, David Argue, John Ley, Angelo D'Angelo; **D:** Brian Trenchard-Smith; **W:** Patrick Edgeworth. **VHS $79.95** *IMP*

The Boatniks 𝄞𝄞𝄞

Accident-prone Coast Guard ensign finds himself in charge of the "Times Square" of waterways, Newport Harbor. Adding to his already "titanic" problems is a gang of ocean-going jewel thieves who lose their loot overboard and try to get it back. Shipshape Disney comedy.
1970 *(G/Family)* 99m/C Robert Morse, Stefanie Powers, Phil Silvers, Norman Fell, Wally Cox, Don Ameche; **D:** Norman Tokar. **VHS, Beta $69.95** *DIS*

Bob the Quail

Taken from the "Fables of the Green Forest," this tale follows Bob's hunt for a good tree that will safely house his family.
1978 *(Preschool-Primary)* 60m/C **VHS, Beta** *FHE*

Bobby Goldsboro's Easter Egg Mornin'

The entertainer hosts a special holiday program of fun and music.
1992 *(Family)* 27m/C **VHS $12.98** *FHE*

Bobby Raccoon

Bobby learns to trust and respect his friendly neighborhood forest critters in this cartoon program.
1985 *(Family)* 60m/C **VHS, Beta** *FHE*

Bobobobs: Around the Galaxy in 80 Days

Peace-loving cartoon-show creatures journey to the weirdest, most remote parts of the galaxy. Additional volumes available.
1987 *(Preschool-Primary)* 120m/C **VHS $39.95** *JFK, WTA*

The Bollo Caper

Cartoon story of Bollo and his mate Nefertiti who are the last golden leopards; all the others have been killed for their pelts. He saves himself and his species from extinction with the help of the President of the United States and the King of his own country. An ABC Weekend Special and adaptation of the book by the acclaimed humorist and columnist Art Buchwald.
1992 *(Family)* 23m/C **VHS $295.00** *AIM*

Bon Voyage, Charlie Brown 𝄞𝄞𝄞

Selected members of the "Peanuts" comic strip kids become exchange students in France, but Charlie Brown and Linus can't figure out why they have to sleep in the stables outside their unseen host's mysterious chateau. Untypical travelogue for the series, perhaps explained by the fact that cartoonist Charles M. Schultz himself relocated to France. Plot reveals some of Charlie Brown's family background, but Snoopy and Woodstock easily steal the show.
1980 *(G/Family)* 76m/C **D:** Bill Melendez; **W:** Charles M. Schulz. **VHS, Beta, LV $14.95** *PAR, WTA*

Bonanza: The Return 𝄞𝄞

Made for TV update to the classic television series has sons of original cast members Michael Landon and Dan Blocker portraying the sons of the original cast members, a novel premise. In 1905, the children of various members of the Cartwright clan fight among themselves before uniting to keep the Ponderosa from falling into the hands of an unscrupulous businessman. Rather bland, though cast and nostalgia (and the occasional film clip from the series) keep it somewhat interesting. **Hound Advisory:** Violence.
1993 *(PG/Family)* 96m/C Michael Landon Jr., Dirk Blocker, Emily Warfield, Alistair MacDougall, Brian Leckner, Dean Stockwell, Ben Johnson, Richard Roundtree, Linda Gray, Jack Elam. **VHS, LV $92.95** *VMK*

Bongo 𝄞𝄞

Originally a part of the Disney cartoon anthology "Fun and Fancy Free." Follows the adventures of a circus bear who flees the big time for the wonders of the forests. Narrated by Dinah Shore. Also available with "Ben and Me" on laserdisc.
1947 *(Family)* 36m/C Bill Roberts, Hamilton Luske; **D:** Jack Kinney. **VHS, Beta $12.99** *DIS, BVV, WTA*

Boo-Busters

Selection of recent Disney cartoon shorts with spooky themes: The Goof Troup discover a haunted house that's home to a Dixieland band of ghosts in "Hallow-Weenies." Chip 'n' Dale head off to jolly old England in "Ghost of a Chance" and find a prankish spook. See also "Monster Bash" and "Witcheroo," released simultaneously.
1993 *(Family)* 44m/C **VHS $12.99** *DIS, WTA*

Book of Love 🐾🐾

"Zany" hijinks as a teenager struggles with friendship, girls, and those all-important hormones when he moves to a new neighborhood in the mid-50's. Average rehash of every 50's movie cliche in existence. Surprise! There's a classic rock 'n' roll soundtrack. Adapted by Kotzwinkle from his novel "Jack in the Box." **Hound Advisory:** Sex talk.
1991 (PG-13/*Jr. High-Adult***)** 88m/C Chris Young, Keith Coogan, Aeryk Egan, Josie Bisset, Tricia Leigh Fisher, Danny Nucci, Michael McKean, John Cameron Mitchell, Lewis Arquette; ***D:*** Robert Shaye; ***W:*** William Kotzwinkle; ***M:*** Stanley Clarke. **VHS, LV, 8mm $19.95** *COL*

Bopha! 🐾🐾🐾

Father-son strife set against the anti-apartheid movement as the Senior township police officer Mikah takes pride in his peaceful community, particularly in light of the growing unrest in the other townships. Son Zweli has become an activist and wife Rosie must be the family peacemaker. Then a prominent freedom movement member is arrested and two officers of the secret police make their sinister appearance. Directorial debut of Freeman is well acted. Adapted from the play by Percy Mtwa, although the hopeful ending has been changed in the movie. The title, a Zulu word, stands for arrest or detention. Filmed on location in Zimbabwe. **Hound Advisory:** Violence; mature themes.
1993 (PG-13/*Jr. High-Sr. High***)** 121m/C Danny Glover, Maynard Eziashi, Alfre Woodard, Malcolm McDowell, Marius Weyers, Malick Bowens, Robin Smith, Michael Chinyamurindi, Christopher John Hall, Grace Mahlaba; ***D:*** Morgan Freeman; ***W:*** Brian Bird, John Wierick; ***M:*** James Horner. **VHS, Beta, LV** *PAR*

Boris and Natasha: The Movie 🐾🐾

Long unreleased oddity that premiered on cable. The inept spies from the classic "Rocky and Bullwinkle" TV 'toon star in a mediocre live-action plot about the nogoodniks sent by "Fearless Leader" to America to capture a time weapon. Main actors are perfect in their incarnations of Boris Badenov and Natasha Fatale (Kellerman even sings the closing theme), but slow-starting script never really takes off, even with a cameo, sort of, by Agents Moose and Squirrel. The original animated versions are also widely available on cassette. **Hound Advisory:** Salty language, alcohol use, cartoonish violence. Believe it or not, Boris and Natasha end the platonic phase of their relationship, but discreetly offscreen.
1992 (PG/*Jr. High-Adult***)** 88m/C Sally Kellerman, Dave Thomas, Paxton Whitehead, Andrea Martin, Alex Rocco, Larry Cedar, Arye Gross, Christopher Neame, Anthony Newley; ***Cameos:*** John Candy, John Travolta, Charles Martin Smith; ***D:*** Charles Martin Smith. **VHS $19.95** *ACA, NLC*

Born Free 🐾🐾🐾

The touching story of a game warden and his wife in Kenya raising Elsa the orphaned lion cub. When the cub reaches maturity, they work to return her to life in the wild. Great family entertainment based on Joy Adamson's book. Theme song became a hit.
1966 *(Family)* 95m/C Virginia McKenna, Bill Travers; ***D:*** James Hill; ***M:*** John Barry. **VHS, Beta, LV $14.95** *COL, HMV*

Born to Run 🐾🐾

Young Australian boy dreams of restoring his grandfather's run-down horse farm to its former glory. Made-for-TV Disney feature, filmed on location.
1977 *(Family)* 87m/C **VHS, Beta $69.95** *DVT*

Born Yesterday 🐾🐾

Remake of the 1950 classic suffers in comparison, particularly Griffith, who has the thankless task of surpassing (or even meeting) Judy Holliday's Oscar-winning mark as not-so-dumb blonde Billie Dawn. Her intellectual inadequacies are glaring when she hits the political world of D.C. with obnoxious tycoon boyfriend Goodman. To save face, he hooks her up with a journalist (Johnson) willing to coach her in Savvy 101, a la Eliza Doolittle. What worked well in post-WWII America seems sadly outdated today; stick with the original. **Hound Advisory:** Profanity; sex talk.
1993 (PG/*Jr. High-Adult***)** 102m/C Melanie Griffith, John Goodman, Don Johnson, Edward Herrmann, Max Perlich, Fred Dalton Thompson, Nora Dunn, Benjamin C. Bradlee, Sally Quinn, Michael Ensign, William Frankfather, Celeste Yarnall, Meg Wittner; ***D:*** Luis Mandoki; ***W:*** Douglas McGrath; ***M:*** George Fenton. **VHS, Beta, LV $94.95** *BVV, HPH*

Bound for Glory 🐾🐾🐾🐾

The award-winning biography of American folk singer Woody Guthrie set against the backdrop of the Depression. Superb portrayal of the spirit and feelings of the period featuring many of his songs encased in the incidents that inspired them. Haskell Wexler's award-winning camera work is superbly expressive.
1976 (PG/*Jr. High-Adult***)** 149m/C David Carradine, Ronny Cox, Melinda Dillon, Randy Quaid; ***D:*** Hal Ashby; ***W:*** Robert Getchell. **Award Nominations:** Academy Awards '76: Best Adapted Screenplay, Best Costume Design, Best Film Editing, Best Picture; Cannes Film Festival '77: Best Film; **Awards:** Academy Awards '76: Best Adapted Score, Best Cinematography; National Board of Review Awards '76: Best Actor (Carradine). **VHS, Beta, LV $19.98** *MGM*

The Bounty 🐾🐾🐾

Cinematically impressive new version of "Mutiny on the Bounty" takes on water at times, but still sails with integrity. Emphasis is on a more realistic relationship between Fletcher Christian and Captain Bligh - and a more sympathetic portrayal of the captain, too. As the conflict-ridden captain, Hopkins delivers a first-rate performance eclipsing that of his shipmate Gibson as Christian. The sensuality of Christian's relationship with a Tahitian beauty also receives greater importance. **Hound Advisory:** Violence; brief nudity; mature themes.

1984 (PG/*Family*) 130m/C Mel Gibson, Anthony Hopkins, Laurence Olivier, Edward Fox, Daniel Day-Lewis, Bernard Hill, Philip Davis, Liam Neeson; *D:* Roger Donaldson; *W:* Robert Bolt. **VHS, Beta, LV $29.98** *VES, LIV*

Bowery Blitzkrieg 🦴

This lesser "East Side Kids" entry has Gorcey opting to enter the boxing ring rather than turn to crime.
1941 (*Jr. High-Adult*) 62m/B Leo Gorcey, Huntz Hall, Bobby Jordan, Warren Hull, Charlotte Henry, Keye Luke; *D:* Wallace Fox. **VHS $19.95** *NOS, VEC, HEG*

Bowery Buckaroos 🦴🦴

The Bowery Boys take their act west in search of gold, meeting up with the usual amounts of goofy characters and hilarious misunderstandings.
1947 (*Family*) 66m/B Leo Gorcey, Huntz Hall, Bobby Jordan, Gabriel Dell, Billy Benedict, David Gorcey, Julie Briggs, Bernard Gorcey, Chief Yowlachie, Iron Eyes Cody; *D:* William Beaudine. **VHS $14.98** *WAR*

Box of Delights 🦴🦴🦴 ◁

English TV treat (based on the novel by John Masefield) about a schoolboy on Christmas Eve assigned to protect a small box, "the greatest magical device of all time," from a cabal of crooks led by an evil wizard. The Box of Delights lets the boy shrink to minuscule size, talk to animals, fly and travel to the past in a long, twisting plot that's not exactly easy to follow and filled with Briticisms (give yourself a Christmas cracker if you know who Herne the Hunter is). Abundant special effects mix animation with live-action and computer-generated visuals; this might have done better as a feature cartoon -where are Hanna-Barbera Studios when you need them?
1983 (*Family*) 120m/C Jon Pertwee. **VHS $19.98** *PAR*

The Boy Friend 🦴🦴🦴

Russell pays tribute to the Busby Berkeley Hollywood musical. Lots of charming dance numbers and clever parody of plot lines in this adaptation of Sandy Wilson's stage play. Fun! ♫The Boy Friend; I Could Be Happy; Won't You Charleston With Me?; Fancy Forgetting; Sur La Plage; A Room in Bloomsbury; Safety in Numbers; It's Never Too Late to Fall in Love; Poor Little Pierette.
1971 (G/*Family*) 135m/C Twiggy, Christopher Gable, Moyra Fraser, Max Adrian, Vladek Sheybal, Georgina Hale, Tommy Tune; *D:* Ken Russell; *W:* Ken Russell. **VHS $19.95** *MGM*

The Boy God WOOF!

Philippines-made loser about a pudgy kid descended from magical beings, in battle against monsters and fiends. Shabby takeoff on Greek mythology, good only for laughs. That ultra-sexy girl on the cassette box never appears in the film. **Hound Advisory:** Fantasy violence.
1986 (*Jr. High-Adult*) 100m/C Nino Muhlach; *D:* Erastheo J. Navda. **VHS, Beta $39.95** *VCD*

Boy of Two Worlds 🦴🦴

The petty prejudice of people in a small town compels a fatherless boy to embark on the adventurous life of a junior Robinson Crusoe.

1970 (G/*Family*) 103m/C Jimmy Sternman, Edvin Adolphson; *D:* Astrid Henning Jensen. **VHS, Beta $29.95** *GEM*

Boy Takes Girl 🦴🦴

Adolescent girl finds hardship and romance when she's left to work on an Australian farming cooperative over the summer recess.
1983 (*Family*) 93m/C Gabi Eldor, Hillel Neeman, Dina Limon; *D:* Michal Bat-Adam. **VHS, Beta $59.95** *MGM*

The Boy Who Could Fly 🦴🦴🦴 ◁

After a plane crash kills his parents, Eric withdraws into a trance state, pretending to fly. The girl next door befriends him, tries to prevent his incarceration in a loony bin - then events hint that Eric can really fly after all. Sentimental drama, rather like the troubled "Radio Flyer"; you either accept intrusion of fantasy in a somewhat grim reality, or you don't. There's no in between, though fine cast works hard to limit the sap. **Hound Advisory:** Salty language, alcohol use, mature themes.
1986 (PG/*Jr. High-Adult*) 120m/C Lucy Deakins, Jay Underwood, Bonnie Bedelia, Colleen Dewhurst, Fred Savage, Fred Gwynne, Louise Fletcher, Jason Priestly; *D:* Nick Castle; *W:* Nick Castle; *M:* Bruce Broughton. **VHS, Beta, LV $14.95** *WAR, LHV*

The Boy Who Drew Cats

Actor Hurt narrates a Japanese folktale about a young artist whose skills come in handy when black magic threatens. Not animated, but told against vivid (and in this case, a little scary) storybook illustrations; from the award-winning series "Rabbit Ears: We All Have Tales," first aired on Showtime cable TV.
1991 (*Family*) 35m/C *M:* Mark Isham. **VHS $19.95** *MVD*

The Boy Who Left Home to Find Out About the Shivers

From "Faerie Tale Theatre" comes a lesser known Brothers Grimm tale about Martin, a young resident of Transylvania who never learned fear. Tossed out by his superstitious father, Martin accepts an offer to spend three nights at a haunted castle. Cast of horror movie vets make this a cute retelling that actually improves on the original's ending. Some zombie ghosts turn out to be playful, Addams-Family level ghouls.
1981 (*Family*) 60m/C Peter MacNicol, Christopher Lee, Vincent Price; *D:* Graeme Clifford. **VHS, Beta, LV $14.98** *KUI, FOX*

The Boy Who Loved Trolls

Paul's fantastic dreams come true when he meets Ofoeti, a real, live troll. The only problem is Ofoeti only has a day to live, and Paul must find a way to save him. Aired on PBS as part of the "Wonderworks" series.
1984 (*Family*) 58m/C Sam Waterston, Susan Anton, Matt Dill; *D:* Harvey Laidman. **VHS $29.95** *PME, HMV, FCT*

The Boy with the Green Hair 🦴🦴 ◁

When young Peter learns his relief-worker parents were killed in an air raid, his hair turns green overnight. He

declares he's become a living reminder of war's terrible cost, but town adults don't want his message and other kids chase and harass him. Considered a thought-provoking statement in its day; now seems outmoded and simplistic (with an utterly pointless musical number early on). Still worth seeing for child-actor Stockwell's haunted determination.
1948 (*Family*) 82m/C Pat O'Brien, Robert Ryan, Barbara Hale, Dean Stockwell; **D:** Joseph Losey. **VHS, Beta, LV** $29.95 *IME*

Boyd's Shadow 🐾🐾

Boy learns about preconceptions and acceptance through the town recluse, who was thought to "boil children and feed them to his snakes." In actuality, the recluse is an accomplished folk musician and friend of the boy's dead father. Filmed adaptation of a play by William Stevens who, along with his family, stars in the production (directed by his brother John).
1992 (*Preschool-Primary*) 45m/C Bill Stevens, Becca Stevens, Katie Stevens, Carolyn Stevens, William Stevens; **D:** John Stevens; **W:** John Stevens; **M:** William Stevens. **VHS** $29.95 *BTV*

Boys of the City 🐾🐾

The East Side Kids run amuck in an eerie mansion while trying to solve the murder of a judge.
1940 (*Family*) 63m/B Leo Gorcey, Bobby Jordan; **D:** Joseph H. Lewis. **VHS, Beta** $24.95 *NOS, SNC, DVT*

Boys Town 🐾🐾🐾

Hollywood's famous, righteous portrayal of the soft-spoken but two-fisted Father Flanagan, who founded Boys Town as a progressive, self-governing community for disadvantaged boys and juvenile delinquents, just outside Omaha. Plot covers the struggling, early years of the facility, underfunded and facing public skepticism. Somewhat slow until the incandescent Rooney shows up as Whitey Marsh, nervy punk who poses a challenge to Father Flanagan's assertion that "There's no such thing as a bad boy." You'll be cheering by the finish. Sequelized in "Men of Boys Town" and "Miracle of the Heart: A Boys Town Story." **Hound Advisory:** Alcohol use; roughhousing.
1938 (*Family*) 93m/B Spencer Tracy, Mickey Rooney, Henry Hull, Gene Reynolds, Sidney Miller, Frankie Thomas Jr.; **D:** Norman Taurog. **Award Nominations:** Academy Awards '38: Best Director (Taurog), Best Picture, Best Screenplay; **Awards:** Academy Awards '38: Best Actor (Tracy), Best Original Screenplay. **VHS, Beta, LV** $19.98 *MGM, BTV, IGP*

Boyz N the Hood 🐾🐾🐾

Extraordinary drama (Singleton's debut as a writer and director) explains with chilling clarity what a lot of America still can't grasp; how ghetto kids end up becoming their own criminal predators. In South Central L.A., four young black high school students with different backgrounds, aims, and abilities grow up in a neighborhood terrorized by crime, gangs and racist cops. Of the quartet, Tre has the best chance of reaching adulthood, because he's the only one with a strong and deeply concerned father. Raw language and brutality, but all in the service of a nonviolent, pro-family message. Singleton was the youngest director ever nominated for an

Oscar. The laserdisc version includes two extra scenes and an interview with him. **Hound Advisory:** Brutality, profanity, sex talk, drug talk, mature themes.
1991 (**R**/*College-Adult*) 112m/C Laurence "Larry" Fishburne, Ice Cube, Cuba Gooding Jr., Nia Long, Morris Chestnut, Tyra Ferrell, Angela Bassett; **D:** John Singleton; **W:** John Singleton; **M:** Stanley Clarke. **Award Nominations:** Academy Awards '91: Best Director (Singleton), Best Original Screenplay; **Awards:** Chicago Film Critics Awards '91: Most Promising Actor (Ice Cube); MTV Movie Awards '92: Best New Filmmaker Award (Singleton); National Board of Review Awards '91: 10 Best Films of the Year. **VHS, Beta, LV, 8mm** $19.95 *COL, CRC, FCT*

Bozo the Clown: Ding Dong Dandy Adventures

Animated adventures of the world's most famous clown, compiled from TV. Additional volumes available.
1959 (*Family*) 90m/C Larry Harmon. **VHS, LV** $24.95 *JFK, IME, WTA*

Brain Donors 🐾🐾🐾

Goofy and uneven effort reminiscent of the Marx Brothers stars Turturro as a sleazy lawyer trying to take over the Oglethorpe Ballet Company by sweet talking its aged patroness. He is helped by two eccentric friends, and together they have plentiful opportunities to crack bad but witty jokes. The action culminates with an hilarious ballet scene featuring someone giving CPR to the ballerina playing the dying swan, an actor in a duck suit, duck hunters, and a pack of hounds. Occasionally inspired silliness. **Hound Advisory:** Sex talk; brief nudity.
1992 (**PG**/*Jr. High-Adult*) 79m/C John Turturro, Bob Nelson, Mel Smith, Nancy Marchand, John Savident, George de la Pena, Juli Donald, Spike Alexander, Teri Copley; **D:** Dennis Dugan; **W:** Pat Proft; **M:** Ira Newborn. **VHS, Beta, LV** $14.95 *PAR*

Brain 17 🐾🐾

10-year-old lad named Stevie helps a giant robot, "Brain 17," battle an evil scientist who is bent on world domination.
1982 (*Preschool-Primary*) 72m/C **VHS, Beta** *FHE*

The Brave Little Toaster 🐾🐾🐾

When a young boy leaves his cottage, the electrical appliances grow concerned and journey to the big city in search of him. Disney released (but didn't animate) this clever cartoon takeoff on "Incredible Journey" type stories, with a lamp, radio, electric blanket, vacuum and, of course, toaster, in lieu of the usual loyal housepet. Brilliant character voices, even if the gimmick wears pretty thin at feature length. Based on a novella by Thomas M. Disch.
1988 (*Family*) 90m/C **D:** Jerry Rees; **V:** Jon Lovitz, Phil Hartman. **VHS, Beta, LV** $19.99 *DIS, BVV, FCT*

Bravestarr: The Legend Returns

Animated series finds a western marshal upholding the law on a barren, outlaw planet. In this epiosde Bravestarr and his pals take on Tex Hex and his evil gang in a battle for New Texas. Additional volumes available.
1987 (*Family*) 120m/C **VHS** $39.95 *JFK, WTA*

The Breakfast Club 🐾🐾🐾

Five students from different cliques at a Chicago suburban high school spend a Saturday together in detention, learn more about each other than they ever did in regular class. Rather well done teenage culture study; these characters delve a little deeper than the standard adult view of adolescent stereotypes. One of Hughes' best movies. Soundtrack features Simple Minds and Wang Chung. **Hound Advisory:** Profanity, sex talk, drug use.

1985 (R/*Sr. High-Family*) 97m/C Ally Sheedy, Molly Ringwald, Judd Nelson, Emilio Estevez, Anthony Michael Hall, Paul Gleason, John Kapelos; **D:** John Hughes; **W:** John Hughes; **M:** Gary Chang, Keith Forsey. **VHS, Beta, LV $19.95** *MCA, FCT*

Breakin' Through 🐾

Disney TV-movie based around the less-than-evergreen breakdancing craze, in which the choreographer of a troubled Broadway musical decides to energize his shows with a troupe of street dancers.

1984 (*Family*) 73m/C Ben Vereen, Donna McKechnie, Reid Shelton; **D:** Peter Medak. **VHS, Beta $69.95** *DIS*

Breaking Away 🐾🐾🐾🐾

Fine coming-of-age drama about a working-class high school graduate, crazy over bicycle racing, whose dreams are tested against the realities of a crucial tournament. An honest, open look at present Americana with tremendous insight into the minds of average youth; shot on location at Indiana University. Great performances, touching family relationships. Writer Steve Tesich revisited the bike-racing motif in "American Flyers." **Hound Advisory:** Roughhousing.

1979 (PG/*Family*) 100m/C Dennis Christopher, Dennis Quaid, Daniel Stern, Jackie Earle Haley, Barbara Barrie, Paul Dooley, Amy Wright; **D:** Peter Yates; **W:** Steve Tesich. **Award Nominations:** Academy Awards '79: Best Director (Yates), Best Picture, Best Supporting Actress (Barrie), Best Original Score; **Awards:** Academy Awards '79: Best Original Screenplay; Golden Globe Awards '80: Best Film—Musical/Comedy; National Board of Review Awards '79: 10 Best Films of the Year, Best Supporting Actor (Dooley). **VHS, Beta, LV $59.98** *FOX, HMV*

Breaking the Ice 🐾🐾

Outdated combination of music and ice-skating spectacle stars child crooner Breen as a boy whose vocal talents are going to waste in his strict, rural religious community. He runs away from the farm and winds up a singing star at a Philadelphia ice show.

1938 (*Family*) 79m/B Bobby Breen, Charlie Ruggles, Dolores Costello, Billy Gilbert, Margaret Hamilton. **VHS, Beta $19.95** *NOS, VYY, DVT*

Breaking the Rules 🐾🐾🐾

Predictable buddy-road movie with a tearjerking premise and comedic overtones. Rob, Gene, and Phil were best buds growing up in Cleveland but young adulthood has separated them. They're reunited by Phil, who is dying of leukemia, and whose last wish is a cross-country road trip to California so he can appear as a contestant on "Jeopardy" (the game show last figured prominently in a movie in "White Men Can't Jump"). Along the way they meet brassy waitress Mary, who impulsively decides to join them and winds up bringing the

trio's shaky friendship back together. Potts sparkles as the big-haired, big-hearted Mary, the rest of the crew is tuned and ready, but script goes down the road well travelled. **Hound Advisory:** Profanity and suggested sex.

1992 (PG-13/*Jr. High-Adult*) 100m/C Jason Bateman, C. Thomas Howell, Jonathan Silverman, Annie Potts, Kent Bateman, Shawn Phelan; **D:** Neal Israel; **W:** Paul Shapiro; **M:** David Kitay. **VHS, LV $92.99** *HBO*

Brenda Starr 🐾🐾

While the long unreleased adaptation of the comic strip by Dale Messick is hardly as bad as the critics said, it's still a notch below average. Shields is well cast as fictional glamour girl reporter Brenda Starr, who declares she's quitting the funnies. A cartoonist (not Dale Messick, one of the first female comics creators - that would have been interesting) jumps into the page, a la "Last Action Hero," and trails Brenda on a typically campy adventure in the South American jungle searching for a scientist with a secret rocket fuel. Accurately conveys the silly, two-dimensional feel of the original strip, for what good that does. **Hound Advisory:** Roughhousing.

1986 (PG/*Jr. High-Adult*) 94m/C Brooke Shields, Timothy Dalton, Tony Peck, Diana Scarwid, Nestor Serrano, Jeffrey Tambor, June Gable, Charles Durning, Eddie Albert, Henry Gibson, Ed Nelson; **D:** Robert Ellis Miller; **W:** James David Buchanan. **VHS** *COL*

Brer Rabbit and Boss Lion

An adaptation of the American folk tale about how brains always overcome brawn, told through delightful illustrations and narration with a lilting musical score by Dr. John. Part of the "Rabbit Ears: American Heroes and Legends" series.

1992 (*Preschool-Primary*) 34m/C **VHS $9.98** *UND,, MVD*

Brer Rabbit and the Wonderful Tar Baby

"Great-grandfather of Bugs Bunny" outwits Brer Fox again in this delightful classic American tale.

1991 (*Preschool-Primary*) 30m/C **VHS, LV $15.99** *KUI, NLC*

Brer Rabbit Tales

Story collection includes "Tar Baby" and "The Laughing Place."

1991 (*Primary*) 48m/C **VHS $12.98** *WEA, FHE*

Brewster's Millions 🐾🐾

An aging minor league baseball player must spend 30 million dollars in order to collect an inheritance of 300 million dollars. He may find that money can't buy happiness. Seventh remake of the story. **Hound Advisory:** Profanity.

1985 (PG/*Jr. High-Adult*) 101m/C Richard Pryor, John Candy, Lonette McKee, Stephen Collins, Jerry Orbach, Pat Hingle, Tovah Feldshuh, Hume Cronyn, Rick Moranis; **D:** Walter Hill; **W:** Herschel Weingrod, Timothy Harris; **M:** Ry Cooder. **VHS, Beta, LV $19.95** *MCA*

Brian's Song 🐾🐾🐾🐾

Affecting and warmly sentimental story of the unique relationship between Gale Sayers, the Chicago Bears' star running back, and his teammate Brian Piccolo. The friendship between the Bears' first interracial roommates ended suddenly when Brian lost his life to cancer. Made for television. **1971** (*G/Family*) 74m/C James Caan, Billy Dee Williams, Jack Warden, Shelley Fabares, Judy Pace; *D:* Buzz Kulik. **VHS, Beta, LV $64.95** *COL*

The Bridge on the River Kwai 🦴🦴🦴🦴

Powerful adaptation of the Pierre Bouelle novel about the folly of war focuses on the battle of wills between a Japanese POW camp commander and the prisoners' leader, a by-the-rules British colonel, portrayed brilliantly by Guinness. Conflict surrounds the construction of a rail bridge by the prisoners, and the parallel efforts by escaped prisoner Holden to destroy it. Holden's role was originally cast for Cary Grant. Memorable too for whistling "Colonel Bogey March." WWII adventure drama is superior on all fronts. Because Wilson and Foreman had been blacklisted, Boulle (who spoke no English) was credited as screenwriter. **Hound Advisory:** Violence. **1957** (*Jr. High-Adult*) 161m/C William Holden, Alec Guinness, Jack Hawkins, Sessue Hayakawa, James Donald, Geoffrey Horne, Andre Morell, Ann Sears; *D:* David Lean; *W:* Michael Wilson, Carl Foreman; *M:* Malcolm Arnold. **Award Nominations:** Academy Awards '57: Best Supporting Actor (Hayakawa); **Awards:** Academy Awards '57: Best Actor (Guinness), Best Adapted Screenplay, Best Color Cinematography, Best Director (Lean), Best Film Editing, Best Picture, Best Original Score; British Academy Awards '57: Best Actor (Guinness), Best Film; Directors Guild of America Awards '57: Best Director (Lean); Golden Globe Awards '58: Best Actor—Drama (Guinness), Best Director (Lean), Best Film—Drama; National Board of Review Awards '57: 10 Best Films of the Year, Best Actor (Guinness), Best Director (Lean), Best Supporting Actor (Hayakawa). **VHS, Beta, LV $19.95** *COL, BTV, HMV*

Bridge to Terabithia

Schoolkids Jesse and Leslie strike up a friendship and create an imaginary fantasy world called Terabithia for themselves in a pine forest near their homes. When Leslie suddenly dies, Jesse is left with the memories and the strength to cope with the tragedy. "WonderWorks" short feature is based on the novel by Katherine Paterson. **1985** (*Family*) 58m/C Annette O'Toole, Julian Coutts, Julie Beaulieu; *D:* Eric Till. **VHS $29.95** *PME, HMV, FCT*

A Bridge Too Far 🦴🦴

A meticulous recreation of one of the most disastrous battles of WWII, the Allied defeat at Arnhem in 1944. Misinformation, adverse conditions, and overconfidence combined to prevent the Allies from capturing six bridges that connected Holland to the German border. **1977** (*PG/Family*) 175m/C Sean Connery, Robert Redford, James Caan, Michael Caine, Elliott Gould, Gene Hackman, Laurence Olivier, Ryan O'Neal, Liv Ullmann, Dirk Bogarde, Hardy Kruger, Arthur Hill, Edward Fox, Anthony Hopkins; *D:* Richard Attenborough; *W:* William Goldman; *M:* John Addison. **VHS, Beta, LV $29.98** *MGM, FOX*

Bright Eyes 🦴🦴◁

Shirley stars as an adorable orphan caught between foster parents in a custody battle; in the meantime she has to live under the same roof with a spoiled brat (played by Withers, another popular kid star of the era). This is the one where Temple performed her signature tune "On the Good Ship Lollipop." Reissued version is rather mysteriously rated PG. **1934** (*PG/Family*) 84m/B Shirley Temple, James Dunn, Lois Wilson, Jane Withers, Judith Allen; *D:* David Butler. **VHS, Beta $14.98** *FOX, MLT*

Brighton Beach Memoirs 🦴🦴◁

Popular (and autobiographical) Neil Simon play takes to the screen. Poignant comedy/drama about a young Jewish boy and his family in 1937 Brooklyn. Not exactly heavy on plot; teenager Eugene wants to see a naked woman at least once before he dies, 16-year old sister Nora wants to be a Broadway dancer etc., but Simon's script endows the characters with keen humanity, even if it worked better on stage. Eugene's story was continued in the plays (and the films) "Biloxi Blues" and "Broadway Bound." **Hound Advisory:** Sex talk, salty language. **1986** (*PG-13/Jr. High-Adult*) 108m/C Blythe Danner, Bob Dishy, Judith Ivey, Jonathan Silverman, Brian Drillinger, Stacey Glick, Lisa Waltz, Jason Alexander; *D:* Gene Saks; *W:* Neil Simon; *M:* Michael Small. **VHS, Beta, LV $19.95** *MCA, FCT*

Bringing Up Baby 🦴🦴🦴🦴

The quintessential screwball comedy, featuring Hepburn as a giddy socialite with a "baby" leopard, and Grant as the unwitting object of her affections. One ridiculous situation after another add up to high-speed entertainment. Hepburn looks lovely, the supporting actors are in fine form, and director Hawks manages the perfect balance of control and mayhem. From a story by Hagar Wilde, who helped Nichols with the screenplay. Also available in a colorized version. **1938** (*Family*) 103m/B Katharine Hepburn, Cary Grant, May Robson, Charlie Ruggles, Walter Catlett, Fritz Feld, Jonathan Hale, Barry Fitzgerald, Ward Bond; *D:* Howard Hawks; *W:* Dudley Nichols. **VHS, Beta, LV $14.98** *TTC, HMV, BTV*

Broadway Danny Rose 🦴🦴🦴◁

One of Woody Allen's best films, a hilarious, heart-rending anecdotal comedy about a third-rate talent agent involved in one of his client's infidelities. The film magically unfolds as show business veterans swap Danny Rose stories at a delicatessen. Allen's Danny Rose is pathetically lovable. **Hound Advisory:** Brief violence. **1984** (*PG/Sr. High-Adult*) 85m/B Woody Allen, Mia Farrow, Nick Apollo Forte, Sandy Baron, Milton Berle, Howard Cosell; *D:* Woody Allen; *W:* Woody Allen. **VHS, Beta, LV $19.98** *VES*

Bronco Billy 🦴🦴◁

Kinder, gentler Eastwood is New Jersey shoe clerk Billy McCoy, who dreams of being a cowboy. One day he fulfills his fantast by becoming the proprietor of a cheapo wild west show. Thin premise occasionally runs dry of charm, which is its chief asset, particularly when focusing on Locke's one-note performance as a spoiled rich girl who joins the show. On the other hand, it's a pleasant enough diversion for Clint and the viewer. **Hound Advisory:** Roughhousing, salty language, mature themes. **1980** (*PG/Family*) 117m/C Clint Eastwood, Sondra Locke, Bill McKinney, Scatman Crothers, Sam Bottoms, Geoffrey Lewis, Dan Vadis, Sierra Pecheur; *D:* Clint Eastwood; *M:* Stephen Dorff. **VHS, Beta, LV $19.98** *WAR, TLF, RXM*

A Bronx Tale 🦴🦴🦴

Vivid snapshot of a young Italian-American boy growing up in the '60s among neighborhood small-time wiseguys. As a 9-

year-old Calogero witnesses mobster Sonny kill a man but doesn't rat to the police, so Sonny takes the kid under his wing. His upright bus-driving father Lorenzo doesn't approve but the kid is drawn to Sonny's apparent glamour and power. At 17, he's gotten both an education in school and on the streets but he needs to make a choice. Good period detail and excellent performances. Palminteri shows both Sonny's charisma and violence and De Niro handles the less-showy father role with finesse. Based on Palminteri's one-man play; De Niro's directorial debut. **Hound Advisory:** Profanity; violence; suggested sex.

1993 (R/*Sr. High-Adult*) 122m/C Robert De Niro, Chazz Palminteri, Lillo Brancato, Frank Capra, Taral Hicks, Kathrine Narducci, Clem Caserta, Alfred Sauchelli Jr., Frank Pietrangolare; *Cameos:* Joe Pesci; *D:* Robert De Niro; *W:* Chazz Palminteri. **VHS, LV** *HBO*

Brother Future

T.J., a black, streetsmart city kid who thinks school and helping others is all a waste of time gets knocked out in a car accident. As he's lying unconscious, he is transported back in time to a slave auction block in the Old South. There the displaced urbanite is forced to work on a cotton plantation, and watch the stirrings of a slave revolt. T.J. sees the light and realizes how much opportunity he's been wasting in his own life. He comes to just a few moments later, but worlds away from who he was before. Part of the "Wonderworks" series.

1991 (*Family*) 110m/C Phill Lewis, Frank Converse, Carl Lumbly, Vonetta McGee. **VHS $29.95** *PME, HMV, BTV*

Brothers Lionheart 🦴🦴

Uneven Scandinavian fantasy about two warrior brothers fighting dragons and tyrants in a mystical Valhalla during the Middle Ages. Director Hellbron also gave the world the "Pippi Longstocking" series.

1985 (G/*Primary-Jr. High*) 120m/C Staffan Gotestam, Lars Soderdahl, Allan Edwall; *D:* Olle Hellbron. **VHS, Beta** *NO*

Brothers O'Toole 🦴🦴

Repeated cases of mistaken identity plague two con-artist brothers in the Old West trying to bring prosperity to a luckless town. Episodic family comedy, atypical for relying on dialogue and characters for the attempted laughs, rather than standard slapstick. Good cast; Carroll later provided the voice of Ursula the Sea Witch in Disney's "The Little Mermaid." **Hound Advisory:** Roughhousing, alcohol use.

1973 (G/*Family*) 94m/C John Astin, Steve Carlson, Pat Carroll, Hans Conried, Lee Meriwether; *D:* Richard Erdman. **VHS, Beta $49.95** *VCI*

Bubbe's Boarding House: Chanukah at Bubbe's

Puppets populate Bubbe's Boarding House and help teach about the traditions of Chanukah and Passover.

1991 (*Family*) 30m/C **VHS $15.98** *MON, MLT*

Buck and the Preacher 🦴🦴🦴

A trail guide and a con man preacher join forces to help a wagon train of former slaves who are seeking to homestead out West. Poitier's debut as a director.

1972 (PG/*Jr. High-Adult*) 102m/C Sidney Poitier, Harry Belafonte, Ruby Dee, Cameron Mitchell, Denny Miller; *D:* Sidney Poitier. **VHS, Beta $14.95** *COL*

Buck Privates 🦴🦴

The wartime comedy that made Abbott & Costello superstars still salutes smartly today. Two streetcorner tie salesmen mistakenly enlist in the army, are naturally assigned to a barracks full of misfits. Needless romantic subplot slows things down, but real fun is at the end when the platoon pulls together to compete in a practice wargame. A more family-friendly alternative to the lewd Bill Murray hit "Stripes."

1941 (*Jr. High-Adult*) 84m/B Bud Abbott, Lou Costello, Shemp Howard, Lee Norman, Alan Curtis, The Andrews Sisters; *D:* Arthur Lubin. **VHS, Beta, LV $14.95** *MCA*

Buck Privates Come Home 🦴🦴🦴

Abbott and Costello return to their "Buck Privates" roles as two soldiers trying to adjust to civilian life after the war. They also try to help a French girl sneak into the United States. Funny antics culminate into a wild chase scene.

1947 (*Family*) 77m/B Bud Abbott, Lou Costello, Tom Brown, Joan Shawlee, Nat Pendleton, Beverly Simmons, Don Beddoe, Don Porter, Donald MacBride; *D:* Charles T. Barton. **VHS $14.98** *MCA*

Buck Rogers Conquers the Universe 🦴🦴

Feature-film condensation of the vintage "Buck Rogers" serial, inspired by Phil Nolan's 25th-century comic-book hero. Buck helps a future Earth break the grasp of the evil Killer Kane, who saps the will of all who oppose him by putting shiny buckets over their heads. Retitled to recall Crabbe's better-known "Flash Gordon Conquers the Universe"; also known as "Buck Rogers: Planet Outlaws."

1939 (*Family*) 91m/B Buster Crabbe, Constance Moore, Jackie Moran; *D:* Ford Beebe, Saul Goodkind. **VHS, Beta $29.95** *FOX*

Buck Rogers in the 25th Century 🦴🦴

American astronaut preserved in space for 500 years is brought back to life by a passing Draconian flagship. Outer space adventures begin when he is accused of being a spy from Earth. Revival of the classic movie serial/'50s TV series/vintage comic strip never would have happened but for the success of "Star Wars" and it looks it, even indulging in the usual cute little robot (voice provided by Mel "Bugs Bunny" Blanc). Made-for-TV movie, subsequently released to theaters, that kicked off a weekly series. Additional series episodes available on tape. **Hound Advisory:** Violence.

1979 (PG/*Family*) 90m/C Gil Gerard, Pamela Hensley, Erin Gray, Henry Silva; *D:* Daniel Haller. **VHS, Beta, LV $14.98** *MCA, MOV*

Bucky O'Hare: Bye-Bye Berserker Baboon

Two episodes from the "Bucky O'Hare" series, which feature the rabbit captain of the space frigate Righteous Indignation and assorted space rip-offs. Additional volumes available.
1991 (*Preschool-Primary*) 47m/C **VHS $12.95** *WTA*

The Buddy Holly Story 𝄞𝄞𝄞♩

Busey, performing Holly's hits himself, lends a stellar performance as the famed 1950s pop icon. Story spans the years from Holly's meteoric career's beginnings in Lubbock to his tragic early death in the now famous plane crash. For that roots of rock 'n' roll double bill, see it with "La Bamba." ♫Rock Around the Ollie Vee; That'll Be the Day; Oh, Boy; It's So Easy; Well All Right; Chantilly Lace; Peggy Sue.
1978 (*PG/Jr. High-Adult*) 113m/C Gary Busey, Don Stroud, Charles Martin Smith, Conrad Janis, William Jordan; *D:* Steve Rash; *M:* Joe Renzetti. **Award Nominations:** Academy Awards '78: Best Actor (Busey), Best Sound; **Awards:** Academy Awards '78: Best Adapted Score; National Society of Film Critics Awards '78: Best Actor (Busey). **VHS, Beta, LV $19.95** *COL*

Buffy the Vampire Slayer 𝄞𝄞♩

Camp-oriented teen genre spoof about a Southern Cal valley girl reluctantly claiming her ancient destiny to slay vampires, specifically ones who have suddenly infested Los Angeles high school hangouts. Canned morality lesson: Buffy fights against the undead even though bimbo cheerleader friends declare her uncool and flee. "Pee Wee Herman" Reubens is unrecognizable and amusing as the vampire king's 1200-year-old henchman, engaging in one of the longer death scenes of film history. **Hound Advisory:** Violence (the vampires get the sharper end of it, naturally), salty language, sex and drug talk.
1992 (*PG-13/Jr. High-Adult*) 98m/C Kristy Swanson, Donald Sutherland, Luke Perry, Paul (Pee Wee Herman) Reubens, Rutger Hauer, Michele Abrams, Randall Batinkoff, Hilary Swank, Paris Vaughan, David Arquette, Candy Clark, Natasha Gregson Wagner; *D:* Fran Rubel Kazui; *W:* Joss Whedon; *M:* Carter Burwell. **VHS, LV $19.98** *FXV, PMS*

Bugs Bunny: All American Hero

Bugs takes a trip back through history, starting in 1492 when Columbus sailed the ocean blue and Bugs was his shipmate. Continues through the American Revolution, WWI, and more with Yosemite Sam, Sylvester and all of your favorites.
1981 (*Family*) 24m/C *V:* Mel Blanc. **VHS $12.95** *WAR, WTA*

Bugs Bunny Cartoon Festival

Four early cartoons starring the nefarious rabbit. One of nine volumes of Bugs and friends on the MGM video label.
1944 (*Family*) 34m/C *D:* Bob Clampett, Chuck Jones, Friz Freleng. **VHS, Beta $14.95** *MGM*

Bugs Bunny: Festival of Fun

Five classic cartoons from the Bugsmeister. Includes "Hare Ribbin," "Rhapsody Rabbit," "Baseball Bugs," "The Wacky Wabbit," and "The Wabbit Who Came to Supper."
194? (*Family*) 35m/C **VHS $12.95** *MGM, WTA*

The Bugs Bunny/Road Runner Movie 𝄞𝄞𝄞

Worthy compilation of classic Warner Brothers cartoons, starring Bugs Bunny, Daffy Duck, Elmer Fudd, the Road Runner, Wile E. Coyote, Porky Pig, and Pepe Le Pew, bookended by Bugs in some all-new animated narration sequences. Also available with Spanish dubbing.
1979 (*G/Family*) 98m/C *D:* Chuck Jones, Phil Monroe; *V:* Mel Blanc. **VHS, Beta $14.95** *WAR, WTA, APD*

Bugs Bunny Superstar 𝄞𝄞♩

A look at the wild characters onscreen and off at the Warner Brothers cartoon studio that created the classic Looney Tunes/Merrie Melodies series in general and Bugs Bunny in particular. Bits and pieces from great cartoons are shown, along with some amazing home movies and behind-the-drawing-board footage, but the low-budget presentation leans toward the haphazard.
1975 (*G/Family*) 91m/C *D:* Larry Jackson, Bob Clampett, Tex Avery, Friz Freleng; *V:* Mel Blanc. **VHS, LV $19.95** *MGM, WTA*

Bugs Bunny's 3rd Movie: 1,001 Rabbit Tales 𝄞𝄞♩

Compilation of old and new classic cartoons featuring Bugs, Daffy, Sylvester, Porky, Elmer, Tweety, Speedy Gonzalez and Yosemite Sam. Favorites all, but a lot of this is better in small doses.
1982 (*G/Family*) 74m/C *D:* Chuck Jones, Robert McKimson, Friz Freleng. **VHS, Beta $14.95** *WAR, FCT, WTA*

Bugsy Malone 𝄞𝄞♩

Oddball musical spoof of 1930s mobster movies with an all-children cast. Plot loosely details a gangland war between sarsaparilla bootlegger Fat Sam and an upstart named Dandy Dan, who raids Sam's speakeasies with newfangled 'splurge guns' shooting whipped cream; evidently a pie in the face in this fantasy world is lethal, yet the what-do-we-do-now ending has the creamed casualties rising to sing together about love and brotherhood. It's hard to say what the point of it all is, but watch young Jodie Foster, as a vampy moll, acting circles around the rest of the cast. Fun but unmemorable songs by Paul Williams. **Hound Advisory:** Cream-pie killings are so stylized and silly that it could be called violence.
1976 (*G/Family*) 94m/C Jodie Foster, Scott Baio, Florrie Augger, John Cassisi, Martin Lev; *D:* Alan Parker; *W:* Alan Parker; *M:* Paul Williams. **VHS, Beta, LV $14.95** *PAR*

The Bulldozer Brigade 𝄞𝄞♩

Irish children's comedy (with serious undertones) set in Belfast; two schoolgirl friends, one Catholic, one Protestant, start a petition to save their secret wooded playground from land developers. But grownups misunderstand, and a simple kiddie protest snowballs into a terrorist scare. The low-budget yarn tends to meander, but offbeat settings and unforced good humor make it worth a look.
1985 (*Family*) 86m/C **VHS $39.98** *FHE, BTV*

Bunnicula: Vampire Rabbit

Strange things happen after a family adopts a bunny. The other pets, a dog and a cat, team up to prove that their furry cohort is a vampire in disguise. "ABC Weekend Special" 'toon, based on the popular children's book by Deborah and James Howe.
1982 *(Family)* 23m/C **VHS, Beta $19.95** *WOV, GKK, WTA*

The 'Burbs 🐾💤

A tepid satire about suburbanites suspecting their creepy new neighbors of murderous activities. Well-designed and sharp, but light on story. **Hound Advisory:** Violence and profanity.
1989 (PG/Jr. High–Adult) 101m/C Tom Hanks, Carrie Fisher, Rick Ducommun, Corey Feldman, Brother Theodore, Bruce Dern, Gale Gordon, Courtney Gains; **D:** Joe Dante; **M:** Jerry Goldsmith. **VHS, Beta, LV $14.95** *MCA, CCB*

Burn 'Em Up Barnes

Mascot Studios was a serial-production outfit that later formed serial powerhouse Republic Pictures, but before that their output was generally unmemorable. This one depicts Barnes, the "Speed Racer" of the era, as he and a buddy battle gangsters. In twelve episodes.
1934 *(Family)* 40m/B Frankie Darro, Lola Lane, Jack Mulhall. **VHS, Beta $26.95** *SNC, NOS, VCN*

The Bushbaby 🐾💤

Simple-minded stuff built around the title animal, a huge-eyed, raccoon-like denizen of the African jungle that's too cute for words. The little heroine is given a mischievous bush baby while visiting her father on the dark continent. When the critter makes her miss her ship home, she gets a ride with a former family servant (future Oscar-winner Louis Gossett Jr.), but authorities mistake him for a kidnapper, and the two - along with the trouble-causing pet - are pursued by cops.
1970 *(Family)* 100m/C Margaret Brooks, Louis Gossett Jr., Donald Houston, Laurence Naismith, Marne Maitland, Geoffrey Bayldon, Jack Gwillim; **D:** John Trent. **VHS $14.98** *MGM, FCT*

Bustin' Loose 🐾🐾💤

Con man on probation is ordered to drive a bus filled with problem children cross-country to a group home. Their comical and 'uplifting' misadventures on the way are standard stuff, improved immeasurably by the talented Pryor; it's no surprise when the star scores with the comedy, but he even makes the sentimental schmaltz seem better than it is. **Hound Advisory:** The R rating is for Pryor's occasionally foul language - mild by 1994 standards, more like a PG13. Sex talk in a subplot about one of the kids having been a teen prostitute. Roughhousing.
1981 (R/Adult) 94m/C Richard Pryor, Cicely Tyson, Robert Christian, George Coe, Bill Quinn; **D:** Oz Scott; **W:** Richard Pryor. **VHS, Beta, LV $14.95** *MCA*

Butch and Sundance: The Early Days 🐾🐾💤

Traces the origins of the famous outlaw duo. It contains the requisite shoot-outs, hold-ups, and escapes. A "prequel" to "Butch Cassidy and the Sundance Kid" is no match for the classic, but may prove of interest to fans of the original. **Hound Advisory:** Salty language; roughhousing.
1979 (PG/Family) 111m/C Tom Berenger, William Katt, John Schuck, Jeff Corey, Jill Eikenberry, Brian Dennehy, Peter Weller; **D:** Richard Lester. **VHS, Beta $19.98** *FOX*

Butch Cassidy and the Sundance Kid 🐾🐾🐾🐾

Two legendary outlaws at the turn of the century take it on the lam with a beautiful, willing ex-school teacher. With a clever script, humanly fallible characters, and warm, witty dialogue, this film was destined to become a box-office classic. Featured the hit song, "Raindrops Keep Falling on My Head" and renewed the buddy film industry, as Newman and Redford trade insult for insult. Look for the great scene where Newman takes on giant Ted Cassidy in a fist fight.
1969 (PG/Family) 110m/C Paul Newman, Robert Redford, Katharine Ross, Jeff Corey, Strother Martin, Cloris Leachman, Kenneth Mars, Ted Cassidy, Henry Jones, George Furth, Sam Elliott; **D:** George Roy Hill; **W:** William Goldman; **M:** Burt Bacharach. **Award Nominations:** Academy Awards '69: Best Director (Hill), Best Picture, Best Sound; **Awards:** Academy Awards '69: Best Cinematography, Best Song ("Raindrops Keep Fallin' on My Head"), Best Story & Screenplay, Best Original Score; British Academy Awards '70: Best Actor (Redford), Best Actress (Ross), Best Director (Hill), Best Film; Golden Globe Awards '70: Best Score. **VHS, Beta, LV $19.98** *FOX, TLF*

The Butcher's Wife 🐾🐾💤

Semi-charming tale of young psychic Moore who brings romance to a Greenwich Village neighborhood. As the clairvoyant married to butcher Dzundza, Moore wields mystical powers that bring magic into the lives of everyone around her, though local psychiatrist Daniels has his doubts. Talented cast works above hamburger script. **Hound Advisory:** Profanity.
1991 (PG-13/Jr. High–Adult) 107m/C Demi Moore, Jeff Daniels, George Dzundza, Frances McDormand, Margaret Colin, Mary Steenburgen, Max Perlich, Miriam Margolyes, Christopher Durang, Diane Salinger; **D:** Terry Hughes; **W:** Ezra Litwack, Marjorie Schwartz; **M:** Michael Gore. **VHS, Beta, LV $14.95** *PAR*

Butterflies Are Free 🐾🐾🐾

Fast-paced humor surrounds the Broadway play brought to the big screen. Blind youth Albert is determined to be self-sufficient. A next-door-neighbor actress helps him gain independence from his over-protective mother (Heckart).
1972 (PG/Jr. High–Adult) 109m/C Goldie Hawn, Edward Albert, Eileen Heckart, Michael Glaser; **D:** Milton Katselas. **Award Nominations:** Academy Awards '72: Best Cinematography, Best Sound; **Awards:** Academy Awards '72: Best Supporting Actress (Heckart). **VHS, Beta $9.95** *GKK*

Buttons and Rusty Series

Selections from the popular children's animated show from the Disney Channel; Buttons the bear cub and Rusty the fox pup have comical adventures, usually with seasonal connections. Episodes include "The Easter Bunny," "The Turkey Gang," "The Halloween Party," "A Special Christmas," "The Adventure Machine," and "The Wildbird Caper."
1988 *(Family)* 25m/C **VHS, Beta $14.99** *BFV*

Bye, Bye, Birdie 🎻🎻🎻

Energized and sweet film version of the Broadway musical about a teen rock and roll idol (Pearson doing Elvis) coming to a small town to see one of his fans (Ann Margret) in a public relations ploy before he leaves for the army. 22-year-old Ann-Margret emerged from role as a bonafide star, and it's easy to see why. ♫Bye Bye Birdie; The Telephone Hour; How Lovely to be a Woman; Honestly Sincere; One Boy; Put on a Happy Face; Kids; One Last Kiss; A Lot of Livin' to Do.
1963 (*Family*) 112m/C Dick Van Dyke, Janet Leigh, Ann-Margret, Paul Lynde, Bobby Rydell, Maureen Stapleton, Ed Sullivan, Trudi Ames; *D:* George Sidney. VHS, Beta, LV $19.95 *COL*

The Cabbage Patch Kid's First Christmas

Hanna-Barbera cartoon TV special tied to the Cabbage Patch Kids dolls, who in their heyday caused near-riots at stores. The popular playthings learn the Christmas spirit when they befriend a disabled little girl (crippled in a stampede for toys, perhaps?).
1991 (*Family*) 30m/C VHS, Beta $9.95 *TTC, WTA*

Cabin Boy WOOF!

Obnoxious "fancy lad" Elliott mistakenly boards the wrong boat and becomes the new cabin boy for a ridiculous bunch of mean, smelly sailors who sail the dangerous seas on what looks to be a giant tank of water. Fish out of water saga sags from the start, so don't kid yourself that it will get better. Surprisingly produced by Tim Burton, who must have owed a favor to somebody. The good news is - it's mercifully short. Look for real-life dad Bob as the lad's dad; good friend Letterman appears briefly as nasty "Old Salt," but uses the alias Earl Hofert in the final credits. As usual, the acerbic Letterman gets the best line, one that viewers will understand all too well: "Man, oh, man do I hate them fancy lads." **Hound Advisory:** Salty language; scatological humor; suggested sex.
1994 (PG-13/*Jr. High-Adult*) 80m/C Chris Elliott, Ann Magnuson, Ritch Brinkley, James Gammon, Brian Doyle-Murray, Russ Tamblyn, Brion James, Ricki Lake, Bob Elliott; *Cameos:* David Letterman; *D:* Adam Resnick; *W:* Adam Resnick; *M:* Steve Bartek. VHS, LV *TOU*

Caddie Woodlawn

Title character is a tomboy in a pioneer family, building their homestead in 1864 Wisconsin. During that eventful year Caddie copes with school, resentful Dakota Indians, the tragic loss of a friend, and a visit from a snooty cousin from the East. She also tries to prevent her dad from hunting animals, a politically correct anachronism in this adaptation of the more realistic young adult novel by Carol Ryie Brink.
1988 (*Family*) 104m/C Parker Stevenson, Emily Schulman, Season Hubley; *D:* George McQuilkin, Noel Resnick. VHS, Beta $375.00 *CHF, RHU*

The Caddy 🎻🎻

Lewis plays frantic caddy prone to slapstick against Martin's smooth professional golfer with a bent toward singing. Mostly a series of Martin and Lewis sketches that frequently land in the rough. Introduces several songs, including a classic Martin and Lewis rendition of "That's Amore." Look for cameos by a host of professional golfers.
1953 (*Family*) 95m/C Dean Martin, Jerry Lewis, Donna Reed, Barbara Bates, Joseph Calleia, Marshall Thompson, Fred Clark; *Cameos:* Ben Hogan, Sam Snead, Byron Nelson, Julius Boros, Jimmy Thomson, Harry E. Cooper; *D:* Norman Taurog. VHS, Beta $14.95 *PAR*

Caddyshack 🎻🎻🎻🎿

Inspired performances by Murray and Dangerfield drive this sublimely moronic comedy onto the green. The action takes place at Bushwood Country Club, where caddy O'Keefe is bucking to win the club's college scholarship. Characters involved in various sophomoric set pieces include obnoxious club president Knight, a playboy who is too laid back to keep his score (Chase), a loud, vulgar, and extremely rich golfer (Dangerfield), and Murray as a filthy gopher-hunting groundskeeper. Occasional dry moments are followed by scenes of pure (and tasteless) anarchy, so watch with someone immature. Does for golf what "Major League" tried to do for baseball. **Hound Advisory:** Nudity, sex, profanity.
1980 (R/*Sr. High-Adult*) 99m/C Chevy Chase, Rodney Dangerfield, Ted Knight, Michael O'Keefe, Bill Murray, Sarah Holcomb, Brian Doyle-Murray; *D:* Harold Ramis; *W:* Brian Doyle-Murray, Doug Kenney, Harold Ramis. VHS, Beta, LV $19.98 *WAR*

Cahill: United States Marshal 🎻🎻

Graying Duke in one of his lesser moments, portraying a marshal who comes to the aid of his sons, mixed up with a gang of outlaws. Turns out that the boys harbor a grudge against pa Cahill due to years of neglect. Will Duke reconcile with the delinquents? Parenting skills mixed with traditional western gunplay. **Hound Advisory:** Violence.
1973 (PG/*Jr. High-Adult*) 103m/C John Wayne, Gary Grimes, George Kennedy, Neville Brand, Marie Windsor, Harry Carey Jr.; *D:* Andrew V. McLaglen; *M:* Elmer Bernstein. VHS, Beta, LV $19.98 *WAR, TLF*

Caldecott Collection

Video series of Caldecott award-winning children's books. Includes "The Polar Express," "The Relatives Game," and "King Bidgood's in the Bathtub." Another video, "Caldecott at Fifty," looks back on the history of the Caldecott Medal.
1988 (*Preschool-Primary*) 30m/C VHS *NO*

Calendar Girl 🎻🎻

In 1962 three high-school best friends borrow a convertible and travel from their Nevada homes to Hollywood to meet their pinup idol, Marilyn Monroe. Priestly portrays Roy the rebel, while Ned's (Olds, in his film debut) the sensitive one, and Scott (O'Connell) is just a regular guy. They stay with Roy's Uncle Harvey (Pantoliano), an aspiring actor, and work to meet their dream girl. Which they finally do, in a notably weak sequence which fits in with this notably uninspired effort basically directed at fans of Priestly. The three actors at least have enough comradery to make realistic buddies - one of the few true touches in the film. **Hound Advisory:** Profanity; brief nudity.

1993 (PG-13/Jr. High-Adult) 86m/C Jason Priestly, Gabriel Olds, Jerry O'Connell, Joe Pantoliano, Stephen Tobolowsky, Kurt Fuller, Steve Railsback, Emily Warfield, Stephanie Anderson; *Cameos:* Chubby Checker; *D:* John Whitesell; *W:* Paul Shapiro; *M:* Hans Zimmer. **VHS, LV, 8mm** *COL*

The California Raisins: Meet the Raisins

Vinton's dancing, singing, rhythm'n'blues raisins became a hit with a series of cereal commercials and brought long-overdue appreciation of his Claymation art. Covers the Raisin characters (yes, they've all got names) and offers their best songs; continued in a followup video "Raisins Sold Out."
1989 (*Family*) 30m/C The California Raisins. **VHS, Beta $12.95** *TMG, WTA*

Call of the Wild 🐾🐾

Parents who have never read Jack London's vivid Gold Rush tale may think it's a kiddies' animal adventure, but even this clunky European version (filmed cheaply in Finland) preserves the harshness and violence of a bloody novel. The Klondike sled dog Buck passes from one master to another, but fate returns him to the only good-hearted one, played nobly by Heston, until finally Buck must give in fully to his feral side. **Hound Advisory:** Brutality (more extreme among beasts than humans), salty language, alcohol use, offscreen sex.
1972 (PG/Jr. High-Adult) 105m/C Charlton Heston, Michele Mercier, George Eastman; *D:* Ken Annakin. **VHS, Beta $14.95** *KUI, SIM, MPI*

Camel Boy 🐾🐾

Yoram Gross, better known for his endearing series of Australian cartoons starring the outback girl Dot, turned to a different part of the world for this animated feature about an Arabian lad and his camel pal who cross the deserts of the Mideast together.
1984 (*Family*) 78m/C *D:* Yoram Gross; *V:* Michael Pate, Ron Haddrick, John Meillon. **VHS, Beta $69.95** *VES, LIV, WTA*

Camelot 🐾🐾

The long-running Lerner and Loewe Broadway musical about King Arthur, Guinevere, and Lancelot was adapted from T.H. White's book, "The Once and Future King." Redgrave and Nero have chemistry as the illicit lovers, Harris is strong as the king struggling to hold together his dream, but muddled direction undermines the effort. Laserdisc edition contains 28 minutes of previously edited footage, trailers and backstage info. ♫I Wonder What the King is Doing Tonight; The Simple Joys of Maidenhood; Camelot; C'est Moi; The Lusty Month of May; Follow Me; How To Handle a Woman; Then You May Take Me to the Fair; If Ever I Would Leave You. **Hound Advisory:** Suggested sex.
1967 (*Family*) 150m/C Richard Harris, Vanessa Redgrave, David Hemmings, Franco Nero, Lionel Jeffries; *D:* Joshua Logan; *M:* Frederick Loewe, Alan Jay Lerner. **Award Nominations:** Academy Awards '67: Best Cinematography, Best Sound; **Awards:** Academy Awards '67: Best Art Direction/Set Decoration, Best Costume Design, Best Score; Golden Globe Awards '68: Best Actor—Musical/Comedy (Harris), Best Song ("If Ever I Should Leave You"), Best Score. **VHS, Beta, LV $29.98** *WAR, RDG, HMV*

Camp Nowhere 🐾🐾

Bland Hollywood Pictures/Disney comedy in which enterprising youngsters, sick of being shipped to dull summer camps,

concoct a phony camp of their own (renting an abandoned commune out in the countryside) and trick the dumb parents into sending them there instead. Funny idea, but when plot finally arrives at Camp Nowhere, it (like the kids) doesn't quite know what to do. Lloyd is the token sympathetic adult, as a deadbeat drama teacher blackmailed into helping pull off the scam. **Hound Advisory:** Alcohol talk; sex talk; drug talk.
1994 (PG/*Family*) 95m/C Christopher Lloyd, Wendy Makkena, M. Emmet Walsh, Peter Scolari, Peter Onorati, Ray Baker, Kate Mulgrew, Jonathan Jackson, Romy Walthall, Maryedith Burrell, Tom Wilson, Nathan Cavaleri, Andrew Keegan, Melody Kay; *D:* Jonathan Prince; *W:* Andrew Kurtzman, Eliot Wald. **VHS** *NYR*

Cancel My Reservation 🐾

New York talk show host Hope sets out for a vacation on an Arizona ranch, but winds up in trouble due to a mysterious corpse, a rich rancher, and an enigmatic mystic. Even more muddled than it sounds. Based on the novel "Broken Gun" by Louis L'Amour, with pointless cameos by Crosby, Wayne, and Wilson.
1972 (G/*Family*) 99m/C Bob Hope, Eva Marie Saint, Ralph Bellamy, Anne Archer, Forrest Tucker, Keenan Wynn, Flip Wilson, Noriyuki "Pat" Morita, Chief Dan George; *Cameos:* John Wayne, Bing Crosby, Doodles Weaver; *D:* Paul Bogart; *W:* Arthur Marx. **VHS, Beta $14.95** *COL, FCT*

Candleshoe 🐾🐾🐾🎵

Los Angeles street urchin poses as an English matron's long lost granddaughter in order to steal a fortune hidden in Candleshoe, her country estate. Great cast, particularly Niven as the foxy butler, breathes life into a gimmicky plot, based on "Christmas at Candleshoe" by Michael Innes.
1978 (G/*Family*) 101m/C Vivian Pickles, Helen Hayes, David Niven, Jodie Foster, Leo McKern; *D:* Norman Tokar. **VHS, Beta $19.99** *DIS*

Canine Commando

Three wartime Pluto cartoons from Disney: "The Army Mascot," "Dog Watch" and "Canine Patrol."
1945 (G/*Family*) 23m/C **VHS, Beta $14.95** *DIS*

Cannon Movie Tales: The Emperor's New Clothes 🐾🐾🐾🎵

Only mediocre but still probably the best of the terminally lame "Cannon Movie Tales" series of would-be Shelley Duvall rivals. Caesar is the vain, clotheshorse despot and Morse is the con-artist tailor who figures out how to swindle the royal treasury by weaving a nonexistent suit that 'only those fit for office can see.' Lively mugging by the talented stars keep this one going.
1989 (*Family*) 85m/C Sid Caesar, Robert Morse, Clive Revill; *D:* David Irving. **VHS** *WAR*

Cannonball 🐾🐾

Assorted ruthless people leave patches of rubber across the country competing for grand prize in less than legal auto race. Not top drawer New World but nonetheless a cult fave. Inferior to Bartel's previous cult classic, "Death Race 2000." Most interesting for plethora of cult cameos, including Scorsese, Dante, and grandmaster Corman. **Hound Advisory:** Violence.

1976 (PG/*Primary-Adult*) 93m/C David Carradine, Bill McKinney, Veronica Hamel, Gerrit Graham, Robert Carradine, Sylvester Stallone, Jonathan Kaplan; *Cameos:* Martin Scorsese, Roger Corman, Joe Dante; **D:** Paul Bartel. **VHS, Beta** *NO*

Cannonball Run 🐾⏹

So many stars, so little plot. Reynolds and sidekick DeLuise disguise themselves as paramedics to foil cops while they compete in cross-country Cannonball race. Shows no sign of having been directed by an ex-stuntman. One of 1981's top grossers-go figure. Followed by equally languid sequel "Cannonball Run II." **Hound Advisory:** Profanity.
1981 (PG/*Jr. High-Adult*) 95m/C Burt Reynolds, Farrah Fawcett, Roger Moore, Dom DeLuise, Dean Martin, Sammy Davis Jr., Jack Elam, Adrienne Barbeau, Peter Fonda, Molly Picon, Bert Convy, Jamie Farr; **D:** Hal Needham. **VHS, Beta, LV $29.98** *VES*

Cannonball Run 2 🐾

More mindless cross-country wheel spinning with gratuitous star cameos. Director Needham apparently subscribes to the two wrongs make a right school of sequels.
1984 (PG/*Sr. High-Adult*) 109m/C Burt Reynolds, Dom DeLuise, Jamie Farr, Marilu Henner, Shirley MacLaine, Jim Nabors, Frank Sinatra, Sammy Davis Jr., Dean Martin, Telly Savalas, Susan Anton, Catherine Bach, Sid Caesar, Ricardo Montalban, Charles Nelson Reilly; *Cameos:* Henry Silva, Tim Conway, Don Knotts, Molly Picon; **D:** Hal Needham; **M:** Stephen Dorff. **VHS, Beta, LV $19.98** *WAR*

Can't Buy Me Love 🐾🐾

High school nerd Ronald buys a month of dates with teen babe Cindy for a grand, in order to win friends and influence people. The gambit works too well; Ronald turns into a popular party guy and ignores his old pals - including Cindy, who was falling for him. Youth morality play commits the cardinal sin of not offering believable situations or dialogue. Released through Disney's Touchstone division. **Hound Advisory:** Sex talk that soon turns into the real thing, salty language.
1987 (PG-13/*Jr. High-Adult*) 94m/C Patrick Dempsey, Amanda Peterson, Dennis Dugan, Courtney Gains; **D:** Steve Rash; **M:** Robert Folk. **VHS, Beta, LV $19.99** *TOU*

The Canterville Ghost 🐾🐾

Sir Simon de Canterville (Laughton) is a coward haunting his family home until a kinsman performs an act of bravery. After 300 years of successfully scaring Britons, Sir Simon faces a visiting platoon of brash American soldiers who aren't spooked by his moaning and groaning. Oscar Wilde's classic short story, in a way the original "Beetlejuice," was heavily padded here by styling it a WWII propaganda vehicle, as a yankee Canterville descendant gains courage to combat the Axis. Leading lady is the popular child star O'Brien, as the 6-year-old 'Lady Jessica,' mistress of the castle. **Hound Advisory:** Brief battlefield violence.
1944 (*Jr. High-Adult*) 95m/B Charles Laughton, Robert Young, Margaret O'Brien, William Gargan, Reginald Owen, Rags Ragland, Una O'Connor, Peter Lawford, Mike Mazurki; **D:** Jules Dassin. **VHS, Beta $19.98** *MGM*

The Canterville Ghost

During an American family's vacation in an old English manor, they run into an ineffective ghost, doomed to haunt the place until he can redeem himself. Mom and dad are unmoved by the spook and their son pulls pranks on him. Only daughter Virginia feels sorry for Simon de Canterville. Substandard entry in the "Wonderworks" series, hurt by fuzzy, cheap-looking cinematography and ill-conceived re-writes of the original Oscar Wilde tale.
1991 (*Family*) 58m/C Richard Kiley, Mary Wickes. **VHS $14.95** *PME, FCT*

Cantinflas

Delightful cartoon character Cantinflas (based on the great Mexican comedian who co-starred in "Around the World in 80 Days") takes young viewers on a trip through history to meet King Tut, Daniel Boone, Madame Curie, and many other famous people.
1984 (*Preschool-Primary*) 60m/C **VHS, Beta** *FHE*

Captain America

Republic serial that was the first film version of the patriotic comic-book character. May infuriate Marvel fans because the character here has no real superpowers. He's just a lawyer who, like Batman, adopts a disguise to fight crime - in this case an evil mastermind masquerading as a respected doctor. Plenty of action; in fact, one authority called this the most violent serial ever. In 15 chapters. **Hound Advisory:** Violence.
1944 (*Family*) 240m/B Dick Purcell, Adrian Booth, Lionel Atwill; **D:** John English; **W:** Elmer Clifton. **VHS, Beta $109.95** *VCN, MLB, VTR*

Captain America 🐾⏹

The Marvel Comics superhero got his own movie (not counting previous made-for-TV incarnations) in time for his 50th anniversary, but this low-cost epic doesn't make the grade despite the wide ranging plot. In 1941 a secret serum turns polio-stricken Steve Rogers into a superstrong superhero, but he's matched by a Nazi counterpart known as the Red Skull. Their battle leaves Captain America frozen in the Arctic for 40 years, but he thaws out to battle the Red Skull again, now a world gangster and anti-environmental meanie. Possibly amusing for kids; adults may note ruefully that this Captain America movie was made in...Yugoslavia. **Hound Advisory:** Violence (sometimes intense, even by comic-book standards). Profanity.
1989 (PG-13/*Jr. High-Adult*) 103m/C Matt Salinger, Scott Paulin, Ronny Cox, Ned Beatty, Darren McGavin, Melinda Dillon; **D:** Albert Pyun; **W:** Stephen Tolkin. **VHS, LV $19.95** *COL*

Captain America 2: Death Too Soon 🐾

Terrorists hit America where it hurts, threatening to use age accelerating drug. Sequelized superhero fights chronic crow lines and series dies slow, painful death. Made for TV.
1979 (*Family*) 98m/C Reb Brown, Connie Sellecca, Len Birman, Christopher Lee, Katherine Justice, Lana Wood, Christopher Carey; **D:** Ivan Nagy. **VHS, Beta $14.98** *MCA*

Captain Blood 🦴🦴🦴◁

Adventure that launched then-unknown Flynn to fame is one of the best pirate swashbucklers ever. Exiled into slavery by a tyrannical governor, physician Peter Blood becomes a chivalrous buccaneer, a sort of seagoing Robin Hood. Finally, his heroics in battle against enemies of the Crown earn him a royal pardon. Based on the novel by Rafael Sabatini. Also available in a computer-colorized version. **Hound Advisory:** Violence.

1935 *(Family)* 120m/B Errol Flynn, Olivia de Havilland, Basil Rathbone, J. Carroll Naish, Guy Kibbee, Lionel Atwill; *D:* Michael Curtiz. **VHS, Beta $19.98** MGM, FCT, MLB

Captain Harlock, Vol. 1

Captain Harlock, the space pirate, is left alone to protect Earth from invasion by the queen of the marauding alien planet Millenia. Strung together episodes of a syndicated cartoon TV series. Additional volumes available.

1981 *(Primary)* 60m/C **VHS, Beta $29.95** FHE, TPV

Captain January 🦴🦴◁

Crusty old lighthouse keeper rescues little orphan girl with curly hair from drowning, and everyone breaks into cutesy song and dance, interrupted only when the authorities try to separate the loving twosome. Popular Temple vehicle of the day, but check out her charming dance partner Ebsen, who was originally cast as Tin Man in "The Wizard of Oz" - but turned out to have a violent allergy to the makeup. ♫At the Codfish Ball; Early Bird; The Right Somebody to Love.

1936 *(Family)* 74m/B Shirley Temple, Guy Kibbee, Buddy Ebsen, Slim Summerville, Jane Darwell, June Lang, George Irving, Si Jenks; *D:* David Butler. **VHS, Beta $19.98** FOX

Captain Kangaroo & His Friends

Compilation of short segments from Captain Kangaroo's long-running TV show, with the Captain's favorite cohorts in kidvid and some surprising celebrity guests. Additional volumes available.

1985 *(Preschool-Primary)* 60m/C Bob Keeshan, Phil Donahue, Joan Rivers, Dolly Parton. **VHS, Beta** MPI

Captain Kangaroo's Merry Christmas Stories

The Captain narrates a selection of animated and live-action tales to lift the Christmas spirits, including: "The Gift of the Little Juggler," "The Fir Tree," and Clement Moore's "A Christmas Carol."

1985 *(Preschool-Primary)* 58m/C Bob Keeshan. **VHS, Beta $39.95** MPI

Captain Planet & the Planeteers: A Hero for Earth

Environmentally conscious TV cartoon launched with mighty fanfare by Ted Turner, though once you get past the eco-propaganda (which just about every kids' show since "Lassie's Rescue Rangers" has been pushing anyway) the Captain and his little buddies look a lot like any old superbunch. In this one they must keep the evil Dr. Blight and his cronies from polluting the Earth. Additional volumes available.

1990 *(Family)* 45m/C **VHS $12.98** TTC, WTA, WSH

Captain Pugwash

Collection of animated shorts from English TV starring the bumbling pirate and his crew, aimed at a very young audience but worth a look for all animation fans; "Pugwash" is brought to life with stop-motion photography of cut-out paper characters, rather than drawings.

1975 *(Preschool-Primary)* 80m/C **VHS, Beta $14.95** FHE

Captain Ron 🦴◁

The Harveys inherit a large boat docked in the West Indies, so they take a Caribbean vacation to pilot her back to the US. Knowing nothing about sailing, they hire the title character, a one-eyed, Long John Silver-talking sea dog whose salty manner hides the fact that he's an irresponsible bumbler. Numerous accidents, embarrassments, and navigational errors culminate in a battle with modern pirates. Pseudo-Disney comedy (through their more 'mature' Touchstone label) sinks instead of floats, and might be retitled "Captain Raunch" for a few of its gags. **Hound Advisory:** Salty language, fittingly enough. Sex, nudity, and Captain Ron both boozes and gambles with the Harvey's adolescent son.

1992 *(PG-13/ Jr. High-Adult)* 104m/C Kurt Russell, Martin Short, Mary Kay Place, Meadow Sisto, Benjamin Salisbury; *D:* Thom Eberhardt; *W:* Thom Eberhardt. **VHS, Beta, LV $94.95** TOU

Captain Scarlet vs. The Mysterons

When Captain Scarlet's expeditionary team mistakenly fires upon an extraterrestrial military complex, the humorless aliens retaliate by setting out to destroy the world. Feature-length compilation of episodes from Gerry Anderson's British TV series done in "Super Marionation," a technique using plastic models operated by very fine wires, matched with some dashing good spacecraft f/x.

1967 *(Family)* 90m/C Alan Perry, Desmond Saunders, Ken Turner; *D:* David Lane. **VHS, Beta $39.95** FHE

Captains Courageous 🦴🦴🦴

Rich, spoiled Harvey falls over the side of a luxury ocean liner. Picked up by a Portuguese fishing boat, the boy has to spend three months at sea, enduring the same rigors as the humble sailors. Gradually he learns the value of hard work and friendship through service with the captain's young son (Rooney) and a fatherly crewman (Tracy, in an Oscar-winning performance). A fine voyage through adventure, triumph and tragedy, based on the Rudyard Kipling novel. Director Fleming went on to "Gone With the Wind" and "The Wizard of Oz." Recently very loosely remade with Chris Elliot in the eminently forgettable "Cabin Boy."

1937 *(Family)* 116m/B Spencer Tracy, Lionel Barrymore, Freddie Bartholomew, Mickey Rooney, Melvyn Douglas, Charley Grapewin, John Carradine, Bobby Watson, Jack LaRue; *D:* Victor Fleming. **Award Nominations:** Academy Awards '37: Best Film Editing, Best Picture, Best Screenplay; **Awards:** Academy Awards '37: Best Actor (Tracy); National Board of Review Awards '37: 10 Best Films of the Year. **VHS, Beta $19.98** MGM, BMV, BTV

The Capture of Grizzly Adams 🦮🦮

TV-movie reunion for the "Grizzly Adams" program, in which the mountain man is framed for murder. He and his bear companion must not only clear his name but outwit a band of outlaws holding Adams' young daughter captive.
1982 *(Family)* 96m/C Dan Haggerty, Chuck Connors, June Lockhart, Kim Darby, Noah Beery Jr., Keenan Wynn. **VHS $89.95** *WOV*

Car 54, Where Are You? WOOF!

Exceedingly lame remake of the exceedingly lame (though strangely beloved) television series, which ran for only two seasons, 1961-63. This time, Toody (Johansen) and Muldoon (McGinley) are protecting a Mafia stool pigeon (Piven), while vampy Velma Velour (Drescher) sets her sights on Muldoon. Not many laughs and a waste of a talented cast. Sat on the shelf at Orion for three years (with good reason). **Hound Advisory:** Profanity; sex talk.
1994 (PG-13/*Jr. High-Adult*) 89m/C David Johansen, Fran Drescher, Rosie O'Donnell, John C. McGinley, Nipsey Russell, Al Lewis, Daniel Baldwin, Jeremy Piven; *D:* Bill Fishman; *W:* Ebbe Roe Smith, Erik Tarloff, Peter McCarthy, Peter Crabbe; *M:* Bernie Worrell, Pray For Rain. **VHS, LV** *ORI*

Car Wash 🦮🦮🦮

L.A. carwash provides a soap-opera setting for disjointed comic bits about owners of dirty cars and people who hose them down for a living. Econo budget and lite plot, but serious comic talent. A sort of disco carwash version of "Grand Hotel."
1976 (PG/*Jr. High-Adult*) 97m/C Franklin Ajaye, Sully Boyer, Richard Brestoff, George Carlin, Richard Pryor, Melanie Mayron, Ivan Dixon, Antonio Fargas; *D:* Michael A. Schultz; *W:* Joel Schumacher. **VHS, Beta $14.98** *MCA, FCT*

Carbon Copy 🦮🦮

Successful white executive who's secretly a Jew has life turned inside out when his seventeen-year old illegitimate son, who happens to be black, decides it's time to look up dear old dad. Typical comedy-with-a-moral strains to state the obvious.
1981 (PG/*Jr. High-Adult*) 92m/C George Segal, Susan St. James, Jack Warden, Paul Winfield, Dick Martin, Vicky Dawson, Tom Poston, Denzel Washington; *D:* Michael A. Schultz; *W:* Stanley Shapiro; *M:* Bill Conti. **VHS, Beta, LV $9.95** *COL, SUE*

Care Bears: Family Storybook

Collection of animated adventures featuring the huggable, buyable, toy-products bear clan. Additional volumes available.
1987 *(Preschool-Primary)* 85m/C **VHS, Beta $39.95** *WTA, LHV*

The Care Bears Movie 🦮🦮

Feature-length cartoon treacle to promote the Care Bears line of toys and tie-ins. Plot has the cuddly commodities leaving their cloud home in Care-a-lot to save Nicolas, a careless boy magician under control of an evil spirit. Song contributions from the likes of Carole King, John Sebastian and NRBQ don't bring this respectability, though Rooney's narration almost does.
1984 (G/*Family*) 75m/C *D:* Arna Selznick; *V:* Mickey Rooney, Georgia Engel, Harry Dean Stanton. **VHS, Beta $14.98** *LIV, VES, VTR*

The Care Bears Movie 2: A New Generation 🦮🦮

More sugary Care Bear fare involving offspring of the likes of Tender Heart Bear, Love-a-Lot Bear, Wish Bear, and Bedtime Bear. Too bad Script Bear never shows up.
1986 (G/*Jr. High-Adult*) 77m/C *D:* Dale Schott; *V:* Maxine Miller, Pam Hyatt, Hadley Key. **VHS, Beta $14.95** *COL, WTA*

Careful, He Might Hear You 🦮🦮🦮

Abandoned by his widowed father, six-year-old P.S. becomes a prize in a tug-of-war custody fight between his two aunts, one working class and the other wealthy. The boy's world is further shaken by the sudden reappearance of that prodigal father. Set in Depression-era Australia, it's a touching and keenly observed child's-eye-sense of the adult world, its hypocrisies and often cruel manipulation. Hardly uplifting, but worthwhile. Based on a novel by Sumner Locke Elliott. **Hound Advisory:** Mature themes, salty language.
1984 (PG/*Family*) 113m/C Nicholas Gledhill, Wendy Hughes, Robyn Nevin, John Hargreaves; *D:* Carl Schultz. **VHS, Beta $59.98** *FOX*

Carnival of the Animals

Poetry comes to life in this story of the animals at the zoo to the music of Saint-Saens. Performance filmed in 1984 features outstanding musicians and the narration of Close and Irons.
1984 *(Family)* 30m/C *D:* Jon Stone. **VHS, Beta $19.95** *VAI, FCT, MVD*

Carousel 🦮🦮🦮🦮

Much-loved Rodgers & Hammerstein musical based on Ferenc Molnar's play "Liliom" (filmed by Fritz Lang in 1935) about a swaggering carnival barker (MacRae) who tries to change his life after he falls in love with a good woman. Killed while attempting to foil a robbery he was supposed to help commit, he begs his heavenly hosts for the chance to return to the mortal realm just long enough to set things straight with his teenage daughter. Jones and MacRae never sounded better. Now indisputably a classic, the film lost $2 million when first released. ♫If I Loved You; Soliloquy; You'll Never Walk Alone; What's the Use of Wond'rin; When I Marry Mister Snow; When the Children Are Asleep; A Real Nice Clambake; Carousel Ballet; Carousel Waltz.
1956 *(Family)* 128m/C Gordon MacRae, Shirley Jones, Cameron Mitchell, Gene Lockhart, Barbara Ruick, Robert Rounseville, Richard Deacon, Tor Johnson; *D:* Henry King; *M:* Richard Rodgers, Oscar Hammerstein. **VHS, Beta, LV $19.98** *FOX, RDG, HMV*

Cartoons for Big Kids

Movie historian and cartoon buff Leonard Maltin holds an animation appreciation collection for all ages, featuring the likes of Bugs Bunny and others.
1989 *(Adult)* 44m/C *D:* Mark Lamberti. **VHS $19.95** *TTC, WTA*

Casablanca 🦮🦮🦮🦮

Can you see George Raft as Rick? Jack Warner did, but producer Hal Wallis wanted Bogart. Considered by many to be the best film ever made and one of the most quoted movies

of all time, it rocketed Bogart from gangster roles to romantic leads as he and Bergman (who never looked lovelier) sizzle on screen. Bogart runs a gin joint in Morocco during the Nazi occupation, and meets up with Bergman, an old flame, but romance and politics do not mix, especially in Nazi-occupied French Morocco. Greenstreet, Lorre, and Rains all create memorable characters, as does Wilson, the piano player to whom Bergman says the oft-misquoted, "Play it, Sam." Without a doubt, the best closing scene ever written; it was scripted on the fly during the end of shooting, and actually shot several ways. Written from an unproduced play. See it in the original black and white. Laserdisc edition features restored imaging and sound and commentary by film historian Ronald Haver about the production, the play it was based on, and the famed evolution of the screenplay on audio track two. 50th Anniversary Edition contains a restored and remastered print, the original 1942 theatrical trailer, a film documentary narrated by Lauren Bacall, and a booklet.
1942 (PG/*Family*) 102m/B Humphrey Bogart, Ingrid Bergman, Paul Henreid, Claude Rains, Peter Lorre, Sydney Greenstreet, Conrad Veidt, S.Z. Sakall, Dooley Wilson, Marcel Dalio, John Qualen, Helmut Dantine; *D:* Michael Curtiz; *W:* Julius J. Epstein, Philip C. Epstein, Howard Koch; *M:* Max Steiner. **Award Nominations:** Academy Awards '43: Best Actor (Bogart), Best Black and White Cinematography, Best Film Editing, Best Supporting Actor (Rains), Best Original Score; **Awards:** Academy Awards '43: Best Director (Curtiz), Best Picture, Best Screenplay; National Board of Review Awards '45: 10 Best Films of the Year. **VHS, Beta, LV, 8mm $19.98** *MGM, FOX, VYG*

Casey at the Bat

From Shelley Duvall's made for cable television "Tall Tales and Legends" series, in which the immortal poem is brought to life. Rousing comedy for the whole family.
1985 (*Family*) 52m/C Bill Macy, Hamilton Camp, Elliott Gould, Carol Kane, Howard Cosell; *D:* David Steinberg. **VHS, Beta $19.98** *FOX*

Casey's Shadow 🦴🦴

Eight-year-old Casey is the youngest of three boys being raised by their impoverished horse-trainer dad after mom walks out. Then Casey raises a quarter horse with championship potential. Can a first-place finish at the world's richest race help this struggling family to survive? Can this plot be any more predictable? **Hound Advisory:** Salty language.
1978 (PG/*Family*) 116m/C Walter Matthau, Alexis Smith, Robert Webber, Murray Hamilton; *D:* Martin Ritt. **VHS, Beta $19.95** *COL*

Casper's Halloween

The friendly ghost entertains with four Halloween treats: "To Boo or Not to Boo," "Which is Witch?," "Fright Day the 13th," and "The Witching Hour." Additional volumes available.
19?? (*Preschool-Primary*) 25m/C **VHS $9.98** *MCA*

The Castaway Cowboy 🦴🦴

Shanghaied cowboy becomes partners with a widow and helps turn her Hawaiian potato farm into a cattle ranch, but a bad guy wants the land for himself. Without the tropical settings it wouldn't be anything special. In fact, it's nothing special with them either.

1974 (G/*Family*) 91m/C James Garner, Robert Culp, Vera Miles; *D:* Vincent McEveety. **VHS, Beta** *DIS, OM*

The Cat 🦴

Boy and tame cougar become friends while on the run from a murderous poacher. Simple-minded animal tale, as generic as the title.
1966 (*Family*) 95m/C Peggy Ann Garner, Roger Perry, Barry Coe; *D:* Ellis Kadison. **VHS, Beta $14.95** *COL, NLC*

Cat City

Creative feature cartoon from Hungary, a rodent James Bond spoof in which heroic agent Grabowski is sent by the worldwide mouse intelligence organization ('Intermaus') to thwart a diabolical weapon developed by a cabal of evil cats. Dubbed into English.
1987 (*Family*) 90m/C *D:* Bela Ternovsky. **VHS $39.95** *JTC, WTA*

The Cat from Outer Space 🦴🦴

Extraterrestrial cat crashes his spaceship on Earth and leads a group of civilians, military types and spies on merry chases. Unspectacular close encounter of the '70s Disney kind.
1978 (G/*Family*) 103m/C Ken Berry, Sandy Duncan, Harry Morgan, Roddy McDowall, McLean Stevenson; *D:* Norman Tokar. **VHS, Beta** *DIS, OM*

The Cat in the Hat

Dr. Seuss classic about a feline freeloader comes to life in a cartoon TV version.
1972 (*Primary*) 25m/C **VHS, Beta $14.98** *BFA, WTA*

The Cat in the Hat Comes Back

Dr Seuss' lovable cat makes another chaotic visit. Two other stories are included.
1990 (*Family*) 30m/C **VHS $9.95** *RAN, VEC*

The Cat in the Hat Gets Grinched

Two Dr. Seuss characters, the Cat in the Hat and the Grinch, meet on a summer's day and begin a crazy rivalry.
1991 (*Primary*) 30m/C **VHS $9.95** *RAN, BTV*

Catch Me. . .If You Can 🦴🦴

Here's school spirit for you: class president Melissa doesn't want the school torn down, so she enlists the homeroom rebel, a drag racer, to compete for cash in the local gambling syndicate. Don't expect greatness and you'll find this far-fetched stuff entertaining. Director Sommers' touch with the youthful performers shows; he later did Disney's 1993 "Adventures of Huck Finn." **Hound Advisory:** Salty language, reckless driving.
1989 (PG/*Jr. High-Adult*) 105m/C Matt Lattanzi, Loryn Locklin, M. Emmet Walsh, Geoffrey Lewis; *D:* Stephen Sommers. **VHS, LV $89.95** *MCG*

Cat's Eye 🦴🦴

Lame anthology of three Stephen King short stories connected by a stray cat who wanders through each tale. **Hound Advisory:** Violence.

1985 (PG-13/*Jr. High-Adult*) 94m/C Drew Barrymore, James Woods, Alan King, Robert Hays, Candy Clark, Kenneth McMillan, James Naughton, Charles S. Dutton; *D:* Lewis Teague; *W:* Stephen King; *M:* Alan Silvestri. **VHS, Beta, LV** $19.99 *FOX, FCT*

Challenge To Be Free 🐾🐾

Historical action adventure geared toward nature lovers. Depicts the struggles of a fugitive trapper and his wolf ally, pursued by 12 men and 100 dogs across a thousand miles of frozen wilderness. Made in 1972 (under the portentous title "Mad Trapper of the Yukon"), but released to the family marketplace in 1976. **Hound Advisory:** Violence.
1976 (G/*Family*) 90m/C Mike Mazurki, Jimmy Kane; *Cameos:* Tay Garnett; *D:* Tay Garnett. **VHS, Beta** $9.98 *MED, VTR*

Challenge to Lassie 🐾🐾🐾

When Lassie's Scottish master dies, the faithful pup remains at his grave. An unsympathetic policeman orders Lassie to leave the premises, inspiring a debate among the townsfolk as to the dog's fate. Based on a true story (although the original hero was a Skye Terrier); remade by Disney as "Greyfriar's Bobby."
1949 (G/*Family*) 76m/C Edmund Gwenn, Donald Crisp, Geraldine Brooks, Reginald Owen, Alan Webb, Henry Stephenson, Alan Napier, Sara Allgood; *D:* Richard Thorpe; *M:* Andre Previn. **VHS, Beta** $14.95 *MGM, FCT*

Challenge to White Fang 🐾🐾

Italian-made Jack London takeoff, no relation to the Disney "White Fang" pics. Courageous wolf-dog prevents a scheming businessman from taking over an old man's gold mine. **Hound Advisory:** Roughhousing.
1986 (PG/*Jr. High-Adult*) 89m/C Harry Carey Jr., Franco Nero; *D:* Lucio Fulci. **VHS, Beta** $69.95 *TWE*

Chances Are 🐾🐾🐾

After her loving husband dies in a chance accident, a pregnant woman remains unmarried, keeping her husband's best friend as her only close male companion. Years later, her now teenage daughter brings a friend home for dinner, but due to an error in heaven, the young man begins to realize that this may not be the first time he and this family have met. A wonderful love-story hampered only minimally by the unbelievable plot. **Hound Advisory:** Mild profanity.
1989 (PG/*Jr. High-Adult*) 108m/C Cybill Shepherd, Robert Downey Jr., Ryan O'Neal, Mary Stuart Masterson, Josef Sommer, Christopher McDonald, Joe Grifasi, James Noble, Susan Ruttan, Fran Ryan; *D:* Emile Ardolino; *W:* Perry Howze, Randy Howze; *M:* Maurice Jarre. **VHS, Beta, LV, 8mm** $19.95 *COL, FCT*

Change of Habit 🐾🐾

Three novitiates undertake to learn about the world before becoming full-fledged nuns. While working at a ghetto clinic a young doctor forms a strong, affectionate relationship with one of them. Presley's last feature film. ♫Change of Habit; Let Us Pray; Rubberneckin'.
1969 (G/*Family*) 93m/C Elvis Presley, Mary Tyler Moore, Barbara McNair, Ed Asner, Ruth McDevitt, Regis Toomey; *D:* William A. Graham; *M:* Billy Goldenberg. **VHS, Beta** $14.95 *MCA, GKK*

Chaplin 🐾🐾🐾

The life and career of "The Little Tramp" is chronicled by director Attenborough and brilliantly portrayed by Downey, Jr, as Chaplin. A flashback format traces his life from its poverty-stricken Dickensian origins in the London slums through his directing and acting career, to his honorary Oscar in 1972. Slow-moving at parts, but captures Chaplin's devotion to his art and also his penchant towards jailbait. In a clever casting choice, Chaplin's own daughter from his fourth marriage to Oona O'Neill, Geraldine Chaplin, plays her own grandmother who goes mad. **Hound Advisory:** Profanity and nudity.
1992 (PG-13/*Jr. High-Adult*) 135m/C Robert Downey Jr., Dan Aykroyd, Geraldine Chaplin, Kevin Dunn, Anthony Hopkins, Milla Jovovich, Moira Kelly, Kevin Kline, Diane Lane, Penelope Ann Miller, Paul Rhys, John Thaw, Marisa Tomei, Nancy Travis, James Woods, David Duchovny, Deborah Maria Moore, Bill Paterson, John Standing, Robert Stephens; *D:* Richard Attenborough; *W:* Bryan Forbes, William Boyd; *M:* John Barry. **Award Nominations:** Academy Awards '92: Best Actor (Downey), Best Art Direction/Set Decoration, Best Original Score; **Awards:** British Academy Awards '93: Best Actor (Downey). **VHS, LV** $19.98 *LIV, MOV, FCT*

Charade 🐾🐾🐾🐾

After her husband is murdered, a young woman finds herself on the run from crooks and double agents who want the $250,000 her husband stole during WWII. Hepburn and Grant are charming and sophisticated as usual in this stylish intrigue filmed in Paris. Based on the story "The Unsuspecting Wife" by Marc Behm and Peter Stone.
1963 (*Jr. High-Adult*) 113m/C Cary Grant, Audrey Hepburn, Walter Matthau, James Coburn, George Kennedy; *D:* Stanley Donen; *W:* Peter Stone; *M:* Henry Mancini. **Award Nominations:** Academy Awards '63: Best Song ("Charade"); **Awards:** British Academy Awards '64: Best Actress (Hepburn); Edgar Allan Poe Awards '63: Best Screenplay. **VHS, Beta** $8.95 *CNG, MRV, MCA*

The Charge of the Model T's 🐾🐾

Regionally made low-budgeter about a German spy during the First World War and his schemes to derail the U.S. army using a souped-up automobile. Always knew we couldn't trust that Herbie in wartime.
1976 (G/*Family*) 90m/C Louis Nye, John David Carson, Herb Edelman, Carol Bagdasarian, Arte Johnson; *D:* Jim McCullough. **VHS, Beta** $9.99 *SUE*

Chariots of Fire 🐾🐾🐾

Lush, if slightly arcane telling of the parallel stories of Harold Abraham and Eric Liddell, real-life English runners who competed in the 1924 Paris Olympics. Abraham, a Jew, strove for excellence to defy widespread bigotry, while the Christian Liddell sprints because he believes he's following the will of God. Outstanding performances in a tale that addresses the universality (and limitations) of sports, with memorable score by Vangelis.
1981 (PG/*Family*) 123m/C Ben Cross, Ian Charleson, Nigel Havers, Ian Holm, Alice Krige, Brad Davis, Dennis Christopher, Patrick Magee, Cheryl Campbell, John Gielgud, Lindsay Anderson, Nigel Davenport; *D:* Hugh Hudson; *W:* Colin Welland; *M:* Vangelis. **Award Nominations:** Academy Awards '81: Best Director (Hudson), Best Supporting Actor (Holm); **Awards:** Academy Awards '81: Best Costume Design, Best Original Screenplay, Best Picture, Best Score; British Academy Awards '81: Best Film, Best Supporting Actor (Holm). **VHS, Beta, LV** $19.98 *WAR, FCT, BTV*

Charley and the Angel 🎬🎬

Heavily sentimental Disney comedy about hardworking Charlie who tries to change his cold ways with his family after being informed by an angel that he hasn't long to live. Set in a warmly nostalgic version of the Great Depression.
1973 (*G/Family*) 93m/C Fred MacMurray, Cloris Leachman, Harry Morgan, Kurt Russell, Vincent Van Patten, Kathleen Cody; *D:* Vincent McEveety. **VHS** *DIS, OM*

Charlie and the Great Balloon Chase 🎬🎬

When grandfather takes Charlie on a cross-country balloon trip to Virginia they're hotly pursued by mom's stuffy fiancee, who wants to send the boy to military-school, as well as by the FBI, a reporter, and the Mafia. Airy made-for-TV movie.
1982 (*Family*) 98m/C Jack Albertson, Adrienne Barbeau, Slim Pickens, Moosie Drier; *D:* Larry Elikann. **VHS, Beta** $59.95 *TLF*

The Charlie Brown and Snoopy Show: Vol. 1

Video compilation from a mid-80s weekly TV cartoon series, starring the "Peanuts" characters in various short subjects like "Snoopy and the Beanstalk." Vol. 2 includes the vintage prime-time special "It's the Great Pumpkin, Charlie Brown."
1983 (*Family*) 44m/C *D:* Bill Melendez, Sam Jaimes. **VHS, Beta** $14.95 *BAR, KAR, APD*

A Charlie Brown Christmas

This is the one — the very first of the splendidly realized Lee Mendelson/Bill Melendez translations of Charles M. Schulz's "Peanuts" cartoons to prime-time TV in cartoon form. Virtually all of the "Peanuts" specials are now on video on various labels, in addition to the theatrical feature cartoons.
1965 (*Family*) 30m/C *D:* Bill Melendez. **VHS, Beta** $9.95 *MED, SHV, VTR*

Charlie, the Lonesome Cougar 🎬🎬

Orphaned mountain lion finds a home with the rough-and-tumble loggers in a timber camp. Enjoyable, if ambling Disney nature drama.
1967 (*G/Family*) 75m/C Linda Wallace, Jim Wilson, Ron Brown, Brian Russell, Clifford Peterson; *D:* Winston Hibler. **VHS, Beta** $69.95 *DIS*

Charlotte's Web 🎬🎬🎬

E.B. White's classic story (adapted by Earl Hamner Jr., creator of TV's "The Waltons") of a friendship between a spider named Charlotte and the pig she manages to save from being turned into bacon. In a touching finale Wilbur has to face the fact that pigs live a lot longer than spiders. This bigscreen treatment by Hanna-Barbera studios rates way above their TV cartoons, and the just-okay songs come to life when performed by Reynolds and other superb character voices.
1973 (*G/Family*) 94m/C *D:* Charles A. Nichols; *V:* Debbie Reynolds, Agnes Moorehead, Paul Lynde, Henry Gibson. **VHS, Beta, LV** $14.95 *KUI, PAR, FCT*

Charmkins

Animated adventures of Lady Slipper and her friends in Charm World where they battle the evil Dragonweed. Designed to charm children into lusting after Charmkins-related toys.
1983 (*Primary-Jr. High*) 60m/C *V:* Ben Vereen, Sally Struthers, Aileen Quinn. **VHS, Beta** $9.95 *FHE, WTA*

Chasing Dreams 🎬🎬

Sickly melodrama about a farmboy who finds fulfillment as a baseball player. Lame, amateur family drama was widely revived on tape when supporting actor Costner became a star (he sued over the plastering of his face all over the video box). Not to be confused with "Field of Dreams," naturally.
1981 (*PG/Jr. High-Adult*) 96m/C David G. Brown, John Fife, Jim Shane, Lisa Kingston, Matt Clark, Kevin Costner; *D:* Sean Roche, Therese Conte. **VHS, Beta** $79.95 *PSM*

Chatterer the Squirrel

Two "Fables of the Green Forest," adapted from works of Thornton W. Burgess. Chatterer the Squirrel learns a much needed lesson in humility in "The Big Boast." In "Captive Chatterer," the farmer's son tries to make a house pet out of Chatterer, but a new home and plenty of food are no substitute for freedom!
1983 (*Preschool-Primary*) 60m/C **VHS, Beta** $29.95 *FHE*

The Cheap Detective 🎬🎬🎬

Neil Simon's parody of the "Maltese Falcon" gloriously exploits the resourceful Falk in a Bogart-like role. Vast supporting cast—notably Brennan, DeLuise, and Kahn—prove equally game for fun in this consistently amusing venture.
1978 (*PG/Jr. High-Adult*) 92m/C Peter Falk, Ann-Margret, Eileen Brennan, Sid Caesar, Stockard Channing, James Coco, Dom DeLuise, Louise Fletcher, John Houseman, Madeline Kahn, Fernando Lamas, Marsha Mason, Phil Silvers, Vic Tayback, Abe Vigoda, Paul Williams, Nicol Williamson; *D:* Robert Moore; *W:* Neil Simon. **VHS** $19.95 *CSM, COL*

Cheetah 🎬🎬🎬

California kids Ted and Susan, visiting their parents in Kenya, embark on the adventure of their lives when, with the help of a young Masai tribesman, they adopt and care for an orphaned cheetah. Based on "The Cheetahs" by Alan Caillou.
1989 (*G/Family*) 80m/C Keith Coogan, Lucy Deakins, Collin Mothupi; *D:* Jeff Blyth. **VHS, LV** $89.98 *DIS*

The Cheyenne Social Club 🎬🎬

Stewart inherits a brothel and Fonda helps him operate it. Kelly directs, sort of. Some laughs, but this effort is beneath this trio.
1970 (*PG/Jr. High-Adult*) 103m/C Henry Fonda, James Stewart, Shirley Jones, Sue Ane Langdon, Elaine Devry; *D:* Gene Kelly. **VHS** $14.95 *WAR*

The Chicken Chronicles 🎬

With only days before graduation and an uncertain future, a high school senior goes nuts with crazy pranks and a campaign to get horizontal with his dream girl. Set in the

1960s, with pretenses of insight into the teen mind, an indecipherable scientific puzzle. **Hound Advisory:** Sex talk, salty language.
1977 (PG/*Sr. High-Adult*) 94m/C Phil Silvers, Ed Lauter, Steve Guttenberg, Lisa Reeves, Meredith Baer; *D:* Francis Simon. **VHS, Beta $14.95** *COL, SUE*

Child of Glass 🎬🎬

Thirteen-year-old Alexander and his family move into a New Orleans mansion. Soon the boy encounters the spirit of a girl killed there during the Civil War, who puts Alexander on the trail of missing treasure. Disney feature, based on the novel "The Ghost Belonged to Me" by Richard Peck.
1978 (G/*Family*) 93m/C Barbara Barrie, Biff McGuire, Anthony Zerbe, Nina Foch, Steve Shaw, Katy Kurtzman, Olivia Barash; *D:* John Erman. **VHS, Beta $69.95** *DIS*

Children's Heroes of the Bible: Story of Jesus

Animated series depicting the lives of famous biblical figures. In this epiosde, the first in a two-part presentation, the actions and teachings of Jesus are chronicled. Additional volumes available.
1986 (*Preschool-Primary*) 23m/C **VHS, Beta $12.99** *VGD, IGP*

Child's Christmas in Wales

Dylan Thomas' prose-poem of Christmas memories in his boyhood village is vividly dramatized in this lyrical, lightly plotted short feature. It doesn't have to be Noel (and you don't need to be Welsh) to savor the sights, sounds and flavors of a traditional British Christmas, circa 1910, recounted by a nice old chap to his grandson. **Hound Advisory:** alcohol use
1988 (*Family*) 55m/C Mathonwy Reeves, Denholm Elliott; *D:* Don McBrearty. **VHS, Beta $9.98** *LIV, VES, HMV*

A Child's Garden of Verses

Fact-based animated short features the young Robert Louis Stevenson ill and bed-ridden, letting his imagination run free and composing the verses that are now familiar favorites among children.
1992 (*Primary*) 20m/C **VHS** *FHE, AMB*

Chip 'n' Dale Animated Antics Series

Chip 'n' Dale star with Donald Duck in a compilation of hilarious adventures from the Disney archives. Individual titles: "Chips Ahoy," "The Lone Chipmunks," "Out on a Limb," "Test Pilot Donald," "Three For Breakfast," and "Winter Storage."
1990 (*Preschool-Primary*) 7m/C **VHS, Beta $160.00** *MTI, DSN*

Chip 'n' Dale Rescue Rangers: Crimebusters

Disney syndicated TV cartoon placing the two chipmunk favorites in a series of wild adventures with their squad of crime-fighting friends. Joining Chip 'n' Dale in this original episode are Zipper the housefly, Monterey Jack (an Australian mouse) and the inventor Gadget. Together they form the Rescue Rangers. Additional volumes available.
1989 (*Family*) 44m/C *D:* John Kimball, Bob Zamboni. **VHS, Beta $12.99** *DIS, WTA*

Chipmunk and His Bird Friends

While a chipmunk is storing his winter supply of acorns, a chickadee and a pygmy nuthatch search in vain for insects. Suddenly they discover a feeding shelf which children have filled for them.
1967 (*Primary*) 10m/C **VHS, Beta** *BFA*

Chips the War Dog 🎬🎬

Disney made-for-TV movie about the friendship that develops under fire between a young soldier and the title canine during WWII.
1990 (*Family*) 90m/C Brandon Douglas, Ned Vaughn, Paxton Whitehead, Ellie Cornell, Robert Miranda, William Devane; *D:* Ed Kaplan. **VHS** *DIS*

Chitty Chitty Bang Bang 🎬🎬

Eccentric inventor spruces up an old car and, in fantasy, takes his kids to a land where the evil rulers have forbidden children. Imitation-Disney cast and imitation-Disney charm is okay for a while, but certainly not for over two hours. Poor special effects and so-so musical numbers stall this vehicle. Loosely adapted by Roald Dahl and Hughes from an Ian Fleming story. ♫Chitty Chitty Bang Bang; Hushabye Mountain; Truly Scrumptious; You Two; Toot Sweet; Me Ol' Bam-Boo; Lovely Lonely Man; Posh; The Roses of Success.
1968 (G/*Family*) 142m/C Dick Van Dyke, Sally Ann Howes, Lionel Jeffries, Gert Frobe, Anna Quayle, Benny Hill; *D:* Ken Hughes; *W:* Ken Hughes, Roald Dahl. **VHS, Beta, LV $19.98** *FOX, MGM, TLF*

Chocolate Fever

Henry's lust for candy lands him in sickbay with a case of "measles" made of pure chocolate. Cartoon entry from the CBS "Storybreak" series, based on the book by Robert Kinnel Smith; nicely animated by Hanna-Barbera's Australian studios.
1985 (*Family*) 25m/C **VHS $14.99** *FOX, KUI, WTA*

C.H.O.M.P.S. 🎬🎬

Comedy about a youthful inventor who builds a robot guard dog -the Canine Home Protection System - who performs super feats to save the town from burglars and win the girl for his master. Harmlessly unfunny, with a mechanical mutt that's a deliberate lookalike for B.E.N.J.I.
1979 (G/*Jr. High-Adult*) 90m/C Jim Backus, Valerie Bertinelli, Wesley Eure, Conrad Bain, Chuck McCann, Red Buttons; *D:* Don Chaffey. **VHS, Beta** *NO*

Christian the Lion 🎬🎬🎬

Travers and McKenna, the stars of "Born Free," are committed animal-rights activists in real life. They portray themselves in this true story of an exploited zoo lion (shades of "Free Willy") and how two students, the actors, and "Born Free" subject George Adamson, help send it to Africa to live with wild lions.

1976 (G/*Family*) 87m/C Virginia McKenna, Bill Travers, George Adamson, James Hill; *D:* Bill Travers. **VHS, Beta $29.95** *UNI*

A Christmas Carol 🎵🎵🎵

MGM version of Dickens' eternal tale of miserly Scrooge, instilled with the Christmas spirit of generosity after an evening with the ghosts of Christmas Past, Present and Future. Lockhart does a nice turn as Ebenezer, though overall production has a by-the-numbers feel. Unfortunate dialogue: Bob Crachit's line at dinner, "I don't think there's anyone who can touch my buns!"

1938 (*Family*) 70m/B Reginald Owen, Gene Lockhart, Terence Kilburn, Leo G. Carroll, Lynne Carver, Ann Rutherford; *D:* Edwin L. Marin. **VHS, Beta, LV $19.95** *MGM*

A Christmas Carol 🎵🎵🎵🎵

If you weigh your "Christmas Carol" by the quality of its Scrooge, then this British retelling wins out over them all. Gaunt, glaring Alastair Sim, who could wither mistletoe with one scowl, portrays the penny-pinching holiday hater who learns appreciation of Christmas following a frightful, revealing evening with supernatural visitors; and he takes Ebenezer credibly from cruelty to contrition. "And God bless Tiny Tim!"

1951 (*Family*) 86m/B Alastair Sim, Kathleen Harrison, Jack Warner, Michael Hordern, Patrick Macnee, Mervyn Johns, Hermione Baddeley, Clifford Mollison, George Cole, Carol Marsh, Miles Malleson, Ernest Thesiger, Hattie Jacques, Peter Bull, Hugh Dempster; *W:* Noel Langley; *M:* Richard Addinsell. **VHS, Beta, LV $19.95** *MLB, HMV*

A Christmas Carol 🎵🎵

Chuck Jones-style cartoon version of Charles Dickens' classic tale. The story of how Ebenezer Scrooge changed from a tyrant to a joyous human being one Christmas Eve.

1984 (*Preschool*) 23m/C *D:* Chuck Jones. **VHS, Beta $19.95** *CHI*

Christmas Cartoons

Collection of children's favorite Christmas cartoons including "Rudolph the Red-Nosed Reindeer," "Santa's Surprise," "Christmas Comes But Once a Year," and more.

19?? (*Preschool-Primary*) 60m/C **VHS $9.95** *SIM*

The Christmas Collection

Three-volume set of the best-known stories, folk songs, and hymns associated with the season.

1992 (*Primary*) 60m/C **VHS $132.00** *SVE, BTV*

Christmas Comes to Willow Creek 🎵🎵

Mutually antagonistic brothers are enlisted to deliver Christmas gifts to an isolated Alaskan community. Can brotherly love be far off? Made-for-TV holiday cheer taking advantage (if that's the word) of the fact that the leads played together in the rowdy series "Dukes of Hazzard."

1987 (*Family*) 96m/C John Schneider, Tom Wopat, Hoyt Axton, Zachary Ansley, Kim Delaney; *D:* Richard Lang; *M:* Charles Fox. **VHS, Beta $14.98** *LIV, FHE*

Christmas Eve on Sesame Street

Particularly outstanding episode of the PBS series, lyrical, funny, and touching; Big Bird and the "Sesame Street" gang go ice skating, Ernie and Bert act out O. Henry's classic "Gift of the Magi," and Oscar the Grouch upsets everybody by posing the puzzle: How does Santa get down those skinny urban chimneys?

1990 (*Family*) 60m/C Big Bird, Oscar the Grouch. **VHS $14.95** *RAN, MLT*

A Christmas Fantasy

Lonely old toymaker and two children take a magical journey on Christmas Eve. Featuring guest appearances by the miming team Shields and Yarnell, plus the music of the Vienna Boys Choir and Toller Cranston.

1989 (*Family*) 50m/C **VHS, Beta $195.00**

The Christmas Messenger

Brilliantly colored animation in this tale of a young boy who realizes the true meaning of Christmas when joins a group of carolers with a secret identity. TV cartoon special produced in part by the Reader's Digest folks.

1975 (*Family*) 25m/C *V:* Richard Chamberlain. **VHS, Beta $195.00** *PYR*

The Christmas Party

The Little Dog and his friend Kitten must confront a greedy alley cat who has stolen Santa's bag of presents. From the "Little Dog" series.

1982 (*Primary*) 6m/C **VHS, Beta** *BFA*

Christmas Stories

Four animated Christmas stories for kids: "The Clown of God," "Morris's Disappearing Bag," "The Little Drummer Boy," and "The Twelve Days of Christmas." Part of the "Children's Circle" series from Weston Woods.

1986 (*Preschool-Primary*) 100m/C **VHS, Beta $19.95** *FCT*

Christmas Stories

Four brief stories which highlight sharing and caring in the holiday season. In "Morris's Disappearing Bag" the title character discovers a very unusual Christmas gift. "The Clown of God" has an Italian juggler performing in front of baby Jesus. "Max's Christmas" details a child's curiosity about Santa. "The Little Drummer Boy" is highlighted by music by the St. Paul Choir School.

1992 (*Family*) 30m/C **VHS $14.95** *WKV, CCC, BTV*

A Christmas Story

Hanna-Barbera Christmas 'toon in which Goober the mutt and Gumdrop the mouse embark on a quest to deliver young Timmy's errant letter to Santa. Yes, it's the same Goober who was recast as a cut-rate Scooby-Doo for the Saturday-morning series "Goober and the Ghost Chasers."

1971 (*Family*) 30m/C **VHS, Beta $9.95** *TTC*

A Christmas Story

Fat Albert and the gang help new neighbors by giving them a temporary home in their clubhouse, forgetting about mean junkyard owner Tightwad Tyrone. Tyrone has other plans for the clubhouse and is about to demolish it until finally he has a change of heart.
1979 (*Primary-Jr. High*) 23m/C **VHS, Beta, LV** *BAR*

A Christmas Story ✄✄✄

Unlikely but winning comedy centering around a boy's single-minded obsession to acquire a Red Ryder BB-gun for Christmas, woven in with nostalgic little vignettes about his eccentric 1940s family preparing for the holiday. Fun for everyone. Based on an autobiographical story by Jean Shepherd from his book "In God We Trust, All Others Pay Cash."
1983 (**PG**/*Jr. High-Adult*) 95m/C Peter Billingsley, Darren McGavin, Melinda Dillon, Ian Petrella; *D:* Bob (Benjamin) Clark; *W:* Bob (Benjamin) Clark, Leigh Brown, Jean Shepherd. **VHS, Beta, LV $19.98** *MGM*

The Christmas That Almost Wasn't ✄✄

Scrooge-like Phineas T. Prune decides to destroy Christmas forever by evicting Santa Claus from the North Pole, where his rent payments have fallen behind. Crude Italian-made children's musical film makes one yearn for Ernest. ♫The Christmas That Almost Wasn't; Christmas is Coming; Hustle Bustle; I'm Bad; Kids Get All the Breaks; The Name of the Song is Prune; Nothing to do But Wait; Santa Claus; Time For Christmas.
1966 (**G**/*Jr. High-Adult*) 95m/C Rossano Brazzi, Paul Tripp, Lidia Brazzi, Sonny Fox, Mischa Auer; *D:* Rossano Brazzi. **VHS, Beta $9.99** *HBO*

A Christmas to Remember ✄✄✄

Depression-era Minnesota farmer who has lost his son in WWI is not too happy hosting his city-bred grandson, visiting the farm for the holidays. Gradually they reach an armistice. Somber, occasionally poignant made-for-TV film ornamented by the stars' presence.
1978 (**G**/*Family*) 96m/C Jason Robards Jr., Eva Marie Saint, Joanne Woodward; *D:* George Englund. **VHS, Beta $69.95** *NO*

The Christmas Toy

Kermit the Frog hosts this Muppet tale about Christmas at the Joneses. All the toys in the playroom come alive to enjoy the holiday, even Rugby, a stuffed tiger who decides he wants to be Jamie's special present again. He sets out to find the family Christmas tree and all the gifts beneath it.
1993 (*Family*) 50m/C **VHS $12.99** *JHV, BTV*

The Christmas Tree

Wordless pantomime story of a fir tree, played by mime Julian Chagrin, that gets cut down to be sold as a Christmas tree.
1975 (*Family*) 12m/C Julian Chagrin. **VHS, Beta $11.95** *PYR*

The Christmas Tree

Yuletide cartoon about children at an orphanage who love a wondrous pine tree on the grounds, but the nasty superintendent plans to cut it down and spoil Christmas. Luckily Santa sides with the children.
1990 (*Family*) 49m/C **VHS $14.95** *FHE, WTA*

A Christmas Tree/Puss-In-Boots

Animated TV double feature from the Rankin-Bass factory: "A Christmas Tree" features two young children who return a stolen Christmas tree from an evil giant. Magical cat helps his master woo a princess in "Puss-In-Boots."
1972 (*Preschool-Primary*) 60m/C **VHS, Beta** *PSM, WTA*

Christmas Video Sing-Along

Sing along with children's favorite Christmas songs.
1992 (*Preschool-Primary*) 30m/C **VHS $6.98** *SMV, MVD*

Christopher's Xmas Mission

Satirical story of a wealthy young boy working in a post office who decides to play Robin Hood and redirect the gifts addressed to rich people to the poor. When the scheme is uncovered, the rich thank him and his parents praise him. Just like real life?
1992 (*Primary-Jr. High*) 23m/C **VHS $195.00**

Christy ✄✄✄

Pilot movie for the TV series finds 19-year-old Christy Huddleston (Martin) leaving her privileged Southern life to teach school in the Great Smoky Mountains. It's 1912 in Cutter Gap, Tennessee and her students are literally dirt poor, with ignorance and superstition the norm. Christy's inspiration is Miss Alice (Daly), a middle-aged Quaker who runs the mission school. And Christy needs encouragement as she struggles to cope with her new life and responsibilities. Based on the novel by Catherine Marshall, which is a fictional biography of her mother.
1994 (*Family*) 90m/C Kellie Martin, Tyne Daly, Tess Harper, Randall Batinkoff, Annabelle Price, Stewart Finlay-McLennan; *D:* Michael Rhodes; *M:* Ron Ramin. **VHS $19.95** *GKK*

The Chronicles of Narnia ✄✄✄

Multicassette BBC production of the C.S. Lewis fantasy series, spanning the first four of the seven interconnected books. Narnia is a country in parallel world of mythical beasts and talking animals, and a group of English children repeatedly find their way there at the right times to save Narnia from danger throughout its history. These scrupulously faithful adaptations sometimes mix animation jarringly with live-action while trying to bring Lewis' vision to life; to see how well an all-animated version would have worked, see the Bill Melendez production of the first book, "Lion, the Witch and the Wardrobe," also on tape. Titles in this BBC set, part of the "Wonderworks" series, include: "The Lion, the Witch and the Wardrobe," "Prince Caspian/Voyage of the Dawn Treader," and "The Silver Chair."

1989 (*Family*) 180m/C Barbara Kellerman, Jeffery Perry, Richard Dempsey, Sophie Cook, Jonathan Scott, Sophie Wilcox, David Thwaites, Tom Baker; **D:** Alex Kirby. VHS $29.95 *FCT, PME, TVC*

Chuck Amuck: The Movie

Made-for-video release chronicling the fifty-year career of Warner Brothers animator Chuck Jones, with highlights from his most famous Bugs Bunny/Daffy Duck cartoons. **1991** (*Family*) 51m/C Chuck Jones. VHS $14.95 *WAR, FCT, WTA*

Cinderella 🦴🦴🦴🦴

Classic Disney animated fairytale about the slighted beauty who outshines her evil stepsisters at a royal ball, then returns to her grim existence before the handsome prince finds her again. Engaging film, with a wicked stepmother, kindly fairy godmother, and singing mice. Songs include: Cinderella; Bibbidy-Bobbidi-Boo; So This is Love; A Dream is a Wish Your Heart Makes; The Work Song; Oh Sing, Sweet Nightingale. ♫Cinderella; Bibbidy-Bobbidi-Boo; So This Is Love; A Dream Is a Wish Your Heart Makes; The Work Song; Oh Sing, Sweet Nightingale. **1950** (*Family*) 76m/C **D:** Wilfred Jackson; **V:** Ilene Woods, William Phipps, Verna Felton, James MacDonald. **Award Nominations:** Academy Awards '50: Best Song ("Bibbidy-Bobbidi-Boo"), Best Sound, Best Original Score; **Awards:** Venice Film Festival '50: Special Jury Prize. VHS, Beta $26.99 *DIS, KUI*

Cinderella 🦴🦴

Network TV special retelling the classic fairy tale of the girl with the mean stepsisters and the missing glass slipper, accompanied by original musical numbers from Broadway giants Richard Rodgers and Oscar Hammerstein. Without that asset it would be rather pedestrian. **1964** (*Family*) 83m/C Lesley Ann Warren, Ginger Rogers, Walter Pidgeon, Stuart Damon, Celeste Holm; **D:** Charles S. Dubin; **M:** Richard Rodgers, Oscar Hammerstein. VHS, Beta, LV $19.98 *FOX, FCT*

Cinderfella 🦴🦴🦴

This twist on the classic children's fairy tale features Lewis as the hapless, orphaned buffoon guided by his fairy godfather to win the hand of the fair, singing maiden over his selfish stepbrothers. Somewhat overdone, with extended talking sequences and gratuitous musical interludes. Lewis, though, mugs effectively, and kids will relate. **1960** (*Preschool-Family*) 88m/C Jerry Lewis, Ed Wynn, Judith Anderson, Anna Maria Alberghetti, Henry Silva, Count Basie, Robert Hutton; **D:** Frank Tashlin; **W:** Frank Tashlin. VHS, Beta $59.95 *LIV*

Cindy Eller

ABC Afterschool Special does a cute job of modernizing the fairy tale of Cinderella, here a wallflower named Cindy who finally gets to meet the handsome "Greg Prince" thanks to her fairy godmother, a magical bag lady. In keeping with the political correctness, Cindy's stepmother is perfectly kind and understanding. **1991** (*Family*) 44m/C Pearl Bailey, Jennifer Grey, Kyra Sedgwick, Melanie Mayron, Kelly Wolf; **D:** Lee Grant. VHS $12.98 *SVI*

Cinema Paradiso 🦴🦴🦴

Salvatore, a fatherless little boy in postwar Italy, spends all his time at his small village's movie palace, where Alfredo the projectionist is a surrogate papa. Salvatore becomes an apprentice projectionist himself, but Alfredo doesn't want the boy following in his lowly footsteps and urges Salvatore to leave and seek his fortune elsewhere. Story unreels in flashbacks as the adult Salvatore, a famous movie director, returns to his roots; it's partly an autobiographical effort by Tornatore, who captures both the sweep of the times and the poignancy of the central father-son relationship. Original Italian version runs even longer, however, and calls into question whether Alfredo's actions enriched the boy's later life - or ruined it. **Hound Advisory:** Sex, alcohol use, brief nudity (in old movie clips), profanity. **1988** (*College-Adult*) 123m/C Philippe Noiret, Jacques Perrin, Salvatore Cascio, Mario Leonardi, Agnes Nano, Leopoldo Trieste; **D:** Giuseppe Tornatore; **W:** Giuseppe Tornatore; **M:** Ennio Morricone. VHS, LV, 8mm $89.99 *HBO, APD, INJ*

Circus Angel 🦴🦴🦴

Glorious, all-ages delight from French director Lamorisse, creator of "The Red Balloon." Petty thief hides in a circus where the ringmaster uses the fugitive in experiments to create a "birdman" act. With wings sewn in his back, the rogue learns to fly, and in a nightdress he looks positively angelic. Fluttering around the land, 'Fifi la Plume' (pic's original title) convinces folks he's indeed a heavenly visitor and performs dubious good deeds - like making a robber gang 'repent' and turn their loot over to him! It's all to win the love of a beautiful trapeze girl, and the hero has a hilarious fight with his romantic rival, the lion tamer, in which all weapons are ornamental clocks. A genuine treasure, long unseen in the US, a rewarding discovery on video. English-language dubbing is awkward, but much of the story needs no dialogue anyway. **Hound Advisory:** Slapstick roughhousing. **1965** (*Family*) 80m/B Philippe Avron, Mirielle Negre; **D:** Albert Lamorisse. VHS, Beta $14.98 *SUE, NLC*

Citizen Kane 🦴🦴🦴🦴

Extraordinary American tragedy of a newspaper tycoon (based loosely on William Randolph Hearst) from his humble beginnings to the solitude of his final years. Widely regarded as one of the greatest films ever made - a stunning tour-de-force in virtually every aspect, from the fragmented narration to breathtaking, deep-focus cinematography; from a vivid soundtrack to fabulous ensemble acting. Wonderkid Welles was only 25 when he co-wrote, directed, and starred. Three-disc laser edition was reproduced from a superior negative and features liner notes and running commentary from film historian Robert J. Carringer. Watch for Ladd and O'Connell as reporters. **1941** (*Jr. High-Adult*) 119m/B Orson Welles, Joseph Cotten, Everett Sloane, Dorothy Comingore, Ruth Warrick, George Coulouris, Ray Collins, William Alland, Paul Stewart, Erskine Sanford, Agnes Moorehead, Alan Ladd, Gus Schilling, Philip Van Zandt, Harry Shannon, Sonny Bupp, Arthur O'Connell; **D:** Orson Welles; **W:** Orson Welles, Herman J. Mankiewicz; **M:** Bernard Herrmann. **Award Nominations:** Academy Awards '41: Best Actor (Welles), Best Black and White Cinematography, Best Director (Welles), Best Film Editing, Best Interior

Decoration, Best Picture, Best Sound, Best Original Score; **Awards:** Academy Awards '41: Best Original Screenplay; National Board of Review Awards '41: 10 Best Films of the Year; New York Film Critics Awards '41: Best Film. **VHS, Beta, LV, 8mm $19.98** *RKO, VYG, CRC*

Citizens Band 🐾🐾🐾

Episodic, low-key comedy about people united by their CB use in a midwestern community. Notable performance from Clark as a soft-voiced guide for truckers passing through. Demme's first comedy is characteristically idiosyncratic.
1977 (PG/*Jr. High-Adult*) 98m/C Paul LeMat, Candy Clark, Ann Wedgeworth, Roberts Blossom, Charles Napier, Marcia Rodd, Bruce McGill, Ed Begley Jr., Alix Elias; *D:* Jonathan Demme; *W:* Paul Brickman; *M:* Bill Conti. **VHS, Beta $59.95** *PAR*

City Boy 🐾🐾

At the turn of the century, orphaned Nick goes from Chicago to the Pacific Northwest, takes a job guarding an old-growth forest, and is torn between the ideals of two new friends. Tom sees the forest as timber that will build homes and provide jobs, while Angelica sees the forest as an irreplaceable sanctuary. This adaptation of "Freckles" by Gene Stratton Porter is a sequel to "The Girl of the Limberlost"; both done for the PBS collection "WonderWorks."
1993 (*Family*) 120m/B Christian Campbell, James Brolin, Sarah Chalke, Wendel Meldrum, Christopher Bolton; *D:* John Kent Harrison; *W:* John Kent Harrison. **VHS $29.95** *PME, BTV, HMV*

City Lights 🐾🐾🐾🐾

Masterpiece that was Chaplin's last silent film is an eloquent and graceful romance, keenly balancing comedy and tragedy. The "Little Tramp" falls in love with a blind flower seller. A series of lucky accidents permits him to get the money she needs for a sight-restoring surgery.
1931 (*Family*) 86m/B Charlie Chaplin, Virginia Cherrill, Florence Lee, Hank Mann, Harry Myers, Henry Bergman, Jean Harlow; *D:* Charlie Chaplin. **VHS, Beta, LV $19.98** *FOX*

City Slickers 🐾🐾🐾

Box-office winner about three men with mid-life crises who leave NYC for a cattle-ranch vacation that turns into an arduous, sometimes dangerous character-building stint. Many hilarious (and some emotional) moments supplied by leads, but Palance steals the cattle drive as a crusty, wise cowpoke. Cuteness factor is provided by a newborn calf named Norman; on the other hand, black and female characters are tokens with nearly nothing to do. Followed by a sequel. **Hound Advisory:** Violence followed by rare cinematic regret: milquetoast Stern gets out of a scrape by pulling a gun, and breaks down about it afterwards. Salty language, sex talk.
1991 (PG-13/*Jr. High-Adult*) 114m/C Billy Crystal, Daniel Stern, Bruno Kirby, Patricia Wettig, Helen Slater, Jack Palance, Noble Willingham, Tracy Walter, Josh Mostel, David Paymer, Bill Henderson, Jeffrey Tambor, Phill Lewis, Kyle Secor, Yeardley Smith, Jayne Meadows; *D:* Ron Underwood; *W:* Lowell Ganz, Babaloo Mandel; *M:* Marc Shaiman. **VHS, Beta, LV, 8mm $19.95** *COL, NLC*

City Slickers 2: The Legend of Curly's Gold 🐾🐾🐾⊲

Mid-life crisis meets the wild west, part deux. Crystal and his fellow urban dudes discover a treasure map in the hat of

departed trail boss Curly and decide to go a-huntin'. Palance is back as Curly's evil twin. Lovitz occupies the screen as Crystal's ne'er-do-well brother, replacing sidekick Bruno Kirby. A bit of a rehash, formulaic and occasionally straining for a punchline, it's still pretty darn funny, especially when the boys start to improvise. **Hound Advisory:** Salty language; sex talk.
1994 (PG-13/*Jr. High-Adult*) 116m/C Billy Crystal, Daniel Stern, Jon Lovitz, Jack Palance, Patricia Wettig, Pruitt Taylor Vince, Bill McKinney, Lindsay Crystal, Noble Willingham, David Paymer, Josh Mostel; *D:* Paul Weiland; *W:* Billy Crystal, Lowell Ganz, Babaloo Mandel; *M:* Marc Shaiman. **VHS** *NYR*

Clara's Heart 🐾

Jamaican maid enriches the lives of her insufferable, bourgeois employers and their particularly repellent son. Kinder, gentler waste of film proves that Goldberg continues to be better than her material. Sentimental clap-trap occasionally lapses into comedy. Young children may appreciate the simplistic message. **Hound Advisory:** Profanity.
1988 (PG-13/*Jr. High-Adult*) 108m/C Whoopi Goldberg, Michael Ontkean, Kathleen Quinlan, Neil Patrick Harris, Spalding Gray, Beverly Todd, Hattie Winston; *D:* Robert Mulligan; *W:* Mark Medoff; *M:* Dave Grusin. **VHS, Beta, LV $19.98** *WAR, FCT*

Clarence 🐾🐾

"When you hear a bell, TV does a se-quel." But it can't make them as memorable; this would-be decades-late followup to "It's a Wonderful Life" finds Clarence the benevolent angel back on the job, risking his wings for a beautiful young woman. Made for cable.
1991 (G/*Family*) 92m/C Robert Carradine, Kate Trotter; *D:* Eric Till. **VHS $79.98** *REP*

Clarence, the Cross-eyed Lion 🐾🐾

Widowed veterinarian and his critter-loving daughter work in the African bush, minister to the title feline and fight marauding poachers. Lighthearted, loosely plotted theatrical release from the creators of "Flipper" looks more like strungtogether TV episodes. No wonder - it was the inspiration for the program "Daktari." **Hound Advisory:** Violence, alcohol use.
1965 (*Family*) 98m/C Marshall Thompson, Betsy Drake, Richard Haydn, Cheryl Miller, Rockne Tarkington, Maurice Marsac; *D:* Andrew Marton. **VHS $19.98** *MGM, FCT*

Clash of the Titans 🐾🐾

Epic stew of Greek legends about heroic Perseus, who does mighty deeds to win a kingdom and the love of a princess, with the gods of Mt. Olympus observing and meddling. Deliberately, almost stubbornly old-fashioned adventure stuff, with plenty of slow stretches despite such creatures as the snake-haired Medusa, winged horse Pegasus and the sea monster Kraken. Ray Harryhausen's stop-motion visuals vary surprisingly in quality, sometimes good, sometimes wretched. **Hound Advisory:** Violence, but the PG rating - rare in a Harryhausen fantasy -derives from brief nudity, sex talk.
1981 (PG/*Primary-Adult*) 118m/C Laurence Olivier, Dame Maggie Smith, Claire Bloom, Ursula Andress, Burgess Meredith, Harry Hamlin, Sian Phillips, Judi Bowker; *D:* Desmond Davis; *W:* Beverly Cross. **VHS, Beta, LV $69.95** *MGM, MLB*

Class Act 🦴🦴◁

Rappers Kid 'N' Play team up once again in this role reversal comedy. A straight-laced brain and a partying, macho bully find their school records and identifications switched when they enroll in a new high school. This turns out to be good for the character of both young men, as the egghead learns to loosen up and the bully learns what it feels like to be respected for his ideas rather than a fierce reputation. Comedy is very uneven but the duo are energetic and likable. **Hound Advisory:** Profanity; sex talk.
1991 (PG-13/*Jr. High-Adult*) 98m/C Christopher Reid, Christopher Martin, Meshach Taylor, Karyn Parsons, Doug E. Doug, Rick Ducommun, Lamont Jackson, Rhea Perlman; *D:* Randall Miller; *M:* Vassal Benford. **VHS, LV** $19.98 *WAR*

Classic Fairy Tales

A collection of Hans Christian Anderson tales, presented in animated form by Canadian cartoon artists.
1982 (*Preschool-Primary*) 62m/C **VHS** $14.95 *FHE*

Classic Fairy Tales

Six classic fairy tales are brought to life for children.
1990 (*Family*) 62m/C **VHS, Beta** $14.95 *FHE*

The Classic Tales Collection

Well-known works of literature are presented in animated form. See individual listings for details; titles include "Alice in Wonderland," "Around the World in 80 Days," "Black Beauty," "The Canterville Ghost," "Hiawatha," "Peter Pan," "The Prisoner of Zenda," "A Tale of Two Cities," "Treasure Island," and "The Wind in the Willows."
1988 (*Family*) 51m/C **VHS** $14.95 *FHE, WTA*

Clean Slate 🦴🦴

Private-eye Maurice Pogue (Carvey) sustains injuries that cause a rare type of amnesia making every day seem like the first day of his life. As the only witness to a crime, he bumbles through mix-ups with the mob and his job as a bodyguard. Lightweight comedy fare is good for a few yuks but doesn't work as well as the similar "Groundhog Day." Barkley the sight-impaired dog steals nearly every scene he's in; but then, he's a show-biz vet, having appeared in two "Ernest" adventures —knowwhatImean?. **Hound Advisory:** Profanity.
1994 (PG-13/*Jr. High-Adult*) 106m/C Dana Carvey, Valeria Golino, James Earl Jones, Kevin Pollak, Michael Murphy, Michael Gambon, Jayne Brook, Vyto Ruginis, Olivia D'Abo; *D:* Mick Jackson; *W:* Robert King; *M:* Alan Silvestri. **VHS, Beta, LV** *MGM*

The Client 🦴🦴◁

Another legal thriller from the Grisham factory. Sarandon is the troubled attorney hired by an 11-year-old boy who witnessed the suicide of a Mafia attorney and now knows more than he should. Jones is the ambitious federal prosecutor who's willing to risk the boy's life in exchange for career advancement. Lacks the mega-big Hollywood names of "The Firm" and "The Pelican Brief" but gains solid acting in

return. No frills, near-faithful adaptation by Schumacher basically travels down the path of least resistance. Filmed on location in Memphis. **Hound Advisory:** Profanity; violence; alcohol talk.
1994 (PG-13/*Jr. High-Adult*) 120m/C Susan Sarandon, Tommy Lee Jones, Brad Renfro, Mary-Louise Parker, Anthony LaPaglia, Bradley Whitford, Anthony Edwards, Ossie Davis, Walter Olkewicz, J.T. Walsh, Will Patton, Anthony Heald; *D:* Joel Schumacher; *W:* Robert Getchell, Akiva Goldsman. **VHS**

Clifford WOOF!

Short plays a 10-year-old in an effort delayed by Orion's financial crisis. Creepy little Clifford's uncle Martin (Grodin) rues the day he volunteered to babysit his nephew to prove to his girlfriend (Steenburgen) how much he likes kids. Clifford terrorizes Grodin in surprisingly nasty ways when their plans for visiting Dinosaurworld fall through, although Grodin sees to well-deserved revenge. Not just bad in the conventional sense, but bad in a bizarre sort of alien fashion that raises questions about who was controlling the bodies of the producers. To create the effect of Short really being short, other actors stood on boxes and sets were built slightly larger. **Hound Advisory:** Profanity and violence.
1992 (PG/*Family*) 90m/C Martin Short, Charles Grodin, Mary Steenburgen, Dabney Coleman, Sonia Jackson; *D:* Paul Flaherty; *W:* Bobby Von Hayes, Jay Dee Rock, Steven Kampmann; *M:* Richard Gibbs. **VHS, LV** *ORI*

Clifford's Fun with Numbers

That lovable red hound is back to entertain the kids and teach them about the numeric system in this fully animated instructional video. A work book is part of the video package. Additional volumes available.
1988 (*Preschool-Primary*) 30m/C **VHS** $12.95 *FHE, FCT*

Clifford's Singalong Adventure

Made for video cartoon/live action film for children, leading them through 17 songs. A few of the many favorites included are, "Row, Row, Row Your Boat" and the ever-classic "Old McDonald."
1986 (*Preschool-Primary*) 30m/C **VHS, Beta** $14.95 *WAR*

Clipped Wings 🦴🦴◁

The Bowery Boys are at their best as they inadvertently join the army while visiting a friend and, in the process of their usual bumblings, uncover a Nazi plot.
1953 (*Family*) 62m/B Leo Gorcey, Huntz Hall, Bernard Gorcey, David Condon, Bennie Bartlett, June Vincent, Mary Treen, Philip Van Zandt, Elaine Riley, Jeanne Dean, Lyle Talbot; *D:* Edward L. Bernds. **VHS** $14.98 *WAR*

Cloak & Dagger 🦴🦴

Thomas followed his starring role in "E.T." with this trifle about little David, a video-game fan who can't convince adults he's stumbled on a very real (and deadly) spy ring. Running for his life, the boy gets survival tips from his imaginary pal, a super-cool commando who's a lookalike for David's own joyless dad. Done like a mid-'70s Disney flick - no great compliment -with violence upped a notch. **Hound Advisory:** Violence.

1984 (PG/*Family*) 101m/C Dabney Coleman, Henry Thomas, Michael Murphy, John McIntire, Jeanette Nolan; *D:* Richard Franklin; *W:* Tom Holland. **VHS, Beta, LV $19.95** *MCA*

Close Encounters of the Third Kind 🐾🐾🐾🐾

Ordinary Americans are swept up in awesome, sometimes frightening phenomena - the result of benevolent aliens trying to contact earthlings. A forerunner to E.T., this Spielberg epic is a stirring achievement, studded with classic sequences, especially a subplot of a tiny boy the visitors want to abduct; he coos with delight as his mother cringes in uncomprehending terror. An exhilarating experience of majestic f/x and uplifting (literally!) themes. Laserdisc includes formerly edited scenes, live interviews with Spielberg and visual wizard Douglas Trumbull and publicity materials.
1977 (PG/*Family*) 152m/C Richard Dreyfuss, Teri Garr, Melinda Dillon, Francois Truffaut, Bob Balaban, Cary Guffey; *D:* Steven Spielberg; *W:* Steven Spielberg; *M:* John Williams. **Award Nominations:** Academy Awards '77: Best Art Direction/Set Decoration, Best Director (Spielberg), Best Film Editing, Best Sound, Best Supporting Actress (Dillon), Best Original Score; **Awards:** Academy Awards '77: Best Cinematography, Best Sound Effects Editing; National Board of Review Awards '77: 10 Best Films of the Year. **VHS, Beta, LV $14.95** *COL, CRC, FUS*

Clowning Around 🐾🐾🐾

Simon, who has lived in foster homes all his life, dreams of becoming a famous circus clown. When he's sent to a new home, his foster parents think his idea is silly, so he runs away and joins the circus. Part of the "Wonderworks" series.
1992 (*Family*) 165m/C Clayton Williamson, Jean-Michel Dagory, Ernie Dingo. **VHS $29.95** *PME, HMV, BTV*

Clowning Around 2 🐾🐾🐾

Continuing story of Sim, whose dream is to become a world-famous clown. Now a member of the Winter Circus in Paris, he is still training with his mentor Anatole. But Sim is dissatisfied and follows another greasepaint cohort Eve to her home in Montreal, then returns to his home in Australia where a surprise is in store.
1993 (*Family*) 120m/C Clayton Williamson, Jean-Michel Dagory, Ernie Dingo, Frederique Fouche; *D:* George Whaley. **VHS $29.95** *PME, BTV*

Club Med 🐾🐾

An insecure comedian and his goofy friend try to make the most of a ski vacation. Perhaps your only chance to see Thicke, Killy, and Coolidge together.
1983 (PG/*Family*) 60m/C Alan Thicke, Jim Carrey, Jean-Claude Killy, Rita Coolidge, Ronnie Hawkins; *D:* David Mitchell, Bob Giraldi; *M:* Peter Bernstein. **VHS, Beta $39.95** *AHV*

Club Paradise 🐾🐾🐾

Chicago fireman flees the big city for a faltering tropical resort and tries to develop some night life. Somewhat disappointing with Williams largely playing the straight man. Most laughs provided by Martin, particularly when she is assaulted by a shower, and Moranis, who gets lost while windsurfing. **Hound Advisory:** Salty language and drug talk.

1986 (PG-13/*Jr. High-Adult*) 96m/C Robin Williams, Peter O'Toole, Rick Moranis, Andrea Martin, Jimmy Cliff, Brian Doyle-Murray, Twiggy, Eugene Levy, Adolph Caesar, Joanna Cassidy, Mary Gross, Carey Lowell, Robin Duke, Simon Jones; *D:* Harold Ramis; *W:* Harold Ramis, Brian Doyle-Murray; *M:* David Mansfield, Van Dyke Parks. **VHS, Beta, LV $19.98** *WAR*

Clue 🐾🐾

Enduring board game takes to the screen as characters must unravel a night of murder at a spooky Victorian mansion. Seemingly clueless as to how to overcome an uneven script, the cast resorts to wild eyes and frantic movements. Butler Curry best survives the evening, while Warren is appealing as well. Theatrical version played with three alternative endings, and the video version shows all three successively.
1985 (PG/*Jr. High-Adult*) 96m/C Lesley Ann Warren, Tim Curry, Martin Mull, Madeline Kahn, Michael McKean, Christopher Lloyd, Eileen Brennan, Howard Hesseman, Lee Ving, Jane Wiedlin, Colleen Camp, Bill Henderson; *D:* Jonathan Lynn; *W:* Jonathan Lynn, John Landis; *M:* John Morris. **VHS, Beta, LV $19.95** *PAR*

Clue You In: The Case of the Mad Movie Mustacher

Fran and Nick are two 13-year-olds who enter a movie screen to help the celluloid detective solve his case. Similarity to "The Last Action Hero" is purely coincidental. Additional volumes available.
19?? (*Primary-Jr. High*) 28m/C **VHS $200.00** *CFV*

The Clutching Hand 🐾🐾

The Clutching Hand seeks a formula that will turn metal into gold and detective Craig Kennedy is out to prevent him from doing so. Serial in 15 chapters on 3 cassettes.
1936 (*Family*) 268m/B Jack Mulhall, Rex Lease. **VHS, Beta $26.95** *SNC, NOS, VDM*

C.L.U.T.Z.

Charming tale about a futuristic family with a slightly outdated robot. Meet George Jetson? No, it's part of the CBS/Storybreak TV specials hosted by Captain Kangaroo, Bob Keeshan.
1985 (*Family*) 25m/C **VHS $14.98** *FOX, KUI*

Coach 🐾🐾

Sexy woman is unintentionally hired to coach a high school basketball team. Despite obvious temptations, her savvy and teamwork mold rookies into young champions. Low-grade roundball fever. **Hound Advisory:** Salty language, sex.
1978 (PG/*Sr. High-Adult*) 100m/C Cathy Lee Crosby, Michael Biehn, Keenan Wynn, Sidney Wicks; *D:* Bud Townsend. **VHS, Beta $9.95** *MED*

Coal Miner's Daughter 🐾🐾🐾

A strong bio of country singer Loretta Lynn, who rose from Appalachian poverty to Nashville riches. Spacek is perfect in the lead, and she even provides acceptable rendering of Lynn's tunes. Band drummer Helm shines as Lynn's father, and Jones is strong as Lynn's downhome husband. Uneven melodrama toward the end, but the film is still a good one.
♫Coal Miner's Daughter; Sweet Dreams of You; I'm a Honky-Tonk

Girl; You're Lookin' at Country; One's On the Way; You Ain't Woman Enough to Take My Man; Back in My Baby's Arms.
1980 (PG/*Jr. High-Adult*) 125m/C Sissy Spacek, Tommy Lee Jones, Levon Helm, Beverly D'Angelo; *D:* Michael Apted. **Award Nominations:** Academy Awards '80: Best Adapted Screenplay, Best Art Direction/Set Decoration, Best Cinematography, Best Film Editing, Best Picture; **Awards:** Academy Awards '80: Best Actress (Spacek); Golden Globe Awards '81: Best Actress—Musical/Comedy (Spacek), Best Film—Musical/Comedy; Los Angeles Film Critics Association Awards '80: Best Actress (Spacek); National Board of Review Awards '80: 10 Best Films of the Year, Best Actress (Spacek); National Society of Film Critics Awards '80: Best Actress (Spacek). **VHS, Beta, LV $14.95** *MCA, BTV*

The Cocoanuts 🦴🦴🦴⌐

The Marx Brothers' first movie, an adaptation of the Broadway show that made them stars, with Groucho as a hotel manager in Florida trying to get rich through a real-estate deal. Technically crude early-sound film, hardly more than radio with pictures; most all the humor is dialogue. But with the Marx Brothers in their prime, the verbal gymnastics are still funnier than most any other picture from the era.
1929 (*Family*) 96m/B Groucho Marx, Chico Marx, Harpo Marx, Zeppo Marx, Margaret Dumont, Kay Francis, Oscar Shaw, Mary Eaton; *D:* Robert Florey, Joseph Santley; *W:* George S. Kaufman, Morrie Ryskind; *M:* Irving Berlin. **VHS, Beta, LV $14.98** *MCA*

Cocoon 🦴🦴🦴

Sci-fi fantasy in which Florida senior citizens discover a watery nest of ancient, dormant aliens that serves effectively as the Fountain of Youth, restoring their health (and sexual virility). Warm-hearted and humane, even if the f/x-crammed finale rips off "Close Encounters of the Third Kind" in every way. Youngsters may want to watch it for the luminous E.T.s, but will also be charmed by elderly performers Ameche, Brimley, Gilford, Cronyn, and Tandy. **Hound Advisory:** Sex talk, and an instance of alien-human lovemaking (with moans and glowing lights but apparently no touching). Salty language.
1985 (PG-13/*Family*) 117m/C Wilford Brimley, Brian Dennehy, Steve Guttenberg, Don Ameche, Tahnee Welch, Jack Gilford, Hume Cronyn, Jessica Tandy, Gwen Verdon, Maureen Stapleton, Tyrone Power Jr., Barret Oliver, Linda Harrison, Herta Ware, Clint Howard; *D:* Ron Howard; *W:* Tom Benedek; *M:* James Horner. **VHS, Beta, LV $19.98** *FOX, FCT, BTV*

Cocoon: The Return 🦴

"Cocoon": The Rerun, as old timers who left with aliens revisit to Earth and basically go through the same stuff all over again. Filmmakers desperately push familiar emotional buttons in search of the fragile magic of the first film. You may find yourself fast-forwarding to the special f/x, or away from the schmaltz. **Hound Advisory:** Sex talk, profanity, alcohol use, mature themes.
1988 (PG/*Jr. High-Adult*) 116m/C Don Ameche, Wilford Brimley, Steve Guttenberg, Maureen Stapleton, Hume Cronyn, Jessica Tandy, Gwen Verdon, Jack Gilford, Tahnee Welch, Courteney Cox, Brian Dennehy, Barret Oliver; *D:* Daniel Petrie; *M:* James Horner. **VHS, Beta, LV $19.98** *FOX*

Cold River 🦴🦴⌐

Experienced guide takes his two children on an extended trip through the Adirondacks. For the children, it's a fantasy vacation - until their father succumbs to a heart attack and the boy and girl must fend for themselves in the chilly mountains. More hard-edged than the typical wilderness-family fare. **Hound Advisory:** Salty language, mature themes.
1981 (PG/*Family*) 94m/C Pat Petersen, Richard Jaeckel, Suzanne Weber; *D:* Fred G. Sullivan. **VHS, Beta $59.98** *FOX*

Collision Course 🦴🦴

Wise-cracking cop from Detroit teams up with Japan's best detective to nail a ruthless gang leader. Release was delayed until 1992 due to a lawsuit, but it was resolved in time to coordinate the release with Leno's debut as the host of "The Tonight Show." Of marginal interest, though Leno fans may appreciate. Filmed on location in Motown.
1989 (PG/*Family*) 99m/C Noriyuki "Pat" Morita, Jay Leno, Chris Sarandon, Al Waxman. **VHS, Beta, LV $89.99** *HBO*

Comeback Kid 🦴🦴

An ex-big league baseball player is conned into coaching an urban team of smarmy street youths, and falls for their playground supervisor. Made for TV.
1980 (*Family*) 97m/C John Ritter, Susan Dey; *D:* Peter Levin. **VHS, Beta $9.98** *SUE, NLC*

Comfort and Joy 🦴🦴🦴⌐

After his kleptomaniac girlfriend deserts him, a Scottish disc jockey is forced to reevaluate his life. He becomes involved in an underworld battle between two mob-owned local ice cream companies. Another odd comedy gem from Forsyth, who did "Gregory's Girl" and "Local Hero". Music by Dire Straits guitarist Knopfler.
1984 (PG/*Sr. High-Adult*) 93m/C Bill Paterson, Eleanor David, C.P. Grogan, Alex Norton, Patrick Malahide, Rikki Fulton, Roberto Berrardi; *D:* Bill Forsyth; *M:* Mark Knopfler. **VHS, Beta $69.95** *MCA*

Comic Book Kids 🦴⌐

Two youngsters enjoy visiting their friend's comic strip studio, since they have the power to project themselves into the cartoon stories. It wasn't an outstanding premise in the blockbuster "Last Action Hero" and it isn't too impressive in this obscure production.
1982 (G/*Family*) 90m/C Joseph Campanella, Mike Darnell, Robyn Finn, Jim Engelhardt, Fay De Witt. **VHS, Beta** *GEM*

The Commitments 🦴🦴🦴

Convinced that they can bring soul music to Dublin, a group of working-class youth form a band. High-energy production paints an interesting, unromanticized picture of modern Ireland and refuses to follow standard showbiz cliches, even though its lack of resolution hurts. Honest, whimsical dialog laced with poetic obscenities, delivered by a cast of mostly unknowns. Very successful soundtrack features the music of Wilson Pickett, James Brown, Otis Redding, Aretha Franklin, Percy Sledge, and others, and received a Grammy nomination. Based on the book "The Commitments" by Roddy Doyle, part of a trilogy which includes "The Snapper" (also out on video) and "The Van." **Hound Advisory:** Profanity.

1991 (R/*Sr. High-Adult*) 116m/C Andrew Strong, Bronagh Gallagher, Glen Hansard, Michael Aberne, Dick Massey, Ken McCluskey, Robert Arkins, Dave Finnegan, Johnny Murphy, Angeline Ball, Felim Gormley, Maria Doyle, Colm Meaney; **D:** Alan Parker; **W:** Dick Clement, Roddy Doyle, Ian LaFrenais. **Award Nominations:** Academy Awards '91: Best Film Editing; **Awards:** British Academy Awards '92: Best Director (Parker), Best Film. **VHS, Beta, LV** $19.98 *FXV, CCB, IME*

Computer Wizard 🎬

Boy genius builds a powerful electronic device. His intentions are good, but the invention disrupts the town and lands him in big trouble. Not the "Thomas Edison Story."
1977 (G/*Family*) 91m/C Henry Darrow, Kate Woodville, Guy Madison, Marc Gilpin; **D:** John Florea. **VHS, Beta** *NO*

The Computer Wore Tennis Shoes 🎬🎬

Slow-witted college student turns into a genius after a "shocking" encounter with the campus computer. His new brains give the local gangster headaches and help save the school. One of a series of awfully cloying Disney campus comedies that seemed singularly out of step with the times. Sequel: "Now You See Him, Now You Don't."
1969 (G/*Family*) 87m/C Kurt Russell, Cesar Romero, Joe Flynn, William Schallert, Allan Hewitt, Richard Bakalayan; **D:** Robert Butler. **VHS, Beta** *DIS, OM*

Conan the Barbarian 🎬🎬🎬

Vicious sword-and-sorcery tale, hearkening back to the original fantasy novels of Robert E. Howard - and not for kids despite the proliferation of Conan comics, cartoons, and of course, Uncle Arnold, ideally cast here as the young slave in an ancient land who embarks on a bloody path to avenge his murdered parents. Sequel, "Conan the Destroyer," is much better suited to the younger fans. **Hound Advisory:** Brutality; sex; nudity.
1982 (R/*Sr. High-Adult*) 115m/C Arnold Schwarzenegger, James Earl Jones, Max von Sydow, Sandahl Bergman, Mako, Ben Davidson, Valerie Quennessen, Cassandra Gaviola, William Smith; **D:** John Milius; **W:** John Milius, Oliver Stone; **M:** Basil Poledouris. **VHS, Beta, LV** $14.95 *MCA*

Conan the Destroyer 🎬🎬🎬

Conan is duped by sorceress Queen Tamaris into searching for a treasure and guarding a virgin maiden. In fact, the girl is to be a human sacrifice and Conan assassinated, but the muscleman acquires an Amazonian warrior ally (Jones) who helps out in their climactic battle against the forces of evil. Frequent action, excellent special f/x, monsters and a silly finale, with an cartoony campiness overall, in contrast to the darkness of the first film. **Hound Advisory:** Violence; sex talk.
1984 (PG/*Jr. High-Adult*) 101m/C Arnold Schwarzenegger, Grace Jones, Wilt Chamberlain, Sarah Douglas, Mako, Olivia D'Abo, Jeff Corey; **D:** Richard Fleischer; **M:** Basil Poledouris. **VHS, Beta, LV** $14.95 *MCA*

Condorman 🎬🎬

Woody Wilkins, an inventive comic book writer, adopts the identity of his own character, Condorman, in order to help a beautiful Russian spy defect. Disney strictly for the small fry. **Hound Advisory:** Roughhousing.

1981 (PG/*Family*) 90m/C Michael Crawford, Oliver Reed, Barbara Carrera, James Hampton, Jean-Pierre Kalfon, Dana Elcar; **D:** Charles Jarrott; **M:** Henry Mancini. **VHS, Beta** $69.95 *DIS*

Coneheads 🎬🎬

Comedy inspired by once popular characters from "Saturday Night Live" coasts in on the coattails of "Wayne's World." Aykroyd and Curtin reprise their roles as Beldar and Prymaat, the couple from the planet Remulak who are just trying to fit in on Earth. Newman, who created the role of teenage daughter Connie, appears as Beldar's sister, while Burke takes over as Connie (toddler Connie is Aykroyd's daughter, in her film debut). One-joke premise is a decade late and a dime short, though cast of comedy all-stars provides a lift. **Hound Advisory:** Alcohol use.
1993 (PG/*Jr. High-Adult*) 86m/C Dan Aykroyd, Jane Curtin, Laraine Newman, Jason Alexander, Michelle Burke, Chris Farley, Michael Richards, Lisa Jane Persky, Sinbad, Shishir Kurup, Michael McKean, Phil Hartman, David Spade, Dave Thomas, Jan Hooks, Chris Rock, Adam Sandler, Julia Sweeney, Danielle Aykroyd; **D:** Steven Barron; **W:** Dan Aykroyd, Tom Davis, Bonnie Turner, Terry Turner. **VHS, Beta** *PAR, BTV*

A Connecticut Yankee 🎬🎬🎬

Charming version of Twain's "A Connecticut Yankee in King Arthur's Court," adapted to the special talents of legendary American humorist Will Rogers. He even teaches King Arthur his famous rope tricks when he's transported back to the days of the Round Table. Humor is mostly verbal (Rogers tells the King of a new 'magic' called advertising: "It makes folks spend what they haven't got on things they don't want"), but the sight of telephones in Camelot and armored knights riding to the rescue in early automobiles make up for the slow spots. **Hound Advisory:** Violence, since the Connecticut Yankee gives the King's men machine guns.
1931 (*Family*) 96m/B Will Rogers, Myrna Loy, Maureen O'Sullivan, William Farnum; **D:** David Butler. **VHS** $19.98 *FOX, FCT*

A Connecticut Yankee in King Arthur's Court 🎬🎬🎬

Pleasant musicalized version of the Twain novel, here about a 1912 American blacksmith transported to Camelot of 538 A.D., where he passes himself off as a powerful wizard and tries to advise King Arthur about democracy. Crosby is his own easygoing self, though the storyline (generally faithful to the original) stops in its tracks to accommodate the inevitable songs. 🎵Once and For Always; Busy Doin' Nothin'; If You Stub Your Toe on the Moon; When Is Sometime?; Twixt Myself and Me.
1949 (*Family*) 108m/C Bing Crosby, Rhonda Fleming, William Bendix, Cedric Hardwicke, Henry Wilcoxon, Murvyn Vye, Virginia Field; **D:** Tay Garnett. **VHS, Beta, LV** $14.98 *MCA*

A Connecticut Yankee in King Arthur's Court 🎬🎬

Animated feature from Europe based on the classic Twain novel about an American transported to Camelot, where his modern inventions and Yankee ingenuity cause more problems than they solve. This version takes numerous liberties

with Sam Clemens' story, including updating the tale to the space age rather than the original's Industrial Revolution era.
1970 (*Family*) 74m/C *D:* Zoran Janjic. **VHS, Beta $19.95** *MGM*

Conquest of the Planet of the Apes 𝄞𝄞

More of a prequel than sequel as the simian series moves into film number four with a look back at how the Planet of the Apes developed. In the distant year of 1990, the apes turn the tables on the human Earth population when they lead a revolt against their cruel homo sapian masters. Trite and cliched at times, but of interest to fans of the series. Followed by "Battle for the Planet of the Apes." **Hound Advisory:** Violence.
1972 (*PG/Jr. High-Adult*) 87m/C Roddy McDowall, Don Murray, Ricardo Montalban, Natalie Trundy, Severn Darden, Hari Rhodes; *D:* J. Lee Thompson. **VHS, Beta, LV $19.98** *FOX*

Conrack 𝄞𝄞𝄞

True story of writer Pat Conroy, who tried to teach a group of illiterate black children, isolated and ignored on a South Carolina island. Through caring and common-sense teaching techniques, Mr. "Conrack" (how the kids pronounced his name) inspired the kids but rocked the boat too much for white authorities. Earnest, if a little bit formulaic. Based on Conroy's book "The Water Is Wide." **Hound Advisory:** Salty language, mature themes.
1974 (*PG/Family*) 111m/C Jon Voight, Paul Winfield, Madge Sinclair, Hume Cronyn, Martin Ritt; *D:* Martin Ritt; *W:* Harriet Frank Jr., Irving Ravetch; *M:* John Williams. **VHS, Beta $59.98** *FOX*

Conspiracy of Love 𝄞

TV drama about the strain of divorce within a family. The irresponsible husband walks out, though the careerist ex-wife still lives with his sympathetic parents. But she can't compete with an easygoing grandpa for the affections of her small daughter (Barrymore). Result: a court order to keep the old folks away. Good premise about how decent people can end up hurting each other, but not above sugary cliches.
1987 (*Jr. High-Adult*) 93m/C Robert Young, Drew Barrymore, Glynnis O'Connor, Elizabeth Wilson, Michael Laurence, John Fujioka, Alan Fawcett; *D:* Noel Black. **VHS $19.95** *STE, NWV*

Cool As Ice 𝄞𝄐

Creativity stopped with the apt casting of rapper Vanilla Ice (his 15 minutes are long gone) as a super-cool biker who motors into a conservative town, eventually winning a local girl's love via heroism. Several so-so musical segments in this mainly inoffensive juvenile exercise in wish-fulfillment, for teenage romantics only. **Hound Advisory:** Roughhousing.
1991 (*PG/Jr. High-Adult*) 92m/C Vanilla Ice, Kristin Minter, Michael Gross, Sydney Lassick, Dody Goodman, Naomi Campbell, Candy Clark; *D:* David Kellogg; *M:* Stanley Clarke. **VHS, Beta, LV $79.95** *MCA*

Cool Change 𝄞𝄞𝄐

Wonderfully scenic Australian drama from the director of "The Man From Snowy River," about a young park ranger used as a pawn in a government conspiracy to rob cattlemen of their land. It's been peddled as a family-oriented video, though between the politics and romance there seems little to really interest kids. Refreshing touch: environmentalists are bad guys, for once. **Hound Advisory:** Sex, alcohol use.
1986 (*PG/Jr. High-Adult*) 79m/C **VHS $39.98** *FHE, BTV*

Cool Runnings 𝄞𝄞𝄐

Bright, slapstick comedy based on the true story of the Jamaican bobsled team's quest to enter the 1988 Winter Olympics in Calgary. Candy is recruited to coach four unlikely athletes who don't quite exemplify the spirit of the Games. He accepts the challenge not only because of its inherent difficulty but because he needs to reconcile himself to past failures as a former sledder. When our heroes leave their sunny training ground for Calgary, their mettle is tested by serious sledders from more frigid climes who pursue the competition with a stern sense of mission. An upbeat story which will appeal to children, its target audience. **Hound Advisory:** Salty language, roughhousing.
1993 (*PG/Jr. High-Adult*) 98m/C Leon, Doug E. Doug, John Candy, Marco Brambilla, Malik Yoba, Rawle Lewis, Raymond J. Barry, Peter Outerbridge, Larry Gilman, Paul Coeur; *D:* Jon Turteltaub; *W:* Tommy Swerdlow, Lynn Siefert, Michael Goldberg; *M:* Hans Zimmer. **VHS, LV** *DIS*

Cooley High 𝄞𝄞𝄞

Likeable comedy-drama about black high school students in Chicago experiencing the rites of passage in their senior year. Funny, streetwise, but with a tragic finale that prevents it from going sitcom. Set in the '60s (great soundtrack features Motown hits of the era) but very much a funky relic of the '70s, right down to a 1976 Godzilla flick playing at the heroes' cinema hangout. **Hound Advisory:** Violence, sex, mature themes.
1975 (*PG/Jr. High-Adult*) 107m/C Glynn Turman, Lawrence Hilton-Jacobs, Garrett Morris, Cynthia Davis; *D:* Michael A. Schultz; *W:* Eric Monte. **VHS, LV $79.98** *ORI, FCT, PTB*

Cop and a Half 𝄞𝄞

Eight-year-old cop groupie Devon witnesses a Miami mob murder and talks police into putting him on the force for a day -otherwise he'll withhold information. His short-term partner is kid-hating detective Reynolds, but bad guys are after Devon, and we know the action hero will adore his little pal by the end. Predictable comedy gets a bone for staying kid-friendly all the way (unlike the violent "Kindergarten Cop"), and Sharkey's ham villain is a treat. Grownup viewers will likely be bored. **Hound Advisory:** Roughhousing.
1993 (*PG/Family*) 87m/C Norman D. Golden II, Burt Reynolds, Ruby Dee, Ray Sharkey, Holland Taylor, Frank Sivero, Marc Macaulay, Rocky Giordani, Sammy Hernandez; *D:* Henry Winkler; *W:* Arne Olsen; *M:* Alan Silvestri. **VHS, LV $19.98** *MCA*

Cops and Robbersons 𝄞

Bored, dim-witted dad Chase, a TV cop-show junkie, wishes his life had a little more danger and excitement. How lucky for him when hard-nosed cop Palance sets up a command post in his house to stake out the mobster living next door (Davi). Predictable plot isn't funny and drags Chase's bumbling idiot persona on for too long. Wiest and Davi are two bright spots, but their talents are wasted, while Palance does little more than reincarnate his "City Slickers" character. Poor effort for otherwise notable director Ritchie. **Hound Advisory:** Profanity; brief nudity.

1994 (PG/ *Jr. High-Adult* **)** 93m/C Chevy Chase, Jack Palance, Dianne Wiest, Robert Davi, Jason James Richter, Fay Masterson, Miko Hughes, Richard Romanus, David Barry Gray; **D:** Michael Ritchie; **W:** Bernie Somers; **M:** William Ross. **VHS** *NYR*

COPS: Crime Doesn't Pay

Lineup of episodes from the syndicated TV cartoon series, as Special Agent "Bulletproof" Vess assembles a team of specialized hi-tech heroes to bust the baddies of Empire City. Additional volumes available.

1989 (*Primary*) 120m/C **VHS, Beta** $39.95 *JFK, WTA*

Corduroy and Other Bear Stories

Collection of three children's films, live action and animated: "Corduroy," "Panama," and "Blueberries for Sal."

1985 (*Preschool-Primary*) 37m/C **VHS, Beta** $19.95 *CCC, FCT, MLT*

The Corn is Green 🎞️🎞️🎞️

Touching story of a school teacher in a poor Welsh village who nurtures a clever boy from a mining family and eventually sends her pupil to a glorious future at Oxford. Davis makes a fine teacher, though a little young, while the on-site photography provides atmosphere. Based on the play by Emlyn Williams.

1945 (*Family*) 115m/B Bette Davis, John Dall, Nigel Bruce, Joan Lorring, Arthur Shields, Mildred Dunnock, Rhys Williams, Rosalind Iven; **D:** Irving Rapper; **M:** Max Steiner. **VHS, Beta** $19.95 *MGM, FCT*

Corrina, Corrina 🎞️🎞️

Whoopi brings humanity again to a white family struggling to find itself. Newly widowed jingle-writer Liotta needs someone to care for his withdrawn eight year-old daughter. Enter Whoopi, as housekeeper and eventual love interest. Sweet, nostalgic romance set in the 1950's rests squarely on the charm of its leads, with Liotta playing against type and Whoopi doing Whoopi. Goldberg also found off-screen romance (again), this time with the film's union organizer Lyle Trachtenberg. Last role for Ameche. **Hound Advisory:** Mature themes; salty language.

1994 (PG/ *Sr. High-Adult* **)** 115m/C Whoopi Goldberg, Ray Liotta, Don Ameche, Tina Majorino, Wendy Crewson, Jenifer Lewis, Larry Miller, Erica Yohn; **Cameos:** Anita Baker; **D:** Jessie Nelson; **W:** Jessie Nelson. **VHS** *NYR*

The Cosmic Eye 🎞️🎞️🎞️

Critically acclaimed, abstract cartoon about three musicians from outer space who come to Earth to spread messages of global peace and harmony. Much of the film consists of representations of various creation stories from different cultures, with tribal imagery (including human sacrifice) and music - great fun for kids who are budding anthropologists, arcane and confusing if they're not. Portions are really inserts from shorter pieces by animator Hubley, like "Moonbird,"

"Cockaboody" and "Voyage to Next," available on cassette by themselves and quite charming.

1971 (*Family*) 71m/C **D:** Faith Hubley; **V:** Dizzy Gillespie, Maureen Stapleton, Benny Carter. **VHS, Beta, LV** $59.98 *LTY, WTA, DIS*

The Count of Monte Cristo 🎞️🎞️🎞️

Alexander Dumas classic about an innocent man (Chamberlain) who is imprisoned, escapes, and finds the treasure of Monte Cristo, which he uses to bring down those who wronged him. Good version of the historical costumer. Originally shown in theaters in Europe, but broadcast on television in the U.S.

1974 (*Family*) 104m/C Richard Chamberlain, Kate Nelligan, Donald Pleasence, Alessio Orano, Tony Curtis, Louis Jourdan, Trevor Howard, Taryn Power; **D:** David Greene. **VHS, Beta** $19.98 *LIV, FUS*

Country 🎞️🎞️🎞️

Strong story with a message about an Iowan farm family in crisis when the government attempts to foreclose on their land. Good performances all around and an excellent portrayal of the wife by Lange. "The River" and "Places In the Heart," both released in 1984, also dramatized the plight of many American farm families in the early 1980s.

1984 (PG/ *Family* **)** 109m/C Jessica Lange, Sam Shepard, Wilford Brimley, Matt Clark, Therese Graham, Levi L. Knebel; **D:** Richard Pearce; **W:** Bill Wittliff. **VHS, Beta, LV** $79.95 *TOU*

Country Girl 🎞️🎞️🎞️🎞️

In the role that completely de-glamorized her (and won her an Oscar), Kelly plays the wife of alcoholic singer Crosby who tries to make a comeback with the help of director Holden. One of Crosby's four dramatic parts, undoubtedly one of his best. Seaton won an Oscar for his adaptation of the Clifford Odets play. Remade in 1982. 🎵The Search is Through; Dissertation on the State of Bliss; It's Mine, It's Yours; The Land Around Us. **Hound Advisory:** Alcohol use.

1954 (*Jr. High-Adult*) 104m/B Bing Crosby, Grace Kelly, William Holden, Gene Reynolds, Anthony Ross; **D:** George Seaton; **W:** George Seaton. **Award Nominations:** Academy Awards '54: Best Actor (Crosby), Best Black and White Cinematography, Best Director (Seaton), Best Picture; Academy Awards '56: Best Art Direction/Set Decoration (B & W); **Awards:** Academy Awards '54: Best Actress (Kelly), Best Screenplay; Golden Globe Awards '55: Best Actress—Drama (Kelly); National Board of Review Awards '54: 10 Best Films of the Year, Best Actress (Kelly). **VHS, Beta** $14.95 *PAR, BTV*

Country Music with the Muppets

Rowlf the Dog plays some of his favorite country music and stars in this collection of highlights from "The Muppet Show."

1985 (*Family*) 55m/C Johnny Cash, Roy Clark, Crystal Gayle, Jim Henson, Frank Oz, Roger Miller. **VHS, Beta** *FOX*

Country Rock

Collection of fun-lovin' Hanna-Barbera cartoon characters entertaining their way through a video filled with country tunes.

1984 (*Preschool-Primary*) 30m/C **VHS, Beta** *TTC*

Coupe de Ville 🦴🦴🦴🎔

Three very different, squabbling young brothers are ordered by their father to drive the title vehicle (mom's birthday gift), from Detroit to Florida in the summer of '63. By the journey's end, all three have grown up a little and come to appreciate each other better - and you've seen it coming from miles away. Convivial cast chauffeurs this sibling comedy-drama script with some panache. **Hound Advisory:** Much sex talk on the road, plus profanity, roughhousing.

1990 (*PG-13*/*Jr. High-Adult*) 98m/C Patrick Dempsey, Daniel Stern, Arye Gross, Joseph Bologna, Alan Arkin, Annabeth Gish, Rita Taggart, James Gammon; *D:* Joe Roth; *W:* Mike Binder; *M:* James Newton Howard. VHS, Beta, LV $19.95 *MCA*

Courage Mountain 🦴🎔

Would-be sequel to Johanna Spyri's classic "Heidi." Europe is on the brink of WWI when Heidi leaves her mountain for an exclusive boarding school in Italy. When armies take over, the kids are sent to an orphanage run by nasties. The girls escape to the mountains and are saved by Heidi's pal Peter (the twentysomething Sheen miscast as a teenager) Ridiculous sequel to the classic tale may appeal to kids, but post-adolescents beware.

1989 (*PG*/*Primary-Adult*) 92m/C Juliette Caton, Joanna Clarke, Nicola Stapleton, Charlie Sheen, Jan Rubes, Leslie Caron, Jade Magri, Kathryn Ludlow, Yorgo Voyagis; *D:* Christopher Leitch; *W:* Weaver Webb; *M:* Sylvester Levay. VHS, Beta, LV $14.95 *COL, FCT*

Courage of Black Beauty 🦴🎔

Another, rather weak trot around the track for the classic stallion character created by Anna Sewell, and his friendship with a boy master.

1957 (*Family*) 80m/C Johnny Crawford, Mimi Gibson, John Bryant, Diane Brewster, J. Pat O'Malley; *D:* Harold Schuster. VHS, Beta $12.95 *LIV*

Courage of Lassie 🦴🦴🎔

Fourteen-year-old Taylor is the heroine in this girl loves dog tale. In this case, the dog is actually called Bill, not Lassie, in spite of the film's title. Bill is found wounded by Taylor and she nurses him back to health. He proves to be loving, loyal, and useful, so much so that, through a complicated plotline, he winds up in the Army's K-9 division and returns home with the doggie version of shell-shock. Taylor's still there to nurse him back to his own kind self again.

1946 (*G*/*Family*) 93m/C Elizabeth Taylor, Frank Morgan, Tom Drake, Selena Royle, Harry Davenport; *D:* Fred M. Wilcox. VHS $14.95 *MGM*

Courage of the North 🦴🎔

The Mounties break up a fur-stealing ring with the help of Captain Dog and Dynamite Horse.

1935 (*Family*) 55m/B John Preston, June Love, William Desmond, Tom London, Jimmy Aubrey, Dynamite Horse, Captain Dog. VHS, Beta *NO*

The Court Jester 🦴🦴🦴🎔

Swashbuckling comedy stars Danny Kaye as a former circus clown who teams up with a band of outlaws trying to dethrone a tyrant king. Kaye poses as the court jester so he can learn more of the evil king's intentions. Filled with more color, more song, and more truly funny lines than any three comedies put together, this is Kaye's best performance. ♫They'll Never Outfox the Fox; Baby, Let Me Take You Dreaming; My Heart Knows a Lovely Song; The Maladjusted Jester.

1956 (*Family*) 101m/C Danny Kaye, Glynis Johns, Basil Rathbone, Angela Lansbury, Cecil Parker, John Carradine, Mildred Natwick, Robert Middleton; *D:* Norman Panama, Melvin Frank; *W:* Norman Panama. VHS, Beta, LV $14.95 *PAR*

The Courtship of Eddie's Father 🦴🦴🦴

Clever nine-year-old boy plays matchmaker for his widowed dad in this rewarding family comedy-drama, the inspiration for the TV series. Some plot elements are outdated, but young Howard's performance is terrific; he would later excel at direction. Based on the novel by Mark Toby.

1962 (*Family*) 117m/C Glenn Ford, Shirley Jones, Stella Stevens, Dina Merrill, Ron Howard, Jerry Van Dyke; *D:* Vincente Minnelli; *W:* John Gay. VHS $19.98 *MGM, FCT*

The Cowboys 🦴🦴🦴

Wayne stars as an Old West cattle rancher who is forced to hire 11 schoolboys to help him drive his cattle 400 miles to market. The roughness - and violence - of the trail helps make men out of the kids, while a clever script makes this one of Duke's better late westerns. Laserdisc available in widescreen letterbox edition. **Hound Advisory:** Violence, plus sex talk with a wagonload of prostitutes.

1972 (*PG*/*Jr. High-Adult*) 128m/C John Wayne, Roscoe Lee Browne, A. Martinez, Bruce Dern, Colleen Dewhurst, Slim Pickens, Robert Carradine; *D:* Mark Rydell; *W:* Harriet Frank Jr., Irving Ravetch; *M:* John Williams. VHS, Beta, LV $19.98 *WAR, TLF*

Cracking Up 🦴🎔

Accident-prone misfit's mishaps on the road to recovery create chaos for everyone he meets. Lewis plays a dozen characters in this overboard comedy with few laughs.

1983 (*PG*/*Jr. High-Adult*) 91m/C Jerry Lewis, Herb Edelman, Foster Brooks, Milton Berle, Sammy Davis Jr., Zane Buzby, Dick Butkus, Buddy Lester; *D:* Jerry Lewis. VHS, Beta $19.98 *WAR*

Crazy Moon 🦴🦴🎔

Eccentric high schooler Brooks falls in love with a deaf girl, and must struggle against his domineering father's and older brother's prejudices. The viewer must struggle against the romantic cliches and heavy-handed message to enjoy a basically tender tale of romance. Noteworthy for showcasing a fashion trend that didn't quite catch on in real life; Brooks is a 'retro' kid, dressing in 1930s fashions and relishing vintage music. **Hound Advisory:** Salty language, mature themes.

1987 (*PG-13*/*Jr. High-Adult*) 89m/C Kiefer Sutherland, Vanessa Vaughan, Peter Spence, Ken Pogue, Eve Napier; *D:* Allan Eastman; *W:* Tom Berry, Stefan Wodoslowsky; *M:* Lou Forestieri. VHS, Beta, LV $14.95 *SUE, NLC*

Cria 🦴🦴🦴

Award-winning story of 9-year-old Ana, who struggles to comprehend her mother's terminal cancer. Ultimately she holds her father responsible; later his death leaves her feeling like a murderer. No less an eminence than "Peanuts" creator Charles Schulz has recommended this somber drama for its portrayal of a child's mind. In Spanish with English subtitles. **Hound Advisory:** Mature themes.

1976 (PG/*Jr. High-Adult*) 115m/C Geraldine Chaplin, Ana Torrent, Conchita Perez; **D:** Carlos Saura. **Award Nominations:** Cannes Film Festival '76: Best Film; **Awards:** National Board of Review Awards '77: 5 Best Foreign Films of the Year. **VHS, Beta, LV $59.95** *INT, TPV, APD*

The Cricket in Times Square

Cat, mouse, boy, and cricket help revive a failing newsstand in this modern fantasy adapted for TV 'toons from George Selden's book.

1973 (*Primary*) 30m/C **D:** Chuck Jones. **VHS, Beta $14.95** *KUI, FHE, CHI*

The Crimson Ghost

Republic Pictures serial named after its villain, a respected university faculty member disguised in a robe and a skull mask (with bad teeth). With his gangster henchmen, the CG schemes to steal the newly invented 'cyclotrode' ray gun and hold the world hostage, unless a heroic criminologist can stop him. Silly chapter play antics, with the Ghost's identity revealed in the final of its 12 episodes. 93-minute colorized condensed version is also available. **Hound Advisory:** Violence.

1946 (*Family*) 100m/B Charles Quigley, Linda Stirling, I. Stanford Jolley, Clayton Moore, Kenne Duncan; **D:** William Witney, Fred Brannon. **VHS, Beta $29.98** *VCN, REP, MLB*

Critters 🐾🐾🐾

One of the better "Gremlins" clones. In fact, it's the only better "Gremlins" clone. Fast-growing, faster-eating little alien beasts crash to Earth with a pair of blast-'em-on-sight galactic bounty hunters right behind them. Both terrorize a farm family in a small Kansas community. Smart and sarcastic sci-fi action that doesn't push gore to extremes. Followed by several inferior sequels. **Hound Advisory:** Violence, but mostly committed upon monsters and bowling alleys - and one E.T. doll, enthusiastically devoured in a priceless moment. One alien swear word, translated thanks to subtitles.

1986 (PG-13/*Jr. High-Adult*) 86m/C Dee Wallace Stone, M. Emmet Walsh, Billy Green Bush, Scott Grimes, Nadine Van Der Velde, Terrence Mann, Billy Zane; **D:** Stephen Herek; **W:** Stephen Herek; **M:** David Newman. **VHS, Beta, LV $14.95** *COL*

Crocodile Dundee 🐾🐾🐾🐾

New York reporter Sue Charlton is assigned to the Outback to interview living legend Mike Dundee. When she finally locates the man, she is so taken with him that she brings him back to New York with her. There, the naive Aussie wanders about, amazed at the wonders of the city and unwittingly charming everyone he comes in contact with, from high-society transvestites to street hookers. One of the surprise hits of 1986. **Hound Advisory:** Roughhousing; salty language.

1986 (PG-13/*Jr. High-Adult*) 98m/C Paul Hogan, Linda Kozlowski, John Meillon, David Gulpilil, Mark Blum; **D:** Peter Faiman. **Award Nominations:** Academy Awards '86: Best Original Screenplay; **Awards:** Golden Globe Awards '87: Best Actor—Musical/Comedy (Hogan). **VHS, Beta, LV, 8mm $14.95** *PAR*

Crocodile Dundee 2 🐾🐾🐾

Mike Dundee, the loveable rube, returns to his native Australia looking for new adventure, having "conquered" New York City. He inadvertently gets involved in stopping a gang of crooks active in Australia and New York. Sequel to original box office smash lacks its charm and freshness. **Hound Advisory:** Violence; mild profanity.

1988 (PG/*Family*) 110m/C Paul Hogan, Linda Kozlowski, Kenneth Welsh, John Meillon, Ernie Dingo, Juan Fernandez, Charles S. Dutton; **D:** John Cornell; **W:** Paul Hogan. **VHS, Beta, LV $14.95** *PAR*

Crooklyn 🐾🐾🐾

Director Lee turns from the life of Malcolm X to the early lives of Generation X in this profile of an African-American middle class family growing up in 1970's Brooklyn. Lee's least politically charged film to date is a joint effort between him and sibs Joie and Cinque, and profiles the only girl in a family of five children coming of age. Tender and real performances from all, especially newcomer Harris, propel the sometimes messy, music-laden trip to nostalgia land. **Hound Advisory:** Profanity; mature themes.

1994 (PG-13/*Jr. High-Adult*) 112m/C Alfre Woodard, Delroy Lindo, Zelda Harris, David Patrick Kelly, Carlton Williams, Sharif Rashed, Tse-March Washington, Christopher Knowings, Jose Zuniga, Isaiah Washington, Ivelka Reyes, N. Jeremi Duru, Frances Foster, Norman Matlock, Patriece Nelson, Joie Lee, Vondie Curtis-Hall, Tiasha Reyes, Spike Lee; **D:** Spike Lee; **W:** Joie Lee, Cinque Lee; **M:** Terence Blanchard. **VHS, LV** *MCA*

Cross Creek 🐾🐾🐾

Based on the life of Marjorie Kinnan Rawlings, author of "The Yearling," who, after 10 years as a frustrated reporter/writer, moves to the remote and untamed Everglades. There she meets colorful local characters and receives the inspiration to write numerous bestsellers. Well acted though overtly sentimental at times. Produced by "Sounder" creator Robert B. Radnitz. **Hound Advisory:** Salty language; brief violence.

1983 (PG/*Family*) 115m/C Mary Steenburgen, Rip Torn, Peter Coyote, Dana Hill, Alfre Woodard, Malcolm McDowell; **D:** Martin Ritt. **VHS, Beta $14.98** *REP*

Crossing Delancey 🐾🐾🐾

Jewish woman (Bozyk), in old world style, plays matchmaker to her independent thirtysomething granddaughter. Charming modern-day NYC fairy tale deftly manipulates cliches and stereotypes. Lovely performance from Irving as the woman whose heart surprises her. Riegert is swell playing the pickle vender who's the gentle but never wimpy suitor. Bozyk, a star on the Yiddish vaudeville stage, is perfectly cast in her film debut. Appealing music by the Roches, with Suzzy Roche giving a credible performance as Irving's friend. Adapted for the big screen by Sandler from her play of the same name. **Hound Advisory:** Salty language; sex talk.

1988 (PG/*Jr. High-Adult*) 97m/C Amy Irving, Reizl Bozyk, Peter Riegert, Jeroen Krabbe, Sylvia Miles, Suzzy Roche, George Martin, John Bedford Lloyd, Rosemary Harris, Amy Wright, Claudia Silver; **D:** Joan Micklin Silver; **W:** Suzzy Roche, Susan Sandler. **VHS, Beta, LV, 8mm $19.98** *WAR, FCT, JCF*

The Crow 🐾🐾🐾◁

Martial arts meets the supernatural, spawning a box office winner and a hit soundtrack. Revenge-fantasy finds Eric Draven (Lee) resurrected on Devil's Night, a year after his death, in order to avenge his own murder and that of his girlfriend. 90% of the scenes are at night, in the rain, or both, and it's not easy to tell what's going on (a blessing considering the violence level). Very dark, but with good performances, particularly from Lee (son of Bruce), in his last role before an unfortunate accident on the set killed him. That footage has been destroyed, but use of a stunt double and camera trickery allowed for the movie's completion. Film was dedicated to Lee and his fiance Eliza. Based on the comic strip by James O'Barr. The video release includes Lee's final interview. **Hound Advisory:** Profanity; brutality; drug use.
1993 (R/*Sr. High-Adult*) 100m/C Brandon Lee, Ernie Hudson, Michael Wincott, David Patrick Kelly, Rochelle Davis, Angel David, Michael Massee, Bai Ling, Lawrence Mason, Bill Raymond, Marco Rodriguez, Anna Thomson, Sofia Shinas, Jon Polito, Tony Todd; *D:* Alex Proyas; *W:* David J. Schow, John Shirley; *M:* Graeme Revell. **VHS, LV** *BVV*

The Crush 🐾◁

Wealthy 14-year-old temptress Silverstone (in her debut) develops an obsessive crush on handsome 28-year-old Elwes, who rents her family's guest house. In an attempt to win his heart, she rewrites his poorly composed magazine articles. This doesn't convince him they should mate for life, so she sabotages his apartment to vent her rage. Sound familiar? The plot's lifted right out of "Fatal Attraction" and Shapiro doesn't offer viewers anything inventively different. He does manage to substitute new methods for the spurned lover to snare her prey. Limp plot might have been exciting if we hadn't seen it so many times before. **Hound Advisory:** Profanity; violence; brief nudity.
1993 (R/*Sr. High-Adult*) 89m/C Cary Elwes, Alicia Silverstone, Jennifer Rubin, Kurtwood Smith, Gwynyth Walsh, Amber Benson; *D:* Alan Shapiro; *W:* Alan Shapiro; *M:* Graeme Revell. **VHS, Beta, LV** *WAR*

Crusoe 🐾🐾◁

Lushly photographed version of the Daniel Defoe adventure classic that rethinks its title character; Crusoe is now an arrogant 1808 slave trader - disliked by even his own crew - who gets shipwrecked on an African island populated by unfriendly natives. When one warrior (not nicknamed Friday) saves his life, Crusoe adjusts his attitude a bit toward the darker-skinned races. With long, dialogue-free passages, it's a thoughtful, occasionally harsh spectacle. From the cinematographer of "The Black Stallion," but child viewers could be alternately bored or alarmed. **Hound Advisory:** Brutality, with human sacrifice (featuring slit throats and decapitation) are among the rituals of a hostile tribe.
1989 (PG-13/*Jr. High-Adult*) 94m/C Aidan Quinn, Ade Sapara, Jimmy Nail, Timothy Spall, Colin Bruce, Michael Higgins, Shane Rimmer, Hepburn Grahame; *D:* Caleb Deschanel; *W:* Walon Green, Christopher Logue; *M:* Michael Kamen. **VHS, Beta, LV** *NO*

Cry-Baby 🐾🐾🐾

Hilarious homage and spoof of "Grease" - stained '50s teen-rock-rebel melodramas. Waters made his name via strange cult faves rather than general audience efforts, but if you've got a weird and savvy family try this high-energy musical about the school delinquent (Depp, with a nearly full-scale electric chair tattooed on his chest) who romances a blonde debutante princess. Sure, the story's weak, but dig the dancing, cute/grotesque cast and the tribute to Elvis. **Hound Advisory:** Sicko touches in the Waters manner, from a romantic opening set during a class vaccination to a finale that glorifies the deadly auto competition of 'chicken.' Loving teen couple has babies out of wedlock at awkward moments and the lone swear word is the centerpiece of a great gag.
1990 (PG-13/*Jr. High-Adult*) 85m/C Johnny Depp, Amy Locane, Polly Bergen, Traci Lords, Ricki Lake, Iggy Pop, Susan Tyrrell, Patty Hearst, Kim McGuire, Darren E. Burrows, Troy Donahue, Willem Dafoe, David Nelson, Mink Stole, Joe Dallesandro, Joey Heatherton, Robert Walsh; *D:* John Waters; *W:* John Waters; *M:* Patrick Williams. **VHS, Beta, LV** $19.95 *MCA*

Cry from the Mountain 🐾🐾

Family drama from the Billy Graham ministry shows a father and teen son on an Alaskan kayak trip so adulterous dad can break the news of his impending divorce. Mishap strands them with a mountain man who relies on his faith to get by in the wilderness. Meanwhile back in the city, bitter mom has her own turmoil. Truncated pic raises important issues, but leaves the resolution up to the viewer; instead of an ending, Graham appears with words of inspiration.
1985 (PG/*Family*) 78m/C James Cavan, Wes Parker, Rita Walter, Chris Kidd, Coleen Gray, Jerry Ballew, Allison Argo, Glen Alsworth, Myrna Kidd; *D:* James F. Collier. **VHS, Beta, LV** $59.95 *LIV*

A Cry in the Wild 🐾🐾🐾

Fourteen-year-old Brian, still hurting from his parents' splitup, is about to visit his father when the chartered plane crashes, leaving the boy as the lone survivor. He must learn to sustain himself alone in the wilderness. Strong acting from Rushton, good pacing, and fine nature photography make a well-used story work again. Award-winning writer Gary Paulsen helped adapt his elemental novel "Hatchet." Sequel: "White Wolves: A Cry in the Wild 2." **Hound Advisory:** Salty language, violence, mature themes.
1990 (PG/*Jr. High-Adult*) 93m/C Jared Rushton, Ned Beatty, Pamela Sue Martin, Stephen Meadows; *D:* Mark Griffiths. **VHS** $14.95 *MGM*

Crystalstone 🐾🐾

In 1908 coastal Spain two kids seek a legendary gem but realize their long-lost father is their real treasure. Handsome but stiff children's adventure, sorely lacking in personality and spontaneity, with some real gloom and doom elements. **Hound Advisory:** Violence, macabre stuff includes a shot of bugs erupting from the face of an exhumed corpse.
1988 (PG/*Family*) 103m/C Frank Grimes, Kamlesh Gupta, Laura Jane Goodwin, Sydney Bromley; *D:* Antonio Pelaez. **VHS, Beta** $79.98 *MCG*

Culpepper Cattle Co. 🐾🐾◁

Sometimes harsh but instructive, realistic western adventure about a naive teenager who wants to be a cowboy. He gets his chance, joining a cattle drive as a cook's helper, but the truth about life on the range turns out to be rougher and less romantic than he expected. Compare/contrast with "City Slickers." **Hound Advisory:** Violence; mature themes.
1972 (PG/*Jr. High-Adult***)** 92m/C Gary Grimes, Billy Green Bush, Bo Hopkins, Charles Martin Smith, Geoffrey Lewis; **D:** Dick Richards; **M:** Jerry Goldsmith. **VHS, Beta $19.98** *FOX*

Curious George

Each of the two tapes in this set contain six five-minute stories featuring the lovable monkey created by H. A. and Margaret Rey. Additional volumes available.
1988 (*Primary***)** 30m/C VHS **$49.95** *RHU*

Curley 🐾🐾

After Hal Roach's "Our Gang" series was phased out in the early '40s (by new owners MGM), Roach launched another kiddie comedy team - in color now - with this very minor short feature in which Curley and his Little Rascals lookalikes play pranks on a teacher. Also known as "The Adventures of Curley and His Gang"; follow-up "Curley and His Gang in the Haunted Mansion" is also on video as "Who Killed Doc Robbin?"
1947 (*Family***)** 53m/C Larry Olsen, Frances Rafferty, Eilene Janssen, Walter Abel; **D:** Bernard Carr. **VHS, Beta $19.95** *DVT, NOS, HHT*

Curly Sue 🐾🐾

Adorable, homeless waif Curly Sue and her con-man guardian Bill plot to rip off a prosperous female attorney for extra cash. But all heartstrings are tugged, and the trio develop a warm, caring relationship. Throwback to the Depression era's Shirley Temple formula films, done by the very modern family filmmaker John Hughes ("Uncle Buck," "Home Alone"), whose wit trails off once the schmaltz starts showing. Available in widescreen format on laserdisc. **Hound Advisory:** Salty language.
1991 (PG/*Family***)** 102m/C James Belushi, Kelly Lynch, Alison Porter, John Getz, Fred Dalton Thompson; **D:** John Hughes; **W:** John Hughes; **M:** Georges Delerue. **VHS, Beta, LV, 8mm $19.98** *WAR, CCB*

Curly Top 🐾🐾◁

Aptly named title character is an orphan (no occupation was deadlier than being one of Shirley's biological parents in a '30s film) who charms a millionaire, then plays matchmaker between the rich man and her beautiful sister. Along the way the heroine sings one of her standards, "Animal Crackers in My Soup."
1935 (*Family***)** 74m/B Shirley Temple, John Boles, Rochelle Hudson, Jane Darwell, Esther Dale, Arthur Treacher, Rafaela Ottiano; **D:** Irving Cummings. **VHS, Beta $19.98** *FOX, MLT*

Curse of the Pink Panther 🐾🐾

Clifton Sleigh, an inept New York City detective played by Wass, is assigned to find the missing Inspector Clouseau. His efforts are complicated by an assortment of gangsters and aristocrats who cross paths with the detective. So-so attempt to keep popular series going after Seller's death. Niven's last film. **Hound Advisory:** Profanity, violence, nudity, scatalogical humor.
1983 (PG/*Jr. High-Adult***)** 110m/C Ted Wass, David Niven, Robert Wagner, Herbert Lom, Joanna Lumley, Capucine, Robert Loggia, Harvey Korman, Leslie Ash, Denise Crosby; **D:** Blake Edwards; **W:** Blake Edwards; **M:** Henry Mancini. **VHS, Beta $14.95** *MGM*

The Cutting Edge 🐾🐾◁

Kate's a spoiled figure skater who can't keep a partner. Doug's a cocky ex-hockey player who thinks figure skating is for wimps. Naturally they team up together and fall in love. Plot's on thin ice as it revolves around their quest for Olympic gold, but the sparks fly between the actors, allowing the upbeat sports romance to work. You'll be tempted to utter "Toepick," at an appropriate moment.
1992 (PG/*Jr. High-Family***)** 101m/C D.B. Sweeney, Moira Kelly, Roy Dotrice, Terry O'Quinn, Dwier Brown, Rachelle Ottley, Jo Jo Starbuck; **D:** Paul Michael Glaser; **W:** Tony Gilroy; **M:** Patrick Williams. **VHS, LV $19.98** *MGM*

Cyrano de Bergerac 🐾🐾🐾🐾

Depardieu brings to exhilarating life Rostand's well-loved play about the brilliant but grotesque-looking swordsman/poet, afraid of nothing - except declaring his love to the beautiful Roxanne. One of France's costliest modern productions, a multi-award winner for its cast, costumes, music and sets. English subtitles (by Anthony Burgess) brilliantly capture the intricate rhymes of the original French dialogue. A rollicking, swashbuckling exploration of emotions at their most noble. **Hound Advisory:** Mature themes, violence.
1990 (PG/*Jr. High-Adult***)** 135m/C Gerard Depardieu, Jacques Weber, Anne Brochet, Vincent Perez, Roland Bertin, Josiane Stoleru, Phillipe Volter, Philippe Morier-Genoud, Pierre Maguelon; **D:** Jean-Paul Rappeneau; **W:** Jean-Claude Carriere, Jean-Paul Rappeneau. **Award Nominations:** Academy Awards '90: Best Actor (Depardieu), Best Art Direction/Set Decoration, Best Foreign Language Film, Best Makeup; **Awards:** Academy Awards '90: Best Costume Design; Cannes Film Festival '90: Best Actor (Depardieu); Cesar Awards '91: Best Actor (Depardieu), Best Director (Rappeneau), Best Film, Best Supporting Actor (Weber). **VHS, LV $19.98** *ORI, FCT, BTV*

D2: The Mighty Ducks 🐾🐾

When an injury forces Gordon (Estevez) out of the minor leagues, he is tapped by promotor Tibbles (Tucker) to coach Team U.S.A. in the Junior Goodwill Games. Upon arriving in LA, the coach's head is turned by the money to be made in endorsements, and he soon gets a lesson in character building (hey, it's Disney). The duck redux premise is lame, but kids will appreciate the hockey action that made the first "Bad News Bears" on ice a hit. **Hound Advisory:** Roughhousing; salty language.
1994 (PG/*Jr. High-Adult***)** 107m/C Emilio Estevez, Michael Tucker, Jan Rubes, Kathryn Erbe, Shaun Weiss, Kenan Thompson, Ty O'Neal; *Cameos:* Kristi Yamaguchi, Kareem Abdul-Jabbar, Wayne Gretzky; **D:** Sam Weisman; **W:** Steven Brill; **M:** J.A.C. Redford. **VHS $19.99** *DIS*

Da 🐾🐾◁

A middle-aged man returns to Ireland for his father's funeral. As he sorts out his father's belongings, his father returns as a ghostly presence to chat with him about life, death, and their own relationship. Based on the Hugh Leonard play with Hughes recreating his Tony-award winning role. **Hound Advisory:** Profanity.

1988 (**PG**/*Jr. High-Adult*) 102m/C Barnard Hughes, Martin Sheen, William Hickey, Hugh O'Conor; **D:** Matt Clark; **W:** Hugh Leonard; **M:** Elmer Bernstein. **VHS, Beta, LV** *NO*

Dad 𝄞𝄞◁

Hoping to make up for lost time, a busy executive rushes home to take care of his father who has just had a heart attack. What could have easily become sappy is made bittersweet by the convincing performances of Lemmon and Danson. Based on the novel by William Wharton.

1989 (**PG**/*Jr. High-Adult*) 117m/C Jack Lemmon, Ted Danson, Ethan Hawke, Olympia Dukakis, Kathy Baker, Zakes Mokae, J.T. Walsh, Kevin Spacey, Chris Lemmon; **D:** Gary David Goldberg; **W:** Gary David Goldberg; **M:** James Horner. **Award Nominations:** Academy Awards '89: Best Makeup; **Awards:** National Media Owl Awards '90: First Prize. **VHS, Beta, LV** **$19.95** *MCA*

Daddy Long Legs

Animated version of Jean Webster's story about an orphaned girl who is sent to school by an anonymous benefactor.

1982 (*Preschool-Primary*) 60m/C **VHS, Beta** *VES, LIV*

Daffy Duck's Movie: Fantastic Island 𝄞𝄞

Fourth of a series of feature-length collections of classic Warner Brothers cartoons, starring Daffy Duck, Speedy Gonzales, Bugs Bunny, Porky Pig, Sylvester and Tweety, the Professor and Mary Anne - wait a minute, that's the wrong island. Daffy adopts the format of the TV show "Fantasy Island" to present these clips, but it's clear that the supply of above-average material is running dry.

1983 (**G**/*Family*) 78m/C **D:** Friz Freleng. **VHS, Beta, LV** **$14.95** *WAR, FCT, WTA*

Daffy Duck's Quackbusters 𝄞𝄞𝄞

Daffy, with help from pals Bugs and Porky, sets up his own "ghostbusting" service. Good compilation of old classics such as "Night of the Living Duck," plus a new feature, "The Duxcorcist," horror spoofs all, but never in bad taste. Video is also available in Spanish.

1989 (**G**/*Family*) 79m/C **D:** Greg Ford, Terry Lennon; **V:** Mel Blanc. **VHS, Beta, LV** **$14.95** *WAR, FCT, APD*

Dakota 𝄞𝄞

Trouble-prone teen biker is released to the custody of a farmer who needs extra help. Dakota proves his worth, fixing the car, romancing the daughter, and lending confidence to a crippled 12-year-old boy. Aspires to wholesome, positive values, but it's still bland melodrama. **Hound Advisory:** Roughhousing, alcohol use.

1988 (**PG**/*Jr. High-Adult*) 96m/C Lou Diamond Phillips, Dee Dee Norton, Eli Cummins, Herta Ware; **D:** Fred Holmes. **VHS, Beta, LV** **$89.99** *HBO*

Dances with Wolves 𝄞𝄞𝄞◁

The story of a U.S. Army soldier, circa 1870, whose heroism in battle allows him his pick of posts. His choice, to see the West before it disappears, changes his life. He meets, understands and eventually becomes a member of a Lakota Sioux tribe in the Dakotas. Costner's first directorial attempt proves him a talent of vision and intelligence. This sometimes too objective movie lacks a sense of definitive character, undermining its gorgeous scenery and interesting perspective on the plight of Native Americans. Lovely music and epic proportions. Adapted by Blake from his novel. **Hound Advisory:** Violence; salty language; mature themes.

1990 (**PG-13**/*Jr. High-Adult*) 181m/C Kevin Costner, Mary McDonnell, Graham Greene, Rodney Grant, Floyd "Red Crow" Westerman, Tantoo Cardinal, Robert Pastorelli, Charles Rocket, Maury Chaykin, Jimmy Herman, Nathan Lee Chasing His Horse, Wes Studi; **D:** Kevin Costner; **W:** Michael Blake; **M:** John Barry. **Award Nominations:** Academy Awards '90: Best Actor (Costner), Best Art Direction/Set Decoration, Best Costume Design, Best Supporting Actor (Greene), Best Supporting Actress (McDonnell), Best Original Score; **Awards:** Academy Awards '90: Best Adapted Screenplay, Best Cinematography, Best Director (Costner), Best Film Editing, Best Picture, Best Sound, Best Score; Directors Guild of America Awards '90: Best Director (Costner); Golden Globe Awards '91: Best Director (Costner), Best Film—Drama, Best Screenplay; National Board of Review Awards '90: 10 Best Films of the Year, Best Director (Costner). **VHS, Beta, LV** **$14.98** *ORI, FCT, IME*

The Dancing Frog

Animation of Quentin Blake's story of George the dancing frog.

1989 (*Preschool-Primary*) 30m/C **VHS** **$14.95** *WTA*

Danger Mouse, Vol. 1

British cartoon takeoff on the BBC secret-agent series of yore, "Danger Man." Here it's a fearless rodent (with an eyepatch) who matches wits against the wicked Baron Greenback. Additional volumes available.

1982 (*Family*) 60m/C **VHS, Beta** **$14.95** *HBO, WTA*

Daniel and the Towers 𝄞𝄞𝄞◁

Part of the "Wonderworks" PBS TV series, this semi-factual tale spotlights the incredible, enigmatic glass towers built in Watts, California, by resident Sam Rodia. Through the device of a (fictional) boy Daniel who goes to work for Sam, the story teaches valuable lessons about beauty and determination - though not much about the real-life Rodia, who remains something of a mystery.

199? (*Family*) 58m/C Allan Arbus, Michael McKean, Carmen Zapata, Miguel Alamo. **VHS** **$29.95** *PME, BTV*

Danny 𝄞𝄞

Predictable girl-and-her-horse drama with a few charms, as a lonely 12-year-old stable hand who cares for an injured show-jumping steed spurned by a spoiled rich child.

1979 (**G**/*Family*) 90m/C Rebecca Page, Janet Zarish, Barbara Jean Earhardt, Gloria Maddox, George Luce; **D:** Gene Feldman. **VHS, Beta** **$59.95** *MON, WOM, HHE*

Darby O'Gill & the Little People 𝄞𝄞𝄞◁

Roguish old Darby tumbles into a well and visits the King of the Leprechauns, who agrees to grant him three wishes. Wonderful Disney production, and the first done by longtime Disney live-action director Stevenson; he gives it a rich Irish

flavor (leading man Sharpe was recruited from the Broadway cast of "Finian's Rainbow"), terrific special effects, wit, charm and an ounce or two of genuine chills. **Hound Advisory:** Alcohol use, and scary stuff - the Death Coach and the Banshee are not soon forgotten.
1959 (G/*Family*) 93m/C Albert Sharpe, Janet Munro, Sean Connery, Estelle Winwood; *D:* Robert Stevenson. **VHS, Beta, LV $19.99** *DIS*

Daredevils of the Red Circle

Three stunt flyers set out to free a man held captive by an escaped convict in this 12-episode Republic serial.
1938 (*Family*) 195m/B Charles Quigley, Bruce (Herman Brix) Bennett, Carole Landis; *D:* John English, William Witney. **VHS $59.95** *REP, VCN, MLB*

Daring Dobermans 🐾🐾

In this sequel to "The Doberman Gang," the barking bank robbers have a new set of outlaw masters. Young Indian boy who loves the dogs enters the picture and may thwart their perfect crime. Dobermaniacs may also want to check out the G-rated "Amazing Dobermans."
1973 (PG/*Family*) 88m/C Charles Robinson, Tim Considine, David Moses, Claudio Martinez, Joan Caulfield; *D:* Byron Ross Chudnow. **VHS, Beta $59.98** *FOX*

The Dark Crystal 🐾🐾🐾

In the 1980s many filmmakers tried to do the ultimate fantasy epic set in a world like no other but combining the mythology of all others etc. Funny thing is, all ended up looking like "Star Wars" anyway. Here's the Jim Henson creature-factory contribution, acted entirely by original Muppets. To defeat the vulture-like Skesis, whose sorcery rules their land, the two surviving Gelflings (elf/fairy/Rebecca DeMornay lookalikes) must insert shard A in slot B on the title gem. An ancient prophecy tells you up front they'll succeed, so there's nothing to do but boggle at the imaginative sets and incredible creature designs by Brian Froud. **Hound Advisory:** Emphasis is on the strange and grotesque rather than the truly frightening. Various characters get killed but are magically resurrected straightaway.
1982 (PG/*Primary-Adult*) 93m/C *D:* Jim Henson; *M:* Trevor Jones. **VHS, Beta, LV** *NO*

Dark Horse 🐾🐾🐾

Gushy, sentimental family film about troubled teen Allison, sentenced after a reckless-driving mishap to community service on a horse farm. She enjoys it, and bonds with a seemingly untameable show-jumping steed. Midway through, however, tragedy strikes, and a girl-and-her-horse tale turns into a tearjerker about trauma and recovery. Meyers holds on gracefully astride the bucking bronco of a plot, playing a demanding (and sometimes unsympathetic) role. **Hound Advisory:** Salty language, alcohol use.
1992 (PG/*Jr. High-Adult*) 98m/C Ari Meyers, Mimi Rogers, Ed Begley Jr., Donovan Leitch, Samantha Eggar; *D:* David Hemmings. **VHS $19.98** *LIV, MOV, FCT*

Darkest Africa

The very first Republic Pictures serial, and regarded by some as the best, a vehicle for real-life animal trainer Clyde Beatty. He plays himself, an adventurer/explorer on the trail of a lost city and strange, prehistoric creatures (including 'batmen' who have nothing to do with Bruce Wayne). In 15 fast-paced chapters.
1936 (*Family*) 270m/B Clyde Beatty, Manuel King, Elaine Shepard; *D:* Joseph Kane, B. Reeves Eason. **LV $49.98** *REP, MOV*

Darkman 🐾🐾🐾

Raimi's tale of a disfigured man who seeks revenge is comicbook kitsch cross-pollinated with a strain of gothic horror. Neeson plays a scientist who's on the verge of discovering the key to cloning body parts; brutally attacked by the henchmen of a crooked politico, his lab is destroyed and he's left for dead. Turns out he's not dead - just horribly disfigured and a wee bit chafed - and he stalks his deserving victims from the shadows, using his lab know-how to disguise his rugged bad looks. Exquisitely violent. Montage by Pablo Ferro. **Hound Advisory:** Brutality and violence.
1990 (R/*Sr. High-Adult*) 96m/C Liam Neeson, Frances McDormand, Larry Drake, Colin Friels, Nelson Mashita, Jenny Agutter, Rafael H. Robledo; *D:* Sam Raimi; *W:* Sam Raimi, Ivan Raimi; *M:* Danny Elfman. **VHS, Beta, LV $19.95** *MCA, CCB*

D.A.R.Y.L. 🐾🐾🐾

Boy found by the side of the road is too polite, too honest, and too smart. Taken in by a childless couple, Daryl is told by a kid pal the necessities of imperfection (if you don't want the grownups to bother you too much), and he becomes more like a real child. But he's actually a lost top-secret military project, a computer brain in a cloned body. Intriguing parental "Twilight Zone" situation doesn't hold up to the finale, but offers some thrills thanks to straightfaced treatment by "Free Willy" director Wincer. **Hound Advisory:** Salty language, sex talk.
1985 (PG/*Family*) 100m/C Mary Beth Hurt, Michael McKean, Barret Oliver, Colleen Camp; *D:* Simon Wincer; *W:* David Ambrose, Allan Scott; *M:* Marvin Hamlisch. **VHS, Beta, LV $14.95** *PAR*

Date with an Angel 🐾🐾🐾

Angel with busted wing crash lands into a swimming pool. Aspiring musician about to marry into rich stuffy family fishes her out and is soon overwhelmed by her grace and beauty, though certainly not by the manuscript masquerading as a script. Soon he finds himself questioning his upcoming wedding to Cates, a cosmetic mogul's daughter. Annoying surplus of sentiment and cuteness, though beauteous Beart is convincingly angelic. **Hound Advisory:** Profanity.
1987 (PG/*Jr. High-Adult*) 114m/C Emmanuelle Beart, Michael E. Knight, Phoebe Cates, David Dukes, Bibi Besch, Albert Macklin, David Hunt, Michael Goodwin; *D:* Tom McLoughlin. **VHS, Beta, LV $19.99** *HBO*

Dave 🐾🐾🐾

Regular guy Dave Kovic (Kline) is a dead ringer for hypocritical (politically sensitive) President (Kline), launching him into the White House after the prez suffers a stroke in

Muppet magic in "The Dark Crystal" (1982)

embarrassing (adultery) circumstances. Langella is the evil political chief of staff who's arranged the switch and hopes to be the power behind the throne, while Grodin is the little guy accountant who helps Dave write the national budget. Weaver is just fine as the first lady hardened to her husband's personal and political deficiencies who is slowly attracted by his sudden aspirations to goodness. Timely fable is a seamless comedy prompting small chuckles and the occasional hearty laugh, inspiring the feel-good faith that as long as we subvert the standard political process, government works. Political cameos abound: look for real-life Senators Alan Simpson, Paul Simon, Howard Metzenbaum, Tom Harkin, and Christopher Dodd as well as the commentators from TV's "The McLaughlin Group," and Stone, poking fun at himself on "Larry King Live," as he tries to convince the public about the conspiracy. **Hound Advisory:** Profanity; sex talk; brief nudity.
1993 (PG-13/*Jr. High-Adult*) 110m/C Kevin Kline, Sigourney Weaver, Frank Langella, Kevin Dunn, Ving Rhames, Ben Kingsley, Charles Grodin, Faith Prince, Laura Linney, Bonnie Hunt, Parley Baer, Stefan Gierasch, Anna Deavere Smith, Bonnie Bartlett; *Cameos:* Oliver Stone, Arnold Schwarzenegger, Jay Leno, Larry King; *D:* Ivan Reitman; *W:* Gary Ross; *M:* James Newton Howard. **VHS, Beta, LV** $95.99 *WAR, BTV, FCT*

Davey and Goliath

Vintage television stars young Davey and his talking dog Goliath star in five stop-motion adventures that convey moral teachings. Additional volumes available.
19?? (*Preschool-Primary*) 70m/C **VHS** $34.95 *WTA,*

David and Goliath

Animated biblical tale of the young shepherd and future kind, and his battle with a giant is retold.
1992 (*Preschool-Primary*) 30m/C **VHS** $12.98 *MVD, BMG*

David and Lisa 🎬🎬🎬

Director Perry won an Oscar for this sensitive independently produced adaption of Theodore Isaac Rubin's fact-based novel. In a halfway house for mentally ill kids, a schizophrenic young man and a childlike teenage girl form a delicate bond that strengthens each one on the path to recovery. Excellent performances throughout in this sleeper. **Hound Advisory:** Mature themes, sex talk.
1962 (*Jr. High-Adult*) 94m/B Keir Dullea, Janet Margolin, Howard da Silva, Neva Patterson, Clifton James; *D:* Frank Perry. **VHS, Beta, LV** $69.95 *COL, MRV*

David and the Magic Pearl 🎬🎬

Animated feature follows David, a Chicago kid, who finds himself in the middle of a jungle, creating a different kind of anxiety for him.
1990 (*Preschool-Primary*) 75m/C *D:* Wieslaw Zieba. **VHS** $39.95 *CEL, WTA*

David Copperfield 🎬🎬🎬🎬

Superior and faithful adaptation of Charles Dickens' great novel. David, an orphan grows to manhood in Victorian England as a wide variety of mentors, friends and foes help and harm. Terrific acting by Bartholomew (one of the best child actors of the '30s), not to mention Fields, Rathbone, and

all the rest. Lavish production, lovingly filmed - a fine example of what happens when the Hollywood system actually worked right.
1935 (*Family*) 132m/B Lionel Barrymore, W.C. Fields, Freddie Bartholomew, Maureen O'Sullivan, Basil Rathbone, Lewis Stone, Frank Lawton, Madge Evans, Roland Young, Edna May Oliver, Lennox Pawle, Elsa Lanchester, Una O'Connor, Arthur Treacher; *D:* George Cukor; *W:* Howard Estabrook, Hugh Walpole; *M:* Herbert Stothart. **Award Nominations:** Academy Awards '35: Best Film Editing; Academy Awards '36: Best Picture; **Awards:** National Board of Review Awards '35: 10 Best Films of the Year. **VHS, Beta, LV** $19.98 *MGM*

David Copperfield 🎬🎬🎬

British made-for-TV production of the Dickens classic takes a more mature approach to the material. Begins with the melancholy, grownup David, then flashes back to the childhood friendships, rivalries, loves and disappointments that made him such a mopey young man. The added material, however, fails to highlight any one character as had the successful 1935 MGM version. Exceptional cast and photography do much to redeem the effort.
1970 (*Family*) 118m/C Richard Attenborough, Cyril Cusack, Edith Evans, Pamela Franklin, Susan Hampshire, Wendy Hiller, Ron Moody, Laurence Olivier; *D:* Delbert Mann; *M:* Malcolm Arnold. **VHS** *FOX*

David the Gnome

Animated series about a gnome teaching various anthropomorphic animals important lessons about life, based on the bestselling gnome tomes by Rien Poortvliet and Wil Huygen. See "The World of David the Gnome" for complete episodes of this cable-TV series.
1987 (*Preschool-Primary*) 45m/C **VHS, Beta** $14.95 *LIV, FHE*

Davy Crockett

Tall tale about frontier hero Davy Crockett—half alligator, half snapping turtle, and a little bit of earthquake. Part of the "Rabbit Ears: American Heroes and Legends" storytelling series.
1992 (*Family*) 30m/C **VHS** $9.95 *BTV*

Davy Crockett and the River Pirates 🎬🎬🎬🎬

After "Davy Crockett, King of the Wild Frontier" became a surprise sensation Disney delivered a sequel (despite having killed off their hero in the original!) by splicing together more TV episodes covering Davy's life long before the Alamo. So maybe it's a prequel, but whatever - adventure is a much more coherent and grandly entertaining effort, chronicling the friendly rivalry between our frontier hero and blustery Mike Fink, the King of the Ohio River. The bigger-than-life pair duel in a furious keelboat race, and then unite against a bandit gang masquerading as Indians and threatening the territories. **Hound Advisory:** Violence, alcohol use.
1956 (G/*Family*) 81m/C Fess Parker, Buddy Ebsen, Jeff York; *D:* Norman Foster. **VHS, Beta, LV** *DIS, OM*

Davy Crockett, King of the Wild Frontier 🎬🎬🎬

Walt Disney himself was surprised when special episodes of his TV show devoted to the life of Davy Crockett -

technically, the very first miniseries - became a smash with '50s kids. Still rousing, this theatrical version blends the segments, covering Davy's days as an Indian fighter (some queasy moments, by modern standards, as the hero wipes out swarms of "those red hornets"), his days in Congress (fighting for, ironically, Indian rights), to his last gallant stand in defense of the Alamo (note how Davy's demise was edited out, by popular demand). Ebsen was to play the lead, then got reassigned to sidekick when Disney discovered the then-unknown Parker. Soundtrack includes the million-selling "Ballad of Davy Crockett," plus a lesser-known love song actually written by the frontiersman. **Hound Advisory:** Abundant violence makes the retroactive PG rating well-earned.
1955 (PG/*Family*) 93m/C Fess Parker, Buddy Ebsen, Hans Conried, Ray Whiteside, Pat Hogan, William "Billy" Bakewell, Basil Ruysdael, Kenneth Tobey; **D:** Norman Foster. **VHS, Beta $19.99** DIS, BTV

A Day at the Races 🎬🎬🎬♪

Marx Brothers madness, with the congenitally lame and way overlong plot concerning veterinarian Groucho's attempt to buy his own hospital by making a fortune betting on the horse races. Some absolutely sidesplitting comic scenes, but also slow spots and numerous boring musical numbers that require the use of the fast-forward button. ♫A Message from the Man in the Moon; On Blue Venetian Waters; Tomorrow is Another Day; All God's Chillun Got Rhythm.
1937 (*Family*) 111m/B Groucho Marx, Harpo Marx, Chico Marx, Sig Rumann, Douglass Dumbrille, Margaret Dumont, Allan Jones, Maureen O'Sullivan; **D:** Sam Wood. **VHS, Beta, LV $19.95** MGM, CCB

A Day for Thanks on Walton's Mountain 🎬🎬

Many of the original television-show cast members returned for this sentimental Thanksgiving reunion on Walton's Mountain.
1982 (*Family*) 97m/C Ralph Waite, Ellen Corby, Judy Norton-Taylor, Eric Scott, Jon Walmsley, Robert Wightman, Mary McDonough, David W. Harper, Kami Cotler, Joe Conley, Ronnie Clair Edwards, Richard Gilliland, Melinda Naud; **D:** Harry Harris. **VHS $19.98** WAR

A Day in October 🎬🎬♪

Niels Jensen (Sweeney) is a Danish resistance fighter fighting in Copenhagen as the Nazis prepare to invade Denmark in 1943. During a sabotage attempt he's injured and rescued by Sara, a young Jewish woman. Her family reluctantly hides the young man as they finally face up to the Nazi reality. Based on historical fact. Good performances help what is otherwise an average script. Filmed on location in Denmark. **Hound Advisory:** Violence; mature themes.
1992 (PG-13/*Jr. High-Adult*) 96m/C D.B. Sweeney, Kelly Wolf, Tovah Feldshuh, Daniel Benzali, Ole Lemmeke, Kim Romer, Anders Peter Bro, Lars Oluf Larsen; **D:** Kenneth Madsen; **W:** Damian F. Slattery; **M:** Jens Lysdal. **VHS $89.95** ACA, FOX

The Day Jimmy's Boa Ate the Wash and Other Stories

Contains four animated stories adapted from popular children's books. The title story finds Jimmy bringing his favorite pet on a class trip. "Monty" features an overworked alligator who needs a rest from his taxi service. "The Great White Man-Eating Shark" and "Fourteen Rats and a Rat-Catcher" impart life's little lessons in a humorous way.
1992 (*Preschool-Primary*) 35m/C **VHS $14.95** CCC, WKV, BTV

The Day of the Dolphin 🎬🎬

Research scientist, after successfully working out a means of teaching dolphins to talk, finds his animals kidnapped; espionage and assassination are involved. Dolphin voices by Henry, who also wrote the screenplay. **Hound Advisory:** Salty language.
1973 (PG/*Family*) 104m/C George C. Scott, Trish Van Devere, Paul Sorvino, Fritz Weaver, Jon Korkes, John Dehner, Edward Herrmann, Severn Darden; **D:** Mike Nichols; **W:** Buck Henry; **M:** Georges Delerue; **V:** Buck Henry. **Award Nominations:** Academy Awards '73: Best Sound; **Awards:** National Board of Review Awards '73: 10 Best Films of the Year. **VHS, Beta, LV $14.98** SUE, NLC

Daydreamer 🎬🎬🎬

Setting is 1801 Vienna, where young Hans Christian Anderson, always in trouble, runs away from home. In daydreams he imagines - and enters - the fairy tales he would later write down, like "Thumbelina" and "The Emperor's New Clothes." Early Arthur Rankin Jr./Jules Bass production, somewhat crudely integrating live-action and stop-motion animation. Puppet characters lack expression and humanity to match the celebrity voices. One nice touch: animated Hans takes unheroic parts in his fantasies (he's a faithless prince who jilts the Little Mermaid), confronting his own personal flaws.
1966 (*Family*) 98m/C Paul O'Keefe, Ray Bolger, Jack Gilford, Margaret Hamilton; **D:** Jules Bass; **V:** Tallulah Bankhead, Boris Karloff, Burl Ives, Terry-Thomas, Ed Wynn, Victor Borge, Patty Duke. **VHS, Beta $19.98** SUE

Dazed and Confused 🎬🎬🎬

Day in the life of a bunch of high school seniors should prove to be a trip back in time for those coming of age in the 70's. Eight students faced with life after high school have one last hurrah, as they search for Aerosmith tickets and haze the incoming freshmen. Keen characterization by writer/director Linklater captures the spirit of a generation shaped by Watergate, the Vietnam War, feminism, and marijuana. Groovy soundtrack features Alice Cooper, Deep Purple, KISS, and Foghat. **Hound Advisory:** Profanity; marijuana smoking (they inhale); alcohol use; poor role modeling; roughhousing.
1993 (R/*Sr. High-Adult*) 97m/C Jason London, Rory Cochrane, Sasha Jensen, Wiley Wiggins, Michelle Burke, Adam Goldberg, Anthony Rapp, Marissa Ribisi; **D:** Richard Linklater; **W:** Richard Linklater. **VHS, LV** MCA

Dead Men Don't Wear Plaid 🎬🎬♪

Martin is frequently hilarious as a private detective who encounters a bizarre assortment of suspects while trying to find out the truth about a scientist's death. Ingeniously interspliced with clips from old Warner Brothers films, including snippets with Humphrey Bogart, Bette Davis, Alan Ladd, Burt Lancaster, Ava Gardner, Barbara Stanwyck, Ray

Milland and others. With nowhere in particular to go, novel whodunit is lightweight amusement.
1982 (PG/*Primary-Adult*) 89m/B Steve Martin, Rachel Ward, Reni Santoni, George Gaynes, Frank McCarthy, Carl Reiner; **D:** Carl Reiner; **W:** Steve Martin, Carl Reiner; **M:** Miklos Rozsa. **VHS, Beta, LV $14.95** *MCA, FCT, HMV*

Dead Poets Society 🐾🐾🐾

Quirky English teacher inspires boys in a dry 1950s' prep school to pursue inner truth and beauty, resulting in clashes with administrative tyrants and hateful parents. Williams is offscreen more than you'd think; story belongs to the student characters. While their struggles with individuality and creative endeavor are enormously moving, pic sends some really mixed messages (advancing teen suicide as a preferable alternative to a military academy) that make this Disney/ Touchstone release very iffy viewing for youngsters. On the other hand, what other pic even tries to show poetry class as interesting? **Hound Advisory:** Salty language, sex talk, mature themes, roughhousing, alcohol use.
1989 (PG/*Jr. High-Adult*) 128m/C Robin Williams, Ethan Hawke, Robert Sean Leonard, Josh Charles, Gale Hansen, Kurtwood Smith, James Waterson, Dylan Kussman, Lara Flynn Boyle, Melora Hardin; **D:** Peter Weir; **W:** Tom Schulman; **M:** Maurice Jarre. **Award Nominations:** Academy Awards '89: Best Actor (Williams), Best Director (Weir), Best Picture; **Awards:** Academy Awards '89: Best Original Screenplay; British Academy Awards '89: Best Film; Cesar Awards '91: Best Foreign Film. **VHS, Beta, LV, 8mm $19.99** *TOU*

Dear Brigitte 🐾🐾

American boy genius ("Lost in Space" tyke Mumy) has a crush on international sex symbol Brigitte Bardot. He and his flustered family journey to Paris to meet her in person. Outdated early '60s screen sitcom/travelogue, putting a charming cast to a sore test. Based on the novel "Erasmus with Freckles" by John Haase.
1965 (*Family*) 100m/C James Stewart, Billy Mumy, Glynis Johns, Fabian, Cindy Carol, John Williams, Jack Kruschen, Brigitte Bardot, Ed Wynn, Alice Pearce; **D:** Henry Koster; **W:** Hal Kanter. **VHS, Beta $19.98** *FOX*

Death Becomes Her 🐾🐾🐾⊲

Aging actress Streep will do anything to stay young and beautiful, especially when childhood rival Hawn shows up, 200 pounds lighter and out to revenge the loss of her fiance, Streep's henpecked hubby. Doing anything arrives in the form of a Faustian pact and a potion that stops the aging process (and keeps her alive forever). Watch for the hilarious party filled with dead celebrities who all look as good as the day they died. Great special effects and fun performances by Streep and Hawn playing their glamour-girl roles to the hilt add merit to heavy-handed commentary on Hollywood's obsession with beauty and youth. **Hound Advisory:** Profanity; nudity; violence; alcohol use; sex talk.
1992 (PG-13/*Jr. High-Adult*) 105m/C Meryl Streep, Bruce Willis, Goldie Hawn, Isabella Rossellini, Sydney Pollack, Michael Caine, Ian Ogilvy, Adam Storke, Nancy Fish, Alaina Reed Hall, Michelle Johnson, Mimi Kennedy, Jonathan Silverman; **Cameos:** Fabio Lanzoni; **D:** Robert Zemeckis; **W:** Martin Donovan, David Koepp; **M:** Alan Silvestri. **VHS, Beta, LV $95.00** *MGM, PMS*

Death of a Goldfish

Mister Rogers explores with children the difficult subject of death. In the Neighborhood of Make Believe, Lady Aberlin and Bob Dog learn that only living things die.

1974 (*Preschool-Primary*) 30m/C Mr. Rogers. **VHS, Beta $29.95**

Death of the Incredible Hulk 🐾⊲

Last of a series of TV movies based on the Marvel Comics superhero, aired after a "Hulk" TV series had run its course. Here scientist David Banner may have a cure to stop his periodic transformations into the big green guy (Ferrigno). But terrorists are also after the Hulk. Despite the portentous title there was to be a follow-up feature reviving the Hulk, but actor/director Bixby became a real-life casualty of terminal cancer. **Hound Advisory:** Violence.
1990 (*Jr. High-Adult*) 96m/C Bill Bixby, Lou Ferrigno, Elizabeth Gracen, Philip Sterling; **D:** Bill Bixby. **VHS $79.95** *RHI*

Death on the Nile 🐾🐾⊲

Agatha Christie's fictional detective, Hercule Poirot, is called upon to interrupt his vacation to uncover who killed an heiress aboard a steamer cruising down the Nile. Ustinov's first stint as the Belgian sleuth is engaging, though story is overlong and poorly paced. Anthony Powell's costume design won an Oscar.
1978 (PG/*Jr. High-Adult*) 135m/C Peter Ustinov, Jane Birkin, Lois Chiles, Bette Davis, Mia Farrow, David Niven, Olivia Hussey, Angela Lansbury, Jack Warden, Dame Maggie Smith, George Kennedy, Simon MacCorkindale, Harry Andrews, Jon Finch; **D:** John Guillermin; **W:** Anthony Shaffer; **M:** Nino Rota. **VHS, Beta, LV $14.98** *REP*

Deathcheaters 🐾🐾⊲

Proof that a tough-guy action-adventure need not be a profane bloodbath; two Aussie stuntmen accept a Secret Service mission to destroy a warlord's fortress in the Philippines. The twist; both heroes are Vietnam vets - and have since sworn never to kill again. So they don't, and the mission stays well within 'G' territory. Try peddling that concept today! Repetitive, but the punchline is worth it. **Hound Advisory:** Violence, only serious in one Vietnam flashback.
1976 (G/*Family*) 96m/C John Hargreaves, Grant Page, Noel Ferrer; **D:** Brian Trenchard-Smith; **W:** Michael Cove. **VHS, Beta $69.98** *VES*

December 🐾⊲

Four prep-school boys in 1941 New Hampshire hear the first reports of Japanese bombing Pearl Harbor. In one night they debate loyalty, friendship, patriotism, censorship, etc. They never make it to national health policy and the ozone layer, but almost; this terribly stagy and earnestly unconvincing drama signals it's about Big Issues with every anachronistic line, and young protagonists are symbols more than people. **Hound Advisory:** Profanity.
1991 (PG/*Jr. High-Adult*) 92m/C Wil Wheaton, Chris Young, Brian Krause, Balthazar Getty, Jason London; **D:** Gabe Torres; **W:** Gabe Torres. **VHS, LV** *NO*

Defenders of the Earth: The Story Begins

Saturday-morning cartoon compilation bringing together heroic characters from the classic newspaper comic-strip characters syndicated through King Features; Flash Gordon,

Ming the Merciless, the Phantom, and Mandrake the Magician. Additional volumes available.
1986 (*Preschool*) 90m/C **VHS, Beta** *FHE*

Defenders of the Vortex

Animated movie follows the Galaxy Legion as it tries to stop the evil Zoa from gaining control of the Vortex.
1990 (*Family*) 92m/C **VHS, Beta $14.99** *JFK, WTA*

Defense Play ♂♂

Espionage tale about two teens who uncover a Soviet agent stealing plans for advanced helicopter technology (with radio-controlled models as the prototypes; movie budget was cheaper that way). Fair throwback to the Hardy-Boys tradition. **Hound Advisory:** Violence.
1988 (*PG/Primary-Jr. High*) 95m/C David Oliver, Susan Ursitti, Monte Markham, William Frankfather, Patch MacKenzie; *D:* Monte Markham. **VHS, Beta $19.98** *TWE*

The Delicate Delinquent ♂♂♂♂

Lewis (in his first film without longtime partner Dean Martin) plays a naive young bumbler under heavy peer pressure to join the street hoods in his part of town. But with the guidance of a brotherly police officer, the delicate delinquent decides to become a cop instead. Message-laden comedy manages to deliver the laughs anyway; keep in mind this came out in the era of "Rebel Without a Cause," (back when gang members wore suits and ties) and its preachier moments can be forgiven. **Hound Advisory:** Roughhousing.
1956 (*Family*) 101m/B Jerry Lewis, Darren McGavin, Martha Hyer, Robert Ivers, Horace McMahon; *D:* Don McGuire; *W:* Don McGuire. **VHS, Beta, LV $24.95** *PAR*

Delirious ♂♂

A writer for a television soap opera wakes from a bash on the head to find himself inside the story where murder and mayhem are brewing. Can he write himself back to safety, and find romance along the way? Engaging premise is done in by less than radiant writing.
1991 (*PG/Jr. High-Adult*) 96m/C John Candy, Mariel Hemingway, Emma Samms, Raymond Burr, David Rasche, Dylan Baker, Charles Rocket, Jerry Orbach, Renee Taylor, Robert Wagner; *D:* Tom Mankiewicz; *M:* Cliff Eidelman. **VHS, Beta, LV, 8mm $14.95** *MGM*

Dennis the Menace ♂♂♂♂

John Hughes adaptation of the Hank Ketcham comic strip unfairly derided by critics as a "Home Alone" ripoff. Emphasis is instead on the relationship between crafty five-year-old Dennis Mitchell and his cranky neighbor Mr. Wilson (Matthau, perfectly cast), whose every pain and pratfall originates with the well-meaning tyke. This gets the epic treatment usually given Moby Dick and Ahab, and it's often hilarious. Dennis then turns his mischief against a nasty, knife-wielding burglar dubbed Switchblade Sam, featuring some really cruel slapstick of the "Home Alone" variety that's not quite as funny as the director would like it to be. Still better than either "Problem Child." **Hound Advisory:**

Cartoonish violence; child kidnapping; sinister villain with dental problems.
1993 (*PG/Family*) 96m/C Walter Matthau, Mason Gamble, Joan Plowright, Christopher Lloyd, Lea Thompson, Robert Stanton, Billie Bird, Paul Winfield, Amy Sakasitz, Kellen Hathaway, Arnold Stang; *D:* Nick Castle; *W:* John Hughes; *M:* Jerry Goldsmith. **VHS, Beta, LV, 8mm $24.96** *WAR*

Dennis the Menace: Dinosaur Hunter WOOF!

Opportunistic video distributors dug up a best-forgotten 1987 TV feature of Hank Ketchum's comic-strip character, tacked on the subtitle "Dinosaur Hunter," and released it on tape to rip off both "Jurassic Park" and John Hughes' "Dennis the Menace." Even without the deception (the listed running time is phony too!), this is still a loser, a dimwit sitcom with horrid kid actors and no dinosaurs - just prehistoric bones Dennis digs up that threaten to make his neighborhood an archaeological site.
1987 (*G/Family*) 93m/C Victor Dimattia, William Windom, Pat Estrin, Jim Jansen, Patsy Garrett. **VHS, LV $89.95** *VMK*

Dennis the Menace in Mayday for Mother

Animated short that brought Hank Ketcham's comic strip to cartoon life for the first time, centering on Dennis' efforts to celebrate Mother's Day.
1980 (*Family*) 24m/C **VHS, Beta $9.98** *MCA*

Dennis the Menace: Spies, Robbers and Ghosts

"Ghost Blusters" has Dennis wanting to make a club house out of a spooky old home. "The Monster of Mudville Flats" is tracked by Dennis, Tommy, and Margaret, and in "Young Sherlock Dennis," The Menace sets out to find who's been eating all the chocolates. "The Defective Detector" features Dennis and friends hunting treasure on the beach with a metal detector. Additionla volumes available.
1993 (*Family*) 35m/C **VHS $9.98** *FOX, WTA*

Dennis the Movie Star

Dennis the Menace stars in his own group of movies when he is able to convince a director that his old star is no good.
1988 (*Family*) 65m/C **VHS, Beta $14.98** *FOX, WTA*

A Dentist and a Toothfairy

Mr. Rogers explains to kids that visiting the dentist can be a pleasant experience.
1986 (*Primary*) 30m/C Fred Rogers. **VHS, Beta** *NO*

Denver the Last Dinosaur

Magical, gentle dinosaur hatches from a giant egg into the 20th century and makes friends with some skateboarding kids who love rock music. Syndicated cartoon that scored big in the ratings and prompted a series. Additional volumes available.
1988 (*Family*) 45m/C **VHS $19.95** *FRH, WTA*

Desert Bloom 🎬🎬🎬

On the eve of a nuclear bomb test nearby, an alcoholic veteran and his Las Vegas family struggle through tensions brought on by a promiscuous visiting aunt, a mother with a gambling habit, and the chaotic, rapidly changing world. Gish shines as Rose, the teenage daughter through whose eyes the story unfolds. **Hound Advisory:** Mature themes, sex talk, roughhousing, salty language.
1986 (PG/Sr. High-Adult**)** 103m/C Jon Voight, JoBeth Williams, Ellen Barkin, Annabeth Gish, Allen (Gooritz) Garfield, Jay Underwood; **D:** Eugene Corr; **W:** Eugene Corr; **M:** Brad Fiedel. VHS, Beta, LV NO

Desperately Seeking Susan 🎬🎬🎬

Bored New Jersey housewife Arquette gets her kicks reading the personals. When she becomes obsessed with a relationship between two lovers who arrange their meetings through the columns, she decides to investigate the Big Apple and find out for herself who they are. But after a timely whack in the head, she takes on the identity of Susan, the free-spirited woman in the personals. Unfortunately, Susan (Madonna, of course) is in a lot of trouble with all sorts of unsavory folk. Soon our innocent and confused housewife finds herself caught in the middle. Terrific characters, with special appeal generated by Arquette and Madonna. Quinn winningly plays the romantic interest. **Hound Advisory:** Violence; profanity; sex; brief nudity.
1985 (PG-13/Jr. High-Adult**)** 104m/C Rosanna Arquette, Madonna, Aidan Quinn, Mark Blum, Robert Joy, Laurie Metcalf, Steven Wright, John Turturro, Richard Hell, Annie Golden, Ann Magnuson; **D:** Susan Seidelman; **M:** Thomas Newman. VHS, Beta, LV $14.98 FCT

Destroy All Monsters 🎬🎬🎬

When alien babes take control of Godzilla and his monstrous colleagues, it looks like all is lost for Earth. Adding insult to injury, Ghidra is sent in to take care of the loose ends. Can the planet possibly survive this madness? Classic Toho monster slugfest also features Mothra, Rodan, Son of Godzilla, Angila, Varan, Baragon, Spigas and others.
1968 (G/Jr. High-Adult**)** 88m/C Akira Kubo, Jun Tazaki, Yoshio Tsuchiya, Kyoko Ai, Yukiko Kobayashi, Kenji Sahara, Andrew Hughes; **D:** Inoshiro Honda. VHS $18.00 FRG

The Devil & Max Devlin 🎬🎬

Recently deceased Max, a Scroogish landlord, strikes a hellish bargain to be restored to life if he gets three honest young folk to sell their souls to the devil. Targets are an aspiring singer, a motorbike racer, and a kid husband-hunting for his widow mom. But hanging with the goodie-goodies gives Max a change of heart. With a script by "Freaky Friday" author Mary Rodgers, a Disney pedigree and Cosby in a dual role (as a dapper demon and his satanic boss), this should have been fun but instead resides in lethargic limbo.
1981 (PG/Family**)** 95m/C Elliott Gould, Bill Cosby, Susan Anspach, Adam Rich, Julie Budd; **D:** Steven Hilliard Stern; **W:** Jimmy Sangster; **M:** Marvin Hamlisch, Buddy Baker. VHS, Beta DIS, OM

Devil Horse 🎬🎬

A boy's devotion to a wild horse marked for destruction as a killer leads him into trouble. A 12-chapter serial; 13 minutes each.
1932 (Family**)** 156m/B Frankie Darro, Harry Carey Sr., Noah Beery Sr.; **D:** Otto Brower, Richard Talmadge. VHS, Beta $14.95 GPV, VCN, DVT

Dial "M" for Murder 🎬🎬🎬

An unfaithful husband devises an elaborate plan to murder his wife for her money, but when she accidentally stabs the killer-to-be, with scissors no less, he alters his methods. Part of the "A Night at the Movies" series, this tape simulates a 1954 movie evening with a Daffy Duck cartoon, "My Little Duckaroo," a newsreel, and coming attractions for "Them" and "A Star Is Born." Filmed in 3-D. Based on the play by Frederick Knotts.
1954 (Jr. High-Adult**)** 123m/C Ray Milland, Grace Kelly, Robert Cummings, John Williams, Anthony M. (Antonio Margheretti) Dawson; **D:** Alfred Hitchcock; **M:** Dimitri Tiomkin. VHS, Beta, LV $19.98 WAR, TLF

Diamonds are Forever 🎬🎬🎬

For a then record-setting salary of $1.25 million, Connery returned to his Bond role after a one-film absence, delivering an entertaining espionage epic. Agent 007 once again battles his nemesis Blofeld, this time in Las Vegas. Bond must prevent the implementation of a plot to destroy Washington through the use of a space-orbiting laser. Fabulous stunts include Bond's wild drive through the streets of Vegas in a '71 Mach 1. Theme sung by Shirley Bassey. **Hound Advisory:** Violence, alcohol use, suggested sex.
1971 (PG/Jr. High-Adult**)** 120m/C Sean Connery, Jill St. John, Charles Gray, Bruce Cabot, Jimmy Dean, Lana Wood, Bruce Glover, Putter Smith, Norman Burton, Joseph Furst, Bernard Lee, Desmond Llewelyn, Laurence Naismith, Leonard Barr, Lois Maxwell, Margaret Lacey, Joe Robinson, Donna Garrat, Trina Parks; **D:** Guy Hamilton; **W:** Tom Mankiewicz; **M:** John Barry. VHS, Beta, LV $19.98 MGM, TLF

Diamond's Edge 🎬🎬🎬

Adolescent private eye and his brother snoop into the affairs of the late master criminal the Falcon, and find intrigue surrounding his box of malteser candies. Based on scripter Anthony Horowitz's book "The Falcon's Malteser" (ouch!), a sample of the puns and genre-parodying gags to be found in this sly English sendup of hardboiled detective tales, set somewhat jarringly in London and brimming with Briticisms despite the Bogart attitude. A real video hidden treasure, worth investigating. Watch the clue-packed, cartoon opening credits carefully. Originally titled "Just Ask For Diamond." **Hound Advisory:** Roughhousing.
1988 (PG/Family**)** 83m/C Susannah York, Peter Eyre, Patricia Hodge, Nickolas Grace; **D:** Stephen Bayly; **W:** Anthony Horowitz; **M:** Trevor Jones. VHS, Beta $79.99 HBO

Diamonds on Wheels 🎬🎬

A Disney film about three British teenagers, amid a big road rally, discovering stolen diamonds and getting pursued by gangsters.
1973 (Family**)** 84m/C VHS, Beta $69.95 DIS

Dick Deadeye 🦴🦴🦴✄

Offbeat animated feature from the creators of the "Charlie Brown" cartoons but based on the operas of Gilbert and Sullivan and drawings by Ronald Searle. Dick Deadeye sports an I.Q. of zero, but nevertheless is hired to wipe out pirates, thieves, and a sorcerer. Along the way, various G & S songs are presented in rock'n'roll arrangements.
1976 (*Family*) 80m/C *D:* Bill Melendez. VHS, Beta **$29.95** *FHE, WTA, PRS*

Dick Tracy

Comic-strip detective first came to the screen in this early Republic serial, the studio's first of many raids on the funny pages. But they deliberately left out nearly all the supporting cast of Chester Gould's characters - even Tess Trueheart - and the results are mixed, as Tracy takes on a typical bizarrely costumed serial fiend called the Spider. Longer than usual in 15 episodes; exciting first chapter is 30 minutes, the tedious remainders are 20 minutes apiece. Hang on long enough to see the Spider's way-cool airplane.
1937 (*Family*) 310m/B Ralph Byrd, Smiley Burnette, Irving Pichel, Jennifer Jones; *D:* John English. VHS, Beta, LV **$29.95** *SNC, VYY, VCI*

Dick Tracy 🦴🦴🦴

Beatty, as producer/director/star, brings Chester Gould's comic-strip detective to life, outdoing other recent mega-bucks funny-pages adaptations due to amazing art direction. Shot in only seven colors, using timeless sets that capture the printed page rather than the reality of the NYC setting, Beatty gives viewers a memorable spectacle. Alas, plot is a fairly ordinary feud between Tracy and crazed mobster Big Boy Caprice (other classic bad guys like Pruneface, Flattop and the Brow have bit parts). Villains are encased in exaggerated makeup, but Tracy isn't, guaranteeing that he's the least interesting guy onscreen - though a similarly unencumbered Madonna gives a fine performance as the femme fatale Breathless Mahoney, belting out Sondheim's musical numbers. Young Korsmo out acts them both as the nameless 'Kid' the hero adopts. Produced through Disney's Touchstone division. Ironically, though this strives for camp appeal, Gould's work was considered stark and realistic for its time, as the first comic strip to depict dead bodies. **Hound Advisory:** Violence - gunfights and death, but not one drop of blood shown.
1990 (**PG**/*Jr. High-Adult*) 105m/C Warren Beatty, Madonna, Charlie Korsmo, Glenne Headly, Al Pacino, Dustin Hoffman, James Caan, Mandy Patinkin, Paul Sorvino, Charles Durning, Dick Van Dyke, R.G. Armstrong, Catherine O'Hara, Estelle Parsons, Seymour Cassel, Michael J. Pollard, William Forsythe, Kathy Bates, James Tolkan; *D:* Warren Beatty; *W:* Jim Cash, Jack Epps Jr.; *M:* Danny Elfman, Stephen Sondheim. **Award Nominations:** Academy Awards '90: Best Cinematography, Best Costume Design, Best Sound, Best Supporting Actor (Pacino); **Awards:** Academy Awards '90: Best Art Direction/Set Decoration, Best Makeup, Best Song ("Sooner or Later"). VHS, Beta, LV **$19.99** *TOU, FCT, IME*

Dick Tracy, Detective 🦴🦴

The first Dick Tracy feature film, in which Splitface is on the loose, a schoolteacher is murdered, the Mayor is threatened, and a nutty professor uses a crystal ball to give Tracy the clues needed to connect the crimes.
1945 (*Family*) 62m/B Morgan Conway, Anne Jeffreys, Mike Mazurki, Jane Greer, Lyle Latelle; *D:* William Burke. VHS, Beta **$16.95** *SNC, MED, VYY*

Dick Tracy Meets Gruesome 🦴🦴

Gruesome and his partner in crime, Melody, stage a bank robbery using the secret formula of Dr. A. Tomic. Tracy has to solve the case before word gets out and people rush to withdraw their savings, destroying civilization as we know it. One of the RKO "Dick Tracy" series that came closer than the serials to matching the comic strip. **Hound Advisory:** Violence.
1947 (*Family*) 66m/B Boris Karloff, Ralph Byrd, Lyle Latelle; *D:* John Rawlins. VHS, Beta **$14.95** *NOS, MRV, SNC*

Dick Tracy Returns

Republic Pictures serial sequel to their original "Dick Tracy" is marginally better. Middleton, who played the nefarious Ming the Merciless in the "Flash Gordon" chapter plays, guest-stars as Pa Stark, patriarch of a family criminal clan that goes up against the great detective. In 15 episodes. **Hound Advisory:** Violence.
1938 (*Family*) 100m/B Ralph Byrd, Charles Middleton; *D:* William Witney. VHS, Beta, LV **$79.95** *VCI, IME, MLB*

Dick Tracy vs. Crime Inc.

The last of the Republic Pictures Dick Tracy serials, with the comic-strip crime-fighter contending with a gangster master-mind who can make himself invisible. **Hound Advisory:** Violence.
1941 (*Family*) 100m/B Ralph Byrd, Ralph Morgan, Michael Owen; *D:* William Witney; *W:* John English. VHS, Beta, LV **$79.95** *VCI, IME, MLB*

Dick Tracy vs. Cueball 🦴🦴

One of the lesser RKO "Dick Tracy" spectacles, with Chester Gould's top cop in pursuit of a bald strangler known as Cueball. **Hound Advisory:** Violence.
1946 (*Family*) 62m/B Morgan Conway, Anne Jeffreys; *D:* Gordon Douglas. VHS, Beta **$14.95** *NOS, VCI, VYY*

Dick Tracy's Dilemma 🦴🦴

Vintage RKO feature in which police detective Dick Tracy tracks down a masked villain known as the Claw. **Hound Advisory:** Violence.
1947 (*Family*) 60m/B Ralph Byrd, Lyle Latelle, Kay Christopher, Jack Lambert, Ian Keith, Jimmy Conlin; *D:* John Rawlins. VHS, Beta *MRV, VCI, VYY*

Did I Ever Tell You How Lucky You Are?

Two Dr. Seuss stories narrated by John Cleese. Includes "Did I Ever Tell You How Lucky You Are?" and "Scrambled Eggs Super."
1993 (*Family*) 30m/C VHS **$9.95** *BTV, RAN*

Die Laughing 🎬🎵

Cab driver/aspiring rock musician unwittingly becomes involved in murder, intrigue, and the kidnapping of a monkey that has memorized a scientific formula capable of destroying the world. Benson wrote, produced, scored, and acted in lame comedy with supposed youth-appeal. **Hound Advisory:** Violence, salty language, sex talk

1980 (PG/*Jr. High-Adult*) 108m/C Robby Benson, Charles Durning, Bud Cort, Elsa Lanchester, Peter Coyote; **D:** Jeff Werner; **W:** Robby Benson, Scott Parker; **M:** Robby Benson. **VHS, Beta $19.98** *WAR*

Digby, the Biggest Dog in the World 🎬

Strained comedy-fantasy from Britain about Digby, an English sheepdog, who wanders around a scientific laboratory, drinks an experimental fluid, and grows to giant size, bringing out the army. Even with hounds, bigger is not always better.

1973 (G/*Family*) 88m/C Jim Dale, Angela Douglas, Spike Milligan, Dinsdale Landen; **D:** Joseph McGrath. **VHS, Beta $59.95** *PSM*

Dimples 🎬🎬🎵

Shirley enlivens this Depression-era rags-to-riches tale as a singing and dancing orphan whose pickpocket grandfather, threatened with jail, gives her up to wealthy adoptive parents. But the girl misses the simple life and returns to the old man. 🎵Hey, What Did the Bluebird Say?; He Was a Dandy; Picture Me Without You; Oh Mister Man Up in the Moon; Dixie-Anna; Get On Board; Swing Low Sweet Chariot.

1936 (PG/*Family*) 78m/B Shirley Temple, John Carradine, Frank Morgan, Helen Westley, Berton Churchill, Robert Kent, Delma Byron; **D:** William A. Seiter. **VHS, Beta $14.98** *FOX*

Dinky: Dinky Finds a Home

Video reissue of Dinky Duck, a cartoon star of the Terrytoons series devised by classic animator Paul Terry; this example in glorious Technicolor.

1946 (*Preschool-Primary*) 36m/C **VHS $5.99** *VTR*

Dinky: Much Ado About Nothing

Shakespeare doesn't have much in common with this wild and crazy duck from the Terrytoon archives.

1940 (*Preschool-Primary*) 36m/C **VHS $5.99** *VTR*

Dinosaurs, Dinosaurs, Dinosaurs

Overexposure to dinosaur lore is turning dino-fan Owens into a dinosaur, so partner Boardman must learn all he can in order to stop the changes. Entertaining, educational program which re-creates the world of dinosaurs.

1987 (*Family*) 30m/C Gary Owens, Eric Boardman. **VHS, Beta $12.98** *MPI, KAR*

Dirt Bike Kid 🎬

Adolescent Jack buys a used motorbike with a mind of its own (a fact everyone accepts without question). Both battle a stuffy banker trying to close a favorite hot dog shop. Billingsley still shows the appeal he had in "A Christmas Story"; otherwise this moronic, low-budget comedy com-

pletely wipes out. At least Jack always wears his helmet. **Hound Advisory:** Sex talk, drug talk, alcohol use.

1986 (PG/*Primary-Sr. High*) 91m/C Peter Billingsley, Anne Bloom, Stuart Pankin, Patrick Collins, Sage Parker, Chad Sheets; **D:** Hoite C. Caston; **W:** Lewis Colick, David Brandes. **VHS, Beta, LV, 8mm $14.95** *COL, NLC*

Dirty Dancing 🎬🎬🎬

Innocent 17-year-old Frances, tellingly nicknamed 'Baby,' is vacationing with her parents in the Catskills in 1963. Bored with the program at the hotel, she finds the real fun at the staff dances, falling for the sensitive-hunk dance instructor (Swayze). The same old story of bittersweet first love, jazzed by fun dance sequences, catchy music, and a terrifically likeable cast. **Hound Advisory:** Sex, mature themes, profanity.

1987 (PG-13/*Jr. High-Adult*) 97m/C Patrick Swayze, Jennifer Grey, Cynthia Rhodes, Jerry Orbach, Jack Weston, Jane Brucker, Kelly Bishop, Lonny Price, Charles "Honi" Coles, Bruce Morrow; **D:** Emile Ardolino; **W:** Eleanor Bergstein; **M:** John Morris. **VHS, Beta, LV $19.98** *LIV, VES*

Dirty Rotten Scoundrels 🎬🎬🎬

A remake of the 1964 "Bedtime Story," in which two confidence tricksters on the Riviera endeavor to rip off a suddenly rich American woman, and each other. Caine and Martin are terrific, Martin has some of his best physical comedy ever, and Headly is charming as the prey who's always one step ahead of them. Fine direction from Oz, the man who brought us the voice of Yoda in "The Empire Strikes Back." **Hound Advisory:** Profanity.

1988 (PG/*Jr. High-Adult*) 112m/C Steve Martin, Michael Caine, Glenne Headly, Anton Rodgers, Barbara Harris, Dana Ivey; **D:** Frank Oz; **W:** Dale Launer, Stanley Shapiro; **M:** Miles Goodman. **VHS, Beta, LV $9.98** *ORI*

Disney's Adventures in Wonderland

Segments from the Disney Channel TV series featuring a new, hip Alice and friends in live-action musical adventures and sketches in Wonderland. Each video includes two exciting full episodes.

1993 (*Family*) 58m/C **VHS, Beta $12.99** *BVV*

Disney's Darkwing Duck: His Favorite Adventures

Join Darkwing Duck on his favorite adventures from the 1991-92 Emmy nominated cartoon series. Each video includes an "MTV-style" Darkwing Duck music video plus feature presentations.

1993 (*Preschool-Primary*) 48m/C **VHS, Beta $12.99** *BVV*

Disney's Greatest Lullabies

Each tape in this series includes five or so bedtime ballads, culled from classic Disney films, designed to bring somnolent bliss to the kiddies.

1986 (*Preschool-Primary*) 25m/C **VHS, Beta** *DIS*

Disney's Haunted Halloween

Goofy helps students learn the origins of this crazy holiday. Superstitions and traditions are discussed.

1984 (*Preschool-Primary*) 10m/C Goofy. **VHS, Beta $205.00** *MTI, DSN*

Disney's Sing-Along Songs: The Twelve Days of Christmas

Get into the holiday spirit with Mickey, Minnie, Donald, and all their friends while singing traditional Christmas carols and new songs too.
1993 (*Family*) 30m/C **VHS $12.99** *DIS*

Disney's Sing-Along Songs, Vol. 1: Heigh-Ho

Professor Ludwig von Drake again narrates a sing-a-long fest for the kids. This volume is one of the best, featuring "Heigh Ho" and "The Dwarfs' Yodel Song" from "Snow White and the Seven Dwarfs."
1988 (*Family*) 28m/C **VHS, Beta, LV $12.99** *DIS, WTA*

Disney's Sing-Along Songs, Vol. 2: Zip-A-Dee-Doo-Dah

Host Ludwig von Drake returns to take the kids through a musical tour of classic Disney movies. Selections from "Peter Pan," "Cinderella," "Song of the South," and others are included.
1988 (*Family*) 26m/C **VHS, Beta, LV $12.99** *DIS, WTA*

Disney's Sing-Along Songs, Vol. 3: You Can Fly!

Great addition to the series features Professor Ludwig von Drake narrating popular songs from "Peter Pan," "Dumbo," "The Jungle Book," "Mary Poppins," and many others.
1988 (*Family*) 28m/C **VHS, Beta, LV $12.99** *DIS, WTA*

Disney's Sing-Along Songs, Vol. 4: The Bare Necessities

Children sing along with the characters and songs from Disney's "The Jungle Book."
1988 (*Family*) 27m/C **VHS, Beta, LV $12.99** *DIS, WTA*

Disney's Sing-Along Songs, Vol. 5: Fun with Music

Sing-a-long fun from 12 Disney movies highlights this animated program narrated by Professor Ludwig von Drake. Billy Joel sings "Why Should I Worry," and selections from "Snow White and the Seven Dwarfs," "Alice in Wonderland," and "Oliver and Company" are included.
1988 (*Family*) 28m/C **M:** Billy Joel. **VHS, Beta $12.99** *DIS, WTA*

Disney's Sing-Along Songs, Vol. 6: Under the Sea

Professor Ludwig von Drake narrates a sing-a-long fest for the kids in this addition to the series. Featured are selections from "The Little Mermaid," "Twenty Thousand Leagues Under the Sea," and other Disney favorites.
1990 (*Family*) 28m/C **VHS, Beta, LV $12.99** *DIS, WTA*

Disney's Sing-Along Songs, Vol. 7: Disneyland Fun

Live actors appear in this series for the first time, marching around the Disneyland grounds with colorful characters in tow. More great fun for the kids.
1990 (*Family*) 29m/C **VHS, Beta $12.99** *DIS, WTA*

Disney's Sing-Along Songs, Vol. 8: Very Merry Christmas Songs

Christmas fun as Professor Ludwig von Drake takes the kids through a whirl of holiday songs. Disney characters perform in selected cartoons to the accompaniment of "Deck the Halls," "Silent Night," "The Twelve Days of Christmas," and nine other tunes.
1988 (*Family*) 27m/C **VHS, Beta $12.99** *DIS, WTA*

Disney's Sing-Along Songs, Vol. 9: I Love to Laugh!

Professor Ludwig von Drake will have you in stitches as you sing along with a variety of silly songs set to classic Disney animation.
1988 (*Family*) 29m/C **VHS, Beta, LV $12.99** *DIS*

Disney's Sing-Along Songs, Vol. 10: Be Our Guest

Musical moments from Disney classic movies with words on screen for viewers to sing-along with the characters. Features "Be Our Guest" and "Beauty and The Beast" from "Beauty and The Beast" as well as "Chim Chim Cheree" and "Spoonful of Sugar" from "Mary Poppins," "Bella Notte" from "Lady and the Tramp," "Little Wooden Head" from "Pinocchio," "Once Upon a Dream" from "Sleeping Beauty," "Hefalumps and Woozles" from "Winnie the Pooh and the Blustery Day," and "The World's Greatest Criminal Mind" from "The Great Mouse Detective."
1992 (*Family*) 30m/C **VHS, Beta $12.99** *DIS*

Disney's Sing-Along Songs, Vol. 11: Friend Like Me

Musical moments from Disney movies, including "Aladdin," "Fox and the Hound," "Song of the South," "Beauty and the Beast," "The Parent Trap," and "The Jungle Book." ♫Friend Like Me; Best of Friends; How Do You Do; Something There; Friendship; In Harmony; Let's Get Together; That's What Friends Are For; A Whole New World.
1993 (*Family*) 30m/C **VHS, LV $12.99** *DIS, WTA*

Disney's TaleSpin, Vol. 1: True Baloo

Acclaimed made-for-TV Disney cartoon show that revives the classic "Jungle Book" character Baloo the Bear as a daring courier pilot. He and his cohorts fly into adventure, danger, and fun. Additional volumes available.
1991 (*Family*) 46m/C **VHS, Beta $12.99** *DIS, BVV*

Disney's Wonderful World of Winter

Stanley the Snowman, Professor of Winterology, teaches Goofy about Thanksgiving, Christmas, and New Years.
1990 (*Preschool-Jr. High*) 10m/C **VHS, Beta $205.00** *MTI, DSN*

Disorderlies 🎵

Members of the popular rap group cavort as incompetent hospital orderlies assigned to care for a cranky millionaire. Fat jokes abound with performances by the Fat Boys.
1987 (**PG**/*Jr. High-Adult*) 86m/C The Fat Boys, Ralph Bellamy; **D:** Michael A. Schultz; **M:** Anne Dudley. **VHS, Beta, LV $19.98** *WAR*

The Disorderly Orderly 🎵

When Lewis gets hired as a hospital orderly, nothing stands upright for long. Vintage slapstick with Lewis running amuck in a nursing home.
1964 (*Family*) 90m/C Jerry Lewis, Glenda Farrell, Everett Sloane, Kathleen Freeman, Susan Oliver; **D:** Frank Tashlin. **VHS, Beta, LV $14.95** *PAR*

Diving In 🎵

Have you heard the one about the acrophobic diver? A paralyzing fear of heights is the only thing between Wayne and a gold medal. While facing his phobia, the teen hero endures romantic travails, bullying from meanie rival divers, and music videos. Cliched underdog jock drama was a longtime project for Indiana film producers, but it bellyflops. **Hound Advisory:** Teen hero has sex with his gorgeous (adult) lady phys.ed instructor. Profanity, nudity.
1990 (**PG-13**/*Jr. High-Adult*) 92m/C Burt Young, Matt Adler, Kristy Swanson, Matt Lattanzi, Richard Johnson, Carey Scott, Yolanda Jilot; **D:** Strathford Hamilton. **VHS, Beta $89.95** *PAR, FCT*

The Doberman Gang 🎵🎵

Criminal mastermind doesn't trust his cohorts, so for a string of bank robberies he turns to man's best friend, a sextet of trained dogs. The dogs steal the movie as well, and return for more Doberman drama in "The Daring Dobermans" and "The Amazing Dobermans."
1972 (**PG**/*Family*) 85m/C Byron Mabe, Hal Reed, Julie Parrish, Simmy Bow, JoJo D'Amore; **D:** Byron Ross Chudnow; **W:** Frank Ray Perilli. **VHS, Beta $59.98** *FOX*

Doc Hollywood 🎵🎵🎵

Hotshot young physician on his way to a lucrative California practice gets stranded in a small Southern town. Will the wacky woodsy inhabitants persuade the city doctor to stay? There aren't many surprises in this fish-out-of-water comedy, but the cast injects it with considerable charm. Adapted from Neil B. Shulman's book "What?...Dead Again?" **Hound Advisory:** Brief nudity; salty language.
1991 (**PG-13**/*Sr. High-Adult*) 104m/C Michael J. Fox, Julie Warner, Woody Harrelson, Barnard Hughes, David Ogden Stiers, Frances Sternhagen, Bridget Fonda, George Hamilton, Roberts Blossom, Helen Martin, Macon McCalman, Barry Sobel; **D:** Michael Caton-Jones; **W:** Daniel Pyne, Jeffrey Price, Peter S. Seaman; **M:** Carter Burwell. **VHS, Beta, LV, 8mm $19.98** *WAR*

Doc Savage 🎵🎵

Doc, superhero of a series of novels (by various authors under the pseudonym Kenneth Robeson) that excited boys since the '30s, finally came to the screen with the campy attitude of TV's "Batman." The muscular Doc and his Fabulous Five fight (without killing - that's a rule) an arch-villain out for gold. There had been 181 Doc Savage books, and the filmmakers announced plans to do all of them. That fell through when this bombed badly on first release, but it has its admirers. **Hound Advisory:** Roughhousing.
1975 (**PG**/*Family*) 100m/C Ron Ely, Pamela Hensley, **D:** Michael Anderson Sr. **VHS, Beta $19.98** *WAR*

Doctor Doolittle 🎵🎵

And it did do little, at the box office. All the sets and talent money could buy went into this big-budget musical version of Hugh Lofting's tale about the Victorian adventurer able to converse with the beasts, but the weak script mutes the entertainment value. Plot has to do with Dr. D pursuing a legendary giant snail to a remote floating island. Features one decent song, "Talk to the Animals." 🎵Doctor Dolittle; My Friend the Doctor; Talk to the Animals; I've Never Seen Anything Like It; Beautiful Things; When I Look in Your Eyes; After Today; Fabulous Places; Where Are the Words?.
1967 (*Family*) 144m/C Rex Harrison, Samantha Eggar, Anthony Newley, Richard Attenborough, Geoffrey Holder, Peter Bull; **D:** Richard Fleischer; **M:** Leslie Bricusse. **Award Nominations:** Academy Awards '66: Best Cinematography, Best Sound, Best Original Score; Academy Awards '67: Best Film Editing, Best Picture; **Awards:** Academy Awards '67: Best Song ("Talk to the Animals"), Best Visual Effects; Golden Globe Awards '68: Best Supporting Actor (Attenborough); National Board of Review Awards '67: 10 Best Films of the Year. **VHS, Beta, LV $14.98** *FOX, FCT, MLT*

Dr. No 🎵🎵🎵

Bond, James Bond. The world is introduced to British secret agent 007 when it is discovered that a mad scientist is sabotaging rocket launchings from his hideout in Jamaica. Notable as the first of the Bond adventures, it's far less glitzy than any of its successors but boasts the sexiest "Bond girl" of them all in Andress, and promptly made stars of her and Connery. Laserdisc version includes interviews with principals as well as movie bills, publicity photos, location pictures, and the British and American trailers. **Hound Advisory:** Violence, alcohol use, suggested sex.
1962 (**PG**/*Jr. High-Adult*) 111m/C Sean Connery, Ursula Andress, Joseph Wiseman, Jack Lord, Zena Marshall, Eunice Gayson, Margaret LeWars, John Kitzmiller, Lois Maxwell, Bernard Lee, Anthony M. (Antonio Marghereti) Dawson; **D:** Terence Young; **M:** John Barry. **VHS, Beta, LV $19.98** *MGM, VYG, CRC*

Dr. Otto & the Riddle of the Gloom Beam 🎵🎵

The first 'Ernest' epic, though Ernest P. Worrell only puts in a guest appearance. Instead comic-actor Varney plays Dr. Otto von Schnick, bizarre supervillain whose ray weapon can wreck the economy. Bankers hire an overconfident hero (his lady sidekick does all the work) to stop Otto, and the best scenes show how the two foes grew up side-by-side in the same town. Rest of the film is a way-weird combo of wacky

sets, costumes, f/x, comic-book cliffhangers. Original, anyway, but very confusing for kids - or adults. **Hound Advisory:** Roughhousing.
1986 (PG/*Adult*) 92m/C Jim Varney; *D:* John R. Cherry III. **VHS, Beta $59.95** *GKK*

Dr. Seuss' ABC

Dr. Seuss classic plus two more of his charming, discombobulating tales.
1990 (*Family*) 30m/C **VHS $9.95** *KUI, RAN, VEC*

Dr. Seuss' Butter Battle Book

Durning narrates Seuss' socially conscious animated allegory of the nuclear arms race.
1989 (*Family*) 30m/C **VHS, Beta $9.95** *GKK*

Dr. Seuss' Caldecotts

Three of Dr. Seuss's Caldecott Award books, "Bartholomew and the Oobleck," "If I Ran the Zoo," and "McElligot's Pool" are gathered together in read-along (rather than animated) form.
1988 (*Primary*) 90m/C **VHS** *RHU*

Dr. Seuss' Cat in the Hat

Everyone's favorite cat helps save two children from the boredom of a rainy day in this classic cartoon.
1971 (*Preschool-Primary*) 30m/C **VHS $14.95** *TVC*

Dr. Seuss' Hoober-Bloob Highway

Cleverly animated Dr. Seuss metaphor for life itself, in which Mr. Hoober-Bloob, a dispatcher from a laboratory in space, sends infants down his highway to Earth. Not adapted from an existing Dr. Seuss book but written specifically for TV.
1975 (*Primary*) 24m/C **VHS, Beta $14.95** *TVC, BFA*

Dr. Seuss' Horton Hears a Who/How the Grinch Stole Christmas

Duo of animated Dr. Seuss classics.
1966 (*Family*) 52m/C **VHS, Beta, LV $29.95** *MGM, WTA*

Dr. Seuss: I Am NOT Going to Get Up Today!

A young boy decides that NOTHING will force him out of bed! Also includes the stories "The Shape of Me and other Stuff," "Great Day for Up," and "In a People House."
1991 (*Family*) 25m/C **VHS, Beta $9.95** *RAN*

Dr. Seuss on the Loose

Combines three short stories including "The Sneetches," "The Zax," and "Green Eggs and Ham," in a thematic trio which explores the often fickle and flexible world of attitudes.
1974 (*Family*) 25m/C **VHS, Beta $14.98** *BFA, WTA*

Dr. Seuss Sleep Book

Animated tale of a long journey from day to night as well as the Seuss story "Hunches in Bunches."
1993 (*Preschool-Primary*) 30m/C **VHS $9.95** *RAN, BTV*

Dr. Seuss' The Lorax

Environmentalist Dr. Seuss cartoon about a creature who emerges from a tree stump and tries to convince a voracious industrial society from greedily cutting down the last of the all-purpose Truffala trees. Strong stuff in kid terms; communities involved with the timber industry have even banned this video and the source book.
1971 (*Family*) 48m/C *D:* Hawley Pratt; *V:* Bob Holt, Athena Lorde. **VHS $14.95** *FOX, TVC*

Dr. Strange 🎭♨

One of numerous disappointing attempts to bring Marvel comic book characters to network TV; this time it's the turn of Dr. Strange, a playboy sorcerer who uses his magical powers to combat the malevolent witch Morgan Le Fey. Pilot for a "Dr. Strange" series that never materialized.
1978 (*Jr. High-Adult*) 94m/C Peter Hooten, Clyde Kusatsu, Jessica Walter, Eddie Benton, John Mills; *D:* Philip DeGuere. **VHS, Beta $39.95** *MCA*

Dr. Syn, Alias the Scarecrow 🎭🎭♨

Mild-mannered clergyman is, in reality, a smuggler and pirate who dresses up in a creepy scarecrow outfit and avenges King George III's injustices upon the English people. Atmospheric Disney swashbuckler (an adaptation of an oft-filmed Russell Thorndyke novel) was originally a miniseries on the "Wonderful World of Disney" TV show.
1964 (G/*Family*) 129m/C Patrick McGoohan, George Cole, Tony Britton, Michael Hordern, Geoffrey Keen, Kay Cole; *D:* James Neilson. **VHS, Beta $69.95** *DIS*

Doctor Who: An Unearthly Child

British sci-fi TV show is one of the longest continuously running programs in history. The title character is a whimsical time-traveller who, in this initial B&W episode from long ago, is a wizardlike old man who takes his granddaughter to prehistoric times to witness the discovery of fire. Though conceived as a kiddie show, "Doctor Who" evolved over two decades into a straightfaced sci-fi program for all ages, with enough aliens, planets, friends and enemies to match "Star Trek" trivia. With eight separate actors portraying the far-wandering Doctor, different editions of the Doctor would occasionally meet each other in the timestream. Apart from the two "Doctor Who" theatrical films, three dozen feature-length episodes of the TV program have been released to tape to date (they were originally aired a chapter at a time, with cliffhanger endings just like the great serials). While never graphically violent, some episodes dwell on grotesque mutations and fairly serious horror. The good news is that parents who preview the tapes beforehand may find themselves on the edge of their seats, just like the kids.
1963 (*Family*) 98m/B William Hartnell, William Russell; *D:* Waris Hussein. **VHS $19.98** *FXV, MOV*

Doctor Who and the Daleks

First feature film based on the popular British TV character, in a broader vein than the BBC program. Though Cushing plays the time-travelling hero for the first time, the movie was done to showcase his most popular foes, a race of cruel, conquest-crazed cyborgs, shaped rather oddly like salt shakers rallying-cry of "Exterminate! Exterminate!" has been a catch phrase among Commonwealth kids for decades. If you can't get enough, the more lavish sequel "Daleks - Invasion Earth 2150 A.D." is also on cassette.
1965 (*Family*) 78m/C Peter Cushing, Roy Castle; **D:** Gordon Flemyng. VHS, Beta $9.98 *REP*

Doctor Zhivago 🐾🐾🐾

Sweeping adaptation of the Nobel Prize-winning Boris Pasternak novel. An innocent Russian poet-intellectual is caught in the furor and chaos of the Bolshevik Revolution. Essentially a poignant love story filmed as a historical epic. Panoramic film popularized the song "Lara's Theme." Overlong, with often disappointing performances, but gorgeous scenery. Lean was more successful in "Lawrence of Arabia," where there was less need for ensemble acting.
1965 (*Sr. High-Adult*) 197m/C Omar Sharif, Julie Christie, Geraldine Chaplin, Rod Steiger, Alec Guinness, Klaus Kinski, Ralph Richardson, Rita Tushingham, Siobhan McKenna, Tom Courtenay; **D:** David Lean; **W:** Robert Bolt; **M:** Maurice Jarre. **Award Nominations:** Academy Awards '65: Best Director (Lean), Best Film Editing, Best Picture, Best Sound, Best Supporting Actor (Courtenay); **Awards:** Academy Awards '65: Best Adapted Screenplay, Best Art Direction/Set Decoration (Color), Best Color Cinematography, Best Costume Design (Color), Best Original Score; Golden Globe Awards '66: Best Actor—Drama (Sharif), Best Director (Lean), Best Film—Drama, Best Screenplay, Best Score; National Board of Review Awards '65: 10 Best Films of the Year, Best Actress (Christie). VHS, Beta, LV $29.98 *MGM, RDG, HMV*

The Dog Days of Arthur Cane

When spoiled, selfish Arthur Cane is transformed into a shaggy dog for a short time, he becomes a much better person for the experience. ABC-TV Weekend Special based on the book by T. Ernesto Bethancourt.
1992 (*Primary-Jr. High*) 29m/C VHS $295.00 *AIM*

A Dog of Flanders 🐾🐾◁

Sentimental tale, based on an 1872 children's novel by Ouida, about a struggling Dutch milk-delivery boy and his grandfather, who find a severely beaten dog and restore it to health. The old man's demise leaves the dog and the kid to fend for themselves. If the canine hero looks familiar that's because it's the same animal thespian who acted in Disney's faithful "Old Yeller."
1959 (*Family*) 96m/C David Ladd, Donald Crisp, Theodore Bikel, Max Croiset, Monique Ahrens; **D:** James B. Clark. VHS, Beta $14.95 *PAR*

Dog Pound Shuffle 🐾🐾

Two drifters, a young man and old showbiz has-been, form a song-and-dance act in order to raise the funds necessary to win their dog's freedom from the pound. Unexceptional little Canadian production. Fans may remember Moody as Fagin from "Oliver!" **Hound Advisory:** Salty language, roughhousing, alcohol use.

1975 (PG/*Primary-Adult*) 98m/C Ron Moody, David Soul; **D:** Jeffrey Bloom; **W:** Jeffrey Bloom. VHS, Beta $59.98 *FOX*

The Dog Who Dared

Cautionary cartoon about Ralph the dog, who saves the day when troublemaker Darryl pressures his friends into trying drugs and alcohol. When Darryl laces Ralph's milk with booze, Ralph gets drunk and realizes the dangers of substance abuse. His experience gets the kids to swear off intoxicants.
1992 (*Primary*) 25m/C VHS $395.00

The Dog Who Stopped the War 🐾🐾🐾◁

Charming Canadian effort was the first of producer Rock Demers' acclaimed "Tales for All" series. Bunch of schoolkids spend Christmas break playing war; one side builds a giant snow fort, the other attacks it. Their tactics, weapons, and homemade battle armor grow more and more elaborate, until a fateful skirmish on the last day of vacation when one boy's St. Bernard gets involved and things turn serious. Even with the clear antiwar message tacked on, it's a captivating, credible look at childhood values and mischief. Dubbed from French into English. **Hound Advisory:** Despite the happy hound on the cassette box, Cleo the dog is more of a martyr than a heroine.
1984 (G/*Family*) 90m/C **D:** Andre Melancon. VHS, Beta *NO*

Doin' Time on Planet Earth 🐾🐾◁

Grab bag of comic ideas, some wrongheaded, some on-target and even touching. Young Ryan feels out of place with his obnoxious family and tacky community. Two wacko UFO nuts give him an explanation; the kid is descended from a long-lost race of spacemen - teenage alienation, get it? If he can recall the right coordinates, Ryan and outcasts like him can blast off for their true home planet. The ending just doesn't follow through on one of the more intriguing ideas for a coming-of-age farce. **Hound Advisory:** Sex, profanity.
1988 (PG-13/*Jr. High-Adult*) 83m/C Adam West, Candice Azzara, Hugh O'Brian, Matt Adler, Timothy Patrick Murphy, Roddy McDowall, Maureen Stapleton, Andrea Thompson; **D:** Charles Matthau. VHS, Beta $19.98 *WAR*

Dominick & Eugene 🐾🐾🐾

Dominick is a little slow, but he makes a fair living as a garbageman-good enough to put his brother through medical school. Both men struggle with the other's faults and weaknesses, as they learn the meaning of family and friendship. Well-acted, especially by Hulce, never melodramatic or weak.
1988 (PG-13/*Jr. High-Adult*) 96m/C Ray Liotta, Tom Hulce, Jamie Lee Curtis, Todd Graff, Bill Cobbs, David Strathairn; **D:** Robert M. Young; **W:** Alvin Sargent, Corey Blechman; **M:** Trevor Jones. VHS, Beta, LV $19.98 *ORI, FCT*

Don Cooper: Sing-Along Story Songs

Cooper sings about the Little Pigs and others in this animated, live action, puppet special.
1990 (*Family*) 30m/C Don Cooper. VHS $9.95 *RAN*

Don Winslow of the Coast Guard

13-episode serial features comic-strip character Winslow as he strives to keep the waters of America safe for democracy. **1943** (*Adult-Family*) 234m/B Don Terry, Elyse Knox; *D:* Ford Beebe, Ray Taylor. **VHS, Beta** $49.95 *NOS, MED, VDM*

Don Winslow of the Navy

13-episode serial centered around the evil Scorpion, who plots to attack the pacific Coast, but is thwarted by comic-strip hero Winslow. **1943** (*Family*) 234m/B Don Terry, Walter Sande, Anne Nagel; *D:* Ford Beebe, Ray Taylor. **VHS, Beta** $39.95 *VYY, MED, MLB*

Donny Deinonychus: The Educational Dinosaur, Vol. 1

Two debut episodes of a series which shares the story of prehistory while teaching basic morals, values, judgments, and courtesies. In "Donny Deinonychus," an experiment turns Donny the Parrot into his prehistoric ancestor, Donny Deinonychus (Dine-non-i-kus), whose bird memory is erased and replaced by that of a dinosaur. In "Stormy, the Long Lost Friend," Donny introduces Stormy the Triceratops and explains that even though someone may be scary looking, they may not necessarily be bad. Additional volumes available. **1993** (*Preschool-Primary*) 30m/C **VHS** $9.95

Don't Change My World 🎵🎵

To preserve the natural beauty of the Appalachian Mountains, wildlife photographer Eric, along with his trusty dog and pet raccoon, oppose a villainous land developer and reckless poachers. Eco-correct. **1983** (*G/Family*) 89m/C Roy Tatum, Ben Jones. **VHS, Beta** $59.98 *LIV*

Don't Eat the Pictures: Sesame Street at the Metropolitan Museum of Art

The Sesame Street Gang wind up locked in New York's Metropolitan Museum of Art after hours. While Cookie Monster learns that paintings of fruit are not for snacks, Big Bird helps the 4,000-year-old spirit of an Egyptian boy solve his ancient riddle. **1987** (*Family*) 60m/C Fritz Weaver, James Mason, Paul Dooley. **VHS** $24.95 *AAI, KUI, RAN*

Don't Tell Mom the Babysitter's Dead 🎵🎵

Mom, travelling abroad, leaves a strict old lady in charge of the household. When she suddenly expires, the kids have the summer to themselves - if they can pay the bills. Daughter Sue Ellen cons her way into an office job and accidentally skyrockets to an exec-level position in the fashion biz, but she has to hide her true age and situation. Somewhere inside this wish-fulfillment comedy is a nice depiction of a teenage girl suddenly thrust into 'the Real World' (pic's original title) and finding she actually enjoys adult responsibility. But emphasis is on quick laughs, preposterous plot twists. **Hound Advisory:** Sue Ellen's lazy brother just wants to relax with beer and pot. Profanity. **1991** (*PG-13/Jr. High-Adult*) 105m/C Christina Applegate, Keith Coogan, Joanna Cassidy, John Getz, Josh Charles, Concetta Tomei, Eda Reiss Merin; *D:* Stephen Herek. **VHS, Beta, LV, 8mm** $19.98 *HBO*

Don't Wake Your Mom

Shari Lewis and her world famous puppets Lambchop, Charlie Horse, and Hush Puppy entertain children 3 to 8, so Mom can get her beauty sleep. **1988** (*Preschool-Primary*) 43m/C **VHS, Beta** $14.95 *BAR, KAR*

The Donut Repair Club: On Tour

Donut Man (Rob Evans) and the lively Donut Repair Club engage in fun, music, and lessons about God. Additional volumes available. **1993** (*Preschool-Primary*) 30m/C **VHS** $14.95 *SPW*

Dorothy in the Land of Oz

Province of Oz faces invasion by the Terrible Toy Maker in these further animated adventures of L. Frank Baum's characters from published sequels to the "Wizard of Oz." This particular one began life as a network TV special "Thanksgiving in the Land of Oz." **1981** (*Preschool-Jr. High*) 60m/C **VHS, Beta** $29.95 *FHE, PMS*

Dot & Keeto

Honey, they shrunk Dot! The star of the Australian cartoon features gets reduced to insect size and has exciting entomological adventures with her mosquito friend Keeto. **1986** (*Preschool-Primary*) 73m/C Robin Moore, Keith Scott. **VHS, Beta** *WTA*

Dot & Santa Claus

The cartoon heroine has lost her kangaroo. Suddenly a bush ranger turns into Santa Claus, and (with a sleigh pulled by kangaroos), they literally travel the world in search of the missing joey. An ambitious outing for Dot, including visits to the U.N. and the Moscow Circus, and twin tributes to Mickey Mouse and Henry Kissinger (!?). **1979** (*Preschool-Primary*) 73m/C **VHS, Beta** $14.95 *WTA, FOX*

Dot & the Kangaroo

First entry in the Australian "Dot," series of semi-musical cartoon features, quite unique in the way they put cleverly animated characters against filmed wildlife footage for nature-themed adventures. Here Dot, the small daughter of a settler, wanders into the outback and gets lost. She meets a friendly kangaroo who takes her on a fabulous journey. **1977** (*Preschool-Primary*) 75m/C **VHS, Beta** *FOX*

Dot & the Koala

Another animated adventure finds young Dot teaming with cartoon animals from the outback to halt environmentally damaging progress. **1988** (*Preschool-Primary*) 75m/C *D:* Yoram Gross. **VHS, Beta** $14.95 *FHE, WTA*

Dot & the Smugglers

Dot's Australian-made adventures continue. This time the cartoon outback girl and her animated animal friends stop a secret wildlife smuggling ring.

1987 (*Preschool-Primary*) 75m/C **VHS, Beta $14.95** *FHE, WTA*

Dot & the Whale

Popular Australian theatrical feature for kids, about how Dot helps a stranded whale and gains a valuable lesson in marine life.

1987 (*Preschool-Primary*) 75m/C **VHS, Beta $14.95** *FHE, WTA*

The Double McGuffin 🐾🐾

So-so attempt by "Benji" creator Camp to do an equally smart flick with two-legged actors, specifically a group of mischievous schoolboys who discover a plot of international intrigue when a sexy prime minister and her security guard pay a visit to a small Virginia community. Vintage Disney in style - or should we say, out of style? **Hound Advisory:** Salty language, sex talk, alcohol use.

1979 (*PG/Jr. High-Adult*) 100m/C Ernest Borgnine, George Kennedy, Elke Sommer, Ed "Too Tall" Jones, Lisa Whelchel, Vincent Spano; *D:* Joe Camp; *V:* Orson Welles. **VHS, Beta $69.95** *VES*

The Double O Kid 🐾

Lance, a 17-year-old office boy at the CIA, has to rush a package to Los Angeles, putting him in the midst of an evil scheme by a crazed computer virus designer. Aided by the prerequisite pretty girl, the boy must avoid all the hazards sent his way. You can safely avoid this worn-out teen-spy spoof, redeemed only by some cool computer graphics. **Hound Advisory:** Salty language, violence.

1992 (*PG-13/Jr. High-Adult*) 95m/C Corey Haim, Wallace Shawn, Brigitte Nielsen, Nicole Eggert, John Rhys-Davies, Basil Hoffman, Karen Black; *Cameos:* Anne Francis; *D:* Duncan McLachlan; *W:* Andrea Buck, Duncan McLachlan. **VHS, Beta $89.95** *PSM*

Doug, Vol. 1: How Did I Get Into This Mess?

Doug Funnie, age 11, encounters toothaches, power failures, and video-game addiction in "Doug's Lost Weekend," "Doug's Dental Disaster," and "Doug on His Own." Includes two original music videos based on the series. Additional volumes available.

1993 (*Primary-Jr. High*) 40m/C **VHS $9.98** *SMV, FCT, WTA*

The Doughnuts

Homer Price is up to his ears in doughnuts, thanks to a doughnut machine that has gone berserk. One of the two-tape set of Homer Price stories from the "Children's Circle" series.

1963 (*Primary*) 26m/C **VHS, Beta**

The Dove 🐾🐾🐾

True story based on the popular book by Robin Lee Graham, of his adventures as a 16-year-old sailing around the world in a 23-foot sloop. The trip takes the boy not only to exotic locales but into manhood, and he falls in love with a girl and becomes a father. Lyrical, mellow, with magnificent photography and scenery. **Hound Advisory:** Sex, nudity, mature themes.

1974 (*PG-13/Jr. High-Adult*) 105m/C Joseph Bottoms, Deborah Raffin, Dabney Coleman, Peter Gwynne; *D:* Charles Jarrott. **VHS, Beta $14.95** *PAR, BMV*

Downhill Racer 🐾🐾🐾

An undisciplined American skier locks ski-tips with his coach and his new-found love while on his way to becoming an Olympic superstar. Character study on film. Beautiful ski and mountain photography keep it from sliding downhill.

1969 (*PG/Jr. High-Adult*) 102m/C Robert Redford, Camilla Sparv, Gene Hackman, Dabney Coleman; *D:* Michael Ritchie. **VHS, Beta, LV $14.95** *PAR*

Dragnet 🐾🐾

Semi-parody of the vintage '60s television cop show. Sgt. Joe Friday's straight-laced nephew and his sloppy partner take on the seamy crime life of Los Angeles. Neither Aykroyd nor Hanks can save this big-budget but lackluster spoof that's full of holes. **Hound Advisory:** Profanity and violence.

1987 (*PG-13/Jr. High-Adult*) 106m/C Dan Aykroyd, Tom Hanks, Christopher Plummer, Harry Morgan, Elizabeth Ashley, Dabney Coleman; *D:* Tom Mankiewicz; *W:* Dan Aykroyd, Tom Mankiewicz, Alan Zweibel; *M:* Ira Newborn. **VHS, Beta, LV $14.95** *MCA*

Dragon: The Bruce Lee Story 🐾🐾🐾

Entertaining, inspiring account of the life of Chinese-American martial-arts legend Bruce Lee. Jason Scott Lee (no relation) is great as the talented artist, exuding his joy of life and gentle spirit, before his mysterious death of a brain disorder at age 32. Ironically, this release coincided with son Brandon's accidental death on the set of "The Crow." The martial arts sequences in "Dragon" are extraordinary, but there's also romance as Lee meets and marries his wife (Holly, who acquits herself well). Based on the book "Bruce Lee: The Man Only I Knew" by his widow, Linda Lee Caldwell. **Hound Advisory:** Violence; profanity; mature themes.

1993 (*PG-13/Jr. High-Adult*) 121m/C Jason Scott Lee, Lauren Holly, Robert Wagner, Michael Learned, Nancy Kwan, Kay Tong Lim, Sterling Macer, Ric Young, Sven Ole-Thorsen; *D:* Rob Cohen; *W:* Edward Khmara, John Raffo, Rob Cohen; *M:* Randy Edelman. **VHS, LV $19.98** *MCA, BTV, FCT*

Dragonslayer 🐾🐾🐾

Sorcerer's youthful apprentice is the only person who can save the kingdom of Urland from its last and worst fire-breathing dragon. Not a fairy-tale treatment, but a genuinely primordial and scary attempt at oft-told material, overlong but memorable. The Industrial Light and Magic f/x workshop created one of the screen's most fearsome dragons - plus gore that would have undoubtedly earned this at least a PG-13 today. **Hound Advisory:** Brutality, nudity, mature themes.

1981 (*PG/Jr. High-Adult*) 110m/C Peter MacNicol, Caitlin Clarke, Ralph Richardson, John Hallam, Albert Salmi, Chloe Salaman; *D:* Matthew Robbins; *W:* Matthew Robbins; *M:* Alex North. **VHS, Beta, LV $19.95** *PAR, COL*

Dragonworld 🦖🦖🦖

Creators of the direct-to-video family hit "Prehysteria" put extra effort into this fantasy and it shows. Five-year-old orphan Johnny McGowan, sent to remote Scottish Highlands to live with relatives, wishes for a friend and gets a baby dragon he names Yowler. Years later, outsiders discover the now giant-sized Yowler, and adult Johnny reluctantly rents his monster pal to an amusement park. But Dragonworld's owner has a Scrooge McDuck disposition, and Johnny and friends soon mount a "Free Willy" rescue of homesick Yowler. Cliches are bearable thanks to carefully calculated sentiment and an overriding gentleness. Dragon f/x are more whimsical than realistic. **Hound Advisory:** Yowler breathes fire a little, but why this isn't rated G is as big a mystery as where the beast came from in the first place.
1994 (PG/Primary-Adult**)** 86m/C Sam Mackenzie, Courtland Mead, Brittney Powell, John Calvin, Andrew Keir, Lila Kaye, John Woodvine; **D:** Ted Nicolaou; **W:** Ted Nicolaou, Suzanne Glazener Naha; **M:** Richard Band. VHS, Beta *PAR*

Dream a Little Dream 🦖🦖

If originality is what you're looking for, you must be dreaming. Elderly couple habitually meditate, trying mystically to regain their youth. When they collide bikes with the teenagers down the street, minds are exchanged, and the young folks with senior souls must figure out how to get back to their rightful bodies. Overly familiar brain exchange made bearable by cast. **Hound Advisory:** Salty language, alcohol use.
1989 (PG-13/Jr. High-Adult**)** 114m/C Corey Feldman, Corey Haim, Meredith Salenger, Jason Robards Jr., Piper Laurie, Harry Dean Stanton, Victoria Jackson, Alex Rocco, Billy McNamara; **D:** Marc Rocco; **W:** Marc Rocco. VHS, Beta, LV $89.98 *LIV, VES, HHE*

Dream Date 🦖🦕

Race change doesn't improve the obsessed-dad comedy formula earlier attempted (and failed) in "She's Out of Control." When Danielle goes on a hot date with the high school football captain, her overly protective father Bill tags along to spy and gets caught in one disaster after another. Much of the humor has a surprisingly cruel edge in this TV movie. **Hound Advisory:** Roughhousing, alcohol use.
1993 (PG-13/Jr. High-Adult**)** 96m/C Tempestt Bledsoe, Clifton Davis, Kadeem Hardison, Anne-Marie Johnson, Pauly Shore, Richard Moll; **D:** Anson Williams. VHS $89.95 *TRI, PMS*

A Dream for Christmas 🦖🦖🦖

Earl Hamner Jr., best known for creating "The Waltons," wrote this moving TV drama of faith and family. Black minister moves with his wife, mother and children from their native rural Arkansas to sunny Los Angeles in December, 1950. Their difficulty in making the transition is capped by the belated discovery that the church the Rev. Douglas is to take over has been slated for demolition. He tries to boost church attendance by Noel.
1973 (Family**)** 100m/C Hari Rhodes, Beah Richards, George Spell, Juanita Moore, Joel Fluellen, Robert DoQui, Clarence Muse; **D:** Ralph Senesky. VHS $19.98 *LIV, HBO, WAR*

Dream Machine 🦖🦕

Childish teen comedy with one of the Coreys is based on that old urban legend of the lucky kid given a free Porshe by the vengeful wife of a wealthy philanderer. The gimmick is that the husband's body is in the trunk; a murderer is in pursuit. Driver's Ed looms in near future as reckless motoring dominates action. To compensate for poor driving tips, the tape includes an anti-drug public service announcement. **Hound Advisory:** Violence, salty language, bad driving.
1991 (PG/Jr. High-Adult**)** 88m/C Corey Haim, Evan Richards, Jeremy Slate, Randall England, Tracy Fraim, Brittney Lewis, Susan Seaforth Hayes; **D:** Lyman Dayton. VHS, LV $89.95 *LIV*

The Dream Team 🦖🦖🦕

On their way to a ball game, four patients from a mental hospital find themselves lost in NYC after their doctor is knocked out by murderers. Scary enough for anyone in their right mind, but among the four of them, these guys lack a right mind. Even though you know the quartet will prove to be more sane than many of the people they encounter outside the hospital, effort still derives some fine moments from a cast of dependable comics. Watch for numerous nods to "One Flew Over the Cuckoo's Nest" (in which Lloyd had a memorable part). Maybe not the most authentic spin on the state of mental illness, but a lark nonetheless. **Hound Advisory:** Profanity; violence.
1989 (PG-13/Jr. High-Adult**)** 113m/C Michael Keaton, Christopher Lloyd, Peter Boyle, Stephen Furst, Lorraine Bracco, Milo O'Shea, Dennis Boutsikaris, Philip Bosco, James Remar, Cynthia Belliveau; **D:** Howard Zieff; **W:** Jon Connolly, David Loucka; **M:** David McHugh. VHS, Beta, LV $19.95 *MCA*

Dreamchild 🦖🦖🦖

Poignant story of the autumn years of Alice Hargreaves, the model for Lewis Carroll's "Alice in Wonderland." As an old woman she makes a much-publicized visit to New York in the 1930s, where media attention inspires flashbacks to her childhood meetings with the eccentric, obsessive Reverend Dodgson (alias Carroll). Fantasy sequences feature Wonderland characters created by Jim Henson's Creature Shop. A most unusual approach to the "Through the Looking-Glass" material, perhaps better appreciated by grownups than kid viewers.
1985 (PG/Jr. High-Adult**)** 94m/C Coral Browne, Ian Holm, Peter Gallagher, Jane Asher, Nicola Cowper, Amelia Shankley, Caris Corfman, Shane Rimmer, James Wilby; **D:** Gavin Millar; **W:** Dennis Potter; **M:** Max Harris, Stanley Myers. VHS, Beta $14.95 *MGM*

Dreaming of Paradise

Award-winning animated feature presents a tale of both caution and hope regarding Earth's future. Spike and her friends live below the planet's surface due to pollution and dream of a place with blue skies and green pastures. Environmentalism and children's cartoons are longtime (almost tiresome) companions, and with everyone from Aquaman to Widget evangelizing for The Cause, the topic weighs heavy. Imaginative animation makes this title distinct.
1987 (Family**)** 75m/C VHS $24.99 *JFK, WTA*

Driving Miss Daisy 𝄞𝄞𝄞♩

Tender and sincere portrayal of a 25-year friendship between an aging Jewish woman and the black chauffeur forced upon her by her son. Humorous and thought-provoking, skillfully acted and directed, it subtly explores the effects of prejudice in the South. The development of Aykroyd as a top-notch character actor is further evidenced here. Part of the fun is watching the changes in fashion and auto design. Adapted from the play by Alfred Uhry. **Hound Advisory:** Profanity.
1989 (PG/*College-Adult*) 99m/C Jessica Tandy, Morgan Freeman, Dan Aykroyd, Esther Rolle, Patti LuPone; *D:* Bruce Beresford; *W:* Alfred Uhry; *M:* Hans Zimmer. **Award Nominations:** Academy Awards '89: Best Actor (Freeman), Best Costume Design, Best Film Editing, Best Supporting Actor (Aykroyd); **Awards:** Academy Awards '89: Best Actress (Tandy), Best Adapted Screenplay, Best Makeup, Best Picture; British Academy Awards '90: Best Actress (Tandy); Golden Globe Awards '90: Best Actor—Musical/Comedy (Freeman), Best Actress—Musical/Comedy (Tandy), Best Film—Musical/Comedy; National Board of Review Awards '89: 10 Best Films of the Year, Best Actor (Freeman). **VHS, Beta, LV, 8mm $19.98** *WAR, FCT, BTV*

Drop Dead Fred WOOF!

As a little girl, Lizzie had an impish imaginary playmate named Fred, who protected her from her domineering mother. When her husband dumps her twenty years later, Fred suddenly materializes to "help" as only he can. Misused cast, poor writing, and indifferent direction make this a truly dismal affair. Gutter humor and mean-spirited pranks throw the whole "heartwarming" premise out the window. **Hound Advisory:** Salty language, roughhousing, general grossness with dog droppings, garbage, and worse.
1991 (PG-13/*Jr. High-Adult*) 103m/C Phoebe Cates, Rik Mayall, Tim Matheson, Marsha Mason, Carrie Fisher, Daniel Gerroll, Ron Eldard; *D:* Ate De Jong; *M:* Randy Edelman. **VHS, LV $92.95** *LIV*

Duck Soup 𝄞𝄞𝄞𝄞

Marx Brothers satiric masterpiece failed at the box office but remains a sterling achievement for the madcap brothers. Mrs. Teasdale (Dumont) promises $20 million to the duchy of Freedonia if Rufus T. Firefly (Groucho) becomes the dictator. His rival shows classic bad management tendencies and hires Chico and Harpo as spies. Jam-packed with the classic anarchic and irreverent Marx shtick; watch for the mirror scene. Zeppo plays a love-sick tenor, in this, his last film with the brothers.
1933 (*Family*) 70m/B Groucho Marx, Chico Marx, Harpo Marx, Zeppo Marx, Louis Calhern, Margaret Dumont, Edgar Kennedy, Raquel Torres, Leonid Kinskey, Charles Middleton; *D:* Leo McCarey; *W:* Harry Ruby, Nat Perrin, Bert Kalmar, Arthur Sheekman; *M:* Harry Ruby, Bert Kalmar. **VHS, Beta, LV $14.98** *MCA, FCT*

DuckTales: Accidental Adventurers

Scrooge McDuck and his nephews Huey, Dewey, and Louie star in a series of cassette adventures excerpted from the Disney Studio's first daily TV cartoon series. Additional volumes available.
1989 (*Family*) 44m/C **VHS, Beta, LV $12.99** *DIS, WTA*

DuckTales the Movie: Treasure of the Lost Lamp 𝄞𝄞♩

Uncle Scrooge and company embark on a lost-ark quest, ala Indiana Jones, for misplaced treasure (a lamp that can make the sky rain ice cream). Based on the daily Disney cartoon of the same name, it's more like an extended-version Saturday morning entertainment than bigscreen spectacle, but still worthy of the Disney name.
1990 (G/*Family*) 74m/C *D:* Bob Hathcock; *W:* Alan Burnett; *M:* David Newman; *V:* Alan Young, Christopher Lloyd, Rip Taylor, June Foray, Chuck McCann, Richard Libertini, Russi Taylor, Joan Gerber, Terence McGovern. **VHS, Beta, LV $22.99** *DIS, WTA*

Dumbo 𝄞𝄞𝄞𝄞

Disney classic about a baby elephant growing up in the circus who is ridiculed for his large ears, until he discovers he can fly. Then he becomes a circus star and, eventually, a hero. Expressively and imaginatively animated, highlighted by the hallucinatory dancing pink elephants sequence. Endearing songs by Frank Churchill, Oliver Wallace, and Ned Washington, including "Baby Mine," "Pink Elephants on Parade," and "I See an Elephant Fly."
1941 (*Family*) 63m/C *D:* Ben Sharpsteen; *W:* Joe Grant, Dick Huemer; *M:* Frank Churchill, Oliver Wallace; *V:* Sterling Holloway, Edward Brophy, Verna Felton, Herman Bing, Cliff Edwards. **Award Nominations:** Academy Awards '41: Best Song ("Baby Mine"); **Awards:** Academy Awards '41: Best Score; National Board of Review Awards '41: 10 Best Films of the Year. **VHS, Beta, LV $24.99** *DIS, KUI, APD*

Duncan's World

Twelve-year-old Duncan helps dad run a wildlife museum and agonizes over who threw a cherry bomb into the duck pond. That's about it for plot in this slow-creeping kiddie obscurity, made on a low budget in North Carolina. Based on a book by Helen Masson Copeland.
1977 (G/*Adult*) 93m/C Larry Tobias, Billy Tobias, Calvin Brown Jr.; *D:* John Clayton. **VHS** *BFV*

Dusty 𝄞𝄞

Touching story of a wild dingo dog raised by an Australian rancher and trained to herd sheep. Filmed in the Australian bush and based on the children's book by Frank Dalby Davison.
1985 (*Family*) 89m/C Bill Kerr, Noel Trevarthen, Carol Burns, Nicholas Holland, John Stanton; *D:* John Richardson. **VHS, Beta $19.95** *MED, FCT, FHE*

Dutch 𝄞♩

Another suburban-contemporary family comedy scripted by John Hughes. Earthy, working-class guy picks up his girlfriend's stuck- up son from boarding school, and their trip together gives them plenty of chances to connect, if they don't kill each other first. Little innovation, obvious sentiment, and type-casting instead of acting. **Hound Advisory:** Salty language, sex talk.
1991 (PG-13/*Jr. High-Adult*) 107m/C Ed O'Neill, Ethan Randall, JoBeth Williams; *D:* Peter Faiman; *W:* John Hughes. **VHS $19.98** *FXV, IME*

Earthling 🎬🎬◁

Terminally ill old fellow helps a ten-year-old boy survive in the Australian wilderness after the kid's parents are killed in a tragic accident. Lessons of life and the power of the human heart are passed on in this panoramic, sentimental drama.
1980 (**PG**/*Family*) 102m/C William Holden, Rick Schroder, Jack Thompson, Olivia Hamnett, Alwyn Kurts; **D:** Peter Collinson. **VHS, Beta $69.98** *LIV, VES*

East of Eden 🎬🎬🎬🎬

Steinbeck's contemporary retelling of the biblical Cain and Abel story receives superior treatment from Kazan and his excellent cast. Dean, in his first starring role, gives a reading of a young man's search for love and acceptance that defines adolescent pain. Though filmed in the 1950s, this story still rivets today's viewers with its emotional message. **Hound Advisory:** Roughhousing.
1954 (*Family*) 115m/C James Dean, Julie Harris, Richard Davalos, Raymond Massey, Jo Van Fleet, Burl Ives, Albert Dekker; **D:** Elia Kazan; **W:** Paul Osborn; **M:** Leonard Rosenman. **Award Nominations:** Academy Awards '55: Best Actor (Dean), Best Director (Kazan), Best Screenplay; **Awards:** Academy Awards '55: Best Supporting Actress (Van Fleet); Golden Globe Awards '56: Best Film—Drama; National Board of Review Awards '55: 10 Best Films of the Year. **VHS, Beta, LV $19.98** *WAR, BTV, HMV*

East of the Sun, West of the Moon

Beautifully illustrated storytelling adaptation of the traditional Norwegian folktale. Young girl leaves her family to go and live with a polar bear in his castle. The bear is really a bewitched handsome prince under the spell of a troll queen. The brave girl then seeks to break the spell. Part of the acclaimed "Rabbit Ears" series of tapes.
1991 (*Primary*) 28m/C **VHS $9.95** *MLT*

Easter Bunny is Coming to Town

Stop-motion 'Animagic' TV special from the Rankin-Bass group focusing on Sunny the Easter Bunny and how he got into the egg habit.
1977 (*Family*) 50m/C **VHS, Beta, LV $14.95** *WTA, VES, IME*

Easter Egg Mornin'

It's up to Picasso "Speedy" Cottontail, the egg-painter, and his friends to save Easter as they go on various bunny adventures.
1993 (*Preschool-Primary*) 27m/C **VHS $12.95** *FHE*

Easter Parade 🎬🎬🎬

Big musical star (Astaire) splits with his partner (Miller) claiming that he could mold any girl to replace her in the act. He tries and finally succeeds after much difficulty. Classic song and dance fest has numerous highlights, including "Drum Crazy" and "A Couple of Swells." Astaire, back after his first "retirement" (Gene Kelly was up first for the role, but broke an ankle and persuaded his reluctant friend to replace him), is in peak form with Garland, aided by a classic Irving Berlin score. ♫Happy Easter; Drum Crazy; It Only Happens When I Dance With You; Everybody's Doin' It; I Want to Go Back to Michigan; Beautiful Faces Need Beautiful Clothes; A Fella With an Umbrella; I Love a Piano; Snookey Ookums.
1948 (*Family*) 103m/C Fred Astaire, Judy Garland, Peter Lawford, Ann Miller, Jules Munshin, Joi Lansing; **D:** Charles Walters; **W:** Sidney Sheldon; **M:** Irving Berlin. **VHS, Beta, LV $19.98** *MGM, HMV*

Eat My Dust 🎬🎬

Teenage son of a California sheriff steals the best stock cars from a race track to take the town's heartthrob for a joy ride. Subsequently he leads the town on a wild car chase. Brainless but fast-paced, serving as a demonstration on how to properly demolish a car. Plenty of Howards, with star Ron supported by dad Rance and brother Clint.
1976 (**PG**/*Jr. High-Adult*) 89m/C Ron Howard, Christopher Norris, Warren Kemmerling, Rance Howard, Clint Howard, Corbin Bernsen; **D:** Charles B. Griffith. **VHS, Beta $9.98** *SUE*

Eddie and the Cruisers 🎬🎬◁

In the early 1960s, rockers Eddie and the Cruisers score with one hit album. Amid their success, lead singer Pare dies mysteriously in a car accident. Years later, a reporter decides to write a feature on the defunct group, prompting a former band member to begin a search for missing tapes of the Cruisers' unreleased second album. Questions posed at the end of the movie are answered in the sequel. Enjoyable soundtrack by John Cafferty and the Beaver Brown Band.
1983 (**PG**/*Jr. High-Adult*) 90m/C Tom Berenger, Michael Pare, Ellen Barkin, Joe Pantoliano, Matthew Laurance; **D:** Martin Davidson. **VHS, Beta, LV, 8mm $14.95** *MVD, SUE, NLC*

Edison Twins

Two youngsters get into a series of predicaments, and use instructive scientific concepts to get themselves out. Series produced for the Disney channel. Additional volumes available.
1985 (*Family*) 45m/C Andrew Sabiston, Marnie McPhail. **VHS, Beta $24.95** *COL*

Educating Rita 🎬🎬🎬◁

Walters and Caine team beautifully in this adaptation of the successful Willy Russell play which finds an uneducated hairdresser determined to improve her knowledge of literature. In so doing, she enlists the aid of a tutor: a disillusioned alcoholic, adeptly played by Caine. Together, the two find inspiration in one another's differences and experiences. Ultimately, the teacher receives a lesson in how to again appreciate his work and the classics as he observes his pupil's unique approach to her studies. Some deem this a "Pygmalion" for the '80s. **Hound Advisory:** Profanity.
1983 (**PG**/*Jr. High-Adult*) 110m/C Michael Caine, Julie Walters, Michael Williams, Maureen Lipman; **D:** Lewis Gilbert; **W:** Willy Russell. **Award Nominations:** Academy Awards '83: Best Actor (Caine), Best Actress (Walters), Best Adapted Screenplay; **Awards:** British Academy Awards '83: Best Actor (Caine), Best Actress (Walters), Best Film; Golden Globe Awards '84: Best Actor—Musical/Comedy (Caine), Best Actress—Musical/Comedy (Walters). **VHS, Beta, LV, 8mm $14.95** *COL*

Edward Scissorhands 🎬🎬🎬

Edward's a synthetic teenager created by an eccentric inventor who dies before he can attach hands to his boy-

creature. With scissors in place of hands, Edward is taken in by a sweetly oblivious Avon Lady but has more trouble fitting into suburbia than most new kids; his finger-blades can create delicate works of art, or maim and even kill. Visually captivating fairy tale full of splash and color, however predictable the Hollywood-prefab denouement. **Hound Advisory:** Like many a classic fairy tale, this one has darker undertones, made manifest in violence, mature themes.
1990 (PG-13/*Jr. High-Adult*) 100m/C Johnny Depp, Winona Ryder, Dianne Wiest, Vincent Price, Anthony Michael Hall, Alan Arkin, Kathy Baker, Conchata Ferrell, Caroline Aaron, Dick Anthony Williams, Robert Oliveri, John Davidson; *D:* Tim Burton; *W:* Caroline Thompson, Tim Burton; *M:* Danny Elfman. **VHS, Beta, LV $19.98** *FOX, FCT*

The Effect of Gamma Rays on Man-in-the-Moon Marigolds 🐾🐾🐾

Wonderful drama based on the Pulitzer-Prize winning play by Paul Zindel. Little Beatrice is preparing her experiment for the school science fair, showing how radiation sometimes kills the helpless marigolds and occasionally causes them to grow into even more beautiful mutations. This mirrors Beatrice, who flowers even amidst the drunkenness of her mother and the dullness of her sister. **Hound Advisory:** Alcohol use, mature themes.
1973 (PG/*Adult*) 100m/C Joanne Woodward, Nell Potts, Roberta Wallach, Judith Lowry, Richard Venture; *D:* Paul Newman. **Award Nominations:** Cannes Film Festival '73: Best Film; **Awards:** Cannes Film Festival '73: Best Actress (Woodward). **VHS** *NO*

8 Seconds 🐾🐾🐾

Love, not sports, dominates the true-life story of rodeo star Lane Frost (Perry), a world champion bull rider killed in the ring at the age of 25 in 1990. A decent guy, he finds quick success on the rodeo circuit, marries (to Geary), and finds his career getting in the way of their happiness. Bull-riding sequences are genuinely stomach churning, the performances low-key. Title refers to the amount of time a rider must stay aboard his animal. **Hound Advisory:** Profanity.
1994 (PG-13/*Jr. High-Adult*) 104m/C Luke Perry, Cynthia Geary, Stephen Baldwin, James Rebhorn, Carrie Snodgress, Red Mitchell, Ronnie Clair Edwards; *D:* John G. Avildsen; *W:* Monte Merrick; *M:* Bill Conti. **VHS, LV** *NLC*

8 Sesame Street Stories

Including: "Everyone Makes Mistakes," "The City Worm and the Country Worm," "Wanted: The Great Cookie Thief," "Big Bird Brings Spring to Sesame Street," and four adventures of "Super Grover."
1985 (*Family*) 60m/C Big Bird, The Cookie Monster. **VHS, Beta $9.95**

18 Again! 🐾🐾🐾

After a bump on the head, an 81-year-old man and his 18-year-old grandson mentally switch places, giving each a new look at his life. Lightweight romp with Burns in especially good form, but not good enough to justify redoing this tired theme.
1988 (PG/*Jr. High-Adult*) 100m/C George Burns, Charlie Schlatter, Anita Morris, Jennifer Runyon, Tony Roberts, Red Buttons, Miriam Flynn, George DiCenzo; *D:* Paul Flaherty; *W:* Jonathan Prince, Josh Goldstein; *M:* Billy Goldenberg. **VHS, Beta, LV $19.95** *STE, NWV*

Electric Dreams 🐾🐾🐾

A young man buys a computer that yearns to do more than sit on a desk. First it takes over his apartment, then it sets its sights on the man's cello-playing neighbor-the same woman his owner is courting. To win her affections, the over-eager computer tries to dazzle her with a variety of musical compositions from his unique keyboard. Cort supplies the voice of Edgar the computer in this film that integrates a rock-music video format. **Hound Advisory:** Profanity.
1984 (PG/*Sr. High-Adult*) 95m/C Lenny Von Dohlen, Virginia Madsen, Maxwell Caulfield, Bud Cort, Koo Stark; *D:* Steven Barron. **VHS, Beta, LV $79.95** *MGM*

The Electric Horseman 🐾🐾🐾

Journalist Fonda sets out to discover the reason behind the kidnapping of a prized horse by an ex-rodeo star. The alcoholic cowboy has taken the horse to return it to its native environment, away from the clutches of corporate greed. As Fonda investigates the story she falls in love with rebel Redford. Excellent Las Vegas and remote western settings.
1979 (PG/*Family*) 120m/C Robert Redford, Jane Fonda, John Saxon, Willie Nelson, Valerie Perrine, Wilford Brimley, Nicholas Coster, James B. Sikking; *D:* Sydney Pollack; *M:* Dave Grusin. **VHS, Beta, LV $14.98** *MCA*

Elephant Boy 🐾🐾🐾

Triumphant British adaptation of Rudyard Kipling's "Toomai of the Elephants." Stay patient during child star Sabu's long, confusing speech at the start - his acting and diction improve straightaway, as he plays a boy taken on an wild elephant roundup in the jungles of India. Tragedy strikes, and the safari looks like a failure when Toomai runs away to the underbrush. There he finds a mythical haven of the great beasts, in astonishing nature scenes that probably couldn't be duplicated today at any cost. Minor classic, worth rediscovery on tape, even with its patronizing, colonial attitudes toward the natives.
1937 (*Family*) 80m/B Sabu, Walter Hudd, W.E. Holloway; *D:* Robert Flaherty, Zoltan Korda. **VHS, Beta, LV $19.98** *HBO, SUE, WAR*

The Elephant Man 🐾🐾🐾🐾

A biography of John Merrick, a severely deformed man who, with the help of a sympathetic doctor, moved from freak shows into posh London society. Lynch's first mainstream film, shot in black and white, it presents a startlingly vivid picture of the hypocrisies evident in the social moves of the Victorian era. Moving performance from Hurt in title role.
1980 (PG/*Jr. High-Adult*) 125m/B Anthony Hopkins, John Hurt, Anne Bancroft, John Gielgud, Wendy Hiller, Freddie Jones, Kenny Baker; *D:* David Lynch; *W:* Eric Bergren, Christopher DeVore, David Lynch; *M:* John Morris, Samuel Barber. **Award Nominations:** Academy Awards '80: Best Actor (Hurt), Best Art Direction/Set Decoration, Best Costume Design, Best Director (Lynch), Best Film Editing, Best Picture, Best Original Score; **Awards:** British Academy Awards '80: Best Actor (Hurt), Best Film; Cesar Awards '82: Best Foreign Film; National Board of Review Awards '80: 10 Best Films of the Year. **VHS, Beta, LV $14.95** *PAR*

The ElmChanted Forest

Yugoslavian cartoon feature about how painter Peter Pallette sleeps under a mystical elm in the Fantasy Forest and gains

Johnny Depp is "Edward Scissorhands" (1990)

the power to bring his art to life. This annoys the local dictator (who's a cross between a circus clown and a cactus). Loud, off-putting mixture of old-style animation and frantic gag heroics.
1986 (*Preschool-Primary*) 90m/C **VHS, Beta $14.95** *CEL, WTA*

Elmer 🦴🦴

Follows the adventures of a temporarily blinded youth and a loyal hound dog together in the wilderness.
1976 (*G/Family*) 82m/C Elmer Swanson, Phillip Swanson; *D:* Christopher Cain. **VHS, Beta $59.98** *LIV, WTA*

Emil and the Detective 🦴🦴🦴

A German ten-year-old is robbed of his grandmother's money by gangsters, and subsequently enlists the help of pre-adolescent detectives to retrieve it. Good Disney dramatization of the Erich Kastner children's novel. Remake of the 1931 German film starring Rolf Wenkhaus.
1964 (*Family*) 99m/C Bryan Russell, Walter Slezak, Roger Mobley; *D:* Peter Tewkesbury. **VHS, Beta $69.95** *DIS*

Emmet Otter's Jug-Band Christmas

Emmet Otter and his Ma enter the Frog Town Hollow talent contest and try to beat out a rock group called the Riverbottom Nightmares for the prize money, which will enable them to have a merry Christmas.
1977 (*Family*) 50m/C **VHS, Beta** *NO*

The Emperor's New Clothes

Classic tale from Hans Christian Andersen about two sly tailors and a vain king, read by master thespian Gielgud as part of the "Rabbit Ears: We All Have Tales" series.
1991 (*Preschool-Primary*) 30m/C **VHS, LV $15.99** *KUI, NLC,*

The Emperor's New Clothes and Other Folktales

Two con-artists make the emperor a new set of clothes that nobody can see. Also includes "Why Mosquitoes Buzz in People's Ears" and "Suho and the White Horse," all from the "Children's Circle" series.
1992 (*Preschool-Primary*) 30m/C **VHS $19.95** *CCC, WKV, BTV*

Empire of the Sun 🦴🦴🦴🦴

Extraordinarily vivid film of J.G. Ballard's autobiographical novel. Young, wealthy British boy is living in Shanghai when Japan invades China at the onset of World War II. Separated from his family, Jim adapts to a brutal (yet exhilarating) life of poverty, discomfort, betrayal, and survival at any cost when he is interred in a prison camp and befriends a scheming American black marketeer. A breathtaking work, in which Steven Spielberg's romantic child's-eye-view of the world has a heartrending context, as the sky fills with wonderful flying things - warplanes - and mysterious, mystical light - the atom bomb. **Hound Advisory:** Brutality, mature themes, sex.

1987 (**PG**/*Jr. High-Adult*) 153m/C Christian Bale, John Malkovich, Miranda Richardson, Nigel Havers, Joe Pantoliano, Leslie Phillips, Rupert Frazer, Ben Stiller, Robert Stephens, Burt Kwouk, Masato Ibu, Emily Richard; *Cameos:* J.G. Ballard; *D:* Steven Spielberg; *W:* Tom Stoppard; *M:* John Williams. **Award Nominations:** Academy Awards '87: Best Art Direction/Set Decoration, Best Cinematography, Best Costume Design, Best Film Editing, Best Sound, Best Original Score; **Awards:** National Board of Review Awards '87: 10 Best Films of the Year, Best Director (Spielberg). **VHS, Beta, LV, 8mm $19.98** *WAR, INJ*

The Empire Strikes Back 🦴🦴🦴🦴

Second in the "Star Wars" trilogy finds Luke Skywalker and the Rebel Alliance on the run from Darth Vader and the forces of the Dark Side. Luke learns the ways of a Jedi knight from master Yoda (a creation of Jim Henson's creature factory), while Han Solo and Princess Leia find romance and adventures of their own. Continues the excellent tradition set by 1977's "Star Wars" with the same superb special effects and a hearty plot, though viewers at the time were frustrated by the cliffhanger ending (followed up in "Return of the Jedi" in 1983). Also available on Laserdisc with "The Making of 'Star Wars'." **Hound Advisory:** Galactic violence.
1980 (**PG**/*Family*) 124m/C Mark Hamill, Carrie Fisher, Harrison Ford, Billy Dee Williams, Alec Guinness, David Prowse, Kenny Baker, Frank Oz, Anthony Daniels, Peter Mayhew, Clive Revill, Julian Glover, John Ratzenberger; *D:* Irvin Kershner; *W:* Leigh Brackett, Lawrence Kasdan; *M:* John Williams; *V:* James Earl Jones. **Award Nominations:** Academy Awards '80: Best Art Direction/Set Decoration, Best Original Score; **Awards:** Academy Awards '80: Best Sound, Best Visual Effects; People's Choice Awards '81: Best Film. **VHS, Beta, LV $19.98** *FOX, FCT, RDG*

Encino Man 🦴🦴

While excavating for a pool, two California high-school dudes dig up a 10,000-year old 'teenaged' caveman. After a makeover and teaching him the necessities like the four basic food groups (Milk Duds in the dairy group, Sweet Tarts in the fruit group), they take the bewildered guy to class where he becomes a hit, for some reason. Juvenile humor supposedly appealing to adolescents has its moments for adults, though the laughs are limited. Encino guy Fraser emotes little but somehow steals the show. Course, he's up against master thespians like Shore, so like, be forewarned, dude. Produced through Disney's Hollywood Pictures division. **Hound Advisory:** Alcohol use, sex talk.
1992 (**PG**/*Jr. High-Adult*) 88m/C Sean Astin, Brendan Fraser, Pauly Shore, Megan Ward, Robin Tunney, Rick Ducommun, Mariette Hartley, Richard Masur, Michael DeLuise; *D:* Les Mayfield; *W:* Shawn Schepps. **VHS, Beta $19.99** *HPH*

Encyclopedia Brown: Case of the Missing Time Capsule

Before a precious time capsule can be opened during the centennial celebration of a small town, the container is stolen. The boy detective sets out to solve the case, in a tale that amalgamates several of Donald J. Sobol's "Encyclopedia Brown" stories (some better than others). Additional volumes available.
1988 (*Family*) 55m/C Steve Holland, Scott Bremner, D. David Scheerer. **VHS $9.98** *VTR, MED*

The Endless Summer 𝄞𝄞𝄞

Classic surfing documentary about the freedom and sense of adventure that surfing symbolizes. Director Brown follows two young surfers around the world in search of the perfect wave. (They finally find it at a then-unknown break off Cape Saint Francis in South America.) Besides the excellent surfing photography, Big Kahuna Brown provides the amusing tongue-in-cheek narrative. Considered by many to be the best surf movie ever. Followed by a sequel nearly 30 years later. **1966** (*Jr. High-Adult*) 90m/C Mike Hynson, Robert August; *D:* Bruce Brown; *W:* Bruce Brown. **VHS, Beta, LV $24.95** *FCT, HMV, PBS*

The Endless Summer 2 𝄞𝄞𝄞

You don't have to personally hang ten to get stoked about this long-awaited sequel that once again follows two surfer dudes in their quest for the perfect wave. This time out pro surfers O'Connell and Weaver circle the globe seeking adventure and the world's best waves. Traces the evolution of surfing, from the lazy, golden days of the '60s to the worldwide phenomenon it is today, complete with its own pro tour circuit. Breathtaking scenery and spectacular surfing sequences highlight this look at a unique subculture. Thirty years later and it's still a great ride, though the travelogue wears thin and the sub-culture's now fairly well exploited. **Hound Advisory:** Nudity.
1994 (**PG**/*Jr. High-Adult*) 107m/C Robert "Wingnut" Weaver, Pat O'Connell, Robert August; *D:* Bruce Brown; *W:* Bruce Brown, Dana Brown. **VHS, LV** *COL*

Enemy Mine 𝄞𝄞

A space fantasy in which two pilots from warring planets, one an Earthling, the other an asexual reptilian Drac, crash land on a barren planet and are forced to work together to survive. **Hound Advisory:** Violence and profanity.
1985 (**PG-13**/*Jr. High-Adult*) 108m/C Dennis Quaid, Louis Gossett Jr., Brion James, Richard Marcus, Lance Kerwin; *D:* Wolfgang Petersen; *M:* Maurice Jarre. **VHS, Beta, LV $19.98** *FOX*

EPIC: Days of the Dinosaurs

From the creators of the Australian "Dot" series of cartoon movies comes this animated fable about two cave-kids separated from their prehistoric tribe, fighting for survival amidst savage dinosaurs. Animation is only slightly better than the prehistory.
1987 (*Family*) 75m/C *D:* Yoram Gross. **VHS, Beta $39.95** *FHE, WTA*

Erik the Viking 𝄞𝄞

Mediocre farce about a Viking who grows dissatisfied with his barbaric way of life and sets out to find mythical Asgaard, where Norse gods dwell. Great cast of character actors in an insubstantial fairytale that flirts with the Monty Python style. That's no coincidence; script was loosely based on stories the director - Python alumnus Jones - wrote to amuse his small son. That this material could somehow wind up with a PG-13 is one of his better jokes.
1989 (**PG-13**/*Jr. High-Adult*) 104m/C Tim Robbins, Terry Jones, Mickey Rooney, John Cleese, Imogen Stubbs, Anthony Sher, Gordon John Sinclair, Freddie Jones, Eartha Kitt; *D:* Terry Jones; *W:* Terry Jones. **VHS, Beta, LV $89.98** *ORI*

Ernest Goes to Camp 𝄞𝄞

The first Ernest hit (not counting cameos and video compilations) with Varney's TV commercial pitchman Ernest P. Worrell, here a fool handyman at a summer camp. For a gag he's promoted to counselor to a loser troop of juvenile delinquents, but of course the dope's upbeat attitude unites the boys to save Camp Kakakee from developers. Really, really poor jokes, with slobbery sentiment and quite a lesson at the climax for kid viewers: If you're unafraid of bullets, they won't hurt you. **Hound Advisory:** Roughhousing, stupid behavior.
1987 (**PG**/*Jr. High-Adult*) 92m/C Jim Varney, Victoria Racimo, John Vernon, Iron Eyes Cody, Lyle Alzado, Gailard Sartain, Daniel Butler, Hakeem Abdul-Samad; *D:* John R. Cherry III. **VHS, Beta $19.99** *TOU*

Ernest Goes to Jail 𝄞𝄞

One of the better "Ernest" outings, thanks to creative gags and slam-bang plotting. Still, after 81 minutes you've had enough, knowwhutImean? Electromagnetized bank janitor Ernest P. Worrell gets switched for a lookalike hardcore convict and winds up in the felon's cell, while the bad guy, on the outside, schemes a heist. Get a load of Ernest's gadget-filled home - it looks like he inherited Pee Wee Herman's old place, as well as his audience. **Hound Advisory:** Roughhousing.
1990 (**PG**/*Jr. High-Adult*) 81m/C Jim Varney, Gailard Sartain, Randall "Tex" Cobb, Bill Byrge, Barry Scott, Charles Napier; *D:* John R. Cherry III. **VHS, LV $89.95** *BVV, TOU*

The Ernest Green Story 𝄞𝄞𝄞

One of the newer breed of Disney made-for-TV features, a true story of the racial hatred and rage endured by Green, the first black teenager to attend an all-white Arkansas high school in the 1950s. Well-acted and uncompromising in its subject matter, and ultimately optimistic and triumphant. **Hound Advisory:** Violence, mature themes.
1993 (*Jr. High-Adult*) 92m/C Morris Chestnut, CCH Pounder, Gary Grubbs, Tina Lifford, Avery Brooks, Ruby Dee, Ossie Davis; *D:* Eric Laneuville. **VHS** *DIS*

Ernest Rides Again 𝄞𝄞

Ernest P. "KnowwhutImean?" Worrell is now aiding a professor who thinks the British crown jewels (the real ones) were hidden in a Revolutionary War cannon. Ernest uncovers the massive wheeled weapon, and the plot is a long slapstick chase between him, British agents and a greedy antiquities collector. Redundant slapstick targeted strictly for Ernest fans in which the star gets comedically upstaged by a couple of goofball vacuum cleaner salesmen. **Hound Advisory:** Roughhousing.
1993 (**PG**/*Jr. High-Adult*) 93m/C Jim Varney, Ron James, Duke Ernsberger, Jeffrey Pillars, Linda Kash, Tom Butler; *D:* John Cherry; *W:* John Cherry, William M. Akers; *M:* Bruce Arnstson, Kirby Shelstad. **VHS $94.95** *MNC*

Ernest Saves Christmas 𝄞𝄞

Ernest P. Worrell is back in the second of the series. When Santa decides that it's time to retire, cabbie Ernest must help recruit a handpicked successor - a has-been children's show

host who is a bit reluctant. Starts off with promise, then succumbs to the Ernest brand of slapstick tedium. For youngest fans only. **Hound Advisory:** Roughhousing.
1988 (PG/*Primary-Adult*) 91m/C Jim Varney, Douglas Seale, Oliver Clark, Noelle Parker, Billie Bird; **D:** John R. Cherry III. **VHS, Beta, LV** $14.99 *TOU*

Ernest Scared Stupid 🎬🎬

Pea-brained Ernest P. Worrell returns yet again in this silly comedy. When he accidentally releases a demon from a sacred tomb, a 200-year-old curse threatens to destroy his hometown, unless Ernest and a friendly witch-lady come to the rescue. Again, the Ernest level of slapstick crosses the line into being annoying, so ensure you're in the mood.
1991 (PG/*Jr. High-Adult*) 93m/C Jim Varney, Eartha Kitt, Austin Nagler, Jonas Moscartolo, Shay Astar; **D:** John R. Cherry III; **M:** Bruce Arnstson. **VHS, Beta** $14.99 *TOU*

The Errand Boy 🎬🎬🎬

Lewis' distinct schnook character hits Hollywood in search of a job. He wins a position as a movie-studio errand boy, but his assignment is really to spy on other employees. That's the slender hook on which hangs some of the comic's brightest slapstick. Imagine the apocalypse if Jerry and Ernest P. Worrell ever met.
1961 (*Preschool*) 92m/B Jerry Lewis, Brian Donlevy, Dick Wesson, Howard McNear, Felicia Atkins, Fritz Feld, Sig Rumann, Renee Taylor, Doodles Weaver, Mike Mazurki, Lorne Greene, Michael Landon, Dan Blocker, Pernell Roberts, Snub Pollard, Kathleen Freeman; **D:** Jerry Lewis; **W:** Jerry Lewis. **VHS, Beta, LV** $59.95 *LIV*

Escapade in Florence 🎬🎬

Two young art students practice their technique in Italy, only to discover that a criminal gang of forgers is passing on their classical-painting reproductions as the real thing. Generally artless Disney adventure.
1962 (*Family*) 81m/C Tommy Kirk, Ivan Desny; **D:** Steve Previn. **VHS, Beta** $69.95 *DIS*

Escapade in Japan 🎬🎬

A Japanese youth helps an American boy frantically search the city of Tokyo for his parents. Shot in Japan.
1957 (*Family*) 93m/C Cameron Mitchell, Teresa Wright, Jon Provost, Roger Nakagawa, Philip Ober, Clint Eastwood; **D:** Arthur Lubin; **M:** Max Steiner. **VHS, Beta** $15.95 *VCI*

Escape Artist 🎬🎬🎬

"Black Stallion" cinematographer Deschanel's first directorial effort was this quirky film about a teenage escape artist (played by the son of Ryan O'Neal, Tatum's brother) who sets out to uncover the identity of his magician-father's killers by using his own illusions and trickery. A more family-friendly alternative to the often rough "F/X" movies. Script co-authored by the writer of "E.T.," based on a novel by David Wagoner. **Hound Advisory:** Salty language.
1982 (PG/*Jr. High-Adult*) 96m/C Griffin O'Neal, Raul Julia, Teri Garr, Joan Hackett, Desi Arnaz Sr., Gabriel Dell, Huntz Hall, Jackie Coogan; **D:** Caleb Deschanel; **W:** Melissa Mathison; **M:** Georges Delerue. **VHS, Beta, LV** $79.98 *LIV, VES*

Escape from the Planet of the Apes 🎬🎬🎬

Reprising their roles as intelligent, English-speaking apes, McDowall and Hunter flee their world before it's destroyed, and travel back in time to present-day America. In L.A. they become the subjects of a relentless search by the fearful population, much like humans Charlton Heston and James Franciscus were targeted for experimentation and destruction in simian society in the earlier "Planet of the Apes" and "Beneath the Planet of the Apes." Best of the "Planet of the Apes" sequels is followed by "Conquest of the Planet of the Apes." **Hound Advisory:** Violence.
1971 (G/*Family*) 98m/C Roddy McDowall, Kim Hunter, Sal Mineo, Ricardo Montalban, William Windom, Bradford Dillman, Natalie Trundy, Eric (Hans Gudegast) Braeden; **D:** Don Taylor; **M:** Jerry Goldsmith. **VHS, Beta, LV** $19.98 *FOX, FUS*

Escape of the One-Ton Pet

When her beloved calf grows into a full-grown steer, a young girl is ordered by her father to find a new pet.
1978 (*Preschool-Primary*) 73m/C **D:** Richard Bennett; **V:** Stacy Swor, James Callahan, Michael Morgan, Richard Yniguez. **VHS, Beta** *FHE, TLF*

Escape to Witch Mountain 🎬🎬🎬

Two young orphans with supernatural powers know their destiny lies at Witch Mountain, but on the way they're chased by a greedy millionaire who wants to exploit their amazing abilities. One of the better 1970s live-action Disney features, diverting and genuinely mysterious at times. Adapted from a novel by Alexander Key.
1975 (G/*Family*) 97m/C Kim Richards, Ike Eisenmann, Eddie Albert, Ray Milland, Donald Pleasence; **D:** John Hough. **VHS, Beta, LV** $19.99 *DIS, BTV*

E.T.: The Extra-Terrestrial 🎬🎬🎬🎬

Spielberg's famous fantasy, one of the most popular films in history, portrays a homely, limpid-eyed little alien stranded on Earth. While trying desperately to signal to his mothership UFO, he forms a special relationship with Elliott, a young boy who literally stumbles across him. Modern fairy tale provides warmth, humor, pathos, and sheer wonder. Held first place as the highest grossing movie of all time for years until a new Spielberg hit replaced it - "Jurassic Park." Debra Winger contributed to the voice of E.T. **Hound Advisory:** Occasional salty language; death, dying and rejuvenation.
1982 (PG/*Family*) 115m/C Henry Thomas, Dee Wallace Stone, Drew Barrymore, Robert MacNaughton, Peter Coyote, C. Thomas Howell, Sean Frye, K.C. Martel; **D:** Steven Spielberg; **W:** Melissa Mathison; **M:** John Williams. **Award Nominations:** Academy Awards '81: Best Film Editing; Academy Awards '82: Best Cinematography, Best Director (Spielberg), Best Picture, Best Sound; **Awards:** Academy Awards '82: Best Sound, Best Visual Effects, Best Original Score; Golden Globe Awards '83: Best Film—Drama, Best Score; People's Choice Awards '83: Best Film. **VHS, Beta, LV** $24.95 *MCA, APD, RDG*

Evil Under the Sun 🎬🎬

Poor Agatha Christie outing in spite of all-star cast makes "Death on the Nile" look much better by comparison. An opulent beach resort is the setting as Hercule Poirot attempts to unravel a murder mystery.

1982 (PG/*Jr. High-Adult*) 112m/C Peter Ustinov, Jane Birkin, Dame Maggie Smith, Colin Blakely, Roddy McDowall, Diana Rigg, Sylvia Miles, James Mason, Nicholas Clay; *D:* Guy Hamilton; *W:* Anthony Shaffer. **VHS, Beta, LV $14.98** *REP*

The Ewok Adventure

Those adorable, friendly creatures from "Return of the Jedi" go from film to made-for-TV in an utterly generic adventure by George Lucas. The teddy-bear Ewoks befriend two kids whose spaceship crashed, then journey to free their parents from "the dreaded giant Gorax." Little of the "Star Wars" lore is present, and the slow-moving plot may as well have taken place anywhere - but LucasFilm has the special-effects moxie like nobody else and the visuals, at least, do not disappoint. Followed by "Ewoks: The Battle for Endor." **Hound Advisory:** Violence.
1984 (G/*Family*) 96m/C Warwick Davis, Eric Walker, Aubree Miller, Fionnula Flanagan; *D:* John Korty; *M:* Elmer Bernstein. **VHS, Beta, LV $14.95** *MGM, FCT*

The Ewoks: Battle for Endor

Made-for-TV follow-up to "The Ewok Adventure" is notably better, if you can get past the jolt at the start - the massacre of the happy human family so laboriously rescued in the last movie. Lone survivor, cute daughter Cindel, accompanies her furry friend Wicket (now speaking English) on a mission to free Ewoks from a monster warlord. They meet more creatures, allies and enemies. Ends with a thrilling battle, reminiscent of the Ewok skirmish at the end of "Return of the Jedi," which is praise indeed; it's the beginning of this that might upset tykes. **Hound Advisory:** Violence.
1985 (*Family*) 98m/C Wilford Brimley, Warwick Davis, Aubree Miller, Sian Phillips, Paul Gleason, Eric Walker, Carel Struycken, Niki Botholo; *D:* Jim Wheat, Ken Wheat. **VHS, Beta, LV $14.95** *MGM, FCT*

Experience Preferred. . . But Not Essential

English schoolgirl Annie gets her first job at a seaside resort where she meets assorted strange characters and learns about life. Gentle tale, often compared to "Gregory's Girl." **Hound Advisory:** Nudity, sex talk, mature themes.
1983 (PG/*Jr. High-Adult*) 77m/C Elizabeth Edmonds, Sue Wallace, Geraldine Griffith, Karen Meagher, Ron Bain, Alun Lewis, Robert Blythe; *D:* Peter Duffell; *W:* June Roberts. **VHS, Beta $59.95** *MGM*

Explorers

What if, in the middle of "E.T.," the classic alien suddenly took off his mask and revealed himself as ... Mork from Ork? That's more or less what happens to this delicate, promising sci-fi tale that takes a galactic detour into gonzo comedy. Three boys, prompted by strange dreams, build a circuit that allows them to turn a scrapped carnival ride into a real spaceship. Zooming into space, they discover who invited them. Recommended more for kid viewers who may better appreciate -and forgive - the punchline. From the director of "Gremlins." **Hound Advisory:** Salty language, roughhousing, alcohol use.

1985 (PG/*Family*) 107m/C Ethan Hawke, River Phoenix, Jason Presson, Amanda Peterson, Mary Kay Place, Dick Miller, Robert Picardo, Dana Ivey, Meshach Taylor, Brooke Bundy; *D:* Joe Dante; *W:* Eric Luke; *M:* Jerry Goldsmith. **VHS, Beta, LV $14.95** *PAR*

Eye on the Sparrow

Winningham and Carradine are a couple who desperately want to raise a child of their own, but the system classifies them as unfit parents since they are both blind. Together they successfully fight the system in this inspiring made for television movie that was based on a true story.
1991 (PG/*Jr. High-Adult*) 94m/C Mare Winningham, Keith Carradine, Conchata Ferrell, Sandy McPeak, Karen Lee, Bianca Rose; *D:* John Korty. **VHS $89.98** *REP*

The Ezra Jack Keats Library

The Children's Circle Studios present animated versions of six of Keats' children's books: "The Snowy Day," "Peter's Chair," "Goggles," "Apt. 3," "Pet Show," and "The Trip." Also included is an interview with Keats.
1992 (*Family*) 45m/C Ezra Jack Keats. **VHS $19.95** *CCC, MLT, WKV*

F/X

Hollywood special effects expert is contracted by the government to fake an assassination to protect a mob informer. After completing the assignment, he learns that he's become involved in a real crime and is forced to reach into his bag of F/X tricks to survive. Twists and turns abound in this fast-paced story that was the sleeper hit of the year. Followed by a sequel. **Hound Advisory:** Profanity; violence; suggested sex.
1986 (R/*Sr. High-Adult*) 109m/C Bryan Brown, Cliff DeYoung, Diane Venora, Brian Dennehy, Jerry Orbach, Mason Adams, Martha Gehman; *D:* Robert Mandel; *W:* Robert T. Megginson, Gregory Fleemand; *M:* Bill Conti. **VHS, Beta, LV $14.98** *HBO, FCT*

F/X 2: The Deadly Art of Illusion

Weak follow-up finds the special-effects specialist set to pull off just one more illusion for the police. Once again, corrupt cops use him as a chump for their scheme, an over-complicated business involving a stolen Vatican treasure. **Hound Advisory:** Violence, nudity, profanity.
1991 (PG-13/*Sr. High-Adult*) 107m/C Bryan Brown, Brian Dennehy, Rachel Ticotin, Philip Bosco, Joanna Gleason; *D:* Richard Franklin. **VHS, LV $14.98** *ORI, IME*

Fabulous Joe

A talking dog named Joe gets involved in the life of a henpecked husband.
1947 (*Family*) 54m/C Walter Abel, Donald Meek, Margot Grahame, Marie Wilson; *D:* Bernard Carr. **VHS, Beta $19.95** *NOS*

Face the Music

Ringwald and Dempsey were once stormily married and pursuing successful, collaborative careers as singer/songwriters for the movies. But they've abandoned the work, along with the marriage, until a movie producer makes them a very

lucrative offer for a new song. Only Dempsey's new girlfriend has some voracious objections.
1992 (PG-13/*Jr. High-Adult*) 93m/C Patrick Dempsey, Molly Ringwald, Lysette Anthony. **VHS $89.98** *LIV*

Faeries

The legendary hero Oisin finds himself enlisted in the fight to save the mystical inhabitants of faerie world from a tyrant king. Elaborate cartoon based on Brian Froud and Alan Lee's best-selling book.
1981 (*Preschool-Primary*) 30m/C *V:* Morgan Brittany, Hans Conried, June Foray. **VHS, Beta $195.00** *FHE, PYR, WTA*

Fame 🐾🐾🐾

The progress of eight talented teens, from freshmen year through graduation from New York's High School of Performing Arts. Untraditional plot opens with their audition, ends simply with their graduation; in between director Parker allows the students to mature on screen, revealing the pressures of constantly trying to prove themselves. A faultless parallel is drawn between these "special" kids and the pressures felt by high schoolers everywhere. Great dance and music sequences are skillfully woven into the realistic narrative, and you'd never detect the epic running time. Inspiration for the popular TV series. There's no shortage of profanity, lewdness and streetwise ambiance, and that R is well deserved. ♫ Fame; Red Light; I Sing the Body Electric; Dogs in the Yard; Hot Lunch Jam; Out Here On My Own; Is It OK If I Call You Mine?. **Hound Advisory:** Profanity, nudity, violence, mature themes.
1980 (R/*Sr. High-Adult*) 133m/C Irene Cara, Barry Miller, Paul McCrane, Anne Meara, Joanna Merlin, Richard Belzer, Maureen Teefy; *D:* Alan Parker; *M:* Michael Gore. **Award Nominations:** Academy Awards '80: Best Film Editing, Best Film Editing, Best Original Screenplay, Best Song ("Out Here on My Own"), Best Sound; **Awards:** Academy Awards '80: Best Song ("Fame"), Best Original Score; Golden Globe Awards '81: Best Song ("Fame"). **VHS, Beta, LV $19.99** *MGM, FCT*

A Family Circus Christmas

Characters of Bill Keane's comic strip, "Family Circus," celebrate Christmas in a cartoon approach. The hysterics begin when one of the children asks Santa for a very unusual present, which he delivers.
1984 (*Family*) 30m/C *D:* Al Kouzel. **VHS, Beta $9.95** *FHE, WTA*

Family Circus Easter

"Family Circus" kids Billy, Dolly, and Jeffy celebrate Easter by trying to catch that celebrated bunny (whose voice is provided by jazz great Gillespie).
1980 (*Family*) 30m/C **VHS, Beta $9.95** *WTA, FHE*

Family Jewels 🐾🐾

Child heiress has to choose her adoptive father from among her six vastly different uncles, all played by Lewis. If you like Lewis you can't miss this. In addition to the six-pack of uncles, he's the chauffeur, plus (offscreen) producer, director, and co-author of the script. He may have also catered and provided transportation. Slapstick shtick and goofy guises will appeal to young viewers.

1965 (*Family*) 100m/C Jerry Lewis, Donna Butterworth, Sebastian Cabot, Robert Strauss; *D:* Jerry Lewis; *W:* Jerry Lewis. **VHS, Beta $19.95** *PAR*

Family Prayers 🐾🐾◁

Coming-of-age drama, set in 1969 Los Angeles, about 13-year-old Andrew and his family troubles. Dad is a compulsive gambler which causes friction with his wife and the sister-in-law who has bailed the couple out of their money problems more than once. Meanwhile, Andrew tries to look out for his younger sister and prepare for his bar-mitzvah. A little too much of a nostalgic golden glow surrounds what is essentially a family tragedy. **Hound Advisory:** Mature themes.
1991 (PG/*Jr. High-Adult*) 109m/C Tzvi Ratner-Stauber, Joe Mantegna, Anne Archer, Patti LuPone, Paul Reiser, Allen (Gooritz) Garfield, Conchata Ferrell, David Margulies; *D:* Scott Rosenfelt; *W:* Steven Ginsburg. **VHS $89.95** *COL*

Famous Five Get into Trouble 🐾🐾

Four precocious youngsters and a dog get involved with a criminal plot and cutely wile their way out of it. Scandinavian; dubbed in English.
1987 (*Preschool-Jr. High*) 90m/C Astrid Villaume, Ove Sprogoe, Lily Broberg; *D:* Trine Hedman. **VHS, Beta $69.95** *TWE*

Fandango 🐾🐾◁

Five college friends (including Costner in an early role) take a wild weekend drive across the Texas Badlands for one last fling before graduation and the prospect of military service. Expanded by Reynolds with assistance from Steven Spielberg, from his student film. Provides an interesting look at college and life during the '60s Vietnam crisis. **Hound Advisory:** Profanity.
1985 (PG/*Sr. High-Adult*) 91m/C Judd Nelson, Kevin Costner, Sam Robards, Chuck Bush, Brian Cesak, Elizabeth Daily, Suzy Amis, Glenne Headly, Pepe Serna, Marvin J. McIntyre; *D:* Kevin Reynolds; *W:* Kevin Reynolds; *M:* Alan Silvestri. **VHS, Beta $19.98** *WAR*

Fangface

Scraps from old Saturday-morning network TV shows feature the adventures of Sherman Fangsworth, a teenager who changes into Fangface the werewolf and fights crime with friends Biff, Kim, and Puggsy. For what little it's worth, the premise actually predates the popular "Teen Wolf" movies and cartoon spinoffs.
1983 (*Family*) 60m/C **VHS, Beta $19.95** *WOV, WTA*

Fangface Spooky Spoofs

Unearthed episodes of the teenage-werewolf TV cartoon, "Great Ape Escape" and "Dinosaur Daze."
1978 (*Preschool-Primary*) 44m/C **VHS $19.95** *WTA*

Fantasia 🐾🐾🐾🐾

An array of classic sequences, from Mickey Mouse as a sorcerer's apprentice to the life-cycle of dinosaurs set to Stravinsky concludes with the mighty occult visuals of "A Night on Bald Mountain." Walt Disney's most personal animation feature first bombed at the box office and irked purists who couldn't take the plotless, experimental mix of classical music and cartoons. It became a cult item, embraced by later, more liberal generations of filmgoers, particularly the Woodstock Nation. Video release was painstakingly restored to match the original version. That's the good news. Bad news is, Disney's distribution of it has ceased because of their planned remake. Note also the Italian "Allegro Non Troppo." ♫ Toccata & Fugue in D; The Nutcracker Suite; The Sorcerer's Apprentice; The Rite of Spring; Pastoral Symphony; Dance of the Hours; Night on Bald Mountain; Ave Maria; The Cossack Dance. **1940** (*Family*) 116m/C Mickey Mouse; *Performed by:* Philadelphia Symphony Orchestra. **VHS, LV $24.99** *DIS, FCT, RDG*

The Fantastic Adventures of Unico

Japanese animated cartoon compilation about a unicorn with the magical ability to make people happy — except critics; one singled out this tape as being especially grotesque and scary, as cuddly Unico battles a monstrous living statue, skewers a bad guy on a spike, and combats a hideous demon. Maybe something got lost in the translation. For those who haven't had enough, "Unico in the Island of Magic" is also available. **1984** (*Family*) 89m/C **VHS, Beta $19.95** *WTA*

Fantastic Planet 🐾🐾🐾

A critically acclaimed French, animated, sci-fi epic based on the drawings of Roland Topor. A race of small humanoids are enslaved and exploited by a race of giants on a savage planet, until one of the small creatures manages to unite his people and fight for equality. **Hound Advisory:** Mature themes, some violence. **1973** (*PG/Family*) 68m/C *D:* Rene Laloux; *V:* Barry Bostwick. **VHS, Beta $24.95** *VYY, MRV, SNC*

The Fantastic World of D.C. Collins 🐾🐾

Little D.C. constantly daydreams of action and adventure. Finally he gets to live out some TV-level James Bond exploits when he obtains a vital videotape lost by the bad guys. Mediocre telefilm designed as a vehicle for "Diff'rent Strokes" star Coleman. **1984** (*Jr. High-Adult*) 100m/C Gary Coleman, Bernie Casey, Shelley Smith, Fred Dryer, Marilyn McCoo, Phillip Abbott, George Gobel, Michael Ansara; *D:* Leslie Martinson. **VHS $19.95** *STE, NWV*

Far and Away 🐾🐾◁

Meandering old-fashioned epic about immigrants, romance, and settling the American West. In the 1890s, Joseph Donelly (Cruise) is forced to flee his Irish homeland after threatening the life of his landlord, and emigrates to America in the company of the landlord's daughter, feisty Shannon Christie (Kidman). Particularly brutal scenes of Cruise earning his living as a bare-knuckled boxer contrast with the expansiveness of the land rush ending. Slow, spotty, and a little too slick for its own good, though real-life couple Cruise and Kidman are an attractive pair. Filmed in 70-mm Panavision on location in Ireland and Montana with a soundtrack contributed to by The Chieftains. Also available in a letter boxed version. **Hound Advisory:** Violence and profanity.

1992 (*PG-13/Jr. High-Adult*) 140m/C Tom Cruise, Nicole Kidman, Thomas Gibson, Robert Prosky, Barbara Babcock, Colm Meaney, Eileen Pollock, Michelle Johnson, Cyril Cusack, Clint Howard, Rance Howard; *D:* Ron Howard; *W:* Bob Dolman; *M:* John Williams. **VHS, Beta, LV $19.98** *MCA*

A Far Off Place 🐾🐾◁

In Africa two mismatched youngsters struggle to survive after poachers slaughter a herd of elephants, and then their parents. The boy and girl face peril during a trek across the Kalahari desert in the company of a teenage bushman. Witherspoon and Randall carry their end well, though Bok steals the show. Collaboration between Spielberg's Amblin Entertain and Disney studios is more violent that most productions bearing the Magic Kingdom stamp, though careful editing reduces the bloodshed. Based on the books "A Story Like the Wind" and "A Far Off Place" by Laurens van der Post. **Hound Advisory:** Elephants slaughtered, parents slaughtered, little blood shed. **1993** (*PG-13/Jr. High-Adult*) 107m/C Reese Witherspoon, Ethan Randall, Sarel Bok, Jack Thompson, Maximilian Schell, Robert Burke, Patricia Kalember, Daniel Gerroll, Miles Anderson; *D:* Mikael Salomon; *W:* Robert Caswell, Jonathan Hensleigh, Sally Robinson; *M:* James Horner. **VHS, Beta, LV $94.95** *DIS*

Farmer Alfalfa Show & Play Your Hunch

Variety of Terrytoon cartoons from the children's show and an episode of Merv Griffin's "Play Your Hunch." **19??** (*Preschool-Primary*) 60m/C **VHS $24.95** *WTA, VRS*

The Farmer's Daughter 🐾🐾🐾

Young portrays Katrin Holmstrom, a Swedish farm girl who becomes a maid to Congressman Cotten and winds up running for office herself (not neglecting to find romance as well). The outspoken and multi-talented character charmed audiences and was the basis of a television series in the 1960s. **1947** (*Jr. High-Adult*) 97m/B Loretta Young, Joseph Cotten, Ethel Barrymore, Charles Bickford, Harry Davenport, Lex Barker, James Arness, Rose Hobart; *D:* H.C. Potter. **Award Nominations:** Academy Awards '47: Best Supporting Actor (Bickford); **Awards:** Academy Awards '47: Best Actress (Young). **VHS, Beta $59.98** *FOX, BTV*

Fast Break 🐾🐾

New York deli clerk who is a compulsive basketball fan talks his way into a college coaching job. He takes a team of street players (including a girl) with him, with predictable results on and off the court. **Hound Advisory:** Profanity, sex talk. **1979** (*PG/Primary-Adult*) 107m/C Gabe Kaplan, Harold Sylvester, Randee Heller; *D:* Jack Smight; *M:* David Shire. **VHS, Beta $19.95** *GKK*

Fast Forward 🐾◁

Group of eight teenagers from Ohio learn how to deal with success and failure when they enter a national dance contest in New York City. Break-dancing variation on the old show business chestnut. ♫ Fast Forward; How Do You Do; As Long As We Believe; Pretty Girl; Mystery; Curves; Showdown; Do You Want It Right Now?; Hardrock. **1984** (*PG/Jr. High-Adult*) 110m/C John Scott Clough, Don Franklin, Tracy Silver, Cindy McGee; *D:* Sidney Poitier; *W:* Richard Wesley; *M:* Tom Bahler. **VHS, Beta, LV $79.95** *COL*

Fast Getaway ♫♫

Chase scenes galore as a teen criminal mastermind plots bank heists for his outlaw father. But dad's karate-kicking new girlfriend/accomplice is jealous of the kid and schemes against him. Adolescent action-comedy, cleverly acted - but your enjoyment may be tempered by the portrayal of bank robbers as heroes. **Hound Advisory:** Profanity, roughhousing, sex talk.
1991 (**PG**/*Jr. High-Adult*) 91m/C Corey Haim, Cynthia Rothrock, Leo Rossi, Ken Lerner, Marcia Strassman; *D:* Spiro Razatos. **VHS, LV, 8mm $89.95** *COL*

Fast Times at Ridgemont High ♫♫♫♫

Parents be forewarned: depicts high school as den of breeding anarchy. Teens at a Southern California high school revel in sex, drugs, and rock 'n' roll. A full complement of student types meet at the mall - that great suburban microcosm percolating with angst-ridden teen trials - to contemplate losing their virginity, plot skipping homeroom, and move inexorably closer to the end of their adolescence. Talented young cast became household names, led by Penn as the California surfer dude who antagonizes teacher, Walston, aka "Aloha Mr. Hand." Based on the best-selling book by Crowe, who at 22 returned to high school to acquire necessary adolescent confidential. One of the best of the "escape from hell high school" genre, bettered only by "Rock 'N' Roll High School." **Hound Advisory:** Profanity; drug use; nudity; sex.
1982 (**R**/*Sr. High-Adult*) 91m/C Sean Penn, Jennifer Jason Leigh, Judge Reinhold, Robert Romanus, Brian Backer, Phoebe Cates, Ray Walston, Scott Thomson, Vincent Schiavelli, Amanda Wyss, Forest Whitaker, Kelli Maroney, Eric Stoltz, Pamela Springsteen, James Russo, Martin Brest, Anthony Edwards; *D:* Amy Heckerling; *W:* Cameron Crowe. **VHS, Beta, LV $14.95** *MCA*

Fat Albert & the Cosby Kids, Vol. 1

The message of this Fat Albert series emphasizes communication: talking, listening, and sharing as important aspects of expression. The Cosby Kids develop these ideas through humorous situations. In this episode, two members of the gang drive an entire hospital crazy when they have to have their tonsils removed. Additional volumes available.
1973 (*Primary-Jr. High*) 60m/C *V:* Bill Cosby. **VHS, Beta $9.95** *BAR, WTA*

Fatal Instinct ♫♫

Spoof on erotic thrillers such as "Fatal Attraction" and "Basic Instinct" is sort of funny without really being funny. Suave Assante plays a guy with dual careers - he's both cop and attorney, defending the criminals he's arrested. Young plays a lovelorn psycho who's lost her panties. Plot is worth mentioning only in passing, since the point is to mercilessly skewer the entire film noir tradition. The gags occasionally hit deep-chuckle level, though for every good joke there's at least three that misfire. Clemmons of "E Street Band" fame wanders around with sax for background music purposes, typical of the acute self-consciousness. **Hound Advisory:** Profanity and sex talk.
1993 (**PG-13**/*Jr. High-Adult*) 90m/C Armand Assante, Sean Young, Sherilyn Fenn, Kate Nelligan, Christopher McDonald, James Remar, Tony Randall; *Cameos:* Clarence Clemmons, Doc Severinsen; *D:* Carl Reiner; *W:* David O'Malley; *M:* Richard Gibbs. **VHS, LV** *MGM*

Father Figure ♫♫♫♫

When a divorced man attends his ex-wife's funeral, he discovers that he must take care of his estranged sons. Based on young adult writer Richard Peck's novel; well-done made-for-TV movie.
1980 (*Sr. High-Adult*) 94m/C Hal Linden, Timothy Hutton, Cassie Yates, Martha Scott, Jeremy Licht; *D:* Jerry London; *M:* Billy Goldenberg. **VHS, Beta** *NO*

Father Hood ♫

Family drama has Swayze playing a small-time criminal whose daughter tracks him down after leaving the foster-care shelter where she and her brother are being abused. The family takes to the road, running from both the police and a journalist (Berry) who wants to expose the corrupt foster-care system. The children are obnoxious, Swayze is miscast, and the entire film is a misfire. **Hound Advisory:** Roughhousing; salty language.
1993 (**PG-13**/*Jr. High-Adult*) 94m/C Patrick Swayze, Halle Berry, Sabrina Lloyd, Brian Bonsall, Diane Ladd, Michael Ironside, Bob Gunton; *D:* Darrell Roodt; *W:* Scott Spencer. **VHS, LV** *BVV*

Father of the Bride ♫♫♫♫

Classic, quietly hilarious comedy about the tribulations of a father preparing for his only daughter's wedding. Tracy is suitably overwhelmed as the loving father and Taylor radiant as the bride. A warm vision of American family life, accompanied by the 1940 MGM short "Wedding Bills." Also available in a colorized version. Followed by "Father's Little Dividend" and later a television series. Remade in 1991.
1950 (*Family*) 94m/C Spencer Tracy, Elizabeth Taylor, Joan Bennett, Billie Burke, Leo G. Carroll, Russ Tamblyn, Don Taylor, Moroni Olsen; *D:* Vincente Minnelli; *W:* Francis Goodrich, Albert Hacket. **VHS, Beta, LV $19.98** *MGM*

Father of the Bride ♫♫♫

Remake of the 1950 comedy classic falls short of the original, but still manages to charm. Nice house, nice neighborhood, nice family. Martin is adequately confused about the upcoming nuptials and reluctant to cut the ties that bind with his daughter, played nicely by Williams in her film debut (later she appeared in a TV ad as a young bride-to-be calling her dad long distance to tell him she's engaged). Keaton is little more than attractive window dressing as the bride's mom, while Short gobbles up the screen and the first row of seats vamping as a pretentious wedding coordinator. Actual wedding is one of the more extravagant in recent film history. Adapted from a novel by Edward Streeter. **Hound Advisory:** Brief profanity.
1991 (**PG**/*Jr. High-Adult*) 105m/C Steve Martin, Diane Keaton, Kimberly Williams, Kieran Culkin, George Newbern, Martin Short, B.D. Wong, Peter Michael Goetz, Kate McGregor Stewart, Martha Gehman; *Cameos:* Eugene Levy; *D:* Charles Shyer; *W:* Charles Shyer, Nancy Meyer; *M:* Alan Silvestri. **VHS, Beta, LV $94.95** *TOU*

Father's Little Dividend ♫♫♫

Tracy expects a little peace and quiet now that he's successfully married off Taylor in this charming sequel to "Father of the Bride." However, he's quickly disillusioned by

Steve Martin contemplates losing his daughter in "Father of the Bride" (1991)

the news he'll soon be a grandfather - a prospect that causes nothing but dismay. Reunited the stars, director, writers, and producer from the successful first film.
1951 (*Family*) 82m/B Spencer Tracy, Joan Bennett, Elizabeth Taylor, Don Taylor, Billie Burke, Russ Tamblyn, Moroni Olsen; **D:** Vincente Minnelli; **W:** Francis Goodrich, Albert Hacket. **VHS, Beta, LV $9.95** *CNG, MRV, NOS*

Fatty Finn 🎵♪

A children's gagfest about young kids and bullies during the Depression, based on Syd Nicholls' comic strip.
1984 (*Family*) 91m/C Ben Oxenbould, Bart Newton; **D:** Maurice Murphy. **VHS, Beta** *NO*

Federal Agents vs. Underworld, Inc.

Super G-Man Dave Worth goes up against Nila, a greedy villainess bent on finding the golden hands of Kurigal so she may rule the world. 12-episode serial.
1949 (*Family*) 167m/B Kirk Alyn, Rosemary La Planche, Roy Barcroft, Carol Forman, James Dale, Bruce Edwards; **D:** Fred Brannon. **VHS $29.98** *REP, MLB*

Felix the Cat: An Hour of Fun

The funny feline delves into his bag of tricks for a compilation of vintage cartoon adventures. Additional volumes available.
1989 (*Family*) 60m/C **VHS, LV $14.95** *IME, WTA*

Felix the Cat: The Movie 🎵♪

Classic cartoon creation Felix returns in a trite feature. The feline and his bag of tricks enter a dimension filled with He-Man/Mutant Ninja Turtles leftovers; new-age princess, comic reptiles, robots and a Darth Vadar clone who's defeated with ridiculous ease. Strictly for undemanding kids. Numerous vintage "Felix" short subjects are also available on separate tapes.
1991 (*Family*) 83m/C **D:** Tibor Hernadi; **V:** Chris Phillips, Alice Playten, Maureen O'Connell. **VHS, Beta $19.99** *BVV, FCT, WTA*

Ferdy

European cartoon based on the books by Ondrej Sekora, centering on the multi-legged inhabitants of Bugville.
1984 (*Family*) 50m/C **VHS, Beta $14.95** *FHE, WTA*

Ferngully: The Last Rain Forest 🎵🎵♪

Cartoon eco-musical about sprites and talking critters who inhabit a rain forest kingdom beset by developers. When fairy Crysta spies a handsome lug helping to cut down trees, she shrinks him to her size to show him the error of his ways. Brilliant visuals and character voices save a preachy script (based on stories by Diane Young) that doesn't even have the courage of its environmental convictions; villain turns out to be not the human polluters but an evil spirit their bulldozers set free. He sure is well drawn, though.
1992 (*G/Family*) 72m/C **D:** Bill Kroyer; **M:** Alan Silvestri; **V:** Samantha Mathis, Christian Slater, Robin Williams, Tim Curry, Jonathan Ward, Grace Zabriskie, Richard "Cheech" Marin, Thomas Chong, Tone Loc, Jim Cox. **VHS $24.98** *FXV, MLT*

Ferris Bueller's Day Off 🎵🎵🎵

Writer/director/producer Hughes fashioned one of his most congenial screen teens in Ferris, a popular high school guy who knows all the angles and goes to elaborate lengths to cut class. Faking sickness, he sneaks his girlfriend and best buddy out of school to spend a grand day enjoying Chicago. Broderick is charming, sharing his philosophy of life with the viewer. Gray amuses as his tattle-tale sister doing everything she can to see him caught and getting Bueller's arch-enemy on the school faculty to hunt the renegade (he's a jerk, as are all the adults). Led to a Ferris Bueller TV series that quickly died and a shameless imitator, "Parker Lewis Can't Lose," that ran for years. Go figure. **Hound Advisory:** Roughhousing, certain anti-authoritarian flavor.
1986 (*PG-13/Jr. High-Sr. High*) 103m/C Matthew Broderick, Mia Sara, Alan Ruck, Jeffrey Jones, Jennifer Grey, Cindy Pickett, Edie McClurg, Charlie Sheen, Del Close, Virginia Capers, Max Perlich, Louis Anderson; **D:** John Hughes; **W:** John Hughes; **M:** Ira Newborn. **VHS, Beta, LV, 8mm $14.95** *PAR, TLF*

Fiddler on the Roof 🎵🎵🎵♪

Poignant story of Tevye, a poor Jewish milkman at the turn of the century in a small Ukrainian village, and his five daughters, his lame horse, his wife, and his companionable relationship with God. Based on the long-running Broadway musical with finely detailed set decoration and choreography. Strong performances from the entire cast create a sense of intimacy in spite of near epic proportions of the production. The play was based on the stories of Sholem Aleichem. 🎵Tradition; Matchmaker, Matchmaker; If I Were a Rich Man; Sabbath Prayer; To Life; Miracle of Miracles; Tevye's Dream; Sunrise, Sunset; Wedding Celebration. **Hound Advisory:** Roughhousing, alcohol use.
1971 (*G/Family*) 184m/C Chaim Topol, Norma Crane, Leonard Frey, Molly Picon; **D:** Norman Jewison; **M:** John Williams. **Award Nominations:** Academy Awards '71: Best Actor (Topol), Best Art Direction/Set Decoration, Best Director (Jewison), Best Picture, Best Supporting Actor (Frey); **Awards:** Academy Awards '71: Best Cinematography, Best Sound, Best Score; Golden Globe Awards '72: Best Actor—Musical/Comedy (Topol), Best Film—Musical/Comedy. **VHS, Beta, LV $29.97** *FOX, MGM, TLF*

Field of Dreams 🎵🎵🎵♪

Based on W. P. Kinsella's novel "Shoeless Joe," this uplifting mythic fantasy depicts an Iowa corn farmer who, following the directions of a mysterious voice, cuts a baseball diamond in his crops. Neighbors doubt his sanity, but soon the ballfield hosts the spirit of Joe Jackson and other ballplayers who were caught up and disgraced in the notorious 1919 "Black Sox" World Series scandal. It's all about chasing a dream, paying debts, maintaining innocence in spite of adulthood, finding redemption, reconciling the child with the man, and of course, celebrating baseball; but avoids excess hokiness through Costner and Madigan's strong, believable characters.
1989 (*PG/Jr. High-Adult*) 106m/C Kevin Costner, Amy Madigan, James Earl Jones, Burt Lancaster, Ray Liotta, Timothy Busfield, Frank Whaley, Gaby Hoffman; **D:** Phil Alden Robinson; **W:** Phil Alden Robinson; **M:** James Horner. **VHS, Beta, LV $19.95** *MCA, FCT, HMV*

The Fiendish Plot of Dr. Fu Manchu WOOF!

A sad farewell from Sellers, who in his last film portrays Dr. Fu in his desperate quest for the necessary ingredients for his secret life-preserving formula. Sellers portrays both Dr. Fu and the Scotland Yard detective on his trail, but it's not enough to save this picture, flawed by poor script and lack of direction.
1980 (PG/Jr. High-Adult) 100m/C Peter Sellers, David Tomlinson, Sid Caesar, Helen Mirren; D: Piers Haggard. VHS, Beta, LV $19.98 WAR, FCT

Fievel's American Tails: A Mouse Known as Zorrowitz/Aunt Sophie's Visit

Two episodes from the animated television series featuring adventures in the Old West. In "A Mouse Known as Zorrowitz," Fievel foils the actions of a stagecoach heist and saves a cheese shipment. "Aunt Sophie's Visit" has Fievel thinking he'll have to miss the rodeo when Aunt Sophie shows up for a visit. Additional volumes available.
1994 (Preschool-Primary) 48m/C D: Lawrence Jacobs; V: Dom DeLuise, Phillip Glasser, Dan Castellaneta, Cathy Cavadini, Kenneth Mars, Lloyd Baattista, Gemt Graham, Susan Silo. VHS, LV $12.98 MCA

The Fifth Monkey 🎬🎬

Brazilian man embarks on a journey to sell four monkeys in order to fill a dowry for his sexy bride, but throughout various obstacles and adventures he comes to view the captive beasts as more than mere property. Often dull, didactic lesson in animal rights that could have used a lighter touch and less raunchier elements. Based on a novel by Jacques Zibi. **Hound Advisory:** Nudity, violence.
1990 (PG-13/Sr. High-Adult) 93m/C Ben Kingsley; D: Eric Rochant; W: Eric Rochant. VHS, LV $89.98 COL, FCT

The Fifth Musketeer 🎬🎬

A campy adaptation of Dumas's "The Man in the Iron Mask," wherein a monarch's evil twin impersonates him while imprisoning the true king. A good cast and rich production shot in Austria make for a fairly entertaining swashbuckler.
1979 (PG/Jr. High-Adult) 90m/C Beau Bridges, Sylvia Kristel, Ursula Andress, Cornel Wilde, Ian McShane, Alan Hale Jr., Helmut Dantine, Olivia de Havilland, Jose Ferrer, Rex Harrison, Helmut Dantine; D: Ken Annakin; W: David Ambrose. Beta $19.95 COL

50 Classic All-Star Cartoons, Vol. 1

A feast for fans, a cassette collection totalling six hours worth of vintage cartoons featuring Popeye, Woody Woodpecker, Felix the Cat, Porky Pig, Casper, Superman, and many more all time (non- Disney) favorites.
1991 (Family) 60m/C VHS $9.99 VTR

50 Classic All-Star Cartoons, Vol. 2

A second volume of great cartoon classics featuring Casper, Little Lulu, Superman, Popeye, Betty Boop, Daffy Duck, Bugs Bunny, and many others.
1991 (Family) 60m/C VHS $9.99 VTR

50 Degrees Below Zero

Two wintery 'toons; in the title tale Jason finds creepy things happening in his house like objects getting moved and his father starting to sleepwalk. Jason wonders if everything is connected to his bad dreams. In "Thomas' Snow Suit," a young boy is teased at school for wearing a drab brown snow suit.
1993 (Primary) 25m/C VHS $12.99

50 Simple Things Kids Can Do to Save the Earth, Parts 1 & 2

Children implementing the ideas listed in David Javna's book of the same title are the focus of this two-video set. Part one, "Water and Resources," explains how kids have cleaned up Pigeon Creek, and part two, "Greenlife, Wildlife, Energy and Air" answers questions kids have on a variety of environmental subjects.
1992 (Primary-Jr. High) 44m/C VHS $149.00 FHS

The Fig Tree

After her mother passes away, grief-stricken Miranda is tormented by fear of death. A visit to her aunts helps her cope with this difficult stage of life. Introspective childhood drama from the "WonderWorks" series has little plot (it's based on a Katherine Anne Porter story, after all), but acting and mood are beyond reproach in this evocation of one girl's anguished state of mind.
1987 (Family) 58m/C Olivia Cole, William Converse-Roberts, Doris Roberts, Teresa Wright, Karron Graves; D: Calvin Skaggs. VHS $14.95 PME, FCT, BTV

Fighting Devil Dogs

Exciting Republic serial about two Marine officers roaming the globe as they unravel the identity of the masked evildoer known as the Lightning. In 12 chapters. **Hound Advisory:** Violence.
1938 (Family) 195m/B Lee Powell, Herman Brix; D: John English, William Witney. VHS $29.98 REP, VCN, MLB

Fighting Marines 🎬🎬

The last of the mostly mediocre serials made by the Mascot studio before they merged to form Republic. Throughout 12 episodes those Marines fight Tiger Shark, a modern-day pirate out to stop the leathernecks from establishing an airstrip on and island in the Pacific.
1936 (Jr. High-Adult) 69m/B Jason Robards Sr., Grant Withers, Ann Rutherford, Pat O'Malley; D: Joseph Kane, B. Reeves Eason. VHS, Beta $24.95 VYY, VCN, VDM

The Fighting Prince of Donegal 🎬🎬🎬

Irish prince battles the invading British in 16th Century Ireland. Escaping their clutches, he leads his clan in rescuing his mother and his beloved in this Disney swashbuckler. Based on the novel "Red Hugh, Prince of Donegal" by Robert T. Reilly.
1966 (Family) 110m/C Peter McEnery, Susan Hampshire, Tom Adams, Gordon Jackson, Andrew Keir; D: Michael O'Herlihy. VHS, Beta $69.95 DIS

Fighting with Kit Carson

Famous guide and Indian fighter leads bands of settlers westward. 12-chapter serial. **Hound Advisory:** Violence.
1933 (Family) 230m/B Johnny Mack Brown, Noah Beery Sr., Noah Beery Jr., Betsy King Ross; *D:* Armand Schaefer, Colbert Clark. **VHS, Beta $24.95** *VYY, VCN, VDM*

A Fine Mess 🎵🎵🎵

Two buffoons cash in when one overhears a plan to dope a racehorse, but they are soon fleeing the plotters' slapstick pursuit. The plot is further complicated by the romantic interest of a gangster's wife. The television popularity of the two stars did not translate to the big screen; perhaps it's Edwards' fault.
1986 (PG/Jr. High-Adult) 100m/C Ted Danson, Howie Mandel, Richard Mulligan, Stuart Margolin, Maria Conchita Alonso, Paul Sorvino; *D:* Blake Edwards; *W:* Blake Edwards; *M:* Henry Mancini. **VHS, Beta, LV $19.95** *COL*

Finian's Rainbow 🎵🎵🎵🎵

Og the leprechaun (Steele) comes to America to retrieve his pot of gold taken by Irish immigrant Finian; meanwhile the magic ore stirs up a southern community by changing a bigoted landowner black. Fanciful musical comedy based on a Broadway hit worked notably better onstage (and in 1947). The terrific cast heroically performs the overlong material with enough sheer zest to prevent this from becoming Finian's wake instead. 🎵How Are Things in Glocca Morra?; Look To the Rainbow; That Old Devil Moon; If This Isn't Love; Something Sort of Grandish; The Be-Gat; This Time of Year; The Great Come and Get It Day; When I'm Not Near the Girl I Love.
1968 (G/Family) 141m/C Fred Astaire, Petula Clark, Tommy Steele, Keenan Wynn, Al Freeman Jr., Don Francks, Susan Hancock, Dolph Sweet; *D:* Francis Ford Coppola. **VHS, Beta, LV $19.98** *WAR, MVD*

Finn McCoul

Legendary Irish hero Finn McCoul and his wife Oonagh battle against the giant Cucullin. Part of the terrific "Rabbit Ears" series of video storybooks, with music by the Celtic band Boys of the Lough.
1992 (Preschool-Primary) 30m/C **VHS $14.99** *MOV, BTV*

Fire and Ice 🎵🎵

Cartoonist Bakshi collaborated with eminent fantasy and comic-book creators for this under-imaginative animated fantasy about warriors fighting the evil conqueror Nekron, whose psychic control of glaciers is the script's one touch of originality. Devoid of humor, film's in a netherworld between adult and kiddie entertainment. Bakshi's rotoscope technique -tracing live, filmed actors - enables his human characters to move, fight, die and, in the case of the sexy, near-naked princess, jiggle realistically. **Hound Advisory:** If this hadn't been a 'mere' cartoon, it would have gotten a stronger rating than PG for nonstop skull-bashing, slashing and spearing. Salty language; alcohol use.
1983 (PG/Jr. High-Adult) 81m/C Randy Norton, Cynthia Leake; *D:* Ralph Bakshi; *V:* Susan Tyrrell, William Ostrander. **VHS, Beta, LV $12.98** *COL, WTA*

Fire in the Sky 🎵🎵

Mysterious disappearance of Sweeney sparks a criminal investigation, until he returns, claiming he was abducted by aliens. Though everybody doubts his story, viewers won't, since the alleged aliens have already made an appearance, shifting the focus to Sweeney as he tries to convince skeptics that his trauma is genuine. Perhaps this mirrors what director Lieberman went through while trying to convince backers the film should be made. He could have benefitted by understanding the difference between what he was telling viewers and what he was showing them. Captivating special effects are one of the few bright spots. Based on a story that might be true. **Hound Advisory:** Profanity; nudity.
1993 (PG-13/Sr. High-Adult) 98m/C D.B. Sweeney, Robert Patrick, Craig Sheffer, Peter Berg, James Garner, Henry Thomas; *D:* Robert Lieberman; *W:* Tracy Torme; *M:* Mark Isham. **VHS, Beta, LV** *PAR*

The Fire in the Stone 🎵🎵

A young boy discovers an opal mine and dreams of using the treasure to reunite his family. However, when the jewels are stolen from him, he enlists his friends to help get them back. Based on the novel by Colin Thiele.
1985 (Family) 97m/C Paul Smith, Linda Hartley, Theo Pertsindis. **VHS, Beta $39.95** *WAR*

Fireman Sam: Hero Next Door

British stop-motion animated short about how Fireman Sam does his best to keep the town of Pontypandy flame free, with the help of his truck, Jupiter.
1989 (Preschool-Primary) 30m/C **VHS $9.95** *FHE*

First Born 🎵🎵🎵

Divorced mother rushes blindly into romance with an intriguing stranger. Teen son Jake takes a stand when Prince Charming turns out to be a drug-pushing creep who gets mom hooked. Fresh, intriguing premise of a child having to take charge over a wayward parent, but eventually the patented Hollywood formula of chases and fights dilutes what should have been hard-hitting drama. **Hound Advisory:** Drug use, mature themes, sex, violence.
1984 (PG-13/Sr. High-Adult) 100m/C Teri Garr, Peter Weller, Christopher Collet, Corey Haim, Sarah Jessica Parker, Robert Downey Jr.; *D:* Michael Apted. **VHS, Beta, LV $14.95** *PAR*

The First Christmas

Rankin-Bass TV holiday cartoon special, about a blind boy cared for by nuns in a small abbey in France, who is divinely rewarded for his kind heart.
1975 (Family) 23m/C *V:* Angela Lansbury, Cyril Ritchard. **VHS, Beta $12.95** *WAR, WTA*

The First Easter Rabbit

Rankin-Bass animated tale of a child's stuffed toy who, through magic, becomes the first Easter bunny. Very loose adaptation of the oft-told "Velveteen Rabbit" tale.
1982 (Primary) 25m/C **VHS $12.95** *WAR, WTA*

First Men in the Moon 🦴🦴

Colorful, fun spectacle depicts a private 19th-century mission to the moon by British scientists who have a secret anti-gravity formula. They rise up through space in a sealed sphere, land on the moon and discover it inhabitant by a civilization of giant insects. Ray Harryhausen contributed the grandiose stop-motion f/x, including a giant caterpillar. Based on a novel by H.G. Wells.
1964 (*Family*) 103m/C Martha Hyer, Edward Judd, Lionel Jeffries, Erik Chitty, Peter Finch; **D:** Nathan Juran; **W:** Nigel Kneale, Jan Read. **VHS, Beta, LV** $14.95 *COL, MLB*

Fish Hawk 🦴🦴

Canadian drama set at the turn of the century, about an alcoholic Indian named Fish Hawk befriending a young boy and going clean and sober. He gets a job at the boy's family's ranch, but finds winning the trust of white adults isn't so easy. While Fish Hawk defeats the bottle, this well-intentioned family film can't swear off the cliches. Based on a novel by Mitchell Jayne. **Hound Advisory:** Alcohol use.
1979 (G/*Family*) 95m/C Will Sampson, Charlie Fields; **D:** Donald Shebib. **VHS, Beta** $19.95 *MED, VTR*

The Fish that Saved Pittsburgh 🦴🦴

Sometimes you can tell just by the title. Lemon, of the Harlem Globetrotters, is among real-life basketball stars adding sparkle to a silly comedy about a loser team that hires an astrologer to change their luck. She makes sure all the team members' zodiac signs are compatible with Pisces (the fish). **Hound Advisory:** Salty language.
1979 (PG/*Jr. High-Adult*) 104m/C Jonathan Winters, Stockard Channing, Flip Wilson, Julius Erving, Margaret Avery, Meadowlark Lemon, Nicholas Pryor, James Bond III, Kareem Abdul-Jabbar, Jack Kehoe, Debbie Allen; **D:** Gilbert Moses. **VHS, Beta** $59.95 *LHV, WAR*

Fisher-Price Grimm's Fairy Tales: Briar Rose

The classic tale of Briar Rose is told here for two- to five-year-olds. Other volumes include "Frog Prince," "Hansel and Gretel," "Little Red Riding Hood," and "The Travelling Musicians of Bremen."
1990 (*Preschool-Primary*) 25m/C **VHS** $9.98 *MED*

Fisherman's Wharf 🦴🦴

Breen stars as an orphan adopted by a San Francisco fisherman who runs away when his aunt and bratty cousin come to live with them.
1939 (*Jr. High-Adult*) 72m/B Bobby Breen, Leo Carrillo, Henry Armetta, Lee Patrick, Rosina Galli, Leon Belasco; **D:** Bernard Vorhaus. **VHS** $19.95 *NOS*

Five Lionni Classics

Children's writer Lionni and famed cut-out animator Giulio Gianini combine their talents to tell five original fairy tales for the young: "Frederick," "Fish Is Fish," "Swimmy," "Cornelius," and "It's Mine!"
1987 (*Preschool-Primary*) 30m/C Leo Lionni. **VHS, Beta** $14.95 *KUI, RAN, WTA*

Five Sesame Street Stories

Five animated Sesame Street tales are presented featuring Super Grover, Big Bird, and the rest of the Sesame Street gang.
198? (*Preschool-Primary*) 30m/C **VHS** $7.95

The 5000 Fingers of Dr. T 🦴🦴🦴

In Dr. Seuss's only non-animated movie, a boy tries to evade piano lessons and dreams of the surreal castle of Dr. Terwilliger, where hundreds of captive boys are held for piano practice and forced to wear silly beanies with "happy fingers" waving on top. Luckily, the trusted family plumber is on hand to save the day with an atom bomb. Marvelous anti-authoritarian satire may mean a bit more to adults than kids, but if only the music had been more memorable this would be in the top league with "The Wizard of Oz." As is, it's a weird, one-of-a-kind treat that, sadly, failed to score with '50s audiences.
1953 (*Family-Family*) 88m/C Peter Lind Hayes, Mary Healy, Tommy Rettig, Hans Conried; **D:** Roy Rowland; **W:** Theodore (Dr. Seuss) Geisel, Allan Scott. **VHS, Beta, LV** $59.95 *COL, XVC, FCT*

The Flame Trees of Thika 🦴🦴🦴

In 1913, a British family relocates to East Africa to start a coffee plantation, and their struggles to adapt to the new environment are shown through the eyes of the youngest daughter. Her childhood includes the local Masai and Kikuyu tribes, plus eccentric and sometimes unhappy white neighbors, and the wild animals that roam the plains. Lovingly-made miniseries based on the memoirs of Elspeth Huxley. Originally broadcast on PBS-TV's "Masterpiece Theatre" and later The Disney Channel. On four cassettes. **Hound Advisory:** Violence - some human, some animal.
1981 (*Family*) 366m/C Hayley Mills, Holly Aird, David Robb, Ben Cross. **VHS** $129.95 *SIG, TVC*

Flaming Frontiers

Frontier scout matches wits against gold thieves and Indians in this Universal serial western, in 15 chapters.
1938 (*Family*) 300m/B Johnny Mack Brown, Eleanor Hanson, Ralph Bowman; **D:** Ray Taylor. **VHS, Beta** $39.95 *VYY, VCN, NOS*

The Flamingo Kid 🦴🦴🦴

Brooklyn teenager Jeffrey gets a summer job at a fancy beach club on Long Island. Suddenly making lots of easy money, the kid is attracted to the flashy style of the local car dealer/gin rummy king, and finds his plumber dad's solid life a bore. By the end of the season, Jeffrey's learned the true worth of both father figures, and the kind of adult he wants to be. Excellent performances all around in an intelligent coming-of-age comedy drama set in 1963, with a soundtrack of early '60s favorites. **Hound Advisory:** Brief sex (overstressed in the ad campaign). Roughhousing, salty language, alcohol use.
1984 (PG-13/*Sr. High-Adult*) 100m/C Matt Dillon, Hector Elizondo, Molly McCarthy, Martha Gehman, Richard Crenna, Jessica Walter, Carole Davis, Janet Jones, Fisher Stevens, Bronson Pinchot; **D:** Garry Marshall. **VHS, Beta, LV** $29.98 *LIV, VES*

The Flash 🎭🎭

Police scientist Barry Allen is doused with chemicals and struck by lightning, which turns him into a super strong, super speedy superhero. With the aid of a pretty researcher cohort, he uses his new identity to nail the biker gang leader who caused his brother's death. Based on a comic-book character from the same stable as Superman, this is the pilot episode for the short-lived network TV series. Obviously influenced by the Tim Burton "Batman" epics, the look is dark, stylized and not played for camp. **Hound Advisory:** Violence.

1990 (*Jr. High-Adult*) 94m/C John Wesley Shipp, Amanda Pays, Michael Nader; *M:* Danny Elfman. **VHS, Beta, LV** $19.98 *WAR*

Flash Gordon 🎭🎭🎭

Gaudy candy-colored version of Flash Gordon's first adventure in outer space. His mission: go to far-off Mongo, where the tyrant Ming the Merciless is threatening the destruction of Earth. Deserves credit for aspiring to the 1930s flavor of the original "Flash" serials and Alex Raymond's comic strip rather than being another "Star Wars" ripoff (like 1979's "Buck Rogers in the 25th Century"). One glaring anachronism: the pounding, glam-rock musical score by the group Queen. **Hound Advisory:** Violence, salty language.

1980 (**PG**/*Jr. High-Adult*) 111m/C Sam Jones, Melody Anderson, Chaim Topol, Max von Sydow, Ornella Muti, Timothy Dalton, Brian Blessed; *D:* Mike Hodges; *M:* Queen, Howard Blake. **VHS, Beta, LV** $14.98 *MCA*

Flash Gordon Conquers the Universe

Third and last of the hit "Flash Gordon" serials made by Universal Pictures, adapting Alex Raymond's famous comic-strip character. A plague called the purple death is devastating Earth. Flash Gordon and Dr. Zarkov discover that arch-villain Ming the Merciless is responsible. They follow his spaceship all the way back to Mars to put a stop to the interplanetary crime. Not quite as good as earlier adventures of the space hero, but diverting, and it does have those odd sets and curious touches peculiar to this series. The strange language of the Rock Men is really recorded English played backwards. In 12 chapters. **Hound Advisory:** Roughhousing.

1940 (*Family*) 240m/B Buster Crabbe, Carol Hughes, Charles Middleton, Frank Shannon. **VHS, Beta** $39.95 *VYY, MRV, SNC*

Flash Gordon: Rocketship 🎭🎭🎭

Re-edited from the original Flash Gordon serial in which Flash and company must prevent the planet Mongo from colliding with Earth. Good character acting and good clean fun.

1936 (*Family*) 97m/B Buster Crabbe, Jean Rogers, Frank Shannon, Charles Middleton, Priscilla Lawson, Jack Lipson; *D:* Frederick Stephani. **VHS, Beta** $29.95 *VYY, PSM, CAB*

Flash Gordon: Vol. 1

Three one-hour volumes of episodes from the cheapo 1950s Flash Gordon TV series are available on video, not to be confused with the classic serials.

1953 (*Family*) 60m/B Steve Holland, Irene Champlin. **VHS, Beta** $29.95 *DVT*

Flash, the Teenage Otter

The adventures of a teenaged (non-mutant, non-ninja) otter, as first televised on "The Wonderful World of Disney" TV program.

1976 (*Preschool-Primary*) 48m/C **VHS, Beta** $250.00 *MTI, DSN*

Flashdance 🎭🎭

18-year-old Alex wants to dance classical ballet, even though she's from the blue-collar side of the tracks. Welder by day, exotic dancer by night (non-explicit), she tries to get up the confidence to audition for the stuffed shirts; complicating matters is her hot affair with her young boss. Silly, souped-up music-video fairy tale, not to be confused with the superficially similar but far more realistic "Fame" (or for that matter, "It's Flashbeagle, Charlie Brown"). Made a mint at the box office anyway, and more off the hit soundtrack album. ♫Flashdance...What a Feeling; I Love Rock 'n Roll; Manhunt; Gloria; Lady, Lady, Lady; Seduce Me Tonight. **Hound Advisory:** Profanity; brief nudity; mature themes; sex. For what it's worth, Alex goes to confession regularly.

1983 (**R**/*Sr. High-Adult*) 95m/C Jennifer Beals, Michael Nouri, Belinda Bauer, Lilia Skala, Cynthia Rhodes, Sunny Johnson, Lee Ving, Kyle T. Heffner, Ron Karabatsos, Robert Wuhl, Elizabeth Sagal; *D:* Franca Pasut. **Award Nominations:** Academy Awards '83: Best Cinematography, Best Film Editing, Best Song ("Maniac"); **Awards:** Academy Awards '83: Best Song ("Flashdance...What a Feeling"); Golden Globe Awards '84: Best Song ("Flashdance...What a Feeling"), Best Score. **VHS, Beta, LV, 8mm** $14.95 *PAR*

Fletch 🎭🎭🎭

Newspaper journalist Fletch is a smart-mouthed guy with a talent for disguises. When he goes undercover to get the scoop on the local drug scene, a wealthy young businessman who claims to be dying enlists his help in helping him reach the here after. Something's rotten in Denmark when the man's doctor knows nothing of the illness and Fletch comes closer to the drug scene than he realizes. Charming comedy, particularly if you're a Chase fan. Based on Gregory McDonald's novel. **Hound Advisory:** Violence and profanity.

1985 (**PG**/*Jr. High-Adult*) 98m/C Chevy Chase, Tim Matheson, Joe Don Baker, Dana Wheeler-Nicholson, M. Emmet Walsh, Kenneth Mars, Geena Davis, Richard Libertini, George Wendt, Kareem Abdul-Jabbar, Alison La Placa; *D:* Michael Ritchie; *W:* Andrew Bergman; *M:* Harold Faltermeyer. **VHS, Beta, LV** $14.95 *MCA*

Fletch Lives 🎭🎭

In this sequel to "Fletch," Chase is back again as the super-reporter. When Fletch learns of his inheritance of a Southern estate he is eager to claim it. During his down-home trip he becomes involved in a murder and must use his disguise skills to solve it before he becomes the next victim. Based on the novels of Gregory MacDonald.

1989 (**PG**/*Jr. High-Adult*) 95m/C Chevy Chase, Hal Holbrook, Julianne Phillips, Richard Libertini, R. Lee Ermey, Cleavon Little; *D:* Michael Ritchie; *W:* Leon Capetanos; *M:* Harold Faltermeyer. **VHS, Beta, LV** $14.95 *MCA*

Flight of Dragons 🎭🎭🎭

Possibly the best of the many fantasies of Arthur Rankin Jr. and Jules Bass, this animated TV feature combines magical

adventure with weighty themes on science and myth. Peter, a modern chemist fond of legendary lore, is magically transported to the world of his own D&D-style board game, where benign sorcery is losing out to logic, and a demon (yes, that's the voice of "Darth Vadar" Jones) schemes to take over. Complicated plot has Peter accidentally turned into a dragon himself, and we get an ingenious physiological explanation for the fire-breathing monsters. A fairy tale for bright kids and adults, it pretends to be based on its own hero's memoirs but is really from "The Dragon and the George," by Gordon R. Dickinson.
1982 *(Primary)* 98m/C **D:** Arthur Rankin Jr., Jules Bass; **V:** John Ritter, Victor Buono, James Earl Jones, Don Messick, Larry Storch. **VHS, Beta $19.98** *WAR, WTA*

Flight of the Grey Wolf 🦴🦴

Tame, innocent wolf is mistaken for a killer and must run for his life with the help of a boy owner. Standard Disney adventure, made for the Magic Kingdom's long-running weekly TV show.
1976 *(Family)* 82m/C Bill Williams, Barbara Hale, Jeff East. **VHS, Beta $69.95** *DIS*

Flight of the Navigator 🦴🦴🦴

Twelve-year-old David comes back from a walk in the woods to find that eight years have passed for his family and the rest of the world. Meanwhile, NASA finds a parked UFO nearby but can't open it. The bewildered boy is the key and has an incredible adventure in time and space. Disney sci-fi starts with a real sense of awe and mystery, which it later abandons for comedy, as Reubens, in character as Pee Wee Herman, does the voice of the alien intelligence. Good fun nonetheless. **Hound Advisory:** Salty language, without which this would have qualified for a G.
1986 *(PG/Family)* 90m/C Joey Cramer, Veronica Cartwright, Cliff DeYoung, Sarah Jessica Parker, Matt Adler, Howard Hesseman; **D:** Randal Kleiser; **W:** Michael Burton, Matt MacManus; **M:** Alan Silvestri; **V:** Paul (Pee Wee Herman) Reubens. **VHS, Beta, LV $19.99** *DIS*

The Flintstone Kids

Collection of 12 episodes revealing the childhood antics of such prehistoric favorites as Fred, Barney, Wilma, Betty, and even Nick (as in Mr.) Slate.
1984 *(Preschool-Primary)* 92m/C **VHS, Beta** *TTC*

The Flintstone Kids: "Just Say No"

Video adventures of the lead Flintstone characters as children, designed in this particular episode to teach young viewers the dangers of drugs. See also "What's Wrong with Wilma?"
1989 *(Family)* 22m/C **VHS, Beta $14.95** *TTC, WTA*

The Flintstones

The foibles of the those modern Stone Age families (and blatant "Honeymooners" imitations, let's face it), the Flintstones and the Rubbles, are chronicled in these two animated episodes of the classic Hanna-Barbera series. Numerous other

Flintstone deposits, both from the original series and later revivals, can be mined on tape.
1960 *(Family)* 50m/C **V:** Alan Reed, Mel Blanc, Jean Vander Pyl, Bea Benadaret. **VHS, Beta $29.95** *TTC*

The Flintstones 🦴🦴⌐

Preceded by massive hype, popular '60s cartoon comes to life thanks to a huge budget and creative sets and props. Seems that Fred's being set up by evil corporate types MacLachlan and Barry to take the fall for their embezzling scheme. Soon he gives up dining at RocDonald's for Cavern on the Green and cans best buddy Barney (Moranis). Forget the lame plot (32 writers took a shot at it) and sit back and enjoy the spectacle. Goodman's an amazingly true-to-type Fred, O'Donnell has Betty's giggle down pat, and Perkins looks a lot like Wilma. Wilma's original voice, VanderPyl, has a cameo; listen for Korman's voice as the Dictabird. Add half a bone if you're under 12. **Hound Advisory:** Mild innuendos.
1994 *(PG/Jr. High-Adult)* 92m/C John Goodman, Rick Moranis, Elizabeth Perkins, Rosie O'Donnell, Elizabeth Taylor, Kyle MacLachlan, Halle Berry, Jonathan Winters, Richard Moll, Irwin Keyes, Dann Florek; **Cameos:** Laraine Newman, Jean VanDerPyl, Jay Leno; **D:** Brian Levant; **W:** Tom S. Parker, Jim Jennewein, Steven E. de Souza; **M:** David Newman; **V:** Harvey Korman. **VHS, LV $19.98** *MCA*

The Flintstones: Fred Flintstone Woos Again

Fred and Wilma take off on a second honeymoon in search of romance and adventure.
1989 *(Family)* 60m/C **V:** Mel Blanc. **VHS, Beta $9.95** *TTC, WTA*

The Flintstones: Rappin' n' Rhymin'

Hanna-Barbera cartoon characters join real kids for an exciting thirty minutes of rappin' and dancin'!
1991 *(Family)* 30m/C **VHS, Beta $9.95** *TTC, WTA*

Flipper 🦴🦴⌐

Sandy, a fisherman's 12-year-old son, saves an injured porpoise, earning the animal's gratitude. Flipper later repays the favor by rescuing Sandy from sharks. This pleasant but formula kiddie entertainment was later spun off into the popular aquatic TV series. You'd better enjoy the "Flipper" theme song because it encores mercilessly.
1963 *(Family)* 87m/C Chuck Connors, Luke Halpin, Kathleen Maguire, Connie Scott; **D:** James B. Clark. **VHS, Beta $19.98** *MVD, MGM*

Flipper's New Adventure 🦴🦴⌐

Believing they are to be separated, Flipper and Sandy travel to a remote island. Little do they know, a British family is being held for ransom on the island they have chosen. It's up to the duo to save the day. Enjoyable, nicely done family adventure.
1964 *(Family-Family)* 103m/C Luke Halpin, Pamela Franklin, Tom Helmore, Francesca Annis, Brian Kelly, Joe Higgins, Ricou Browning; **D:** Leon Benson. **VHS, Beta $19.98** *MGM, FCT*

Flipper's Odyssey 🦴🦴

Flipper has disappeared and his adopted family goes looking for him, but when one of the boys gets trapped in a cave, the marine mammal is his only hope.
1966 (*Family*) 77m/C Flipper, Luke Halpin, Brian Kelly, Tommy Norden; **D:** Paul Landres. **VHS, Beta $14.95** *CNG, PSM*

Flirting 🦴🦴🦴

In 1965 rural Australia, romantic misfit Danny Embling is enrolled at St. Albans boys boarding school next to a similar institution for girls. Male and female students are permitted to mix, under strict adult supervision, and Danny finds a soulmate in Thandi, bright, beautiful daughter of an African diplomat, whose black skin makes her as much of an outcast as Danny. Their defiant love affair is tender, amusing, sad and wise. Followup to "The Year My Voice Broke" is the second installment of director Duigan's coming-of-age trilogy, to be completed once actor Taylor is old enough for the concluding chapter. **Hound Advisory:** Sex, nudity, alcohol use, mature themes, roughhousing.
1989 (**R**/*Sr. High-Adult*) 100m/C Noah Taylor, Thandie Newton, Nicole Kidman, Bartholomew Rose, Felix Nobis, Josh Picker, Kiri Paramore, Marc Gray, Joshua Marshall, David Wieland, Craig Black, Leslie Hill; **D:** John Duigan; **W:** John Duigan. **VHS, LV $94.95** *VMK, BTV*

Flower Angel

Blue-eyed girl named Angel does good deeds during her globetrotting adventures in search of the Flower of Seven Colors. Dismal Japanese animation that makes the Care Bears look like Eugene O'Neill. Also available on tape with a compilation of Yankee cartoon castoffs, under the umbrella title "Angel."
1980 (*Family*) 46m/C **VHS, Beta $29.95** *FHE*

Flower Drum Song 🦴🦴

Rodgers and Hammerstein musical played better on Broadway than in this overblown adaptation of life in San Francisco's Chinatown. Umeki plays the young girl who arrives from Hong Kong for an arranged marriage. Her intended (Soo) is a fast-living nightclub owner already enjoying the love of singer Kwan. Meanwhile Umeki falls for the handsome Shigeta. Naturally, everything comes together in a happy ending. ♫I Enjoy Being A Girl; Don't Marry Me; Grant Avenue; You Are Beautiful; A Hundred Million Miracles; Fan Tan Fanny; Chop Suey; The Other Generation; I Am Going to Like It Here.
1961 (*Family*) 133m/C Nancy Kwan, Jack Soo, James Shigeta, Miyoshi Umeki, Juanita Hall; **D:** Henry Koster; **M:** Richard Rodgers, Oscar Hammerstein. **VHS, Beta, LV $39.98** *MCA, FCT*

The Flying Deuces 🦴🦴🦴

Ollie's broken heart lands Laurel and Hardy in the Foreign Legion. The comic pair escape a firing squad only to suffer a plane crash that results in Hardy's reincarnation as a horse. A musical interlude with a Laurel soft shoe while Hardy sings "Shine On, Harvest Moon" is one of the highlights.
1939 (*Family*) 65m/B Stan Laurel, Oliver Hardy, Jean Parker, Reginald Gardiner, James Finlayson; **D:** Edward Sutherland. **VHS, Beta, LV $9.95** *CNG, MRV, NOS*

Flying Wild 🦴🦴

A gang of saboteurs is out to steal top-secret airplane blueprints. Who else but the Bowery Boys could conceivably stop them?
1941 (*Adult*) 62m/B Leo Gorcey, Bobby Jordan, Donald Haines, Joan Barclay, David Gorcey, Bobby Stone, Sammy Morrison; **D:** William West. **VHS $19.95** *NOS, LOO*

Follow Me, Boys! 🦴🦴🦴

Disney film set in the 1930s about a simple man who decides to put down roots and enjoy the quiet life, after one year too many on the road with a ramshackle jazz band. That life is soon interrupted when he volunteers to lead a high-spirited boy scout troop. Effective mix of warmth, inspiration and rowdiness. Future adult star Russell plays a town delinquent reformed by the discipline of scouting.
1966 (*Family*) 120m/C Fred MacMurray, Vera Miles, Lillian Gish, Charlie Ruggles, Elliott Reid, Kurt Russell, Luanna Patten, Ken Murray; **D:** Norman Tokar. **VHS, Beta $69.95** *DIS*

Follow that Bunny!

Clay-animated musical about a magic egg stolen while on its way to the Easter Bunny. If the egg isn't found, spring will never arrive and the video will run eternally.
1993 (*Preschool-Primary*) 27m/C **VHS $12.98** *FHE, WTA*

Follow That Sleigh!

Seasonal TV cartoon wherein Santa's sleigh is hijacked by two children, and Elf Control sends Elvis, the Rockin' Reindeer, to save the day. A hunka hunka burning snow.
1990 (*Family*) 25m/C **VHS $9.99** *VTR, WTA*

Follow the Fleet 🦴🦴🦴

Song-and-dance man joins the Navy and meets two sisters in need of help in this Rogers/Astaire bon-bon featuring a classic Berlin score. Look for Grable, Ball, and Martin in minor roles. Hilliard went on to be best known as the wife of Ozzie Nelson in TV's "The Adventures of Ozzie and Harriet." ♫Let's Face the Music and Dance; We Saw the Sea; I'm Putting All My Eggs In One Basket; Get Thee Behind Me, Satan; But Where Are You?; I'd Rather Lead a Band; Let Yourself Go.
1936 (*Family*) 110m/B Fred Astaire, Ginger Rogers, Randolph Scott, Harriet Hilliard Nelson, Betty Grable, Lucille Ball; **D:** Mark Sandrich; **M:** Irving Berlin, Max Steiner. **VHS, Beta, LV $14.98** *RKO, MED, TTC*

Follow the Leader 🦴🦴

Wartime "Bowery Boys" adventure. On leave from the Army, Slip and Satch discover that one of their pals has been jailed on a trumped-up charge and set about finding the real culprit. Also known as "East of the Bowery." ♫Now and Then; All I Want to Do Play the Drums.
1944 (*Jr. High-Adult*) 65m/B Leo Gorcey, Huntz Hall, Gabriel Dell, Jack LaRue, Joan Marsh, Billy Benedict, Mary Gordon, Sammy Morrison; **D:** William Beaudine; **M:** Gene Austin, Sherrill Sisters. **VHS $19.95** *NOS*

"The Flintstones" - the modern Stone-Age family (1994)

Foofur & His Friends

Leader of the pack Foofur gets into trouble as usual in this animated compilation from the Hanna-Barbera series. Additional volumes available.

1988 *(Preschool-Primary)* 110m/C **VHS, Beta $39.95** *JFK, WTA*

Footloose 🎵🎵🎵

When a city boy moves to a small Midwestern town, he discovers some disappointing news: rock music and dancing have been forbidden because parents blame such fun for a past drunk-driving tragedy. Determined to bring some life into the place, he enlists the help of the daughter of the minister responsible for the law. Rousing music, talented young cast, and plenty of trouble make an entertaining musical drama. 🎵Footloose; Let's Hear it for the Boy; The Girl Gets Around; Dancing in the Sheets; Somebody's Eyes; Almost Paradise; I'm Free; Never; Holding Out for a Hero. **Hound Advisory:** Brief nudity, mature themes, roughhousing, salty language.

1984 (PG/*Jr. High-Adult)* 107m/C Kevin Bacon, Lori Singer, Christopher Penn, John Lithgow, Dianne Wiest, John Laughlin, Sarah Jessica Parker; *D:* Herbert Ross; *M:* Miles Goodman. **VHS, Beta, LV, 8mm $14.95** *PAR*

For Better and For Worse 🎵🎵

Nice young couple is planning to have your average nice wedding when one of their friends gets hold of an invitation and decides to jokingly invite the Pope to attend. But the joke is on them when the Pope accepts. Talk about upstaging the bride.

1992 (PG/*Jr. High-Adult)* 94m/C Patrick Dempsey, Kelly Lynch. **VHS, LV $89.98** *LIV*

For Better or For Worse: The Bestest Present

Fully animated Canadian TV special based on Lynn Johnston's popular and realistic newspaper comic strip, about a crusty widower who teaches the Patterson's boy the true meaning of Christmas.

1985 *(Family)* 23m/C *D:* Lynn Johnston. **VHS, Beta $9.95** *FHE, WTA*

For Keeps 🎵🎵

Two high school sweethearts on the verge of graduating get married after the girl becomes pregnant and rejects the option of abortion (that her own mother prefers). Ringwald was America's Sweetheart when this was made, and putting her through a realistic depiction of teenage parenthood and

marital woes could have worked brilliantly. Alas, it's a muddled, missed opportunity, mixing cheap laughs with sentiment. The screenwriters later disavowed the heavily revamped script. **Hound Advisory:** Sex, mature themes, alcohol use, salty language.
1988 (PG-13/*Sr. High-Adult*) 98m/C Molly Ringwald, Randall Batinkoff, Kenneth Mars; *D:* John G. Avildsen; *W:* Tim Kazurinsky, Denise DeClue; *M:* Bill Conti. VHS, Beta, LV $14.95 *COL*

For Love or Money 🐾🐾

Struggling hotel concierge with a heart of gold finds himself doing little "favors" for a slimy entrepreneur who holds the key to his dreams - the cash to open an elegant hotel of his own. Romantic comedy is reminiscent of the classic screwball comedies of the '30s and '40s, but lacks the trademark tight writing and impeccable timing. Fox is appealing and likable as the wheeling and dealing concierge, a role undermined by a mediocre script offering too few laughs and holes big enough for the entire cast to jump through. Anwar is effectively attractive. **Hound Advisory:** Profanity and sex talk.
1993 (PG/*Jr. High-Adult*) 89m/C Michael J. Fox, Gabrielle Anwar, Isaac Mizrahi, Anthony Higgins, Michael Tucker, Bobby Short, Dan Hedaya, Bob Balaban, Udo Kier, Patrick Breen, Paula Laurence; *D:* Barry Sonnenfeld; *W:* Mark Rosenthal, Larry Konner; *M:* Bruce Broughton. VHS, LV *MCA*

For Our Children: The Concert

Disney music video that assembles a galaxy of star talent, performing children's music in a benefit for the Pediatric AIDS Foundation. Segments include Paula Abdul doing "Zip-A-Dee-Doo-Dah," Michael Bolton with "You Are My Sunshine," Salt'N'Pepa rapping "This Old Man," and Bobby McFerrin's a cappella "Wizard of Oz" medley.
1992 (*Family*) 85m/C VHS $19.99 *BVV*

For the Love of Benji 🐾🐾🐾

In the second "Benji" the small but clever dog accompanies his owners on a Greek vacation. Murky spy subplot has Benji dognapped for ready-made adventure involving a secret code, but never mind that; the brilliant move was putting Benji abroad without the benefit of English subtitles. Now the viewer sees the world from a canine perspective, as Benji sizes up various human friends and foes not on the basis of what they say (it's all Greek to him - and us) but what they do. Benji's expressive acting, if anything, has improved since last time.
1977 (G/*Family*) 85m/C Benji, Patsy Garrett, Cynthia Smith, Allen Finzat, Ed Nelson; *D:* Joe Camp. VHS, Beta $19.99 *FCT, APD, BFV*

For Your Eyes Only 🐾🐾🐾

In this James Bond adventure, 007 must keep the Soviets from getting hold of a valuable instrument aboard a sunken British spy ship. Sheds the gadgetry of its more recent predecessors in the series in favor of some spectacular stunt work and the usual beautiful girl and exotic locale. Glen's first outing as director, though he handled second units on previous Bond films. Sheena Easton sang the hit title tune. **Hound Advisory:** Violence, alcohol use, suggested sex.

1981 (PG/*Jr. High-Adult*) 136m/C Roger Moore, Carol Bouquet, Chaim Topol, Lynn-Holly Johnson, Julian Glover, Cassandra Harris, Jill Bennett, Michael Gothard, John Wyman, Jack Hedley, Lois Maxwell, Desmond Llewelyn, Geoffrey Keen, Walter Gotell, Charles Dance; *D:* John Glen; *W:* Michael G. Wilson; *M:* Bill Conti. VHS, Beta, LV $19.98 *MGM, FOX, TLF*

Forbidden Games 🐾🐾🐾🐾

Excellent French antiwar drama about Paulette, a Parisian girl who sees her parents and dog killed during WWII air raid. Taken in by a well-meaning but rather petty farm family, she befriends their youngest son Michel. The two make a game of burying dead animals, in imitation of the constant war casualties around them, and soon have their own secret garden of crosses and memorials, borrowed from local cemeteries. Ultimately heartrending, but not the relentless downer it sounds; there's a lacing of ironic wit, coupled with the screen's shrewdest observation on how kids concoct their own fantasy worlds, and what happens when those clash with grownups. Winner of numerous awards; available in both subtitled and English-dubbed versions. **Hound Advisory:** Salty language, alcohol use, mature themes, brief brutality.
1952 (*Family*) 90m/B Brigitte Fossey, Georges Poujouly, Amedee, Louis Herbert; *D:* Rene Clement. **Award Nominations:** Academy Awards '54: Best Story; **Awards:** Academy Awards '52: Best Foreign Language Film; British Academy Awards '53: Best Film; National Board of Review Awards '52: 5 Best Foreign Films of the Year; New York Film Critics Awards '52: Best Foreign Film; Venice Film Festival '52: Best Film. VHS, Beta, LV $29.98 *NOS, SUE, APD*

Force on Thunder Mountain 🐾

Father and son go camping and encounter peculiar stuff, the work of an old man from a flying saucer (the UFO looks just like clips from "Lost in Space"). Benign but dull mess of a family sci-fi flick that sometimes spontaneously turns into a nature documentary.
1977 (*Family*) 93m/C Christopher Cain, Todd Dutson. VHS, Beta $19.95 *VCI*

Foreign Correspondent 🐾🐾🐾🐾

Classic Hitchcock tale of espionage and derring-do. A reporter is sent to Europe during WWII to cover a pacifist conference in London, where he becomes romantically involved with the daughter of the group's founder and befriends an elderly diplomat. When the diplomat is kidnapped, the reporter uncovers a Nazi spy-ring headed by his future father-in-law.
1940 (*Family*) 120m/B Joel McCrea, Laraine Day, Herbert Marshall, George Sanders, Robert Benchley, Albert Basserman, Edmund Gwenn, Eduardo Ciannelli, Harry Davenport, Martin Kosleck, Charles Halton; *D:* Alfred Hitchcock; *W:* Robert Benchley, Charles Bennett, Joan Harrison, James Hilton; *M:* Alfred Newman. **Award Nominations:** Academy Awards '40: Best Black and White Cinematography, Best Interior Decoration, Best Original Screenplay, Best Picture, Best Supporting Actor (Basserman); **Awards:** National Board of Review Awards '40: 10 Best Films of the Year. VHS, Beta, LV $59.95 *WAR*

Forever Young 🐾🐾🐾

When test pilot Gibson's girlfriend is hit by a car and goes into a coma, he volunteers to be cryogenically frozen for one year. As luck would have it, he's left frozen for fifty years, and when he finally thaws, he finds that he's a frozen fish out of water. He befriends a couple of kids, and the adventure begins. Predictable, though supported nicely by Wood, and designed to be a tear jerker, though it serves mostly as a star

vehicle for Gibson who bumbles with 90s technology, finds his true love, and escapes from government heavies, adorable as ever. Schmaltzy but entertaining romantic drama. **Hound Advisory:** Mild profanity.
1992 (PG/*Jr. High-Adult*) 102m/C Mel Gibson, Jamie Lee Curtis, Elijah Wood, Isabel Glasser, George Wendt, Joe Morton, Nicolas Surovy, David Marshall Grant, Art LaFleur; *D:* Steve Miner; *W:* Jeffrey Abrams; *M:* Jerry Goldsmith. **VHS, LV, 8mm** $19.98 *WAR, BTV*

Forrest Gump 𝄪𝄪𝄪𝄪

Director Zemeckis once again stretches the technological boundaries of film with this strange, satirically dark tale that became a smash at the box office. Intellectually challenged man from a small Southern town has a positive outlook on life so strong that he succeeds at whatever career he attempts, bringing him celebrity status over a span of four decades. Hanks turns in another great performance as the innocent Gump who becomes an All-American football player and decorated war hero, among other things. Historic events surround a tale of enduring love and friendship. Incredible special effects by Industrial Light & Magic put Forrest right into the footage of actual events. But while the special effects certainly entertain, it's Gump's good-heartedness and decency that stick with you. Hanks, in a role reminiscent of Peter Seller's simpleton in "Being There," manages to make Gump one of the great screen characters. Sinise offers stellar support as the disgruntled handicapped Vietnam vet, while Field is effective as Gump's beloved mother. From the novel by Winston Groom. **Hound Advisory:** Violence and gore during Vietnam episode; mature language and themes; brief nudity.
1994 (PG-13/*Sr. High-Adult*) 142m/C Tom Hanks, Robin Wright, Sally Field, Gary Sinise, Mykelti Williamson; *D:* Robert Zemeckis; *W:* Eric Roth. **VHS** *NYR*

Foul Play 𝄪𝄪𝄪

Hawn is a librarian who picks up a hitchhiker which leads to nothing but trouble. She becomes involved with San Francisco detective Chase in an effort to expose a plot to kill the Pope during his visit to the city. Also involved is Moore as an English orchestra conductor with some kinky sexual leanings. Chase is charming (no mugging here) and Hawn both bubbly and brave. A big winner at the box office; features Barry Manilow's hit tune "Ready to Take a Chance Again."
1978 (PG/*Jr. High-Adult*) 116m/C Goldie Hawn, Chevy Chase, Dudley Moore, Burgess Meredith, Billy Barty, Rachel Roberts, Eugene Roche, Brian Dennehy, Chuck McCann, Bruce Solomon; *D:* Colin Higgins; *M:* Charles Fox. **VHS, Beta, LV, 8mm** $19.95 *PAR*

Four Babar Classics

Babar, the witty, clever and charming elephant created by Jean de Brunhoff, is involved in four different engaging adventures on one cassette.
1987 (*Family*) 60m/C **VHS** $149.95 *RHU*

Four by Dr. Seuss

Four Dr. Seuss classics, "Yertle the Turtle," "Gertrude McFuzz," "Thidwick, the Big-Hearted Moose," and "The Big Brag" are in this collection.

1987 (*Primary*) 46m/C **VHS** $99.95 *RHU*

The 400 Blows 𝄪𝄪𝄪𝄪

Truffaut created one of the most memorable alienated screen teens with this semi-autobiographical drama. Schoolboy Antoine Doinel cuts class, shoplifts, goes to movies, and does basically anything he can to help avoid his unhappy home life. Even when he seriously applies himself to studying for a vital exam, he fails anyway. Eventually he's sent to a seaside juvenile detention camp, supposedly escape-proof, where he gains an exhilarating sense of freedom. There are no easy solutions or convenient wrap-ups, and Truffaut was to follow the character into manhood in four later films (all done with Leaud). In French with English subtitles.
1959 (*Jr. High-Adult*) 97m/B Jean-Pierre Leaud, Claire Maurier, Albert Remy, Guy Decomble, Georges Flament, Patrick Auffay, Jeanne Moreau, Jean-Claude Brialy, Jacques Demy, Francois Truffaut; *D:* Francois Truffaut; *W:* Marcel Moussey, Francois Truffaut; *M:* Jean Constantin. **Award Nominations:** Academy Awards '59: Best Story & Screenplay; **Awards:** Cannes Film Festival '59: Best Director (Truffaut); New York Film Critics Awards '59: Best Foreign Film. **VHS, Beta, LV** $39.95 *HMV, MRV, APD*

The Four Musketeers 𝄪𝄪𝄪

Fun-loving continuation of Lester's "The Three Musketeers," filmed simultaneously. Lavish swashbuckler jaunts between France, England, and Italy, in following the adventures of D'Artagnan, Athos, Aramis and Porthos, fighting the treacheries of the seductive Milady DeWinter. Like its predecessor, a saucy and amusing romp, more for adults than other tellings of the Dumas classic. Gets serious near the end with the deaths of prominent characters. Followed, in 1989, by "The Return of the Musketeers." **Hound Advisory:** Swashbuckling violence, tipping of pints, medieval sex.
1975 (PG/*Jr. High-Adult*) 108m/C Michael York, Oliver Reed, Richard Chamberlain, Frank Finlay, Raquel Welch, Christopher Lee, Faye Dunaway, Jean-Pierre Cassel, Geraldine Chaplin, Simon Ward, Charlton Heston, Roy Kinnear, Nicole Calfan; *D:* Richard Lester. **VHS, Beta** *LIV, OM*

Four Weddings and a Funeral 𝄪𝄪𝄪𝄪

Refreshing, intelligent adult comedy filled with upper-class sophistication and wit. Thirtyish Brit bachelor Charles (Grant) attends the weddings of his friends, but won't take the plunge himself-even as he falls in love with Carrie (MacDowell). Great beginning offers loads of laughs as the first two weddings unfold, then becomes decidedly bittersweet. Grant is terrific as the romantic bumbler, but MacDowell seems slightly out of place. Supporting characters are superb, especially Coleman as the "flirty" Scarlett and Atkinson as a new minister. Surprising box office hit found a broad audience. **Hound Advisory:** Mature teens may appreciate the charming love story, though film has fairly tame sexual situations and frequent usage of the "F" word.
1993 (R/*Sr. High-Adult*) 118m/C Hugh Grant, Andie MacDowell, Simon Callow, Kristin Scott Thomas, James Fleet, John Hannah, Charlotte Coleman, David Bower, Corin Redgrave, Rowan Atkinson; *D:* Mike Newell; *W:* Richard Curtis; *M:* Richard Rodney Bennett. **VHS, LV** *PGV*

1492: Conquest of Paradise 𝄪𝄪

Large-scale Hollywood production striving for political correctness is a drawn-out account of Columbus's (Depardieu) discovery and subsequent exploitation of the "New World." Skillful directing by Ridley Scott and impressive scenery add interest, yet don't make up for a script which chronicles events but tends towards trite dialogue and characterization. Available in both pan-and-scan and letterbox formats. **Hound Advisory:** Violence and nudity.

1992 (PG-13/*Jr. High-Adult*) 142m/C Gerard Depardieu, Sigourney Weaver, Armand Assante, Frank Langella, Loren Dean, Angela Molina, Fernando Rey, Michael Wincott, Steven Waddington, Tcheky Karyo, Kario Salem; *D:* Ridley Scott; *W:* Roselyne Bosch; *M:* Vangelis. **VHS, Beta, LV $95.95** *PAR, BTV*

The Fourth King

Animated presentation in which animals of the world, seeing the Christmas Star, gather and choose one among them to represent the beasts to the Christ child. Italian-American TV cartoon co-production for Noel.

1977 (*Family*) 24m/C **VHS $9.95** *WTA, JTC*

The Fourth Wish 🎬🎬🎬

Australian father learns his 12-year-old son is dying of leukemia. He vows to make Sean's last months meaningful, quitting work to grant the lad's three wishes: owning a dog, reuniting with a divorced, drunkard mom, and meeting Queen Elizabeth. Bring lots of hankies; this effective tearjerker grips the heartstrings thanks to Meillon's prize-winning portrayal of a rough-hewn but devoted dad. **Hound Advisory:** Salty language, mature themes, alcohol use.

1975 (*Family*) 107m/C John Meillon, Robert Bettles, Robyn Nevin; *D:* Don Chaffey. **VHS, Beta $49.95** *SUE*

The Fox and the Hound 🎬🎬🎬

Sweet story of the friendship shared by a fox and hound. Young and naive, the critters become pals, but a season later the hound has become his master's best hunting dog and may have to track down his former playmate. There's a convenient happy ending, though (for a lesson on how Disney sanitizes and homogenizes story material, read the original, grim novel by Daniel P. Mannix). Considered the final bow for remnants of the original Magic Kingdom animation team; it was the next generation who brought a new vigor with the likes of "The Little Mermaid" and "Beauty and the Beast."

1981 (G/*Family*) 83m/C *D:* Art Stevens, Ted Berman, Richard Rich; *W:* Art Stevens, Peter Young, Steve Hulett, Earl Kress, Vance Gerry, Laury Clemmons, Dave Michener, Burny Mattinson; *M:* Buddy Baker; *V:* Mickey Rooney, Kurt Russell, Pearl Bailey, Jack Albertson, Sandy Duncan, Jeanette Nolan, Pat Buttram, John Fiedler, John McIntire, Richard Bakalayan, Paul Winchell, Keith Mitchell, Corey Feldman. **VHS, Beta $24.99** *DIS, WTA, BTV*

Foxes 🎬🎬🎬

Four teenage California valley girls get by with little supervision from their divorced, distracted parents (still in need of maturity themselves). Awash in sex and drugs, the youthful quartet look for a good time and try - with varying degrees of success - to avoid tragic mistakes. Loose, not always clear storyline, but there's a sobering look at kids relying on each other in a world where they have to make adult choices, yet aren't considered grown up. **Hound Advisory:** Sex, profanity, drug use, mature themes, violence.

1980 (R/*Sr. High-Adult*) 106m/C Jodie Foster, Cherie Currie, Marilyn Kagan, Scott Baio, Sally Kellerman, Randy Quaid, Laura Dern; *D:* Adrian Lyne. **VHS, Beta $14.95** *MGM, FOX*

Fraggle Rock: A Festive Fraggle Holiday

Two holiday tales with the Fraggles. "The Bells of Fraggle Rock" features Gobo not believing the Great Bell used in the Festival of the Bells really exists, but he's proven wrong. In "Perfect Blue Rollie," Wembley and Boober find a riverbed full of smoothies and rollies and every Fraggle knows that a perfect blue rollie is the best gift you can give a friend.

199? (*Preschool-Primary*) 52m/C **VHS $12.99** *JHV*

Fraggle Rock, Vol. 1: Meet the Fraggles

Special series of Jim Henson's "Fraggle" videos with two episodes per tape. "Beginnings" introduces the playful Muppet characters, and "A Friend in Need" features Doc's misunderstood dog, and how a Fraggle comes to his rescue. Additional volumes available.

1993 (*Preschool-Primary*) ?m/C **VHS $12.99** *BVV*

Francis Goes to the Races 🎬🎬🎬

The second in the talking-mule series finds O'Connor and Francis taking up residence on Kellaway's failing horse ranch. When mobsters seize control of the property to pay off a debt, Francis decides to check with the horses at the Santa Anita race track and find a sure winner to bet on.

1951 (*Family*) 88m/B Donald O'Connor, Piper Laurie, Cecil Kellaway, Jesse White, Barry Kelley, Hayden Rorke, Vaughn Taylor, Larry Keating; *D:* Arthur Lubin; *W:* Oscar Brodney; *M:* Frank Skinner; *V:* Chill Wills. **VHS** *MCA*

Francis Joins the WACs 🎬🎬🎬

The fifth entry in the series finds O'Connor working as a bank clerk when he is mistakenly drafted back into the military-and sent to a WAC base. Francis tries to keep him out of trouble with the ladies. Wills, the voice of Francis, also turns up as a general.

1954 (*Family*) 94m/B Donald O'Connor, Julie Adams, Chill Wills, Mamie Van Doren, Lynn Bari, ZaSu Pitts, Joan Shawlee, Mara Corday, Allison Hayes; *D:* Arthur Lubin; *V:* Chill Wills. **VHS** *MCA*

Francis the Talking Mule 🎬🎬🎬

The first of the silly but funny series about, what else, a talking mule. Peter Stirling (O'Connor) is the dim-bulb G.I. who hooks up with Francis while fighting in Burma. Francis helps Peter become a war hero but of course everyone thinks he's crazy when Peter insists the mule can talk. The joke is that Francis is smarter than any of the humans. O'Connor starred in six of the films, with Mickey Rooney taking over the final adventure. Director Lubin went on to create the television series "Mr. Ed," about a talking horse.

1949 (*Family*) 91m/B Donald O'Connor, Patricia Medina, ZaSu Pitts, Ray Collins, John McIntire, Eduard Franz, Howland Chamberlin, Frank Faylen, Tony Curtis; *D:* Arthur Lubin; *M:* Frank Skinner; *V:* Chill Wills. **VHS $14.98** *MCA*

Remember: Life is like a box of chocolates—"Forrest Gump" (1994)

Frankenweenie

Before he became a star director with "Pee Wee's Big Adventure," Burton made this offbeat short subject for Disney that went unreleased for years. Little Victor Frankenstein, a suburban science buff, is heartbroken when his dog is hit by a car. Boy resurrects pet through electricity, but neighborhood adults panic at the friendly but bolt-necked pooch. Affectionate, if mildly predictable parody of "Frankenstein" from a kid's eye view, with great B&W photography. Note the "Batman" kite and other elements prophetic of Burton's later career.

1984 (PG/Family**)** 27m/B Shelley Duvall, Daniel Stern, Barret Oliver, Paul Bartel; **D:** Tim Burton; **W:** Tim Burton. **VHS, Beta $14.99** *BVV*

Freaked 🎬🎬

Bizarre little black comedy throws everything at the screen, hoping some of the gross-out humor will prove amusing (and some does). Greedy TV star Ricky Coogin (Winter) agrees to be the spokesman for E.E.S. Corporation, which markets a toxic green slime fertilizer to the Third World. He's sent to South America to promote the product and is captured by the mad scientist proprietor (Quaid) of a mysterious sideshow, who douses him with the fertilizer. Before you know it he's an oozing half-man, half-beast, perfect to join other freaks as the latest attraction. Lots of yucky makeup. Reeves has an uncredited cameo as the Dog Boy. **Hound Advisory:** Profanity and violence.

1993 (PG-13/Jr. High-Adult**)** 80m/C Alex Winter, Randy Quaid, Megan Ward, Michael Stoyanov, Brooke Shields, William Sadler, Derek McGrath, Mr. T, Alex Zuckerman, Karyn Malchus; **Cameos:** Keanu Reeves; **D:** Alex Winter, Tom Stern; **W:** Alex Winter, Tim Burns, Tom Stern; **M:** Kevin Kiner; **V:** Bob(cat) Goldthwait. **VHS** *FXV*

Freaky Friday 🎬🎬🎬

Housewife and her teenage daughter inadvertently switch bodies and each then tries to carry on the other's normal routine. Mary Rodgers' popular book is brought to the screen with great charm in this above average Disney film, a good ten years ahead of the plague of similar body-exchanging plots in the late 1980s. Note also the father-son variation "Summer Switch."

1976 (G/Family**)** 95m/C Barbara Harris, Jodie Foster, Patsy Kelly, Dick Van Patten, Ruth Buzzi; **D:** Gary Nelson. **VHS, Beta $19.99** *DIS*

Free to Be. . .You and Me

Acclaimed, all-star joyful celebration of childhood through song, story, comedy, and poetry that was created to let children feel "free to be who they are and who they want to be" with a gentle emphasis on equality between the sexes.

1983 (Primary**)** 45m/C Marlo Thomas, Alan Alda, Harry Belafonte, Mel Brooks, Diana Ross, Roosevelt Grier. **VHS, Beta $14.98** *LIV*

Free Willy 🎬🎬🎬

Hit film about 12-year-old runaway Jesse, sentenced to clean up his graffiti at an amusement park. Unexpectedly he befriends Willy, a moody, captive killer whale in a cramped tank. What eventually happens is as predictable as the title, and the same story's been done many times before (with every possible critter). What helps this is young Richter as the bad boy who makes good; Hollywood suits reportedly wanted the main character to be an angelic little girl, but the filmmakers went with a tough kid instead, and it made a difference. Madsen adds a nice touch as a concerned parent, while whales handle aquatic chores effortlessly. Closing theme performed by Michael Jackson. **Hound Advisory:** Touches lightly on juvenile delinquency, makes positive statement about self esteem and responsibility.

1993 (PG/Jr. High-Adult**)** 112m/C Jason James Richter, Lori Petty, Jayne Atkinson, August Schellenberg, Michael Madsen; **D:** Simon Wincer; **W:** Keith A. Walker, Corey Blechman; **M:** Basil Poledouris. **Award Nominations:** MTV Movie Awards '94: Breakthrough Performance (Richter), Best Kiss (Jason James Richter/Willy); **Awards:** MTV Movie Awards '94: Best Song ("Will You Be There"). **VHS, LV, 8mm $24.95** *WAR, BTV*

French Postcards 🎬🎬◁

Misadventures of three American students studying all aspects of French culture during their junior year of college at the Institute of French Studies in Paris. By the same writers who penned "American Graffiti" a few years earlier, and like that classic, has its share of young soon-to-be stars.

1979 (PG/Sr. High-Adult**)** 95m/C Miles Chapin, Blanche Baker, Valerie Quennessen, Debra Winger, Mandy Patinkin, Marie-France Pisier; **D:** Willard Huyck; **W:** Gloria Katz, Willard Huyck. **VHS, Beta $59.95** *PAR*

The Freshman 🎬🎬◁

Brando, in an incredible parody of his Don Corleone character, makes this work. Broderick is a college student in need of fast cash, and innocent enough to believe that any work is honest. A good supporting cast and a twisty plot keep things interesting. Sometimes heavy handed with its sight gags, but Broderick and Brando push the movie to hilarious conclusion. Don't miss Burt Parks' musical extravaganza.

1990 (PG/Jr. High-Adult**)** 102m/C Marlon Brando, Matthew Broderick, Penelope Ann Miller, Maximilian Schell, Bruno Kirby, Frank Whaley, Jon Polito, Paul Benedict, Richard Gant, B.D. Wong, Bert Parks; **D:** Andrew Bergman; **W:** Andrew Bergman; **M:** David Newman. **VHS, Beta, LV, 8mm $19.95** *COL, FCT*

Friendly Persuasion 🎬🎬🎬

Earnest, solidly acted tale about a peaceful Quaker family struggling to remain true to its ideals in spite of the Civil War which touches their farm life in southern Indiana. Cooper and McGuire are excellent as the parents with Perkins fine as the son worried he's using his religion to hide his cowardice. Based on a novel by Jessamyn West.

1956 (Jr. High-Adult**)** 140m/C Gary Cooper, Dorothy McGuire, Anthony Perkins, Marjorie Main, Charles Halton; **D:** William Wyler; **M:** Dimitri Tiomkin. **Award Nominations:** Academy Awards '56: Best Adapted Screenplay, Best Director (Wyler), Best Picture, Best Song ("Friendly Persuasion (Thee I Love)"), Best Sound, Best Supporting Actor (Perkins); **Awards:** Cannes Film Festival '57: Best Film. **VHS, Beta, LV $59.98** *FOX*

A Friendship in Vienna 🎬🎬◁

Serious-minded Disney TV drama set in Nazi-occupied Austria, about the daughter of a collaborator who struggles to help her friend, a Jewish teenager, escape to freedom with her family. Based on the book "Devil in Vienna" by Doris Orgel.

Boy meets whale in "Free Willy" (1993)

1988 (*Jr. High-Adult*) 100m/C Jenny Lewis, Ed Asner, Jane Alexander, Stephen Macht, Rosemary Forsyth, Ferdinand "Ferdy" Mayne, Kamie Harper; **D:** Arthur Seidelman; **W:** Richard Alferi. **VHS** *DIS*

Frog 🐸🐸🐸

Fun tale of the nerdy Arlo who adds a frog to his reptile collection but finds it's really an enchanted Italian prince. With the help of the talkative frog, Arlo tries to ace his school science fair and get a fair maiden to kiss the creature. Duvall's Platypus Productions, responsible for her great "Faerie Tale Theatre" and other classics, contributed this to the PBS "Wonderworks" series. Followed by "Frogs!"
1989 (*Family*) 55m/C Paul Williams, Scott Grimes, Shelley Duvall, Elliott Gould, David Grossman. **VHS, Beta, LV $9.98** *ORI, IME*

Frog and Toad are Friends

Animated film of Arnold Lobel's Caldecott Honor-winning children's book about Frog, who cheerfully welcomes each day, and his best friend Toad, who moans and groans each morning.
1985 (*Preschool-Primary*) 30m/C **VHS $12.99** *CHF*

Frog and Toad Together

Four of Arnold Lobel's classic children's stories are featured together.

1988 (*Primary*) 18m/C **VHS, Beta $295.00** *CHF,*

Frog Goes to Dinner

While out to dinner, a little boy's frog jumps out of his pocket, disrupting all the guests in the fancy restaurant.
1985 (*Primary*) 12m/C **D:** Gary Templeton. **VHS, Beta** *BFA*

The Frog Prince

Delightful musical Muppet version, originally made for TV, of the classic fairy tale, abounding with frogs. Kermit discovers that the new frog at the pond is really a handsome prince who has been turned into an amphibian by a witch's spell, and only the kiss of a beautiful princess can cure him.
1981 (*Family*) 54m/C **V:** Jim Henson, Frank Oz. **VHS, Beta** *JHV, BVV*

Frog Prince

Excruciatingly awful musical rendering of the classic fairy tale, one of the Cannon Movie Tales. Paragon gives the role of the prince-turned-amphibian some panache, but even he can't survive lyrics like "Ever since I was a tadpole/I was such a sad pole."
1988 (*Family*) 86m/C Aileen Quinn, Helen Hunt, John Paragon; **D:** Jackson Hunsicker. **VHS, LV $9.98** *NO*

Frogs!

Lengthy "WonderWorks" sequel to "Frog" is one too many trips to the well, though it imaginatively inverts the plot of the earlier tale. Arlo is now the most popular (and conceited) kid in school. His plans to be prom king are interrupted when he and Gus are both reverted to froghood by a witch. When they discover the pond is being poisoned, their only hope is Hannah, a brainy classmate Arlo previously scorned as a nerd. **199?** (*Family*) 55m/C Shelley Duvall, Elliott Gould, Paul Williams, Scott Grimes, Judith Ivey. **VHS $29.95** *PME, HMV, BTV*

From Russia with Love 🎬🎬🎬✄

Bond is back and on the loose in exotic Istanbul looking for a super-secret coding machine. He's involved with a beautiful Russian spy and has the SPECTRE organization after him, including villainess Rosa Klebb (she of the killer shoe). Lots of exciting escapes but no over-reliance on the gadgetry of the later films. Second 007 adventure is considered by many to be the best. Laserdisc edition includes interviews with director Terence Young and others on the creative staff. **Hound Advisory:** Violence, alcohol use, suggested sex. **1963** (PG/*Jr. High-Adult*) 125m/C Sean Connery, Daniela Bianchi, Pedro Armendariz Sr., Lotte Lenya, Robert Shaw, Eunice Gayson, Walter Gotell, Lois Maxwell, Bernard Lee, Desmond Llewelyn, Nadja Regin, Alizia Gur, Martine Beswick, Leila; **D:** Terence Young; **M:** John Barry. **VHS, Beta, LV $19.98** *MGM, VYG, CRC*

The Front Page 🎬🎬✄

A remake of the Hecht-MacArthur play about the managing editor of a 1920s Chicago newspaper who finds out his ace reporter wants to quit the business and get married. But first an escaped convicted killer offers the reporter an exclusive interview. **Hound Advisory:** Profanity. **1974** (PG/*Family*) 105m/C Jack Lemmon, Walter Matthau, Carol Burnett, Austin Pendleton, Vincent Gardenia, Charles Durning, Susan Sarandon; **D:** Billy Wilder; **W:** Billy Wilder, I.A.L. Diamond. **VHS, LV $89.95** *MCA*

Frosty Returns

Frosty the Snowman returns in another 'toon, befriending a little girl named Holly. But the evil Mr. Twitchell has an invention that sprays the snow away. Frosty and Holly must stop him if they want to save winter. **1992** (*Family*) 25m/C **V:** John Goodman, Andrea Martin, Brian Doyle-Murray, Jan Hooks. **VHS $12.98** *FHE, MOV, BTV*

Frosty the Snowman

The original Rankin-Bass holiday classic cartoon about the snowman who comes to life when crowned with the hat of a magician, making him a friend to children. **1969** (*Family*) 30m/C **D:** Arthur Rankin Jr., Jules Bass; **V:** Billy DeWolfe, Jackie Vernon. **VHS $12.98** *FHE, BTV, WTA*

Frosty's Winter Wonderland/The Leprechauns' Christmas Gold

Features two Rankin-Bass holiday cartoons. In the first Jack Frost (no relation) threatens a certain Snowman and his newly-created wife, while in the second story a young boy discovers a magical island of leprechauns at Christmas.

1981 (*Preschool-Primary*) 50m/C **D:** Arthur Rankin Jr., Jules Bass; **V:** Andy Griffith, Shelley Winters, Art Carney, Peggy Cass. **VHS, Beta $14.98** *LIV, WTA*

The Fugitive 🎬🎬🎬✄

Exciting big-screen version of the '60s TV series with the same basic storyline: Dr. Richard Kimble's wife is murdered and he's implicated, so he goes on the lam to find the real killer, the mysterious one-armed man. Meanwhile, he's being pursued by relentless federal marshall Jones, who seems to have enormous fun throughout the show. Lots of mystery and action, particularly a spectacular train/bus crash sequence, keeps the tension high. Due to illness, Richard Jordan was replaced by Krabbe after production had begun. Alec Baldwin was originally slated to star as Kimble, but backed out and Ford was cast. Sound familiar? Ford also replaced Baldwin as Jack Ryan in "Patriot Games." The second highest grossing movie of 1993. **Hound Advisory:** Fair amount of profanity and violence, plus implied sexual situations. **1993** (PG-13/*Sr. High-Adult*) 127m/C Harrison Ford, Tommy Lee Jones, Jeroen Krabbe, Julianne Moore, Sela Ward, Joe Pantoliano, Andreas Katsulas, Daniel Roebuck; **D:** Andrew Davis; **W:** David N. Twohy, Jeb Stuart; **M:** James Newton Howard. **Award Nominations:** Academy Awards '93: Best Cinematography, Best Film Editing, Best Original Screenplay, Best Picture, Best Sound, Best Sound Effects Editing; British Academy Awards '93: Best Supporting Actor (Jones); Directors Guild of America Awards '93: Best Director (Davis); Golden Globe Awards '94: Best Actor—Drama (Ford), Best Director (Davis); **Awards:** Academy Awards '93: Best Supporting Actor (Jones); Golden Globe Awards '94: Best Supporting Actor (Jones); Los Angeles Film Critics Association Awards '93: Best Supporting Actor (Jones); MTV Movie Awards '94: Best On-Screen Duo (Harrison Ford/Tommy Lee Jones), Best Action Sequence. **VHS $24.96** *WAR*

Fun & Fancy Free

Part-animated, part-live-action feature is split into two segments: "Bongo" with Dinah Shore narrating the story of a happy-go-lucky circus bear; and "Mickey and the Beanstalk"—a "new" version of an old fairly tale. **1947** (*Family*) 96m/C Edgar Bergen, Charlie McCarthy, Jiminy Cricket, Mickey Mouse, Donald Duck, Goofy, Dinah Shore. **VHS, Beta** *DIS*

Funny Face 🎬🎬🎬

Musical satire on beatniks and the fashion scene also features the May-December romance between Astaire and the ever-lovely Hepburn. He's a high-fashion photographer (based on Richard Avedon); she's a Greenwich Village bookseller fond of shapeless, drab clothing. He decides to take her to Paris and show her what modeling's all about. Elegant musical score features classic Gershwin. Laserdisc includes the original theatrical trailer and is available in widescreen. ♫Let's Kiss and Make Up; He Loves and She Loves; Funny Face; How Long Has This Been Going On?; Clap Yo' Hands; S'Wonderful; Bonjour Paris; On How To Be Lovely; Marche Funebre. **1957** (*Jr. High-Adult*) 103m/C Fred Astaire, Audrey Hepburn, Kay Thompson, Suzy Parker; **D:** Stanley Donen; **M:** George Gershwin, Ira Gershwin. **VHS, Beta, LV, 8mm $14.95** *PAR, FCT*

Funny Farm 🎬🎬

Chase as a New York sportswriter finds that life in the country is not quite what he envisioned. Uneven but almost engaging, and worth a laugh or two. **Hound Advisory:** Salty language.

1988 (*PG*/*Jr. High–Adult*) 101m/C Chevy Chase, Madolyn Smith, Joseph Maher, Jack Gilpin, Brad Sullivan, MacIntyre Dixon; **D:** George Roy Hill; **W:** Jeffrey Boam; **M:** Elmer Bernstein. **VHS, LV $19.98** *WAR, STE*

Funny Girl 🎬🎬🎬

Follows the early career of comedian Fanny Brice, her rise to stardom with the Ziegfeld Follies and her stormy romance with gambler Nick Arnstein in a fun and funny look at back stage music hall life in the early 1900s. Streisand's film debut followed her auspicious performance of the role on Broadway. Score was augmented by several tunes sung by Brice during her performances. Excellent performances from everyone, captured beautifully by Wyler in his musical film debut. Followed by "Funny Lady." ♫My Man; Second Hand Rose; I'd Rather Be Blue Over You; People; Don't Rain On My Parade; I'm The Greatest Star; Sadie, Sadie; His Love Makes Me Beautiful; You Are Woman, I Am Man.

1968 (*G*/*Family*) 151m/C Barbra Streisand, Omar Sharif, Walter Pidgeon, Kay Medford, Anne Francis; **D:** William Wyler. **Award Nominations:** Academy Awards '68: Best Cinematography, Best Film Editing, Best Picture, Best Song ("Funny Girl"), Best Sound, Best Supporting Actress (Medford), Best Original Score; **Awards:** Academy Awards '68: Best Actress (Streisand); Golden Globe Awards '69: Best Actress—Musical/Comedy (Streisand). **VHS, Beta, LV $19.95** *COL, BTV*

Funny Lady 🎬🎬🎬¼

A continuation of "Funny Girl," recounting Fanny Brice's tumultuous marriage to showman Billy Rose in the 1930s and her lingering affection for first husband Nick Arnstein. One of the rare sequels which are just as good, or at least almost, as the original. ♫How Lucky Can You Get?; Great Day; More Than You Know; Blind Date; So Long, Honey Lamb; Isn't This Better; Let's Hear It For Me; I Like Him/I Like Her; It's Only a Paper Moon.

1975 (*PG*/*Jr. High–Adult*) 137m/C Barbra Streisand, Omar Sharif, James Caan, Roddy McDowall, Ben Vereen, Carole Wells, Larry Gates, Heidi O'Rourke; **D:** Herbert Ross; **W:** Jay Presson Allen, Arnold Schulman. **VHS, Beta, LV $19.95** *COL, FCT*

Further Adventures of the Wilderness Family, Part 2 🎬🎬🎬¼

More of the same scenic nature shots and low-intensity survival drama involving the Robinson clan of the Colorado wilderness, earlier depicted in "The Adventures of the Wilderness Family." Next sequel: "Mountain Family Robinson."

1977 (*G*/*Family*) 104m/C Heather Rattray, Ham Larsen, George Flower, Robert F. Logan, Susan Damante Shaw; **D:** Frank Zuniga. **VHS, Beta $9.98** *MED, VTR*

The Further Adventures of Wil Cwac Cwac

Ten new episodes featuring the trouble-prone duckling and his farm-animal playmates from Welsh TV.

1987 (*Preschool-Primary*) 40m/C **VHS, Beta** *LIV, FHE*

G-Men Never Forget

Moore, former stuntman and future Lone Ranger, stars in the 12-part serial about FBI agents battling the bad guys. **Hound Advisory:** Violence.

1948 (*Family*) 167m/B Clayton Moore, Roy Barcroft, Ramsay Ames, Drew Allen, Tommy Steele, Eddie Acuff; **D:** Fred Brannon, Yakima Canutt. **VHS $29.98** *REP, MLB*

G-Men vs. the Black Dragon

Re-edited serial of "Black Dragon of Manzanar" stars Cameron as a Fed who battle Asian Axis agents during WWII. **Hound Advisory:** Violence.

1943 (*Adult*) 244m/B Rod Cameron, Roland Got, Constance Worth, Nino Pipitone, Noel Cravat; **D:** William Witney. **VHS, LV $29.98** *REP, MED, MLB*

Gabby Cartoonies

Compilation of seven short Max Fleischer cartoons starring the determined but bumbling Gabby, first seen as the town crier in Fleischer's feature "Gulliver's Travels."

1941 (*Family*) 49m/C **VHS, LV $14.95** *WTA*

Gaiking

The mighty flying robot, Gaiking, becomes earth's strongest and most heroic defense against the cunning Davius. Japanimation.

1982 (*Primary*) 100m/C **VHS, Beta $17.98** *FHE, WTA, TPV*

Galaxy Express 🎬🎬

Japanese animated adventure about young boy who sets out to find immortality by traveling on The Galaxy Express, an ultra-modern 35th century space train that carries its passengers in search of their dreams.

1982 (*PG*/*Primary-Adult*) 91m/C **D:** Taro Rin; **V:** Booker Bradshaw, Corey Burton. **VHS, Beta $39.98** *NO*

Galaxy High School: Welcome to Galaxy High

Melded-together episodes of the TV cartoon about the first two Earth kids to enroll in Galaxy High, meeting all manner of wacky, other-worldly creatures.

1988 (*Family*) 91m/C **VHS $39.95** *FHE, WTA*

Gallavants 🎬🎬

Full-length animated fantasy about an ant society whose youngsters must demonstrate responsibility and maturity to earn their "kabumps" — bulges on their little ant rearends that prove they're adults and ready to take their places in insect society. Stop snickering, you.

1984 (*Preschool-Primary*) 100m/C **VHS, Beta $14.95** *CEL, WTA*

Gandy Goose: One Man Navy

Video revival time for the vintage Terrytoons shorts about the silly goose and his Jimmy Durante-style companion Sourpuss the cat.

1941 (*Preschool-Primary*) 38m/C **VHS $5.99** *VTR*

The Gang's All Here Series

Mickey Mouse, Donald Duck, and Goofy star together in some hilarious misadventures on separate tapes: "Lonesome Ghosts," "Mickey's Trailer," and "Tugboat Mickey."
1990 *(Preschool-Primary)* 8m/C **VHS, Beta $170.00** *MTI, DSN*

The Garbage Pail Kids Movie WOOF!

Once upon a time there was a set of grotesque bubblegum cards that parodied the ever-so-cute Cabbage Patch Kids toys. The hit cards inspired this bad movie, with the Kids just little actors in stiff, ugly masks. Public reaction was, well ... TV stations subsequently refused to air a tie-in "Garbage Pail Kids" cartoon series. Any questions?
1987 (PG/Jr. High-Adult) 100m/C Anthony Newley, MacKenzie Astin, Katie Barberi; **D:** Rod Amateau. **VHS, Beta, LV $14.95** *PAR, BAR, IME*

Garfield

Series of well-received prime-time animated specials featuring the cranky, self-possessed feline of comic strip fame. Episodes include "Here Comes Garfield," "Garfield on the Town," and "Garfield Goes Hollywood," all done by the "Peanuts" TV cartoon team.
1989 *(Preschool)* 30m/C **VHS, Beta $12.98** *FOX*

A Garfield Christmas

The rotund feline spends Christmas down on the farm with Jon's family.
1991 *(Family)* 24m/C **VHS $9.98** *FXY, WTA*

Garfield Goes Hollywood

Garfield tries out for Hollywood's TV show, "Pet Search." Under the name Johnny Bop and the Two-Steps, he, his owner Jon, and dog Odie have a shot at stardom.
1990 *(Family)* 30m/C **V:** Lorenzo Music. **VHS, LV $12.98** *FOX, WTA*

Garfield: His 9 Lives

Litter of TV cartoons in which Garfield dreams about his past, present, and future lives, including his time as a Pharaoh's prized cat, a laboratory animal, and a space-age cat battling aliens.
1993 *(Family)* 60m/C **VHS $12.98** *FOX, WTA*

Garfield in Paradise

Jon, Garfield, and Odie are on vacation at a cheap tropical resort where they meet a lost tribe who decides to sacrifice man and cat to their volcano god.
1986 *(Family)* 30m/C **VHS $9.95** *WTA, FOX*

Garfield on the Town

Seeking refuge from a gang of cats ("The Claws"), Garfield hides in a restaurant. Lo and behold as luck and coincidence would have it, Garfield discovers his family owns the joint and that it is the site of his very own birth. All of this conspires to remind him of many of his past misdeeds.
1990 *(Family)* 24m/C **V:** Lorenzo Music. **VHS $12.98** *FOX, WTA*

Garfield's Feline Fantasy

Animated spoof of Indiana Jones adventures with Garfield and Odie in search of the Banana of Bombay.
1993 *(Family)* 35m/C **VHS $9.98** *FOX, WTA*

Garfield's Halloween Adventure

Garfield and Odie dress up as pirates for trick-or-treat fun but the trick may be on them when they find themselves at a haunted house.
1985 *(Family)* 30m/C **VHS $9.95** *WTA, FOX*

Garfield's Thanksgiving

Garfield goes on a pre-Thanksgiving diet and Jon ruins dinner but Grandma arrives in time to save the day. Whew; what a relief.
1989 *(Family)* 30m/C **VHS $9.95** *WTA, FOX*

The Gate 🦴🦴

Left alone for the weekend (uh-oh!), youngster Glen and his playmates discover a large hole in the backyard that turns out to be the gateway to Hell - and the natives are restless. Lowbrow but effective kids-eye-view horror indulges in wild special effect thrills rather than tasteless bloodletting and gore. Followed by a sequel. **Hound Advisory:** Demon violence, but they're dead already, aren't they? Zero humans are killed, which could be a world's record for the genre.
1987 (PG-13/Jr. High-Adult) 85m/C Christa Denton, Stephen Dorff, Louis Tripp; **D:** Tibor Takacs. **VHS, Beta, LV $14.98** *LIV, VES*

Gateway to the Mind

The five senses are explored in this animated video from "Bugs Bunny" animator Chuck Jones. Many revelations for children, including the ability of grasshoppers to hear with the stomach.
199? *(Primary-Jr. High)* 58m/C **D:** Chuck Jones; **W:** Chuck Jones. **VHS $19.98** *FCT, WTA, RHI*

Gay Purr-ee 🦴🦴

Cartoon feature (co-written by Chuck Jones) in which provincial cat Mewsette goes to Paris in search of love and adventure. She winds up in the paws of suave scoundrel Meowrice and must be rescued by her tomcat boyfriend from home. Lushly animated parody of romantic melodramas, unevenly mixing kid stuff with clever touches for grownups. Gets an extra half-bone for the cast of voices, who make the songs much better than they are.
1962 *(Family)* 85m/C **D:** Abe Levitow; **W:** Chuck Jones; **M:** Harold Arlen; **V:** Judy Garland, Robert Goulet, Red Buttons, Hermione Gingold, Mel Blanc. **VHS, LV $14.95** *WAR, FCT, WTA*

The Geisha Boy 🦴🦴🦴

Jerry is a floundering magician who joins the USO and tours the Far East finding romance with a Japanese widow after her small son claims him as a father. But it's the slapstick that will win kid viewers over, much of it involving the conjuror's tricky white rabbit, one of the screen's most memorable

bunnies since Bugs. Special appearance by the Los Angeles Dodgers.
1958 *(Family)* 98m/C Jerry Lewis, Marie McDonald, Sessue Hayakawa, Barton MacLane, Suzanne Pleshette, Nobu McCarthy; *D:* Frank Tashlin. **VHS $14.95** *PAR*

General Spanky 🦴🦴

The only "Our Gang" feature with the original cast goofed by transplanting the Little Rascals from their accustomed 1920s/30s environment into a Civil War setting popular with Hollywood at the time. Spanky and Alfalfa are unlikely Confederate kids who play soldier, outsmarting Union troops. Some funny stuff, but Buckwheat's role as an eager slave is pretty disturbing today.
1936 *(Family)* 73m/B George "Spanky" McFarland, Phillips Holmes, Ralph Morgan, Irving Pichel, Rosina Lawrence, Billie "Buckwheat" Thomas, Carl "Alfalfa" Switzer, Louise Beavers; *D:* Fred Newmeyer. **VHS, LV $19.98** *MGM, FCT*

Gentle Ben

Episodes from the late '60s television show about the son of an Everglades game warden and the family's adopted bear. Derived from the film "Gentle Giant" (also on video), both from "Flipper" creator Ivan Tors.
1969 *(Preschool)* 60m/C Dennis Weaver, Beth Brickell, Clint Howard, Rance Howard, Angelo Rutherford, Burt Reynolds. **VHS, Beta $14.95** *CNG*

Gentle Giant 🦴🦴

An orphaned bear is taken in by a boy and his family and grows to be a 750 pound giant who must be returned to the wild. "Gentle Ben" TV series was derived from this feature.
1967 *(Family)* 93m/C Dennis Weaver, Vera Miles, Ralph Meeker, Clint Howard, Huntz Hall; *D:* James Neilson. **VHS $14.98** *REP*

George! 🦴◁

Carefree bachelor inherits the title St. Bernard and has to take both the clumsy 250-pound animal and his girlfriend on a Swiss Alps trip. George proves his worth when his new master gets caught in an avalanche. Low-budget ancestor of "Beethoven" combines unfunny gags with muddy travel footage. Originally 87 minutes.
1970 *(G/Family)* 70m/C Marshall Thompson, Jack Mullaney, Inge Schoner; *D:* Wallace C. Bennett; *W:* Wallace C. Bennett. **VHS, Beta $39.95** *VCI*

George Balanchine's The Nutcracker 🦴🦴◁

Pas de deux redux. Tchaikovsky's classic ballet about the magic of Christmas and a little girl (Cohen) who dreams on Christmas Eve that she is in an enchanted kingdom. Culkin lamely grins through his wooden performance as the Nutcracker Prince, but the talent of the Sugarplum Fairy (Kistler) and the other dancers is such that conventional camera techniques sometimes fail to keep up with their exacting moves. Adapted from the 1816 book by E.T.A. Hoffmann.
1993 *(G/Family)* 93m/C Macaulay Culkin, Jessica Lynn Cohen, Bart Robinson Cook, Darci Kistler, Damian Woetzel, Kyra Nichols, Wendy Whelan, Gen Horiuchi, Margaret Tracey; *D:* Emile Ardolino; *W:* Susan Cooper. **VHS, LV, 8mm $19.99** *WAR*

George of the Jungle

"Rocky and Bullwinkle" producer Jay Ward also created the inept animated TV hero "George of the Jungle" in these Tarzan spoofs that initially failed with audiences but have since become cult items for their snide humor (great moments in marketing: for video reissue they've been dubbed "greentoons" to catch the environmentalist wave). Also includes 'toons with the race-car driver Tom Slick and Super Chicken. Each tape is available individually: "Gullible Travels," "Jungle Mutants," "There's No Place Like Jungle," and "The World According to George."
1967 *(Family)* 30m/C **VHS $9.98** *FXV, WTA*

George's Island 🦴🦴

When young George is placed with the worst foster parents in the world, his eccentric grandfather helps him and a little girl escape. They wind up on an island where hammy ghosts of Captain Kidd and his crew still guard buried treasure. Canadian kids' film, cute in parts but too often scuttled by overacting and cheesy f/x. Filmed in Nova Scotia.
1991 *(PG/Family)* 89m/C Ian Bannen, Sheila McCarthy, Maury Chaykin, Nathaniel Moreau, Vicki Ridler, Brian Downey, Gary Reineke; *D:* Paul Donovan; *W:* J. William Ritchie; *M:* Marty Simon. **VHS, LV $19.95** *COL, NLC*

Gerald McBoing-Boing

Classic Dr. Seuss story of a boy who can only communicate through the title sound effect but finds fame, fortune, happiness, and self-fulfillment in spite of being "different." Considered in its day to be a breakthrough of sorts in "sophisticated" cartoon style.
1950 *(Family)* 55m/B **VHS, Beta** *CHF*

Gerald McBoing Boing, Vol. 1: Favorite Sing-Along Songs

Episodes from the first cartoon show made for television which includes educational aspects. Includes "Turned Around Clown," "The Unenchanted Princess," "The Freezee Yum Story," "The Little Boy Who Ran Away," and "Matador and the Troubador." Additional volumes available.
1956 *(Preschool-Jr. High)* 20m/C *D:* Ernie Pintoff. **VHS $9.95** *PAR, FCT, WTA*

Geronimo 🦴🦴🦴

Not to be confused with the big screen version, this made for cable television drama uses three actors to portray the legendary Apache warrior (1829-1909) at various stages of his life. The intrepid teenager who leads attacks on Mexican troops, the adult fighting the duplicitous bluecoats, and the aged man witnessing the destruction of his way of life. The true story is told from the point of view of Native American culture and historical records.
1993 *(Jr. High-Adult)* 120m/C Joseph Runningfox, Jimmy Herman, Ryan Black, Nick Ramus, Michelle St. John, Michael Greyeyes, Tailinh Forest Flower, Kimberly Norris, August Schellenberg, Geno Silva, Harrison Lowe; *D:* Roger Young; *W:* J.T. Allen; *M:* Patrick Williams. **VHS** *TTC*

Geronimo: An American Legend 🎬🎬🎬◁

Well-intentioned bio-actioner about the legendary Apache leader who fought the U.S. Army over forcing Native Americans onto reservations is often too noble for its own good, leading to some slow spots. Narrator is young Army officer Gatewood (Patric), whose division is to round up the renegades led by Geronimo (Studi), whom he naturally comes to admire. Hackman and Duvall (as a general and a scout respectively) steal any scene they're in although the leads manage to hold their own. Great location filming around Moab, Utah. **Hound Advisory:** Violence, profanity.

1993 (PG-13/Jr. High-Adult) 115m/C Wes Studi, Jason Patric, Robert Duvall, Gene Hackman, Matt Damon, Rodney Grant, Kevin Tighe, Carlos Palomino, Stephen McHattie; **D:** Walter Hill; **W:** John Milius, Larry Gross; **M:** Ry Cooder. **VHS, LV, 8mm** *COL*

The Get Along Gang, Vol. 1

Get Along Gang members are cartoon critters traveling the country in their Clubhouse Caboose, leaving worthwhile moral lessons in their wake. Additional volumes available.
198? *(Family)* 44m/C **VHS $24.95** *LHV, KAR, WTA*

Getting Even with Dad 🎬◁

Crook Danson can't find the money he stole in his last heist. Why? because his precocious son has hidden it with the intention of blackmailing dear old dad into going straight and acting like a real father. Title is unintentionally funny in light of Mac's domineering dad Kit, who, as they say, drives a hard bargain. Fairly bland family film squanders charm of Danson and Culkin, running formulaic plot into ground. Headly is likewise wasted as district attorney who prosecutes and then falls for Pops, behaving like any good lawyer would. Macaulay's precocious days are down to a precious few. **Hound Advisory:** Roughhousing; salty language.

1994 (PG/Jr. High-Adult) 108m/C Macaulay Culkin, Ted Danson, Glenne Headly, Hector Elizondo, Saul Rubinek, Gailard Sartain, Kathleen Wilhoite, Sam McMurray; **D:** Howard Deutch; **W:** Tom S. Parker, Jim Jennewein. **VHS** *NYR*

Gettysburg 🎬🎬🎬🎬◁

Civil War buff Ted Turner (who has a cameo as a Confederate soldier) originally intended Michael Shaara's Pulitzer Prize-winning novel "The Killer Angels" to be adapted as a three-part miniseries for his "TNT" network, but the lure of the big screen prevailed, marking the first time the battle has been committed to film and the first time a film crew has been allowed to film battle scenes on the Gettysburg National Military Park battlefield. The greatest battle of the war and the bloodiest in U.S. history is realistically staged by more than 5,000 Civil War re-enactors. The all-male cast concentrates on presenting the human cost of the war, with Daniels particularly noteworthy as the scholarly Colonel Chamberlain, determined to hold Little Big Top for the Union. Last film role for Jordan, to whom the movie is co-dedicated. The full scale recreation of Pickett's Charge is believed to be the largest period scale motion-picture sequence filmed in North America since D.W. Griffith's "Birth of a Nation." **Hound Advisory:** Violence.

1993 (PG/Jr. High-Adult) 254m/C Jeff Daniels, Martin Sheen, Tom Berenger, Sam Elliott, Richard Jordan, Stephen Lang, Kevin Conway, C. Thomas Howell, Maxwell Caulfield, Andrew Prine, James Lancaster, Royce D. Applegate, Brian Mallon; **Cameos:** Ken Burns, Ted Turner; **D:** Ronald Maxwell; **W:** Ronald Maxwell; **M:** Randy Edelman. **VHS** *TTC*

Ghost 🎬🎬🎬

Zucker, known for overboard comedies like "Airplane!" and "Ruthless People," changed tack and directed this undemanding romantic thriller, which was the surprising top grosser of 1990. Swayze is a murdered investment consultant attempting (from somewhere near the hereafter) to protect his lover, Moore, from imminent danger when he learns he was the victim of a hit gone afoul. Goldberg is the medium who suddenly discovers that the powers she's been faking are real. A winning blend of action, special effects (from Industrial Light and Magic) and romance. **Hound Advisory:** Violence; profanity; suggested sex.

1990 (PG-13/Sr. High-Adult) 127m/C Patrick Swayze, Demi Moore, Whoopi Goldberg, Tony Goldwyn, Rick Aviles, Vincent Schiavelli, Gail Boggs, Armelia McQueen, Phil Leeds; **D:** Jerry Zucker; **W:** Bruce Joel Rubin; **M:** Maurice Jarre. **Award Nominations:** Academy Awards '90: Best Film Editing, Best Picture, Best Original Score; **Awards:** Academy Awards '90: Best Original Screenplay, Best Supporting Actress (Goldberg); Golden Globe Awards '91: Best Supporting Actress (Goldberg); People's Choice Awards '91: Best Film—Drama. **VHS, Beta, LV, 8mm $14.95** *PAR, SUP, FCT*

The Ghost Belonged to Me

Alexander Armsworth has an encounter with the spirit world and learns self-confidence. This live-action Walt Disney short was adapted for the Magic Kingdom's TV program from the book by Richard Peck.
1990 *(Primary-Sr. High)* 11m/C **VHS, Beta $220.00** *MTI, DSN*

Ghost Chasers 🎬🎬

The Bowery Boys become mixed up in supernatural hijinks when a seance leads to the appearance of a ghost that only Sach can see.
1951 *(Family)* 70m/B Leo Gorcey, Huntz Hall, Billy Benedict, David Gorcey, Buddy Gorman, Bernard Gorcey, Jan Kayne, Philip Van Zandt, Lloyd Corrigan; **D:** William Beaudine. **VHS $14.98** *WAR*

Ghost Dad 🎬🎬

Widowed workaholic Elliot Hopper dies in an auto mishap (well, not really, but that's getting ahead of ourselves). He returns in phantom form to help his kids prepare for life without him. The "Dad" theme of this movie is nice and sweet, as Cosby plays the belated family man. Alas, stress is on the "Ghost" part, with poor f/x trying to compete with "Beetlejuice" as Elliot masters walking through walls, flying, and general spooking. Booed at the box office, spectral flop might interest households with elementary fry.

1990 (PG/Primary-Adult) 84m/C Bill Cosby, Denise Nicholas, Ian Bannen, Christine Ebersole, Dana Ashbrook, Arnold Stang; **D:** Sidney Poitier; **W:** S.S. Wilson, Brent Maddock; **M:** Henry Mancini. **VHS, Beta, LV $19.95** *MCA*

Wes Studi is "Geronimo: An American Legend" (1993)

Ghost Fever WOOF!

Two bumbling cops try to evict the inhabitants of a haunted house and tangle with both good and evil spirits. Childish humor, on the level of "Scooby-Doo" but tarred with racism and sex gags that may make it a turnoff for kids, or at least their parents. Alan Smithee is a pseudonym used when a director does not want his or her name on a film - no wonder. **Hound Advisory:** Sex talk, salty language.
1987 (PG/*Jr. High*) 86m/C Sherman Hemsley, Luis Avalos; *D:* Alan Smithee; *W:* Oscar Brodney. **VHS, Beta, LV** $19.98 *NLC*

The Ghost Goes West 🦴🦴🦴

Antiquated but still fun fantasy about 200-year-old Murdoch Glourie cursed to haunt his Scottish castle. The kilt-clad ghost gets rattled when an American tycoon decides to buy Glourie Castle and move it brick-by-brick to Florida, turning the spook into a media gimmick for his grocery store chain. Special f/x are nothing special by modern standards, but overall pic is pleasant and satisfying. Available in digitally remastered stereo with the original theatrical trailer. **Hound Advisory:** Alcohol use.
1936 (*Family*) 85m/B Robert Donat, Jean Parker, Eugene Pallette, Elsa Lanchester; *D:* Rene Clair; *W:* Robert Sherwood. **VHS, Beta** $19.98 *HBO, SUE*

Ghost in the Noonday Sun WOOF!

Home video salvaged this derelict comedy that never got theatrical release. Sellers is bizarre as super-superstitious pirate Dick Scratcher (off-color puns abound), unable to remember a treasure site. He kidnaps a boy he imagines to be psychic in hopes of locating the loot. Marvelous silent-movie opening sequence, and lots of childish slapstick, but adults who aren't Sellers completists should look elsewhere. Based on the children's book by Sid Fleischman.
1974 (*Family*) 90m/C Peter Sellers, Spike Milligan, Anthony (Tony) Franciosa, Clive Revill, Rosemary Leach, Peter Boyle; *D:* Peter Medak. **VHS, Beta** *NO*

The Ghost of Thomas Kempe

When James Harrison unwittingly frees a mischievous ghost from a bottle, he's blamed for the many pranks pulled by the spook. Adaptation of the book by Penelope Lively.
1979 (*Primary-Jr. High*) 60m/C **VHS, Beta** $12.98 *MTT, SVI*

Ghost Stories

Three lesser-known Charles Dickens ghost stories, "The Ghost in the Wardrobe," "The Mail Coach Ghosts," and "The Goblin & The Gravedigger," (this last surprisingly reminiscent of "A Christmas Carol"), derived from Dickens' "Pickwick Papers." Quite spooky and entertaining, in spite of limited low-budget animation.
1988 (*Primary-Jr. High*) 60m/C **VHS** $29.95 *WTA*

Ghostbusters 🦴🦴🦴

After losing their scholastic funding, a group of paranormal investigators go into business for themselves, aiding NYC citizens in removing ghosts, poltergeists, and other supernatural pests, climaxing in a titanic battle with an ancient demon-

god. Comedy-thriller with great special effects, zany characters, and some of the best laughs of the decade. Also available in a laserdisc version with letterboxing, analysis of all special effects, complete screenplay, and original trailer. The inspiration for two competing cartoon shows also on video. **Hound Advisory:** Salty language, sex talk with the possessed, roughhousing.
1984 (PG/*Family*) 103m/C Bill Murray, Dan Aykroyd, Harold Ramis, Rick Moranis, Sigourney Weaver, Annie Potts, Ernie Hudson, William Atherton; *D:* Ivan Reitman; *W:* Dan Aykroyd, Harold Ramis, Harold Ramis; *M:* Elmer Bernstein. **VHS, Beta, LV, 8mm** $19.95 *COL, VYG, APD*

Ghostbusters 2 🦴🦴

Fun opening finds the Ghostbusters out of work, reduced to doing Barney-the-Dinosaur-type birthday parties for kids. When a river of slime threatens NYC just so a long-dead baddie can reincarnate himself in Weaver's baby, the paranormal investigators are back in action. One priceless gag with the Statue of Liberty; otherwise a dispirited affair that offers music-videos in place of plot. **Hound Advisory:** Sex talk, profanity.
1989 (PG/*Adult*) 102m/C Bill Murray, Dan Aykroyd, Sigourney Weaver, Harold Ramis, Rick Moranis, Ernie Hudson, Peter MacNicol, David Margulies, Wilhelm von Homburg, Harris Yulin, Annie Potts; *D:* Ivan Reitman; *W:* Harold Ramis; *M:* Randy Edelman. **VHS, Beta, LV, 8mm** $19.95 *COL*

Ghostbusters: Back to the Past

TV cartoon collection based not on the Bill Murray movies but an earlier Sid & Marty Krofft live-action kids' comedy that happened to bear that suddenly-sellable title "Ghostbusters." These 'toons cashed in on the name recognition by reviving the premise of two paranormal investigators and their gorilla friend, who can now travel back in time to take on ectoplasmic evildoers. Additional volumes available.
1991 (*Family*) 75m/C **VHS** $19.99 *JFK, CEL*

Ghostwriter, Vol. 1: Ghost Story

Carefully conceived and quite enchanting educational series from PBS-TV; six urban children solve mysteries with the help of a special partner, an amnesiac ghost who can only communicate by reading and writing. Someone in the neighborhood is stealing backpacks, and clues point to a weird gang with monster masks, who leave coded messages. Lenni, Jamal, Alex, and Gaby, with a lesson in logic from their new friend Ghostwriter, crack the code and figure out what's up. Feature-length, five-episode compilation from the program, which is entertaining enough to give learning a good name. Supplementary materials, like exercise books and even a fan magazine, are also available. Additional volumes available.
1993 (*Primary-Jr. High*) 105m/C **VHS** $34.98 *REP,*

Ghoulies 🦴

"Gremlins" recycled as young man gets more than he bargained for when he conjures up a batch of evil creatures when dabbling in the occult. Ridiculous but successful. Followed by two sequels. **Hound Advisory:** Violence and sex talk.

Surfer girl "Gidget" with Moondoggie (1959)

1985 (PG-13/*Jr. High-Adult*) 81m/C Lisa Pelikan, Jack Nance, Scott Thomson, Tamara DeTreaux, Mariska Hargitay, Bobbie Bresee; **D:** Luca Bercovici; **M:** Richard Band. **VHS, Beta $29.98** *LIV, VES, HHE*

G.I. Joe, Vol. 1: A Real American Hero

G.I. Joe and his army must fight off Cobra for control of a device that reduces people and objects to a molecular level. Additional volumes available.

1983 (*Family*) 94m/C **VHS, Beta $9.95** *FHE, WTA*

Giant 𝄢𝄢𝄢𝄢

Based on the Edna Ferber novel, this epic saga covers two generations of a wealthy Texas cattle baron (Hudson) who marries a strong-willed Virginia woman (Taylor) and takes her to live on his vast ranch. It explores the problems they have adjusting to life together, as well as the politics and prejudice of the time. Dean plays the resentful ranch hand (who secretly loves Taylor) who winds up striking oil and beginning a fortune to rival that of his former boss. Dean's last movie -he died in a car crash shortly before filming was completed.

1956 (*Family*) 201m/C Elizabeth Taylor, Rock Hudson, James Dean, Carroll Baker, Chill Wills, Dennis Hopper, Rod Taylor, Earl Holliman, Jane Withers, Sal Mineo, Mercedes McCambridge; **D:** George Stevens. **Award Nominations:** Academy Awards '56: Best Actor (Dean), Best Actor (Hudson), Best Adapted Screenplay, Best Art Direction/Set Decoration (Color), Best Costume Design (Color), Best Film Editing, Best Picture, Best Supporting Actress (McCambridge), Best Original Score; **Awards:** Academy Awards '56: Best Director (Stevens); Directors Guild of America Awards '56: Best Director (Stevens). **VHS, Beta, LV $29.98** *WAR, BTV*

Gidget 𝄢𝄢

Plucky, boy-crazy teenage girl (whose nickname means girl midget) discovers romance and wisdom on the beaches of Malibu when she becomes involved with a group of college-aged surfers. First in a series of Gidget/surfer films also served as the basis for two television series. Based on a novel by Frederick Kohner about his daughter.

1959 (*Family*) 95m/C Sandra Dee, James Darren, Cliff Robertson, Mary Laroche, Arthur O'Connell, Joby Baker; **D:** Paul Wendkos. **VHS, Beta, LV $9.95** *COL*

Gidget Goes Hawaiian 𝄢𝄢

Gidget is off to Hawaii with her parents and is enjoying the beach (and the boys) when she is surprised by a visit from boyfriend "Moondoggie." Sequel to "Gidget" and followed by "Gidget Goes to Rome."

1961 (*Family*) 102m/C Deborah Walley, James Darren, Carl Reiner, Peggy Cass, Michael Callan, Eddie Foy Jr.; *D:* Paul Wendkos. **VHS, Beta $14.95** *COL*

Gidget Goes to Rome ♪♫

Darren returns in his third outing as boyfriend "Moondoggie" to yet another actress playing "Gidget" as the two vacation in Rome and find themselves tempted by other romances. Second sequel to "Gidget."
1963 (*Family*) 104m/C Cindy Carol, James Darren, Jeff Donnell, Cesare Danova, Peter Brooks, Jessie Royce Landis; *D:* Paul Wendkos; *M:* John Williams. **VHS, Beta $19.95** *COL*

The Gift of Amazing Grace

Twelve-year-old Grace Wheeler is the only member of her gospel-singing family without vocal talent. After much pain and frustration, she finally discovers how (besides lip-syncing) she can contribute to the act. ABC Afterschool Special is filled with great gospel tunes.
1986 (*Family*) 48m/C Tempestt Bledsoe. **VHS $12.95** *SVI, FCT, MLT*

Gift of the Whales

Makah Indian boy gains meaning in life by watching a pod of humpbacked whales frolic in the sea, their activities explained by a beachside researcher. One of the award-winning "Legend" videos from Miramar Home Video, concerned with wildlife and native culture of the Pacific Northwest. Others in the series: "Spirit of the Eagle" and "Winter Wolf."
1989 (*Primary-Jr. High*) 30m/C *D:* Kathleen Phelan. **VHS, Beta, LV $19.98** *BMG, AAI, MIR*

Gift of Winter

Canadian cartoon with future "Saturday Night Live" comics lending voiceovers to the tale of Mr. Winter taking complaints from some small town residents who feel he failed to deliver on a promise for snow.
1974 (*Preschool-Primary*) 30m/C *V:* Gilda Radner, Dan Aykroyd. **VHS, Beta $12.95** *FHE, WTA,*

Gigglesnort Hotel, Vol. 1

Puppets inhabiting the Gigglesnort Hotel teach kids to cope with the foibles of growing up. Two episodes here are "Puppy Parenthood" and "Tender is the Man." Additional volumes available.
1985 (*Preschool-Primary*) 50m/C **VHS, Beta** *LHV, WAR*

Gilligan's Planet

Episode from the animated Saturday-morning cartoon of the well-known sitcom, finding the castaway gang stranded in outer space thanks to the Professor's rocket ship. Episode title: "Let Sleeping Minnows Lie."
1982 (*Preschool-Primary*) 23m/C **VHS, Beta $14.95** *MGM, WTA*

A Gingerbread Christmas

As goodwill ambassadors from the North Pole, a gingerbread boy and girl are sent to bring the spirit of Christmas to Gloomsbury.
1992 (*Preschool-Primary*) 30m/C **VHS $9.95** *UND,*

The Gingerbread Man and Other Nursery Stories

The famed Gingerbread Man once again is on the run from those who seek only nourishment from his being. Also included are several other entertaining shorts.
1990 (*Preschool-Primary*) 30m/C **VHS $7.95**

The Gingham Dog and the Calico Cat

The recording artist narrates the classic tale of antagonistic toyroom cohabitants, in this tape in the "Rabbit Ears" series, first aired on Showtime.
1991 (*Family*) 30m/C *M:* Chet Atkins. **VHS $9.95**

Girl Crazy ♪♫♫

Wealthy young playboy is sent to an all-boy school in Arizona to get his mind off girls. Once there, he still manages to fall for a local girl who can't stand the sight of him. George and Ira Gershwin provide the tunes, while Rooney and Garland sing and dance up a storm in their eighth film pairing. Adapted from the Broadway hit starring Ethel Merman.
♫Sam and Delilah; Embraceable You; I Got Rhythm; Fascinating Rhythm; Treat Me Rough; Bronco Busters; Bidin' My Time; But Not For Me; Do.
1943 (*Family*) 99m/B Mickey Rooney, Judy Garland, Nancy Walker, June Allyson; *D:* Norman Taurog; *M:* George Gershwin, Ira Gershwin. **VHS, Beta, LV $19.98** *MGM, TTC, FCT*

The Girl Who Spelled Freedom ♪♫♫

Cambodian war refugee girl, speaking little English, strives to adjust with her adoptive American family in Tennessee. She faces her challenges by becoming a national spelling bee champ. Genuinely inspirational Disney TV movie, handled without mawkishness by "Free Willy" director Wincer.
1986 (*Primary-Jr. High*) 90m/C Wayne Rogers, Mary Kay Place, Jade Chinn, Kieu Chinh, Kathleen Sisk; *D:* Simon Wincer. **VHS, Beta $59.95** *DIS*

Girlfriends ♪♫♫

Bittersweet story of a young Jewish photographer learning to make it on her own. Directorial debut of Weill reflects her background in documentaries as the true-to-life episodes unfold.
1978 (*PG/Sr. High-Adult*) 87m/C Melanie Mayron, Anita Skinner, Eli Wallach, Christopher Guest, Amy Wright, Viveca Lindfors, Bob Balaban; *D:* Claudia Weill; *W:* Vicki Polon. **VHS, Beta $19.98** *WAR*

Girls Just Want to Have Fun ♪♫

Teen army brat and her friends pull out all the stops and defy their parents for a chance to dance on a national TV program. Low-flying, but harmless; based loosely upon Cyndi Lauper's '80s hit song of the same name, so don't expect well-developed storyline.
1985 (*PG/Sr. High-Adult*) 90m/C Sarah Jessica Parker, Helen Hunt, Ed Lauter, Holly Gagnier, Morgan Woodward, Lee Montgomery, Shannen Doherty, Biff Yeager; *D:* Alan Metter; *M:* Thomas Newman. **VHS, Beta, LV $9.95** *NWV, STE*

Give My Regards to Broad Street 𝄢𝄢

McCartney film made for McCartney fans. Film features many fine versions of the ex-Beatle's songs that accompany his otherwise lackluster portrayal of a rock star in search of his stolen master recordings. ♫Eleanor Rigby; Ballroom Dancing; Good Day, Sunshine; Silly Love Songs; No Values; No More Lonely Nights; Yesterday; Not Such a Bad Boy; The Long and Winding Road. **Hound Advisory:** Mild violence.
1984 (PG/*Family*) 109m/C Paul McCartney, Bryan Brown, Ringo Starr, Barbara Bach, Tracey Ullman; Ralph Richardson, Linda McCartney; **D:** Peter Webb. **VHS, Beta, LV $19.95** *MVD, FOX*

The Glacier Fox

Feature nature documentary on the wild cousins of the domestic dog in their natural northern habitat.
1979 (G/*Preschool-Primary*) 90m/C **VHS, Beta** *FHE*

Gleaming the Cube 𝄢𝄢⊲

Teenage Brian's brother's death is ruled a suicide by the cops, but Brian knows better. Using his skateboarding skills the rebellious young hero unmasks the murderer. Adolescent-minded action impresses with stunt footage only. Title is a fictional bit of kid slang dreamt up by the filmmakers, meaning 'way cool' or something. **Hound Advisory:** Violence, profanity.
1989 (PG-13/*Jr. High-Adult*) 102m/C Christian Slater, Steven Bauer, Min Luong, Art Chudabala, Le Tuan; **D:** Graeme Clifford; **W:** Michael Tolkin; **M:** Jay Michael Ferguson. **VHS, Beta, LV $14.98** *LIV, VES*

The Glenn Miller Story 𝄢𝄢𝄢

The music of the Big Band Era lives again in this warm biography of the legendary Glenn Miller, following his life from the late '20s to his untimely death in a WWII plane crash. Stewart's likably convincing and even fakes the trombone playing well. ♫Moonlight Serenade; In the Mood; Tuxedo Junction; Little Brown Jug; Adios; String of Pearls; Pennsylvania 6-5000; Stairway to the Stars; American Patrol.
1954 (G/*Family*) 113m/C James Stewart, June Allyson, Harry Morgan, Gene Krupa, Louis Armstrong, Ben Pollack; **D:** Anthony Mann; **W:** Oscar Brodney; **M:** Henry Mancini. **Award Nominations:** Academy Awards '54: Best Story & Screenplay, Best Original Score; **Awards:** Academy Awards '54: Best Sound. **VHS, Beta, LV $19.95** *MCA, RDG*

The Gnome-Mobile 𝄢𝄢⊲

Lumber baron and his two grandchildren attempt to free a pair of forest gnomes from a sideshow and return them to their gnome colony. Disney adventure filled with f/x is fun but no match for "Darby O'Gill and the Little People." Brennan has a dual role as both a human and a gnome grandfather. Based on a children's novel by Upton Sinclair.
1967 (*Family*) 84m/C Walter Brennan, Richard Deacon, Ed Wynn, Karen Dotrice, Matthew Garber; **D:** Robert Stevenson; **M:** Buddy Baker. **VHS, Beta** *DIS, OM*

The Go-Between 𝄢𝄢𝄢⊲

Young boy acts as a messenger between an aristocratic beauty and her former lover, a mere farmer. But tragedy befalls them all when the lovers are discovered. The story is told as the elderly messenger (now played by Redgrave) recalls his younger days as this secret courier, himself secretly infatuated with the lady. Excellent, bittersweet tale of youthful innocence and loss, based on a story by L. P. Hartley and adapted by playwright Harold Pinter. **Hound Advisory:** Mature themes.
1971 (PG/*Jr. High-Adult*) 116m/C Julie Christie, Alan Bates, Dominic Guard, Margaret Leighton, Michael Redgrave, Michael Gough, Edward Fox; **D:** Joseph Losey; **W:** Harold Pinter. **Award Nominations:** Academy Awards '71: Best Supporting Actress (Leighton); **Awards:** British Academy Awards '71: Best Supporting Actor (Fox), Best Supporting Actress (Leighton). **VHS** *CSM, MGM*

Go Go Gophers: Up in the Air

Col. Coyote stars in this cartoon tape that includes episodes of "Underdog."
1966 (*Family*) 60m/C **VHS** *WTA*

Go West 𝄢𝄢𝄢⊲

The brothers Marx help in the making and un-making of the Old West. Weak, late Marx Bros., but always good for a few yucks.
1940 (*Family*) 80m/B Groucho Marx, Chico Marx, Harpo Marx, John Carroll, Diana Lewis; **D:** Edward Buzzell. **VHS, Beta, LV $19.95** *MGM, CCB*

Gobots

TV cartoon series in which the heroic Gobots battle the evil Renegades. Anyone here tell the difference between a Gobot and a Transformer?
1985 (*Family*) 48m/C **VHS $29.95** *WTA*

Gobots: Battle of the Rock Lords 𝄢

Another theatrical cartoon designed to sell toys, in this case the mechanized Gobots. They strive to save the planet Quartex from the Rocklords and the Renegades. 75 minutes of merchandising may prove to be too much.
1985 (*Preschool-Jr. High*) 75m/C **D:** Ray Patterson; **V:** Margot Kidder, Roddy McDowall, Michael Nouri, Telly Savalas. **VHS, LV $14.98** *BAR, IME*

The Gods Must Be Crazy 𝄢𝄢𝄢⊲

Charming comedy from South Africa that became a world-wide hit. Natives of the Kalihari desert make first contact with the 20th century via an empty Coke bottle dropped from a plane. The strange object "from the gods" sparks greed and envy in the tribe, so Xixo the bushman vows to walk to the edge of the world and throw the evil thing off. On the way he meets assorted representatives of civilization, including an oafish biologist, bureaucratic lawmen, and terrorists; soon their behavior seems as ridiculous to us as it is to the simple, sensible Xixo. Crammed with slapstick and broad humor of every sort, yet secretly gentle and profound. **Hound Advisory:** Roughhousing, salty language. Native nudity and some risque stuff, but nothing distasteful at all.
1984 (PG/*Jr. High-Adult*) 109m/C N!xau, Marius Weyers, Sandra Prinsloo, Louw Verwey, Jamie Uys, Michael Thys, Nic de Jager; **D:** Jamie Uys. **VHS, Beta, LV $19.39** *FOX, FCT, TVC*

The Gods Must Be Crazy 2 𝄞𝄞𝄞◁

Winning sequel to the 1981 hit, doesn't have the fable-like quality of the original - this is more like a string of gags -but what splendid gags! Children of Xixo accidentally stow away in a poacher's truck, and the heroic Kalihari bushman follows their trail to more slapstick encounters with so-called civilized people (including two opposing soldiers who repeatedly take each other hostage). Not as celebrated as its predecessor, but worthwhile nonetheless. **Hound Advisory:** Salty language, roughhousing, alcohol use.
1989 (PG/*Jr. High-Adult*) 90m/C N!xau, Lena Farugia, Hans Strydom, Eiros Nadies, Eric Bowen; **D:** Jamie Uys; **M:** Charles Fox. **VHS, Beta, LV $19.95** COL, TTC, FCT

Godzilla vs. Megalon 𝄞◁

Godzilla's creators show their gratitude to misguided but faithful American audiences by transforming the giant monster into a good guy. This time, the world is threatened by Megalon, the giant cockroach, and Gigan, a flying metal creature, simultaneously. Fortunately, the slippery hero's robot pal Jet Jaguar is on hand to slug it out side by side with Tokyo's ultimate defender. Dubbed in the usual incompetent manner. **Hound Advisory:** Mild salty language; monstrous roughhousing.
1976 (G/*Family*) 80m/C Katsuhiko Sasakai, Hiroyuki Kawase, Yutaka Hayashi, Robert Dunham; **D:** Jun Fukuda. **VHS $19.95** NOS, MRV, NWV

Godzilla vs. the Cosmic Monster 𝄞𝄞

Godzilla's worst nightmares become a reality as he is forced to take on the one foe he cannot defeat - a metal clone of himself! To make matters worse, Earth is in dire peril at the hands of cosmic apes. We all need friends, and Godzilla is never more happy to see his buddy King Seeser, who gladly lends a claw. Released originally as "Godzilla Vs. the Bionci Monster" until TV's "Bionic Man" served cease and desist papers.
1974 (G/*Family*) 80m/C Masaaki Daimon, Kazuya Aoyama, Reiko Tajima, Barbara Lynn, Akihiko Hirata; **D:** Jun Fukuda. **VHS $9.95** NWV, MRV, VYY

Godzilla vs. the Smog Monster 𝄞

One of those campy Godzilla movies that reinvented the radioactive monster reptile (originally a metaphor for the devastating atom bomb) as a friend to all kids. Little Ken summons the Big G to battle a creature born of pollution, a 400-foot sludge blob named Hedora. Great (we're being sarcastic here) opening song: "Save the Earth" that you'll keep humming whether you want to or not. **Hound Advisory:** Monster violence, but some humans (including Ken's father) also wind up hurt by Hedora's acid-burning slime.
1972 (G/*Preschool-Jr. High*) 87m/C Akira Yamauchi, Hiroyuki Kawase, Toshio Shibaki; **D:** Yoshimitu Banno. **VHS, Beta $19.98** ORI

Goin' Coconuts 𝄞

Donny and Marie play Donny and Marie in this smarmy comedy of crooks and jewels and Hawaiian travel scenes. Aimed at family audiences, and indeed on the level of a Saturday-morning cartoon - but without Scooby-Doo and a half-hour running time, it's a big bore on the big island.
1978 (PG/*Jr. High-Adult*) 93m/C Donny Osmond, Marie Osmond, Herb Edelman, Kenneth Mars, Ted Cassidy, Marc Lawrence, Harold Sakata; **D:** Howard Morris. **VHS** NO

Goin' South 𝄞𝄞𝄞

An outlaw is saved from being hanged by a young woman who agrees to marry him in exchange for his help working a secret gold mine. They try to get the loot before his old gang gets wind of it. A tongue-in-cheek western that served as Nicholson's second directorial effort. Movie debuts of Steenburgen and Belushi. **Hound Advisory:** Salty language, violence.
1978 (PG/*Family*) 109m/C Jack Nicholson, Mary Steenburgen, John Belushi, Christopher Lloyd, Veronica Cartwright, Richard Bradford, Danny DeVito, Luana Anders, Ed Begley Jr., Anne Ramsey; **D:** Jack Nicholson; **W:** Charles Shyer. **VHS, Beta, LV $19.95** PAR

Going Ape! 𝄞𝄞

Danza inherits a bunch of orangutans. If the apes are treated well, a legacy of $5 million will follow. This is all you need to know.
1981 (PG/*Jr. High-Adult*) 87m/C Tony Danza, Jessica Walter, Danny DeVito, Art Metrano, Rick Hurst; **D:** Jeremy Joe Kronsberg; **M:** Elmer Bernstein. **VHS, Beta $49.95** PAR

Going Bananas 𝄞𝄞

Strictly-for-kids adventure about a talking chimp being chased throughout Africa by a villain who wants to sell the critter to the circus. To the monkey's aid comes a boy, his caretaker, and a guide. **Hound Advisory:** Salty language.
1988 (PG/*Adult-Family*) 95m/C Dom DeLuise, Jimmie Walker, David Mendenhall, Herbert Lom; **D:** Boaz Davidson. **VHS, Beta $19.95** MED, VTR

Going in Style 𝄞𝄞𝄞◁

Three elderly gentlemen, tired of doing nothing, decide to liven up their lives by pulling a daylight bank stick-up. They don't care about the consequences because anything is better than sitting on a park bench all day long. The real fun begins when they get away with the robbery. Great cast makes this a winner.
1979 (PG/*Family*) 91m/C George Burns, Art Carney, Lee Strasberg; **D:** Martin Brest. **VHS, Beta $19.98** WAR

Going My Way 𝄞𝄞𝄞◁

Classic musical comedy about a progressive young Father O'Malley (the Bingster) assigned to a downtrodden parish. He works to get the parish out of debt, but clashes with his elderly curate Fitzgibbon (Fitzgerald, Oscar-nominated for both best actor and best supporting actor) who's set in his ways. A little music creates a lot of magic, however, helping O'Malley save the church and appease the cranky Fitzgibbon. Followed by "The Bells of St. Mary's." ♫The Day After Forever; Swingin' On a Star; Too-ra-loo-ra-loo-ra; Going My Way; Silent Night; Habanera; Ave Maria.
1944 (*Family*) 126m/B Bing Crosby, Barry Fitzgerald, Rise Stevens, Frank McHugh, Gene Lockhart, Porter Hall; **D:** Leo McCarey; **W:** Frank Butler, Frank Cavett, Leo McCarey. **Award Nominations:** Academy Awards '44: Best Actor (Fitzgerald), Best Black and White Cinematography, Best Film Editing; **Awards:**

Academy Awards '44: Best Actor (Crosby), Best Director (McCarey), Best Picture, Best Song ("Swinging on a Star"), Best Story & Screenplay, Best Supporting Actor (Fitzgerald); National Board of Review Awards '44: 10 Best Films of the Year; New York Film Critics Awards '44: Best Actor (Fitzgerald), Best Director (McCarey), Best Film. **VHS, Beta, LV $14.98** *MCA, IGP, BTV*

Going to the Doctor

Mr. Rogers shows kids how to deal with and even enjoy a trip to the doctor's. Also available in a version for pediatricians. **1986** *(Primary)* 15m/C Fred Rogers. **VHS, Beta**

The Gold Bug 🐛

Young Frank searches for treasure on what he thought was a deserted island only to confront a mysterious recluse. Badly conceived and none-too-faithful adaptation of a classic Edgar Allan Poe adventure. Gone is the ingenious code-breaking subplot better explored in the PBS series "Ghostwriter." **1990** *(Family)* 45m/C Roberts Blossom, Geoffrey Holder, Anthony Michael Hall; *D:* Robert Fuest. **VHS, Beta $19.95** *KUI, NWV, BTV*

The Gold Rush 🏆🏆🏆🏆

Chaplin's most critically acclaimed film and the best definition of his simple approach to film form: adept maneuvering of visual pathos. The "Little Tramp" searches for gold and romance in the Klondike in the mid-1800s. Includes the dance of the rolls, pantomime sequence of eating the shoe, and Chaplin's lovely music. **1925** *(Family)* 85m/B Charlie Chaplin, Mack Swain, Tom Murray, Georgina Hale; *D:* Charlie Chaplin. **VHS, Beta, LV, 8mm $9.95** *CNG, NOS, CAB*

The Golden Child 🏆🏆

Title refers to a mystic Tibetan boy kidnapped by minions of Satan and transported to Los Angeles. The child's guardians contact a streetwise, ever-skeptical investigator to come to the rescue. Big-budget fantasy adventure was originally cast with Mel Gibson in mind; when Murphy took over aspects of his comic persona were plugged into the script, including sex talk, drug talk, and profanity. Result is a lively, but quite charmless escapist adventure. **Hound Advisory:** Profanity, drug talk (no usage), sex talk. More than a little violent, but naturally the Golden Child can restore life to any important casualties. **1986** *(PG-13/Jr. High-Adult)* 94m/C Eddie Murphy, Charlotte Lewis, Charles Dance, Victor Wong, Randall "Tex" Cobb, James Hong; *D:* Michael Ritchie; *M:* Michel Colombier. **VHS, Beta, LV, 8mm $19.95** *PAR*

The Golden Seal 🏆🏆

Well-meaning but somewhat facile tale of little Eric, dwelling on an island off Alaska, who finds a rare golden-haired seal and her pup - animals prophesied by the native Aleuts as coming to bring peace and understanding. Trouble is, every adult (Eric's dad included) wants to shoot the seals for their hides, and the boy ends up throwing himself between gun and mammal so often that the drama loses its impact. Based on the novel "A River Ran From Eden," by Vance Marshall. **Hound Advisory:** Salty language, roughhousing. **1983** *(PG/Family)* 94m/C Steve Railsback, Michael Beck, Penelope Milford, Torquil Campbell; *D:* Frank Zuniga; *M:* John Barry. **VHS, Beta, LV, 8mm $19.98** *SUE*

Golden Voyage of Sinbad 🏆🏆🏆

Worthwhile high adventure, as Sinbad races the usual evil wizard to the mysterious land of Lemuria, where the power of ultimate good or evil can be had among the ruins. Along the way the valiant sailor combats the customary horde of magical creatures, from a ship's living figurehead to a giant one-eyed centaur, that rank among the best of Ray Harryhausen's stop-motion special effects. **Hound Advisory:** Note to multiculturalists: this is one of the few Sinbad tales that makes any attempt to reflect Arab/Hindi civilization - and that includes a blink-and-you'll-miss-it reference to recreational hashish use. Violence, and a sexy slave girl who finds many excuses to bend over in her scant costume. **1973** *(G/Family)* 105m/C John Phillip Law, Caroline Munro, Tom Baker, Douglas Wilmer, Martin Shaw, John David Garfield, Gregoire Aslan; *D:* Gordon Hessler; *W:* Brian Clemens; *M:* Miklos Rozsa. **VHS, Beta, LV $14.95** *COL, MLB*

Goldie Gold & Action Jack II

Two more adventures with Goldie Gold (whose parents must not have had much imagination) in "Island of Terror" and "Revenge of the Ancient Astronauts." **19??** *(Preschool-Primary)* 40m/C **VHS $19.95** *WTA*

Goliath 2

The tiniest elephant in the world is the shame of his parents until he does a gigantic deed, showing that size isn't everything. A Disney short cartoon that earned an Oscar nomination. **1960** *(Preschool-Primary)* 15m/C **VHS, Beta $250.00** *DSN, MTI*

Gone are the Days 🏆🏆

Government agent Korman is assigned to protect a family who witnessed an underworld shooting, but the family would like to get away from both the mob and the police. Made-for-cable Disney comedy is well-acted but done in by cliches. **1984** *(Family)* 90m/C Harvey Korman, Susan Anspach, Robert Hogan; *D:* Gabrielle Beaumont. **VHS, Beta $69.95** *DIS*

Gone with the Wind 🏆🏆🏆🏆

Epic Civil War drama focuses on the life of petulant southern belle Scarlett O'Hara. Starting with her idyllic lifestyle on a sprawling plantation, the film traces her survival through the tragic history of the South during the Civil War and Reconstruction, and her tangled love affairs with Ashley Wilkes and Rhett Butler. Classic Hollywood doesn't get any better than this; one great scene after another, equally effective in intimate drama and sweeping spectacle. The train depot scene, one of the more technically adroit shots in movie history, involved hundreds of extras and dummies, and much of the MGM lot was razed to simulate the burning of Atlanta. Based on Margaret Mitchell's novel, screenwriter Howard was assisted by producer Selznick and novelist F. Scott Fitzgerald. For its 50th anniversary, a 231-minute restored version was released that included the trailer for "The Making of a Legend: GWTW." The laserdisc is available in a limited, numbered edition, fully restored to Technicolor from

G g

the original negative, with an enhanced soundtrack and seven minutes of rare footage, including the original trailer. **Hound Advisory:** Violence; suggested sex.

1939 (*Family*) 231m/C Clark Gable, Vivien Leigh, Olivia de Havilland, Leslie Howard, Thomas Mitchell, Hattie McDaniel, Butterfly McQueen, Evelyn Keyes, Harry Davenport, Jane Darwell, Ona Munson, Barbara O'Neil, William "Billy" Bakewell, Rand Brooks, Ward Bond, Laura Hope Crews, Yakima Canutt, George Reeves, Marjorie Reynolds, Ann Rutherford, Victor Jory, Carroll Nye, Paul Hurst, Isabel Jewell, Cliff Edwards, Eddie Anderson, Oscar Polk, Eric Linden, Violet Kemble-Cooper; *D:* Victor Fleming; *W:* Sidney Howard; *M:* Max Steiner. **Award Nominations:** Academy Awards '39: Best Actor (Gable), Best Sound, Best Special Effects, Best Supporting Actress (de Havilland), Best Original Score; **Awards:** Academy Awards '39: Best Actress (Leigh), Best Color Cinematography, Best Director (Fleming), Best Film Editing, Best Interior Decoration, Best Picture, Best Screenplay, Best Supporting Actress (McDaniel); New York Film Critics Awards '39: Best Actress (Leigh). **VHS, Beta, LV $19.98** *MGM, FUS, BTV*

Gonzo Presents Muppet Weird Stuff

Rare "Muppet Show" showcase for that strange but friendly turkey-creature Gonzo. With the dubious assistance of celebrity guest stars, he catches a cannonball and wrestles a brick blindfolded on a guided tour of his mansion.

1985 (*Family*) 55m/C Frank Oz, Jim Henson, John Cleese, Julie Andrews, Vincent Price, Madeline Kahn. **VHS, Beta** *FOX*

Goober & the Ghost Chasers

Scrawny, semi-visible cartoon dog goes ghost-huntin' with his buddies in this short-lived Saturday-morning show that didn't give "Scooby-Doo" any serious competition, even with the Partridge Family as semi-regular guests. Both Goober and Scooby came from the Hanna-Barbera assembly line.

1974 (*Preschool-Primary*) 50m/C **VHS, Beta $19.95** *WOV, GKK, WTA*

The Good Son ⅛⅛

In a grand departure from cute, Culkin tackles evil as a 13-year-old obsessed with death and other unseemly hobbies. During a stay with his uncle, Mark (Wood) watches as his cousin (Culkin) gets creepier and creepier, and tries to alert the family. But will they listen? Nooo - they, like most good Hollywood families, choose to ignore the little warning signs like the doll hanging by a noose in Culkin's room. And then there's the untimely death of a sibling. Hmmm. Culkin isn't as bad as expected, but doesn't quite get all the way down to bone-chilling terror either. Original star Jesse Bradford was dropped when Papa Culkin threatened to pull Mac off "Home Alone 2" if he wasn't cast in the lead. **Hound Advisory:** Violence and profanity.

1993 (*R/Sr. High-Adult*) 87m/C Macaulay Culkin, Elijah Wood, Wendy Crewson, David Morse, Daniel Hugh-Kelly, Quinn Culkin; *D:* Joseph Ruben; *W:* Ian McEwan; *M:* Elmer Bernstein. **VHS, LV** *FXV*

The Good Time Growing Show

In this children's series from the Episcopal Radio-TV Foundation, two young boys, a tiger, and a dragon discover basic biblical principles about a variety of topics in an entertaining way. Tapes available individually.

1986 (*Preschool-Primary*) 24m/C **VHS, Beta $119.70** *VBL,,*

The Goodbye Bird ⅛⅛

Frank is accused of stealing the school's prized talking parrot. With the aid of a kindly veterinarian, the boy tries to discover who the thief really is. Featherweight.

1993 (*G/Family*) 91m/C Cindy Pickett, Concetta Tomei, Wayne Rogers, Christopher Pettiet; *D:* William Clark. **VHS $89.95** *WOV*

The Goodbye Girl ⅛⅛⅛⅟

Top-notch original Neil Simon story of a former actress, her precocious nine-year-old daughter and the aspiring actor who moves in with them. The daughter serves as catalyst for the other two to fall in love, with the requisite Simonized pull and tug. Mason is believable in a tough role, while Dreyfuss delivers one of his classic performances.

1977 (*PG/Jr. High-Adult*) 110m/C Richard Dreyfuss, Marsha Mason, Quinn Cummings, Barbara Rhoades, Marilyn Sokol; *D:* Herbert Ross; *W:* Neil Simon; *M:* Dave Grusin. **Award Nominations:** Academy Awards '76: Best Picture; Academy Awards '77: Best Actress (Mason), Best Original Screenplay, Best Supporting Actress (Cummings); **Awards:** Academy Awards '77: Best Actor (Dreyfuss); British Academy Awards '78: Best Actor (Dreyfuss); Golden Globe Awards '78: Best Actor—Musical/Comedy (Dreyfuss), Best Actress—Musical/Comedy (Mason), Best Film—Musical/Comedy, Best Screenplay; Los Angeles Film Critics Association Awards '77: Best Actor (Dreyfuss). **VHS, Beta, LV $19.98** *MGM, BTV*

Goodbye, Miss 4th of July ⅛⅛⅟

Disney TV-movie from "Man From Snowy River" director Miller about an American family who moves to Greece and must overcome the suspicion and mistrust the locals have for outsiders, especially Yankees. Based on the book by Christopher G. Janus.

1988 (*Family*) 89m/C Roxana Zal, Louis Gossett Jr., Chris Sarandon, Chantal Contouri, Chynna Phillips, Mitchell Anderson, Conchata Ferrell, Ed Lauter; *D:* George Miller. **VHS $39.99** *DIS*

Goof Troop: Goin' Fishin'

Goofy and his friends go fishing in two episodes of TV's Disney kids' show. In "Slightly Dinghy," Max and Pete go fishing with their dads for sunken treasure. "Wrecks, Lies, and Videotape" features Max and P.J. trying to win a Hawaiian vacation for the best new home video by making Goofy their subject. Ah, you have to love the wordplay in those titles. Additional volumes available.

1992 (*Preschool-Primary*) ?m/C **VHS $12.99** *DIS, WTA*

A Goofy Look at Valentine's Day

The history and meaning of Valentine's Day is taught to Goofy by Cupid.

1990 (*Preschool-Primary*) 10m/C **VHS, Beta $205.00** *MTI, DSN*

Goofy's Field Trip Series

Goofy teaches children the various parts of a plane, a ship and a train.

1989 (*Preschool-Primary*) 15m/C **VHS, Beta $280.00** *MTI, DSN*

The Goonies ⅛⅛

Two brothers, members of a band of outcast kids called the Goonies, are about to lose their family home to creditors but conveniently pick up an old pirate's treasure map. They muster the Goonies and head for the 'X,' finding caves filled with bones, ancient booby-traps and pursuing criminals. Producer Spielberg and "Superman" director Donner joined to do this high- energy action fantasy that shows what the Little Rascals might have looked like with million-dollar f/x and leftover sets and stunts from "Indiana Jones and the Temple of Doom" (which also starred Ke Huy Quan). Big, loud, dizzying, and not as cute as it thinks it is. Laserdisc edition comes in a widescreen format. **Hound Advisory:** Profanity that would make a pirate blush. Violence continually threatened, seldom carried out.

1985 **(PG/**Family) 114m/C Sean Astin, Josh Brolin, Jeff B. Cohen, Corey Feldman, Martha Plimpton, John Matuszak, Robert Davi, Anne Ramsey, Mary Ellen Trainor, Jonathan Ke Quan, Kerri Green, Joe Pantoliano; **D:** Richard Donner; **W:** Chris Columbus, Steven Spielberg; **M:** Dave Grusin. **VHS, Beta, LV $14.95** WAR

The Goosehill Gang and the Gold Rush Treasure Map

Goosehill Gang finds a treasure map hidden in an old diary. But instead of treasure, the Gang only finds greed, in this live-action morality tale. Additional volumes available.

1980 (Primary-Jr. High) 20m/C **VHS, Beta $14.95** VBL,

Gorillas in the Mist 🎬🎬🎬

The life of Dian Fossey, animal rights activist and world-renowned expert on the African Gorilla, from her pioneering contact with mountain gorillas to her murder at the hands of poachers. Weaver is totally appropriate as the increasingly obsessed Fossey, but the character moves away from us, just as we need to see and understand more about her. Excellent special effects. **Hound Advisory:** Profanity, violence, suggested sex.

1988 **(PG-13/**Jr. High-Adult) 117m/C Sigourney Weaver, Bryan Brown, Julie Harris, Iain Cuthbertson, John Omirah Miluwi, Constantin Alexandrov, Waigwa Wachira; **D:** Michael Apted; **W:** Anna Hamilton Phelan; **M:** Maurice Jarre. **Award Nominations:** Academy Awards '88: Best Actress (Weaver), Best Adapted Screenplay, Best Film Editing, Best Sound, Best Original Score; **Awards:** Golden Globe Awards '88: Best Actress—Drama (Weaver); Golden Globe Awards '89: Best Score. **VHS, Beta, LV $19.95** MCA, HMV

Gotcha! 🎬🎬◁

The mock assassination game "Gotcha!" abounds on the college campus and sophomore Edwards is one of the best. What he doesn't know is that his "assassination" skills are about to take on new meaning when he meets up with a female Czech graduate student who is really an international spy. **Hound Advisory:** Brief nudity; profanity; violence.

1985 **(PG-13/**Jr. High-Adult) 97m/C Anthony Edwards, Linda Fiorentino, Alex Rocco, Nick Corri, Marla Adams, Klaus Loewitsch, Christopher Rydell; **D:** Jeff Kanew; **W:** Dan Gordon; **M:** Bill Conti. **VHS, Beta, LV $14.98** MCA

Government Agents vs. the Phantom Legion

Agent Hal Duncan must stop an evil group that is stealing shipments from under the government's nose Edited from 12 episodes of the original serial.

1951 (Family) 167m/B Walter Reed, Mary Ellen Kay, Dick Curtis, John Pickard. **VHS, Beta $29.98** REP, MLB

Grandizer

Japanese animation with toy connections, as a samurai-looking mechanical superhero tries to protect his adopted homeland, the planet Earth.

1982 (Primary) 101m/C **VHS, Beta $17.98** FHE, WTA, TPV

The Grass is Always Greener Over the Septic Tank 🎬🎬

Based on Erma Bombeck's best-seller. A city family's flight to the supposed peace of suburbia turns out to be a comic compilation of complications. Made for TV.

1978 (Family) 98m/C Carol Burnett, Charles Grodin, Linda Gray, Alex Rocco, Robert Sampson, Vicki Belmonte, Craig Richard Nelson, Anrae Walterhouse, Eric Stoltz; **D:** Robert Day. **VHS, Beta** NO

The Grasshopper and the Ants

Animated Aesop fable pounds home the necessity of hard work.

1979 (Preschool-Primary) 8m/C **VHS, Beta $165.00** DSN,, MTI

Grease 🎬🎬◁

Stage to screen musical sendup of '50s teens and rock'n'roll regarded by some as an unintentional camp classic. After a summer romance Danny and Sandy break up under high-school peer pressure; he's supposed to act macho and mean, she's urged to behave like a bad girl. Ultimately she does to get him back. There's also a makeout scene with an anti-condom punchline. With a likeable cast (all about ten years too old for their roles), and good dancing, this was a megahit among adolescent audiences in the '70s. That explains a lot. Dig that animated title sequence - this was once planned as a cartoon feature. ♫Grease; Summer Nights; Hopelessly Devoted To You; You're the One That I Want; Sandy; Beauty School Dropout; Look at Me, I'm Sandra Dee; Greased Lightnin'; It's Raining on Prom Night. **Hound Advisory:** Alcohol use, salty language, much sex talk.

1978 **(PG/**Family) 110m/C John Travolta, Olivia Newton-John, Jeff Conaway, Stockard Channing, Eve Arden, Sha-Na-Na, Frankie Avalon, Sid Caesar; **D:** Randal Kleiser. **Award Nominations:** Academy Awards '78: Best Song ("Hopelessly Devoted to You"); **Awards:** People's Choice Awards '79: Best Film. **VHS, Beta, LV $14.95** PAR, FCT

Grease 2 🎬🎬

Continuing saga of the T-Birds, the Pink Ladies, and young love at Rydell High. Newton-John and Travolta have graduated, leaving newcomer Pfeiffer to lead on love-struck bookneb Caulfield as the fresh romantic characters. Some okay tunes, lame story.

1982 **(PG/**Jr. High-Adult) 115m/C Maxwell Caulfield, Michelle Pfeiffer, Adrian Zmed, Lorna Luft, Didi Conn, Eve Arden, Sid Caesar, Tab Hunter; **D:** Patricia Birch. **VHS, Beta, LV $14.95** PAR

Greased Lightning 🎬🎬◁

The story of the first black auto racing champion, Wendell Scott, who had to overcome racial prejudice to achieve his success. Slightly-better-than-average Pryor comedy vehicle.

1977 **(PG/**Jr. High-Adult) 95m/C Richard Pryor, Pam Grier, Beau Bridges, Cleavon Little, Vincent Gardenia; **D:** Michael A. Schultz; **W:** Leon Capetanos, Melvin Van Peebles. **VHS, Beta $59.95** WAR

Great Adventure 🦴🦴

In the severe environment of the gold rush days in the rugged Yukon territory, a touching tale unfolds of a young orphan boy and his eternal bond of friendship with a great northern dog. Italian-made adaption of a Jack London story.
1975 (PG/*Jr. High-Adult*) 90m/C Jack Palance, Joan Collins, Fred Romer, Elisabetta Virgili, Remo de Angelis, Manuel de Blas; **D:** Paul Elliotts. **VHS, Beta $19.95** *MED, VTR*

Great Bible Stories: Abraham

One of a series of animated volumes relating well-known (and not so well-known) stories from the Bible in cartoon form; this tape covers the saga of Abraham's unyielding faith, as well as the tale "Naaman and the Slave Girl." Additional volumes available.
1986 (*Preschool-Primary*) 30m/C **VHS, Beta $14.99** *BFV*

The Great Cheese Conspiracy

Two mice plus one rat in a New York City cinema watch so many spy and gangster movies that they get the crime bug and plan a cheese-stealing caper. Animation based on a book by Jan van Leewen.
1991 (*Preschool-Primary*) 60m/C **D:** Vaclav Bedrick. **VHS $19.99** *JFK*

The Great Harbor Rescue

Cartoon tale depicting a compassionate choo-choo's rescue of defenseless animals stuck on a sinking barge.
1984 (*Preschool-Primary*) 30m/C **VHS $7.95**

The Great Land of Small 🦴🗐

A rare misstep in the superb "Tales for All" series by Canadian producer Rock Demers; this is a strange mixture of dream imagery, circus stunts, and forced whimsy centering on a bag of magic gold stolen from a fairy kingdom. The elf responsible befriends two human children and takes them to visit the Great Land of Small, where a sad-eyed muck monster/mediator/god called Slimo both rewards and punishes the inhabitants by swallowing them. Huh? Maybe kids can explain it better.
1986 (G/*Preschool-Jr. High*) 94m/C Karen Elkin, Michael Blouin, Michael Anderson Jr., Ken Roberts; **D:** Vojtech Jasny. **VHS, Beta $19.95** *STE, NWV, HHE*

Great Love Experiment 🦴🦴

Everyone in a high school learns a valuable lesson about beauty and friendship when four popular students try to change the personality of an awkward classmate.
1984 (*Jr. High-Sr. High*) 52m/C Tracy Pollan, Esai Morales, Kelly Wolf, Scott Benderer. **VHS, Beta** *NO*

The Great Mike 🦴🦴🗐

Unlikely but moving story of a young boy who convinces track management that his work horse has a chance against the touted thoroughbred. Sentimental, with little innovation, but generally well-acted.
1944 (*Jr. High-Adult*) 72m/B Stuart Erwin, Robert "Buzzy" Henry, Pierre Watkin, Gwen Kenyon, Carl "Alfalfa" Switzer, Edythe Elliott, Marion Martin; **D:** Wallace Fox. **VHS $19.95** *NOS*

The Great Mouse Detective 🦴🦴🗐

Disney animated version of the "Basil of Baker Street" stories by Eve Titus, with the exploits of a crime-fighting mouse who also resides at 221B Baker Street and styles himself as a Sherlock Holmes of the mouse world. Here he foils a plot against the rodent royal family. Not classic Disney - we defy you to remember one song afterwards - but Vincent Price lends terrific vocals to the insidious Professor Ratigan.
1986 (G/*Family*) 74m/C **D:** John Musker, Ron Clements, Dave Michener, Burny Mattinson; **W:** Dave Michener; **M:** Henry Mancini; **V:** Vincent Price, Barrie Ingham, Val Bettin, Susanne Pollatschek, Candy Candido, Eve Brenner, Alan Young, Melissa Manchester. **VHS, Beta, LV $24.99** *DIS, OM*

The Great Muppet Caper 🦴🦴🦴

The followup to the original "Muppet Movie" is more like an extended musical parody skit from TV's "Muppet Show." And what's wrong with that? Writing is clever and filled with gag movie references for grownups, as Kermit the Frog and Fozzie Bear play twin brothers (!) investigating a jewel heist in London. Watch for Jim Henson's cameo in the supper club.
1981 (G/*Family*) 95m/C Jim Henson's Muppets, Charles Grodin, Diana Rigg; **Cameos:** John Cleese, Robert Morley, Peter Ustinov, Peter Falk, Jack Warden; **D:** Jim Henson; **W:** Jack Rose; **V:** Frank Oz. **VHS, Beta, LV $22.99** *JHV, FOX*

The Great Outdoors 🦴🦴

John "Home Alone" Hughes has a reputation for writing movies in a weekend. This one must have taken a lunch hour, as a family's peaceful summer vacation is disturbed by uninvited, trouble-making relatives. Aykroyd and Candy are two funny guys done in by a lame script that awkwardly examines friendship and growing up, then throws in a marauding bear when things get unbearably slow. **Hound Advisory:** Salty language.
1988 (PG/*Primary-Adult*) 91m/C Dan Aykroyd, John Candy, Stephanie Faracy, Annette Bening, Chris Young, Lucy Deakins; **D:** Howard Deutch; **W:** John Hughes; **M:** Thomas Newman. **VHS, Beta, LV $14.95** *MCA*

Great Race 🦴🦴🗐

A dastardly villain, a noble hero and a spirited suffragette are among the competitors in an uproarious New York-to-Paris auto race circa 1908, complete with pie fights, saloon brawls, and a confrontation with a feisty polar bear. Road epic is jam-packed with stars but too long and only sporadically funny.
1965 (*Family*) 160m/C Jack Lemmon, Tony Curtis, Natalie Wood, Peter Falk, Keenan Wynn, George Macready; **D:** Blake Edwards; **M:** Henry Mancini. **Award Nominations:** Academy Awards '65: Best Color Cinematography, Best Film Editing, Best Song ("The Sweetheart Tree"), Best Sound; **Awards:** Academy Awards '65: Best Sound Effects Editing. **VHS, Beta, LV $19.98** *WAR, FCT*

The Great Rupert 🦴🦴🦴

Durante and family are befriended by a helpful squirrel (a puppet) in obtaining a huge fortune. Good fun; Durante shines.
1950 (*Family*) 86m/B Jimmy Durante, Terry Moore, Tom Drake, Frank Orth, Sara Haden, Queenie Smith; **D:** Irving Pichel. **VHS, Beta $19.98** *DVT, HEG, VYY*

Great St. Trinian's Train Robbery 🎬🎬

Train robbers hide their considerable loot in an empty country mansion only to discover, upon returning years later, that the mansion has been converted into a girls' boarding school. When they try to recover the money, the thieves run up against a band of pestiferous adolescent girls, with hilarious results. Based on the cartoon by Ronald Searle. Sequel to "The Pure Hell of St. Trinian's."
1966 (Jr. High-Adult) 90m/C Dora Bryan, Frankie Howerd, Reg Varney, Desmond Walter Ellis; **D:** Sidney Gilliat, Frank Launder; **M:** Malcolm Arnold. VHS, Beta NO

The Great Santini 🎬🎬🎬

Lt. Col. Bull Meechum, a Marine pilot stationed stateside in a '60s southern town, fights private battles involving his frustrated career goals and repressed emotions. His kids become his platoon, as he abuses them in the name of discipline and allows himself no other way to show affection. Duvall stands out in successful blend of warm humor, tenderness, and the harsh cruelties inherent with dysfunctional families. Based on Pat Conroy's autobiographical novel, the movie was virtually undistributed at first, then re-released due to critical acclaim. Also known as "The Ace." **Hound Advisory:** Violence, mature themes, salty military language.
1980 (PG/Jr. High-Adult) 118m/C Robert Duvall, Blythe Danner, Michael O'Keefe, Julie Ann Haddock, Lisa Jane Persky, David Keith; **D:** Lewis John Carlino; **M:** Elmer Bernstein. **Award Nominations:** Academy Awards '80: Best Actor (Duvall), Best Supporting Actor (O'Keefe); **Awards:** Montreal World Film Festival '80: Best Actor (Duvall); National Board of Review Awards '80: 10 Best Films of the Year. VHS, Beta, 8mm $19.98 WAR

The Great Train Robbery 🎬🎬🎬

A dapper thief arranges to heist the Folkstone bullion express in 1855, the first moving train robbery. Well-designed, fast-moving costume piece based on Crichton's best-selling novel.
1979 (PG/Jr. High-Adult) 111m/C Sean Connery, Donald Sutherland, Lesley-Anne Down, Alan Webb; **D:** Michael Crichton; **W:** Michael Crichton; **M:** Jerry Goldsmith. VHS, Beta, LV $14.95 MGM, FCT, HMV

The Great Waldo Pepper 🎬🎬🎬

Low key and (for Hill) less commercial film about a WWI pilot-turned-barnstormer who gets hired as a stuntman for the movies. Features spectacular vintage aircraft flying sequences.
1975 (PG/Family) 107m/C Robert Redford, Susan Sarandon, Margot Kidder, Bo Svenson, Scott Newman, Geoffrey Lewis, Edward Herrmann; **D:** George Roy Hill; **W:** William Goldman; **M:** Henry Mancini. VHS, Beta, LV $19.95 MCA

The Great White Hope 🎬🎬🎬

A semi-fictionalized biography of boxer Jack Johnson, played by Jones, who became the first black heavyweight world champion in 1910. Alexander makes her film debut as the boxer's white lover, as both battle the racism of the times. Two Oscar-nominated performances in what is essentially an "opened-out" version of the Broadway play.
1970 (PG/Jr. High-Adult) 103m/C James Earl Jones, Jane Alexander, Lou Gilbert, Joel Fluellen, Chester Morris, Robert Webber, Hal Holbrook, R.G. Armstrong, Moses Gunn, Scatman Crothers; **D:** Martin Ritt. VHS, Beta $39.98 FOX, FCT

The Greatest 🎬🎬

Autobiography of Cassius Clay, the fighter who could float like a butterfly and sting like a bee. Ali plays himself, and George Benson's hit "The Greatest Love of All" is introduced.
1977 (PG/Family) 100m/C Muhammad Ali, Robert Duvall, Ernest Borgnine, James Earl Jones, John Marley, Roger E. Mosley, Dina Merrill, Paul Winfield; **D:** Tom Gries; **W:** Ring Lardner Jr. VHS, Beta $14.95 COL

The Greatest Show on Earth 🎬🎬🎬

Hollywood's most lavish vision of the circus, a wildly melodramatic and kitschy spectacle that will nonetheless keep you watching as a love triangle develops between the no-nonsense ringmaster (Heston), his tightrope-walking girl-friend, and an arrogant new trapeze artist. Numerous subplots include a clown with a guilty past (Jimmy Stewart's underneath all that greasepaint), and a train wreck and spectacular fire. But no matter what, the show must go on. Emmett Kelly, one of the most celebrated big top clowns in real life, has a supporting role. **Hound Advisory:** Roughhousing.
1952 (Jr. High-Adult) 149m/C Betty Hutton, Cornel Wilde, James Stewart, Charlton Heston, Dorothy Lamour, Lawrence Tierney; **D:** Cecil B. DeMille. **Award Nominations:** Academy Awards '52: Best Costume Design (Color), Best Director (DeMille), Best Film Editing; **Awards:** Academy Awards '52: Best Picture, Best Story; Golden Globe Awards '53: Best Director (DeMille), Best Film—Drama. VHS, Beta, LV $29.95 PAR, BTV

The Greatest Stories Ever Told: The Creation

Amy Grant recounts the story of creation for youngsters, as it is told in Genesis.
1993 (Preschool-Primary) 30m/C VHS $12.98

Greedy 🎬🎬

Money-grubbing family suck up to elderly millionaire uncle Douglas when they fear he'll leave his money to d'Abo, the sexy, young former pizza delivery girl he's hired as his nurse. Fox is the long-lost nephew who comes to the rescue. Wicked comedy from veterans Ganz and Mandel should zing, but instead falls flat thanks to a descent into the maudlin. Fox bares his backside and Douglas has fun as the mean old miser, but check out Hartman, a riot as a snarky relative. **Hound Advisory:** Profanity; brief nudity; suggested sex.
1994 (PG-13/Jr. High-Adult) 109m/C Kirk Douglas, Michael J. Fox, Olivia D'Abo, Phil Hartman, Nancy Travis, Ed Begley Jr., Bob Balaban, Colleen Camp, Jere Burns, Khandi Alexander; **Cameos:** Jonathan Lynn; **D:** Jonathan Lynn; **W:** Lowell Ganz, Babaloo Mandel; **M:** Randy Edelman. VHS, LV MCA

Green Archer

15 episode serial featuring a spooky castle complete with secret passages and tunnels, trapdoors, and the mysterious masked figure of the Green Archer.
1940 (Family) 283m/B Victor Jory, Iris Meredith, James Craven, Robert Fiske; **D:** James W. Horne. VHS, Beta $39.95 VYY, NOS, VCN

Green Card ♫♫♪

Some marry for love, some for money, others for an apartment in the Big Apple. Refined, single MacDowell covets a rent-controlled apartment in Manhattan, but the lease stipulates that the apartment be let to a married couple. Enter brusque and burly Depardieu, a foreigner who covets the elusive green card from the government allowing him to permanently stay in the States. A marriage of convenience will give them both what they want. Will this practical arrangement between two distinctly different people turn into something more romantic? Engaging romantic comedy was written by Director Weir with Depardieu, making his English-language debut, in mind. **Hound Advisory:** Profanity.
1990 (PG-13/*Jr. High–Adult*) 108m/C Gerard Depardieu, Andie MacDowell, Bebe Neuwirth, Gregg Edelman, Robert Prosky, Jessie Keosian, Ann Wedgeworth, Ethan Phillips, Mary Louise Wilson, Lois Smith, Simon Jones; **D:** Peter Weir; **W:** Peter Weir; **M:** Hans Zimmer. **Award Nominations:** Academy Awards '90: Best Original Screenplay; Golden Globe Awards '91: Best Actress—Musical/Comedy (MacDowell); **Awards:** Golden Globe Awards '91: Best Actor—Musical/Comedy (Depardieu), Best Film—Musical/Comedy. **VHS, Beta, LV** $19.99 *TOU*

Green Eggs and Ham from Dr. Seuss on the Loose

Story unfolds in classical cumulative rhyme as "Sam I Am" tries to share his "Green Eggs and Ham" with an unwilling acquaintance from the book by Dr. Seuss
1974 (*Primary*) 9m/C **VHS, Beta** *BFA*

The Green Hornet

Cheapo production values stung this fast-paced serial adaptation of the famous radio superhero - a blood relative of the Lone Ranger, no less - who made "Flight of the Bumblebee" famous as his theme song. News editor Britt Reid uses the Green Hornet disguise for the first time in his fight against racketeers, but cops initially think the masked avenger is a villain himself. Oriental valet Cato, who comes up with the Hornet's gadgets, is here loudly identified as Korean; his race kept changing depending on the war situation in the Pacific. In 13 episodes. **Hound Advisory:** Violence.
1939 (*Family*) 100m/B Gordon Jones, Keye Luke, Anne Nagel, Wade Boteler, Walter McGrail, Douglas Evans, Cy Kendall. **VHS, Beta** $49.95 *NOS, GKK, GPV*

Greenstone

Micro-budgeted obscurity about a 12-year-old boy who finds the title gem near a forbidden forest. Lots of pointless chases as assorted giants, dwarfs and leprechauns seek the Greenstone; they're all played by normal-sized actors in Merrie Men costumes. Orson Welles narrates in overly-poetic style.
1985 (G/*Family*) 48m/C Joseph Corey, John Riley, Kathleen Irvine, Jack Mauck; **D:** Kevin Irvine. **VHS, Beta** $19.95 *AHV*

Gregory's Girl ♫♫♫♪

Sweet, disarming comedy established Forsyth. An awkward young Scottish schoolboy falls in love with the female goalie of his soccer team. He turns to his ten-year-old sister for advice, but she's more interested in ice cream than love. His best friend is no help, either, since he has yet to fall in love. Perfect mirror of teen-agers and their instantaneous, raw, and all-consuming loves. Very sweet scene with Gregory and his girl lying on their backs in an open space illustrates the simultaneous simplicity and complexity of young love.
1980 (*Jr. High–Adult*) 91m/C Gordon John Sinclair, Dee Hepburn, Jake D'Arcy, Chic Murray, Alex Norton, John Bett, Clare Grogan; **D:** Bill Forsyth; **W:** Bill Forsyth. **VHS, Beta** $69.98 *SUE, TVC*

Gremlins ♫♫♫

Comedy horror with deft satiric edge, produced by Spielberg. Fumbling gadget salesman Rand Peltzer is looking for something really special to get his son Billy. He finds a small, adorable creature in Chinatown, but the "mogwai" mutates into a gang of nasty gremlins who tear up the town on Christmas Eve. The switch from cuteness to terror is jarring, but be ready for it and enjoy the ride. **Hound Advisory:** Violence (the worst committed against non-humans, of course), salty language.
1984 (PG/*Jr. High–Adult*) 106m/C Zach Galligan, Phoebe Cates, Hoyt Axton, Polly Holliday, Frances Lee McCain, Keye Luke, Dick Miller, Corey Feldman, Judge Reinhold; **D:** Joe Dante; **W:** Chris Columbus; **M:** Jerry Goldsmith. **VHS, Beta, LV, 8mm** $14.95 *WAR, TLF*

Gremlins 2: The New Batch ♫♫♫

Sequel to "Gremlins" sets the little monsters loose in a futuristic skyscraper in New York, where they overrun the empire and ambitions of a greedy real-estate/cable-TV magnate who plans to exploit them. Less violent and far more campy than the last infestations, with director Dante paying myriad surreal tributes to scores of movies, including "The Wizard of Oz" plus slams against modern urban living. Great fun, with Tony Randall as the voice of the Gremlin leader heading a long list of celebrity cameos. **Hound Advisory:** Gremlin violence.
1990 (PG-13/*Sr. High–Adult*) 107m/C Phoebe Cates, Christopher Lee, John Glover, Zach Galligan; *Cameos:* Jerry Goldsmith; **D:** Joe Dante; **M:** Jerry Goldsmith. **VHS, Beta, LV, 8mm** $14.95 *WAR, HHE*

Grendel, Grendel, Grendel ♫♫

Urbane, ogre-like monster wants to be friends, but people are just terrified of Grendel. The tale sounds like "Casper the Friendly Ghost," but the intent is more serious (unfortunately, the animation is still Saturday-morning level) in this revision of the Beowulf legend, based on the novel by John Gardner.
1982 (*Family*) 90m/C **D:** Alexander Stitt; **M:** Bruce Smeaton; **V:** Peter Ustinov, Arthur Dignam, Julie McKenna, Keith Michell. **VHS, Beta** $29.95 *FHE*

The Grey Fox ♫♫♫♪

A gentlemanly old stagecoach robber tries to pick up his life after thirty years in prison. Unable to resist another heist, he tries train robbery, and winds up hiding out in British Columbia where he meets an attractive photographer, come to document the changing West. Farnsworth is perfect as the man who suddenly finds himself in the 20th century trying to work at the only craft he knows. Based on the true story of

Gremlin relaxing (1984)

Canada's most colorful and celebrated outlaw, Bill Miner. **Hound Advisory:** Brief violence.

1983 (PG/*Jr. High-Adult***)** 92m/C Richard Farnsworth, Jackie Burroughs, Wayne Robson, Timothy Webber, Ken Pogue; **D:** Phillip Borsos; **M:** Michael Conway Baker. **VHS, Beta, LV $19.95** *MED*

Greyfriars Bobby 🐾🐾🐾

True story of a Skye terrier named Bobby who, after his pauper master dies, refuses to leave the grave. Even after being coaxed by the local children into town, he still returns to the cemetery each evening. Eventually the loyal Bobby becomes the pet of 19th century Edinburgh. Nicely done by the Disney crew, with fine location photography and good acting. Great for children and animal lovers, and if you prefer collies, the same plot was used for earlier "Challenge to Lassie."

1961 (*Preschool-Family***)** 91m/C Donald Crisp, Laurence Naismith, Kay Walsh; **D:** Don Chaffey. **VHS $69.95** *DIS*

Greystoke: The Legend of Tarzan, Lord of the Apes 🐾🐾

The seventh Earl of Greystoke becomes a shipwrecked orphan and is raised by apes. Ruling the ape-clan in the vine-swinging persona of Tarzan, he is discovered by an anthropol-ogist and returned to his ancestral home in Scotland, where he is immediately recognized by his grandfather. The contrast between the behavior of man and ape is interesting, and Tarzan's introduction to society is fun, but there's no melodrama or vine-hanging action, as we've come to expect of the Tarzan genre. Due to her heavy southern accent, MacDowell (as Jane) had her voice dubbed by Glenn Close. **Hound Advisory:** Brief nudity; violence.

1984 (PG/*Jr. High-Adult***)** 130m/C Christopher Lambert, Ralph Richardson, Ian Holm, James Fox, Andie MacDowell, Ian Charleson, Cheryl Campbell, Nigel Davenport; **D:** Hugh Hudson. **VHS, Beta, LV $19.98** *WAR*

Grimm's Fairy Tales: Beauty and the Beast

Animated retelling of the classic French story of the beautiful maiden and the fearsome beast, teaching "Don't judge a book by its cover." Additional fairytales available.

1990 (*Preschool-Primary***)** 27m/C **VHS $9.99** *VTR*

Grizzly Adams: The Legend Continues 🐾🐾

Obscure attempt to revive the popular mountain man character but without original actor Dan Haggerty. A small

town is saved from three desperadoes by Grizzly and his huge bear pet Martha.
1990 *(Family)* 90m/C Gene Edwards, Link Wyler, Red West, Tony Caruso, Acquanetta, L.Q. Jones; *D:* Ken Kennedy. **VHS** *NO*

Gross Anatomy 𝄞𝄞◁

Lightweight comedy/drama centers on the trials and tribulations of medical students. Modine is the very bright, but somewhat lazy, future doctor determined not to buy into the bitter competition among his fellow students. His lack of desire inflames Lahti, a professor dying of a fatal disease who nevertheless believes in modern medicine. She pushes and inspires him to focus on his potential, and his desire to help people. Worth watching, in spite of cheap laughs. Interesting cast of up-and-comers. **Hound Advisory:** Profanity.
1989 *(PG-13 / Sr. High-Adult)* 107m/C Matthew Modine, Daphne Zuniga, Christine Lahti, John Scott Clough, Alice Carter, Robert Desiderio, Zakes Mokae, Todd Field; *D:* Thom Eberhardt; *W:* Ron Nyswaner; *M:* David Newman. **VHS, Beta, LV $19.99** *TOU*

Groundhog Day 𝄞𝄞𝄞

Phil, (Murray) an obnoxious weatherman, is in Punxatawney, PA to cover the annual emergence of the famous rodent from its hole. After he's caught in a blizzard that he didn't predict, he finds himself trapped in a time warp, doomed to relive the same day over and over again until he gets it right. Lighthearted romantic comedy takes a funny premise and manages to carry it through to the end. Murray has fun with the role, although he did get bitten by the groundhog during the scene where they're driving. Elliott, who has been missed since his days as the man under the seats on "Late Night with David Letterman" (forget "Cabin Boy") is perfectly cast as a smart-mouthed cameraman. **Hound Advisory:** Profanity.
1993 *(PG / Jr. High-Adult)* 103m/C Bill Murray, Andie MacDowell, Chris Elliott, Stephen Tobolowsky, Brian Doyle-Murray, Marita Geraghty, Angela Paton; *D:* Harold Ramis; *W:* Harold Ramis, Daniel F. Rubin; *M:* George Fenton. **VHS, LV $19.95** *COL, FCT, BTV*

Grumpy Old Men 𝄞𝄞𝄞

Lemmon and Matthau team for their seventh movie, in parts that seem written just for them. Boyhood friends and retired neighbors, they have been feuding for so long that neither of them can remember why. Doesn't matter much, when it provides a reason for them to spout off at each other every morning and play nasty practical jokes every night. This, and ice-fishing, is life as they know it, until feisty younger woman Ann-Margret moves into the neighborhood and lights some long dormant fires. Eighty-three-year old Meredith is a special treat playing Lemmon's extremely feisty ninetysomething father. Filmed in Wabasha, Minnesota, and grumpy, in the most pleasant way. **Hound Advisory:** Salty language, roughhousing.
1993 *(PG-13 / Jr. High-Adult)* 104m/C Jack Lemmon, Walter Matthau, Ann-Margret, Burgess Meredith, Daryl Hannah, Kevin Pollak, Ossie Davis, Buck Henry, Christopher McDonald; *D:* Donald Petrie; *W:* Mark Steven Johnson; *M:* Alan Silvestri. **VHS, LV, 8mm** *WAR*

Gryphon

New substitute teacher at Ricky's inner-city school can do all sorts of magical things, like materializing angels and seeing dragons. Hidden among her tricks are lessons in creativity, beauty and imagination. New-Age spaciness intrudes in this family drama, aired on PBS as part of the "WonderWorks" series.
1988 *(Family)* 58m/C Amanda Plummer, Sully Diaz, Alexis Cruz; *D:* Mark Cullingham. **VHS $14.95** *PME, FCT, BTV*

Gulliver in Lilliput 𝄞𝄞𝄞

Live-action British TV adaptation of the Jonathan Swift classic that effectively preserves the stinging satire of the original, as gentleman castaway Gulliver deals with the petty rivalries rampant amidst the arrogant Lilliputian royalty. Tale is told largely from the point of the little people, who treat the giant Gulliver as a social inferior even as he defeats their enemies (scenes done through storybook illustrations rather than special f/x). Themes may be a bit complex for very young viewers, but those who stick with it will be rewarded. **Hound Advisory:** Mildly risque, as a married lady in the palace makes the big guy the object of her (platonic) affections.
1982 *(Family)* 107m/C Andrew Burt, Linda Polan, Jonathan Cecil; *D:* Barry Letts. **VHS, Beta $19.98** *FOX*

Gulliver's Travels 𝄞𝄞◁

Max and Dave Fleischer, animation pioneers best known for "Popeye," tried to follow Walt Disney into the cartoon-feature arena with this version of castaway Gulliver's adventure in Lilliput, the island where the squabbling inhabitants average about two inches tall. Not up to "Snow White" standards, and certainly not Jonathan Swift, but still a 'toon treat thanks to glorious artwork. Gulliver, a live actor inked over in the rotoscope process, is awesome. The hilarious Gabby ("There's a giant on the beach!") was popular enough to get his own series of short subjects.
1939 *(Family)* 74m/C *D:* Dave Fleischer; *V:* Lanny Ross, Jessica Dragonette. **VHS, LV $8.95** *CNG, MRV, NOS*

Gulliver's Travels 𝄞𝄞

Partially animated Commonwealth version of Jonathan Swift's classic finds Lemuel Gulliver shipwrecked in the miniature land of Lilliput, but in real life the movie was all at sea when the filmmakers ran out of money for a time. The low-budget blues show onscreen; see instead the all-animated 1939 feature or better still, "Gulliver in Lilliput."
1977 *(G / Family)* 80m/C Richard Harris, Catherine Schell; *D:* Peter Hunt. **VHS, Beta $19.95** *VCI, VTR, HHE*

Gulliver's Travels 𝄞𝄞

Jonathan Swift's tale about a sailor whose voyage takes him to an unusual island populated by tiny people. As with most kid-minded adaptations, it leaves out the majority of the book and sugars the abundantly sour elements of Swift's satire. This Hanna-Barbera retelling is still more accurate than their '60s Saturday-morning series "The Adventures of Gulliver."

1979 (*Family*) 52m/C VHS, Beta $9.95 *WOV, GKK, KUI*

Gulliver's Travels

Yet another animated interpretation of Jonathan Swift's 18th century satire, done in "classics illustrated" fashion.
1992 (*Primary-Jr. High*) 47m/C VHS $295.00 *BAR*

Gumball Rally 🦴🦴

An unusual assortment of people converge upon New York for a cross country car race to Long Beach, California where breaking the rules is part of the game. **Hound Advisory:** Salty language.
1976 (**PG**/*Sr. High-Adult*) 107m/C Michael Sarrazin, Gary Busey, Raul Julia, Nicholas Pryor, Tim McIntire, Susan Flannery; *D:* Chuck Bail; *W:* Leon Capetanos. VHS, Beta $59.95 *WAR*

Gumby Adventures

Those timeless clay animation heroes, Gumby and Pokey, originally guests on the "Howdy Doody" program, battle evil and the Blockheads in this series of tapes. Each cassette includes 8 or 9 episodes of this TV staple.
1956 (*Preschool-Primary*) 50m/C VHS, Beta *FHE*

Gumby and the Moon Boggles

Five episodes featuring the memorable green stop-motion character, in imaginative shorts that still stand up well today: "Indian Trouble," "Weight and See," "Mystic Magic," "Gabby Auntie," and the title episode.
1956 (*Family*) 30m/C VHS, Beta $14.95 *FHE, WTA*

Gumby, Vol. 1: The Return of Gumby

Nine episodes featuring the little green guy and his pal Pokey. Includes "Witty Witch," "Hot Rod Granny," and much more! Additional volumes available.
1956 (*Family*) 50m/C Gumby; *D:* Art Clokey. VHS $14.95 *FHE, WTA*

Gumby's Holiday Special

Gumby, Pokey, Prickle, and Goo celebrate the holidays in their own special way.
1956 (*Family*) 60m/C Gumby. VHS $14.95 *FHE, WTA*

Gumby's Supporting Cast

Series featuring the clay-animated adventures of Gumby's buddies, with six 6-minute episodes per program.
1986 (*Family*) 42m/C VHS, Beta $14.95 *FHE, WTA*

Gung Ho 🦴🦴◁

Ethnic stereotyping is the order of the day as a Japanese firm takes over a small-town U.S. auto factory, causing major cultural collisions. Keaton plays the go-between for employees and management while trying to keep both groups from killing each other. From the director of "Splash" and "Night Shift." Made into a short-lived television series. **Hound Advisory:** Salty language.

1985 (**PG-13**/*Sr. High-Adult*) 111m/C Michael Keaton, Gedde Watanabe, George Wendt, Mimi Rogers, John Turturro, Clint Howard, Michelle Johnson, So Yamamura, Sab Shimono; *D:* Ron Howard; *W:* Babaloo Mandel, Lowell Ganz; *M:* Thomas Newman. VHS, Beta, LV, 8mm $14.95 *PAR*

Guns of the Magnificent Seven 🦴🦴◁

The third remake of "The Seven Samurai." Action-packed western in which the seven free political prisoners and train them to kill. The war party then heads out to rescue a Mexican revolutionary being held in an impregnable fortress.
1969 (**G**/*Jr. High-Adult*) 106m/C George Kennedy, Monte Markham, James Whitmore, Reni Santoni, Bernie Casey, Joe Don Baker, Scott Thomas, Michael Ansara, Fernando Rey; *D:* Paul Wendkos; *M:* Elmer Bernstein. VHS $19.98 *MGM*

Gus 🦴🦴◁

The California Atoms football team has the worst record in the league until they begin winning games with the help of their field-goal kicking mule of a mascot, Gus. Gridiron rivals then plot a donkey-napping. Wackier than usual premise and a good comic ensemble breathe life into this predictable Disney farce.
1976 (**G**/*Family*) 96m/C Ed Asner, Tim Conway, Dick Van Patten, Ronnie Schell, Bob Crane, Tom Bosley; *D:* Vincent McEveety. VHS, Beta, LV *COL, DIS*

Guys and Dolls 🦴🦴🦴

New York gambler Sky Masterson takes a bet that he can romance a Salvation Army lady. Based on the stories of Damon Runyon with Blaine, Kaye, Pully, and Silver recreating their roles from the Broadway hit. Brando's not-always-convincing musical debut. ♫More I Cannot Wish You; My Time of Day; Guys and Dolls; Fugue for Tinhorns; Follow the Fold; Sue Me; Take Back Your Mink; If I Were a Bell; Luck Be a Lady.
1955 (*Family*) 150m/C Marlon Brando, Jean Simmons, Frank Sinatra, Vivian Blaine, Stubby Kaye, Sheldon Leonard, Veda Ann Borg; *D:* Joseph L. Mankiewicz; *W:* Joseph L. Mankiewicz; *M:* Frank Loesser. **Award Nominations:** Academy Awards '55: Best Art Direction/Set Decoration (Color), Best Color Cinematography, Best Costume Design (Color), Best Original Score; **Awards:** Golden Globe Awards '56: Best Actress—Musical/Comedy (Simmons), Best Film—Musical/Comedy. VHS, Beta, LV $19.98 *FOX, FCT*

Gypsy Colt 🦴🦴◁

"Lassie" with a species change; Gypsy is the horse beloved by the young Meg. But drought forces her family to sell the animal to a racing stable 500 miles away. Gypsy escapes and starts out on a journey to be reunited with Meg.
1954 (**G**/*Family*) 72m/C Donna Corcoran, Ward Bond, Frances Dee, Lee Van Cleef, Larry Keating; *D:* Andrew Marton. VHS $14.98 *MGM, FCT*

Hadley's Rebellion 🦴🦴

Shy Georgia farm boy adjusts to life at an elitist California boarding school by flaunting his wrestling abilities. Eventually he realizes it takes more than that to be a man. Middling blend of low-key sports drama and coming-of-age tale. **Hound Advisory:** Salty language, roughhousing.
1984 (**PG**/*Jr. High-Adult*) 96m/C Griffin O'Neal, Charles Durning, William Devane, Adam Baldwin, Dennis Hage, Lisa Lucas; *D:* Fred Walton; *W:* Fred Walton. VHS, Beta $59.98 *FOX*

Hair Bear Bunch

Hanna-Barberian collection of five cartoons about a trio of bears who are always devising ways to escape from the zoo in which they live.
1984 *(Preschool-Primary)* 85m/C **VHS, Beta $19.95** *TTC, WTA*

Hairspray 🎝🎝🎝

Waters, a cult filmmaker infamous for sleazo spoofs, pleased and surprised everyone with this wild comedy detailing 1962 Baltimore and teen rivals after the top spot in a local TV dance show. Deals with racism and stereotypes, as well as typical youth problems - like hair-do's and "hair-don'ts." Filled with refreshingly tasteful, subtle social satire, but not without demented touches. Only a movie rebel like Waters would create heroine like Ricki Lake's, an appealing girl who's fat and not ashamed by it. Her mom is played by a Waters mainstay, hefty transvestite actor Divine. Watch for the writer/director's cameo as a crazed shrink, listen for great 60s music. **Hound Advisory:** Salty language.
1988 (PG/ *Sr. High-Adult)* 94m/C Ricki Lake, Divine, Jerry Stiller, Colleen Fitzpatrick, Sonny Bono, Deborah Harry, Ruth Brown, Pia Zadora, Ric Ocasek, Michael St. Gerard, Leslie Ann Powers, Shawn Thompson; *Cameos:* John Waters; *D:* John Waters; *W:* John Waters. **VHS, Beta, LV $14.95** *COL, FCT*

Halloween is Grinch Night

Dr. Seuss TV cartoon that serves as a follow-up to the classic "How the Grinch Stole Christmas." On Halloween night a lad named Eukariah saves Whoville from the schemes of the ever-unsociable Grinch.
1977 *(Family)* 25m/C **VHS $9.95** *WTA*

Hambone & Hillie 🎝🎝◁

Elderly woman traveller is separated from her dog during an airport transfer. Hambone makes a heroic 3000-mile trek across the United States to return to her. Sometimes entertaining, sometimes dull as the pooch stumbles into one subplot after another. **Hound Advisory:** Brief and quite out-of-place violence.
1984 (PG/ *Family)* 97m/C Lillian Gish, Timothy Bottoms, Candy Clark, O.J. Simpson, Robert Walker Jr., Jack Carter, Alan Hale Jr., Anne Lockhart; *D:* Roy Watts. **VHS, Beta $19.95** *STE*

Hammerman: Nobody's Perfect

Excerpt from the animated TV adventure series starring a 'toonerized version of the popular rap star.
199? *(Primary)* 25m/C *V:* M.C. Hammer. **VHS $9.98** *BMG, WTA*

Hang Your Hat on the Wind

A Navajo boy finds a renegade horse and is forced to choose whether to keep it or return it. The parish priest helps him to make the right choice in this episode from TV's "Wonderful World of Disney."
1990 *(Preschool-Primary)* 46m/C **VHS, Beta $250.00** *MTI, DSN*

Hanna-Barbera Storybook Classics

Animated series of short features adapted from great works and characters of literature, given generally unspectacular renderings by the Hanna-Barbera 'toon factory. Individual titles: "Black Beauty," "The Count of Monte Cristo," "Cyrano," "Daniel Boone," "Davy Crockett on the Mississippi," "Gulliver's Travels," "Heidi's Song," "Jack and the Beanstalk," "Last of the Mohicans," "Oliver and the Artful Dodger," "The Three Musketeers," and "20,000 Leagues Under the Sea."
1973 *(Family)* 50m/C **VHS, Beta $19.95** *TTC, WTA*

Hans Brinker 🎝🎝◁

Made-for-TV version of the 1865 novel by Mary Mapes Dodge, about Dutch youth Hans who enters an ice-skating race across Holland's frozen canals to earn money for his father's operation. Musical numbers don't add much, but the tale (nicely filmed in Amsterdam) comes to an exciting conclusion nonetheless.
1969 *(Family)* 103m/C Robin Askwith, Eleanor Parker, Richard Basehart, Cyril Ritchard, John Gregson; *D:* Robert Scheerer. **VHS, Beta $19.98** *WAR, OM*

Hap Palmer's Follow Along Songs

Young viewers are encouraged to sing along with their homemade musical instruments with "Baby Songs" singer Hap Palmer and his songs about colors and the alphabet.
1991 *(Preschool-Primary)* 30m/C **VHS $12.95** *BTV*

The Happiest Millionaire 🎝🎝◁

Colorful period piece with musical interludes, about a newly immigrated lad who finds a job as butler in the home of an eccentric millionaire. Notable as the last Disney production personally okayed by Walt before his death, it's based on the book "My Philadelphia Father," by Kyle Chrichton. 🎝What's Wrong With That?; Watch Your Footwork; Valentine Candy; Strengthen the Dwelling; I'll Always Be Irish; Bye-Yum Pum Pum; I Believe in This Country; Detroit; There Are Those.
1967 *(Family)* 118m/C Fred MacMurray, Tommy Steele, Greer Garson, Geraldine Page, Lesley Ann Warren, John Davidson; *D:* Norman Tokar. **VHS, Beta** *DIS, OM*

Happily Ever After 🎝🎝

Non-Disney cartoon sequel to "Snow White" was long in the making, short in the theaters. Snow White and her Prince plan their wedding, but the Wicked Queen's brother, Lord Maliss, avenges his sister by kidnapping the groom. Because Disney has legal rights to the classic Seven Dwarfs, Snow White here seeks aid from their female cousins, the Dwarfelle. Matchless cast supplies voices to this tepid entertainment for the kiddies.
1993 (G/ *Family)* 80m/C *D:* John Howley; *W:* Martha Moran, Robby London; *V:* Dom DeLuise, Phyllis Diller, Zsa Zsa Gabor, Ed Asner, Sally Kellerman, Irene Cara, Carol Channing, Tracey Ullman. **VHS $24.95** *WOV, WTA*

Happy Holidays with Darkwing Duck and Goofy

Two Christmas tales from recent made-for-TV Disney cartoons. Goofy gets carried away with decorations while son Max learns that silly family traditions really make the holiday special in "Have Yourself a Goofy Little Christmas." In "It's

a Wonderful Leaf,'' Darkwing Duck saves Christmas for the citizens of St. Canard.
1993 *(Family)* 47m/C **VHS $12.99** *DIS, WTA*

The Happy Prince

Reader's Digest presentation of Oscar Wilde's classic, tragic fable of the self-sacrificing statue and the loyal swallow, in full animation.
1974 *(Preschool-Primary)* 25m/C **VHS, Beta $14.95** *PYR, ECU*

Hard-Boiled Mahoney 🎭🎭◁

Slip, Sach, and the rest of the Bowery Boys try to solve a mystery involving mysterious women and missing men. The last film in the series for Bobby Jordan, whose career was ended when he was injured in an accident involving a falling elevator.
1947 *(Family)* 64m/B Leo Gorcey, Huntz Hall, Bobby Jordan, Billy Benedict, David Gorcey, Gabriel Dell, Teala Loring, Dan Seymour, Bernard Gorcey, Patti Brill, Betty Compson; **D:** William Beaudine. **VHS $14.98** *WAR*

Hard Country 🎭🎭◁

Caught between her best friend's success as a country singer and the old values of a woman's place, a small town girl questions her love and her life style. Warm and intelligent rural drama is Basinger's debut.
1981 *(PG/Jr. High-Adult)* 104m/C Jan-Michael Vincent, Kim Basinger, Michael Parks, Gailard Sartain, Tanya Tucker, Ted Neeley, Daryl Hannah, Richard Moll; **D:** David Greene; **W:** Michael Kane; **M:** Michael Martin Murphy. **VHS, LV** *NO*

Hardly Working 🎭🎭

Unemployed circus clown finds it difficult to adjust to real life, fumbling (well, he's a clown, right?) from one job to another. Continually threatens to dissolve into a disconnected series of skits, but some of them are funny, a few almost charming. Fans of Lewis and slapstick will appreciate it, but others need not bother. **Hound Advisory:** Alcohol use.
1981 *(PG/Family)* 90m/C Jerry Lewis, Susan Oliver, Roger C. Carmel, Gary Lewis, Deanna Lund; **D:** Jerry Lewis; **W:** Jerry Lewis. **VHS, Beta $59.98** *FOX*

The Hare and the Hedgehog

One of the Grimm Brothers' lesser-known fairy tales, brought to animated life. One in a series of Grimm tales from the Nickelodeon cable TV channel.
1991 *(Family)* 40m/C **VHS $9.99** *VTR*

Harley 🎭🎭

Harley, an L.A. motorcycle delinquent, is sent to a Texas rehabilitation community. There, he bonds with an ex-biker, and may just find his way back down the straight and narrow path to virtue. But local citizens regard him with suspicion. Say, didn't Phillips do the same plot already as "Dakota?"
1990 *(PG/Jr. High-Adult)* 80m/C Lou Diamond Phillips, Eli Cummins, DeWitt Jan, Valentine Kim; **D:** Fred Holmes; **W:** Frank Kuntz, Sandy Kuntz. **VHS $89.95** *VMK*

Harold and His Amazing Green Plants

This botanical bonanza explores the life cycle of the green plant, using a fun story line and bright animation.
1990 *(Preschool-Primary)* 8m/C **VHS, Beta $170.00** *MTI, DSN*

Harold and the Purple Crayon and Other Harold Stories

Harold and his magic purple crayon in three animated adventures based on the books by author/illustrator George Crockett. Also includes a brief documentary about Crockett from animator Gene Deitch.
1993 *(Preschool-Primary)* 27m/C **VHS $14.95** *CCC, WKV, BTV*

Harper Valley P.T.A. 🎭🎭

Eden raises hell in Harper Valley after the PTA questions her parental capabilities. Brain candy was adapted from a hit song; TV series followed.
1978 *(PG/Jr. High-Adult)* 93m/C Barbara Eden, Nanette Fabray, Louis Nye, Pat Paulsen, Ronny Cox, Ron Masak, Audrey Christie, John Fiedler, Bob Hastings; **D:** Richard Bennett; **W:** Barry Schneider. **VHS, Beta $19.98** *VES*

Harry & Son 🎭🎭

Crusty, widowed construction worker faces the problems of raising his teenaged offspring. Has Newman trademark all over it; he directed, co-wrote, and co-directed, making it a labor of love but less than stunning for all its parts and participants. Character-acting fest is potentially insightful; main complaint is we've seen this sort of plot plenty of times before. **Hound Advisory:** Salty language, sex talk, mature themes.
1984 *(PG/Jr. High-Adult)* 117m/C Paul Newman, Robby Benson, Ellen Barkin, Wilford Brimley, Judith Ivey, Ossie Davis, Morgan Freeman, Joanne Woodward; **D:** Paul Newman; **M:** Henry Mancini. **VHS, Beta, LV $79.98** *VES*

Harry and the Hendersons 🎭🎭◁

Seattle family man accidentally runs down Bigfoot with his station wagon. Thinking the hairy giant dead, he brings home the body. But the man-beast revives, bewildered but friendly, though he's a tad rough on the furniture. Like any hairy, good-natured giant, he endears himself to the Hendersons, who do their best to conceal the big guy's presence from snoopy neighbors and a gun-toting hunter. Producer Steven Spielberg raided his own "E.T.," for this formula comedy about yet another middle-class household invaded by the fantastic. Well, better that Spielberg rip himself off than someone else, right? Nice little tale efficiently told, with Oscar-winning makeup and a fine performance from Lithgow as the frustrated dad. Eventually premise was used for a short-lived TV series. **Hound Advisory:** Sasquatch rough-housing.
1987 *(PG/Jr. High-Adult)* 111m/C John Lithgow, Melinda Dillon, Don Ameche, David Suchet, Margaret Langrick, Joshua Rudoy, Kevin Peter Hall, Lainie Kazan, M. Emmet Walsh; **D:** William Dear; **W:** William Dear, William E. Martin, Ezra D. Rappaport; **M:** Bruce Broughton. **VHS, Beta, LV $14.98** *MCA, APD*

Harry & Walter Go to New York 𝄢𝄢

At the turn of the century, two vaudeville performers are hired by a crooked British entrepreneur for a wild crime scheme. The cast and crew try their hardest, but it's not enough to save this boring comedy. The vaudeville team of Caan and Gould perhaps served as a model for Beatty and Hoffman in "Ishtar."
1976 (*PG*/*Family*) 111m/C James Caan, Elliott Gould, Michael Caine, Diane Keaton, Burt Young, Jack Gilford, Charles Durning, Lesley Ann Warren, Carol Kane; *D:* Mark Rydell; *M:* David Shire. **VHS, Beta, LV $9.95** *COL*

Hashimoto: Hashimoto San

A Terrytoon introducing the character of a Japanese mouse, recounting his adventures and folktales to a G.I. reporter.
1959 (*Preschool-Primary*) 35m/C **VHS $5.99** *VTR*

Hashimoto: Strange Companion

More American-made cartoons about a Japanese mouse.
1961 (*Preschool-Primary*) 35m/C **VHS $5.99** *VTR*

Hatari 𝄢𝄢𝄢

Adventure-loving team of professional big game hunters ventures to East Africa to round up animals for zoos around the world. Led by Wayne, they get into a couple of scuffs along the way, including one with a lady photographer doing a story on the expedition. Extraordinary footage of Africa and the animals brought to life by a fantastic musical score, including the debut of Mancini's famous "Baby Elephant" tune.
1962 (*Family*) 158m/C John Wayne, Elsa Martinelli, Red Buttons, Hardy Kruger, Gerard Blain, Bruce Cabot; *D:* Howard Hawks; *M:* Henry Mancini. **VHS, Beta, LV $49.95** *PAR*

Haunted Mansion Mystery

ABC-TV production in which two children search for a million dollars in cash in a haunted mansion.
1983 (*Family*) 42m/C **VHS, Beta $9.98** *MTT, SVI*

The Haunting of Barney Palmer

New Zealand kid Barney fears he's inherited the family curse of magic powers after the death of a great-uncle, when he's suddenly tormented by eerie apparitions. Or something like that. This is surely the weirdest of the "WonderWorks" series, with some authentically chilling (non-gory) special f/x but a frantic, nearly incomprehensible plot, adapted by Margaret Mahy from her novel "The Haunting."
199? (*Family*) 58m/C Ned Beatty, Alexis Banas, Eleanor Gibson. **VHS $29.95** *PME, FCT, BTV*

Have Picnic Basket, Will Travel

Vacation plans go haywire for Yogi Bear and the rest of the Hanna-Barbera gang.
19?? (*Preschool-Primary*) 90m/C **VHS $29.95** *WTA*

Hawk of the Wilderness

A man, shipwrecked as an infant and reared on a remote island by native Indians, battle modern day pirates. 12-episode serial.
1938 (*Family*) 195m/B Herman Brix, Mala, William Boyle; *D:* William Witney. **VHS, Beta $29.95** *VCN, MLB*

Hawmps! 𝄢𝄢

Old-west comedy from the makers of the "Benji" series focuses on a klutzy Civil War lieutenant ordered to try camels instead of horses in the American desert terrain. (You can hear the concept meeting on this one - we've done dogs to death; how about camels?) When the soldiers and animals begin to grow fond of each other, Congress orders the camels to be set free. Based on some sort of vague historical incident, and you'll quickly find out why there are a lot more movies about loyal dogs than camels. Course, it does have both Pickens and Pyle collaborating on old ham fest. Edited on video from an original length of 126 minutes.
1976 (*G*/*Family*) 98m/C James Hampton, Christopher Connelly, Slim Pickens, Denver Pyle; *D:* Joe Camp. **VHS, Beta $79.95** *VES*

Hazel's People 𝄢𝄢◁

When a bitter student radical attends a friend's funeral in Mennonite country, the religious community's simple lifestyle soothes him and he tries to join. Despite a low budget approach and seriously dated 1960s elements, this drama of faith and doubt works more often than not, and it avoids simplifying a difficult subject. Based on the Merle Good novel "Happy as the Grass Was Green."
1975 (*G*/*Family*) 105m/C Geraldine Page, Pat Hingle, Graham Beckel. **VHS, Beta $29.95** *VCI, VGD*

HBTV: Old Time Rock & Roll

Hanna-Barbera TV, get it? The Flintstones star in this animated music video for kids. Songs include Bob Seger's "Old Time Rock & Roll," "Teddy Bear" by Elvis, The Beach Boys' "Catch a Wave," "Da Doo Run Run" by Dave Edmunds, "See You Later Alligator" by Bill Haley & the Comets, and plenty more.
1986 (*Family*) 30m/C **VHS, Beta $14.95** *TTC*

He is My Brother 𝄢𝄢

Boy and his brother survive a shipwreck, but the South Seas island they wash up upon may not be much of an improvement; it contains an isolated leper colony, racked by fear and superstition. Missionary-themed drama.
1975 (*G*/*Family*) 90m/C Keenan Wynn, Bobby Sherman, Robbie Rist; *D:* Edward Dmytryk. **VHS, Beta** *NO*

He-Man & the Masters of the Universe, Vol. 1

He-Man and his friends from Eternia battle the evil Skeletor. "The Dragon Invasion" and "Curse of the Spellstone" are included. Additional volumes available.
1985 (*Primary-Jr. High*) 45m/C **VHS, Beta, LV, 8mm $24.95** *COL,, WTA*

Harry and the Hendersons (1987)

Head 🦴🦴🦴

Infamously plotless musical comedy co-written by Nicholson starring the television fab four of the '60s, the Monkees, in their only film appearance. A number of guest stars appear and a collection of old movie clips are also included. ♫Circle Sky; Can You Dig It; Long Title: Do I Have To Do This All Over Again; Daddy's Song; As We Go Along; The Porpoise Song.
1968 (G/*Family*) 86m/C Peter Tork, Mickey Dolenz, Davy Jones, Michael Nesmith, Frank Zappa, Annette Funicello, Teri Garr; **D:** Bob Rafelson; **W:** Jack Nicholson, Bob Rafelson. **VHS, Beta, LV $19.95** *MVD, COL*

Heart and Souls 🦴🦴🦴

Romantic comedy involving reincarnation casts Downey, Jr. as a mortal whose body is inhabited by four lost souls who died in a bus accident on the night he was born. Now a frustrated, self-centered adult, he must finish what they could not, no matter how outrageous the request. And his dead soulmates have only so much time before the big bus from the sky descends and takes them away. Talented cast carries the sometime creaky story (Sizemore particularly shines), creating a little magic amid the sentimentality. Downey, who demonstrated strong mimicry and physical comedy skills in "Chaplin," again displays his considerable talents. **Hound Advisory:** Profanity, sex talk.
1993 (PG-13/*Jr. High-Adult*) 104m/C Robert Downey Jr., Charles Grodin, Tom Sizemore, Alfre Woodard, Kyra Sedgwick, Elisabeth Shue, David Paymer; **D:** Ron Underwood; **W:** Brent Maddock, S.S. Wilson, Gregory Hansen, Erik Hansen; **M:** Marc Shaiman. **VHS, LV $19.98** *MCA, BTV*

Heart Like a Wheel 🦴🦴🦴

The story of Shirley Muldowney, who rose from the daughter of a country-western singer to the leading lady in drag racing. The film follows her battles of sexism and choosing whether to have a career or a family. Bedelia's performance is outstanding. Fine showings from Bridges and Axton in supporting roles.
1983 (PG/*Jr. High-Adult*) 113m/C Bonnie Bedelia, Beau Bridges, Bill McKinney, Leo Rossi, Hoyt Axton, Dick Miller, Anthony Edwards; **D:** Jonathan Kaplan; **W:** Ken Friedman. **VHS, Beta, LV $59.98** *FOX*

Heartbeeps 🦴🦴

Sci-fi fare set in 1995 (ha!), about two humanoid robot servants who fall in love at the factory and run off together. Listless and apparently aimed at the very young, though kids may enjoy the romantic electroplated duo (makeup effects by Stan Winston) of Kaufman and Peters.
1981 (PG/*Jr. High-Adult*) 79m/C Andy Kaufman, Bernadette Peters, Randy Quaid, Kenneth McMillan, Christopher Guest, Melanie Mayron, Jack Carter; **D:** Allan Arkush; **M:** John Williams. **VHS, Beta $39.95** *MCA*

Heartbreak Hotel 🦴🦴🦴

Johnny Wolfe kidnaps Elvis Presley from his show in Cleveland and drives him home to his mother, a die-hard Elvis fan. Completely unbelievable, utterly ridiculous, and still a lot of fun. **Hound Advisory:** Profanity and violence.
1988 (PG-13/*Jr. High-Adult*) 101m/C David Keith, Tuesday Weld, Charlie Schlatter, Angela Goethals, Jacque Lynn Colton, Chris Mulkey, Karen Landry, Tudor Sherrard, Paul Harkins; **D:** Chris Columbus; **W:** Chris Columbus; **M:** Georges Delerue. **VHS, Beta, LV $89.95** *TOU*

The Heartbreak Kid 🦴🦴🦴

Director May's comic examination of love and hypocrisy. Grodin embroils himself in a triangle with his new bride and a woman he can't have, an absolutely gorgeous and totally unloving woman he shouldn't want. Walks the fence between tragedy and comedy, with an exceptional performance from Berlin. Based on Bruce Jay Friedman's story.
1972 (PG/*Jr. High-Adult*) 106m/C Charles Grodin, Cybill Shepherd, Eddie Albert, Jeannie Berlin, Audra Lindley, Art Metrano; **D:** Elaine May; **W:** Neil Simon. **VHS, Beta, LV $19.95** *MED, VTR*

Heartland 🦴🦴🦴🦴

In 1910 a widow from Back East journeys west with her little daughter to a new life on the Wyoming frontier, working for (and eventually marrying) a laconic homesteader. The hazards she faces, her courage and spirit get an unprettified, stunningly realistic treatment, worth comparing to the later "Sarah, Plain and Tall." Based on the diaries of Elinore Randall Stewart.
1981 (PG/*Jr. High-Adult*) 95m/C Conchata Ferrell, Rip Torn, Barry Primus, Lilia Skala, Megan Folson; **D:** Richard Pearce. **VHS, Beta $79.99** *HBO*

Hearts of the West 🦴🦴🦴🦴

Fantasy-filled farm boy travels to Hollywood in the 1930s and seeks a writing career. Instead, he finds himself an ill-suited western movie star in this small offbeat comedy-drama that's a tribute to the cowboy serials and early "B" flicks. Under appreciated little gem is sure to charm.
1975 (PG/*Jr. High-Adult*) 103m/C Jeff Bridges, Andy Griffith, Donald Pleasence, Alan Arkin, Blythe Danner; **D:** Howard Zieff; **W:** Rob Thompson. **VHS, Beta $19.98** *MGM*

Heathcliff & Cats & Co., Vol. 1

Four cartoons from Heathcliff and the gang stitched together from TV episodes: "The Great Pussini," "Kitty Kat Kennels," "Chauncey's Big Escape," and "Carnival Caper." Additional volumes available.
1986 (*Primary-Jr. High*) 45m/C **VHS, Beta $24.95** *WTA*

Heathcliff & Marmaduke

Saturday-morning animated adventures with the long-running comic-strip great dane Marmaduke sharing a time slot with his newspaper cohort Heathcliff the cat.
1983 (*Family*) 60m/C **VHS, Beta $5.99** *WOV, WTA*

Heathcliff: The Movie 🦴🦴

Title is a severe misnomer, as this full-length animated film, released to theaters, merely scrapes together episodes from the TV cartoon featuring the newspaper comic-strip cat. For more and better Heathcliff, see the various kidvid releases. Or read "Wuthering Heights."
1988 (*Family*) 73m/C **VHS, Beta, LV $9.95** *BAR, IME, WTA*

Heathcliff's Double & Other Tails

Ten episodes from the animated series starring the hostile comic-strip feline.
1987 (*Preschool-Primary*) 110m/C **VHS, Beta $59.95** *WTA*

Shirley Temple in "Heidi" (1937)

The Heavenly Kid 🦴

Leather-jacketed "cool" guy who died in a '60s hot rod crash gets an offer to exit limbo and enter heaven if he tutors a dull 1980s teen on how to be a hip and worldly dude. Lessons include booze, marijuana, and boorish behavior. Less than heavenly youth-appeal comedy. **Hound Advisory:** Drug use, roughhousing, profanity.

1985 (**PG-13**/*Jr. High-Adult*) 92m/C Lewis Smith, Jane Kaczmarek, Jason Gedrick, Richard Mulligan; *D:* Cary Medoway. **VHS, Beta** *NO*

Hector's Bunyip

What's a bunyip? It's a traditional Australian bogeyman/ dragon, and little Hector keeps an invisible one around as an imaginary friend. Welfare authorities are not amused, as they consider taking Hector from his large, eccentric family. Then Hector gets kidnapped - by his supposedly imaginary friend. A Down Under TV production aired on "WonderWorks," this veers toward sentimental slush, then turns around and becomes something absolutely fresh and delightful in the end, the hallmark of the justly acclaimed PBS series.

1986 (*Family*) 58m/C Scott Bartle, Robert Coleby, Barbara Stephens, Tushka Hose; *D:* Mark Callan. **VHS** $14.95 *PME, FCT, BTV*

Heidi 🦴🦴🦴⊲

Sentimental adaptation of German writer Johanna Spyri's 1881 novel. Heidi is an orphan shuttled from relative to relative until she happily ends up with her crotchety grandfather in his mountain cabin. But the child is taken off to the city to be a companion to an unpleasant invalid girl Klara. Will Heidi triumph over the household's mean governess and return to grandfather? Does Shirley have curls? Also available colorized. Available on laserdisc with another Temple treat, "Poor Little Rich Girl."

1937 (*Family*) 88m/B Shirley Temple, Jean Hersholt, Helen Westley, Arthur Treacher; *D:* Allan Dwan. **VHS, Beta** $14.98 *FXV, HMV, MLT*

Heidi 🦴🦴

Made-for-TV adaptation of the classic Johanna Spyri novel of an orphaned girl who goes to the Swiss Alps to live with her grandfather. This is the one that interrupted the Jets football game on TV.

1967 (*Family*) 100m/C Maximilian Schell, Jennifer Edwards, Michael Redgrave, Jean Simmons; *D:* Delbert Mann; *M:* John Williams. **VHS, Beta** $19.98 *LIV, VES, GLV*

Heidi 🦴🦴🦴

Made-for-TV Disney version of the children's classic by Johanna Spyri. Thornton is charming as the orphan shuttled from taken from her simple, mountain-dwelling grandfather and whisked off to the city to a rich relative's unhappy household. Seymour is the snobbish, scowling governess. This "Heidi" is spunky enough to keep the sugar level tolerable. Filmed on location in Austria.

1993 (G/*Family*) 167m/C Noley Thornton, Jason Robards Jr., Jane Seymour, Lexi Randall, Sian Phillips, Patricia Neal, Benjamin Brazier, Michael Simkins, Andrew Bicknell, Jane Hazlegrove; **D:** Michael Rhodes; **W:** Jeanne Rosenberg; **M:** Lee Holdridge. **VHS $19.99** *DIS*

Hell Hounds of Alaska 🦴🦴

Yukon nature adventure in which a frontiersman goes searching for a kidnapped boy during the gold rush days of Alaska.

197? (G/*Family*) 90m/C Doug McClure. **VHS, Beta** *NO*

Hello, Dolly! 🦴🦴

Widow Dolly Levi, while matchmaking for her friends, finds a match for herself. Based on the hugely successful Broadway musical adapted from Thornton Wilder's play "Matchmaker." Lightweight story needs better actors with stronger characterizations. Original Broadway score helps. ♫Hello Dolly; Just Leave Everything to Me; Love is Only Love; Dancing; Walter's Gavotte; It Only Takes a Moment; Ribbons Down My Back; Elegance; It Takes a Woman.

1969 (G/*Family*) 146m/C Barbra Streisand, Walter Matthau, Michael Crawford, Louis Armstrong, E.J. Peaker, Marianne McAndrew, Tommy Tune; **D:** Gene Kelly; **W:** Ernest Lehman; **M:** Jerry Herman. **Award Nominations:** Academy Awards '69: Best Cinematography, Best Costume Design, Best Film Editing, Best Picture; **Awards:** Academy Awards '69: Best Art Direction/Set Decoration, Best Sound, Best Score. **VHS, Beta, LV $19.98** *FOX, FCT*

The Hellstrom Chronicle 🦴🦴🦴

A powerful quasi-documentary about insects, their formidable capacity for survival, and the conjectured battle man will have with them in the future.

1971 (G/*Family*) 90m/C Lawrence Pressman; **D:** Walon Green; **W:** David Seltzer. **VHS, Beta** *COL, OM*

Help! 🦴🦴🦴

Ringo Starr's ruby ring is the object of a search by a human-sacrifice cult who chase the Beatles all over the globe in order to acquire the bauble. Zany, fun-filled satire pokes fun at the Fab Four's own superstardom with a mixture of satire and great music that still holds up. Tell the kids that if they enjoy "The Monkees" they'll like these foreign imitators. The laserdisc version includes a wealth of Beatles memorabilia, rare footage behind the scenes and at the premiere, and extensive publicity material. ♫Help!; You're Gonna Lose That Girl; You've Got To Hide Your Love Away; The Night Before; Another Girl; Ticket To Ride; I Need You.

1965 (G/*Jr. High-Adult*) 90m/C John Lennon, Paul McCartney, Ringo Starr, George Harrison, Leo McKern, Eleanor Bron; **D:** Richard Lester; **W:** Charles Wood. **VHS, Beta, LV $19.98** *MPI, MVD, CRC*

Henry Hamilton: Graduate Ghost

This junior specter of a Civil War soldier is too nice to haunt a modern family effectively, the way he was taught in ghost school. Instead he urges the mortals to believe in themselves and their dreams. Live-action comedy, based on a book by Marilyn Redmond.

1990 (*Primary-Jr. High*) 45m/C Larry Gelman, Stu Gilliam. **VHS $99.95** *SVI, AIM*

Henry's Cat

TV's cartoon bear tells tales and conveys acceptable human principles in the process.

1986 (*Primary-Jr. High*) 60m/C **VHS, Beta $19.95** *HBO, WTA*

Her Alibi 🦴🦴

When successful murder-mystery novelist Phil Blackwood runs out of ideas for good books, he seeks inspiration in the criminal courtroom. There he discovers a beautiful Romanian immigrant named Nina who is accused of murder. He goes to see her in jail and offers to provide her with an alibi. Narrated by Blackwood in the tone of one of his thriller novels. Uneven comedy, with appealing cast and arbitrary plot. **Hound Advisory:** Profanity, comic violence.

1988 (PG/*Jr. High-Adult*) 95m/C Tom Selleck, Paulina Porizkova, William Daniels, James Farentino, Hurd Hatfield, Patrick Wayne, Tess Harper, Joan Copeland; **D:** Bruce Beresford; **W:** Charlie Peters; **M:** Georges Delerue. **VHS, Beta, LV, 8mm $14.95** *WAR*

Herbie Goes Bananas 🦴🦴◁

While Herbie the VW is racing in Rio de Janeiro he is bugged by the syndicate, a pickpocket, and a raging bull. The fourth and final entry in the Disney "Love Bug" movies shows a definite drop in gag mileage, but Herbie later turned up in a TV series.

1980 (G/*Family*) 93m/C Cloris Leachman, Charles Martin Smith, Harvey Korman, John Vernon, Alex Rocco, Richard Jaeckel, Fritz Feld; **D:** Vincent McEveety. **VHS, Beta $69.95** *DIS*

Herbie Goes to Monte Carlo 🦴🦴

While participating in a Paris-to-Monte-Carlo race, Herbie the VW gets detoured by jewel thieves and falls in love with a Lancia motorcar. Third in the Disney "Love Bug" series seems in need of a tune up.

1977 (G/*Family*) 104m/C Dean Jones, Don Knotts, Julie Sommars, Roy Kinnear; **D:** Vincent McEveety. **VHS, Beta $69.95** *DIS*

Herbie Rides Again 🦴🦴◁

In this "Love Bug" sequel, Herbie comes to the aid of elderly Widow Steinmetz, threatened by a ruthless tycoon determined to raise a skyscraper on her property. Humorous Disney fare with a rousing conclusion.

1974 (G/*Family*) 88m/C Helen Hayes, Ken Berry, Stefanie Powers, John McIntire, Keenan Wynn; **D:** Robert Stevenson. **VHS, Beta, LV $19.99** *DIS*

Hercules 🦴🦴◁

The one that started it all, Reeves is perfect as the mythical hero Hercules who encounters many dangerous situations

while trying to win over his true love. Dubbed in English. Cinematography by Mario Bava. **Hound Advisory:** Violence.
1958 *(Family)* 107m/C Steve Reeves, Sylva Koscina, Fabrizio Mioni, Giana Maria Canale, Arturo Dominici; *D:* Pietro Francisci. **VHS, Beta, LV $14.98** *MRV, IME, VDM*

Hercules 🐾

Poor superhero saga finds legendary muscle guy Hercules in the person of TV's "Incredible Hulk" Ferrigno, fighting the evil King Minos for his own survival and the love of Cassiopeia, a rival king's daughter. The script makes a mess of the myths. **Hound Advisory:** Muscle-stretching violence.
1983 *(PG/Primary-Adult)* 100m/C Lou Ferrigno, Sybil Danning, William Berger, Brad Harris, Ingrid Anderson; *D:* Lewis (Luigi Cozzi) Coates; *W:* Lewis (Luigi Cozzi) Coates; *M:* Pino Donaggio. **VHS, Beta, LV $79.95** *MGM, IME*

Hercules 2 WOOF!

Muscle-bound demi-god returns to do battle with more evil foes amidst the same stunningly cheap special effects. At one point he turns into a cartoon of himself, which must've saved some bucks. Also known as "Adventures of Hercules." **Hound Advisory:** Violence.
1985 *(PG/Jr. High-Adult)* 90m/C Lou Ferrigno, Claudio Cassinelli, Milly Carlucci, Sonia Viviani, William Berger, Carlotta Green; *D:* Lewis (Luigi Cozzi) Coates; *M:* Pino Donaggio. **VHS $79.95** *MGM*

Hercules in New York 🐾◁

Cheapo motion picture debut of Schwarzenegger, here christened 'Arnold Strong' (with his voice terribly dubbed into English) resurfaced on home video to cash in on his action-hero superstardom. But Arnold's acting muscles in particular weren't developed when he did this charmless farce of the Greek demigod sent by Zeus to Manhattan, where he eventually becomes a professional wrestler. Also known as "Hercules Goes Bananas."
1970 *(G/Family)* 93m/C Arnold Schwarzenegger, Arnold Stang, Deborah Loomis, James Karen, Ernest Graves; *D:* Arthur Seidelman. **VHS, Beta $59.98** *MPI*

Hercules Unchained 🐾🐾

Sequel to "Hercules" finds superhero Reeves must use all his strength to save the city of Thebes and the woman he loves from the giant Antaeus. **Hound Advisory:** Violence.
1959 *(Jr. High-Adult)* 101m/C Steve Reeves, Sylva Koscina, Silvia Lopel, Primo Carnera; *D:* Pietro Francisci. **VHS, Beta, LV $14.95** *VDM, SUE, MRV*

Here Comes Droopy 🐾🐾

TV revival of the sad-eyed bloodhound sheriff created by Tex Avery, in which he once again saves the day in spite of himself. A little bit of Droopy-ness goes a long way.
1990 *(G/Family)* 60m/C **VHS $12.98** *MGM, WTA*

Here Comes Garfield

Comic-strip cat Garfield's first step from newspaper to TV cartoon has the lazy feline rousing himself enough to save his dumb dog pal Odie from the pound. Animated by the same team responsible for the successful "Charlie Brown" series.
1990 *(G/Family)* 24m/C *V:* Lorenzo Music. **VHS $12.98** *FOX, WTA*

Here Comes Peter Cottontail

Arthur Rankin-Jules Bass "Animagic" seasonal TV special that chronicles a scheme by an ambitious rabbit to dethrone Peter Cottontail, the reigning Head Easter Bunny.
1971 *(Family)* 53m/C *V:* Danny Kaye, Casey Kasem, Vincent Price. **VHS $12.98** *FHE, WTA*

Here Comes Santa Claus 🐾◁

Yes, even the French can make crummy children's films. This slushy holiday tale involves two kids whose parents are held prisoner by African rebels. They visit the North Pole and get Santa's help. The sight of Pere Noel schlepping through the tropics is funny at first, but awful dialogue (English-dubbed) and production values melt any xmas spirit.
1984 *(Family)* 78m/C Karen Cheryl, Armand Meffre; *D:* Christian Gion. **VHS, Beta $14.95** *NWV, STE*

The Hero 🐾◁

Popular soccer player agrees to throw a game for big cash, and then worries about losing the respect of a young boy who idolizes him. Nothing new in this overly sentimental sports drama.
1971 *(PG/Jr. High-Adult)* 97m/C Richard Harris, Romy Schneider, Kim Burfield, Maurice Kaufman; *D:* Richard Harris. **VHS, Beta $59.98** *SUE*

Hero 🐾🐾🐾

Interesting twist on Cinderella fable and modern media satire has television reporter Davis looking for the man who saved her life, expecting a genuine hero, and accepting without question the one who fits her vision. Critically considered disappointing, but wait-Garcia and Hoffman make a great team, and Davis is fetching as the vulnerable media person. Strong language and dark edges may keep away some of the kids, but otherwise this is a fine fable. **Hound Advisory:** Profanity.
1992 *(PG-13/Jr. High-Adult)* 116m/C Geena Davis, Dustin Hoffman, Andy Garcia, Joan Cusack, Kevin J. O'Connor, Chevy Chase, Maury Chaykin, Stephen Tobolowsky, Christian Clemenson, Tom Arnold, Janis Paige, Warren Berlinger, Susie Cusack, James Madio, Richard Riehle, Don Yesso, Darrell Larson; *D:* Stephen Frears; *W:* David Peoples; *M:* George Fenton. **VHS, LV, 8mm $19.95** *COL*

A Hero Ain't Nothin' But a Sandwich 🐾🐾🐾

The creators of the hit family film "Sounder" also made this under appreciated, ahead-of-its-time adaptation of Alice Childress' novel about Benjie, a smart, black 13-year-old in South Central L.A. who starts slipping into drugs. Teachers, preachers, counselors and family (especially his single mother's no-nonsense boyfriend) try to stop the boy's downward spiral, but in the end it's up to Benjie himself. Not a finger-wagging junkie horror story, but a sometimes wrenching drama that doesn't simplify either the rehab/recovery process or the alienation of its young main character. Though obviously meant to connect with younger viewers, there's much here of concern to grownups. **Hound Advisory:** Sex, some very raw language, explicit drug use, nudity - when this

came out the PG rating was considered a lot stronger than it is today - but none of it in an exploitive manner.
1978 (PG/*Jr. High-Adult*) 107m/C Cicely Tyson, Paul Winfield, Larry B. Scott, Helen Martin, Glynn Turman, David Groh; *D:* Ralph Nelson. **VHS, Beta $14.95** *PAR, FCT*

Hero at Large 🎬🎬⏴

Good-natured, unemployed actor foils a robbery while dressed in a promotional "Captain Avenger" suit, and instant celebrity follows, although he has no superpowers. When politicians exploit his popularity, Captain Avenger has to decide what he stands for. Lightweight, yet enjoyable tale with a moral. **Hound Advisory:** Roughhousing.
1980 (PG/*Jr. High-Adult*) 98m/C John Ritter, Anne Archer, Bert Convy, Kevin McCarthy, Kevin Bacon; *D:* Martin Davidson. **VHS, Beta $59.95** *MGM*

Hero High's Supermagic Adventures

Six cartoon episodes of the series involving a group of scientifically precocious high school kids.
1981 (*Primary*) 80m/C **VHS, Beta** *SUE*

Heroes on Hot Wheels, Vol. 1

Animated series derived from a certain line of toy cars you may have heard of, with Michael Valiant and his racing team travelling the world in search of action-packed racing adventures. This video features the episodes "Valiant vs. Valiant" and "Highway Pirate." Additional volumes available.
1991 (*Primary-Jr. High*) 45m/C **VHS** *NO*

Hey, Cinderella!

One of the oldest Muppet presentations available on tape, this TV special displays all the characteristic sly wit and post-modern whimsy of the Jim Henson workshop, as Cinderella arrives at the ball in a coach pulled by a purple beast named Splurge (a Muppet character who never did quite catch on) and driven by Kermit the singing frog (one who did).
1969 (*Family*) 54m/C *V:* Jim Henson, Frank Oz. **VHS, Beta $20.00** *JHV, BVV, BTV*

Hey There, It's Yogi Bear 🎬🎬

Bill Hanna and Joseph Barbera's first feature-length 'toon stars Yogi Bear, who comes out of hibernation and learns that his girlfriend Cindy has been taken away by the Chizzling Brothers Circus. With his pal Boo Boo, Yogi leaves Jellystone Park and journeys to the big city to rescue her. On the level of the TV show, with several musical numbers.
1964 (*Family*) 98m/C *D:* William Hanna; *V:* Daws Butler, James Darren, Mel Blanc, J. Pat O'Malley, Julie Bennett. **VHS, Beta, LV $19.95** *WOV, IME, WTA*

The Hideaways 🎬🎬🎬⏴

Twelve-year-old Claudia and her younger brother run away and hide in New York's Metropolitan Museum of Art, dodging night watchmen and living a seemingly grand adventure. Claudia ponders a marble angel that may or may not be a work by Michelangelo. Her search for the truth takes her to confront the wealthy, mysterious recluse who donated it. Only then does the issue of running away from home come up; previously it isn't even mentioned and hovers uneasily in the shadows of this sunny family tale. Based on the kids' novel "From the Mixed-Up Files of Mrs. Basel E. Frankweiler" by E.L. Konigsburg.
1973 (G/*Family*) 105m/C Richard Mulligan, George Rose, Ingrid Bergman, Sally Prager, Johnny Doran, Madeline Kahn; *D:* Fielder Cook. **VHS, Beta $14.95** *WAR, VHE, FCT*

Hiding Out 🎬🎬

Young stockbroker testifies against the Mafia and must find a place to hide from their revenge. He winds up at his cousin's high school in Delaware, masquerading as an inmate, and reliving all the usual teenage troubles (repressive teachers, student cliques). Mediocre comedy that doesn't take too many opportunities for insight into youth culture. **Hound Advisory:** Salty language, violence.
1987 (PG-13/*Jr. High-Adult*) 99m/C Jon Cryer, Keith Coogan, Gretchen Cryer, Annabeth Gish, Tim Quill; *D:* Bob Giraldi; *M:* Anne Dudley. **VHS, Beta $19.99** *HBO*

High Anxiety 🎬🎬

As always, Brooks tries hard to please in this low-brow parody of Hitchcock employing dozens of references to films like "Psycho," "Spellbound," "The Birds," and "Vertigo" (including the looping, revealing camera and the massive orchestral movements). Tells the tale of a height-fearing psychiatrist caught up in a murder mystery. The title song performed a la Sinatra by Brooks is one of the brighter moments in a uneven but generally amusing tribute.
1977 (PG/*Jr. High-Adult*) 92m/C Mel Brooks, Madeline Kahn, Cloris Leachman, Harvey Korman, Ron Carey, Howard Morris, Dick Van Patten; *D:* Mel Brooks; *W:* Mel Brooks, Ron Clark, Barry Levinson, Rudy DeLuca. **VHS, Beta, LV $14.98** *FOX*

High Country Calling 🎬🎬

Wolf pups escape captivity and set off on a cross-country chase. Canine nature adventure narrated, suitably enough, by onetime Alpo representative Greene.
1975 (G/*Family*) 84m/C **VHS, Beta $29.95** *GEM, CNG*

High Noon 🎬🎬🎬🎬

Landmark western about Hadeyville town marshal Will Kane (Cooper) who faces four professional killers alone, after being abandoned to his fate by the gutless townspeople who profess to admire him. Cooper is the ultimate hero figure, his sheer presence overwhelming. Note the continuing use of the ballad written by Dimitri Tamkin, "Do Not Forsake Me, Oh My Darlin'" (sung by Tex Ritter) to heighten the tension and action. Laserdisc includes the original trailer, an essay by Howard Suber on audio 2, a photo essay of production stills, Carl Foreman's original notes of the film and the complete text of "The Tin Star," the story on which the film is based. **Hound Advisory:** Violence.
1952 (*Jr. High-Adult*) 85m/B Gary Cooper, Grace Kelly, Lloyd Bridges, Lon Chaney Jr., Thomas Mitchell, Otto Kruger, Katy Jurado, Lee Van Cleef, Henry Morgan, Robert J. Wilke, Sheb Wooley; *D:* Fred Zinneman; *W:* Carl Foreman; *M:* Dimitri Tiomkin. **Award Nominations:** Academy Awards '52: Best Director (Zinneman), Best Picture, Best Screenplay; **Awards:** Academy Awards '52: Best Actor (Cooper), Best Film Editing, Best Song ("High Noon (Do Not Forsake Me, Oh My Darlin')"), Best Score; Golden Globe Awards '53: Best Actor—Drama

(Cooper), Best Supporting Actress (Jurado), Best Score; National Board of Review Awards '52: 10 Best Films of the Year; New York Film Critics Awards '52: Best Director (Zinneman), Best Film. **VHS, LV $19.98** *REP, VYG, TLF*

High Society 🎬🎬♪

Wealthy man attempts to win back his ex-wife who's about to be remarried in enjoyable remake of "The Philadelphia Story" that's most notable for the score by Cole Porter. Some memorable musical moments, including Frank, Bing, and Satchmo (playing himself) working together. Letterboxed laserdisc format also includes the original movie trailer. ♪High Society Calypso; Little One; Who Wants to Be a Millionaire?; True Love; You're Sensational; I Love You, Samantha; Now You Has Jazz; Well, Did You Evah?; Mind if I Make Love to You?.

1956 (*Jr. High-Adult*) 107m/C Frank Sinatra, Bing Crosby, Grace Kelly, Louis Armstrong, Celeste Holm, Sidney Blackmer, Louis Calhern; **D:** Charles Walters; **M:** Cole Porter. **VHS, Beta, LV, 8mm $14.95** *MGM*

Highlander 🎬🎬🎬

Strange tale about an immortal 16th-century Scottish warrior who has had to battle his evil immortal enemy through the centuries. The feud comes to blows in modern-day Manhattan. Connery makes a memorable appearance as the good warrior's mentor. Spectacular battle and death scenes. A cult favorite which spawned a weak sequel and a television series. Based on a story by Gregory Widen. **Hound Advisory:** Violence.

1986 (**R**/*Jr. High-Adult*) 110m/C Christopher Lambert, Sean Connery, Clancy Brown, Roxanne Hart, Beatie Edney, Alan North, Sheila Gish, Jon Polito; **D:** Russell Mulcahy; **W:** Gregory Widen, Peter Bellwood, Larry Ferguson; **M:** Michael Kamen. **VHS, Beta, LV $14.98** *REP*

Highlander 2: The Quickening 🎬♪

The saga of Connor MacLeod and Juan Villa-Lobos continues in this sequel set in the year 2024. An energy shield designed to block out the sun's harmful ultraviolet rays has left planet Earth in perpetual darkness, but there is evidence that the ozone layer has repaired itself. An environmental terrorist and her group begin a sabotage effort and are joined by MacLeod and Villa-Lobos in their quest to save Earth. Stunning visual effects don't make up for ozone hole in script. **Hound Advisory:** Violence.

1991 (**R**/*Sr. High-Adult*) 90m/C Christopher Lambert, Sean Connery, Virginia Madsen, Michael Ironside, John C. McGinley; **D:** Russell Mulcahy; **W:** Peter Bellwood; **M:** Stewart Copeland. **VHS, LV, 8mm $14.95** *COL*

Highlander: The Gathering 🎬🎬

Re-edited episodes from the syndicated television series finds good immortals Connor MacLeod (Lambert) and distant relative Duncan (Paul) battling against an evil immortal (Moll as a particularly nasty villain) and a misguided human (Vanity). Lots of sword-play and a little bit of romance (courtesy of Vandernoot). **Hound Advisory:** Violence.

1993 (**PG-13**/*Jr. High-Adult*) 98m/C Christopher Lambert, Adrian Paul, Richard Moll, Vanity, Alexandra Vandernoot, Stan Kirsh; **D:** Thomas J. Wright, Ray Austin; **W:** Lorain Despres, Dan Gordon. **VHS $89.95** *HMD*

Hillbilly Bears

Cartoon adventures of a backwoods clan of bruins, from the Hanna-Barbera territories.

197? (*Family*) 51m/C **VHS, Beta $19.95** *TTC, WTA*

Hiroshima Maiden

Idealistic family man in 1955 opens his house to a Japanese girl who survived the atom bomb, in the US for surgery to her radiation scars. But his son believes she's an enemy spy and won't be friends. Were American kids really this stupid? Maybe, but only the adult characters really come to life as sympathetic characters in this plea for tolerance from the "WonderWorks" series.

1988 (*Family*) 58m/C Susan Blakely, Richard Masur, Tamlyn Tomita; **D:** Joan Darling. **VHS $29.95** *PME, WNE, HMV*

His Girl Friday 🎬🎬🎬🎬

Classic, unrelentingly hilarious war-between-the-sexes comedy in which a reporter and her ex-husband editor help a condemned man escape the law-while at the same time furthering their own ends as they try to get the big scoop on political corruption in the town. One of Hawks' most furious and inventive screen combats in which women are given uniquely equal (for Hollywood) footing, with staccato dialogue and wonderful performances. Based on the Hecht-MacArthur play "The Front Page," which was originally filmed in 1931. Remade again in 1974 as "The Front Page," and in 1988 as "Switching Channels." Also available colorized.

1940 (*Family*) 92m/B Cary Grant, Rosalind Russell, Ralph Bellamy, Gene Lockhart, John Qualen, Porter Hall, Roscoe Karns, Abner Biberman, Cliff Edwards, Billy Gilbert, Helen Mack, Ernest Truex, Clarence Kolb, Frank Jenks; **D:** Howard Hawks; **W:** Charles Lederer; **M:** Morris Stoloff. **VHS, Beta $9.95** *CNG, MRV, NOS*

The Hobbit 🎬🎬🎬

Somewhat simplified but still the best animated interpretation of J.R.R. Tolkien. Hobbit Bilbo Baggins is persuaded to leave his comfortable Shire and help a tribe of dwarfs recover their gold from Smaug the evil dragon. In the process Bilbo discovers a magic Ring of Power, and its tale continues in Ralph Bakshi's "Lord of the Rings." This version can be enjoyed complete in itself, however. Good character voices, artwork, pleasant songs. Made for TV by Arthur Rankin Jr. and Jules Bass, who revisited Middle Earth with "The Return of the King."

1978 (*Family-Family*) 76m/C **D:** Arthur Rankin Jr., Jules Bass; **V:** Orson Bean, John Huston, Otto Preminger, Richard Boone. **VHS, Beta, 8mm $14.95** *WAR, CHI, FCT*

The Hoboken Chicken Emergency 🎬🎬♪

Arthur is sent to buy a holiday turkey, but a mad scientist instead persuades the boy to purchase a live, 6-foot tall 266-lb. chicken. Father won't have the friendly, freakish fowl around the house, but when Henrietta and Arthur are separated the devoted bird runs wild throughout the town. Slight but funny "WonderWorks" adaptation of the absurdist

kids' novel by D. Manus Pinkwater. The amusing Henrietta was fabricated by Sid & Marty Krofft puppeteers.
1984 (*Family*) 55m/C Dick Van Patten, Peter Billingsley, Gabe Kaplan, Arlene Golonka; **D:** Peter Baldwin. **VHS $14.95** *PME, FCT, BTV*

Hobo's Christmas 🎞🎞

A man who left his family to become a hobo comes home for Christmas 25 years later. Hughes turns in a delightful performance as the hobo in this made for TV special.
1987 (*Preschool*) 94m/C Barnard Hughes, William Hickey, Gerald McRaney, Wendy Crewson; **D:** Will MacKenzie. **VHS, Beta** *NO*

Hockey Night 🎞🎞◁

Follows takes a break from her "Anne of Green Gables" persona to do a grittier Canadian-content drama, about hockey-loving Kathy who becomes the first girl on a kid's team in a provincial town. The team's offended adult sponsor turns up the heat to have her removed from the ice. Nice drama with superb young actors, but surprisingly dull hockey scenes, apparently filmed from the cheap seats. **Hound Advisory:** Alcohol use.
1984 (*Primary-Jr. High*) 77m/C Megan Follows, Rick Moranis, Gail Youngs, Martin Harburg, Henry Ramer; **D:** Paul Shapiro. **VHS, Beta** *FHE*

Hocus Pocus 🎞🎞◁

Midler, Najimy, and Parker are executed 17th-century witches accidentally conjured up by 20th century teenagers on Halloween in Salem, Massachusetts. They (the witches, that is) plot to take revenge on the town by sucking life from its children. Given the Disney label, pic is surprisingly gruesome (compare it with "Bedknobs and Broomsticks" to see how times change), but the pumpkin-pageant-performances of the three stars - they rant, rave, sing, fly - make up for the lack of substance with comedy sorcery. Production values and f/x are awesome even by lofty Magic Kingdom standards. **Hound Advisory:** Supernatural violence, including a comic zombie who gets temporarily dismembered (just like Scarecrow in "The Wizard of Oz"). Sex talk, since the witches need to kill a virgin -giggle, giggle.
1993 (*PG/Jr. High-Adult*) 95m/C Bette Midler, Kathy Najimy, Sarah Jessica Parker, Thora Birch, Doug Jones, Omri Katz, Vinessa Shaw, Stephanie Faracy, Charles Rocket; **Cameos:** Penny Marshall, Garry Marshall; **D:** Kenny Ortega; **W:** Neil Cuthbert, Mick Garris; **M:** John Debney. **VHS, Beta, LV $96.03** *DIS, BVV, BTV*

Holiday Inn 🎞🎞◁

Astaire and Crosby are rival song-and-dance men who decide to work together to turn a Connecticut farm into an inn, open only on holidays. Remade (and improved) in 1954 as "White Christmas." ♫White Christmas; Be Careful, It's My Heart; Plenty to Be Thankful For; Abraham, Abraham; Let's Say It With Firecrackers; I Gotta Say I Love You Cause I Can't Tell A Lie; Let's Start the New Year Right; Happy Holidays; Song of Freedom.
1942 (*Family*) 101m/B Bing Crosby, Fred Astaire, Marjorie Reynolds, Walter Abel, Virginia Dale; **D:** Mark Sandrich. **Award Nominations:** Academy Awards '42: Best Story, Best Original Score; **Awards:** Academy Awards '42: Best Song ("White Christmas"). **VHS, Beta, LV $14.98** *MCA*

Hollywood on Parade

A collection of several "Hollywood on Parade" shorts produced by Paramount Studios between 1932 and 1934. Nearly every big star of the era is featured singing, dancing, or taking part in bizarre sketches.
1934 (*Family*) 59m/B Fredric March, Ginger Rogers, Jean Harlow, Jeanette MacDonald, Maurice Chevalier, Mary Pickford, Jackie Cooper. **VHS, Beta $24.95** *NOS, HEG, DVT*

Hollywood or Bust 🎞🎞◁

The zany comedy duo of Martin and Lewis (making the last of many successful appearances together) take off for the motion picture capital, where Jerry expects to meet his dream girl, screen siren Anita Ekberg. Lots of loose slapstick episodes ensue. Kid viewers will especially enjoy the antics of 'Mr. Bascombe,' Jerry's "Marmaduke"-sized great dane.
1956 (*Family*) 95m/C Dean Martin, Jerry Lewis, Anita Ekberg, Pat Crowley, Maxie "Slapsie" Rosenbloom, Willard Waterman; **D:** Frank Tashlin. **VHS $14.95** *PAR, CCB*

Holt of the Secret Service

Secret Service agent runs afoul of saboteurs and fifth columnists in this 15-chapter serial.
1942 (*Family*) 290m/B Jack Holt, Evelyn Brent, Montague Shaw, Tristram Coffin, John Ward, George Cheseboro; **D:** James W. Horne. **VHS $39.95** *VYY, MED, DVT*

Holy Matrimony 🎞🎞◁

Mild-mannered and pleasant comedy in spite of its potentially salacious plot. Thieves Peter (Donovan) and Havana (Arquette) take off to Canada to hide out in the Hutterite religious community where Peter grew up and where he's welcomed as the prodigal son. Peter hides their stolen loot but neglects to pass the word on before he's killed in an accident. Wanting to stay and search for the money, Havana uses the colony's reliance on biblical law to marry Peter's brother, Zeke (Gordon-Levitt). Only problem is Zeke is 12 and doesn't even like girls. Strictly brother-sister affection develops between the two. Amusing performances by both. **Hound Advisory:** Profanity; sexual situations.
1994 (*PG-13/Jr. High-Adult*) 93m/C Patricia Arquette, Joseph Gordon-Levitt, Armin Mueller-Stahl, Tate Donovan, John Schuck, Lois Smith, Courtney B. Vance, Jeffrey Nordling, Richard Riehle; **D:** Leonard Nimoy; **W:** David Weisberg, Douglas S. Cook; **M:** Bruce Broughton. **VHS** *BVV*

Home Alone 🎞🎞🎞

Eight-year-old Kevin is sent to his room for innocently misbehaving, and is forgotten the next day when his large family rushes to catch a plane to France. Left alone - and believing he somehow wished all his relatives into nonexistence - the tyke learns to survive on his own in a wintery suburban neighborhood haunted by suspicious grownups, a scary old man and two bumbling burglars planning to rob the house. One of John Hughes' most pleasing and successful films, thanks to Culkin's terrific, star-making performance and the slapstick siege pitting the crooks against the boy's many domestic booby-traps. Much-imitated; in fact Hughes reworked his earlier, more adult-oriented script "Career

Opportunities" for the premise. Critics complained that the pratfalls bordered on real violence, but the main beef is the contrived Christmas sentiment. **Hound Advisory:** Cartoonish violence bordering on the severe but funny nonetheless.
1990 (PG/*Jr. High-Adult*) 105m/C Macaulay Culkin, Catherine O'Hara, Joe Pesci, Daniel Stern, John Heard, Roberts Blossom, John Candy, Catherine O'Hara, Billie Bird, Angela Goethals, Devin Ratray, Kieran Culkin; *D:* Chris Columbus; *W:* John Hughes; *M:* John Williams. **VHS, Beta, LV $24.98** *FXV, IME, RDG*

Home Alone 2: Lost in New York 🦴🦴

Overlong, near-exact duplication of the original blockbuster. One year later the harebrained McCallisters again lose Kevin in the shuffle to catch a plane to Florida for their Yuletide vacation. The boy instead lands in NYC, scams his way into a luxury hotel, and goes through a rerun routine with returning burglars Pesci and Stern, who plot to steal a toy store's charity proceeds (you could call this "Kevin Saves Christmas"). Loaded with cartoon violence and shameless holiday pathos, all as fresh as December fruitcake in May. Culkin is as adorable, but his patented scream act wears out about the fiftieth time or so. Tape includes a banal breakfast cereal commercial, a fitting companion. **Hound Advisory:** Violence, bordering on brutality and Kevin hits the burglars with even nastier, bone-cracking booby-traps.
1992 (PG/*Family*) 120m/C Macaulay Culkin, Joe Pesci, Daniel Stern, Catherine O'Hara, John Heard, Tim Curry, Brenda Fricker, Devin Ratray, Hillary Wolf, Eddie Bracken, Dana Ivey, Rob Schneider, Kieran Culkin, Gerry Bamman; *Cameos:* Donald Trump; *D:* Chris Columbus; *W:* John Hughes; *M:* John Williams. **VHS, LV $24.98** *FXV, BTV*

Home at Last

Billy, an orphaned street punk in turn-of-the-century New York, avoids jail by shipping to Nebraska and settles on the farm of a family whose own son has just died. After many difficulties the troublesome Billy and his Scandinavian foster father finally come to terms at a local horse-pulling contest. Somewhat plodding "WonderWorks" entry that nonetheless has you caring for its characters by the close.
1988 (*Family*) 58m/C Adrien Brody, Frank Converse, Caroline Lagerfelt, Sascha Radetsky. **VHS $29.95** *PME, HMV, FCT*

Home for Christmas 🦴🦴◁

An elderly homeless man, with the love of a young girl, teaches a wealthy family the spirit of Christmas.
1990 (*Family*) 96m/C Mickey Rooney, Joel Kaiser; *D:* Peter McCubbin. **VHS $79.95** *RHI*

Home Movies 🦴◁

Blockbuster Hollywood director DePalma and his film students at Sarah Lawrence College devised this loose, sloppy comedy that got a theatrical release. Tells the story of a neurotic 16-year-old boy who uses moviemaking as a way to cope with (and wreak havoc on) his awful family. Pretty distasteful at times. **Hound Advisory:** Profanity, mature themes, sex.
1979 (PG/*Jr. High-Adult*) 89m/C Kirk Douglas, Nancy Allen, Keith Gordon, Gerrit Graham, Vincent Gardenia, Harry Davenport; *D:* Brian DePalma; *W:* Brian DePalma; *M:* Pino Donaggio. **VHS, Beta, LV $69.98** *LIV, VES, IME*

A Home of Our Own 🦴🦴◁

Semi-autobiographical tearjerker based on screenwriter Duncan's childhood. Widowed and poor mother of six is fired from her job at a Los Angeles potato chip factory. So she packs up the tribe and heads for a better life, landing in Idaho, in a ramshackle house owned by lonely Mr. Moon. What follows is a winter of discontent. Bates provides an intense performance as a poor but proud woman with a tough exterior. Furlong supplies the story's narration as the eldest son.
1993 (PG-13/*Jr. High-Adult*) 104m/C Kathy Bates, Edward Furlong, Soon-Teck Oh, Amy Sakasitz, Tony Campisi; *D:* Tony Bill; *W:* Patrick Duncan. **VHS, LV $94.99** *PGV*

Home to Stay 🦴🦴🦴

Gentle, affecting made-for-TV family drama centered around a farm family whose aging patriarch Fonda insists on overseeing business affairs, even though his memory is clearly faltering. When the frustrated dad talks about putting the old man in a nursing home, the teenage daughter sneaks away with her beloved grandpa on an extended road trip so they can spend more time together. Based on the book "Grandpa and Frank" by Janet Marjerus.
1979 (*Jr. High-Adult*) 74m/C Henry Fonda, Frances Hyland, Michael McGuire; *D:* Delbert Mann; *M:* Hagood Hardy. **VHS, Beta $59.95** *TLF*

Homecoming: A Christmas Story 🦴🦴🦴

Made-for-television heart tugger that inspired the enduring television series "The Waltons." Depression-era Virginia mountain family struggles to celebrate Christmas although the whereabouts and safety of their father are unknown. Adapted by Earl Hamner, Jr. from his own autobiographical novel.
1971 (*Family*) 98m/C Richard Thomas, Patricia Neal, Edgar Bergen, Cleavon Little, Ellen Corby; *D:* Fielder Cook. **VHS, Beta $14.98** *FOX*

Homer Price Stories

Live-action filmizations of the popular children's stories.
1985 (*Primary*) 40m/C **VHS, Beta $19.95** *CCC, WKV, BTV*

Homeward Bound 🦴🦴◁

Terminally ill teenager tries to reunite his long-estranged father and grandfather. Made-for-TV tearjerker with effective performances triumphing over formula script.
1980 (G/*Family*) 96m/C David Soul, Moosie Drier, Barnard Hughes; *D:* Richard Michaels. **VHS, Beta $59.95** *HMV*

Homeward Bound: The Incredible Journey 🦴🦴🦴

Remake of the 1963 Disney flick tells the tried-and-true tale with a "Look Who's Talking" approach; now you can hear the lost animals talking, via celebrity voiceovers, as they try to find the way home after their owners relocate. The gimmick works (even though some of Fox's topical wisecracks may mean nothing to future generations), and it's hard not to shed

a tear for the brave trio who develop a trusting bond through assorted misadventures. Stirring animalistic tale.
1993 (G/*Family*) 85m/C Robert Hays, Kim Greist, Jean Smart, Benj Thall, Veronica Lauren, Kevin Timothy Chevalia; *D:* Duwayne Dunham; *W:* Linda Woolverton, Carolyn Thompson; *M:* Bruce Broughton; *V:* Don Ameche, Michael J. Fox, Sally Field. **VHS, LV $22.99** *DIS, BTV*

Honey, I Blew Up the Kid 🐾🐾◁

Big-budget sequel to Disney's surprise hit "Honey, I Shrunk the Kids" cleverly turns the plot formula 180 degrees. Now screwball suburban inventor Wayne Szalinski works on an enlarging ray that accidentally zaps his two-year-old into a rambunctious, rampaging giant who gets bigger every time he comes in contact with electricity. Loaded with great f/x, tale gets a bit thin in places but remains charming and funny enough. Accompanied on cassette by a comic Little Richard music video "On Top of Spaghetti." **Hound Advisory:** This could easily have been a G.
1992 (PG/*Family*) 89m/C Rick Moranis, Marcia Strassman, Robert Oliveri, Daniel Shalikar, Joshua Shalikar, Lloyd Bridges, John Shea, Keri Russell, Gregory Sierra, Julia Sweeney, Kenneth Tobey, Peter Elbling; *D:* Randal Kleiser; *W:* Thom Eberhardt, Garry Goodrow; *M:* Bruce Broughton. **VHS, Beta, LV $19.99** *DIS*

Honey, I Shrunk the Kids 🐾🐾◁

Not one of the greats, but an amicably gimmicky Disney fantasy that became a giant hit with audiences, about a suburban inventor whose raygun accidentally reduces his kids to 1/4 inch tall. When dad accidentally throws them out with the garbage, they must journey back to the house through the perilous jungle that was once the lawn. Accompanied by "Tummy Trouble," the first of a series of Roger Rabbit 'Maroon Cartoon' short subjects spun off from his own hit debut feature. **Hound Advisory:** The shrunken kids befriend a loyal ant who dies defending them; not exactly "Old Yeller," but the filmmakers milk the sacrifice for all possible sentiment.
1989 (G/*Family*) 101m/C Rick Moranis, Matt Frewer, Marcia Strassman, Kristine Sutherland, Thomas Wilson Brown, Jared Rushton, Amy O'Neill, Robert Oliveri; *D:* Joe Johnston, Rob Minkoff; *W:* Tom Schulman, Stuart Gordon; *M:* James Horner; *V:* Charles Fleischer, Kathleen Turner, Lou Hirsch, April Winchell. **VHS, Beta, LV $19.99** *DIS, MOV, RDG*

Honeymoon in Vegas 🐾🐾◁

Romantic comedy turns frantic after Cage loses his fiancee to wealthy but essentially criminal Caan in a high stakes Vegas poker game. So he has to get her back, providing Cage with more than an hour's worth of manic comedy in the classic Cage manic comedy vein. As the distraught young groom-to-be who encounters numerous obstacles on his way to the altar, Cage does his best to keep the juice going with basic economy script. Lightweight comedy features a bevy of Elvis impersonators in every size, shape, and color (including Elvis sky divers) and new versions of favorite Elvis tunes. **Hound Advisory:** Profanity; adult situations; sex talk.
1992 (PG-13/*Jr. High-Adult*) 95m/C James Caan, Nicolas Cage, Sarah Jessica Parker, Noriyuki "Pat" Morita, John Capodice, Robert Costanzo, Anne Bancroft, Peter Boyle, Seymour Cassel, Tony Shalhoub; *D:* Andrew Bergman; *W:* Andrew Bergman; *M:* David Newman. **VHS, LV $19.95** *COL, NLC, IME*

Honkytonk Man 🐾🐾

Unsteady change-of-pace vehicle for action star Eastwood, set during the Depression. An aging, whoring, alcoholic country singer tries one last time to make it to Nashville, hoping to perform at the Grand Ole Opry. This time he takes his 14-year-old nephew (played by Eastwood's real-life son) with him, and a father-son relationship develops. **Hound Advisory:** Mature themes, sex, alcohol use, profanity.
1982 (PG/*Jr. High-Adult*) 123m/C Clint Eastwood, Kyle Eastwood, John McIntire, Alexa Kenin, Verna Bloom; *D:* Clint Eastwood; *M:* Stephen Dorff. **VHS, Beta, LV $19.98** *WAR*

Hook 🐾🐾◁

Peter Banning, an uptight executive who puts work before family, is on a trip to London when his children are kidnapped by a supernatural force. This can happen on those transatlantic trips. However, it seems yuppie Banning is really Peter Pan, who did grow up and forgot Neverland. But his ancient enemy Captain Hook remembers, and has the kids. Tinkerbell drags the frantic, nonbelieving Banning back to the fantasy realm for a showdown. Spielberg's take on the J.M. Barrie stories - what if they were true? - is a rich but unwieldy bag of treats, mixing action, huge sets, and superb f/x with serious themes of parenthood and rediscovery, literally, of one's inner child. But it's way too long, and the 'final' duel with the pompous Hook (Hoffman, in a dandy piece of ham acting) is unsatisfying and clearly open to a sequel. That proved wishful thinking; this was one of Stevie's few box-office disappointments. Still, there's a lot worthwhile here for youngsters and adults, especially when they can stop the VCR once or twice for a breather. **Hound Advisory:** Lots of roughhousing between the pirates and the Lost Boys, and one of Peter's playmates is killed - but the plot soft pedals all violence.
1991 (PG/*Jr. High-Adult*) 142m/C Dustin Hoffman, Robin Williams, Julia Roberts, Bob Hoskins, Dame Maggie Smith, Charlie Korsmo, Caroline Goodall, Amber Scott, Phil Collins, Arthur Malet, Dante Basco, Gwyneth Paltrow; *Cameos:* Glenn Close, David Crosby; *D:* Steven Spielberg; *W:* Nick Castle; *M:* John Williams. **VHS, Beta, LV, 8mm $19.95** *COL*

Hoosiers 🐾🐾🐾

In 1951 Indiana, a small-town high school basketball team gets a new, unorthodox coach. Despite public skepticism, he makes the team, and each person on it, better than they thought possible. Classic, uplifting plot rings true because of Hackman's complex and sensitive performance coupled with Hopper's touching portrait of an alcoholic ex-hoops star who becomes a winner again. **Hound Advisory:** Alcohol use, salty language.
1986 (PG/*Jr. High-Adult*) 115m/C Gene Hackman, Barbara Hershey, Dennis Hopper, David Neidorf, Sheb Wooley, Fern Parsons, Brad Boyle, Steve Hollar, Brad Long; *D:* David Anspaugh; *W:* Angelo Pizzo; *M:* Jerry Goldsmith. **VHS, Beta, LV $14.98** *LIV*

Hop on Pop

Cartoon version of the Dr. Seuss classic plus two more, "Marvin K. Mooney Will You Please Go Now" and "Oh Say Can You Say?"
1990 (*Family*) 30m/C **VHS $9.95** *RAN, VEC*

Macaulay Culkin discovers he's "Home Alone"

Hope and Glory 🎬🎬🎬🎬

Boorman turns memories of WWII into a complex and sensitive family saga of suburban Londoners surviving the Battle of Britain. While father's away fighting, mother must cope with a mischief-prone son, the awakening sexuality of the teenage daughter, plus those pesky nightly air raids. Tale unfurls largely through the small boy's eyes, and such scenes are priceless: war becomes a giant, abstract game, sometimes tragic, but mostly an opportunity for grand fun. "Thank you Adolf!" shouts a child when a Nazi bomb levels their hated school. No real violence, but an abundance of mature themes (like the daughter's promiscuity and resulting pregnancy) skew this more toward adult viewers. **Hound Advisory:** Mature themes, alcohol use, sex. The son joins a club of kid vandals in the bombed-out ruins; their admission ceremony is a recitation of swear words - all but one of which seems utterly inoffensive today.
1987 (PG-13/*Sr. High-Adult*) 97m/C Sebastian Rice Edwards, Geraldine Muir, Sarah Miles, Sammi Davis-Voss, David Hayman, Derrick O'Connor, Susan Wooldridge, Jean-Marc Barr, Ian Bannen, Jill Baker, Charley Boorman, Annie Leon, Katrine Boorman, Gerald James; **D:** John Boorman. **Award Nominations:** Academy Awards '87: Best Art Direction/Set Decoration, Best Cinematography, Best Director (Boorman), Best Original Screenplay, Best Picture; **Awards:** British Academy Awards '87: Best Film, Best Supporting Actress (Wooldridge); Los Angeles Film Critics Association Awards '87: Best Director (Boorman), Best Film; National Board of Review Awards '87: 10 Best Films of the Year. **VHS, Beta, LV, 8mm** $14.98 *SUE, FCT, HMV*

Hoppity Goes to Town

Full-length animated feature from the Fleischer Brothers, the "Popeye" and "Betty Boop" animators, who sought to become cartoon tycoons on the scale of Disney but never earned "Snow White" scale profits at the box office. Their work is still well worth a look, and in this inventive modern tale the fun-loving inhabitants of Bugville, who live in a patch of weeds in NYC, try to avoid careless extermination by humans.
1941 (*Family*) 77m/C **D:** Dave Fleischer; **M:** Frank Loesser, Hoagy Carmichael. **VHS, LV** $14.98 *REP, MRV, FCT*

The Horn Blows at Midnight 🎬🎬🎬

Lavish comedy-fantasy starring comedian Benny as a band trumpeter who falls asleep and dreams he's an archangel, who must earn his wings not by helping some earthly soul like Clarence did in "It's a Wonderful Life" - but by sounding the mystical note that destroys the world. Sent to the doomed Earth on New Year's Eve, he's soon distracted by pretty faces and other temptations. Funny, and a little subversive; you really root for Benny and hope he'll blow that note to please his employers!
1945 (*Family*) 78m/B Jack Benny, Alexis Smith, Dolores Moran, Allyn Joslyn, Reginald Gardiner, Guy Kibbee, John Alexander, Margaret Dumont; **D:** Raoul Walsh. **VHS** $19.98 *MGM, FCT*

Horse Feathers 🎬🎬🎬🎬

Marx Brothers madness with Groucho sidesplitting as Professor Wagstaff, new president of Huxley College, who'll stop at nothing to win a big football match. He mistakes Harpo and Chico for championship athletic talent and recruits them as students. Terrific slapstick game finale that violates every known rule of sportsmanship, and a short running time that's just right. **Hound Advisory:** Alcohol use.
1932 (*Family*) 67m/B Groucho Marx, Chico Marx, Harpo Marx, Zeppo Marx, Thelma Todd, David Landau, Nat Pendleton; **D:** Norman Z. McLeod. **VHS, Beta, LV** $14.98 *MCA*

The Horse in the Gray Flannel Suit 🎬🎬🎬

Disney diversion about a harried advertising man whose daughter wants a horse and whose client wants to boost sales of his aspirin pills. Our hero tries to combine the best of both worlds with an ad campaign built around a beer-drinking steed. **Hound Advisory:** Alcohol use.
1968 (G/*Family*) 114m/C Dean Jones, Ellen Janov, Fred Clark, Diane Baker, Lloyd Bochner, Kurt Russell; **D:** Norman Tokar. **VHS, Beta** *DIS, OM*

The Horse That Played Center Field

A horse is installed on the roster of a losing baseball team to motivate the players into performing up to their potential. The beast proves to be a phenomenal fielder and leads the team to the World Series. An ABC Afterschool Special.
197? (*Primary-Jr. High*) 48m/C **VHS, Beta** *MTT*

The Horse Without a Head 🎬🎬🎬

Stolen loot has been hidden in a discarded toy horse which is now the property of a group of poor children. The thieves, however, have different plans. Good family fare originally shown on the Disney television show.
1963 (*Family*) 89m/C Jean-Pierre Aumont, Herbert Lom, Leo McKern, Pamela Franklin, Vincent Winter; **D:** Don Chaffey. **VHS, Beta** $69.95 *DIS*

Horsemasters 🎬🎬

A group of young riders enter a special training program in England to achieve the ultimate equestrian title of horsemaster, with Annette having to overcome her fear of jumping. Originally a two-part Disney television show, and released as a feature film in Europe.
1961 (*Family*) 85m/C Tommy Kirk, Annette Funicello, Janet Munro, Tony Britton, Donald Pleasence, Jean Marsh, John Fraser, Millicent Martin; **D:** William Fairchild. **VHS, Beta** $69.95 *DIS*

Horton Hatches the Egg

Cartoon version of the Dr. Seuss tale of big-hearted Horton the Elephant who helps out a friend by sitting on the little egg in her nest. Also includes the story "If I Ran the Circus."
1991 (*Primary*) 30m/C **VHS** $9.95 *RAN, BTV*

Horton Hears a Who!

Horton, the whimsical rhyming elephant, tries to rescue the tiny Whos of Whoville after realizing that their microscopic world resides on a dust speck, in this musicalized Dr. Seuss fable.
1970 (*Family*) 26m/C **VHS, Beta** $19.95 *MGM, KUI, WTA*

Hot Lead & Cold Feet 🎬🎬

In the Old West contrasting twin brothers (one a gunfighter, the other a missionary) compete in a train race where the winner will take ownership of a small western town. Dale plays both brothers and their curmudgeony father. Standard vintage-70s Disney comedy barely avoids Apple Dumpling gang territory.

1978 (G/*Family*) 89m/C Jim Dale, Don Knotts, Karen Valentine; **D:** Robert Butler; **M:** Buddy Baker. **VHS, Beta $69.95** *DIS*

Hot Shot 🎬🎬

Jimmy defies his wealthy parents to qualify as a soccer player. When his attitude threatens his pro career, though, the young man seeks training from a Brazilian champ, portrayed by Pele. Old story, different sport, new swear words, yellow cards. **Hound Advisory:** Profanity.

1986 (PG/*Primary-Sr. High*) 90m/C Pele, Jim Youngs, Billy Warlock, Weyman Thompson, Mario Van Peebles, David Groh; **D:** Rick King. **VHS, Beta $14.95** *WAR, MVD*

Hot Shots! Part Deux 🎬🎬

Second "Hot Shots" outing doesn't live up to the first, but it's not bad either. Admiral Tug Benson (Bridges) is elected President (yes, of the U.S.) and calls on Sheen's newly pumped-up Topper to take on Saddam Hussein Rambo-style. Love interest Ramada (Golino), returns but this time she's competing with Michelle (Bakke), a sexy CIA agent. Crenna spoofs his role in the "Rambo" films as Sheen's mentor; look for real-life dad Martin in a take-off of "Apocalypse Now." Shtick flies as fast and furious as the bullets and bodies, with Bridges getting a chance to reprise his glory days of "Sea Hunt." Don't miss the credits. **Hound Advisory:** Brief nudity; profanity; violence; sex talk.

1993 (PG-13/*Jr. High-Adult*) 89m/C Charlie Sheen, Lloyd Bridges, Valeria Golino, Brenda Bakke, Richard Crenna, Miguel Ferrer, Rowan Atkinson, Jerry Haleva, Mitchell Ryan, Gregory Sierra, Ryan Stiles, Michael Colyar; **Cameos:** Martin Sheen, Bob Vila; **D:** Jim Abrahams; **W:** Pat Proft, Jim Abrahams; **M:** Basil Poledouris. **VHS $96.98** *FXV, BTV*

Hot to Trot! 🎬

Babbling idiot inherits a talking horse who's full of stock-market tips, in an updated, downtrodden version of the "Francis, the Talking Mule" comedies, with a scent of Mr. Ed. The equine voice is provided by Candy. Some real funny guys are wasted here. **Hound Advisory:** Salty language, sex talk.

1988 (PG/*Preschool*) 90m/C Bob(cat) Goldthwait, Dabney Coleman, Virginia Madsen, Jim Metzler, Cindy Pickett, Tim Kazurinsky, Santos Morales, Barbara Whinnery, Garry Kluger; **D:** Michael Dinner; **W:** Charlie Peters; **M:** Danny Elfman; **V:** John Candy. **VHS, Beta, LV $19.95** *WAR*

The Hound that Thought He was a Raccoon

Nubbin the hound refuses to chase raccoons because he wants to be one. A live-action tale from the TV series "The Wonderful World of Disney."

1990 (*Preschool-Primary*) 48m/C **VHS, Beta $250.00** *MTI, DSN*

House 🎬🎬🎬

Horror novelist moves into his dead aunt's supposedly haunted house only to find that the monsters don't necessarily stay in the closets. His worst nightmares come to life as he writes about his Vietnam experiences and is forced to relive the tragic events, but these aren't the only visions that start springing to life. It sounds depressing, but is actually a funny, intelligent "horror" flick. Followed by several lesser sequels. **Hound Advisory:** Profanity, violence.

1986 (R/*Sr. High-Adult*) 93m/C William Katt, George Wendt, Richard Moll, Kay Lenz, Michael Ensign, Mary Stavin, Susan French; **D:** Steve Miner; **W:** Ethan Wiley; **M:** Harry Manfredini. **VHS, Beta, LV $19.95** *NWV, STE*

House of Cards 🎬🎬🎬

Six-year-old Sally suddenly stops talking and even reacting in normal ways after her father is killed in an accident at an archeological site in Mexico. Mom Ruth fights with conventional therapists to drag her daughter out of the fantasy realm, and her unorthodox treatment includes virtual-reality computer technology, Mexican mysticism, and an elaborate tower of cards. Coming out right after the thematically similar "Lorenzo's Oil," this couldn't help suffering by comparison; it's a melange of dubious psychology and arresting visual surprises, held together by Turner's intractable performance and little Menina's ethereal presence in her acting debut. **Hound Advisory:** Mature themes, salty language.

1992 (PG-13/*Jr. High-Adult*) 109m/C Kathleen Turner, Asha Menina, Tommy Lee Jones, Shiloh Strong, Esther Rolle, Park Overall, Michael Horse, Anne Pitoniak; **D:** Michael Lessac; **W:** Michael Lessac. **VHS, LV $92.98** *LIV, BTV, FCT*

The House of Dies Drear

A modern-day African American family moves into an old house that turns out to be haunted by the ghost of a long dead abolitionist. The family is transported back to the days of slavery as they interact with the ghost. Based on the story by Virginia Hamilton. Part of the "Wonderworks" series.

1988 (*Family*) 107m/C Howard E. Rollins Jr., Moses Gunn, Shavar Ross, Gloria Foster, Clarence Williams III; **D:** Allan Goldstein. **VHS $29.95** *HMV, PME, FCT*

House of Wax 🎬🎬🎬

Deranged sculptor (Price, who else?) builds a sinister wax museum which showcases creations that were once alive. A remake of the early horror flick "Mystery of the Wax Museum," and one of the 50s' most popular 3-D films. This one still has the power to give the viewer the creeps, thanks to another chilling performance by Price. Look for a very young Bronson, as well as Carolyn "Morticia Addams" Jones as a victim. **Hound Advisory:** Violence.

1953 (PG/*Sr. High-Adult*) 88m/C Vincent Price, Frank Lovejoy, Carolyn Jones, Phyllis Kirk, Paul Cavanagh, Charles Bronson; **D:** Andre de Toth. **VHS, Beta, LV $19.98** *WAR, MLB*

House Party 🎬🎬🎬

Light-hearted, black hip-hop version of a '50s teen comedy with rap duo Kid 'n' Play. After his father grounds him for fighting, a high-schooler attempts all sorts of wacky schemes to get to his friend's party. Sleeper hit features real-life music rappers and some dynamite dance numbers. **Hound Advisory:** Profanity.

1990 (R/*College-Adult*) 100m/C Christopher Reid, Christopher Martin, Martin Lawrence, Tisha Campbell, Paul Anthony, A.J. Johnson, Full Force, Robin Harris; **D:** Reginald Hudlin; **W:** Reginald Hudlin; **M:** Marcus Miller. **VHS, Beta, LV** $14.95 COL, FCT, NLC

House Party 2: The Pajama Jam 🎬🎬◁

Rap stars Kid 'N' Play are back in this hip-hop sequel to the original hit. At Harris University Kid 'N' Play hustle up overdue tuition by holding a campus "jammie jam jam." A stellar cast shines in this rap-powered pajama bash. **Hound Advisory:** Profanity.

1991 (R/*Sr. High-Adult*) 94m/C Christopher Reid, Christopher Martin, Tisha Campbell, Iman, Queen Latifah, Georg Stanford Brown, Martin Lawrence, Eugene Allen, George Anthony Bell, Kamron, Tony Burton, Helen Martin, William Schallert; **D:** Doug McHenry, George Jackson; **W:** Rusty Cundieff, Daryl G. Nickens; **M:** Vassal Benford. **VHS, LV** $19.95 COL, NLC

House Party 3 🎬

Kid is engaged to be married and Play tries to set up a blowout bachelor party. The duo are also working on their record producer careers by trying to sign a feisty female rap group (real life TLC). Strikes out early for easy profanity while never coming within spitting distance of first two flicks. **Hound Advisory:** Profanity; sex talk.

1994 (R/*Sr. High-Adult*) 93m/C Christopher Reid, Christopher Martin, Angela Means, Tisha Campbell, Bernie Mac, Barbara Edwards, Michael Colyar, David Edwards, Betty Lester, Christopher Tucker; **D:** Eric Meza; **W:** Takashi Bufford; **M:** David Allen Jones. **VHS, LV** COL, IME

The House with a Clock in Its Walls

Eerie 'toon tale about a man with a plan to destroy the world. Lots of spooky imagery including a gothic house, a graveyard, an orphan, and magic. Based on the novel by John Bellairs. 1991 (*Primary-Jr. High*) 24m/C VHS $50.00 BAR

A House Without a Christmas Tree 🎬🎬◁

Father with a sour attitude toward the holidays repeatedly denies his small daughter what she most desires — a real indoor Christmas tree. Will dad come around by fadeout? Charming, if slightly predictable, made-for-TV movie. 1972 (*Family*) 90m/C Jason Robards Jr., Lisa Lucas, Mildred Natwick; **D:** Paul Bogart. **VHS, Beta** $14.98 FXV, FCT

Housekeeping 🎬🎬🎬

Quiet, offbeat and sensitive comedy by "Gregory's Girl" Forsyth. Young sisters (orphaned by their mother's suicide) are cared for by their eccentric, free-spirited aunt in a small and small-minded '50s Oregon community. Soon it's clear that Aunt Sylvie is not only unorthodox but mentally ill, and the girls' relationship with her defies public disapproval. Acting showcase for Lahti receives generous support from young Walker and Burchill. Based on the novel "Sylvie's Ark" by Marilynne Robinson. **Hound Advisory:** Mature themes.

1987 (PG/*Jr. High-Adult*) 117m/C Christine Lahti, Sarah Walker, Andrea Burchill; **D:** Bill Forsyth; **W:** Bill Forsyth; **M:** Michael Gibbs. **VHS, Beta** $89.95 COL

Housesitter 🎬🎬◁

Martin is an architect/dreamer who builds his high school sweetheart Delany a beautiful house and surprises her with a marriage proposal. After she says no, he has no choice but to have a one-night stand with Hawn, which changes his life. Hawn moves into Martin's empty dream house and assumes the position of his wife, unbeknownst to him. Soon she's spinning whoppers of lies and soon has the entire town, including Davis's parents and ex-girlfriend, believing her wacky stories, while she struggles to keep with the twists and turns of her story. Romantic screwball comedy is uneven and not exactly plotted with reality in mind, but Martin and Hawn give it a go. **Hound Advisory:** Sex.

1992 (PG/*Jr. High-Adult*) 102m/C Steve Martin, Goldie Hawn, Dana Delany, Julie Harris, Donald Moffatt, Peter MacNicol, Richard B. Shull, Laurel Cronin, Christopher Durang; **D:** Frank Oz; **W:** Mark Stein, Brian Grazer; **M:** Miles Goodman. **VHS, Beta, LV** $19.98 MCA, PMS, BTV

How Green was My Valley 🎬🎬🎬🎬

Saga of the triumphs and tribulations of a Welsh mining family, from the youthful perspective of the youngest child (played by a 13-year-old McDowall). Setting is turn of the century, when coal mining was a difficult but fair-paying way of life, and ends, after unionization, strikes, fatalities, romance, and the boy hero's ordeals at the hands of cruel schoolmaster. Splendid entertainment will leave you nostalgic for a time and place you never even knew. Based on the novel by Richard Llewellyn.

1941 (*Jr. High-Adult*) 118m/C Walter Pidgeon, Maureen O'Hara, Donald Crisp, Anna Lee, Roddy McDowall, John Loder, Sara Allgood, Barry Fitzgerald, Patric Knowles, Rhys Williams, Arthur Shields, Ann Todd, Mae Marsh; **D:** John Ford; **W:** Philip Dunne; **M:** Alfred Newman. **Award Nominations:** Academy Awards '41: Best Film Editing, Best Screenplay, Best Sound, Best Supporting Actress (Allgood), Best Original Score; **Awards:** Academy Awards '41: Best Black and White Cinematography, Best Director (Ford), Best Interior Decoration, Best Picture, Best Supporting Actor (Crisp). **VHS, Beta** $19.98 FOX, FUS, BTV

How I Got into College 🎬🎬

Underachieving but mainly inoffensive satire about a high school senior and the desperate measures he takes to qualify for admission to a ritzy local college (inspired by Wesleyan College) so he can pursue the girl of his dreams. **Hound Advisory:** Profanity.

1989 (PG-13/*Jr. High-Adult*) 87m/C Corey Parker, Lara Flynn Boyle, Christopher Rydell, Anthony Edwards, Phil Hartman, Brian Doyle-Murray, Nora Dunn, Finn Carter, Charles Rocket; **D:** Steve Holland; **W:** Terrel Seltzer. **VHS, Beta, LV** $89.98 FOX

How the Rhino Got His Skin/How the Camel Got His Hump

Nicholson narrates these two tales from Kipling's Just So stories. Part of the "Rabbit Ears" series of marvelous storytelling videos.

1991 (*Preschool-Primary*) 30m/C VHS $15.99 KUI, COL

How the West was Won 🦴🦴🦴

A panoramic view of the American West, focusing on the trials, tribulations and travels of three generations of one family, set against the background of wars and historical events. Particularly notable for its impressive cast list and expansive western settings. **Hound Advisory:** Violence; alcohol use.

1963 (G/*Jr. High-Adult*) 165m/C John Wayne, Carroll Baker, Lee J. Cobb, Spencer Tracy, Gregory Peck, Karl Malden, Robert Preston, Eli Wallach, Henry Fonda, George Peppard, Debbie Reynolds, Carolyn Jones, Richard Widmark, James Stewart, Walter Brennan, Andy Devine, Raymond Massey, Agnes Moorehead, Henry Morgan, Thelma Ritter, Russ Tamblyn; *D:* John Ford, Henry Hathaway, George Marshall; *W:* James R. Webb. **Award Nominations:** Academy Awards '63: Best Art Direction/Set Decoration (Color), Best Color Cinematography, Best Costume Design (Color), Best Picture, Best Original Score; **Awards:** Academy Awards '63: Best Film Editing, Best Sound, Best Story & Screenplay; National Board of Review Awards '63: 10 Best Films of the Year. **VHS, Beta, LV $29.98** *MGM*

How the Whale Got His Throat

From Kipling's "Just So Stories" comes this tale of what happens after a whale lets a man go free after he tried to eat him.

1984 (*Primary-Jr. High*) 10m/C **VHS, Beta** *MTI*

How to Be a Perfect Person in Just Three Days

Fun comedy for the whole family shows the efforts of a kid striving for perfection before realizing that individuality is more fun. Based on the book by Stephen Mane. Part of the "Wonderworks" series.

1984 (*Family*) 58m/C Wallace Shawn, Ilan Mitchell-Smith, Hermione Gingold, Joan Micklin Silver. **VHS $29.95** *PME, FCT, HMV*

How to Eat Fried Worms

One of the CBS Storybreak series, an animated version of Thomas Rockwell's book about a boy named Billy who bets $50 that he can eat a worm a day for 15 days.

1985 (*Preschool-Jr. High*) 25m/C **VHS $9.95** *WTA, KUI*

How to Play Baseball

Disney cartoon comedy in which a whole team of Goofballs take to the field to play a hilarious game of baseball.

1977 (*Preschool-Primary*) 8m/C **VHS, Beta $155.00** *MTI, DSN*

How to Stuff a Wild Bikini 🦴🦴

Tired next to last feature in the overlong tradition of Frankie and Annette doing the beach thing, featuring a pregnant Funicello (though this is hidden and not part of the plot). Avalon actually has only a small role as the jealous boyfriend trying to see if Annette will remain faithful while he's away on military duty. Keaton is the witch doctor who helps Frankie keep Annette true. "Playboy" playmates wander about in small swimsuits, garage band extraordinare "The Kingsmen" play themselves, and Brian Wilson of the "Beach Boys" makes a rare public appearance. Followed by "Ghost in the Invisible Bikini," the only movie in the series that isn't on video. ♫After the Party; Better Be Ready; Follow Your Leader; Give Her Lovin'; How About Us?; How to Stuff a Wild Bikini; I'm the Boy Next Door; Madison Avenue; The Perfect Boy.

1965 (*Family*) 90m/C Annette Funicello, Dwayne Hickman, Frankie Avalon, Beverly Adams, Buster Keaton, Harvey Lembeck, Mickey Rooney, Brian Donlevy, Jody McCrea, John Ashley, Marianne Gaba, Len Lesser, Irene Tsu, Bobbi Shaw, Luree Holmes; *D:* William Asher; *W:* William Asher, Leo Townsend; *M:* Les Baxter. **VHS, Beta** *NO*

Howard the Duck 🦴

Quack if you've seen it. Megabucks Lucasfilm adaptation of a short-lived Marvel Comics superhero spoof. Alien resembling a talking duck accidentally beams to Earth - Cleveland, in fact. First half has Howard trying to fit into human society, and when those fowl gags run dry, the filmmakers give him space demons to fight in a climactic f/x barrage. Plus an all-girl rock band! Overstuffed screen turkey's premise has appeal for kids (it does have a talking duck) and a decent cast but it's feathered with birdbrained sex 'n' drug jokes. The stiff, mask-like duck face makes one appreciate the fine job the Jim Henson Creature Shop did for the Teenage Mutant Ninja Turtles. **Hound Advisory:** Sex talk, drug talk, violence, salty language, brief duck nudity (you think we're kidding?).

1986 (PG/*Jr. High-Adult*) 111m/C Lea Thompson, Jeffrey Jones, Tim Robbins; *D:* Willard Huyck; *W:* Willard Huyck, Gloria Katz; *M:* Sylvester Levay, John Barry. **VHS, Beta, LV $14.98** *MCA*

Howard's End 🦴🦴🦴🦴

E.M. Forster's 1910 novel about property, privilege, class differences, and Edwardian society is brought to enchanting life by the Merchant Ivory team. A tragic series of events occurs after two impulsive sisters become involved with a working class couple and a wealthy family. Tragedy aside, this is a visually beautiful effort with subtle performances where a glance or a gesture says as much as any dialog. The winner of numerous awards and wide critical acclaim. Thompson is especially notable as the compassionate Margaret, while Hopkins plays the repressed English gentleman brilliantly.

1992 (PG/*Jr. High-Adult*) 143m/C Anthony Hopkins, Emma Thompson, Helena Bonham Carter, Vanessa Redgrave, James Wilby, Sam West, Jemma Redgrave, Nicola Duffett, Prunella Scales, Joseph Bennett; *Cameos:* Simon Callow; *D:* James Ivory; *W:* Ruth Prawer Jhabvala. **Award Nominations:** Academy Awards '92: Best Cinematography, Best Costume Design, Best Director (Ivory), Best Picture, Best Supporting Actress (Redgrave), Best Original Score; Cannes Film Festival '92: Best Film; **Awards:** Academy Awards '92: Best Actress (Thompson), Best Adapted Screenplay, Best Art Direction/Set Decoration; British Academy Awards '93: Best Actress (Thompson); Chicago Film Critics Awards '92: Best Actress (Thompson); Golden Globe Awards '93: Best Actress—Drama (Thompson); Los Angeles Film Critics Association Awards '92: Best Actress (Thompson); National Board of Review Awards '92: 10 Best Films of the Year, Best Actress (Thompson), Best Director (Ivory); National Society of Film Critics Awards '92: Best Actress (Thompson). **VHS, LV, 8mm $19.95** *COL, CRC, MOV*

The Howdy Doody Show (Puppet Playhouse)/The Gabby Hayes Show

Buffalo Bill, Clarabell, and the Peanut Gallery help Howdy Doody with a nostalgic circus of fun in this popular and pioneering children's program. On the same tape, Gabby Hayes sings the Quaker Oats song and tells a tale of the old west.

1948 (*Preschool-Jr. High*) 60m/B **VHS, Beta $19.00** *IHF, MVC*

The Howling *♪♪♪*

Pretty television reporter takes a rest at a clinic and discovers slowly that its denizens are actually werewolves. Crammed with inside jokes, this horror comedy pioneered the use of the body-altering prosthetic make-up (by Rob Bottin) now essential for on-screen man-to-wolf transformations. At last count, followed by five sequels. **Hound Advisory:** Horror violence.

1981 (*R/Sr. High-Adult*) 91m/C Dee Wallace Stone, Patrick Macnee, Dennis Dugan, Christopher Stone, Belinda Balaski, Kevin McCarthy, John Carradine, Slim Pickens, Elisabeth Brooks, Robert Picardo, Dick Miller; **D:** Joe Dante; **W:** John Sayles, Terence H. Winkless; **M:** Pino Donaggio. **VHS, Beta, LV $14.95** COL, SUE

H.R. Pufnstuf, Vol. 1

Compilation of the famous surreal Sid & Marty Krofft production. The friendly dragon Mayor of Magic Island, H.R. Pufnstuf, and his friend Jimmy battle the evil Witchie-poo and her bumbling henchmen as they struggle to find the Secret Path of Escape. Additional volumes available.

1969 (*Primary-Jr. High*) 46m/C Billie Hayes, Jack Wild, Joan Gerber, Felix Silla, Jerry Landon. **VHS, Beta $9.95** NLC, SUE

Huck and the King of Hearts *♪♪*

Nice banter between the title characters is the best part of this trifle. Huck's a resourceful modern-day Hannibal boy fleeing a broken home to find his grandpa. He becomes buddies out west with a homeless Indian cardshark - named Jim, of course - who's (yawn) chased by gangsters. Insubstantial Twain takeoff, loses half a bone for the miserable, crotch-kicking finale. **Hound Advisory:** Roughhousing, salty language, alcohol use, (anti)drug talk.

1993 (*PG/Jr. High-Adult*) 103m/C Chauncey Leopardi, Graham Greene, Dee Wallace Stone, Joe Piscopo, John Astin, Gretchen Becker; **D:** Michael Keusch; **W:** Christopher Sturgeon; **M:** Chris Saranec. **VHS, Beta, LV $92.95** PSM

Huckleberry Finn *♪♪*

Followup to the 1973 Readers Digest musical version of "Tom Sawyer" is a forgettable concoction, nowhere near as fun. East reprises his role as the adventurous Huck, and the storyline sticks to Mark Twain's novel of a boy and a runaway slave along the Mississippi, but tiresome songs stop the story deader'n'a riverboat on a sandbar.

1974 (*G/Family*) 114m/C Jeff East, Paul Winfield, Harvey Korman, David Wayne, Arthur O'Connell, Gary Merrill, Natalie Trundy, Lucille Benson; **D:** J. Lee Thompson. **VHS, Beta, LV $14.95** MGM, FOX, FCT

Huckleberry Finn *♪♪*

Whitewashed version of the Twain classic features Andy Griffith's onetime 'Opie' Howard among the miscastings as the footloose Huck. Stars three more members of the Howard clan; they should have let Ron direct instead. Made for TV.

1975 (*G/Family*) 74m/C Ron Howard, Donny Most, Royal Dano, Antonio Fargas, Jack Elam, Merle Haggard, Rance Howard, Jean Howard, Clint Howard, Shug Fisher, Sarah Selby, Bill Erwin; **D:** Robert Totten. **VHS, Beta $14.98** KUI, FXV, FCT

Hugo the Hippo *♪♪*

Animated feature from Hungary (with a plethora of Hollywood celebrity voices) about a fugitive baby hippo struggling to save his family from starvation in Zanzibar. Conservation-minded cartoon boasting songs by Donnie and Marie Osmond.

1976 (*G/Family*) 90m/C **V:** Paul Lynde, Burl Ives, Robert Morley, Marie Osmond. **VHS, Beta $49.98** FOX

Hulk Hogan's Rock 'n' Wrestling

Three episodes per tape of the World Wrestling Federation's cartoon counterparts as they battle evil and injustice. Lots of pro-wrestling stars are depicted, but all the voices are studio actors. Additional volumes available.

1987 (*Primary*) 50m/C **VHS, Beta $39.98** LHV

The Human Comedy *♪♪♪♪*

Straight, unapologetically sentimental version of the episodic William Saroyan novel. Focuses on Homer Macauley, messenger-boy son in a small-town family during WWII and how he and they cope with day-to-day life and an eventual battlefield tragedy. Well-acted and warm, but not a laugh riot; title is an allusion to Dante's "Divine Comedy."

1943 (*Family*) 117m/B Mickey Rooney, Frank Morgan, James Craig, Fay Bainter, Ray Collins, Donna Reed, Van Johnson, Barry Nelson, Robert Mitchum, Jackie "Butch" Jenkins; **D:** Clarence Brown; **W:** William Saroyan. **Award Nominations:** Academy Awards '43: Best Actor (Rooney), Best Black and White Cinematography, Best Director (Brown), Best Picture; **Awards:** Academy Awards '43: Best Story. **VHS, Beta, LV $24.98** MGM

The Hunchback of Notre Dame *♪♪♪*

It's not often that a classic novel is remade into a classic movie that's remade into a made-for-TV reprise, and survives its multiple renderings. But it's not often a cast so rich in stage trained actors is assembled on the small screen. Hopkins gives a textured, pre-Hannibal Lecter interpretation of Quasimodo, the Hunchback in Hugo's eponymous novel. Impressive model of the cathedral by production designer John Stoll.

1982 (*PG/Jr. High-Adult*) 102m/C Anthony Hopkins, Derek Jacobi, Lesley-Anne Down, John Gielgud, Tim Pigott-Smith, Rosalie Crutchley, Robert Powell; **D:** Michael Tuchner. **VHS $89.95** VMK

The Hunchback of Notre Dame

Animated version of the Victor Hugo classic about the deformed bell-ringer in love with a gypsy girl.

1985 (*Family*) 60m/C **VHS, Beta $12.98** LIV, FHE, WTA

A Hungarian Fairy Tale *♪♪*

Title, packaging and plot outline makes this look likes a kids' picture, but it's a surreal, dense mass of symbolism about bureaucracy and Mozart's "The Magic Flute." After his single mother is killed, a boy searches for his real father, though the name and address he's got are fictions, concocted to satisfy government paperwork. For the art-film crowd. In Hungarian with English subtitles. **Hound Advisory:** Violence; alcohol use.

1987 (*College-Adult*) 97m/B Arpad Vermes, Maria Varga, Frantisek Husak, Eszter Csakanyi, Szilvia Toth, Judith Pogany, Geza Balkay; **D:** Gyula Gazdag. **VHS $59.95** EVD, INJ

The Hunt for Red October 🐾🐾🐾

Based on Tom Clancy's blockbuster novel, a high-tech Cold War yarn about a Soviet nuclear sub turning rogue and heading straight for U.S. waters, as both the U.S. and the U.S.S.R. try to stop it. Complicated, ill-plotted potboiler that succeeds breathlessly due to the cast and McTiernan's tommy-gun direction. Introduces the character of CIA analyst Jack Ryan who returns in "Patriot Games," though in the guise of Harrison Ford. **Hound Advisory:** Brief violence. **1990** (*PG/Jr. High-Adult*) 137m/C Sean Connery, Alec Baldwin, Richard Jordan, Scott Glenn, Joss Ackland, Sam Neill, James Earl Jones, Peter Firth, Tim Curry, Courtney B. Vance, Jeffrey Jones, Fred Dalton Thompson; **D:** John McTiernan; **W:** Larry Ferguson, Donald Stewart; **M:** Basil Poledouris. **Award Nominations:** Academy Awards '90: Best Film Editing, Best Sound; **Awards:** Academy Awards '90: Best Sound Effects Editing. **VHS, Beta, LV, 8mm, CD-I $14.95** *PAR, SUP*

Hurricane Express

One of the Wayne serials done by Mascot, a studio that later helped form Republic Pictures. But serial greatness was far away when Mascot did this tedious 12-chapter yarn in which the young Duke tries to find out the identity of The Wrecker, a villain whose acts of railroad sabotage cost the hero his father. **Hound Advisory:** Violence. **1932** (*Family*) 223m/B John Wayne, Joseph Girard, Conway Tearle, Shirley Grey; **D:** J.P. McGowan, Armand Schaefer. **VHS, Beta $16.95** *SNC, NOS, RHI*

Hyper-Sapien: People from Another Star 🐾◁

Two alien kids run away from UFO-sweet-UFO, accompanied by a space pal who looks like a big furry starfish. They befriend a Wyoming farmboy and get mistaken for assassins but don't worry, there's a happy - and illogical - ending. Haphazard pic, dedicated "to the young in spirit throughout the Universe," had a messy production history and it shows. **1986** (*PG/Family*) 93m/C Sydney Penny, Keenan Wynn, Gail Strickland, Ricky Paull Goldin, Peter Jason, Talia Shire; **D:** Peter Hunt. **VHS, Beta, LV $14.95** *WAR*

I Am a Fugitive from a Chain Gang 🐾🐾🐾🐾

WWI veteran Muni returns home with dreams of traveling across America. After a brief stint as a clerk, he strikes out on his own. Near penniless, Muni meets up with a tramp who takes him to get a hamburger. He becomes an unwilling accomplice when the bum suddenly robs the place. Convicted and sentenced to a Georgia chain gang, he's brutalized and degraded, though he eventually escapes and lives the life of a criminal on the run. Based on the autobiography by Robert E. Burns, timeless and thought-provoking classic combines brutal docu-details with powerhouse performances. Not a pretty picture and one that kids may have trouble hanging with, but an uncompromising expose worth the time for the mature. **1932** (*Jr. High-Adult*) 93m/B Paul Muni, Glenda Farrell, Helen Vinson, Preston Foster, Edward Ellis, Allen Jenkins; **D:** Mervyn LeRoy; **W:** Howard J. Green. **Award Nominations:** Academy Awards '33: Best Actor (Muni), Best Picture, Best Sound; **Awards:** National Board of Review Awards '32: 10 Best Films of the Year. **VHS, Beta $19.98** *MGM, FOX, CCB*

I am the Cheese 🐾🐾

An institutionalized boy undergoes psychiatric treatment; with the aid of his therapist (Wagner) he relives his traumatic childhood and finds out the truth about the death of his parents. A bit muddled, but has its moments. Adapted from a Robert Cormier teen novel. **Hound Advisory:** Salty language, mature themes. **1983** (*Jr. High-Adult*) 95m/C Robert MacNaughton, Hope Lange, Don Murray, Robert Wagner, Sudie Bond; **D:** Robert Jiras. **VHS, Beta $69.98** *LIV, VES*

I Confess 🐾🐾◁

When a priest (Clift) hears a murderer's confession, the circumstances seem to point to him as the prime suspect. Tepid, overly serious and occasionally interesting mid-career Hitchcock. Adapted from Paul Anthelme's 1902 play. **1953** (*Sr. High-Adult*) 95m/B Montgomery Clift, Anne Baxter, Karl Malden, Brian Aherne; **D:** Alfred Hitchcock. **VHS, Beta, LV $19.98** *WAR, FCT, MLB*

I Live with Me Dad 🐾◁

A vagrant drunk and his son fight the authorities for the right to be together. **1986** (*Family*) 86m/C Peter Hehir, Haydon Samuels; **D:** Paul Maloney. **VHS, Beta $79.98** *FOX*

I Love Trouble 🐾🐾◁

Veteran reporter Peter Brackett (sexy veteran Nolte) and ambitious cub reporter Sabrina Petersen (young and sexy Roberts) are competitors working for rival Chicago newspapers. When they begin to secretly exchange information on a big story, they find their lives threatened and their rivalry turning to romance. Some action, simplistic retro script, one big star, one sorta big star, and you've got the perfect movie package for the Prozac decade. Written, produced and directed by husband/wife team Meyers and Shyer. **Hound Advisory:** Violence. **1994** (*PG/Sr. High-Adult*) 123m/C Julia Roberts, Nick Nolte, Saul Rubinek, Robert Loggia, James Rebhorn; **D:** Charles Shyer; **W:** Nancy Myers, Charles Shyer. **VHS** *NYR*

I Never Sang For My Father 🐾🐾🐾◁

A devoted son must choose between caring for his cantankerous but well-meaning father, and moving out West to marry the divorced doctor whom he loves. While his mother wants him to stay near home, his sister, who fell out of her father's favor by marrying out of the family faith, argues that he should do what he wants. An introspective, stirring story based on the Robert Anderson play. **1970** (*PG/Jr. High-Adult*) 90m/C Gene Hackman, Melvyn Douglas, Estelle Parsons, Dorothy Stickney; **D:** Gilbert Cates; **W:** Robert Anderson. **Award Nominations:** Academy Awards '70: Best Actor (Douglas), Best Adapted Screenplay, Best Supporting Actor (Hackman); **Awards:** National Board of Review Awards '70: 10 Best Films of the Year. **VHS, Beta, LV $69.95** *COL*

I Ought to Be in Pictures 🐾🐾

After hitchhiking from New York to Hollywood to break into the movies, a teen-aged actress finds her father, a screenwriter, turned alcoholic and gambler. Far from the best Neil Simon comedies to hit the screen, but it does make points

about the perils of parenthood. **Hound Advisory:** Salty language, sex talk, alcohol use.
1982 (**PG**/*Jr. High-Adult*) 107m/C Walter Matthau, Ann-Margret, Dinah Manoff, Lance Guest, Michael Dudikoff; **D:** Herbert Ross; **W:** Neil Simon; **M:** Marvin Hamlisch. **VHS, Beta $59.98** *FOX*

I Remember Mama 🐾🐾🐾🎵

True Hollywood heart tugger chronicling the life of a Norwegian immigrant family living in San Francisco during the early 1900s. Dunne triumphs as the self-sacrificing mother, providing her family with wisdom and inspiration. A kindly father, four children, three high-strung aunts and an eccentric doctor who treats a live-in uncle round out this nuclear family. Adapted from John Van Druten's stage play, based on Kathryn Forbes memoirs, "Mama's Bank Account." A TV series came later.
1948 (*Family*) 95m/B Irene Dunne, Barbara Bel Geddes, Oscar Homolka, Ellen Corby, Cedric Hardwicke, Edgar Bergen, Rudy Vallee, Barbara O'Neil, Florence Bates; **D:** George Stevens. **Award Nominations:** Academy Awards '48: Best Actress (Dunne), Best Black and White Cinematography, Best Supporting Actor (Homolka), Best Supporting Actress (Corby, Bel Geddes); **Awards:** Golden Globe Awards '49: Best Supporting Actress (Corby). **VHS, Beta, LV $19.98** *CCB, RKO, TTC*

I Wanna Hold Your Hand 🐾🐾🐾

Funny slapstick recounting of the craziness surrounding the Beatle's first appearance on the "Ed Sullivan Show." Allen's about to be married but wants a night with one of the Liverpool lads, while Saldana is a photographer looking for the one great shot of the band to launch her career. Sperber and Deezen steal the show as groupies of the highest order. Warm and witty Spielberg production effectively captures craziness of the era. **Hound Advisory:** Roughhousing.
1978 (**PG**/*Jr. High-Adult*) 104m/C Nancy Allen, Bobby DiCicco, Wendie Jo Sperber, Marc McClure, Susan Kendall Newman, Theresa Saldana, Eddie Deezen, William Jordan; **D:** Robert Zemeckis; **W:** Robert Zemeckis. **VHS, Beta, LV $19.98** *WAR, FCT*

Ice Castles 🐾🐾

Teen figure skater's Olympic dreams are dimmed when she is blinded in an accident, but her boyfriend gives her the strength, encouragement, and love necessary to perform a small miracle. Way too schmaltzy.
1979 (**PG**) 110m/C Robby Benson, Lynn-Holly Johnson, Tom Skerritt, Colleen Dewhurst, Jennifer Warren, David Huffman; **D:** Donald Wrye; **M:** Marvin Hamlisch. **VHS, Beta $64.95** *COL*

Ice Pirates 🐾🎵

Space pirates in the far future steal blocks of ice to fill the needs of a thirsty galaxy. Cool plot has its moments. **Hound Advisory:** Violence, profanity, suggested sex.
1984 (**PG**/*Family*) 91m/C Robert Urich, Mary Crosby, Michael D. Roberts, John Matuszak, Anjelica Huston, Ron Perlman, John Carradine, Robert Symonds; **D:** Stewart Raffill; **W:** Stewart Raffill; **M:** Bruce Broughton. **VHS, Beta, LV $14.95** *MGM*

Ice Station Zebra 🐾🐾🎵

A nuclear submarine races Soviet seamen to find a downed Russian satellite under a polar ice cap. Suspenseful Cold War adventure based on the novel by Alistair MacLean.

1968 (**G**/*Family*) 148m/C Rock Hudson, Ernest Borgnine, Patrick McGoohan, Jim Brown, Lloyd Nolan, Tony Bill; **D:** John Sturges; **M:** Michel Legrand. **VHS, Beta, LV $19.98** *MGM*

Iceman 🐾🐾🐾

Frozen prehistoric man is brought back to life, after which severe culture shock takes hold. Sympathetic scientist Hutton tries to help. Underwritten but nicely acted, especially by Lone as the primal man. **Hound Advisory:** Violence and profanity.
1984 (**PG**/*Jr. High-Adult*) 101m/C Timothy Hutton, Lindsay Crouse, John Lone, David Strathairn, Josef Sommer, Danny Glover; **D:** Fred Schepisi; **W:** Chip Proser; **M:** Bruce Smeaton. **VHS, Beta, LV $69.95** *MCA*

Ida Fanfanny and Three Magical Tales

Three animated children's tales: "Louis James Hates School," "The Lightning and Thunder Case," "How to Dig a Hole to the Other Side of the World," and the title short.
1981 (*Preschool-Primary*) 49m/C **VHS, Beta $14.95** *NWV, WTA*

If Looks Could Kill 🐾🐾🎵

High school cutup travels to France with his class, gets mistaken for a CIA agent, and stumbles into a James-Bondish plot to take over all the money in the world. Much implausible action and I-was-a-teenaged-007 bits follow, but it's agreeably lightweight and leads to a rousing incendiary conclusion. **Hound Advisory:** Profanity, violence, and sex talk, but no extremes in those departments.
1991 (**PG-13**/*Jr. High-Adult*) 89m/C Richard Grieco, Linda Hunt, Roger Rees, Robin Bartlett, Gabrielle Anwar, Roger Daltrey, Geraldine James, Carole Davis; **D:** William Dear; **W:** Fred Dekker; **M:** David Foster. **VHS, Beta, LV, 8mm $19.98** *WAR*

I'll Do Anything 🐾🐾🎵

Struggling actor lands a job as chauffeur to a powerful Hollywood producer, but even that doesn't seem to boost his thespian career. Meanwhile his small daughter - left with him when his ex-wife went to prison - gets a dream role as kiddie star of a TV sitcom. Sharply written comedy (which once was a musical with songs by the guy who used to be called Prince) suffers from a distinctly split personality; half is a satire of showbiz with a heavy 'insider' feel (and heavier profanity), while the rest is a truly touching picture of a man coping with emergency fatherhood, to a somewhat spooky girl trained since infancy by her unstable mother to distrust him. Uneven (it should be, having been completely recut after previews) but worthwhile. **Hound Advisory:** Profanity, brief nudity, sex, mature themes.
1993 (**PG-13**/*Jr. High-Adult*) 115m/C Nick Nolte, Albert Brooks, Julie Kavner, Whittni Wright, Joely Richardson, Tracey Ullman; **D:** James L. Brooks; **W:** James L. Brooks; **M:** Hans Zimmer. **VHS, LV, 8mm** *COL*

I'm a Little Teapot

Includes the title song plus a host of other children's nursery songs and rhyme actions to encourage children to play along.
1993 (*Preschool*) 40m/C **VHS $9.98** *FFF, SVI*

I'm Not Oscar's Friend Anymore...and Other Stories

Animated tale of friendship and differences along with the stories "Creole," "Hug Me," and "Birds of a Feather."
1991 *(Primary)* 30m/C **VHS $7.95** *BTV*

Immediate Family

Childless couple contact a pregnant, unmarried girl and her boyfriend in hopes of adoption. As the pregnancy advances, the girl has doubts about giving up her baby. Good acting from a big screen cast elevates this to about the level of the usual surrogate-motherhood TV-movie. **Hound Advisory:** Sex talk, mature themes, profanity.
1989 **(PG-13/***Jr. High-Adult)* 112m/C Glenn Close, James Woods, Kevin Dillon, Mary Stuart Masterson, Kevin Dillon, Linda Darlow, Jane Greer, Jessica James, Mimi Kennedy; *D:* Jonathan Kaplan; *W:* Barbara Benedek; *M:* Brad Fiedel. **VHS, Beta, LV $19.95** *COL*

Improper Channels

Mediocre comedy about a subject that's less and less a basis for family gags - child abuse. Zealous social worker snatches a six-year-old from the hospital, falsely thinking she's being beaten at home. Dad loses his job and his credit, and the lawyers smell blood. There's a point being made here about mindless bureaucracy, if you can get over the queasy premise. **Hound Advisory:** Salty language.
1982 **(PG/***Jr. High-Adult)* 91m/C Monica Parker, Alan Arkin, Mariette Hartley; *D:* Eric Till. **VHS, Beta, LV $69.95** *VES*

The In Crowd

Bright high school guy crashes a Philadelphia TV dance-party show circa 1965, and must choose between uncertain broadcast fame and going to college. Rose-colored look at the era, with swell dancing but a central romance that sputters because the girl character gets a bimbo treatment. Nonetheless, a more wholesome alternative to "Grease." Leitch is the son of folk singer Donovan. **Hound Advisory:** Mild roughhousing. Nice detail has feuding young men work out their differences not through fights but impromptu dance contest.
1988 **(PG/***Jr. High-Adult)* 96m/C Donovan Leitch, Jennifer Runyon, Scott Plank, Joe Pantoliano; *D:* Mark Rosenthal; *W:* Mark Rosenthal. **VHS, Beta, LV $19.98** *ORI*

In Search of a Golden Sky

Following their mother's death, a group of city-bred children move to the mountains and join their secluded, cabin-dwelling uncle, much to the righteous chagrin of the welfare department. Wholesome but unexceptional nature drama.
1984 **(PG/***Jr. High-Adult)* 94m/C Charles Napier, George Flower, Cliff Osmond; *D:* Jefferson Richard. **VHS, Beta $79.98** *FOX*

In Search of the Castaways

Stirring adventure tale of a teenage girl and her younger brother searching for their father, a ship's captain lost at sea years earlier. Powerful special effects and strong cast make this a winning Disney effort. Based on a story by Jules Verne.

1962 *(Family)* 98m/C Hayley Mills, Maurice Chevalier, George Sanders, Wilfrid Hyde-White, Michael Anderson Jr.; *D:* Robert Stevenson. **VHS, Beta $19.99** *DIS*

In the Army Now

Pauly dude gets his head shaved, man. Service comedy about a slacker who joins the Army hoping to cash in on military benefits but who winds up in combat instead. Shore drops the Valley Guy shtick and ventures into the land of action when he gets sent on a mission to the Sahara. Strictly for Shore's fans. **Hound Advisory:** Profanity and sex talk.
1994 **(PG/***Jr. High-Adult)* 93m/C Pauly Shore, Esai Morales, Lori Petty, David Alan Grier, Ernie Hudson, Andy Dick; *D:* Dan Petrie Jr.; *W:* Dan Petrie Jr., Ken Kaufman, Fax Bahr, Stu Krieger, Adam Small. **VHS**

Incident at Hawk's Hill

The Allen Eckert book comes to life in this TV drama from Disney about Ben, a lonely boy who finds it difficult to talk to people and finds peace, love and understanding as he befriends animals.
1990 *(Preschool-Primary)* 29m/C **VHS, Beta $250.00** *MTI, DSN*

Incredible Agent of Stingray

Captain Troy Tempest and the Stingray crew take an underwater voyage to rescue a beautiful woman kept prisoner in Titanica. Compilation of the British "Stingray" puppet sci-fi series.
1980 *(Preschool-Primary)* 93m/C **VHS, Beta** *FHE*

The Incredible Hulk

Bixby is a scientist who achieves superhuman strength after he is exposed to a massive dose of gamma rays. But his personal life suffers, as does his wardrobe. Ferrigno is the Hulkster. The pilot for the TV series is based on the Marvel Comics character. Later TV feature film specials were broadcast and released to video; they include "The Incredible Hulk Returns," "The Trial of the Incredible Hulk," and "The Death of the Incredible Hulk." **Hound Advisory:** Violence.
1977 *(Family)* 94m/C Bill Bixby, Susan Sullivan, Lou Ferrigno, Jack Colvin; *D:* Kenneth Johnson. **VHS, Beta, LV $19.95** *MCA*

The Incredible Hulk Returns

The muscular green mutant is back, and in this TV movie he meets another of the Marvel Comics superheroes, the mild-mannered guy who changes into the Viking warrior named Thor. Paper-thin fantasy was designed as the pilot for a Thor TV series that never took flight on its own. The next feature, "The Trial of the Incredible Hulk," attempted to do the same for the comic character Daredevil. **Hound Advisory:** Roughhousing.
1988 *(Family)* 100m/C Bill Bixby, Lou Ferrigno, Jack Colvin, Lee Purcell, Charles Napier, Steve Levitt; *D:* Nick Corea. **VHS, LV $19.95** *STE, NWV*

The Incredible Journey

Labrador retriever, bull terrier and Siamese cat mistake their caretaker's intentions when he leaves for a hunting trip. Believing he's gone forever, the trio set out on a 250-mile, peril filled trek across Canada's rugged terrain to find their

master. Told straightforwardly from the critters' point of view, this entertaining Disney adventure from Sheila Burnford's book suffers mainly from being copied and ripped off so often. Still stands up well, even next to the same studio's own clever remake "Homeward Bound."
1963 (*Family*) 80m/C *D:* Fletcher Markle. **VHS, Beta $69.95** *DIS*

The Incredible Mr. Limpet 𝄞𝄞◁

Reverse of "The Little Mermaid" has Knotts perfectly cast as a henpecked, nebbish bookkeeper who falls into the sea and transforms into a fish, fulfilling his aquatic dreams. Eventually he falls in love with another fish and helps the U.S. Navy find Nazi subs during WWII. Partially animated (by Warner Brothers), beloved by some, particularly those under the age of seven. Based on Theodore Pratt's novel.
1964 (*Family*) 99m/C Don Knotts, Jack Weston, Carole Cook, Andrew Duggan, Larry Keating, Elizabeth McRae; *D:* Arthur Lubin. **VHS, Beta, LV $14.95** *WAR, WTA*

The Incredible Rocky Mountain Race 𝄞𝄞

Townspeople of St. Joseph, fed up with Mark Twain's destructive feud with neighbor Mike Fink, devise a shrewd scheme to rid the town of the troublemakers by sending them on a road race through the west. A tall tale of short stature, made-for TV and starring recruits of the sitcom "F-Troop."
1977 (*Family*) 97m/C Christopher Connelly, Forrest Tucker, Larry Storch, Mike Mazurki; *D:* James L. Conway. **VHS, Beta $19.95** *STE*

The Incredible Shrinking Woman 𝄞𝄞◁

"Kids, I shrunk Honey!" Inoffensive social satire finds household cleaners (that daddy advertises) producing some strange side effects on a housewife, slowly shrinking her to doll size. She tries to get on with life as normal, but gets kidnapped by evil scientists, befriends lab gorilla. Sight gags and fancy sets abound but the cuteness wears thin by the end. **Hound Advisory:** Salty language, sex talk.
1981 (PG/*Jr. High-Adult*) 89m/C Lily Tomlin, Charles Grodin, Ned Beatty, Henry Gibson; *D:* Joel Schumacher; *W:* Jane Wagner. **VHS, Beta, LV $14.98** *MCA*

The Incredible Two-Headed Transplant WOOF!

Mad scientist Dern has a criminal head transplanted on to the shoulder of big John Bloom and the critter runs amuck. Low-budget special effects guaranteed to give you a headache or two. Watch for onetime Pat "Marilyn Munster" Priest in a bikini.
1971 (PG/*Jr. High-Adult*) 88m/C Bruce Dern, Pat Priest, Casey Kasem, Albert Cole, John Bloom, Berry Kroeger; *D:* Anthony M. Lanza. **VHS** *NO*

The Incredible Voyage of Stingray 𝄞𝄞

A marionette adventure spinoff of Gerry Anderson's British "Thunderbirds" series, about the crew of the undersea vessel Stingray and their quest to save the beautiful Marina from captivity in the land of Titanica.
1980 (*Family*) 93m/C **VHS, Beta, LV $39.95** *FHE*

Indian Paint 𝄞𝄞

Okay children's adventure set amid Plains Indian tribes before contact with the white man (though everybody speaks English anyway). Young brave Nishko forms a friendship with a newborn colt that later saves his life. Nishko's chieftain father is played by Silverheels, the great Native American actor who was Tonto in the "Lone Ranger" movies and TV show. Based on the novel by Glenn Balch. **Hound Advisory:** Violence in battles with an enemy tribe.
1964 (*Primary*) 90m/C Jay Silverheels, Johnny Crawford, Pat Hogan, Robert Crawford Jr., George Lewis; *D:* Norman Foster. **VHS, Beta $19.95** *VCI*

Indian Summer 𝄞𝄞◁

Yet another addition to the growing thirtysomething nostalgia genre. Delete the big house, add a crusty camp director (Arkin), change the characters' names (but not necessarily their lives) and you feel like you're experiencing deja vu. This time seven friends and the requisite outsider reconvene at Camp Tamakwa, the real-life summer camp to writer/director Binder. The former campers talk. They yearn. They save Camp Tamakwa and experience personal growth. A must see for those who appreciate listening to situational jokes that are followed by "I guess you had to be there." Good cast works hard, though the standout is probably Raimi as a camp maintenance guy. **Hound Advisory:** Profanity; brief nudity; drug use; sex.
1993 (PG-13/*Jr. High-Adult*) 108m/C Alan Arkin, Matt Craven, Diane Lane, Bill Paxton, Elizabeth Perkins, Kevin Pollak, Sam Raimi, Vincent Spano, Julie Warner, Kimberly Williams, Richard Chevolleau; *D:* Mike Binder; *W:* Mike Binder; *M:* Miles Goodman. **VHS, Beta, LV $19.99** *TOU, FCT*

Indiana Jones and the Last Crusade 𝄞𝄞𝄞

In the third Indiana Jones adventure, we find the fearless archaeologist once again up against the Nazis in a race to find a powerful religious artifact, this time the Holy Grail. Rerun syndrome is not entirely cured by the added attraction of Connery as Indy's domineering father. Splendid opening setup goes back to the hero's boyhood (he's played by Phoenix) and his first adventure; Indy fans even get the origin of the infamous fedora. More chases, exotic places, dastardly villains, and daring escapes. **Hound Advisory:** Violence, sex talk.
1989 (PG/*Jr. High-Adult*) 126m/C Harrison Ford, Sean Connery, Denholm Elliott, Alison Doody, Julian Glover, John Rhys-Davies, River Phoenix, Michael Byrne, Alex Hyde-White; *D:* Steven Spielberg; *W:* Jeffrey Boam; *M:* John Williams. **VHS, Beta, LV, 8mm $14.95** *PAR, SUP, TLF*

Indiana Jones and the Temple of Doom 𝄞𝄞𝄞◁

Daredevil archaeologist Jones is back and literally dropped into a quest for a magic stone and a ruthless cult in India that enslaves hundreds of children. Enough action for ten movies,

f/x galore, and less regard for plot than original "Raiders of the Lost Ark." That actually helps the roller-coaster ride of nearly nonstop thrills. Stirred a debate over movie gore; nightmarish heart-removal/human-sacrifice scene is unrealistic but still too much for tot viewers. On the other hand, Indy has a terrific rapport with kid companion Quan, more believable than his romance with the prissy showgirl heroine. **Hound Advisory:** Violence, occasional profanity, foreign stereotypes, alcohol use.
1984 (PG/*Primary-Adult*) 118m/C Harrison Ford, Kate Capshaw, Ke Huy Quan, Amrish Puri; **D:** Steven Spielberg; **W:** Willard Huyck, Gloria Katz; **M:** John Williams. **Award Nominations:** Academy Awards '84: Best Original Score; **Awards:** Academy Awards '84: Best Visual Effects. **VHS, Beta, LV, 8mm** $14.95 *PAR, APD*

Infra-Man WOOF!

If you're looking for a movie as good/bad as the Mighty Morphin Power Rangers, this Japanese import is it. Infra-Man, who seems to be Ultraman but with more side paneling, is a superhero rescuing the galaxy from evil Princess Dragon Mom and her army of mutant monsters. Outlandish dialogue, garish special f/x and costumes, plus kung fu, all badly dubbed in English. What more could you ask for? **Hound Advisory:** Violence.
1976 (PG/*Family*) 92m/C Li Hsiu-hsien, Wang Hsieh, Yuan Man-tzu, Terry Liu, Tsen Shu-yi, Huang Chien-lung, Lu Sheng; **D:** Hua-Shan; **W:** Peter Fernandez. **VHS, Beta** $49.95 *PSM*

Innerspace 🦴🦴◁

Space pilot, miniaturized for a journey through a lab rat a la "Fantastic Voyage," is accidentally injected into a nebbish supermarket clerk, and together they nab some bad guys and get the girl. Award-winning special effects support some funny moments between micro Quaid and nerdy Short, with Ryan producing the confused romantic interest. **Hound Advisory:** Profanity; violence.
1987 (PG/*Jr. High-Adult*) 120m/C Dennis Quaid, Martin Short, Meg Ryan, Kevin McCarthy, Fiona Lewis, Henry Gibson, Robert Picardo, John Hora, Wendy Schaal, Orson Bean, Chuck Jones, William Schallert, Dick Miller, Vernon Wells, Harold Sylvester, Kevin Hooks, Kathleen Freeman, Kenneth Tobey; **D:** Joe Dante; **W:** Jeffrey Boam, Chip Proser; **M:** Jerry Goldsmith. **VHS, Beta, LV, 8mm** $14.95 *WAR*

Inspector Clouseau: Ape Suzette

Five cartoons from the Pink Panther's peerless pursuer, an accident-prone French detective and his gendarme pal, Deaux-Deaux. Included are "Ape Suzette," "The Pique Poquette of Paris," "Sicque! Sicque! Sicque!," "Unsafe and Seine," and "That's No Lady, That's Notre Dame."
1966 (*Family*) 35m/C **V:** Pat Harrington. **VHS** $29.98 *MGM, WTA*

Inspector Clouseau: Napoleon Blown-Aparte

Four more cartoons from the bumbling French detective and his little Spanish buddy. Included are "Cirrhosis of the Louvre," "Napoleon Blown-Apart," "Reaux Reaux Reaux Your Boat," "Plastered in Paris," and "Cock-a-Doodle Deaux Deaux."
1966 (*Family*) 35m/C **V:** Pat Harrington. **VHS** $29.98 *MGM, WTA*

Inspector Gadget, Vol. 1

Comedian Adams lends his voice to the versatile cartoon Inspector Gadget, who, along with his trusted companions Penny and Brain, go up against the evil Dr. Claw. Additional volumes available.
1983 (*Preschool-Primary*) 60m/C **V:** Don Adams. **VHS, Beta** *FHE, LIV*

International Velvet 🦴🦴◁

In this belated sequel to "National Velvet," adult Velvet, with live-in companion, grooms her orphaned niece (O'Neal) to become an Olympic champion horsewoman. Good photography and performances by Plummer and Hopkins manage to keep the sentiment at a trot.
1978 (PG/*Primary-Adult*) 126m/C Tatum O'Neal, Anthony Hopkins, Christopher Plummer; **D:** Bryan Forbes. **VHS, Beta** $59.95 *MGM*

Into the West 🦴🦴🦴◁

Seamless mix of magic and gritty reality in present-day Ireland. Shattered by his wife's death, gypsy Riley quits his caravan and moves with his small sons to a Dublin housing project, where the boys have a hard time hiding a mystical white horse that suddenly appears. Cops seize the champion-grade animal to sell to a businessman, but the children liberate the horse and hightail it on a wild cross-country chase. Outstanding all-ages entertainment, a hit in Britain that never found a proper audience in US theaters but was released widely on video through Disney. **Hound Advisory:** Alcohol use, roughhousing.
1992 (PG/*Jr. High-Adult*) 92m/C Gabriel Byrne, Ellen Barkin, Ciaran Fitzgerald, Ruaidhri Conroy, David Kelly, Colm Meaney; **D:** Mike Newell; **W:** Jim Sheridan; **M:** Patrick Doyle. **VHS, LV** $96.83 *TOU*

Invaders from Mars 🦴🦴◁

Sci-fi juvie favorite about little David seeing a flying saucer bury itself behind his house. He can't convince grownups, though, and parents and playmates are soon possessed by the alien beings. Though a cheapo budget shows (note the balloons bobbing on walls of the Martians' 'glass' cave stronghold), this tale can be enjoyed as both a basic kid adventure and on a deeper level as a small boy's viewpoint of adult society -dominant, threatening and sometimes hostile as any green space invader. Video release includes previews of coming attractions from classic science fiction films. **Hound Advisory:** Violence.
1953 (*Jr. High-Adult*) 78m/C Helena Carter, Arthur Franz, Jimmy Hunt, Leif Erickson; **D:** William Cameron Menzies. **VHS, Beta** $19.95 *MED, MLB*

Invaders from Mars 🦴🦴

Adequate but pointless remake of the 1953 semi-classic about a Martian invasion perceived only by one young boy and a sympathetic school nurse (played by mother and son Black and Carson). Jimmy Hunt, child star of the first flick, cameos here as an adult cop; otherwise Stan Winston's colorful creature f/x are the attractions of this timekiller. **Hound Advisory:** Salty language, violence.

1986 (PG/Jr. High-Adult) 102m/C Hunter Carson, Karen Black, Louise Fletcher, Laraine Newman, Timothy Bottoms, Bud Cort; *D:* Tobe Hooper; *W:* Dan O'Bannon, Don Jakoby. **VHS, Beta, LV** $39.95 *MED, IME*

Invasion of the Body Snatchers 🐾🐾🐾◁

One of the few instances where a remake is an improvement on the original, which was itself a classic. This time, the "pod people" are infesting San Francisco, with only a small group of people aware of the invasion. A ceaselessly inventive, creepy version of the alien-takeover paradigm, with an intense and winning performance by Sutherland. **Hound Advisory:** Violence.
1978 (PG/Jr. High-Adult) 115m/C Donald Sutherland, Brooke Adams, Veronica Cartwright, Leonard Nimoy, Jeff Goldblum, Kevin McCarthy, Don Siegel, Art Hindle; *D:* Philip Kaufman; *W:* W.D. Richter. **VHS, Beta, LV** $14.95 *MGM*

The Invisible Boy 🐾🐾◁

Vintage sci-fi was conceived as an encore for the 'Robby the Robot' character created for the sci-fi classic "Forbidden Planet." This is a more juvenile but still worthwhile adventure in which a kid named Timmie builds and befriends a mighty mechanical man. An evil supercomputer takes control of Robby, and the robot must decide whether to lead a machine takeover or defend his young master. **Hound Advisory:** Roughhousing.
1957 (G/Family) 89m/C Richard Eyer, Diane Brewster, Phillip Abbott, Harold J. Stone; *D:* Hermann Hoffman; *W:* Cyril Hume; *M:* Les Baxter. **VHS** $19.98 *MGM, FCT*

The Invisible Monster

Special investigators Lane Carlson and Carol Richards battle a mad scientist ready to take over the world with this invisible army. 12-episode serial.
1950 (Family) 167m/B Richard Webb, Aline Towne, Lane Bradford, Stanley Price, John Crawford, George Meeker; *D:* Fred Brannon. **VHS** $29.98 *REP*

Invitation to the Dance 🐾🐾◁

The MGM musical studio gave Kelly free reign to make his dream project, and this is it; three exuberant, dialogue-free short pieces, pure dancing. First two are bittersweet love stories, one set in a circus, the other following a ring that passes between several sets of (unfaithful) partners. Kids may or may not get those, but viewers of all ages will be enthralled by the concluding "Sinbad the Sailor" segment, in which Kelly dances with two animated palace guards, fearsomely drawn by the Hanna-Barbera cartoonists. Colorful, vastly underrated film that was, sadly, a commercial disappointment in its day.
1956 (Family) 93m/C Gene Kelly, Igor Youskevitch, Tamara Toumanova; *D:* Gene Kelly. **VHS, Beta** $19.98 *MGM, CCB*

Ira Sleeps Over

Young boy is invited to sleep over at his friend's house for the first time, and must decide whether to bring his teddy bear or brave it alone.
1988 (Primary-Jr. High) 13m/C **VHS** *FHE,*

Iron Will 🐾🐾

Disney movie based on a true story and a script that had sat around since the early '70s. Maybe if they waited another 20 years its cliches would be back in style. In 1917 newly fatherless South Dakota teen Will Stoneman needs money for college. He enters a 500-mile dogsled race, becoming a nationwide media sensation as he mushes through a treacherous route that daunts professional racers. Successfully evokes the physical danger in dogsledding, but the canned sentiment, a villain seemingly inspired by Scrooge McDuck, and plenty of pilferings from other movies dog the plot all the way to the finish line. **Hound Advisory:** Roughhousing.
1993 (PG/Jr. High-Adult) 109m/C MacKenzie Astin, Kevin Spacey, David Ogden Stiers, August Schellenberg, George Gerdes, John Terry; *D:* Charles Haid; *W:* John Michael Hayes, Jeffrey Arch, Djordje Milicevic; *M:* Joel McNeely. **VHS, LV** *DIS*

Irreconcilable Differences 🐾🐾◁

When her Beverly Hills parents spend more time working and fretting than giving hugs and love, a ten-year-old girl sues them for divorce on the grounds of "irreconcilable differences." Media has a field day when they hear that she would rather go live with the maid. Well cast, with solid characterizations, but goes for the humanely comical rather than uproarious gags.
1984 (PG/Jr. High-Adult) 112m/C Ryan O'Neal, Shelley Long, Drew Barrymore, Sam Wanamaker, Allen (Gooritz) Garfield, Sharon Stone, Luana Anders; *D:* Charles Shyer; *W:* Charles Shyer, Nancy Meyers. **VHS, Beta, LV** $29.98 *LIV, VES*

The Island at the Top of the World 🐾🐾

Rich Englishman, in search of his missing son, travels to the Arctic Circle in 1908 via a fantastic balloon (the dirigible is the real star of the show). The rescue party discovers a lost Viking kingdom in a fairly workaday Jules Verne-style adventure from Disney. Based on the novel "The Lost Ones" by Ian Cameron. **Hound Advisory:** Viking roughhousing.
1974 (G/Family) 93m/C David Hartman, Donald Sinden, Jacques Marin, Mako, David Gwillim; *D:* Robert Stevenson; *M:* Maurice Jarre. **VHS, Beta** $69.95 *DIS*

Island of Dr. Moreau 🐾🐾◁

This remake of the "Island of the Lost Souls" (1933) is a bit disappointing but worth watching for Lancaster's solid performance as the scientist who has isolated himself on a Pacific island in order to continue his chromosome research-he can transform animals into near-humans and humans into animals. Neat-looking critters. Adaptation of the H.G. Wells novel of the same title.
1977 (PG/Jr. High-Adult) 99m/C Burt Lancaster, Michael York, Nigel Davenport, Barbara Carrera, Richard Basehart; *D:* Don Taylor. **VHS, Beta** $19.98 *WAR, OM*

Island of the Blue Dolphins 🐾🐾◁

From the award-winning children's book by Scott O'Dell, this tells the tale of Karana, a young native girl left behind with her little brother on a Pacific island when their tribe abruptly leaves. The brother is killed by wild dogs, and Karana must

survive on her own. Ironically, the leader of the dog pack becomes her loyal companion. Early production from Robert Radnitz, later to do "Sounder" and other fine family fare of the '70s. This isn't in that league due to stilted performances and conventional handling, but what remains of O'Dell's story is occasionally stirring. **Hound Advisory:** Violence.
1964 (*Family*) 99m/C Celia Kaye, Larry Domasin, Ann Daniel, George Kennedy; **D:** James B. Clark. VHS, Beta $59.95 *MCA*

Islands 𝄩𝄩

Minor Canadian made-for-TV short feature about trouble-prone teen punk Lacey left with motherly island-dweller Maureen, in hopes that a rustic lifestyle will teach the girl responsibility. They fight, they make up, and when you hear Lacey is adopted it's no brilliant deduction why Maureen is so interested in her. Broadcast on PBS-TV's "WonderWorks," but issued on a separate video label from the others in that exceptional series. **Hound Advisory:** Roughhousing, in a rather unnecessary subplot about an obsessed boy stalking Lacey.
1987 (*Jr. High-Adult*) 55m/C Louise Fletcher. VHS, Beta $19.95 *NWV*

It Came from Hollywood

A compilation of scenes from "B" horror and science fiction films of the 1950s, highlighting the funny side of these classic schlock movies. Some sequences in black and white. **Hound Advisory:** Sexual references, scatological humor.
1982 (**PG**/*Jr. High-Adult*) 87m/C **D:** Malcolm Leo. VHS, Beta, LV $59.95 *PAR*

It Came Upon a Midnight Clear 𝄩𝄩

A heavenly miracle enables a retired (and dead) New York policeman to keep a Christmas promise to his grandson. Made for TV.
1984 (*Family*) 96m/C Mickey Rooney, Scott Grimes, George Gaynes, Annie Potts, Lloyd Nolan, Barrie Youngfellow; **D:** Peter Hunt. VHS, Beta $9.95 *GKK*

It Could Happen to You 𝄩𝄩𝄩

NYC cop Charlie Lang (Cage) doesn't have any change to leave coffee shop waitress Yvonne (Fonda) a tip, so he promises to drop by the next day and either double the tip or split his lottery ticket with her. When he nets four million dollars that evening, he makes good on the promise, much to the chagrin of his upwardly mobile wife (Perez). Feel-good romantic comedy is led by Cage's charm as the cop with a heart of gold and Fonda's winning waitress, but is nearly capsized by Perez's stereotypical Latin golddigger. Don't look for the diner on your next trip to NYC; it was specially built in TriBeCa and dismantled after the shoot. **Hound Advisory:** Roughhousing; salty language.
1994 (**PG**/*Sr. High-Adult*) 101m/C Bridget Fonda, Nicolas Cage, Rosie Perez, Red Buttons, Isaac Hayes, Seymour Cassel, Stanley Tucci, J.E. Freeman, Richard Jenkins, Ann Dowd, Wendell Pierce; **D:** Andrew Bergman; **W:** Jane Anderson, Andrew Bergman. VHS *NYR*

It Happened at the World's Fair 𝄩𝄩𝄩

Fun and light romance comedy has Elvis and a companion (O'Brien) being escorted through the Seattle World's Fair by a fetching Chinese girl. ♫I'm Falling In Love Tonight; They Remind Me Too Much Of You; Take Me To The Fair; Relax; How Would You Like To Be; Beyond the Bend; One Broken Heart For Sale; Cotton Candy Land; A World Of Our Own.
1963 (*Family*) 105m/C Elvis Presley, Joan O'Brien, Gary Lockwood, Kurt Russell, Edith Atwater, Yvonne Craig; **D:** Norman Taurog. VHS, Beta $14.95 *MGM*

It Happened in New Orleans 𝄩𝄩

Vehicle for boy actor/singer Breen, regarded at the time as a sort of male counterpart to Shirley Temple. Except Breen's flicks haven't aged as well, and in this sentimental example he's cared for by a faithful former slave in post-Civil War New Orleans. His grandmother finally takes him to his resentful family in New York, but the kid's charm overcomes all hostilities.
1936 (*Family*) 86m/B Bobby Breen, May Robson, Alan Mowbray, Benita Hume. VHS, Beta $24.95 *VYY*

It Happened One Night 𝄩𝄩𝄩𝄩

Classic Capra comedy about an antagonistic couple determined to teach each other about life. Colbert is an unhappy heiress who runs away from her affluent home in search of contentment. On a bus she meets newspaper reporter Gable, who teaches her how "real" people live. She returns the favor in this first of the 1930s screwball comedies. The plot is a framework for an amusing examination of war between the sexes. Colbert and Gable are superb as affectionate foes. Remade as the musicals "Eve Knew Her Apples" and "You Can't Run Away From It."
1934 (*Family*) 105m/B Clark Gable, Claudette Colbert, Roscoe Karns, Walter Connolly, Alan Hale, Ward Bond; **D:** Frank Capra; **W:** Robert Riskin. VHS, Beta, LV $19.95 *COL, BTV, HMV*

It's a Dog's Life 𝄩𝄩𝄩

The hero and narrator of this story is a wily bull terrier called Wildfire. He's a tough dog on the mean streets of the Bowery in turn-of-the-century New York and his master has him in dog fights in the local saloon but then abandons him. Wildfire is taken in by the kindly employee of the rich and dog-hating Jagger but naturally manages to win the codger over. Based on the short story "The Bar Sinister" by Richard Harding Davis.
1955 (*Family*) 87m/C Jeff Richards, Edmund Gwenn, Dean Jagger; **D:** Hermann Hoffman; **W:** John Michael Hayes; **M:** Elmer Bernstein. VHS $19.98 *FCT*

It's a Short Summer, Charlie Brown

A "Peanuts" TV cartoon special: Charlie, Lucy, and the gang go off to camp for the summer.
19?? (*Family*) 25m/C VHS $9.99 *VTR*

It's a Wonderful Life 🦴🦴🦴🦴

American classic about downtrodden George Bailey, saved from suicide by Clarence the Angel, who then shows the hero how secretly important he's been to his loved ones and community. Corny but inspirational and heartwarming, with endearing characters and performances. Christmas-themed, but perfect year-round for people who want to feel good, joyfully teetering on the border between Hollywood schmaltz and genuine heartbreak. Also available colorized. Laserdisc version includes production and publicity stills, the theatrical trailer, and commentary by film professor Jeanine Basinger. Also available in a 160-minute Collector's Edition with original preview trailer, "The Making of 'It's a Wonderful Life,'" and a new digital transfer from the original negative. **Hound Advisory:** Alcohol use, roughhousing. **1946** (*Family*) 125m/B James Stewart, Donna Reed, Henry Travers, Thomas Mitchell, Lionel Barrymore, Samuel S. Hinds, Frank Faylen, Gloria Grahame, H.B. Warner, Ellen Corby, Sheldon Leonard, Beulah Bondi, Ward Bond, Frank Albertson, Todd Karns, Mary Treen, Charles Halton; **D:** Frank Capra; **W:** Francis Goodrich, Albert Hacket, Jo Swerling; **M:** Dimitri Tiomkin. **Award Nominations:** Academy Awards '46: Best Actor (Stewart), Best Director (Capra), Best Film Editing, Best Picture, Best Sound; **Awards:** Golden Globe Awards '47: Best Director (Capra). **VHS, LV** $9.95 *IGP, MRV, CNG*

It's Not Easy Being Green

Children's sing-along presentation features Kermit, Miss Piggy, Fozzie, and Gonzo singing thirteen of the Muppets most popular tunes. ♪Kokomo; Splish Splash; Octopus' Garden; Pass It On; Movin' Right Along; Somewhere Over the Rainbow; Bein' Green; BBQ; Frog Talk. **1994** (*Preschool-Primary*) 37m/C Jim Henson's Muppets. **VHS** $12.99 *JHV, BVV*

It's the Great Pumpkin, Charlie Brown (triple feature)

In addition to Linus' telling of the "Great Pumpkin" legend, this three-episode collection includes "What a Nightmare Charlie Brown," and "It Was A Short Summer, Charlie Brown." **1966** (*Family*) 77m/C **VHS, Beta** $14.95 *SHV*

It's the Muppets, Vol. 1: Meet the Muppets

Comedy bits gathered from TV's "Muppet Show," including Kermit and Miss Piggy, Pigs in Space, piano-playing chickens, and lots of production numbers. Additional volumes available. **1992** (*Family*) 37m/C **VHS** $12.99 *JHV*

It's the Wolf

Collection of 12 cartoon episodes featuring Hanna-Barbera less-than-headliners like Lambsy, Mildew Wolf, and Bristle Hound. **1984** (*Preschool-Primary*) 80m/C **VHS, Beta** $19.95 *TTC, WTA*

Jabberjaw

Four episodes from the Saturday-morning Hanna-Barbera cartoon about a friendly blue shark and his seagoing human friends in the year 2021. **1978** (*Preschool-Primary*) 85m/C **VHS, Beta** $19.95 *TTC, WTA*

Jabberwocky 🦴🦴

Chaos prevails in the medieval kingdom of King Bruno the Questionable, who rules with cruelty, stupidity, lust, and dust. Jabberwocky is the big dragon mowing everything down in its path until a hero decides to take it on. Uneven, undisciplined work by remnants of the Monty Python team who would subsequently do such wonderfully warped fairy tales as "Time Bandits" and "The Adventures of Baron Munchausen." **Hound Advisory:** Violence, sex talk. **1977** (*PG/Jr. High-Adult*) 104m/C Michael Palin, Eric Idle, Max Wall, Deborah Fallender, Terry Jones, John Le Mesurier; **D:** Terry Gilliam; **W:** Terry Gilliam. **VHS, Beta, LV** $19.95 *COL*

Jack & the Beanstalk 🦴🦴

While babysitting, Costello falls asleep and dreams he's Jack in this weak spoof of the classic fairy tale. In keeping with the low budget, the 'giant' (Baer) seems unusually small for a member of the fe-fi-fo-fum crowd. **1952** (*Family*) 78m/C Bud Abbott, Lou Costello, Buddy Baer; **D:** Jean Yarborough. **VHS, Beta, LV** $19.95 *NOS, VCI, VTR*

Jack & the Beanstalk 🦴🦴

Animated musical version of the familiar story of Jack, the young boy who climbs a magic beanstalk up into the clouds, where he meets a fearsome giant. **1976** (*Family*) 80m/C **D:** Peter J. Solmo; **W:** Peter J. Solmo. **VHS, Beta** *COL*

Jack and the Beanstalk

Michael Palin (Monty Python, "A Fish Called Wanda") and the Eurythmics' own Dave Stewart team up for a memorable rendition of this classic tale. Fi, Fye, Fo, Fum! Part of the "Rabbit Ears" series of recited tales (against lush, painted illustrations) from different countries and cultures. **1991** (*Family*) 30m/C **M:** Dave Stewart. **VHS, Beta** $9.95 *MCA, FCT*

Jack Frost

Made-for-television Christmas special tells of the spritely Jack Frost's love for a human maiden via stop-motion model animation ("Animagic") perfected by the Rankin-Bass group. **1979** (*Family*) 48m/C **V:** Buddy Hackett, Robert Morse, Dave Garroway. **VHS, Beta, 8mm** $14.98 *LIV, WTA*

Jack the Bear 🦴◁

Exercise in neuroses centering on a father and his two boys, trying to pick up the pieces after the death of mom. Dad, who hosts a late-night horror show, is cuddly as a bear - when he's not drinking. While the talent and circumstances might have been enough to create a sensitive study, the emotion is completely overwrought by contrived plot, including a kidnapping by the local Nazi. It's like a cement block dropped on a card house. Point made, but so much for subtlety. Based on a novel by Dan McCall. **Hound Advisory:** Alcohol use, mature themes, violence.

1993 (PG-13/*Jr. High-Adult*) 98m/C Danny DeVito, Robert J. Steinmiller Jr., Miko Hughes, Gary Sinise, Art LaFleur, Andrea Marcovicci, Julia Louis-Dreyfus, Reese Witherspoon; *D:* Marshall Herskovitz; *W:* Steven Zaillian; *M:* James Horner. **VHS, LV $19.98** *FXV*

Jack the Giant Killer 📽📽

Brave young farmer, aided by a leprechaun, journeys to rescue a princess from an evil wizard. Along the way Jack fights giants and monsters, who unfortunately get cuter and cuddlier, not scarier, as the fairytale plot progresses. Economy-minded imitation of the classic Ray Harryhausen stop-motion adventures, this has school-pageant-level dialogue, costumes and mentality, with just adequate special effects from "Gumby" animator Jim Danforth. Filmed in 'Fantascope.' Right. **Hound Advisory:** Monster roughhousing.
1962 (G/*Family*) 95m/C Kerwin Mathews, Judi Meredith, Torin Thatcher, Walter Burke, Roger Mobley, Barry Kelley, Don Beddoe, Anna Lee, Robert Gist; *D:* Nathan Juran. **VHS, Beta, LV $14.95** *MGM, FCT*

Jacob Have I Loved

Award-winning offering from PBS-TV's "WonderWorks" vividly dramatizes the pain felt by Louise, a hardworking teenage girl in an isolated, deeply religious Chesapeake Bay community during WWII. All her life Louise has seen her simpering sister Caroline get all the attention and advantages. Then Louise takes a stand and befriends an outcast fisherman — and when he too seems to favor Caroline, the heroine feels more cheated than ever. Tale is flawed mainly by its short running time; you don't want this emotional family saga to end so suddenly. An abridgment of the source novel by Katherine Paterson.
1988 (*Family*) 57m/C Bridget Fonda, Jenny Robertson, John Kellogg; *D:* Victoria Hochberg. **VHS $29.95** *PME, WNE, RHU*

Jacob Two: Two Meets the Hooded Fang

Engaging, one-of-a-kind family film from Canada, based on a Mordecai Richter story. Jacob Two-Two (who has to say everything twice, since adults never listen to a kid the first time) dreams he's taken to a gloomy prison just for youngsters who give grief to grownups. The Hooded Fang is the bumbling, child-hating warden, an ex-pro wrestler. Fortunately Jacob has friends on the outside in the shape of zany superheroes who will rescue him if only he can get a message out. Production difficulties and deficiencies of a modest budget hold back tale somewhat, though it's still richly deserving and worth hunting up on tape.
1979 (*Primary*) 90m/C Alex Karras; *D:* Theodore J. Flicker. **VHS, Beta $69.98** *LIV*

Jamaica Inn 📽📽

In old Cornwall, an orphan girl becomes involved with smugglers. Below-average Hitchcock, though stellar cast makes it interesting. Based on the story by Daphne Du Maurier and remade for British TV in 1982.
1939 (*Jr. High-Adult*) 98m/B Charles Laughton, Maureen O'Hara, Leslie Banks, Robert Newton; *D:* Alfred Hitchcock. **VHS, Beta $16.95** *SNC, NOS, CAB*

James Bond, Jr.

The animated adventures of this young hero as he battles deranged criminals to save the world from disaster. Despite his name, the junior version of the suave James Bond is actually the nephew of the randy spy. James, Jr. attends a British boarding school with progeny of other characters from 007 movies and battles an evil organization known as S.C.U.M.
1992 (*Family*) ?m/C **VHS $9.95** *MGM*

James Hound: Give Me Liberty

Terrytoon series (created by Ralph Bakshi) in which a dog secret agent goes through James Bondesque perils and adventures.
1967 (*Preschool-Primary*) 42m/C **VHS $5.99** *VTR*

James Hound: Mr. Winlucky

The cunning 007 of the dog world stars in another collection of TV episodes.
1967 (*Preschool-Primary*) 30m/C **VHS $5.99** *VTR*

Jane & the Lost City 📽📽📽📷

A surprise, a comedy from a comic strip that could have been an ordeal but isn't. "Jane" was a British newspaper heroine meant to titillate WWII-era soldiers; during her adventures she constantly loses her clothes. This spritely, farcical version stays away from raunch (in her old-style undergarments Jane shows less skin than the Little Mermaid) and offers great spoofs of "Raiders"-type jungle flicks, as Jane races the Germans for African treasure.
1987 (PG/*Jr. High-Adult*) 94m/C Kristen Hughes, Maud Adams, Sam Jones; *D:* Terry Marcel; *W:* Mervyn Haisman; *M:* Harry Robertson. **VHS, Beta $14.95** *NWV, STE*

Jane Eyre 📽📽📽

Excellent adaptation of the Charlotte Bronte novel about the plain governess with the noble heart and her love for the mysterious and tragic Mr. Rochester. Fontaine has the proper backbone and yearning in the title role but to accommodate Welles' emerging popularity the role of Rochester was enlarged. Excellent bleak romantic-Gothic look. Taylor, in her third film role, is seen briefly in the early orphanage scenes.
1944 (*Jr. High-Adult*) 97m/B Joan Fontaine, Orson Welles, Margaret O'Brien, Peggy Ann Garner, John Sutton, Sara Allgood, Henry Daniell, Agnes Moorehead, Aubrey Mather, Edith Barrett, Barbara Everest, Hillary Brooke, Elizabeth Taylor; *D:* Robert Stevenson; *W:* John Houseman, Aldous Huxley, Robert Stevenson; *M:* Bernard Herrmann. **VHS $19.98** *FXV, FCT, BTV*

Janosch: Fables from the Magic Forest

Storytelling bear spins a few more yarns about his mystical wooded homeland.
1990 (*Family*) 115m/C **VHS $39.95** *JFK, WTA*

Jason and the Argonauts 🦴🦴🦴🦴

Jason, son of King of Thessaly, sails on the Argo to the land of Colchis. He and his valiant crew - including Hercules - encounter numerous perils and wonders during their quest for the magical Golden Fleece, guarded by a seven-headed hydra. Superb. Ray Harryhausen's special effects are at their best, and robust characters bring the classic figures of Greek legend to life, but myth buffs will note that the script brings the adventure to a close in time to skip the less-than-heroic tragedy of Jason and his lady love Medea. **Hound Advisory:** Violence, alcohol use (or nectar of the gods, anyway, that gets the crew drunk). The famous battle between Jason and a horde of reanimated skeleton warriors blends horror, swashbuckling, and grisly humor.

1963 (G/*Family*) 104m/C Todd Armstrong, Nancy Kovack, Gary Raymond, Laurence Naismith, Nigel Green, Michael Gwynn, Honor Blackman; **D:** Don Chaffey; **W:** Jan Read, Beverly Cross. **VHS, Beta, LV, 8mm $14.95** COL, MLB, FUS

Jayce & the Wheeled Warriors, Vol. 1

Line of toy products provided this syndicated TV cartoon series with a reason for existing; Jayce, the son of a space scientist, and his gang of heroic freedom-fighters roll off on a long saga to overthrow a galactic vegetable tyrant. Episodes here are entitled "Ghostship" and "Escape from the Garden." Additional volumes available.

1985 (*Preschool-Jr. High*) 45m/C **VHS, Beta $24.95** COL, WTA

Jazz Time Tale

Funky, animated story of a young girl who meets jazz great Fats Waller.

19?? (*Primary*) 29m/C **D:** Michael Sporn. **VHS $9.98** LIV, FFF, WTA

Jean de Florette 🦴🦴🦴🦴

The first of two films (with "Manon of the Spring") based on Marcel Pagnol's novel. A single spring in drought-ridden Provence, France is blocked by two scheming countrymen (Montand and Auteuil). They await the imminent failure of the farm nearby, inherited by a city-born hunchback, whose chances for survival fade without water for his crops. A devastating story with a heartrending performance by Depardieu as the hunchback. Lauded and awarded; in French with English subtitles. **Hound Advisory:** Mature themes.

1987 (PG/*Jr. High-Adult*) 122m/C Gerard Depardieu, Yves Montand, Daniel Auteuil, Elisabeth Depardieu, Ernestine Mazurowna; **D:** Claude Berri; **W:** Gerard Brach, Claude Berri. **VHS, Beta, LV $19.98** ORI, IME, FCT

Jem, Vol. 1: Truly Outrageous

Saturday-morning TV cartoon series from Hanna-Barbera about Jem, a futuristic rock star, who is also a superheroine/ businesswoman/philanthropist/toy-store product. Additional volumes available.

1986 (*Preschool-Primary*) 90m/C **VHS, Beta $14.95** FHE, WTA

Jeremiah Johnson 🦴🦴🦴

Hollywood's concession to mountain man mania of the '70s is notably rougher than "Grizzly Adams" or the "Wilderness Family," but deserves mention for its sheer beauty and realistic portrayal of the American frontier. Based on a real character, Johnson turns his back on civilization, circa 1850, and learns a new code of survival amid isolated mountains, hostile Indians, and rival trappers. **Hound Advisory:** Frontier violence.

1972 (PG/*Jr. High-Adult*) 107m/C Robert Redford, Will Geer; **D:** Sydney Pollack; **W:** Edward Anhalt, John Milius. **VHS, Beta, LV $19.98** WAR, FCT

Jersey Girl 🦴🦴🦴

Toby Mastellone (Gertz) is a bright single gal from the Jersey shore who wants something better in her life. Her hard-working dad (Bologna) has fixed her up with an apprentice plumber but she wants a Manhattan guy. And then Toby meets cute Sal (McDermott), who seems just the ticket, but can you really take the Jersey out of the girl?

1992 (PG-13/*Jr. High-Adult*) 95m/C Jami Gertz, Dylan McDermott, Joseph Bologna, Aida Turturro, Star Jasper, Sheryl Lee, Joseph Mazzello, Molly Price; **D:** David Burton Morris; **W:** Gina Wendkos. **VHS** COL

Jesse James Rides Again

Republic serial giving the hero treatment to one of the west's most famous outlaws (played by "Lone Ranger" actor Moore), making him a sort of Robin Hood of the frontier.

1947 (*Jr. High-Adult*) 181m/B Clayton Moore, Linda Stirling, Roy Barcroft, Tristram Coffin; **D:** Fred Brannon, Thomas Carr. **VHS $29.98** REP, MLB

Jesus Christ, Superstar 🦴🦴🦴

A rock opera that portrays, in music, the last seven days in the earthly life of Christ, as reenacted by young tourists in Israel. Outstanding musical score was the key to the success of the film. Based on the stage play by Tim Rice and Andrew Lloyd Weber, film is sometimes stirring while exhibiting the usual heavy-handed Jewison approach. ♫Jesus Christ, Superstar; I Don't Know How To Love Him; What's The Buzz?; Herod's Song; Heaven On Their Minds; Strange Thing, Mystifying; Then We Are Decided; Everything's Alright; This Jesus Must Die.

1973 (G/*Adult-Family*) 108m/C Ted Neeley, Carl Anderson, Yvonne Elliman, Josh Mostel; **D:** Norman Jewison. **VHS, Beta, LV $19.98** MCA

Jesus of Nazareth 🦴🦴🦴

All-star cast vividly portrays the life of Christ in this made-for-television mini-series. Skillfully directed and sensitively acted. On three cassettes.

1977 (*Family*) 371m/C Robert Powell, Anne Bancroft, Ernest Borgnine, Claudia Cardinale, James Mason, Laurence Olivier, Anthony Quinn; **D:** Franco Zeffirelli; **M:** Maurice Jarre. **VHS, Beta $69.98** LIV, FOX, ECU

A Jetson's Christmas Carol

Even Mr. Spacely gets into the spirit in this holiday special derived from the Hanna-Barbera cartoon series. Nine more volumes of Jetson flotsam are available on tape, plus the occasional feature-length production.

1989 (*Family*) 30m/C **V:** George O'Hanlon, Penny Singleton, Daws Butler, Mel Blanc. **VHS, Beta, LV $9.95** TTC, IME, WTA

The Jetsons Meet the Flintstones 🎬🎬

They said it couldn't be done: a melding of the space age with the stone age. Made-for-TV double-dose of Hanna-Barbera franchises, when young Elroy Jetson's time machine takes him and his family back to the 25th century B.C. There they meet the Flintstones and the Rubbles, who accidentally get transported into the future. Will either family ever get back home?
1988 (*Family-Family*) 100m/C **V:** Mel Blanc, Daws Butler, Jean VanDerPyl, George O'Hanlon, Penny Singleton. **VHS, Beta, LV $19.95** *TTC, IME, WTA*

The Jetsons: The Movie 🎬🎬

Ill-starred version of TV's outer space family is like an average episode with a half-hour plot stretched to feature length: George Jetson gets promoted in charge of an extraterrestrial factory that hurts the ecosystem of some furry Ewok lookalikes. 1990 environmental sermons make the 21st century story seem 100 years behind the times, and you might want to subtract a bone for the treatment of Janet Waldo, the original Judy Jetson, booted off the project at the last minute and replaced with the voice of teen crooner Tiffany. Other sad news: Mel Blanc (Mr. Spacely) and George O'Hanlon (George Jetson) died before the movie's release, and it's dedicated to them.
1990 (*G/Family*) 82m/C **D:** William Hanna, Joseph Barbera; **M:** John Debney; **V:** George O'Hanlon, Mel Blanc, Penny Singleton, Tiffany, Patric Zimmerman, Don Messick, Jean VanDerPyl, Ronnie Schell, Patti Deutsch, Dana Hill, Russi Taylor, Paul Kreppel, Rick Dees. **VHS, Beta, LV $14.98** *MCA, APD, WTA*

The Jewel of the Nile 🎬🎬🎬

Sequel to "Romancing the Stone" with the same cast but new director. Romance novelist Joan thought she found her true love in Jack but finds that life doesn't always end happily ever. After they part ways, Jack realizes that she may be in trouble and endeavors to rescue her from the criminal hands of a charming North African president. Of course, he can always check out this "jewel" at the same time. Chemistry is still there, but the rest of the film isn't quite up to the "Stone's" charm. **Hound Advisory:** Violence; sex talk; profanity.
1985 (*PG/Jr. High-Adult*) 106m/C Michael Douglas, Kathleen Turner, Danny DeVito, Avner Eisenberg, The Flying Karamazov Brothers, Spiros Focas, Holland Taylor; **D:** Lewis Teague; **W:** Mark Rosenthal, Larry Konner; **M:** Jack Nitzsche. **VHS, Beta, LV $19.98** *FOX*

Jiminy Cricket's Christmas

Yuletide collection of Disney cartoons, featuring Donald Duck, Chip 'n' Dale, Goofy, Jiminy Cricket; includes the rare "Mickey's Good Deed" (1932).
1932 (*G/Family*) 47m/C **VHS, Beta, LV $12.99** *DIS, WTA*

Jimmy the Kid 🎬🎬

Jimmy is kidnapped by a bumbling gang of crooks and held for ransom, but the clever tyke both befriends and outsmarts them. Screen vehicle for TV sitcom star Coleman ("Diff'rent Strokes"), based on a caper novel by Donald E. Westlake. **Hound Advisory:** Roughhousing, salty language.

1982 (*PG/Family*) 95m/C Gary Coleman, Cleavon Little, Fay Hauser, Ruth Gordon, Dee Wallace Stone, Paul LeMat, Don Adams; **D:** Gary Nelson; **W:** Sam Bobrick. **VHS, Beta** *NO*

Joe Panther 🎬🎬🎬

Well-intentioned family drama about a young Seminole Indian who wants to ship out on a fishing boat but instead stakes his claim in the white man's world by wrestling alligators.
1976 (*G/Family*) 110m/C Brian Keith, Ricardo Montalban, Alan Feinstein, Cliff Osmond, A. Martinez, Robert Hoffman; **D:** Paul Krasny. **VHS** *WAR*

Joe Versus the Volcano 🎬🎬

The answer to the question: In what other movie besides "Sleepless in Seattle" have Hanks and Ryan co-starred? Shanley's directorial debut is an expressionistic goofball comedy about a dopey guy who, after finding out he has only months to live, contracts with a millionaire to leap into a volcano alive. Then of course, romance enters picture as Tom meets Meg, who plays not one, but three roles. Imaginatively styled farce displays great "Metropolis"-pastiche visuals but is undermined by a fairly stupid script caught between satire and sentiment, though youngsters seem to enjoy the fairy tale atmosphere and sheer charm of the stars. Special effects courtesy of Industrial Light and Magic. **Hound Advisory:** Slight salty language.
1990 (*PG/Jr. High-Adult*) 106m/C Tom Hanks, Meg Ryan, Lloyd Bridges, Robert Stack, Amanda Plummer, Abe Vigoda, Dan Hedaya, Barry McGovern, Ossie Davis; **D:** John Patrick Shanley; **W:** John Patrick Shanley; **M:** Georges Delerue. **VHS, Beta, LV, 8mm $19.98** *WAR*

Joey 🎬🎬

Daddy, a former doo-wopper, looks back on his years of musical success as a waste of time. His son takes to the world of rock guitar with blind fervor. Their argument plays against the backdrop of the "Royal Doo-Wopp Show" at New York City's Radio Music Hall. Features multi-generational rock songs.
1985 (*PG/Primary-Adult*) 90m/C Neill Barry, James Quinn. **VHS, Beta** *NO*

Joey Runs Away and Other Stories

Little Kangaroo Joey leaves his mother's pouch for better accommodations, but discovers that it really is hard to beat home. Selection of animated kids' books from the "Children's Circle" lineup also includes "The Cow Who Fell in the Canal," "The Bear and the Fly," and "The Most Wonderful Egg in the World."
1989 (*Preschool-Primary*) 28m/C **VHS $19.95** *CCC, FCT, WKV*

Johann's Gift to Christmas

TV cartoon story of a young mouse who inspires the writing of the beloved Christmas carol "Silent Night." For a live action version, see "Silent Mouse."
1991 (*Preschool-Primary*) 25m/C **VHS $12.98** *FHE, FFF*

John & Julie 🎬🎬

Vintage British kids' film about two six-year-old children who set out by themselves on an eventful journey to London to see the coronation of the new Queen Elizabeth.

1957 (*Preschool-Primary*) 82m/C Colin Gibson, Lesley Dudley. **VHS, Beta** **$29.95** *FHE*

John Henry

Legend of John Henry, who singlehandedly defeats a steam drill in a steel driving competition, is illustrated in storybook fashion and read by thespian Washington as part of the "Rabbit Ears" collection of tall tales.
1993 (*Primary*) 30m/C **M:** B.B. King. **VHS $9.95** *PMS, BTV*

John the Fearless 🐾🐾🐾

In Europe, 1410 A.D., John is a brawny young peasant, jobless because he refuses to cringe before any master (some things never change). Exiled from his hometown, John becomes a freelance hero, fighting deadly foes to see if he can ever truly experience fear. Belgian animated feature has a great premise (based on the novel by Constant De Kinder) and pro animation that looks like a medieval woodcut come to life. But after awhile the story gets very predictable and surprisingly short on action. **Hound Advisory:** Roughhousing.
1987 (*Primary-Jr. High*) 80m/C **VHS $14.95** *WTA*

Johnny Appleseed

Recitation of the story of Johnny Appleseed, the American naturalist who roamed the Ohio Valley in the early 1800s, with artwork by Stan Olson. Part of the "Rabbit Ears: American Heroes and Legends" series.
1993 (*Preschool-Primary*) 30m/C **VHS $9.95** *BTV*

Johnny Dangerously 🐾🐾

Gangster spoof about Johnny Dangerously, who turned to crime in order to pay his mother's medical bills. Now, Dangerously wants to go straight, but competitive crooks would rather see him dead than law-abiding and his mother requires more and more expensive operations. In spite of the talent, this crime only pays in near-comic ways. **Hound Advisory:** Violence and profanity.
1984 (PG-13/*Jr. High-Adult*) 90m/C Michael Keaton, Joe Piscopo, Danny DeVito, Maureen Stapleton, Marilu Henner, Peter Boyle, Griffin Dunne, Glynnis O'Connor, Dom DeLuise, Richard Dimitri, Ray Walston, Dick Butkus, Alan Hale Jr., Bob Eubanks; **D:** Amy Heckerling; **W:** Norman Steinberg. **VHS, Beta** **$79.98** *FOX*

Johnny Shiloh 🐾🐾

Orphan youth becomes a heroic drummer during the Civil War. Originally a two-part Disney television show, somewhat lacking in spectacle.
1963 (*Family*) 90m/C Kevin Corcoran, Brian Keith, Darryl Hickman, Skip Homeier; **D:** James Neilson. **VHS, Beta $69.95** *DIS*

Johnny the Giant Killer

When Johnny is reduced to miniature size by the giant, he befriends a bird and a queen bee who help him to even the score.
1954 (*Family*) 68m/C **VHS, Beta $19.95** *DVT, WTA*

Johnny Tremain & the Sons of Liberty 🐾🐾

Disney adaptation of the Esther Forbes novel, depicting the beginnings of the American Revolution from the viewpoint of a teenage apprentice silversmith in 1773 Boston. Johnny eventually meets Paul Revere and Samuel Adams, joins the Boston Tea Party, and fights in the Battle of Lexington. Like the smash "Davy Crockett," this historical tale was made as a miniseries for Disney's network TV show and released to theaters. Scope, characters and production values remain small-screen-sized, however.
1958 (*Family*) 85m/C Sebastian Cabot, Hal Stalmaster, Luanna Patten, Richard Beymer; **D:** Robert Stevenson. **VHS, Beta $69.95** *DIS*

Johnny Woodchuck's Adventures

Little Johnny Woodchuck is more precocious than his well-behaved brothers. One day, he leaves home and family behind and sets out on an adventure.
1978 (*Preschool-Primary*) 60m/C **VHS, Beta** *FHE*

The Jolson Story 🐾🐾🐾

Smash Hollywood bio of Jolson, from his childhood to super-stardom, runs amuck with cliches but who cares? Parks, doing Jolson as seen by Jolson, delivers. Features dozens of vintage songs from Jolson's parade of hits. Jolson himself dubbed the vocals for Parks, rejuvenating his own career in the process. 🎵Swanee; You Made Me Love You; By the Light of the Silvery Moon; I'm Sitting On Top of the World; There's a Rainbow Round My Shoulder; My Mammy; Rock-A-Bye Your Baby With a Dixie Melody; Liza; Waiting for the Robert E. Lee.
1946 (*Family*) 128m/C Larry Parks, Evelyn Keyes, William Demarest, Bill Goodwin, Tamara Shayne, John Alexander, Jimmy Lloyd, Ludwig Donath, Scotty Beckett; **D:** Alfred E. Green; **M:** Morris Stoloff. **Award Nominations:** Academy Awards '46: Best Actor (Parks), Best Color Cinematography, Best Film Editing, Best Supporting Actor (Demarest); **Awards:** Academy Awards '46: Best Sound, Best Score. **VHS, Beta, LV $19.95** *COL*

Jonah and the Whale

Animated version of the biblical tale of Jonah, assigned by God to tell the people of Ninevah to renounce their evil ways, then swallowed by a whale.
1992 (*Preschool-Primary*) 30m/C **VHS $12.98** *MVD, RIN*

Jonathan Livingston Seagull 🐾🐾

Imagine how "Homeward Bound: The Incredible Journey" or "The Adventures of Milo and Otis" would have been if the animal characters mainly sat and talked philosophy all the time. Based on the best-seller by Richard Bach, this finds a vaguely Christlike nonconformist seabird banished by his flock for seeking a higher purpose. Hardly featherbrained, but the awkwardness of putting Bach's book on the screen made this a box-office turkey. Introspective songs on the soundtrack by Neil Diamond.
1973 (G/*Family*) 99m/C James Franciscus, Juliet Mills; **D:** Hall Bartlett; **M:** Neil Diamond. **Award Nominations:** Academy Awards '73: Best Cinematography, Best Film Editing; **Awards:** Golden Globe Awards '74: Best Score. **VHS, Beta** **$29.95** *PAR, WSH*

Joni

Inspirational story based on the real life of Joni Tada (playing herself) who was severely paralyzed in a diving accident, but found the strength to cope. She took up painting, writing, and finally evangelizing her born again faith (Billy Graham helped produce the film and lends a Hitchcock-style cameo appearance). Wholesome drama based on the autobiography by Tada.
1979 (G/Family) 75m/C Joni Eareckson Tada, Bert Remsen, Katherine De Hetre, Cooper Huckabee; D: James F. Collier. VHS, Beta $59.95 LIV

Josh and S.A.M.

Road movie with a twist: the driver can barely see over the dashboard. Josh and Sam are brothers whose parents are splitting. They cope by taking off on their own. Sam, meanwhile has been convinced by the older Josh that he's not a real boy at all, but rather a military S.A.M.: Strategically Altered Mutant (sounds like Josh saw "D.A.R.Y.L"). Lightweight tale in search of deeper significance will appeal to kids, but adults will see over the dashboard and through the transparent plot.
1993 (PG-13/Jr. High-Adult) 97m/C Jacob Tierney, Noah Fleiss, Martha Plimpton, Joan Allen, Christopher Penn, Stephen Tobolowsky, Ronald Guttman; D: Billy Weber; W: Frank Deese; M: Thomas Newman. VHS, LV NLC

Josie & the Pussycats in Outer Space

Three Saturday-morning episodes of the '70s all-girl cartoon rock group. None of the original, earthbound "Josie & the Pussycats" shows are currently available on tape (so suffer!), just this sci-fi spinoff in which the caterwaulers take off on a spaceship into the far corners of the galaxy. Additional volumes available.
197? (Family) 58m/C VHS, Beta $19.95 TTC, WTA

Journey Back to Oz

Animated musical sequel to "The Wizard of Oz" sat on the shelf for several years after its completion. Not bad, with some scenes quite nicely designed, but nothing is particularly magical about the story apart from the casting of Minelli (daughter of Judy Garland) to provide the voice for Dorothy. The Kansas girl and her little dog Toto return to visit their friends in the magical land of Oz, only to find the land hostage to the forces of evil witch Mombi.
1964 (Preschool-Primary) 90m/C V: Liza Minnelli, Ethel Merman, Paul Lynde, Milton Berle, Mickey Rooney, Danny Thomas. VHS, Beta $14.95 FHE, KAR, HHE

Journey for Margaret

Young and Day star as an expectant American couple living in London during WWII. Day miscarries during an air raid and heads back to the States while Young stays in London where he meets two orphans and takes them under his wing. He decides to take them back to the U.S. but problems arise. Tearjerker with good story that shows the war through the eyes of children. O'Brien's first film. Based on the book by William L. White.

1942 (Family) 81m/B Robert Young, Laraine Day, Fay Bainter, Signe Hasso, Margaret O'Brien, Nigel Bruce, G.P. Huntley Jr., William Severn, Doris Lloyd, Halliwell Hobbes, Jill Esmond; D: Woodbridge S. Van Dyke. VHS $19.98 MGM, FCT

The Journey of Natty Gann

With the help of a guardian wolf and a young hobo, 14-year-old Natalie travels across Depression-era America disguised as a boy to find her father. Warm and winning Disney family feature with memorable characters and an excellent sense of time and place. From the scriptwriter of "The Black Stallion."
1985 (PG/Family) 101m/C Meredith Salenger, John Cusack, Ray Wise, Scatman Crothers, Lainie Kazan, Verna Bloom; D: Jeremy Paul Kagan; W: Jeanne Rosenberg; M: James Horner. VHS, Beta, LV $29.95 DIS

Journey to Spirit Island

Maria, a present-day Makah Indian girl, has mysterious dreams of her ancestors buried on Spirit Island, now the potential site of a resort. Eventually she, a friend and two visiting Chicago boys are stranded on the island and try to save the sacred ground from underhanded developers. Not just a solid kiddie adventure but a fresh, stereotype-busting look at a modern Native American community, filled with nice little character surprises. Deserves more recognition. Filmed in the Neah Bay area of Washington state.
1992 (PG/Jr. High-Adult) 93m/C Brandon Douglas, Gabriel Damon, Tony Acierto, Nick Ramus, Marie Antoinette Rodgers, Tarek McCarthy; D: Laszlo Pal. VHS $89.95 ACA

Journey to the Center of the Earth

Enjoyable fantasy based on the Jules Verne novel about a scientist who, following an ancient map, leads an expedition into the crater of an extinct Icelandic volcano and descends to a prehistoric world deep beneath the Earth, where both dinosaurs and the remains of Atlantis can be found. Dinos are just lizards filmed in closeup, and the romantic subplot is a silly trifle, but the sense of epic-scale adventure and discovery remain intact, though shrunken on video. Hound Advisory: Violence.
1959 (Family) 132m/C James Mason, Pat Boone, Arlene Dahl, Diane Baker, Thayer David; D: Henry Levin. VHS, Beta, LV $19.98 FOX, FCT, FUS

Journey to the Center of the Earth WOOF!

Young nanny and two teenage boys discover Atlantis while exploring a volcano. Embarrassment has next to nothing to do with Jules Verne and aborts itself in mid-plot, presumably when money ran out. MTV sets, costumes, film clips actually came from numerous other low-grade fantasies made around the same time. Hound Advisory: Alcohol use, profanity, roughhousing.
1988 (PG/Jr. High-Adult) 83m/C Nicola Cowper, Paul Carafotes, Ilan Mitchell-Smith; D: Rusty Lemorande; W: Rusty Lemorande, Kitty Chalmers. VHS, Beta, LV $79.95 CAN

The Joy Luck Club 🐾🐾🐾

Universal themes in mother/daughter relationships are explored in a context Hollywood first rejected as too narrow, but which proved to be a modest sleeper hit. Tan skillfully weaves the plot of her 1989 best-seller into a screenplay which centers around young June's going-away party. Slowly the stories of four Chinese women, who meet weekly to play mah-jongg, are unraveled. Each vignette reveals life in China for the four women and the tragedies they survived, before reaching into the present to capture the relationships between the mothers and their daughters. Powerful, relevant, and moving. **Hound Advisory:** Salty language; sexual situations.
1993 (**R**/*Sr. High-Adult*) 136m/C Tsai Chin, Kieu Chinh, France Nuyen, Rosalind Chao, Tamlyn Tomita, Lisa Lu, Lauren Tom, Ming-Na Wen, Michael Paul Chan, Andrew McCarthy, Christopher Rich, Russell Wong, Victor Wong, Vivian Wu, Jack Ford, Diane Baker; **D:** Wayne Wang; **W:** Amy Tan. **VHS, LV** *BVV, HPH*

Judgment at Nuremberg 🐾🐾🐾🐾

It's 1948 and a group of high-level Nazis are on trial for war crimes. Chief Justice Tracy must resist political pressures as he presides over the trials. Excellent performances throughout, especially by Dietrich and Garland. Considers to what extent an individual may be held accountable for actions committed under orders of a superior officer. Consuming account of the Holocaust and WWII is deeply moving and powerful. Based on a "Playhouse 90" television program. **Hound Advisory:** Mature themes.
1961 (*Jr. High-Adult*) 178m/B Spencer Tracy, Burt Lancaster, Richard Widmark, Montgomery Clift, Maximilian Schell, Judy Garland, Marlene Dietrich, William Shatner; **D:** Stanley Kramer; **W:** Abby Mann; **M:** Ernest Gold. **Award Nominations:** Academy Awards '61: Best Actor (Tracy), Best Art Direction/Set Decoration (B & W), Best Black and White Cinematography, Best Costume Design (B & W), Best Director (Kramer), Best Film Editing, Best Picture, Best Supporting Actor (Clift), Best Supporting Actress (Garland); **Awards:** Academy Awards '61: Best Actor (Schell), Best Adapted Screenplay; Golden Globe Awards '62: Best Actor—Drama (Schell), Best Director (Kramer); New York Film Critics Awards '61: Best Actor (Schell). **VHS, Beta, LV** *$29.98 MGM, FOX, BTV*

The Jungle Book 🐾🐾

Lavish, live-action British version of Rudyard Kipling's stories about Mowgli, the child raised by wolves in the jungles of India, who can talk to the beasts, both friendly and hostile, and develops a mortal enemy in Shere Khan the tiger. Animals are sometimes unconvincing puppets, but Sabu makes a fine boy hero and pic maintains a rich storybook flavor throughout. From the makers of another Kipling great, "Elephant Boy."
1942 (*Family*) 109m/C Sabu, Joseph Calleia, Rosemary DeCamp, Ralph Byrd, John Qualen; **D:** Zoltan Korda; **M:** Miklos Rozsa. **VHS, LV** *$9.95 CNG, MRV, REP*

The Jungle Book 🐾🐾🐾

Based on Kipling's classic, a young boy raised by wolves must choose between his jungle friends and human "civilization." Along the way he meets a variety of jungle characters including zany King Louie, kind-hearted Baloo, wise Bagherra and the evil Shere Khan. Great, classic songs including "Trust in Me," "I Wanna Be Like You," and Oscar-nominat-

ed "Bare Necessities." Last Disney feature overseen by Uncle Walt himself and a must for kids of all ages.
1967 (*Family*) 78m/C **D:** Wolfgang Reitherman; **V:** Phil Harris, Sebastian Cabot, Louis Prima, George Sanders, Sterling Holloway, J. Pat O'Malley, Verna Felton, Darlene Carr. **VHS, Beta, LV** *$24.99 DIS, BVV, FCT*

Jungle Book: Mowgli Comes to the Jungle

The first installment in the series of animated stories based on Rudyard Kipling's characters. This episode introduces Mowgli to green wilderness and his adoption by Alexander's wolf pack. Additional volumes available.
1990 (*Family*) 30m/C **VHS** *$9.98 SVI, WTA*

Jungle Drums of Africa

Dull Republic serial, one of their last. Moore, better known for portraying the Lone Ranger, encounters lions, wind tunnels, a heroine in jeopardy, voodoo and enemy agents in deepest Africa. 12 episodes, on two cassettes.
1953 (*Family*) 167m/B Clayton Moore, Phyllis Coates, Roy Glenn, John Cason; **D:** Fred Brannon. **VHS** *REP, MLB*

A Jungle for Joey

Orangutan named Joey is separated from his family in Borneo.
1989 (*Preschool-Primary*) 14m/C **VHS, Beta** *$245.00 AIM*

Junior Bonner 🐾🐾🐾

A rowdy modern-day western about a young drifting rodeo star who decides to raise money for his father's new ranch by challenging a formidable bull. **Hound Advisory:** Alcohol use.
1972 (**PG**/*Jr. High-Adult*) 100m/C Steve McQueen, Robert Preston, Ida Lupino, Ben Johnson, Joe Don Baker, Barbara Leigh; **D:** Sam Peckinpah. **VHS, Beta** *$19.98 FOX*

Jurassic Park 🐾🐾🐾🐾

Michael Crichton's bestseller translates well to the big screen due to its main attraction: realistic, rampaging dinosaurs, brought to life with state-of-the-art special effects. In the plot, however, they're cloned from prehistoric cells, and all seems fine until the carnivores escape from their island pens and prove smarter and less controllable than expected. Spielberg's saurians knocked Spielberg's (!!) lovable alien E.T. out of first place as the highest grossing movie of all time, and launched a noisy debate over whether this was too intense for the kiddie viewers (whom advertisers and toy manufacturers mercilessly courted all the same). Our verdict: no problem. The script features two child characters - less bratty than the novel's, thankfully - who get chased, tossed, crushed, even electrocuted, and always bounce back, alive and well. Plenty of PG films put youngsters in worse danger than this blockbuster escapism. **Hound Advisory:** Violence, salty language.
1993 (**PG-13**/*Jr. High-Adult*) 126m/C Sam Neill, Laura Dern, Jeff Goldblum, Richard Attenborough, Bob Peck, Martin Ferrero, B.D. Wong, Joseph Mazzello, Ariana Richards, Samuel L. Jackson, Wayne Knight; **D:** Steven Spielberg; **W:** David Koepp, Michael Crichton; **M:** John Williams; **V:** Richard Kiley. **Award Nominations:** MTV Movie Awards '94: Best Film, Best Villain (T-Rex), Best Action Sequence; **Awards:** Academy Awards '93: Best Sound, Best Sound Effects Editing, Best Visual Effects. **VHS, LV** *$24.98 MCA*

The Jungle Book (1967)

Just Around the Corner 🦴🦴

With the aid of song and dance, Temple helps her Depression-poor father get a job after she befriends a cantankerous millionaire. ♫This Is A Happy Little Ditty; I'm Not Myself Today; I'll Be Lucky With You; Just Around the Corner; I Love To Walk in the Rain; Brass Buttons and Epaulets.
1938 (*Family*) 70m/B Shirley Temple, Charles Farrell, Bert Lahr, Joan Davis, Bill Robinson, Cora Witherspoon, Franklin Pangborn; *D:* Irving Cummings. VHS, Beta $19.98 *FOX*

Just One of the Guys 🦴🦴

When a high school newspaper refuses to accept the work of an attractive girl, she pulls a gender switch, dressing as a guy to prove her intrinsic worth. In this disguise she befriends a sensitive outcast boy and helps him outgrow his awkward stage, falling for him in the process. Very cute, but predictable tale. **Hound Advisory:** Sex talk, roughhousing, brief nudity.
1985 (**PG-13**/*Jr. High-Adult*) 100m/C Joyce Hyser, Clayton Rohner, Billy Jacoby, Toni Hudson, Leigh McCloskey, Sherilyn Fenn; *D:* Lisa Gottlieb. VHS, Beta, LV $79.95 *COL*

Just Tell Me You Love Me 🦴

Unappealing youth-appeal tale about three runaway teens - two boys and a girl - on their own in Hawaii and plotting to make easy money as con artists.
1980 (**PG**/*Family*) 90m/C Robert Hegyes, Debralee Scott, Lisa Hartman, Ricci Martin, June Lockhart; *D:* Tony Mordente. VHS, Beta $69.98 *LIV, VES*

Just the Way You Are 🦴🦴🦴💧

Attractive musician struggles to overcome a physical handicap and winds up falling in love while on vacation in the French Alps. Uneven but charming romantic comedy.
1984 (**PG**/*Jr. High-Adult*) 96m/C Kristy McNichol, Robert Carradine, Kaki Hunter, Michael Ontkean, Alexandra Paul, Lance Guest, Timothy Daly, Patrick Cassidy; *D:* Edouard Molinaro; *M:* Vladimir Cosma. VHS, Beta $14.95 *MGM*

Just William's Luck 🦴🦴

Precocious English brat sneaks into an old mansion, which happens to be the headquarters of a fur-thieving gang. Belated followup to 1939's "Just William" (not on video), the only two features based on Richmal Crompton's storybook hero, a sort of British Dennis the Menace. In fact, Dennis has been retitled "Just Dennis" for UK consumption.
1947 (*Family*) 87m/B William A. Graham, Garry Marsh; *D:* Val Guest. VHS, Beta $24.95 *VYY*

Justin Morgan Had a Horse 🦴🦴

True story of a colonial school teacher in post-Revolutionary War Vermont who first bred the Morgan horse, the first and most versatile American breed.
1981 (*Family*) 91m/C Don Murray, Lana Wood, Gary Crosby; *D:* Hollingsworth Morse. VHS, Beta $69.95 *DIS*

K-9 🦴🦴

After having his car destroyed by a drug dealer, a lone-wolf cop is forced to take another type of canine as partner - a German Shepherd. Together they work to round up the bad guys and maybe chew on their shoes a little. Sometimes amusing one-joke comedy done in by a paper-thin script, though both the dog and Belushi are good. **Hound Advisory:** Salty language and violence, barely worse than an average TV show.
1989 (**PG-13**/*Jr. High-Adult*) 111m/C James Belushi, Mel Harris, Kevin Tighe, Ed O'Neill, Cotter Smith, James Handy, Jerry Lee; *D:* Rod Daniel; *W:* Steven Siegel, Scott Myers; *M:* Miles Goodman. VHS, Beta, LV $19.95 *MCA*

K-9000 🦴🦴

A cyberdog fights the forces of evil with the aid of a cop, a lady reporter, and the usual cliches. Made for TV.
1989 (*Jr. High-Adult*) 96m/C Chris Mulkey, Catherine Oxenberg; *D:* Kim Manners; *M:* Jan Hammer. VHS $64.95 *FRH*

The Karate Kat: Aristokratic Kapers

Spelling-impaired feline uses the ancient martial arts to take on bad guys in this cartoon.
1987 (*Family*) 33m/C VHS, Beta $14.95 *LHV, WAR, WTA*

The Karate Kid 🦴🦴🦴

Cliches stack up like split bricks at a karate demo, but it's all done with grace and understated performances. New boy in town Danny is instantly victimized by sadistic bullies, because he's the new boy in town. As luck would have it, his apartment is blessed with a Japanese handyman/Zen master, who agrees to teach grasshopper martial arts. Hence, a friendship (and a movie) develops between boy and life tutor that is deep and sincere. The karate is really only an afterthought here; not so in the many sequels and ripoffs - including a Saturday-morning cartoon - that followed this popular crowd pleaser. From the director of the original "Rocky." **Hound Advisory:** Violence, drug use, salty language.
1984 (**PG**/*Family*) 126m/C Ralph Macchio, Noriyuki "Pat" Morita, Elisabeth Shue, Randee Heller, Martin Kove, Chad McQueen; *D:* John G. Avildsen; *W:* Robert Mark Kamen; *M:* Bill Conti. VHS, Beta, LV, 8mm $19.95 *COL*

The Karate Kid: Part 2 🦴🦴

Sequel in which Daniel accompanies his friend and teacher back to Japan. Instantly the two face Miyagi's old hometown enemy who holds a longstanding, dangerous grudge. Formula of the original is slavishly rerun; warm scenes between Macchio and Morita sandwiched between repetitious episodes of karate threats and revenge. Travelogues of Okinawa and Japanese culture are a minor bonus. **Hound Advisory:** Violence.
1986 (**PG**/*Jr. High*) 95m/C Ralph Macchio, Noriyuki "Pat" Morita, Danny Kamekona, Martin Kove, Tamlyn Tomita, Nobu McCarthy, Yuji Okumoto; *D:* John G. Avildsen; *W:* Robert Mark Kamen; *M:* Bill Conti. VHS, Beta, LV, 8mm $19.95 *COL*

The Karate Kid: Part 3 🦴

The psycho Vietnam vet karate teacher from Part 1 teams up with a psycho Vietnam vet mobster to split up and smash Daniel and Miyagi. Somehow, bonsai trees are involved. Genuinely terrible sequel magnifies stupid elements of earlier chapters -overacting villains, asinine dialogue, violent revenge

A T.Rex looks for lunch in "Jurassic Park"

- and what's with Macchio? Daniel babbles nearly nonstop (best line: "Why am I so stupid?"). Lone bone is for Morita maintaining serene dignity. **Hound Advisory:** Profanity (the worst in the series), violence.

1989 (**PG**/*Jr. High-Sr. High*) 105m/C Ralph Macchio, Noriyuki "Pat" Morita, John G. Avildsen, Thomas Ian Griffith, Martin Kove, Sean Kanan, Robyn Elaine; *D:* John G. Avildsen; *W:* Robert Mark Kamen; *M:* Bill Conti. **VHS, Beta, LV, 8mm $19.95** *COL*

Katy and the Katerpillar Kids 🦴🦴

Cartoon feature about a beautiful butterfly named Katy who must deal with her two caterpillar children who are anxious to become butterflies and fly.

1987 (*Preschool-Primary*) 85m/C *D:* Jose Luis, Santiago Moro. **VHS $19.99** *JFK, WTA*

Kavik, the Wolf Dog 🦴🦴

TV-movie spins a Yukon variant of "Lassie Come Home," with the bad guy taking loyal Kavik from his young master and transporting the canine to Alaska to pull a sled. Kavik escapes, and tries to return to his beloved boy in Seattle.

1984 (*Family*) 99m/C Ronny Cox, Linda Sorensen, Andrew Ian McMillian, Chris Wiggins, John Ireland; *D:* Peter Carter. **VHS, Beta $19.95** *MED*

Kermit and Piggy Story

Romantic story of how a pig rose from the chorus line to superstardom and finds the frog of her dreams along the way.

1985 (*Family*) 57m/C Cheryl Ladd, Tony Randall, Loretta Swit, Raquel Welch, Jim Henson, Frank Oz. **VHS, Beta $14.98**

Key Largo 🦴🦴🦴

Gangster melodrama set in Key West, Florida, where hoods take over a hotel in the midst of a hurricane. Cynical WWII vet Frank McCloud (Bogart) visits the hotel owned by the family of a dead war buddy, and finds a tempest brewing both inside and out. Based on a play by Maxwell Anderson. Star-studded classic delivers great performances and a compelling story.

1948 (*Sr. High-Adult*) 101m/B Humphrey Bogart, Lauren Bacall, Claire Trevor, Edward G. Robinson, Lionel Barrymore; *D:* John Huston; *W:* Richard Brooks, John Huston; *M:* Max Steiner. **VHS, Beta, LV $19.98** *MGM, FOX, TLF*

Kid Colter 🦴🦴

12-year-old Boston-bred Justin Colter goes to the Pacific Northwest to visit his divorced dad, played with great warmth by Stafford - who unfortunately drops from the story entirely when Justin gets kidnapped by "Home Alone"-style crooks (would you believe they're working for the Russians?).

Abandoned in the wilderness, Justin has a mystic epiphany, becoming a junior mountain man. Messy family adventure never stays on one track long enough. **Hound Advisory:** Roughhousing, salty language.
1985 (*Family*) 101m/C Jim Stafford, Jeremy Shamos, Hal Terrance, Greg Ward, Jim Turner; *D:* David O'Malley; *W:* David O'Malley. **VHS, Beta $79.98** *FOX*

Kid Dynamite

Boxer Gorcey is kidnapped to prevent his participation in a major fight. The real fighting occurs when his brother substitutes for him.
1943 (*Sr. High-Adult*) 73m/B Leo Gorcey, Huntz Hall, Bobby Jordan, Gabriel Dell, Pamela Blake; *D:* Wallace Fox. **VHS $19.95** *NOS, HEG*

A Kid for Two Farthings 🦴🦴◁

Episodic, sentimental portrait of life in the Jewish quarter of London's East End, centered on a little boy taught by his old-country grandfather about unicorns and their power to grant wishes. When the boy finds a malformed goat with only one horn, he uses his few coins to buy the animal in the hopes it will indeed bring his family what they most need - a steam press for their cleaning and tailoring business. Enjoyable but heavily sentimental family saga, adapted by scripter Wolf Mankowitz from his own novel. Severely condensed 30-minute version is also on tape under the title "The Unicorn."
1955 (*Preschool-Jr. High*) 96m/C Jonathan Ashmore. **VHS $39.95** *HMV, FCT*

The Kid from Left Field 🦴🦴

Bat boy for the San Diego Padres transforms the team from losers to champions when he passes on the advice of his father, a has-been ballplayer, to the team members. A made-for-TV remake of the 1953 classic (not yet on video), here styled as a vehicle for prime-time child star Coleman.
1979 (*Family*) 80m/C Gary Coleman, Robert Guillaume, Ed McMahon, Tab Hunter; *D:* Adell Aldrich. **VHS, Beta $69.95** *VES*

Kid from Not-So-Big 🦴🦴

Family film that was a foray into feature making by the Six Flags amusement park company. Title refers to Jenny, a young girl left to carry on her grandfather's frontier-town newspaper. When two con men come to town, the newskid sets out to expose them.
1978 (*G/Family*) 87m/C Jennifer McAllister, Veronica Cartwright, Robert Viharo, Paul Tulley; *D:* Bill Crain. **VHS, Beta $39.98** *WAR, OM*

The Kid Who Loved Christmas 🦴🦴

After his adoptive mother is killed in a car crash, little Reggie is taken from his loving musician stepfather by a Scrooge-like social worker, who believes showbiz and parenthood don't mix. Reggie writes to Santa for help. Mushy Yuletide TV movie works hard to be touching, sometimes succeeds thanks to that once-in-a-lifetime ensemble cast gathered by producer Eddie Murphy. Last film for Sammy.
1990 (*Family*) 118m/C Cicely Tyson, Michael Warren, Sammy Davis Jr., Gilbert Lewis, Ken Page, Della Reese, Esther Rolle, Ben Vereen, Vanessa Williams, John Beal, Trent Cameron, Arthur Seidelman. **VHS $14.95** *PAR*

The Kid with the 200 I.Q. 🦴🦴

When an earnest boy genius enters college at age 13, predictable comic situations arise that involve his attempts at impressing his idolized astronomy professor (Guillaume), as well as an equally unrequited bout of first love. Harmless comedy, one of a series of squeaky-clean made for TV family fare starring Coleman.
1983 (*Family*) 96m/C Gary Coleman, Robert Guillaume, Harriet Hilliard Nelson, Dean Butler, Karli Michaelson, Christina Murrull, Mel Stewart; *D:* Leslie Martinson. **VHS, Beta $49.95** *LIV*

The Kid with the Broken Halo 🦴🦴

Coleman and Guillaume are paired again in this unsuccessful pilot for a TV series. A young angel, out to earn his wings, must try to help three desperate families, with the help of an experienced angel.
1982 (*Jr. High-Adult*) 100m/C Gary Coleman, Robert Guillaume, June Allyson, Mason Adams, Ray Walston, John Pleshette, Kim Fields, Georg Stanford Brown, Telma Hopkins; *D:* Leslie Martinson. **VHS** *NO*

Kidco 🦴🦴◁

Fact-based story of a toothpaste-making corporation headed and run by children ranging in age from nine to sixteen. Quite engaging, as the kids learn the ropes of capitalism, prosper - then get crushed by government regulations. Good Republican Party primer.
1983 (*PG/Family*) 104m/C Scott Schwartz, Elizabeth Gorcey, Cinnamon Idles, Tristine Skyler; *D:* Ronald F. Maxwell. **VHS, Beta $59.98** *FOX*

Kidnapped 🦴🦴◁

Scottish heir David Balfour is sold by his scheming uncle into servitude as a cabin boy to get him out of the way. By chance David meets Highland rebel Alan Stewart, who helps him regain his inheritance amidst much rather draggy historical background detail. Disney film based on the Robert Louis Stevenson classic, directed by no-relation namesake Robert Stevenson, long the Magic Kingdom's specialist in the production of live-action features.
1960 (*Family*) 94m/C Peter Finch, James MacArthur, Peter O'Toole; *D:* Robert Stevenson. **VHS, Beta $19.99** *DIS*

Kidnapped 🦴🦴

Animated adaptation of the Robert Louis Stevenson adventure in which a young heir is kidnapped on the orders of a wicked uncle. Made for TV as part of the "Famous Classic Tales" series.
1973 (*Preschool-Jr. High*) 49m/C **VHS, Beta $19.95** *MGM, WTA*

Kindergarten Cop 🦴🦴◁

Schwarzenegger spoofs his screen image (again) as one-man-army police officer Kimble, hunting a particularly vicious drug lord by staking out his ex-wife and six-year-old son. When Kimble's lady partner gets sick, he's forced to take her place masquerading as a kindergarten teacher in the school district where mother and son reside. Classroom of uncontrollable tykes (almost all of them the products of broken homes, by the way) manage to thoroughly unnerve the undercover

tough man. Blockbuster hit covers all bases; it's got cutesy kiddie comedy and romance on one hand - and some really serious violence and killing on the other. Even Arnold called this unsuitable for very young viewers. **Hound Advisory:** Profanity, violence bordering on brutality.
1990 (PG-13/ *Jr. High-Adult*) 111m/C Arnold Schwarzenegger, Penelope Ann Miller, Pamela Reed, Linda Hunt, Richard Tyson, Carroll Baker, Cathy Moriarty, Park Overall, Richard Portnow, Jayne Brook; **D:** Ivan Reitman; **W:** Murray Salem, Herschel Weingrod, Timothy Harris; **M:** Randy Edelman. **VHS, Beta, LV** **$19.95** *MCA, CCB*

The King and I 🎞🎞🎞🎞

Wonderful adaptation of Rogers and Hammerstein's Broadway play based on the novel "Anna and the King of Siam" by Margaret Landon. English governess Kerr is hired to teach the King of Siam's many children and bring them into the 20th century. She has more of a job than she realizes, for this is a king, a country, and a people who value tradition above all else. Features one of Rodgers and Hammerstein's best-loved scores. Brynner made this role his, playing it over 4,000 times on stage and screen before his death. Kerr's voice was dubbed when she sang; the voice you hear is Marni Nixon, who also dubbed the star's singing voices in "West Side Story" and "My Fair Lady." ♫ Shall We Dance?; Getting To Know You; Hello, Young Lovers; We Kiss in a Shadow; I Whistle a Happy Tune; March of the Siamese Children; I Have Dreamed; A Puzzlement; Something Wonderful.
1956 *(Family)* 133m/C Deborah Kerr, Yul Brynner, Rita Moreno, Martin Benson, Terry Saunders, Rex Thompson, Alan Mowbray, Carlos Rivas; **D:** Walter Lang; **W:** Ernest Lehman; **M:** Richard Rodgers, Oscar Hammerstein. **Award Nominations:** Academy Awards '56: Best Actress (Kerr), Best Color Cinematography, Best Director (Lang), Best Picture; **Awards:** Academy Awards '56: Best Actor (Brynner), Best Art Direction/Set Decoration (Color), Best Costume Design (Color), Best Sound, Best Score; Golden Globe Awards '57: Best Actress—Musical/Comedy (Kerr), Best Film—Musical/Comedy. **VHS, Beta, LV** **$19.98** *FOX, BTV, RDG*

King Arthur & the Knights of the Round Table, Vol. 1

Tale of King Arthur is told beginning with his birth to the mighty sword Excalibur. Additional volumes available.
1981 *(Family)* 60m/C **VHS, Beta** **$29.95** *FHE*

King Kong 🎞🎞🎞🎞

Original beauty and beast classic tells the story of Kong, a giant ape captured in Africa and brought to New York as a sideshow attraction. Kong falls for Wray, escapes from his captors and rampages through the city, ending up on top of the newly built Empire State Building. Moody Steiner score adds color, and Willis O'Brien's stop-motion animation still holds up well. Remade numerous times. **Hound Advisory:** Violence.
1933 *(Family)* 105m/B Fay Wray, Bruce Cabot, Robert Armstrong, Frank Reicher, Noble Johnson, Sam Hardy, James Flavin; **D:** Ernest B. Schoedsack; **M:** Max Steiner. **VHS, Beta, LV, 8mm** **$16.98** *TTC, RKO, MED*

King Kong 🎞🎞

Bloated, expensive remake of the 1933 classic, updates the storyline but otherwise follows it pretty closely, as an oil company discovering the fabled giant ape on a remote island.

Kong becomes infatuated with a pretty shipwreck survivor, is captured and brought to New York, where he breaks loose and climbs the World Trade Center. The elaborate monkey suit, created and acted by makeup ace Rick Baker, is impressive, as are the sets, but the ponderous plot gains nothing from being a half-hour longer than the original. PG-13 sequel "King Kong Lives," from 1986, isn't worth anybody's time. **Hound Advisory:** Violence; salty language; alcohol use.
1976 (PG/ *Family*) 135m/C Jeff Bridges, Charles Grodin, Jessica Lange, Rene Auberjonois, John Randolph, Ed Lauter, Jack O'Halloran; **D:** John Guillermin; **M:** John Barry. **Award Nominations:** Academy Awards '76: Best Cinematography, Best Sound; **Awards:** Academy Awards '76: Best Visual Effects. **VHS, Beta, LV, 8mm** **$24.95** *PAR, HMV*

King Kong: Rocket Island

King Kong, Prof. Bond, and Bobby meet on a prehistoric island and battle evil villains in these caged TV cartoon reruns from Rankin-Bass. Originally a prime-time show rather than the usual Saturday-morning timeslots.
196? *(Primary-Jr. High)* 30m/C **VHS** **$9.95** *WTA*

King Kong: Treasure Trap

Another adventure with King Kong, Prof. Bond, and Bobby on the island of Mondo.
196? *(Primary-Jr. High)* 30m/C **VHS** **$9.95** *WTA*

King of the Grizzlies 🎞🎞

Mystical relationship between a Cree Indian and a grizzly cub is put to the test when the full grown bear troubles a ranch at which the man is foreman. Just bear-able Disney nature drama, based on the book "Biography of a Grizzly" by Ernest Thompson Seton.
1969 (G/ *Family*) 93m/C Chris Wiggins, John Yesno; **D:** Ron Kelly. **VHS, Beta** **$69.95** *DIS*

King of the Hill 🎞🎞🎞◁

Excellent depression-era drama focuses on Aaron, a 12-year-old in St. Louis whose family is barely intact; mother is in a tuberculosis sanitarium, younger brother is with relatives, and the exceedingly self-centered father travels the countryside as a salesman. Left by himself, Aaron desperately guards the family's precious apartment and property, under ceaseless threat of eviction. Sadly overlooked at the box office, this suspenseful and exhilarating tale for all ages doesn't glorify its era but admires the main character's resourcefulness and imagination during hard times. Based on the book by A.E. Hochner describing his own childhood. **Hound Advisory:** Violence, mature themes. As poverty closes in on Aaron and his neighbors, one commits suicide, another is engulfed in a police riot.
1993 (PG-13/ *Jr. High-Adult*) 102m/C Jesse Bradford, Jeroen Krabbe, Lisa Eichhorn, Karen Allen, Spalding Gray, Elizabeth McGovern, Joseph Chrest, Adrien Brody, Cameron Boyd, Chris Samples, Katherine Heigl, Amber Benson, John McConnell, Ron Vawter, John Durbin, Lauryn Hill, David Jensen; **D:** Steven Soderberg; **W:** Steven Soderberg; **M:** Cliff Martinez. **VHS, LV** *MCA*

King of the Rocketmen

Republic serial that created their most emblematic character, Rocket Man. Mystery villain 'Dr. Vulcan' is knocking off eminent scientists, so researcher Jeff King (mustachioed actor Coffin, usually seen in bad-guy roles) fights back in disguise, using a newly invented jet backpack and metal mask to become the flying hero. In 12 chapters; first is 20 minutes long, the rest are 13 minutes each. The Rocket Man suit was re-used by Republic for two later, non-sequel serials, "Radar Men from the Moon" and "Zombies of the Stratosphere." And of course it inspired Disney's "The Rocketeer." **Hound Advisory:** Roughhousing. More often than not, the Rocket Man and his allies will shoot the guns out of enemies' hands. **1949** (*Family*) 156m/B Tristram Coffin, Mae Clarke, I. Stanford Jolley; **D:** Fred Brannon. **VHS, LV** $29.98 *MED, VCN, REP*

King of the Wind 𝄞𝄞𝄞♩

Magnificent stallion is given as a gift by Arabs to the King of France in 1729. Agba, a mute stable boy, won't be parted from the horse; he and his beast pass from one mean-spirited owner to another throughout Europe. Based on Marguerite Henry's novel, this should be a stirring tale, but its episodic narrative grows repetitive, with poor Agba seeing the white infidels at their worst again and again. Gets an extra half-bone for being one of the few English-speaking family films (with "The Black Stallion Returns") to portray Arabs and Islam in a positive light. **1993** (*PG/Family*) 101m/C Richard Harris, Glenda Jackson. **VHS** $89.98 *FHE*

King Ralph 𝄞𝄞

When the rest of the royal family passes away in a freak accident, lounge lizard Ralph finds himself the only heir to the throne. O'Toole is the long-suffering valet who tries to train him for the job, while Hurt provides a certain touch of ham in cheek evil. Sporadically funny semi-satire flutters on the good graces of Goodman, making it a pleasant if not particularly memorable 96 minutes. **Hound Advisory:** Brief profanity. **1991** (*PG/Jr. High-Adult*) 96m/C John Goodman, Peter O'Toole, Camille Coduri, Joely Richardson, John Hurt; **D:** David S. Ward; **W:** David S. Ward; **M:** James Newton Howard. **VHS, Beta, LV** $19.95 *MCA, CCB*

Kipperbang 𝄞𝄞

During the summer of 1948 a 13-year-old boy wishes he could kiss the girl of his dreams. He finally gets the chance in a school play. Not unsatisfying, but falls short of being the bittersweet comedy-drama it could have been. Title is a nonsense word the kids throw back and forth. **1982** (*PG/Jr. High-Adult*) 85m/C John Albasiny, Abigail Cruttenden, Alison Steadman; **D:** Michael Apted. **VHS, Beta** $59.95 *MGM*

Kismet 𝄞𝄞♩

Big budget Arabian Nights musical drama of a Baghdad street poet who manages to infiltrate himself into the Wazir's harem. Based on the Broadway play (which was based on an earlier film version). Indifferently directed but still fun to watch. Music was adapted from Borodin by Robert Wright and George Forrest. Original trailer and letterboxed screen available in special laserdisc edition. ♫Fate; Not Since Ninevah; Baubles, Bangles, and Beads; Stranger in Paradise; Bored; Night of My Nights; The Olive Tree; And This Is My Beloved; Sands of Time. **1955** (*Family*) 113m/C Howard Keel, Ann Blyth, Dolores Gray, Vic Damone; **D:** Vincente Minnelli; **M:** Andre Previn. **VHS, Beta, LV** $19.98 *MGM, FCT*

Kiss Me Goodbye 𝄞𝄞

Young widow Fields can't shake the memory of her first husband, a charismatic but philandering Broadway choreographer, who's the antithesis of her boring but devoted professor fiance. She struggles with the charming ghost of her first husband, as well as her domineering mother, attempting to understand her own true feelings. Harmless but two-dimensional remake of "Dona Flor and Her Two Husbands." **Hound Advisory:** Profanity; sexual situations. **1982** (*PG/Jr. High-Adult*) 101m/C Sally Field, James Caan, Jeff Bridges, Paul Dooley, Mildred Natwick, Claire Trevor; **D:** Robert Mulligan; **W:** Charlie Peters; **M:** Ralph Burns. **VHS, Beta** $59.98 *FOX*

Kissyfur!: Hugs and Kissyfur

Animated antics of a pair of former circus bears, Kissyfur and his widowed papa bear Gus. Escapees from big top captivity, the two inhabit a marshful of wild characters, and the TV series placed an emphasis on a single parent raising a child — or cub, as the case may be. In this denful of episodes a vulture and a slithery snake try to corrupt the young animals. Will Kissyfur and friends be won over by their bad ways? Additional volumes available. **1991** (*Preschool-Primary*) 75m/C **VHS** $19.99 *JFK, CEL*

Knights & Emeralds 𝄞𝄞𝄞♩

In a modern British factory town, cross-cultural rivalries and romances develop between members of two high school marching bands, one all white and one black, as the national band championships draw near. Familiar but effective pleas for teen tolerance, mixed with mediocre music. **Hound Advisory:** Sex talk. **1987** (*PG/Jr. High-Adult*) 90m/C Christopher Wild, Beverly Hills, Warren Mitchell; **D:** Ian Emes; **M:** Colin Towns. **VHS, Beta** $19.98 *WAR*

Knute Rockne: All American 𝄞𝄞𝄞

Life story of Notre Dame football coach Knute Rockne, who inspired many victories with his powerful speeches. Reagan, as the dying George Gipp, utters that now-famous line, "Tell the boys to win one for the Gipper." **1940** (*Family*) 96m/B Ronald Reagan, Pat O'Brien, Gale Page, Donald Crisp, John Qualen; **D:** Lloyd Bacon. **VHS, Beta** $19.98 *MGM, FHE*

Koi and the Kola Nuts

Koi, the son of an African chief, finds his place in the world with the help of a snake, an alligator and an army of ants in this African folktale from the "Rabbit Ears" series of recitations starring celebrity narrators and well-known musicians. **1992** (*Primary*) 30m/C **M:** Herbie Hancock. **VHS** $9.95 *BTV,*

Konrad 🦴🦴🦴⋅

Prototype "instant" child, born and trained to perfection in a high-tech factory, is mistakenly delivered (in a can) to an eccentric woman. She makes room in her life for the unusual eight-year-old and grows to love him, and as Konrad attends school with real kids he learns that perfection isn't always appropriate. This is too much for the factory director, who tries to 'recall' the boy. Warm, witty and wry family satire, with a cast that's likewise perfect. Based on "Konrad oder Das Kind aus der Konservenbu echse" by Christine Noestlinger (but you knew that already, right?). Part of the "Wonderworks" series.
1985 *(Family)* 110m/C Ned Beatty, Polly Holliday, Max Wright, Huckleberry Fox. **VHS $29.95** *PME, HMV, BTV*

Kotch 🦴🦴🦴

An elderly man resists his children's attempts to retire him. Warm detailing of old age with a splendid performance by Matthau. Lemmon's directorial debut.
1971 *(PG/Jr. High-Adult)* 113m/C Walter Matthau, Deborah Winters, Felicia Farr; *D:* Jack Lemmon; *M:* Marvin Hamlisch. **Award Nominations:** Academy Awards '71: Best Actor (Matthau), Best Film Editing, Best Song ("Life Is What You MaKe It"), Best Sound; **Awards:** Golden Globe Awards '72: Best Song ("Life Is What You Make It"). **VHS $59.98** *FOX*

Kramer vs. Kramer 🦴🦴🦴🦴⋅

Highly acclaimed family drama about an ad executive husband and his small son left behind when the wife leaves on a quest to find herself. Formerly neglectful of his kid, Mr. Kramer wrestles with the newfound art of fatherhood - and the subsequent courtroom battle when Mrs. Kramer returns demanding custody. The entire cast gives exacting performances, successfully moving you from tears to laughter and back again. Based on the novel by Avery Corman. **Hound Advisory:** Brief nudity, sex talk, mature themes, salty language.
1979 *(PG/Jr. High-Adult)* 105m/C Dustin Hoffman, Meryl Streep, Jane Alexander, Justin Henry, Howard Duff, JoBeth Williams; *D:* Robert Benton. **Award Nominations:** Academy Awards '79: Best Cinematography, Best Film Editing, Best Supporting Actor (Henry); **Awards:** Academy Awards '79: Best Actor (Hoffman), Best Adapted Screenplay, Best Director (Benton), Best Picture, Best Supporting Actress (Streep); Golden Globe Awards '80: Best Actor—Drama (Hoffman), Best Film—Drama, Best Screenplay, Best Supporting Actress (Streep); National Board of Review Awards '79: 10 Best Films of the Year, Best Supporting Actress (Streep); National Society of Film Critics Awards '79: Best Actor (Hoffman), Best Director (Benton), Best Supporting Actress (Streep). **VHS, Beta, LV $19.95** *COL, BTV*

Krull 🦴🦴

Overly familiar mid-'80s attempt to do the Ultimate Fantasy Adventure Set in a World Peopled by Creatures of Myth and Magic. Prince embarks on a quest to find the Glaive (a magical weapon) and joins with Robin-Hood types to rescue his princess bride, taken by a giant Beast who travels in a spacegoing Black Fortress and controls endless hordes of "Star Wars" style armored stormtroopers. Wild special f/x, but the fun is labored. **Hound Advisory:** Supernatural violence.
1983 *(PG/Jr. High-Adult)* 121m/C Ken Marshall, Lysette Anthony, Freddie Jones, Francesca Annis, Liam Neeson; *D:* Peter Yates; *M:* James Horner. **VHS, Beta, LV $14.95** *GKK*

Kuffs 🦴🦴

Slater stars as George Kuffs, a young guy who reluctantly joins his brother's highly respected private security team in this original action comedy. After his brother is gunned down in the line of duty, George finds himself the new owner of the business. Out to avenge his brother, George pursues a crooked art dealer as he battles crime on the streets of San Francisco. Thin on plot and with the predictable awaiting him at every turn, Slater mugs as best as can be expected. **Hound Advisory:** Violence and profanity.
1992 *(PG-13/Jr. High-Adult)* 102m/C Christian Slater, Tony Goldwyn, Milla Jovovich, Bruce Boxleitner, Troy Evans, George de la Pena, Leon Rippy; *D:* Bruce A. Evans; *W:* Bruce A. Evans, Raynold Gideon; *M:* Harold Faltermeyer. **VHS, Beta, LV $19.98** *MCA*

La Bamba 🦴🦴🦴

Romantic biography of the late 1950s pop idol Ritchie Valens, concentrating on his stormy relationship with his half-brother, his love for his WASP girlfriend, and his tragic, sudden death in the famed plane crash that also took the lives of Buddy Holly and the Big Bopper. Soundtrack features Setzer, Huntsberry, Crenshaw, and Los Lobos as, respectively, Eddie Cochran, the Big Bopper, Buddy Holly, and a Mexican bordello band. **Hound Advisory:** Salty language; references to drug taking.
1987 *(PG-13/Jr. High-Adult)* 99m/C Lou Diamond Phillips, Esai Morales, Danielle von Zernaeck, Joe Pantoliano, Brian Setzer, Marshall Crenshaw, Howard Huntsberry, Rosana De Soto, Elizabeth Pena, Rick Dees; *D:* Luis Valdez; *W:* Luis Valdez; *M:* Carlos Santana, Miles Goodman. **VHS, Beta, LV, 8mm $14.95** *COL*

L.A. Story 🦴🦴🦴

Livin' ain't easy in the city of angels. Harris K. Telemacher (Martin), a weatherman in a city where the weather never changes, wrestles with emptiness while consorting with beautiful people, distancing from significant other Henner, cavorting with valley girl Parker, falling for newswoman Tennant (Martin's real-life wife), and taking messages from an electronic freeway information sign. Written by the comedian, the story's full of keen insights into the everyday problems and ironies of living in the Big Tangerine. (It's no wonder the script's full of so much thoughtful detail: Martin is said to have worked on it intermittently for seven years.) Charming story of life and love on the fault line and the semi-fast lane. **Hound Advisory:** Profanity.
1991 *(PG-13/Sr. High-Adult)* 98m/C Steve Martin, Victoria Tennant, Richard E. Grant, Marilu Henner, Sarah Jessica Parker, Sam McMurray, Patrick Stewart, Iman, Kevin Pollak; *D:* Mick Jackson; *W:* Steve Martin; *M:* Peter Melnick. **VHS, Beta, LV $92.95** *LIV, WAR*

Labyrinth 🦴🦴🦴

Imaginative adventure directed by Muppeteer Henson, produced by "Star Wars" creator George Lucas, and written by Monty Python's Jones. While baby-sitting her baby brother, Sara, a modern teen absorbed in fairy-tale lore, gets frustrated and asks goblins to take the troublesome kid. The Goblin King (rock star Bowie) complies, and Sara can regain the tyke only by finding her way through the fantastic maze to the goblin castle. As she befriends odd creatures along the way, the narrative often loses momentum, but wild Muppet characters, production design, and musical numbers make this trip worth taking. **Hound Advisory:** Solving the labyrinth is nothing compared with figuring out where the PG rating came from. Danger level is low, though creatures are often grotesque.

1986 (PG/_Family_**)** 90m/C David Bowie, Jennifer Connelly, Toby Froud; **D:** Jim Henson; **W:** Terry Jones; **M:** David Bowie, Trevor Jones. **VHS, Beta, LV, 8mm $14.98** _SUE, NLC_

Lady and the Tramp 🐾🐾🐾🐾

Animated Disney classic about two dogs who fall in love. Tramp is wild and carefree; Lady is a spoiled pedigree who runs away from home after her owners have a baby. They just don't make dog romances like this one anymore, based on a novel by Ward Greene. Songs by Sonny Burke and Peggy Lee; decades later she sued and won a lucrative judgment against the Disney corporation for the royalties. ♫He's a Tramp; La La Lu; Siamese Cat Song; Peace on Earth; Bella Notte. **1955 (G/**_Family_**)** 76m/C **D:** Hamilton Luske; **M:** Peggy Lee, Sonny Burke; **V:** Larry Roberts, Peggy Lee, Barbara Luddy, Stan Freberg, Alan Reed, Bill Thompson, Bill Baucon, Verna Felton, George Givot, Dallas McKennon, Lee Millar. **VHS, Beta, LV $29.95** _DIS, APD_

The Lady in White 🐾🐾🐾

Small-town ghost story, nicely done from a kid's perspective. Schoolboy Frankie is accidentally locked in the classroom on Halloween and encounters the restless spirit of a murdered little girl. He sorts out clues to her killer, who's still very much at large. Well-developed characters, atmospheric style compensate for a whodunit plot that's almost as transparent as the spooks. A rarity among serious horror flicks: one suitable for the family. **Hound Advisory:** Violence, mature themes, alcohol use.

1988 (PG-13/_Jr. High-Adult_**)** 92m/C Lukas Haas, Len Cariou, Alex Rocco, Katherine Helmond, Jason Presson, Renato Vanni, Angelo Bertolini, Jared Rushton; **D:** Frank Laloggia; **W:** Frank Laloggia; **M:** Frank Laloggia. **VHS, Beta, LV** _NO_

Lady Lovelylocks & the Pixietails, Vol. 1

First of a mangy cartoon series pushing the Lady Lovelylocks toys onto brainwashable kids. Ms. Lovelylocks must save the inhabitants of her kingdom from villains Ravenwaves, Snarla, and Hairball. Additional volumes available.

1986 (_Primary_**)** 30m/C **VHS, Beta $12.95** _WTA_

The Lady Vanishes 🐾🐾🐾🐾

When a kindly old lady disappears from a fast-moving train, her young friend finds an imposter in her place and a spiraling mystery to solve. Hitchcock's first real winner, a smarmy, wit-drenched British mystery that precipitated his move to Hollywood. Along with "39 Steps," considered an early Hitchcock classic. From the novel "The Wheel Spins," by Ethel Lina White. Special edition contains short subject on Hitchcock's cameos in his films. Remade in 1979.

1938 (_Adult-Family_) 99m/B Margaret Lockwood, Paul Lukas, Michael Redgrave, May Whitty, Googie Withers, Basil Radford, Naunton Wayne, Cecil Parker, Linden Travers, Catherine Lacey, Sidney Gilliat; **Cameos:** Alfred Hitchcock; **D:** Alfred Hitchcock; **W:** Frank Launder, Louis Levy, Alma Reville. **VHS, Beta, LV $16.95** _SNC, NOS, SUE_

Ladybugs 🐾◁

Hangdog salesman Dangerfield would like to move up the corporate ladder, but must first turn the company-sponsored girl's soccer team into winners. Routine Dangerfield vehicle exploits nearly everything for laughs, including dressing an athletic boy as a girl so he can play on the team. Obvious fluff that will likely engage the youngsters. **Hound Advisory:** Profanity; mature themes; sex talk.

1992 (PG-13/_Jr. High-Adult_**)** 91m/C Rodney Dangerfield, Jackee, Jonathan Brandis, Ilene Graff, Vinessa Shaw, Tom Parks, Jeanetta Arnetta, Nancy Parsons, Blake Clark, Tommy Lasorda; **D:** Sidney J. Furie; **M:** Richard Gibbs. **VHS, Beta $19.95** _PAR_

Ladyhawke 🐾🐾🐾

In medieval France, a young pickpocket meets a nomadic warrior and his lady love, separated by a cruel spell. At night he turns into a wolf, while by day she is a hawk; they travel together, yet cannot meet in human form. More successful than many modern screen fantasies because it doesn't try to be the Ultimate Fairy Tale (f/x are virtually nonexistent), just a magically romantic adventure. Still, it's way too long, and Broderick unwisely falls back on his "Ferris Bueller" persona for the youthful knave. **Hound Advisory:** Violence.

1985 (PG-13/_Jr. High-Adult_**)** 121m/C Matthew Broderick, Rutger Hauer, Michelle Pfeiffer, John Wood, Leo McKern, Alfred Molina, Ken Hutchison; **D:** Richard Donner; **W:** Edward Khmara, Michael Thomas, Tom Mankiewicz; **M:** Andrew Powell. **VHS, Beta, LV $19.98** _WAR_

Lamb Chop's Play Along: Action Songs

Shari Lewis and Lamb Chop sing songs that kids can interact with. Additional volumes available.

1992 (_Preschool-Primary_**)** ?m/C **VHS $9.95** _A&M, TVC, FFF_

Lamb Chop's Sing-Along Play-Along

Shari Lewis and her puppets joke and sing, and young viewers can join in.

1990 (_Family_**)** 45m/C Shari Lewis. **VHS, Beta $14.95** _FRH_

The Land Before Time 🐾🐾🐾

Before his dinosaur tales "Jurassic Park" and "We're Back!," Steven Spielberg helped produce this lushly animated children's adventure about five orphaned baby dinos near the end of the Age of Reptiles. They band together and try to find the Great Valley, a green paradise where they can avoid extinction. Charming, coy, and often shamelessly tearjerking; for adult viewers who can't shake the idea that there was no Great Valley in real life, it's unusually melancholy. One of the more successful efforts from the Don Bluth Studios. **Hound Advisory:** Littlefoot, the baby brontosaurus hero, sees his mother die, though there's later a glimpse of her in dino-heaven.

Lady and the Tramp (1955)

1988 (G/*Family*) 70m/C *D:* Don Bluth; *W:* Stu Krieger; *M:* James Horner; *V:* Pat Hingle, Helen Shaver, Gabriel Damon, Candice Houston, Burke Barnes, Judith Barsi, Will Ryan. **VHS, LV $19.98** *MCA, FCT, APD*

The Land of Faraway

Mediocre international spectacle (dubbed into English) in which a boy is whisked from his dreary everyday existence to the magical Land of Faraway, where he does battle with evil knights and flies on winged horses. Based on a novel by Pippi Longstocking's creator Astrid Lindgren.
1987 (G/*Family*) 95m/C Timothy Bottoms, Christian Bale, Susannah York, Christopher Lee, Nicholas Pickard; *D:* Vladimir Grammatikov. **VHS, Beta $9.99** *PSM*

Land of the Lost

1990s revival of one of the better Saturday-morning shows of the '70s. Tom Porter and his children Kevin and Annie are transported back to the prehistoric land, where they are joined by a mysterious jungle girl and a monkey-boy named Stink. They fight for survival against the familiar gigantic dinosaurs, evil lizard-men, and other dangers, with slightly upscale special f/x in this go-around. Two episodes per tape.
1992 (*Primary*) ?m/C Timothy Bottoms. **VHS** *WOV*

Land of the Lost, Vol. 1

Forest ranger Rick Marshall and his two teenaged children Will and Holly become trapped in a strange prehistoric world populated by dinosaurs, "sleestax," futuristic ruins and other enigmas. Minor classic Saturday-morning kids' series with cool stop-motion animation dinosaurs and innovative, occasionally mind-expanding plot lines. No coincidence, because some classic "Star Trek" scriptwriters were contributors. The show was revived a decade later. Additional volumes available.
1974 (*Family*) 46m/C Wesley Eure, Ron Harper, Kathy Coleman, Spencer Milligan, Phillip Paley. **VHS, Beta $9.95** *NLC, SUE*

Land That Time Forgot

Dinosaur adventure worth noting mainly for how much better special effects technology has improved in a few decades. WWI submarine goes off course into Antarctica and surfaces in a land outside time, filled with cavepersons and prehistoric monsters (mostly non-threatening puppets). Based on the 1918 novel by Tarzan's creator, Edgar Rice Burroughs. Followed in 1977 by "The People that Time Forgot." **Hound Advisory:** Violence.
1975 (PG/*Jr. High-Adult*) 90m/C Doug McClure, John McEnery, Susan Penhaligon; *D:* Kevin Connor. **VHS, Beta $59.98** *LIV, VES*

Lantern Hill 🐾🐾🐾⌐

During the Depression, 12-year-old Jane reluctantly goes to live with her long-absent father, liking him in spite of herself. She then attempts to reconcile both estranged parents. Gentle family drama from the pen of Lucy Maud Montgomery, done by the same high-quality Canadian filmmakers responsible for the "Anne of Green Gables" series. Released on tape in the US as part of the PBS Wonderworks series.
1990 (*G/Family*) 112m/C Sam Waterston, Colleen Dewhurst, Sarah Polley, Marion Bennett, Zoe Caldwell; *D:* Kevin Sullivan. **VHS, LV $29.95** *BVV, FCT*

Lassie 🐾🐾🐾⌐

Everyone's favorite collie returns as the Turner family moves to Virginia's Shenandoah Valley to take up sheep ranching. However, because this is the '90s, Dad meets financial disaster, and junior can't stand his stepmom. Can Lassie meet the challenges of dysfunctional family living? "What is it girl? Call a therapist?" This Lassie is a direct descendant of Pal, the original 1943 star, and every bit as beautiful. **Hound Advisory:** Mature themes; salty language.
1994 (*PG/Family*) 92m/C Helen Slater, Jon Tenney, Tom Guiry, Brittany Boyd, Richard Farnsworth, Frederic Forrest; *D:* Daniel Petrie; *W:* Matthew Jacobs, Gary Ross, Elizabeth Anderson. **VHS** *NYR*

Lassie: Adventures of Neeka 🐾🐾

America's best friend joins her Native American buddy, Neeka, for a journey through a forest in the Pacific Northwest. They camp in a deserted settlement, pull an elderly gent out of a frigid pond, and risk their lives to release horses from a burning stable. Adapted from the collie's long-running TV series.
1968 (*Family*) 75m/B Jed Allan, Mark Miranda, Robert Rockwell, Lassie; *D:* Richard Moder, Jack B. Hively. **VHS, Beta** *NO*

Lassie, Come Home 🐾🐾🐾

In the first of the Lassie features, the famed collie is reluctantly sold by their impoverished owners to a rich guy. But the canine knows where she really belongs and makes an arduous treacherous cross-country journey back to her rightful family. Material has gotten a little familiar with the years, but you can't beat that cast. Nicely based on the novel by Eric Knight. Followup "Son of Lassie" is also on tape. Remade as both "The Magic of Lassie" and, with a species change, "The Gypsy Colt."
1943 (*G/Family*) 90m/C Roddy McDowall, Elizabeth Taylor, Donald Crisp, Edmund Gwenn, May Whitty, Nigel Bruce, Elsa Lanchester, J. Pat O'Malley, Lassie; *D:* Fred M. Wilcox. **Award Nominations:** Academy Awards '43: Best Color Cinematography; **Awards:** National Board of Review Awards '43: 10 Best Films of the Year. **VHS, Beta, LV $14.95** *MGM*

Lassie: The Miracle 🐾

Lassie's weekly TV show, which ran more or less continually for nearly 20 years, was barely retired when the heroic collie encored with this made-for-TV-movie featuring the photogenic canine saving newborn pups and befriending a mute boy.
1975 (*Primary*) 90m/C Lassie. **VHS, Beta $29.95** *MGM*

Lassie: Well of Love 🐾🐾

Various installments of the durable TV series featuring the heroic collie are combined. Lassie takes two pups under her paw and, in the process, loses her way. As she tries to get home, she brings joy back into the lives of two despondent children. Finally, the canine faces death when she tumbles into an abandoned well and must depend on humans for rescue.
1990 (*Family*) 76m/C Lassie, Mary Gregory, Robert Donner. **VHS, Beta** *NO*

Lassie's Great Adventure 🐾🐾🐾⌐

Lassie and her master Timmy are swept away from home by a runaway balloon. After they land in the Canadian wilderness, they learn to rely on each other through peril and adventure. Condensed from the long-running "Lassie" TV series.
1962 (*Family*) 104m/C June Lockhart, Jon Provost, Hugh Reilly, Lassie; *D:* William Beaudine. **VHS, Beta $29.99** *MGM*

Lassie's Rescue Rangers

Cartoon version of the courageous collie, who tries to save the environment with the help of the brave Rescue Rangers animal friends. These repackaged Saturday-morning animated adventures are unrelated to the later Chip'n'Dale Rescue Rangers. Additional volumes available.
1973 (*Preschool-Jr. High*) 60m/C *D:* Hal Sutherland; *V:* Ted Knight. **VHS, Beta $29.95** *FHE*

Last Action Hero 🐾🐾🐾⌐

Adolescent boy addicted to action movies gets a magic movie ticket that lets him enter a bombastic Hollywood slam-bang sequel starring his idol Jack Slater, the kind of cop who never loses a fight, survives gunfire and explosions, has a cool car, and a great big gun. Expensive action/spoof of movies within a movie is tremendous fun for about the first half or so, then the not so original premise wears thin. Arnold possesses his usual self-mocking charm and exploits his rapport with the youngster to the fullest. Since the make-believe violence is really supposed to be make-believe violence (mostly, anyway), it's pretty inoffensive. Look for lots of big stars in small roles and cameos, plus tons of inside Hollywood gags. **Hound Advisory:** Violence, but a lot of it is admittedly unreal. Swearing, meanwhile, never exceeds a very soft PG-13 (the subject of a brilliant gag). Sex talk.
1993 (*PG-13/Jr. High-Adult*) 131m/C Arnold Schwarzenegger, Austin O'Brien, Mercedes Ruehl, F. Murray Abraham, Charles Dance, Anthony Quinn, Robert Prosky, Tommy Noonan, Frank McRae, Art Carney, Brigitte Wilson; *Cameos:* Sharon Stone, M.C. Hammer, Chevy Chase, Jean-Claude Van Damme, Tori Spelling, Joan Plowright, Adam Ant, James Belushi, James Cameron, Tony Curtis, Timothy Dalton, Tony Danza, Edward Furlong, Little Richard, Damon Wayans, Robert Patrick; *D:* John McTiernan; *W:* Shane Black, David Arnott; *M:* Michael Kamen. **VHS, Beta, LV, 8mm $96.95** *COL, BTV*

The Last American Hero 🐾🐾🐾

The true story of how former moonshine runner Junior Johnson became one of the fastest race car drivers in the history of the sport. Entertaining slice of life chronicling whiskey running and stock car racing, with Bridges superb in

Everybody's favorite collie..."Lassie"

the lead. Based on a series of articles written by Tom Wolfe.
Hound Advisory: Profanity and sex.
1973 (PG/*Jr. High-Adult*) 95m/C Jeff Bridges, Valerie Perrine, Gary Busey, Art Lund, Geraldine Fitzgerald, Ned Beatty; **D:** Lamont Johnson; **W:** William Roberts; **M:** Charles Fox. **VHS, Beta $59.98** *FOX*

The Last Flight of Noah's Ark 🐾🐾◁

Disney adventure with story input from aviation novelist Ernest K. Gann. Result is a scenic diversion about an old B-29 bomber filled with animals and stowaway orphans that crash lands on a Pacific island, where two Japanese holdouts haven't yet heard that the war is over. Hey, it could happen. Major complaint is the high whine factor of the two obligatory kids.
1980 (G/*Family*) 97m/C Elliott Gould, Genevieve Bujold, Rick Schroder, Vincent Gardenia, Tammy Lauren; **D:** Charles Jarrott; **M:** Maurice Jarre. **VHS, Beta $69.95** *DIS*

The Last of the Mohicans

The first talking pictures version of the famous James Fenimore Cooper novel was this stiff, low-budget serial from the Mascot studios, depicting the life-and-death struggle of the Mohican tribe during the French and Indian was in 12 chapters of 13 minutes each. **Hound Advisory:** Violence.
1932 (*Family*) 230m/B Edwina Booth, Harry Carey Sr., Hobart Bosworth, Frank "Junior" Coghlan; **D:** Ford Beebe, B. Reeves Eason. **VHS, Beta $39.95** *VYY, VCN, NOS*

The Last of the Mohicans 🐾🐾

So-so adaptation of the well-known novel, about the scout Hawkeye and his companions Natty Bumpo, Uncas and Chingachgook during the French and Indian Wars, done in unimaginative fashion for prime-time TV. **Hound Advisory:** Violence.
1985 (R/*Family*) 97m/C Steve Forrest, Ned Romero, Andrew Prine, Don Shanks, Robert Tessier, Jane Actman; **D:** James L. Conway. **VHS, Beta $19.95** *STE, VCI*

The Last of the Mohicans 🐾🐾🐾

It's 1757, at the height of the French and English war in the American colonies, with native American tribes allied to each side. Hawkeye, a white frontiersman raised by the Mohicans, wants nothing to do with either side until he rescues Cora, an English officer's beautiful daughter, from the revenge-minded Huron Magua. The real pleasure in this adaptation, which draws from both the Cooper novel and the 1936 film, is in its lush look and attractive stars. Hawkeye's foster-father. Released in a letterbox format to preserve the original integrity of the film. **Hound Advisory:** The Indian wars are dramatized in all their historically accurate brutality, and this gets an R for its violence.
1992 (R/*Sr. High-Adult*) 114m/C Daniel Day-Lewis, Madeleine Stowe, Wes Studi, Russell Means, Eric Schweig, Jodhi May, Steven Waddington, Maurice Roeves, Colm Meaney, Patrice Chereau; **D:** Michael Mann; **W:** Christopher Crowe, Michael Mann; **M:** Trevor Jones, Randy Edelman. **VHS, LV $24.98** *FXV, BTV*

The Last Prostitute 🐾🐾

Two teenage boys search for a legendary prostitute to initiate them into manhood, only to discover that she has retired.

They hire on as workers on her horse farm, and one of them discovers the meaning of love. Well cast but somewhat labored coming-of-age saga, made for cable TV. **Hound Advisory:** Mature themes, sex, profanity.
1991 (PG-13/*Sr. High-Adult*) 93m/C Sonia Braga, Wil Wheaton, David Kaufman, Woody Watson, Dennis Letts, Cotter Smith; **D:** Lou Antonio. **VHS $89.95** *MCA*

The Last Starfighter 🐾🐾🐾◁

Bored with his small-town job at the family motel, teen Alex masters an arcade video game - then gets a visit from fast-talking "Music Man" type alien (Preston, of course), who informs him that he's just qualified to fight for the good guys in a distant intergalactic war. Infectiously high-spirited space adventure almost helps you forget the frequent "Star Wars" mimicry. Computer-generated f/x were considered revolutionary at the time. **Hound Advisory:** Violence, salty language.
1984 (PG/*Jr. High-Adult*) 100m/C Lance Guest, Robert Preston, Barbara Bosson, Dan O'Herlihy, Catherine Mary Stewart, Cameron Dye, Kimberly Ross, Wil Wheaton; **D:** Nick Castle. **VHS, Beta, LV $19.95** *MCA*

The Last Unicorn 🐾🐾🐾◁

Upon hearing she's the last of her kind in the world, Unicorn ventures forth with an incompetent magician and a bandit queen to find out what became of the rest. Too-literal adaptation of Peter S. Beagle dense fantasy novel (with a script by the author) has a great gallery of voices but its fragile spell is strained, though not broken, by budget-minded animation from Rankin-Bass studio. Unremarkable songs.
1982 (G/*Family*) 95m/C **D:** Jules Bass; **M:** Jim Webb; **V:** Alan Arkin, Jeff Bridges, Tammy Grimes, Angela Lansbury, Mia Farrow, Robert Klein, Christopher Lee, Keenan Wynn. **VHS, Beta, LV $14.98** *FOX, KAR, WTA*

Law of the Wild

Mascot serial showcasing the son of the original movie dog hero Rin Tin Tin. Junior sniffs along the trail of a magnificent stallion, horsenapped by racketeers just before a championship sweepstakes race. In 12 chapters.
1934 (*Family*) 230m/B Bob Custer, Ben Turpin, Lucille Browne, Lafe McKee; **D:** B. Reeves Eason, Armand Schaefer. **VHS $24.95** *GPV, NOS, VCN*

Lawrence of Arabia 🐾🐾🐾🐾

Lean at the height of his epic period directs this exceptional biography of T.E. Lawrence, a British military "observer" who strategically helps the Bedouins battle the Turks during WWI. Lawrence, played masterfully by O'Toole in his first major film, is a hero consumed more by a need to reject British tradition than to save the Arab population. Stunning photography of the desert in all its harsh reality. Laser edition contains 20 minutes of restored footage and a short documentary about the making of the film. Available in letterboxed format. **Hound Advisory:** Violence.
1962 (PG/*Family*) 221m/C Peter O'Toole, Omar Sharif, Anthony Quinn, Alec Guinness, Jack Hawkins, Claude Rains, Anthony Quayle, Arthur Kennedy, Jose Ferrer; **D:** David Lean; **W:** Robert Bolt; **M:** Maurice Jarre. **Award Nominations:** Academy Awards '62: Best Actor (O'Toole), Best Adapted Screenplay, Best Supporting Actor (Sharif); **Awards:** Academy Awards '62: Best Art Direction/Set Decoration (Color), Best Color Cinematography, Best Director (Lean), Best Film Editing, Best Picture, Best Sound, Best Original Score; British Academy Awards

'62: Best Actor (O'Toole), Best Film; Directors Guild of America Awards '62: Best Director (Lean); Golden Globe Awards '63: Best Director (Lean), Best Film—Drama, Best Supporting Actor (Sharif). **VHS, Beta, LV $34.95** *COL, VYG, CRC*

The Lawrenceville Stories 🎬🎬◁

Chronicles the life and times of a group of young men at the prestigious Lawrenceville prep school in 1905. Galligan plays William Hicks, alias "The Prodigious Hickey," the ringleader of their obnoxious stunts. Based on the stories of Owen Johnson, which originally ran in the Saturday Evening Post. **198?** *(Family)* 180m/C Zach Galligan, Edward Herrmann, Nicholas Rowe, Allan Goldstein, Robert Joy, Stephen Baldwin; *D:* Robert Iscove. **VHS $69.95** *MON, BTV*

Lazer Tag Academy: The Movie

The toy line comes to animated life in this movie-length commercial, made of strung-together TV episodes from the short-lived cartoon series about present-day kids armed with futuristic weapons to make this a better world. Right. **1990** *(Family)* 95m/C **VHS, Beta $39.95** *JFK, WTA*

Leader of the Band 🎬🎬

Wayward big-city musician takes a job in rural Georgia trying to train the world's worst high school band. The twist on the "Music Man" formula becomes evident in the farfetched finale. Good cast helps this comedy march along, if not always in step. **Hound Advisory:** Profanity, sex. **1987** *(PG/Jr. High-Adult)* 90m/C Steve Landesburg, Gailard Sartain, Mercedes Ruehl, James Martinez, Calvert Deforest; *D:* Nessa Hyams; *M:* Dick Hyman. **VHS, Beta, LV $14.95** *LIV*

A League of Their Own 🎬🎬🎬

Charming segment of baseball history - the real-life All American Girls Professional Baseball League, formed in the 1940s when the men were off at war. Loose plot focuses on sibling rivalry between two farm-bred sisters; Dottie, a beautiful, crackerjack catcher wise enough to appreciate when the game is and isn't important, and Kit, the younger, insecure pitcher with a chance to shine outside her sister's shadow. A great cast of characters rounds out the film, including Hanks as a hard-drinking, reluctant coach and Madonna as a happily promiscuous wench. But director Marshall ("Big") keeps everything agreeably sunny, sweet, and nostalgic. Enjoyable family outing at the ballpark with a positive message for young girls. **Hound Advisory:** Ballpark-spiced pepper, sex talk, alcohol use, wads of chewing tobacco. **1992** *(PG/Jr. High-Adult)* 127m/C Tom Hanks, Geena Davis, Madonna, Lori Petty, Jon Lovitz, David Strathairn, Garry Marshall, Bill Pullman, Rosie O'Donnell, Megan Cavanagh, Tracy Reiner, Bitty Schram, Ann Cusack, Anne Elizabeth Ramsay, Freddie Simpson, Renee Coleman; *D:* Penny Marshall; *W:* Lowell Ganz, Babaloo Mandel; *M:* Hans Zimmer. **VHS, Beta, LV, 8mm $19.95** *COL*

Lean on Me 🎬🎬🎬

Dramatization of the true story of Joe Clark, a tough New Jersey teacher who takes charge as principal of the state's worst school and enforces strict discipline. He weeds out punk kids all right, but also fires teachers and insults even his supporters when they question his tactics. Well-acted and rousing, obviously favoring its controversial hero, yet doesn't hesitate in showing his tyrannical and egomaniac sides. **Hound Advisory:** Roughhousing, profanity, drug use, but nothing gratuitous as Mr. Clark cleans house. **1989** *(PG-13/Jr. High-Adult)* 109m/C Morgan Freeman, Robert Guillaume, Beverly Todd, Alan North, Lynne Thigpen, Robin Bartlett, Michael Beach, Ethan Phillips, Regina Taylor; *D:* John G. Avildsen; *W:* Michael Schiffer; *M:* Bill Conti. **VHS, Beta, LV, 8mm $19.98** *WAR, FCT*

Leap of Faith 🎬🎬◁

Jonas Nightengale (Martin) is a traveling evangelist/scam artist whose tour bus is stranded in an impoverished farm town. Nevertheless he sets up his show and goes to work, aided by the technology utilized by accomplice Winger. Both Martin and Winger begin to have a change of heart after experiencing love-Winger with local sheriff Neeson and Martin after befriending a waitress (Davidovich) and her crippled brother (Haas). Martin is in his element as the slick revivalist with the hidden heart but the film is soft-headed as well as soft-hearted. **Hound Advisory:** Profanity. **1992** *(PG-13/Jr. High-Adult)* 110m/C Steve Martin, Debra Winger, Lolita Davidovich, Liam Neeson, Lukas Haas, Meatloaf, Philip S. Hoffman, M.C. Gainey, La Chanze, Delores Hall, John Toles-Bey, Albertina Walker, Ricky Dillard; *D:* Richard Pearce; *W:* Janus Cercone; *M:* Cliff Eidelman. **VHS, Beta, LV $19.95** *PAR, BTV*

The Learning Tree 🎬🎬◁

Uneven adaptation of Gordon Parks' autobiographical novel about Newton, a black teenager in the 1920s south, who matures while finding himself at the center of numerous racially-explosive situations, including witnessing a murder. Preachy but often hard- hitting. Major problem is that Johnson looks quite a bit older than Newt's 14 years. **Hound Advisory:** Brutality, profanity, alcohol use, mature themes. **1969** *(PG/Jr. High-Adult)* 107m/C Kyle Johnson, Alex Clarke, Estelle Evans, Dana Elcar; *D:* Gordon Parks. **VHS, Beta $19.98** *WAR, FCT, AFR*

The Left-Handed Gun 🎬🎬🎬

Offbeat version of the exploits of Billy the Kid, which portrays him as a 19th-century Wild West juvenile delinquent. Director Penn's movie debut is a psychological western that attempts to shed frontier myth and portray Billy as a dimwitted menace considerate of his few friends and deadly to his enemies. Stranger yet, The Kid was originally written for James Dean (who died before filming), and the screen version is based on a 1955 Philco teleplay written by Gore Vidal (and directed by Penn), which featured wild homosexual Billy. **1958** *(Family)* 102m/B Paul Newman, Lita Milan, John Dehner; *D:* Arthur Penn. **VHS, Beta $19.98** *WAR, TLF*

Legend 🎬🎬◁

Epic fantasy evokes a rich visual landscape of unicorns, elves, goblins, fairies, swamps, mists, snows, forests, and castles. Too bad the Prince of Darkness (Curry, under awesome makeup) is the only character with personality, as he devilishly tilts the balance between good and evil. He also steals young Jack's girlfriend, and the nature-boy hero, accompanied by bumbling dwarfs, schleps to the rescue. Picture can't help looking impressive, but in the end it's just

another pompous '80s try at the Ultimate Fairy Tale, never mind that one had already been done in 1977 - "Star Wars." **Hound Advisory:** Violence, but on a fantasy level.
1986 **(PG/***Family***)** 89m/C Tom Cruise, Mia Sara, Tim Curry, David Bennent, Billy Barty, Alice Playten; *D:* Ridley Scott; *M:* Jerry Goldsmith. **VHS, Beta, LV** $14.95 *MCA*

Legend of Billie Jean 🎬🔊

Texas girl and her brother have some violent scrapes with thieving bullies and a would-be rapist. Now fugitives from the law, the pair become heroes to the local teen population. Likeable young actors, seen to better advantage elsewhere, make the most of this weightless brew of juvenile rebellion and sappy political symbolism. **Hound Advisory:** Violence, profanity, mature themes.
1985 **(PG-13/***Jr. High-Adult***)** 92m/C Helen Slater, Peter Coyote, Keith Gordon, Christian Slater, Richard Bradford, Yeardley Smith, Dean Stockwell; *D:* Matthew Robbins; *W:* Mark Rosenthal. **VHS, Beta** $79.98 *FOX*

The Legend of Black Thunder Mountain 🎬🔊

Children's adventure courtesy of the Beemans in the mold of "Grizzly Adams" and "The Wilderness Family."
1979 **(G/***Family***)** 90m/C Holly Beeman, Steve Beeman, Ron Brown, F.A. Milovich; *D:* Tom Beeman. **VHS, Beta** *NO*

Legend of Boggy Creek 🎬🔊

Peculiar mixture of fact, fiction and eerie ambiance, dramatizing various Arkansas Bigfoot sightings. Followed by a couple of sasquatch sequels that were entirely scripted kiddie-oriented adventures, like "Return to Boggy Creek"; stick with "Harry and the Hendersons." **Hound Advisory:** Some scary moments, and visuals include cats and dogs allegedly slain by the Boggy Creek creature.
1975 **(G/***Family***)** 87m/C Willie E. Smith, John P. Nixon, John W. Gates, Jeff Crabtree, Buddy Crabtree; *D:* Charles B. Pierce; *W:* Charles B. Pierce. **VHS, Beta** $59.98 *LIV, MRV*

The Legend of Hiawatha

Hiawatha must confront a demon who casts a plague on his people. This animated program is loosely based on Henry Wadsworth Longfellow's poem.
1982 **(***Family***)** 35m/C **VHS, Beta** $29.95 *FHE, WTA*

Legend of Lobo 🎬🎬

Crafty wolf Lobo seeks to free his mate from the clutches of greedy hunters. A Disney wildlife adventure.
1962 **(***Family***)** 67m/C **VHS, Beta** $69.95 *DIS*

The Legend of Manxmouse 🎬🎬🔊

Japanese-animated feature (based on a Paul Gallico story) looks childish and silly on the surface but addresses some deep philosophical concerns, as a Pinocchio-type mouse, who comes to life from a carved figurine, is told that by tradition he must be eaten in public by the last of the Manx cats. But Thomas J. Manxcat is a happy fellow, also troubled by the deadly ritual. Should the duo submit to destiny? Artwork is frankly crude at times, but this fate-vs-free-will fable is a lot

easier to take than its literary soulmate, Shirley Jackson's "The Lottery." **Hound Advisory:** Violence
1991 **(***Preschool-Primary***)** 85m/C **VHS** $14.99 *JFK, WTA*

The Legend of Sleepy Hollow 🎬🎬

Washington Irving's classic tale of the Headless Horseman of Sleepy Hollow features Goldblum well cast as Ichabod Crane but otherwise stretches the short story to tedious length. Made for television. **Hound Advisory:** Roughhousing. The legendary headless spook is unimpressive, scare-wise, compared to the Disney cartoon incarnation.
1979 **(G/***Family***)** 100m/C Jeff Goldblum, Dick Butkus, Paul Sand, Meg Foster, James Griffith, John S. White. **VHS, Beta, LV** $9.99 *STE, VCI*

The Legend of Sleepy Hollow

Classic Washington Irving tale is given the classy Duvall treatment in her "Tall Tales and Legends" series. When a snooty teacher goes too far, the town blacksmith decides to play the ultimate Halloween trick on him. Made for cable television.
1986 **(***Family***)** 51m/C Ed Begley Jr., Beverly D'Angelo, Charles Durning, Tim Thomerson. **VHS** $19.98 *FOX*

Legend of the Lone Ranger 🎬🔊

Fabled Lone Ranger's first meeting with his Indian companion, Tonto, is brought almost to life in this weak and vapid version that tried to revive interest in the western hero. The narration by Merle Haggard leaves something to be desired as do most of the performances. **Hound Advisory:** Violence, salty language.
1981 **(PG/***Family***)** 98m/C Klinton Spilsbury, Michael Horse, Jason Robards Jr., Richard Farnsworth, Christopher Lloyd, Matt Clark; *D:* William A. Fraker; *W:* William Roberts, Ivan Goff, Michael Kane; *M:* John Barry. **VHS, Beta** $29.98 *FOX*

Legend of the Northwest 🎬🎬

The loyalty of a dog is evidenced in the fierce revenge he has for the drunken hunter who shot and killed his master. Jack London-esque wilderness adventure starring "Grizzly Adams" regular Pyle **Hound Advisory:** Violence.
1978 **(G/***Family***)** 83m/C Denver Pyle. **VHS, Beta** $19.95 *STE, GEM, HHE*

Legend of the White Horse 🎬🔊

Scientist and his son travel to a faraway land where the magical white horse reigns. Botched internationally produced fantasy for the family market, with some past Spielberg thespians horsing around in the cast.
1985 **(***Family***)** 91m/C Christopher Lloyd, Dee Wallace Stone, Allison Balson, Soon-Teck Oh, Luke Askew; *D:* Jerzy Domaradzki, Janusz Morgenstern. **VHS** $59.98 *FXV*

The Legend of Wolf Mountain 🎬

Three kids are held hostage by prison escapees in the Utah mountains. But 11-year-old Kerry has a guardian angel in the form of a native medicine-man's ghost who helps the kids vanquish the bad guys. Terrible mixture of New-Age mysticism with a woodsy ripoff of "Home Alone." Wastes a decent

cast of new and veteran performers, and Rooney's role is very small indeed. **Hound Advisory:** Roughhousing.
1992 (PG/*Jr. High-Adult*) 91m/C Mickey Rooney, Bo Hopkins, Don Shanks, Vivian Schilling, Robert Z'Dar, David Shark, Nicole Lund, Natalie Lund, Matthew Lewis, Jonathan Best; **D:** Craig Clyde. VHS, LV $9.95 HMD

The Legend of Young Robin Hood

Dramatization on how the early life of the Sherwood Forest outlaw might have gone. He learns to use a longbow, and forms his convictions as his fellow Saxons struggle with their Norman conquerors.
197? (G/*Family*) 60m/C VHS, Beta $19.95 GEM

The Legend of Zelda: Missing Link

Nick and Zelda, teen adventurers, protect the kingdom of Hyrule from the evil wizard Ganon. The TV cartoon based on the Nintendo Game, originally paired on the tube with a "Super Mario Brothers" cartoon for maximum marketing. Additional volumes available.
1988 (*Primary-Jr. High*) 30m/C VHS $9.95 GKK

Lend a Paw

One of those Academy Award-winning cartoon shorts that made Walt Disney owner of more Oscars than any other individual in history. Jealousy is overcome as Pluto deals with Mickey's newly adopted kitten.
1941 (*Preschool-Primary*) 8m/C VHS, Beta $170.00 DSN, MTI

Leonard Part 6

Expensive, inexplicable, ill-conceived 'family comedy' about super secret agent Leonard Parker (with five undiscussed missions behind him), who comes out of retirement to save San Francisco from killer animals controlled by an evil vegetarian, and patch up his collapsing personal life - not in that order. You're in trouble when the funniest actors are a trout and a bunch of frogs, rather than Cosby (who produced and co-scripted). **Hound Advisory:** Violence, sex talk.
1987 (PG/*Jr. High-Adult*) 83m/C Bill Cosby, Gloria Foster, Tom Courtenay, Joe Don Baker; **D:** Paul Weiland; **W:** Bill Cosby, Jonathan Reynolds; **M:** Elmer Bernstein. VHS, Beta, LV $89.95 COL

Les Miserables

Victor Hugo's classic novel of injustice (the basis for the international hit musical) is adapted in this Japanese-animated family feature about Inspector Javert's long, pitiless pursuit of peasant petty thief Jean Valjean.
1979 (*Family*) 70m/C VHS, Beta $29.95 FHE, APD, WTA

Let the Balloon Go

Based on the international children's bestseller by Ivan Southall, the story is set in the year 1917 and centers around the struggle of a handicapped boy in Australia to win independence and respect.
1976 (*Preschool-Primary*) 92m/C Robert Bettles, Sally Whiteman, Matthew Wilson, Terry McQuillan. VHS, Beta MCA

Let's Go to the Zoo with Captain Kangaroo

Composed of short clips from the Captain's Library of shows, this program features segments introducing youngsters to many great zoo beasts.
1985 (*Preschool-Primary*) 60m/C Bob Keeshan. VHS, Beta MPI

Let's Pretend with Barney

Dinosaurs Barney and BJ use their imaginations to have adventures.
1994 (*Preschool*) 30m/C VHS $14.95 LGV

Let's Sing Again

Eight-year-old singing sensation Breen made his debut in this dusty musical vehicle, as a runaway orphan who becomes the pal of a washed-up opera star in a traveling show. ♫Let's Sing Again; Lullaby; Farmer in the Dell; La Donna e Mobile.
1936 (*Family*) 70m/B Bobby Breen, Henry Armetta, George Houston, Vivienne Osborne, Grant Withers, Inez Courtney, Lucien Littlefield; **D:** Kurt Neumann. VHS $15.95 NOS, LOO, DVT

Liar's Moon

Local boy woos and weds the town's wealthiest young lady, only to be trapped in family intrigue. Standard soaper elevated by talented cast. **Hound Advisory:** Salty language.
1982 (PG/*Jr. High-Adult*) 106m/C Cindy Fisher, Matt Dillon, Christopher Connelly, Susan Tyrrell; **D:** David Fisher. VHS, Beta $29.98 VES

License to Drive

When Les fails his first driver's license test, the kid steals the family auto for a hot date with the girl of his dreams. Bad Example #1. The evening leads to slam-bang danger, including drunken driving. Bad Example #2. If you rented this inane teen-speed comedy instead of Haim's excellent "Lucas" make that Bad Example #3. **Hound Advisory:** Alcohol use, profanity, roughhousing, extremely poor driving.
1988 (PG-13/*Jr. High-Adult*) 90m/C Corey Feldman, Corey Haim, Carol Kane, Richard Masur; **D:** Greg Beeman; **M:** Jay Michael Ferguson. VHS, Beta, LV $19.98 FOX

Lies My Father Told Me

All-ages drama about growing up in the 1920s in a Jewish ghetto in Montreal, Canada. Young David's father has no time for him, so the boy's gentle, immigrant grandfather takes over the role of parent, steering the impressionable kid through adolescence. Quiet and moving. **Hound Advisory:** Sex talk, mature themes.
1975 (PG/*Jr. High-Adult*) 102m/C Yossi Yadin, Len Birman, Marilyn Lightstone, Jeffery Lynas; **D:** Jan Kadar; **W:** Ted Allan. **Award Nominations:** Academy Awards '75: Best Original Screenplay; **Awards:** Golden Globe Awards '76: Best Foreign Film. VHS NO

Life & Times of Grizzly Adams

Grizzly is mistakenly chased for a crime he didn't commit and along the way befriends a big bear. Lightweight family adventure based on the rugged life of legendary frontiersman, Grizzly Adams. Served as the launching pad for the TV series

and locked the ursine Haggerty into a series of friendly mountain-man roles.
1974 (G/ *Family*) 93m/C Dan Haggerty, Denver Pyle, Lisa Jones, Marjorie Harper, Don Shanks; **D:** Richard Friedenberg. **VHS, Beta $19.95** *VCI*

Life Begins for Andy Hardy 🦴🦴🦴

Andy gets a job in New York before entering college and finds the working world to be a sobering experience. Surprisingly downbeat and hard-hitting for the Hardy series, and better for it. Garland's last appearance in the series.
1941 (*Family*) 100m/B Mickey Rooney, Judy Garland, Lewis Stone, Ann Rutherford, Fay Holden, Gene Reynolds, Ralph Byrd; **D:** George B. Seitz. **VHS, Beta $19.95** *MGM*

Life on the Mississippi

Beautifully photographed production for PBS-TV based on selections from Mark Twain's memoir of the same title. Flavorful narrative follows the adolescent Samuel Clemens, already spinning tall tales during his pre-Civil War apprenticeship as a steamboat pilot on the mighty river; in his escapades and mischievous outlook we can see the roots of Tom Sawyer and Huck Finn. Preston is outstanding as usual as Mr. Bixby, the boy's mentor in navigating both sand bars and life. Introduction by novelist Kurt Vonnegut, who looks startlingly like Twain himself. An abridged 54-minute version is also available.
1980 (*Family*) 120m/C Robert Lansing, David Knell, James Keane. **VHS, Beta $19.95** *KUI, MCA, FLI*

Life with Father 🦴🦴🦴🦴

Based on the autobiographical writings of Clarence Day, Jr. and a long-running Broadway play, recalling a childhood spent in New York City during the 1880s. A delightful saga about stern but loving father Powell and his relationship with his knowing wife Dunne and four red-headed sons. Powell creates one of the great father figures of film in this heavily lauded classic that was followed by "Life with Mother."
1947 (*Family*) 118m/C William Powell, Irene Dunne, Elizabeth Taylor, Edmund Gwenn, ZaSu Pitts, Jimmy Lydon, Martin Milner; **D:** Michael Curtiz; **M:** Max Steiner. **Award Nominations:** Academy Awards '47: Best Actor (Powell), Best Art Direction/Set Decoration (Color), Best Color Cinematography; **Awards:** Golden Globe Awards '48: Best Score; New York Film Critics Awards '47: Best Actor (Powell). **VHS, Beta $9.95** *CNG, MRV, NOS*

Life with Mikey 🦴🦴🦴

Fox is well cast as a once-beloved former TV child actor who as a grownup runs a struggling talent agency for other juvenile thespians. Looking for a new kid superstar to turn business around, he thinks he's found it in Angie, a 10-year-old Brooklyn pickpocket. Light comedy, low on urgency and generally predictable, but agreeably sweet-spirited. **Hound Advisory:** Salty language.
1993 (PG/ *Jr. High-Adult*) 92m/C Michael J. Fox, Christina Vidal, Cyndi Lauper, Nathan Lane, David Huddleston, Victor Garber, David Krumholtz, Tony Hendra; **Cameos:** Ruben Blades; **D:** James Lapine; **W:** Marc Lawrence; **M:** Alan Menken. **VHS, Beta, LV $39.99** *TOU, BTV*

The Light in the Forest 🦴🦴🦴

Disney adaptation of the Conrad Richter novel about a young man, kidnapped by Indians when he was a pioneer child and raised within the tribe. Years later he's forcibly returned to his original family. His problems coping with white society are a bit sentimentalized and familiar, but still effective drama.
1958 (*Family*) 92m/C James MacArthur, Fess Parker, Carol Lynley, Wendell Corey, Joanne Dru, Jessica Tandy, Joseph Calleia, John McIntire; **D:** Herschel Daugherty. **VHS, Beta $69.95** *DIS*

Light of Day 🦴🦴

Confused family drama with a rock 'n roll background. Working class siblings Joe and Patti escape their dreary lives through their bar band in Cleveland. Their parents disapprove, and Joe ends up torn between the prodigal sister and their sick mother. Script falls flat, although Jett is utterly believable (helps to have real-life experience) and Fox works up a sweat in uncharacteristic hard-edged role. Title song written by Bruce Springsteen. **Hound Advisory:** Profanity, mature themes, alcohol use.
1987 (PG-13/ *Sr. High-Adult*) 107m/C Michael J. Fox, Joan Jett, Gena Rowlands, Jason Miller, Michael McKean, Michael Rooker, Michael Dolan; **D:** Paul Schrader; **W:** Paul Schrader; **M:** Thomas Newman. **VHS, Beta, LV $29.98** *LIV, VES*

The Light Princess

Charming British made-for-TV fairy tale fetchingly combines live actors with animated backgrounds and creatures in George MacDonald's 1862 story of how a wicked witch curses a princess, literally and figuratively, with lightness; she has zero gravity and never takes anything seriously, a trial for her royal parents who must keep her from floating away.
1979 (*Family*) 56m/C Stacey Dorning, John Fortune; **D:** Andrew Gosling. **VHS, Beta $19.98** *FOX, WTA, HMV*

Lightning Jack 🦴🦴

Alleged western comedy about Lightning Jack Kane (Hogan), an aging second-rate outlaw who desperately wants to become a western legend. Mute store clerk Ben (Gooding) winds up as his partner in crime, adept at rolling his eyes while running smack into criticism of Stepin Fetchitism. Saddlebags are full of cliches and the running gags (including Kane's surreptitious use of his eyeglasses so he can see his shooting targets) frequently fall flat. **Hound Advisory:** Violence.
1994 (PG-13/ *Jr. High-Adult*) 101m/C Paul Hogan, Cuba Gooding Jr., Beverly D'Angelo, Kamala Dawson, Pat Hingle, Richard Riehle, Frank McRae, Roger Daltrey, L.Q. Jones, Max Cullen; **D:** Simon Wincer; **W:** Paul Hogan; **M:** Bruce Rowland. **VHS** *HBO*

Lightning: The White Stallion 🦴🦴

Can Mickey Rooney's megawatts of talent save a whole movie? The answer is ... almost, but not quite, as he narrates this forgettable compendium of girl-and-her-horse cliches, right down to the heroine's urgent need for an operation. Meanwhile, she tries to train a racing steed to be a show-jumper, then has to reclaim the animal from thieves. **Hound Advisory:** Alcohol use.

1986 (**PG**/*Jr. High-Adult*) 93m/C Mickey Rooney, Susan George, Isabel Lorca; **D:** William A. Levey. **VHS, Beta $19.98** *MED*

Like Father, Like Son ♫♪

First and least of several body-switch movies that cluttered Hollywood in the late '80s. Magic potion makes Dr. Hammond and his small son Chris switch personalities, with predictable hijinks. The few good moments go to the impish Moore, at the top of his form as an adolescent spirit in a bigshot surgeon's body. **Hound Advisory:** Profanity, sex.
1987 (**PG-13**/*Jr. High-Adult*) 101m/C Dudley Moore, Kirk Cameron, Catherine Hicks, Margaret Colin, Sean Astin; **D:** Rod Daniel; **M:** Miles Goodman. **VHS, Beta, LV $19.95** *COL*

Like Jake and Me

Sensitive boy wonders what his new siblings will be like in this Mavis Jukes tale distributed through Disney.
1989 (*Primary-Jr. High*) 16m/C **VHS, Beta $280.00** *MTI, DSN*

Lili ♫♫♫

Delightful musical romance about a 16-year-old orphan who joins a traveling carnival and falls in love with a crippled, embittered puppeteer. Heartwarming and charming, if occasionally cloying. Leslie Caron sings the films's song hit, "Hi-Lili, Hi-Lo."
1953 (*Family*) 81m/C Leslie Caron, Jean-Pierre Aumont, Mel Ferrer, Kurt Kasznar, Zsa Zsa Gabor; **D:** Charles Walters; **M:** Bronislau Kaper. **Award Nominations:** Academy Awards '53: Best Actress (Caron), Best Art Direction/Set Decoration (Color), Best Color Cinematography, Best Director (Walters), Best Screenplay; **Awards:** Academy Awards '53: Best Score; British Academy Awards '53: Best Actress (Caron); Golden Globe Awards '54: Best Screenplay; National Board of Review Awards '53: 10 Best Films of the Year. **VHS, Beta $19.98** *MGM*

Lilies of the Field ♫♫♫

Five East German nuns running a farm in the Southwest enlist the aid of a free-spirited U.S. Army veteran, persuading him to build a chapel for them and teach them English. As the itinerant laborer, Poitier helps limit the inherent saccharine, bringing an engaging honesty and strength to his role. Skala is fine as the mother superior; prior to this opportunity, she had been struggling to make ends meet in a variety of day jobs. Warm and engaging drama certified Poitier as a superstar, as he became the first black man to win an Oscar, and the first African American nominated since Hattie MacDaniel in 1939. Followed by "Christmas Lilies of the Field" (1979).
1963 (*Family*) 94m/B Sidney Poitier, Lilia Skala, Lisa Mann, Isa Crino, Stanley Adams; **D:** Ralph Nelson; **M:** Jerry Goldsmith. **Award Nominations:** Academy Awards '63: Best Adapted Screenplay, Best Black and White Cinematography, Best Picture, Best Supporting Actress (Skala); **Awards:** Academy Awards '63: Best Actor (Poitier); Berlin International Film Festival '63: Best Actor (Poitier); Golden Globe Awards '64: Best Actor—Drama (Poitier); National Board of Review Awards '63: 10 Best Films of the Year. **VHS, Beta $19.98** *MGM, FOX, BTV*

The Lion in Winter ♫♫♫♫

Medieval monarch Henry II and his wife, Eleanor of Aquitane, match wits over the succession to the English throne and much else in this fast-paced film version of James Goldman's play. The family, including three grown sons, and visiting royalty are united for the Christmas holidays fraught with tension, rapidly shifting allegiances, and layers of psychological manipulation. Superb dialogue and perfectly realized characterizations. O'Toole and Hepburn are triumphant. Screen debuts for Hopkins and Dalton. Shot on location, this literate costume drama surprised the experts with its box-office success.
1968 (**PG**/*Jr. High-Adult*) 134m/C Peter O'Toole, Katharine Hepburn, Jane Merrow, Nigel Terry, Timothy Dalton, Anthony Hopkins, John Castle, Nigel Stock; **D:** Anthony Harvey; **W:** Jim Goldman; **M:** John Barry. **Award Nominations:** Academy Awards '68: Best Actor (O'Toole), Best Costume Design, Best Director (Harvey); **Awards:** Academy Awards '68: Best Actress (Hepburn), Best Adapted Screenplay, Best Score; Directors Guild of America Awards '68: Best Director (Harvey); Golden Globe Awards '69: Best Actor—Drama (O'Toole), Best Film—Drama; National Board of Review Awards '68: 10 Best Films of the Year; New York Film Critics Awards '68: Best Film. **VHS, LV $19.95** *COL, BTV, TVC*

The Lion King ♫♫♫♪

Epic animated African adventure once again does Disney proud. Lion cub Simba is destined to be king of the beasts, until evil uncle Scar (Irons) plots against him. Growing up in the jungles of Africa he learns about life and responsibility as he returns to reclaim his throne. Heartwarming combo of crowd-pleasing songs, a story with depth, emotion, and politically correct multiculturalism, and stunning animation created in painstaking detail with lifelike creatures and beautiful landscapes. 32nd Disney animated film is the first without human characters, the first based on an original story, and the first to use the voices of a well-known, ethnically diverse cast. Scenes of violence in the animal kingdom may be too much for younger viewers. ♫Can You Feel the Love Tonight; The Circle of Life; I Just Can't Wait to Be King; Be Prepared; Hakuna Matata. **Hound Advisory:** Simba's father dies tragically, a scene which may be too much for very young children.
1994 (**G**/*Family*) 87m/C Jim Cummings; **D:** Rob Minkoff, Roger Allers; **W:** Jonathan Roberts, Irene Mecchi; **M:** Elton John, Hans Zimmer, Tim Rice; **V:** Matthew Broderick, Jeremy Irons, James Earl Jones, Madge Sinclair, Robert Guillaume, Jonathan Taylor Thomas, Richard "Cheech" Marin, Whoopi Goldberg, Rowan Atkinson, Nathan Lane, Ernie Sabella, Niketa Calame, Moira Kelly. **VHS** *NYR*

The Lion, the Witch and the Wardrobe ♫♫♫

The classic C.S. Lewis fantasy (with religious overtones) about four children who find a doorway to the mystical land of Narnia, under the icy spell of the White Witch. The animators of the TV "Peanuts" series and the Children's Television Workshop joined with the Episcopal Radio/TV Foundation to produce this made-for-TV cartoon adaptation (good news: the commercial-break blackouts are nearly unnoticeable) that starts off a little stiffly but improves and enchants as it goes along. Winner of an Emmy award for Best Animated Special.
1979 (*Family*) 95m/C **VHS $12.98** *BTV, REP, WTA*

Lionheart ♫♫

Boy warrior in 12th-century France runs away from his first serious battle. Mistaken for one of Richard the Lionhearted noble Crusaders, the bland teen is joined by hundreds of orphaned and homeless children, seeking protection from the

evil slave-trader known as the Black Prince. Played by Byrne, the BP's a terrific villain, and the major reason for watching this bogus, kiddie rewrite of medieval history, barely released in theaters. **Hound Advisory:** Violence.
1987 (PG/ *Preschool)* 105m/C Eric Stoltz, Talia Shire, Nicola Cowper, Dexter Fletcher, Nicholas Clay, Deborah Barrymore, Gabriel Byrne; **D:** Franklin J. Schaffner; **W:** Richard Outten; **M:** Jerry Goldsmith. **VHS, Beta, LV $19.98** *WAR*

Lisa 🦴🦴

Teen psychothriller that almost works. Title character is a 14-year-old who plays prank phone calls on a handsome new guy in town, enticing him into a rendezvous. Little does Lisa realize he's a serial killer. Well-built suspense evaporates in violent climax, and the single mother/growing daughter relationship doesn't go very deep. **Hound Advisory:** Mature themes, sex talk, profanity, violence.
1990 (PG-13/ *Jr. High-Adult)* 95m/C Staci Keanan, Cheryl Ladd, D.W. Moffett, Tanya Fenmore, Jeffrey Tambor, Julie Cobb; **D:** Gary Sherman. **VHS $19.98** *FOX*

Little Big League 🦴🦴🦴

12-year-old baseball nut inherits the Minnesota Twins baseball team from his grandfather, appoints himself manager when everyone else declines, and becomes the youngest owner-manager in history. He finds the sledding tough, losing contact with his friends and discovering the challenge of managing unruly pro ballplayers. Nothing new about the premise, but kids and America's favorite pastime add up to good clean family fun. Edwards is engaging as the mini exec. Features several real-life baseball players, including the Mariners' Griffey. Good cast features TV's Busfield at first base. Screenwriting debut from Pincus, and directorial debut from the executive producer of "Seinfeld," Scheinman. **Hound Advisory:** Salty ballpark language.
1994 (PG/ *Jr. High-Adult)* 119m/C Luke Edwards, Jason Robards Jr., Kevin Dunn, Dennis Farina, John Ashton, Jonathan Silverman, Wolfgang Bodison, Timothy Busfield, Ashley Crow, Scott Patterson, Billy L. Sullivan, Miles Feulner, Kevin Elster, Leon "Bull" Durham, Brad "The Animal" Lesley; **Cameos:** Don Mattingly, Ken Griffey Jr., Paul O'Neill; **D:** Andrew Scheinman; **W:** Gregory Pincus, Adam Scheinman. **VHS** *NYR*

Little Big Man 🦴🦴🦴🦴

Based on Thomas Berger's picaresque novel, this is the story of 121-year-old Jack Crabb and his quixotic life as gunslinger, charlatan, Indian, ally to George Custer, and the only white survivor of Little Big Horn. Told mainly through flashbacks. Hoffman provides a classic portrayal of Crabb, as fact and myth are jumbled and reshaped. **Hound Advisory:** Violence; alcohol use; sex.
1970 (PG/ *Jr. High-Adult)* 135m/C Dustin Hoffman, Faye Dunaway, Chief Dan George, Richard Mulligan, Martin Balsam, Jeff Corey, Aimee Eccles; **D:** Arthur Penn; **W:** Calder Willingham. **VHS, Beta, LV $19.98** *FOX, HMV*

Little Boy Lost 🦴🦴

True story of the hunt for a lost young boy in Australia. Complicating matters; the child has been taught never to talk to strangers, so he avoids search parties.
1978 (G/ *Family)* 92m/C John Hargreaves, Tony Barry, Lorna Lesley; **D:** Alan Spires. **VHS, Beta** *NO*

Little Buddha 🦴🦴

Tibetan Lama Norbu informs the Seattle Konrad family that their 10-year-old son Jesse may be the reincarnation of a respected monk. He wants to take the boy back to Tibet to find out and, with some apparently minor doubts, the family head off on their spiritual quest. In an effort to instruct Jesse in Buddhism, this journey is interspersed with the story of Prince Siddhartha, who will leave behind his worldly ways to follow the path towards enlightenment and become the Buddha. The two stories are an ill-fit, the acting awkward (with the exception of Ruocheng as the wise Norbu), but boy, does the film look good (from cinematographer Vittorio Storaro). Filmed on location in Nepal and Bhutan. **Hound Advisory:** Salty language.
1993 (PG/ *Jr. High-Adult)* 123m/C Keanu Reeves, Alex Wiesendanger, Ying Ruocheng, Chris Isaak, Bridget Fonda; **D:** Bernardo Bertolucci; **W:** Mark Peploe, Rudy Wurlitzer; **M:** Ryuichi Sakamoto. **VHS** *NYR*

Little Critter Series: Just Me and My Dad

Little Critter and his ever-patient father go on a camping trip, where dad rescues his son and teaches him the lessons of life. Based on the 1977 book by Mercer Mayer.
1993 (*Preschool-Primary)* 25m/C **VHS $12.99**

The Little Crooked Christmas Tree

At a Christmas tree farm, one spruce grows crooked from bending branches to protect a mother dove and her babies. When the other trees are cut down at Christmastime, the little crooked tree is left behind, and the tree farmer has a special plan in mind. Holiday cartoon.
1993 (*Family)* 30m/C **D:** Michael Cutting; **W:** Michael Cutting. **VHS** *BAR*

Little Darlings WOOF!

Distasteful premise has summer campers Kristy and Tatum in a race to lose their virginity. Kristy is better (at acting, that is); but who cares? And just who is meant to be the market for this movie, anyway?
1980 (R/ *Sr. High-Adult)* 95m/C Tatum O'Neal, Kristy McNichol, Matt Dillon, Armand Assante, Margaret Blye; **D:** Ronald F. Maxwell; **M:** Charles Fox. **VHS, Beta, LV $14.95** *PAR*

Little Dog Lost

Abused dog Candy searches for and finally finds a kind master in this live-action adaptation of the book by Meindert de Jong. From TV's "Wonderful World of Disney" show.
1990 (*Preschool-Primary)* 48m/C **VHS, Beta $250.00** *MTI, DSN*

The Little Drummer Boy

The classic Rankin-Bass rendering of the tale of the drummer who played for the Christ Child in the manger, one of their most successful stop-motion animated TV specials. Background vocals by the Vienna Boys Choir.
1968 (*Family)* 30m/C **D:** Takeya Nakamura; **V:** Teddy Eccles, Jose Ferrer, Paul Frees. **VHS, Beta $12.98** *FHE, WTA*

The Little Engine That Could

Classic children's tale by Watty Piper comes to vivid animated life. The tiny engine comes upon the stranded Birthday Train and with a cheerful "I think I can..." refrain manages to haul the trainload of toys over a steep mountain pass.
1991 (Preschool-Primary) 30m/C **D:** Dave Edwards. **VHS, LV** $12.98 MCA, WTA

The Little Fox ♫♫

Cartoon feature from Europe following the adventures of an orphaned young fox named Vic, growing up in a forest.
1987 (Preschool-Primary) 80m/C **VHS, Beta** $39.95 CEL, WTA

The Little Girl Who Lives Down the Lane ♫♫♫

Engrossing, offbeat thriller about a strangely mature 13-year-old who apparently lives all by herself - her father never seems to be home, and she's hiding something (guess what) in the basement. Foster is excellent, not playing a psycho but a sympathetic, self-possessed youngster who'll do anything, including murder, to maintain her independence in a world hostile to kids. Based on the novel by Laird Koenig. **Hound Advisory:** Mature themes, sex.
1976 (PG/Sr. High-Adult) 90m/C Jodie Foster, Martin Sheen, Alexis Smith, Scott Jacoby; **D:** Nicolas Gessner. **VHS, Beta, LV** $29.98 LIV, VES

Little Heroes ♫♫♫

Impoverished little girl gets through hard times with the aid of her loyal dog and eventually his memory helps her cope with tragedy. Low-budget family tearjerker that nonetheless works, it claims to be based on a true story.
1991 (G/Family) 78m/C Raeanin Simpson, Katherine Willis, Keith Christensen, Hoover the Dog; **D:** Craig Clyde; **W:** Craig Clyde; **M:** John McCallum. **VHS** $14.95 HMD

Little Hiawatha

Playing fair is the name of the game as children win support and true friendship in this vintage Disney "Silly Symphony."
1937 (Preschool-Primary) 8m/C **VHS, Beta** $170.00 DSN, MTI

The Little House

The story of a house whose peace and quiet comes to an end when the city moves into its neighborhood. Disney adaptation of Virginia Lee Burton's book.
1988 (Preschool-Primary) 8m/C **VHS, Beta** $170.00 DSN,, MTI

Little House on the Prairie ♫♫♫

Pilot for the fine network television series based on the life and books of Laura Ingalls Wilder and her family's struggles on the American plains in the 1860s. Other episodes are also available on tape, including Patricia Neal's Emmy-winning guest role as a dying widow seeking a home for her children. Rosy and warm, rendered with care by series creator Michael Landon.
1974 (Family) 98m/C Michael Landon, Karen Grassle, Victor French, Melissa Gilbert, Melissa Sue Anderson; **D:** Michael Landon. **VHS, Beta** $19.98 WAR, OM

Little Lord Fauntleroy ♫♫♫♫

The vintage Hollywood version of the Frances Hodgson Burnett story of fatherless Brooklyn boy Cedric Errol, who discovers he's the heir to a English dukedom and must win the affections of his nobleman grandfather. Charming and beautifully cast. Also available in a computer colorized edition. C. Aubrey Smith, the boy's crusty old guardian, was a grand British character actor who may be familiar to American audiences as a visual inspiration for the pipe-smoking, tale-telling Commander McBragg from the vintage "Tennessee Tuxedo" cartoon series.
1936 (Family) 102m/B Freddie Bartholomew, Sir C. Aubrey Smith, Mickey Rooney, Dolores Costello, Jessie Ralph, Guy Kibbee; **D:** John Cromwell; **M:** Max Steiner. **VHS, Beta** $19.95 NOS, MRV, VEC

Little Lord Fauntleroy ♫♫♫

Poor boy in New York suddenly finds himself the heir to his grandfather's estate in England. Lavish remake of the 1936 classic, adapted from Frances Hodgson Burnett's novel. Guinness is his usual old-pro self; newcomer Schroder an appealing counterpoint as the Little Lord. Made for TV.
1980 (Family) 98m/C Rick Schroder, Alec Guinness, Victoria Tennant, Eric Porter, Colin Blakely, Connie Booth, Rachel Kempson; **D:** Jack Gold. **VHS, Beta** $14.95 FHE, STE

Little Man Tate ♫♫♫

Seven-year-old Fred Tate has a genius IQ and a close rapport with his streetwise, single parent Dede. But he's lonely and bored in school, so Dede reluctantly surrenders him to a (childless) woman academic specializing in gifted children. Enrolled in college and torn between competing mothers, the boy feels more of a misfit than ever. Compelling all-ages drama, thoughtful but never dry or dull; main complaint is it finishes with more than a few loose ends. Interesting to note Foster (making her directing debut) and musician/supporting actor Harry Connick, Jr. were both child prodigies themselves. **Hound Advisory:** Fred catches a college-age pal in bed with a co-ed, and there's realistically salty language, alcohol talk.
1991 (PG/Jr. High-Adult) 99m/C Jodie Foster, Dianne Wiest, Harry Connick Jr., Adam Hann-Byrd, George Plimpton, Debi Mazar, Celia Weston, David Pierce, Danitra Vance, Josh Mostel, P.J. Ochlan; **D:** Jodie Foster; **W:** Scott Frank; **M:** Mark Isham. **VHS** $19.98 ORI, CCB

The Little Match Girl ♫♫♫

Adults more than small children should watch - and watch out for - this British TV redo of Hans Christian Andersen. Set in Victorian London, musical captures a "Les Miserables" sense of heroic melancholy with the story of a nameless urchin peddling matches in the icy streets on Christmas Eve. Unlike Andersen's sad waif, this match girl has a relatively stable home life, a rich playmate and a gainfully employed boyfriend. But yearnings for her deceased mother drive her to the fate recounted in the original unhappy tale. Finale is rendered in theatrical, highly fantasized terms, and kid viewers may or may not sense the intimations of suicide. Recommended for grownup Andrew Lloyd-Webber fans; songs here derive from a Jeremy Paul/Leslie Stewart stage production "Scraps." **Hound Advisory:** Alcohol use, mature themes, salty language. 1987 *(Family)* 90m/C John Rhys-Davies, Rue McClanahan, Roger Daltrey, Twiggy, Natalie Morse; *D:* Michael Lindsay-Hogg. **VHS, Beta $19.95** *ACA*

The Little Match Girl

Hans Christian Andersen goes politically correct in this jazzy cartoon adaptation, set in poverty-wracked NYC in 1899. Angela is a freezing street urchin peddling matches to rich snobs on New Year's Eve, and her bittersweet tale (still cheerier than the original) is heavy on help-the-homeless themes. 1990 *(Family)* 30m/C **VHS, Beta $14.98** *FHE, WTA*

Little Men 🎵◁

Movie version of Louisa May Alcott's own sequel to her oft-filmed "Little Women" is a tepid tale that finds the grownup Jo March running an orphanage for boys. 1940 *(Family)* 86m/B Jack Oakie, Jimmy Lydon, Kay Francis, George Bancroft; *D:* Norman Z. McLeod. **VHS, Beta $19.95** *NOS, MRV, VCN*

The Little Mermaid 🎵🎵

Animated version of Hans Christian Andersen's tale about a little mermaid who rescues a prince whose boat has capsized. She immediately falls in love and wishes that she could become a human girl. Not to be confused with the 1989 Disney version. 1978 *(G/Primary)* 71m/C *D:* Tim Reid. **VHS, Beta $19.95** *STE, GEM*

The Little Mermaid 🎵🎵🎵◁

Teenage mermaid Ariel falls in love with a human prince and longs to be a land-dweller too. She makes a pact with Ursula the Sea Witch to trade her voice for a pair of legs. Charming family musical, which harks back to the days of classic Disney animation, and hailed a new era of superb Disney animated musicals. Sebastian the calypso crab nearly steals the show with his wit and musical numbers "Under the Sea" and "Kiss the Girl." Based on the Hans Christian Anderson fairy tale - but severely altering his original bittersweet ending. 🎵Under the Sea; Kiss the Girl; Daughters of Triton; Part of Your World; Poor Unfortunate Souls; Les Poissons. 1989 *(G/Family)* 82m/C *D:* John Musker, Ron Clements; *M:* Alan Menken, Howard Ashman; *V:* Jodi Benson, Christopher Daniel Barnes, Pat Carroll, Rene Auberjonois, Samuel E. Wright, Buddy Hackett, Jason Marin, Edie McClurg, Kenneth Mars, Nancy Cartwright. **Award Nominations:** Academy Awards '89: Best Song ("Kiss the Girl"); **Awards:** Academy Awards '89: Best Song ("Under the Sea"), Best Original Score; Golden Globe Awards '90: Best Song ("Under the Sea"), Best Score. **VHS, Beta, LV, 8mm** *DIS, OM*

Little Miss Broadway 🎵🎵

Orphan Temple brings the residents of a theatrical boarding house together in hopes of getting them into show business. Awfully cliched, but worth seeing just for Shirley and Jimmy combining talents. Also available in computer colorized version. 🎵Be Optimistic; How Can I Thank You; I'll Build a Broadway For You; If All the World Were Paper; Thank You For the

Use of the Hall; We Should Be Together; Swing Me an Old-Fashioned Song; When You Were Sweet Sixteen; Happy Birthday to You. 1938 *(Family)* 70m/B Shirley Temple, George Murphy, Jimmy Durante, Phyllis Brooks, Edna May Oliver, George Barbier, Donald Meek, Jane Darwell; *D:* Irving Cummings. **VHS, Beta $19.98** *FOX*

Little Miss Marker 🎵🎵🎵

Heartwarming semi-musical based on the oft-filmed Damon Runyon tale. Little girl left with lowlifes as an IOU for a gambling debt charms her way into everyone's heart (always the hazard around Shirley), especially when her father's death makes her an orphan (always the hazard around Shirley). Great supporting cast. 1934 *(Family)* 88m/B Adolphe Menjou, Shirley Temple, Dorothy Dell, Charles Bickford, Lynne Overman; *D:* Alexander Hall. **VHS $49.99** *MCA*

Little Miss Marker 🎵◁

Mediocre remake of the often retold story of a bookie who accepts a little girl as a security marker for a $10 bet. Disappointing performance from Curtis adds to an already dull affair. **Hound Advisory:** Salty language. 1980 *(PG/Primary-Adult)* 103m/C Walter Matthau, Julie Andrews, Tony Curtis, Bob Newhart, Lee Grant, Sara Stimson, Brian Dennehy; *D:* Walter Bernstein; *M:* Henry Mancini. **VHS, Beta $14.98** *MCA*

Little Miss Millions 🎵🎵

Twelve-year-old heiress Heather has run away from the wicked stepmom who's siphoning off her fortune. Her family hires bounty hunter Nick Frost to bring her back. How much do you want to bet that cold-hearted Nick will warm to Heather before the movie's end? (Hint: plot takes place around Christmas.) Slow, sentimental timekiller with a good cast. **Hound Advisory:** Roughhousing, alcohol use. 1993 *(PG/Jr. High-Adult)* 90m/C Howard Hesseman, Anita Morris, Love Hewitt; *D:* Roger Corman. **VHS $89.98** *NHO*

Little Monsters 🎵🎵◁

Young Brian discovers that kid brother Eric's complaints are true: there really is a monster - named Maurice - under his bed. The blue-faced, horned prankster takes Brian on tours of the wild world beneath the bed in a plotline mildly reminiscent of Dr. Seuss but less successful, especially when it turns serious. But juvenile monster fest has its moments. Mandel plays Maurice; he and his creepy cohorts bear a more-than-coincident resemblance to the spooks in "Beetlejuice." Savage and Stern both served subsequent time on TV's "The Wonder Years" (Stern was the narrative voice). **Hound Advisory:** Salty language among the monster-beset kids. 1989 *(PG/Jr. High-Sr. High)* 100m/C Fred Savage, Howie Mandel, Margaret Whitton, Ben Savage, Daniel Stern, Rick Ducommun, Frank Whaley; *D:* Richard Alan Greenberg; *W:* Ted Elliot, Terry Rossio; *M:* David Newman. **VHS, Beta, LV $14.95** *MGM*

Little Nemo: Adventures in Slumberland 🎵🎵

Animators had planned for years to bring Winsor McKay's surreal turn-of-the-century comic strip to life, but this bland Japanese cartoon barely hints at the fun a truly inspired

Ariel and Flounder pose for underwater camera in "The Little Mermaid"

production might have been. Nemo is a young boy whose dreams take him to Slumberland. There, Nemo unwittingly unleashes a nightmare creature who kidnaps good King Morpheus. Nemo leads the rescue mission, but dull songs and tired gags don't save the film. Visually accomplished, but that's it.

1992 (G/*Family*) 85m/C *D:* William T. Hurtz, Masami Hata; *W:* Chris Columbus, Richard Outten; *M:* Tom Chase, Steve Rucker; *V:* Gabriel Damon, Mickey Rooney, Rene Auberjonois, Daniel Mann, Laura Mooney, Bernard Erhard, William E. Martin. **VHS, LV $24.95** *HMD, WTA*

Little Nikita 🎵🎵

California boy is shocked to learn that his parents are actually Soviet spies, planted long ago as American citizens to wait for an eventual call to duty. Now the FBI is closing in. What should the kid do? Poitier provides about the only spark in this somewhat incoherent thriller. **Hound Advisory:** Salty language, violence.

1988 (PG/*Jr. High-Adult*) 98m/C River Phoenix, Sidney Poitier, Richard Bradford, Richard Lynch, Caroline Kava, Lucy Deakins; *D:* Richard Benjamin; *W:* Bo Goldman; *M:* Marvin Hamlisch. **VHS, Beta, LV $14.95** *COL*

Little Orphan Annie 🎵🎵

Long before she became a Broadway musical extravaganza, Annie went from Harold Gray's newspaper comic-strip to the

silver screen with this unpretentious short feature, still worth a look for the curious.

1932 (*Family*) 60m/B May Robson, Buster Phelps, Mitzie Green, Edgar Kennedy; *D:* John S. Robertson; *M:* Max Steiner. **VHS, Beta $29.98** *CCB*

The Little Prince 🎵🎵

Disappointing adaptation of the classic metaphor-choked story by Antoine de Saint-Exupery, about an aviator stranded in the desert who encounters a thoughtful little boy from asteroid B-612 longing away for his distant love, a rose. Despite interesting efforts by Gene Wilder (as a fox) and Bob Fosse (miming a snake), the forgettable Lerner and Loewe score emphasizes a general lack of magic or spontaneity. 🎵It's a Hat; I Need Air; I'm On Your Side; Be Happy; You're a Child; I Never Met a Rose; Why Is the Desert (Lovely to See)?; Closer and Closer and Closer; Little Prince (From Who Knows Where).

1974 (G/*Family*) 88m/C Richard Kiley, Bob Fosse, Steven Warner, Gene Wilder; *D:* Stanley Donen; *W:* Alan Jay Lerner; *M:* Frederick Loewe, Alan Jay Lerner. **Award Nominations:** Academy Awards '74: Best Song ("Little Prince"), Best Original Score; **Awards:** Golden Globe Awards '75: Best Score. **VHS, Beta, LV $14.95** *PAR*

The Little Prince & Friends

Will Vinton's brand of clay animation is at its finest in this collection of short subjects: St. Exupery's "The Little

Prince," Washington Irving's "Rip Van Winkle," and Leo Tolstoy's "Martin the Cobbler."

1987 *(Family)* 90m/C **VHS, Beta, LV $19.95** *IME*

The Little Prince, Vols. 1-5

Each program in this series adapts Antoine de Saint Exupery's beloved, thoughtful little character into different adventures designed to teach basic lessons and morals. Additional volumes available.

1985 *(Primary-Jr. High)* 60m/C **VHS, Beta $14.98** *LIV*

The Little Princess 🐾🐾🐾🐾

Perhaps the best of Shirley's films and her first in color. The moppet's a schoolgirl in Victorian London sent to a harsh boarding school when her Army officer father is posted abroad. With dad missing in action, the penniless girl must work as a mistreated servant at the institution to pay her keep, all the while haunting the hospitals for her lost papa. Classic tearjerker, even with the obligatory song and dance numbers. Based on the Frances Hodgson Burnett children's classic.

1939 *(Family)* 91m/B Shirley Temple, Richard Greene, Anita Louise, Ian Hunter, Cesar Romero, Arthur Treacher, Sybil Jason, Miles Mander, Marcia Mae Jones, E.E. Clive; *D:* Walter Lang. **VHS, Beta, LV $9.95** *CNG, MRV, NOS*

The Little Princess 🐾🐾🐾

Multi-cassette adaptation of Frances Hodgson Burnett's book. In Victorian England, kind-hearted Sara is a star pupil (and thus much-resented) at Miss Minchin's Select Seminary for Young Ladies. She's forced into poverty when her father suddenly dies. Can his longtime friend find her and restore her happiness? British production originally aired in the US on PBS as part of the "Wonderworks" family movie series.

1987 *(Family)* 180m/C Amelia Shankley, Nigel Havers, Maureen Lipman; *D:* Carol Wiseman. **VHS $29.95** *FCT, PME, SIG*

The Little Rascals 🐾🐾🐾

Alfalfa runs afoul of the membership requirements for the "He-Man Woman Haters Club" when he starts to fall for Darla. If you like cute kids doing cute stuff, you'll likely be charmed by this remake of the original series. which included silent shorts and more than 80 talking episodes eventually syndicated for television. Director Spheeris currently holds "Queen of the Remakes" title, having rendered TV's "The Beverly Hillbillies" and "Wayne's World" for the big screen. **Hound Advisory:** Salty language.

1994 *(PG/Family)* 80m/C Daryl Hannah, Courtland Mead, Travis Tedford, Brittany Ashton Holmes, Bug Hall, Zachary Mabry, Kevin Jamal Woods, Ross Bagley, Sam Saletta, Blake Collins, Jordan Warkol, Blake Ewing, Juliette Brewer, Heather Karasek; *Cameos:* Whoopi Goldberg; *D:* Penelope Spheeris; *W:* Penelope Spheeris, Paul Guay, Steve Mazur; *M:* David Foster, Linda Thompson. **VHS** *NYR*

Little Rascals Christmas Special

Spanky and the "Our Gang" kids try to raise money to buy a winter coat for Spanky's mom and learn the true meaning of Christmas along the way. One-shot attempt to remake the vintage Little Rascals children in cartoon form (unrelated to a

later Hanna-Barbera "Little Rascals" on Saturday-morning TV), even features two of the original performers, Darla and Stymie, lending their voiceovers to adult characters. Included on the cassette are also some brief 1930s Yuletide cartoons: "Jack Frost," "Rudolph the Red-Nosed Reindeer," "Christmas Comes But Once a Year," and "Somewhere in Dreamland."

1979 *(Family)* 60m/C Darla Hood, Matthew "Stymie" Beard; *D:* Fred Wolf, Charles Swenson. **VHS, Beta $29.95** *FHE*

A Little Romance 🐾🐾🐾

American girl living in Paris falls in love with a French boy; eventually they run away, to seal their love with a kiss beneath a bridge. Olivier gives a wonderful, if hammy, performance as the old pickpocket who encourages her. Gentle, agile comedy based on the novel by Patrick Cauvin. **Hound Advisory:** Salty language.

1979 *(PG/Jr. High-Adult)* 110m/C Laurence Olivier, Diane Lane, Thelonious Bernard, Sally Kellerman, Broderick Crawford; *D:* George Roy Hill; *M:* Georges Delerue. **Award Nominations:** Academy Awards '79: Best Adapted Screenplay; **Awards:** Academy Awards '79: Best Original Score. **VHS, Beta, LV $14.95** *WAR, INJ*

Little Shop of Horrors 🐾🐾🐾

Screen version of the hit stage musical (based on a 1960 horror cheapie of the same title). Nerd florist Seymour finds a mystery plant that talks, sings like one of the Four Tops -and thrives on drops of human blood. As it gets bigger (and it does get bigger), the persuasive plant increasingly demands "Feed me!" so poor Seymour must turn to murder to appease his carnivorous green friend. Lively, darkly humorous, and not unduly gory. Trouble is, the storyline gets awfully thin for the big-budget Hollywood treatment. Kids will adore the voracious vegetable, brought to writhing, roaring life by the Jim Henson creature factory. In fact, a short-lived TV cartoon grew out of this. Songs by Alan Menken and Howard Ashman, who also collaborated on Disney classics like "Beauty and the Beast" and "The Little Mermaid." ♫Mean Green Mother From Outer Space; Some Fun Now; Your Day Begins Tonight. **Hound Advisory:** Violence, serious gore only hinted. The stage production's original grim climax has been altered (rather awkwardly) into a cheery, upbeat finale.

1986 *(PG-13/Jr. High-Adult)* 94m/C Rick Moranis, Ellen Greene, Vincent Gardenia, Steve Martin, James Belushi, Christopher Guest, Bill Murray, John Candy; *D:* Frank Oz; *M:* Miles Goodman, Howard Ashman. **VHS, Beta, LV $14.95** *WAR, HMV, MVD*

Little Sister 🐾🐾

Prankster Silverman, on a dare, dresses up as a girl and joins a sorority. Problems arise when he falls in love with his "big sister" (Milano) in the sorority. What will happen when she finds out the truth? Will we care? **Hound Advisory:** Brief nudity and sexual situations.

1992 *(PG-13/Jr. High-Adult)* 94m/C Jonathan Silverman, Alyssa Milano. **VHS $89.98** *LIV*

Little Sister Rabbit

Animated tale of Big Brother Rabbit left to babysit his little sister, demonstrating the responsibility of caring for a child.

Adapted from the children's book by Ulf Nilsson and Eva Eriksson.
1992 (*Primary*) 23m/C **VHS $245.00** *LME, WTA*

The Little Thief 🐾🐾

Touted as Francois Truffaut's final legacy, this French drama is actually based on a story he co-wrote with Claude de Givray about a post-WWII adolescent girl who reacts to the world around her by stealing and getting involved in petty crime. The artistry of Truffaut's "The 400 Blows" and "Small Change" is markedly absent. **Hound Advisory:** Mature themes, sex.
1989 (**PG-13**/ *Sr. High-Adult*) 108m/C Charlotte Gainsbourg, Simon de la Brosse, Didier Bezace, Raoul Billerey, Nathalie Cardone; *D:* Claude Miller; *W:* Annie Miller, Claude Miller; *M:* Alain Jonny. **VHS, Beta, LV $89.99** *HBO, INJ*

Little Toot

Little Toot the tugboat welcomes Plato Pelican, Donna Dolphin, and temperamental waterspout, Typhoon Tina.
1992 (*Preschool-Primary*) 52m/C **VHS $12.95** *WTA*

Little Tough Guys 🐾🐾

The Little Tough Guys (AKA The Dead End Kids) come to the rescue of Halop, a young guy gone bad to avenge his father's unjust imprisonment. First of the series by the former Dead End Kids, who later become the East Side Kids before evolving into the Bowery Boys.
1938 (*Family*) 84m/B Helen Parrish, Billy Halop, Leo Gorcey, Marjorie Main, Gabriel Dell, Huntz Hall; *D:* Harold Young. **VHS, Beta $19.95** *NOS, MRV, VYY*

The Little Troll Prince

Hanna-Barbera Christmas special produced in association with the Lutheran Laymen's League depicts Bu, prince of gnomes, saved from a dreary, backwards existence when he discovers God's love.
1990 (*Family*) 46m/C *V:* Vincent Price, Jonathan Winters, Cloris Leachman, Don Knotts. **VHS, Beta $14.95** *TTC*

Little Wizards: The Singing Sword

First episode of in the Marvel network Saturday-morning cartoon fantasy: The Singing Sword could give Prince Dexter the magic he needs to reclaim his crown from the evil king.
1987 (*Preschool-Primary*) 23m/C **VHS $14.95** *WTA*

Little Women 🐾🐾🐾🐾

Louisa May Alcott's Civil War story of the four March sisters -Jo, Beth, Amy, and Meg - approaching womanhood who share their young loves, their joys, and their sorrows. Everything about this classic works, from the lavish period costumes to the excellent script, and particularly the captivating performances by the cast. A must-see for fans of Alcott and Hepburn, and others will find it enjoyable. Remade several times, but this version remains definitive.
1933 (*Family*) 107m/B Katharine Hepburn, Joan Bennett, Paul Lukas, Edna May Oliver, Frances Dee, Spring Byington, Jean Parker, Douglass Montgomery; *D:* George Cukor; *W:* Andrew Solt, Sarah Y. Mason, Victor Heerman; *M:* Adolph Deutsch, Max Steiner. **Award Nominations:** Academy Awards '33: Best Director (Cukor), Best Picture; **Awards:** Academy Awards '33: Best Adapted

Screenplay; Venice Film Festival '34: Best Actress (Hepburn). **VHS, Beta, 8mm $19.98** *MGM, KUI, IGP*

Little Women 🐾🐾🐾

Stylish, no-expense-spared color version of Louisa May Alcott's classic. Star power triumphs over genetics in casting the likes of Allyson, O'Brien, Taylor and Leigh as teenage sisters growing up against the backdrop of the Civil War.
1949 (*Family*) 121m/C June Allyson, Peter Lawford, Margaret O'Brien, Elizabeth Taylor, Janet Leigh, Mary Astor; *D:* Mervyn LeRoy. **Award Nominations:** Academy Awards '49: Best Color Cinematography; **Awards:** Academy Awards '49: Best Art Direction/Set Decoration (Color). **VHS $19.98** *MGM*

Little Women 🐾🐾

Louisa May Alcott's classic tale of four loving sisters who face the joys and hardships of 19th-century America comes to life in this animated program hailing from Japan.
1983 (*Family*) 60m/C **VHS, Beta $59.98** *LIV, WTA*

Little Women Series

Seven episodes of an animated version of Louisa May Alcott's story about the four March sisters and their youth in Civil War New England.
1985 (*Primary-Jr. High*) 30m/C **VHS, Beta, 8mm $14.95** *KAR*

The Littlest Angel 🐾🐾

Well-cast but mediocre made-for-TV musical about a shepherd boy who dies falling off a cliff and wants to become an angel. He learns a valuable lesson in the spirit of giving.
1969 (*Family*) 77m/C Johnny Whitaker, Fred Gwynne, E.G. Marshall, Cab Calloway, Connie Stevens, Tony Randall. **VHS, Beta $14.98** *SUE, CNG, KAR*

The Littlest Horse Thieves 🐾🐾🐾

Wholesome Disney film about three turn-of-the-century British children and their efforts to save 'pit ponies,' much-abused horses put to dangerous work in mines. Filmed on location in England, with the change of scenery doing well for the Magic Kingdom folks.
1976 (**G**/ *Family*) 109m/C Alastair Sim, Peter Barkworth; *D:* Charles Jarrott. **VHS, Beta $69.95** *DIS*

The Littlest Outlaw 🐾🐾🐾

Mexican peasant boy steals a beautiful stallion to save it from being destroyed. Together, they ride off on a series of adventures. Decent Disney effort filmed on location in Mexico.
1954 (*Family*) 73m/C Pedro Armendariz Sr., Joseph Calleia, Andres Velasquez; *D:* Roberto Gavaldon. **VHS, Beta $69.95** *DIS*

The Littlest Rebel 🐾🐾🐾

Shirley showcases this well-done piece set during the Civil War in the Old South. She befriends a Union officer while protecting her Confederate father at the same time. She even goes to Washington to plea with President Lincoln. Nice dance sequences by Temple and Robinson. Available in computer-colored version.
1935 (*Family*) 70m/B Shirley Temple, John Boles, Jack Holt, Bill Robinson, Karen Morley, Willie Best; *D:* David Butler. **VHS, Beta $19.98** *FOX*

Littlest Warrior 🦴🦴

Japanese cartoon feature in which Zooshio, the littlest warrior, is forced to leave his beloved forest and experiences many adventures before he is reunited with his family.
1975 (*Preschool-Primary*) 70m/C **VHS, Beta $24.95** *FHE*

Live and Let Die 🦴🦴

Agent 007 is out to thwart the villainous Dr. Kananga, a black mastermind who plans to control western powers with voodoo and hard drugs. Moore's first appearance as Bond makes you nostalgic for Connery. Title song by Paul McCartney. **Hound Advisory:** Violence, alcohol use, suggested sex.
1973 (PG/*Jr. High-Adult***)** 131m/C Roger Moore, Jane Seymour, Yaphet Kotto, Clifton James, Julius W. Harris, Geoffrey Holder, David Hedison, Gloria Hendry, Bernard Lee, Lois Maxwell, Madeleine Smith, Roy Stewart; *D:* Guy Hamilton; *W:* Tom Mankiewicz; *M:* George Martin. **VHS, Beta, LV $19.98** *MGM, FOX, TLF*

The Living Desert 🦴🦴🦴

Life cycle of animals and plants in the American desert is shown through the seasons in this Disney documentary. The painstaking care that went into getting rare nature footage set a high mark that outdoor documentaries have tried to follow ever since.
1953 (*G/Family*) 69m/C *D:* James Algar. **VHS, Beta $69.95** *DIS*

Living Free 🦴🦴◁

Sequel to "Born Free," based on the nonfictional books by Joy Adamson. Recounts the travails of Elsa the lioness, who is now dying, with three young cubs that need care. Nice and pleasant, but could you pick up the pace?
1972 (*G/Family*) 91m/C Susan Hampshire, Nigel Davenport; *D:* Jack Couffer. **VHS, Beta, LV $9.95** *COL, GKK*

Local Hero 🦴🦴🦴🦴

Riegert is a yuppie representative of a huge oil company who endeavors to buy a sleepy Scottish fishing village for excavation, and finds himself hypnotized by the place and its crusty denizens. Back in Texas at company headquarters, tycoon Lancaster deals with a psycho therapist and gazes at the stars looking for clues. A low-key, charmingly offbeat Scottish comedy with its own sense of logic and quiet humor, poetic landscapes, and unique characters, epitomizing Forsyth's original style. **Hound Advisory:** Salty language.
1983 (PG/*Jr. High-Adult***)** 112m/C Peter Riegert, Denis Lawson, Burt Lancaster, Fulton Mackay, Jenny Seagrove, Peter Capaldi, Norman Chancer; *D:* Bill Forsyth; *W:* Bill Forsyth; *M:* Mark Knopfler. **VHS, Beta, LV $19.98** *WAR*

Locke the Superpower 🦴🦴

Japanese-animated feature about male and female superheroes fighting an intergalactic war against each other. **Hound Advisory:** Violence.
1986 (*Family*) 92m/C **VHS, Beta $14.99** *JFK, WTA*

Lollipop Dragon: Magic Lollipop Adventure

Cartoon adventures of a kindly dragon opposing the evil Baron Bad Blood, who's dragon-napped three reptilian babies and taken them to Blood Castle.
1987 (*Preschool-Primary*) 30m/C **VHS, Beta $5.99** *JFK, WTA*

Lollipop Dragon: The Great Christmas Race

Animated fantasy for the very young about a dragon and his buddies who battle Baron Bad Blood for the welfare of lollipopdom.
1985 (*Preschool-Primary*) 25m/C **VHS, Beta $19.95** *WTA, JFK*

The Lone Ranger

Theatrical feature spun off into the TV series that made Moore the classic Kemosabe and Silverheels the definitive faithful Indian sidekick. And, of course, there's that "William Tell Overture." Still, it's pretty cliched stuff initially, as the Lone Ranger and Tonto try to prevent a war between ranchers and natives, with an outlaw gang behind all the trouble. **Hound Advisory:** Violence.
1956 (*Family*) 87m/C Clayton Moore, Jay Silverheels, Lyle Bettger, Bonita Granville; *D:* Stuart Heisler. **VHS, Beta $29.95** *MGM*

The Lone Ranger

Two volumes of three cartoons each depict the Saturday-morning TV adventures of the western hero. These episodes came from a "Tarzan/Lone Ranger Adventure Hour" 'toon show of the late '70s, rather than the "Lone Ranger" animated series of the 1960s.
1980 (*Preschool-Jr. High*) 60m/C **VHS, Beta $29.95** *FHE*

The Lone Ranger and the Lost City of Gold 🦴🦴◁

Another movie edition starring the duo from the well-remembered "Lone Ranger" TV show. Three Indian braves are found dead, and the Lone Ranger and Tonto ride into action to find the murderer and prevent plundering of a treasure-laden sacred ground. Colorful photography, good action, and the heroic duo at their best. **Hound Advisory:** Violence.
1958 (*Family*) 80m/C Clayton Moore, Jay Silverheels, Douglas Kennedy; *D:* Lesley Selander; *M:* Les Baxter. **VHS** *NO*

The Lone Ranger: Code of the Pioneers 🦴

The Masked Man and Tonto hang around a town to make sure that local elections stay honest, in this B&W episode of the TV western series. Several other volumes of episodes are available; each tape in this series begins with a trivia quiz to test your knowledge of Lone Ranger-ology.
1955 (*Jr. High-Adult*) 55m/B Clayton Moore, Jay Silverheels. **VHS $19.99** *RHI*

Lone Star Kid

Eleven-year-old Brian realizes that his tiny community of Crabb, Texas, should incorporate as a town to survive. When no grownup is willing to push the idea, Brian runs for the (non-paying) job of mayor and learns a few important lessons. Slow-moving but pleasant "WonderWorks" drama based on a true story, done by "Happy Days" alumni Williams and exec producer Ron Howard. Country-music star Daniels performs the soundtrack music and portrays Brian's loyal opposition. **1988** *(Family)* 55m/C James Earl Jones, Chad Sheets; *M:* Charlie Daniels. **VHS** **$29.95** *PME, HMV, BTV*

The Lone Wolf

Boy learns kindness by befriending an old military dog which villagers think is mad and responsible for killing their sheep. After a brush with death, the boy convinces the villagers of the dog's good qualities.
1972 *(Family)* 45m/C **VHS, Beta $39.98** *SUE*

The Loneliest Runner 🎬🎬🎬

Writer/director Landon based this made-for-TV story on a wrenching true story - his own. Teenager with a miserable home life suffers humiliation as a bed-wetter. Nonetheless, he perseveres as an athlete, eventually becoming an Olympics track star. Touching and sensitive, and more effective than Landon's theatrical film "Sam's Son," with much the same story.
1976 *(Sr. High-Adult)* 74m/C Michael Landon, Lance Kerwin, DeAnn Mears, Brian Keith, Melissa Sue Anderson; *D:* Michael Landon. **VHS, Beta $19.98** *WAR, OM*

The Loneliness of the Long Distance Runner 🎬🎬🎬

Courtenay, in his film debut, turns in a powerful performance as an angry teenager, a hopeless product of the British slums. His first attempt at crime lands him in the reformatory, where the headmaster recruits him for the running team. The adult is obsessed with winning the big race, but the kid is indifferent, locking the two in a seemingly one-sided power struggle. One of the best teen-angst dramas of the '60s, a riveting depiction of one boy's difficult passage into manhood.
1962 *(Jr. High-Adult)* 104m/B Tom Courtenay, Michael Redgrave, Avis Bunnage, Peter Madden, James Bolam, Julia Foster, Topsy Jane, Frank Finlay; *D:* Tony Richardson; *M:* John Addison. **VHS, Beta $19.98** *WAR, SNC*

The Long Day Closes 🎬🎬🎬

Nearly plotless, but surrender to its rhythms and experience the lyrical memories of Bud, an 11-year-old in 1950s Liverpool. He enters a parochial school (so strict that all kids are beaten on the first day, as a warning of what will come if they really do misbehave!), attends movies and church with equal devotion, and sadly leaves childhood behind. Nostalgic view of family life via sweet, small everyday moments in an impoverished postwar England made magical and musical in the dreamy youth's mind. A followup to Davies's "Distant Voices, Still Lives" (also on video) which similarly chronicled earlier generations in Bud's troubled household. **Hound Advisory:** Violence.
1992 *(PG/Sr. High-Adult)* 84m/C Leigh McCormack, Marjorie Yates, Anthony Watson, Ayse Owens; *D:* Terence Davies; *W:* Terence Davies. **VHS $89.95** *COL*

The Longshot WOOF!

Four bumblers try to raise cash to put on a sure-bet racetrack tip in this sorry comedy. Mike Nichols is the executive producer.
1986 *(PG-13/Jr. High-Adult)* 89m/C Tim Conway, Harvey Korman, Jack Weston, Ted Wass, Jonathan Winters, Stella Stevens, Anne Meara; *D:* Paul Bartel; *W:* Tim Conway, John Myhers; *M:* Charles Fox. **VHS, Beta $59.95** *HBO, CNG*

Look Who's Talking 🎬🎬🎬

When a woman bears the child of a married man, she sets her sights elsewhere in search of the perfect stepfather; Travolta is the cabbie who tries to prove he's the best candidate. All the while, the baby gives us his views via the sarcastic voice of Willis. Disarming, often raunchy comedy that took a silly gimmick and made it thoroughly entertaining; two sequels and several TV imitations have failed to repeat the trick. **Hound Advisory:** Bawdy stuff, including an early sex scene revealing the rock 'n' rolling action inside the woman's womb as the chatty tyke is conceived. Profanity.
1989 *(PG-13/Jr. High-Adult)* 90m/C John Travolta, Kirstie Alley, Olympia Dukakis, George Segal, Abe Vigoda; *D:* Amy Heckerling; *W:* Amy Heckerling; *M:* David Kitay; *V:* Bruce Willis. **VHS, Beta, LV $19.95** *COL, RDG*

Look Who's Talking Now 🎬🎬

Continuing to wring revenue from a tired premise, the family dogs throw in their two cents in the second sequel to "Look Who's Talking." Sparks, Alpo, and butt jokes fly as the dogs mark their territory. Meanwhile, dimwit wife Alley is worried that husband Travolta is having an affair, and is determined to get him back. **Hound Advisory:** Sex talk, profanity.
1993 *(PG-13/Jr. High-Adult)* 95m/C John Travolta, Kirstie Alley, Olympia Dukakis, George Segal, Lysette Anthony; *D:* Tom Ropelewski; *W:* Tom Ropelewski, Leslie Dixon; *M:* William Ross; *V:* Diane Keaton, Danny DeVito. **VHS, LV, 8mm** *COL*

Look Who's Talking, Too 🎬

If Academy Awards for Stupidest Sequel and Lamest Dialogue existed, this diaper drama would have cleaned up. Second infant talkfest throws the now married accountant-cabbie duo into a marital tailspin and husband Travolta moves out. Meanwhile, the baby, still voiced by Willis, smartmouths incessantly. A once-clever gimmick now unencumbered by plot; not advised for linear thinkers. The voice of Arnold, though, is a guarantee you'll get one laugh for your rental. **Hound Advisory:** Profanity galore, sex, and raunch.
1990 *(PG-13/Jr. High-Adult)* 81m/C Kirstie Alley, John Travolta, Olympia Dukakis, Elias Koteas; *D:* Amy Heckerling; *V:* Bruce Willis, Mel Brooks, Damon Wayans, Roseanne (Barr) Arnold. **VHS, LV, 8mm $19.95** *COL*

Looking for Miracles 🎬🎬

Sixteen-year-old Ryan lands a precious job at a summer camp during the Depression, but mom won't allow him to go unless he brings his kid brother along. In spite of themselves, the pair learn to get along. Fine Canadian TV production (released in the US through the PBS Wonderworks series) from the reliable "Anne of Green Gables" gang, based on the second volume of A.E. Hochner's fictionalized memoirs. The first book, "King of the Hill," was made into a splendid theatrical feature in 1993; these two are worth comparing. **1990 (G/**Family**)** 104m/C Zachary Bennett, Greg Spottiswood, Joe Flaherty. **VHS, LV $29.95** BVV, DIS, FCT

Looney Looney Looney Bugs Bunny Movie 𝄞𝄞𝄞

Followup to "The Bugs Bunny/Road Runner Movie" does a more imaginative job of tying together a feature-length compilation of classic Warner Brothers cartoons. Watch for favorites Bugs Bunny, Elmer Fudd, Porky Pig, Yosemite Sam, Daffy Duck and Foghorn Leghorn. **1981 (G/**Family**)** 80m/C **D:** Friz Freleng, Chuck Jones, Bob Clampett; **V:** Mel Blanc, June Foray. **VHS, Beta $14.95** WAR, FCT, WTA

Lord of the Flies 𝄞𝄞𝄞𝄞

In a society racked with gang violence and youth crime, William Golding's allegorical novel about castaway schoolboys, free from adult supervision, degenerating into barbarism is more relevant than ever. Not a children's film by any means, but since the novel is a fixture in many classrooms it warrants inclusion here. This stark, straightforward British adaptation is certainly the more faithful and tasteful version, though it makes no effort to humanize the characters, and the acting is sub-par. **Hound Advisory:** Violence; mature themes. **1963 (**Sr. High-Adult**)** 91m/B James Aubrey, Tom Chapin, Hugh Edwards, Roger Elwin, Tom Gamen; **D:** Peter Brook. **VHS, Beta, LV $29.95** HMV, FUS

Lord of the Flies 𝄞𝄞

Second filming of the harrowing novel tries to turn William Golding's highly symbolic characters into real people, as castaway boys on a deserted island split into factions - those who go savage, and the dwindling few determined to stay civilized. But the filmmakers give personalities to the kids by making them foulmouthed and sexually sophisticated (one brat even has a police record!), completely losing Golding's point about innocence gone bad. Violence also enters R territory. **Hound Advisory:** Brutality; profanity; sex talk; mature themes. **1990 (R/**Sr. High-Adult**)** 90m/C Balthazar Getty, Danuel Pipoly, Chris Furrh, Badgett Dale, Edward Taft, Andrew Taft; **D:** Harry Hook. **VHS, Beta, LV, 8mm $19.95** COL, SUE, TVC

The Lord of the Rings 𝄞𝄞

Murky - in more ways than one - interpretation of J.R.R. Tolkien's classic tale of the fantasy folk who inhabit Middle Earth. Animator Ralph Bakshi used rotoscoping (painting animated characters over live-action footage of actors, birds and horses) to give his characters lifelike motion and characteristics. Too bad nobody did the same for the script. Adapting Tolkien's highly detailed and lengthy works is a mighty task, and non-readers may feel confused by the

beginning, confounded in the middle, and cheated at the ending, which leads straight to a next chapter, not yet filmed. **Hound Advisory:** Violence. **1978 (PG/**Primary-Adult**)** 128m/C **D:** Ralph Bakshi; **V:** Christopher Guard, John Hurt. **VHS, Beta $14.98** REP, FCT, WTA

The Lords of Flatbush 𝄞𝄞𝄞

Four street toughs battle against their own maturation and responsibilities in 1950s Brooklyn. Winkler introduces the leather-clad hood he's made a career of and Stallone introduces a character not unlike Rocky. Interesting slice of life. **Hound Advisory:** Violence. **1974 (PG/**Jr. High-Adult**)** 88m/C Sylvester Stallone, Perry King, Henry Winkler, Susan Blakely, Armand Assante, Paul Mace; **D:** Stephen Verona, Martin Davidson; **M:** Joseph Brooks. **VHS, Beta, LV $14.95** COL

Lords of Magick 𝄞𝄞

Medieval wizard brothers, disciples of Merlin the Magician himself, pursue an evil sorcerer with a kidnapped princess across time to 20th century L.A. Low-budget fantasy with a modest share of thrills and a climactic magical duel that's a hoot. **Hound Advisory:** Violence, profanity, alcohol use. The older brother is a lusty libertine, the younger chaste and virtuous, and much is made of the contrast. **1988 (PG-13/**Jr. High-Adult**)** 98m/C Jarrett Parker, Matt Gauthier, Brendan Dillon Jr.; **D:** David Marsh. **VHS, Beta $79.95** PSM

Lorenzo's Oil 𝄞𝄞𝄞

Wrenching family drama based on the true story of Augusto and Michaela Odone's efforts to cure their 5-year-old son, Lorenzo, diagnosed with a rare and incurable neurological disorder. Confronted by a medical community slow moving and clinically cold in character, the parents painstakingly research their own treatment. Sarandon delivers an outstanding and emotionally charged performance as Lorenzo's ferociously loving mother. The devastating disease is depicted in all its cruel progression, and Miller's operatic direction could never be described as subtle, but neither are any reason to pass up this emotional wringer of a film. **Hound Advisory:** Profanity. **1992 (PG-13/**Jr. High-Adult**)** 135m/C Nick Nolte, Susan Sarandon, Zach O'Malley-Greenberg, Peter Ustinov, Kathleen Wilhoite, Gerry Bamman, Margo Martindale, James Rebhorn, Ann Hearn; **D:** George Miller; **W:** Nick Enright, George Miller. **VHS, Beta, LV $19.98** MCA, MOV, BTV

The Lost Boys 𝄞𝄞𝄞

Teenaged Michael, new in town, falls for a pretty girl with some hard-living friends. These partying punks are actually a delinquent gang of kid vampires. And if Michael can't beat them, he'll have to join them. The R rating derives from blood-gushing violence - undead get the worst of it - but attitude overall is one of scary fun (including the pint-sized vampire-busting 'Frog Brothers'), making it acceptable for youngsters no longer afraid of the dark. The eerie Peter Pan parallel implied by the title is never really fleshed out. **Hound Advisory:** Carnage (though the recipients are already dead), profanity.

1987 (*R*/*Sr. High-Adult*) 97m/C Jason Patric, Kiefer Sutherland, Corey Haim, Jami Gertz, Dianne Wiest, Corey Feldman, Barnard Hughes, Edward Herrmann, Billy Wirth; *D:* Joel Schumacher; *W:* Jeffrey Boam; *M:* Thomas Newman. **VHS, Beta, LV, 8mm $14.95** *WAR, FUS*

Lost in a Harem 🦴🦴⊲

Abbott & Costello play magicians in a theatrical troupe stranded in a desert kingdom ruled by an evil sheik. The sheik's nephew (and rightful heir) hires the two to steal some magic rings and the pretty Maxwell to play footsie with his susceptible uncle in an attempt to regain his kingdom. Average comedy with musical numbers by Jimmy Dorsey and His Orchestra.
1944 (*Family*) 89m/B Bud Abbott, Lou Costello, Marilyn Maxwell, John Conte, Douglass Dumbrille, Lottie Harrison; *D:* Charles Riesner. **VHS $19.98** *MGM*

Lost in Dinosaur World

Ten-year old boy and his seven-year old sister have the experience of a lifetime when they get lost in a dinosaur park (where DO they get these clever story ideas?). Tension mounts as their parents are warned that it's almost feeding time for the dinosaurs. Strives to offer scientific facts about dinosaurs and the world in which they lived.
1993 (*Primary-Jr. High*) 30m/C **VHS $14.95** *PSS*

Lost in the Barrens 🦴🦴⊲

Two young boys, one a Canadian Indian and the other a rich white boy, get lost in the wilderness of the Canadian north. Out of necessity and common need they become close and form a lifelong friendship. Based on a book by "Never Cry Wolf" author Farley Mowat.
1991 (*Family*) 95m/C Graham Greene, Nicholas Shields. **VHS** *NO*

Lost in Yonkers 🦴🦴⊲

Arty and Jay are two teenage brothers who, while their widowed father looks for work, are sent to live with their stern grandmother, small-time gangster uncle, and childlike aunt in 1942 New York. Ruehl reprises her Tony award-winning performance as Aunt Bella, who loses herself in the movies while trying to find a love of her own, out from under the oppressive thumb of her domineering mother (Worth). Performances by the adults are more theatrical than necessary but the teenagers do well in their observer roles. Based on the play by Neil Simon, which again chronicles his boyhood. **Hound Advisory:** Salty language.
1993 (*PG*/*Jr. High-Adult*) 114m/C Mercedes Ruehl, Irene Worth, Richard Dreyfuss, Brad Stoll, Mike Damus, David Strathairn, Robert Miranda, Jack Laufer, Susan Merson; *D:* Martha Coolidge; *W:* Neil Simon; *M:* Elmer Bernstein. **VHS, LV, 8mm $95.95** *COL, FCT*

The Lost Jungle

Circus legend Beatty searches for his girl and her dad in the jungle. Animal stunts keep it interesting. 12-chapter serial.
1934 (*Family*) 156m/B Clyde Beatty, Cecilia Parker, Syd Saylor, Warner Richmond, Wheeler Oakman; *D:* Armand Schaefer, David Howard. **VHS, Beta $19.95** *NOS, VCN, VDM*

Lost Legacy: A Girl Called Hatter Fox 🦴🦴⊲

Tradition and technology are at odds in the life of a young Indian girl. Strong cast makes this work. Made for TV and better than average. Originally broadcast under the title "A Girl Called Hatter Fox."
1977 (*Adult*) 100m/C Ronny Cox, Joanelle Romero, Conchata Ferrell; *D:* George Schaefer. **VHS $59.95** *GEM*

Lots of Luck 🦴⊲

Nice to see Annette working for the Magic Kingdom again, though this is a weak feature sitcom (with a good cast) for the Disney Channel. The hardworking Maris family goes on a nonstop winning streak, taking the prize in a million-dollar lottery. Their loser friends, peers and parasites are jealous and cause them much misery; somehow it all ends up in a car race featuring a "Love Bug" lookalike.
1985 (*Family*) 88m/C Martin Mull, Annette Funicello, Fred Willard, Polly Holliday; *D:* Peter Baldwin; *M:* William Goldstein. **VHS, Beta $69.95** *DIS*

Love and Death 🦴🦴🦴

In 1812 Russia, a condemned man reviews the follies of his life. Woody Allen's satire on "War and Peace," and every other major Russian novel.
1975 (*PG*/*Jr. High-Adult*) 89m/C Woody Allen, Diane Keaton, Georges Adel, Despo Diamantidou, Frank Adu, Harold Gould; *D:* Woody Allen; *W:* Woody Allen. **VHS, Beta, LV $14.95** *MGM, FOX*

Love at First Bite 🦴🦴⊲

Intentionally campy spoof of the vampire film. Dracula is forced to leave his Transylvanian home as the Rumanian government has designated his castle a training center for young gymnasts. Once in New York, the Count takes in the night life and falls in love with a woman whose boyfriend embarks on a campaign to warn the city of Dracula's presence. Hamilton of the never-fading tan is appropriately fang-in-cheek in a role which briefly resurrected his film career.
1979 (*PG*/*Jr. High-Adult*) 93m/C George Hamilton, Susan St. James, Richard Benjamin, Dick Shawn, Arte Johnson, Sherman Hemsley, Isabel Sanford; *D:* Stan Dragoti; *M:* Charles Bernstein. **VHS, Beta, LV $9.98** *ORI, WAR*

The Love Bug 🦴🦴⊲

Race car driver is befriended by Herbie, a cute little white Volkswagen with a mind of its own. Soon he and Herbie prove a winning combination at the track. Trendsetting Disney fun that had enough gas in it for several sequels.
1968 (*G*/*Family*) 110m/C Dean Jones, Michele Lee, Hope Lange, Robert Reed, Bert Convy; *D:* Robert Stevenson. **VHS, Beta, LV $19.99** *DIS*

Love Finds Andy Hardy 🦴🦴🦴

Young Andy Hardy finds himself torn between three girls before returning to the girl next door. Garland's first appearance in the acclaimed Andy Hardy series features her singing "In Between" and "Meet the Best of my Heart." Also available with "Andy Hardy Meets Debutante" on laserdisc.

1938 (*Family*) 90m/B Mickey Rooney, Judy Garland, Lana Turner, Ann Rutherford, Fay Holden, Lewis Stone, Marie Blake, Cecilia Parker, Gene Reynolds; **D:** George B. Seitz. **VHS, Beta, LV** $19.95 *MGM*

Love Happy 🎬🎬

Impoverished troupe of actors accidentally gains possession of some stolen diamonds, and Groucho is the detective assigned to retrieve them. If the Marx Brothers had made this a decade or two earlier it might have been a classic, but this was late in their careers, and, except for the endearing pantomimes of Harpo, the comedy team seems awfully tired. Young Monroe has Groucho drooling over her in a brief cameo.
1950 (*Family*) 85m/B Groucho Marx, Harpo Marx, Chico Marx, Vera-Ellen, Ilona Massey, Marion Hutton, Raymond Burr, Marilyn Monroe; **D:** David Miller. **VHS, LV** $19.98 *REP*

Love Laughs at Andy Hardy 🎬🎬

Andy Hardy, college boy, is in love and in trouble. Financial and romantic problems come to a head when Andy is paired with a six-foot tall blind date. Sixth in the series.
1946 (*Family*) 93m/B Mickey Rooney, Lewis Stone, Sara Haden, Lina Romay, Bonita Granville, Fay Holden; **D:** Willis Goldbeck. **VHS, Beta** $19.95 *NOS, MRV, HHT*

Love Leads the Way 🎬🎬

Disney TV movie retelling how Morris Frank established the Seeing-Eye Dog program for the blind in the 1930s. Heavily sentimentalized adaptation of Frank's own book "First Lady of the Seeing Eye."
1984 (*Family*) 99m/C Timothy Bottoms, Eva Marie Saint, Arthur Hill, Susan Dey, Ralph Bellamy, Ernest Borgnine, Patricia Neal; **D:** Delbert Mann. **VHS, Beta** $69.95 *DIS*

Love Your Mama 🎬🎬🎬

Independently made, worthwhile urban family drama about the strong Lucia, whose religious faith and sheer refusal to give up help her bear many crosses, including a drunken husband, car thief son, and pregnant teenage daughter. Believable role models and uniquely good performances help out occasionally amateur film technique. **Hound Advisory:** Profanity, alcohol use, sex talk.
1989 (PG-13/*Jr. High-Adult*) 93m/C Audrey Morgan, Carol E. Hall, Andre Robinson, Ernest Rayford, Kearo Johnson, Jacqueline Williams; **D:** Ruby L. Oliver; **W:** Ruby L. Oliver. **VHS** $89.95 *HMD, BTV, FCT*

Lt. Robin Crusoe, U.S.N. 🎬

Navy pilot crash lands on a tropical island, falls hard for an island babe and schemes intensely against the local evil ruler. Lackluster Disney debacle.
1966 (G/*Family*) 113m/C Dick Van Dyke, Nancy Kwan, Akim Tamiroff; **D:** Byron Paul. **VHS, Beta** *DIS, OM*

Lucas 🎬🎬🎬

Small but brainy Lucas is a classroom misfit, having skipped a few grades at high school. But when he falls in love with the new girl in town, the pint-sized hero tries to win her through the seemingly hopeless stunt of trying out for the football team. Humorous, sympathetic, and affectionate view of

youthful infatuation and the perils of growing up. Outstanding performances and characterizations, with Sheen as the gridiron jock who's not a dumb villain but Lucas' close friend, even as he develops into a romantic rival. **Hound Advisory:** Salty language and sex talk, but there's not one swear word or locker-room jibe that's needless or gratuitous in context.
1986 (PG-13/*Jr. High-Adult*) 100m/C Corey Haim, Kerri Green, Charlie Sheen, Winona Ryder, Courtney Thorne-Smith, Thomas E. Hodges; **D:** David Seltzer; **W:** David Seltzer; **M:** Dave Grusin. **VHS, Beta** $14.98 *FXV, FOX*

Lucky Luke: Ballad of the Daltons

Easygoing cowboy hero Lucky Luke gets involved in a wild feud with the bumbling Dalton Brothers gang in this animated feature.
1978 (*Family*) 82m/C **D:** Rene Goscinny. **VHS, Beta, LV** $49.95 *DIS, WTA*

Lucky Luke: Daisy Town

Comic-strip cowboy Lucky Luke is virtually unknown in the US, but in France he's been a favorite for generations. In this rather spoofy feature cartoon from "Asterix" animator Goscinny, the all-American French cowboy saves the little community of Daisy Town from his perennial enemies, the hot-headed Dalton Gang. Dubbed into English.
1971 (*Family*) 75m/C **D:** Rene Goscinny; **M:** Claude Bolling. **VHS, Beta, LV** $49.95 *DIS, WTA*

Luggage of the Gods 🎬🎬

Lost tribe of cave people are confronted with civilization when suitcases fall from an airplane. Low-budget comedy reminiscent of "The Gods Must Be Crazy" was filmed - and mainly seen - in upstate New York.
1987 (G/*Family*) 78m/C Mark Stolzenberg, Gabriel Barre, Gwen Ellison; **D:** David Kendall. **VHS, Beta** $29.95 *ACA*

Lumpkin the Pumpkin

Animated Halloween tale of a witch and her friend, narrated by pop- and country-music star Goldsboro.
19?? (*Primary*) 25m/C **VHS** $12.98 *FHE*

Mac and Me 🎬🎬

Heavy backing by McDonalds created merchandising opportunity that turns out to be a subplot-by-subplot ripoff of "E.T." Here a whole family of Chaplinesque aliens are brought to Earth by a Mars probe. The tiniest escapes government captivity and befriends a wheelchair-bound boy. If you can forgive rampant Spielberg pillaging, some truly lively stuff occurs under guidance of "Wilderness Family" director Raffill that's sure to please young kids, and dig that wild final scene. **Hound Advisory:** Alcohol talk.
1988 (PG/*Primary-Sr. High*) 94m/C Christine Ebersole, Jonathan Ward, Katrina Caspary, Lauren Stanley, Jade Calegory; **D:** Stewart Raffill; **W:** Stewart Raffill; **M:** Alan Silvestri. **VHS, Beta, LV** $9.98 *ORI*

MacArthur 🎬🎬

General Douglas MacArthur's life from Corregidor in 1942 to his dismissal a decade later in the midst of the Korean conflict. Episodic sage with forceful Peck but weak supporting characters. Fourteen minutes were cut from the original

version; intended to be Peck's "Patton," it falls short of the mark.
1977 (PG/*Jr. High-Adult*) 130m/C Gregory Peck, Ivan Bonar, Ward Costello, Nicholas Coster, Dan O'Herlihy; **D:** Joseph Sargent; **W:** Matthew Robbins; **M:** Jerry Goldsmith. **VHS, Beta, LV $19.95** *MCA, TLF*

Macron 1: Dark Discovery in a New World

Intergalactic animation! An unfortunate mishap switches the good and evil sides to opposite universes and the result is a battle to restore order. Major Chance and Dark Star fight to the end in this episode compilation. Additional volumes available.
1986 (*Primary-Family*) 115m/C **VHS, Beta $9.95** *JFK, WTA*

Mad Max: Beyond Thunderdome 🎬🎬◁

Max drifts into evil town ruled by Turner and becomes gladiator, then gets dumped in desert and is rescued by band of feral orphans. Third in a bleak, extremely violent, often exhilarating series. **Hound Advisory:** Violence; profanity; mature themes.
1985 (PG-13/*Jr. High-Adult*) 107m/C Mel Gibson, Tina Turner, Helen Buday, Frank Thring, Bruce Spence, Robert Grubb, Angelo Rossitto, Angry Anderson, George Spartels, Rod Zuanic; **D:** George Miller, George Ogilvie; **W:** George Miller, Terry Hayes; **M:** Maurice Jarre. **VHS, Beta, LV, 8mm $19.98** *WAR*

Mad Monster Party 🎬🎬◁

One of the cute but brittle stop-motion puppet animation features Arthur Rankin Jr. and Jules Bass did for theatrical release before turning their efforts primarily to TV. Aging Dr. Frankenstein wants to retire from being the senior monster, so he calls a convention of famous movie creatures to decide whether Mummy, Wolfman, Dracula or whatever should take his place. Rest assured that never have so many fiends been rendered in such a nonthreatening manner.
1968 (*Family*) 94m/C **D:** Jules Bass; **V:** Boris Karloff, Ethel Ennis, Phyllis Diller. **VHS, Beta $9.95** *COL, SUE*

Mad Scientist

Mattel produced this 'toon about Dr. Sy N. Tist, who must eat his words when his Mad Lab is programmed to take his language seriously, even when it is figurative. Soon the Doctor learns to think before he talks. This might be educational.
1988 (*Family*) 30m/C **VHS, Beta $14.95** *FHE, WTA*

Madame Rosa 🎬🎬🎬

Elderly Rosa, a retired hooker and Holocaust survivor, tends other prostitutes' offspring in the Parisian ghetto. Her spirit is revived by one of her charges - an abandoned Arab boy, and she determines to make a better life for him in the short time she has left. Warmhearted and award-winning, in French with English subtitles. **Hound Advisory:** Sex talk, mature themes.
1977 (PG/*Sr. High-Adult*) 105m/C Simone Signoret, Claude Dauphin; **D:** Moshe Mizrahi. **VHS, Beta $59.95** *HTV, VES*

Madame Sousatzka 🎬🎬🎬

Eccentric, extroverted London piano teacher demands complete control over her students' lives, which is why they inevitably leave her. She meets her match in a strong-willed, ferociously talented Indian boy who seems destined for symphonic stardom. MacLaine's flamboyant acting helps carry this mixture of character study and coming-of-age drama. **Hound Advisory:** Salty language, sex, mature themes, alcohol use.
1988 (PG-13/*Jr. High-Adult*) 113m/C Shirley MacLaine, Peggy Ashcroft, Shabana Azmi, Twiggy, Leigh Lawson, Geoffrey Bayldon, Navin Chowdhry, Lee Montague; **D:** John Schlesinger; **W:** Ruth Prawer Jhabvala, John Schlesinger; **M:** Gerald Gouriet. **VHS, Beta, LV $19.95** *MCA*

Made in America 🎬🎬

High-energy, lightweight comedy stars Whoopi as a single mom whose daughter Long discovers her birth was the result of artificial insemination. More surprising is her biological dad: white, obnoxious, country-western car dealer Danson. Overwrought with obvious gags and basically a one-joke movie. Nonetheless, Goldberg and Danson chemically connect onscreen (and for a short time offscreen as well) while supporting actor Smith grabs comedic attention as Teacake, Long's best friend. **Hound Advisory:** Profanity.
1993 (PG-13/*Jr. High-Adult*) 111m/C Whoopi Goldberg, Ted Danson, Will Smith, Nia Long, Paul Rodriguez, Jennifer Tilly, Peggy Rea, Clyde Kusatsu; **D:** Richard Benjamin; **W:** Holly Goldberg Sloan; **M:** Mark Isham. **VHS, Beta, LV $34.98** *WAR*

Madeline

Musical cartoon adaptation of the classic Ludwig Bemelmans tale of the smallest, bravest, and wildest of a dozen French schoolgirls, and her friends' concern when Madeline has to have her appendix taken out. Simple but charming animation faithfully reproduces the original books' whimsical style, and it kicked off a series of "Madeline" shows first broadcast on HBO cable.
1989 (*Primary-Jr. High*) 30m/C **VHS $9.99** *KUI, VTR, SIG*

Madeline's Christmas

Madeline learns an important lesson about giving when she is forced to care for her sick friends on Christmas morning. Cartoon based on the books by Ludwig Bemelman. Additional volumes available.
1991 (*Family*) 30m/C **VHS, Beta $14.95** *SIG, TVC*

Madhouse 🎬◁

New homeowners find themselves unable to expel loathsome, boorish guests. Presumably, a comedy cashing in on two of sitcom's brightest lights. **Hound Advisory:** Profanity; sex.
1990 (PG-13/*Jr. High-Adult*) 90m/C John Larroquette, Kirstie Alley, Alison La Placa, John Diehl, Jessica Lundy, Bradley Gregg, Dennis Miller, Robert Ginty; **D:** Tom Ropelewski; **W:** Tom Ropelewski; **M:** David Newman. **VHS, Beta, LV $9.98** *ORI*

Magic Kid 🎬◁

Filmmakers who usually do violent action B-pics tried a family feature with this. Don't quit your day jobs, fellas. Kevin,

Michigan's youngest martial-arts champ, visits Uncle Bob, a shady L.A. talent agent in debt to the mob. Plot switches between Kevin kicking around bad guys, boring pep talks to boost Bob's self-esteem, and lots of Hollywood travel footage (including a big promo for the Universal City Studios "Backdraft" tour). **Hound Advisory:** Violence, sex talk, alcohol use. Also, coming-attractions for non-kiddie movies at the start of the tape contribute extra sex, brutality.
1992 (PG/Jr. High-Adult) 91m/C Ted Jan Roberts, Shonda Whipple, Stephen Furst, Joseph Campanella, Billy Hufsey, Sondra Kerns, Pamela Dixon, Lauren Tewes, Don "The Dragon" Wilson; *D:* Joseph Merhi; *W:* Stephen Smoke; *M:* Jim Halfpenny. VHS, LV $89.95 *PMH*

Magic of Lassie 🐾🐾

Attempt to revive the classic collie in the 1970s turned out to be a box office dog. Innocuous but simple-minded remake of 1943's "Lassie Come Home" has Jimmy Stewart as a singing grandpa who won't sell Lassie to an evil millionaire, so the bad guy dognaps the animal.
1978 (G/Family) 100m/C James Stewart, Mickey Rooney, Stephanie Zimbalist, Alice Faye, Pernell Roberts, Lassie; *D:* Don Chaffey. VHS, Beta $19.98 *MGM*

Magic Pony 🐾🐾

Obscure US-Soviet cartoon co-production, blending Russian folklore with the voices of Yankee capitalist TV stars. With the help of a beautiful flying horse, Ivan battles a greedy emperor to become a kind-hearted prince and live happily ever after with a beautiful princess.
1978 (Preschool-Primary) 80m/C *D:* Ivan Ivanov-vano; *V:* Jim Backus, Erin Moran, Hans Conried, Johnny Whitaker. VHS, Beta, LV *GEM*

Magic Snowman 🐾◁

Young Jamie builds a snowman that starts talking, with the urbane voice of Roger Moore (yet with its spiky hair and glaring red eyes, the thing looks more like a snow-punk). The snowman tells Jamie where his fisherman father can find the best waters, but the boy misuses the information. Extremely awkward Yugoslavian fantasy slush, unconvincingly acted. **Hound Advisory:** Roughhousing.
1988 (Family) 85m/C VHS $39.98 *FHE, BTV*

The Magic Sword 🐾🐾

Fantasy adventure about a young man raised by a doting sorceress stepmother, who sets out to rescue a beautiful princess from being the next meal for an evil wizard's dragon. Low-budget but fitfully imaginative tale that, in its better moments, achieves a smart mixture of fairy tale and satire. **Hound Advisory:** The hero's magical posse of the six mightiest knights of all time get killed one by one. But hey, they were dead to begin with, and return unhurt at the finale.
1962 (Family) 80m/C Basil Rathbone, Estelle Winwood, Gary Lockwood; *D:* Bert I. Gordon. VHS, Beta $14.95 *MGM, MRV, VYY*

The Magic Voyage 🐾🐾

Animated tale of a friendly woodworm named Pico who voyages with Columbus to the new world and convinces him that the world is indeed round. He then comes to the aid of a magical firefly named Marilyn who helps Columbus find gold to bring back to Spain.
1993 (G/Family) 82m/C *V:* Dom DeLuise, Mickey Rooney, Corey Feldman, Irene Cara, Dan Haggerty, Samantha Eggar. VHS, LV $19.95 *HMD*

The Magical Princess Gigi

Spliced-together episodes from an imported Japanese cartoon from 1984, about an extraterrestrial princess coming to Earth disguised as an ordinary 12-year-old and working her magic to do good deeds.
1989 (Family) 80m/C *D:* Hiroshi Watanabe. VHS, Beta $14.99 *JFK, WTA*

Maid to Order 🐾◁

Rich girl Sheedy's fairy godmother puts her in her place by turning her into a maid for a snooty Malibu couple. Good-natured and well-acted if rather mindless Cinderella story. **Hound Advisory:** Salty language; brief nudity.
1987 (PG/Jr. High-Adult) 92m/C Ally Sheedy, Beverly D'Angelo, Michael Ontkean, Dick Shawn, Tom Skerritt, Valerie Perrine; *D:* Amy Holden Jones; *W:* Perry Howze; *M:* Georges Delerue. VHS, Beta, LV $14.95 *LIV*

The Main Event 🐾🐾

Streisand plays a wacky-and bankrupt—cosmetic executive who must depend on the career of washed-up boxer O'Neal to rebuild her fortune. Desperate (and more than a little smitten), she badgers and bullies him back into the ring. Lame, derivative screwball comedy desperate to suggest chemistry of Streisand and O'Neal's "What's Up, Doc?" (1972). Streisand sings the title song.
1979 (PG/Jr. High-Adult) 109m/C Barbra Streisand, Ryan O'Neal; *D:* Howard Zieff. VHS, Beta $14.95 *WAR*

Major League 🐾🐾◁

Comedy about a pathetic major league baseball team whose new owner schemes to lose the season and relocate the team to Miami. Sheen is okay as the pitcher with control problems (both on and off the field), while Bernsen seems to be gazing affectionately at "L.A. Law" from a distance. Predictable sports spoof is good for a few laughs, particularly those scenes involving Haysbert as a slugger with voodoo on his mind (and in his locker) and Snipes as a base stealer whose only problem is getting on base. Followed by a sequel outside the strike zone. **Hound Advisory:** Profanity and violence.
1989 (R/Jr. High-Adult) 107m/C Tom Berenger, Charlie Sheen, Corbin Bernsen, James Gammon, Margaret Whitton, Bob Uecker, Rene Russo, Wesley Snipes, Dennis Haysbert, Charles Cyphers; *D:* David S. Ward; *W:* David S. Ward; *M:* James Newton Howard. VHS, Beta, LV, 8mm $14.95 *PAR*

Major League 2 🐾◁

It's been five years since they won the series, and this plodding sequel finds the wacky championship Cleveland Indians ruined by success and once again struggling in last place. Limited charm of original is lost; dull and filled with such lame jokes that you won't care if they manage to make it to the top again. Cast returns with the exception of Wesley Snipes as Willie Mae Hays (now played by Epps). **Hound Advisory:** Profanity.

1994 (PG/*Jr. High-Adult*) 105m/C Charlie Sheen, Tom Berenger, Corbin Bernsen, James Gammon, Dennis Haysbert, Omar Epps, David Keith, Bob Uecker, Alison Doody, Michelle Burke, Margaret Whitton, Eric Bruskotter, Takaaki Ishibashi; *D:* David S. Ward; *W:* R.J. Stewart; *M:* Michel Colombier. **VHS, LV** *WAR*

Making Contact 🎬🎬

Oddball German production is one long tribute/ripoff of the imagery of George Lucas and Steven Spielberg. Joey (pic's original title), a small boy with a pet R2D2 robot, is assailed by poltergeists. Can his Jedi window curtains save him? How about his E.T. drinking glass? What about his Goonie friends? Harmless but annoyingly unoriginal. **Hound Advisory:** Fantasy violence. One death, followed by "E.T." style resurrection, amid much tears and pathos.
1986 (PG/*Jr. High-Adult*) 83m/C Joshua Morrell, Eve Kryll; *D:* Roland Emmerich. **VHS, Beta $14.95** *NWV, STE*

Making Mr. Right 🎬🎬🎬

Offbeat satire about a high-powered marketing and image consultant who falls in love with the android that she's supposed to be promoting. Unbelievable comedy is shaky at times, but Magnuson and Malkovich create some magic.
1986 (PG-13/*Jr. High-Adult*) 95m/C John Malkovich, Ann Magnuson, Glenne Headly, Ben Masters, Laurie Metcalf, Polly Bergen, Hart Bochner, Polly Draper, Susan Anton; *D:* Susan Seidelman. **VHS, Beta, LV $19.99** *HBO*

Making the Grade 🎬🎬

Jersey tough kid owes the mob. For vital cash he attends prep school in place of a rich boy who can't be bothered, and shows preppie teens the view from the other side of the tracks. Better than similar '80s youth flicks, but not by much. Note the presence of actor Clay, before he assumed the persona of an ultra-offensive stand-up comic. **Hound Advisory:** Salty language.
1984 (PG/*Jr. High-Adult*) 105m/C Judd Nelson, Joanna Lee, Dana Olsen, Ronald Lacey, Scott McGinnis, Gordon Jump, Carey Scott, Andrew Dice Clay; *D:* Dorian Walker; *W:* Gene Quintano; *M:* Basil Poledouris. **VHS, Beta $79.95** *MGM*

Malcolm X 🎬🎬🎬

Stirring tribute to the controversial black activist, a leader in the struggle for black liberation. Hitting bottom during his imprisonment in the 50s, he became a Black Muslim and then a leader in the Nation of Islam. His assassination in 1965 left a legacy of black nationalism, self-determination, and racial pride. Marked by strong direction from Lee and good performances (notably Freeman Jr. as Elijah Muhammad), it is Washington's convincing performance in the title role that truly brings the film alive. Based on "The Autobiography of Malcolm X" by Malcolm X and Alex Haley. **Hound Advisory:** Violence, profanity, suggested sex.
1992 (PG-13/*Jr. High-Adult*) 201m/C Denzel Washington, Angela Bassett, Albert Hall, Al Freeman Jr., Delroy Lindo, Spike Lee, Theresa Randle, Kate Vernon, Lonette McKee, Tommy Hollis, James McDaniel, Ernest Thompson, Jean LaMarre, Giancarlo Esposito, Craig Wasson, John Ottavino, David Patrick Kelly, Shirley Stoler; *Cameos:* Christopher Plummer, Karen Allen, Peter Boyle, William Kunstler, Bobby Seale, Al Sharpton; *D:* Spike Lee; *W:* Spike Lee, Arnold Perl, James Baldwin; *M:* Terence Blanchard. **Award Nominations:** Academy Awards '92: Best Actor (Washington), Best Costume Design; **Awards:** Chicago Film Critics Awards '93: Best Actor (Washington), Best Film; MTV Movie Awards '93: Best Actor (Washington); New York Film Critics Awards '93: Best Actor (Washington). **VHS, Beta, LV, 8mm $24.98** *WAR, MOV, BTV*

The Maltese Falcon 🎬🎬🎬🎬

After the death of his partner, detective Sam Spade finds himself enmeshed in a complicated, intriguing search for a priceless statuette. "It's the stuff dreams are made of," says Bogart of the Falcon. Excellent, fast-paced film noir with outstanding performances, great dialogue, and concentrated attention to details. Huston makes giant debut, Greenstreet appears in a nonsilent for the first time, and Bogart secures leading man status. First of several films by Bogart and Astor. Third version based on the novel by Dashiell Hammett. Also available colorized.
1941 (*Sr. High-Adult*) 101m/B Humphrey Bogart, Mary Astor, Peter Lorre, Sydney Greenstreet, Ward Bond, Barton MacLane, Gladys George, Lee Patrick, Elisha Cook Jr., Jerome Cowan; *Cameos:* Walter Huston; *D:* John Huston; *W:* John Huston; *M:* Adolph Deutsch. **VHS, Beta, LV $19.98** *MGM, FOX, TLF*

Man & Boy 🎬🎬

Delicate and beautiful family film goes very wrong in its third act. Cosby is a homesteader in old Arizona whose horse is stolen while in the care of his young son. Man and boy follow the trail of the lost animal, a thoughtful and seriocomic odyssey throughout the west that abruptly turns violent, with an ugly, bloody shootout between a black outlaw and a white sheriff bringing the tale to a pointless end. What were these filmmakers thinking? Don't trust the G rating. **Hound Advisory:** Brutality, alcohol use, mature themes.
1971 (G/*Family*) 98m/C Bill Cosby, Gloria Foster, George Spell, Henry Silva, Yaphet Kotto; *D:* E.W. Swackhamer; *M:* Quincy Jones. **VHS, Beta $59.95** *COL*

Man and His World 🎬🎬🎬

Italian-made cartoon for kids depicting the major landmarks in man's development over the centuries in the pointed style of the "Allegro Non Troppo" animator Bozzetto.
1990 (*Family*) 90m/C *D:* Bruno Bozzetto. **VHS, Beta $59.95** *PSM, WTA*

The Man Called Flintstone 🎬🎬

Long before "Stephen Spielrock's" mammoth-budget 1994 Flintstones epic, this feature-length theatrical release appeared in which Fred Flintstone spoofs James Bond cliches that were terribly in vogue in the mid-'60s (A.D.) and already getting stale. During the intrigues, Fred takes his family and the Rubbles to Paris and Rome.
1966 (*Family*) 87m/C *D:* William Hanna, Joseph Barbera; *V:* Alan Reed, Mel Blanc, Jean VanDerPyl, Gerry Johnson, Don Messick, Janet Waldo, Paul Frees, Harvey Korman, John Stephenson, June Foray. **VHS, Beta, LV $29.95** *TTC, IME, APD*

A Man for All Seasons 🎬🎬🎬🎬

Sterling, heavily Oscar-honored biographical drama concerning the life and subsequent martyrdom of 16th-century Chancellor of England, Sir Thomas More (Scofield). Story revolves around his personal conflict when King Henry VIII (Shaw) seeks a divorce from his wife, Catherine of Aragon, so he can wed his mistress, Anne Boleyn-events that ultimately lead the King to bolt from the Pope and declare himself head of the Church of England. Remade for television in 1988 with Charlton Heston in the lead role.

1966 (G/*Family*) 120m/C Paul Scofield, Robert Shaw, Orson Welles, Wendy Hiller, Susannah York, John Hurt, Nigel Davenport, Vanessa Redgrave; *D:* Fred Zinneman; *W:* Constance Willis, Robert Bolt; *M:* Georges Delerue. **Award Nominations:** Academy Awards '66: Best Supporting Actor (Shaw), Best Supporting Actress (Hiller); **Awards:** Academy Awards '66: Best Actor (Scofield), Best Adapted Screenplay, Best Color Cinematography, Best Costume Design (Color), Best Director (Zinneman), Best Picture; British Academy Awards '67: Best Actor (Scofield), Best Film; Directors Guild of America Awards '66: Best Director (Zinneman); Golden Globe Awards '67: Best Actor—Drama (Scofield), Best Director (Zinneman), Best Film—Drama, Best Screenplay; National Board of Review Awards '66: 10 Best Films of the Year, Best Actor (Scofield), Best Director (Zinneman), Best Supporting Actor (Shaw). **VHS, Beta, LV $19.95** *COL, BTV, TVC*

Man from Button Willow 🦴🦴

Cowboy star Robertson basically had his western hero personality 'toonerized for this animated adventure. He lends his voice to Justin Eagle, a singing rancher/government secret agent in 1869 who joins with his wonder horse to save a kidnapped senator and an imperiled railroad. Strictly for young'uns with stetsons and popguns.
1965 (G/*Family*) 79m/C *V:* Dale Robertson, Edgar Buchanan, Barbara Jean Wong, Howard Keel. **VHS, Beta** *NO*

Man from Clover Grove 🦴🦴

Nutty inventor stirs up the community with his supersonic gadgets and the spies they attract. Alternate title, "The Absent- Minded Man From Clover Grove," is a hint of where the filmmakers got their inspiration.
1978 (G/*Family*) 96m/C Ron Masak, Cheryl Miller, Jed Allan, Rose Marie. **VHS, Beta $19.95** *MED*

The Man from Snowy River 🦴🦴🦴

Stunning cinematography highlights this popular but otherwise fairly ordinary adventure story set in 1888 Australia's cowboy territory. Young Jim Craig tries to prove himself worthy while working on the ranch of a rich American and taming a destructive herd of wild horses ("brumbies"). Douglas plays a dual role as estranged twin brothers. Based on an epic Aussie poem by A.B. "Banjo" Paterson, and with enough loose ends left at the end for the sequel, "Return to Snowy River." **Hound Advisory:** Roughhousing, salty language, mature themes, alcohol use.
1982 (PG/*Family*) 104m/C Kirk Douglas, Tom Burlinson, Sigrid Thornton, Terence Donovan, Tommy Dysart, Jack Thompson, Bruce Kerr; *D:* George Miller. **VHS, Beta, LV $14.98** *FOX, TVC, HMV*

The Man in the Iron Mask 🦴🦴🦴

Swashbuckling tale about twin brothers separated at birth. One turns out to be King Louis XIV of France, and the other a carefree wanderer and friend of the Three Musketeers. Their eventual clash leads to action-packed adventures and royal revenge.
1939 (*Family*) 110m/B Louis Hayward, Alan Hale, Joan Bennett, Warren William, Joseph Schildkraut, Walter Kingsford, Marion Martin; *D:* James Whale. **VHS, Beta $9.99** *CCB, MED*

The Man in the Iron Mask 🦴🦴🦴

Made for TV remake finds the tyrannical French king kidnapping his twin brother and imprisoning him on a remote island. Chamberlain, king of the miniseries, is excellent in the dual role. Adapted from the Dumas classic.
1977 (*Jr. High-Adult*) 105m/C Richard Chamberlain, Patrick McGoohan, Louis Jourdan, Jenny Agutter, Ian Holm, Ralph Richardson; *D:* Mike Newell. **VHS, Beta $19.98** *LIV, FUS, FOX*

The Man in the Moon 🦴🦴🦴🦴

Beautifully rendered coming-of-age tale. On a farm outside a small Louisiana town in the 1950s, 14 year-old Dani wonders if she will ever be as pretty and popular as her older sister Maureen. Dani is beginning to notice boys, particularly Court, a teenager she meets when swimming, and a rift develops between the sisters after Court meets Maureen. Intelligently written, excellent direction, lovely cinematography, and exceptional acting make this a particularly recommended film.
1991 (PG-13/*Jr. High-Adult*) 100m/C Reese Witherspoon, Emily Warfield, Jason London, Tess Harper, Sam Waterston, Gail Strickland; *D:* Robert Mulligan. **VHS $19.98** *MGM*

The Man in the Santa Claus Suit 🦴🦴

A costume shop owner has an effect on three people who rent Santa Claus costumes from him. Astaire plays seven different roles in this made for TV film. Average holiday feel-good movie.
1979 (*Family*) 96m/C Fred Astaire, Gary Burghoff, John Byner, Nanette Fabray, Bert Convy; *D:* Corey Allen. **VHS, Beta $69.95** *MED*

Man of La Mancha 🦴🦴

Arrested by the Inquisition and thrown into prison, Miguel de Cervantes relates the story of Don Quixote. Not nearly as good as the Broadway musical it is based on. ♫It's All the Same; The Impossible Dream; Barber's Song; Man of La Mancha; Dulcinea; I'm Only Thinking of Him; Little Bird, Little Bird; Life as It Really Is; The Dubbing.
1972 (PG/*Jr. High-Adult*) 129m/C Peter O'Toole, Sophia Loren, James Coco, Harry Andrews, John Castle, Brian Blessed; *D:* Arthur Hiller. **Award Nominations:** Academy Awards '72: Best Original Score; **Awards:** National Board of Review Awards '72: 10 Best Films of the Year, Best Actor (O'Toole). **VHS, Beta, LV $19.99** *FOX, FCT*

The Man Who Skied Down Everest 🦴🦴🦴

Documentary about a Japanese athlete who undertakes a demanding downhill run, and the cost (human and financial) of getting there.
1975 (G/*Family*) 86m/C **VHS** *NO*

The Man Who Wagged His Tail 🦴🦴🦴

A mean slumlord is turned into a dog as the result of a curse cast upon him. In order to regain his human form, he must be loved by someone. Mildly amusing fantasy filmed in Spain and Brooklyn, New York.
1957 (*Jr. High-Adult*) 91m/B Peter Ustinov, Pablito Calvo, Aroldo Tieri, Silvia Marco; *D:* Ladislao Vajda. **VHS $16.95** *SNC, VYY*

The Man Who Would Be King 🦴🦴🦴🦴

Grand, old-fashioned adventure based on the classic story by Rudyard Kipling about two mercenary soldiers who travel from India to Kafiristan in order to conquer it and set

themselves up as kings. Splendid characterizations by Connery and Caine, and Huston's royal directorial treatment provides it with adventure, majestic sweep, and well-developed characters. **Hound Advisory:** Violence.
1975 (PG/*Jr. High-Adult***)** 129m/C Sean Connery, Michael Caine, Christopher Plummer, Saeed Jaffrey, Shakira Caine; **D:** John Huston; **W:** Gladys Hill, John Huston; **M:** Maurice Jarre. VHS, Beta, LV $19.98 *FOX*

The Man with One Red Shoe 🎬🎬

Hanks is a lovable clod of a violinist who ensnares himself in a web of intrigue when CIA agents, both good and evil, mistake him for a contact by his wearing one red shoe. Sporadically funny remake (even Hanks is not too crazy about this one) of the French "The Tall Blond Man with One Black Shoe." **Hound Advisory:** Profanity and violence.
1985 (PG/*Jr. High-Adult***)** 92m/C Tom Hanks, Dabney Coleman, Lori Singer, Carrie Fisher, James Belushi, Charles Durning, Edward Herrmann, Tommy Noonan, Gerrit Graham, David Lander, David Ogden Stiers; **D:** Stan Dragoti; **M:** Thomas Newman. VHS, Beta $14.98 *FXV, FOX*

The Man with the Golden Gun 🎬🎬🎬

Moore is the debonair secret agent 007 in this ninth of the Bond series. Assigned to recover a small piece of equipment which can be utilized to harness the sun's energy, Bond engages the usual bevy of villains and beauties. **Hound Advisory:** Violence, alcohol use, suggested sex.
1974 (PG/*Jr. High-Adult***)** 134m/C Roger Moore, Christopher Lee, Britt Ekland, Maud Adams, Herve Villechaize, Clifton James, Soon-Teck Oh, Richard Loo, Marc Lawrence, Bernard Lee, Lois Maxwell, Desmond Llewelyn; **D:** Guy Hamilton; **W:** Tom Mankiewicz; **M:** John Barry. VHS, Beta, LV $19.98 *MGM, FOX*

The Man Without a Face 🎬🎬🎬

For his directorial debut Gibson chooses melodrama, playing a badly scarred recluse in Maine who develops a mentor relationship with a lonely, fatherless boy. Chuck (Stahl) wants to go away to military school, but flunks the entrance exam, and enlists former teacher McLeod as a tutor. Adapted from a novel by Isabelle Holland. **Hound Advisory:** Mature themes; sex talk; profanity.
1993 (PG-13/*Jr. High-Adult***)** 115m/C Mel Gibson, Nick Stahl, Margaret Whitton, Fay Masterson, Richard Masur, Gaby Hoffman, Geoffrey Lewis, Jack DeMave; **D:** Mel Gibson; **W:** Malcolm MacRury; **M:** James Horner. VHS, Beta, LV *WAR*

Man, Woman & Child 🎬🎬

Close, upscale California family is shocked when a child from the husband's long-ago affair with a Frenchwoman appears at their door. Pure sentimentalism, as the family tries to do the right thing in confronting this unexpected development. Two hankies—one each for fine performances by Sheen and Danner. Based on a sentimental novel by Erich Segal of "Love Story" fame, who co-wrote the script.
1983 (PG/*Sr. High-Adult***)** 99m/C Martin Sheen, Blythe Danner, Craig T. Nelson, David Hemmings; **D:** Dick Richards; **W:** Erich Segal; **M:** Georges Delerue. VHS, Beta $59.95 *PAR*

The Manhattan Project 🎬🎬

For a science fair project, a high school genius builds a functional nuclear bomb, complete with plutonium swiped from a government lab, and a manhunt for him begins.

Lithgow is excellent as a flippant weapons scientist who belatedly realizes the destructive power held by the boy (and, by extension, anyone with nukes). Teen technothriller has a splendid concept, but too many implausibilities disarm it. **Hound Advisory:** Profanity, mild sex talk.
1986 (PG-13/*Jr. High-Adult***)** 112m/C John Lithgow, Christopher Collet, Cynthia Nixon, Jill Eikenberry, John Mahoney, Sully Boyer, Richard Council, Robert Schenkkan, Paul Austin; **D:** Marshall Brickman; **W:** Marshall Brickman. VHS, Beta, LV $14.98 *REP*

Mannequin 🎬🎬

Nerd creates store window displays for a living. One plaster mannequin turns out to be an enchanted maiden of old, who comes to life only once she's alone with the hero. Whenever they start to kiss, someone walks in and catches the guy in a romantic embrace with a now-lifeless, life-size doll. Not as lewd as it sounds, but jokes and dialogue were written seemingly for ... well, dummies. **Hound Advisory:** Sex talk.
1987 (PG/*Jr. High-Adult***)** 90m/C Andrew McCarthy, Kim Cattrall, Estelle Getty, James Spader, Meshach Taylor, Carole Davis, G.W. Bailey; **D:** Michael Gottlieb; **W:** Ed Rugoff; **M:** Jefferson Starship. VHS, Beta, LV $9.99 *CCB, MED, VTR*

Mannequin 2: On the Move WOOF!

Less of a sequel, more of a witless rerun, with yet another lovesick princess frozen for 1,000 years and reviving as a department store dummy. Wild overacting in the cast suggest that everyone is auditioning for the Cannon Movie Tales. **Hound Advisory:** Roughhousing.
1991 (PG/*Jr. High-Adult***)** 95m/C Kristy Swanson, William Ragsdale, Meshach Taylor, Terry Kiser, Stuart Pankin; **D:** Stewart Raffill; **W:** Ed Rugoff. VHS, LV $92.98 *LIV*

Manny's Orphans 🎬

Out-of-work teacher takes on a lovable home for orphaned boys. Dull retread of "Bad News Bears" - from a director who later made his name with bloody horror flicks like "Friday the 13th."
1978 (PG/*Family***)** 92m/C Richard Lincoln, Malachy McCourt, Sel Skolnick; **D:** Sean S. Cunningham. VHS, Beta $69.98 *LIV, VES, CNG*

Manon of the Spring 🎬🎬🎬

Sequel to "Jean de Florette" is an outstanding morality play based on a Marcel Pagnol novel. The adult daughter of the dead hunchback, Jean, discovers who blocked up the spring on her father's land. She plots her revenge, which proves greater than she could ever imagine. As the villain of the piece, Montand is outstanding, while Beart brings a rare beauty to the screen. In French with English subtitles. **Hound Advisory:** Mature themes, nudity.
1987 (PG/*Jr. High-Adult***)** 113m/C Yves Montand, Daniel Auteuil, Emmanuelle Beart, Hippolyte Girardot; **D:** Claude Berri; **W:** Gerard Brach, Claude Berri. VHS, Beta, LV $19.98 *ORI, APD, INJ*

Man's Best Friend

Collection of nine cartoons, featuring such lovable but lesser-known cartoon canines like Cuddles, Snoozer, Duffy Dog and Dizzy, all from "Woody Woodpecker" creator Lantz.
1964 (*Family***)** 51m/C VHS, Beta $14.95 *MCA, WTA*

Maple Town

Animated series about anthropomorphic animals living in a tiny town, acting out vital life lessons for kids. Based on a Tonka toy line, which is a lesson in itself. Episodes include "The Stolen Necklace," "The Pot That Wouldn't Hold Water," and "Welcome to Maple Town."
1987 *(Preschool-Primary)* 86m/C **VHS, Beta $19.95** *FHE, WTA*

Maple Town: Case of the Missing Candy

Animated adventure featuring the toy-store figurines. When their parents come down hard on them, Bobby Bear, Patty Rabbit, and others decide to run away. Things are swell until Wilde Wolf turns up to make things interesting. Also included is the episode, "Teacher, Please Don't Go."
1987 *(Family)* 51m/C **VHS $14.95** *FHE, WTA*

March of the Wooden Soldiers 🎵🎵🎵

Hal Roach produced this classic combo of Mother Goose tale and Victor Herbert musical about the secret life of Christmas toys, with clowns Laurel and Hardy as Santa's helpers, who must save Toyland and Bo Peep from the wicked Barnaby and his apelike Bogeymen. Less than grandiose, but still way charming by modern standards, and a Yuletide "must see." Don't be surprised if Barnaby looks familiar; actor Kleinbach (later Henry Brandon) was the model for Disney's Gepetto in "Pinocchio." Also known as "Babes in Toyland" and available in a colorized version.
1934 *(Adult)* 73m/B Stan Laurel, Oliver Hardy, Charlotte Henry, Henry Kleinbach (Brandon), Felix Knight, Jean Darling, Johnny Downs, Marie Wilson; **D:** Charles "Buddy" Rogers, Gus Meins. **VHS, LV $29.95** *NOS, GKK, IME*

Marco Polo, Jr. 🎵

Marco Polo, Jr., the daring descendant of the legendary explorer, travels to Xanadu himself in this song-filled but cheaply animated feature from Australia.
1972 *(Preschool-Jr. High)* 82m/C **D:** Eric Porter; **V:** Bobby Rydell. **VHS, Beta $24.95** *FHE, WTA*

Maricela

Young Maricela Flores and her mother come to the US from El Salvador to escape the civil war that killed her brother. Living with a Southern California family, Maricela has a hard time adjusting to life in a free society. Another solid entry in the PBS "WonderWorks" anthology, this offers good, complicated characters and doesn't simplify the issues.
1988 *(Family)* 55m/C Linda Lavin, Carlina Cruz. **VHS $29.95** *PME, HMV, BTV*

Mario

Autistic 10-year-old Mario can only be drawn out of catatonia by teen brother Simon, with whom he plays imagination games on their island home. When Simon finds first love with a tourist girl, the lifelong burden of caring for Mario becomes too clear. Dreamlike Canadian drama, more for adults than kids. Ending is pure tragedy, wrapped in a wishful fantasy

sequence. Based on the novel "La Sabliere" by Claude Jasmin. **Hound Advisory:** Salty language; mature themes.
1974 (PG) *(Primary-Jr. High)* 98m/C Francis Reddy, Xavier Normann Petemann, Nathalie Chalifour; **D:** Jean Beudin. **VHS, Beta** *NFB, HHE*

Mark Twain and Me 🎵🎵🎵

Disney TV movie in which Robards portrays the aging and irascible Samuel Clemens, attended by a devoted adult daughter who nonetheless seems distant to him. On a sea voyage the writer forms a closer attachment with an adolescent girl named Dorothy. Based on a true story, recounted by Dorothy Quick in her book "Enchantment."
1991 *(Family)* 93m/C Jason Robards Jr., Talia Shire, Amy Stewart, Chris Wiggins, R.H. Thomson, Fiona Reid; **D:** Daniel Petrie. **VHS $19.99** *DIS, BTV*

Mark Twain's A Connecticut Yankee in King Arthur's Court

Low-budget (shot on videotape) but worthwhile TV version of the Mark Twain novel. New England industrialist is magically teleported from the 19th century back to Arthurian England, where he becomes a knight ("Sir Boss") and tries to put his all-American know-how to work in Camelot. Interesting revision: Merlin the Magician, a bad guy in the book, is here benevolent, wise — and African.
1978 *(Family)* 60m/C Richard Basehart, Roscoe Lee Browne, Paul Rudd. **VHS, Beta, LV $64.95** *MAS*

Martians Go Home! 🎵🎵

Joke-loving Martians come to Earth and pester a nerdy composer with one-liners. Low-budget sci-fi satire proves extraterrestrials have lousy comic timing. **Hound Advisory:** Profanity.
1990 (PG-13) *(Jr. High-Adult)* 89m/C Randy Quaid, Margaret Colin, Anita Morris, John Philbin, Ronny Cox, Gerrit Graham, Barry Sobel, Vic Dunlop; **D:** David Odell. **VHS, Beta, LV** *NO*

Marvelous Land of Oz 🎵🎵🎵

One of a series of cartoon Oz adventures generally faithful to the L. Frank Baum original novels, and amusing for young and old. Here Dorothy makes her first return visit to the magic land in time to foil an Emerald City takeover by General Ginger, her all-schoolgirl army, and bumbling witch Mombi. Canadian animation (oddly Japanese-looking) is simplistic but effective, though character voices tend to be dull.
1988 *(Family)* 90m/C **VHS, Beta $39.95** *COL, WTA*

Marvin & Tige 🎵🎵🎵

Sentimental drama about the deep friendship that develops between an aging alcoholic and a streetwise 11-year-old black boy he talks out of committing suicide after they meet one night in an Atlanta park. **Hound Advisory:** Salty language, mature themes.
1984 (PG) *(Family)* 104m/C John Cassavetes, Gibran Brown, Billy Dee Williams, Fay Hauser, Denise Nicholas-Hill; **D:** Eric Weston. **VHS, Beta $24.98** *SUE*

Mary Poppins 🎞🎞🎞🎞

Wonder-working English nanny descends one day via the East Wind and takes over the household of stuffy Londoner Mr. Banks. She introduces the Banks kids to such characters as Bert, the chimney sweep (Van Dyke) and a host of cartoon penguins. From Mary Poppins (Andrews, in her movie debut) the entire family learns that life can always be happy and joyous - not to mention supercalifragilisticexpialidocious - if you take the proper perspective. Based on the books by P.L. Travers, this is a tuneful Disney perennial that hasn't lost any of its magic over the years. ♫Chim Chim Cheree; A Spoonful of Sugar; The Perfect Nanny; Sister Suffragette; The Life I Lead; Stay Awake; Feed the Birds; Fidelity Feduciary Bank; Let's Go Fly a Kite. **1964** (*Family*) 139m/C Ed Wynn, Hermione Baddeley, Julie Andrews, Dick Van Dyke, David Tomlinson, Glynis Johns; **D:** Robert Stevenson. **Award Nominations:** Academy Awards '64: Best Adapted Screenplay, Best Art Direction/Set Decoration (Color), Best Color Cinematography, Best Costume Design (Color), Best Director (Stevenson), Best Picture, Best Sound, Best Original Score; **Awards:** Academy Awards '64: Best Actress (Andrews), Best Film Editing, Best Song ("Chim Chim Cher-ee"), Best Visual Effects, Best Score; Golden Globe Awards '65: Best Actress—Musical/Comedy (Andrews). **VHS, Beta, LV $24.99** *DIS, APD, BTV*

The Marzipan Pig

An animated children's story about a lovable swine who brings joy to a desolate mouse, a languishing owl, an exhausted flower, and a bee with a thirst for knowledge. **1990** (*Family*) 30m/C **VHS, Beta $14.98** *FHE, FCT, WTA*

M*A*S*H 🎞🎞🎞🎞

Hilarious, irreverent, and well-cast black comedy about a group of surgeons and nurses at a Mobile Army Surgical Hospital in Korea. The horror of war is set in counterpoint to their need to create havoc with episodic late-night parties, practical jokes, and sexual antics. An all-out anti-war festival, highlighted by scenes that starkly uncover the chaos and irony of war, and establish Altman's influential style. Watch for real-life football players Fran Tarkenton, Ben Davidson, and Buck Buchanan as they make an appearance in the squad football game. Loosely adapted from the novel by the pseudonymous Richard Hooker (Dr. H. Richard Hornberger and William Heinz). Subsequent hit TV series moved even further from the source novel. **Hound Advisory:** Mature themes, nudity, suggested sex, profanity, alcohol use. **1970** (**R**/*Sr. High-Adult*) 116m/C Donald Sutherland, Elliott Gould, Tom Skerritt, Sally Kellerman, JoAnn Pflug, Robert Duvall, Rene Auberjonois, Roger Bowen, Gary Burghoff, Fred Williamson, John Schuck, Bud Cort, G. Wood; **D:** Robert Altman; **W:** Ring Lardner Jr.; **M:** Johnny Mandel. **Award Nominations:** Academy Awards '70: Best Director (Altman), Best Film Editing, Best Picture, Best Supporting Actress (Kellerman); **Awards:** Academy Awards '70: Best Adapted Screenplay; Cannes Film Festival '70: Best Film; Golden Globe Awards '71: Best Film—Musical/Comedy. **VHS, Beta, LV $19.98** *FOX*

Mask 🎞🎞🎞

Fact-based story of Rocky Dennis, a bright teenager struck by a rare disease that grotesquely warped his head and face. Shunned by strangers, he's accepted and nurtured by the rambunctious motorcycle gang who hang out with his no-nonsense single mom, but her habitual drug use soon wears on him. Sounds gimmicky but it isn't thanks to Stoltz's

magnificent performance and unintrusive direction by Bogdanovich that rarely slips into maudlin territory. Depiction of a rowdy biker gang as a bunch of cuddly aunts and uncles takes some getting used to. **Hound Advisory:** Drug abuse is winked at by the bikers but opposed by Rocky, as is mom's promiscuity. She also brings home a young prostitute to make her son feel less lonely; Rocky and the girl just talk instead. Salty language. **1985** (**PG-13**/*Jr. High-Adult*) 120m/C Cher, Sam Elliott, Eric Stoltz, Estelle Getty, Richard Dysart, Laura Dern, Harry Carey Jr., Lawrence Monoson, Marsha Warfield, Barry Tubb, Andrew (Andy) Robinson, Alexandra Powers; **D:** Peter Bogdanovich; **W:** Anna Hamilton Phelan. **VHS, Beta, LV $19.95** *MCA*

The Mask 🎞🎞🎞

Adolescent supernatural horror comedy with lollapalooza special effects is Carrey's follow-up to "Ace Ventura." Mild-mannered bank clerk Carrey discovers an ancient mask that has supernatural powers. Based on the Dark Horse comic book series and originally conceived as a horror flick. Director Russell, who gave Freddy Krueger a sense of humor, recast this one as a cartoon-action black comedy. Carrey's rubber face is an asset combined with the breakthrough special effects courtesy of Industrial Light and Magic. The dog is good, too. **Hound Advisory:** Violence; sex talk. **1994** (**PG-13**/*Jr. High-Adult*) 100m/C Jim Carrey, Peter Riegert, Peter Greene, Amy Yasbeck; **D:** Chuck Russell; **W:** Mike Werb. **VHS** *NYR*

The Masked Marvel

Wartime serial in which the title hero saves America's industries from Axis saboteur Sakima. Unusual gimmick in this one is that the identity of the Masked Marvel is a secret until the final chapter; usually that's how the serials treated their costumed bad guys. In 12 episodes. **Hound Advisory:** Violence. **1943** (*Family*) 195m/B William Forrest, Louise Currie, Johnny Arthur; **D:** Spencer Gordon Bennet. **VHS $29.98** *VCN, REP, MLB*

Masters of the Universe 🎞🎞

Action-choked movie of the cartoon character/toy franchise is of the it-could-have-been-worse variety; pitching it at a high school audience was a definite mistake. Muscular He-Man (actors actually say that name without giggling) and friends fight Skeletor for supremacy on the planet Eternia. A Cosmic Key teleports the heroes to Anytown USA, where they continue sword and laser battles in the conveniently deserted streets. Big-budget adventure wasn't Master of the Box Office, so you can disregard the promised sequel at the close. **Hound Advisory:** Violence. Salty language that's wholly inappropriate to He-Man's rugrat fans. **1987** (**PG**/*Primary-Adult*) 109m/C Dolph Lundgren, Frank Langella, Billy Barty, Courteney Cox, Meg Foster; **D:** Gary Goddard; **M:** Bill Conti. **VHS, Beta, LV $19.98** *WAR*

Matilda 🎞🎞

Family fare about an entrepreneur who decides to manage a boxing kangaroo, which nearly succeeds in defeating the world heavyweight champion. Uneven and seldom engaging, partly because the kangaroo is so obviously a man in a silly animal suit. Based on Paul Gallico's novel.

1978 (PG/*Primary-Adult*) 103m/C Elliott Gould, Robert Mitchum, Harry Guardino, Clive Revill; **D:** Daniel Mann. **VHS, Beta $69.98** *LIV, VES*

Matinee 𝄞𝄞◁

Comic look at fantasy/sci-fi cheapies and the youthful audiences raised on them in bygone days. Setting is Key West, Florida, during the 1962 Cuban Missile Crisis; while the rest of the country fears nuclear annihilation, a gimmick-crazed Hollywood producer (Goodman, based on more than one actual movie mogul) test screens his radioactive-monster movie "MANT: Half-man, Half-ant, All Terror!" for a teen audience. Meanwhile, kids in the crowd have their own little romantic subplots and intrigues going. Trouble is, none of that is ever as hip or funny as the too-brief "Mant" sequences, re-created in impeccable B&W by director Dante (who's had offers to finish "Mant" and release that on its own!). Note the brief coming-attractions spoof "The Screwy Shopping Cart," a poke at hopelessly square Disney flicks - like the "Herbie" series -that only drove smart kids to the creature features instead.

1992 (PG/*Jr. High-Adult*) 98m/C John Goodman, Cathy Moriarty, Simon Fenton, Omri Katz, Lisa Jakub, Kellie Martin, Jesse Lee, Lucinda Jenney, James Villemaire, Robert Picardo, Dick Miller, John Sayles, Mark McCracken, Jesse White, David Clennon, Luke Halpin; **D:** Joe Dante; **M:** Jerry Goldsmith. **VHS, Beta, LV $19.98** *MCA, BTV*

Matt the Gooseboy 𝄞𝄞

Boy seeks revenge against an evil baron who stole his prize goose. Animated feature from a Hungarian folk tale.

198? (*Family***) 77m/C **VHS $39.98** *FHE, WTA*

Maurice Sendak Library

Three of Sendak's popular children's books are brought to the screen in animated form, plus an interview with Sendak himself in which he talks about his work.

1990 (*Family***) 35m/C Maurice Sendak; **V:** Carole King, Prof. Peter Schickele. **VHS, Beta $14.95** *FCT, CCC, MLT*

Maurice Sendak's Really Rosie

Animated tale of Rosie, who gets the entire neighborhood into her pretend movie and into her private spotlight. King provides the voice of Rosie and the songs.

1975 (*Primary***) 26m/C **M:** Carole King. **VHS, Beta $14.95** *CCC,, MVD*

Maverick 𝄞𝄞◁

Entertaining remake of the popular ABC series is fresh and funny, with sharp dialogue and a good cast. Everybody looks like they're having a great time, not difficult for the charming Gibson, but a refreshing change of pace for the usually serious Foster and Greene. In a fun bit of casting, Garner, the original Maverick, shows up as Marshal Zane Cooper. Lightweight, fast-paced comedy was reportedly highly improvised, though Donner retained enough control to keep it coherent. The end is left wide open so a sequel seems likely. Keep your eyes peeled for cameos from country stars, old

time Western actors, and an unbilled appearance from Glover. **Hound Advisory:** Salty language.

1994 (PG/*Jr. High-Adult*) 129m/C Mel Gibson, Jodie Foster, James Garner, Graham Greene, James Coburn, Alfred Molina, Paul Smith, Geoffrey Lewis, Max Perlich; **Cameos:** Dub Taylor, Dan Hedaya, Robert Fuller, Doug McClure, Bert Remsen, Denver Pyle, Will Hutchins, Waylon Jennings, Kathy Mattea, Danny Glover, Clint Black; **D:** Richard Donner; **W:** William Goldman; **M:** Randy Newman. **VHS** *NYR*

Max Dugan Returns 𝄞𝄞

A Simon comedy about an ex-con trying to make up with his daughter by showering her with presents bought with stolen money. Sweet and light, with a good cast.

1983 (PG/*Jr. High-Adult*) 98m/C Jason Robards Jr., Marsha Mason, Donald Sutherland, Matthew Broderick, Kiefer Sutherland; **D:** Herbert Ross; **W:** Neil Simon; **M:** David Shire. **VHS, Beta, LV $59.98** *FOX*

Max Fleischer's Cartoon Capers, Vol. 1: Playin' Around

Three vintage titles from the Fabulous Fleischer Studios: "Play Safe," "Small Fry," and "Ants in the Plants." Additional volumes available.

1941 (*Family***) 25m/C **VHS, Beta $9.95** *DIS, WTA*

Maxie's World: Dancin' & Romancin'

Antics of a modern teen queen, cartoon-style; fashionable Maxie has her own television program and leads a busy social life at Surfside High School. Such stuff as dreams are made of, repackaged for home video. Additional volumes available.

1989 (*Preschool-Primary***) 120m/C **VHS $39.95** *JFK, WTA*

Max's Chocolate Chicken and Other Stories for Young Children

Three charming children's stories. "Max's Chocolate Chicken" by Rosemary Wells finds Max the bunny and his big sister Ruby in an Easter story which features a moral about playing fair. "Each Peach Pear Plum" by Janet and Allan Ahlberg has familiar Mother Goose and folklore characters hiding in colorful pictures and waiting to be found by eagle-eyed youngsters. "The Circus Baby" by Maud and Miska Petersham finds a baby elephant with bad manners learning a lesson from his mother.

1992 (*Preschool***) 30m/C **VHS $14.95** *CCC, WKV, BTV*

Meatballs 𝄞𝄞

The Activities Director at kiddie Camp North Star is a sarcastic goof, and...that's about it really, as Murray breezes through comic routines and a bit of sentimental schmaltz in the role that made him a sensation and inspired some many stinkaroo imitations - especially its own numerous sequels (all done without Murray or director Reitman). **Hound Advisory:** Brief nudity, sex, profanity.

1979 (PG/*Jr. High-Adult*) 92m/C Bill Murray, Harvey Atkin, Kate Lynch; **D:** Ivan Reitman; **W:** Len Blum, Harold Ramis; **M:** Elmer Bernstein. **VHS, Beta, LV $24.95** *PAR*

Julie Andrews levitates as "Mary Poppins" (1964)

Meet Me in St. Louis 🦴🦴🦴⌐

Charming tale of a St. Louis family during the 1903 World's Fair has plenty of period detail. One of Garland's better musical performances as one of four daughters who become anxious when dad is told he needs to relocate to New York. Future husband Minnelli directs superbly. And the songs are great: "Meet Me in St. Louis" and "Have Yourself a Merry Christmas" among them. ♫You and I; Skip to My Lou; Over the Bannister; Meet Me In St. Louis; Brighten the Corner; Summer In St. Louis; All Hallow's Eve; Ah, Love; The Horrible One.

1944 (*Family*) 113m/C Judy Garland, Margaret O'Brien, Mary Astor, Lucille Bremer, Tom Drake, June Lockhart, Harry Davenport; **D:** Vincente Minnelli. **Award Nominations:** Academy Awards '44: Best Color Cinematography, Best Screenplay, Best Song ("The Trolley Song"), Best Original Score; **Awards:** National Board of Review Awards '44: 10 Best Films of the Year. **VHS, Beta, LV, 8mm $19.98** *MGM, TLF, HMV*

Meet the Hollowheads 🦴⌐

Miscalculated 'family' situation comedy set in a foul future society of tubes, drains, pipes and drippy conduits. There a harried father must prepare his awful, slime-ridden household for a visit from the tyrannical boss. Directorial debut of makeup expert Burnam not surprisingly emphasizes grossness and f/x. **Hound Advisory:** The Hollowhead daughter is a sex-crazed nymphet, and the boss who lusts after her gets what he deserves in a violent finale. Salty language.

1989 (PG-13/*Sr. High-Adult*) 89m/C John Glover, Nancy Mette, Richard Portnow, Matt Shakman, Juliette Lewis, Anne Ramsey; **D:** Tom Burman. **VHS, LV $39.95** *MED, IME*

Melody 🦴🦴⌐

Melody is a 12-year-old girl in love with 11-year-old Daniel; so much so that they petition adults to allow them to marry. Sweet-natured British production (not at all the raunch it might have been a few decades later) slightly soured by slow narrative and severely outdated '60s-era 'Swinging London' ambiance. Frequent musical interludes by the Bee Gees.

1971 (G/*Family*) 106m/C Tracy Hyde, Jack Wild, Mark Lester, Colin Barrie, Roy Kinnear; **D:** Waris Hussein; **W:** Alan Parker. **VHS, Beta $69.98** *SUE*

The Member of the Wedding 🦴🦴

Setting is Georgia in 1945, where Frankie Addams, awkwardly straddling gawky adolescence and young womanhood, builds unrealistic, romantic hopes around the marriage of her big sister to a serviceman. Touching performances (though the agonized, androgynous Harris is clearly way past 12!), but heavy going. Carson McCullers's play (based on her novel) is just too talky and introspective to sustain a close-up screen treatment. 1983 TV movie rehash is also on tape. **Hound Advisory:** Alcohol use, mature themes.

1952 (*Jr. High-Adult*) 90m/C Ethel Waters, Julie Harris, Brandon de Wilde, Arthur Franz; **D:** Fred Zinneman; **W:** Edward Anhalt; **M:** Alex North. **VHS, Beta** *NO*

Memoirs of an Invisible Man 🦴🦴

Nick Halloway, a slick and shallow stock analyst, is rendered invisible by a freak accident. When he is pursued by a CIA agent-hit man who wants to exploit him, Nick turns for help to Alice, a documentary filmmaker he has just met. Naturally, they fall in love along the way. Effective sight gags, hardworking cast can't overcome pitfalls in script, which indecisively meanders between comedy and thrills. **Hound Advisory:** Violence; mature themes.

1992 (PG-13/*Jr. High-Adult*) 99m/C Chevy Chase, Daryl Hannah, Sam Neill, Michael McKean, Stephen Tobolowsky, Jim Norton, Patricia Heaton, Rosalind Chao; **D:** John Carpenter. **VHS, LV $19.98** *WAR*

Men Don't Leave 🦴🦴🦴

Newly widowed, Beth has to sell her home and move to an urban apartment to take a full-time job. Her two sons start drifting away, the younger one staying with his best friend's family, the older a live-in lover for an older woman in the building. Muted, often painful family drama with a ring of truth - it doesn't tie up things neatly at the end and offers characters of unexpected depth and emotion. Great performances by all in drama deserving of more recognition. **Hound Advisory:** Profanity, mature themes as Beth slips into pill-popping manic depression. Brief sex.

1989 (PG-13/*Jr. High-Adult*) 115m/C Jessica Lange, Arliss Howard, Joan Cusack, Kathy Bates, Charlie Korsmo, Corey Carrier, Chris O'Donnell, Tom Mason, Jim Haynie; **D:** Paul Brickman; **W:** Barbara Benedek, Paul Brickman; **M:** Thomas Newman. **VHS, Beta, LV, 8mm $19.98** *WAR*

Men of Boys Town 🦴🦴⌐

Sequel to 1938's "Boys Town" has the same sentimentality, even more if that's possible. Father Flanagan's reformatory faces closure, while the kids reach out to an embittered new inmate. Worth seeing for the cast reprising their roles.

1941 (*Family*) 106m/B Spencer Tracy, Mickey Rooney, Darryl Hickman, Henry O'Neill, Lee J. Cobb, Sidney Miller; **D:** Norman Taurog. **VHS $19.98** *MGM, FCT*

Menace on the Mountain 🦴🦴

Family-oriented drama about a father and son facing hardship during the Civil War.

1970 (G/*Family*) 89m/C Patricia Crowley, Albert Salmi, Charles Aidman. **VHS, Beta $69.95** *DIS*

Menace II Society 🦴🦴🦴⌐

Portrayal of black teens lost in inner-city hell is realistically captured by 21-year-old twin directors, in their big-screen debut. Caine (Turner) lives with his grandparents and peddles drugs for spending money, from the eve of his high school graduation to his decision to escape south-central Los Angeles for Atlanta. Bleak and haunting, with unsettling, bloody violence at the core of this urban tragedy. Based on a story by the Hughes' and Tyger Williams. **Hound Advisory:** Very mature teens may withstand the heavy violence, obscenity, drug taking, sexual situations, and so on that occur. On the other hand, lots of fairly mature adults have trouble sitting through this one.

1993 (**R**/*Sr. High-Adult*) 104m/C Tyrin Turner, Larenz Tate, Samuel L. Jackson, Glenn Plummer, Julian Roy Doster, Bill Duke, Charles S. Dutton; **D:** Allen Hughes, Albert Hughes; **W:** Tyrin Turner. **Award Nominations:** Independent Spirit Awards '94: Best Actor (Turner), Best Cinematography, Best First Feature; **Awards:** MTV Movie Awards '94: Best Film. **VHS, LV** COL, NLC, IME

Merlin and the Sword 🦴

Poor use of a good cast in this hokey, made-for-TV treatment of the legend of King Arthur, as a 20th-century gal tumbles back through time and finds herself in Camelot, caught up between intrigues with Merlin and the witch Morgan Le Fey. **1985** (*Family*) 94m/C Malcolm McDowell, Edward Woodward, Candice Bergen, Dyan Cannon; **D:** Clive Donner. **VHS, Beta $69.98** LIV, VES

Mermaids 🦴🦴🦴

Mrs. Flax is a flamboyant single mother of two who leaves town every time a relationship threatens to turn serious. Having moved some eighteen times, her daughters, Charlotte, 15, and Kate, 8, are a little worse for the wear, psychologically. The former aspiring to be a nun though they're not Catholic. Amusing, well-acted comedy-drama of multi-generational maturity (or lack of it), based on a novel by Patty Dann. **Hound Advisory:** Mature themes, sex talk, profanity. **1990** (**PG-13**/*Jr. High-Adult*) 110m/C Cher, Winona Ryder, Bob Hoskins, Christina Ricci, Michael Schoeffling, Caroline McWilliams, Jan Miner; **D:** Richard Benjamin; **W:** June Roberts; **M:** Jack Nitzsche. **VHS, Beta, LV $9.98** ORI

A Merry Mirthworm Christmas

The animated annelids known as Mirthworms get together to celebrate Christmas and that's when the alleged fun begins. **1984** (*Family*) 30m/C **V:** Rachel Rutledge, Jerry Reynolds, Peggy Nicholson. **VHS, Beta $9.95** FHE, WTA

Merry Mother Goose

Several Mother Goose favorites are featured. **1990** (*Preschool-Primary*) 30m/C **VHS $7.95**

The Meteor Man 🦴🦴🦴

Initially gentle superhero spoof about a D.C. teacher acquiring semi-super powers after being hit by a meteor. Fun stuff; Meteor Man flies only four feet off the ground (because he's afraid of heights) and tries on ludicrous costumes sewn by his mother. Plot sags, though, in a prolonged knockabout showdown with a gang terrorizing the neighborhood. Theme of black citizens standing up against crime, but, as in the first Ninja Turtles feature, bad guys are ultra-cool, and one wonders what message kid viewers are getting. Special f/x by Industrial Light and Magic; interesting cameo by Cosby. **Hound Advisory:** Violence. **1993** (**PG**/*Jr. High-Adult*) 100m/C Robert Townsend, Robert Guillaume, Marla Gibbs, James Earl Jones, Frank Gorshin; **Cameos:** Bill Cosby, Sinbad, Luther Vandross, LaWanda Page; **D:** Robert Townsend; **W:** Robert Townsend. **VHS, LV $94.99** MGM

Metropolitan 🦴🦴🦴

Brittle comedy of manners among upper-class teenagers of Manhattan, during Christmas break. Middle-class Tom is drawn into a nightly circle of friends who debate socialism, Jane Austin heroines, the existence of God, and who's going out with whom with equal civility and precocious world-weary wit. After the monosyllabic grunts that pass for 'realistic' dialogue in other flirting-with-adulthood movies, this intelligent talkfest comes as a welcome change, though viewers who aren't hooked right off will inevitably be bored. Released to theaters unrated; on video its PG-13 is inexplicable. **Hound Advisory:** Sex talk, with shades of drug use, and widely scattered profanity. **1990** (**PG-13**/*Sr. High-Adult*) 98m/C Carolyn Farina, Edward Clements, Taylor Nichols, Christopher Eigeman, Allison Rutledge-Parisi, Dylan Hundley, Isabel Gillies, Bryan Leder, Will Kempe, Elizabeth Thompson; **D:** Whit Stillman; **W:** Whit Stillman; **M:** Mark Suozzi. **Award Nominations:** Academy Awards '90: Best Original Screenplay; **Awards:** Independent Spirit Awards '91: Best First Feature; New York Film Critics Awards '90: Best Director (Stillman). **VHS, LV $19.95** COL, FCT

Mickey Mouse Club, Vol. 1

Each cassette in this series features three episodes from the popular 1950s' television series, with a newly filmed introduction by Annette Funicello. These lively programs, starring the "Mouseketeers," include song, dance, cartoons, documentary newsreels, and continuing serialized adventures. Additional volumes available. **195?** (*Preschool-Primary*) 90m/B Annette Funicello. **VHS, Beta** DIS

Mickey Mouse: The Early Years Series

The world's best-loved animated mouse stars in some very early Disney adventures on separate tapes, including his very first, "Steamboat Willie" from 1928. Others are "The Band Concert" (1935) and "Thru the Mirror" (1936). In all three, Walt Disney himself lends his voice to the trademark creation. **1990** (*Preschool-Primary*) 9m/C **VHS, Beta $195.00** MTI, DSN

Mickey's Birthday Party

It's Mickey's birthday, and the whole Disney cartoon gang celebrates with a cake made by Goofy. **1942** (*Preschool-Primary*) 8m/C **VHS, Beta $160.00** MTI, DSN

Mickey's Christmas Carol 🦴🦴🦴

Mickey Mouse returns along with all the other Disney characters in this adaptation of the Charles Dickens classic that marked the legendary rodent's first all-new cartoon in decades; an added documentary describes how the featurette was made. **1983** (**G**/*Family*) 25m/C **VHS, Beta, LV $12.99** DIS, MTI, DSN

Mickey's Crazy Careers

Outstanding collection from Disney with five bonafide classics, and one early black and white cartoon. The classics are Mickey's first Technicolor adventure "The Band Concert," plus "Clock Cleaners," "Tugboat Mickey," "Magician Mickey," and "Mickey's Fire Brigade." **1940** (*Family*) 48m/C Mickey Mouse. **VHS, Beta** BVV

Mickey's Field Trips Series

Mickey takes children on trips to a fire station, hospital, police station and the United Nations, where he teaches the importance of each and their various functions and value.
1988 (*Preschool-Primary*) 12m/C **VHS, Beta $230.00** *MTI, DSN*

A Midnight Clear 🦴🦴🦴

Sensitive war drama takes place in the Ardennes Forest, near the French-German border in December 1944. It's Christmas time and six of the remaining members of a 12-member squad are sent on a dangerous mission to an abandoned house to locate the enemy. Filmed in a dreamy surreal style, the setting is somewhat reminiscent of a fairytale, although a sense of anguish is present throughout. Solid script, excellent direction, and a good cast make this more than another WWII fly by night. Adapted from the novel by William Wharton. **Hound Advisory:** Violence; profanity; mature themes.
1992 (**PG**/*Sr. High-Adult*) 107m/C Peter Berg, Kevin Dillon, Arye Gross, Ethan Hawke, Gary Sinise, Frank Whaley, John C. McGinley, Larry Joshua, Curt Lowens; *D:* Keith Gordon; *W:* Keith Gordon; *M:* Mark Isham. **VHS, LV $19.95** *COL, PMS*

Midnight Madness 🦴

Five teams of college students chase all over the city of Los Angeles for clues in an all-night scavenger hunt. This insipid, no-brainer comedy's lone claim to fame (aside from an early Michael J. Fox appearance) was being among the Disney Studio's first PG-rated pics.
1980 (**PG**/*Family*) 110m/C David Naughton, Stephen Furst, Debra Clinger, Eddie Deezen, Michael J. Fox, Maggie Roswell; *D:* David Wechter; *W:* David Wechter. **VHS, Beta** *BVV, OM*

The Mighty Ducks 🦴🦴🦴

Bad News Bears (Disney-style) on skates. Selfish lawyer Gordon Bombay is arrested for drunk driving, and his sentence is to coach juvenile hockey players, the usual misfits, slobs and underachievers. Dual themes of teamwork and redemption are hammered constantly and heavily, but there's exciting rink action and good ensemble work from the kids. Scored with young fans thanks to the phenomenon of peewee hockey, and a real-life team, the Mighty Ducks of Anaheim, was founded as a result/promo of this hit. Followed by more hockey shenanigans in "D2 - The Mighty Ducks." **Hound Advisory:** Alcohol use, roughhousing.
1992 (**PG**/*Jr. High-Adult*) 114m/C Emilio Estevez, Joss Ackland, Lane Smith, Heidi Kling, Josef Sommer, Matt Doherty, Steven Brill, Joshua Jackson, Elden Ratliff, Shaun Weiss; *D:* Stephen Herek; *W:* Steven Brill, Brian Hohlfield; *M:* David Newman. **VHS, Beta, LV $94.95** *TOU, BTV*

Mighty Hercules: Champion of the People!

Hercules champions justice, fights for truth, and punishes evil-doers in these early '60s syndicated TV cartoons brought back from the Underworld.
1963 (*Family*) 60m/C **VHS $14.95** *VMK, WTA*

Mighty Hercules: Conqueror of Evil!

When a magic ring is exposed to lightning it changes a mere mortal into...the Mighty Hercules!
1963 (*Family*) 60m/C **VHS $14.95** *VMK, WTA*

The Mighty Hercules: Mightiest Mortal!

He's very mighty! But wait! If the Mighty Hercules is so great(!), why can't he do something about all these exclamation points?! Just asking!
1963 (*Family*) 60m/C **VHS $14.95** *VMK, WTA*

Mighty Joe Young 🦴🦴🦴

Creators of the original "King Kong" and "Son of Kong" returned with more kid-friendly monkeyshines in this tale about yet another giant ape brought from the African wilds to civilization and exploited in a silly nightclub act. Bullied and gaining the key to the liquor cabinet, the sweet-tempered Joe goes on a drunken rampage but redeems himself by rescuing orphans from a convenient fire. Stop-motion special f/x courtesy of Willis O'Brien and the great Ray Harryhausen are probably the film's best feature. Also available colorized. Laserdisc includes commentary on the technical wizardry involved. **Hound Advisory:** Roughhousing, primate alcohol use.
1949 (*Family*) 94m/B Terry Moore, Ben Johnson, Robert Armstrong, Frank McHugh; *D:* Ernest B. Schoedsack. **VHS, Beta, LV $19.95** *TTC*

Mighty Mouse

Moon-dwelling mouse stars in this tape in a vintage Terrytoon, along with a few other animated creations. Titles include "Wolf! Wolf!," "Christmas Comes but Once a Year," "Porky's Railroad," and "Timid Toreador." Additional volumes available.
19?? (*Family*) 30m/C *V:* Tom Morrison. **VHS** *CNG*

Mighty Mouse in the Great Space Chase

Feature-length adventure starring the moon-dwelling rodent hero of Terrytoon fame, in which Mighty Mouse battles the nefarious Harry the Heartless in order to save Queen Pureheart and the galaxy. Additional volumes available.
1983 (*Family*) 88m/C **VHS, Beta $59.98** *WTA*

Mighty Orbots: Devil's Asteroid

Cartoon sci-fi; if you're old enough to decipher the anagram "orbot" you may be too old to watch. Evil lord creates an imposter killer Orbot, causing the real Orbots to be sentenced for murder to the Devil's Asteroid for 999 years.
1984 (*Preschool-Primary*) 26m/C **VHS, Beta $14.95** *MGM*

The Mighty Pawns

To keep inner city junior-high kids off the streets, a progressive teacher starts a chess club and tricks some unruly students into joining. The logic and discipline of the

MICKEY MOUSE

Mm

Mickey goes jogging

ancient game motivates most of them to improve in and out of the classroom. Familiar but uplifting "WonderWorks" episode, based on the true story of the "Bad Bishops" of Robert Vaux Junior High School in Philadelphia.
1987 *(Family)* 58m/C Paul Winfield, Alfonso Ribeiro, Terence Knox, Rosalind Cash, Teddy Wilson; **D:** Eric Laneuville. **VHS $29.95** *PME, HMV, FCT*

Mighty Thor: Enter Hercules

TV cartoons in which the Marvel Comics hero Thor fights for his girl in "Enter Hercules" and travels to the 30th Century in "The Tomorrow Man." Additional volumes available.
1966 *(Primary-Jr. High)* 35m/C **VHS $14.95** *WTA*

Mike Mulligan and His Steam Shovel

Thanks to modern technology, Mike's trusty steamshovel Mary Anne is becoming obsolete. They still, however, manage to dig themselves into a number of dilemmas. A typically hip cartoon version of the Virginia Lee Burton book from animator Michael Sporn.
1992 *(Preschool-Primary)* 25m/C **VHS $12.95** *WTA*

Million Dollar Duck 🎦🎦

Family duck is doused with radiation and begins to lay gold eggs. Does this make him a Mighty Duck? It did for Disney - movie sure wasn't art but became one of the Magic Kingdom's bigger hits of the '70s.
1971 *(G/Family)* 92m/C Dean Jones, Sandy Duncan, Joe Flynn, Tony Roberts; **D:** Vincent McEveety; **M:** Buddy Baker. **VHS, Beta** *DIS, OM*

Million Dollar Kid 🎦🎦

When a group of thugs wreak havoc in the neighborhood, the East Side Kids try to help a wealthy man put a stop to it. They face an even greater dilemma when they discover that the man's son is part of the gang.
1944 *(Jr. High-Adult)* 65m/B Leo Gorcey, Huntz Hall, Gabriel Dell, Louise Currie, Noah Beery Jr., Iris Adrian, Mary Gordon; **D:** Wallace Fox. **VHS $19.95** *VYY, DVT, NOS*

The Mini-Monsters: Adventures at Camp Mini-Mon

Summer camp cartoon adventure for young monster admirers.
1987 *(Family)* 33m/C **VHS $14.98** *LHV, WAR, WTA*

A Minor Miracle 🎦🎦

Minor movie about a group of orphaned children who band together under the loving guidance of a dying priest (famed movie director/actor Huston) to save St. Francis School from closure. Their plan: a big soccer match. And yes, that is soccer legend Pele in a supporting role. Also known as "Young Giants."
1983 *(G/Family)* 100m/C John Huston, Pele, Peter Fox; **D:** Terrell Tannen. **VHS, Beta, LV $9.95** *COL, SUE*

The Miracle 🎦🎦◁

Irish teens, whose strong friendship is based upon their equally unhappy home lives, find both tested when a secretive

American woman turns up in town and intrigues the boy. Excellent debuts from the young actors, though the dreamy script tends to tell too much too soon. **Hound Advisory:** Roughhousing, alcohol use, Irish profanity, mature themes, sex talk.
1991 *(PG/Jr. High-Adult)* 97m/C Beverly D'Angelo, Donal McCann, Niall Byrne, Lorraine Pilkington, J.G. Devlin; **D:** Neil Jordan; **W:** Neil Jordan; **M:** Anne Dudley. **VHS, LV $89.98** *LIV*

Miracle at Moreaux

Three Jewish children fleeing from Nazis find sanctuary in a French convent school with a kindly nun. But some of the Catholic kids have been raised in anti-Semitic households and don't easily accept the newcomers. Touching "Wonder-Works" drama, based on Clare Huchet Bishop's book "Twenty and Ten." **Hound Advisory:** Brief violence.
1986 *(Family)* 58m/C Loretta Swit, Marsha Moreau, Robert Joy, Ken Pogue, Robert Kosoy, Talya Rubin; **D:** Paul Shapiro. **VHS $29.95** *PME, HMV, IGP*

Miracle Down Under 🎦🎦◁

"Man from Snowy River" Miller (not fellow Australian "Mad Max" Miller) directs inoffensive Disney-produced drama. Family endures arduous times in 1890s Australia before a Christmas miracle changes their fortunes.
1987 *(Family)* 101m/C Dee Wallace Stone, John Waters, Charles Tingwell, Bill Kerr, Andrew Ferguson; **D:** George Miller. **VHS, Beta $29.95** *BVV, IGP*

Miracle of Our Lady of Fatima 🎦🎦◁

Lush, big-budget adaptation of the supposedly true events surrounding a vision of the Virgin Mary witnessed by three children in Portugal during WWI. Some of the pic's cliches owe more to the gods of Hollywood than the Catholic faith, but there are some undeniably touching and stirring moments.
1952 *(Jr. High-Adult)* 102m/C Gilbert Roland, Susan Whitney, Sherry Jackson, Sammy Ogg, Angela Clark, Frank Silvera, Jay Novello; **D:** John Brahm; **M:** Max Steiner. **VHS, Beta, LV $19.98** *WAR, IGP, KEP*

Miracle of the Heart: A Boys Town Story 🎦🎦

TV movie based on the story of Boys Town and an old priest who stick up for Boys Town's principles in the face of a younger priest with rigid ideas.
1986 *(Family)* 100m/C Art Carney, Casey Siemaszko, Jack Bannon; **D:** Georg Stanford Brown. **VHS, Beta $19.95** *COL*

Miracle of the White Stallions 🎦◁

A disappointing Disney adventure about the director of a Viennese riding academy who guides his prized Lippizan stallions to safety when the Nazis occupy Austria in WWII.
1963 *(Family)* 92m/C Robert Taylor, Lilli Palmer, Eddie Albert, Curt Jurgens; **D:** Arthur Hiller. **VHS, Beta $69.95** *DIS*

Miracle on Ice 🎦🎦◁

Occasionally stirring TV film recounts the surprise triumph of the American hockey team over the touted Soviet squad during the 1980 Winter Olympics at Lake Placid.

Miracle on 34th Street (1947)

1981 (*Family*) 150m/C Karl Malden, Steve Guttenberg, Andrew Stevens, Lucinda Dooling, Jessica Walter; *D:* Steven Hilliard Stern. **VHS, Beta** *NO*

Miracle on 34th Street 🦴🦴🦴🦴

Nice old man named Kris Kringle is hired as Santa Claus for the Macy's Thanksgiving parade and claims to be the real thing. All New York is enchanted by the idea, but the parade sponsor's cynical little daughter refuses to be convinced. Eventually, Kringle goes on trial for his sanity and must prove himself to the law as well as the child. Hollywood classic that never fades, with terrific performances (especially by youngster Wood) and as satisfying an ending as has ever been done. Also available colorized.

1947 (*Family*) 97m/B Maureen O'Hara, John Payne, Edmund Gwenn, Natalie Wood, William Frawley, Porter Hall, Gene Lockhart, Thelma Ritter, Jack Albertson; *D:* George Seaton; *W:* George Seaton; *M:* Cyril Mockridge. **Award Nominations:** Academy Awards '47: Best Picture; **Awards:** Academy Awards '47: Best Story & Screenplay, Best Supporting Actor (Gwenn). **VHS, Beta, LV** **$9.98** *CCB, FOX, HMV*

The Miracle Worker 🦴🦴🦴⅟

True story of the famous struggle by teacher Anne Sullivan to break through to the deaf, blind, mute girl Helen Keller. Helen's family allowed the (literally) senseless child to rampage willfully around the estate, until Sullivan took over and sought to communicate sign language to the crafty, but seemingly uncontrollable youngster - by force if necessary. An intense, moving experience adapted by William Gibson from his own play. **Hound Advisory:** Roughhousing.

1962 (*Family*) 107m/B Anne Bancroft, Patty Duke, Victor Jory, Inga Swenson, Andrew Prine, Beah Richards; *D:* Arthur Penn. **Award Nominations:** Academy Awards '62: Best Adapted Screenplay, Best Costume Design (B & W), Best Director (Penn); **Awards:** Academy Awards '62: Best Actress (Bancroft), Best Supporting Actress (Duke); National Board of Review Awards '62: 10 Best Films of the Year, Best Actress (Bancroft). **VHS, Beta** **$19.98** *MGM, BTV, CCB*

The Miracle Worker 🦴🦴🦴

Remade for television story of blind, deaf and mute Helen Keller and her teacher, Annie Sullivan, whose patience, perseverance - and ability to swing with the punches - finally enables the child to learn to communicate with the world. Nice bit of casting has Duke, who played Keller in the 1962 original, as the teacher here. She teams splendidly with "Little House on the Prairie" pioneer Gilbert as Keller.

1979 (*Family*) 98m/C Patty Duke, Melissa Gilbert; *D:* Paul Aaron; *M:* Billy Goldenberg. **VHS, Beta** **$59.95** *WAR, OM*

A Mirthworm Masquerade

Animated short from Hanna-Barbera featuring those "lovable" Mirthworms throwing Wormingham's annual costume

ball. Who will win, Wormaline Wiggler or Crystal Crawler? Who wrote this stuff? Mirthworm fans will also want to see "A Merry Mirthworm Christmas."
1986 *(Preschool)* 24m/C **VHS, Beta** $12.95 *FHE, WTA*

The Misadventures of Merlin Jones *𝄞𝄞*

Episodic comedy about college goof Merlin, who experiments with raising the intelligence of chimpanzees and athletes. Wacky adventures ensue. Some of the hardware is funny (like Merlin's wired-up football helmet) but most of this is bland, dated Disney. A sequel, "The Monkey's Uncle," followed.
1963 *(G/Family)* 90m/C Tommy Kirk, Annette Funicello, Leon Ames, Stuart Erwin, Connie Gilchrist; *D:* Robert Stevenson; *M:* Buddy Baker. **VHS, Beta** $69.95 *DIS*

Miss Annie Rooney *𝄞𝄞*

Annie is a poor Irish girl who falls in love with a wealthy young man, with the usual family disapproval and ponderous plot twists. The maturing child starlet receives her first screen kiss.
1942 *(G/Family)* 86m/B Shirley Temple, Dickie Moore, William Gargan, Guy Kibbee, Peggy Ryan, June Lockhart; *D:* Edwin L. Marin. **VHS, Beta** $12.95 *LIV, MED*

Miss Firecracker *𝄞𝄞𝄞*

Hunter, longing for love and self-respect, decides to change her promiscuous image by entering the local beauty pageant in her conservative southern hometown. The somewhat drippy premise is transformed by a super script and cast into an engaging and upbeat film. Henley's script was adapted from her own Off-Broadway play where Hunter created the role. Actress Lahti, wife of director Schlamme, makes a brief appearance.
1989 *(PG/Jr. High-Adult)* 102m/C Holly Hunter, Scott Glenn, Mary Steenburgen, Tim Robbins, Alfre Woodard, Trey Wilson, Bert Remsen, Ann Wedgeworth, Christine Lahti, Amy Wright; *D:* Thomas Schlamme; *W:* Beth Henley; *M:* David Mansfield. **VHS, Beta, LV** $89.99 *HBO*

Mrs. Doubtfire *𝄞𝄞𝄞*

Williams is an unemployed voiceover actor going through a messy divorce. When his wife gets custody, the distraught father dresses as a woman and become a nanny to his own children. He also has to deal with the old flame who re-enters his ex-wife's life. Vintage Williams shtick extraordinaire with more than a little sugary sentimentality. Based on the British children's book "Madame Doubtfire" by Anne Fine. **Hound Advisory:** Sex talk.
1993 *(PG-13/Jr. High-Adult)* 120m/C Robin Williams, Sally Field, Pierce Brosnan, Harvey Fierstein, Robert Prosky, Mara Wilson; *D:* Chris Columbus; *W:* Randi Mayem Singer, Leslie Dixon; *M:* Howard Shore. **Award Nominations:** MTV Movie Awards '94: Best Actor (Williams); **Awards:** Academy Awards '93: Best Makeup; Golden Globe Awards '94: Best Actor—Musical/Comedy (Williams), Best Film—Musical/Comedy; MTV Movie Awards '94: Best Comedic Performance (Williams). **VHS** $19.98 *FXV*

Mr. & Mrs. Bridge *𝄞𝄞𝄞𝄞*

Set in '30s and '40s in Kansas City, this adaptation of two overlapping Evan S. Connell novels painstakingly portrays an upper middle-class family in an emotional vacuum. Father is stuffy and domineering; Mother has repressed all traces of willfulness and personality in total submission to her husband. Quiet, yet enormously moving, with real-life acting couple Newman and Woodward delivering two of their best, most subtle, and nuanced performances.
1991 *(PG-13/Jr. High-Adult)* 127m/C Joanne Woodward, Paul Newman, Kyra Sedgwick, Blythe Danner, Simon Callow, Diane Kagan, Robert Sean Leonard, Saundra McClain, Margaret Welsh, Austin Pendleton, Gale Garnett, Remak Ramsay; *D:* James Ivory; *W:* Ruth Prawer Jhabvala. **VHS, LV** $92.99 *HBO, FCT*

Mr. & Mrs. Condor

Life as a big bird in a big forest has its ups and downs. This cartoon series follows the fun-loving Condor family at work and play. Each tape includes three episodes.
1979 *(Preschool-Primary)* 60m/C **VHS, Beta** $29.95 *FHE, WTA*

Mr. & Mrs. Quack

Two episodes of the obscure cartoon series.
198? *(Family)* ?m/C **VHS, Beta** $29.95 *FHE, WTA*

Mr. & Mrs. Smith *𝄞𝄞𝄞𝄞◁*

Hitchcock's only screwball comedy, an underrated, endearing farce about a bickering but happy modern couple who discover their marriage isn't legitimate and go through courtship all over again. Vintage of its kind, with inspired performances and crackling dialogue.
1941 *(Family)* 95m/B Carole Lombard, Robert Montgomery, Gene Raymond, Jack Carson, Lucile Watson, Charles Halton; *D:* Alfred Hitchcock; *W:* Norman Krasna. **VHS, Beta, LV** $19.95 *MED, TTC*

Mr. Baseball *𝄞𝄞*

Washed-up American baseball player tries to revive his career by playing in Japan and experiences cultures clashing under the ballpark lights. Semi-charmer swings and misses often enough to warrant return to minors. Film drew controversy during production when Universal was bought by the Japanese Matsushita organization and claims of both Japan- and America-bashing were thrown about. **Hound Advisory:** Profanity.
1992 *(PG-13/Jr. High-Adult)* 109m/C Tom Selleck, Ken Takakura, Toshi Shioya, Dennis Haysbert, Aya Takanashi; *D:* Fred Schepisi; *W:* Gary Ross, Kevin Wade, Monte Merrick; *M:* Jerry Goldsmith. **VHS, Beta, LV** $19.98 *MCA*

Mr. Bill Looks Back Featuring Sluggo's Greatest Hits

Compilation of Williams' notorious "Mr. Bill" shorts from "Saturday Night Live." Mr. Bill is a parody of a little clay kiddie-show host - not animated; he just stands there - who gets mashed and dismembered within the course of each cutesy short subject. Sidesplitting (literally) stuff for adults and kids who've had too much Barney. Williams supplies new footage as well as old favorites in this collection. A new Mr. Bill short can also be found at the start of "Ernest Rides Again."
1983 *(Sr. High-Adult)* 31m/C **VHS, Beta** *NO*

Mrs. Doubtfire (1993)

Mr. Bill's Real-Life Adventures

One of Shelley Duvall's stranger productions, a gag that doesn't quite come off. Live-action sitcom (done for cable TV) with kiddie-show host Mr. Bill and his normally clay family impersonated by live actors, though they're still miniature people dwelling in a full-sized world. No serious violence or dismemberment, but flesh-and-blood Bill still takes a lot of slapstick abuse. A lengthy featurette hosted by Duvall shows how the f/x were done.
1986 (*Jr. High-Adult*) 43m/C Peter Scolari, Valerie Mahaffey, Lenore Kasdorf, Michael McManus; *D:* Jim Drake. **VHS, Beta $29.95** *PAR*

Mr. Destiny 𝄞𝄞

Mid-level businessman Belushi has a mid-life crisis of sorts when his car dies. Wandering into an empty bar, he encounters bartender Caine who serves cocktails and acts omniscient before taking him on the ten-cent tour of life as it would've been if he hadn't struck out in a high school baseball game. Less than wonderful rehash of "It's a Wonderful Life."
Hound Advisory: Profanity.
1990 (PG-13/*Sr. High-Adult*) 110m/C James Belushi, Michael Caine, Linda Hamilton, Jon Lovitz, Bill McCutcheon, Hart Bochner, Rene Russo, Jay O. Sanders, Maury Chaykin, Pat Corley, Douglas Seale, Courteney Cox, Kathy Ireland; *D:* James Orr; *W:* James Orr, Jim Cruickshank. **VHS, Beta, LV $19.99** *TOU, FCT*

Mr. Hulot's Holiday 𝄞𝄞𝄞

Superior slapstick details the misadventures of a dullard's seaside holiday. Inventive French comedian Tati at his best. Light-hearted and natural, with magical mime sequences.
1953 (*Family*) 86m/B Jacques Tati, Natalie Pascaud, Michelle Rolla; *D:* Jacques Tati. **Award Nominations:** Academy Awards '55: Best Story & Screenplay; **Awards:** National Board of Review Awards '54: 5 Best Foreign Films of the Year. **VHS, Beta, LV, 8mm $24.95** *NOS, MRV, VYY*

Mr. Magoo: 1001 Arabian Night's Dream

Magoo appears as Aladdin's uncle, the lamp dealer, in this classic tale of genies and palaces.
1959 (*Family*) 75m/C **VHS $19.95** *WTA*

Mr. Magoo: Cyrano De Bergerac/A Midsummer Night's Dream

The near-sighted Mr. Magoo stars in a compilation of theatrical cartoons that featured the character in whimsical (and sometimes quite straightforward) adaptations of great works of literature. Here he appears first as the large-nosed Cyrano De Bergerac, then as the silly Puck in the Shakespeare comedy.
1964 (*Primary-Jr. High*) 50m/C *V:* Jim Backus. **VHS $12.95** *PAR, WTA*

Mr. Magoo: Don Quixote de la Mancha

Myopic Mr. Magoo portrays the famous knight in an adaptation of Cervantes' novel.
1964 (*Preschool-Jr. High*) 50m/C *V:* Jim Backus. **VHS $12.95** *PAR, FCT, WTA*

Mr. Magoo in Sherwood Forest 𝄞𝄞𝄞

As Friar Tuck, the nearsighted Mr. Magoo takes a role with Robin Hood and his Merry Men in their struggle against the Sheriff of Nottingham. Feature-length Magoo adventure does a generally faithful job in retelling the Sherwood Forest legend.
1964 (*Family*) 83m/C *V:* Jim Backus. **VHS, Beta, LV $12.95** *PAR, WTA*

Mr. Magoo in the King's Service 𝄞𝄞𝄞

Mr. Magoo is off on the King's business in this wacky full-length cartoon compilation of theatrical Magoo short subjects, all adaptations of famous characters with royal connections. Magoo portrays D'Artagnan (cohort of the Three Musketeers), Cyrano de Bergerac, and Merlin the Magician.
1966 (*Family*) 92m/C *V:* Jim Backus. **VHS, Beta $24.95** *PAR, WTA*

Mr. Magoo: King Arthur/The Count of Monte Cristo

Mr. Magoo plays King Arthur and the Count of Monte Cristo in this double feature.
1964 (*Preschool-Jr. High*) 50m/C *V:* Jim Backus. **VHS $12.95** *PAR, FCT, WTA*

Mr. Magoo: Little Snow White

Mr. Magoo plays all of the seven dwarfs in this adaptation of the classic fairy tale.
1964 (*Preschool-Jr. High*) 50m/C *V:* Jim Backus. **VHS $12.95** *PAR, FCT, WTA*

Mr. Magoo: Sherlock Holmes/Dr. Frankenstein

Mr. Magoo first plays Sherlock Holmes's sidekick Watson and then the mad Dr. Frankenstein.
1964 (*Primary-Jr. High*) 50m/C *V:* Jim Backus. **VHS $12.95** *PAR, WTA*

The Mr. Magoo Show, Vol. 1

Five episodes from the 1960 juvenile cartoon series. Included are "Magoo's Last Stand," "Short Order Magoo," "Lost Vegas," "Cupid Magoo," and "Cuckoo Magoo." Additional volumes available.
1960 (*Preschool-Jr. High*) 25m/C *V:* Jim Backus. **VHS $9.95** *PAR, FCT, WTA*

Mr. Magoo: The Three Musketeers

Mr. Magoo stars in a cartoon adaptation of the Dumas swashbuckling epic.
1964 (*Preschool-Jr. High*) 50m/C *V:* Jim Backus. **VHS $12.95** *PAR, FCT, WTA*

Mr. Magoo's Christmas Carol 𝄞𝄞𝄞

Nearsighted Mr. Magoo, in character as Ebenezer Scrooge, receives Christmas visits from three ghosts in an entertaining and quite effective version of the classic tale. No less an authority than Sir Alistair Cooke has recommended this as

one of the best of the many, many adaptations of the Charles Dickens original.
1962 *(Family)* 52m/C **V:** Jim Backus. **VHS, Beta, LV** $12.95 *PAR, WTA*

Mr. Magoo's Storybook 🎾🎾🎾

Mr. Magoo acts out all the parts in versions of three famous tales of literature: "Snow White and the Seven Dwarfs," "Don Quixote," and "A Midsummer Night's Dream." Entertaining and surprisingly instructional compilation of Magoo theatrical short subjects.
1964 *(Family)* 113m/C **V:** Jim Backus. **VHS, Beta** $14.95 *PAR, WTA*

Mr. Mom 🎾🎾🎾

Auto exec loses his job and stays home with the kids while his wife becomes the breadwinner. He's forced to cope with the rigors of housework and child care, resorting to alcohol and soap operas for relief. Keaton's funny as homebound dad chased by amok appliances and poker buddy to the ladies in the neighborhood. Written by John Hughes. **Hound Advisory:** Alcohol use, near sexual situations.
1983 **(PG/***Jr. High-Adult)* 92m/C Michael Keaton, Teri Garr, Christopher Lloyd, Martin Mull, Ann Jillian, Jeffrey Tambor, Edie McClurg, Valri Bromfield; **D:** Stan Dragoti; **W:** John Hughes. **VHS, Beta, LV** $29.98 *LIV, VES*

Mr. Nanny 🎾🎾

For those who fear change, this predictable plot should be comforting. Hulkster plays nanny/bodyguard to a couple of bratty kids. Meanwhile, his arch rival schemes to gain world dominance by holding the kids for the ransom of their father's top secret computer chip. Never fear - in this world, the good guys kick butt, naturally, and everyone learns a lesson. **Hound Advisory:** Roughhousing.
1993 **(PG/***Jr. High-Adult)* 85m/C Hulk Hogan, Sherman Hemsley, Austin Pendleton, Robert Gorman, Madeline Zima, Mother Love, David Johansen; **D:** Michael Gottlieb; **W:** Ed Rugoff, Michael Gottlieb; **M:** David Johansen, Brian Koonin. **VHS** *NLC, COL*

Mr. North 🎾🎾◁

Capra-corn fable about a charming, bright Yale graduate who encounters admiration and disdain from upper-crust Rhode Island residents when news of his miraculous "cures" spreads. Marks the directorial debut of Danny Huston, son of John Huston, who co-wrote the script and served as executive producer before dying several weeks into shooting. Set in the 1920s and adapted from Thornton Wilder's "Theophilus North."
1988 **(PG/***Jr. High-Adult)* 90m/C Anthony Edwards, Robert Mitchum, Lauren Bacall, Harry Dean Stanton, Anjelica Huston, Mary Stuart Masterson, Virginia Madsen, Tammy Grimes, David Warner, Hunter Carson, Christopher Durang, Mark Metcalf, Katherine Houghton; **D:** Danny Huston; **W:** John Huston, Janet Roach; **M:** David McHugh. **VHS, Beta, LV** *NO*

Mister Rogers Meets an Astronaut

Apollo 15 astronaut, Major Alfred Worden, discusses moon flights and astronauts by answering questions submitted by children.
1971 *(Primary)* 29m/C Mr. Rogers.*NO*

Mister Rogers: Music and Feelings

Specially edited Mr. Rogers program focusing on the importance and enjoyment of music for kids.
1986 *(Preschool-Primary)* 65m/C Fred Rogers. **VHS, Beta** $14.98 *FOX*

Mister Rogers: Musical Stories

Two musical fables by Rogers, starring his TV show's coterie of puppets: "Potato Bugs and Cows" and "Granddad for Daniel."
1987 *(Preschool-Primary)* 59m/C Fred Rogers. **VHS, Beta** $14.98 *FOX, HMV*

Mister Rogers: When Parents Are Away

The renowned children's television host instructs kids in how to manage at home alone (in the pre-Macauley Culkin era, anyway).
1987 *(Preschool-Primary)* 66m/C **VHS, Beta** $14.98 *FOX, HMV*

Mr. Rossi Looks For Happiness 🎾🎾

Aided by a magic whistle, Mr. Rossi travels through the past and future, only to learn that there's no time like the present. Italian animation from the creator of the classic "Allegro Non Troppo."
1986 *(Preschool-Primary)* 80m/C **D:** Bruno Bozzetto. **VHS, Beta** $39.95 *FHE, WTA*

Mr. Rossi's Dreams 🎾🎾

Mr. Rossi gets to act out his fantasies of being Tarzan, Sherlock Holmes, and a famous movie star in this cartoon feature from the "Allegro Non Troppo" animation maestro.
1983 *(Family)* 80m/C **D:** Bruno Bozzetto. **VHS, Beta** $39.95 *FHE, WTA*

Mr. Rossi's Vacation 🎾🎾🎾

Mr. Rossi and his dog Harold go off in search of quiet on a "let's get away from it all" vacation. More well-done Italian 'toonage from the animator behind "Allegro Non Troppo."
1983 *(Family)* 82m/C **D:** Bruno Bozzetto. **VHS, Beta** $39.95 *FHE, WTA*

Mr. Smith Goes to Washington 🎾🎾🎾🎾

Another classic from Hollywood's golden year of 1939. Jimmy Stewart is an idealistic and naive young man selected to fill in for an ailing Senator. Upon his arrival in Washington, he is inundated by a multitude of corrupt politicians. He takes a stand for his beliefs and tries to denounce many of those he feels are unfit for their positions, meeting with opposition from all sides. Great cast is highlighted by Stewart in one of his most endearing performances. Quintessential Capra tale sharply adapted from Lewis Foster's story. Outstanding in every regard.
1939 *(Family)* 130m/B James Stewart, Jean Arthur, Edward Arnold, Claude Rains, Thomas Mitchell, Beulah Bondi, Eugene Pallette, Guy Kibbee, Harry Carey Sr., H.B. Warner, Porter Hall, Jack Carson, Charles Lane; **D:** Frank Capra; **W:** Sidney Buchman; **M:** Dimitri Tiomkin. **Award Nominations:** Academy Awards '39: Best Actor (Stewart), Best Director (Capra), Best Interior Decoration, Best Picture, Best Screenplay, Best Sound, Best Supporting Actor (Rains, Carey), Best

Score; **Awards:** Academy Awards '39: Best Story; National Board of Review Awards '39: 10 Best Films of the Year; New York Film Critics Awards '39: Best Actor (Stewart). **VHS, Beta, LV** $19.95 *COL, HMV*

Mr. Superinvisible ♫♫

Searching to cure the common cold, a bumbling scientist invents an invisibility serum. He and his loyal (of course) sheepdog try to keep the formula from falling into the wrong hands. European production is a mid-'70s Disney clone in style and content. Is that the good news or the bad news? **1973 (G/** *Family***)** 90m/C Dean Jones, Ingeborg Schoener, Gastone Moschin; *D:* Anthony M. (Antonio Margheriti) Dawson. **VHS, Beta** *NO*

Mr. Wise Guy ♫♫

The East Side Kids break out of reform school to clear one of the Kids' brother's of a murder charge. Typical pre-Bowery Boys vehicle. **1942** (*Family*) 70m/B Leo Gorcey, Huntz Hall, Billy Gilbert, Guinn Williams, Benny Rubin, Douglas Fowley, Ann Doran, Jack Mulhall, Warren Hymer, David Gorcey; *D:* William Nigh. **VHS, Beta** $19.95 *NOS, DVT, HEG*

Mr. Wizard's World: Air and Water Wizardry

Before "Beakman's World" and Bill Nye the Science Guy there was Don Herbert, quintessential science instructor better known as Mr. Wizard. In a compilation from his Nickelodeon cable show, he conducts a slew of entertaining but simple experiments with air pressure and water. Companion tape, "Mr. Wizard's World: Puzzles, Problems & Impossibilities," is also available. **1983** (*Family*) 44m/C **VHS, Beta** $19.98 *FOX*

Mr. Wonderful ♫♫◁

Bittersweet (rather than purely romantic) look at love and romance. Divorced Con Ed worker Gus (Dillon) is hard up for cash and tries to marry off ex-wife Lee (Sciorra) so he can use her alimony to invest in a bowling alley with his buddies. Routine effort is elevated by the cast, who manage to bring a small measure of believability to a transparent plot. Minghella was a critical hit with his debut, "Truly, Madly, Deeply" but may find that fame can be fleeting. **Hound Advisory:** Profanity and sex. **1993 (PG-13/** *Jr. High-Adult***)** 99m/C Matt Dillon, Annabella Sciorra, William Hurt, Mary-Louise Parker, Luis Guzman, Dan Hedaya, Vincent D'Onofrio; *D:* Anthony Minghella; *W:* Amy Schor, Vicki Polon; *M:* Michael Gore. **VHS, Beta, LV** *WAR*

Misunderstood ♫♫◁

Former black market merchant in Tunisia has to learn how to relate to his neglected sons after his wife dies. The father, now a legitimate businessman, is more concerned with running his shipping firm than growing closer to the boys. Fine acting by Hackman and "E.T."'s Thomas grapples with a transparent tearjerker plot. **1984 (PG/** *Jr. High-Adult***)** 92m/C Gene Hackman, Susan Anspach, Henry Thomas, Rip Torn, Huckleberry Fox; *D:* Jerry Schatzberg. **VHS, Beta** $79.95 *MGM*

Modern Problems ♫♫

Man involved in a nuclear accident discovers he has acquired telekinetic powers, which he uses to turn the tables on his professional and romantic rivals. A fine cast but an unsuccessful fission trip. **Hound Advisory:** Brief nudity; suggested sex. **1981 (PG/** *Jr. High-Adult***)** 93m/C Chevy Chase, Patti D'Arbanville, Mary Kay Place, Brian Doyle-Murray, Nell Carter, Dabney Coleman; *D:* Ken Shapiro. **VHS, Beta** $14.98 *FOX*

Mom and Dad Save the World ♫♫◁

Attempt to do "a so dumb it's funny" comedy for all ages only gets the dumb part right. Planet Spengo, populated entirely by idiots, plans to destroy Earth. But nasty King Tod spies through his telescope an average suburban housewife and falls in love. He teleports Mr. and Mrs. Nelson to Spengo, and postpones death-raying their world until he can marry Mom, dispose of Dad. Highlights are the goofy playpen sets; lowlight is the misuse of an excellent cast, especially Idle and Shawn. Very young kid viewers might be amused. **Hound Advisory:** Roughhousing, sex talk. **1992 (PG/** *Primary-Adult***)** 87m/C Teri Garr, Jeffrey Jones, Jon Lovitz, Eric Idle, Wallace Shawn, Dwier Brown, Kathy Ireland, Thalmus Rasulala; *D:* Greg Beeman; *M:* Jerry Goldsmith. **VHS, LV** $92.99 *HBO*

Mommie Dearest ♫♫

Based on Christina Crawford's memoirs of her incredibly abusive and violent childhood at the hands of her adoptive mother, actress Joan Crawford. More appreciated for its campiness than artistic merit, as Dunaway works up a lather in over-the-top performance as Lady Joan. **1981 (PG/** *Jr. High-Adult***)** 129m/C Faye Dunaway, Diana Scarwid, Steve Forrest, Mara Hobel, Rutanya Alda, Harry Goz, Howard da Silva; *D:* Frank Perry; *W:* Robert Getchell; *M:* Henry Mancini. **VHS, Beta, LV** $59.95 *PAR*

The Money Pit ♫♫◁

Often hilarious urban nightmare comedy about a young yuppie couple encountering sundry problems when they attempt to renovate their newly purchased, seemingly self-destructive, Long Island home. Both home and relationship suffer in the ensuing domestic crisis. Never has a house fallen apart with such gusto. While the stunts tend to overwhelm the story and cast, both Hanks and Long are appealing as the young couple plunged into mortgage hell. A Spielberg production somewhat modeled after "Mr. Blandings Builds His Dream House." **Hound Advisory:** Profanity and suggested sex. **1986 (PG/** *Jr. High-Adult***)** 91m/C Tom Hanks, Shelley Long, Alexander Godunov, Maureen Stapleton, Philip Bosco, Joe Mantegna, Josh Mostel; *D:* Richard Benjamin; *M:* Michel Colombier. **VHS, Beta, LV** $14.95 *MCA*

Monkees, Volume 1

The notorious 'mod' '60s band, fabricated as a response to the Beatles, turned out to have undeniable and enduring appeal, and episodes of their anything-goes network comedy series have gained them a new generation of young viewers thanks to rebroadcasts on MTV. Monkee fans will flip for these six videocassette volumes, each holding two music-filled

episodes each. The Monkees' daringly abstract (G-rated) feature film "Head," as bizarre an experience as Hollywood ever produced, is also on tape, mainly of interest to film scholars and non-linear thinkers.
1966 (*Jr. High-Adult*) 50m/C Michael Nesmith, Davy Jones, Peter Tork, Mickey Dolenz. **VHS, Beta, LV** $14.95 *MVD, COL*

Monkey Business 🎬🎬🎬🎬

A scientist invents a fountain-of-youth potion, a lab chimpanzee mistakenly dumps it into a water cooler, and then grownups start turning into adolescents. Monroe is the secretary sans skills, while absent-minded Grant and sexy wife Rogers race hormonally as teens. Occasionally labored but comic moments do shine.
1931 (*Family*) 77m/B Groucho Marx, Harpo Marx, Chico Marx, Zeppo Marx, Thelma Todd, Ruth Hall, Harry Woods; **D:** Norman Z. McLeod. **VHS, Beta, LV** $14.98 *MCA*

Monkey Business 🎬🎬🎬

Scientist invents a fountain-of-youth potion, a lab chimpanzee mistakenly dumps it into a water cooler, and then grown-ups start turning into adolescents. Top-flight crew occasionally labors in this screwball comedy, though comic moments shine. Monroe is the secretary sans skills, while absent-minded Grant and sexy wife Rogers race hormonally as teens.
1952 (*Family*) 97m/B Cary Grant, Ginger Rogers, Charles Coburn, Marilyn Monroe, Hugh Marlowe, Larry Keating, George Winslow; **D:** Howard Hawks; **W:** Ben Hecht, Charles Lederer, I.A.L. Diamond. **VHS, Beta, LV** $14.98 *FOX*

The Monkey People

South American folktale about a lazy village and an industrious boy who figures out a way to get work done. As a result of not working, the villagers become indistinguishable from animals, and the boy moves away to continue his trade. Great multicultural storytelling from the "Rabbit Ears: We All Have Tales" series.
1991 (*Primary*) 30m/C **M:** Lee Ritenour. **VHS** $9.95 *UND, MCA,*

Monkey Trouble 🎬🎬🎬

Crummy title, surprisingly good movie. Girl feels abandoned when mom and stepdad shower attention on a new baby brother and won't let her get a pet. Then Dodger, a Capuchin monkey trained as a Venice Beach pickpocket, seeks refuge in her house from his conniving gypsy master. The little heroine goes to great lengths hiding Dodger from parent and gypsy alike, and the flick stakes a lot of its entertainment wallop on the talents of the slippery fingered simian, who steals the show (among other things). Formula abounds, but gags are fun and freshly paced, with a nice aside about the divorced family conferring amicably over the daughter's welfare. **Hound Advisory:** Alcohol use.
1994 (**PG**/*Primary-Adult*) 95m/C Thora Birch, Finster, Harvey Keitel, Mimi Rogers, Christopher McDonald; **D:** Franco Amurri; **W:** Franco Amurri, Stu Krieger; **M:** Mark Mancina. **VHS** *NYR*

Monkeys, Go Home! 🎬🎬

Dumb Disney yarn about young American who inherits a badly neglected French olive farm. When he brings in four chimpanzees to pick the olives, the local townspeople go on strike. First this, then Euro-Disneyland. Based on "The Monkeys" by G. K. Wilkinson.
1966 (*Family*) 89m/C Dean Jones, Yvette Mimieux, Maurice Chevalier, Clement Harari, Yvonne Constant; **D:** Andrew V. McLaglen. **VHS, Beta** $69.95 *DIS*

Monkey's Uncle 🎬🎬

Sequel to Disney's "The Misadventures of Merlin Jones" and featuring more bizarre antics and scientific hoopla, including teaching chimps with a flying machine.
1965 (*Family*) 90m/C Tommy Kirk, Annette Funicello, Leon Ames, Arthur O'Connell; **D:** Robert Stevenson; **M:** Buddy Baker. **VHS, Beta** $69.95 *DIS*

Monster Bash

Selection of Disney TV comedy cartoons parodying spooky plots. "Frankengoof" features Goofy inheriting a castle and encountering the Frankengoof monster. In "Ducky Horror Picture Show," the Monsters Unanimous Convention comes to Duckberg and Huey, Dewey, and Louie have a monstrously good time. Released along with two similar compilations, "Boo-Busters" and "Witcheroo."
1993 (*Family*) 44m/C **VHS** $12.99 *DIS, WTA*

The Monster Squad 🎬🎬

School-age monster enthusiasts battle the real thing, the famous Universal Pictures horror icons, led by Dracula. Commanding the Wolf Man, Mummy and Black Lagoon gillman, the vampire invades their community in search of a magic amulet, while the childlike Frankenstein monster becomes the kids' ally. Frank's also the only character with the right mix of innocence and menace. Meeting of classic creatures, high-tech special effects and typical foulmouthed movie youngsters is more of a collision than collusion. **Hound Advisory:** Salty language, violence (mostly against monsters), sex talk in abundance when the kids learn they need a virgin girl - giggle giggle - to recite a spell.
1987 (**PG-13**/*Jr. High*) 82m/C Andre Gower, Stephen Macht, Tommy Noonan, Duncan Regehr; **D:** Fred Dekker; **W:** Fred Dekker, Shane Black; **M:** Bruce Broughton. **VHS, Beta, LV** $19.98 *LIV, VES*

Monty Python and the Holy Grail 🎬🎬🎬🎬

Britain's famed comedy band assaults the Arthurian legend in a cult classic replete with a Trojan rabbit and an utterly dismembered, but inevitably pugnacious, knight. Fans of manic comedy - and goofy but graphic violence - should get more than their fill here. Teens with mature funny bone may appreciate. **Hound Advisory:** Assault by killer rabbit; non-fatal dismemberment; salty language (though mostly in French).
1975 (**PG**/*Jr. High-Adult*) 90m/C Graham Chapman, John Cleese, Terry Gilliam, Eric Idle, Terry Jones, Michael Palin, Carol Cleveland, Connie Booth, Neil Innes, Patsy Kensit; **D:** Terry Gilliam, Terry Jones; **W:** Graham Chapman, John Cleese, Terry Gilliam, Eric Idle, Terry Jones, Michael Palin. **VHS, Beta, LV, 8mm** $19.95 *COL, SIG, TVC*

Moon Pilot 🦴🦴

First astronaut scheduled to orbit the moon is followed prior to the launch by an enticing mystery woman. She turns out to be a (French-accented) alien who's only trying to help, but government security forces panic and chase them both. Outdated, rather dull Disney romantic comedy with no f/x whatsoever. Notable for inspiring a feud between Walt Disney and FBI Director J. Edgar Hoover, who was upset at the depiction of a federal agent character as a pompous blowhard. It's said Disney made sure the feds were bumbling boobs in all his subsequent productions.
1962 (*Family*) 98m/C Tom Tryon, Brian Keith, Edmond O'Brien, Dany Saval, Tommy Kirk; *D:* James Neilson. **VHS, Beta $69.95** *DIS*

Moon-Spinners 🦴🦴

Lightweight Disney mystery (based on a Mary Stewart novel) about a young Englishwoman travelling through Crete who meets up with a wounded man accused of being a jewel thief. The pair work together to unmask the real evildoers.
1964 (*PG/Family*) 118m/C Hayley Mills, Peter McEnery, Eli Wallach, Pola Negri; *D:* James Neilson. **VHS, Beta** *DIS, OM*

The Moon Stallion 🦴🦴🦴

Professor Purwell leads an excavation to uncover evidence of the mythical King Arthur, but it's his daughter Diana, sightless and psychic, who holds the key to strange apparitions of a legendary white horse. Interesting British-German TV production of the novel by Brian Hayles, attempts to be a tale of fantasy and mystery for all ages.
1985 (*Family*) 95m/C Sarah Sutton, David Haig, James Greene, John Abineri, Caroline Goodall; *D:* Dorothea Brooking. **VHS $29.95** *BFS, HMV*

Mooncussers 🦴🦴

Details the exploits of a precocious 12-year-old determined to exact revenge upon a band of ruthless pirates.
1962 (*Family*) 85m/C Kevin Corcoran, Rian Garrick, Oscar Homolka; *D:* James Neilson. **VHS, Beta $69.95** *DIS*

Moondreamers, Vol. 1

Moondreamer adventures take place in a land where dreams come true. Included on this animation compilation are "All in a Night's Sleep," "The Star of Stars," and "The Poobah of Pontoon." Additional volumes available.
19?? (*Preschool-Primary*) 30m/C **VHS, Beta $9.95**

Moonraker 🦴🦴

Uninspired Bond fare has 007 unraveling intergalactic hijinks. Bond is aided by a female CIA agent, assaulted by a giant with jaws of steel, and captured by Amazons when he sets out to protect the human race. Moore, Chiles, and Lonsdale all seem to be going through the motions only. **Hound Advisory:** Violence, alcohol use, suggested sex.
1979 (*PG/Jr. High-Adult*) 136m/C Roger Moore, Lois Chiles, Richard Kiel, Michael Lonsdale, Corinne Clery, Geoffrey Keen, Emily Bolton, Walter Gotell, Bernard Lee, Lois Maxwell, Desmond Llewelyn; *D:* Lewis Gilbert; *M:* John Barry. **VHS, Beta, LV $19.98** *MGM, TLF*

Moonstruck 🦴🦴🦴🦴

Winning romantic comedy about widow engaged to one man but falling in love with his younger brother in Little Italy. Excellent performances all around, with Cher particularly fetching as attractive, hapless widow. Unlikely casting of usually dominating Aiello as unassuming mama's boy also works well, and Cage is at his best as a tormented one-handed opera lover/baker. **Hound Advisory:** Salty language; sexual situations.
1987 (*PG-13/Jr. High-Adult*) 103m/C Cher, Nicolas Cage, Olympia Dukakis, Danny Aiello, Vincent Gardenia, Julie Bovasso, Louis Guss, Anita Gillette, Feodor Chaliapin, John Mahoney; *D:* Norman Jewison; *W:* John Patrick Shanley. **Award Nominations:** Academy Awards '87: Best Director (Jewison), Best Picture, Best Supporting Actor (Gardenia); **Awards:** Academy Awards '87: Best Actress (Cher), Best Original Screenplay, Best Supporting Actress (Dukakis); Golden Globe Awards '88: Best Actress—Musical/Comedy (Cher), Best Supporting Actress (Dukakis). **VHS, Beta, LV $19.98** *MGM, BTV, HMV*

More Adventures of Roger Ramjet

Join Roger and his crew as they once again take on N.A.S.T.Y. Cartoons are "Monster Masquerade" and "Coffee House."
1965 (*Family*) 30m/C *V:* Gary Owens. **VHS $14.99** *RHI, WTA*

More American Graffiti 🦴🦴

George Lucas is not be found in this sequel to 1973's acclaimed early '60s homage "American Graffiti." Charts the various teenagers' experiences in the more radical late '60s. Gimmicky style shifts elaborately between the different guys and gals in different years (the nerdy Terry the Toad, for example, now bumbles through Vietnam). Sorely lacking the warmth and empathy of the first film; of interest only to fans desperate to see what became of the great characters. **Hound Advisory:** Violence, mature themes.
1979 (*PG/Jr. High-Adult*) 111m/C Candy Clark, Bo Hopkins, Ron Howard, Paul LeMat, MacKenzie Phillips, Charles Martin Smith, Anna Bjorn, Richard Bradford, Cindy Williams, Scott Glenn; *D:* B.W.L. Norton. **VHS, LV $14.98** *MCA*

More Dinosaurs

Companion to other Owens/Boardman dinosaur videos like the aptly named "Dinosaurs, Dinosaurs, Dinosaurs." Our intrepid co-hosts go on an African safari to investigate reports of a living dinosaur and tour Dinosaur National Monument and the Smithsonian to learn more.
1985 (*Family*) 30m/C **VHS, Beta $12.98** *MPI, KAR, MPI*

More Song City U.S.A.

Features rock videos for the kids such as "Clean Up My Room Blues" and "La Bamba."
1989 (*Family*) 30m/C **VHS, Beta $14.95** *FHE*

More Stories for the Very Young

The Children's Circle Studios present five films animated from children's books. Includes "Max's Christmas," "The Little Red Hen," "Petunia," "Not So Fast, Songololo," and "The Napping House."
1992 (*Preschool-Primary*) 36m/C **VHS $19.95** *CCC, MLT, WKV*

Morgan Stewart's Coming Home 🐾◁

When Dad needs to project a 'family values' image to the media in his political race, he brings son Morgan home from boarding school. But the boy doesn't approve of how his parents are using him as a prop and turns their lives upside down. Trite, sitcom-level stuff.
1987 (**PG-13**/*Jr. High-Adult*) 96m/C Jon Cryer, Lynn Redgrave, Nicholas Pryor, Viveka Davis, Paul Gleason, Andrew Duncan, Savely Kramorov, John Cullum, Robert Sedgrave, Waweru Njenga, Sudhir Rad; **D:** Alan Smithee; **M:** Peter Bernstein. **VHS, Beta, LV $34.95** *HBO*

Mosby's Marauders 🐾🐾

Disney historical adventure about a boy during the Civil War who learns the meaning of courage, gallantry and love when he joins General Mosby's famous Confederate raiding company. **Hound Advisory:** Violence.
1966 (*Family*) 79m/C Kurt Russell, James MacArthur, Jack Ging, Peggy Lipton, Nick Adams; **D:** Michael O'Herlihy. **VHS, Beta $69.95** *DIS*

Moschops: Adventures in Dinosaurland

British stop-motion animated series (from the animator of the puppet Paddington Bear) about a cute baby dinosaur who offers a whimsical lizard's-eye-view of the Age of Giant Reptiles. Four episodes lurk on the tape.
1983 (*Preschool-Primary*) 44m/C **D:** Barry Leith. **VHS, Beta** *FHE*

Mother Goose Rock 'n' Rhyme 🐾🐾🐾◁

Another all-star kidvid romp with a cast that only Duvall could corral, as assorted prominent musicians and thespians hunt for a missing Mother Goose and return her to her rightful position in Rhymeland.
1990 (*Family*) 96m/C Shelley Duvall, Teri Garr, Howie Mandel, Jean Stapleton, Ben Vereen, Bobby Brown, Art Garfunkel, Dan Gilroy, Deborah Harry, Cyndi Lauper, Little Richard, Paul Simon, Stray Cats, ZZ Top, Harry Anderson, Elayne Boosler, Woody Harrelson, Richard "Cheech" Marin, Garry Shandling. **VHS, Beta $79.98** *MED*

Mountain Family Robinson 🐾🐾

Another retread of "The Adventures of the Wilderness Family," with the urban Robinsons trying to maintain their back-to-nature lifestyle in the Rockies despite multiple disasters and opposition from the US Forest Service. Scenic, though slow-moving.
1979 (**G**/*Family*) 102m/C Robert F. Logan, Susan Damante Shaw, Heather Rattray, Ham Larsen, William Bryant, George Flower; **D:** John Cotter. **VHS, Beta $9.98** *MED, VTR*

Mountain Man 🐾🐾◁

Historically accurate drama about Galen Clark's successful fight in the 1860s to save the magnificent wilderness area that is now Yosemite National Park. Together with naturalist John Muir, he fought a battle against the lumber companies who wanted the timber and won President Lincoln's support for his cause.
1977 (*Family*) 96m/C Denver Pyle, John Dehner, Ken Berry, Cheryl Miller, Don Shanks, Cliff Osmond, Jack Kruschen, Ford Rainey; **D:** David O'Malley; **W:** David O'Malley. **VHS, Beta** *LME*

The Mouse and the Motorcycle

A double feature of TV specials based on Beverly Cleary's best-selling books about Ralph the talking (and motorcycle riding) mouse, who stars in "The Mouse and the Motorcycle" and its sequel "Runaway Ralph." Delightful stop-motion animation combined with well-known actors bring the unlikely rodent to life. For another Cleary classic, see the "Ramona" series.
198? (*Family*) 90m/C Fred Savage, Ray Walston, Sara Gilbert, Philip Waller; **V:** Billy Barty, Zelda Rubinstein. **VHS $24.95** *SVI*

Mouse on the Mayflower

William Mouse accompanies the Pilgrims on board the Mayflower to the New World in this Thanksgiving-related animated special from the Rankin-Bass TV show factory.
1968 (*Preschool-Primary*) 48m/C **V:** Tennessee Ernie Ford, Eddie Albert, June Foray. **VHS $12.98** *FHE, WTA, BTV*

The Mouse That Roared 🐾🐾🐾

With its wine export business going down the drain, tiny, desperate Grand Fenwick decides to declare war on the United States in hopes that the U.S., after its inevitable triumph, will revive the conquered nation with massive aid. So off to New York go 20 chain-mail clad warriors armed with bow and arrow. Off-the-wall farce features the great Sellers in three roles: army leader, Duchess of Grand Fenwick, and the prime minister. Based on "The Wrath of the Grapes" by Leonard Wibberley and followed by a humbler sequel, "Mouse on the Moon."
1959 (*Family*) 83m/C Peter Sellers, Jean Seberg, Leo McKern, David Kossoff, William Hartnell, Timothy Bateson, MacDonald Parke, Monte Landis; **D:** Jack Arnold; **W:** Roger MacDougall, Stanley Mann; **M:** Edwin Astley. **VHS, Beta $19.95** *COL*

Movie, Movie 🐾🐾◁

Acceptable spoof of 1930s films features Scott in twin-bill of black and white "Dynamite Hands," which lampoons boxing dramas, and "Baxter's Beauties," a color send-up of Busby Berkeley musicals. There's even a parody of coming attractions. Wholesome, mildly entertaining.
1978 (**PG**/*Jr. High-Adult*) 107m/B Stanley Donen, George C. Scott, Trish Van Devere, Eli Wallach, Red Buttons, Barbara Harris, Barry Bostwick, Harry Hamlin, Art Carney; **D:** Stanley Donen; **W:** Larry Gelbart; **M:** Ralph Burns. **VHS** *FOX*

Moving Violations 🐾◁

This could be entitled "Adventures in Traffic Violations School." Wise-cracking tree planter is sent to traffic school after accumulating several moving violations issued to him by a morose traffic cop. Lightweight comedy has Bill Murray's little brother in feature role. **Hound Advisory:** Profanity and suggested sex.
1985 (**PG-13**/*Jr. High-Adult*) 90m/C John Murray, Jennifer Tilly, James Keach, Brian Backer, Sally Kellerman, Fred Willard, Clara Peller, Wendie Jo Sperber; **D:** Neal Israel; **W:** Pat Proft; **M:** Ralph Burns. **VHS, Beta, LV $79.98** *FOX*

Mowgli's Brothers

Cartoon story, selected from Rudyard Kipling's "The Jungle Book," tells of a boy raised in jungle nobility by a pair of

wolves. One of a trio of Kipling tales beautifully animated for TV by Chuck Jones; see also "Rikki-Tikki-Tavi" and "The White Seal."
1973 (*Preschool-Primary*) 25m/C **D:** Chuck Jones. **VHS, Beta $9.95** *FHE, CHI, WTA*

Much Ado About Nothing 🦴🦴🦴🦴

Shakespeare for the masses details romance between two sets of would-be lovers - the battling Beatrice and Benedick (Thompson and Branagh) and the ingenuous Hero and Claudio (Beckinsdale and Leonard). Washington is the noble warrior leader, Reeves his evil half-dressed half-brother, and Keaton serves brilliant comic relief as the officious, bumbling Dogberry. Sunlit, lusty, and revealing about all the vagaries of love, Branagh brings passion to his quest of making Shakespeare more approachable. His second attempt after "Henry V" at breaking the stuffy Shakespearean tradition. Filmed on location in Tuscany, Italy. **Hound Advisory:** Mature themes; brief nudity; suggested sex.
1993 (**PG-13/*Sr. High-Adult***) 110m/C Kenneth Branagh, Emma Thompson, Robert Sean Leonard, Kate Beckinsale, Denzel Washington, Keanu Reeves, Michael Keaton, Brian Blessed, Phyllida Law, Imelda Staunton, Gerard Horan, Jimmy Yuill, Richard Clifford, Ben Elton; **D:** Kenneth Branagh; **W:** Kenneth Branagh; **M:** Patrick Doyle. **VHS, LV** *COL*

Munchie 🦴🦴

A stiff-looking puppet - oops, we mean a magical dwarf creature, is discovered in a mine shaft by young Gage. Munchie turns out to be a friend, driving off bullies and an obnoxious potential stepfather. So-called sequel has nothing to do with 1987's "Munchies" (a dimwit "Gremlins" ripoff from the same filmmakers). That's the good news. Bad news is, it's uninspired and inane. **Hound Advisory:** Alcohol use.
1992 (**PG/*Family***) 80m/C Loni Anderson, Andrew Stevens, Arte Johnson, Jamie McEnnan; **D:** Jim Wynorski; **V:** Dom DeLuise. **VHS $89.98** *NHO*

Munchies 🦴

"Gremlins" rip-off about tiny aliens who love beer and fast food, and invade a small town. Lewd and ribald. **Hound Advisory:** Sex talk; alcohol use.
1987 (**PG/*Jr. High-Adult***) 83m/C Harvey Korman, Charles Stratton, Nadine Van Der Velde; **D:** Bettina Hirsch. **VHS, Beta $14.98** *MGM*

Muppet Babies: Explore with Us

"The New Adventures of Kermo Polo" showcases the Muppet Babies on the high seas, discovering the Mountain of Youth and meeting the Great Gonzo Khan and Fozzie de Leon. "Transcontinental Whoo-Whoo" has the Muppet Babies helping to build the Transcontinental railroad.
1992 (*Preschool-Primary*) 44m/C **VHS $12.99** *JHV, WTA*

Muppet Babies: Let's Build

In "Six to Eight Weeks," the Muppet Babies are expecting their new playhouse to come in the mail and dream about what it will be like. "Eight Flags Over the Nursery" features the Muppet Babies, using Scooter's computer, to build an amusement park called Babyland.
1992 (*Preschool-Primary*) 44m/C **VHS $12.99** *JHV, WTA*

Muppet Babies: Time to Play

Two stories: "The Next Generation" has Baby Kermit commanding the Starship Booby Prize on a space adventure. In "Beauty and the Schnoz," Baby Gonzo and Baby Piggy act out their favorite fairy tales.
1992 (*Preschool-Primary*) 44m/C **VHS $12.99** *JHV, WTA*

Muppet Babies Video Storybook, Vol. 1

Jim Henson's classic Muppet characters are depicted romping together as children. Or cubs. Or pups. Or whatever (especially Gonzo). Segments include: "Meet the Muppet Babies," "Baby Piggy and the Giant Bubble," and "What's a Gonzo?" Additional volumes available.
1988 (*Family*) 30m/C **VHS, LV $9.95** *GKK, WTA*

The Muppet Christmas Carol 🦴🦴🦴

Christmas classic features all the Muppet favorites together in Victorian garb. Gonzo the Great as Dickens narrates the tale as Scrooge (Caine, a younger-seeming miser than usual) takes his legendary Christmas Eve journey escorted by three (flannel) spirits. Directed by Brian Henson, Jim's son, and as heartwarming as Kermit/Bob Cratchit's crackling fire, walking a very narrow line between sincerity and parody. Also features some sappy songs by Paul Williams.
1992 (**G/*Family***) 120m/C Michael Caine; **D:** Brian Henson; **M:** Paul Williams, Miles Goodman; **V:** Dave Goelz, Steve Whitmire, Jerry Nelson, Frank Oz. **VHS, Beta $22.99** *JHV*

The Muppet Movie 🦴🦴🦴

Seeking fame and footlights, Kermit the Frog and his pal Fozzie Bear trek to Hollywood, and along the way are joined by the Muppet characters who make up the classic "Muppet Show" ensemble. Delightful, with enough side references to keep adults interested though pitched at the kids. Paul Williams contributes uniformly pleasant songs. Numerous celebrity cameos include the one and only Big Bird. 🎵The Rainbow Connection; Frog's Legs So Fine; Movin Right Along; Can You Picture That?; Never Before; Something Better; This Looks Familiar; I'm Going Back There Someday.
1979 (**G/*Family***) 94m/C Jim Henson's Muppets; **Cameos:** Edgar Bergen, Milton Berle, Mel Brooks, Madeline Kahn, Steve Martin, Carol Kane, Paul Williams, Charles Durning, Bob Hope, James Coburn, Dom DeLuise, Elliott Gould, Cloris Leachman, Telly Savalas, Orson Welles; **D:** James Frawley; **M:** Paul Williams; **V:** Jim Henson, Frank Oz. **VHS, Beta, LV $22.99** *JHV, FOX*

Muppet Musicians of Bremen

Kermit the Frog narrates this Muppet-ized Brothers Grimm story of a group of jazz-playing animals who want to escape from their masters and seek freedom and fame.
1982 (*Family*) 50m/C **V:** Frank Oz, Jim Henson. **VHS, Beta, LV** *NO*

Muppet Revue

Join Kermit the Frog and Fozzie Bear as they go down Muppet Memory Lane to remember some of the best moments from "The Muppet Show."

Bob Cratchit and Tiny Tim in "The Muppet Christmas Carol"

1985 (*Family*) 56m/C Frank Oz, Harry Belafonte, Linda Ronstadt, Paul Williams; *D:* Jim Henson. **VHS, Beta** $14.98 *FOX*

Muppet Treasures

Kermit and Fozzie discover some unexpected treasures in the "Muppet Show" attic archives, including cooking lessons with the Swedish Chef and episodes of "Pigs in Space" and "Veterinarian's Hospital."
1985 (*Family*) 55m/C Frank Oz, Jim Henson, Peter Sellers, Zero Mostel, Buddy Rich, Paul Simon, Ethel Merman. **VHS, Beta** *FOX*

Muppet Video Series

Highlights of Muppet specials, including "Country Music with the Muppets," "Muppet Weird Stuff," and "Muppet Treasures."
1984 (*Family*) 60m/C *V:* Jim Henson, Frank Oz. **VHS, Beta** $59.98 *FOX*

Muppets Moments

Kermit and Fozzie uncover classic segments from "Veterinarian's Hospital" and "Pigs in Space" while doing their annual spring cleaning. Great stuff excerpted from "The Muppet Show" television series.
1985 (*Family*) 55m/C Frank Oz, Jim Henson, Liza Minnelli, Zero Mostel, Lena Horne; *D:* Jim Henson. **VHS, Beta** $14.98 *FOX*

Muppets Take Manhattan 🐾🐾🐾

Following a smashing success with an amateur musical, the Muppets take their show and talents to Broadway, only to face ruin. Among the New York crises: composer Kermit the Frog gets amnesia and takes a job in an all-frog ad agency. Great fun, if a bit skittish in the plot department. Flashback introduces the Muppet Babies, and it culminates in the wedding of Kermit and Miss Piggy (attended by "Sesame Street" characters, among others).
1984 (G/*Family*) 94m/C Jim Henson's Muppets; *Cameos:* Dabney Coleman, James Coco, Art Carney, Joan Rivers, Gregory Hines, Linda Lavin, Liza Minnelli, Brooke Shields, John Landis; *D:* Frank Oz; *M:* Ralph Burns; *V:* Jim Henson, Frank Oz. **VHS, Beta, LV** $14.98 *FOX, HMV*

Murphy's Romance 🐾🐾🐾

Young divorced mother with an urge to train horses pulls up the stakes and heads for Arizona with her son. There she meets a pharmacist who may be just what the doctor ordered to help her build a new life. **Hound Advisory:** Mature themes; sex.
1985 (PG-13/*Jr. High–Adult*) 107m/C James Garner, Sally Field, Brian Kerwin, Corey Haim, Dennis Burkley, Charles Lane, Georgann Johnson; *D:* Martin Ritt; *W:* Harriet Frank Jr., Irving Ravetch; *M:* Carole King. **VHS, Beta, LV** $14.95 *COL, HMV*

Muscle Beach Party 🐾🐾

Sequel to "Beach Party" finds Frankie and Annette romping in the sand again. Trouble invades teen nirvana when a new gym opens and the hardbodies try to muscle in on surfer turf. Meanwhile, Paluzzi tries to muscle in on Funicello's turf. Good clean corny fun, with the usual lack of script and plot. Lorre appeals in a cameo, his final screen appearance. Watch for "Little" Stevie Wonder in his debut. Rickles' first appearance in the "BP" series; Lupus was credited as Rock

Stevens. Followed by "Bikini Beach." 🎵Muscle Beach Party; Runnin' Wild; Muscle Bustle; My First Love; Surfin' Woodie; Surfer's Holiday; Happy Street; A Girl Needs a Boy; A Boy Needs a Girl.
1964 (*Jr. High–Adult*) 94m/C Frankie Avalon, Annette Funicello, Buddy Hackett, Lucianna Paluzzi, Don Rickles, John Ashley, Jody McCrea, Morey Amsterdam, Peter Lupus, Candy Johnson, Dolores Wells, Stevie Wonder, Donna Loren, Amadee Chabot; *Cameos:* Peter Lorre; *D:* William Asher; *W:* Robert Dillon; *M:* Les Baxter. **VHS, Beta, LV** $29.95 *VTR*

The Music Man 🐾🐾🐾🐾

Con man Henry Hill gets off the train in River City, Iowa, where there are plans to build a pool hall. Hill declares billiards would destroy family values (sound familiar?) and convinces adults to instead finance a wholesome children's marching band. Although the huckster plans to take their money and run before the instruments arrive, his love for the spinsterish town librarian makes him think twice about fleeing the Heartland. This musical isn't just a slice of Americana; it's a whole pie. Acting and singing are terrific "with a capital 'T' and that rhymes with 'P' and that stands for" Preston, who epitomizes the charismatic pitchman (for an encore, see "The Last Starfighter"). Future filmmaker Howard once again proves to be one of the screen's best child actors. Grabbed multiple Oscars, including Best Picture. 🎵Seventy-six Trombones; Trouble; If You Don't Mind; Till There Way You; The Wells Fargo Wagon; Being in Love; Goodnight, My Someone; Rock Island; Iowa Stubborn.
1962 (G/*Family*) 151m/C Robert Preston, Shirley Jones, Buddy Hackett, Hermione Gingold, Paul Ford, Pert Kelton, Ron Howard; *D:* Morton DaCosta; *W:* Marion Hargrove. **Award Nominations:** Academy Awards '62: Best Art Direction/Set Decoration (Color), Best Costume Design (Color), Best Film Editing, Best Picture, Best Sound; **Awards:** Academy Awards '62: Best Adapted Score; Golden Globe Awards '63: Best Film—Musical/Comedy. **VHS, Beta, LV** $19.98 *WAR, MVD, TLF*

My American Cousin 🐾🐾🐾

Canadian comedy-drama set in 1959. Bored 12-year-old Sandy and her girlfriends are excited by a surprise summer visit from Butch, a 17-year-old California cousin with a red sportscar and a James Dean attitude. Sandy figures out he's run away from home; she's had the same idea and hopes he'll take her away with him. Likeable and sympathetic, if mildly simplistic (who wouldn't flee from Butch's grotesque parents?). Sandy's romantic misadventures continued in sequel "American Boyfriends." **Hound Advisory:** Sex talk, salty language, mature themes, roughhousing, alcohol use.
1985 (PG/*Jr. High–Adult*) 94m/C Margaret Langrick, John Wildman, Richard Donat, Jane Mortifee; *D:* Sandy Wilson; *W:* Sandy Wilson. **VHS, Beta, LV** $19.95 *MED, VTR*

My Best Friend Is a Vampire 🐾🐾

Compare/contrast with "Buffy the Vampire Slayer." Average high schooler gets bitten, turns into a nice-guy vampire. It seems the undead are just another oppressed minority, and Leonard needs both his supernatural and normal pals to protect him when a fanatical vampire-exterminator shows up. Not exactly the most effective plea for social tolerance, but among the mildest teen-vampire fables you'll find. **Hound Advisory:** Salty language.

1988 (PG/Jr. High-Adult) 90m/C Robert Sean Leonard, Evan Mirand, Cheryl Pollak, Rene Auberjonois, Cecilia Peck, Fannie Flagg, Kenneth Kimmins, David Warner, Paul Wilson; *D:* Jimmy Huston; *M:* Stephen Dorff. **VHS** $14.99 *HBO*

My Bodyguard 🎬🎬🎬

Undersized high school student fends off attacking bullies by hiring a hulking, withdrawn classmate as his bodyguard. Their "business" arrangement develops into true friendship. An acclaimed adolescent-underdog tale with realistic characters, intelligence, and sensitivity, even if a lot of the plot hinges on paybacks and revenge. **Hound Advisory:** Roughhousing, salty language.
1980 (PG/Jr. High-Adult) 96m/C Chris Makepeace, Adam Baldwin, Martin Mull, Ruth Gordon, Matt Dillon, John Houseman, Joan Cusack, Craig Richard Nelson; *D:* Tony Bill; *W:* Alan Ormsby; *M:* Dave Grusin. **VHS, Beta** $14.98 *FOX*

My Boyfriend's Back 🎬

Embarrassingly dumb horror comedy about a teenage boy who wants to take the prettiest girl in the school to the prom. The only problem is that he's become a zombie. Bits of him keep falling off (she thoughtfully glues them back on) and if he wants to stay "alive" long enough to get to the dance he has to munch on human flesh. Distasteful. Director Balaban seems to have a fixation on cannibals and kids; he also did the adult-oriented "Parents." **Hound Advisory:** Violence juggles the gore quota within a PG-13 rating.
1993 (PG-13/Jr. High-Adult) 85m/C Andrew Lowery, Traci Lind, Edward Herrmann, Mary Beth Hurt, Danny Zorn, Austin Pendleton, Jay O. Sanders, Paul Dooley, Bob Dishy, Matthew Fox, Paxton Whitehead; *D:* Bob Balaban; *W:* Dean Lorey. **VHS, LV** *BVV*

My Dear Uncle Sherlock

Little boy and his uncle enjoy playing detective. One day they get to solve a real-life mystery when a neighbor is robbed. ABC-TV kid-sized adaptation of a short story by thriller writer Hugh Pentacost.
197? (Primary-Jr. High) 24m/C **VHS, Beta** *MTT*

My Dog, the Thief 🎬🎬

Disney's entry in the adorable St.Bernard sweepstakes is the story of a helicopter weatherman unaware that the pooch he has adopted is a kleptomaniac. When the beast steals a necklace from a gang of jewel thieves, the alleged fun begins.
1969 (Family) 88m/C Joe Flynn, Elsa Lanchester, Roger C. Carmel, Mickey Shaughnessy, Dwayne Hickman, Mary Ann Mobley; *D:* Robert Stevenson. **VHS, Beta** $69.95 *DVT*

My Father the Hero 🎬🎬

Another adaptation of a French film ("Mon Pere, Ce Heroes") finds 14-year-old Heigl on an island paradise with divorced dad Depardieu, passing him off as her boyfriend (without his knowledge) to impress a cute boy, causing obvious misunderstandings. Depardieu shows a flair for physical comedy, but his talent is superior to a role that's vaguely disturbing; one of the funnier moments finds him unwittingly singing "Thank Heaven For Little Girls" to a horrified audience. Best for the pre-teen set. Top notch actress Thompson's surprising (uncredited) cameo is due to

her friendship with Depardieu. **Hound Advisory:** Salty language; sex talk.
1993 (PG/Jr. High-Adult) 90m/C Gerard Depardieu, Katherine Heigl, Dalton James, Lauren Hutton, Faith Prince; *Cameos:* Emma Thompson; *D:* Steve Miner; *W:* Francis Veber, Charlie Peters; *M:* David Newman. **VHS, LV** *TOU*

My Father's Glory 🎬🎬🎬

Based on Marcel Pagnol's tales of his childhood, this is a sweet, beautiful memory of a young boy's favorite summer in the French countryside of the early 1900s. Not much happens, yet the film is such a perfect evocation of the place and time that you're carried into the dreams and thoughts of all the characters. One half of a duo, followed by "My Mother's Castle." In French with English subtitles.
1991 (G/Adult-Family) 110m/C Julien Ciamaca, Philippe Caubere, Nathalie Roussel, Therese Liotard, Didier Pain; *D:* Yves Robert; *W:* Lucette Andrei; *M:* Vladimir Cosma. **VHS** $19.98 *INJ, ORI, BTV*

My Favorite Brunette 🎬🎬🎬◁

Detective parody starring Hope as a photographer turned grumbling private eye. He becomes involved with a murder, a spy caper, and a dangerous brunette (Lamour).
1947 (Family) 85m/B Bob Hope, Dorothy Lamour, Peter Lorre, Lon Chaney Jr., Alan Ladd, Reginald Denny, Bing Crosby; *D:* Elliott Nugent. **VHS, Beta, LV** $9.95 *CNG, MRV, NOS*

My Favorite Year 🎬🎬🎬

A young writer on a popular live television show in the 1950s is asked to keep a watchful eye on the week's guest star-his favorite swashbuckling movie hero. Through a series of misadventures, he discovers his matinee idol is actually a drunkard and womanizer who has trouble living up to his cinematic standards. Sterling performance from O'Toole, with memorable portrayal from Bologna as the show's host, King Kaiser (a take-off of Sid Caesar from "Your Show of Shows"). **Hound Advisory:** Salty language, sexual situations, alcohol use.
1982 (PG/Jr. High-Adult) 92m/C Peter O'Toole, Mark Linn-Baker, Joseph Bologna, Jessica Harper, Lainie Kazan, Bill Macy, Anne DeSalvo, Lou Jacobi, Adolph Green, Cameron Mitchell, Gloria Stuart; *D:* Richard Benjamin; *W:* Norman Steinberg; *M:* Ralph Burns. **VHS, Beta, LV** $19.95 *MGM*

My Friend Flicka 🎬🎬🎬

Colorado Rockies boy makes friends with a colt of dubious value. His rancher dad thinks the horse is full of wild oats, but young Roddie trains diligently until Flicka is the best gosh darned horse in pre-Disney family faredom. Based on Mary O'Hara's book, followed by "Thunderhead, Son of Flicka," and TV series.
1943 (Family) 89m/C Roddy McDowall, Preston Foster, Rita Johnson, James Bell, Jeff Corey; *D:* Harold Schuster. **VHS, Beta** $14.98 *FXV, FCT, HMV*

My Friend Walter 🎬🎬◁

Ten-year-old Bess Throckmorten is visiting the Tower of London when the 400-year old ghost of her distant ancestor, Sir Walter Raleigh, asks to follow her home to see how the family is doing. With the Throckmortens about to lose their farm, the gallant spook hatches a plan. Elements of this "WonderWorks Family Movie" seem overly familiar at first (only the charming little heroine can see the meddling ghost, etc.), but stick with it to the end and you'll be rewarded, and yankee kids unfamiliar with Sir Walter will gain a painless history lesson. Based on the book by Michael Morpurgo. **1993** (*Family*) 87m/C Polly Grant, Ronald Pickup, Prunella Scales, Louise Jameson, James Hazeldine, Lawrence Cooper, Constance Chapman; *D:* Gavin Millar. **VHS $29.95** *PME, BTV*

My Girl 🐾🐾◁

Chlumsky is delightful in her debut as 11-year old tomboy Veda, who must come to grips with the realities of life - and death. Best friend Thomas (Culkin) understands her better than her widowed mortician father and his nice girlfriend, the new makeup artist at the funeral parlor, but the kids' budding romance is derailed by tragedy. Comedy-drama script battles between very real warmth and forced eccentricity, rewards the viewer in the end. **Hound Advisory:** Salty language, sex talk. The demise of a certain lead character stirred a debate as to whether this was suitable for youngsters to see, but death is handled with dignity - and is no worse than any tearjerker of past eras anyway. Very young kids ought to be somewhat prepared. **1991** (**PG**/*Primary-Adult*) 102m/C Dan Aykroyd, Jamie Lee Curtis, Macaulay Culkin, Anna Chlumsky, Griffin Dunne, Raymond Buktenica, Richard Masur, Ann Nelson, Peter Michael Goetz, Tom Villard; *D:* Howard Zieff; *W:* Laurice Elehwany; *M:* James Newton Howard. **VHS, LV, 8mm $19.95** *COL*

My Girl 2 🐾🐾◁

Chlumsky is back as Vada (this time without Culkin) in this innocent coming-of-ager. Portly Ackroyd and flaky Curtis return as parental window dressing who encourage Vada's search for information on her long-dead mother. She tracks down old friends of her mom's (Masur and Rose) who are having difficulties with their obnoxious adolescent son (O'Brien). Predictable, but enjoyable. Certain to fail the credibility test of nit-pickers who may wonder why the only thing Ackroyd can remember of his first wife is that she left behind a paper bag with a date scribbled on it. Set in 1974. **Hound Advisory:** Mature themes. **1994** (**PG**/*Jr. High-Adult*) 99m/C Anna Chlumsky, Dan Aykroyd, Jamie Lee Curtis, Austin O'Brien, Richard Masur, Christine Ebersole; *D:* Howard Zieff; *W:* Janet Kovalcik; *M:* Cliff Eidelman. **VHS, LV, 8mm** *COL*

My Grandpa is a Vampire 🐾

When 12 year-old Lonny and his pal visit nice old Grandpa Cooger in New Zealand, they discover a long-hidden family secret - Grandpa's a vampire "of innocent origin." The boys help Grandpa elude some frightened locals, and that's about it. Also known as "Moonrise," uneventful tale needed to be "My Grandpa is a Scriptwriter." Terrible f/x; main attraction is Lewis recreating his character from TV's "The Munsters." **Hound Advisory:** Sex talk; alcohol use; salty language; roughhousing. **1992** (**PG**/*Jr. High-Adult*) 90m/C Al Lewis, Justin Gocke, Milan Borich, Noel Appleby; *D:* David Blyth. **VHS $89.98** *REP*

My Heroes Have Always Been Cowboys 🐾🐾◁

An aging rodeo rider returns to his hometown to recuperate and finds himself forced to confront his past. His ex-girlfriend, his dad and his sister all expect something from him. He learns how to give it, and gains the strength of purpose to get back on the bull that stomped him. Excellent rodeo footage, solid performances, but the story has been around the barn too many times to hold much interest. **Hound Advisory:** Brief profanity, violence. **1991** (**PG**/*Jr. High-Adult*) 106m/C Scott Glenn, Kate Capshaw, Ben Johnson, Balthazar Getty, Mickey Rooney, Gary Busey, Tess Harper, Clarence Williams III, Dub Taylor, Clu Gulager, Dennis Fimple; *D:* Stuart Rosenberg; *W:* Joel Don Humphreys; *M:* James Horner. **VHS, Beta, LV $9.99** *VTR, FXV, COL*

My Life 🐾🐾◁

Maudlin, sometimes depressing melodrama preaches the power of a well-examined life. Public relations exec Keaton is diagnosed with cancer and the doctors predict he will most likely die before the birth of his first child. Film follows his transition from uncommunicative and angry to acceptance, a role to which Keaton brings a sentimental strength. Kidman is window dressing as the ever-patient, nobly suffering wife, a cardboard character notable mainly for her beauty. **Hound Advisory:** Mature themes; profanity. **1993** (**PG-13**/*Jr. High-Adult*) 114m/C Michael Keaton, Nicole Kidman, Haing S. Ngor, Bradley Whitford, Queen Latifah, Michael Constantine, Toni Sawyer, Rebecca Schull, Lee Garlington; *D:* Bruce Joel Rubin; *W:* Bruce Joel Rubin; *M:* John Barry. **VHS, LV, 8mm** *COL*

My Life as a Dog 🐾🐾🐾🐾

12-year-old Ingmar doesn't mean to be troublesome, but calamities follow him everywhere. After he innocently burns down most of the neighborhood, his dying mother sends Ingmar to the country to live with an eccentric uncle's family, separating the boy from his beloved dog. Unhappy and confused, Ingmar gradually makes new friends as he struggles to find security, acceptance and love. Extraordinary, compassionate comedy drama, sometimes agonizing to watch, sometimes agonizingly funny as the hapless young hero faces a range of crushing disappointments and wild mishaps with the all-purpose attitude: "It could have been worse." Swedish film is geared to adults but by no means off limits to bright kid viewers who can take its rougher elements. Based on a novel by Reidar Jonsson, available in both subtitled and (badly) English-dubbed versions. **Hound Advisory:** Brief nudity, mature themes. If this were to be rated it would probably qualify as a PG13. **1985** (*Jr. High-Adult*) 101m/C Anton Glanzelius, Tomas Van Bromssen, Anki Liden, Melinda Kinnaman, Kicki Rundgren, Ing-mari Carlsson; *D:* Lasse Hallstrom. **Award Nominations:** Academy Awards '87: Best Adapted Screenplay, Best Director (Hallstrom); **Awards:** Golden Globe Awards '88: Best Foreign Film; Independent Spirit Awards '88: Best Foreign Film. **VHS, Beta, LV $79.95** *PAR, INJ, HMV*

My Little Pony

My Little Pony is - guess what - a children's toy, here starring in a cartoon production pitting the adorable Ponyland

A first kiss in "My Girl" (1991)

playthings against the evil centaur Tirac. Additional volumes available.
1984 (*Family*) 30m/C *V:* Tony Randall, Sandy Duncan. **VHS, Beta $29.98** *LIV*

My Little Pony: The Movie 🦴◁

Animated theatrical horsefeathers designed to promote "My Little Pony" playthings, about little Megan helping defend Ponyland from Hydia the witch. Series of short cassettes from the inevitable Saturday-morning TV show are also available.
1986 (*Family*) 87m/C *D:* Michael Joens; *V:* Danny DeVito, Cloris Leachman, Tony Randall, Madeline Kahn. **VHS, Beta $9.99** *VTR, WTA*

My Mom's a Werewolf 🦴◁

Dizzy suburban housewife is bitten by a dashing pet-shop owner and soon begins to turn into a werewolf. Her teenage daughter must come up with a plan to regain dear, sweet mom. First-rate cast grapples with third-rate jokes and f/x. Werewolf faces are clearly store-bought masks; at least there's little chance of kid viewers being seriously scared.
1989 (**PG**/*Jr. High-Adult*) 90m/C Susan Blakely, John Saxon, John Schuck, Katrina Caspary, Ruth Buzzi, Marilyn McCoo, Marcia Wallace, Diana Barrows; *D:* Michael Fischa; *W:* Mark Pirro. **VHS, Beta, LV $79.95** *PSM*

My Mother's Castle 🦴🦴🦴

Second half of the two-part French film series based on the boyhood memoirs of Marcel Pagnol that started with "My Father's Glory." Again, the story is loose, lyrical, and warm, as the Pagnol family spend free time at a home in the countryside. Some mild adventures confirm the young narrator's admiration for his father. Tenderly directed, charming, and suitable for the entire family, particularly if the kids are into subtitles (in French).
1991 (**PG**/*Jr. High-Adult*) 98m/C Philippe Caubere, Nathalie Roussel, Didier Pain, Therese Liotard, Julien Ciamaca, Victorien Delmare; *D:* Yves Robert; *M:* Vladimir Cosma. **VHS $19.98** *INJ, ORI, BTV*

My Name is Nobody 🦴🦴◁

Fast-paced spaghetti-western wherein a cocky, soft-hearted gunfighter is sent to kill the famous, retired outlaw he reveres, but instead they band together.
1974 (**PG**/*Family*) 115m/C Henry Fonda, Terence Hill, R.G. Armstrong; *D:* Tonino Valerii; *M:* Ennio Morricone. **VHS, Beta $14.95** *BAR, HHE*

My Neighbor Totoro 🦴🦴◁

Hit Japanese children's cartoon (dubbed into English) about two little girls who move to the countryside and meet magical forest denizens, especially the clan of furry Totoros, who look like a cross between the Tasmanian Devil and Barney the Dinosaur, though fortunately with the sweet temperament of the latter. Well-tuned to the bedtime-story crowd; animation is slow but pleasant, creatures fresh and endearing.

1993 (G/Family) 76m/C **D:** Hayao Miyazaki; **W:** Hayao Miyazaki. **VHS $19.98** FXV

My Old Man 🎬🎬🎵

Plucky teenaged girl and her seedy horsetrainer father come together over important horse race. Oates makes this one worth watching on a slow evening. A Hemingway story made for television. **Hound Advisory:** Alcohol use.

1979 (Family-Family) 102m/C Kristy McNichol, Warren Oates, Eileen Brennan; **D:** John Erman. **VHS, Beta $9.95** CAF

My Pet Monster, Vol. 1

Another toy-inspired series of live-action fantasies about a boy who turns into a shaggy monster when he's hungry. From the same minds who brought you the Care Bears. Additional volumes available.

1986 (Preschool-Primary) 60m/C **VHS, Beta $14.95** MED, WTA

My Science Project 🎬🎵

Teenager Stockwell stumbles across a crystal sphere with a funky light. Unaware that it is an alien time-travel device, he takes it to school to use as a science project in a last-ditch effort to avoid failing his class. Chaos follows and Stockwell and his chums find themselves battling gladiators, mutants, and dinosaurs. Plenty of special effects and a likeable enough, dumb teenage flick. **Hound Advisory:** Profanity.

1985 (PG/Jr. High-Adult) 94m/C John Stockwell, Danielle von Zernaeck, Fisher Stevens, Raphael Sbarge, Richard Masur, Barry Corbin, Ann Wedgeworth, Dennis Hopper, Candace Silvers, Beau Dremann, Pat Simmons, Pamela Springsteen; **D:** Jonathan Betuel; **M:** Peter Bernstein. **VHS, Beta, LV $79.95** TOU

My Side of the Mountain 🎬🎬🎬🎵

Thirteen-year-old Teddy, at odds with his parents, decides to give up his home to live in the Canadian mountains. There a kindly folk-singer neighbor helps Teddy along with his unpracticed wilderness survival skills and eventual family reconciliation. Above-average adaptation of the novel by Jean Craighead George.

1969 (G/Family) 100m/C Teddy Eccles, Theodore Bikel; **D:** James B. Clark. **VHS, Beta $29.95** KUI, PAR

My Stepmother Is an Alien 🎬🎬

Eccentric astronomer sends a greeting to another galaxy on a stormy night; his answer is an inquisitive extraterrestrial in luscious human form. Of course, the scientist doesn't realize her origins (plot is rather farfetched) and courts the enticing visitor; only his young daughter notices the stepmom's strange ways. Fairly dim fantasy-comedy features a good cast and makes a very slight improvement over "My Mom's a Werewolf." **Hound Advisory:** Salty language, sex talk, as alien has to learn all about human lovemaking.

1988 (PG-13/Jr. High-Adult) 108m/C Dan Aykroyd, Kim Basinger, Jon Lovitz, Alyson Hannigan, Joseph Maher, Seth Green, Wesley Mann, Adrian Sparks, Juliette Lewis, Tanya Fenmore; **D:** Richard Benjamin; **W:** Herschel Weingrod, Timothy Harris, Jonathan Reynolds; **M:** Alan Silvestri. **VHS, Beta, LV $14.95** COL

Mysterious Doctor Satan 🎬🎬

Republic serial in which a mad scientist tries to conquer the world with his tin-can robots. Opposing him is Copperhead, a hero guy in a chain-mail mask and a business suit. If that sounds uninspired, there's a reason; this had been scripted as an Superman adventure, but Republic couldn't get legal rights to the Man of Steel, so writers hastily concocted Copperhead. Watch the 15 episodes and consider what might have been. Also available as an edited feature "Dr. Satan's Robot." **Hound Advisory:** Roughhousing.

1940 (Family) 250m/B Eduardo Ciannelli, Robert Wilcox, Ella Neal; **D:** William Witney. **VHS $29.95** REP, VCN, MLB

Mysterious Island 🎬🎬🎬🎵

Exhilarating sci-fi classic adapted from Jules Verne's novel about escaping Civil War soldiers who go up in a balloon and come down on a Pacific Island populated by giant animals. Adopting a Robinson Crusoe in Jurassic Park lifestyle, they encounter two shipwrecked English ladies (how very convenient), pirates, and eventually the notorious Captain Nemo and his sub. Ray Harryhausen's stop-motion animation brings mammoth crabs, turtles and bees to life. **Hound Advisory:** Violence.

1961 (Family) 101m/C Michael Craig, Joan Greenwood, Michael Callan, Gary Merrill, Herbert Lom, Beth Rogan, Percy Herbert, Dan Jackson, Nigel Green; **D:** Cy Endfield; **M:** Bernard Herrmann. **VHS, Beta, LV $19.95** COL, MLB

Mysterious Tadpole and Other Stories

Louis gets a curious birthday gift from his uncle. The tape from Weston Woods' acclaimed "Children's Circle" series also includes "Five Chinese Brothers," "Jonah and the Great Fish," and "The Wizard."

1989 (Preschool-Primary) 34m/C **VHS $19.95** CCC, WKV

Mystery Date 🎬🎬

Another teen date-from-hell comedy, in which a shy college guy gets a date with the girl of his dreams, only to be mistaken for a master criminal and pursued by gangsters, police, and a crazed florist. Not terrible, but if you're old enough to drive, you're probably too old to watch with great amusement. **Hound Advisory:** Violence.

1991 (PG-13/Jr. High-Adult) 98m/C Ethan Hawke, Teri Polo, Brian McNamara, Fisher Stevens, B.D. Wong; **D:** Jonathan Wacks; **W:** Terry Runte; **M:** John Du Prez. **VHS $92.98** ORI

Mystery Island 🎬🎬🎵

Beautifully filmed underwater scenes in this children's film about four youths who discover a deserted island, which they name Mystery Island, and the retired pirate who lives there. When the children find counterfeit money and the bad guys return for it, the old pirate's clever plans keep the kids safe.

1981 (Family) 75m/C **VHS, Beta** NO

Mystery Mansion 🐾🐾

Made-in-Utah family film with a surprisingly dark undertone. Little girl exploring a spooky old house realizes she's the reincarnation of a pioneer child murdered a century ago, and thus knows where a fortune in gold is hidden. **Hound Advisory:** Violence is implied rather than shown, but it's still significant.

1983 (PG/*Jr. High-Adult***)** 95m/C Dallas McKennon, Greg Wynne, Jane Ferguson. **VHS, Beta** $19.95 *MED*

Nadia 🐾🐾🐾

Japanese-animated kids' series is a gadget-filled Jules Verne pastiche featuring Nadia, a 19th-century girl of unknown origin, pursued by villains and protected by French boy inventor Jean. Eventually they meet Captain Nemo himself, in five initial volumes of 25-minutes each.

1989 (*Family***)** 100m/C Talia Balsam, Jonathan Banks, Simone Blue, Johann Carlo, Carrie Snodgress; **D:** Alan Cooke. **VHS, Beta** $19.95 *FHE, STP*

The Naked Gun: From the Files of Police Squad 🐾🐾🐾

More hysterical satire from the creators of "Airplane!" The short-lived television cop spoof "Police Squad" moves to the big screen and has Lt. Drebin uncover a plot to assassinate Queen Elizabeth while she is visiting Los Angeles. Nearly nonstop gags and pratfalls provide lots of laughs. Nielsen is perfect as Drebin and the supporting cast is strong; cameos abound. **Hound Advisory:** Salty language; sex talk.

1988 (PG-13/*Jr. High-Adult***)** 85m/C Leslie Nielsen, Ricardo Montalban, Priscilla Presley, George Kennedy, O.J. Simpson, Nancy Marchand, John Houseman; **Cameos:** Weird Al Yankovic, Reggie Jackson, Dr. Joyce Brothers; **D:** David Zucker; **W:** Jerry Zucker, Jim Abrahams, Pat Proft, David Zucker; **M:** Ira Newborn. **VHS, Beta, LV, 8mm** $14.95 *PAR*

Naked Gun 2 1/2: The Smell of Fear 🐾🐾🐾

Lt. Drebin returns to rescue the world from a faulty energy policy devised by the White House and oil-lords. A notch down from the previous entry but still hilarious cop parody. Nielsen has this character down to a tee, and there's a laugh every minute. Laserdisc version is letterboxed and features dolby surround sound. **Hound Advisory:** Profanity; adult humor.

1991 (PG-13/*Jr. High-Adult***)** 85m/C Leslie Nielsen, Priscilla Presley, George Kennedy, O.J. Simpson, Robert Goulet, Richard Griffiths, Jacqueline Brookes, Lloyd Bochner, Tim O'Connor, Peter Mark Richman; **Cameos:** Mel Torme, Eva Gabor, Weird Al Yankovic; **D:** David Zucker; **W:** David Zucker, Pat Proft; **M:** Ira Newborn. **VHS, Beta, LV, 8mm, CD-I** $14.95 *PAR*

Naked Gun 33 1/3: The Final Insult 🐾🐾🐾

Ever dumb, crass, and crude, Lt. Drebin returns to the force from retirement to lead an investigation into terrorist activities in Hollywood. Lots of current events jokes - dated as soon as they hit the screen, and one of Simpson's last screen efforts for the moment. Sure to satisfy genre fans with a taste for bad puns. Fans of previous "Naked Gun" epics will

best appreciate. Watch for the cameos, especially at the "Oscars." **Hound Advisory:** Vulgarity, sex talk.

1994 (PG-13/*Jr. High-Adult***)** 90m/C Leslie Nielsen, Priscilla Presley, O.J. Simpson, Fred Ward, George Kennedy, Gary Cooper, Kathleen Freeman, Raquel Welch; **Cameos:** Pia Zadora, James Earl Jones, Weird Al Yankovic, Ann B. Davis; **D:** Peter Segal; **W:** Robert Locash, David Zucker, Pat Proft; **M:** Ira Newborn. **VHS, Beta** *PAR*

Nancy Drew, Reporter 🐾🐾

The young sleuth gets to play reporter after winning a newspaper contest. In no time at all, she's involved in a murder mystery.

1939 (*Family***)** 68m/B Bonita Granville, John Litel, Frankie Thomas Jr., Mary Lee, Sheila Bromley, Betty Amann, Dick Jones, Olin Howland, Charles Halton; **D:** William Clemens. **VHS** $19.95 *HTV, NOS*

Napoleon and Samantha 🐾🐾🐾

Disney adventure written by "Wilderness Family" filmmaker Stewart Raffill. Napoleon is an orphan befriended by college guy Danny (Douglas, early in his career). After the death of his grandfather, Napoleon doesn't want to be locked in an institution, so he runs away, taking Major - an elderly pet lion - in pursuit of Danny, who like many college students on summer break, is goat herding in Oregon's mountain country. So who's Samantha? She's Major's co-owner, played by Foster, making her film debut and good as always. Pleasant and worth watching.

1972 (*Family***)** 91m/C Jodie Foster, Johnny Whitaker, Michael Douglas, Will Geer, Henry Jones; **D:** Bernard McEveety; **W:** Stewart Raffill; **M:** Buddy Baker. **VHS, Beta** $69.95 *DIS*

Nate and Hayes 🐾🐾🐾

Set during the mid-1800s in the South Pacific, the notorious real-life swashbuckler Captain "Bully" Hayes ("good pirate") helps young missionary Nate recapture his fiancee from a cutthroat gang of evil slave traders. Entertaining "jolly rogers" film. **Hound Advisory:** Violence.

1983 (PG/*Sr. High-Adult***)** 100m/C Tommy Lee Jones, Michael O'Keefe, Max Phipps, Jenny Seagrove; **D:** Ferdinand Fairfax; **M:** Trevor Jones. **VHS, Beta, LV** $14.95 *PAR*

National Lampoon's Christmas Vacation 🐾🐾🐾

Third vacation for the Griswold family finds them hosting repulsive relatives for Yuletide. Predictable sight gags and pratfalls, plot-by-numbers plot still produce a Yuletide chuck-lefest sure to have you laughing even as you resist. **Hound Advisory:** Profanity.

1989 (PG-13/*Jr. High-Adult***)** 93m/C Chevy Chase, Beverly D'Angelo, Randy Quaid, Diane Ladd, John Randolph, E.G. Marshall, Doris Roberts, Julia Louis-Dreyfus, Mae Questel, William Hickey, Brian Doyle-Murray, Juliette Lewis, Johnny Galecki, Nicholas Guest, Miriam Flynn; **D:** Jeremiah S. Chechik; **W:** John Hughes; **M:** Angelo Badalamenti. **VHS, Beta, LV, 8mm** $19.98 *WAR*

National Lampoon's European Vacation 🐾🐾

Sappy sequel to "Vacation" that has witless Chase and his family bumbling around in the land "across the pond." The

Griswolds nearly redefine the term "ugly American." Stonehenge will never be the same. **Hound Advisory:** Profanity.
1985 (PG-13/*Jr. High-Adult*) 94m/C Chevy Chase, Beverly D'Angelo, Dana Hill, Jason Lively, Victor Lanoux, John Astin; *D:* Amy Heckerling; *W:* John Hughes, Robert Klane, Eric Idle; *M:* Charles Fox. **VHS, Beta, LV, 8mm** $19.98 *WAR*

National Lampoon's Loaded Weapon 1 𝄞◁

Cop Jack Colt (Estevez) and partner Wes Luger (Jackson) attempt to recover a microfilm which contains a formula for turning cocaine into cookies. Essentially a sendup of the popular "Lethal Weapon" series, although other movies and themes receive passing attention. Short on plot and long on slapstick as the jokes come fast and furious, but a tired formula creates nostalgia for the granddaddy of them all, "Airplane." Lots of cameos, including one from sibling spoof star Sheen. The magazine folded while the movie was in production, an ominous sign. **Hound Advisory:** Salty language and violence.
1993 (PG-13/*Jr. High-Adult*) 83m/C Emilio Estevez, Samuel L. Jackson, Jon Lovitz, Tim Curry, Kathy Ireland, William Shatner; *Cameos:* Dr. Joyce Brothers, James Doohan, Richard Moll, F. Murray Abraham, Denis Leary, Corey Feldman, Phil Hartman, J.T. Walsh, Erik Estrada, Larry Wilcox, Allyce Beasley, Charlie Sheen; *D:* Gene Quintano; *W:* Gene Quintano, Don Holley. **VHS, LV** *NLC, IME*

National Velvet 𝄞𝄞𝄞𝄞

1920s English girl Velvet Brown wins a horse named Pie in a village raffle and is determined to enter it in the Grand National Steeplechase. Fortunately her family's tenant is a washed-up ex-jockey, and he helps train the animal for championship competition. The only question is, who will ride the Pie? 12-year-old Taylor is superb in her first starring role, and receives excellent supported from future "Black Stallion" co-star Rooney and the rest of the cast. Filmed with a loving eye for the bucolic locations, this inspirational story of a girl and her steed may have become cliched over the years but it still runs beautifully. Based on the novel by Enid Bagnold and followed many years later by "International Velvet" in 1978.
1944 (*Family*) 124m/C Elizabeth Taylor, Mickey Rooney, Arthur Treacher, Donald Crisp, Anne Revere, Angela Lansbury, Reginald Owen, Norma Varden, Jackie "Butch" Jenkins, Terence Kilburn; *D:* Clarence Brown; *W:* Helen Deutsch, Theodore Reeves; *M:* Herbert Stothart. **Award Nominations:** Academy Awards '45: Best Color Cinematography, Best Director (Brown); **Awards:** Academy Awards '45: Best Film Editing, Best Supporting Actress (Revere). **VHS, Beta, LV, 8mm** $19.98 *MGM, KUI, TLF*

The Natural 𝄞𝄞𝄞

A beautifully filmed movie about baseball as myth. A young man, whose gift for baseball sets him apart, finds that trouble dogs him, particularly with a woman. In time, as an aging rookie, he must fight against his past to lead his team to the World Series, and win the woman who is meant for him. From the Bernard Malamud story. **Hound Advisory:** Brief violence.
1984 (PG/*Jr. High-Adult*) 134m/C Robert Redford, Glenn Close, Robert Duvall, Kim Basinger, Wilford Brimley, Barbara Hershey, Richard Farnsworth, Robert Prosky, Darren McGavin, Joe Don Baker, Michael Madsen; *D:* Barry Levinson; *M:* Randy Newman. **VHS, Beta, LV** $14.95 *COL*

The Navigator 𝄞𝄞𝄞

Creative time-travel story of a 14th-century boy with visionary powers who leads the residents of his medieval English village away from a plague by burrowing through the earth's core and into late 20th-Century New Zealand. Original and refreshing.
1988 (PG/*Jr. High-Adult*) 92m/C Hamish McFarlane, Bruce Lyons, Chris Haywood, Marshall Napier, Noel Appleby, Paul Livingston, Sarah Pierse; *D:* Vincent Ward; *W:* Vincent Ward. **VHS** *NO*

Nearly No Christmas

This bittersweet family tale depicts a Christmas that almost didn't come off.
1981 (*Preschool-Primary*) 60m/C Michael Haigh, Mildred Woods, John Banas. **VHS, Beta** *FHE*

'Neath Brooklyn Bridge 𝄞𝄞

The Bowery Boys get tangled up in crime when they try to help a young girl whose guardian was murdered.
1942 (*Jr. High-Adult*) 61m/B Leo Gorcey, Huntz Hall, Bobby Jordan, Sammy Morrison, Anne Gillis, Noah Beery Jr., Marc Lawrence, Gabriel Dell; *D:* Wallace Fox. **VHS** $19.95 *NOS, MRV, PME*

Neptune Factor 𝄞

Scientists board a special new deep-sea sub to search for their colleagues lost in an undersea earthquake. Diving ever deeper into the abyss, they gawk at giant sea monsters - which anybody who's ever visited a pet shop will recognize as ordinary salt-water critters photographed in closeup. Underachieving, underwater, and undistinguished.
1973 (G/*Family*) 94m/C Ben Gazzara, Yvette Mimieux, Walter Pidgeon, Ernest Borgnine; *D:* Daniel Petrie; *W:* Jack DeWitt. **VHS, Beta** $59.98 *FOX*

Nestor the Long-Eared Christmas Donkey

Sort of a biblical variation of "Rudolph the Red-Nosed Reindeer" finds Nestor, the long-eared donkey scorned and unable to join in any donkey games. Then one foggy Christmas Eve, he's chosen to lead Mary and Joseph into Bethlehem. A Rankin-Bass production.
1977 (*Family*) 23m/C *V:* Paul Frees, Brenda Vaccaro. **VHS, Beta** $12.95 *WAR, WTA*

Never a Dull Moment 𝄞𝄞

Disney comedy coasts along on the considerable charm of Van Dyke as an actor mistaken by mobsters for an accomplished assassin and thief. Naturally he has to play along with the heist of a valuable painting, and improvise wildly when the real crook shows up. **Hound Advisory:** Roughhousing.
1968 (G/*Family*) 90m/C Dick Van Dyke, Edward G. Robinson, Dorothy Provine, Henry Silva, Joanna Moore, Tony Bill, Slim Pickens, Jack Elam; *D:* Jerry Paris. **VHS, Beta, LV** $39.95 *DIS*

Never Cry Wolf 𝄞𝄞𝄞◁

Tenderfoot biologist is dropped off alone in Arctic territory on an ill-conceived mission to study the behavior and habitation of wolves. As he adapts to the freezing climate and the ways of the wolf society, the assignment becomes a journey of self-

discovery and awareness of nature. Beautifully photographed but unevenly paced adaptation of Farley Mowat's book. In one instant director Ballard will jolt your breath away, at another point he'll nearly lull you to sleep. Splendid scenery and images can never have impact on video that they do on the big screen, but this Disney release comes highly recommended all the same. **Hound Advisory:** Non-exploitive nudity, as the hero literally runs naked with the wolf pack through a caribou herd. Alcohol talk.
1983 (PG/*Jr. High-Adult*) 105m/C Charles Martin Smith, Brian Dennehy, Samson Jorah; *D:* Carroll Ballard; *W:* Curtis Hanson, Sam Hamm. **VHS, Beta, LV** $19.99 *DIS*

Never Say Never Again 🐾🐾◁

James Bond matches wits with a charming but sinister tycoon who is holding the world nuclear hostage as part of a diabolical plot by SPECTRE. Connery's return to the world of Bond after 12 years is smooth in this remake of "Thunderball" hampered by an atrocious musical score. Carrera is stunning as Fatima Blush. **Hound Advisory:** Violence, sex, alcohol use.
1983 (PG/*Jr. High-Adult*) 134m/C Sean Connery, Klaus Maria Brandauer, Max von Sydow, Barbara Carrera, Kim Basinger, Edward Fox, Bernie Casey, Pamela Salem, Rowan Atkinson, Valerie Leon, Prunella Gee, Saskia Cohen Tanugi; *D:* Irvin Kershner. **VHS, Beta, LV** $19.98 *WAR, TLF*

The NeverEnding Story 🐾🐾◁

Dreamy schoolkid Bastian is roughed up daily by bullies, failing his classes, etc. He cowers and reads a magical storybook that lets him share adventures of a boy warrior on a quest to save the imaginary world of Fantasia from destruction by a creeping Nothingness. Big-scale f/x and wild characters in a thematically obscure European production (based on the novel by Michael Ende) that made the Hound recall that old Groucho joke: "It's so simple a ten-year-old child could figure it out... Somebody find me a ten-year-old child." In any case, it was popular enough with those ten-year-olds to spawn NeverEnding sequels. **Hound Advisory:** Violence.
1984 (PG/*Family*) 94m/C Barret Oliver, Noah Hathaway, Gerald McRaney, Moses Gunn, Tami Stronach, Patricia Hayes, Sydney Bromley; *D:* Wolfgang Petersen; *W:* Wolfgang Petersen; *M:* Klaus Doldinger, Giorgio Moroder. **VHS, Beta, LV, 8mm** $14.95 *WAR, GLV, APD*

The NeverEnding Story 2: Next Chapter 🐾🐾

Redundant-titled sequel to the first journey that didn't end suffers from rerun fatigue. Last time the land of Fantasia was threatened by the Nothing; now the menace is the Emptiness. Existential trauma like this is to be avoided. Only wimp kid Bastian can stop that empty feeling, so he enters the storybook realm again. Whimsical creatures and grandiose f/x return, and a witch villainess at least provides a more prosaic explanation for what's going on. The Warner Brothers videocassette also includes "Box Office Bunny," the first Bugs theatrical cartoon in 26 years. **Hound Advisory:** Roughhousing.

1991 (PG/*Jr. High-Adult*) 90m/C Jonathan Brandis, Kenny Morrison, Clarissa Burt, John Wesley Shipp, Martin Umbach; *D:* George Miller; *M:* Robert Folk. **VHS, LV, 8mm** $14.95 *WAR, APD*

The New Adventures of Pippi Longstocking 🐾◁

Decent cast clowns in a buffoon musical rehash of Astrid Lindgren's children's books, no improvement over the Swedish-German "Pippi Longstocking" that it follows fairly closely. Separated in a storm from her sea-captain father, the spunky red-headed little girl returns to the deserted family mansion, where her spirited stunts and independent ways delight kids and outrage the grownups. Grates less as it goes on, but only slightly. **Hound Advisory:** Roughhousing
1988 (G/*Preschool-Primary*) 100m/C Tami Erin, Eileen Brennan, Dennis Dugan, Dianne Hull, George DiCenzo, John Schuck, Dick Van Patten; *D:* Ken Annakin. **VHS, Beta, LV** $19.95 *COL, TVC*

The New Adventures of Winnie the Pooh, Vol. 1: Great Honey Pot Robbery

More adventures of A.A. Milne's Pooh and the other inhabitants of the 100-Acre Woods, from Disney but made for network Saturday mornings. Additional volumes available.
1987 (*Family*) 44m/C **VHS, Beta** $12.99 *DIS, WTA*

New Adventures of Zorro, Vol. 1

Daring swordplay highlights these three animated tales of the swashbuckling swordsman of Old California. He's foppish Don Diego one moment, fearless hero Zorro the other, and Saturday-morning TV leftovers always. Episodes are "Three's a Crowd," "Flash Flood," and "The Blockade." Additional volumes available.
1981 (*Preschool-Jr. High*) 60m/C **VHS, Beta** $29.95 *FHE, WTA*

New Archies: Stealing the Show

Those animated teenage zanies are back. This time they are serving up a high school performance of Cinderella. But Reggie and Veronica can't let things roll smoothly and are determined to undermine the show. Will they succeed in dousing the stage ambitions of their more ernest teen brethren?
1977 (*Family*) 23m/C **VHS** $9.95

New Zoo Revue, Vol. 1

Each episode of this entertaining, educational children's series stars costumed animals like Freddie the Frog and Henrietta Hippo teaching youngsters the importance of peace, friendship, and compassion in daily interaction with others. Additional volumes available.
1973 (*Family*) 60m/C Emily Peden, Doug Momary. **VHS, Beta** *FHE*

Newsies 🐾🐾

Disney attempt at a grand-scale musical, but songs are forgettable and dance numbers just get in the way. Pic would have worked better straight, minus tunes, since it vividly

evokes a true incident, the 1899 New York newsboys strike against newspaper baron Joseph Pulitzer (imagine Scrooge as a publisher) to get him to lower unfair prices. Lavish, turn-of-the-century NYC atmosphere, with much made of the city's immigrant kids overcoming their gang-like ethnic divisions. **Hound Advisory:** Some serious violence as Pulitzer lets his goons loose on the youthful picketers. Alcohol use.
1992 (PG/*Jr. High-Adult***)** 121m/C Christian Bale, Bill Pullman, Robert Duvall, Ann-Margret, Michael Lerner, Kevin Tighe, Charles Cioffi, Luke Edwards, Max Casella, David Moscow; **D:** Kenny Ortega; **M:** Alan Menken, Jack Feldman. **VHS, Beta $19.99** *DIS*

The Next Karate Kid 𝄞𝄞

Fourth installment in the "Kid" series finds martial arts expert Miyagi (Morita) training Julie Pierce (Swank), the orphaned tomboy daughter of an old war buddy who saved his life 50 years earlier. He even teaches her the waltz, just in time for the prom, but she's still tough enough to scrap with a guy. Must-see for "Karate Kid" fans, though many of them may now be too old to appreciate. **Hound Advisory:** Some mild language and violence.
1994 (PG/*Jr. High-Adult***)** 104m/C Noriyuki "Pat" Morita, Hilary Swank; **D:** Christopher Cain; **W:** Mark Lee; **M:** Bill Conti. **VHS**

A Night at the Opera 𝄞𝄞𝄞𝄞

The Marx Brothers get mixed up with grand opera in their first MGM-produced pic, their first without Zeppo, and perhaps their last truly great comedy, even with the usual romantic subplot about young lovers in a opera touring company. Groucho, Chico and Harpo try to get the kids a contract, and in the process they deflate and devastate a pompous production. Immortal comic moments include the famous scene aboard ship, in which the Marxes welcome more and more visitors to their small stateroom until it's literally packed to the ceiling with goofballs.
1935 (*Family***)** 92m/B Groucho Marx, Chico Marx, Harpo Marx, Allan Jones, Kitty Carlisle Hart, Sig Rumann, Margaret Dumont, Walter Woolf King; **D:** Sam Wood; **W:** George S. Kaufman, Morrie Ryskind, Bert Kalmar, Harry Ruby, Al Boasberg; **M:** Herbert Stothart. **VHS, Beta, LV $19.95** *MGM, VYG, CRC*

The Night Before 𝄞𝄞

Snobby high school beauty Tara loses a bet and has to go to the prom with geek Winston. They get lost on the wrong side of the tracks and become involved with pimps, crime, and the police. Drunken Winston loses his virginity, as well as his father's car, but somehow wins Tara's heart, which is more than this obscure teen comedy will do with the viewer. Reeves later became a star in the "Bill & Ted" adventures. **Hound Advisory:** Sex, roughhousing, alcohol use, mature themes.
1988 (PG-13/*Jr. High-Sr. High***)** 90m/C Keanu Reeves, Lori Loughlin, Trinidad Silva, Michael Greene, Theresa Saldana, Suzanne Snyder, Morgan Lofting, Gwil Richards; **D:** Thom Eberhardt; **W:** Gregory Scherick, Thom Eberhardt. **VHS, Beta $79.99** *HBO*

The Night Before Christmas

Christmas spirit is in the air in this Disney cartoon retelling of the eternal Clement Moore poem, complete with an appearance by Santa himself.

1933 (*Family***)** 9m/C **VHS, Beta $170.00** *MTI, DSN*

The Night Before Christmas and Best-Loved Yuletide Carols

Collection of Christmas classics combined with beautiful artwork and narration by Streep set the holiday spirit in this heartwarming program. Also featured are favorite Christmas carols performed by George Winston, the Edwin Hawkins Singers, and the Christ Church Cathedral Choir.
1992 (*Preschool-Primary***)** 30m/C **VHS $9.95**

Night Crossing 𝄞𝄞𝄞

Fact-based Disney drama of two East German families who attempted a dangerous escape over the Berlin Wall to freedom in a homemade hot air balloon. Fairly exciting in spite of the bland dialogue and characters. **Hound Advisory:** Violence.
1981 (PG/*Family***)** 106m/C John Hurt, Jane Alexander, Glynnis O'Connor, Doug McKeon, Beau Bridges; **D:** Delbert Mann; **W:** John McGreevey; **M:** Jerry Goldsmith. **VHS, Beta $69.95** *DIS*

A Night in Casablanca 𝄞𝄞𝄞

The Marx Brothers find themselves in the luxurious Hotel Casablanca, going after some leftover Nazis searching for treasure. One of the later films, but still loaded with wisecracks and mayhem.
1946 (*Family***)** 85m/B Groucho Marx, Harpo Marx, Chico Marx, Charles Drake, Dan Seymour, Sig Rumann; **D:** Archie Mayo. **VHS, Beta** *NO*

Night of the Comet 𝄞𝄞𝄞

After surviving the explosion of a deadly comet, two California girls discover that they are the last people on Earth. When zombies begin to chase them, things begin to lose their charm. Cute and funny, but the script runs out before the movie does.
1984 (PG-13/*Jr. High-Adult***)** 90m/C Catherine Mary Stewart, Kelli Maroney, Robert Beltran, Geoffrey Lewis, Mary Woronov, Sharon Farrell, Michael Bowen; **D:** Thom Eberhardt; **W:** Thom Eberhardt. **VHS, Beta $19.98** *FOX*

The Night the Lights Went Out in Georgia 𝄞𝄞

Loosely based on the popular hit song, the film follows a brother and sister as they try to cash in on the country music scene in Nashville. McNichol is engaging.
1981 (PG/*Jr. High-Adult***)** 112m/C Kristy McNichol, Dennis Quaid, Mark Hamill, Don Stroud; **D:** Ronald F. Maxwell; **M:** David Shire. **VHS, Beta $69.95** *SUE, TWE*

The Night They Saved Christmas 𝄞𝄞

Made-for-TV musical in which Santa's North Pole headquarters is endangered by the progress of an expanding oil company. Will a petroleum geologist's children be able save the day? Carney is a treat as the businesslike Kris Kringle, but otherwise this stiff production would have worked better as a (shorter) Rankin/Bass animated special.
1987 (*Family***)** 94m/C Art Carney, Jaclyn Smith, Paul Williams, Paul LeMat; **D:** Jackie Cooper. **VHS, Beta $9.95** *CAF, PSM*

Nightingale

Animated version of the Hans Christian Andersen classic fairy tale of the Emperor of China and his little nightingale.
1988 (*Preschool-Primary*) 30m/C **VHS, Beta $14.95** *HSE, WTA*

The Nightmare Before Christmas 🦴🦴🦴

Grandiose and grotesque tour de force of joyous stop-motion animation that manages to bag two holidays in one. Jack, the friendly but ghoulish Pumpkin King of Halloween Town, discovers neighboring Christmas Town for the first time and decides to put a fresh face on Noel by kidnapping Santa and take the old guy's place, delivering ghastly gifts to unsuspecting children on December 24. Outstanding modelwork, terrific Elfman musical score (Elfman also provide's Jack's singing voice), and a marvelously macabre sense of humor. This is the sort of kid movie the Addams Family would keep ready for a sunny day. Based on an idea (and co-produced) by Tim Burton. Distributed by Disney/Touchstone - but don't believe their advertising boast that this is the first ever puppet-animated theatrical feature; see 1954's "Hansel and Gretel." **Hound Advisory:** Halloween Town is a nonstop cavalcade of monsters and weirdos; still, that PG seems a little extreme.
1993 (PG/*Jr. High-Adult***)** 75m/C **D:** Henry Selick; **W:** Caroline Thompson; **M:** Danny Elfman; **V:** Danny Elfman, Chris Sarandon, Catherine O'Hara, William Hickey, Ken Page, Ed Ivory, Paul (Pee Wee Herman) Reubens, Glenn Shadix. **VHS $19.99** *BVV*

Nikki, the Wild Dog of the North 🦴🦴🦴

Malamute pup tethered to an orphaned bear cub are separated from their frontiersman master. In a charming series of semi-documentary scenes, the critters learn cooperation to survive. Second half of the story finds the dog, now fully grown, captured by an evil trapper. Swell Disney outdoor adventure set in 1890s Canada. Adapted from the novel "Nomads of the North" by James Oliver Curwood. **Hound Advisory:** Violence, especially when Nikki's nasty owner forces him into a dogfight.
1961 (G/*Family***)** 73m/C Jean Coutu; **D:** Jack Couffer, Don Haldane. **VHS, Beta $69.95** *DIS*

The Nine Lives of Elfego Baca 🦴🦴⌐

Disney TV miniseries, part of a "True Heroes of the West" series done in the afterglow of the Davy Crockett craze. Baca was a Mexican-American who became an instant legend when he survived an incredible 33-hour gun battle with a mob of galoots. The plot follows up his later career as New Mexico's numero uno lawman. Loggia is an ever-smiling and polite hero, and the action never gets unduly harsh. **Hound Advisory:** Violence, alcohol use.
1958 (*Family*) 78m/C Robert Loggia, Robert Simon, Lisa Montell, Nestor Paiva; **D:** Norman Foster. **VHS, Beta $69.95** *DIS*

1994 Winter Olympics Highlights Video

The best of the Winter Olympics from Lillehammer, Norway, including opening ceremonies and sporting events from luge to ice hockey.
1994 (*Jr. High-Adult*) 60m/C **VHS $19.95** *FOX*

No Big Deal 🦴⌐

Dillon is a streetwise teenager who makes friends at his new school. Blah premise; bad acting makes this no big deal.
1983 (PG-13/*Sr. High-Adult***)** 86m/C Kevin Dillon, Sylvia Miles, Tammy Grimes, Jane Krakowski, Christopher Gartin, Mary Joan Negro; **D:** Robert Charlton. **VHS $79.95** *BTV*

No Deposit, No Return 🦴🦴

No awards either, but the cast does what they can with this Disney action comedy about rich brats who persuade bumbling crooks to kidnap them so they can all share a ransom from their irascible millionaire grandfather (Niven).
1976 (G/*Family***)** 115m/C David Niven, Don Knotts, Darren McGavin, Barbara Feldon, Charles Martin Smith; **D:** Norman Tokar; **M:** Buddy Baker. **VHS, Beta $69.95** *DIS*

No Drums, No Bugles 🦴⌐

West Virginia farmer and conscientious objector leaves his family to live alone in a cave for three years during the Civil War. Interesting decision but not particularly cinematic.
1971 (G/*Family***)** 85m/C Martin Sheen, Davey Davidson, Denine Terry, Rod McCary; **D:** Clyde Ware. **VHS, Beta $39.95** *CNG, VTR*

No Holds Barred 🦴⌐

Cheesy camp about big-time professional wrestler Rip, who grapples not only with bestial opponents but an evil TV magnate who'll stop at nothing to make Rip do his wrestling show. The first feature to showcase WWF favorite 'Hulk' Hogan is obviously aimed at kids but went far enough with the violence that some commentators called foul. Fortunately, Hogan hasn't made that mistake in his subsequent vehicles like "Suburban Commando" and "Mr. Nanny." **Hound Advisory:** Violence, alcohol use.
1989 (PG-13/*Jr. High***)** 98m/C Hulk Hogan, Kurt Fuller, Joan Severance, Tiny Lister; **D:** Thomas J. Wright. **VHS, Beta, LV $19.95** *COL*

No Man's Valley

When the encroaching civilization endangers their homes, a flock of condors send a scout to find a safe place to colonize. Ecologically minded cartoon from the producer of TV's "Peanuts" series.
1981 (*Preschool-Primary*) 30m/C **V:** Barney Phillips, Richard Deacon, Art Metrano, Arnold Stang, Joe E. Ross. **VHS, Beta** *FHE*

No Time for Sergeants 🦴🦴🦴⌐

Young Griffith is excellent as the Georgia farm boy who gets drafted into the service during a war lull and creates mayhem among his superiors and colleagues. Hilarious film version written by John Lee Mahin from the Broadway play by Ira Levin, which was based on the novel by Mac Hyman and an

earlier television special (and eventually became a TV series). Note eventual sidekick Knotts and Benny Baker in small roles along with Jameel Farah, who went on to star in TV's M*A*S*H after changing his name to Jamie Farr.
1958 (*Family*) 119m/B Andy Griffith, Nick Adams, Murray Hamilton, Don Knotts, Jamie Farr, Myron McCormick; **D:** Mervyn LeRoy. **VHS, Beta, LV** $19.98 *WAR*

Noah's Animals and Other Stories

Three animated children's tales, unrelated to the other "Noah's Animals." Segments include the title story, "King of the Beasts," and "Last of the Red Hot Dragons."
1986 (*Preschool-Primary*) 78m/C **VHS, Beta $29.95** *WTA*

Nobody's Boy

Japanese cartoon saga about an 8-year-old boy's search for his missing mother.
1971 (*Preschool-Jr. High*) 80m/C **D:** Jim Flocker; **V:** Jim Backus. **VHS, Beta** *MPI*

Noel

Romer Muller's story about a Christmas ornament that comes to life.
1993 (*Family*) 25m/C **VHS $12.95** *PGV*

The Norfin Adventures: The Great Egg Robbery

Magical trolls help a girl clear her father of stealing a golden egg.
1994 (*Primary*) 29m/C **VHS $12.98** *WEA*

Norma Rae 🎬🎬🎬

A poor, uneducated textile worker joins forces with a New York labor organizer to unionize the reluctant workers at a Southern mill. Field was a surprise with her fully developed character's strength, beauty, and humor; her Oscar was well-deserved. Ritt's direction is top-notch. Jennifer Warnes sings the theme song, "It Goes Like It Goes," which also won an Oscar. **Hound Advisory:** Salty language; minor violence.
1979 (PG/*Jr. High-Adult*) 114m/C Sally Field, Ron Leibman, Beau Bridges, Pat Hingle; **D:** Martin Ritt; **W:** Harriet Frank Jr., Irving Ravetch; **M:** David Shire. **Award Nominations:** Academy Awards '79: Best Adapted Screenplay, Best Picture; Cannes Film Festival '79: Best Film; **Awards:** Academy Awards '79: Best Actress (Field), Best Song ("It Goes Like It Goes"); Golden Globe Awards '80: Best Actress—Drama (Field); Los Angeles Film Critics Association Awards '79: Best Actress (Field); National Board of Review Awards '79: Best Actress (Field); New York Film Critics Awards '79: Best Actress (Field). **VHS, Beta, LV** $19.98 *FOX, BTV*

Norman the Doorman and Other Stories

"Lentil," "Brave Irene," and "Norman the Doorman" are seen in their animated version from the "Children's Circle" collection.
1989 (*Family*) 30m/C **VHS $19.95** *CCC, BTV*

Norman's Awesome Experience 🎬🎬

The distributor would like you to confuse this with "Bill & Ted's Excellent Adventure." In fact the Canadian comedy sported the original title "A Stitch in Time," referring to some modern teenagers time trippin' back to the days of the Roman Empire. All hail Caesar, dude.
1988 (PG-13/*Jr. High-Adult*) 90m/C Tom McCamus, Laurie Paton, Jaques Lussier; **D:** Paul Donovan. **VHS, Beta** *NO*

North 🎬🎬

Some laughs with a message in disappointing family fare from Reiner. Eleven-year old Wood divorces his workaholic parents ("Seinfeld" costars Alexander and Louis-Dreyfus) and searches the world for a functional family (good luck). Instead, he becomes the poster boy for a fascist children's political organization while running into all manner of ethnic and class stereotypes (including Vigoda as an elderly Eskimo about to be set adrift at sea). Willis, who's a treat in a pink bunny suit among other costumes, acts as guardian angel/narrator and subtly helps the kid find what's the most important thing. Premise sags in spite of great sets and illustrious comedic cast. Based on a book by original "Saturday Night Live" screenwriter (and "Gary Shandling Show" co-creator) Zweibel, who put things in motion ten years ago when he asked Reiner to write a book jacket quote for the novel. **Hound Advisory:** Salty language.
1994 (PG/*Jr. High-Adult*) 88m/C Elijah Wood, Jason Alexander, Julia Louis-Dreyfus, Bruce Willis, Jon Lovitz, Alan Arkin, Dan Aykroyd, Kathy Bates, Faith Ford, Graham Greene, Reba McEntire, John Ritter, Abe Vigoda, Kelly McGillis, Alexander Godunov, Noriyuki "Pat" Morita; **D:** Rob Reiner; **W:** Andrew Scheinman, Alan Zweibel; **M:** Marc Shaiman. **VHS** *NYR*

The North Avenue Irregulars 🎬🎬🎬

Priest and three members of the local ladies' club try to bust a crime syndicate when the corrupt cops won't. Outstanding cast brings sufficient laughter to a silly Disney production, based on a true story, chronicled in the book by the Rev. Albert Fay Hill.
1979 (G/*Family*) 99m/C Edward Herrmann, Barbara Harris, Susan Clark, Karen Valentine, Michael Constantine, Cloris Leachman, Melora Hardin, Alan Hale Jr., Ruth Buzzi, Patsy Kelly, Virginia Capers; **D:** Bruce Bilson. **VHS $69.95** *DIS*

North by Northwest 🎬🎬🎬🎬

Self-assured Madison Avenue ad exec Grant inadvertently gets involved with international spies when they mistake him for someone else. His problems are compounded when he's framed for murder. The movie where Grant and Saint dangle from the faces of Mount Rushmore and a plane chases Grant through farm fields. Exceptional performances, particularly Grant's. Plenty of plot twists are mixed with tongue-in-cheek humor. Considered by many to be one of Hitchcock's greatest films. Laserdisc includes letterboxing, digital soundtrack, Hitchcock interview, production and publicity photos, storyboards, and the original trailer.
1959 (*Jr. High-Adult*) 136m/C Cary Grant, Eva Marie Saint, James Mason, Leo G. Carroll, Martin Landau, Jessie Royce Landis, Philip Ober, Adam Williams, Josephine Hutchinson, Edward Platt; **D:** Alfred Hitchcock; **W:** Ernest Lehman; **M:** Bernard Herrmann. **Award Nominations:** Academy Awards '59: Best Art Direction/Set Decoration (Color), Best Film Editing, Best Story & Screenplay; **Awards:** Edgar Allan Poe Awards '59: Best Screenplay. **VHS, Beta, LV** $19.98 *MGM, VYG, CRC*

Not My Kid 🦴🦴◁

The 15-year-old daughter of a surgeon brings turmoil to her family when she becomes heavily involved in drugs. Producer Polson, along with Dr. Miller Newton, wrote the original book for this emotional story. Made for TV. **Hound Advisory:** Drug use.

1985 (*Family*) 120m/C George Segal, Stockard Channing, Viveka Davis, Andrew (Andy) Robinson, Gary Bayer, Nancy Cartwright, Tate Donovan; **D:** Michael Tuchner; **W:** Christopher Knopf. **VHS, Beta $79.95** *SVE*

Not Quite Human 🦴🦴

Okay but standard Disney TV comedy about an inventor who builds a robot teenage boy, named Chip, who's almost indistinguishable from the real thing. The doctor grows emotionally close to his creation as he tries to conceal Chip's secret from a rival. Based on a book series by Seth McEvoy, and followed by sequels "Not Quite Human II" and "Still Not Quite Human."

1987 (*Family*) 91m/C Alan Thicke, Robin Lively, Robert Harper, Joseph Bologna, Jay Underwood; **D:** Steven Hilliard Stern. **VHS, Beta $39.99** *DIS*

Nothing in Common 🦴🦴◁

In his last film, Gleason plays the abrasive, diabetic father of immature advertising agency worker Hanks. After his parents separate, Hanks learns to be more responsible and loving in caring for his father. Comedy and drama are blended well here with the help of satirical pokes at the ad business and Hanks turns in a fine performance, but the unorganized, lengthy plot may lose some viewers. **Hound Advisory:** Profanity; suggested sex.

1986 (*PG/Sr. High-Adult*) 119m/C Tom Hanks, Jackie Gleason, Eva Marie Saint, Bess Armstrong, Hector Elizondo, Barry Corbin, Sela Ward, John Kapelos, Jane Morris, Dan Castellaneta, Tracy Reiner; **D:** Garry Marshall; **W:** Rick Podell; **M:** Patrick Leonard. **VHS, Beta, LV $19.98** *WAR, HBO*

Notorious 🦴🦴🦴🦴

Post-WWII story of a beautiful playgirl sent by the US government to marry a suspected spy living in Brazil. Grant is the agent assigned to watch her. Duplicity and guilt are important factors in this brooding, romantic spy thriller. Suspenseful throughout, with a surprise ending. The acting is excellent all around and Hitchcock makes certain that suspense is maintained throughout this classy and complex thriller. Laser edition contains original trailer, publicity photos, and additional footage.

1946 (*Jr. High-Adult*) 101m/B Cary Grant, Ingrid Bergman, Claude Rains, Louis Calhern, Madame Konstantin, Reinhold Schunzel, Moroni Olsen; **D:** Alfred Hitchcock; **W:** Ben Hecht. **VHS, Beta, LV $19.98** *FOX, VYG, CRC*

Now You See Him, Now You Don't 🦴🦴

Featherweight Disney comedy involving a college guy who accidentally invents an invisibility formula to win a science fair and save his school. Of course, a gang of crooks want to use the stuff to rob a bank. Sequel to Disney's "The Computer Wore Tennis Shoes."

1972 (*G/Family*) 85m/C Kurt Russell, Joe Flynn, Cesar Romero, Jim Backus; **D:** Robert Butler. **VHS, Beta $69.95** *DIS*

Nukie 🦴

E.T. phone lawyer! European ripoff of the Spielberg favorite has not one, but two alien potato-heads crashing to Earth. One is tortured in the lab by heartless scientists, while his brother Nukie lands in Africa and spooks the silly natives. Don't worry, everyone utters their awful dialogue in English - even monkeys. **Hound Advisory:** Alcohol use.

1993 (*PG/Family*) 99m/C Glynis Johns, Steve Railsback; **D:** Sias Odendal. **VHS $92.95** *VMK*

Nursery Rhymes

Pages of a nursery rhyme book come to cartoon life as a youngster leafs through them. Features all-time nursery rhyme favorites "Simple Simon," "Little Bo Peep," "Old King Cole," and many more.

1982 (*Preschool-Primary*) 60m/C **V:** Isla St. Clair, Michael Berry, Valentine Dyall. **VHS, Beta $9.95** *FHE*

Nutcase 🦴🦴

A trio of young children in New Zealand attempt to thwart a group of terrorists who threaten to reactivate a large city's volcanoes unless they are given a large sum of money. Novel twist here.

1983 (*Family*) 49m/C Nevan Rowe, Ian Watkin, Michael Wilson; **D:** Roger Donaldson. **VHS, Beta** *NO*

Nutcracker Fantasy 🦴🦴

Rather confused Japanese stop-motion animated adaptation of E.T.A. Hoffman's classic tells the tale (using English-speaking actors) of little Clara, who must rescue a beautiful sleeping princess from wicked mice. Set to the music of Tchaikovsky.

1979 (*Family*) 60m/C **V:** Melissa Gilbert, Roddy McDowall. **VHS, Beta $19.95** *COL, WTA*

The Nutcracker Prince 🦴🦴

Animated treatment of the E.T.A. Hoffman tale that inspired the classic ballet, but this Canadian cartoon feature has more in common with Tom & Jerry than Tchaikovsky as the enchanted Nutcracker Prince battles the thuglike Mouse King 'round and 'round the toyroom at Christmas. Good character voices. **Hound Advisory:** Violence

1991 (*Family*) 75m/C **D:** Paul Schibli; **V:** Kiefer Sutherland, Megan Follows, Michael MacDonald, Phyllis Diller, Peter O'Toole. **VHS, LV, 8mm $19.98** *WAR, WTA*

The Nutty Professor 🦴🦴🦴

Clumsy scientist creates a potion that turns him from a homely but good-natured nerd-geek-dweeb into a handsome but cold-hearted ladies' man. One of Lewis' best comedies, though skewed more toward adult viewers; small kids accustomed to his goofy slapstick may want more of bumbling Professor Kelp and less of his subtle alter ego 'Buddy Love.'

1963 (*Family*) 107m/C Jerry Lewis, Stella Stevens, Howard Morris, Kathleen Freeman; **D:** Jerry Lewis; **W:** Jerry Lewis. **VHS, Beta, LV $14.95** *PAR*

Nuzzling with the Noozles

Collection of Down Under TV cartoons starring koalas Blinky and Pinky, seen on American cable. They befriend Sandy, a little girl, and have many adventures. For the bulk of them, see "The Noozles" listing.
1990 (*Family*) 110m/C **VHS, Beta $19.99** *CEL, WTA*

Nyoka and the Tigermen

Adventurous scientist's daughter Nyoka, last seen (played by a different actress) in the serial "Jungle Girl," returns for more Republic action. This time evil princess Vultura and her pet gorilla Satan are seeking the fabled Lost Tablets of Hippocrates, artifacts of pure gold that hold a secret cancer cure. Loads of stunts and chases, and Nyoka is one vintage heroine who gets to use her fists. Elements of this serial in particular show exactly where George Lucas and Steven Spielberg got the notion for Indiana Jones. Originally called "Perils of Nyoka." In 15 episodes. **Hound Advisory:** Violence.
1942 (*Family*) 250m/B Kay Aldridge, Clayton Moore; *D:* William Witney. **VHS, LV $29.98** *VCN, REP, MLB*

Octopussy *♫♫*

Bond saga continues as Agent 007 is on a mission to prevent a crazed Russian general from launching a nuclear attack against the NATO forces in Europe. Lots of special effects and gadgets keep weak plot moving. **Hound Advisory:** Violence, sex, alcohol use.
1983 (PG/*Jr. High-Adult*) 140m/C Roger Moore, Maud Adams, Louis Jourdan, Kristina Wayborn, Kabir Bedi; *D:* John Glen; *W:* Michael G. Wilson; *M:* John Barry. **VHS, Beta, LV $19.98** *MGM, FOX, TLF*

The Odd Couple *♫♫♫♫*

Two divorced men with completely opposite personalities move in together. Lemmon's obsession with neatness drives slob Matthau up the wall, and their inability to see eye-to-eye results in many hysterical escapades. A Hollywood rarity, it is actually better in some ways than Neil Simon's original Broadway version. Basis for the hit television series.
1968 (G/*Family*) 106m/C Jack Lemmon, Walter Matthau; *D:* Gene Saks; *W:* Neil Simon. **VHS, Beta, LV $14.95** *PAR*

Odd Jobs *♫♫*

When five college friends look for jobs during summer break, they wind up running their own moving business with the help of the mob. Good comic talent, but a silly slapstick script results in only a passable diversion.
1985 (PG-13/*Jr. High-Adult*) 89m/C Paul Reiser, Scott McGinnis, Rick Overton, Robert Townsend; *D:* Mark Story; *M:* Robert Folk. **VHS, Beta $79.95** *HBO*

Ode to Billy Joe *♫♫*

1967 Bobby Gentry hit song of the same title is expanded to tell why a young man jumped to his death off the Tallahatchie Bridge. The problems of growing up in the rural South, sex and teenage romance don't match the mournful appeal (and

brevity!) of the theme music, but the youthful leads work well together. **Hound Advisory:** Sex talk, mature themes.
1976 (PG/*Jr. High-Adult*) 106m/C Robby Benson, Glynnis O'Connor, Joan Hotchkis, Sandy McPeak, James Best; *D:* Max Baer Jr. **VHS, Beta $19.98** *CCB, WAR*

Of Mice and Men *♫♫♫*

Somber retelling of John Steinbeck's classic as adapted by Horton Foote. Set on the migratory farms of California, it follows the friendship of the simple-minded Lennie (Malkovich) with his reluctant protector George (Sinise). Interesting performances from both, well-supported by cinematographer Kenneth MacMillan. Director Sinise received permission from Steinbeck's widow to film the novel (actually the third adaptation). **Hound Advisory:** Profanity; violence; mature themes.
1992 (PG-13/*Jr. High-Adult*) 110m/C John Malkovich, Sherilyn Fenn, Casey Siemaszko, Joe Morton, Ray Walston, Gary Sinise, John Terry, Richard Riehle; *D:* Gary Sinise; *W:* Horton Foote. **VHS, LV $19.98** *MGM, PMS, BTV*

Off Beat *♫♫*

Shy librarian unluckily wins a spot in a police benefit dance troupe, and then falls in love with a tough police woman. With a screenplay by playwright Medoff, and a good supporting cast, it still manages to miss the mark.
1986 (PG/*Sr. High-Adult*) 92m/C Judge Reinhold, Meg Tilly, Cleavant Derricks, Fred Gwynne, John Turturro, Jacques D'Amboise, James Tolkan, Joe Mantegna, Harvey Keitel, Amy Wright; *D:* Michael Dinner; *W:* Mark Medoff; *M:* James Horner. **VHS, Beta, LV $79.95** *TOU*

An Officer and a Duck

Donald goes to war in this classic compilation of Donald Duck WWII episodes narrating his military adventures as a private, a paratrooper, and more. Component of Disney's Limited Gold Edition 2.
1943 (*Family*) 45m/C **VHS, Beta** *DIS*

Oh, God! *♫♫♫*

God, incarnated as a wizened, wisecracking senior citizen, recruits an average guy (Denver, in his film debut) as his herald in a plan to save the world. Society questions the man's sanity, but he keeps faith and is rewarded. It's not exactly a substitute for divinity school (the question of Jesus' parenthood is gingerly sidestepped), but sincere performances and optimism make for a satisfying, ecumenical parable. Based on the novel by Avery Corman.
1977 (PG/*Family*) 104m/C George Burns, John Denver, Paul Sorvino, Ralph Bellamy, Teri Garr, William Daniels, Donald Pleasence, Barnard Hughes, Barry Sullivan, Dinah Shore, Jeff Corey, David Ogden Stiers; *D:* Carl Reiner; *W:* Larry Gelbart. **VHS, Beta, LV $19.98** *WAR*

Oh, God! Book 2 *♫*

Burns returns as the "Almighty One" in strained sequel to "Oh God!" This time He enlists the help of a young girl to remind others of His existence. The slogan she concocts saves God's image, but not the movie. Followed by "Oh, God! You Devil."
1980 (PG/*Family*) 94m/C George Burns, Suzanne Pleshette, David Birney, Louanne, Conrad Janis, Wilfrid Hyde-White, Hans Conried, Howard Duff; *D:* Gilbert Cates; *M:* Charles Fox. **VHS, Beta $19.98** *WAR*

Oh, God! You Devil 🐾🐾

During his third trip to earth, Burns plays both the Devil and God as he first takes a struggling musician's soul, then gives it back. A few verbal zingers and light atmosphere spell salvation for an unoriginal plot. **Hound Advisory:** Salty language.
1984 (PG/*Family*) 96m/C George Burns, Ted Wass, Roxanne Hart, Ron Silver, Eugene Roche, Robert Desiderio; **D:** Paul Bogart; **W:** Andrew Bergman; **M:** David Shire. **VHS, Beta, LV $19.98** *WAR*

Oh, Heavenly Dog! 🐾🐾

Pairing of animal superstar Benji and 'sophisticated' comic Chase is an ungainly tale. Private eye returns from the dead as the dog and tries to solve his own murder. The canine is terrific, as ever, and kid viewers probably won't mind his use in such an inane gimmick. **Hound Advisory:** Profanity, sex talk, salty barking.
1980 (PG/*Family*) 104m/C Chevy Chase, Jane Seymour, Omar Sharif, Robert Morley, Susan Kellerman; **D:** Joe Camp. **VHS, Beta $19.98** *FOX*

Oh, What a Night 🐾🐾

Bittersweet coming of age tale about lonely 17-year-old Haim. He's moved with his father and stepmother to a chicken farm in 1955 Ontario, where he falls in love with an older woman who has a husband and two kids. Features a great fifties soundtrack and beautiful scenes of the Canadian countryside. **Hound Advisory:** Mature themes.
1992 (PG-13/*Jr. High-Adult*) 93m/C Corey Haim, Barbara Williams, Keir Dullea, Genevieve Bujold, Robbie Coltrane; **D:** Eric Till. **VHS, LV $89.95** *COL, NLC*

Oklahoma! 🐾🐾🐾⬩

Cowboy and country girl fall in love, but she is tormented by another unwelcomed suitor. Throughout their travails, they sing, dance, and create a little movie magic. Arizona substitutes for Oklahoma in the screen adaptation of Rodgers and Hammerstein's Broadway hit, complete with original, culturally imprinted score. Agnes de Mille choreographed, replacing Jones and MacRae in the Dream Ballet with dancers Bambi Linn and James Mitchell. The 19-year-old Jones in her film debut is a must-see for musical fans. ♫Oh, What a Beautiful Morning; Surrey with the Fringe on Top; I Cain't Say No; Many a New Day; People Will Say We're in Love; Poor Jud Is Dead; All 'Er Nuthin'; Everything's Up to Date in Kansas City; The Farmer and the Cowman.
1955 (G/*Family*) 145m/C Gordon MacRae, Shirley Jones, Rod Steiger, Gloria Grahame, Eddie Albert, Charlotte Greenwood, James Whitmore, Gene Nelson, Barbara Lawrence, Jay C. Flippen; **D:** Fred Zinneman; **W:** Sonya Levien, William Ludwig; **M:** Richard Rodgers, Oscar Hammerstein. **Award Nominations:** Academy Awards '55: Best Color Cinematography, Best Film Editing; **Awards:** Academy Awards '55: Best Sound, Best Score. **VHS, Beta, LV $19.98** *FOX, RDG, HMV*

Oklahoma Crude 🐾🐾⬩

Sadistic oil trust rep Palence battles man-hating Dunaway for her well. Drifter Scott helps her resist on the promise of shared profits. In this 1913 setting, Dunaway tells Scott she wishes she could avoid men altogether, but later settles for him.
1973 (PG/*Jr. High-Adult*) 108m/C George C. Scott, Faye Dunaway, John Mills, Jack Palance, Harvey Jason, Woodrow Parfrey; **D:** Stanley Kramer; **W:** Marc Norman; **M:** Henry Mancini. **VHS** *FOX*

The Old Curiosity Shop 🐾🐾

After plundering Mark Twain with mixed results for their musicals "Tom Sawyer" and "Huckleberry Finn," the Readers Digest group tried this British musicalization of Charles Dickens, in vain hopes of repeating the success of "Oliver!" Story concerns a Scroogish scoundrel who wants to take over a small antique shop run by an elderly man and his granddaughter. Also known as "Mr. Quilp." Songs written by Anthony Newley. ♫When a Felon Needs a Friend; Somewhere; Love Has the Longest Memory; Happiness Pie; The Sport of Kings; What Shouldn't Happen to a Dog; Quilp.
1975 (G/*Family*) 118m/C Anthony Newley, David Hemmings, David Warner, Jill Bennett, Peter Duncan, Michael Hordern; **D:** Michael Tuchner; **M:** Elmer Bernstein. **VHS, Beta $14.98** *REP, SUE*

The Old Curiosity Shop 🐾🐾

Animated adaptation of the classic Dickens story about little Nell and her grandfather, who are evicted from their antique shop by evil landlord Quilp.
1984 (G/*Family*) 72m/C **VHS, Beta $19.98** *LIV*

Old Enough 🐾🐾

Slow-moving comedy-drama about the clique-crossing friendship of two NYC teenagers, one from a rich family, the other a streetwise Italian-American with plenty to teach about makeup, sex, and shoplifting. Independently made. **Hound Advisory:** Sex talk, salty language.
1984 (PG/*Sr. High-Adult*) 91m/C Sarah Boyd, Rainbow Harvest, Neill Barry, Danny Aiello, Susan Kingsley, Roxanne Hart, Alyssa Milano, Fran Brill, Anne Pitoniak; **D:** Marisa Silver; **W:** Marisa Silver. **VHS, Beta $59.95** *MED*

Old MacDonald's Farm and Other Animal Tales

Gripping story of Old MacDonald is recounted along with various other animated tales featuring a variety of animals.
1990 (*Preschool-Primary*) 30m/C **VHS $7.95**

The Old Mill

An Oscar-winning Disney "Silly Symphony": a run-down building, housing an array of animals, withstands a nasty storm and the animals learn the value of teamwork.
1937 (*Preschool-Primary*) 9m/C **VHS, Beta $170.00** *DSN, MTI*

Old Yeller 🐾🐾🐾⬩

Disney Studios' first and best boy-and-his-dog adventure. Fourteen-year-old Travis is left in charge of the family farm while Pa is away. When his younger brother brings home a stray dog, Travis is displeased but lets him stay. Yeller saves the boy's life, but contracts rabies in the process. Keep tissue handy, especially for the kids. Strong acting, effective scenery - all good stuff. Based on the novel by Fred Gipson. Sequel "Savage Sam" released in 1963. **Hound Advisory:** Violence. Just about every Disney animal movie ever (even "The

Shaggy Dog") has that scene in which someone threatens to shoot the dog/cow/deer/elephant, but this is the heartbreaker in which the deed is truly done.
1957 (G/*Family*) 84m/C Dorothy McGuire, Fess Parker, Tommy Kirk, Kevin Corcoran, Jeff York, Beverly Washburn, Chuck Connors; **D:** Robert Stevenson. **VHS, Beta, LV $19.99** *DIS*

Old Yeller

A condensed version of the heartbreaking 1957 Disney classic based on Fred Gipson's timeless tale; the ill-fated relationship between a boy and his mongrel dog cause the boy to become a man.
1990 (*Preschool-Jr. High*) 28m/C **VHS, Beta, LV $250.00** *MTI, DSN*

The Olden Days Coat

"Anne of Green Gables" leading lady Follows stars in this minor Canadian time-travel short about a city girl who doesn't like visiting her grandmother for the holidays. Sally changes her attitude when a magical garment transports her to the old woman's own childhood.
1981 (*Preschool-Primary*) 30m/C Megan Follows, Doris Petrie; **D:** Bruce Pittman. **VHS, Beta** *NWV*

Oliver! 🦴🦴🦴🦴

Cinephiles were scandalized when this beat out "2001: A Space Odyssey" for a Best Picture Oscar, but face it - which movie made more people happy? Lush, big-budget musical adaptation of "Oliver Twist" does a grand job with London locations and a peerless cast in the classic story of the innocent orphan expelled from a Victorian workhouse and into a gang of boy pickpockets. Moody's Fagin is a more loveable rogue than Charles Dickens could ever have imagined. ♫Food, Glorious Food; Oliver; Boy For Sale; Where Is Love?; Consider Yourself; Pick a Pocket or Two; I'd Do Anything; Be Back Soon; As Long As He Needs Me. **Hound Advisory:** Violence, alcohol use.
1968 (G/*Family*) 145m/C Mark Lester, Jack Wild, Ron Moody, Shani Wallis, Oliver Reed, Hugh Griffith; **D:** Carol Reed. **Award Nominations:** Academy Awards '68: Best Actor (Moody), Best Adapted Screenplay, Best Cinematography, Best Costume Design, Best Film Editing, Best Supporting Actor (Wild); **Awards:** Academy Awards '68: Best Art Direction/Set Decoration, Best Director (Reed), Best Picture, Best Sound, Best Score; Golden Globe Awards '69: Best Actor—Musical/Comedy (Moody), Best Film—Musical/Comedy; National Board of Review Awards '68: 10 Best Films of the Year. **VHS, Beta, LV $19.95** *COL, BTV, HMV*

Oliver Twist 🦴🦴

The first talking version of Dickens' classic (Jackie Coogan's 1922 silent is also on video), looks genuinely 19th-century and poverty-wracked — or is that a reflection of the primitive budget? English accents come and go, and Oliver's not even onscreen much in this one. Note Boyd, later a hero to millions as cowboy star Hopalong Cassidy, here cast as the murderous Bill Sykes. **Hound Advisory:** Violence.
1933 (*Family*) 70m/B Dickie Moore, Irving Pichel, William Boyd, Barbara Kent; **D:** William J. Cowan. **VHS, Beta $19.95** *NOS, MRV, HHT*

Oliver Twist 🦴🦴🦴🦴

Charles Dickens' immortal story of a Victorian workhouse orphan, tricked into a life of crime with a gang of juvenile pickpockets, then finding a home with a wealthy Londoner. The best of the many film adaptations, with excellent portrayals. But if you're expecting something fun and cuddly, try the musical "Oliver!" - this is a stark, deadly serious version of the novel, accurately reflecting the author's concern over poverty, cruel injustice and exploitation of children. And Fagin (Guinness) sure isn't the lovable rascal of the stage show. An earlier dramatization from 1933 is also on video. **Hound Advisory:** Violence, alcohol use.
1948 (*Family*) 116m/C Robert Newton, John Howard Davies, Alec Guinness, Francis L. Sullivan, Anthony Newley, Kay Walsh, Diana Dors, Henry Stephenson; **D:** David Lean; **W:** David Lean. **VHS, Beta, LV $19.95** *PAR, DVT, FHS*

Oliver Twist 🦴🦴🦴

Made-for-TV version of the classic tale of a Victorian orphan boy's rescue from a London pickpocket gang. Cut too short to capture Dicken's intricate narrative, and Scott's Fagin, though a treat, is of the heart-of-gold variety. Historical period details are on the mark.
1982 (*Family*) 72m/C George C. Scott, Tim Curry, Michael Hordern, Timothy West, Lysette Anthony, Eileen Atkins, Cherie Lunghi; **D:** Clive Donner; **W:** James Goldman; **M:** Nick Bicat. **VHS, Beta $14.98** *REP, VES*

Oliver Twist

British TV miniseries adaptation crams more of Charles Dickens' original novel into its narrative than any other — you can do that when you're 5.5 hours long. Oliver the orphan boy plunges into the underworld of Victorian London and assorted villains seek to profit off the secret of his birth. On two tapes. **Hound Advisory:** Violence.
1985 (*Family*) 333m/C Ben Rodska, Eric Porter, Frank Middlemass, Gillian Martell. **VHS, Beta $29.98** *FOX, SIG, HMV*

Oliver Twist

Animated musical TV version of the Charles Dickens tale of the roguish Fagin, the Artful Dodger, and the orphaned Oliver (who has a pet toad named Squeaker in this none-too faithful adaptation).
19?? (*Family*) 95m/C **V:** Davy Jones, Larry Storch. **VHS $19.98** *WAR*

Ollie Hopnoodle's Haven of Bliss 🦴🦴🦴

Jean Shepherd, the humorist whose work inspired "A Christmas Story," scripted and narrates this Disney made-for-TV comedy about a family man taking his unruly brood on an accident-fraught vacation.
1988 (*Family*) 90m/C James B. Sikking, Dorothy Lyman, Jerry O'Connell; **D:** Dick Bartlett. **VHS, Beta $39.99** *DIS*

Olly Olly Oxen Free 🦴🦴

Junkyard owner Hepburn helps two boys fix up and fly a hot-air balloon, once piloted by McKenzie's grandfather, as a surprise for the man's birthday. Beautiful airborne scenes over California and a dramatic landing to the tune of the

Old Yeller (1957)

"1812 Overture," but not enough to make the whole film interesting.
1978 *(Family)* 89m/C Katharine Hepburn, Kevin McKenzie, Dennis Dimster, Peter Kilman; **D:** Richard A. Colla. **VHS, Beta** *TLF*

The Olympic Champ
Walt Disney's Goofy is a contestant at the Olympic games where he proceeds to demonstrate his athletic prowess.
1981 *(Preschool-Primary)* 8m/C   **VHS, Beta $155.00** *MTI, DSN*

On a Clear Day You Can See Forever 🐾🐾
A psychiatric hypnotist helps a girl stop smoking and finds that in trances she remembers previous incarnations. He falls in love with one of the women she used to be. Alan Jay Lerner of "My Fair Lady" and "Camelot" wrote the lyrics and the book. Based on a musical by Lerner and Burton Lane. ♫On a Clear Day, You Can See Forever; Come Back to Me; What Did I Have That I Don't Have?; He Isn't You; Hurry, It's Lovely Up Here; Go To Sleep; Love with All the Trimmings; Melinda.
1970 (G/*Family*) 129m/C Barbra Streisand, Yves Montand, Bob Newhart, Jack Nicholson, Simon Oakland; **D:** Vincente Minnelli. **VHS, Beta, LV $14.95** *PAR*

On Golden Pond 🐾🐾🐾🐾
Henry Fonda won his only Oscar for his role as the curmudgeonly patriarch of the Thayer family. He and his wife grudgingly agree to look after their adolescent grandson while at their summer home in Maine. Through his gradually affectionate relationship with the boy, Thayer comes to terms with his own old age and gains an understanding of his semi-estranged daughter, played by real-life offspring Jane. Deeply moving, often funny adaptation of Ernest Thompson's play.
1981 (PG/*Family*) 109m/C Henry Fonda, Jane Fonda, Katharine Hepburn, Dabney Coleman, Doug McKeon, William Lanteau; **D:** Mark Rydell; **W:** Ernest Thompson; **M:** Dave Grusin. **Award Nominations:** Academy Awards '81: Best Actor (Fonda), Best Cinematography, Best Director (Rydell), Best Film Editing, Best Sound, Best Supporting Actress (Fonda), Best Original Score; **Awards:** Academy Awards '81: Best Actor (Fonda), Best Actress (Hepburn), Best Adapted Screenplay; British Academy Awards '82: Best Actress (Hepburn); Golden Globe Awards '82: Best Actor—Drama (Fonda), Best Film—Drama, Best Screenplay. **VHS, Beta, LV $14.95** *FHE, SUP, KAR*

On Her Majesty's Secret Service 🐾🐾🐾
In the sixth 007 adventure, Bond again confronts the infamous Blofeld, who is planning a germ-warfare assault on the entire world. Australian Lazenby took a crack at playing the super spy, with mixed results. Many feel this is the best-written of the Bond films and might have been the most famous, had Sean Connery continued with the series. Includes the song "We Have All the Time In the World," sung by Louis Armstrong. **Hound Advisory:** Violence, alcohol use, sex.
1969 (PG/*Jr. High-Adult*) 144m/C George Lazenby, Diana Rigg, Telly Savalas, Gabriel Ferzetti, Ilse Steppat, Bernard Lee, Lois Maxwell, Desmond Llewelyn, Catherine Schell, Julie Ege, Joanna Lumley, Mona Chong, Anouska Hempel, Jenny Hanley; **D:** Peter Hunt; **M:** John Barry. **VHS, Beta, LV $19.98** *MGM, FOX, TLF*

On the Comet 🐾🐾🐾
Lesser-known sci-fi fantasy by Jules Verne brought to life by Czech filmmaker Karl Zeman, with his trademark meld of whimsical animation and live action. Wandering planetoid brushes past 19th-century Earth and takes part of the Mediterranean coast with it. Drifting through the solar system, assorted Europeans, Arabs, soldiers, lovers and scalawags slowly realize their old nationalistic squabbles are pointless now that they're on their own. Adults more than kid viewers may get the sly satire of human nature, though there are some memorable dinosaur f/x (stop motion and puppets) as well. English-language dubbing is on the clunky side. **Hound Advisory:** Alcohol use.
1968 *(Family)* 76m/C Emil Horvath Jr., Magda Vasarykova, Frantisek Filipovsky; **D:** Karel Zeman. **VHS, Beta $19.99** *FCT, MRV*

On the Edge: The Survival of Dana 🐾
Hand-wringing TV-movie was intended in its day as a sincere examination of juvenile delinquency, but the results are maudlin and unintentionally silly. Anderson was also residing in "Little House on the Prairie" at the time she was calculatingly cast as Dana, new girl in town who falls in with a bad crowd of mean teens. Her concerned mom is played by Ross, Mrs. Cunningham from "Happy Days." See the similarly titled "Over the Edge" instead for a better treatment of the subject. **Hound Advisory:** Drug use; sex talk; roughhousing.
1979 *(Family)* 92m/C Melissa Sue Anderson, Robert Carradine, Marion Ross, Talia Balsam, Michael Pataki, Kevin Breslin, Judge Reinhold, Barbara Babcock; **D:** Jack Starrett. **VHS, Beta** *GEM*

On the Right Track 🐾🐾
Young orphan living in Chicago's Union Station has the gift of being able to pick winning race horses. May be appealing to fans of Coleman and "Different Strokes" television show, but lacks the momentum to keep most viewers from switching tracks.
1981 (PG/*Family*) 98m/C Gary Coleman, Lisa Eilbacher, Michael Lembeck, Norman Fell, Maureen Stapleton, Herb Edelman; **D:** Lee Philips. **VHS, Beta $59.95** *FOX*

On the Town 🐾🐾🐾🐾
Kelly's directorial debut is a high-energy wonder about three sailors on a one-day leave searching for romance in the Big Apple. Notable for taking the musical from the soundstage to the street: filmed on location in New York City, with uncompromisingly authentic flavor. Based on the successful Broadway musical, with Leonard Bernstein's stage score modified by Roger Edens. Available in a deluxe collector's laserdisc edition. ♫New York, New York; I Feel Like I'm Not Out of Bed Yet; Come Up to My Place; Miss Turnstiles Ballet; Main Street; You're Awful; On the Town; You Can Count on Me; Pearl of the Persian Sea.
1949 *(Family)* 98m/C Gene Kelly, Frank Sinatra, Vera-Ellen, Ann Miller, Betty Garrett; **D:** Gene Kelly, Stanley Donen; **W:** Betty Comden, Adolph Green. **VHS, Beta, LV $19.98** *MGM*

On Vacation with Mickey and Friends

Disney mouse and his pals star in a number of misadventures including, "Canine Caddy," "Bubble Bee," "Goofy and Wilbur," "Dude Duck," "Mickey's Trailer," and "Hawaiian Holiday."
19?? *(Family)* 47m/C **VHS, Beta, LV** *DIS*

Once a Hero 🐕🐕

Fictional Captain Justice's powers fade because readers are losing interest in his superhero comic book. He leaps out of the fantasy realm to complain to his human creator, and has to deal with the drawbacks and problems of dwelling in the real world. Fascinating, not entirely successful idea, slightly reminiscent of "The Last Action Hero," formed the pilot for a short-lived network TV series.
1988 *(Adult)* 74m/C Jeff Lester, Robert Forster, Milo O'Shea; *D:* Claudia Weill. **VHS $9.99** *NWV, STE*

Once Upon a Brothers Grimm 🐕🐕

An original musical fantasy in which the Brothers Grimm meet a succession of their most famous storybook characters, including Hansel and Gretel, the Gingerbread Lady, Little Red Riding Hood, and Rumpelstiltskin.
1977 *(Family)* 102m/C Dean Jones, Paul Sand, Cleavon Little, Ruth Buzzi, Chita Rivera, Teri Garr. **VHS, Beta $39.95** *VCI*

Once Upon a Crime 🐕⋖

Extremely disappointing comedy featuring a high profile cast set in Europe. The plot centers around Young and Lewis finding a dachshund and travelling from Rome to Monte Carlo to return the stray and collect a $5,000 reward. Upon arrival in Monte Carlo, they find the dog's owner dead and are implicated for the murder. Other prime suspects include Belushi, Candy, Hamilton, and Shepherd. Weak script is made bearable only by the comic genius of Candy. **Hound Advisory:** Roughhousing and profanity.
1992 *(PG/Jr. High-Adult)* 94m/C John Candy, James Belushi, Cybill Shepherd, Sean Young, Richard Lewis, Ornella Muti, Giancarlo Giannini, George Hamilton, Joss Ackland, Elsa Martinelli; *D:* Eugene Levy; *M:* Richard Gibbs. **VHS $14.95** *MGM*

Once Upon a Forest 🐕🐕

Cartoon about young woodland creatures whose forest is slimed by a toxic spill. To save a chemically burned badger baby, the animals race to gather medicinal ingredients. Ecologically correct feature by Hanna-Barbera and "American Tail" creator David Kirschner is light on plot, heavy on sentiment about oppressive humans and their big, bad machines. Serviceable animation, undistinguished songs, put this well behind the similar "Ferngully."
1993 *(G/Family)* 80m/C *D:* Charles Grosvenor; *W:* Mark Young, Kelly Ward; *V:* Michael Crawford, Ben Vereen. **VHS, LV $24.98** *FXV, FUS, WTA*

Once Upon a Scoundrel 🐕🐕⋖

Mostel's delicious, larger-than-life bluster brightens this tale of ruthless Mexican land baron whose villainy finally goes too far. Villagers stage a ghostly hoax to make him reform in Scrooge-like fashion.
1973 *(G/Family)* 90m/C Zero Mostel, Katy Jurado, Tito Vandis, Priscilla Garcia, A. Martinez; *D:* George Schaefer; *M:* Alex North. **VHS, Beta $9.99** *PSM*

Once Upon a Time

Case of an adults-mainly Japanese cartoon that might easily be mistaken for a kiddie picture, which this isn't. Re-edited Japanimation feature "Windaria" still has many disturbing elements, including violence, sex and murder-suicide, as a prince and princess from rival futuristic fantasy kingdoms try desperately to avert a devastating war. **Hound Advisory:** Mature themes, brutality, sex.
1987 *(Family)* 92m/C **VHS, Beta $39.95** *MED*

Once Upon a Time in the West 🐕🐕🐕⋖

The uncut version of Leone's sprawling epic about a band of ruthless gunmen who set out to murder a mysterious woman waiting for the railroad to come through. Filmed in John Ford's Monument Valley, it's a revisionist western with some of the longest opening credits in the history of the cinema. Fonda is cast against type as an extremely cold-blooded villain. Brilliant musical score.
1968 *(PG/Jr. High-Adult)* 165m/C Henry Fonda, Jason Robards Jr., Charles Bronson, Claudia Cardinale, Keenan Wynn, Lionel Stander, Woody Strode, Jack Elam; *D:* Sergio Leone; *W:* Sergio Leone, Bernardo Bertolucci, Dario Argento; *M:* Ennio Morricone. **VHS, Beta, LV $24.95** *PAR*

The One and Only, Genuine, Original Family Band 🐕🐕⋖

Harmonious musical family becomes divided when various members take sides in the 1888 presidential battle between Benjamin Harrison and Grover Cleveland. Semi-musical nostalgic Americana from Disney, best for those whose favorite section of Disney World is Main Street USA.
1968 *(G/Family)* 110m/C Walter Brennan, Buddy Ebsen, Lesley Ann Warren, Kurt Russell, Goldie Hawn, Wally Cox, Richard Deacon, Janet Blair; *D:* Michael O'Herlihy. **VHS, Beta, LV $9.99** *DIS*

One Crazy Summer 🐕🐕⋖

Group of teens spend a fun-filled summer on Nantucket Island in New England. This follow-up to "Better Off Dead" is offbeat and fairly charming, led by Cusack's perplexed-about-his-future cartoonist (whose drawings come to animated life) and with comic moments delivered by Goldthwait. **Hound Advisory:** Sex talk, salty language, roughhousing.
1986 *(PG/Jr. High-Adult)* 94m/C John Cusack, Demi Moore, William Hickey, Curtis Armstrong, Bob(cat) Goldthwait, Mark Metcalf, Joel Murray, Tom Villard, Joe Flaherty; *D:* Steve Holland; *W:* Steve Holland; *M:* Cory Lerios. **VHS, Beta, LV $19.98** *WAR*

One Fish, Two Fish, Red Fish, Blue Fish

The Dr. Seuss classic cartoon is paired with two other stories, "Oh, the Thinks You Can Think" and "The Foot Book" on one tape.
1990 *(Family)* 30m/C **VHS $9.95** *VEC, RAN*

101 Dalmatians 🦴🦴🦴⊲

Disney classic and one of the highest-grossing animated films in Hollywood history centers around Roger and Anita, and their respective dalmatians, Pongo and Perdita, whose purebred puppies are kidnapped by callous Cruella de Vil to make a spotted coat. When the canine parents go to the rescue, they find not only their own litter, but 84 more puppies. You can expect a happy ending in this adaptation of the children's book by Dodie Smith. Technically notable for the first time use of the Xerox process to transfer the animator's drawings onto celluloid, which made the opening sequence of dots evolving into 101 barking dogs possible and was a major step toward computerizing the Magic Kingdom's animation works. ♫Remember When; Cruella de Vil; Dalmation Plantation; Kanine Krunchies Kommercial.
1961 (G/*Family*) 79m/C **D:** Clyde Geronomi, Wolfgang Reitherman, Hamilton Luske; **V:** Rod Taylor, Betty Lou Gerson, Lisa Davis, Ben Wright, Frederick Worlock, J. Pat O'Malley. **VHS, Beta $24.99** *DIS, OM*

101 Problems of Hercules

Not a self-help tape; Disney version of the Hercules saga.
1966 (*Family*) 50m/C **VHS $24.95** *DSN, DIS*

One Little Indian 🦴🦴

AWOL cavalry man and his 12-year-old Indian ward team up with a widow and her daughter in an attempt to cross the New Mexican desert via camel. Tepid presentation from the Disney studio.
1973 (*Family*) 90m/C James Garner, Vera Miles, Jodie Foster, Clay O'Brien, Andrew Prine, Bernard McEveety; **D:** Bernard McEveety; **M:** Jerry Goldsmith. **VHS, Beta $69.95** *DIS*

One Magic Christmas 🦴🦴

Holiday tearjerker from Disney about an depressed lady hit with multiple calamities at Yuletime. Her little daughter restores her spirits with the help of Santa and a seedy-looking guardian angel. Jarring juxtaposition of fantasy and realistic elements - one moment a robbery and murder, the next moment the North Pole toy factory. It won't make anyone forget "Miracle on 34th Street." **Hound Advisory:** Mature themes.
1985 (G/*Family*) 88m/C Mary Steenburgen, Harry Dean Stanton, Gary Basaraba, Michelle Meyrink, Arthur Hill, Elisabeth Harnois, Robbie Magwood; **D:** Phillip Borsos; **M:** Michael Conway Baker. **VHS, Beta, LV $14.99** *DIS*

One of Our Dinosaurs Is Missing 🦴🦴

English nanny and her cohorts help British Intelligence retrieve a dinosaur skeleton from Red Chinese spies who stole it to obtain a secret microfilm formula. No "Jurassic Park," this calcified Disney comedy was shot on location in England. Based on the novel "The Great Dinosaur Robbery" by David Forrest.
1975 (G/*Family*) 101m/C Peter Ustinov, Helen Hayes, Derek Nimmo, Clive Revill, Robert Stevenson, Joan Sims; **D:** Robert Stevenson. **VHS, Beta $69.95** *DIS*

One on One 🦴🦴⊲

"Rocky"-esque story about a high school basketball star from the country who accepts an athletic scholarship to a big city university. He encounters a demanding coach and intense competition. Lightweight drama that occasionally scores, written by Benson and his own father. **Hound Advisory:** Salty language, sex talk.
1977 (PG/*Primary-Adult*) 100m/C Robby Benson, Annette O'Toole, G.D. Spradlin, Gail Strickland, Melanie Griffith; **D:** Lamont Johnson; **M:** Charles Fox. **VHS, Beta $39.98** *WAR*

Only the Lonely 🦴🦴⊲

Middle-aged cop Candy lives with his ma O'Hara, in her first role in years. Then he falls in love with Sheedy, a shy undertaker's assistant and is torn between love and dear old Mom. Sentimental, tender, and uneven, supported by fine performances, particularly Candy's as the sincere Danny Muldoon. **Hound Advisory:** Profanity.
1991 (PG/*Jr. High-Adult*) 104m/C John Candy, Ally Sheedy, Maureen O'Hara, Anthony Quinn, Kevin Dunn, James Belushi, Milo O'Shea, Bert Remsen, Macaulay Culkin, Joe V. Greco; **D:** Chris Columbus; **W:** Chris Columbus; **M:** Maurice Jarre. **VHS, Beta, LV $19.98** *FXV*

Only You 🦴⊲

Shy guy has always searched for true romance. But his cup runneth over when he meets, and must choose between, two beautiful women - your basic beach babe and a sensible beauty. What's a guy to do? Lightweight romantic comedy fails to satisfy. **Hound Advisory:** Salty language.
1992 (PG-13/*Jr. High-Adult*) 85m/C Andrew McCarthy, Kelly Preston, Helen Hunt. **VHS $89.98** *LIV*

Opportunity Knocks 🦴🦴⊲

Dana's a small-time hood on the run from a vengeful gangster. Opportunity knocks and he begins impersonating a wealthy man, falls in tight with a rich suburbanite family, and has a go at romance with the comely daughter. Comedic capers then ensue. Basic sitcom is lightweight and obvious, but Carvey's first starring feature has its charms, particularly for young fans. **Hound Advisory:** Salty language; violence.
1990 (PG-13/*Jr. High-Adult*) 105m/C Dana Carvey, Robert Loggia, Todd Graff, Milo O'Shea, Julia Campbell, James Tolkan, Doris Belack, Sally Gracie, Del Close; **D:** Donald Petrie; **W:** Mitchel Katlin, Nat Bernstein; **M:** Miles Goodman. **VHS, Beta, LV $19.95** *MCA*

The Original Fabulous Adventures of Baron Munchausen 🦴🦴🦴

To avoid mixups with a 1979 European cartoon (also on video, in a version that doesn't even spell "Munchausen" correctly) distributors retitled "The Fabulous Adventures of Baron Munchausen," from Czech animation master Karl Zeman. Under any name it's worth a search. Cosmonaut reaches the moon - only to find all the fictional greats who made the trip centuries ago, like Cyrano de Bergerac and Baron Munchausen. These legends mistake their visitor for an alien (!), and the slightly vain Baron volunteers to take 'moon man' on an explanatory tour of Earth, circa the 1700s. There follows familiar Munchausen escapades: rescuing a

Pongo plays with pups in "101 Dalmations" (1961)

maiden from a sultan, riding through a battle on a cannonball, and circling the world inside a whale. Told with tinted live-action footage, stop-motion, and cutouts. Cumulative effect is lyrical, actually soothing - a true bedtime story in movie form. **1961** (*Adult-Family*) 84m/C Milos Kopecky, Jana Brejchova, Rudolph Jelinek, Jan Werich; *D:* Karel Zeman. **VHS, LV** *NO*

Orphan Train 🐾🐾🐾

A woman realizes her New York soup kitchen can't do enough to help the neighborhood orphans, so she takes a group of children out West in hopes of finding families to adopt them. Their journey is chronicled by a newspaper photographer an a social worker. Based on the orphans trains of the mid- to late 1800s. From the novel by Dorothea G. Petrie. Made for TV. **1979** (*Family*) 150m/C Jill Eikenberry, Kevin Dobson, Glenn Close, Linda Manz; *D:* William A. Graham. **VHS $14.95** *PSM, KAR, HHE*

Oscar 🐾🐾

The improbable casting of Stallone in a 1930s style crime farce (an attempt to change his image) is hard to imagine, and harder to believe. Stallone has little to do as he plays the straight man in this often ridiculous story of a crime boss who swears he'll go straight. Cameos aplenty, with Curry's the most notable. Based on a French play by Claude Magnier. **Hound Advisory:** Salty language.
1991 (PG/*Sr. High-Adult*) 109m/C Sylvester Stallone, Ornella Muti, Peter Riegert; *Cameos:* Tim Curry, Chazz Palminteri; *D:* John Landis; *M:* Elmer Bernstein. **VHS, LV $19.99** *COL, IME, TOU*

The Other Side of the Mountain 🐾🐾

Tear-jerking true story of Olympic hopeful skier Jill Kinmont, paralyzed in a fall. Bridges helps her pull her life together. A sequel followed two years later. Based on the book "A Long Way Up" by E. G. Valens.
1975 (PG/*Jr. High-Adult*) 102m/C Marilyn Hassett, Beau Bridges, Dabney Coleman, John David Garfield, Griffin Dunne; *D:* Larry Peerce; *W:* David Seltzer; *M:* Charles Fox. **VHS, Beta $14.98** *MCA*

The Other Side of the Mountain, Part 2 🐾🐾

Quadriplegic Jill Kinmont, paralyzed in a skiing accident that killed her hopes for the Olympics, overcomes depression and the death of the man who helped her to recover. In this chapter, she falls in love again and finds happiness. More tears are jerked.
1978 (PG/*Jr. High-Adult*) 99m/C Marilyn Hassett, Timothy Bottoms; *D:* Larry Peerce. **VHS, Beta $14.98** *MCA*

Our Little Girl 🐾🐾

Precocious little tyke tries to reunite her estranged parents by running away to their favorite vacation spot. Sure to please Temple fans, despite a lackluster script.
1935 (*Family*) 63m/B Shirley Temple, Joel McCrea, Rosemary Ames, Lyle Talbot, Erin O'Brien Moore; *D:* John S. Robertson. **VHS, Beta $19.98** *FOX*

Out of Time

ABC Afterschool Special about two kids who travel back in time to solve a mystery about one of their ancestors.

1985 (**PG**/*Primary-Jr. High*) 60m/C Adam Baldwin, Amy Locane, R.D. Robb. **VHS, Beta** *NO*

Out on a Limb 🐾

Lame comedy follows the misadventures of financial whiz Bill Campbell (Broderick). His young sister is convinced their stepfather is a criminal and persuades her brother to return home. On his way, Bill is robbed and abandoned by a woman hitchhiker, then found by two moronic brothers. It also turns out his stepfather has a twin brother who wants revenge for past crimes. Frantic chase scenes and lots of noise do not a comedy make. Broderick and Jones also appeared together in "Ferris Bueller's Day Off." **Hound Advisory:** Violence; some profanity.
1992 (PG/*Jr. High-Adult*) 82m/C Matthew Broderick, Jeffrey Jones, Heidi Kling, John Reilly, Marian Mercer, Larry Hankin, David Margulies; *D:* Francis Veber. **VHS, Beta, LV $19.98** *MGM*

The Outlaw Josey Wales 🐾🐾🐾🐾

Eastwood plays a farmer with a motive for revenge - his family was killed and for years he was betrayed and hunted. His desire to play the lone killer is, however, tempered by his need for family and friends. He kills plenty, but in the end finds happiness. Considered one of the last great Westerns, with many superb performances. Eastwood took over directorial chores during filming from Kaufman, who co-scripted. Adapted from "Gone To Texas" by Forest Carter. **Hound Advisory:** Violence.
1976 (PG/*Jr. High-Adult*) 135m/C Clint Eastwood, Chief Dan George, Sondra Locke, Matt Clark, John Vernon, Bill McKinney, Sam Bottoms; *D:* Clint Eastwood, Philip Kaufman; *W:* Philip Kaufman. **VHS, Beta, LV $19.98** *WAR, TLF*

Outside Chance of Maximillian Glick 🐾🐾🐾

Terrific, heartfelt comedy from Canada. Max Glick is a 12-year-old Jewish boy in the early 1960s who feels smothered by his tradition-bound family. He considers cancelling his bar mitzvah when they forbid his friendship with a gentile girl, but Max finds an unexpected ally in the free-thinking new rabbi who scandalizes the community. Viewers of any age - and any faith - will be rewarded by hunting up this delightful tale, based on a novel by Morley Torgov. Look closely at the cassette box art; ironically (for a film that celebrates ethnic identity), the video distributor retouched Max's yarmulke into a baseball cap. It's a shonda!
1988 (G/*Jr. High-Adult*) 94m/C Noam Zylberman, Fairuza Balk, Saul Rubinek; *D:* Allan Goldstein. **VHS, Beta $14.95** *HMD*

The Outsiders 🐾🐾

S.E. Hinton book (written when the author was just 17!) changed the tone of young adult fiction forever; still, it seems slender material smothered under this grandiose, melodramatic, all the talent money can buy treatment from Coppola. Simple story of a teen gang from the wrong side of the tracks in 1966 Tulsa, and how their feuding with upper-class young hoods brings on both tragedy and heroism. Many characters are reduced to one-scene star cameos. Only Dillon has the

chance to create a full personality as the hotheaded Dallas. **Hound Advisory:** Brutality, alcohol use, sex talk, mature themes, salty language.
1983 (PG/*Sr. High-Adult*) 91m/C C. Thomas Howell, Matt Dillon, Ralph Macchio, Patrick Swayze, Diane Lane, Tom Cruise, Emilio Estevez, Rob Lowe, Tom Waits, Leif Garrett; **D:** Francis Ford Coppola; **W:** Kathleen Rowell; **M:** Carmine Coppola. VHS, Beta, LV $19.98 *WAR*

Over the Edge 🎬🎬🎬♫

Updated "Rebel Without a Cause" highlighted by music from 70's icons Cheap Trick, The Cars, and The Ramones. Realistic tale of bored, alienated suburban kids on violence and vandalism binges that escalate to tragedy. Intent is insight, not exploitation, and the dialogue is excellent. Shelved for several years and finally released after Dillon, making his screen debut, became a star. **Hound Advisory:** Violence, drug use, sex, mature themes, profanity.
1979 (PG/*Jr. High-Adult*) 91m/C Michael Kramer, Matt Dillon, Pamela Ludwig, Vincent Spano; **D:** Jonathan Kaplan. VHS, Beta $19.98 *WAR*

Over the Top 🎬♫

"Heavy handed" takes on a whole new meaning in this drama of parenthood and arm-wrestling. "Rocky"-type trucker (Stallone in a stretch) named Linc Hawk decides the only way he can gain custody of his little boy from a rich-creep stepfather, as well as win the boy's respect, is through triumph in big-time professional arm-wrestling. Contrived beyond belief, and an example of why arm-wrestling never edged out the World Wrestling Federation in terms of visual thrills. **Hound Advisory:** Salty language, violence.
1986 (PG/*Jr. High-Adult*) 94m/C Sylvester Stallone, Susan Blakely, Robert Loggia, David Mendenhall; **D:** Menahem Golan; **W:** Sylvester Stallone, Gary Conway, Sterling Silliphant. VHS, Beta, LV $19.98 *WAR*

Overboard 🎬🎬

Wealthy, spoiled woman falls off of her yacht and into the arms of a low-class carpenter who picks her up and convinces her she is in fact his wife, and mother to his four brats. Just when she learns to like her life, the tables are turned again. Even though it's all been done before, you can't help but laugh at the screwy gags.
1987 (PG/*Jr. High-Adult*) 112m/C Goldie Hawn, Kurt Russell, Katherine Helmond, Roddy McDowall, Edward Herrmann; **D:** Garry Marshall; **W:** Leslie Dixon; **M:** Alan Silvestri. VHS, Beta, LV $14.95 *MGM, HMV, FOX*

Ovide and the Gang

Compilation of cartoon episodes featuring a cast of marsupials and other fantastic pals on their South Seas tropical island. Additional volumes available.
1987 (*Preschool-Primary*) 120m/C **VHS** $39.98 *JFK, WTA*

The Owl and the Pussycat

Animated version of Edward Lear's beloved children's poem with an original musical score.
19?? (*Family*) ?m/C **VHS, Beta** $14.95 *COL, GKK*

Owl Moon and Other Stories

Collection of animated tales from the "Children's Circle" of books carefully and gracefully brought to cartoon life. Includes "Owl Moon" by Jane Yolen, "The Caterpillar and the Polliwog" by Jack Kent, "Hot Hippo" by Mwenye Hadithi, and "Time of Wonder" by Robert McCloskey.
1991 (*Preschool-Primary*) 35m/C **VHS** $14.95 *FCT, CCC*

Ox Tales

Another animal species proves that nobody is above TV animation, in this selection of Ollie the ox episodes. Additional volumes available.
1989 (*Preschool-Primary*) 120m/C **VHS** $39.95 *JFK, WTA*

Oxford Blues 🎬🎬

An American finagles his way into England's Oxford University and onto the rowing team in pursuit of the girl of his dreams. Beautiful scenery, but the plot is wafer-thin. Remake of "Yank at Oxford."
1984 (PG-13/*Sr. High-Adult*) 98m/C Rob Lowe, Ally Sheedy, Amanda Pays, Julian Sands, Michael Gough, Gail Strickland; **D:** Robert Boris; **M:** John Du Prez. **VHS, Beta, LV** $19.98 *FOX*

Ozma of Oz 🎬🎬

Dorothy and her pals encounter Ozma, the beautiful Princess of Oz, and together they venture into Nomeland. Another in a worthwhile Canadian series that renders some of the many, many Oz books written by L. Frank Baum long after "The Wizard of Oz"; see also "The Marvelous Land of Oz" and "Emerald City of Oz."
1988 (*Family*) 90m/C **VHS, Beta** $59.95 *COL, WTA*

Paco 🎬♫

South American lad from the mountains of Columbia journeys alone to Bogota in hopes of retrieving his mule, gambled away by his shifty uncle. Potentially delightful material takes a wrong turn and shifts focus to a subplot about an actor forced by mobsters to participate in a jewel heist. Murky, low-cost look doesn't help either. **Hound Advisory:** Alcohol use, roughhousing.
1975 (G/*Family*) 89m/C Jose Ferrer, Panchito Gomez, Allen (Gooritz) Garfield, Pernell Roberts, Andre Marquis; **D:** Robert Vincent O'Neil. VHS, Beta *GHV*

Paddington Bear

Michael Bond's internationally famous ursine creation gets into a variety of adventures after his adoption into the Brown family. Each volume of this two-dimensional and stop-motion animation production includes 11 vignettes.
1985 (*Family*) 50m/C **VHS, Beta** *DIS*

Paddington Goes to the Movies

The loveable, stuffed English bear visits the movies, in animated fashion.
1983 (*Family*) 21m/C **VHS, Beta** *NO*

Paddy Beaver

Paddy Beaver teaches the residents of the Green Forest how to depend upon each other in this animated edition of Thornton Burgess' "Fables of the Green Forest."
1984 (*Family*) 60m/C **VHS, Beta $29.95** *FHE*

Paint Your Wagon 🎵🎵♩

Big-budget western musical-comedy lurches about, occasionally providing stellar moments. In No-Name City, a gold mining boom town, two prospectors share the same Mormon wife while struggling with a classic Lerner and Loewe score. Marvin chews up the sagebrush and, along with Eastwood, attempts to sing, although Seberg was mercifully dubbed. Presnell, who can sing, stands out. Overlong and occasionally engrossing, with pretty songs warbled plainly and plenty of panoramic scenery. Adapted from the Broadway play. ♫I Talk To the Trees; I Still See Elisa; I'm On My Way; Hand Me Down That Can O' Beans; Whoop-Ti-Ay; They Call the Wind Maria; There's a Coach Comin' In; Wandrin' Star; Best Things. **Hound Advisory:** Suggested sex.
1969 (*PG/Family*) 164m/C Lee Marvin, Clint Eastwood, Jean Seberg, Harve Presnell; *D:* Joshua Logan; *W:* Paddy Chayefsky; *M:* Frederick Loewe, Andre Previn, Alan Jay Lerner. **VHS, Beta, LV $29.95** *PAR*

Pajama Party 🎵🎵

Follow-up to "Bikini Beach" takes the party inside in this fourth entry in the popular "Beach Party" series. Plot is up to beach party realism. Funicello is Avalon-less (although he does have a cameo) so she falls for Martian Kirk instead. He's scouting for an alien invasion, but after he falls into Annette's lap decides to save the planet instead. Typical fluff with the usual beach movie faces present; look for a young Garr as a dancer. Followed by the classic "Beach Blanket Bingo." ♫It's That Kind of Day; There Has to Be a Reason; Where Did I Go Wrong?; Pajama Party; Beach Ball; Among the Young; Stuffed Animal.
1964 (*Family*) 82m/C Tommy Kirk, Annette Funicello, Elsa Lanchester, Harvey Lembeck, Jesse White, Jody McCrea, Donna Loren, Susan Hart, Bobbi Shaw, Cheryl Sweeten, Luree Holmes, Candy Johnson, Dorothy Lamour, Toni Basil, Teri Garr, Ben Lessy; *Cameos:* Buster Keaton, Frankie Avalon, Don Rickles; *D:* Don Weis; *W:* Louis M. Heyward; *M:* Les Baxter. **VHS, LV** *NO*

Palooka 🎵🎵♩

Counterjab to night of watching "Rocky" numbers 1 through 33 is this movie version of Ham Fisher's long-running comic strip "Joe Palooka." Jimmy Durante is at his very best as the fast-talking boxing manager who discovers Joe and coaches him for the big fight against the champ. Dated, but Durante will never fade. **Hound Advisory:** Roughhousing, alcohol use.
1934 (*G/Family*) 86m/B Jimmy Durante, Stuart Erwin, Lupe Velez, Robert Armstrong, Thelma Todd, William Cagney; *D:* Ben Stoloff. **VHS, Beta $19.95** *NOS, RXM, VYY*

Panda and the Magic Serpent 🎵🎵

Japanese cartoon feature based on a Chinese legend about a boy who finds a white snake his parents won't let him keep. The reptile is really an enchanted maiden, who falls in love with the boy when he grows up, though an evil wizard strives to keep them apart. Enter one heroic panda.
1975 (*Preschool-Primary*) 78m/C **VHS, Beta $29.00** *FHE*

The Paper 🎵🎵🎵

Another crowd pleaser from director Howard follows a red letter day in the life of an editor at the tabloid New York Sun (modeled on the trashy Post). Fresh, fast-moving script by the Koepp brothers (who appear as reporters) offers a fairly accurate portrayal of the business of journalism (including the "brisk" language), with a few Hollywood exceptions. Pace suffers from cutaways to life outside, while script and direction sometimes coast past targets. Propelled by a fine cast, with Keaton the focus as he juggles his personal and professional lives. Close is amusing as a managing editor married to her work, while Duvall is solid as the old newsroom warhorse. Tons of cameos, though those outside of the business may not notice them. **Hound Advisory:** Profanity; roughhousing.
1994 (*R/Sr. High-Adult*) 112m/C Michael Keaton, Robert Duvall, Marisa Tomei, Glenn Close, Randy Quaid, Jason Robards Jr., Jason Alexander, Spalding Gray, Catherine O'Hara, Lynne Thigpen; *D:* Ron Howard; *W:* David Koepp, Steven Koepp; *M:* Randy Newman. **VHS, LV** *MCA*

The Paper Bag Princess

Animated tale of a young girl who sets out to rescue the neighboring prince from a fierce dragon. Only the dragon turns out to be a lot more likeable than the boy-prince. Gentle lesson in not judging people based on outward appearance.
1993 (*Preschool-Primary*) 25m/C **VHS $12.95**

The Paper Chase 🎵🎵🎵

Students at Harvard Law School suffer and struggle through their first year. A realistic, sometimes acidly humorous look at Ivy League ambitions, with Houseman stealing the show as the tough professor. Wonderful adaptation of the John Jay Osborn novel which later became the basis for the acclaimed television series.
1973 (*PG/Jr. High-Adult*) 111m/C Timothy Bottoms, Lindsay Wagner, John Houseman, Graham Beckel, Edward Herrmann, James Naughton, Craig Richard Nelson, Bob Lydiard; *D:* James Bridges; *W:* James Bridges; *M:* John Williams. **Award Nominations:** Academy Awards '73: Best Adapted Screenplay, Best Sound; **Awards:** Academy Awards '73: Best Supporting Actor (Houseman); Golden Globe Awards '74: Best Supporting Actor (Houseman); National Board of Review Awards '73: Best Supporting Actor (Houseman). **VHS, Beta, LV $19.98** *FOX, BTV*

Paper Moon 🎵🎵🎵♩

Winning story set in 1930s Kansas, with Bible-wielding con artist Moses Pray stuck with a nine-year-old orphan who can see right through his scams. But little Addie (star O'Neal's daughter, Tatum) also watches out for him, and soon a paternal relationship develops in spite of their antagonism. Irresistible chemistry between the O'Neals helped Tatum grab the Oscar (she was the youngest actor at the time to take home a statue). Cinematically picturesque and cynical enough to keep overt sentimentalism away. Based on Joe David Brown's novel, "Addie Pray." **Hound Advisory:**

Addie chainsmokes; plus alcohol use, mature themes, offscreen sex, and violence.
1973 (PG/*Jr. High-Adult*) 102m/B Ryan O'Neal, Tatum O'Neal, Madeline Kahn, John Hillerman, Randy Quaid; **D:** Peter Bogdanovich; **W:** Alvin Sargent. **Award Nominations:** Academy Awards '73: Best Adapted Screenplay, Best Sound, Best Supporting Actress (Kahn); **Awards:** Academy Awards '73: Best Supporting Actress (O'Neal); National Board of Review Awards '73: 10 Best Films of the Year. **VHS, Beta, LV $49.95** *PAR, BTV*

Papillon 🎞🎞🎞

McQueen is a criminal sent to Devil's Island in the 1930s determined to escape from the Lemote prison. Hoffman is the swindler he befriends. A series of escapes and recaptures follow. Box-office winner based on the autobiographical writings of French thief Henri Charriere. Excellent portrayal of prison life and fine performances from the prisoners. Certain segments would have been better left on the cutting room floor. The film's title refers to the lead's butterfly tattoo.
1973 (PG/*Jr. High-Adult*) 150m/C Steve McQueen, Dustin Hoffman, Victor Jory, George Coulouris, Anthony Zerbe; **D:** Franklin J. Schaffner; **M:** Jerry Goldsmith. **VHS, Beta, LV $19.98** *FOX, WAR*

Parade 🎞🎞🎞

French comic filmmaker and mime artist Jacques Tati fashioned this as a loving tribute to the circus that can be savored by all ages, though grownups might better appreciate the rhythms and magical transformations of its show-within-a-show format. A European troupe puts on a three-ring circus, with Tati (refreshingly agile and limber compared to his trudging Mr. Hulot character) as both ringmaster and performer in a series of acts. Highlight: a portly gentleman from the audience tries again and again to mount a bucking donkey.
1974 (*Adult*) 85m/C Jacques Tati; **D:** Jacques Tati; **W:** Jacques Tati. **VHS, LV $29.95** *HMV, VYG, CRC*

The Paradine Case 🎞🎞🎞⊲

Passable Hitchcock romancer about a young lawyer who falls in love with the woman he's defending for murder, not knowing whether she is innocent or guilty. Script could be tighter and more cohesive. $70,000 of the $3 million budget were spent recreating the original Bailey courtroom. Based on the novel by Robert Hichens.
1947 (*Jr. High-Adult*) 125m/B Gregory Peck, Alida Valli, Ann Todd, Louis Jourdan, Charles Laughton, Charles Coburn, Ethel Barrymore, Leo G. Carroll; **D:** Alfred Hitchcock. **VHS, Beta, LV $19.98** *FOX*

Paradise 🎞🎞🎞

Ten-year-old Willard goes to the country to stay with his pregnant mother's married friends (real-life husband and wife Johnson and Griffith). From the outset it's clear that the couple's relationship is on the rocks, making the boy's assimilation all the more difficult, until he forms a charming relationship with a little girl who helps reconcile the adults. Largely predictable, this remake of the French film "Le Grand Chemin" works thanks to the surprisingly good work of its ensemble cast and gorgeous South Carolina scenery.

Hound Advisory: Mature themes - source of the couple's unhappiness is the recent death of their own child.
1991 (PG-13/*Jr. High-Adult*) 112m/C Melanie Griffith, Don Johnson, Elijah Wood, Thora Birch, Sheila McCarthy, Eve Gordon, Louise Latham, Greg Travis, Sarah Trigger; **D:** Mary Agnes Donoghue; **W:** Mary Agnes Donoghue; **M:** David Newman. **VHS, Beta $92.95** *TOU*

The Parent Trap 🎞🎞🎞⊲

Mills plays twin sisters Susan and Sharon who have never met until an accidental reunion at summer camp in this heartwarming comedy. Posing as each other to visit the other's households, they conspire to bring their divorced parents together again. Well-known Disney fluff, overlong but a source of fond false hopes for a generation of kids from broken homes. Based on the novel by Eric Kastner. Followed by several made-for-TV sequels featuring the now grown-up twins.
1961 (*Family*) 127m/C Hayley Mills, Maureen O'Hara, Brian Keith, Charlie Ruggles, Una Merkel, Leo G. Carroll; **D:** David Swift. **VHS, Beta, LV $19.99** *DIS*

Parenthood 🎞🎞🎞

Grown siblings struggle with various crises of parenthood in the same family; the nervous, newly divorced mother whose teenage daughter dates an irresponsible stock-car driver; a yuppie couple finding that their adolescent boy has deep psychological problems; a super dad who's a lousy husband; and the college drop-out who breezes into town towing a mixed-race son nobody knew about before. Genuinely warm ensemble comedy-drama that makes having children look like a nightmare, then a joy with a careful twist of storyline. Some of it treads sitcom territory (in fact it inspired a fast-faded network sitcom), but some fine family nuances and the life-affirming finale more than compensate. **Hound Advisory:** Profanity, mature themes, sex talk (including an incident with a vibrator), drug talk.
1989 (PG-13/*Jr. High-Adult*) 124m/C Steve Martin, Mary Steenburgen, Dianne Wiest, Martha Plimpton, Keanu Reeves, Tom Hulce, Jason Robards Jr., Rick Moranis, Harley Jane Kozak, Leaf (Joaquin Rafael) Phoenix, Paul Linke, Dennis Dugan; **D:** Ron Howard; **W:** Lowell Ganz, Babaloo Mandel, Ron Howard; **M:** Randy Newman. **VHS, Beta, LV $19.95** *MCA*

The Party 🎞🎞🎞

Somewhat overlooked Peter Sellers vehicle that looks like a preview of the spectacular damage the star would wreak in Blake Edwards' "Pink Panther" pics of the 1970s. Here he plays an Indian (as in Bombay) movie actor of colossal clumsiness, who is mistakenly invited to a lavish Hollywood party. Some brilliantly choreographed slapstick occurs as he bumbles around the posh mansion, compensating for outdated hippie-era references and a general lack of any other sort of plot. **Hound Advisory:** Alcohol use.
1968 (*Jr. High-Adult*) 99m/C Peter Sellers, Claudine Longet, Marge Champion, Sharron Kimberly, Denny Miller, Gavin MacLeod, Carol Wayne; **D:** Blake Edwards; **W:** Blake Edwards; **M:** Henry Mancini. **VHS $14.95** *MGM, TVC*

Pastime 🎞🎞🎞

Bittersweet baseball elegy set in the minor leagues in 1957. Roy, a boyish 41-year-old pitcher, can't face his impending

retirement and pals around with the team outcast, a 17-year-old rookie who's the franchise's first black player. The old pro ends up teaching the kid his championship moves. Beautifully written and acted, though quite sad as the likeable Roy enters his final inning. **Hound Advisory:** Ballpark profanity, alcohol use, roughhousing.
1991 (PG/*Sr. High-Adult*) 94m/C William Russ, Scott Plank, Glenn Plummer, Noble Willingham, Jeffrey Tambor, Deidre O'Connell; *D:* Robin B. Armstrong. VHS, LV $19.95 *COL*

Pat and Mike 𝄞𝄞𝄞

War of the sexes rages in this comedy about a leathery sports promoter who futilely attempts to train a woman for athletic competition. Tracy and Hepburn have fine chemistry, but supporting players contribute too. Watch for the first on-screen appearance of Bronson (then Charles Buchinski) as a crook.
1952 (*Family*) 95m/B Spencer Tracy, Katharine Hepburn, Aldo Ray, Jim Backus, William Ching, Sammy White, Phyllis Povah, Charles Bronson, Chuck Connors, Mae Clarke, Carl "Alfalfa" Switzer; *D:* George Cukor; *W:* Ruth Gordon, Garson Kanin. VHS, Beta, LV $19.98 *MGM*

Paul Bunyan

Paul and his huge blue ox Babe were the greatest pair of loggers in the west. Here Disney animation retells their tall tale in appropriate larger-than-life fashion.
1958 (*Primary-Jr. High*) 17m/C VHS, Beta $250.00 *DSN,, MTI*

P.C.U. 𝄞𝄞

Satire on campus political correctness follows freshman Tom Lawrence's (Young) adventures as he navigates the treacherous waters of Port Chester University (PCU). He falls in with the gang from the Pit, the militantly non-PC dorm, who encourage bizarre and offensive behavior. Essentially a modern update of "National Lampoon's Animal House," but without the brilliance; add half a bone for tackling the thorny sensitivity issue in a humorous way that parodies, but shouldn't offend. Actor Bochner's directorial debut. **Hound Advisory:** Profanity.
1994 (PG-13/*Sr. High-Adult*) 81m/C Jeremy Piven, Chris Young, David Spade, Sarah Trigger, Jessica Walter, Jon Favreau, Megan Ward, Jake Busey; *Cameos:* George Clinton; *D:* Hart Bochner; *W:* Adam Leff, Zak Penn; *M:* Steve Vai. VHS *FXV*

Peachboy

From Japan comes the story of the boy found living in a gigantic peach. A poor, barren couple discover Peachboy and raise him until he becomes a master warrior who conquers a clan of child- snatching ogres. Part of the "Rabbit Ears" series of worldwide stories read against glorious painted illustrations (rather than animation).
1991 (*Family*) 30m/C *M:* Ryuichi Sakamoto. VHS, Beta $9.95 *MVD, MCA, FCT*

The Peanut Butter Solution 𝄞𝄞𝄞

The second entry in Rock Demers' Tales for All is a wild piece of pure imagination that's slow to get started, then watch out! Eleven-year-old Michael looks in the window of a spooky house and sees something so frightful that his hair

falls out. Helpful ghosts leave a recipe for a magical hair-replacement ointment, but Michael uses too much of the key ingredient -peanut butter - and his follicles sprout at an uncontrollable rate. And that's only the beginning; hop aboard this delightful, all-ages film and enjoy the ride. **Hound Advisory:** One off-color joke about a kid who applies the peanut-butter solution to a more private hairless area.
1985 (PG/*Family*) 96m/C Matthew Mackay, Siluck Saysanasy, Alison Podbrey, Michael Maillot, Griffith Brewer, Michael Hogan, Helen Hughes; *D:* Michael Rubbo; *W:* Michael Rubbo; *M:* Lewis Furey. VHS, Beta $14.95 *NWV, STE, HHE*

Pecos Bill

Meet the man who used the Grand Canyon for a swimmin' hole, dug the Rio Grande and used the Texas panhandle for a fryin' pan. From Shelly Duvall's "Tall Tales and Legends" series. Originally made for cable television.
1986 (*Family*) 50m/C Steve Guttenberg, Martin Mull, Claude Akins, Rebecca DeMornay. VHS $19.98 *FOX, COL*

Pecos Bill

Disney cartoon version of the famous western folk hero raised by coyotes, narrated by another legend of the range. Bill manages to dig the Rio Grande and the Grand Canyon, and ride a cyclone.
1990 (*Preschool-Primary*) 17m/C VHS, Beta $250.00 *DSN, MTI*

Pecos Bill

Williams reads the text of the rollicking tall tales featuring frontier hero Pecos Bill roping cyclones and moving rivers. Musical accompaniment by Ry Cooder.
19?? (*Preschool-Primary*) 30m/C VHS $15.99 *MLT, KUI*

Pee Wee's Big Adventure 𝄞𝄞𝄞𝄞

Zany, endearing comedy about the infamously nerdy children's entertainer and his many adventures while attempting to recover his stolen bicycle. Full of classic sequences, including a barroom encounter between Pee Wee and several ornery bikers that leads to a musical number. A colorful, exhilarating experience, with amusing star cameos.
1985 (PG/*Primary-Jr. High*) 92m/C Paul (Pee Wee Herman) Reubens, Elizabeth Daily, Mark Holton, Diane Salinger, Judd Omen, Cassandra Peterson, James Brolin, Morgan Fairchild, Tony Bill, Jan Hooks; *D:* Tim Burton; *W:* Paul (Pee Wee Herman) Reubens, Phil Hartman, Michael Varhol; *M:* Danny Elfman. VHS, Beta, LV $19.98 *WAR*

Pee Wee's Playhouse Festival of Fun

The TV series had a crazy brilliance all its own, as the man-child Pee Wee romps with such self-mocking characters as the King of Cartoons, grumpy Captain Carl, handsome hunk Tito and the beautiful Miss Yvonne. This tape compilation includes five episodes; 15 volumes of individual half-hour episodes are also available. Note however, that "The Pee Wee Herman Show" on HBO Video, is an early, more risque stand-up comedy special for adults rather than youngsters.
1988 (*Family*) 123m/C Paul (Pee Wee Herman) Reubens. VHS, Beta $79.95 *MED*

Peggy Sue Got Married 🦴🦴🦴🎦

Uneven but entertaining comedy about an unhappily married middle-aged woman who takes a trip back in time. Turner's the Peggy Sue in question, and she's about to divorce her obnoxious hubby Cage. While attending her high school reunion, Turner falls unconscious and awakens to find herself back in school in 1960, with an opportunity to change her life. But will she? Film takes a fairly mature but entertaining look at the question, eschewing most of the ready-made time-traveling woman in a girl's body gimmicks. Turner shows considerable range in the dash from 43 to 17 and back again, while Cage is sufficiently annoying both as a teen and a middle-aged appliance salesman. **Hound Advisory:** Profanity and suggested sex.
1986 (PG-13/*Jr. High-Adult*) 103m/C Kathleen Turner, Nicolas Cage, Catherine Hicks, Maureen O'Sullivan, John Carradine, Helen Hunt, Lisa Jane Persky, Barbara Harris, Joan Allen, Kevin J. O'Connor, Barry Miller, Don Murray, Leon Ames, Sofia Coppola, Sachi Parker, Jim Carrey; *D:* Francis Ford Coppola; *W:* Jerry Leichtling, Arlene Sarner; *M:* John Barry. **VHS, Beta, LV $19.98** FOX

The Pelican Brief 🦴🦴

Tulane law student Darby Shaw (Roberts) writes a speculative brief on the murders of two Supreme Court justices that results in more murder and sends her running for her life. Fairly faithful to the Grisham bestseller, but the multitude of characters is confusing. Pakula adds style and star-power, but much will depend on your tolerance for paranoid political thrillers and ability to accept Roberts as the smart cookie who hits on the right answer and then manages to keep herself alive while bodies are dropping all around her. Washington is sharp as reporter Gray Grantham, the guy Roberts looks like she falls hard for (but the book's romance is nowhere to be seen). **Hound Advisory:** Violence; mature themes.
1993 (PG-13/*Jr. High-Adult*) 141m/C Julia Roberts, Denzel Washington, John Heard, Tony Goldwyn, Stanley Tucci, James B. Sikking, William Atherton, Robert Culp, John Lithgow, Sam Shepard; *Cameos:* Hume Cronyn; *D:* Alan J. Pakula; *W:* Alan J. Pakula; *M:* James Horner. **VHS, LV, 8mm** WAR

Penny Serenade 🦴🦴🦴

Newlyweds adopt a child, but tragedy awaits. Simplistic story nonetheless proves to be a moving experience. They don't make 'em like this anymore, and no one plays Grant better than Grant. Dunne is adequate. Also available colorized.
1941 (*Family*) 120m/B Cary Grant, Irene Dunne, Beulah Bondi, Edgar Buchanan; *D:* George Stevens. **VHS, LV $9.95** CNG, NOS, PSM

The People That Time Forgot 🦴🦴

Sequel to "The Land That Time Forgot" has rescue team returning to a world of prehistoric monsters to bring back a man left there after the first film. Silly adventure; a case of the plot that time forgot. **Hound Advisory:** Violence.
1977 (PG/*Jr. High-Adult*) 90m/C Doug McClure, Patrick Wayne, Sarah Douglas, Dana Gillespie, Thorley Walters, Shane Rimmer; *D:* Kevin Connor. **VHS, Beta $9.98** SUE

Pepper and His Wacky Taxi 🦴🎦

Astin, a favorite character actor thanks to his TV role as Gomez Addams, plays a more conventional father of four who buys a '59 Cadillac and starts a cab company. Mild fun with a curious cast.
1972 (G/*Family*) 79m/C John Astin, Frank Sinatra Jr., Jackie Gayle, Alan Sherman; *D:* Alex Grasshof. **VHS, Beta $19.95** UNI

A Perfect World 🦴🦴🎦

Butch Haynes (Costner) is an escaped con who takes 8-year-old fatherless Phillip (who's also a Jehovah's Witness) as a hostage in 1963 Texas, becoming surrogate father to the lad as they attempt to evade the law on the backroads. Meanwhile, amid the man-boy bonding, crusty Texas Ranger Red Garnett (Eastwood) is hot on their trail in a trailer with Dern as a sidekick. Unusual premise is twist on standard fugitive road picture, as director Eastwood tries to bring something new to the genre. Butch, played with wooden intensity by Costner, is portrayed as a bad guy, though very intelligent, who's blessed with a sense of morality, though a wee bit twisted. He's also very sensitive to the issue of child abuse, based on his relationship with his own father. Lowther is convincing as the needy little boy, one of the drama's strengths. Ambitious, disjointed, but interesting, with one of the longer death scenes in recent film history. Eastwood also cowrote one of the songs. **Hound Advisory:** Violence; salty language; implied attempted child molestation.
1993 (PG-13/*Sr. High-Adult*) 138m/C Kevin Costner, T.J. Lowther, Clint Eastwood, Laura Dern, Keith Szarabajka, Leo Burmester, Paul Hewitt, Bradley Whitford, Ray McKinnon, Wayne Dehart, Jennifer Griffin, Linda Hart; *D:* Clint Eastwood; *W:* John Lee Hancock; *M:* Lennie Niehaus. **VHS, LV $96.03** WAR

The Perils of Penelope Pitstop

Convoy of old Saturday-morning cartoons starring animated motorist Penelope Pitstop, who has to ward off the villainous Sylvester Sneekly while she drives in races around the world. Additional volumes available.
1969 (*Family*) 60m/C *V:* Janet Waldo, Paul Lynde, Mel Blanc, Paul Winchell, Don Messick. **VHS, Beta $19.95** WTA

The Perils of Problemina 🦴🦴

Animated film about ants saving their families from a rampaging anteater.
19?? (*Preschool-Primary*) 90m/C **VHS, Beta $59.98** LIV, WTA

Permanent Record 🦴🦴🎦

Two-years-later sequel to the hit horror-comedy finds eggs of the voracious aliens hatching, and the little monsters chew again on Grovers Bend, Kansas. Grimes, a youngster during the first encounter with the aliens, is back as a likeable teenager unfairly blamed by the community for the chaos, and the shape-changing space bounty hunters also return. Occasionally inspired; "Critters 3" & "4" are just video dead weight. **Hound Advisory:** Profanity, drugs, mature themes, but all for a noble cause. Profanity, brief nudity, occasionally gruesome violence.
1988 (PG-13/*Jr. High-Adult*) 92m/C Alan Boyce, Keanu Reeves, Michelle Meyrink, Jennifer Rubin, Pamela Gidley, Michael Elgart, Richard Bradford, Barry Corbin, Kathy Baker; *D:* Marisa Silver; *W:* Jarre Fees, Alice Liddle, Larry Ketron; *M:* Joe Strummer. **VHS, Beta, LV $89.95** PAR

Peter and the Magic Egg

Cartoon story of Amish farmers Mama and Papa Doppler who avoid losing their farm to greedy Tobias Tinwhiskers thanks to their mysterious foundling Peter Paas. Narrator Bolger was the Scarecrow from the classic "Wizard of Oz," is that why Tinwhiskers looks just like the Tin Woodman? Also on the tape with this animated TV special are two vintage Tex Avery 'toons, "Jerky Turkey" and Casper in "The Friendly Ghost."
1983 (*Preschool-Primary*) 60m/C *V:* Ray Bolger. **VHS, Beta $14.95** *FHE, MTI, WTA*

Peter and the Wolf

Puppeteer Jim Gamble uses a variety of marionettes to portray people, animals, and instruments in this tale based on Sergei Prokofiev's musical work. Prokofiev himself appears in puppet form to explain how a composer writes. Music performed by the Hamburg Symphony Orchestra.
1992 (*Preschool-Primary*) 30m/C **VHS $14.95** *BTV*

Peter and the Wolf

Animated version of the classic tale, narrated by "Wizard of Oz" Scarecrow Ray Bolger.
19?? (*Preschool-Jr. High*) 82m/C **VHS, Beta** *VES*

Peter Cottontail: How He Got His Hop

Puppet tale in which Peter wants to enter the Meadowlands Spring Talent Show but can't figure out what he's good at. An assortment of animals try to help him out (most amusing is a Bob Dylanesque dog poet). Marionette production from Jim Gamble, whose string creations can ride skateboards and even juggle, making them more clever than most people we know.
1993 (*Preschool-Primary*) 30m/C **VHS $14.95**

Peter Cottontail's Adventures

Peter loves to play practical jokes until no one wants to be his friend anymore, teaching him the importance of his Green Forest cohorts like Johnny and Polly Woodchuck, Jimmy Skunk, Chatterer Chipmunk, Reddy and Granny Fox, and Sammy Bluejay, all cartoon adaptations of the classic characters from Thornton W. Burgess. See also "Fables of the Green Forest."
1978 (*Preschool-Primary*) 70m/C **VHS, Beta $24.95** *FHE*

Peter Lundy and the Medicine Hat Stallion 🦴🦴◁

A teenaged Pony Express rider must outrun the Indians and battle the elements in order to carry mail from the Nebraska Territory to the West Coast in this made for TV film.
1977 (*Family*) 85m/C Leif Garrett, Mitchell Ryan, Bibi Besch, John Quade, Milo O'Shea; *D:* Michael O'Herlihy. **VHS, Beta $69.98** *LIV, VES, VTR*

Peter-No-Tail 🦴🦴◁

Tail-less kitten wins the Cats Mastership and the heart of Molly Cream-Nose. Animation with an all-star gallery of voices.
1983 (*Family*) 82m/C *V:* Ken Berry, Dom DeLuise, Richard Kline, Tina Louise, Larry Storch, June Lockhart. **VHS, Beta $59.95** *WTA*

Peter Pan 🦴🦴🦴

Disney classic about the great Pan, the boy who never grew up, who takes the younger members of the Darling family to Never Never Land for perilous adventures fighting Captain Hook. Wonderful animation and action, forgettable tunes (not to be confused with the Mark Charlap-Jule Stein songs popularized by Mary Martin on Broadway). Based on J.M. Barrie's book and play.
1953 (*G*/*Family*) 76m/C *D:* Hamilton Luske; *V:* Bobby Driscoll, Kathryn Beaumont, Hans Conried, Heather Angel, Candy Candido. **VHS, Beta, LV $24.99** *DIS, APD, HMV*

Peter Pan 🦴🦴🦴◁

A TV classic, this videotape of a performance of the 1954 Broadway musical, adapted from the J.M. Barrie classic, feature Martin in one of her most famous incarnations, as the boy who never wants to grow up. Songs include: "I'm Flying," "Neverland," and "I Won't Grow Up."
1960 (*Family*) 100m/C Mary Martin, Cyril Ritchard, Sondra Lee, Heather Halliday, Luke Halpin; *D:* Vincent J. Donehue. **VHS, Beta, LV $24.99** *GKK, COL, MLT*

Peter Pan & the Pirates: Demise of Hook

In an attempt to cash in on Peter Pan-a-mania (which never quite happened) with the release of Spielberg's movie "Hook," the Fox Television Networks aired this cartoon adventure series based on the J.M. Barrie characters battling Captain Hook in Neverland.
1992 (*Preschool-Primary*) 23m/C *V:* Tim Curry. **VHS $9.98** *FXV, WTA*

Peter Pan/Hiawatha

Two-volume set containing the classic fairy tales "Peter Pan" and "Hiawatha" in short animated form.
1990 (*Family*) 63m/C **VHS $14.95** *FHE*

Peter Rabbit and Other Tales

That crazy rabbit who gets his kicks out of invading farmer John's garden is back, along with some other classic children's stories from Beatrix Potter.
1990 (*Preschool-Primary*) 30m/C **VHS $7.95**

Pete's Dragon 🦴🦴◁

Elliott, an enormous, sometimes-invisible dragon with a penchant for clumsy heroics, accompanies poor orphan Pete, newly arrived in a fishing village while on the run from his nasty stepfamily. Energetic but hopelessly juvenile Disney epic, crammed full of forgettable songs (and one not so forgettable - Reddy's hit "Candle on the Water") and large-scale slapstick. Elliott the dragon appears in cartoon form,

"Peter Pan" arrives (1953)

while everything else is live-action, a technique perfected over a decade later with "Who Framed Roger Rabbit?" Main animator here is Disney dissident Don Bluth, who later formed his own 'toon studio. **Hound Advisory:** Alcohol use - lots of it early on, apparently in the belief that public drunkenness is the cutest thing. Even Elliott drains a flask.
1977 (G/*Family*) 128m/C Helen Reddy, Shelley Winters, Mickey Rooney, Jim Dale, Red Buttons, Sean Marshall, Jim Backus, Jeff Conaway; **D:** Don Chaffey; **W:** Malcolm Marmorstein; **V:** Charlie Callas. **VHS, Beta, LV $24.99** DIS, FCT, WTA

The Phantom Creeps

Evil Dr. Zorka, armed with a meteorite chunk which can bring an army to a standstill, provides the impetus for this enjoyable 12-episode serial. **Hound Advisory:** Violence.
1939 (*Family*) 235m/B Bela Lugosi, Dorothy Arnold, Robert Kent, Regis Toomey; **D:** Ford Beebe, Saul Goodkind. **VHS, Beta $19.95** NOS, SNC, VCN

The Phantom Empire

One of the strangest serials ever made. Publicity at the time claimed the writer dreamed up the story while doped with anesthesia at the dentist's! That's as good as any explanation, as singing cowboy Autry, playing himself, discovers that deep under his radio station/dude ranch is the lost kingdom of Murania, ruled by an evil queen and patrolled by robots (who look like the "Oz" Tin Man in aluminum stetsons). Gene fights life-or-death battles to prevent world conquest by the cloaked 'Thunder Riders' - but no matter how bad things get, Autry always manages to escape above ground in time for another song cue on his radio variety program. Really must be seen to be believed. In 12 episodes.
1935 (*Family*) 245m/B Gene Autry, Frankie Darro, Betsy King Ross, Smiley Burnette; **D:** B. Reeves Eason, Otto Brower. **VHS, Beta $19.95** NOS, SNC, VYY

Phantom of the Opera

Deformed, skull-faced masked man who lives under the Paris Opera House wants a young soprano to sing just for him in a cut-rate cartoon adaptation of the oft-redone Gaston Leroux novel.
1987 (*Family*) 60m/C **VHS, Beta, LV $9.99** JFK, WTA

Phantom Tollbooth 🦴🦴🦴

Milo, a live-action boy, drives his car into a cartoon world where the numbers are at war with the letters, and he has been chosen to save Rhyme and Reason to bring stability back to the Land of Wisdom. Completely unique; the first feature film from Warner Brothers animator Chuck Jones, it combines his Bugs-Bunny sense of mischief with more surreal and intellectual interests. Don't rule out adult viewers by any means. Based on Norman Justers' metaphorical novel.
1969 (G/*Family*) 89m/C **D:** Chuck Jones; **V:** Mel Blanc, Hans Conried. **VHS, Beta $19.95** MGM, WTA

Phar Lap 🦴🦴◁

"Free Willy" director Wincer made this factual saga of a legendary Australian racehorse who rose from obscurity to win nearly 40 races in just three years before tragically - and

suspiciously - dying in 1932 (Aussies still blame American gambling syndicates for the deed). **Hound Advisory:** Mature themes.
1984 (PG/*Family*) 107m/C Ron Leibman, Tom Burlinson, Judy Morris, Celia de Burgh; **D:** Simon Wincer; **W:** David Williamson. **VHS, Beta $14.98** FOX

Philadelphia 🦴🦴🦴◁

AIDS goes Hollywood as hot-shot corporate attorney Andrew Beckett (Hanks), fired because he has the disease, hires brilliant but homophobic personal injury attorney Washington as his counsel when he sues for discrimination with the support of his mate and close-knit family. Hanks claims the title as hottest actor in America with his moving, dignified portrayal of a dying man denied his basic rights and determined to fight. Washington is superb as well as the lawyer forced to acknowledge his own prejudices in order to present his client's case. Woodward and Robards lead an expert supporting cast. Criticized by some for sterilizing its homosexual element, drama doesn't probe deeply into the gay lifestyle, focusing instead on the human search for justice and compassion. Emotional operatic set piece with Hanks and Washington will likely land in classic vault. Demme directs with confidence in taking AIDS issue into mainstream entertainment, complete with soundtrack contributions from Neil Young and Bruce Springsteen. **Hound Advisory:** Derogatory slang for homosexuals; mature themes.
1993 (PG-13/*Jr. High-Adult*) 125m/C Tom Hanks, Denzel Washington, Antonio Banderas, Jason Robards Jr., Joanne Woodward, Mary Steenburgen, Ron Vawter, Robert Ridgely, Obba Babatunde, Robert Castle, Daniel Chapman, Roger Corman, John Bedford Lloyd, Roberta Maxwell, Warren Miller, Anna Deavere Smith, Kathryn Witt, Andre B. Blake, Ann Dowd, Bradley Whitford, Chandra Wilson, Charles Glenn, Peter Jacobs, Paul Lazar, Dan Olmstead, Joey Perillo, Lauren Roselli, Bill Rowe, Lisa Talerico, Daniel von Bargen, Tracey Walter; **Cameos:** Karen Finley, David Drake, Quentin Crisp; **D:** Jonathan Demme; **W:** Ron Nyswaner; **M:** Howard Shore. **Award Nominations:** Academy Awards '93: Best Makeup, Best Original Screenplay, Best Song ("Philadelphia"); MTV Movie Awards '94: Best Film, Best On-Screen Duo (Tom Hanks/Denzel Washington), Best Song ("Streets of Philadelphia"); **Awards:** Academy Awards '93: Best Actor (Hanks), Best Song ("Streets of Philadelphia"); Golden Globe Awards '94: Best Actor—Drama (Hanks), Best Song ("Streets of Philadelphia"). **VHS, LV, 8mm** COL

The Philadelphia Story 🦴🦴🦴🦴

Woman's plans to marry again go awry when her dashing ex-husband arrives on the scene. Matters are further complicated when a loopy reporter - assigned to spy on the nuptials - falls in love with the blushing bride. Classic comedy, with trio of Hepburn, Grant, and Stewart all serving aces. Based on the hit Broadway play by Philip Barry, and remade as the musical "High Society" in 1956 (stick to the original). Also available colorized.
1940 (*Family*) 112m/B Katharine Hepburn, Cary Grant, James Stewart, Ruth Hussey, Roland Young, John Howard, John Halliday, Virginia Weidler, Henry Daniell, Hillary Brooke, Mary Nash; **D:** George Cukor; **W:** Donald Ogden Stewart; **M:** Franz Waxman. **Award Nominations:** Academy Awards '40: Best Actress (Hepburn), Best Director (Cukor), Best Picture, Best Supporting Actress (Hussey); **Awards:** Academy Awards '40: Best Actor (Stewart), Best Screenplay. **VHS, Beta, LV $19.98** MGM, BTV, HMV

The Pickwick Papers 🦴🦴🦴◁

Feature-length TV cartoon version of the Charles Dickens novel about Samuel Pickwick, a wealthy tale-spinner who

founds a club for similar eccentrics in Victorian England. Pickwick welcomes adventure, but has an undesired one when a lawsuit gets him abruptly thrown into jail. Much of the picture is devoted to recreations of the spooky tales members of the Pickwick Club tell each other; these have been excerpted and expanded for a separate video title "Ghost Stories" (aka "Charles Dickens' Ghost Stories").
1985 *(Family)* 72m/C **VHS, Beta $19.98** *LIV*

Piece of the Action 𝄞𝄞⟁

Good-natured comedy finds an ex-cop tricking a safecracker and a con man (Cosby and Poitier) into supervising teen juvenile delinquents at a Chicago community center. **Hound Advisory:** Salty language
1977 *(PG/Jr. High-Adult)* 135m/C Sidney Poitier, Bill Cosby, James Earl Jones, Denise Nicholas, Hope Clarke, Tracy Reed, Tito Vandis, Ja'net DuBois; *D:* Sidney Poitier; *M:* Curtis Mayfield. **VHS, Beta $19.98** *WAR*

The Pied Piper/Cinderella

Double-feature of short puppet-animated tales by British stop-motion specialists. First is an excellent adaptation of Robert Browning's poem about the mystery minstrel who rids Hamlin town of its rats, then exacts a terrible price. Next is an attempt to do "Cinderella" entirely in wordless puppet pantomime, but the puppets aren't expressive enough, and this seg comes truly to life only when the fairy godmother is at large.
1981 *(Family)* 70m/C **VHS, Beta** *HBO*

The Pied Piper of Hamelin 𝄞𝄞⟁

Television version of the evergreen classic about the magical piper who rids a village of rats and then disappears with the village children into a mountain when the townspeople fail to keep a promise. Effective score and cast make it worthwhile.
1957 *(Family)* 90m/C Van Johnson, Claude Rains, Jim Backus, Kay Starr, Lori Nelson; *D:* Bretaigne Windust. **VHS, Beta $14.95** *KAR, NOS, MED*

The Pied Piper of Hamelin

Animated version of the Robert Browning poem, recited by Orson Welles.
1985 *(Family)* 18m/C **VHS, Beta** *CHF*

The Pigeon that Worked a Miracle

A pigeon is so loved by a boy that a miracle occurs when the bird forces him to walk again. A live-action episode of TV's "Wonderful World of Disney."
1990 *(Preschool-Primary)* 47m/C **VHS, Beta $250.00** *MTI, DSN*

The Pigs' Wedding and Other Stories

Five stories from the acclaimed "Children's Circle" series, illustrated with non-animated drawings. Includes "Pig's Wedding," "The Selkie Girl," "A Letter to Amy," "The Happy Owls," and "The Owl and the Pussycat."
1991 *(Family)* 39m/C **VHS $14.95** *CCC, FCT, BTV*

The Pinballs

Three displaced youths, in the same foster home, come to learn about understanding themselves and caring for others. An "Afterschool Special" TV adaptation of the novel by Betsy Byars.
1990 *(Primary-Sr. High)* 31m/C Kristy McNichol. **VHS, Beta $495.00** *MTI, DSN*

Pink Cadillac 𝄞𝄞⟁

A grizzled, middle-aged bondsman is on the road, tracking down bail-jumping crooks. He helps the wife and baby of his latest target escape from her husband's more evil associates. Eastwood's performance is good and fun to watch, in this otherwise lightweight film. **Hound Advisory:** Violence, profanity, suggested sex.
1989 *(PG-13/Jr. High-Adult)* 121m/C Clint Eastwood, Bernadette Peters, Timothy Carhart, Michael Des Barres, William Hickey, John Dennis Johnston, Geoffrey Lewis, Jim Carrey, Tiffany Gail Robinson, Angela Louise Robinson; *D:* Buddy Van Horn; *W:* John Eskow; *M:* Stephen Dorff. **VHS, Beta, LV, 8mm $19.98** *WAR*

The Pink Panther 𝄞𝄞𝄞

When the legendary Pink Panther diamond is stolen, disaster-prone Inspector Clouseau descends on a ski resort in search of the professional cat-burglar responsible. Fans of the slapstick epics of the 1970s will be disappointed that this opening installment is really a rather slow-paced romantic comedy, with more love triangles than sight gags. Sellers is a supporting character, with the spotlight on the charming Niven as the thief. Kids will likely be bored. Animated opening sequence originated the Pink Panther cartoon character. **Hound Advisory:** Alcohol use; sex talk.
1964 *(Family)* 113m/C Peter Sellers, David Niven, Robert Wagner, Claudia Cardinale, Capucine, Brenda de Banzie; *D:* Blake Edwards; *W:* Blake Edwards; *M:* Henry Mancini. **VHS, Beta, LV $19.98** *MGM, FOX, TVC*

The Pink Panther

The Pink Panther began life in the opening credits of a 1964 live-action caper comedy of the same name and was immediately judged popular enough for a series himself. This compilation includes his bigscreen outings like "Slink Pink," "Come On In! The Water's Pink," and more.
1988 *(Family)* 60m/C **VHS, Beta, LV $14.95** *MGM*

Pink Panther: Fly in the Pink

Classic cartoons from the debonair Pink Panther include "Pink Flea," "A Fly in the Pink," "Keep our Forest Pink," and "Pink in the Clink."
1966 *(Family)* 57m/C **VHS, Beta, 8mm $12.95** *MGM, WTA*

Pink Panther: Pink Christmas

TV cartoon Christmas special derived from O. Henry's tale "The Cop and the Anthem." This time the Pink Panther is cold and hungry on the streets of New York and, like many city residents, tries to get arrested to enjoy jailhouse food and shelter.
1989 *(Family)* 23m/C **VHS, Beta $14.95** *MGM, WTA*

The Pink Panther Strikes Again 🎵🎵🎵

The wackiest and best in the "Pink Panther" series, and the closest to a live-action cartoon. Incompetent Inspector Clouseau now must fight his former boss from the police force, who has been driven insane thanks to the bumbling sleuth and menaces the entire planet with a death ray. A must for anyone who appreciates slapstick. **Hound Advisory:** Roughhousing, sex talk.
1976 (PG/*Jr. High-Adult*) 103m/C Peter Sellers, Herbert Lom, Lesley-Anne Down, Colin Blakely, Leonard Rossiter, Burt Kwouk; *D:* Blake Edwards; *W:* Edwards Waldman, Frank Waldman; *M:* Henry Mancini. **VHS, Beta, LV** $19.95 *FOX, TVC*

Pink Panther: Tickled Pink

Nine Pink Panther cartoons, including "Tickled Pink," "Pink 8-Ball," and "G.I. Pink" are featured.
1970 (*Family*) 57m/C **VHS, Beta** $12.98 *MGM, WTA*

Pinocchio 🎵🎵🎵🎵

Walt Disney's second animated film is considered by some to be his best. Pinocchio, a little wooden puppet made by the old woodcarver Geppetto, is brought to life by a good fairy. Except Pinocchio isn't content to be just a puppet - he wants to become a real boy. Lured by a sly fox, Pinocchio has a number of adventures as he tries to return safely home. Classic has held up over time, but don't let it make you skip Carlo Collodi's original, often satirical Pinocchio tales. 🎵When You Wish Upon a Star; Give a Little Whistle; Turn on the Old Music Box; Hi-Diddle-Dee-Dee (An Actor's Life For Me); I've Got No Strings. **Hound Advisory:** Several scenes that might chill the wee small ones, like the nightmarish Pleasure Island where naughty boys change into donkeys, and a close encounter with Monstro the Whale.
1940 (G/*Family*) 87m/C *D:* Ben Sharpsteen; *V:* Dick Jones, Cliff Edwards, Evelyn Venable, Walter Catlett, Frankie Darro, Charles Judels, Don Brodie, Christian Rub. **VHS, Beta, LV** $24.99 *DIS, WTA*

Pinocchio

Lonely toymaker's finest creation is magically brought to life in this retelling of Carlo Collodi's story, animated with Brian Ajhar's illustrations. Music by the Les Miserables Brass Band. From the "Rabbit Ears: We All Have Tales" series.
1993 (*Family*) 30m/C **VHS** $9.95 *BTV, PMS*

Pinocchio and the Emperor of the Night 🎵🎵

Fast-forgotten theatrical cartoon sequel to the story of "Pinocchio," not from Disney but by an outfit responsible for plenty of bland Saturday-morning animation. It's Pinocchio's one-year anniversary as a real boy, and Gepetto sends him (and a Jiminy Cricket clone) on an errand. Just like last time, the little hero gets sidetracked, hoodwinked, and takes a long journey with a sinister circus. There are songs, but nothing that can touch "When You Wish Upon a Star."
1987 (*Preschool-Primary*) 91m/C *D:* Hal Sutherland; *V:* William Windom, Tom Bosley, Ed Asner, Don Knotts, James Earl Jones, Rickie Lee Jones. **VHS, Beta, LV** $19.95 *STE, NWV, WTA*

Pinocchio in Outer Space

Dim-witted Belgian-American feature cartoon stars a blond Pinocchio, turned back into a puppet and sent on a musical, rocketship-age rerun of the original plot. Now for instance it's Astro the cosmic whale who swallows him, get it? Not exactly stellar entertainment.
1964 (*Family*) 71m/C *D:* Ray Goosens; *V:* Arnold Stang, Minerva Pious, Peter Lazer, Conrad Jameson. **VHS, Beta** $19.95 *COL, WTA*

Pinocchio's Christmas

Puppet-animated holiday TV special from the Rankin-Bass workshop, wherein Pinocchio finds romance and adventures while trying to raise money for a present for Geppetto.
1983 (*Family*) 60m/C *V:* Alan King, George S. Irving. **VHS, Beta** $14.95 *LIV, VES, WTA*

Pippi Goes on Board 🎵🎵

Fourth and final adventure in the popular Swedish-German series of Pippi Longstocking films of the 1970s finds Pippi's sea captain father arriving to take her to Taka-Kuka, his island kingdom. She can't bear to leave her landlubber friends and jumps ship to return home. Like all the features in the series, it's garishly photographed and poorly dubbed into English, but Pippi partisans probably won't notice; the films did well with small kids. Based on the books by Astrid Lindgren.
1971 (G/*Family*) 83m/C Inger Nilsson; *D:* Olle Hellbron. **VHS, Beta** $19.95 *GEM, MOV, TPV*

Pippi in the South Seas 🎵🎵

The indomitable Pippi Longstocking and her pals Tommy and Anneka journey to rescue Capt. Ephraim Longstocking, Pippi's father, a captive of pirates on a South Sea island. Naturally, clever Pippi saves the day. Badly dubbed and edited Swedish-German production that followed the first "Pippi Longstocking," redubbed for the poor English-speaking market in 1975.
1968 (G/*Family*) 99m/C Inger Nilsson; *D:* Olle Hellbron. **VHS, Beta** $19.95 *GEM, MOV, TPV*

Pippi Longstocking 🎵🎵

This little red-pigtailed tomboy became a favorite with kids thanks to the "Pippie Langstrumpf" books of Astrid Lindgren -and thanks to a garish series of Swedish-German kiddie pictures, released in the U.S. throughout the '70s. Separated from her seagoing father, Pippi descends on her hometown, creating havoc through her pets, pranks and feats of superhuman strength. The story is a rickety affair, f/x are terrible, and bad English dubbing hurts the ears, but one still sees why Pippi captivates kids - she lives just the way she wants and makes even household chores fun. Adults may just find her obnoxious. Followed by "Pippi in the South Seas," "Pippi on the Run," "Pippi Goes on Board," and the Yankee remake "New Adventures of Pippi Longstocking."
1968 (G/*Family*) 99m/C Inger Nilsson; *D:* Olle Hellbron. **VHS, Beta** $19.95 *GEM, MOV, TPV*

Pinocchio meets Jiminy Cricket (1940)

Pippi on the Run 🦴🦴

Third in the Swedish-German Astrid Lindgren adaptations finds Pippi Longstocking on the trail of two friends who have run away from home. The three have many poorly dubbed adventures before deciding home is best.
1970 (G/Family) 99m/C VHS, Beta $19.99 GEM, MOV, TPV

Pippin 🦴🦴🦴

Video version of the stage musical about the adolescent son of Charlemagne finding true love as well as the perils of leadership. Adequate recording of Bob Fosse's Broadway smash features Vereen recreating his original Tony Award-winning role.
1981 (Jr. High-Adult) 120m/C Ben Vereen, William Katt, Martha Raye, Chita Rivera. VHS, Beta, LV $29.95 VCI, FHE, FCT

Pirate Movie 🦴🦴

Gilbert and Sullivan's "The Pirates of Penzance" is combined with new pop songs in this tale of fantasy and romance. Feeble attempt to update a musical that was fine the way it was. **Hound Advisory:** Salty language; sex talk.
1982 (PG/Jr. High-Adult) 98m/C Kristy McNichol, Christopher Atkins, Ted Hamilton, Bill Kerr, Garry McDonald; D: Ken Annakin. VHS, Beta $59.95 FOX

Pirates of Dark Water: The Saga Begins

Feature-length pilot of Hanna-Barbera's original cartoon series for the Fox Network, and it looks like this time they dreamt a fantastic world BEFORE planning the toys. Only Prince Ren and his bandit band can save the ocean-covered planet of Mer from the plague of Black Water (yes, more eco-propaganda), but to gather the antidote they combat the cruel pirate tyrant Bloth. Splendid production design (Asian animators helped out, natch), mediocre characters, pretty confusing story.
1991 (Family) 90m/C VHS, Beta $29.95 TTC, WTA

The Pirates of Penzance 🦴🦴

Gilbert and Sullivan's comic operetta is the story of a band of fun-loving pirates, their reluctant young apprentice, the "very model of a modern major general," and his lovely daughters. Less-than-inspired adaptation of Joseph Papp's award-winning Broadway play.
1983 (G/Family) 112m/C Kevin Kline, Angela Lansbury, Linda Ronstadt, Rex Smith, George Rose; D: Wilford Leach. VHS, Beta, LV $19.98 MCA, FOX

Pistol: The Birth of a Legend 🦴🦴🦴

Wholesome, authorized biography of "Pistol" Pete Maravich, the basketball star who defied age limitations in the 1960s to play on his varsity team. Solidly told, though sadly, Maravich died unexpectedly soon after this was completed.
1990 (G/Family) 104m/C Adam Guier, Nick Benedict, Boots Garland, Millie Perkins; D: Frank C. Schroeder. VHS, Beta $19.95 COL

P.K. and the Kid 🦴🦴

A runaway kid meets up with a factory worker on his way to an arm wrestling competition and they become friends.
1985 (Family) 90m/C Molly Ringwald, Paul LeMat, Alex Rocco, John Madden, Esther Rolle; D: Lou Lombardo; M: James Horner. VHS, Beta, LV $79.95 LHV, WAR

Places in the Heart 🦴🦴🦴🦴

After her lawman husband's sudden murder, a young widow strives to bring in her farm's vital cotton crop in Depression-era Texas. Support comes from her kids, a blind veteran, and a black drifter. Plot threatens to become just one disaster after another (including a scary tornado) but succeeds thanks to strong performances and an unforgettable final scene stressing love and Christian forgiveness. **Hound Advisory:** Violence.
1984 (PG/Jr. High-Adult) 113m/C Sally Field, John Malkovich, Danny Glover, Ed Harris, Lindsay Crouse, Amy Madigan, Terry O'Quinn; D: Robert Benton; W: Robert Benton; M: Howard Shore. **Award Nominations:** Academy Awards '84: Best Costume Design, Best Director (Benton), Best Picture, Best Supporting Actor (Malkovich), Best Supporting Actress (Crouse); **Awards:** Academy Awards '84: Best Actress (Field), Best Original Screenplay; Golden Globe Awards '85: Best Actress—Drama (Field). VHS, Beta, LV $19.98 FOX, BTV, HMV

Plain Clothes 🦴

Though Coolidge directed the surprisingly empathetic teen flick "Valley Girl," this has none of that pic's redeeming qualities. Undercover cop masquerades as a high schooler to free his own kid brother from a charge of murdering a teacher. The student characters are just scenery, while the adult school faculty are crooks and loonies. **Hound Advisory:** The MPAA must have been cutting class the day of the screening, for they assigned a mild PG to this smarmy whodunit despite lots of profanity, sex talk, violence, mature themes.
1988 (PG/Jr. High-Adult) 98m/C Arliss Howard, George Wendt, Suzy Amis, Diane Ladd, Seymour Cassel, Larry Pine, Jackie Gayle, Abe Vigoda, Robert Stack; D: Martha Coolidge; M: Scott Wilk. VHS, Beta $14.95 PAR

Planet of the Apes 🦴🦴🦴🦴

Astronauts crash land on a planet where apes are masters and humans are merely brute animals. Superior science fiction with sociological implications marred only by unnecessary humor. Heston delivers one of his more plausible performances. Superb ape makeup creates realistic pseudo-simians of McDowall, Hunter, Evans, Whitmore, and Daly. Adapted from Pierre Boulle's novel "Monkey Planet." Followed by four sequels and two television series. **Hound Advisory:** Violence.
1968 (G/Family) 112m/C Charlton Heston, Roddy McDowall, Kim Hunter, Maurice Evans, Linda Harrison, James Whitmore, James Daly; D: Franklin J. Schaffner; W: Rod Serling, Michael G. Wilson; M: Jerry Goldsmith. **Award Nominations:** Academy Awards '68: Best Costume Design, Best Original Score; **Awards:** National Board of Review Awards '68: 10 Best Films of the Year. VHS, Beta, LV $19.98 FOX, FUS

Planet of the Dinosaurs 🦴🦴

Spaceship crashes on a prehistoric planet, and the human survivors must put aside their considerable squabbles about what to do next to fight for survival against hungry Earth-

style dinosaurs. Good stop-motion dinosaur f/x done on a minuscule budget; it's the acting and dialogue that seem fossilized. **Hound Advisory:** Violence; alcohol use.
1980 (PG/*Family*) 85m/C James Whitworth; *D:* James K. Shea. **VHS, Beta $39.95** *AHV, VTR*

Plastic Man

With his amazing ability to mold and stretch himself into any shape, Plastic Man stretches himself into new dimensions to fight evil and play with Baby Plas. Standard Saturday-morning cartoon stuff adapted from a well-regarded satirical comic book.
1981 (*Preschool-Primary*) 56m/C **VHS, Beta $5.99** *WOV, WTA*

Play-Along Video: Hey, You're as Funny as Fozzie Bear

Henson's Muppets star in one of a series of humorous, educational videos designed to capture the attention and imagination of pre-school and young children. This one offers a lesson in joketelling.
1989 (*Preschool-Primary*) 30m/C Jim Henson's Muppets. **VHS $14.99** *LHV*

Play-Along Video: Mother Goose Stories

Muppet video for young children that both enlightens and entertains.
1989 (*Preschool-Primary*) 30m/C Jim Henson's Muppets. **VHS $14.99** *LHV*

Play-Along Video: Sing-Along, Dance-Along, Do-Along

Music-oriented edition of the participatory Muppet videocassettes.
1989 (*Preschool-Primary*) 30m/C Jim Henson's Muppets. **VHS $14.99** *LHV*

Play-Along Video: Wow, You're a Cartoonist!

Young children can have lots of fun learning how to draw with the Muppet gang. Basic animation using a flip-book is also covered.
1989 (*Preschool-Primary*) 30m/C Jim Henson's Muppets. **VHS $14.99** *LHV*

Play It Again, Sam 🦴🦴🦴◁

Allen is—no surprise—a nerd, and this time he's in love with his best friend's wife. Modest storyline provides a framework of endless gags, with Allen borrowing heavily from "Casablanca." Bogey even appears periodically to counsel Allen on the ways of wooing women. Superior comedy isn't hurt by Ross directing instead of Allen, who adapted the script from his own play.
1972 (PG/*Adult*) 85m/C Woody Allen, Diane Keaton, Tony Roberts, Susan Anspach, Jerry Lacy, Jennifer Salt, Joy Bang, Viva, Herbert Ross; *D:* Herbert Ross; *M:* Billy Goldenberg. **VHS, Beta, LV, 8mm $19.95** *PAR*

Playbox 1

Elementary entertainment for the very young, consisting of mime and live-action tricks mixed with animation of all shapes and styles.
1982 (*Preschool-Primary*) 30m/C Brian Rix. **VHS, Beta** *FHE*

The Playboys 🦴🦴🦴

In 1957 in a tiny Irish village, unmarried Tara Maguire causes a scandal by having a baby. Her beauty attracts lots of men-there's a former beau who kills himself, the obsessive, middle-aged Sergeant Hegarty, and the newest arrival, Tom Castle, an actor with a rag-tag theatrical troupe called the Playboys. Slow-moving and simple story with particularly good performances by Wright as the strong-willed Tara and Finney as Hegarty, clinging to a last chance at love and family. The Playboys' hysterically hammy version of "Gone With the Wind" is a gem. Directorial debut of Mackinnon. Filmed in the village of Redhills, Ireland, the hometown of co-writer Connaughton. **Hound Advisory:** Profanity and violence.
1992 (PG-13/*Sr. High-Adult*) 114m/C Albert Finney, Aidan Quinn, Robin Wright, Milo O'Shea, Alan Devlin, Niamh Cusack, Ian McElhinney, Niall Buggy, Adrian Dunbar; *D:* Gilles Mackinnon; *W:* Shane Connaughton, Kerry Crabbe; *M:* Jean-Claude Petit. **VHS $92.99** *HBO, FCT*

Playtime 🦴🦴🦴

Leisurely comedy in which bemused Frenchman Mr. Hulot goes to the city to meet relatives living in a see-through apartment, then tries to keep an appointment in a vast, impersonal office building. Mostly pantomime and slapstick, with a small amount of (English) dialogue. Quite slow-paced as it makes the point about an absurd concrete-and-glass modern civilization, and small viewers might be bored, but there are immortal comic whimsies. The traffic circle that turns into a merry-go-round is not to be missed. Third in Tati's Hulot series; see also "Mr. Hulot's Holiday" and "Mon Oncle." **Hound Advisory:** Alcohol use.
1967 (*Family*) 108m/C Jacques Tati, Barbara Dennek, Jacqueline Lecomte, Jack Gautier; *D:* Jacques Tati. **VHS, Beta $29.98** *SUE, INJ, NLC*

Please Don't Eat the Daisies 🦴🦴◁

Drama critic and family flee the Big Apple for the country and are traumatized by flora and fauna. Goofy sixties fluff taken from Jean Kerr's book and play and the basis for the eventual TV series.
1960 (*Family*) 111m/C Doris Day, David Niven, Janis Paige, Spring Byington, Richard Haydn, Patsy Kelly, Jack Weston, Margaret Lindsay; *D:* Charles Walters. **VHS, Beta, LV $19.98** *MGM, FCT*

Pluto

Collection of Plutonian escapades with the Disney cartoon dog include "The Pointer," "Bone Trouble," "Private Pluto," "Camp Dog," and "The Legend of Coyote Rock."
1950 (*Family*) 52m/C **VHS, Beta** *DIS*

Pluto (limited gold edition)

Pluto and pals Dinah the Dachshund and Butch the Bulldog star in a number of adventures including "Pluto at the Zoo" and "Pluto Junior."
1950 *(Family)* 47m/C **VHS, LV** *DIS*

Pluto's Christmas Tree

Pluto is driven batty when the tree that Mickey Mouse chops down for Christmas turns out to be Chip 'n' Dale's home.
1952 *(Preschool-Primary)* 7m/C **VHS, Beta $160.00** *MTI, DSN*

Poetic Justice 𝄞𝄞↲

Justice (Jackson in her movie debut, for better or worse) gives up college plans to follow a career in cosmetology after her boyfriend's brutal murder. She copes with her loss by dedicating herself to poetry writing (provided by no less than poet Maya Angelou) and meets postal worker Shakur. Singleton's second directorial effort is less bleak than his stunning debut but not as assured. Production stopped on the South Central L.A. set during the '92 riots, but the aftermath provided poignant pictures for later scenes. **Hound Advisory:** Profanity; violence; sex.
1993 *(R / Sr. High-Adult)* 109m/C Janet Jackson, Tupac Shakur, Tyra Ferrell, Regina King, Joe Torry; *D:* John Singleton; *W:* John Singleton; *M:* Stanley Clarke. **Award Nominations:** Academy Awards '93: Best Song ("Again"); Golden Globe Awards '94: Best Song ("Again"); **Awards:** MTV Movie Awards '94: Best Actress (Jackson), Most Desirable Female (Jackson). **VHS, LV, 8mm** *COL, BTV*

Pogo for President: "I Go Pogo" 𝄞𝄞↲

Stop-motion animated feature of Walt Kelly's comic-strip character Pogo Possum. He becomes an unlikely and unwilling presidential candidate when ambitious Howland Owl proclaims him the winner of an election. Dull songs, fine cast of voices. Puppetry is exceptionally faithful to Kelly's concepts, but will kids comprehend the heavy-duty political satire? Exists on video in two versions, the original and a later re-edited edition with added narration. Either one could have been G-rated with no problems.
1980 *(PG / Family)* 84m/C *V:* Jonathan Winters, Vincent Price, Ruth Buzzi, Stan Freberg, Jimmy Breslin. **VHS, Beta $49.95** *DIS, WTA*

The Point 𝄞𝄞𝄞↲

Charming, lyrical, and timeless made-for-television animated fable, with a father reading his son the story of Oblio, a round-headed child who's a misfit in his world of pointy-headed people. Exiled to the Pointless Forest, Oblio and his dog Arrow learn that "you don't have to have a point to have a point." Excellent score written and performed by Harry Nilsson.
1971 *(Family)* 74m/C *D:* Fred Wolf; *M:* Harry Nilsson. **VHS, Beta, LV $14.98** *FHE, VES, WTA*

The Polar Bear King 𝄞𝄞

Prince refuses to marry the evil witch of Summerland, so she turns him into a polar bear. Only through the long-term love of a maiden can the Polar Bear King be restored to humanity.

Jim Henson's workshop designed the title beast; too bad they didn't rewrite the script as well, a ponderous tale sorely lacking in traditional Muppet playfulness and humor. Scandinavian co-production based on Norse folklore. **Hound Advisory:** Alcohol use.
1994 *(PG / Jr. High-Adult)* 87m/C Maria Bonnerie, Jack Fjeldstad, Tobias Hoesl, Anna-Lotta Larsson; *D:* Ola Solum. **VHS, LV $19.95** *HMD*

Police Academy 𝄞𝄞

In an attempt to recruit more cops, a big-city police department does away with all its job standards. The producers probably didn't know that they were introducing bad comedy's answer to the "Friday the 13th" series, but it's hard to avoid heaping the sins of its successors on this film. Besides, it's just plain dumb. **Hound Advisory:** Roughhousing, profanity, sex talk.
1984 *(R / Sr. High-Adult)* 96m/C Steve Guttenberg, Kim Cattrall, Bubba Smith, George Gaynes, Michael Winslow, Leslie Easterbrook, Georgina Spelvin, Debralee Scott; *D:* Hugh Wilson; *W:* Hugh Wilson, Pat Proft, Neal Israel; *M:* Robert Folk. **VHS, Beta, LV, 8mm $19.98** *WAR*

Police Academy 2: Their First Assignment 𝄞

More predictable idiocy from the cop shop. This time they're determined to rid the precinct of some troublesome punks. No real story to speak of, just more high jinks in this mindless sequel. **Hound Advisory:** Profanity.
1985 *(PG-13 / Jr. High-Adult)* 87m/C Steve Guttenberg, Bubba Smith, Michael Winslow, Art Metrano, Colleen Camp, Howard Hesseman, David Graf, George Gaynes; *D:* Jerry Paris; *W:* Barry W. Blaustein. **VHS, Beta, LV $19.98** *WAR*

Police Academy 3: Back in Training 𝄞

In yet another sequel, the bumbling cops find their alma mater is threatened by a budget crunch and they must compete with a rival academy to see which school survives. The "return to school" plot allowed the filmmakers to add new characters to replace those who had some scruples about picking up yet another "Police Lobotomy" check. Followed by three more sequels. **Hound Advisory:** Salty language; violence.
1986 *(PG / Jr. High-Adult)* 84m/C Steve Guttenberg, Bubba Smith, David Graf, Michael Winslow, Marion Ramsey, Art Metrano, Bob(cat) Goldthwait, Leslie Easterbrook, Tim Kazurinsky, George Gaynes, Shawn Weatherly; *D:* Jerry Paris; *W:* Gene Quintano; *M:* Robert Folk. **VHS, Beta, LV $19.98** *WAR*

Police Academy 4: Citizens on Patrol 𝄞

The comic cop cutups from the first three films aid a citizen's patrol group in their unnamed, but still wacky, hometown. Moronic high jinks ensue. Fourth in the series of five (or is it six?) that began with "Police Academy". **Hound Advisory:** Mild profanity.
1987 *(PG / Jr. High)* 88m/C Steve Guttenberg, Bubba Smith, Michael Winslow, David Graf, Tim Kazurinsky, George Gaynes, Colleen Camp, Bob(cat) Goldthwait, Sharon Stone; *D:* Jim Drake; *W:* Gene Quintano; *M:* Robert Folk. **VHS, Beta, LV $19.98** *WAR*

Police Academy 5: Assignment Miami Beach WOOF!

The fourth sequel, wherein the misfits-with-badges go to Miami and bumble about in the usual manner. It's about time these cops were retired from the force. **Hound Advisory:** Salty language.
1988 (PG/*Jr. High-Adult*) 89m/C Bubba Smith, David Graf, Michael Winslow, Leslie Easterbrook, Rene Auberjonois, Marion Ramsey, Janet Jones, George Gaynes, Matt McCoy; **D:** Alan Myerson; **M:** Robert Folk. **VHS, Beta, LV $19.98** *WAR*

Police Academy 6: City Under Siege 🦴

In what is hoped to be the last in a series of bad comedies, the distinguished graduates pursue three goofballs responsible for a crime wave. **Hound Advisory:** Violence and profanity.
1989 (PG/*Jr. High-Adult*) 85m/C Bubba Smith, David Graf, Michael Winslow, Leslie Easterbrook, Marion Ramsey, Matt McCoy, Bruce Mahler, G.W. Bailey, George Gaynes; **D:** Peter Bonerz; **M:** Robert Folk. **VHS, LV $89.95** *WAR*

Police Academy, the Series

Purveyors of the animated "Rambo" also coughed up this TV cartoon series based on the profitable, mutton-headed comedy film franchise. Episodes include: "The Good, the Bad, and the Bogus" and "Cops and Robots." Additional volumes available.
1989 (*Primary*) 33m/C **VHS, Beta $12.95** *WAR, WTA*

Pollyanna 🦴🦴🦴⌐

Based on the Eleanor Porter story about an enchanting young girl whose contagious enthusiasm and zest for life touches the hearts of all she meets in her all-American town in the early 1900s. Mills is perfect in the title role and was awarded a special Oscar for outstanding juvenile performance. Distinguished supporting cast is the icing on the cake in this delightful Disney confection. Silent version filmed in 1920 with Mary Pickford is also on tape.
1960 (*Family*) 134m/C Hayley Mills, Jane Wyman, Richard Egan, Karl Malden, Nancy Olson, Adolphe Menjou, Donald Crisp, Agnes Moorehead, Kevin Corcoran; **D:** David Swift. **VHS, Beta, LV $19.99** *DIS, BTV*

Poltergeist 🦴🦴🦴⌐

He's listed only as co-writer and co-producer, but this production has Steven Spielberg written all over it. Young family's home becomes a house of horrors when menacing spirits contact, then abduct their five-year-old daughter...through the TV screen! Rollercoaster thrills and chills, dazzling special effects, perfectly timed humor and a family you care about highlight this stupendous ghost story. **Hound Advisory:** Spooky stuff successfully pushes every panic button ever, from tornadoes to rotting corpses to a child's fear of clowns, but no real casualties result. Mom and dad do smoke marijuana, though.
1982 (PG/*Sr. High-Adult*) 114m/C JoBeth Williams, Craig T. Nelson, Beatrice Straight, Heather O'Rourke, Zelda Rubinstein, Dominique Dunne, Oliver Robbins, Richard Lawson, James Karen; **D:** Tobe Hooper; **W:** Steven Spielberg, Michael Grais, Mark Victor; **M:** Jerry Goldsmith. **VHS, Beta, LV $19.98** *MGM*

Poltergeist 2: The Other Side 🦴🦴

Adequate sequel to the Spielberg-produced venture into the supernatural, where restless ghosts - explained in hackneyed terms as a 19th-century suicide cult - still hunt the Freelings to recapture the clairvoyant little daughter Carol Anne. In the climax, her family dives into the afterlife themselves to rescue her, encountering monsters galore. Script gets credit for attempting to depict the strain of demon attacks on family relationships, but visual effects and measured scares are the point here, not high drama. **Hound Advisory:** Supernatural violence. Flick could actually put people off alcohol; Mr. Freeling swills tequila, and the worm in the bottle gets possessed, causing him to barf up a 'vomit creature.'
1986 (PG-13/*Jr. High-Adult*) 92m/C Craig T. Nelson, JoBeth Williams, Heather O'Rourke, Will Sampson, Julian Beck, Geraldine Fitzgerald, Oliver Robbins, Zelda Rubinstein; **D:** Brian Gibson; **W:** Mark Victor, Michael Grais; **M:** Jerry Goldsmith. **VHS, Beta, LV $14.95** *MGM*

Poltergeist 3 🦴🦴⌐

Wrestling with the supernatural has unnerved little Carol Ann and she's sent to stay with her aunt and uncle in a modern high-rise apartment and attend a school for disturbed children. Evil ghosts follow her, and meanie psychotherapists don't believe her spook stories until it's too late. Flat acting, worn-out premise, paltry f/x finally exorcise the series. Dedicated to 12-year-old child actress O'Rourke, who died from an intestinal disorder before the theatrical release. **Hound Advisory:** Violence, salty language. Climax features many of the supporting characters turned into rotting skeletons, but if they're good guys, they get to change back to normal.
1988 (PG-13/*Jr. High-Adult*) 97m/C Tom Skerritt, Nancy Allen, Heather O'Rourke, Lara Flynn Boyle, Zelda Rubinstein; **D:** Gary Sherman; **W:** Brian Taggert. **VHS, Beta, LV $14.95** *MGM*

Pontoffel Pock, Where Are You?

Dr. Seuss cartoon features the hapless Pontoffel, whose magic piano can transport him though time and space.
1991 (*Primary*) 30m/C **VHS $9.95** *RAN, WTA, BTV*

Pony Express Rider 🦴🦴🦴

Young Jimmy joins up with the Pony Express hoping to bag the varmint responsible for killing his pa. Well-produced script boasts a bevy of veteran western character actors, all lending rugged performances. From the producers of "Where the Red Fern Grows."
1976 (G/*Family*) 100m/C Stewart Peterson, Henry Wilcoxon, Buck Taylor, Maureen McCormick, Joan Caulfield, Ken Curtis, Slim Pickens, Dub Taylor, Jack Elam; **D:** Robert Totten. **VHS** *TPI*

Poochie

Toy-inspired cartoon. Poochie is a pink pup newspaper columnist who travels to Cairo with her robot sidekick Hermes to answer a young boy's distress call. Toy store receipts were apparently insufficient to justify a return visit from Poochie; even the last part of this cassette is devoted to some unrelated 'toons starring the winged horse Luna.
1984 (*Preschool-Primary*) 30m/C **VHS, Beta $29.98** *LIV, WTA*

Pooh Learning: Helping Others

"Owl's Well That Ends Well" has Pooh and Piglet trying to teach Owl to sing. "A Very, Very Large Animal" turns out to be Piglet, at least to some very small ants. In "Caws and Effects," Pooh does his best to help Rabbit's harvest and in "To Dream the Impossible Scheme," Gopher and the gang learn dreams don't always have to come true.
1994 (*Preschool*) 40m/C **VHS** *DIS*

Pooh Learning: Making Friends

In "Cloud, Cloud Go Away," Tigger makes friends with a lonely cloud and in "The Bug Stops Here," Christopher Robin discovers an irresistible insect. Piglet's good work turns out to be its own reward in "Tigger's the Mother of Invention."
1994 (*Preschool*) 45m/C **VHS** *DIS*

Pooh Learning: Sharing and Caring

"Lights Out" has Rabbit borrowing Gopher's head lamp and learning a lesson about sharing. In "The Rats Who Came to Dinner," everyone turns to Pooh for help when there's a big rainstorm, and in "No Rabbit's a Fortress," Rabbit is taught a lesson about trusting his friends.
1994 (*Preschool*) 45m/C **VHS** *DIS*

Pooh Playtime: Cowboy Pooh

"The Good, the Bad and the Tigger" is about a mysterious train robbery that causes Sheriff Piglet to round up some unusual suspects. In "Rabbit Marks the Spot," The Pooh Pirates are tricked into digging for buried treasure.
1993 (*Preschool*) 46m/C **VHS** *DIS*

Pooh Playtime: Detective Tigger

In "Tigger Private Ear," Pooh realizes he's missing some of his honey pots, and Tigger investigates. "Sham Pooh" deals with a case of mistaken identity. "Invasion of the Pooh Snatcher" features more thrills with Pooh in peril and in "Eeyore's Tail Tale," Piglet comes to the rescue.
1993 (*Preschool*) 52m/C **VHS** *DIS*

Pooh Playtime: Pooh Party

Three short tales featuring the A.A. Milne characters. "Party Poohper" features Rabbit finding too many relatives at his party. In "A Bird in the Hand," Pooh gets into trouble and "Pooh Day Afternoon" has Pooh appointed assistant dog-sitter by Christopher Robin.
1993 (*Preschool*) 46m/C **VHS** *DIS*

Pooh's Great School Bus Adventure

Winnie, Piglet, Tigger, and the crowd sing songs about the safety rules for going to school that Christopher Robin has taught them.
1990 (*Preschool-Primary*) 14m/C **VHS, Beta $285.00** *MTI, DSN*

The Poor Little Rich Girl 🎵🎵♪

Motherless rich girl wanders away from home and is "adopted" by a pair of struggling vaudevillians. With her help, they rise to the big time. Also available with "Heidi" on laserdisc. ♫Oh My Goodness; Buy a Bar of Barry's; Wash Your Neck With a Cake of Peck's; Military Man; When I'm with You; But Definitely; You've Gotta Eat Your Spinach, Baby.
1936 (*Family*) 79m/B Shirley Temple, Jack Haley, Alice Faye, Gloria Stuart, Michael Whalen, Sara Haden, Jane Darwell; *D:* Irving Cummings. **VHS, Beta $19.95** *FOX*

Popeye 🎵🎵

Cartoon sailor is brought to life in a search to find his long-lost father. In a seaside town he meets Olive Oyl (Duvall) and adopts little Sweet Pea. Williams accomplishes the near-impossible feat of looking and sounding like the title character, and Duvall and Dooley (as Bluto) are equally splendid -but the big mistake here is putting Popeye not into a great adventure but a landlocked domestic sitcom. Dull songs by Harry Nilsson don't spice up this stale spinach. **Hound Advisory:** Roughhousing.
1980 (**PG**/*Family*) 114m/C Robin Williams, Shelley Duvall, Ray Walston, Paul Dooley, Bill Irwin, Paul Smith, Linda Hunt, Richard Libertini; *D:* Robert Altman; *W:* Jules Feiffer; *M:* Harry Nilsson. **VHS, Beta, LV $14.95** *PAR*

Popi 🎵🎵🎵

Arkin is the heart and soul of this poignant charmer in his role as a Puerto Rican immigrant hell-bent on securing a better life outside the ghetto for his two sons. His zany efforts culminate in one outrageous scheme to set them adrift off the Florida coast in hopes they will be rescued and raised by a wealthy family. Farfetched, but ultimately heartwarming.
1969 (**G**/*Jr. High-Adult*) 115m/C Alan Arkin, Rita Moreno, Miguel Alejandro, Ruben Figueroa; *D:* Arthur Hiller. **VHS, Beta** *NO*

The Popples

Furry toys inspired these cartoon characters who star in a series of tapes, each featuring two short adventures.
1985 (*Preschool-Primary*) 25m/C **VHS, Beta $14.95** *COL*

The Poseidon Adventure 🎵🎵♪

The cruise ship Poseidon is on its last voyage from New York to Athens on New Year's Eve when it is capsized by a tidal wave. The ten survivors struggle to escape the water-logged tomb. Oscar-winning special effects, such as Shelley Winters floating in a boiler room. Created an entirely new genre of film making-the big cast disaster flick.
1972 (**PG**/*Jr. High-Adult*) 117m/C Gene Hackman, Ernest Borgnine, Shelley Winters, Red Buttons, Jack Albertson, Carol Lynley, Roddy McDowall; *D:* Ronald Neame; *W:* Wendell Mayes, Sterling Silliphant; *M:* John Williams. **Award Nominations:** Academy Awards '72: Best Art Direction/Set Decoration, Best Cinematography, Best Costume Design, Best Film Editing, Best Sound, Best Supporting Actress (Winters), Best Original Score; **Awards:** Academy Awards '72: Best Song ("The Morning After"), Best Visual Effects; Golden Globe Awards '73: Best Supporting Actress (Winters). **VHS, Beta, LV $19.98** *FOX*

Posse Impossible

Hanna-Barbera reruns about a bungling group of good guys.
1984 (*Preschool-Primary*) 81m/C **VHS, Beta $19.95** *TTC, WTA*

Possible Possum: Freight Fright

Terrytoon series spun off from "Deputy Dawg" and his associates, centering on a possum character dwelling in the same Happy Hollow. Additional volumes available.
1965 (*Preschool-Primary*) 32m/C **VHS $5.99** *VTR*

Potato Head Kids, Vol. 1

A tater-rific time with the Potato Head Kids in this cartoon series that belatedly brought the toys to animated life for the first time. Additional volumes available.
1986 (*Preschool-Jr. High*) 40m/C **VHS, Beta $19.95** *MCA, WTA*

Potsworth and the Midnight Patrol

Hanna-Barbera cartoon compilation about a heroic squad of dogs.
1991 (*Family*) 84m/C **VHS, Beta $29.95** *TTC, WTA*

Pound Puppies

Saturday-morning cartoon canines organize and help other strays and lost dogs bust out of the prison known to humans as the City Pound. Hanna-Barbera production is once again based on a line of ever-so-cute toy products. Additional volumes available.
1985 (*Preschool-Primary*) 50m/C **V:** Ed Begley Jr., Jo Anne Worley, Jonathan Winters. **VHS, Beta $9.95** *FHE, WTA*

The Power of One 🦴🦴

Set in South Africa during the 1940s, the anti-apartheid drama depicts P.K., a white orphan of British descent sent to a boarding school run by Afrikaaners (South Africans of German descent). Humiliated and bullied, particularly when England and the Axis go to war, P.K. finds friends in a German pianist and a black coach who teach him to fight for rights of all races. Preachy, well-intentioned, and crammed with stereotypes, with "The Karate Kid" director giving it the usual triumphant young underdog treatment. Based on the novel by Bryce Courtenay. **Hound Advisory:** Violence, salty language.
1992 (*PG-13/Jr. High-Adult*) 126m/C Stephen Dorff, Armin Mueller-Stahl, Morgan Freeman, John Gielgud, Fay Masterson, Marius Weyers, Tracy Brooks Swope, John Osborne, Daniel Craig, Dominic Walker, Alois Mayo, Ian Roberts, Maria Marais; **D:** John G. Avildsen; **W:** Robert Mark Kamen. **VHS, LV $19.98** *WAR*

Prancer 🦴🦴◁

Eight-year-old Jessica, motherless and facing a bleak winter in a recession-hit town, finds a sick, oddly docile reindeer. She decides he's one of Santa's flying deer gone astray, and tries to nurse 'Prancer' back to health. Recent revivals suggest this is evolving into a true holiday classic. Elliott's properly somber and gruff as the dad trying to do right, while Harrell is believable as the kid with a reindeer secret. Occasionally contrived and obvious, with an ending that steps too far over the line into fantasy. No wonder folks love it.
1989 (*G/Family*) 102m/C Sam Elliott, Rebecca Harrell, Cloris Leachman, Rutanya Alda, John Joseph Duda, Abe Vigoda, Michael Constantine, Ariana Richards, Mark Rolston; **D:** John Hancock; **M:** Maurice Jarre. **VHS, Beta, LV, 8mm $19.95** *COL, ORI, FCT*

Precious Pupp

Cartoon compilation about the most charming dog alive and his owner, who enjoy some wacky adventures together, Hanna-Barbera style.
198? (*Family*) 51m/C **VHS, Beta $19.95** *TTC, WTA*

Prehysteria 🦴🦴

Family flick deserves bones just for marketing savvy, arriving on tape while "Jurassic Park" cleaned up in theaters. But this dino-clone has 100% non-threatening monsters. Ancient eggs from South America hatch at the farm of a widower archaeologist. His kids are delighted at the resulting brood of tame, pygmy dinosaurs - cat-sized T.Rex, mini brachiosaur, etc. - each named for a different rock star. The puppet f/x beasts are cute, the villain is dumb, and rough stuff (when bumbling burglars go after the creatures) is minimal. Alas, the script is banal and boring, but it didn't prevent this trifle from being, until Disney's "The Return of Jafar," the most profitable straight-to-video feature ever. **Hound Advisory:** Roughhousing, sex talk.
1993 (*PG/Primary-Adult*) 86m/C Brett Cullen, Austin O'Brien, Samantha Mills, Colleen Morris, Tony Longo, Stuart Fratkin, Stephen Lee; **D:** Albert Band, Charles Band; **W:** Greg Suddeth, Mark Goldstein. **VHS, Beta** *PAR*

Prehysteria! 2 🦴🦴◁

The original "Prehysteria" earned piles of money, but evidently none of it went to the f/x budget of this weak sequel, since the dwarf dinosaurs look even more like lifeless puppets. Talented kid actors can't help much with a plot about the monster midgets leaving their ranch and helping a poor little rich boy cope with a nasty nanny and an inattentive yuppie dad. **Hound Advisory:** Roughhousing.
1994 (*Primary-Adult*) 81m/C Kevin R. Connors, Jennifer Harte, Dean Scofield, Bettye Ackerman, Larry Hankin, Greg Lewis, Alan Palo, Michael Hagiwara, Owen Bush; **D:** Albert Band; **W:** Brent Friedman, Michael Paul Davis; **M:** Richard Band. **VHS, Beta** *PAR*

Prelude to a Kiss 🦴🦴

Disappointing screen adaptation of Craig Lucas' hit play features Baldwin and Ryan as young lovers in this romantic fantasy. Ryan is Rita, a free-spirited bartender and Baldwin is Peter, a conservative writer, who decide to marry after a whirlwind courtship. At their wedding reception, Rita obligingly kisses one of their guests, an old man (Walker). Then, on their honeymoon, Peter begins to notice a number of changes to Rita's character and comes to realize this is truly not the girl he married. The delicate fantasy which worked on stage struggles to survive the "opening up" of the screen adaptation though Baldwin (who reprises his stage role) and Ryan are appealing.
1992 (*PG-13/Jr. High-Adult*) 106m/C Alec Baldwin, Meg Ryan, Sydney Walker, Ned Beatty, Patty Duke, Kathy Bates, Stanley Tucci; **D:** Norman Rene; **M:** Howard Shore. **VHS, LV $19.98** *FXV, PMS*

Pretty in Pink 🦴🦴◁

More teen pain from the pen of John Hughes. Working-class girl Andie falls for a rich guy. Their families fret, their friends

are distressed - particularly the boy's snobby clique and Andie's longtime steady. If you can buy into the themes of peer pressure and economic social classes flourishing in high school, then you may be able to accept the premise. Slickly done and adequately, if not enthusiastically, acted (watch for Clay, before his career as a hyper-offensive stand-up comic). In 1987, Hughes remade this film and put himself in the director's chair with much of the same result: see "Some Kind of Wonderful." **Hound Advisory:** Salty language, mature themes.
1986 (PG-13/*Jr. High-Adult*) 96m/C Molly Ringwald, Andrew McCarthy, Jon Cryer, Harry Dean Stanton, James Spader, Annie Potts, Andrew Dice Clay, Margaret Colin, Alexa Kenin, Gina Gershon, Dweezil Zappa; **D:** Howard Deutch; **W:** John Hughes; **M:** Michael Gore. **VHS, Beta, LV, 8mm $14.95** *PAR*

The Pretty Piggies: The Adventure Begins

Four good-lookin' little pigs struggle for survival against pirates, dinosaurs, and a mean woman who acts like a queen. Additional volumes available.
1990 (*Family*) 25m/C **VHS $14.98** *VTR, WTA*

The Prime of Miss Jean Brodie 🎬🎬🎬

Oscar-winning performance by Smith as a forward-thinking teacher in a Scottish girls' school during the 1920's. She captivates her impressionable young students with her fascist ideals and free-thinking attitudes in this adaptation of the play taken from Muriel Spark's novel. **Hound Advisory:** Mature themes.
1969 (PG/*Jr. High-Adult*) 116m/C Dame Maggie Smith, Pamela Franklin, Robert Stephens, Celia Johnson, Gordon Jackson, Jane Carr; **D:** Ronald Neame; **W:** Jay Presson Allen. **Award Nominations:** Academy Awards '69: Best Song ("Jean"); Cannes Film Festival '69: Best Film; **Awards:** Academy Awards '69: Best Actress (Smith); British Academy Awards '69: Best Actress (Smith), Best Supporting Actress (Johnson). **VHS, Beta $79.98** *FOX, BTV*

Primo Baby 🎬🎬

A 15-year-old delinquent is placed with a foster father who happens to raise racehorses. The girl learns responsibility, discipline, and horse-movie cliches by caring for a vision-impaired thoroughbred and entering it in a championship race. Farfetched family horseventure from Canada.
1988 (*Family*) 97m/C **VHS $89.95** *WOV*

The Prince and the Great Race 🎬🎬

Three Australian children search the outback to find their kidnapped horse who is scheduled to run in the big New Year's Day Race.
1983 (*Family*) 91m/C John Ewart, John Howard, Nicole Kidman. **VHS, Beta $14.98** *LIV*

The Prince and the Pauper 🎬🎬🎬

Satisfying version of the classic story of a young street urchin who trades places with the lookalike heir to the throne of England. Flynn's presence as the adult lead guarantees swashbuckling entertainment galore, though not the most accurate rendering of Mark Twain's class-boundary themes. Also available in a computer-colorized version.

1937 (*Family*) 118m/B Errol Flynn, Claude Rains, Alan Hale, Billy Mauch, Montagu Love, Henry Stephenson, Barton MacLane; **D:** William Keighley; **M:** Erich Wolfgang Korngold. **VHS, Beta, LV $19.95** *FOX, MLB, CCB*

The Prince and the Pauper 🎬🎬

Prince and a poor young boy swap their clothes and identities, thus causing understandable confusion in Merrie Englande. Minor-league Disney made-for-TV adaptation of the story by Mark Twain.
1962 (*Primary-Adult*) 93m/C Guy Williams, Laurence Naismith, Donald Houston, Jane Asher, Walter Hudd. **VHS, Beta $12.99** *DIS*

The Prince and the Pauper 🎬🎬🎬

Large-scale redo of the Mark Twain classic, heavily indebted to the "Three Musketeers" swashbucklers of the '70s for its tongue-in-cheek attitude, as an English prince and a street urchin ("Oliver!" star Lester was a bit old for the dual role) see that they have identical appearances and get switched with each other. Enjoyable, but still feels like a smug put-on from time to time. Also known as "Crossed Swords." **Hound Advisory:** Victorian roughhousing.
1978 (PG/*Family*) 113m/C Oliver Reed, Raquel Welch, Mark Lester, Ernest Borgnine, George C. Scott, Rex Harrison, Charlton Heston, Sybil Danning; **D:** Richard Fleischer; **M:** Maurice Jarre. **VHS, Beta $19.98** *MED*

The Prince and the Pauper

Mickey Mouse came out of nearly a decade's retirement to star in this cartoon version of the Twain classic about two lookalikes from opposite ends of the economic scale who trade places.
1991 (*Family*) 24m/C **VHS, Beta $12.99** *DIS, WTA*

The Prince of Central Park 🎬🎬🎬

Two young orphans are forced by circumstance to live in a tree In New York's Central Park until they are befriended by a lonely old woman. Above-average made for TV adaptation of the novel by Evan H. Rhodes; the story was later used for a Broadway play.
1977 (*Jr. High-Adult*) 76m/C Ruth Gordon, T.J. Hargrave, Lisa Richards, Brooke Shields, Marc Vahanian, Dan Hedaya; **D:** Harvey Hart. **VHS, Beta $59.95** *LIV*

Prince Valiant 🎬🎬🎬

Uneven but entertaining swashbuckler based on Hal Foster's newspaper comic strip. Valiant is a Scandinavian prince who journey's to King Arthur's Court to learn to become a knight. First half of the picture gets sidetracked by silly romantic mixups (Princess: "I hate you! I love you!"), but it comes to rousing life in the action-packed second hour, when Val aids Christianized Vikings to rebel against a pagan tyrant. The use of Cinemascope filming suffers badly on the small screen, especially in the climactic duel. **Hound Advisory:** Violence.
1954 (*Family*) 100m/C James Mason, Janet Leigh, Robert Wagner, Debra Paget, Sterling Hayden, Victor McLaglen, Donald Crisp, Brian Aherne, Barry Jones, Mary Philips; **D:** Henry Hathaway; **W:** Dudley Nichols. **VHS, Beta $14.98** *FXV, FCT*

VIDEOHOUND'S FAMILY VIDEO RETRIEVER

Prince Valiant

Animated version of Hal Foster's comic strip, with Prince Valiant undertaking a dangerous journey to find the legendary land of Camelot.
199? (*Family*) 92m/C **V:** Robby Benson, Efrem Zimbalist Jr., Samantha Eggar, Tim Curry. **VHS $59.95** *WTA*

Princes in Exile 𝄞𝄞◁

Made-for-TV movie about young people with life-threatening illnesses at a special summer camp. They find that love and friendship hold the key to dreams about the future. Excellent cast of newcomers. Based on a novel of the same name by Mark Schreiber. **Hound Advisory:** Mature themes.
1990 (*PG-13*/ *Sr. High-Adult*) 103m/C Zachary Ansley, Nicholas Shields, Stacy Mistysyn, Alexander Chapman, Chuck Shamata; **D:** Giles Walker. **VHS, Beta, LV $89.95** *FRH, FCT*

Princess and the Goblin

Story based on the George MacDonald book combines illustration and closeups of Jackson reading. Complete with puzzle.
1992 (*PG*/*Primary-Jr. High*) 60m/C **VHS $19.95** *HMD*

The Princess and the Goblin 𝄞𝄞

Smaller kiddies may enjoy this British-made animated adventure but it's a bland story with mediocre animation. Nasty, underground-dwelling goblins (portrayed as silly rather than scary) plot against the surface kingdom of humans, especially little Princess Irene. Brave boy miner Curdie helps save the day. Based on a book by George MacDonald that's been a favorite with English kids for a century.
1994 (*G*/*Family*) 82m/C **V:** Sally Ann Marsh, Peter Murray, Claire Bloom. **VHS $24.95** *HMD*

The Princess Bride 𝄞𝄞𝄞◁

Smart spoof of the basic bedtime story, crammed with all the cliches. Beautiful maiden is carried off to the kingdom of Florin to be married to its prince, but he plans to do away with her in a diabolical plot. To the rescue comes her swashbuckling true love, at the head of an increasingly strange rescue party. Great dueling scenes and offbeat satire of fairy tales make this fun for adults as well as children. Based on William Goldman's cult novel - and without the book's infuriating open ending. **Hound Advisory:** Swashbuckling violence.
1987 (*PG*/*Family*) 98m/C Cary Elwes, Mandy Patinkin, Robin Wright, Wallace Shawn, Peter Falk, Andre the Giant, Chris Sarandon, Christopher Guest, Billy Crystal, Carol Kane, Fred Savage, Peter Cook, Mel Smith; **D:** Rob Reiner; **W:** William Goldman; **M:** Mark Knopfler. **VHS, Beta, LV, 8mm $14.95** *COL, SUE, SUP*

Princess Scargo and the Birthday Pumpkin

The "Rabbit Ears: We All Have Tales" series retells a Native American legend about a young girl who gives up a precious gift to aid her people.
1992 (*Preschool-Primary*) 30m/C **VHS $9.95** *BTV, PMS*

The Private Eyes 𝄞◁

Airheaded comedic romp with Knotts and Conway as bungling sleuths investigating two deaths. They're led on a merry chase through secret passages to a meeting with a ghostly adversary.
1980 (*PG*/*Family*) 91m/C Don Knotts, Tim Conway, Trisha Noble, Bernard Fox; **D:** Lang Elliott; **W:** Tim Conway, John Myhers. **VHS, Beta, LV $29.98** *VES*

Prize Fighter 𝄞𝄞

The comedy team of Knotts and Conway take on the "Rocky" plot. Depression-era brawler Conway seems to be an underdog on a winning streak to the championship, but neither he nor his nitwit manager realize all their matches have been fixed by a gangster. Scripted by Conway and mainly enjoyable if intelligence is suspended at onset. **Hound Advisory:** Roughhousing.
1979 (*PG*/*Family*) 99m/C Tim Conway, Don Knotts; **D:** Michael Preece; **W:** Tim Conway. **VHS, Beta $9.95** *MED*

Problem Child 𝄞◁

Way-obnoxious comedy that was a popular hit (so much for the Dignity of the Common Man). Junior is a destructive, sadistic brat, the terror of the orphanage. The Healys, childless yuppies, make a big mistake upon adopting Mr. Sweetness and Light. Meek stepdad Ben tries to reform the kid with love and sweetness despite all the vicious pranks Junior and a repetitious, one-note script can unleash on him. In order to make Junior look 'cute,' every character but Ben is a cartoon creep, fully deserving of what they get. **Hound Advisory:** Roughhousing, sex talk. Junior's no role model, that's for sure.
1990 (*PG*/*Jr. High-Family*) 81m/C John Ritter, Michael Oliver, Jack Warden, Amy Yasbeck, Gilbert Gottfried, Michael Richards, Peter Jurasik; **D:** Dennis Dugan; **W:** Scott Alexander, Larry Karaszewski; **M:** Miles Goodman. **VHS, LV $14.98** *MCA*

Problem Child 2 𝄞

Ben Healy and his nasty adopted son Junior move to another town, full of man-hungry divorcees. None is worse than wealthy, witchy Lawanda; in order to stop her marriage plans for Ben, Junior joins forces with his equal in malevolence, a little girl from school. Director Levant went on to do "Beethoven" and "The Flintstones," but he'll not escape responsibility for this lowly slapstick, with a marathon mass-vomiting scene setting a new high in depths. **Hound Advisory:** Sex, slapstick violence, bad-taste gags involving urine and doggie dung, to name but a few.
1991 (*PG-13*/*Jr. High-Adult*) 91m/C John Ritter, Michael Oliver, Laraine Newman, Amy Yasbeck, Jack Warden, Ivyann Schwan, Gilbert Gottfried, James Tolkan, Charlene Tilton, Alan Blumenfeld; **D:** Brian Levant; **W:** Scott Alexander, Larry Karaszewski. **VHS, Beta, LV $19.98** *MCA*

The Prodigal 𝄞𝄞

Born-again family drama in which a sundered family is brought together by the return of a once-estranged son. Filled with Hollywood celebrities, and the Rev. Billy Graham adding his own variation on star power.

1983 (PG/Jr. High-Adult) 109m/C John Hammond, Hope Lange, John Cullum, Morgan Brittany, Ian Bannen, Arliss Howard, Joey Travolta, Billy Graham; **M:** Bruce Broughton. **VHS, Beta, LV $59.95** *LIV*

Professor Iris: Music Mania

Professor Iris teaches preschoolers all about music, song, and dance from around the world with his classroom orchestra. Additional volumes available.
1993 (*Preschool*) 40m/C **VHS $12.95** *BTV*

The Program 🎞🎞🎞🔉

Sensitive tearjerker about college football players getting caught up in the drive for a championship. As the season takes its toll on both mind and body, players prepare for the Big Game. Caan is the team's gruff coach, who's willing to look the other way as long as his boys are winning. Film sparked controversy when the Disney studio pulled and recut it after release because one scene, where Sheffer's character lies down in traffic, sparked copy-cat actions and several deaths. The scene was not restored for the video version. **Hound Advisory:** Profanity.
1993 (R/Sr. High-Adult) 110m/C James Caan, Craig Sheffer, Kristy Swanson, Halle Berry, Omar Epps, Duane Davis, Abraham Benrubi, Jon Maynard Pennell, Andrew Bryniarski; **D:** David S. Ward; **W:** Aaron Latham, David S. Ward; **M:** Michel Colombier. **VHS, Beta $96.03** *TOU*

Project X 🎞🎞🎞

Bemused young Air Force pilot gets a strange assignment - training chimpanzees to fly planes. He grows close to the appealing apes and is shocked to learn the true, cruel purpose of the experiments. High-tech tale falls somewhere between sci-fi and animal drama, but there's more than a touch of real wonder and an emotionally satisfying conclusion. Great performances by the primates. **Hound Advisory:** Salty language, monkey casualties.
1987 (PG/Jr. High-Adult) 107m/C Matthew Broderick, Helen Hunt, William Sadler, Johnny Rae McGhee, Jonathan Stark, Robin Gammell, Stephen Lang, Jean Smart, Dick Miller; **D:** Jonathan Kaplan; **W:** Stanley Weiser, Lawrence Lasker; **M:** James Horner. **VHS, Beta, LV $19.98** *FOX*

The Projectionist 🎞🎞🎞

Fetching and inventive low-budget tale about a misfit who works as a projectionist in a seedy New York movie house. In Walter Mitty-type fantasies, however, he's Captain Flash, a serial superhero who battles against a campy villain called The Bat (Dangerfield), aided by vintage clips of Hollywood heroes like Humphrey Bogart and John Wayne. Made when star McCann was a prominent NYC-area kiddie-show TV personality, though the intended audience is film buffs.
1971 (PG/Jr. High-Adult) 84m/C Rodney Dangerfield, Chuck McCann, Ina Balin; **D:** Harry Hurwitz; **W:** Harry Hurwitz. **VHS, Beta $69.98** *LIV, VES*

Promises in the Dark 🎞🎞🎞🔉

Depressing drama focusing on the complex relationship between a woman doctor and her 17-year-old female patient who is terminally ill with cancer. **Hound Advisory:** Mature themes.

1979 (PG/Jr. High-Adult) 118m/C Marsha Mason, Ned Beatty, Kathleen Beller, Susan Clark, Paul Clemens, Donald Moffatt, Michael Brandon; **D:** Gerome Hellman. **VHS, Beta $59.95** *WAR*

Pssst! Hammerman's After You

A frail 11-year-old, Mouse, provokes the town bully and must face up to the consequences of his actions. Based on the Betsy Byars work "The 18th Emergency," this was originally done for TV's "Afterschool Special."
1990 (*Preschool-Primary*) 28m/C **VHS, Beta $470.00** *MTI, DSN*

Puff and the Incredible Mr. Nobody

Cartoon compilation led by Puff the Magic Dragon and a little boy traveling through the Fantaverse to find an imaginary friend, Mr. Nobody. Does this mean that Nobody likes Puff? One of three TV specials recasting the folk-song dragon as a sort of guidance counselor to the young; musician Peter Yarrow (as in Peter, Paul and Mary) was one of the producers.
1982 (*Primary-Jr. High*) 45m/C **V:** Burgess Meredith. **VHS, Beta $14.98** *LIV, MTI, WTA*

Puff the Magic Dragon

Animated adaptation of the song by Peter Yarrow (who contributes a voiceover) about little Jackie Paper and his friend Puff, The Magic Dragon. Except the boy is now called Jackie Draper (guess why) and Puff is a mentor figure who helps instill the lad with self-confidence through whimsical adventures. Taking up slack on the tape are three "Hector Heathcote" 'toons about a historical time-traveller.
1978 (*Primary*) 45m/C **V:** Burgess Meredith. **VHS, Beta $14.98** *LIV, WTA*

Puff the Magic Dragon in the Land of Living Lies

Puff the Magic Dragon teaches a troubled little girl (caught in the throes of her parents' divorce) that there's a big difference between fantasy and telling a lie.
1979 (*Primary-Jr. High*) 24m/C **V:** Burgess Meredith. **VHS, Beta $14.95** *MTI, WTA*

Punky Brewster: Little Orphan Punky

Punky, Brandon, Cherie and the rest of the youthful ensemble from the short-lived network TV sitcom return for a not ready for prime-time adventure as globetrotting Saturday-morning cartoon kids. Additional volumes available.
1991 (*Family*) 75m/C **V:** Soleil Moon Frye. **VHS $19.99** *JFK*

The Puppetoon Movie 🎞🎞

This begins by comparing stop-motion animation pioneer George Pal to Walt Disney, but when Pal's famous Puppetoon musical shorts from the '30s and '40s unreel it's clear they haven't held their charm like Uncle Walt's cartoons. Included are "Tubby the Tuba," "Tulips Shall Grow" (an anti-Nazi allegory), and perhaps best of all, a modern Sleeping Beauty awakened by swing music. Outdated racial stereotypes too often predominate, though they're mercifully absent in the "John Henry" segment. Gumby, Pokey, Speedy Alka Seltzer

and the Pillsbury Doughboy appear in too-brief prologue and epilogue scenes; for a career history of Pal himself, see "The Fantasy Film Worlds of George Pal."
1987 (*G*/*Family*) 80m/C **D:** Arnold Leibovit; **M:** Buddy Baker. VHS, Beta, LV $19.95 *FHE, WTA*

The Pure Hell of St. Trinian's 🐾🐾🔊

Sequel to "Blue Murder at St. Trinian's" finds a sheik, desiring to fill out his harem, recruiting at the rowdy girls' school. Based on the Ronald Searle carton and followed by "The Great St. Trinian's Train Robbery."
1961 (*Adult*) 94m/B Cecil Parker, Joyce Grenfell, George Cole, Thorley Walters; **D:** Frank Launder; **M:** Malcolm Arnold. VHS *FCT*

Purple People Eater 🐾🔊

The alien of the title, a silly, shaggy cyclops with all the raw realism of Barney the Dinosaur, descends to Earth to mix with teen rock'n'rollers. Based on the novelty song of the same name whose performer, Sheb Wooley, has a small part. Harmless, stupid fun for the whole family.
1988 (*PG*/*Jr. High-Sr. High*) 91m/C Ned Beatty, Shelley Winters, Neil Patrick Harris, Kareem Abdul-Jabbar, Little Richard, Chubby Checker, Peggy Lipton; **D:** Linda Shayne. VHS, Beta, LV $79.95 *MED, VTR*

The Purple Rose of Cairo 🐾🐾🐾

A diner waitress, disillusioned by the Depression and a lackluster life, escapes into a film playing at the local movie house where a blond film hero, tiring of the monotony of his role, makes a break from the celluloid to join her in the real world. The ensuing love story allows director-writer Allen to show his knowledge of old movies and provide his fans with a change of pace. Farrow's film sister is also her real-life sister Stephanie, who went on to appear in Allen's "Zelig." **Hound Advisory:** Violence.
1985 (*PG*/*Sr. High-Adult*) 82m/C Mia Farrow, Jeff Daniels, Danny Aiello, Dianne Wiest, Van Johnson, Zoe Caldwell, John Wood, Michael Tucker, Edward Herrmann, Milo O'Shea, Glenne Headly, Karen Akers, Deborah Rush; **D:** Woody Allen; **W:** Woody Allen; **M:** Dick Hyman. **Award Nominations:** Academy Awards '85: Best Original Screenplay; **Awards:** British Academy Awards '85: Best Film; Cesar Awards '86: Best Foreign Film; Golden Globe Awards '86: Best Screenplay. VHS, Beta, LV $19.98 *LIV, VES, HMV*

Puss in Boots 🐾🐾

Children's Theater Company of Minneapolis presents a jazzed-up, New Orleans-style version of the "Puss in Boots" tale. VHS version is in stereo. **Hound Advisory:** Roughhousing.
1982 (*Family*) 89m/C VHS, Beta *FHE*

Puss in Boots 🐾🔊

Banal and overlong "Cannon Movie Tales" retelling of the famous cat tale, in which the well-meaning intentions of a mischievous feline get his master out of danger again and again. Several songs are yowled.
1988 (*Family*) 96m/C Christopher Walken, Jason Connery; **D:** Eugene Marner. VHS, Beta $19.95 *CAN*

Puss in Boots

When a down-and-out man decides to eat his entire feline inheritance, the cat comes up with a plan to save himself by transforming his owner into a noble prince. Part of the "Rabbit Ears: We All Have Tales" series of great folktales told by terrific narrators against felicitous illustrations.
1992 (*Primary*) 30m/C **M:** Jean Luc Ponty. VHS $9.95 *BTV*

Puss 'n Boots Travels Around the World 🐾🐾

Fairy-tale adaptation of a certain Jules Verne tale finds the feline favorite on a bet to make his way around the globe before eighty days have passed. The evildoer, Rumblehog, tries at every turn to thwart his success.
1983 (*Family*) 70m/C VHS, Beta $19.95 *COL, GKK*

Quark the Dragon Slayer 🐾🐾

Python alumnus Cleese narrates this silly Norse animated feature about a baby giant called Quark (after his first word) who causes a lot of trouble for his adopted village.
1990 (*Preschool-Primary*) 70m/C **V:** John Cleese. VHS $24.95 *CEL, WTA*

Quarterback Princess 🐾🐾

Workaday made-for-TV telling of the real-life girl who goes out for football and becomes homecoming queen. Heartwarming, if you like that kinda stuff, but not exciting.
1985 (*Jr. High-Adult*) 96m/C Helen Hunt, Don Murray, John Stockwell, Daphne Zuniga; **D:** Noel Black. VHS, Beta $59.98 *FOX*

Queen of Hearts 🐾🐾🐾🔊

Whimsy set in early-'60s Britain, about an Italian couple who defied both their families to marry for love. Four children later they're running a diner in England, but the wife's old suitor arrives to launch a devious vendetta to split mama from papa. Told through the eyes of Eddie, the 10-year-old son, who lends the complicated saga a child's-eye-view quality, uniquely blending magic, laughter, tears and the everyday. **Hound Advisory:** Sex talk, mature themes.
1989 (*PG*/*Jr. High-Adult*) 112m/C Anita Zagaria, Joseph Long, Eileen Way, Vittorio Duse, Vittorio Amandola, Ian Hawkes; **D:** Jon Amiel; **M:** Michael Convertino. VHS, Beta, LV *NO*

The Quest 🐾🐾🔊

Orphan Cody leads a carefree life in the Australian outback, under the hands-off parenting style of his adult guardian. Bright and brave, the boy builds wild inventions and investigates a local Aboriginal superstition about a monster in a lake. Sometimes dull, sometimes enthralling tale with an unsatisfying conclusion but an admirable young leading man in "E.T." star Thomas. Originally titled "Frog Dreaming." **Hound Advisory:** Alcohol use, salty language.
1986 (*PG*/*Jr. High-Adult*) 94m/C Henry Thomas, Tony Barry, John Ewart, Rachel Friend, Tamsin West, Dennis Miller, Katya Manning; **D:** Brian Trenchard-Smith. VHS, Beta $9.98 *NLC*

The Quiet Man 🎬🎬🎬🎬

Classic incarnation of Hollywood Irishness, and one of Ford's best. Wayne is Sean Thornton, a weary American ex-boxer who returns to the Irish hamlet of his childhood and tries to take a spirited lass (O'Hara, never lovelier) as his wife, despite the strenuous objections of her brawling brother (McLaglen). Thornton's aided by the leprechaun-like Fitzgerald and the local parish priest, Bond. High-spirited and memorable, brimming with stage Irish characters, witty banter, and shots of the lush countryside. **1952** (*Family*) 129m/C John Wayne, Maureen O'Hara, Barry Fitzgerald, Victor McLaglen, Arthur Shields, Jack MacGowran, Ward Bond, Mildred Natwick, Ken Curtis, Mae Marsh, Sean McClory, Francis Ford; *D:* John Ford; *W:* Frank Nugent; *M:* Victor Young. **Award Nominations:** Academy Awards '52: Best Art Direction/Set Decoration (Color), Best Picture, Best Screenplay, Best Sound, Best Supporting Actor (McLaglen); **Awards:** Academy Awards '52: Best Color Cinematography, Best Director (Ford); National Board of Review Awards '52: 10 Best Films of the Year; Venice Film Festival '52: Best Director (Ford). **VHS, LV $19.98** *REP, TLF, CCB*

Quigley Down Under 🎬🎬🎬

A Western sharpshooter moves to Australia in search of employment. To his horror, he discovers that he has been hired to kill aborigines. Predictable action is somewhat redeemed by the terrific chemistry between Selleck and San Giacomo and the usual enjoyable theatrics from Rickman as the landowner heavy. **Hound Advisory:** Light violence and nudity. **1990** (*PG-13/Sr. High-Adult*) 121m/C Tom Selleck, Laura San Giacomo, Alan Rickman, Chris Haywood, Ron Haddrick, Tony Bonner, Roger Ward, Ben Mendelsohn, Jerome Ehlers, Conor McDermottroe; *D:* Simon Wincer; *W:* John Hill; *M:* Basil Poledouris. **VHS, Beta, LV, 8mm $19.98** *MGM*

Rabbit Ears Storybook Classics Collection

Acclaimed series of tapes in which well-known fairy tales are read by popular celebrities, while beautiful paintings (sometimes with limited animation) help bring the stories to life. See individual listings for details; titles include "The Emperor and His Nightingale," "The Fisherman and His Wife," "How the Leopard Got His Spots," "How the Rhinoceros Got His Skin," "How the Camel Got His Hump," "The Legend of Sleepy Hollow," "Pecos Bill," "The Tale of Gloucester," "The Tale of Mr. Jeremy Fisher," "The Tale of Peter Rabbit," "The Three Billy Goats Gruff," "The Three Little Pigs," "Thumbelina," "Bre'r Rabbit and the Wonderful Tar Baby," "Paul Bunyan," "Red Riding Hood," "Goldilocks," and "The Emperor's New Clothes." **1988** (*Family*) 30m/C **VHS, Beta $9.95** *COL, HMV*

Raccoons: Let's Dance

Canadian TV cartoon characters Melissa, Ralph, and Bert Raccoon perform in six of their own original music videos, designed especially for children. **1984** (*Family*) 30m/C Rita Coolidge, Leo Sayer, John Schneider, Dottie West. **VHS, Beta** *SUE, NLC*

Raccoons on Ice

Two Canadian cartoons featuring Ralph, Melissa, and Bert Raccoon. In "Raccoons on Ice," they play a hockey game against the Brutish Bears. "Christmas Raccoons" finds them fighting to protect Evergreen Forest and their "raccoondominium" home. **1982** (*Family*) 49m/C *M:* Leo Sayer, Rita Coolidge. **VHS, Beta, LV $9.98** *SUE*

Race for Your Life, Charlie Brown 🎬🎬🎬

Third in the feature-length theatrical cartoons based on the "Peanuts" comic strip finds perennial loser Charlie Brown and his companions at summer camp long before Ernest ever set foot there. Traditionally loose plot concerns an anti-boy campaign (led by Lucy) and a white-water raft race. **1977** (*G/Family*) 76m/C *W:* Charles M. Schulz. **VHS, Beta, LV $14.95** *PAR, WTA*

Racing with the Moon 🎬🎬🎬

Sweet, nostalgic film about two buddies awaiting induction into the Marines in 1942. They have their last chance at summer romance. Benjamin makes the most of skillful young actors and conventional story. Great period detail. Keep your eyes peeled for glimpses of many rising young stars including Hannah and Carvey. **Hound Advisory:** Profanity, nudity, suggested sex, brief violence. **1984** (*PG/Sr. High-Adult*) 108m/C Sean Penn, Elizabeth McGovern, Nicolas Cage, John Karlen, Rutanya Alda, Max Showalter, Crispin Glover, Suzanne Adkinson, Page Hannah, Michael Madsen, Dana Carvey, Carol Kane, Michael Talbott; *D:* Richard Benjamin; *W:* Steven Kloves; *M:* Dave Grusin. **VHS, Beta, LV $14.95** *PAR*

Rad 🎬🎬

Flat-tired teenage drama revolving around BMX bicycle racing from stuntmaster Needham. The kid hero neglects his paper route and endangers his SAT scores to show his stuff in the big competition. Real-life BMX Olympics star Bart Conner plays the nasty champ. **Hound Advisory:** Salty junior biker language. **1986** (*PG/Jr. High-Adult*) 94m/C Bill Allen, Bart Conner, Talia Shire, Jack Weston, Lori Loughlin; *D:* Hal Needham. **VHS, Beta, LV $9.98** *SUE, NLC*

Radar Men from the Moon

Republic serial that reused both the Rocket Man costume (last seen in "King of the Rocketmen") and the alien suits (plus some of the plot) from "The Purple Monster Strikes." Space avenger Commando Cody flies into action against Retik, an invader from the moon who allies himself with Earth gangsters. An admirable example of recycling, but nothing special as a plot. In 12 episodes. Also known as "Commando Cody," after the hero who subsequently got his own network TV series. **Hound Advisory:** Violence. **1952** (*Family*) 152m/B George Wallace, Aline Towne, Roy Barcroft, William "Billy" Bakewell, Clayton Moore; *D:* Fred Brannon. **VHS, LV $49.95** *NOS, REP, SNC*

Radio Days 🎬🎬🎬

Lovely, unpretentious remembrance of a NYC childhood during World War II. Allen fashions a series of comic vignettes centering around a youth in Brooklyn, his eccentric extended family, and the radio entertainers who held them spellbound in that pre-TV era. Not strong on plot, but many scenes (like the boy narrator's once-in-a- lifetime glimpse of an Axis spy submarine) won't soon be forgotten. **Hound Advisory:** Sex talk, mature themes.

1987 (PG/Sr. High-Adult) 96m/C Mia Farrow, Dianne Wiest, Julie Kavner, Michael Tucker, Wallace Shawn, Josh Mostel, Tony Roberts, Jeff Daniels, Kenneth Mars, Seth Green, William Magerman, Diane Keaton, Renee Lippin, Danny Aiello, Gina DeAngelis, Kitty Carlisle Hart, Mercedes Ruehl, Tito Puente; **D:** Woody Allen; **W:** Woody Allen. **VHS, Beta, LV** $19.95 HBO

Radio Flyer 🎬🎬

It's 1969 and Mike and Bobby have just moved to northern California with their divorced mom. All would be idyllic except mom marries a drunk who beats Bobby. Mike decides to help Bobby escape by turning their Radio Flyer wagon into a magic flying machine that will carry the boy beyond harm's reach. Infamous box-office flop offers a truly appealing version of childhood dreams and imagination, but its child abuse angle and darker aspects (some commentators interpret the Radio Flyer as a metaphor for suicide) were desperately rewritten and reshot. The unsatisfactory ending cops out with a flight into pure fantasy, followed by a child abuse public service announcement. **Hound Advisory:** Salty language, brutality, mature themes (what's left of them).

1992 (PG-13/Jr. High-Adult) 114m/C Elijah Wood, Joseph Mazzello, Lorraine Bracco, Adam Baldwin, John Heard, Ben Johnson; **D:** Richard Donner. **VHS, LV** $19.95 COL

Radio Patrol

Pinky Adams, radio cop, is assisted by his trusted canine partner Irish. A cop's best friend is his dog in this action-packed 12-chapter serial.

1937 (Family) 235m/B Mickey Rentschler, Adrian Morris, Monte Montague, Jack Mulhall, Grant Withers, Catherine Hughes; **D:** Ford Beebe, Cliff Smith. **VHS, Beta** $21.95 NOS, VDM, MLB

Raft Adventures of Huck & Jim

Loose adaptation of "Huckleberry Finn" puts Mark Twain's adventurous duo down the Mississippi River on a raft.

1978 (Preschool-Primary) 72m/C Timothy Gibbs. **VHS, Beta** $29.95 FHE, WTA

Raggedy Ann and Andy

Two cartoon Raggedy Ann and Andy TV specials from Chuck Jones. In "The Pumpkin Who Couldn't Smile," the pair aid a boy who lost his Halloween pumpkin. "The Great Santa Claus Caper" has them foiling a plot to turn Santa's workshop into a factory.

1979 (Family) 52m/C **D:** Chuck Jones; **V:** June Foray, Daws Butler. **VHS, Beta** $29.95 MPI

Raggedy Ann and Andy: A Musical Adventure 🎬🎬

Cartoon feature adventure of the lookalike dolls Raggedy Ann and Andy, who embark on a song-filled quest to rescue a kidnapped plaything. Animation is lovely but the plot sags like a rag ...well, you know. No fewer than 16 musical numbers ooze by.

1977 (G/Family) 87m/C **D:** Richard Williams; **V:** Didi Conn, Joe Silver. **VHS, Beta** $14.98 FOX

Raiders of the Lost Ark 🎬🎬🎬🎬

Breathless '30s-style adventure made Indiana Jones a household name. The intrepid archeologist battles Nazis, decodes hieroglyphics and tries to avoid snakes in his search for the biblical Ark of the Covenant. Truly hair-raising opening scene starts an avalanche of f/x and fun (with a nagging feeling that the stunts are shaping the story instead of the other way around). Followed by the controversial "Indiana Jones and the Temple of Doom," and later a short-lived TV series. **Hound Advisory:** Violence galore, including melting flesh that pushes the boundaries of a PG rating. Alcohol use, sex talk.

1981 (PG/Family) 115m/C Harrison Ford, Karen Allen, Wolf Kahler, Paul Freeman, John Rhys-Davies, Denholm Elliott, Ronald Lacey, Anthony Higgins, Alfred Molina; **D:** Steven Spielberg; **W:** George Lucas, Philip Kaufman; **M:** John Williams. **Award Nominations:** Academy Awards '81: Best Cinematography, Best Director (Spielberg), Best Picture, Best Original Score; **Awards:** Academy Awards '81: Best Art Direction/Set Decoration, Best Film Editing, Best Sound, Best Visual Effects; People's Choice Awards '82: Best Film. **VHS, Beta, LV, 8mm** $14.95 PAR

Railway Children 🎬🎬🎬

In turn-of-the-century England a father of three children is framed for spying and imprisoned during Christmas. The kids and their mother must survive on a poverty-stricken farm near the railroad tracks. They eventually meet an aristocrat who helps them prove their father's innocence. Pleasantly performed, atmospherically directed entertainment from the classic Evelyn Nesbitt novel.

1970 (Family) 104m/C Jenny Agutter, William Mervyn, Bernard Cribbins, Dinah Sheridan, Iain Cuthbertson; **D:** Lionel Jeffries. **VHS, Beta** NO

The Railway Dragon

Little Emily and her magical friend, a shy dragon who lives under the old railway tunnel, set off for a secret festival of the legendary reptiles in this well-animated adventure.

1988 (Family) 30m/C **VHS, Beta** $14.95 FHE, WTA

Rain Man 🎬🎬🎬🎬

When his wealthy father dies, ambitious and self-centered Charlie Babbit finds he has Raymond, an older autistic brother who's been institutionalized for years. He's also something of a savant, having extraordinary math skills. Needing him to claim an inheritance, Charlie liberates Raymond from the institution and takes to the road, where both brothers undergo subtle changes. Vegas montage, with Raymond and his mathematical wizardry loose in the casinos, is special. Splendid from start to finish, with Hoffman providing a classic performance both funny and touching. Cruise supplies his best

performance to date as he goes from cad to recognizing something wonderfully human in his brother and himself. **Hound Advisory:** Mature themes; profanity.
1988 (R/ *Sr. High-Adult*) 128m/C Dustin Hoffman, Tom Cruise, Valeria Golino, Jerry Molen, Jack Murdock, Michael D. Roberts, Ralph Seymour, Lucinda Jenney, Bonnie Hunt, Kim Robillard, Beth Grant; **D:** Barry Levinson; **W:** Ronald Bass; **M:** Hans Zimmer. **Award Nominations:** Academy Awards '88: Best Art Direction/ Set Decoration, Best Cinematography, Best Film Editing, Best Original Score; **Awards:** Academy Awards '88: Best Actor (Hoffman), Best Director (Levinson), Best Original Screenplay, Best Picture; Berlin International Film Festival '88: Golden Berlin Bear; Directors Guild of America Awards '88: Best Director (Levinson); Golden Globe Awards '89: Best Actor—Drama (Hoffman), Best Film—Drama; People's Choice Awards '89: Best Film—Drama. **VHS, Beta, LV, 8mm $19.98** *MGM, BTV, JCF*

Rainbow Brite: A Horse of a Different Color

Episodes of a TV cartoon about a little girl whose magic rainbow belt allows here to spread joy and color everywhere; it's all sweetness and light and ruthless merchandising of the Rainbow Brite line of toys and accessories. Additional volumes available.
1986 (*Family*) 42m/C **VHS $29.98** *LIV, WTA*

Rambling Rose 🎞🎞🎞

Dern is Rose, a free-spirited young woman in 1935 who's into free love several decades before everyone else. Taken in by a southern family, Rose immediately has an impact on the male members of the clan, father Duvall and son Haas, thanks to her insuppressible sexuality. This causes consternation with the strait-laced patriarch, who attempts to control his desire for the girl. Eventually Rose decides she must try to stick to one man, but this only causes further problems. Dern gives her best performance yet in this excellent period piece, and solid support is offered from the rest of the cast, in particular Duvall and Dern's real-life mother Ladd. **Hound Advisory:** Profanity; nudity; sexual situations.
1991 (R/ *Sr. High-Adult*) 115m/C Laura Dern, Diane Ladd, Robert Duvall, Lukas Haas, John Heard, Kevin Conway, Robert Burke, Lisa Jakub, Evan Lockwood; **D:** Martha Coolidge; **W:** Calder Willingham; **M:** Elmer Bernstein. **Award Nominations:** Academy Awards '91: Best Actress (Dern), Best Supporting Actress (Ladd); **Awards:** Independent Spirit Awards '92: Best Director (Coolidge), Best Film, Best Supporting Actress (Ladd). **VHS, LV $19.98** *LIV*

Rambo: Children for Peace

Two episodes of the movie-based children's animated series. On TV the Rambo character's explicit violence was toned down and the commando himself transformed into little more than G.I. Joe with long hair and less uniform. Episodes herein are "When S.A.V.A.G.E. Stole Santa" and the title segment. Additional volumes available.
1988 (*Preschool-Primary*) 45m/C **VHS, Beta $14.95** *FHE, WTA*

Ramona

Series of live-action children's adventures starring the heroine from the famous Beverly Cleary children's books.
1987 (*Preschool-Primary*) 60m/C **VHS, Beta** *LHV*

Ramona: Goodbye, Hello

Ramona and her sister deal with the death of the pet cat, but life goes on with Mrs. Quimby's pregnancy. Additional episodes featuring Beverly Cleary's heroine are also available.
1988 (*Family*) 26m/C **VHS $29.95** *WAR*

A Rare Breed 🎞🎞

Adventure of a kidnapped horse in Italy and a young girl's quest to retrieve it. Directed by David Nelson, of television's "Ozzie and Harriet" fame, this one's cute and old fashioned, though decidedly on the bland side.
1981 (PG/ *Jr. High-Adult*) 94m/C George Kennedy, Forrest Tucker, Tracy Vaccaro, Tom Hallick, Don DeFore; **D:** David Nelson. **VHS, Beta $19.95** *STE, LIV*

Rascal

Rascal the raccoon teaches a lonely boy responsibility and changes his life. Condensed adaption of the 1969 Disney feature based on the Sterling North book.
1990 (*Preschool-Primary*) 15m/C **VHS, Beta $250.00** *MTI, DSN*

Rascals and Robbers

Subtitled "The Secret Adventures of Tom Sawyer and Huckleberry Finn," the secret being that this isn't taken from Mark Twain's writings but is a pretty standard TV adventure in which Tom and Huck are chased by a villainous embezzler.
1982 (*Family*) 95m/C Anthony James. **VHS, Beta $59.98** *FOX*

Reading Rainbow: A Chair for My Mother

After a tragic fire, family members work together to rebuild their lives. Burton and friends create a song and dance number called "Teamwork" to illustrate this theme.
19?? (*Family*) 30m/C **VHS $39.95**

Reading Rainbow: Abiyoyo

Award winning PBS-TV series is well represented on videocassette. Each episode uses a storytelling session (usually with a well-known celebrity reader) as a springboard for an informative segment hosted by actor Burton, with additional reading materials suggested at the program's conclusion. Here folk singing deity Seeger relates a South African lullaby about a giant which threatens a town and the little boy who comes up with a plan to save his home. Burton reveals the way stories can be told through music.
19?? (*Family*) 30m/C **VHS $39.95**

Reading Rainbow: Alistair in Outer Space

Alistair is on his way to the library when a spaceship captures him and takes him away in this book by Marilyn Sadler. Host Burton visits the Library of Congress in Washington, DC.
19?? (*Family*) 30m/C **VHS $39.95**

Indiana Jones charms snake in "Raiders of the Lost Ark"

Reading Rainbow: Alistair's Time Machine

In Marilyn Sadler's book, Alistair builds his own time machine. Burton learns about inventors and inventions, including some that never quite worked.
19?? *(Family)* 30m/C **VHS $39.95**

Reading Rainbow: Animal Cafe

Maxwell finds that the food in his shop has mysteriously disappeared overnight in this story by John Stadler while Burton learns what happens at night in New York City.
19?? *(Family)* 30m/C **VHS $39.95**

Reading Rainbow: Arthur's Eyes

Narrator Cosby spins a tale about Arthur, who needs glasses to help him see, which leads to an exploration of the many different ways of looking at the world.
1983 *(Family)* 30m/C **VHS, Beta $14.98** *KUI, LIV,*

Reading Rainbow: Barn Dance!

The book by Bill Martin, Jr. and John Archambault inspires Burton to travel to Tennessee for bluegrass music and a lesson in clogging at a real barn dance.
19?? *(Family)* 30m/C **VHS $39.95**

Reading Rainbow: Bea and Mr. Jones

Kindergartner and her father trade places when she wishes she could be someone else.
198? *(Family)* 30m/C **VHS $39.95**

Reading Rainbow: Berlioz the Bear

Jan Brett's funny story about a group of bears who take their show on the road. Burton meets street musicians and the Boys Choir of Harlem.
19?? *(Family)* 30m/C **VHS $39.95**

Reading Rainbow: Best Friends

Steven Kellogg's book tells how two best friends learn to share a newborn puppy. Burton meets eight golden retriever puppies and learns the importance of pet care.
19?? *(Family)* 30m/C **VHS $39.95**

Reading Rainbow: Bored - Nothing to Do!

Peter Spier's story about two boys who build their own plane and actually fly it. Erstwhile host Burton is inspired to take a flying lesson and learns about airplanes and airports.
19?? *(Family)* 30m/C **VHS $39.95**

Reading Rainbow: Brush

Brush comes to life to replace a banished dog in the book by Pere Calders. Burton learns about Macy's Thanksgiving Day parade balloons and floats.
19?? *(Family)* 30m/C **VHS $39.95**

Reading Rainbow: Bugs

Learn all about insects, including where they live and what they're good for. Burton visits Insect World at the Cincinnati Zoo.
19?? *(Family)* 30m/C **VHS $39.95**

Reading Rainbow: Chickens Aren't the Only Ones

Ruth Heller's book explores the age old question—which came first, the chicken or the egg? Burton visits a chicken farm and then travels to Florida to learn about loggerhead turtles which bury their eggs in the beach sands.
19?? *(Family)* 30m/C **VHS $39.95**

Reading Rainbow: Come a Tide

Features Carter reading George Ella Lyon's book about a family coping with a spring flood. Host Burton discusses different kinds of weather, and offers safety tips. Also includes clips from Hurricane Hugo.
199? *(Family)* 30m/C **VHS $33.70** *PBS,*

Reading Rainbow: Desert Giant: The World of the Saguaro Cactus

Barbara Bash's book about Arizona's Sonoran Desert and its inhabitants. Viewers get a close-up look at bobcats, Gila monsters, rattlesnakes, and other creatures.
19?? *(Family)* 30m/C **VHS $39.95**

Reading Rainbow: Digging Up Dinosaurs

Burton takes viewers back in time to do some dinosaur watching in another installment of the award-winning series.
1983 *(Family)* 30m/C *V:* Jerry Stiller. **VHS $14.98** *KUI,, VES*

Reading Rainbow: Dinosaur Bob and His Adventures with the Family Lazardo

While on an African safari with his family, Scotty befriends a dinosaur he names Bob. Bob has a hidden talent—he can play basketball. From the book by William Joyce. Burton gets basketball tips from the pros of the Oakland Athletics while at spring training.
19?? *(Family)* 30m/C **VHS $39.95**

Reading Rainbow: Dive to the Coral Reef/The Magic School Bus Inside the Earth

In "Dive to the Coral Reef," Burton goes on a scuba adventure in the coral reefs off the Florida Keys. "The Magic School Bus Inside the Earth" has a peculiar teacher and her students going on an amazing field trip, with Burton going cave exploring at the California Caverns.
1992 *(Family)* 60m/C **VHS $12.95** *PBS,, BTV*

Reading Rainbow: Duncan and Delores

Barbara Samuels' book about a little girl who's trying to win the affection of a cat. At Marine World Africa USA, Burton learns about the king of beasts and then gives a backstage peek at the Broadway musical "Cats."
19?? *(Family)* 30m/C **VHS $39.95**

Reading Rainbow: Feelings

Burton's look into the world of feelings, including embarrassment, loneliness, happiness, jealousy, and excitement.
19?? *(Family)* 30m/C **VHS $39.95**

Reading Rainbow: Florence and Eric Take the Cake

Case of mistaken identity develops, from the book by Jocelyn Wild. Burton goes behind the scenes at the MovieLand Wax Museum and learns how a wax figure is made.
19?? *(Family)* 30m/C **VHS $39.95**

Reading Rainbow: Fox on the Job

Lazy fox tries to find the perfect job in this story by James Marshall. Burton learns about different jobs, including household chores.
19?? *(Family)* 30m/C **VHS $39.95**

Reading Rainbow: Galimoto

Karen Lynn Williams' book tells the story of an African boy and his search for scraps of wire to complete a special project. Viewers learn the many uses of wire.
19?? *(Family)* 30m/C **VHS $39.95**

Reading Rainbow: Germs Make Me Sick!

Burton uses a microscope to examine pond water and discover all about germs—what they look like, how they're caught, and how the human body fights back.
19?? *(Family)* 30m/C **VHS $39.95**

Reading Rainbow: Gregory the Terrible Eater/Gila Monsters Meet You at the Airport

Gregory the goat worries his family by being a fussy eater as Burton visits a zoo to learn about the eating habits of animals. A young boy wonders what the west and Gila monsters are really like in this exploration of the Arizona desert.
1983 *(Family)* 60m/C **VHS $14.98** *KUI, LIV, VES*

Reading Rainbow: Hot-Air Henry

Cat enjoys(?) adventure in a hot air balloon and Burton visits a national ballooning event held in South Carolina.
19?? *(Family)* 30m/C **VHS $39.95**

Reading Rainbow: Humphrey the Lost Whale: A True Story

California humpback whale loses his way and needs the help of some human friends to get himself back to the ocean. Burton goes whale-watching.
19?? *(Family)* 30m/C **VHS $39.95**

Reading Rainbow: Imogene's Antlers

Young girl wakes up to discover she has grown antlers overnight but manages to put them to practical use. Burton visits the Philadelphia Zoo to get a close-up look at various animals.
19?? *(Family)* 30m/C **VHS $39.95**

Reading Rainbow: Jack, the Seal and the Sea

Gerald Aschenbrenner's tale of a man who finds an ailing seal and discovers how polluted the oceans are. Burton learns about preserving the waters and about marine life.
19?? *(Family)* 30m/C **VHS $39.95**

Reading Rainbow: Kate Shelley and the Midnight Express

Heroic true story by Margaret K. Wetterer finds Burton looking at the history of trains and traveling on Amtrack's Coast Starlight up the California coast.
19?? *(Family)* 30m/C **VHS $38.95**

Reading Rainbow: Keep the Lights Burning, Abbie

Peter and Connie Roop's book is based on the true story of a young girl who kept the lighthouse light burning through a terrible storm. Burton tours a modern lighthouse in Maine and joins a sailing family for a day at sea.
19?? *(Family)* 30m/C **VHS $39.95**

Reading Rainbow: Knots on a Counting Rope

Native American story about a young boy who finds the confidence to deal with his blindness. Burton tests himself when he decides to camp out all alone in the wilderness.
19?? *(Family)* 30m/C **VHS $39.95**

Reading Rainbow: Liang and the Magic Paintbrush

Chinese legend has a young boy finding a magic paintbrush which brings pictures to life. Host Burton explores New York City's Chinatown and the world of computer art.
19?? *(Family)* 30m/C **VHS $39.95**

Reading Rainbow: Little Nino's Pizzeria

Tony loves helping out at the family restaurant. However, when his father opens a fancy new place, Tony only seems to be in the way. From the book by Karen Barbour. Burton learns how to make his own pizza.
19?? *(Family)* 30m/C **VHS $39.95**

Reading Rainbow: Louis the Fish

Story about a man turning into a fish has host Burton exploring exotic marine life, dolphins, and tidal pools.
19?? *(Family)* 30m/C **VHS $39.95**

Reading Rainbow: Ludlow Laughs

Grumpy Ludlow never laughs or smiles until he has the funniest dream ever. Viewers get a look behind the scenes at a comedy club and meet a stand-up comedian.
19?? *(Family)* 30m/C **VHS $39.95**

Reading Rainbow: Mama Don't Allow

Miles gets a saxophone for his birthday and everyone suffers. But then he and his Swamp Band get an invitation to play at the Alligator Ball. Burton visits an alligator farm in Louisiana, takes a riverboat journey in Mississippi, and meets a New Orleans saxophonist.
19?? *(Family)* 30m/C **VHS $39.95**

Reading Rainbow: Meanwhile Back at the Ranch

Rancher Hicks misses some big surprises at home when he travels to Sleepy Gulch in Trinka Hankes Noble's book. Burton learns about the cowboy life when he visits the western town of Old Tucson, Arizona.
19?? *(Family)* 30m/C **VHS $39.95**

Reading Rainbow: Miss Nelson is Back

The book is all about surprises; host Burton finds some surprises of his own while on a birthday treasure hunt.
198? *(Family)* 30m/C **VHS $39.95**

Reading Rainbow: Mrs. Katz and Tush

Friendship between a widowed Jewish woman and her young black friend is explored. As their friendship grows, they share each other's cultures, and note the similarities in their histories. LeVar Burton participates in a seder.
1993 *(Primary)* 28m/C **VHS $39.95**

Reading Rainbow: Mufaro's Beautiful Daughters

Story is an African tale about two very different sisters. Burton learns about African culture and joins the Forces of Nature, an African dance troupe.
19?? *(Family)* 30m/C **VHS $39.95**

Reading Rainbow: Mummies Made in Egypt/Bringing the Rain to Kapiti Plain

"Mummies Made in Egypt" provides a look at the ancient world of mummies, with Burton visiting the Museum of Fine Arts in Boston to learn about conserving Egyptian artifacts. The story "Bringing the Rain to Kapiti Plain" is a tale from the Nandi people of Kenya and has Burton planning an adventurous day around rainy weather.
1992 *(Family)* 60m/C **VHS $12.95** *PBS, BTV,*

Reading Rainbow: My Little Island

Frane Lessac's book concerns a little boy who takes his best friend to visit the Caribbean island where he was born. Burton visits the beautiful tropical island of Montserrat in the West Indies.
19?? *(Family)* 30m/C **VHS $39.95**

Reading Rainbow: OPT: An Illusionary Tale/A Three Hat Day

"OPT: An Illusionary Tale" explores the fool-the-eye world of optical illusions. "A Three Hat Day" has Burton exploring the hats used in different professions, which includes visiting a racetrack and a hockey rink.
1992 *(Family)* 60m/C **VHS $12.95** *PBS, BTV,*

Reading Rainbow: Ox-Cart Man

Account of family life in 19th century New England leads Burton to visit the living history museum at Old Sturbridge, Massachusetts.
19?? *(Family)* 30m/C **VHS $39.95**

Reading Rainbow: Paul Bunyan

Tall tale of woodsman Paul Bunyan is narrated while Burton joins Smokey the Bear in learning about forest conservation.
19?? *(Family)* 30m/C **VHS $39.95**

Reading Rainbow: Perfect the Pig/ Ty's One-Man Band

A look at the ways people view pigs, as contrasted to their real everyday existence — and the episodes guest star, Kermit the Frog, should know a thing or two about pigs. Includes a short, "Ty's One-Man Band," about a mysterious stranger who devises a Rube-Goldbergian one-man band.
1987 *(Family)* 60m/C Kermit the Frog. **VHS, Beta $14.98** *KUI,*

Reading Rainbow: Raccoons and Ripe Corn

Burton joins author/illustrator Jim Arnosky to learn about wildlife watching.
19?? *(Family)* 30m/C **VHS $39.95**

Reading Rainbow: Rechenka's Eggs

traditional Ukrainian egg-painting art called pysanky is demonstrated by author/illustrator Patricia Polacco.
19?? *(Family)* 30m/C **VHS $39.95**

Reading Rainbow: Rumplestiltskin/ Snowy Day: Stories and Poems

In "Rumplestiltskin," Burton visits a Renaissance festival where traveling performers re-enact the classic fairy tale. "Snowy Day: Stories and Poems" has Burton traveling to Jackson Hole, Wyoming to show viewers how to enjoy winter's chills and thrills.
1992 *(Family)* 60m/C **VHS $12.95** *PBS, BTV,*

Reading Rainbow: Sam the Sea Cow

Find out about the manatee, both from Francine Jacobs' book and a trip to Sea World of Florida.
19?? *(Family)* 30m/C **VHS $39.95**

Reading Rainbow: Seashore Surprises

Burton goes beachcombing in southwestern Florida using the reference book by Rose Wyler as his guide. He also talks to naturalist Lisa Satchel and marine scientist Christy Slomer, who share their knowledge about the area and its life. Includes reviews on three books by young readers: "The Seashore Book," "What's Inside? Shells," and "Is This a House for Hermit Crab?"
199? *(Family)* 30m/C **VHS $33.70** *PBS,*

Reading Rainbow: Silent Lotus

Deaf Cambodian girl named Lotus learns to dance by following the vibrations of the music, and becomes the best dancer in the kingdom. LeVar Burton talks with other hearing people, who show how they communicate with sign language.
1993 *(Preschool-Primary)* 28m/C **VHS $39.95**

Reading Rainbow: Simon's Book

Doodled drawings come to scary life in this story while Burton visits a printing plant and meets author/illustrator Henrik Drescher.
19?? *(Family)* 30m/C **VHS $39.95**

Reading Rainbow: Sophie and Lou

Petra Mathers book finds a mouse named Sophie learning to dance to help her overcome her shyness. Dancing is also what Burton practices as viewers get a look at different dances from around the world.
19?? *(Family)* 30m/C **VHS $39.95**

Reading Rainbow: Space Case

One spooky Halloween a young boy gets a special treat when he meets beings from another planet.
19?? *(Family)* 30m/C **VHS $39.95**

Reading Rainbow: Sports Pages

Arnold Adoff's book inspires your man Burton to explore all types of sports, including soccer, basketball, ice skating, swimming, and gymnastics.
19?? *(Family)* 30m/C **VHS $39.95**

Reading Rainbow: Stay Away from the Junkyard!

In Tricia Tusa's book, Theodora wanders into a forbidden junkyard only to find that all the "junk" really isn't useless. Burton meets an artist who uses found objects in his work.
19?? *(Family)* 30m/C **VHS $39.95**

Reading Rainbow: Sunken Treasure

Fearless host Burton is inspired by Gail Gibbons book to go on a treasure hunt at "Pirates' Cove" in California. Also a look at the most famous shipwreck in history, the Titanic.
19?? *(Family)* 30m/C **VHS $39.95**

Reading Rainbow: Tar Beach

When you can't go to a real beach the building roof makes a dandy substitute in this tale from Faith Ringgold. Viewers take a sky-high look at the George Washington Bridge as well as rooftop gardens and a pigeon keeper.
19?? *(Family)* 30m/C **VHS $39.95**

Reading Rainbow: The Bicycle Man/ The Adventures of Taxi Dog

"The Bicycle Man" has Burton exploring all types of wheeled vehicles, including bicycles, skateboards, scooters, and roller blades. "The Adventures of Taxi Dog" follows a day in the life of a dog befriended by a New York City cab driver. Burton becomes a taxi driver for a day and then goes to Colorado to meet a very special dog.
1992 *(Family)* 60m/C **VHS $12.95** *PBS, BTV,*

Reading Rainbow: The Bionic Bunny Show

Wilbur is an ordinary rabbit in real life but his job has him turning into the superhero star of his own television show. Burton takes the viewer behind the scenes of the TV show "Star Trek: The Next Generation," where he happens to have a starring role.
19?? *(Family)* 30m/C **VHS $39.95**

Reading Rainbow: The Day Jimmy's Boa Ate the Wash

School trip to a peaceful farm turns wild when Jimmy's pet boa constrictor escapes. Meanwhile, your faithful host Burton

visits an exotic pet store and a livestock show where he learns about barnyard animals.
19?? *(Family)* 30m/C **VHS $39.95**

Reading Rainbow: The Gift of the Sacred Dog

Folktale from American tribal tradition about a boy who brings horses as a gift to his people. Host Burton visits the Crow Fair powwow in Montana.
19?? *(Family)* 30m/C **VHS $39.95**

Reading Rainbow: The Lady with the Ship on Her Head

Deborah Nurse Lattimore's book inspires a visit to the world's biggest barbershop as well as a wacky news report.
19?? *(Family)* 30m/C **VHS $39.95**

Reading Rainbow: The Legend of the Indian Paintbrush/The Lifecycle of the Honeybee

"The Legend of the Indian Paintbrush" has a young Indian boy searching for a special gift to give his people. Burton visits Taos, New Mexico to talk to three Pueblo artists. "The Lifecycle of the Honeybee" has Burton visiting a bee-keeper to examine a beehive and learn how honey is made.
1992 *(Family)* 60m/C **VHS $12.95** *PBS, BTV,*

Reading Rainbow: The Milk Makers

Learn about one of nature's most nutritious foods, from the dairy cow to the supermarket. Burton visits a farm, learns to milk a cow by hand, and sees how milking machines work.
19?? *(Family)* 30m/C **VHS $39.95**

Reading Rainbow: The Paper Crane

Molly Bang's book about the kindness of a restaurant owner and the magical gift he receives from a stranger. Burton celebrates Japanese culture with the Gasho of Japan in Central Valley, New York.
19?? *(Family)* 30m/C **VHS $39.95**

Reading Rainbow: The Patchwork Quilt

Young girl learns the secrets behind her grandmother's memory quilt in this story by Valerie Flournoy. At the Boston Children's Museum, kids learn to make their own patchwork quilt.
19?? *(Family)* 30m/C **VHS $39.95**

Reading Rainbow: The Piggy in the Puddle

Host Burton visits artists who dramatize the book "Piggy in the Puddle," by Charlotte Pomerantz, through claymation and walks viewers through the process step by step.
199? *(Family)* 30m/C **VHS $33.70** *PBS,*

Reading Rainbow: The Purple Coat

Every year Gabrielle gets a new navy blue coat from her Grandpa but this year she wants him to make her something different. Burton learns about the New York garment district and the world of fashion design.
19?? *(Family)* 30m/C **VHS $39.95**

Reading Rainbow: The Robbery at the Diamond Dog Diner

Eileen Christelow's book concerns a chicken named Gloria Feathers who must outwit a couple of would-be robbers. Burton goes to Rosie's Diner and gets a lesson in becoming a short-order cook.
19?? *(Family)* 30m/C **VHS $39.95**

Reading Rainbow: The Runaway Duck

Carved wooden duck named Egbert goes on a trip around the world in the book by David Lyon. Burton learns about waterfowl while on a trip to Maryland's Chesapeake Bay as well as the art of duck carving.
19?? *(Family)* 30m/C **VHS $39.95**

Reading Rainbow: The Wall

Eve Bunting's book finds Burton at the Vietnam Veteran's Memorial in Washington, DC and meeting the architect, Maya Lin.
19?? *(Family)* ?m/C **VHS $38.95**

Reading Rainbow: Three by the Sea

Burton explores the beach thanks to this episode's story and learns about the sea, sun, and air, and using your imagination.
19?? *(Family)* 30m/C **VHS $39.95**

Reading Rainbow: Three Days on a River in a Red Canoe

Burton goes camping with a group of young friends and experiences some of the same adventures the children in a story have.
19?? *(Family)* 30m/C **VHS $39.95**

Reading Rainbow: Through Moon and Stars and Night Skies

Ann Turner's loving tale of a family formed through adoption leads to a look at family life.
19?? *(Family)* 30m/C **VHS $39.95**

Reading Rainbow: Tight Times

First episode of the PBS "Reading Rainbow" series, with host Burton showing his friends how to have a great time without spending any money, including a visit to the public library.
198? *(Family)* 30m/C **VHS $39.95**

Reading Rainbow: Tooth-Gnasher Superflash

The Popsnorkles need a new car and test drive the amazing Tooth-Gnasher Superflash. From the book by Daniel Pinkwater. Burton learns all about automobiles when he spends the day in a service station.
19?? *(Family)* 30m/C **VHS $39.95**

Reading Rainbow: Tortoise & the Hare/Hill of Fire

Radner narrates "Tortoise & the Hare" while host Burton competes with some of Hawaii's top bicyclists in the Rainbow Mini-Classic race. In "Hill of Fire" a volcano is born in a poor farmer's corn field while Burton visits Volcanoes National Park.
1987 *(Family)* 60m/C **VHS, Beta $14.98** *KUI, LIV,*

Reading Rainbow: Watch the Stars Come Out

Burton explores the plight of immigrants to America and learns about the restoration of the Statue of Liberty.
19?? *(Family)* 30m/C **VHS $39.95**

Real Genius 🎬🎬🎬

Socially awkward teen genius graduates high school early, then attends a technical college and finds friends among brilliant but wild young adults who use their scientific know-how for zany pranks and "Beakman's World"-style fun. When they learn their class-project laser is to be sold as a military weapon, the youths use their cleverness to thwart the illegal scheme. Nice to see a comedy that so clearly celebrates higher intelligence; it's just too bad that the second half dwells on a basic revenge setup. **Hound Advisory:** Sex, some of it quite touching (like the teen hero's affair with lonely girl nerd), some of it smarmy (a seductive blonde plots to sleep with the brightest man she can find). Salty language.
1985 **(PG/**Jr. High-Adult**)** 108m/C Val Kilmer, Gabe Jarret, Jonathan Gries, Michelle Meyrink, William Atherton, Patti D'Arbanville, Severn Darden; **D:** Martha Coolidge; **W:** Peter Torokvei, Neal Israel, Pat Proft; **M:** Thomas Newman. **VHS, Beta, LV $14.95** *COL*

The Real Ghostbusters

Cartoon series based on characters from the blockbuster '80s feature film comedies. Of special interest to kids whose parents want them to be copyright lawyers; it's called the "real" Ghostbusters to distinguish them from "The Original Ghostbusters," a mid-'70s live-action Saturday-morning Sid & Marty Krofft comedy that was later revived in cartoon form (as plain old "Ghostbusters") to take advantage of renewed ghost buster mania. All three titles haunt home video, if you need to compare. Additional volumes available.
1986 *(Preschool)* 25m/C **VHS, Beta $14.95** *COL*

The Real McCoy 🎬🎬

Generally awful crime-caper film about female bank robber Karen McCoy (Basinger). Just out of prison, all Karen wants to do is go straight and raise her young son but her plans are thwarted by former associates who kidnap the child to force her into one last heist. Kilmer is the small-time thief, with a crush on Karen, who tries to help her out. Dumb, slow-moving story with a vapid performance by Basinger. **Hound Advisory:** Violence and profanity.
1993 **(PG-13/**Jr. High-Adult**)** 104m/C Kim Basinger, Val Kilmer, Terence Stamp, Zach English, Gailard Sartain; **D:** Russell Mulcahy; **W:** William Davies. **VHS, LV** *MCA*

The Real Story of Humpty Dumpty

Animated story of good egg Humpty who rescues a princess from an evil witch but winds up scrambled.
1992 *(Preschool-Primary)* 25m/C **V:** Glenda Jackson, Huey Lewis. **VHS $12.95** *BTV, WTA, GBV*

The Real Story of Oh Christmas Tree

Fable of why the pine tree stays green all year and how the tradition of Christmas trees got started.
1992 *(Preschool-Primary)* ?m/C **V:** John Ritter, Deborah Harry, Jason Ritter. **VHS $14.95** *WTA, FFF, GBV*

Reality Bites 🎬🎬🎬

Charming little story about life on the other side of college for four recent grads living, working, and slacking in Houston. Script by newcomer Childress is at its best when highlighting the Generation X artifacts: 7-Eleven Big Gulps, tacky '70s memorabilia, and games revolving around episodes of old TV shows like "Good Times," to name a few. Interesting story about the post-adolescent muddle, with strong performances by Ryder and Hawke as housemates fighting their attraction to each other, though newcomer Garofalo steals the show. Look for a nice bit by Mahoney as a cranky morning show host. Stiller proves adept both behind and in front of the camera. **Hound Advisory:** Fairly tame stuff for mature teens, with a limited semi-sexual situation tastefully exploited. Should not be used as a teaching aid for credit card use. Some profanity; alcohol use; drug talk.
1994 **(PG-13/**Jr. High-Adult**)** 99m/C Winona Ryder, Ethan Hawke, Ben Stiller, Janeane Garofalo, Steve Zahn, Swoosie Kurtz, Joe Don Baker, John Mahoney; **Cameos:** David Pirner, Anne Meara, Jeanne Tripplehorn, Karen Duffy, Evan Dando; **D:** Ben Stiller; **W:** Helen Childress; **M:** Karl Wallinger. **VHS, LV** *MCA*

Really Wild Animals: Deep Sea Dive

Neat new concept from the National Geographic Foundation makes their famed nature documentaries more accessible to MTV-generation kids through the use of animation, bright music, and graphics integrated with usual superb animal footage. Moore hosts (as a cartoon globe named Spin), and here he narrates amazing adventures with some of the ocean's remarkable denizens, including sharks, dolphins, and whales.
1994 *(Primary-Jr. High)* 45m/C **VHS $14.95** *COL, BTV*

Really Wild Animals: Swinging Safari

National Geographic footage takes kids on an African safari from the Serengeti Plain to the Kalahari Desert, with looks at cheetahs, crocodiles, rhinos, and chimpanzees, both through Moore's witty narration and music-video montage. Child-friendly and notably absent of those standard scenes of lions disembowelling prey.
1994 (*Primary-Jr. High*) 44m/C **VHS $14.95** *COL, BTV*

Really Wild Animals: Wonders Down Under

Series goes to Australia and reveals some of the country's strange creatures, including koalas, platypuses, and kangaroos. Moore does the marsupial rap.
1994 (*Primary-Jr. High*) 45m/C **VHS $14.95** *COL, BTV*

Rear Window 🎬🎬🎬🎬

Newspaper photographer with a broken leg (Stewart) passes the time recuperating by observing his neighbors through the window. When he sees what he believes to be a murder, he decides to solve the crime himself. With help from his beautiful girlfriend and his nurse, he tries to catch the murderer without getting killed himself. Top-drawer Hitchcock blends exquisite suspense with occasional on-target laughs. Based on the story "It Had to Be Murder" by Cornell Woolrich.
1954 (*Jr. High-Adult*) 112m/C James Stewart, Grace Kelly, Thelma Ritter, Wendell Corey, Raymond Burr, Judith Evelyn; **D:** Alfred Hitchcock; **W:** John Michael Hayes; **M:** Franz Waxman. **Award Nominations:** Academy Awards '54: Best Director (Hitchcock), Best Screenplay, Best Sound; **Awards:** Edgar Allan Poe Awards '54: Best Screenplay. **VHS, Beta, LV $19.95** *MCA, TLF, HMV*

Rebecca 🎬🎬🎬🎬

Based on Daphne Du Maurier's best-selling novel about a young unsophisticated girl who marries a moody and prominent country gentleman haunted by the memory of his first wife, Rebecca. Fontaine and Olivier turn in fine performances as the unlikely couple. Suspenseful and surprising gothic romance was Hitchcock's first American film and earned his only "best picture" Oscar. Laserdisc features rare screen tests of Vivien Leigh, Anne Baxter, Loretta Young, and Joan Fontaine, footage from Rebecca's winning night at the Academy Awards, original radio broadcasts of film by Orson Welles and David O. Selznick, and commentary of film with interview excerpts with Hitchcock.
1940 (*Family*) 130m/B Joan Fontaine, Laurence Olivier, Judith Anderson, George Sanders, Nigel Bruce, Florence Bates, Gladys Cooper, Reginald Denny, Leo G. Carroll, Sir C. Aubrey Smith, Melville Cooper; **D:** Alfred Hitchcock; **W:** Joan Harrison, Robert Sherwood; **M:** Franz Waxman. **Award Nominations:** Academy Awards '40: Best Actor (Olivier), Best Actress (Fontaine), Best Adapted Screenplay, Best Director (Hitchcock), Best Film Editing, Best Interior Decoration, Best Supporting Actress (Anderson), Best Original Score; **Awards:** Academy Awards '40: Best Black and White Cinematography, Best Picture; National Board of Review Awards '40: 10 Best Films of the Year. **VHS, Beta, LV $19.98** *FOX, VYG, HMV*

Rebecca of Sunnybrook Farm 🎬🎬🎬

Farm girl Rebecca becomes a radio star over her aunt's objections, in this bouncy musical that has next to nothing to do with the famous Kate Douglas Wiggin novel of the title. The curly-topped one performs a medley of her song hits (including "On the Good Ship Lollipop") with future Tin Woodman Haley and dances the finale with Robinson. For purists, Mary Pickford's 1917 silent adaptation of "Rebecca of Sunnybrook Farm," more faithful to the book, is also on tape. 🎵On the Good Ship Lollipop/When I'm With You/Animal Crackers medley; Crackly Corn Flakes; Alone With You; Happy Ending; Au Revoir; An Old Straw Hat; Come and Get Your Happiness; Parade of the Wooden Soldiers.
1938 (*Family*) 80m/B Shirley Temple, Randolph Scott, Jack Haley, Phyllis Brooks, Gloria Stuart, Slim Summerville, Bill Robinson, Helen Westley, William Demarest; **D:** Allan Dwan. **VHS, Beta, LV $19.98** *FOX, MLB, MLT*

Rebel Without a Cause 🎬🎬🎬🎬

James Dean's most memorable screen appearance, as a troubled teen from the right side of the tracks. New kid in town Jim Stark is alienated from both his wealthy parents ("Mr. Magoo" Backus in a dramatic mien as Jim's weak-willed father) and high-school peers. One fateful night he competes with local punks over neighborhood bad girl Wood and tries to save a neurotic boy who trusts Jim as his only friend. Slang, hair and clothes may have changed since 1955, but this in-the-gut story of adolescence still packs a wallop. Peace's original widescreen format suffers severely on trimmed-down videocassette. **Hound Advisory:** Alcohol use, violence, mature themes.
1955 (*Jr. High-Adult*) 111m/C James Dean, Natalie Wood, Sal Mineo, Jim Backus, Nick Adams, Dennis Hopper, Ann Doran, William Hopper, Rochelle Hudson, Corey Allen, Edward Platt; **D:** Nicholas Ray; **W:** Stewart Stern; **M:** Leonard Rosenman. **VHS, Beta, LV $19.98** *WAR*

The Red Balloon 🎬🎬🎬🎬

The story of Pascal, a lonely French boy who befriends a wondrous red balloon which follows him everywhere. Lovely, finely done parable of childhood, imagination, and friendship.
1956 (*Family*) 34m/C Pascal Lamorisse; **D:** Albert Lamorisse. **VHS, Beta, LV, 8mm $14.95** *COL, HHT, DVT*

The Red Pony 🎬🎬🎬

Tommy, small son in a not-so-harmonious ranching family, feels closer to genial hired-hand Billy than to his moody father. Billy gives the boy his first pony to care for, but its tragic illness leaves Tommy feeling betrayed. Somewhat uneven in its mix of adult- and kid-level drama, but effectively tearjerking in the end, with a warm evocation of its time and place. Based on the novel by John Steinbeck.
1949 (*Family*) 89m/C Myrna Loy, Robert Mitchum, Peter Miles, Louis Calhern, Sheppard Strudwick, Margaret Hamilton, Beau Bridges; **D:** Lewis Milestone; **M:** Aaron Copland. **VHS, LV $14.98** *REP, KUI*

The Red Pony 🎬🎬🎬

Award-winning TV redo of the John Steinbeck novel about the troubled farm boy who spends time with a frail pony to help cope with his turbulent home life. Emphasis in this

version is on the family's difficult father, portrayed superbly by Fonda. **Hound Advisory:** Violence.
1976 *(Preschool)* 101m/C Henry Fonda, Maureen O'Hara; **D:** Robert Totten. VHS, Beta, LV $19.98 *BFA*

Red Riding Hood 🦴⬚

Cannon Movie Tale, which should be warning enough, stretches the story of the little girl in red and that nasty wolf to torturous feature length.
1989 *(G/Family)* 84m/C Craig T. Nelson, Isabella Rossellini; **D:** Adam Brooks. VHS *WAR*

Red Riding Hood and Goldilocks

Two classic children's stories are read, not animated, against detailed illustrations and scintillating music, featuring actress Ryan as narrator. Part of the "Rabbit Ears: We All Have Tales" series.
1991 *(Preschool-Primary)* 30m/C VHS, LV $15.99 *KUI, COL*

The Red Shoes 🦴🦴🦴🦴

Beautifully filmed British classic about a young ballerina torn between love and her choreographer's demand that she devote herself completely to her work. What she primarily performs is, in fact, "The Red Shoes," the Hans Christian Andersen story about a pair of shoes that won't stop dancing even when the owner wants to, which is a metaphor for the heroine's dilemma. Only tangentially a children's film, and the climax is tragedy at its most dizzyingly romantic. The same filmmakers went on to do "The Tales of Hoffmann," arguably more kid-friendly. **Hound Advisory:** Mature themes.
1948 *(Family)* 136m/C Anton Walbrook, Moira Shearer, Marius Goring, Leonide Massine, Robert Helpmann, Albert Basserman, Ludmila Tcherina, Esmond Knight, Emeric Pressburger; **D:** Michael Powell; **W:** Emeric Pressburger, Michael Powell. **Award Nominations:** Academy Awards '48: Best Film Editing, Best Picture, Best Story; **Awards:** Academy Awards '48: Best Art Direction/Set Decoration (Color), Best Score; Golden Globe Awards '49: Best Score; National Board of Review Awards '48: 10 Best Films of the Year. VHS, Beta, LV $19.95 *PAR, HMV*

The Red Shoes

An animated modernization of the Hans Christian Andersen tale, involving two present-day girls and a winning lottery ticket as well as that endlessly dancing footwear.
1990 *(Preschool-Primary)* 30m/C **D:** Michael Sporn. VHS, Beta $14.95 *FHE, TVC, WTA*

The Red Stallion 🦴🦴

A young boy raises his pony into an award-winning racehorse that saves the farm when it wins the big race. Good outdoor photography but loses something in the human relationships.
1947 *(Family)* 82m/B Robert Paige, Noreen Nash, Ted Donaldson, Jane Darwell; **D:** Lesley Selander. VHS $19.95 *NOS, MOV, HEG*

Reddy the Fox

Another cartoon character from "Fables of the Green Forest," an episode featuring the most cunning of all forest dwellers, Reddy, who's a sort of vulpine Wile E. Coyote eternally after Peter Cottontail. Available in Spanish as well as English.

1980 *(Family)* 52m/C VHS $29.95 *FHE*

Regarding Henry 🦴🦴🦴

Cold-hearted successful lawyer gets shot in the head during a holdup and becomes warm-hearted unemployed lawyer with no memory of earlier life. During recovery the new Henry displays compassion and conscience the old one never had, bonding with lonely wife and daughter. Too calculated in its yuppie-bashing ironies, it's still a rather sweet good-feeler that works thanks to solid acting. **Hound Advisory:** Ford takes a bullet to the head in opening moments; otherwise, it's a fairly inoffensive affair.
1991 *(PG-13/Jr. High-Adult)* 107m/C Harrison Ford, Annette Bening, Bill Nunn, Mikki Allen, Elizabeth Wilson, Robin Bartlett, John Leguizamo, Donald Moffatt, Nancy Marchand; **D:** Mike Nichols; **W:** Jeffrey Abrams; **M:** Hans Zimmer. VHS, Beta, LV $14.95 *PAR*

Regl'ar Fellers 🦴🦴

Gang of kids save the town and soften the heart of their grandmother, too. Sloppy production redeemed by the presence of Little Rascal fave 'Alfalfa' Switzer. Not coincidentally, the short feature was based on a popular newspaper comic strip of the era that was itself inspired by "Our Gang."
1941 *(Family)* 66m/B Billy Lee, Carl "Alfalfa" Switzer, Buddy Boles, Janet Dempsey, Sarah Padden, Roscoe Ates; **D:** Arthur Dreifuss. VHS $19.95 *NOS, FMT, VYY*

The Reivers 🦴🦴🦴

Young rich boy, his roguish chauffeur and another adult pal journey from small town Mississippi, circa 1905, to the big city of Memphis in a stolen car. Based on William Faulkner's last novel, it's an enjoyable, picaresque road trip. **Hound Advisory:** Alcohol use, sex talk, mature themes.
1969 *(PG/Jr. High-Adult)* 107m/C Steve McQueen, Sharon Farrell, Will Geer, Michael Constantine, Rupert Crosse; **D:** Mark Rydell; **W:** Harriet Frank Jr., Irving Ravetch; **M:** John Williams. VHS, Beta $14.98 *FOX*

The Reluctant Dragon

Sir Giles is called on to rid the town of its worst pest: a dragon who enjoys not fighting, but reading poetry. Abridged version of the Disney classic short.
1990 *(Preschool-Primary)* 19m/C VHS, Beta $250.00 *DSN, MTI, GBV*

The Remains of the Day 🦴🦴🦴

If repression is your cup of tea then this is the film for you. Others may want to shake British butler par excellence Stevens (Hopkins) and tell him to express an emotion. In the 1930s, Stevens is the rigidly traditional butler to Lord Darlington (Fox). When Miss Kenton (Thompson) the almost vivacious new housekeeper expresses a quietly personal interest in Stevens his loyalty to an unworthy master prevents him from a chance at happiness. A quiet movie, told in flashback. Hopkins' impressive performance gets by strictly on nuance with Thompson at least allowed a small amount of natural charm. Based on the novel by Kazuo Ishiguro. **Hound Advisory:** Brief profanity.

1993 (**PG**/*College-Adult*) 135m/C Anthony Hopkins, Emma Thompson, James Fox, Christopher Reeve, Peter Vaughan, Hugh Grant, Michael Lonsdale, Tim Pigott-Smith; **D:** James Ivory; **W:** Ruth Prawer Jhabvala; **M:** Richard Robbins. **Award Nominations:** Academy Awards '93: Best Actor (Hopkins), Best Actress (Thompson), Best Adapted Screenplay, Best Art Direction/Set Decoration, Best Costume Design, Best Director (Ivory), Best Original Screenplay, Best Picture; British Academy Awards '94: Best Actress (Thompson), Best Adapted Screenplay, Best Director (Ivory), Best Film; Directors Guild of America Awards '93: Best Director (Ivory); Golden Globe Awards '94: Best Actor—Drama (Hopkins), Best Actress—Drama (Thompson), Best Director (Ivory), Best Film—Drama, Best Screenplay; **Awards:** British Academy Awards '94: Best Actor (Hopkins); Los Angeles Film Critics Association Awards '93: Best Actor (Hopkins); National Board of Review Awards '93: Best Actor (Hopkins). **VHS, LV, 8mm** *COL*

Remo Williams: The Adventure Begins 🐾🐾

Adaptation of "The Destroyer" adventure novel series with a Bond-like hero who can walk on water and dodge bullets after being instructed by a Korean martial arts master. Funny and diverting, and Grey is excellent (if a bit over the top) as the wizened oriental. The title's assumption is that the adventure will continue. **Hound Advisory:** Profanity and violence.
1985 (**PG-13**/*Jr. High-Adult*) 121m/C Fred Ward, Joel Grey, Wilford Brimley, Kate Mulgrew; **D:** Guy Hamilton. **VHS, Beta, LV $14.99** *HBO*

Remote 🐾🐾

Thirteen-year-old Randy is a whiz designing remote-control gadgets, but his parents have mixed feelings about his constant tinkering. The boy stashes his model planes, helicopters, robots, and cars in a home under construction, and when robbers invade the hideout, Randy fights back with his high-tech army. Innocuous but low-flying ripoff of "Home Alone," from the creators of "Prehysteria." **Hound Advisory:** Roughhousing, though allegedly the PG rating was for salty language, which even the Hound's ears couldn't detect.
1993 (**PG**/*Jr. High-Adult*) 80m/C Chris Carrara, Jessica Bowman, John Diehl, Derya Ruggles, Tony Longo, Stuart Fratkin; **D:** Ted Nicolaou; **W:** Mike Farrow; **M:** Richard Band. **VHS, Beta** *PAR*

Renaissance Man 🐾🐾🐾🐾

Skeptical new teacher inspires a classroom of underachievers and finds his true calling. Based loosely on the experiences of screenwriter Burnstein at a base in Michigan. Civilian Bill Rago (DeVito) is an unemployed ad exec assigned to teach Shakespeare to a group of borderline Army recruits led by Hardison. Add half a bone for the recruits and their Hamlet rap, a breath of fresh air in an otherwise stale plot. Some funny moments, reminiscent of "Stripes," but not quite as wacky. On the other hand, Marshall does endearing better than most. Shot with the cooperation of the Army. **Hound Advisory:** Profanity.
1994 (**PG-13**/*Jr. High-Adult*) 124m/C Danny DeVito, Gregory Hines, James Remar, Stacey Dash, Ed Begley Jr., "Marky" Mark Wahlberg, Lillo Brancato, Kadeem Hardison, Richard T. Jones, Khalil Kain, Peter Simmons, Jenifer Lewis; **Cameos:** Cliff Robertson; **D:** Penny Marshall; **W:** Jim Burnstein, Ned Mauldin; **M:** Hans Zimmer. **VHS** *NYR*

Renfrew of the Royal Mounted 🐾🐾

Canadian Mountie goes after counterfeiters and sings a few songs in this mild adaptation of a popular kid's radio serial. The original Dudley Do-Right, though humor here isn't quite

so intentional. Perhaps Renfrew's dog Lightning should have been the star. Also on video: "Renfrew on the Great White Trail."
1937 (*Family*) 57m/B Carol Hughes, James Newill, Kenneth Harlan; **D:** Al Herman. **VHS, Beta** *DVT, GPV, HEG*

The Rescue 🐾🐾

The Disney folks bought into the 1980s "Rambo" craze (through their Touchstone Pictures division) with this empty-headed mix of firefights and family values. When an elite team of U.S. Navy Seal commandoes is captured by the commies in North Korea, the U.S. government won't do a thing to save them. So their children decide to mount a rescue. Not for cynics. **Hound Advisory:** Violence, salty language.
1988 (**PG**/*Primary-Adult*) 97m/C Marc Price, Charles Haid, Kevin Dillon, Christina Harnos, Edward Albert; **D:** Ferdinand Fairfax; **W:** Jim Thomas, John Thomas; **M:** Bruce Broughton. **VHS, Beta, LV $89.95** *TOU, HHE*

The Rescuers 🐾🐾🐾

Bernard and Miss Bianca, two mice members of the Rescue Aid Society who meet in the walls of the United Nations, attempt to save an orphan named Penny from the evil Madame Medusa, who's after the world's biggest diamond. The heroes are aided by a comic albatross, a dragonfly, and a horde of silly swamp creatures. Cute, not great, Disney animation. Based on the stories of Margery Sharp.
1977 (**G**/*Family*) 76m/C **D:** Wolfgang Reitherman, John Lounsbery; **V:** Bob Newhart, Eva Gabor, Geraldine Page, Jim Jordan, Joe Flynn, Jeanette Nolan, Pat Buttram. **VHS, LV $24.99** *DIS, OM*

The Rescuers Down Under 🐾🐾🐾

The followup to "The Rescuers" places its characters in Australia with only mild results for a Magic Kingdom product. Heroic mice Bernard and Bianca protect a young boy and a rare golden eagle from a poacher. One undeniable asset: a stirring musical score by Bruce Broughton.
1990 (**G**/*Family*) 77m/C **D:** Hendel Butoy, Mike Gabriel; **W:** Jim Cox, Karey Kirkpatrick, Joe Ranft, Byron Simpson; **M:** Bruce Broughton; **V:** Bob Newhart, Eva Gabor, John Candy, Tristan Rogers, George C. Scott, Frank Welker, Adam Ryen. **VHS, Beta, LV $29.99** *DIS, OM*

Return from Witch Mountain 🐾🐾

Sequel to the well-done "Escape to Witch Mountain" wastes a good cast in a rehash ranging from tepid to distressing. Two evil grownups use mind-control drugs to try and harness the psychic kids from the original and use their powers to place Los Angeles in nuclear jeopardy. Note the Disney-cute L.A. street gangs.
1978 (**G**/*Family*) 93m/C Christopher Lee, Bette Davis, Ike Eisenmann, Kim Richards, Jack Soo; **D:** John Hough; **W:** Malcolm Marmorstein. **VHS, Beta** *DIS*

Return of Captain Invincible 🐾🐾

Erratic superhero spoof from Australia, brilliant in some scenes, incredibly inept in others - much like its main character, a washed-up, alcoholic Superman-type trying to make a comeback. Some swell gags are lost simply because of bad editing. Zany (sometimes profane) musical numbers from the "Rocky Horror Picture Show" team are the high points.

Hound Advisory: Profanity, alcohol use, sex talk, rough-housing.
1983 (PG/*Jr. High-Adult*) 90m/C Alan Arkin, Christopher Lee, Kate Fitzpatrick, Bill Hunter, Graham Kennedy, Michael Pate, Hayes Gordon, Max Phipps, Noel Ferrier; *D:* Philippe Mora; *W:* Steven E. de Souza. **VHS, Beta, LV** *NO*

The Return of Jafar 🎬🎬🎬

Clumsy thief Abis Mal inadvertently releases evil sorcerer Jafar from his lamp prison and now the powerful "genie Jafar" plots his revenge. So it's up to Aladdin and friends to save the Sultan's kingdom once again. Contains five new songs. ♫Just Forget About Love; Nothing In the World (Quite Like a Friend); I'm Looking Out for Me; You're Only Second Rate; Arabian Nights.
1994 (G/*Family*) 66m/C *V:* Scott Weinger, Linda Larkin, Gilbert Gottfried, Val Bettin, Dan Castellaneta. **VHS** **$22.99** *DIS*

The Return of Our Gang 🎬🎬

Even kids who are longtime "Our Gang" fans may not be aware that the first Little Rascals adventures were made during the silent film era. This contains three silent Pathe shorts seldom seen today: "The School Play (Stage Fright)," "Summer Daze (The Cobbler)," and "Dog Days."
1925 (*Family*) 57m/B Joe Cobb, Ernie Morrison, Mickey Daniels, Farina Hoskins, Mary Kornman, Jackie Condon, Jack Davis, Jannie Hoskins, Andy Samuels, Eugene Jackson, Pete the Pup. **VHS, Beta, 8mm** **$24.95** *VYY*

The Return of Roger Ramjet

More adventures of the well-remembered '60s animated camp hero, who could attain the power of 20 atom bombs in 20 seconds and fight evil with friends like Yank, Doodle, Dan, and Dee.
1966 (*Family*) 30m/C *V:* Gary Owens. **VHS, Beta** **$9.95** *RHI, WTA*

The Return of Swamp Thing 🎬🎬

The DC Comics creature rises again out of the muck to fight the same mad doctor he killed last time, now breeding a gallery of mutants. Don't ask how or why - it's all tongue-in-cheek, less serious than even the previous entry, let alone the cult comic book that inspired both. Brat alert: beware peripheral characters of two way-obnoxious kids trying to get a photo of Swamp Thing. **Hound Advisory:** Violence, mainly between mutants and people-turned-mutants. Some of the monster designs are nightmarish indeed, but the filmmakers treat just about everything onscreen as a big joke.
1989 (PG-13/*Jr. High-Adult*) 95m/C Louis Jourdan, Heather Locklear, Sarah Douglas, Dick Durock; *D:* Jim Wynorski. **VHS, Beta, LV** **$14.95** *COL*

Return of the Jedi 🎬🎬🎬

Third segment of George Lucas' original "Star Wars" trilogy is the weakest from the standpoint of storyline, but it does the job in wrapping up the space saga. Luke Skywalker and his allies first attempt to rescue the captive Han Solo, then again confront the forces of the Empire in essentially a mightier rerun of the first film's climactic battle, with truly awesome special effects. This introduces the cute-as-can-be Ewoks, teddy bearish forest creatures who were spun off in a cartoon series and made-for-TV features as well as into toy stores. May the force be with you. **Hound Advisory:** Violence.
1983 (PG/*Family*) 132m/C Mark Hamill, Carrie Fisher, Harrison Ford, Billy Dee Williams, David Prowse, James Earl Jones, Kenny Baker, Denis Lawson, Anthony Daniels, Peter Mayhew; *D:* Richard Marquand; *W:* George Lucas, Lawrence Kasdan; *M:* John Williams; *V:* Alec Guinness, Frank Oz. **Award Nominations:** Academy Awards '83: Best Art Direction/Set Decoration, Best Sound, Best Original Score; **Awards:** Academy Awards '83: Best Visual Effects; People's Choice Awards '84: Best Film. **VHS, Beta, LV** **$19.98** *FOX, RDG, HMV*

The Return of the King

The Rankin/Bass follow-up to their excellent TV feature cartoon adaptation of J.R.R. Tolkien's "The Hobbit," skips two whole books in the "Lord of the Rings" trilogy (Ralph Bakshi had already covered the same ground in his theatrical "Rings" movie) right to the final installment, as Samwise tries to rescue his friend Frodo from the orcs and destroy the One Ring in the forges of Mordor before the evil of Sauron conquers Middle Earth. Confused? It's all about as lucid as it could be, given the circumstances, with above-average animation and good character voices.
1980 (*Family*) 120m/C *D:* Arthur Rankin Jr., Jules Bass; *V:* Orson Bean, Roddy McDowall, John Huston, Theodore Bikel, William Conrad, Glen Yarborough, Paul Frees, Casey Kasem, Sonny Melendrez. **VHS** **$9.99** *XVC, VTR, FFF*

The Return of the Musketeers 🎬🎬

Lester's third Musketeers film (after his successful double-act in the '70s) is a good-natured but average costume/comedy/buddy film, based on Dumas' own literary sequel "Twenty Years After." Two decades passed since D'Artagnan, Athos, Porthos, and Aramis saved the French queen from scandal, but now Milady DeWinter's devious daughter Justine is here to take mama's scheming place, and just to add a little more excitement Athos' adopted son Raoul falls for the femme fatale. **Hound Advisory:** Swashbuckling violence.
1989 (PG/*Jr. High-Adult*) 103m/C Michael York, Oliver Reed, Frank Finlay, Richard Chamberlain, Kim Cattrall, C. Thomas Howell, Geraldine Chaplin, Roy Kinnear, Christopher Lee, Philippe Noiret, Jean-Pierre Cassel, Billy Connolly, Eusebio Lazaro; *D:* Richard Lester; *W:* George MacDonald Fraser. **VHS, LV** **$89.98** *MCA, BTV, FCT*

Return of the Pink Panther 🎬🎬

Bumbling Inspector Clouseau is called upon (again) to rescue the Pink Panther diamond stolen from a museum. Clouseau manages to produce mayhem with a vacuum cleaner and other devices that, in his accident-prone hands, become instruments of terror. While technically the fourth installment in the Pink Panther movie series, it revised and energized Clouseau to showcase nearly nonstop shtick and slapstick not seen since the glory days of Chaplin and Keaton.
1974 (G/*Family*) 113m/C Peter Sellers, Christopher Plummer, Catherine Schell, Herbert Lom, Victor Spinetti; *D:* Blake Edwards; *W:* Frank Waldman, Blake Edwards; *M:* Henry Mancini. **VHS, Beta, LV** **$14.98** *FOX, FHE, FCT*

Return to Boggy Creek 🎬🎬

Townspeople in a small fishing village learn from a photographer that a "killer" beast, whom they thought had disappeared, is back and living in Boggy Creek. Curious children follow the shutterbug into the marsh, despite hurricane warnings, and the bigfootish swamp monster reacts with kindliness and compassion. Kiddies-only sequel to allegedly fact-based "Legend of Boggy Creek."

1977 (G/*Jr. High-Adult*) 87m/C Dawn Wells, Dana Plato, Louise Belaire, John Hofeus; **D:** Tom Moore. **VHS, Beta $19.98** *FOX*

Return to Oz

Dorothy returns to you-know-where to find her friends in the wonderful land of Oz have lost their brain, heart, and courage, respectively, and once again she must demonstrate Kansas leadership qualities. Early Rankin-Bass animated TV special.

1964 (*Family*) 60m/C **VHS, Beta $79.95** *PSM*

Return to Oz 🦴🦴◁

Disney and "Star Wars" producer Gary Kurtz united to pick up where "The Wizard of Oz" left off. Dorothy goes to a turn-of-the-century asylum for her "delusions" of a land called Oz. Then a natural disaster takes her back to Oz, where she has much to do - the Emerald City is ruined, Scarecrow is missing, and the Lion and Tin Man have turned to stone. Visually stunning adaptation of later L. Frank Baum books makes no effort to look (or sing) like the 1939 MGM classic. But premise is confused, and it's low on humor; except for a wisecracking hen, attitude is sober, even scary, as Dorothy meets the head-hunting witch Mombi and the rock giant Nome King (astonishing claymation technique by Will Vinton). Definitely worth a look for the curious. That's Jim Henson's son Brian as the voice of Jack Pumpkinhead.

1985 (PG/*Jr. High-Adult*) 109m/C Fairuza Balk, Piper Laurie, Matt Clark, Nicol Williamson, Jean Marsh; **D:** Walter Murch; **M:** David Shire. **VHS, Beta, LV $29.95** *DIS*

Return to Snowy River 🦴🦴◁

Continues the scenic love story of the Australian buckaroo and the rancher's daughter that began in "The Man From Snowy River." Now Jim Craig has his own mountain spread, but city slickers and their roughriders plan to run him and the other mountain ranchers off their land. Sketchy plot indeed - part agriculture, part romance, mostly horses, horses, horses, beautifully filmed. Dennehy takes over from Kirk Douglas as the grouchy American. Distributed by Disney, but with a few harsh moments. **Hound Advisory:** Violence, salty language, alcohol talk.

1988 (PG/*Jr. High-Adult*) 99m/C Tom Burlinson, Sigrid Thornton, Brian Dennehy, Nicholas Eadie, Mark Hembrow, Bryan Marshall; **D:** Geoff Burrowes. **VHS, Beta, LV $19.99** *DIS, TVC*

Return to Treasure Island, Vol. 1

Disney-Channel TV Series based on the Robert Louis Stevenson classic with the continuing adventures of Jim Hawkins and encoring scoundrel Long John Silver. Five feature-length tapes of two episodes apiece are available.

1985 (*Family*) 101m/C Brian Blessed, Kenneth Colley, Christopher Guard, Reiner Schoene; **D:** Piers Haggard. **VHS, Beta $49.95** *DIS*

Reunion 🦴🦴🦴

Jewish businessman, living in the U.S., returns to his family home in Stuttgart, Germany. He hopes to find out what happened to a boyhood school friend, the son of a noble German family. Extensive flashbacks (in muted color; do not adjust your VCR) show the rise of anti-Semitism and how it affects the friendship of both youths. Thoughtful and well-acted though occasionally plodding drama, a more austere and dignified movie on the topic than "Swing Kids." Based on Fred Uhlman's autobiographical novella. **Hound Advisory:** Mature themes, sex, nudity.

1988 (PG-13/*Jr. High-Adult*) 120m/C Jason Robards Jr., Christien Anholt, Sam West, Francoise Fabian, Maureen Kerwin, Barbara Jefford, Alexander Trauner; **D:** Jerry Schatzberg; **W:** Harold Pinter. **VHS, Beta, LV $29.95** *FRH, IME, FCT*

Revenge of Roger Ramjet

Campy-heroic adventures of the vintage TV good guy daredevil, who was using WHACK! and OUCH! title cards during his fights even before the live-action "Batman." See also "The Return of Roger Ramjet" and "Roger Ramjet vs. N.A.S.T.Y."

1966 (*Family*) 30m/C **VHS, Beta $9.95** *RHI, WTA*

Revenge of the Mysterons from Mars

Vicious plunderers arrive from the red planet, so Captain Scarlet and Spectrum rise to the battle. Adapted from the live-action galactic puppet adventure "Captain Scarlet and the Mysterons."

1981 (*Preschool-Primary*) 91m/C **VHS, Beta** *FHE*

Revenge of the Nerds 🦴🦴◁

When nerdy college freshmen are victimized by jocks, frat boys and the school's beauties, they start their own fraternity and seek revenge. Carradine and Edwards team well as the geeks in this better than average teen sex comedy. Guess who gets the girls? Sequel was much worse. **Hound Advisory:** Profanity, sex talk.

1984 (R/*Sr. High-Adult*) 89m/C Robert Carradine, Anthony Edwards, Timothy Busfield, Andrew Cassese, Curtis Armstrong, Larry B. Scott, Brian Tochi, Julia Montgomery, Michelle Meyrink, Ted McGinley, John Goodman, Bernie Casey; **D:** Jeff Kanew; **W:** Tim Metcalfe; **M:** Thomas Newman. **VHS, Beta, LV $14.98** *FOX*

Revenge of the Pink Panther 🦴🦴◁

Inspector Clouseau survives an assassination attempt, but allows the world to think he is dead in order to pursue an investigation of the culprits in his own unique, bumbling way. More laid-back than other "Pink Panther" romps of the '70s (and the last one made by Sellers when he was alive), breaking out with the full-fledged slapstick only in the fiery finale. **Hound Advisory:** Roughhousing, sex talk.

1978 (PG/*Jr. High-Adult*) 99m/C Peter Sellers, Herbert Lom, Dyan Cannon, Robert Webber, Burt Kwouk, Robert Loggia; **D:** Blake Edwards; **W:** Blake Edwards, Ron Clark, Frank Waldman; **M:** Henry Mancini. **VHS, Beta, LV $19.98** *FOX, FCT*

Rhinestone 🦴

A country singer claims she can turn anyone, even a cabbie, into a singing sensation. Stuck with Stallone, Parton prepares her protege to sing at New York City's roughest country-

western club, The Rhinestone. Only die-hard Dolly and Rocky fans need bother with this bunk. Some may enjoy watching the thick, New York accented Stallone learn how to properly pronounce dog ("dawg") in country lingo. Yee-haw. **Hound Advisory:** Profanity, violence, sex talk.
1984 (PG/*Jr. High-Adult*) 111m/C Sylvester Stallone, Dolly Parton, Ron Leibman, Richard Farnsworth, Tim Thomerson; *D:* Bob (Benjamin) Clark; *W:* Sylvester Stallone, Phil Alden Robinson. **VHS, Beta, LV** $79.98 *FOX*

Rich in Love 🦴🦴🦴

Lighthearted look at the changes in a Southern family after its matriarch leaves to pursue her own life. Seen through the eyes of 17-year-old daughter Lucille who assumes the role of "mother" for sister and father while trying to come to terms with her own confused feelings. Nice performances by newcomer Erbe and Finney can't overcome a mediocre script. Based on the novel by Josephine Humphreys.
1993 (PG-13/*Jr. High-Adult*) 105m/C Albert Finney, Jill Clayburgh, Kathryn Erbe, Kyle MacLachlan, Piper Laurie, Ethan Hawke, Suzy Amis, Alfre Woodard; *D:* Bruce Beresford; *W:* Alfred Uhry; *M:* Georges Delerue. **VHS, LV** $19.98 *MGM, BTV, FCT*

Rich Kids 🦴🦴🦴

Drama focusing on the children of divorce, specifically about a girl trying to cope with the split up of her parents, aided by a boyfriend whose parents have already called it quits. Somewhat simplistic screenplay tends to hang on the notion of middle-aged grownups as immature boobs, their kids as wise but vulnerable. Some touching moments nonetheless.
1979 (PG/*Family*) 97m/C John Lithgow, Kathryn Walker, Trini Alvarado, Paul Dooley, David Selby, Jill Eikenberry, Olympia Dukakis; *D:* Robert M. Young. **VHS, Beta** $59.95 *MGM*

Richard Scarry's Best ABC Video Ever

Huckle Cat and his school friends present the alphabet in 26 entertaining stories, each emphasizing a different letter.
1990 (*Family*) 30m/C **VHS** $14.95 *RAN, HMV, MLT*

Richard Scarry's Best Busy People Video Ever

Richard Scarry's animated characters illustrate for children the many jobs that people hold.
1993 (*Family*) 30m/C **VHS** $9.95 *BTV,*

Richard Scarry's Best Counting Video Ever

Learning to count can be darn fun. Lily Bunny counts from 1 to 20 in this numerical adventure. Huckle Cat, Lowly Worm, Bananas Gorilla, and more of the gang find things for Lily to count everywhere they go. Everyone: 1, 2, 3, 4...
1990 (*Family*) 30m/C **VHS** $14.95 *RAN, HMV, MLT*

Richie Rich

World's wealthiest little boy, Richie Rich, with a weekly allowance of $100,000, and his girlfriend Gloria travel around the world to do good deeds. Cash becomes the equivalent of a super power in this Saturday-morning cartoon adaptation of a classic kiddie comic book; enough exposure to this stuff and Malcolm Forbes would've gone communist. A Hanna-Barbera production.
1980 (*Family*) 50m/C **VHS, Beta** $5.99 *TTC, WTA*

Ride a Wild Pony 🦴🦴🦴

In the early 1900s a poor Australian farmer's son is allowed to pick a horse of his own from a rancher's herd. After he trains and grows to love the pony, the rancher's daughter, a handicapped girl, decides to claim it for herself. Determining who should be the animal's master (or mistress) takes a courtroom wrangle and Solomon-like judgment in this slow-moving Disney feature, based on the tale "Sporting Proposition," by James Aldridge.
1975 (G/*Family*) 86m/C John Meillon, Michael Craig, Robert Bettles, Eva Griffith, Graham Rouse; *D:* Don Chaffey; *M:* John Addison. **VHS, Beta** $69.95 *DIS*

The Right Stuff 🦴🦴🦴

Long, rambunctious adaptation of Tom Wolfe's long, rambunctious nonfiction bestseller about the beginnings of the U.S. space program, from Chuck Yeager's breaking of the sound barrier to the last of the Mercury missions. Featuring an all-star cast, sharp performances, and an ambitious script. Rowdy, imaginative, and thrilling, though broadly painted. **Hound Advisory:** Profanity.
1983 (PG/*Jr. High-Adult*) 193m/C Ed Harris, Dennis Quaid, Sam Shepard, Scott Glenn, Fred Ward, Charles Frank, William Russ, Kathy Baker, Barbara Hershey, Levon Helm, David Clennon, Kim Stanley, Mary Jo Deschanel, Veronica Cartwright, Pamela Reed, Jeff Goldblum, Harry Shearer, Donald Moffatt, Scott Paulin, Lance Henriksen, Scott Wilson, John P. Ryan, Royal Dano; *D:* Philip Kaufman; *W:* Philip Kaufman; *M:* Bill Conti. **Award Nominations:** Academy Awards '83: Best Art Direction/Set Decoration, Best Cinematography, Best Picture, Best Supporting Actress (Shepard); **Awards:** Academy Awards '83: Best Film Editing, Best Sound, Best Original Score. **VHS, Beta, LV** $29.98 *WAR*

Rikki-Tikki-Tavi

Derived from Rudyard Kipling's "The Jungle Book," this nicely animated story deals with a domesticated mongoose who saves his human family from two attacking cobras.
1975 (*Preschool-Primary*) 30m/C *D:* Chuck Jones. **VHS, Beta** $9.95 *FHE, WTA, MLT*

Rin Tin Tin, Hero of the West 🦴🦴

In one of his last adventures, the famous German Shepherd proves his courage and hyper-canine intelligence. Colorized.
1955 (*Family*) 75m/C James Brown, Lee Aaker, Rin Tin Tin. **VHS, Beta** $24.95 *MON*

Rin Tin Tin: The Paris Conspiracy

Episode from The Family Channel television series has Hank, Stevie, and Rin Tin Tin investigating the case of some missing diamonds, which leads to a terrorist conspiracy.
199? (*Family*) 92m/C **VHS** *NO*

Ring of Bright Water 🦴🦴🦴

Well-done story from Gavin Maxwell's nonfiction book, an endearing tale of a civil servant with a pet otter who moves to

the country highlands of Scotland. Starring the "Born Free" acting team of Travers and McKenna, broadening their species experience.
1969 (*G/Family*) 107m/C Bill Travers, Virginia McKenna, Peter Jeffrey, Archie Duncan; *D:* Charles Lamont. **VHS, Beta** *FCT, SIG, TVC*

Rip Van Winkle

Washington Irving's tale of settler Van Winkle and his 20-year nap features delightful artwork and music, from the great "Rabbit Ears" series of storytelling videos.
1993 (*Primary*) 30m/C **VHS $9.98** *BTV*

The River 🎞🎞🎙

Hard-luck farmers battle a river whose flood threatens their farm, as well as the wealthy landowner hoping to scoop up their lots at discount prices. Spacek, is strong and believable as the wife and mother, but Gibson less so as the distressed husband and father. Beautiful photography by Vilmos Zsigmond highlights third (following "Country" and "Places in the Heart") in an onslaught of films in the early '80s that dramatized the plight of the small American farmer. **Hound Advisory:** Brief nudity; violence; profanity.
1984 (*PG/Family*) 124m/C Mel Gibson, Sissy Spacek, Scott Glenn, Billy Green Bush; *D:* Mark Rydell; *W:* Julian Barry, Robert Dillon; *M:* John Williams. **VHS, Beta, LV $14.98** *MCA*

The River Rat 🎞🎞🎙

Ex-con is reunited with his 13-year-old daughter after spending that same number of years in prison, and they work together to restore an old Mississippi riverboat. Of course, there's a lesser storyline about stashed loot that should have been jettisoned in favor of more getting-to-know-you father-daughter drama. **Hound Advisory:** Violence, salty language.
1984 (*PG/Family*) 93m/C Tommy Lee Jones, Brian Dennehy, Martha Plimpton, Shawn Smith, Melissa Davis; *D:* Tom Rickman. **VHS, Beta, LV $14.95** *PAR*

A River Runs Through It 🎞🎞🎞

Contemplative exploration of family ties and growing up in Montana during the 1920s. Presbyterian minister raises two sons, trouble-prone and rebellious Paul, and Norman, equally strong-minded, but obedient. No matter how bad things get between the boys and their father, they join together on fly-fishing idylls that quietly relate to life, religion, and responsibility. Slow-moving philosophical fish story, but worthwhile. Based on the autobiographical novel by Norman Maclean. The laser disc version includes commentary by Redford. **Hound Advisory:** Mature themes, sex, alcohol use.
1992 (*PG/Jr. High-Adult*) 123m/C Craig Sheffer, Brad Pitt, Tom Skerritt, Brenda Blethyn, Emily Lloyd, Edie McClurg, Stephen Shellan, Susan Taylor; *D:* Robert Redford; *W:* Richard Friedenberg; *M:* Mark Isham. **Award Nominations:** Academy Awards '92: Best Adapted Screenplay, Best Original Score; **Awards:** Academy Awards '92: Best Cinematography. **VHS, LV, 8mm $19.95** *COL, CRC, BTV*

Road Construction Ahead

Many children seem to be fascinated by the workings of heavy machinery, so this video should keep their attention. It shows every stage of road building from surveying to the first car driving on the completed highway. Machinery includes bulldozers, excavators, rock crushers, bucket loaders, and giant trucks, all explained by a friendly worker named George.
1992 (*Preschool-Primary*) 30m/C **VHS $19.95**

Roald Dahl's: Dirty Beasts

Collection of comic verse from the author whose works inspired "Willy Wonka and the Chocolate Factory" and "The Witches." Dahl's ghastly menagerie of animals do crazy things in comic verse and animation based on the original illustrations by Quentin Blake.
19?? (*Preschool-Primary*) 30m/C *V:* Prunella Scales, Timothy West. **VHS $9.98** *FFF, SVI*

Roald Dahl's The Enormous Crocodile

Crocodile's plot to have a child for lunch is foiled in typical Dahlesque fashion.
1993 (*Primary*) 25m/C **VHS $9.99** *SVI*

Rob Roy - The Highland Rogue 🎞🎙

In the early 18th century, Scottish Highlander Rob Roy must battle against the King of England's secretary, who would undermine the MacGregor clan to enact his evil deeds. Dull Disney drama.
1953 (*Family*) 84m/C Richard Todd, Glynis Johns, James Robertson Justice, Michael Gough; *D:* Harold French. **VHS, Beta $69.95** *DIS*

Robin and Marian 🎞🎞

After a separation of twenty years, an aging, disillusioned Robin Hood is reunited with Maid Marian, who is now a nun. Their dormant feelings for each other are reawakened as Robin spirits her to Sherwood Forest for a reunion with old friends and enemies. Not really for kids, this "mature version" of the legend robs Robin of much magic, spontaneity, and fun (though there is swashbuckling violence). On the other hand, superior cast does what it can to bring some depth and charm to the endeavor. **Hound Advisory:** Violence.
1976 (*PG/Jr. High-Adult*) 106m/C Sean Connery, Audrey Hepburn, Robert Shaw, Richard Harris; *D:* Richard Lester; *M:* John Barry. **VHS, Beta, LV $19.95** *COL, FOX*

Robin Hood: Men in Tights 🎞🎞

Brooksian rendition of the classic legend inspires guffaws, but doesn't hit the bullseye on all it promises. Hood aficionados will appreciate the painstaking effort taken to spoof the 1938 Errol Flynn classic while leaving plenty of room to poke fun at the more recent Costner non-classic "Robin Hood: Prince of Thieves." Elwes, last seen swinging swords in "The Princess Bride," is well cast as the Flynn look-alike. Expect the usual off-color humor that's so prevalent in all Brooks outings. **Hound Advisory:** Profanity and sex talk.
1993 (*PG-13/Jr. High-Adult*) 105m/C Cary Elwes, Richard Lewis, Roger Rees, Amy Yasbeck, Dave Chappelle, Isaac Hayes, Tracey Ullman, Mark Blankfield, Megan Cavanagh, Eric Allen Kramer, Tony Griffin, Dick Van Patten, Mel Brooks; *D:* Mel Brooks; *W:* Mel Brooks, J. David Shapiro; *M:* Hummie Mann. **VHS** *FXV*

Robin Hood: Prince of Thieves 🐾🐾⌐

Revisionist retelling of the Sherwood Forest legends is a strange brew indeed; Costner's obviously American Robin Hood sorely lacks swashbuckling charisma, and Rickman easily overpowers him (dramatically, anyway) as the wicked, crazed Sheriff of Nottingham, just one of a memorable cast of character actors. Great action sequences, a gritty and credible picture of the Middle Ages (blown to shreds at the end when Bryan Adams and his band materialize in the heather to croon the hit music-video love theme!). Still has lots of fun for lovers of romance and fairy tales. **Hound Advisory:** Violence. The Sheriff of Nottingham worships Satan and nearly rapes Maid Marian (or is it the other way around?) but neither act is explicit.

1991 **(PG-13/***Jr. High-Adult***)** 144m/C Kevin Costner, Morgan Freeman, Mary Elizabeth Mastrantonio, Christian Slater, Alan Rickman, Geraldine McEwan, Micheal McShane, Brian Blessed, Michael Wincott, Nick Brimble, Jack Wild, Harold Innocent, Jack Wild; *Cameos:* Sean Connery; *D:* Kevin Reynolds; *W:* Pen Densham, John Watson; *M:* Michael Kamen. **Award Nominations:** Academy Awards '91: Best Song (''(Everything I Do) I Do It for You''); **Awards:** British Academy Awards '92: Best Supporting Actor (Rickman); MTV Movie Awards '92: Best Song (''(Everything I Do) I Do for You''). **VHS, LV $19.98** *WAR, RDG*

Robinson Crusoe

Animated adaptation of the classic Daniel Defoe story about a man marooned on a small island.

1978 *(Family)* 86m/C **VHS, Beta $11.95** *FHE*

Robinson Crusoe & the Tiger 🐾⌐

Ultra-cheapo version of Daniel Defoe's famous story of how Robinson Crusoe became stranded and survived on a desert island. Made in the Philippines.

1972 **(G/***Family***)** 109m/C Hugo Stiglitz, Ahui; *D:* Rene Cardona Jr. **VHS, Beta $29.98** *SUE*

Robocop 🐾🐾🐾

Detroit cop killed in action is used as donor for the brain of a crime-fighting cyborg. Trouble begins when Robocop starts remembering his life as a human. Not just superhero action; there's a bleak, cynical view of the future, an acid satire of corporate America, and an underlying sadness about its main character. Though an inspiration for toys, comics and a later TV series, this one's not for children. Graphic gore nearly earned the picture an X rating. **Hound Advisory:** Carnage, profanity, mature themes, alcohol use.

1987 **(R/***Sr. High-Adult***)** 103m/C Peter Weller, Nancy Allen, Ronny Cox, Kurtwood Smith, Ray Wise, Miguel Ferrer, Dan O'Herlihy, Robert DoQui, Felton Perry, Paul McCrane, Del Zamora; *D:* Paul Verhoeven; *W:* Michael Miner, Edward Neumeier; *M:* Basil Poledouris. **VHS, Beta, LV $14.98** *ORI, SUP*

Robocop 2 🐾🐾

Savagely violent sequel shows a new drug making future Detroit more dangerous yet. Robocop's corporate owners eventually build a bigger, stronger cyborg with the brain of a psycho pusher/addict/cult leader. It goes berserk, and the metal beings fight an epic battle, in between enough subplots for three movies. More comic-bookish than the previous entry, yet perversely unsuitable for kids. Besides gore, there's a sadistic boy drug lord and a scene of a little league

team looting a store ("Harder!" orders one tyke as they beat an old man with a bat they're barely big enough to lift). Movies like this are aimed strictly and properly at jaded grownups, yet youngsters were obviously seen as consumers; note the finger-wagging antidrug PSA at the start of the tape. **Hound Advisory:** Carnage, profanity, drug use.

1990 **(R/***Adult***)** 117m/C Peter Weller, Nancy Allen, Belinda Bauer, Dan O'Herlihy, Tommy Noonan, Gabriel Damon, Galyn Gorg, Felton Perry, Patricia Charbonneau; *D:* Irvin Kershner; *W:* Walon Green. **VHS, Beta, LV $14.98** *ORI*

Robocop 3 🐾⌐

Far from the best of the "Robocop" movies, but certainly the only kid-friendly one. There's a little orphan girl provided as partner and surrogate daughter for the metal hero when corporate mercenaries kill her parents to seize the real estate of their Detroit slum. Robocop joins with the citizens to protect their homes. Violence and swearing have been scaled down from the earlier films (so has the budget, obviously), in what could generally pass for an episode of the subsequent "Robocop" TV series. **Hound Advisory:** Violence, profanity.

1991 **(PG-13/***Jr. High-Adult***)** 104m/C Robert Burke, Nancy Allen, John Castle, CCH Pounder, Bruce Locke, Rip Torn, Remi Ryan, Felton Perry; *D:* Fred Dekker; *W:* Fred Dekker, Frank Miller; *M:* Basil Poledouris. **VHS** *ORI*

Robocop, Vol. 1: Man in the Iron Suit

Rebuilt episodes for the Marvel Comics TV cartoon series "Inhumanoids," based on the cyborg police officer from the ultraviolent movies. In this installment, a jealous villain tests a new powersuit against Robocop. Additional volumes available.

1989 *(Primary-Jr. High)* 22m/C **VHS, LV $14.95** *WTA*

Robot Jox 🐾🐾

In the future, diplomacy means two lone gladiators fight to the finish inside giant robots. Will brotherhood and goodness prevail? Semi-meaningful, semi-ludicrous sci-fi (with uneven quality f/x) isn't strictly aimed at small fry but earns a mention here for the fighting machines' suspicious similarity to popular toys like the Transformers and the Gobots. At least it's better than their cartoons. **Hound Advisory:** Profanity, violence, sex talk.

1989 **(PG/***Jr. High-Adult***)** 84m/C Gary Graham, Anne-Marie Johnson, Paul Koslo, Robert Sampson, Danny Kamekona, Hilary Mason, Michael Alldredge; *D:* Stuart Gordon; *W:* Stuart Gordon. **VHS, LV $14.95** *COL*

Robotech: Southern Cross

The armies of the Southern Cross are left to defend Earth. Although inexperienced, they are smart and energetic. Eight volumes are available individually.

19?? *(Primary-Jr. High)* 66m/C **VHS $29.95** *WTA*

Robotech: The Macross Saga, Vol. 1

First in a series of six videos that recount the struggle of three generations of Earthlings who must fight off an invasion by the alien Zantraedi. Intricately plotted, character crammed, gadget-glutted Japanese TV cartoon adventure

serial has a cult of admirers (plus various imitations and soundalikes) who consider it a cut above the usual toy-peddling 'toons. Additional volumes available.
1987 (*Family*) 80m/C **VHS, Beta $14.95** *FHE, WTA, STP*

Robotech: The New Generation

Contains eight more volumes of the popular Japanese-made space serial.
1985 (*Primary-Jr. High*) 66m/C **VHS $29.95** *WTA, STP, TPV*

Robotech, Vol. 1: Booby Trap

Rookie pilot in the elite Robotech Defense Force battles for his life against more experienced warriors. Ex-Yankees dominate cast. Additional volumes available.
1985 (*Family*) 30m/C Roger Maris, Mickey Mantle, Whitey Ford, Elston Howard, Al Downing. **VHS, Beta $9.95** *FHE*

Robotman and Friends

Animated adventures with several episodes, detailing the TV escapades of Robotman and his pals Stellar and Oops, who repeatedly side with humanity against the evil forces of Roberon. Humanity was also the target for the Robotman line of toy products.
1984 (*Preschool-Primary*) 48m/C **VHS, Beta, LV $29.98** *LIV, WTA*

Rock-a-Doodle 🐾🐾

Boy knocked out during a storm envisions the following: Chanticleer, the fabled rooster whose voice raises the sun, tricked into neglecting his duties by an evil barnyard owl. Humiliated, the fowl flees the farm and winds up in Vegas as an Elvis lookalike, and rock success threatens to spoil the bird. Misconceived melange of mythology and pop-music icons, this was rushed early into theaters to raise vital cash for Don Bluth's studios, and it looks it; note the heavy use of narration to patch over absent scenes.
1992 (*G*/*Family*) 77m/C *D:* Don Bluth; *W:* David A. Weiss; *M:* Robert Folk; *V:* Glen Campbell, Christopher Plummer, Phil Harris, Sandy Duncan, Ellen Greene, Charles Nelson Reilly, Eddie Deezen, Toby Scott Granger, Sorrell Booke. **VHS, LV $24.98** *HBO, MVD*

Rock Music with the Muppets

The Muppets perform their own brand of rock and roll with their special musical guests. The songs featured include "Rock Around the Clock," "Call Me," "Rainbow Connection," and "Disco Frog."
1985 (*Family*) 54m/C *V:* Frank Oz, Jim Henson, Alice Cooper, Deborah Harry, Paul Simon, Helen Reddy, Leo Sayer, Loretta Swit, Ben Vereen. **VHS, Beta $14.98** *FOX*

Rock 'n' Roll High School 🐾🐾🐾

Music of the rockin' Ramones highlights this non-stop high-energy cult classic about high school kids out to thwart the rock-hating principal at every turn. If it had been made in 1957, it would have been the ultimate rock 'n' roll teen movie. The 1970s' milieu works against it, but the performances are perfect for the material, resembling a "Mad Magazine" parody (a good one) come to life. Songs include "Teenage Lobotomy," "Blitzkrieg Bop," "I Wanna Be

Sedated," and the title track, among others. Followed far less successfully by "Rock 'n' Roll High School Forever." **Hound Advisory:** Salty language.
1979 (**PG**/*Sr. High-Adult*) 94m/C The Ramones, P.J. Soles, Vincent Van Patten, Clint Howard, Dey Young, Mary Woronov, Alix Elias, Dick Miller, Paul Bartel; *D:* Allan Arkush. **VHS, Beta $64.95** *MVD*

Rock 'n' Roll High School
Forever WOOF!

Jesse and his band just want to rock 'n' roll, but the new principal (Woronov, caricaturing her caricature from "Rock 'n' Roll High School") opposes them with terror tactics. Way late, way lame sequel misses by miles the spunk and wit that made the original a cult classic. **Hound Advisory:** Profanity, and of course sex, drugs, and rock 'n' roll.
1991 (**PG-13**/*Sr. High-Adult*) 94m/C Corey Feldman, Mary Woronov, Mojo Nixon, Evan Richards, Michael Ceveris, Patrick Malone, Larry Linville, Sarah Buxton; *D:* Deborah Brock; *W:* Deborah Brock. **VHS, Beta, LV $89.95** *LIV, IME*

Rocket Gibraltar 🐾🐾🐾

Large family gathers to celebrate Levi Rockwell's 77th birthday, but his adult children seem preoccupied and awkward around the old guy. Only the grandkids realize what he wants and they conspire to grant his dying wish - a viking-style cremation at sea. Great when the juveniles (including "Home Alone's" Culkin, in his screen debut) and Lancaster are together. Nice little parable about family, inheritance, life, death, sex, and so on. **Hound Advisory:** Sex talk, salty language, mature themes.
1988 (**PG**/*Jr. High-Adult*) 92m/C Burt Lancaster, Bill Pullman, John Glover, Suzy Amis, Macaulay Culkin, Patricia Clarkson, Frances Conroy, Sinead Cusack, Bill Martin, Kevin Spacey; *D:* Daniel Petrie; *W:* Amos Poe; *M:* Andrew Powell. **VHS, Beta $14.95** *COL*

The Rocketeer 🐾🐾🐾

Fun Disney adaptation of Dave Stevens' recent retro-style comic book. Stunt flyer in the 1930s finds a prototype jet backpack sought by Nazi spies. Donning a metal mask, he becomes a flying superhero. Breezy family entertainment with stupendous special effects; even better if you know movie trivia, as it brims with Hollywood references, like a great villain (Dalton) clearly based on Errol Flynn. **Hound Advisory:** Disney-style violence
1991 (**PG**/*Family*) 109m/C Bill Campbell, Jennifer Connelly, Alan Arkin, Timothy Dalton, Paul Sorvino, Melora Hardin, Tiny Ron, Terry O'Quinn, Ed Lauter, James Handy; *D:* Joe Johnston; *W:* Danny Bilson, Paul DeMeo; *M:* James Horner. **VHS, Beta, LV $19.99** *DIS, CCB, IME*

Rockin' with Judy Jetson 🐾🐾

Made-for-TV animated feature starring the Jetsons' teenage daughter, whose crush on future pop star Sky Rocker leads to her own bid for space-age music stardom. Fans of the Hanna-Barbera series will find this politically correct compared to "Jetsons: The Movie," which unceremoniously replaced the longstanding Judy vocalizer, Janet Waldo, with teen diva Tiffany.
1988 (*Preschool-Primary*) 90m/C **VHS, Beta, LV $29.95** *TTC, IME, WTA*

Rocky 🎬🎬🎬◁

Surprising box office smash about a young man from the slums of Philadelphia who dreams of becoming a boxing champion. Then unknown Stallone wrote the script and stars as Rocky, the underdog who gets a shot at fame and self-respect when a conceited champ picks him as an easy opponent for a high-profile bout. Great rags-to-riches story that loses strength in the subsequent (and numerous) rerun sequels. Powerful score by Bill Conti. **Hound Advisory:** Brutality in the dynamic fight scenes. Alcohol use, occasional salty language.
1976 (PG/*Jr. High-Adult*) 125m/C Sylvester Stallone, Talia Shire, Burgess Meredith, Burt Young, Carl Weathers; **D:** John G. Avildsen; **W:** Sylvester Stallone; **M:** Bill Conti. **Award Nominations:** Academy Awards '76: Best Actor (Stallone), Best Actress (Shire), Best Original Screenplay, Best Song ("Gonna Fly Now"), Best Sound, Best Supporting Actor (Meredith, Young); **Awards:** Academy Awards '76: Best Director (Avildsen), Best Film Editing, Best Picture; Directors Guild of America Awards '76: Best Director (Avildsen); Golden Globe Awards '77: Best Film—Drama; Los Angeles Film Critics Association Awards '76: Best Film; National Board of Review Awards '76: 10 Best Films of the Year, Best Supporting Actress (Shire). **VHS, Beta, LV, 8mm $14.95** *MGM, FOX, BTV*

Rocky 2 🎬🎬◁

Time-marking sequel to the box office smash finds Rocky frustrated by the commercialism which followed his match to Apollo, but considering a return bout. Meanwhile, his wife fights for her life. Overall effect is to prepare you for the next sequel. **Hound Advisory:** Violence and profanity.
1979 (PG/*Jr. High-Adult*) 119m/C Sylvester Stallone, Talia Shire, Burt Young, Burgess Meredith, Carl Weathers; **D:** Sylvester Stallone; **W:** Sylvester Stallone; **M:** Bill Conti. **VHS, Beta, LV $14.95** *MGM, FOX*

Rocky 3 🎬🎬◁

Rocky is beaten by big, mean Clubber Lang (played to a tee by Mr. T). He realizes success has made him soft, and has to dig deep to find the motivation to stay on top. Amazingly, Stallone regains his underdog persona here, looking puny next to Mr. T, who is the best thing about the second-best "Rocky" flick. **Hound Advisory:** Violence; salty language.
1982 (PG/*Jr. High-Adult*) 103m/C Sylvester Stallone, Talia Shire, Burgess Meredith, Carl Weathers, Mr. T, Leif Erickson, Burt Young; **D:** Sylvester Stallone; **W:** Sylvester Stallone; **M:** Bill Conti. **VHS, Beta, LV $14.95** *MGM, FOX*

Rocky 4 🎬◁

Rocky travels to Russia to fight the Soviet champ who killed his friend during a bout. Will Rocky knock the Russkie out? Will Rocky get hammered on the head a great many times and sag around the ring? Will Rocky ever learn? Lundgren isn't nearly as much fun as some of Rocky's former opponents and Stallone overdoes the hyper-patriotism and relies too heavily on uplifting footage from earlier "Rocky" movies. **Hound Advisory:** Violence and profanity.
1985 (PG/*Jr. High-Adult*) 91m/C Sylvester Stallone, Talia Shire, Dolph Lundgren, Brigitte Nielsen, Michael Pataki, Burt Young, Carl Weathers; **D:** Sylvester Stallone; **W:** Sylvester Stallone. **VHS, Beta, LV $14.95** *MGM, FOX*

Rocky 5 🎬🎬

Brain damaged and broke, Rocky finds himself back where he started on the streets of Philadelphia. Boxing still very much in his blood, Rocky takes in a protege, training him in the style that made him a champ (take a lickin' and keep on tickin'). However an unscrupulous promoter has designs on the young fighter and seeks to wrest the lad from under the former champ's wing. This eventually leads to a showdown between Rocky and the young boxer in a brutal streetfight. Supposedly the last "Rocky" film, it's clear the formula has run dry.
1990 (PG/*Jr. High-Adult*) 105m/C Sylvester Stallone, Talia Shire, Burt Young, Sage Stallone, Tom Morrison, Burgess Meredith; **D:** John G. Avildsen; **W:** Sylvester Stallone; **M:** Bill Conti. **VHS, Beta, LV, 8mm $14.95** *MGM*

Roger Ramjet vs. N.A.S.T.Y.

Once again Roger must take on the fiendish bunch of N.A.S.T.Y. Cartoons are "Bank Robbers" and "Bathosphere."
1965 (*Family*) 30m/C **VHS $14.99** *RHI, WTA*

Roman Holiday 🎬🎬🎬◁

Hepburn's first starring role is a charmer as a princess bored with her official visit to Rome who slips away and plays at being an "average Jane." A reporter discovers her little charade and decides to cash in with an exclusive story. Before they know it, love calls. Blacklisted screenwriter Trumbo was "fronted" by Ian McLellan Hunter, who accepted screen credit and the Best Story Oscar in Trumbo's stead. The Academy voted to posthumously award Trumbo his own Oscar in 1993.
1953 (*Family*) 118m/B Audrey Hepburn, Gregory Peck, Eddie Albert, Tullio Carminati; **D:** William Wyler; **W:** Dalton Trumbo. **Award Nominations:** Academy Awards '53: Best Art Direction/Set Decoration (B & W), Best Black and White Cinematography, Best Director (Wyler), Best Film Editing, Best Picture, Best Screenplay, Best Supporting Actor (Albert); **Awards:** Academy Awards '53: Best Actress (Hepburn), Best Costume Design (B & W), Best Story; British Academy Awards '53: Best Actress (Hepburn); Golden Globe Awards '54: Best Actress—Drama (Hepburn); New York Film Critics Awards '53: Best Actress (Hepburn). **VHS, Beta, LV, 8mm $14.95** *PAR, BTV, HMV*

Romancing the Stone 🎬🎬🎬

Uptight romance novelist Turner lives out her fantasies after she receives a mysterious map from her murdered brother-in-law and her sister is kidnapped in South America — the ransom being the map. Out to rescue her sister, she's helped and hindered by American soldier of fortune Douglas, whose main concern is himself and the hidden treasure described in the map. Great chemistry between the stars and loads of clever dialogue in this appealing adventure comedy. First outing with Turner, Douglas, and DeVito. Followed by "The Jewel of the Nile." **Hound Advisory:** Violence; brief nudity; profanity.
1984 (PG/*Family*) 106m/C Michael Douglas, Kathleen Turner, Danny DeVito, Zack Norman, Alfonso Arau, Ron Silver; **D:** Robert Zemeckis; **M:** Alan Silvestri. **Award Nominations:** Academy Awards '84: Best Film Editing; **Awards:** Golden Globe Awards '85: Best Actress—Musical/Comedy (Turner), Best Film—Musical/Comedy. **VHS, Beta, LV $19.98** *FOX, HMV*

Romeo and Juliet 🎬🎬🎬◁

Still one of the most heartbreaking and eloquent portrayals of young love ever, and the only one of many, many adaptations of Shakespeare's classic play to underscore such themes by

casting actual teenagers as the adolescent leads. Also available in a 45-minute edited version. **Hound Advisory:** Sex, violence, nudity, mature themes.
1968 (**PG** / *Family*) 138m/C Olivia Hussey, Leonard Whiting, Michael York, Milo O'Shea; **D:** Franco Zeffirelli; **M:** Nino Rota. **Award Nominations:** Academy Awards '68: Best Director (Zeffirelli), Best Picture; **Awards:** Academy Awards '68: Best Cinematography, Best Costume Design; Golden Globe Awards '69: Best Foreign Film; National Board of Review Awards '68: 10 Best Films of the Year, Best Director (Zeffirelli). **VHS, Beta, LV $19.95** *PAR, HMV, PBC*

Romper Room and Friends: Explore Nature

Miss Molly and the Romper Room Gang learn all about nature, including animals and how they live, trees and how soil is made, how important every living thing is. Additional volumes available.
1985 (*Family*) 32m/C **VHS, Beta $14.98** *FOX*

Roobarb

Collection of rambunctious cartoons from British TV about a mongrel named Roobarb and a cat named Custard.
1980 (*Preschool-Primary*) 67m/C **VHS, Beta $14.95** *FHE, WTA*

Rookie of the Year 🎞🎞🎞◁

Twelve-year-old Little Leaguer Henry breaks his arm, and when it heals askew he's blessed with a pitching arm so spectacular he's recruited for the Chicago Cubs, leading them to the World Series. Good-natured sports fantasy is a highly predictable but enjoyable family outing for first-time director Stern (who also plays a goofy, childlike teammate). Keep your eyes peeled for appearances by real-live sluggers Pedro Guerrero, Barry Bonds, and others. **Hound Advisory:** One muffled word that might have been salty, but probably not. This could been a G with no problem.
1993 (**PG** / *Jr. High-Adult*) 103m/C Thomas Ian Nicholas, Daniel Stern, Gary Busey, Dan Hedaya; **D:** Daniel Stern; **W:** Sam Harper; **M:** Bill Conti. **VHS** *FXV*

Room for Heroes

Frontier favorites abound in this animated salute to Johnny Appleseed, Pecos Bill, Casey Jones, and Davey Crockett, with clips from past Disney classics.
1990 (*Preschool-Primary*) 14m/C **VHS, Beta $250.00** *DSN, MTI*

Room Service 🎞🎞🎞◁

Groucho plays a penniless Broadway producer who can't pay his hotel bill. With the help of cronies Harpo and Chico, he schemes to stay in the high-rise suite (staging a fake outbreak of measles, among other pranks) until he can secure funds for the next show. Not as funny as previous Marx Brothers comedies, mainly because it's based on a stage play of the era, with the Marxists following most of the script straight, imposing a minimum of their own personalities.
1938 (*Family*) 78m/B Groucho Marx, Harpo Marx, Chico Marx, Lucille Ball, Ann Miller, Frank Albertson, Donald MacBride, Charles Halton; **D:** William A. Seiter. **VHS, Beta, LV $19.95** *RKO, CCB, MED*

Rooster Cogburn 🎞🎞🎞◁

The sequel to "True Grit" pairs the hard-drinking, hard-fighting marshal with a straightlaced but equally spirited schoolmarm in order to capture a gang of outlaws who killed her father. Typical story, but the fireworks between Wayne and Hepburn are right on target. **Hound Advisory:** Violence.
1975 (**PG** / *Jr. High-Adult*) 107m/C John Wayne, Katharine Hepburn, Richard Jordan, Anthony Zerbe, John McIntire, Strother Martin, Paul Koslo; **D:** Stuart Millar. **VHS, Beta, LV $19.95** *MCA, TLF*

Rose-Petal Place

Animated TV musical fantasy about flowers turning into young girls; foremost among the flower-fairies is Rose-Petal, voiced by Ms. Osmond.
1983 (*Preschool*) 60m/C **V:** Marie Osmond. **VHS, Beta $14.95** *WOV, WTA*

Rosie's Walk

Animated tale of little red hen Rosie, who struts across the barnyard keeping her cool while unknowingly leading a stalking fox into a series of disasters. Also includes "Charlie Needs a Cloak," "The Story about Ping," and "The Beast of Monsieur Racine." Part II of the "Children's Circle" series from Weston Woods.
1970 (*Primary*) 32m/C **VHS, Beta $19.95** *CCC,*

The Rousters 🎞🎞

Descendants of Wyatt Earp run a carnival in a small Western town. Rambling, family-friendly made-for-TV movie that was a pilot for a short-lived TV series, this obscurity was released to home video to capitalize on the popularity of Jim Varney, playing a character almost identical (physically and intellectually) to his hit movie boob Ernest P. Worrell. **Hound Advisory:** Roughhousing.
1983 (**PG** / *Adult*) 72m/C Jim Varney, Mimi Rogers, Chad Everett, Maxine Stuart, Hoyt Axton; **D:** E.W. Swackhamer; **W:** E.W. Swackhamer, Stephen J. Cannell. **VHS, LV $79.95** *VMK*

Rover Dangerfield 🎞🎞

The "Brave Little Toaster" crew also did this cartoon vehicle for comic Rodney Dangerfield that cannily recasts him as the casino-wise pet hound of a Las Vegas showgirl. So far, so good, but then the plot unwisely dumps Rover in a farm setting, far from the glitter and gambling tables and into a worn-out farmboy-and-his-dog plot; you can imagine almost any animated character doing exactly the same tired tale. Dangerfield also wrote the script, incorporating characteristic catchphrases, mannerisms and fire-hydrant jokes. **Hound Advisory:** Violence, surprisingly, in a wolf attack and miscellaneous mayhem.
1991 (**G** / *Family*) 78m/C **W:** Harold Ramis; **M:** David Newman; **V:** Rodney Dangerfield. **VHS, LV, 8mm $19.98** *WAR*

Roxanne 🎞🎞🎞

Modern comic retelling of "Cyrano de Bergerac" dwells on the romantic triangle between a small town fire chief with a very big nose and a fast tongue, a handsome, fairly stupid fireman, and the lovely astronomer they both love. In a complex, enjoyable performance, Martin is a hoot as Chief Bales, utilizing wit as his rapier and chivalrously assisting his dimwitted fireman's courtship of Roxanne while pining for her himself. Don't miss the bar scene where he gets back at a heckler. A wonderful adaptation for the modern age. **Hound Advisory:** Profanity; suggested sex.

1987 (PG/*Jr. High-Adult*) 107m/C Steve Martin, Daryl Hannah, Rick Rossovich, Shelley Duvall, Michael J. Pollard, Fred Willard, John Kapelos, Max Alexander, Damon Wayans, Matt Lattanzi, Kevin Nealon; *D:* Fred Schepisi; *W:* Steve Martin; *M:* Bruce Smeaton. **VHS, Beta, LV, 8mm** $14.95 *COL*

Rubber Tarzan 🦴🦴🦴

Ivan is a gentle, friendless, quiet (and possibly dyslexic) boy bullied daily at school and bossed at home by his workaholic dad, who wants him to be like Tarzan. But a sympathetic dockworker helps Ivan affirm his self-worth. Delicate little Danish film avoids gooey melodrama, but its slow pace and subtleties steer it more toward adult viewers than kids.

1983 (*Family*) 75m/C **VHS, Beta** *SUE, NLC*

Rubik, the Amazing Cube, Vol. 1

One of the unlikeliest toy pandering Saturday-morning TV shows; here are two episodes from the animated series based upon the puzzle cube that became a commercial sensation too profitable for the networks to ignore, and originally broadcast together with a similar crossover concept, the cartoon edition of Pac-Man. "Welcome Back Kotter" character actor Palillo provides the voice of Rubik. Additional volumes available.

1984 (*Family*) 45m/C **VHS, Beta** $24.95 *COL, WTA*

Rudolph the Red-Nosed Reindeer 🦴🦴🦴

Durable Christmas story inspired by the Johnny Marks song about the nasally enhanced reindeer who saved the holiday. Colorful stop-motion animation and character voices bring it to life, with a memorable guest visit from an abominable snowman. Made for television by Arthur Rankin Jr. and Jules Bass.

1964 (*Family*) 53m/C *D:* Larry Roemer. **VHS, Beta, LV, 8mm** $12.98 *FHE, WTA, LME*

Rudy 🦴🦴◁

Inspiring true story about an unlikely legend of Notre Dame football, the small-sized Daniel E. "Rudy" Ruettiger (onetime "Goonie" Astin). A mediocre student, the working-class youth dreams of playing for the prestigious school. Through determination and hard work he makes the practice squad, but still has his mind set on getting into a real game. Likeable sports drama with an engaging hero. **Hound Advisory:** Football mayhem.

1993 (PG/*Jr. High-Adult*) 112m/C Sean Astin, Ned Beatty, Charles S. Dutton, Lili Taylor, Robert Prosky, Jason Miller, Ron Dean, Chelcie Ross, Jon Favreau, Greta Lind, Scott Benjaminson, Christopher Reed; *D:* David Anspaugh; *W:* Angelo Pizzo; *M:* Jerry Goldsmith. **VHS, LV, 8mm** *COL*

Rugrats, Vol. 1: Tales from the Crib

Episodes of the award-winning Nickelodeon cable-TV 'toon show about mischievous toddlers. Tommy and his best friend, Chuckie, star in "Toy Palace," "Real or Robots," and "Beach Blanket Babies." Includes two claymation vignettes of Inside Out Boy, the superhero with the power to save kids by grossing out grownups. Additional volumes available.

1993 (*Preschool-Primary*) 40m/C **VHS** $14.98 *SMV, WTA*

Rumble Fish 🦴🦴🦴

Rusty-James, a young street punk, idolizes his older brother, a cool but weary former gang leader who's become a slum legend known as the Motorcycle Boy. Coppola's second adaptation of a bestselling S.E. Hinton young-adult novel is a much more daring production than "The Outsiders," with stark B&W photography and occasionally muffled sound to reflect the Motorcycle Boy's view of the world (you have to pay close attention to catch the detail that he's color blind and partially deaf). Even with a musical score by rocker Stewart Copeland, this isn't at all a youth-pandering delinquent drama, but one that requires adult patience to get past the alienating style. **Hound Advisory:** Mature themes; profanity; drug talk; alcohol use. Sex and nudity in a very brief but raw orgy scene.

1983 (R/*Sr. High-Adult*) 94m/B Matt Dillon, Mickey Rourke, Dennis Hopper, Diane Lane, Vincent Spano, Nicolas Cage, Diana Scarwid, Christopher Penn, Tom Waits; *D:* Francis Ford Coppola; *W:* Francis Ford Coppola; *M:* Stewart Copeland. **VHS, Beta, LV** $59.95 *MCA*

Rumpelstiltskin

Canadian animated version of the classic Brothers Grimm fairy tale about the maiden ordered to spin straw into gold.

1985 (*Family*) 24m/C **VHS, Beta** $12.95 *FHE, WTA*

Rumpelstiltskin 🦴◁

First of the Cannon Movie Tales, musical retellings of classic fairy tales by the Cannon Film studio, is one of their better efforts, but that's not saying much. A miller brags that his daughter can spin straw into gold, so the greedy King and the scheming Queen (Irving's real-life mother Pointer) threaten to cut off her head unless she succeeds. Irving is lovely, and Barty is a mischievous delight as the rhyme-talking dwarf who helps her, but lackluster direction and uninspired songs make this a yawner; there just isn't enough story for feature length, as Shelley Duvall knew well.

1986 (G/*Family*) 84m/C Amy Irving, Billy Barty, Robert Symonds, Priscilla Pointer, Clive Revill, John Moulder-Brown; *D:* David Irving. **VHS, Beta, LV** $19.98 *MED*

Rumpelstiltskin

Turner reads this classic tale from the Brothers Grimm about a girl who promises her first-born to a mysterious little man in exchange for a magical favor. Vividly illustrated by Peter Sis, with music by Tangerine Dream. A typically outstanding combo of sight and sound from the "Rabbit Ears: We All Have Tales" series.

1992 (*Primary*) 30m/C *M:* Tangerine Dream. **VHS** $9.95 *BTV*

Run, Appaloosa, Run

An Indian girl and Holy Smoke, her stallion, share happiness and tragedy in this adventure excerpted from the long-running Walt Disney TV program.
1966 (*Primary-Jr. High*) 48m/C **VHS, Beta $250.00** *MTI, DSN*

Run for Life: An Olympic Fable

Japanese animated feature delving into the origins of the Olympic Games; a young athlete running to restore support for his country's King in Ancient Greece.
1979 (*Preschool-Primary*) 68m/C **VHS, Beta $39.98** *LIV, WTA*

Run for the Roses 🐾🐾

Young Puerto Rican boy living with a Kentucky step-family tries to make a racetrack winner out a broken-down horse - not to mention the broken-down plot. Cliched underdog-horse tale, also known as "Thoroughbred."
1978 (**PG**/*Family*) 93m/C Lisa Eilbacher, Vera Miles, Stuart Whitman, Sam Groom; **D:** Henry Levin. **VHS, Beta $59.98** *LIV*

Run, Rebecca, Run 🐾🐾🐾

Interesting family adventure yarn about a South American refugee who tries to stop a young girl from leaving an Australian island where both are stranded. She eventually befriends him and attempts to get permission for him to enter the country.
1981 (*Family*) 90m/C Simone Buchanan, Henri Szeps; **D:** Peter Maxwell. **VHS, Beta** *NO*

Runaway

A boy blames himself for his friend's accidental death and runs away to live in the subway tunnels of New York City. After four months of life underground, a disabled veteran and a waitress lend the boy a hand. Adapted from the novel "Slake's Limbo" by Felice Holman. Part of the "Wonderworks" series.
1989 (*Family*) 58m/C Charles S. Dutton, Jasmine Guy, Gavin Allen; **D:** Gilbert Moses. **VHS $29.95** *PME, HMV, COL*

Runaway Ralph

Ralph S. Mouse runs away so he won't have to share his motorcycle anymore. Stop-motion follow-up to "The Mouse and the Motorcycle," both based on Beverly Cleary classics and a quality production for ABC-TV.
1989 (*Primary*) 40m/C Fred Savage; **D:** Ron Underwood. **VHS, Beta $9.98** *MLT, CHF*

The Runaways 🐾🐾

TV movie about a troubled boy who runs away from an unhappy foster-home situation and finds a friend in a kindred spirit — a leopard that has similarly escaped from a zoo. Based on a novel by Victor Canning.
1975 (*Family*) 76m/C Dorothy McGuire, John Randolph, Neva Patterson, Josh Albee; **D:** Harry Harris. **VHS, Beta** *NO*

Running Brave 🐾🐾

True story of Billy Mills, a South Dakota Sioux Indian who won the Gold Medal in the 10,000 meter run at the 1964 Tokyo Olympics. Not bad, but plodding and hokey in the way of many inspirational true-story flicks. **Hound Advisory:** Brief nudity, mature themes, roughhousing.
1983 (**PG**/*Family*) 90m/C Robby Benson, Claudia Cron, Pat Hingle, Denis Lacroix; **D:** D.S. Everett. **VHS, Beta, LV** *DIS*

Running Mates 🐾🐾

Occasionally intriguing drama of two teens who fall in love, but are kept apart by their fathers' local political rivalry. Could have been better, but cardboard characters abound.
1986 (**PG-13**/*Jr. High-Adult*) 90m/C Greg Webb, Barbara Howard, J. Don Ferguson, Clara Dunn; **D:** Thomas L. Neff. **VHS, Beta $19.95** *STE, NWV*

Running on Empty 🐾🐾🐾

Two 1960s radicals are still on the run in 1988 for a long-ago bombing, changing their names and moving from place to place whenever they think the law is closing in. But now their teenage son wants a normal life, even if it means never seeing his parents again. Unimpeachable performances in a compelling, believable drama. **Hound Advisory:** Salty language, mature theme.
1988 (**PG-13**/*Jr. High-Adult*) 116m/C Christine Lahti, River Phoenix, Judd Hirsch, Martha Plimpton, Jonas Arby, Ed Crowley, L.M. Kit Carson, Steven Hill, Augusta Dabney, David Margulies, Sidney Lumet; **D:** Sidney Lumet; **M:** Tony Mottola. **Award Nominations:** Academy Awards '88: Best Original Screenplay, Best Supporting Actor (Phoenix); **Awards:** Golden Globe Awards '89: Best Screenplay; National Board of Review Awards '88: Best Supporting Actor (Phoenix). **VHS, Beta, LV, 8mm $19.95** *WAR*

Running Wild 🐾🐾🐾

Free-lance photographer on assignment in Colorado becomes personally involved in a dispute over the fate of a wild mustang herd. Easygoing, if vaguely dull story, enhanced by good performances, okay script, and modern Western backdrop.
1973 (**G**/*Family*) 102m/C Lloyd Bridges, Dina Merrill, Pat Hingle, Gilbert Roland, Morgan Woodward; **D:** Robert McCahon; **W:** Robert McCahon. **VHS, Beta $19.95** *MED*

Rupert

Popular British character Rupert the Bear stars in 12 adventures told through storybook-style illustrations rather than animation. Rupert is joined by his friends Bill Badger, Tiger-Lily, and Jack Frost.
1988 (*Preschool-Family*) 57m/C **VHS $14.98** *FOX, FCT*

Rupert and the Frog Song

Paul and Linda McCartney produced this impressive music-video animation centered around the popular British cartoon bruin. Also on the tape: "Seaside Woman" and "Oriental Nightfish," two abstract 'toons based on Linda's compositions.
1985 (*Preschool*) 22m/C **VHS, Beta, LV $14.95** *FHE, WTA*

Rupert and the Runaway Dragon

Join Rupert the Bear, Tiger-Lily, and Ping-Pong on a series of seven adventures in their magical wonderland.
1989 (*Preschool-Family*) 37m/C **VHS $14.98** *FOX, FCT*

Russkies 🎬🎬🎬

Tame, outdated comedy about three adorable Florida boys who capture, hide, and eventually grow to like a stranded young sailor off a Russian submarine. Politically correct villain is a meanie US serviceman in hot pursuit of the kids' pet Red. **Hound Advisory:** Salty language.
1987 (*PG/Jr. High*) 98m/C M: Leaf (Joaquin Rafael) Phoenix, Whip Hubley, Peter Billingsley, Stefan DeSalle; *D:* Rick Rosenthal; *M:* James Newton Howard. **VHS, Beta, LV $14.95** *LHV, WAR*

Ryan's Daughter 🎬🎬🎬

Irish woman (Miles) marries a man she does not love and then falls for a shell-shocked British major who arrives during the 1916 Irish uprising to keep the peace. Not surprisingly, she is accused of betraying the local IRA gunrunners to her British lover. Tasteful melodrama with lots of pretty scenery that goes on a bit too long.
1970 (*PG/Sr. High-Adult*) 194m/C Sarah Miles, Robert Mitchum, John Mills, Trevor Howard, Christopher Jones, Leo McKern; *D:* David Lean; *W:* Robert Bolt; *M:* Maurice Jarre. **Award Nominations:** Academy Awards '70: Best Actress (Miles), Best Sound; **Awards:** Academy Awards '70: Best Cinematography, Best Supporting Actor (Mills); National Board of Review Awards '70: 10 Best Films of the Year. **VHS, Beta, LV $29.98** *MGM, BTV*

Saber Rider and the Star Sheriffs: All That Glitters

Japanese-made outer space western cartoon series, distinguished from any other Japanese-made outer space western cartoon series by being the first to use interactive technology; with proper toy equipment, kiddie viewers could supposedly play along with the action onscreen. In this particular episode, the evil, extradimensional Outriders tempt the good citizens with phony trinkets — sounds like an apt metaphor in there somewhere. Additional volumes available.
1990 (*Family*) 45m/C **VHS, Beta $9.95** *FRH, WTA*

Saboteur 🎬🎬🎬

Man wrongly accused of sabotaging an American munitions plant during WWII sets out to find the traitor who framed him, meeting Lane along the way. Hitchcock uses his locations, including Boulder Dam, Radio City Music Hall, and the Statue of Liberty, to greatly intensify the action. Stunning resolution.
1942 (*Family*) 108m/B Priscilla Lane, Robert Cummings, Otto Kruger, Alan Baxter, Norman Lloyd, Charles Halton; *D:* Alfred Hitchcock; *W:* Alfred Hitchcock, Peter Viertel. **VHS, Beta, LV $19.95** *MCA*

Sabrina 🎬🎬🎬

Two wealthy brothers, one an aging businessman and the other a dissolute playboy, vie for the attention of their chauffeur's daughter, who has just returned from a French finishing school. Typically acerbic, in the Wilder manner, with Bogart and Holden cast interestingly against type. Based on the play "Sabrina Fair" by Samuel Taylor.
1954 (*Jr. High-Adult*) 113m/B Audrey Hepburn, Humphrey Bogart, William Holden, Walter Hampden, Francis X. Bushman, John Williams, Martha Hyer, Marcel Dalio; *D:* Billy Wilder; *W:* Billy Wilder, Ernest Lehman. **Award Nominations:** Academy Awards '54: Best Actress (Hepburn), Best Art Direction/Set Decoration (B & W), Best Black and White Cinematography, Best Director (Wilder), Best Screenplay; **Awards:** Academy Awards '54: Best Costume Design (B & W); Directors Guild of America Awards '54: Best Director (Wilder); Golden Globe Awards '55: Best Screenplay; National Board of Review Awards '54: 10 Best Films of the Year, Best Supporting Actor (Williams). **VHS, Beta, LV $19.95** *PAR*

Sabrina, the Teenaged Witch

Spinoff of the "Archie" TV cartoon series, in which one of the girls at Riverdale High is a fun-loving, non-wicked witch. Episodes feature appearances by those regulars Archie Andrews, Jughead, Betty, Veronica and Reggie.
1969 (*Family*) 57m/C *V:* Jane Webb. **VHS, Beta $39.98** *SUE*

Sad Cat: Apprentice Good Fairy

The backwoods adventures of a melancholy feline character created for Terrytoons by Ralph Bakshi. Additional volumes available.
1965 (*Preschool-Primary*) 37m/C **VHS $5.99** *VTR*

The Saga of Windwagon Smith

Disney cartoon short based on folklore about how inventor Smith embarks on a wacky trip across the prairie on his schooner fitted with sails and masts.
1961 (*Preschool-Primary*) 13m/C **VHS, Beta $250.00** *DSN, MTI*

Salem's Lot 🎬🎬🎬

Based on Stephen King's novel about a sleepy New England village which is infiltrated by evil. Mysterious antiques dealer takes up residence in a forbidding hilltop house — and it becomes apparent that a vampire is on the loose. Generally creepy; Mason is good, but Soul only takes up space in the lead as a novelist returning home. Also available in the original television miniseries version at 190 minutes on two cassettes. **Hound Advisory:** Violence.
1979 (*PG/Jr. High-Adult*) 112m/C David Soul, James Mason, Lance Kerwin, Bonnie Bedelia, Lew Ayres, Bo Fanders, Elisha Cook Jr., Reggie Nalder, Fred Willard, Kenneth McMillan, Marie Windsor; *D:* Tobe Hooper. **VHS, Beta, LV $14.95** *WAR*

Salty 🎬🎬

The creators of "Flipper" swam again with this inoffensive but ever-so-familiar tale of another lovable marine mammal, this time a mischievous sea lion who complicates two brothers' lives when they volunteer to renovate a Florida marina threatened with foreclosure.
1973 (*Family*) 93m/C Clint Howard, Mark Slade, Nina Foch; *D:* Ricou Browning. **VHS, Beta** *NO*

A Salute to Chuck Jones

One of a series of cassettes in the "24 Karat Collection," compiling some of the best of the Warner animation works. This tape contains some of the best-known productions by director Jones, including Daffy in "Duck Dodgers in the 24 1/

4 Century," the Bugs-Bunny starrer "Rabbit Seasoning," plus the famous "One Froggy Evening" and more.
1960 *(Family)* 56m/C **D:** Chuck Jones; **V:** Mel Blanc. **VHS, Beta $12.95** *WAR, WTA*

A Salute to Mel Blanc

This compilation of Warner Brothers animation pays tribute to Blanc, man of a thousand voices. Many of the all-time greatest cartoons would simply be unimaginable without him, and Mel's memorable moments here include "The Rabbit of Seville," "Little Boy Boo" and "Robin Hood Daffy." Part of Warner's "24 Karat Collection."
1958 *(Family)* 58m/C **D:** Chuck Jones, Friz Freleng, Bob Clampett; **V:** Mel Blanc. **VHS, Beta $12.95** *WAR, WTA*

Samantha 𝄞𝄞♪

Twenty-one year-old Samantha discovers she was left on her parents' doorstep in a basket and decides to find out where she came from. Good cast and high charm quotient help this film along. **Hound Advisory:** Profanity.
1992 (PG/*Jr. High-Adult***)** 101m/C Martha Plimpton, Dermot Mulroney, Hector Elizondo, Mary Kay Place, Ione Skye; **D:** Steven La Rocque; **W:** John Golden, Steven La Rocque. **VHS, Beta $89.95** *ACA*

Sammy Bluejay

Features two escapades from the world of author Thornton W. Burgess, "Brainy Bluejay" and "Sammy's Revenge," starring Sammy Bluejay, Peter Cottontail, and Reddy the Fox.
1983 *(Preschool-Primary)* 60m/C **VHS, Beta $29.95** *FHE, WTA*

Sammy, the Way-Out Seal 𝄞𝄞

Two young boys bring a mischievous seal to live in their beach house and try to keep it a secret from their parents. Disney in its early '60s phase.
1962 *(Family)* 89m/C Michael McGreevey, Billy Mumy, Patricia Barry, Robert Culp; **D:** Norman Tokar. **VHS, Beta $69.95** *DIS*

Sam's Son 𝄞𝄞

Writer/director Landon rehashed the sentimental themes he explored earlier in the 1979 TV movie "The Loneliest Runner" (also on video). Once again, it's an autobiographical tale about a teen athlete - this time a javelin thrower - in a troubled relationship with his father.
1984 (PG/*Family***)** 107m/C Eli Wallach, Anne Jackson, Timothy Patrick Murphy, Hallie Todd, James Karen, Allan Hayes, Joanna Lee, Michael Landon; **D:** Michael Landon; **W:** Michael Landon. **VHS, Beta $59.95** *WOV*

Samson and Sally: The Song of the Whales 𝄞𝄞𝄞

Two orphaned whales set off in search of Moby Dick; legend has it that the sea giant will save endangered whales from the "iron beasts" — predatory humans in their deadly whaling ships. Environmentally concerned animated feature stands out from the herd of eco-'toons with its well-rendered underwater settings and themes. Tellingly, it hails from Norway, one of the few nations to actively hunt whales in

modern times. Based on the book "Song of the Whales" by Brent Haller. **Hound Advisory:** Violence.
1984 *(Primary)* 58m/C **VHS, Beta $14.99** *CEL, JFK, WTA*

The Sand Castle

Oscar-winning example of superb stop-motion animation shows the gentle Sandman and the whimsical creations and living animals he wordlessly sculpts out of the sand, plus "The Northwind and the Sun," "Alphabet," and "The Owl and the Lemming."
1977 *(Family)* 30m/C **VHS $14.98** *SMA, NFB, SAL*

The Sandlot 𝄞𝄞𝄞

Mom's remarriage takes non-athletic Scotty to a new town in California in 1962. He befriends local boys playing idle baseball at the local sandlot, and plot is a loose set of antics on and off the diamond. Finale is a long, crazy battle with "the Beast," a legendary junkyard dog (shown in glimpses as a monster-sized menace) lurking behind the fence, who's hoarded all their home-run balls. You don't have to be baseball fan - though it helps - to like this offbeat look at childhood, deliberately cast with newcomer young actors. Written and directed by the scripter of the ill-fated "Radio Flyer," in a gentler mode. **Hound Advisory:** Occasional lapses to near-ballpark grammar, mild sex talk.
1993 (PG/*Family***)** 101m/C Tom Guiry, Mike Vitar, Patrick Renna, Chauncey Leopardi, Marty York, Brandon Adams, Karen Allen, James Earl Jones, Maury Wills, Art LaFleur, Marlee Shelton; **Cameos:** Denis Leary, Brooke Adams; **D:** David Mickey Evans; **W:** Robert Gunter, David Mickey Evans; **M:** David Newman; **V:** Arliss Howard. **VHS, LV $19.98** *FXV*

Santa & the 3 Bears 𝄞𝄞

Holiday-oriented cartoon released to theaters. When a mother bear and her cubs discover the magic of Christmas in the forest, they decide to skip hibernation for the winter. Kindly park ranger decides to humor the cubs by impersonating Santa on the crucial night.
1979 *(Preschool-Primary)* 60m/C **VHS, Beta $29.95** *WTA, PSM*

Santa & the Tooth Fairies

When Santa gets Hans' letter too late to deliver his gifts personally, he gives the job to the Tooth Fairies.
1992 *(Preschool-Primary)* ?m/C **VHS $12.95** *WTA*

Santa Claus Conquers the Martians 𝄞

The green-faced Martian children are feeling blue, so to speak, and their parents decide it's because Earth has a Santa Claus and Mars doesn't. So the aliens invade the North Pole and abduct Kris Kringle. Fortunately human kids tag along for a rescue and some awful songs. Celebrated as one of the worst flicks ever made, but it's that kind of awfulness you can have fun with, if you're in the right mood.
1964 *(Family)* 80m/C John Call, Pia Zadora, Leonard Hicks, Vincent Beck, Victor Stiles, Donna Conforti; **D:** Nicholas Webster. **VHS, Beta $19.95** *COL, SNC, SUE*

Santa Claus is Coming to Town 🦴🦴🦴

Classic Arthur Rankin-Jules Bass TV-special biopic of Kris Kringle himself, taking you from his childhood to his marriage to Mrs. Claus to his destiny as the North Pole's magical purveyor of the Christmas spirit, as he give toys to the citizens of Sombertown. An "Animagic" tale done in stop-motion puppet animation.
1970 *(Family)* 53m/C *D:* Arthur Rankin Jr., Jules Bass; *V:* Mickey Rooney, Keenan Wynn, Paul Frees. **VHS, Beta, LV $12.98** *FHE, WTA, LME*

Santa Claus: The Movie 🦴🦴

Uneven holiday spectacle from the makers of the "Superman" pics; first part is a formal, stiff telling of how a child-loving old guy and his wife won the honor of being the immortal Mr. and Mrs. Claus. Rest is a fresher, amusing tale about a well-meaning elf who leaves the North Pole to work for a greedy toy tycoon and almost ruins Christmas. Good cast, tinsel-thin special f/x. **Hound Advisory:** Alcohol use, but nothing naughty enough to deserve that PG.
1985 *(PG/Family)* 112m/C Dudley Moore, John Lithgow, David Huddleston, Judy Cornwell, Burgess Meredith; *D:* Jeannot Szwarc; *W:* David Newman; *M:* Henry Mancini. **VHS, Beta, LV $9.98** *MED*

Santabear's First Christmas

That cuddly little fellow Santabear is back, and just in time for the holidays.
1989 *(Family)* 25m/C **VHS $9.98** *VES, WTA*

Santabear's High Flying Adventure

Network TV cartoon finds Santabear saving Christmas when a rival steals toys from the real Santa Claus.
1987 *(Preschool-Primary)* 23m/C *V:* John Malkovich, Kelly McGillis, Bobby McFerrin, Glenne Headly. **VHS, Beta $9.98** *LIV, VES, WTA*

Santa's First Christmas

Young Santa Claus trains reindeer and finds elves to help out as he begins his Christmas work.
1992 *(Preschool-Primary)* ?m/C **VHS $12.95** *WTA*

Sarafina! 🦴🦴🦴

Part coming-of-age saga, part political drama, part musical, and all emotionally powerful. Sarafina is a young girl in a township school in Soweto, South Africa in the mid-'70s, gradually coming into a political awakening amid the Soweto riots. Khumalo recreates her stage role as the glowing and defiant Sarafina with both Goldberg and Makeba satisfying in their roles as Sarafina's outspoken and inspirational teacher and her long-suffering mother, respectively. Adapted from Ngema's stage musical. **Hound Advisory:** Violence.
1992 *(PG-13/Jr. High-Adult)* 98m/C Leleti Khumalo, Whoopi Goldberg, Miriam Makeba, John Kani, Mbongeni Ngema; *D:* Darrell Roodt; *W:* Mbongeni Ngema, William Nicholson; *M:* Stanley Myers. **VHS, Beta, LV $94.95** *TOU*

Sarah, Plain and Tall 🦴🦴🦴

New England schoolteacher Sarah travels to Kansas circa 1910 to care for the family of a widowed farmer who has advertised for a wife. Of course, a simple business arrange-ment soon blossoms into genuine love. Superior entertainment for the whole family. Adapted for television from Patricia MacLachlan's novel of the same name. Nominated for nine Emmy Awards.
1991 *(G/Family)* 98m/C Glenn Close, Christopher Walken, Lexi Randall, Margaret Sophie Stein, Jon DeVries, Christopher Bell; *D:* Glenn Jordan. **VHS, LV $14.98** *REP*

Satisfaction 🦴

All-girl, high school rock band fool around with instruments the summer before college. The men, drugs and music they sample (and reject, eventually) is supposed to be a growing experience, but overall this teen-appeal tale is smarmy stuff. **Hound Advisory:** Sex, drugs, plus profanity.
1988 *(PG-13/Jr. High-Adult)* 93m/C Justine Bateman, Trini Alvarado, Britta Phillips, Julia Roberts, Scott Coffey, Liam Neeson, Deborah Harry; *D:* Joan Freeman; *W:* Charles Purpura; *M:* Michel Colombier. **VHS, Beta, LV $19.98** *FOX*

Saturday the 14th 🦴🦴◁

Sloppy spoof of haunted houses and horror movies. Goofy family inherits a mansion where a black-magic book is hidden, copes with monster in the bathtub, mummy in refrigerator, cheapo special f/x. Kids might be amused, so were swear words really necessary? Followed by even worse in-name-only sequel: "Saturday the 14th Strikes Back". **Hound Advisory:** Salty language, monster roughhousing.
1981 *(PG/Jr. High-Adult)* 91m/C Richard Benjamin, Paula Prentiss, Severn Darden; *D:* Howard R. Cohen. **VHS, Beta $19.98** *SUE*

Savage Sam 🦴🦴

Disney's sequel to their classic "Old Yeller" isn't anywhere near as effective. Sam is indeed the offspring of the loyal Old Yeller, and he proves his canine courage by assisting in the hunt for children kidnapped by hostile Apaches. Occasionally fun, but nothing more. Based on the novel by Fred Gipson.
1963 *(Preschool-Primary)* 103m/C Tommy Kirk, Kevin Corcoran, Brian Keith, Dewey Martin, Jeff York, Marta Kristen; *D:* Norman Tokar. **VHS, Beta $69.95** *DIS*

Savannah Smiles 🦴🦴🦴◁

Poor little rich girl Savannah, frustrated by her neglectful, careerist parents, runs away. She hides in the car of two harmless escaped convicts, who are hunted as kidnappers. But while on the run the "captive" Savannah gets more love and caring attention than she did at home. Sweet-natured but much too long, sentimental family comedy. **Hound Advisory:** Salty language, without which this could have earned an easy G rating.
1982 *(PG/Jr. High-Adult)* 104m/C Bridgette Anderson, Mark Miller, Donovan Scott, Peter Graves, Chris Robinson, Michael Parks; *D:* Pierre De Moro. **VHS, Beta, LV $14.98** *SUE, NLC*

Save the Lady 🦴🦴

Plucky kids fight city hall to save an old ferry, the Lady Hope, from the scrap heap.
1982 *(Family)* 76m/C Matthew Excell, Robert Clarkson, Miranda Cartledge, Kim Clifford; *D:* Leon Thau. **VHS, Beta** *NO*

Say Anything 🎵🎵🎵

Thoughtful, often sparkling, teen romance about a spirited loner who courts the beautiful, unapproachable valedictorian of his high school. Her father disapproves of their love affair, but he's got problems of his own. Smart comedy-drama works well on both the romantic and serious levels without getting too sticky, and offers young characters well worth your time. **Hound Advisory:** Sex, salty language, mature themes. **1989** (PG-13/*Jr. High-Adult*) 100m/C John Cusack, Ione Skye, John Mahoney, Joan Cusack, Lili Taylor, Richard Portnow, Pamela Segall, Jason Gould, Loren Dean, Bebe Neuwirth, Aimee Brooks, Eric Stoltz, Chynna Phillips, Joanna Frank; *D:* Cameron Crowe; *W:* Cameron Crowe; *M:* Anne Dudley, Richard Gibbs, Nancy Wilson. VHS, Beta, LV $19.98 *FOX*

Scandalous John 🎵🎵◁

Disney comedy western about a last cattle drive devised by an aging rancher in order to save his spread from developers. Good acting carries this one; watch for a young John Ritter. **1971** (G/*Family*) 113m/C Brian Keith, Alfonso Arau, Michele Carey, Rick Lenz, John Ritter, Harry Morgan; *D:* Robert Butler. VHS, Beta $69.95 *DIS*

The Scarlet Pimpernel 🎵🎵🎵

Remake of the classic about a British dandy who saved French aristocrats from the Reign of Terror guillotines during the French Revolution. Made for British television version is almost as good as the original 1935 film, with beautiful costumes and sets and strong performances from Seymour and Andrews. **1982** (*Jr. High-Adult*) 142m/C Anthony Andrews, Jane Seymour, Ian McKellan, James Villers, Eleanor David; *D:* Clive Donner; *M:* Nick Bicat. VHS, Beta, LV $19.98 *LIV, VES, FUS*

School Ties 🎵🎵🎵

David is a talented, likeable quarterback who gets a scholarship to the elite St. Matthew prep school. To conform with the closed-mindedness of the 1950s, both his father and coach suggest that he hide his Jewish religion. David's a big man on campus until his secret comes out, creating an ugly rift in the school. What easily could have been just another teen hunk flick looks at much more than just Fraser's pretty face in successful, unflinching treatment of anti-Semitism. **Hound Advisory:** Salty language, mature themes. **1992** (PG-13/*Jr. High-Adult*) 110m/C Brendan Fraser, Matt Damon, Chris O'Donnell, Randall Batinkoff, Andrew Lowery, Cole Hauser, Ben Affleck, Anthony Rapp, Amy Locane, Peter Donat, Zeljko Ivanek, Kevin Tighe, Michael Higgins, Ed Lauter; *D:* Robert Mandel; *W:* Dick Wolf, Darryl Ponicsan; *M:* Maurice Jarre. VHS, Beta, LV $19.95 *PAR*

Schoolhouse Rock: Grammar Rock

Children get to learn grammar basics through timely rock music and animation in these nine segments from the award-winning network TV series of Saturday-morning short subjects. **1974** (*Primary*) 28m/C VHS, Beta $9.95 *KUI,, CHI*

Schoolhouse Rock: History Rock

ABC-TV network's award-winning educational shorts that teach history using catchy songs and animation. This volume contains "Shot Heard 'Round the World," "Sufferin' Thru Suffrage," and the classic "I'm Just a Bill," plus more. **1974** (*Family*) 32m/C VHS, Beta $9.95 *KUI,, WTA*

Schoolhouse Rock: Science Rock

Complicated scientific concepts are simplified in segments from the ABC-TV series. **1974** (*Primary*) 31m/C VHS, Beta $9.95 *KUI,, CHI*

Scooby-Doo

Collection of the most mysterious adventures Hanna-Barbera's celebrated Scooby-Doo and his teen sidekicks ("...those meddling kids!") have ever encountered. Take a ride in the Mystery Mobile as it takes the mongrel sleuth and his friends to all sorts of spooky venues, with periodic guest star voices. Additional volumes available. **1983** (*Family*) 90m/C *V:* Sonny Bono, Cher, Don Messick, Casey Kasem, Frank Welker, Heather North. VHS, Beta, LV $29.95 *TTC, IME, WTA*

Scout's Honor 🎵🎵

An orphan (Coleman) is determined to become the best Cub Scout ever when he joins a troop led by an executive who dislikes children. Harmless, enjoyable family tale includes several former child stars as Scout parents. Made for television. **1980** (*Family*) 96m/C Gary Coleman, Katherine Helmond, Wilfrid Hyde-White, Pat O'Brien, Joanna Moore, Meeno Peluce, Jay North, Harry Morgan, Angela Cartwright; *D:* Henry Levin. VHS, Beta *NO*

Scrooge 🎵🎵◁

Lavish British musical version of Charles Dickens' classic "A Christmas Carol" obviously aimed to captivate audiences with the Victorian-England On-Broadway magic that "Oliver!" managed to work, but the songs aren't half as good. Still, production values and the energy levels run high, with Finney memorable as the title miser and Guiness a terrific Marley's Ghost. 🎵The Beautiful Day; Happiness; Thank You Very Much; A Christmas Carol; Christmas Children; I Hate People; Farver Chris'mas; See the Phantoms; December the 25th. **1970** (G/*Family*) 86m/C Albert Finney, Alec Guinness, Edith Evans, Kenneth More; *D:* Ronald Neame; *M:* Leslie Bricusse. **Award Nominations:** Academy Awards '70: Best Art Direction/Set Decoration, Best Costume Design, Best Song ("Thank You Very Much"), Best Original Score; **Awards:** Golden Globe Awards '71: Best Actor—Musical/Comedy (Finney). VHS, Beta, LV $14.98 *FOX, FUS*

Scrooge McDuck and Money

Children learn lessons in money and economics through song and dance. **1990** (*Preschool-Primary*) 16m/C VHS, Beta $250.00 *MTI, DSN*

Scrooged 🎵🎵◁

Big-budget but frequently leaden satire of the hallowed holiday classic finds maniacally callous TV executive Murray staging "A Christmas Carol." Suddenly he himself is visited by the traditional three ghosts, but with modern twists; Xmas Past is a ghoulish cabbie, Xmas Present is a sweet-looking fairy who's violently abusive, and Xmas Future is the usual ghoul. Starts on a hysterical pitch and stays there, leaving

Murray to find any number of different ways to display cynicism and insincerity (he's very good at that, less believable upon transformation) and the rest of the all-star cast almost no room to develop their characters. Eye-poppin' f/x, nearly stinging satire in what is at least a fresh take on the Scrooge story. **Hound Advisory:** Sex talk, drug talk, salty language and lots of cartoony violence.

1988 (PG-13/*Jr. High–Adult*) 101m/C Bill Murray, Carol Kane, John Forsythe, David Johansen, Bob(cat) Goldthwait, Karen Allen, Michael J. Pollard, Brian Doyle-Murray, Alfre Woodard, John Glover, Robert Mitchum, Buddy Hackett, Robert Goulet, Jamie Farr, Mary Lou Retton, Lee Majors; *D:* Richard Donner; *W:* Mitch Glazer, Michael O'Donoghue; *M:* Danny Elfman. **VHS, Beta, LV, 8mm $89.95** PAR

Scruffy

Animated feature, actually a linked-together three-part TV special, sort of a mini-miniseries. Orphaned pooch Scruffy looks for a home, first with a vagrant Shakespearean actor, then a pack of other dogs, and finally a little boy.

1980 (*Family*) 72m/C *V:* Alan Young, June Foray, Hans Conried, Nancy McKeon. **VHS, Beta $19.95** WOV, GKK, WTA

Scuffy the Tugboat and Friends

Cartoon in which a magic tugboat is joined by his pals for a seafaring venture. Toot toot.

1989 (*Family*) 30m/C **VHS $7.95**

Sea Gypsies 🦴🦴◁

"Wilderness Family" crew set sail for a different sort of nature adventure in this passable effort about a handful of modern-day adults and kids who get shipwrecked off the Aleutian Islands, near Alaska. They must escape before winter or learn to survive attacks by wolves, bears and killer whales. Allegedly based on a true story.

1978 (G/*Family*) 101m/C Robert F. Logan, Mikki Jamison-Olsen, Heather Rattray, Cjon Damitri; *D:* Stewart Raffill; *W:* Stewart Raffill. **VHS, Beta $14.95** WAR

Sea Hound

Gets extra bone just for the title. Actually, that's the name of the boat commanded by Captain Silver, a popular radio and comic-book hero of the era, who grapples with late-'40s pirates over a sunken treasure in this 15-part Columbia serial.

1947 (*Jr. High–Adult*) ?m/B Buster Crabbe, Jimmy Lloyd, Pamela Blake, Ralph Hodges, Robert Barron; *D:* Walter B. Eason, Mack V. Wright. **VHS** MLB, GPV

Sea Prince and the Fire Child 🦴🦴

Japanese animated film follows two young lovers who set off on an adventure to escape the disapproval of their parents.

1982 (*Family*) 70m/C **VHS, Beta $19.95** COL

Seabert: Good Guys Wear White

Lovable Arctic white seal, accompanied by human friends Tommy and Aura, travel the world from their Greenland HQ to save endangered species and protect the ecosystem. Environmentally minded TV started out on a politically correct foot by recycling its own episodes for video. Additional volumes available.

1988 (*Primary*) 120m/C **VHS, Beta $39.95** JFK, WTA

Searching for Bobby Fischer 🦴🦴🦴◁

Seven-year-old Josh Waitzkin (Pomeranc, in a terrific debut) shows an amazing gift for chess, stunning his parents, who must then try to strike the delicate balance of developing his abilities while also allowing him a "normal" childhood. Excellent cast features Mantegna and Allen as his parents, Kingsley as demanding chess teacher Pandolfini, and Fishburne as an adept speed-chess hustler. Pomeranc is great, and his knowledge of chess (he's a ranked player) brings authenticity to his role. Title comes from Pandolfini's belief that Josh may equal the abilities of chess whiz Bobby Fischer. Underrated little gem based on a true story and adapted from the book by Waitzkin's father. No automatic pull for the kids (unless they're into chess) but a sweet, worthy view. **Hound Advisory:** Salty language.

1993 (PG/*Jr. High–Adult*) 111m/C Joe Mantegna, Max Pomeranc, Joan Allen, Ben Kingsley, Laurence "Larry" Fishburne, Robert Stephens, David Paymer, Robert Stephens, William H. Macy; *D:* Steven Zaillian; *W:* Steven Zaillian; *M:* James Horner. **Award Nominations:** Academy Awards '93: Best Cinematography; **Awards:** MTV Movie Awards '94: Best New Filmmaker Award (Zaillian). **VHS, Beta** PAR

Sebastian's Caribbean Jamboree

Sebastian, the musical crab from "The Little Mermaid," is back with another video. This time he co-hosts a travelogue through Walt Disney World with co-host Sam Wright.

1991 (*Family*) 30m/C *V:* Samuel E. Wright. **VHS $12.99** BVV, WTA

Sebastian's Party Gras

Sebastian, the crab star of "The Little Mermaid," takes his friends on a reggae and calypso fest.

1991 (*Family*) 30m/C **VHS $12.99** DIS, BTV

Secret Admirer 🦴◁

When 16-year-old Michael is slipped an anonymous love letter, he replies with unsigned mash notes of his own. But all the messages go to the wrong people, resulting in car crashes, vandalism, marital infidelity, sexual dysfunction, police brutality, heavy drinking, heavier swearing. Maybe John Hughes could have done something sweet and human with the premise, but foulmouthed romantic farce isn't for kids and may not be of much interest to adults. **Hound Advisory:** Profanity, alcohol use, sex, brief nudity, roughhousing.

1985 (R/*Sr. High–Adult*) 98m/C C. Thomas Howell, Cliff DeYoung, Kelly Preston, Dee Wallace Stone, Lori Loughlin, Fred Ward, Casey Siemaszko, Corey Haim, Leigh Taylor-Young; *D:* David Greenwalt. **VHS, Beta, LV** NO

The Secret Garden 🦴🦴🦴

The beloved Frances Hodgson Burnett story has been remade and even revamped as a Broadway musical, but this early version is especially well-remembered. Orphan Mary Lennox arrives at her uncle's estate on the Yorkshire Moors and finds the household revolves around her screaming, spoiled invalid of a little cousin Colin. But Mary's discovery of a long-hidden garden -and her ability to scream right back - brings about a miraculous change in the boy. The cast is

outstanding, and this telling of the tale concentrates more than the others on Colin's tormented father. Like the "Wizard of Oz," this starts out in beautifully photographed B&W before blazing into Technicolor for the scenes in the blooming garden.
1949 (*Family-Family*) 92m/B Margaret O'Brien, Herbert Marshall, Dean Stockwell, Gladys Cooper, Elsa Lanchester, Brian Roper; *D:* Fred M. Wilcox. **VHS, Beta, LV $19.98** *MGM*

The Secret Garden 🎬🎬🎬

Effective made-for-TV adaptation of the Frances Hodgson Burnett story of the lonely orphan sent to live with her distant uncle in England, who warms up the chilly household - and her own selfish heart - through the discovery and nurturing of a long-neglected garden. A prologue and afterword to the story (depicting the characters as adults during the First World War) are unnecessary additions, but this is a class production with fine performances. **Hound Advisory:** The deaths of the little heroine's parents from plague probably earned this the MPAA's PG. Either that or the coin came up heads.
1987 (*PG/Family*) 100m/C Gennie James, Barret Oliver, Jadrien Steele, Michael Hordern, Derek Jacobi, Billie Whitelaw, Lucy Gutteridge, Julian Glover, Colin Firth, Alan Grint. **VHS, LV $14.98** *REP*

The Secret Garden 🎬🎬🎬

Renewed interest in Frances Hodgson Burnett's classic tale prompted a Broadway musical, two TV movies, and this latest screen version about the orphaned Mary Lennox and the neglected garden she brings back to life, transforming a joyless cavern-like Yorkshire mansion. Stately and visually beautiful but thin on plot; trick the kids into watching this if you can, but it's skewed to adult emotions and attention spans.
1993 (*G/Family*) 102m/C Kate Maberly, Dame Maggie Smith, Haydon Prowse, Andrew Knott, John Lynch; *D:* Agnieszka Holland; *W:* Caroline Thompson; *M:* Zbigniew Preisner. **VHS, Beta, LV $24.96** *WAR, BTV*

Secret Life of Walter Mitty 🎬🎬🎬

An entertaining adaptation of the James Thurber short story about a meek man (Kaye) who lives an unusual fantasy life. Henpecked by his fiancee and mother, oppressed at his job, Walter imagines himself in the midst of various heroic fantasies. Comedic romp for Kaye, though Thurber himself professed to hate the movie.
1947 (*Jr. High-Adult*) 110m/C Danny Kaye, Virginia Mayo, Boris Karloff, Ann Rutherford, Fay Bainter, Florence Bates; *D:* Norman Z. McLeod. **VHS, Beta, LV $19.98** *HBO, SUE*

Secret Lives of Waldo Kitty Volume 1

Saturday-morning TV show takeoff on the James Thurber character Walter Mitty, here re-imagined as a daydreaming cat in perpetual wrangles with a bulldog. The animals are live-action with voiceovers a la "Milo & Otis," while Waldo's fantasies are 'toons.
1975 (*Family*) 48m/C **VHS, Beta** *SUE, OM*

The Secret of El Zorro 🎬🎬

Compilation of Disney TV episodes concerning the swashbuckling swordsman of old California, secretly fighting for freedom while maintaining a deceptive identity as wimpy Don Diego. Here Don Diego's friend Don Ricardo unknowingly threatens to unmask the hero when he challenges the legendary Zorro to a duel. Also available: "The Sign of Zorro."
1957 (*Family*) 75m/B Guy Williams. **VHS, Beta $39.95** *DIS*

The Secret of Navajo Cave 🎬🎬

Low budget adventure, narrated by cowboy star Allen, in which two young friends explore the mysterious title cavern.
1976 (*G/Family*) 84m/C Holger Kasper, Steven Benally Jr., Johnny Guerro; *D:* James T. Flocker. **VHS $39.95** *XVC, VCI*

Secret of NIMH 🎬🎬🎬

Animated tale, produced by a staff of Disney-trained artists led by Bluth, concerns a newly widowed mouse who discovers a secret agency of superintelligent rats (they've escaped from a science lab) who aid her in protecting her family. As is usually the case with Bluth films, animation is superb while socially aware storyline struggles to keep pace. That aside, it's still an interesting treat. Adapted from Robert C. O'Brien's "Mrs. Frisby and the Rats of N.I.M.H."
1982 (*G/Family*) 84m/C *D:* Don Bluth; *W:* Don Bluth; *M:* Jerry Goldsmith; *V:* John Carradine, Derek Jacobi, Dom DeLuise, Elizabeth Hartman, Peter Strauss, Aldo Ray, Edie McClurg, Wil Wheaton. **VHS, Beta, LV, 8mm $14.95** *MGM, WTA*

Secret of the Ice Cave 🎬

Computer whiz kid, on a visit to his jungle-researcher mom, gets a hint of vast fortune hidden in nearby mountains. He ends up pursued by villains and mercenaries of all shapes but only one size - dumb and a half. Basically witless juvenile adventure. **Hound Advisory:** Violence, profanity.
1989 (*PG-13/Jr. High-Adult*) 106m/C Michael Moriarty, Sally Kellerman, David Mendenhall, Virgil Frye, Gerald Anthony, Norbert Weisser; *D:* Radu Gabrea. **VHS, Beta $14.99** *MOV*

Secret of the Seal 🎬🎬

Animated tale of young Tottoi who, while swimming around a beautiful Italian island, finds a mother Mediterranean seal (thought to be extinct) and her little cub. But Tottoi can't keep his discovery a secret and then must fight to save the seals lives.
1993 (*Preschool-Primary*) 90m/C **VHS $24.95** *CEL, BTV, JFK*

Secret Places 🎬🎬

During World War II a German refugee enrolled in an English girls' boarding school finds friendship with a popular classmate, who soon learns the causes of the new girl's unhappy home life. Touching, though not as involving as it could have been. Based on a novel by Janice Elliott. **Hound Advisory:** Brief nudity, salty language, mature themes, drug use.
1985 (*PG/Jr. High-Adult*) 98m/C Maria Therese Relin, Tara MacGowan, Claudine Auger, Jenny Agutter; *D:* Zelda Barron. **VHS, Beta $79.98** *FOX*

See You in the Morning 🦴🦴

Disappointing romantic comedy-drama about a divorced psychiatrist and a widow, both of whom had unhappy marriages, who meet and wed. They must cope with their respective children, family tragedies, and their own expectations in order to make this second chance work for both. About the level of an average TV show, despite the sterling cast and promises of psychological insight. **Hound Advisory:** Mature themes, sex.
1989 (*PG-13/Jr. High-Adult*) 119m/C Jeff Bridges, Alice Krige, Farrah Fawcett, Drew Barrymore, Lukas Haas, Macaulay Culkin, David Dukes, Frances Sternhagen, Theodore Bikel, George Hearn, Linda Lavin; *D:* Alan J. Pakula; *W:* Alan J. Pakula. **VHS, Beta, LV** $14.95 *WAR*

A Separate Peace 🦴🦴◁

The John Knowles novel, a perpetual homework assignment for millions of high schoolers, gets a scrupulously faithful - though not terribly gripping - screen treatment. The quiet Gene and the athletic, boisterous Finny are roommates in a New England prep school during World War II. A tragic accident (or was it an accident?) shows the darker side of their apparent friendship. **Hound Advisory:** Profanity.
1973 (*PG/Jr. High-Adult*) 104m/C John Heyl, Parker Stevenson, William Roerick; *D:* Larry Peerce; *M:* Charles Fox. **VHS, Beta** $45.95 *PAR, HMV*

Serendipity the Pink Dragon 🦴🦴

Boy gets stranded on Paradise Island and meets a gentle dragon.
1990 (*Preschool-Primary*) 90m/C *D:* Jim Terry. **VHS, Beta** $24.95 *JFK, WTA*

Serial Mom 🦴🦴🦴

June Cleaver-like housewife Turner is nearly perfect, except when someone disrupts her orderly life. Didn't rewind your videotape? Chose the white shoes after Labor Day? Uh oh. Stardom reigns after she's caught and the murderer-as-celebrity phenomenon is exploited to the fullest. Darkly funny Waters satire tends toward the mainstream and isn't as perverse as earlier efforts, but still maintains a shocking edge (vital organs are good for an appearance or two). Turner's chameleonic performance as the perfect mom/crazed killer is right on target, recalling "The War of the Roses." Waterston, Lake, and Lillard are terrific as her generic suburban family. **Hound Advisory:** Violence; profanity; nudity.
1994 (*R/Sr. High-Adult*) 93m/C Kathleen Turner, Ricki Lake, Sam Waterston, Matthew Lillard, Mink Stole, Traci Lords; *Cameos:* Suzanne Somers, Joan Rivers, Patty Hearst; *D:* John Waters; *W:* John Waters; *M:* Basil Poledouris. **VHS** *HBO*

Sesame Songs: Dance Along!

Big Bird, Oscar the Grouch, and the Count teach kids new dances and valuable lessons.
1990 (*Family*) 30m/C **VHS** $14.95 *RAN*

Sesame Songs: Elmo's Sing-Along Guessing Game

Elmo plays the host of a very silly game show. Kids will love to try to answer his questions while singing songs like "My

Best Friend," "I Love My Elbows," "Eight Balls of Fur," and more.
1991 (*Family*) 30m/C **VHS, Beta** $14.95 *RAN*

Sesame Songs: Monster Hits!

Favorite monsters from "Sesame Street" sing the hits: "C is for Cookie," "Fuzzy and Blue," and many more.
1990 (*Preschool-Primary*) 30m/C **VHS** $14.95 *RAN*

Sesame Songs: Rock & Roll!

Your favorite Muppets from Sesame Street will have you rockin' and rollin' to the beat in this dynamic sing-a-long video. The Count sings his hit "Count Up to Nine" and Bert knows "It's Hip to Be Square."
1990 (*Family*) 30m/C *V:* Jim Henson. **VHS** $14.95 *RAN*

Sesame Songs: Sing-Along Earth Songs

Sesame Street music videos featuring Grover and friends. ♫Every Bit A'Litter Hurts; Just Throw it My Way; Air; Water Pollution; On My Pond; Little Plant; Box City Recycling Rap; Oscar's Junk Band; Keep the Parks Clean for the Pigeons.
1993 (*Preschool-Primary*) 30m/C **VHS** $9.95 *RAN, BTV*

Sesame Songs: Sing, Hoot & Howl

Big Bird hosts this musical tribute to the animal world, where kids can sing songs like "Proud to Be a Cow," "The Insects in Your Neighborhood," "Cluck around the Clock," and nine more.
1991 (*Family*) 30m/C **VHS, Beta** $14.95 *RAN*

Sesame Songs: Sing Yourself Silly!

Sesame Street stars and special guest stars Pee Wee Herman, Barbara Bush, and John Candy sing your favorites.
1990 (*Preschool-Primary*) 30m/C **VHS** $14.95 *RAN*

Sesame Songs: We All Sing Together

From the Sesame Songs Home Video Series comes more delightful music for children to sing with their favorite Muppets: Elmo, the Count, and Telly. Emphasis is on tolerance and stresses that despite outward appearances, kids are basically the same. ♫Skin; Fixin' My Hair; One Thousand Faces; I Want to be Me; Dancing Shoes; Mom and Me; Different Yet the Same; No Matter What; We All Sing With the Same Voice.
1993 (*Preschool-Primary*) 30m/C **VHS** $9.95 *RAN*

Sesame Street: Bedtime Stories and Songs

Sesame Street characters read favorite bedtime stories.
1990 (*Family*) 30m/C **VHS** $14.95 *KUI, RAN*

Sesame Street: Best of Ernie and Bert

Some of Ernie and Bert's best moments from the acclaimed children's TV series "Sesame Street."
1990 *(Family)* 30m/C **VHS $14.95** *RAN*

Sesame Street: Big Bird's Favorite Party Games

Big Bird shows children a number of fun and easy games they can play together.
1990 *(Family)* 30m/C **VHS $14.95** *RAN*

Sesame Street: Count It Higher

Some of the best music videos from Sesame Street.
1990 *(Family)* 30m/C **VHS $14.95** *RAN*

Sesame Street: Developing Self-Esteem

The Sesame Street gang along with some special friends teach children to take pride in their accomplishments, aptitudes, and abilities.
1984 *(Primary)* 40m/C Lily Tomlin, Marv Albert, Itzhak Perlman, Jim Henson's Muppets. **VHS, Beta** *CHI*

Sesame Street: I'm Glad I'm Me

The PBS Muppets teach children the value of being themselves.
1990 *(Family)* 30m/C **VHS $14.95** *KUI, RAN*

Sesame Street: Play-Along Games and Songs

Children learn while playing interesting games with all their favorite Sesame Street characters.
1990 *(Family)* 30m/C **VHS $14.95** *KUI, RAN*

Sesame Street Presents: Follow That Bird 🎞🎞🎞

Television's Big Bird suffers an identity crisis, and leaves Sesame Street to join a family of real birds. He soon misses his home, and returns, in a danger-filled journey.
1985 *(G/Family)* 92m/C Sandra Bernhard, John Candy, Chevy Chase, Joe Flaherty, Dave Thomas, Waylon Jennings, Jim Henson's Muppets; **D:** Ken Kwapis; **M:** Lennie Niehaus. **VHS, Beta, LV $14.95** *WAR*

Sesame Street Visits the Firehouse

Big Bird, Elmo, and Gordon go to the fire station in this live action adventure. They learn about firefighters and their equipment and even see a real fire.
1990 *(Family)* 30m/C **V:** Jim Henson. **VHS $14.95** *RAN, VEC*

Seven Alone 🎞🎞🎞

Fact-based adventure about a pioneer family on the treacherous 2000-mile journey from Missouri to the newly opened Oregon territory. When tragedy strikes, the trouble-prone eldest boy has to take charge of his brothers and sisters.

Though performances teeter between adequate and amateurish, the young hero's change from wagon-train delinquent to fearless frontiersman is something to behold, and little sugarcoating the harsh 1842 wilderness occurs. The producers of the successful "Where the Red Fern Grows" adapted this from the memoir "On to Oregon" by Honore Morrow. **Hound Advisory:** Violence.
1975 *(G/Family)* 85m/C Dewey Martin, Aldo Ray, Anne Collins, Dean Smith, Stewart Peterson; **D:** Earl Bellamy. **VHS, Beta** *NO*

Seven Brides for Seven Brothers 🎞🎞🎞🎞

Eldest of seven fur-trapping brothers in the Oregon Territory brings home a wife. She begins to civilize the other six, who realize the merits of women and begin to look for romances of their own. Thrilling choreography by Michael Kidd - don't miss "The Barn Raising." Charming performances by Powell and Keel, both in lovely voice. Based on Stephen Vincent Benet's story. Thrills, chills, singin', and dancin' - a classic Hollywood good time. ♫When You're In Love; Spring, Spring, Spring; Sobbin' Women; Bless Your Beautiful Hide; Goin' Co'tin; Wonderful, Wonderful Day; June Bride; Lonesome Polecat Lament.
1954 *(Family)* 103m/C Howard Keel, Jane Powell, Russ Tamblyn, Julie Newmar, Jeff Richards, Tommy Rall, Virginia Gibson; **D:** Stanley Donen. **Award Nominations:** Academy Awards '54: Best Color Cinematography, Best Film Editing, Best Picture, Best Screenplay; **Awards:** Academy Awards '54: Best Score; National Board of Review Awards '54: 10 Best Films of the Year. **VHS, Beta, LV, 8mm $14.95** *MGM, HMV*

Seven Faces of Dr. Lao 🎞🎞🎞

Dr. Lao is an old Chinese man who rides his mule into a town in the old west. Amazingly, he single-handedly sets up a full-fledged carnival, complete with monsters, marvels and magic that come to the aid of squabbling local citizens. Sunny flipside of "Something Wicked This Way Comes," with a heavily made-up Randall playing the buffoonish yet secretly wise Lao plus six other roles, from Merlin the Magician to the Abominable Snowman - admittedly with varied degrees of success (Peter Sellers was originally cast but backed out). Farfetched but winning fantasy, based on the novel by Charles Finney.
1963 *(Family)* 101m/C Tony Randall, Barbara Eden, Arthur O'Connell, Lee Patrick, Noah Beery Jr., John Qualen; **D:** George Pal. **VHS, Beta, LV $59.95** *MGM*

The Seven Little Foys 🎞🎞🎞

Enjoyable musical about Eddie Foy, a turn-of-the-century vaudeville stage star whose wife's unexpected death (while he was away touring) leaves him father to seven kids he barely knows. He tries to be a dutiful dad by taking them on the road as his act. More time could have been spent on the parenthood theme - first hour is all romance and backstage stuff, pretty boring for young viewers - but overall pic is pleasant in the old-Hollywood style, and Hope is at his finest. Narrated by Charlie Foy, one of the real-life kids grown up. ♫Mary's a Grand Old Name; I'm a Yankee Doodle Dandy; I'm the Greatest Father of Them All; Nobody; Comedy Ballet; I'm Tired; Chinatown, My Chinatown. **Hound Advisory:** Alcohol use. Mr. and

Sesame Street's Big Bird

Mrs. Foy turned out to be unmarried during 16 years and seven kids together, a fact handled so gingerly you might miss it.
1955 (*Family*) 95m/C Bob Hope, Milly Vitale, George Tobias, Angela Clark, James Cagney; **D:** Melville Shavelson; **W:** Jack Rose, Melville Shavelson. **VHS, Beta $14.95** COL

Seven Minutes in Heaven 🎜🎜⍦

Sensitive teen love story about a 15-year-old girl who invites her platonic male friend to live in her house, and finds it disturbs her boyfriend, as these things will. Tastefully done, with gentle humor. **Hound Advisory:** Sex talk.
1986 (PG/*Jr. High-Adult*) 90m/C Jennifer Connelly, Byron Thames, Maddie Corman; **D:** Linda Feferman. **VHS, Beta $19.98** WAR

7 Ninja Kids 🎜

Unlike "3 Ninjas" and similar polished Hollywood fare, this is the real thing, a grungy, poorly dubbed Hong Kong production imported on videocassette to take advantage of American karatemania among the kidset. Seven Asian youngsters (who fight and even speak in unison) battle bad guys over a stolen jewel. Obnoxious stuff, but if you must know there are a whole series with this bunch, including "37 Ninja Kids." **Hound Advisory:** Violence, needless profanity.
1989 (PG/*Primary-Adult*) 90m/C **VHS** VTR, HHE, MTX

1776 🎜🎜🎜

Broadway musical comedy about America's first Continental Congress hits the screen straightaway, with many members of the original cast. Delegates battle the English and each other trying to establish a set of laws and the Declaration of Independence, all the while singing and dancing up a storm. Long and bellowing, but at the very least a novel faux-history lesson. Available in widescreen format on laserdisc with additional footage. 🎜The Lees of Old Virginia; He Plays the Violin; But, Mr. Adams; Sit Down John; Till Then; Piddle, Twiddle and Resolve; Yours, Yours, Yours; Mama, Look Sharp; The Egg.
1972 (G/*Family*) 141m/C William Daniels, Howard da Silva, Ken Howard, Donald Madden, Blythe Danner, Ronald Holgate, Virginia Vestoff, Stephen Nathan, Ralston Hill; **D:** Peter Hunt. **Award Nominations:** Academy Awards '72: Best Cinematography; **Awards:** National Board of Review Awards '72: 10 Best Films of the Year. **VHS, Beta, LV $19.95** COL, FCT

The Seventh Voyage of Sinbad 🎜🎜🎜

Honey, he shrunk the Princess! When an evil magician reduces Sinbad's fiancee to tiny size (she hardly seems to object) the fearless sailor journeys to the monster-filled island of Colossa in search of a cure. Never mind that the plot has holes big enough for a cyclops, Ray Harryhausen created some of his best stop-motion animation creatures for this rousing adventure. See also "The Golden Voyage of Sinbad" and "Sinbad and the Eye of the Tiger." **Hound Advisory:** Violence.
1958 (G/*Family*) 94m/C Kerwin Mathews, Kathryn Grant, Torin Thatcher, Richard Eyer; **D:** Nathan Juran; **W:** Kenneth Kolb; **M:** Bernard Herrmann. **VHS, Beta, LV $14.95** COL, MLB, CCB

The Shadow 🎜🎜⍦

Who knows what evil lurks in the hearts of men? Why "The Shadow" of course, as is shown in this highly stylized big screen version of the '30s radio show that once starred Orson Welles. Billionaire playboy Lamont Cranston (Baldwin) is a master of illusion and defender of justice thanks to his alter ego. Aided by companion Margo Lane (Miller), da Shadow battles super-criminal Shiwan Khan (Lone), the deadliest descendant of Ghenghis Khan. Story is not particularly enamoring, but you may not notice due to the wonderful sets. Numerous, elaborate special effects provide icing on the cake for those in the mood for a journey back to the radio past or a quick superhero fix. **Hound Advisory:** Violence.
1994 (PG-13/*Jr. High-Adult*) 107m/C Alec Baldwin, John Lone, Penelope Ann Miller, Peter Boyle, Ian McKellan, Tim Curry, Jonathan Winters; **D:** Russell Mulcahy; **W:** David Koepp. **VHS** NYR

Shadow of a Doubt 🎜🎜🎜⍦

Uncle Charlie has come to visit his relatives in Santa Rosa. Although he is handsome and charming, his young niece slowly comes to realize he is a wanted mass murderer - and he comes to recognize her suspicions. Hitchcock's personal favorite movie; a quietly creepy venture into Middle American menace based on a true story. Terrific performances throughout, distinguished by Cotten as the uncle with a problem and Cronyn as the oddball neighbor. Adapted by Wilder from the story by Gordon McConnell.
1943 (*Jr. High-Adult*) 108m/B Teresa Wright, Joseph Cotten, Hume Cronyn, MacDonald Carey, Henry Travers, Wallace Ford; **D:** Alfred Hitchcock; **W:** Thorton Wilder; **M:** Dimitri Tiomkin. **VHS, Beta, LV $19.95** MCA

Shadow of the Eagle

Wayne saves the day in more ways than one in this creaky Mascot serial. His winning star charisma is the main reason to watch, as members of an aviation corporation are blackmailed by a mystery villain called the Eagle. Suspicion points to a crippled fighter ace, now running a struggling carnival. His loyal stunt pilot Craig McCoy (Wayne) strives to unmask the lethal Eagle, in 12 chapters of 20 minutes each. **Hound Advisory:** Roughhousing.
1932 (*Family*) 226m/B John Wayne, Dorothy Gulliver, Walter Miller; **D:** Ford Beebe. **VHS $24.95** GPV, VYY, VCN

Shadow of the Wolf 🎜🎜

Phillips is Agaguk, the son of the village leader, in this snowbound saga of survival set against the Arctic wilderness. Upset with the intrusion of white men onto his land, he decides to look for better accommodations elsewhere with Eskimo babe Tilly. Together they face the harsh tundra, struggling to stay alive in the Great White North. Big daddy, meanwhile, believes Agaguk's departure to be the ultimate betrayal and casts upon him the "curse of the white wolf." Sweeping cinematography helps make the adventure palatable, but first you must sled past the silliness of the casting (though if Abe Vigoda can play an Eskimo in "North," why not Phillips and Tilly as a cute Eskimo couple here?). Based on the novel "Agaguk" by Yves Theriault. **Hound Advisory:** Violence and profanity.
1992 (PG-13/*Jr. High-Adult*) 108m/C Lou Diamond Phillips, Donald Sutherland, Jennifer Tilly, Toshiro Mifune; **D:** Jacques Dorfman; **W:** Rudy Wurlitzer, Evan Jones. **VHS, LV $14.95** COL

The Shadow Riders 🦴🦴

Two brothers who fought on opposite sides during the Civil War return home to find their brother's fiancee kidnapped by a renegade Confederate officer who plans to use her as ransom in a prisoner exchange, and they set out to rescue the woman. Preceded by "The Sacketts" and based on the works of Louis L'Amour. Made for television.
1982 (PG/Jr. High-Adult) 96m/C Tom Selleck, Sam Elliott, Ben Johnson, Katharine Ross, Jeffery Osterhage, Gene Evans, R.G. Armstrong, Marshall Teague, Dominique Dunne, Jeanetta Arnetta; *D:* Andrew V. McLaglen. VHS $79.98 *VMK*

Shadowlands 🦴🦴🦴

Touching, tragic story of the late-in-life romance between celebrated author and Christian theologian C.S. Lewis (Hopkins) and brash New York divorcee Joy Gresham (Winger). Attenborough's direction is rather stately and sweeping and Winger is really too young for her role but Hopkins is excellent as (another) repressed man who finds more emotions than he can handle. Critically acclaimed adaptation of Nicholson's play will require lots of kleenex. **Hound Advisory:** Brief profanity.
1993 (PG/Jr. High-Adult) 130m/C Anthony Hopkins, Debra Winger, Edward Hardwicke, Joseph Mazzello, Michael Denison, John Wood, Peter Firth, Peter Howell; *D:* Richard Attenborough; *W:* William Nicholson; *M:* George Fenton. **Award Nominations:** Academy Awards '93: Best Actress (Winger), Best Adapted Screenplay; British Academy Awards '94: Best Actor (Hopkins), Best Actress (Winger), Best Adapted Screenplay, Best Director (Attenborough); **Awards:** British Academy Awards '94: Best Film; Los Angeles Film Critics Association Awards '93: Best Actor (Hopkins); National Board of Review Awards '93: Best Actor (Hopkins). VHS *HBO*

Shag: The Movie 🦴🦴🦴

The time is 1963, the setting Myrtle Beach, South Carolina, the latest craze shaggin' when four friends hit the beach for one last weekend together. Carson (Cates) is getting ready to marry staid Harley (Power); Melaina (Fonda) wants to be discovered in Hollywood; and Pudge (Gish) and Luanne (Hannah) are off to college. They encounter lots of music, boys, and dancing in affectionate nod to a more innocent time. Not to be confused with other "teen" movies, this one boasts a good script and an above average cast. **Hound Advisory:** Brief nudity.
1989 (PG/Jr. High-Adult) 96m/C Phoebe Cates, Annabeth Gish, Bridget Fonda, Page Hannah, Scott Coffey, Robert Rusler, Tyrone Power Jr., Jeff Yagher, Carrie Hamilton, Shirley Anne Field, Leilani Sarelle Ferrer; *D:* Zelda Barron; *W:* Robin Swicord, Lanier Laney, Terry Sweeney. VHS, Beta, LV $89.99 *HBO*

The Shaggy D.A. 🦴🦴🦴

The grownup Wilby Daniels is running for District Attorney when his old canine condition recurs. Ouch, did someone say 'curs?.' Fun next-generation sequel to Disney's "The Shaggy Dog" ranks a hair or two above the original.
1976 (G/Family) 90m/C Dean Jones, Tim Conway, Suzanne Pleshette, Keenan Wynn; *D:* Robert Stevenson; *M:* Buddy Baker. VHS, Beta *DIS, OM*

The Shaggy Dog 🦴🦴🦴

When teenager Wilby Daniels utters some magical words from the inscription of an ancient ring he turns into a talking sheepdog. Little brother Moochie is delighted; dog-hating dad nearly goes over the edge. Disney slapstick is on target at times, though it drags in places and brings in a spy subplot even sillier than the one in "For Love of Benji." Tim Burton style stop-motion animation in the opening credits. Followed by "The Shaggy D.A." and "Return of the Shaggy Dog."
1959 (G/Family) 101m/B Fred MacMurray, Jean Hagen, Tommy Kirk, Annette Funicello, Tim Considine, Kevin Corcoran; *D:* Charles T. Barton. VHS, Beta, LV $19.99 *DIS, BTV*

The Shakiest Gun in the West 🦴🦴🦴

Don Knotts isn't Bob Hope, but he's pretty funny in the same bumbling way. Remake of Hope's "Paleface" has Philadelphia dentist Knotts unwittingly taking on bad guys and sultry Rhoades.
1968 (Family) 101m/C Don Knotts, Barbara Rhoades, Jackie Coogan, Donald (Don "Red") Barry, Ruth McDevitt; *D:* Alan Rafkin. VHS, LV *MCA*

Shall We Dance 🦴🦴🦴

And shall we ever! Seventh Astaire-Rogers pairing has a famous ballet dancer and a musical-comedy star embark on a promotional romance and marriage, to boost their careers, only to find themselves truly falling in love. Thin, formula plot is inconsequential, as Astaire and Rogers sing and dance their way to success. Score by the Gershwins includes lots of memorable songs. ♪ Slap That Bass; Beginner's Luck; Let's Call the Whole Thing Off; Walking the Dog; They All Laughed; They Can't Take That Away From Me; Shall We Dance.
1937 (Family) 116m/B Fred Astaire, Ginger Rogers, Edward Everett Horton, Eric Blore; *D:* Mark Sandrich; *M:* George Gershwin, Ira Gershwin. VHS, Beta, LV $14.98 *TTC, RKO, CCB*

Shalom Sesame

Engaging series of children's videos that provide an introduction to the land, people, and culture of Israel with the characters from the Israeli version of Sesame Street. In English with an introduction to Hebrew songs, numbers, and letters.
1990 (Family) 40m/C VHS $19.98 *MLT, FFF, ADL*

Shamu & You: Exploring the World of Birds

With Shamu you'll take a look at such winged creatures as hummingbirds, parrots, owls, flamingos, vultures, oxpeckers, and eagles in a format which features songs, stories, animation, and wildlife footage.
1992 (Family) 30m/C VHS $14.98 *VTR*

Shamu & You: Exploring the World of Fish

Shamu and you or your next of kin can discover the mysteries of undersea life, including sharks, rays, eels, sea horses, clownfish, and batfish. Yes, those darn batfish.
1992 (Family) 30m/C VHS $14.98 *VTR*

Shamu & You: Exploring the World of Mammals

A Sea World introduction to the world of mammals, including killer whales, with footage of life in the wild, animation, talks with kids, and catchy music.
1992 (*Family*) 30m/C **VHS** **$14.98** *VTR*

Shamu & You: Exploring the World of Reptiles

An up-close look at such creatures as alligators, snakes, lizards, and sea turtles.
1992 (*Family*) 30m/C **VHS** **$14.98** *VTR*

Shane 🐾🐾🐾🐾

Retired gunfighter, now a drifter, comes to the aid of a homestead family threatened by a land baron and his hired gun. In the performance of his career, Ladd is the mystery man who becomes the idol of the family's young son, played with great sincerity by de Wilde. Classic, flawless archetypal western is long and stately and worth savoring. Pulitzer prize-winning western novelist A.B. Guthrie, Jr. adapted from the novel by Jack Schaefer. **Hound Advisory:** Violence.
1953 (*Family*) 117m/C Alan Ladd, Jean Arthur, Van Heflin, Brandon de Wilde, Jack Palance, Ben Johnson, Elisha Cook Jr., Edgar Buchanan, Emile Meyer; **D:** George Stevens; **W:** Jack Sher; **M:** Victor Young. **Award Nominations:** Academy Awards '53: Best Director (Stevens), Best Picture, Best Screenplay, Best Supporting Actor (de Wilde, Palance); **Awards:** Academy Awards '53: Best Color Cinematography; National Board of Review Awards '53: 10 Best Films of the Year, Best Director (Stevens). **VHS, Beta, LV** **$14.95** *PAR, TLF*

Shari Lewis & Lamb Chop: In the Land of No Manners

Lewis and her puppet pal teach the value of good manners by visiting a horrible land where there are none.
1991 (*Family*) 44m/C Shari Lewis. **VHS** **$14.95** *A&M, FCT, TVC*

Shari Lewis & Lamb Chop: One Minute Bible Stories, New Testament

Shari and her puppet friend present a number of Biblical tales for children.
1986 (*Family*) 30m/C Shari Lewis, Lambchop, Florence Henderson. **VHS** *NO*

Shari Lewis: Don't Wake Your Mom

Lewis and her puppets Lamb Chop, Hush Puppy, and Charlie Horse sing and tell stories using the book "Is it Time Yet?"
1992 (*Preschool-Primary*) 45m/C **VHS** **$14.95** *PGV, MVD, TVC*

Shari Lewis: Have I Got a Story for You

Lewis and her coterie of puppet characters tell classic stories, including "Rumpelstiltskin" and "The Sorcerer's Apprentice."
1984 (*Preschool-Primary*) 59m/C Shari Lewis. **VHS, Beta** **$9.95** *MGM*

Shari Lewis: Kooky Classics

Lewis, Lambchop, and other puppets take children through the world of classical music, from Brahms to Mozart.
1984 (*Preschool-Primary*) 59m/C Shari Lewis. **VHS, Beta** **$9.95** *MGM*

Shari Lewis: One Minute Bedtime Stories

Puppeteer and ventriloquist Lewis, aided by Lamb Chop and Hush Puppy, reads twenty-six popular children's stories.
1985 (*Preschool-Primary*) 30m/C **VHS, Beta** *WOV, GKK*

Sharon, Lois & Bram at the Young People's Theatre

Three singers perform for and with children to help the youngsters develop an appreciation of music.
1983 (*Primary*) 30m/C **VHS, Beta**

Sharon, Lois & Bram: Back by Popular Demand-Live

A live performance from the children's cable television stars. Songs include "Jelly Jelly in My Belly," "Chugga, Chugga" and more.
1990 (*Preschool-Primary*) 30m/C **VHS** **$14.95** *MVD, A&M*

Sharon, Lois & Bram: Live in Your Living Room

A concert video from the beloved stars of the children's cable television program "Elephant Show."
1990 (*Preschool-Primary*) 30m/C **VHS, LV, 8mm** **$14.95** *MVD, A&M*

Sharon, Lois & Bram: Sing A to Z

Trio of performers use songs, skits, and dances to entertain and teach the spelling and definition of new words.
1992 (*Preschool-Primary*) 50m/C **VHS** **$14.98** *A&M, BTV*

Sharon, Lois & Bram's Elephant Show: Babysitting

Episodes from the popular Nickelodeon cable-TV show starring the three children's entertainers and their faithful pachyderm companion. Due to Elephant's antics, Sharon, Lois & Bram end up babysitting a handful of kids. Juggling team Circus Shmirkus come over to help out. Additional volumes available.
1990 (*Family*) 30m/C **VHS** *MOV*

Shazam!

Young Billy Batson says "shazam" and turns into the mighty Captain Marvel in this cheesy Saturday-morning live-action adaptation of the classic comic-book character whose popularity once exceeded Superman's. Additional episodes available.
1981 (*Preschool-Jr. High*) 60m/C **VHS, Beta** **$29.95** *FHE, WTA*

Shari Lewis and Friends

Shazzan

Arabian adventures, Hanna-Barbera style; modern kids Chuck and Nancy are transported back in time by a magic ring and accompany Shazzan the genie through two tapes of excavated Saturday-morning cartoon adventures. Additional episodes available.

1967 (*Family*) 60m/C **V:** Barney Phillips, Janet Waldo, Don Messick. **VHS, Beta $19.95** *TTC, WTA*

She-Devil 𝄞𝄞

Comic book version of the acidic Fay Weldon novel "The Life and Loves of a She-Devil." Fat, dowdy suburban wife (Arnold) becomes a vengeful beast when a smarmy romance novelist steals her husband. Uneven comedic reworking of a distinctly unforgiving feminist fiction. Arnold is given too much to handle (her role requires an actual range of emotions); Streep's role is too slight, though she displays a fine sense of comedic timing. **Hound Advisory:** Salty language; mature themes.

1989 (*PG-13*/*Jr. High-Adult*) 100m/C Meryl Streep, Roseanne (Barr) Arnold, Ed Begley Jr., Linda Hunt, Elizabeth Peters, Bryan Larkin, A. Martinez, Sylvia Miles; **D:** Susan Seidelman; **W:** Mark Burns, Barry Strugatz; **M:** Howard Shore. **VHS, Beta, LV $9.98** *ORI*

She-Ra, Vol. 1

She-Ra is the twin sister of He-Man, of "Masters of the Universe" and toy store fame, and sometimes the big guy makes guest appearances in these episodes gathered from their cartoon TV series. In "Missing Axe," she saves a woodcutter from Mantenna and in "Crystal Castles," she saves Castle Bright Moon from the Shadow Weaver's energy blasts. Additional volumes available.

1985 (*Primary-Jr. High*) 45m/C **VHS $24.95** *WTA*

Sheena 𝄞

A sportscaster aids a jiggly jungle queen in defending her kingdom from an evil prince. Female Tarzan character (first a vintage comic book, then a '50s TV show) comes to the screen trapped in an ill-wrought effort somewhere between sexy satire and bubble-gum action. **Hound Advisory:** Violence, salty language, and a surprising amount of nudity for a PG. One commentator sagely observed that this premiered just days before the initiation of the PG-13 rating, which it surely would have earned.

1984 (*PG*/*Jr. High-Adult*) 117m/C Tanya Roberts, Ted Wass, Donovan Scott, Elizabeth Toro; **D:** John Guillermin; **W:** David Newman. **VHS, Beta, LV $12.95** *GKK*

Shelley Duvall's Bedtime Stories

Another Shelley Duvall series of stories, here based on popular children's books and narrated by celebrities. Each tape is available individually and contains at least two stories. Originally produced for cable television. Additional episodes available.

1992 (*Preschool-Primary*) 25m/C **VHS, LV $12.98** *MCA*

Shelley Duvall's Rock 'n' Rhymeland

Retelling of classic nursery rhymes done in Shelley Duvall's inimitable style, with guest stars from the pop-music scene.

1990 (*Family*) 77m/C Shelley Duvall, Deborah Harry, Paul Simon, Cyndi Lauper, ZZ Top, Bobby Brown, Little Richard, Stray Cats. **VHS $14.98** *MVD*

Sherlock Hound: Dr. Watson I Presume?

Sherlock Hound searches for his arch-nemesis Professor Moriarty with the help of his pal, Dr. Watson. Additional volumes available.

1991 (*Preschool-Jr. High*) 120m/C **VHS $29.95** *JFK, WTA*

She's Having a Baby 𝄞𝄞 ♩

Newlyweds tread marital waters with difficulty, and an impending baby (after an infertility scare) further complicates their lives. Told from Bacon's viewpoint as the young writer and husband, still grappling with maturity and wondering if the suburban yuppie life traps him. Hughes' first venture into the adult world isn't as satisfying as his teen angst flicks, although the charming leads help. Major drawbacks are the arguably sexist premise and dull resolution. Great soundtrack. **Hound Advisory:** Sex, mature themes, profanity.

1988 (*PG-13*/*Jr. High-Adult*) 106m/C Kevin Bacon, Elizabeth McGovern, William Windom, Paul Gleason, Alec Baldwin, Cathryn Damon, Holland Taylor, James Ray, Isabel Lorca, Dennis Dugan, Edie McClurg, John Ashton; **D:** John Hughes; **W:** John Hughes; **M:** Stewart Copeland. **VHS, Beta, LV, 8mm $19.95** *PAR*

Shinbone Alley 𝄞𝄞

Offbeat, loosely plotted musical hodgepodge about archy (who's name, like e.e. cummings, is never initially capped), a free-verse poet reincarnated as a cockroach, and his wayward lady friend Mehitabel, a loose-living alley cat. With uneven animation, the attractions are the great character voices and songs by "Man of La Mancha" composer Joe Darion. Adapted from a stage musical and a record album production based on the famous story-poems by Don Marquis - all aimed at and appreciated better by adults than small kids. **Hound Advisory:** Mature themes? Yes indeed - the morose archy is no stranger to suicide, and the irresponsible Mehitbel plans to drown her own kittens.

1970 (*G*/*Family*) 83m/C **D:** John D. Wilson; **V:** Carol Channing, Eddie Bracken, John Carradine, Alan Reed. **VHS, Beta $14.95** *SIM, GEM, KAR*

Shining Time Station: Singsongs, Vol. 1

Sixteen music videos written to enhance the themes of various "Shining Time Station" episodes.

1992 (*Preschool-Primary*) ?m/C **VHS $14.98** *FFF, FFF*

Shining Time Station: 'Tis a Gift Holiday Special

Whimsical Christmas tale about a mysterious bearded man named Mr. Nicholas who is waiting for a train a week before Christmas. From the acclaimed PBS series.

1992 (*Preschool-Primary*) 51m/C Ringo Starr, Lloyd Bridges. **VHS** $14.98 *AVE, FFF*

Shipwrecked 🎬🎬⏴

Disney-made kiddie swashbuckler based on an 1873 popular novel "Haakon Haakonsen." Title character is a cabin boy marooned on an island after pirates take over his ship. Familiar but pleasant enough seagoing adventure, with shades of "Home Alone" when the pirates come calling. **Hound Advisory:** Alcohol use, violence threatened but never really shown. The PG is pointless, unless someone at the MPAA thought this unfairly defamed pirates.
1990 (**PG/***Jr. High-Adult*) 93m/C Gabriel Byrne, Stian Smestad, Louisa Haigh, Trond Munch, Bjorn Sundquist, Eva Von Hanno, Kjell Stormoen; *D:* Nils Gaup; *W:* Nick Thiel, Nils Gaup; *M:* Patrick Doyle. **VHS, LV** $19.99 *BVV*

Shirley Temple Baby Berlesques

Before Shirley Temple became a 1930s mainstay in feature films, she started out in these curious short subjects that put all-toddler casts in short parodies of standard Hollywood scenes (example: Shirley's a missionary in Africa, rescued by a pint-sized Tarzan from tiny cannibals). Unusual, sometimes in questionable taste, but entertaining, and even younger than usual, Shirley's star power shines through.
1933 (*Family*) 60m/B Shirley Temple. **VHS, Beta** $19.95 *MVC, VYY*

Shirley Temple Festival

Ramshackle assemblage of Temple material includes two "Baby Berlesks," plus a pair of unrelated comedy shorts in which Shirley has supporting parts (stealing the show, as always). Ends with a newsreel of her teenaged marriage to actor John Agar.
1933 (*Family*) 55m/B Shirley Temple, Andy Clyde. **VHS, Beta** $19.95 *MRV*

Shirley Temple Storybook Theater

Episodes of an irregularly broadcast network TV show hosted by the grownup Shirley, in one-hour re-enactments of classic fairy tales. As with Shelley Duvall, an amazing array of Hollywood celebrities appeared in the casts. 13 volumes are: "Ali Baba & the Forty Thieves," "Dick Whittington & His Cat," "Hiawatha," "Mother Goose," "Rapunzel," "Rip Van Winkle," "Sleeping Beauty," "The Emperor's New Clothes," "The Land of Green Ginger," "The Lame Little Prince," "The Magic Fishbone," "The Nightingale," and "The Wild Swan."
1960 (*Family*) 60m/B Nehemiah Persoff, Sebastian Cabot, Pernell Roberts, Shirley Temple, Agnes Moorehead, E.G. Marshall, Nancy Marchand, Eli Wallach, Jack Albertson, Lorne Greene, Leo G. Carroll, Thomas Mitchell, Melville Cooper. **VHS, Beta** *WKV*

The Shootist 🎬🎬🎬⏴

Wayne, in a supporting last role, plays a legendary gunslinger afflicted with cancer who seeks peace and solace in his final days. Town bad guys Boone and O'Brian aren't about to let him rest and are determined to gun him down to avenge past deeds. One of Wayne's best and most dignified performances about living up to a personal code of honor. Stewart and

Bacall head excellent supporting cast. Based on Glendon Swarthout's novel.
1976 (**PG/***Jr. High-Adult*) 100m/C John Wayne, Lauren Bacall, Ron Howard, James Stewart, Richard Boone, Hugh O'Brian, Bill McKinney, Harry Morgan, John Carradine, Sheree North, Scatman Crothers; *D:* Don Siegel; *M:* Elmer Bernstein. **Award Nominations:** Academy Awards '76: Best Art Direction/Set Decoration; **Awards:** National Board of Review Awards '76: 10 Best Films of the Year. **VHS, Beta, LV** $14.95 *PAR, TLF*

Short Circuit 🎬🎬

Advanced robot designed for the military is hit by lightning and begins to think for itself. The tin man is taken in by a spacey animal lover (who amusingly mistakes it for an "E.T."-style alien), then hides from the meanies at the weapons lab who want their hardware back. Intrinsically kid-friendly premise was apparently designed for short attention spans; everything happens at ultra- high speed, and characters are needlessly lewd and obnoxious. **Hound Advisory:** Profanity, sex talk.
1986 (**PG/***Jr. High-Adult*) 98m/C Steve Guttenberg, Ally Sheedy, Austin Pendleton, Fisher Stevens, Brian McNamara; *D:* John Badham; *W:* S.S. Wilson, Brent Maddock; *M:* David Shire. **VHS, Beta, LV** $19.98 *FOX*

Short Circuit 2 🎬🎬⏴

Sequel to the adorable-robot tale is actually an improvement, with better pacing and funnier gags. The cheerful metal hero, Number Five, arrives in the city to visit old friends, draws the attention of a toy merchant and gang of jewel thieves. Cute stuff; even Stevens' lead human character, a caricatured ethnic stereotype, has been toned down from last time. **Hound Advisory:** Robot roughhousing, salty language.
1988 (**PG/***Jr. High-Sr. High*) 95m/C Fisher Stevens, Cynthia Gibb, Michael McKean, Jack Weston, David Hemblen; *D:* Kenneth Johnson; *W:* S.S. Wilson, Brent Maddock; *M:* Charles Fox. **VHS, Beta, LV** $19.95 *COL*

A Shot in the Dark 🎬🎬🎬⏴

Second and possibly the best in the classic "Inspector Clouseau-Pink Panther" series of comedies. The bumbling Inspector Clouseau (Sellers, of course) investigates the case of a parlor maid (Sommer) accused of murdering her lover. Clouseau's libido convinces him she's innocent, even though all the clues point to her. Classic gags, wonderful music. After this film, Sellers as Clouseau disappears until 1975's "Return of the Pink Panther" (Alan Arkin played him in "Inspector Clouseau," made in 1968 by different folks.) **Hound Advisory:** Sex talk; roughhousing; alcohol use.
1964 (*Family*) 101m/C Peter Sellers, Elke Sommer, Herbert Lom, George Sanders, Bryan Forbes; *D:* Blake Edwards; *W:* William Peter Blatty, Blake Edwards; *M:* Henry Mancini. **VHS, Beta, LV** $19.98 *FOX, FCT*

Shout 🎬🎬

In a sleepy Texas town during the 1950s, Jesse's rebel ways land him in a work farm for delinquent boys. Then a hip new teacher (Travolta) turns the restless kids on to the new poetry called rock 'n' roll. It's all been done before and better. Note the anachronistic dance styles and MTV music videos, 30 years before their time. **Hound Advisory:** Salty language, implied teen sex, roughhousing.

1991 (PG-13/*Jr. High-Adult*) 93m/C John Travolta, James Walters, Heather Graham, Richard Jordan, Linda Fiorentino, Scott Coffey; **D:** Jeffrey Hornaday; **M:** Randy Edelman. **VHS, Beta, LV $19.98** *MCA*

Sidekicks 🎭🎭

Cutesy vehicle for action star/executive producer Norris. Barry has bully problems at school and an ineffectual dad at home. Barry instead worships movie hero Norris, who appears as himself in a series of daydream martial-arts sequences. Plot eventually evolves into a "Karate Kid" clone, predictable and sappy. Directed by the star's brother. **Hound Advisory:** Roughhousing.
1993 (PG/*Family*) 100m/C Chuck Norris, Jonathan Brandis, Beau Bridges, Mako, Julia Nickson-Soul, Danica McKellar, Richard Moll, Joe Piscopo; **D:** Aaron Norris; **W:** Donald W. Thompson, Lou Illar; **M:** Alan Silvestri, David Shire. **VHS, LV, 8mm $19.95** *COL*

Sigmund & the Sea Monsters, Vol. 1

Oceanside pals Johnny and Scott befriend a tentacled sea monster who's been disowned by his grumpy family for his inability to scare humans. Live-action Sid & Marty Krofft Saturday-morning show distinguished by its weird costumes. Additional volumes available.
1973 (*Family*) 46m/C Billy Barty, Johnny Whitaker, Mary Wickes, Rip Torn, Margaret Hamilton, Fran Ryan. **VHS, Beta $9.95** *NLC, SUE*

The Sign of Zorro 🎭🎭

Adventures of the masked swordsman as he champions the cause of the oppressed in early California. Full-length version of the popular late-50s Disney TV series.
1960 (*Family*) 89m/C Guy Williams, Henry Calvin, Gene Sheldon, Romney Brent, Britt Lomond, George Lewis, Lisa Gaye; **D:** Norman Foster, Lewis R. Foster. **VHS, Beta $69.95** *DIS*

Silence 🎭🎭◁

Eric, an autistic boy, gets lost in the wilderness but is found and befriended by a crusty but kindly hermit called Crazy Jack (prompting alternate title "Crazy Jack and the Boy"). The old fellow is played by Geer, best-known as Grandpa on "The Waltons" TV series, but off the tube his whole family pitched in to perform and help write this decent little picture.
1973 (G/*Family*) 82m/C Will Geer, Ellen Geer, Richard Kelton, Ian Geer Flanders, Craig Kelly; **D:** John Korty. **VHS, Beta** *NO*

Silence of the North 🎭🎭◁

Widow with three children struggles to survive under rugged pioneer conditions on the Canadian frontier. The scenery is, not surprisingly, stunning. Based on a true but generic story.
1981 (PG/*Jr. High-Adult*) 94m/C Ellen Burstyn, Tom Skerritt; **D:** Allan Winton King; **M:** Michael Conway Baker. **VHS, Beta $59.95** *MCA*

Silent Movie 🎭🎭◁

A has-been movie director (Brooks) is determined to make a comeback and save his studio from being taken over by a conglomerate. Hilarious at times but uneven. An original idea; not as successful as it could have been. Has music and sound effects, but only one word of spoken dialogue by famous mime Marceau.

1976 (PG/*Family*) 88m/C Mel Brooks, Marty Feldman, Dom DeLuise, Burt Reynolds, Anne Bancroft, James Caan, Liza Minnelli, Paul Newman, Sid Caesar, Bernadette Peters, Harry Ritz, Marcel Marceau; **D:** Mel Brooks; **W:** Mel Brooks, Ron Clark, Rudy DeLuca, Barry Levinson. **VHS, Beta, LV $14.98** *FOX*

The Silver Fox and Sam Davenport

Man and beast come to a mutual respect when a farmer rescues a fox and nurtures it back to health. A live-action tale from TV's "Wonderful World of Disney."
1990 (*Preschool-Primary*) 47m/C **VHS, Beta $250.00** *MTI, DSN*

Silver Stallion 🎭🎭◁

Awe-inspiring all-ages spectacle from Australia tells of Thara, a mighty horse destined to rule a herd of mountain 'brumbies' (cowboy slang for wild horses). As in the "Man From Snowy River" adventures, one cowboy won't rest until he's caught and tamed the king of the brumbies. But this time their duel is told through the animal's eyes, and the result is a nature drama both mystical and heroic, combining "The Black Stallion" with "Prancer" but outdoing them both. Based on stories by Down Under author Elyne Mitchell, and taking place largely in the mind of her onscreen daughter, who checks the manuscript as mum types the tale of Thara and realizes it's more than fiction. Never got the major release on big theater screens a film this visionary deserves, but a must-see on video anyway. **Hound Advisory:** Horse violence.
1941 (*Family*) 59m/C David Sharpe, Carol Hughes, Leroy Mason, Walter Long; **D:** Edward Finney. **VHS, Beta $19.95** *VYY, GPV*

The Silver Stallion: King of the Wild Brumbies 🎭🎭◁

Adolescent Indi is enthralled as her writer-mother relates each new chapter in the saga of Thara, the amazing silver stallion. And she imagines each adventure as the horse triumphs over evil men, other horses, and the elements to become leader of the herd. Based on the Australian children's novel "The Silver Brumby" by Elyne Mitchell.
1994 (G/*Family*) 93m/C Caroline Goodall, Ami Daemion, Russell Crowe; **D:** John Tatoulis; **W:** John Tatoulis, Jon Stephens; **M:** Tassos Ioannides. **VHS, Beta** *PAR*

The Silver Streak 🎭🎭🎭

Pooped exec Wilder rides a train from L.A. to Chicago, planning to enjoy a leisurely, relaxing trip. Instead he becomes involved with murder, intrigue, and a beautiful woman. Energetic Hitchcock parody features successful first pairing of Wilder and Pryor.
1976 (PG/*Jr. High-Adult*) 113m/C Gene Wilder, Richard Pryor, Jill Clayburgh, Patrick McGoohan, Ned Beatty, Ray Walston, Richard Kiel, Scatman Crothers; **D:** Arthur Hiller; **W:** Colin Higgins; **M:** Henry Mancini. **VHS, Beta, LV $14.98** *FOX*

Silverado 🎭🎭🎭

Straightforward plot has four virtuous cowboys rise up against a crooked lawman in a blaze of six guns. Affectionate pastiche of western cliches is not subtle, with the meter running on deep background pieces that explain why our heroes came to be. But it's plenty of fun, with good clean frontier violence (shootings, knifings, etc.) and characters who have populated every western ever made. Laserdisc edition features a wide screen film-to-tape transfer monitored by the photography director, set photos, release trailers, and other publicity hoohah as well as a special time-lapse sequence of the set construction, and interviews with the stars and director Kasdan. Letterboxed laserdisc version is available with Dolby SurroundSound. **Hound Advisory:** Violence and profanity.

1985 (PG-13/*Jr. High-Adult*) 132m/C Kevin Kline, Scott Glenn, Kevin Costner, Danny Glover, Brian Dennehy, Linda Hunt, John Cleese, Jeff Goldblum, Rosanna Arquette, Jeff Fahey; **D:** Lawrence Kasdan; **W:** Lawrence Kasdan; **M:** Bruce Broughton. **VHS, Beta, LV $14.95** *COL, VYG, CRC*

Silverhawks: Sky Shadows

Cartoon sci-fi series about law-enforcement officers on distant planets. The cyborg Silverhawks, under the command of Commander Stargazer, fight a continuing battle with the forces of Mon Star, Intergalactic Public Enemy 1. Not surprisingly, there was a toy-product tie-in. Additional volumes available.

1986 (*Preschool-Primary*) 30m/C VHS, Beta $14.95 *LHV, WTA*

Silverhawks: The Original Story

Full-length "debut film" (actually cobbled together from episodes of the series) delineating the first adventure of the part-metal, part-human, all-toy-promoting superheroes in the year 2839. A Rankin-Bass production.

1986 (*Preschool-Primary*) 101m/C VHS, Beta $19.98 *LHV, WAR, WTA*

Simon 🎬🎬◁

Bored demented scientists looking for something to do brainwash a college professor, convincing him he's an alien from a distant galaxy. Whereupon he begins trying to correct the evil in America. Screwball comedy, or semi-serious satire of some kind? Hard to tell. Some terrific set pieces but as a whole it doesn't quite hold together. Directorial debut of Brickman, who previously worked as a scriptwriter with Woody Allen ("Sleeper," etc.).

1980 (PG/*Jr. High-Adult*) 97m/C Alan Arkin, Madeline Kahn, Fred Gwynne, Adolph Green, Wallace Shawn, Austin Pendleton; **D:** Marshall Brickman; **W:** Marshall Brickman. **VHS, Beta $19.98** *WAR*

The Simpsons Christmas Special

The only episode of TV's hilarious, infamous "Simpsons" clan on video is one of the earliest, a holiday segment in which Bart gets a tattoo, Homer works as a mall Santa, and the unruly household gets the Christmas spirit thanks to the dog they adopt. Devotees of the series will have fun noting the changes made since this aired; mother Marge was subsequently written a lot smarter, dad Homer dumber.

1989 (*Family*) 30m/C V: Dan Castellaneta, Julie Kavner, Harry Shearer, Maggie Roswell, Nancy Cartwright, Yeardley Smith. **VHS $9.98** *FXV, WTA*

Sinbad and the Eye of the Tiger 🎬🎬🎬

Sinbad the Sailor voyages to the Polar regions to restore a prince transformed into a baboon, In pursuit is an evil sorceress, but as in every one of the these Sinbad adventures, the baddies' have a real quality control problem with those black magic spells. Forgive the clumsy opening and closing, and you'll be left with a fine, quite underrated adventure in the Sinbad series that showcased Ray Harryhausen's special effects skills. **Hound Advisory:** Violence, very brief nudity as a curious cave giant (who turns out to be a good guy) catches two girls bathing.

1977 (G/*Family*) 113m/C Patrick Wayne, Jane Seymour, Taryn Power, Margaret Whiting; **D:** Sam Wanamaker; **W:** Beverly Cross. **VHS, Beta, LV $14.95** *COL, CCB*

Sinbad the Sailor 🎬🎬🎬

Old-style Hollywood retelling of Sinbad's eighth voyage - a joke, since the sailor of lore made only seven. Fans of the Ray Harryhausen fantasies will be disappointed, because this one has no magic or special effects, just Sinbad, a princess, and villains trying to outsmart each other over the location of a treasure isle. You can easily imagine crooks going through the same routine over the Maltese Falcon, though Fairbanks has one great swashbuckling chase/fight sequence through a palace. **Hound Advisory:** Violence.

1947 (*Family*) 117m/C Douglas Fairbanks Jr., Maureen O'Hara, Anthony Quinn, Walter Slezak, George Tobias, Jane Greer, Mike Mazurki, Sheldon Leonard; **D:** Richard Wallace. **VHS, Beta, LV $24.95** *RKO, MED, TTC*

Since You Went Away 🎬🎬🎬◁

American family copes with the tragedy, heartache and shortages of wartime in classic mega-tribute to the home front. Be warned: very long and bring your hankies. Colbert is superb, as is the photography. John Derek unobtrusively made his film debut as an extra.

1944 (*Jr. High-Adult*) 172m/B Claudette Colbert, Jennifer Jones, Shirley Temple, Joseph Cotten, Agnes Moorehead, Monty Woolley, Guy Madison, Lionel Barrymore, Robert Walker, Hattie McDaniel, Keenan Wynn, Craig Stevens, Albert Basserman, Alla Nazimova, Lloyd Corrigan, Terry Moore, Florence Bates, Ruth Roman, Andrew V. McLaglen, Dorothy Dandridge, Rhonda Fleming; **D:** John Cromwell; **W:** David O. Selznick; **M:** Max Steiner. **Award Nominations:** Academy Awards '43: Best Supporting Actress (Jones); Academy Awards '44: Best Actress (Colbert), Best Black and White Cinematography, Best Film Editing, Best Interior Decoration, Best Picture, Best Supporting Actor (Woolley); **Awards:** Academy Awards '44: Best Score. **VHS, Beta, LV $39.98** *FOX*

Sing 🎬◁

The students in a Brooklyn public school endure the trials of adolescence while putting together a musical revue. Goes from the doubtful to the preposterous, with way too much cheesy music. From the creator of "Fame" and "Footloose." **Hound Advisory:** Profanity, mature themes.

1989 (PG-13/*Jr. High-Adult*) 111m/C Lorraine Bracco, Peter Dobson, Jessica Steen, Louise Lasser, George DiCenzo, Patti LaBelle; **D:** Richard Baskin; **M:** Jay Gruska. **VHS, Beta, LV $89.95** *COL*

Sing Along with Little Lulu

Vintage Little Lulu comic-book character stars in a special song-filled collection of her nostalgic cartoons.

1983 (*Family*) 86m/C VHS $39.95 *REP, WTA*

Sing, Giggle & Grin

Fun, easy songs for children, captioned so they can sing along.
1986 (*Family*) 30m/C **VHS, Beta $9.95**

Sing, Stretch & Shape Up

Zany, easy to follow songs for children, captioned so they can sing along and exercise.
1986 (*Family*) 30m/C **VHS, Beta $9.95**

Sing Together

Includes eight original songs written by the performers Trick Street Man, Janet and Judy, and Dan Crow, who are sure to engage children in interactive sing-along fun.
19?? (*Preschool-Primary*) 25m/C **VHS $12.95**

Singin' in the Rain 🦴🦴🦴🦴

One of the all-time great movie musicals - an affectionate spoof of the turmoil that afflicted the motion picture industry in the late 1920s during the changeover from silent films to sound. Co-director Kelly and Hagen lead a glorious cast. Music and lyrics by Arthur Freed and Nacio Herb Brown. Served as basis of story by Betty Comden and Adolph Green. Also available on laserdisc with the original trailer, outtakes, behind the scenes footage, and commentary by film historian Ronald Haver. Later a Broadway musical. ♫All I Do is Dream of You; Should I?; Singin' in the Rain; Wedding of the Painted Doll; Broadway Melody; Would You; I've Got a Feelin' You're Foolin'; You Are My Lucky Star; Broadway Rhythm.
1952 (*Family*) 103m/C Gene Kelly, Donald O'Connor, Jean Hagen, Debbie Reynolds, Rita Moreno, King Donovan, Millard Mitchell, Cyd Charisse, Douglas Fowley, Madge Blake, Joi Lansing; **D:** Gene Kelly, Stanley Donen; **W:** Adolph Green, Betty Comden. **Award Nominations:** Academy Awards '52: Best Supporting Actress (Hagen), Best Original Score; **Awards:** Golden Globe Awards '53: Best Actor—Musical/Comedy (O'Connor); National Board of Review Awards '52: 10 Best Films of the Year. **VHS, Beta, LV $19.98** *MGM, VYG, TLF*

Singles 🦴🦴🦴

Seattle's music scene is the background for this lighthearted look at single twentysomethings in the '90s. Hits dead on thanks to Crowe's tight script and a talented cast, and speaks straight to its intended audience - those fine young folks of the "Generation X" crowd. Real life band Pearl Jam portrays alternative band Citizen Dick (that's acting!) and sets the tone for a great soundtrack featuring the hot Seattle sounds of Alice in Chains, Soundgarden, and Mudhoney. The video contains six extra minutes of footage after the credits that was thankfully edited out of the final cut. Look for Horton, Stoltz (as a mime), Skerritt, and Burton in cameos. **Hound Advisory:** Profanity; suggested sex; alcohol use.
1992 (**PG-13**/*Sr. High-Adult*) 100m/C Matt Dillon, Bridget Fonda, Campbell Scott, Kyra Sedgwick, Sheila Kelley, Jim True, Bill Pullman, James LeGros, Ally Walker, Devon Raymond, Camillo Gallardo, Jeremy Piven; **Cameos:** Tom Skerritt, Peter Horton, Eric Stoltz, Tim Burton; **D:** Cameron Crowe; **W:** Cameron Crowe; **M:** Paul Westerberg. **VHS, Beta, LV $19.98** *WAR, PMS*

Sir Prancelot

Cartoon compilation about a medieval inventor and his wife, two children, butler, and others out to find adventure.
1970 (*Preschool-Jr. High*) 94m/C **VHS $14.95** *WTA*

Sister Act 🦴🦴🦴◁

Disney/Touchstone box office hit casts Goldberg as Deloris, a loose-living lounge singer who witnesses a mob murder and hides out in a convent where she's restless in a habit. Much to the dismay of the straightlaced Mother Superior, Deloris takes over the rag-tag choir and molds them into a swinging, religious version of a '60s girls group, singing "My God" to the tune of "My Guy." Predictable in the extreme, but sweet-natured and likeable. **Hound Advisory:** Sex talk.
1992 (**PG**/*Jr. High-Adult*) 100m/C Whoopi Goldberg, Dame Maggie Smith, Harvey Keitel, Bill Nunn, Kathy Najimy, Wendy Makkena, Mary Wickes, Robert Miranda, Richard Portnow, Joseph Maher; **D:** Emile Ardolino; **W:** Joseph Howard; **M:** Marc Shaiman. **VHS, Beta, LV $19.99** *TOU, PMS*

Sister Act 2: Back in the Habit 🦴🦴

Her old convent friends convince Vegas singer Deloris to resume her nun identity to help bring order to a rough San Francisco parochial school. Even among lame excuses for sequels that's a weak one, but the movie improves when Deloris decides to revive the school's once-champion choir, and enters the kids in the World Series equivalent for gospel music. Forget the plot and turn up the soundtrack; Whoopi's opening medley is a hoot.
1993 (**PG**/*Jr. High-Adult*) 107m/C Whoopi Goldberg, Kathy Najimy, James Coburn, Dame Maggie Smith, Wendy Makkena, Barnard Hughes, Mary Wickes, Sheryl Lee Ralph, Michael Jeter, Robert Pastorelli, Thomas Gottschalk, Lauryn Hill, Brad Sullivan; **D:** Bill Duke; **W:** James Orr, Jim Cruickshank, Judi Ann Mason; **M:** Miles Goodman. **VHS, LV** *BVV*

Six Pack 🦴◁

Country-singer Rogers, in his theatrical debut, stars as Brewster Baker, a former stock car driver. When he finds six larcenous (and foulmouthed) orphan kids trying to strip his car. Nevertheless, he becomes their pal and guardian, and they support his return to the racing circuit. A reminder of why it's bad to put sugar in a gas tank. **Hound Advisory:** Profanity, sex talk.
1982 (**PG**/*Jr. High-Adult*) 108m/C Kenny Rogers, Diane Lane, Erin Gray, Barry Corbin, Anthony Michael Hall; **D:** Daniel Petrie; **M:** Charles Fox. **VHS, Beta $14.98** *FOX*

Six Weeks 🦴🦴

Young girl dying of leukemia brings together her work-driven mother and an aspiring married politician. Manipulative hanky-wringer has good acting from both Moores but oddly little substance. **Hound Advisory:** Mature themes.
1982 (**PG**/*Jr. High-Adult*) 107m/C Dudley Moore, Mary Tyler Moore, Katherine Healy; **D:** Tony Bill; **M:** Dudley Moore. **VHS, Beta, LV $12.95** *COL*

Sixteen Candles 🦴🦴🦴

Hughes, in his feature directing debut, gathers his stable of young stars again for one of his best films. Every girl's sixteenth birthday is supposed to be special, but in the rush of

Gene Kelly "Singin' in the Rain" (1952)

her sister's wedding nobody remembers Samantha's - and she had hoped the event would bring her together with the guy of her dreams. Instead a weirdo adolescent named Geek comes calling as part of a bet. Ringwald and Hall are especially charming in this humorous look at teenage traumas. Title song performed by The Stray Cats. **Hound Advisory:** Salty language, sex talk, alcohol use, brief nudity.
1984 (PG/*Jr. High-Adult*) 93m/C Molly Ringwald, Justin Henry, Michael Schoeffling, Haviland Morris, Gedde Watanabe, Anthony Michael Hall, Paul Dooley, Carlin Glynn, Blanche Baker, Edward Andrews, Carole Cook, Max Showalter, Liane Curtis, John Cusack, Joan Cusack, Brian Doyle-Murray, Jami Gertz, Cinnamon Idles, Zelda Rubinstein; **D:** John Hughes; **W:** John Hughes; **M:** Ira Newborn. VHS, Beta, LV $19.95 *MCA*

Skateboard 🐾

Down-and-out Hollywood agent creates a pro skateboarding team and enters them in a race worth $20,000. Quickie premise executed lamely, to take advantage of the brand-new thrasher craze.
1977 (PG/*Jr. High-Adult*) 97m/C Allen (Gooritz) Garfield, Kathleen Lloyd, Chad McQueen, Leif Garrett, Richard Van Der Wyk, Tony Alva, Antony Carbone; **W:** Dick Wolf. VHS, Beta *NO*

The Skateboard Kid WOOF!

Awful amalgam of two earlier lousy kid flicks, ''The Dirt Bike Kid'' and ''Munchie,'' from the same filmmakers. When bullying bad guys break Jack's skateboard, the kid finds a magical replacement that can talk and fly (lousy f/x). Now the villains are in for it! And so are the viewers.
1993 (PG/*Jr. High-Adult*) 90m/C Bess Armstrong, Timothy Busfield; **D:** Larry Swerdlove; **W:** Roger Corman; **V:** Dom DeLuise. VHS $89.98 *NHO*

Skeezer 🐾🐾◁

Stray dog becomes a key factor in a sympathetic doctor's efforts to communicate with emotionally unstable children. Based on a true story, recounted in the book ''Skeezer: Dog with a Mission'' by Elizabeth Yates. Quality done-for-TV family fare, but don't be misled; emphasis is on the therapy rather than the mutt, making this nearer to ''The Miracle Worker'' than ''Lassie.'' **Hound Advisory:** Roughhousing.
1982 (*Family*) 100m/C Karen Valentine, Dee Wallace Stone, Tom Atkins, Mariclare Costello, Leighton Greer, Justine Lord; **D:** Peter Hunt. VHS $39.95 *LIV*

Ski Patrol 🐾🐾

Wacky ski groupies try to stop an evil developer. Good ski action in a surprisingly plotful effort from the crazy crew that brought the world ''Police Academy.'' **Hound Advisory:** Mature themes; profanity.
1989 (PG/*Jr. High-Adult*) 85m/C Roger Rose, Yvette Nipar, T.K. Carter, Leslie Jordan, Ray Walston, Martin Mull; **D:** Richard Correll. VHS, Beta, LV $19.95 *COL*

Skills for the New Technology Series

This three part series deals with learning the technological advances and the skills needed to understand them.
1990 (*Primary-Jr. High*) 10m/C VHS, Beta $205.00 *MTI, DSN*

Skylark 🐾🐾◁

In a sequel to television's hugely successful ''Sarah, Plain and Tall,'' the whole Kansas crew returns for more of their little-farm-on-the-prairie life. After two years in America's squarest state, mail-order bride Sarah loves Jacob but not the scenery and still yearns for the lush greenery of Maine. When drought and fire threaten the farm, Jacob sends the family back east for their safety. Close's ''tough Yankee'' expression grows a bit tiresome in a plot that's a tad predictable, yet the simplistic charm and nostalgia work to propel this quality production.
1993 (G/*Family*) 98m/C Glenn Close, Christopher Walken, Lexi Randall, Christopher Bell, Tresa Hughes, Lois Smith, Lee Richardson, Elizabeth Wilson, Margaret Sophie Stein, Jon DeVries, James Rebhorn, Woody Watson, Lois Smith; **D:** Joseph Sargent; **W:** Patricia MacLachlan. VHS $14.98 *REP, BTV*

Sleeper 🐾🐾🐾◁

Hapless nerd Allen is revived two hundred years after an operation gone bad. Keaton portrays Allen's love interest in a futuristic land of robots and giant vegetables. He learns of the hitherto unknown health benefits of hot fudge sundaes; discovers the truth about the nation's dictator, known as The Leader; and gets involved with revolutionaries seeking to overthrow the government. Hilarious, fast-moving comedy, full of slapstick and satire. Don't miss the ''orgasmatron.''
1973 (PG/*Jr. High-Adult*) 88m/C Woody Allen, Diane Keaton, John Beck, Howard Cosell; **D:** Woody Allen; **W:** Woody Allen, Marshall Brickman; **M:** Woody Allen. VHS, Beta, LV $14.95 *MGM, FOX, FUS*

Sleeping Beauty 🐾🐾🐾

Lavish Walt Disney cartoon feature wasn't just supposed to be any old 'toon; Walt himself promoted it as the most expensive and spectacular animated epic ever, about the handsome prince who must revive the enchanted princess and her frozen realm with a kiss. But the thin storyline and characters hold this back from being top-ranked. Still, the fiery climax doesn't Mickey Mouse around - the battle with Maleficent, the witch-turned-dragon, is one of those sequences that puts the magic into the Magic Kingdom. **Hound Advisory:** The demonic Maleficent rates as one of the scariest Disney villains of all time, without even the saving grace of humor.
1959 (G/*Family*) 75m/C **D:** Clyde Geronomi, Eric Larson, Wolfgang Reitherman, Les Clark. VHS, Beta, LV *DIS, OM*

Sleeping Beauty 🐾◁

''Cannon Movie Tales'' treatment of the Grimm story features Baker, the dwarf actor inside R2D2 in ''Star Wars,'' as a magic little man whose spell allows a childless Queen to bear a daughter at last. But a wicked witch curses the girl with a deep sleep, and only a handsome prince can revive her. Cannon's typically forgettable songs and dances curse the movie with its own brand of somnolence.
1989 (*Family*) 92m/C Tahnee Welch, Morgan Fairchild, Nicholas Clay, Sylvia Miles, Kenny Baker. VHS $14.95 *MGM, PSM, CVC*

"Sleeping Beauty" dancing with admirers (1959)

Sleeping Beauty 🦴◁

A cheap and forgettable Cannon Movie Tale, starring my wife, Morgan Fairchild. Ya, that's the ticket. Semi-musical about a princess, a heroic prince, and an evil witch. Suitable for putting anyone to sleep.
1989 (**G**/*Family*) 90m/C Morgan Fairchild, Tracy Welch, Nicholas Clay, Sylvia Miles, Kenny L. Baker, David Holliday; **D:** David Irving. **VHS** *WAR*

Sleepless in Seattle 🦴🦴🦴◁

Witty, sweet romantic comedy explores the differences between men and women when it comes to love and romance. When widower Hanks talks about his wife on a national talk show, recently engaged Ryan responds. Writer/director Ephron's humorous screenplay is brought to life by a perfectly cast ensemble; it also breathed new life into the classic weepie "An Affair to Remember," comparing it to "The Dirty Dozen" in an unforgettable scene. Full of fine detail, from Sven Nykvist's camera work to the graphic layout of the opening credits to the great score. Captured millions at the box office, coming in as the fourth highest grossing movie of 1993. **Hound Advisory:** Mature themes; sex talk; salty language.
1993 (**PG**/*Jr. High-Adult*) 105m/C Tom Hanks, Meg Ryan, Bill Pullman, Ross Malinger, Rosie O'Donnell, Gaby Hoffman, Victor Garber, Rita Wilson, Barbara Garrick, Carey Lowell, Rob Reiner, Sarah Trigger; **D:** Nora Ephron; **W:** Jeffrey Arch, Larry Atlas, David S. Ward, Nora Ephron; **M:** Marc Shaiman. **VHS, LV, 8mm $99.95** *COL, BTV, FCT*

Sleuth 🦴🦴🦴◁

A mystery novelist and his wife's lover face off in ever shifting, elaborate, and diabolical plots against each other, complete with red herrings, traps, and tricks. Playful, cerebral mystery thriller from top director Mankiewicz. Schaeffer also scripted "Frenzy" for Hitchcock, from his play.
1972 (**PG**/*Jr. High-Adult*) 138m/C Laurence Olivier, Michael Caine; **D:** Joseph L. Mankiewicz; **W:** Anthony Shaffer; **M:** John Addison. **Award Nominations:** Academy Awards '72: Best Actor (Caine), Best Actor (Olivier), Best Director (Mankiewicz), Best Original Score; **Awards:** Edgar Allan Poe Awards '72: Best Screenplay. **VHS, Beta, LV $19.95** *MED, HMV, VTR*

Small Change 🦴🦴🦴🦴

Sweet, nearly plotless record of a school year in a French town where students and instructors live virtually side-by-side in quaint tenements and courtyards. The mischief-prone kids disrupt class, tumble from windows, find first love, and assist their favorite teacher when he becomes a father himself. Ends with the news that one youngster is abused at home (sadly, not the shock today that it was back in 1976) and a direct plea for children's rights. A realistic and tender testament to the great director's belief in childhood as a "state of grace." Original title: "L'Argent de Poche"; on tape in French with English subtitles. **Hound Advisory:** Salty language, nudity, mature themes.
1976 (**PG**/*Jr. High-Adult*) 104m/C Geory Desmouceaux, Philippe Goldman, Jean-Francois Stevenin, Chantal Mercier, Claudio Deluca, Frank Deluca, Richard Golfier, Laurent Devlaeminck, Francis Devlaeminck; **D:** Francois Truffaut; **W:** Suzanne Schiffman. **VHS, Beta, LV $19.99** *MGM, FCT, INJ*

The Small One

Poor boy must sell his beloved donkey, "Small One," on the eve of the first Christmas in Bethlehem. Holiday cartoon short from Disney.
1980 (*Family*) 25m/C **VHS, Beta $12.99** *DIS, MTI, DSN*

Smart Alecks 🦴◁

The Bowery Boys get involved with gangsters when Jordan helps capture a crook. The usual wise-cracking from Hall and Gorcey helps keep things moving.
1942 (*Jr. High-Adult*) 88m/B Leo Gorcey, Huntz Hall, Gabriel Dell, Gale Storm, Roger Pryor Jr., Walter Woolf King, Herbert Rawlinson, Joe Kirk, Marie Windsor; **D:** Wallace Fox. **VHS $19.95** *NOS*

Smile 🦴🦴🦴

Barbed, merciless send-up of small-town America focusing on a group of naive California girls who compete for the "Young American Miss" crown amid rampant commercialism, exploitation and pure middle-class idiocy. Hilarious neglected '70s-style satire. Early role for Griffith.
1975 (**PG**/*Jr. High-Adult*) 113m/C Bruce Dern, Barbara Feldon, Michael Kidd, Nicholas Pryor, Geoffrey Lewis, Colleen Camp, Joan Prather, Annette O'Toole, Melanie Griffith, Denise Nickerson; **D:** Michael Ritchie; **W:** Jerry Belson. **VHS, Beta, LV $19.95** *MGM*

Smile for Auntie and Other Stories

Compilation of animated shorts based on famous children's stories, including the award-winning title segment, plus "Make Way for Ducklings," "The Snowy Day," and "Wynken, Blynken, and Nod." Volume III of the "Children's Circle" series from Weston Woods Studios.
1979 (*Preschool-Primary*) 26m/C **VHS, Beta $19.95** *CCC, WKV, BTV*

Smith! 🦴🦴

Disney picture with a social conscience gets points for trying, but Davy Crockett enthusiastically killing off swarms of 'those red hornets' looms taller in the mind than this treatise on the sad circumstances of modern Indians. Headstrong rancher Smith takes the side of a native American accused of murdering a storekeeper, and it all boils down to courtroom drama. Based on Paul St. Pierre's novel "Breaking Smith's Quarter Horse."
1969 (**G**/*Family*) 101m/C Glenn Ford, Frank Ramirez, Keenan Wynn; **D:** Michael O'Herlihy. **VHS, Beta $69.95** *DIS*

Smoke 🦴🦴◁

A young boy nurses a lost German shepherd back to health with the help of his new stepfather, whom he learns to trust. Then he runs away with the dog when the original owners show up. Made for television Disney fare starring Opie/Richie (and later successful director) Howard.
1970 (*Family*) 89m/C Earl Holliman, Ron Howard, Andy Devine; **D:** Vincent McEveety. **VHS, Beta $69.95** *DIS*

Smokey and the Bandit 🦴🦴◁

If you don't know how to end a movie, you call for a car chase. The first and best of the horrible series about bootlegger

Reynolds is one long car chase. Reynolds makes a wager that he can have a truck load of Coors beer-once unavailable east of Texas—delivered to Atlanta from Texas in 28 hours. Gleason is the "smokey" who tries to stop him. Field is the hitchhiker Reynolds picks up along the way. Great stunts; director Needham was a top stunt man. **Hound Advisory:** Profanity.

1977 (PG/*Jr. High-Adult*) 96m/C Burt Reynolds, Sally Field, Jackie Gleason, Jerry Reed, Mike Henry, Paul Williams, Pat McCormick; *D:* Hal Needham; *W:* Charles Shyer. **VHS, Beta, LV $14.98** *MCA*

Smokey and the Bandit, Part 2 𝄞

Pathetic sequel to "Smokey and the Bandit" proved a box-office winner, grossing $40 million. The Bandit is hired to transport a pregnant elephant from Miami to the Republican convention in Dallas. Sheriff Buford T. Justice and family are in hot pursuit.

1980 (PG/*Jr. High-Adult*) 101m/C Burt Reynolds, Sally Field, Jackie Gleason, Jerry Reed, Mike Henry, Dom DeLuise, Pat McCormick, Paul Williams; *D:* Hal Needham; *W:* Jerry Belson, Michael Kane. **VHS, Beta, LV $14.98** *MCA*

Smokey and the Bandit, Part 3 𝄞

You thought the second one was bad? Another mega car chase, this time sans Reynolds and director Needham. **Hound Advisory:** Profanity and nudity.

1983 (PG/*Adult*) 88m/C Burt Reynolds, Jackie Gleason, Jerry Reed, Paul Williams, Pat McCormick, Mike Henry, Colleen Camp; *D:* Dick Lowry. **VHS, Beta, LV $14.98** *MCA*

Smokey the Bear: Founder's Day Folly

Episode from a Rankin-Bass TV cartoon show starring the furry mascot of the National Forest Fires Commission. Less strident in its environmental themes than later Saturday-morning fare.

1969 (*Preschool-Jr. High*) 30m/C **VHS $9.95** *WTA*

Smokey the Bear: Silliest Show on Earth

Smokey and friends have fun and occasionally teach the importance of wildlife and preventing forest fires.

1969 (*Preschool-Primary*) 30m/C **VHS $9.95** *WTA*

A Smoky Mountain Christmas 𝄞𝄞

Dolly gets away from it all in a secluded cabin that has been appropriated by a gang of orphans, and sings a half dozen songs. Innocuous seasonal country fun.

1986 (*Family*) 94m/C Dolly Parton, Bo Hopkins, Dan Hedaya, Gennie James, David Ackroyd, Rene Auberjonois, John Ritter, Anita Morris, Lee Majors; *D:* Henry Winkler; *W:* Dolly Parton. **VHS, Beta $79.98** *FOX*

Smooth Talk 𝄞𝄞𝄞

Flirtatious teenager Connie is determined to lose both her virginity and her mother's tight reins on her. A shady, possibly dangerous man looks like he may have the solution to at least one of her problems. Disturbing and thought-provoking maturity saga, with Dern giving a brilliant performance as the sheltered girl. Based on the Joyce Carol Oates story.

Hound Advisory: Profanity, alcohol use, mature themes. Frequent sex talk leads to more serious stuff offscreen.

1985 (PG-13/*Jr. High-Adult*) 92m/C Laura Dern, Treat Williams, Mary Kay Place, Levon Helm; *D:* Joyce Chopra. **VHS, Beta, LV $29.98** *LIV, VES*

Smuggler's Cove 𝄞𝄞

Gorcey wrongly believes he has inherited a mansion. He and the Bowery Boys move in, only to stumble across a smuggling ring. Plenty of slapsticks; the boys at their best.

1983 (*Family*) 75m/C **VHS, Beta** *NO*

Smurfs

These blue-hued forest-dwelling dwarfs started out as Disney-esque Belgian comic-strip characters (called 'Schtroumpfs, in Flemish) in the 1950s; only belatedly did American TV stumble across them, and Hanna-Barbera's first Smurf cartoon was a Saturday-morning ratings smash. Two volumes are available here, each containing six episodes per tape.

1984 (*Preschool-Primary*) 90m/C **VHS, Beta $19.95** *TTC, WTA*

Smurfs & the Magic Flute 𝄞𝄞

The Smurfs, longtime Belgian comic-strip characters (known across the Atlantic as 'Schtroumpfs' by the way) were imported and mass-marketed in the U.S. as toys, as a Hanna-Barbera TV series, and as this mediocre feature cartoon, a musical tale about a flute with the magic power to make any listener dance.

1981 (G/*Family*) 72m/C *D:* Jose Dutillieu, Jon Rust. **VHS, Beta, LV $9.99** *VTR*

The Snapper 𝄞𝄞𝄞

Originally made for BBC television, Frears creates a small comic gem based on the second novel of Doyle's Barrytown trilogy. Set in Dublin, 20-year-old Sharon Curley (Kellegher) finds herself unexpectedly pregnant and refuses to name the father. Family and friends are understanding - until they discover the man's identity. Affecting performances, particularly from Meany as Sharon's dad who takes a much greater interest in the birth of his grandchild than he ever did with his own children. Cheerful semi-sequel to "The Commitments" serves up domestic upheavals graced with humor and a strong sense of family loyalty. **Hound Advisory:** Syntactically correct Irish profanity; sexual situations; alcohol use.

1993 (R/*Sr. High-Adult*) 95m/C Tina Kellegher, Colm Meaney, Ruth McCabe, Colm O'Byrne, Pat Laffan, Eanna MacLiam, Ciara Duffy; *D:* Stephen Frears; *W:* Roddy Doyle. **VHS, LV** *TOU*

Sneakers 𝄞𝄞

Nearly competent thriller about five computer hackers with questionable pasts and an equally questionable government job. Of course, nothing is as it seems. Rather slow-going considering the talents and suspense involved and wildly off the map as to plausibility, but otherwise nearly entertaining. Aykroyd's handyman is a pleasant little gem. **Hound Advisory:** Violence; profanity; mature themes.

1992 (PG-13/*Jr. High-Adult*) 125m/C Robert Redford, Sidney Poitier, River Phoenix, Dan Aykroyd, Ben Kingsley, David Strathairn, Mary McDonnell, Timothy Busfield, George Hearn, Eddie Jones, James Earl Jones, Stephen Tobolowsky; *D:* Phil Alden Robinson; *W:* Lawrence Lasker, Walter F. Parkes, Phil Alden Robinson; *M:* James Horner, Branford Marsalis. **VHS, Beta, LV $19.98** *MCA, PMS*

The Sneetches from Dr. Seuss on the Loose

Sneetches are Sneetches. Star-Belly Sneetches are no better or worse than Plain-Belly Sneetches, and Sylvester McMorkey, McBean's mechanical machine, helps to prove this point. 1974 (*Primary*) 14m/C **VHS, Beta** *BFA*

Sniffles Bells the Cat

Sniffles the Mouse (who never did quite catch on) stars in three of his classic Warner Brothers cartoons of the '40s. 1944 (*Family*) 32m/C **VHS, Beta $14.95** *MGM*

Snoopy, Come Home 🦴🦴🦴

Snoopy leaves Charlie Brown to visit his former owner Lila in the hospital and returns with her to her apartment house. Will the Chaplinesque beagle ever return to the hapless boy? That question generates a bit more pathos than usual in this theatrical edition of Charles Schultz's popular comic strip "Peanuts." Director Bill Melendez also did the vocals for Snoopy's distinctive high-pitched barks and guffaws. 1972 (G/*Family*) 80m/C *D:* Bill Melendez; *W:* Charles M. Schulz. **VHS, Beta, LV $14.98** *FOX*

Snorks

These snorkel-headed underwater creatures first came to prominence as a Belgian comic book, so it was only natural that when their countrymen, the Smurfs, made it big in America the Hanna-Barbera folks would import these for the standard Saturday-morning treatment too. Volume one and volume two are available and contain eight episodes per tape. 1984 (*Preschool-Primary*) 90m/C **VHS, Beta $19.95** *TTC, WTA*

The Snow Queen

US-Russian animated version of the Hans Christian Andersen tale about Gerda, off to rescue her friend from the icy grip of the Snow Queen, who has decided to adopt the boy. 1992 (*Preschool-Primary*) 30m/C **VHS $12.98** *MVD, BMG, PMS*

Snow Treasure 🦴🦴

With the help of an underground agent, Norwegian children smuggle gold out of the country right under the noses of the Nazis. Stiff and not terribly interesting international production. Based on the book by Marie McSwigan. 1967 (G/*Family*) 96m/C James Franciscus, Paul Anstad; *D:* Irving Jacoby. **VHS, Beta $29.95** *LIV*

Snow White 🦴🦴

The incomparable Rigg brings some zest to her act as the jealous Evil Queen, who adopts numerous disguises to try to slay Snow White in this lackluster Cannon Movie Tales retelling of the Brothers Grimm story. Real star is Queen's spooky magic mirror, partly because it lends an eerie, "Dorian Grey" type ending, but mainly because it doesn't sing any of the dumb tunes. 1989 (*Family*) 85m/C Diana Rigg, Sarah Patterson, Billy Barty; *D:* Michael Berz. **VHS** *WAR*

Snow White and Rose Red

Snow White and a fellow maiden encounter a prince transformed into a bear in this animated Grimm's tale. 19?? (*Preschool-Primary*) 30m/C **VHS $9.99** *VTR*

Snow White and the Seven Dwarfs 🦴🦴🦴🦴

Classic Disney adaptation of the Grimm Brothers fairy tale about the fairest of them all, who lives with seven hardworking little men ("heigh ho, heigh ho, it's off to work we go"). Beautiful animation, memorable characters, and wonderful songs mark this as the definitive "Snow White." Set the stage for other animated features after Uncle Walt took an unprecedented gamble by attempting the first animated feature-length film, a project which took over two years to create and $1.5 million to make, and made believers out of those who laughed at the concept. Lifelike animation was based on real stars; Margery Belcher (later Champion) posed for Snow, Louis Hightower was the Prince, and Lucille LaVerne gave the Queen her nasty look. As in most Disney animated films, evil is portrayed in a fairly intense way. Songs include "Whistle While You Work," "Heigh Ho," and "Some Day My Prince Will Come." 🎵Some Day My Prince Will Come; One Song; With a Smile and a Song; Whistle While You Work; Bluddle-Uddle-Um-Dum; The Dwarfs' Yodel Song; Heigh Ho; I'm Wishing; Isn't This a Silly Song?. 1937 (G/*Family*) 83m/C *D:* David Hand; *W:* Ted Sears, Otto Englander, Earl Hurd, Dorothy Blank, Richard Creedon, Dick Richard, Merrill De Maris, Webb Smith; *M:* Frank Churchill, Paul Smith, Larry Morey, Leigh Harline; *V:* Adriana Caseloti, Harry Stockwell, Lucille LaVerne, Moroni Olsen, Billy Gilbert, Pinto Colvig, Otis Harlan, Scotty Matraw, Roy Atwell, Stuart Buchanan, Marion Darlington, Jim Macdonald. **VHS $26.99** *DIS*

Snow White and the Three Stooges 🦴

Explain this if you can: The aging Stooges, late in their careers, sub for the dwarfs as miners who discover and protect Snow White. She's played by champion figure-skater Heiss, and much of her screen time involves ice-skating dream ballets of the Snow White saga. Good color photography; otherwise the words 'Dopey' and 'Sleepy' come to mind. 1961 (*Family*) 107m/C Moe Howard, Curly Howard, Larry Fine, Carol Heiss, Patricia Medina; *D:* Walter Lang. **VHS, Beta $14.98** *FOX, FCT*

Snowball Express 🦴🦴

When the New Yorker Baxter family inherit a hotel in the Rocky Mountains, dad decides to move his family west to attempt to make a go of the defunct ski resort, only to find the place falling apart. Run of the mill, fish out of water Disney comedy, based on the novel "Chateau Bon Vivant" by Frankie and John O'Rear.

1972 (G/*Family*) 120m/C Dean Jones, Nancy Olson, Harry Morgan, Keenan Wynn; *D:* Norman Tokar. **VHS, Beta $69.95** *DIS*

The Snowman

A young boy makes his first snowman and at midnight it comes to life and takes the boy on wonderful adventures, including visiting Santa at the North Pole. A highly-rated cartoon without dialogue, based on the book by Raymond Briggs.
1978 (*Family*) 30m/C **VHS $14.95** *COL,, MLT*

Snuffy the Elf Who Saved Christmas

Is there any animal/vegetable/mineral out there who hasn't saved Christmas? It's Snuffy to the rescue when the Sandman puts all the other elves to sleep on the job.
1991 (*Preschool-Primary*) 25m/C **VHS $12.98** *FHE, FFF, WTA*

So Dear to My Heart 𝄞𝄞𝄞⤴

Heartwarming Disney film about a farm boy determined to enter his black sheep at the county fair, who goes to great lengths to earn the entry fee. Several sequences combine live action with superb Disney animation, and musical numbers include standards like "Lavender Blue." Straightforward and likeable but never sentimental. Great vintage Disney, not as well-remembered as some of their other classics but worth rediscovering on tape. Based on "Midnight and Jeremiah" by Sterling North. ♫Sourwood Mountain; Billy Boy; So Dear To My Heart; County Fair; Stick-To-It-Ivity; Ol' Dan Patch; It's Whatcha Do With Watcha Got; Lavender Blue (Dilly Dilly).
1949 (*Family*) 82m/C Bobby Driscoll, Burl Ives, Beulah Bondi, Harry Carey Sr., Luanna Patten; *D:* Harold Schuster. **VHS, Beta, LV $69.95** *DIS, WTA*

So I Married an Axe Murderer 𝄞𝄞

Combination comedy/romance/thriller that's fairly stupid while holding true to its own sense of parody. Charlie is a hip, angst-ridden bookstore owner/poet with a commitment problem. When he finally falls in love with a butcher, he comes to suspect she's a serial killer and he's in line as her next victim. Myers has a dual role: as Charlie and as Scottish dad Stuart, who steals the show with his intense Scottish demeanor. Occasionally inspired, probably too self-conscious, but there are worse ways to spend an evening. **Hound Advisory:** Profanity; violence; brief nudity.
1993 (PG-13/*Jr. High-Adult*) 92m/C Mike Myers, Nancy Travis, Anthony LaPaglia, Amanda Plummer, Brenda Fricker, Matt Doherty, Charles Grodin; *Cameos:* Phil Hartman, Steven Wright, Alan Arkin; *D:* Thomas Schlamme; *W:* Mike Myers, Robbie Fox; *M:* Bruce Broughton. **VHS, LV, 8mm** *COL*

Solarbabies 𝄞

Rollerskating youths in a drought-stricken future vie for a mysterious, friendly ball from the stars who can replenish the Earth's water. Juvenile adventure is like an explosion in a mind-candy factory, raining bits of every sci-fi movie from "Rollerball" to "E.T." Good sets and special effects wasted. **Hound Advisory:** Mild violence, the worst of which is a pain device in the bad guys' torture chamber. But it only creates illusions of mutilating flesh.

1986 (PG-13/*Jr. High-Adult*) 95m/C Richard Jordan, Sarah Douglas, Charles Durning, Lukas Haas, Jami Gertz, Jason Patric; *D:* Alan Johnson; *W:* Walon Green; *M:* Maurice Jarre. **VHS, Beta, LV $14.95** *MGM*

Some Kind of Wonderful 𝄞𝄞

High school tomboy has a crush on a guy who also happens to be her best friend. Her feelings go unrequited as he falls for a rich girl with snobbish friends. Will true love win out in the end? Deutch also directed (and John Hughes also produced) the teen flick "Pretty in Pink," which had much the same plot, with the rich/outcast characters reversed by gender. OK, but completely predictable - whether you've seen its mirror-clone or not. **Hound Advisory:** Salty language.
1987 (PG-13/*Sr. High-Adult*) 93m/C Eric Stoltz, Lea Thompson, Mary Stuart Masterson, Craig Sheffer, John Ashton, Elias Koteas, Molly Hagan; *D:* Howard Deutch; *W:* John Hughes. **VHS, LV $19.95** *PAR*

Someday Me Series

Series of videotapes from Fisher-Price featuring the characters Max and Jennifer, who have fun experiencing what life is like in the adult world.
1988 (*Preschool-Primary*) 30m/C **VHS, Beta $14.98** *HSE*

Something Special 𝄞𝄞

Fourteen-year-old Milly suspects that boys have it easy. She gets to find out when she magically grows a penis (no surprise, as this was the theme of the pic's ad campaign). Taking the name Willy and a male persona, our 'heroine' goes off to find how the other half lives. Not as slimy as it sounds, but could have used more development from the shoulders up. **Hound Advisory:** Mature themes, salty language, sex talk, roughhousing.
1986 (PG-13/*Jr. High-Adult*) 93m/C Pamela Segall, Patty Duke, Eric Gurry, John Glover, Seth Green; *D:* Paul Schneider. **VHS, LV** *NO*

Something Wicked This Way Comes 𝄞𝄞

Two boys discover the evil secret of Mr. Dark's traveling carnival that visits their town once a generation, wreaking havoc by granting folks their secret wishes. Ray Bradbury wrote the screenplay, adapting - and simplifying - his poetic horror novel for Disney, but results are severely stilted and slow-moving, with a storm of f/x at the end barely explained in terms of what it all means. **Hound Advisory:** Some violence (including a severed head), but very stylized and hallucinatory.
1983 (PG/*Jr. High-Adult*) 94m/C Jason Robards Jr., Jonathan Pryce, Diane Ladd, Pam Grier, Richard Davalos, James Stacy; *D:* Jack Clayton; *W:* Ray Bradbury; *M:* James Horner. **VHS, Beta, LV $14.99** *DIS*

Somewhere in Time 𝄞⤴

Playwright Reeve (in his first post-Clark Kent role) falls in love with a beautiful woman in an old portrait. Through self-hypnosis he goes back in time to 1912 to discover what their relationship might have been. Drippy rip-off of the brilliant novel "Time and Again" by Jack Finney at least made a star of the Grand Hotel on Mackinac Island in Michigan, where romantic drama was shot. Probably best appreciated by

Reeves fans with low expectations or friends of Mackinac Island.
1980 (PG/*Jr. High-Adult*) 103m/C Christopher Reeve, Jane Seymour, Christopher Plummer, Teresa Wright; *D:* Jeannot Szwarc; *W:* Richard Matheson; *M:* John Barry. **VHS, Beta, LV** $19.95 *MCA*

Somewhere Tomorrow 🐾🐾◁

Pleasant little romantic fantasy about a lonely, fatherless teenage girl trying to hold onto her horse farm. She receives assistance from the ghost of a young man. Works better than it sounds; charming and moving.
1985 (PG/*Jr. High-Adult*) 91m/C Sarah Jessica Parker, Nancy Addison, Tom Shea; *D:* Robert Wiemer. **VHS, Beta** $59.95 *MED*

Sommersby 🐾🐾◁

Too-good-to-be-true period romance based on the French "The Return of Martin Guerre." Civil War veteran Gere returns to his wife's Foster less-than-open arms. She soon warms up to his kind, sensitive and caring manner, but can't quite believe the change that the war has wrought. Neither can the neighbors, especially Pullman who has his own eye on Laurel Sommersby. So is he really Jack Sommersby or an all too clever imposter? Lots of hankies needed for the tender-hearted. Strong performance by Foster, while Gere's displays an acceptable level of narcissism (that's acting!). Filmed in Virginia (passing for the state of Tennessee.) The laserdisc version is available in letterbox format. **Hound Advisory:** Nudity; violence; mature themes.
1993 (PG-13/*Jr. High-Adult*) 114m/C Richard Gere, Jodie Foster, Bill Pullman, James Earl Jones, William Windom, Brett Kelley, Richard Hamilton, Maury Chaykin, Lanny Flaherty, Frankie Faison, Wendell Wellman, Clarice Taylor, R. Lee Ermey; *D:* Jon Amiel; *W:* Nicholas Meyer, Sarah Kernochan; *M:* Danny Elfman. **VHS, Beta, LV, 8mm** $19.98 *WAR, FCT*

Son-in-Law 🐾🐾

Surfer-dude comic Shore's a laconic fish out of water as a city-boy rock 'n' roller who falls in love with a country beauty, marries her, and visits the family farm to meet the new in-laws. Once there, he weirds out family and neighbors before showing everyone how to live, Pauly style. Silly entertainment best appreciated by Shore fans. **Hound Advisory:** Profanity.
1993 (PG-13/*Jr. High-Adult*) 95m/C Pauly Shore, Carla Gugino, Lane Smith, Cindy Pickett, Mason Adams, Patrick Renna, Dennis Burkley, Dan Gauthier, Tiffani-Amber Thiessen; *D:* Steve Rash; *W:* Shawn Schepps, Fax Bahr, Adam Small; *M:* Richard Gibbs. **VHS, Beta** $96.03 *HPH*

Son of Captain Blood 🐾◁

The son of the famous pirate meets up with his father's enemies on the high seas. The son of the famous actor Errol Flynn—Sean—plays the son of the character the elder Flynn played in "Captain Blood." Let's just say the gimmick didn't work.
1962 (G/*Family*) 90m/C Sean Flynn, Ann Todd; *D:* Tulio Demicheli. **VHS, Beta** $59.95 *PSM, MLB*

Son of Dinosaurs

One of a set of dinosaur videos for kids, in which comical hosts Gary Owens and Eric Boardman drop educational tidbits on the giant lizards, in the background of a farcical plotline. Here the duo defend a dinosaur egg containing a live dino embryo from a villain determined to steal it. Others in the series: "Dinosaurs Dinosaurs Dinosaurs," "More Dinosaurs," "Prehistoric World," and "The World's Greatest Dinosaur Video."
1990 (*Family*) 60m/C Gary Owens, Eric Boardman, Kenneth Mars, Alex Rodine, James Stewart. **VHS** *NO*

Son of Flubber 🐾🐾◁

Sequel to "The Absent Minded Professor" finds Professor Brainard still toying with his prodigious invention, Flubber, now in the form of Flubbergas, causes those who inhale it to float away (why didn't they Just Say No!). Disney's first-ever sequel is high family wackiness.
1963 (*Primary-Adult*) 96m/C Fred MacMurray, Nancy Olson, Tommy Kirk, Leon Ames, Joanna Moore, Keenan Wynn, Charlie Ruggles, Paul Lynde; *D:* Robert Stevenson. **VHS, Beta** *DIS*

Son of Kong 🐾🐾◁

Expedition returns to King Kong's prehistoric island and discovers the great ape's descendant - smaller, cuter and albino. Kong 2 defends his human friends against rampaging dinosaurs, a bear, and other perils. Quickly minted sequel to take advantage of the smash success of the original isn't near as good but still has a spirit of fun and f/x by stop-motion pioneer Willis O'Brien. **Hound Advisory:** Violence.
1933 (*Family*) 70m/B Robert Armstrong, Helen Mack; *D:* Ernest B. Schoedsack; *M:* Max Steiner. **VHS, Beta, LV** $19.98 *NOS, MED, FCT*

Son of the Pink Panther 🐾◁

Lame leftover from the formerly popular comedy series. Director Edwards has chosen not to resurrect Inspector Clouseau, instead opting for his son (Benigni), who turns out to be just as much of a bumbling idiot as his father. Commissioner Dreyfus (Lom), the twitching, mouth-foaming former supervisor of the original Clouseau is looking for a kidnapped princess (Farentino) along with Clouseau, Jr., who himself does not know he is the illegitimate son of his partner's dead nemesis. Many of the sketches have been recycled from previous series entrants. **Hound Advisory:** Violence.
1993 (PG/*Jr. High-Adult*) 115m/C Roberto Benigni, Herbert Lom, Robert Davi, Debrah Farentino, Claudia Cardinale, Burt Kwouk, Shabana Azmi; *D:* Blake Edwards; *W:* Blake Edwards; *M:* Henry Mancini. **VHS, LV** *MGM*

Son of Zorro

Zorro takes the law into his own hands to protect ranchers from bandits. A serial in thirteen chapters. **Hound Advisory:** Violence.
1947 (*Family*) 164m/B George Turner, Peggy Stewart, Roy Barcroft, Edward Cassidy. **VHS** $27.95 *REP, VCN, MLB*

Song City U.S.A.

The Song City crowd dazzles audiences with a slew of wild and wacky music videos down at the diner of the same name.
1989 (*Family*) 30m/C Brian O'Connor. **VHS** $14.95 *FHE, LIV*

The Song of Sacajawea

Story of the 17-year-old Shoshone woman, sister to her people's chief, who leads explorers Lewis and Clark to the Pacific Ocean. Beautifully animated by John Molloy; part of the "Rabbit Ears: American Heroes & Legends" series.
1993 (Preschool-Primary) 30m/C VHS $9.95 UND, MVD

Songs for Us Series

This Disney series features songs that children can learn that relate to life in today's society. Tapes, available separately, are "Appreciating Differences," "Making Friends," and "Sharing and Cooperation."
1989 (Preschool-Primary) 8m/C VHS, Beta $250.00 MTI, DSN

Songs from Mother Goose

Children can sing along with the same happy songs that have delighted youngsters for decades.
1983 (Family) 30m/C VHS $7.95

Sorcerer's Apprentice

In this non-Disney animated version of Jacob Grimm's classic tale, young Hans realizes that his master plans to use magic for evil purposes and tries to motivate the old wizard towards more pleasant prestidigitation. Originally a syndicated TV special.
1985 (Preschool-Primary) 22m/C VHS, Beta $14.95 LHV, WTA

Sorrowful Jones 🎞🎞

A "Little Miss Marker" remake, in which bookie Hope inherits a little girl as collateral for an unpaid bet. Good for a few yuks, but the original is much better.
1949 (Family) 88m/B Bob Hope, Lucille Ball, William Demarest, Bruce Cabot, Thomas Gomez, Mary Jane Saunders; D: Sidney Lanfield; W: Jack Rose, Melville Shavelson. VHS, Beta $14.98 MCA

Soul Man 🎞🎞

Denied the funds he expected for his Harvard tuition, a young white student (Howell) masquerades as a black in order to get a minority scholarship. As a black student at Harvard, Howell learns about racism and bigotry. Pleasant lightweight comedy with romance thrown in (Chong is the black girl he falls for), and with pretensions to social satire that it never achieves. **Hound Advisory:** Profanity; sex; violence.
1986 (PG-13/Sr. High-Adult) 101m/C C. Thomas Howell, Rae Dawn Chong, James Earl Jones, Leslie Nielsen, Arye Gross; D: Steve Miner. VHS, Beta, LV $9.95 NWV, STE

The Sound of Music 🎞🎞🎞🎞

Classic film version of the Rodgers and Hammerstein musical based on the true story of the singing von Trapp family of Austria and their escape from the Nazis just before WWII. Beautiful Salzburg, Austria location photography and an excellent cast. Andrews, fresh from her Oscar for "Mary Poppins," is effervescent, in beautiful voice, but occasionally too good to be true. Not Rodgers & Hammerstein's most innovative score, but lovely to hear and see. Plummer's singing was dubbed by Bill Lee. Marni Nixon, behind-the-scenes songstress for "West Side Story" and "My Fair Lady," makes her on-screen debut as one of the nuns. ♫I Have Confidence In Me; Something Good; The Sound of Music; Preludium; Morning Hymn; Alleluia; How Do You Solve A Problem Like Maria?; Sixteen, Going on Seventeen; My Favorite Things.
1965 (Family) 174m/C Julie Andrews, Christopher Plummer, Eleanor Parker, Peggy Wood, Charmian Carr, Heather Menzies, Marni Nixon, Richard Haydn, Anna Lee, Norma Varden, Nicholas Hammond, Angela Cartwright, Portia Nelson, Duane Chase, Debbie Turner, Kym Karath; D: Robert Wise; W: Ernest Lehman; M: Richard Rodgers, Oscar Hammerstein. **Award Nominations:** Academy Awards '65: Best Actress (Andrews), Best Art Direction/Set Decoration (Color), Best Color Cinematography, Best Costume Design (Color), Best Supporting Actress (Wood); **Awards:** Academy Awards '65: Best Adapted Score, Best Director (Wise), Best Film Editing, Best Picture, Best Sound; Directors Guild of America Awards '65: Best Director (Wise); Golden Globe Awards '66: Best Actress—Musical/Comedy (Andrews), Best Film—Musical/Comedy; National Board of Review Awards '65: 10 Best Films of the Year. VHS, Beta, LV $24.98 FOX, BTV, RDG

Sounder 🎞🎞🎞🎞

The struggles of a family of black sharecroppers in rural Louisiana during the Depression. When David's father is sentenced to jail for stealing to feed his family, they work even harder to survive, and David finds education a path out of poverty. Moving and well made, with little sentimentality and superb acting. Script neatly expands and defines the short source novel by William Armstrong. Sequel, "Part 2, Sounder," is not yet available on tape. **Hound Advisory:** Brief violence, with Sounder, the family hound, wounded by gunfire.
1972 (G/Jr. High-Adult) 105m/C Paul Winfield, Cicely Tyson, Kevin Hooks, Taj Mahal, Carmin Mathews, James Best, Janet MacLachlan; D: Martin Ritt; M: Taj Mahal. **Award Nominations:** Academy Awards '72: Best Actor (Winfield), Best Actress (Tyson), Best Adapted Screenplay, Best Picture; **Awards:** National Board of Review Awards '72: 10 Best Films of the Year; National Society of Film Critics Awards '72: Best Actress (Tyson). VHS, Beta, LV $14.95 KUI, PAR, PTB

Sourdough 🎞🎞

Fur trapper Perry escapes the hustle and bustle of modern life by fleeing to the Alaskan wilderness. Near-plotless travelogue depends heavily on scenery—and there's plenty of that.
1977 (Family) 94m/C Gil Perry, Charles Brock, Slim Carlson, Carl Clark; D: Martin J. Spinelli. VHS, Beta, LV $89.95 IMP

South Pacific 🎞🎞🎞◁

Young American Navy nurse and a Frenchman fall in love during WWII. Expensive production included much location shooting in Hawaii. Based on Rodgers and Hammerstein's musical; not as good as the play, but still pretty darn entertaining. The play in turn was based on James Michener's novel "Tales of the South Pacific." ♫My Girl Back Home; Dites-Moi; Bali Ha'i; Happy Talk; A Cockeyed Optimist; Soliloquies; Some Enchanted Evening; Bloody Mary; I'm Gonna Wash That Man Right Out of My Hair.
1958 (Family) 167m/C Mitzi Gaynor, Rossano Brazzi, Ray Walston, France Nuyen, John Kerr, Juanita Hall, Tom Laughlin; D: Joshua Logan; M: Richard Rodgers, Oscar Hammerstein; V: Giorgio Tozzi. **Award Nominations:** Academy Awards '56: Best Color Cinematography; Academy Awards '58: Best Original Score; **Awards:** Academy Awards '58: Best Sound. VHS, Beta, LV $19.98 FOX, RDG, HMV

Space Angel, Vol. 1

Some folks now look back with nostalgia on this ultra-cheap TV cartoon made with a process called 'Syncro-Vox': live actors' lips were filmed over the faces of the 'toon characters to save drawing the mouth movements when they talked. Similar money-saving touches pervade this tale of Space Agent Scott McCloud attempting to retrieve a solar panel stolen by aliens. Additional volumes available.
1964 *(Primary)* 50m/C **VHS, Beta $29.95** *FHE, WTA, STP*

Space Battleship Yamato

One of Japan's most popular cartoon TV shows is this lavishly animated saga, slightly reminiscent of "Battlestar Galactica," detailing the heroic star cruiser Yamato, in a running battle with alien blue meanies as they search for their lost homeworld of Earth. Available in 77 (aieeee!) half-hour cassettes, plus five two-hour theatrical feature spinoffs.
1983 *(Preschool-Jr. High)* 30m/C **VHS $17.95** *WTA*

Space Firebird 🐾🐾

Peculiar Japanese animated feature, a somewhat unpalatable mix of mysticism, mythology, and Lucasfilm. Greedy rulers of a dying Earth send star pilot Gordo off to capture a dangerous, shape-changing space phoenix, to exploit as an energy source. Some spectacular scenes of destruction, plus overly familiar environmental sermons. Loses half a bone for really lousy English dubbing. **Hound Advisory:** Violence.
1980 *(Family)* 103m/C **VHS, Beta $14.99** *JFK, WTA*

Space Raiders 🐾

Plucky 10-year-old blasts off into a futuristic world of intergalactic desperados, crafty alien mercenaries, starship battles and cliff-hanging dangers. Recycled special effects (from producer Roger Corman's other, better "Battle Beyond the Stars") and plot (lifted near-whole from "Star Wars"). The same producer later filched scenes from this for "Andy and the Airwave Rangers!" **Hound Advisory:** Violence.
1983 *(PG/Jr. High-Adult)* 84m/C Vince Edwards, David Mendenhall; *D:* Howard R. Cohen. **VHS, Beta $19.98** *WAR*

Space Warriors: Battle for Earth Station S/1

Animated space fantasy for kids, from Japanese TV.
1987 *(Family)* 99m/C **VHS, Beta $14.99** *JFK, WTA*

Spaceballs 🐾🐾🐾

Parody of sci-fi blockbusters, especially "Star Wars." The planet Spaceball needs air (so will you, after some of the jokes) and its forces, led by short bad guy Dark Helmet, try to conquer a neighboring world. Insubstantial and sometimes raunchy, but the plethora of sight gags will appeal to kids in "Mad Magazine" style. Crazy characters include Candy as the friendly "mog" -half man, half dog (a Chewbacca takeoff) and Brooks in two roles, one of them puny wise man/wise guy

Yogurt. **Hound Advisory:** Salty space/Brooks language, sex talk.
1987 *(PG/Jr. High-Adult)* 96m/C Mel Brooks, Rick Moranis, John Candy, Bill Pullman, Daphne Zuniga, Dick Van Patten, John Hurt, George Wyner, Joan Rivers, Lorene Yarnell, Sal Viscuso, Stephen Tobolowsky, Dom DeLuise, Michael Winslow; *D:* Mel Brooks; *W:* Mel Brooks, Ronny Graham, Thomas Meehan; *M:* John Morris. **VHS, Beta, LV $14.95** *MGM*

SpaceCamp 🐾🐾

Misfit kids and their adult instructor from the real-life NASA Space Camp in Alabama strap into a genuine space shuttle during a field trip. Suddenly the usual cute little robot friend tricks Ground Control into launching them into space, a field trip indeed. The kids must find the confidence and teamwork to return to Earth, a big challenge for anyone. Potentially exciting plot crashes thanks to hokey treatment, subpar special effects, predictably 'inspirational' moments, but younger kids might enjoy. **Hound Advisory:** Salty space language.
1986 *(PG/Jr. High-Adult)* 115m/C Kate Capshaw, Tate Donovan, Leaf (Joaquin Rafael) Phoenix, Kelly Preston, Larry B. Scott, Tom Skerritt, Lea Thompson, Terry O'Quinn; *D:* Harry Winer; *M:* John Williams. **VHS, Beta, LV $29.98** *LIV, VES, IME*

Spaced Invaders 🐾🐾

Ship full of little green Martians is sent to an alien war but mistakenly lands in rural Illinois. It's Halloween, and the five bumbling would-be conquerors are mistaken for kiddie trick-or-treaters. Earth children know the truth: "They're not bad, just stupid." The same may be said for the film, a Disney co-production (through Touchstone) that undiscriminating kids might like but is just too loud and repetitive for anyone else. **Hound Advisory:** Lots of bathroom/potty jokes; otherwise G-level.
1990 *(PG/Jr. High-Adult)* 102m/C Douglas Barr, Royal Dano, Ariana Richards, Kevin Thompson, Jimmy Briscoe, Tony Cox, Debbie Lee Carrington, Tommy Madden; *D:* Patrick Read Johnson. **VHS, Beta, LV $14.99** *TOU, BVV*

Spaceketeers 🐾🐾

Japanese animation highlights this multi-cassette sci-fi saga in which an army of mutant invaders overrun a peaceful solar system. Opposing them are the lovely Princess Aurora (who looks about as oriental as General Douglas MacArthur) and her kung-fu cyborg sidekick Jesse Dart. Several volumes of individual episodes from the TV show are available. **Hound Advisory:** Roughhousing.
1982 *(Family)* 100m/C **VHS, Beta $17.98** *FHE, WTA, TPV*

Spaceship 🐾🍸

Misguided attempt to spoof creature-features. Mad scientist tries to protect kindly monster from crazed crew. Not very funny, with the exception of the song-and-dance routine by the monster.
1981 *(PG/Jr. High-Adult)* 88m/C Cindy Williams, Bruce Kimmel, Leslie Nielsen, Gerrit Graham, Patrick Macnee, Ron Kurowski; *D:* Bruce Kimmel. **VHS $69.98** *LIV*

The hills are alive with "The Sound of Music" (1965)

Sparky's Magic Piano

Cartoon (adapted from a famous kids' record) in which a magic piano grants a little boy who doesn't practice the ability to play like a master. But in the end Sparky learns a lesson in modesty and tact.

1988 *(Family)* 51m/C **VHS, Beta $14.95** *FHE, WTA*

Speaking of Animals, Vol. 1

Modern compilation of vintage novelty shorts from the '30s and '40s, with different kinds of animals in funny situations — often singing and talking thanks to animated lips expertly superimposed and synced with recordings of famous celebrities. Still quite a riot.

1983 *(Family)* 60m/C **VHS, Beta $19.95** *FHE*

Special Valentine with Family Circus

Cartoonist Bill Keane's comic-strip characters come to life in a special Valentine's Day program that has the kids trying to outdo each other for the best valentine. Also known as "A Family Circus Valentine."

1980 *(Family)* 30m/C **VHS, Beta $9.95** *FHE*

Speed 🐾🐾🐾⟀

Excellent dude Reeves has grown up (and bulked up) as Los Angeles SWAT cop Jack Traven, up against bomb expert Howard Payne (Hopper, bringing a special glee to his usual mania) who's after major ransom money. First it's a rigged elevator in a very tall building. Then it's a rigged bus - if it slows, it will blow, bad enough any day, but a nightmare in LA traffic. And that's still not the end. Terrific directorial debut for cinematographer De Bont, who certainly knows how to keep the adrenaline pumping. Fine support work by Daniels, Bullock, and Morton and enough wit in Yost's script to keep you chuckling. Great nonstop actioner from the "Die Hard" school. **Hound Advisory:** Violence and profanity.

1994 **(R/** *Sr. High-Adult)* 115m/C Keanu Reeves, Dennis Hopper, Sandra Bullock, Joe Morton, Jeff Daniels, Alan Ruck, Glenn Plummer, Richard Lineback, Beth Grant, Hawthorne James, David Kriegel, Carlos Carrasco, Natsuko Ohama, Daniel Villarreal; **D:** Jan De Bont; **W:** Graham Yost; **M:** Mark Mancina. **VHS $19.98** *FXV*

Speed Racer

Adult cult of admirers has lately joined the kiddie fans of this popular cartoon that originated in Japan. Speed Racer drives the fast, futuristic, jumping Mach-5 race car, and competes in various races that get them both in perilous escapades worldwide. Tapes are available individually.

1967 *(Family)* 30m/C **VHS $9.98** *WTA, TPV*

Spellbound 🐾🐾🐾⟀

Psychological thriller stars Peck as an amnesia victim accused of murder. Bergman is the icy psychiatrist who uncovers his past through Freudian analysis and ends up falling in love with him. One of Hitchcock's finest films of the 1940s, with a riveting dream sequence designed by Salvador Dali. Full of classic Hitchcock plot twists and Freudian imagery. Based on Francis Bleeding's novel "The House of Dr. Edwardes."

1945 *(Jr. High-Adult)* 111m/B Ingrid Bergman, Gregory Peck, Leo G. Carroll, Michael Chekhov, Wallace Ford, Rhonda Fleming, Regis Toomey; **D:** Alfred Hitchcock; **M:** Miklos Rozsa. **Award Nominations:** Academy Awards '45: Best Actor (Chekhov), Best Black and White Cinematography, Best Director (Hitchcock), Best Picture; **Awards:** Academy Awards '45: Best Score. **VHS, Beta, LV $19.98** *FOX, IME, TLF*

Spider-Woman

Stan Lee, creator of Spiderman, also came up with this, so that's why there's been no spider-lawsuit. Magazine editor Jessica Drew turns into the heroic Spider-Woman to take on a slew of criminals, super and otherwise, in these respun TV cartoons.

1985 *(Family)* 60m/C **VHS, Beta $19.95** *MCA, WTA*

Spiderman

Two volumes of episodes from a brief prime-time TV series that brought the famous Marvel Comics superhero to very temporary life. Spidey saves the world from global terrorism and thwarts political plots in the sets "Night of the Clones/Escort to Danger" and "Con Caper/Curse of Rava."

1981 *(Preschool-Primary)* 90m/C Nicholas Hammond, Morgan Fairchild, Lloyd Bochner, Barbara Luna, Theodore Bikel. **VHS, Beta** *PSM*

Spiderman & His Amazing Friends: Origin of the Spider Friends

Marvel superheroes meet as teenagers and form a crime-fighting alliance in this Saturday-morning TV cartoon.

1983 *(Family)* 24m/C **VHS $14.95** *WTA*

Spiderman: The Deadly Dust

Feature-length episode from the mediocre "Spiderman" live-action TV program, in which the Marvel Comics superhero tries to save New York from a city-destroying plutonium accident.

1978 *(Family)* 93m/C Nicholas Hammond, Robert F. Simon, Chip Fields; **D:** Ron Satlof. **VHS, Beta** *FOX*

Spiderman, Vol. 1: Dr. Doom

Spiderman takes on the ultimate super villain, Dr. Doom, in this animated adventure. Additional volumes available.

1981 *(Family)* 22m/C **VHS, Beta $14.99** *BFV, WTA*

Spies Like Us 🐾🐾⟀

Space fantasy in which two pilots from warring planets, crash land on a barren planet and are forced to work together to survive. Relationship is further complicated due to one being an Earthling and the other an asexual reptilian Drac. On the surface it's a story of developing friendship and trust between two very different beings; underneath are some muddled big ideas about the nature of it all. **Hound Advisory:** Violence and profanity.

1985 **(PG/** *Jr. High-Adult)* 103m/C Chevy Chase, Dan Aykroyd, Steve Forrest, Bruce Davison, William Prince, Bernie Casey, Tom Hatton, Donna Dixon, Frank Oz; **Cameos:** Michael Apted, Constantin Costa-Gavras, Terry Gilliam, Ray Harryhausen, Joel Coen, Martin Brest, Bob Swaim; **D:** John Landis; **W:** Dan Aykroyd, Lowell Ganz, Babaloo Mandel; **M:** Elmer Bernstein. **VHS, Beta, LV $19.98** *WAR*

Daryl Hannah makes a "Splash" (1984)

Spiral Zone: Ride the Whirlwind

Two episodes of the animated toy-inspired cartoon series, "The Unexploded Pod" and the title episode.
1987 (*Preschool-Primary*) 45m/C **VHS, Beta $14.95** *FHE, WTA*

Spiral Zone: Zone of Darkness

The Spiral Force meets with corruption in sci-fi scoundrels. Includes "Small Packages," "King of the Skies," and "Holographic Zone Battles."
1987 (*Family*) 86m/C **VHS, Beta $29.95** *FHE, WTA*

Spirit of the Eagle 🦴🦴

Man and young son wander in mountains and make friends with feathered creature. Then boy is kidnapped, creating problems for dad. Somnolent nature fare.
1990 (*PG/Jr. High-Adult*) 93m/C Dan Haggerty, Bill Smith, Don Shanks, Jeri Arrendondo, Trever Yarrish; *D:* Boon Collins; *W:* Boon Collins. **VHS, LV** *SGE, IME*

Spirit of the Eagle

In the wilds of Alaska a young boy and his pals witness the beauty and majesty of the American bald eagle. Part of the Miramar "Legends" series about fauna of the Pacific North-

west, accompanied by "Gift of the Whales" and "Winter Wolf."
1990 (*Primary-Sr. High*) 30m/C **VHS, Beta $19.95** *MIR, MLT, VPJ*

Splash 🦴🦴🦴◁

Beautiful mermaid ventures into New York City in search of the grown-up man she encountered at the seashore while they were both children. Growing legs, she seeks out lucky but bewildered Hanks, who can't figure out why his dream girl acts so odd -and eats raw lobsters whole at fancy restaurants. Charming, wide-eyed adult fairy tale (mildly racy content makes it an iffy choice for small kids), a winner that was among the first flicks from Disney's fledgling Touchstone division. **Hound Advisory:** Sex, nudity (none of it truly vulgar), salty language.
1984 (*PG/Family*) 109m/C Tom Hanks, Daryl Hannah, Eugene Levy, John Candy, Dody Goodman, Shecky Greene, Richard B. Shull, Bobby DiCicco, Howard Morris; *D:* Ron Howard; *W:* Babaloo Mandel, Lowell Ganz. **VHS, Beta, LV, 8mm $79.95** *TOU, BVV*

Spook Busters 🦴🦴◁

The Bowery Boys take jobs as exterminators, only to find themselves assigned the unenviable task of ridding a haunted house of ghosts. To make matters worse, the resident mad scientist wants to transplant Sach's brain into a gorilla. Essential viewing for anyone who thought "Ghostbusters" was an original story.

1946 (*Family*) 68m/B Leo Gorcey, Huntz Hall, Douglass Dumbrille, Bobby Jordan, Gabriel Dell, Billy Benedict, David Gorcey, Bernard Gorcey, Tanis Chandler, Maurice Cass, Charles Middleton; **D:** William Beaudine. **VHS $14.98** *WAR, GPV*

Spooks Run Wild 🎞🎞⚁

Early "Bowery Boys" comedy (back when the troupe was also known as the East Side Kids), with the comical band of overgrown urchins seeking refuge in an eerie mansion owned by Lugosi, secretly a Nazi spy. A fun horror-comedy, with the kids' antics playing off Lugosi's menace quite well.

1941 (*Family*) 64m/B Huntz Hall, Leo Gorcey, Bobby Jordan, Sammy Morrison, Dave O'Brien, Dennis Moore, Bela Lugosi; **D:** Phil Rosen; **W:** Carl Foreman. **VHS, Beta $19.95** *NOS, SNC, VYY*

Spot Goes to the Farm

Features Spot the puppy, from the interactive book series by Eric Hill, in five fun stories including "Spot Goes to the Farm," "Spot Sleeps Over," "Spot Goes to the Circus," "Spot's Windy Day," and "Spot Goes to the Park." The cassette box features the trademark hide-and-seek activities from the books. See also "Where's Spot?"

1993 (*Preschool*) 30m/C **VHS $14.99** *BVV, BTV*

Spy Smasher 🎞🎞🎞

Considered by serial fans to be one of the very finest, this stars a popular comic-book hero of the era, a war reporter who used his supposed death in a plane crash (and a convenient twin brother) to go underground and fight Nazi counterfeiters trying to wreck the economy. Most serials end with a cliffhanger; this 12-episode chapter play begins with one, and takes off from there. Fast and stylish, with "Beethoven's Fifth Symphony" as a theme song because the opening notes coincided with the Allied 'V for victory' Morse code signal. "Spy Smasher Returns," also on tape, isn't a sequel but a feature-length condensed version. **Hound Advisory:** Violence.

1942 (*Family*) 185m/B Kane Richmond, Marguerite Chapman, Sam Flint, Hans Schumm, Tristram Coffin; **D:** William Witney. **VHS $29.95** *REP*

The Spy Who Loved Me 🎞🎞

James Bond teams up with female Russian Agent XXX to squash a villain's plan to use captured American and Russian atomic submarines in a plot to destroy the world. The villain's henchman, 7-foot, 2-inch Kiel, is the steel-toothed Jaws. Carly Simon sings the memorable, Marvin Hamlisch theme song, "Nobody Does It Better." **Hound Advisory:** Violence, alcohol use, suggested sex.

1977 (*PG/Sr. High-Adult*) 136m/C Roger Moore, Barbara Bach, Curt Jurgens, Richard Kiel, Caroline Munro, Walter Gotell, Geoffrey Keen, Valerie Leon, Bernard Lee, Lois Maxwell, Desmond Llewelyn; **D:** Lewis Gilbert; **M:** Marvin Hamlisch. **VHS, Beta, LV $19.98** *MGM, FOX, TLF*

Squanto and the First Thanksgiving

More storybook-than-animated version of a true story about the Indian who was sold into slavery in Spain, returned to

North America, and helped the Pilgrims survive their first severe years at the Plymouth colony. Narrated by Native American actor Greene.

1993 (*Family*) 30m/C **VHS $9.98** *BTV,*

Square Dance 🎞🎞⚁

Thirteen-year-old Gemma leaves her childhood Texas farm to live in the city with her promiscuous mother, whose somewhat randy circle of friends test the girl's Bible-quoting innocence. Slow-moving but superbly acted tale of self-discovery, based on a novel by Alan Hines. **Hound Advisory:** Sex, profanity, mature themes.

1987 (*PG-13/Jr. High-Adult*) 118m/C Jane Alexander, Jason Robards Jr., Rob Lowe, Winona Ryder, Deborah Richter, Guich Koock, Elbert Lewis; **D:** Daniel Petrie; **W:** Alan Hines; **M:** Bruce Broughton. **VHS, Beta, LV** *NO*

Squiddly Diddly

Compilation of obscure "Squiddly Diddly" cartoons, about a star-struck squid hoping to break into show business.

196? (*Family*) 55m/C **VHS, Beta $19.95** *TTC, WTA*

Stacking 🎞🎞

1950s Montana family is threatened with losing their farm when father is injured. Mother struggles on, despite conflicting emotions, and the whole thing is told through the eyes of the 14-year-old daughter, played by "Anne of Green Gables" star Follows. Slow-paced agri-drama, aided by acting, blighted by boredom. **Hound Advisory:** Mature themes, alcohol use, salty language.

1987 (*PG/Jr. High-Adult*) 111m/C Christine Lahti, Megan Follows, Frederic Forrest, Peter Coyote, Jason Gedrick; **D:** Martin Rosen; **M:** Patrick Gleeson. **VHS, Beta, LV $14.95** *NLC*

Stage Fright 🎞🎞🎞

Wyman will stop at nothing to clear her old boyfriend, who has been accused of murdering the husband of his mistress, an actress (Dietrich). Disguised as a maid, she falls in love with the investigating detective, and discovers her friend's guilt. Dietrich sings "The Laziest Gal in Town" and "La Vie en Rose." The Master's last film made in England until "Frenzy" (1971).

1950 (*Jr. High-Adult*) 110m/B Jane Wyman, Marlene Dietrich, Alastair Sim, Sybil Thorndike, Michael Wilding, Kay Walsh; **D:** Alfred Hitchcock. **VHS, Beta, LV $19.98** *WAR, MLB*

Stand and Deliver 🎞🎞🎞⚁

True story of Jaime Escalante, a tough but caring teacher who inspired hard-luck students in an East L.A. barrio to take the Advanced Placement Test in calculus. His ghetto pupils score so well that authorities suspect mass cheating, and the class must vindicate themselves. Not just a nudge to do your math homework but a clarion call to excellence and self-esteem, with a wonderful performance from Olmos. **Hound Advisory:** Profanity.

1988 (*PG/Jr. High-Adult*) 105m/C Edward James Olmos, Lou Diamond Phillips, Rosana De Soto, Andy Garcia, Will Gotay, Ingrid Oliu, Virginia Paris, Mark Eliot; **D:** Ramon Menendez; **W:** Tom Musca, Ramon Menendez; **M:** Craig Safan. **Award Nominations:** Academy Awards '88: Best Actor (Olmos); **Awards:** Independent Spirit Awards '89: Best Actor (Olmos), Best Director (Menendez), Best Film, Best

Screenplay, Best Supporting Actor (Phillips), Best Supporting Actress (De Soto).
VHS, LV, 8mm $19.98 *WAR, HMV*

Stand By Me 🎬🎬🎬

Observant adaptation of the Stephen King novella "The Body," one of the bestselling author's few well known non-horror tales. Four 12-year-olds in 1960 trek into the Oregon wilderness to find the body of a missing boy, learning about death and personal courage. Told as a reminiscence by narrator Dreyfuss with solid performances from all four child actors. Much R-rated obscene language may render this a turnoff for most families, which is too bad; there's some fine stuff here, like the riotous fireside discussion about the exact species of Disney's Goofy. **Hound Advisory:** Profanity - loads of it - plus mature themes, threatened violence.
1986 (R/Jr. High-Adult) 87m/C River Phoenix, Wil Wheaton, Jerry O'Connell, Corey Feldman, Kiefer Sutherland, Richard Dreyfuss, Casey Siemaszko, John Cusack; **D:** Rob Reiner; **W:** Raynold Gideon; **M:** Jack Nitzsche. **VHS, Beta, LV, 8mm $14.95** *COL*

Stand Up and Cheer 🎬🎬🎵

The new federal Secretary of Entertainment organizes a huge show to raise the country's depressed spirits. Near-invisible plot, fantastic premise are an excuse for lots of imagery, dancing, and comedy, including four-year-old Temple singing "Baby Take a Bow." Also available colorized. 🎵 I'm Laughing; We're Out of the Red; Broadway's Gone Hillbilly; Baby Take a Bow; This Is Our Last Night Together; She's Way Up Thar; Stand Up and Cheer.
1934 (Family) 80m/B Shirley Temple, Warner Baxter, Madge Evans, Nigel Bruce, Stepin Fetchit, Frank Melton, Lila Lee, James Dunn, John Boles, Scotty Beckett; **D:** Hamilton MacFadden; **W:** Will Rogers, Ralph Spence. **VHS, Beta $19.98** *FOX*

Stanley and the Dinosaurs

Stanley the progressive caveman is banished from his tribe until they see the usefulness of his new inventions. Based on "Stanley" by Syd Hoff.
1989 (Primary) 16m/C **VHS, Beta $325.00** *CHF*

Stanley the Ugly Duckling

Stanley the aesthetically-challenged juvenile waterfowl and his fox friend Nathan learn that what is inside counts more than appearance in this cartoon variant of Hans Christian Andersen, from the portentously-named "I Like Myself Productions."
1982 (Preschool-Primary) 27m/C **V:** Rick Dees, Wolfman Jack. **VHS $12.98** *FHE*

Star Fairies

Sickly sweet Hanna-Barbera cartoon about ethereal beings Spice, Nightsong, Jazz, True Love, and Whisper (sound like colognes) who grant children's wishes under the direction of Princess Sparkle.
1985 (Preschool) 40m/C **V:** Jonathan Winters, Didi Conn, Howard Morris, Arte Johnson. **VHS, Beta $12.95** *FHE, WTA*

Star Street: Adventures of the Star Kids

The Star Kids embark on an exciting new adventure. Cosmic cartoon, not to be confused with either "Star Trek" or "Sesame Street."
1989 (Preschool-Jr. High) 80m/C **VHS $39.95** *WTA*

Star Street: The Happy Birthday Movie

The Star Kids star in a warmed-over cartoon collection.
1989 (Family) 85m/C **VHS $39.95** *JFK, WSH, WTA*

Star Trek: The Motion Picture 🎬🎬🎵

The Enterprise fights a strange alien force that threatens Earth in this first film adaptation of the famous television series. Slow cruise through the universe is best appreciated by fans of the TV series. Twelve additional minutes of previously unseen footage have been added to this home video version of the theatrical feature. Laserdisc edition in widescreen format is also available. Numerous sequels.
1980 (G/Family) 143m/C William Shatner, Leonard Nimoy, DeForest Kelley, James Doohan, Stephen Collins, Persis Khambatta, Nichelle Nichols, Walter Koenig, George Takei; **D:** Robert Wise; **M:** Jerry Goldsmith. **VHS, Beta, LV $14.95** *PAR*

Star Trek 2: The Wrath of Khan 🎬🎬🎬

Picking up from the 1967 Star Trek episode "Space Seed," Admiral James T. Kirk and the crew of the Enterprise must battle Khan, an old foe out for revenge. Warm and comradly in the nostalgic mode of its successors. Introduced Kirk's former lover and unknown son to the series plot, as well as Mr. Spock's "death," which led to the next sequel (1984's "The Search for Spock"). Can be seen in widescreen format on laserdisc. **Hound Advisory:** Violence and gore.
1982 (PG/Family) 113m/C William Shatner, Leonard Nimoy, Ricardo Montalban, DeForest Kelley, Nichelle Nichols, James Doohan, George Takei, Walter Koenig, Kirstie Alley, Merritt Butrick, Paul Winfield; **D:** Nicholas Meyer; **M:** James Horner. **VHS, Beta, LV, 8mm $14.95** *PAR*

Star Trek 3: The Search for Spock 🎬🎬🎵

Captain Kirk hijacks the USS Enterprise and commands the aging crew to go on a mission to the Genesis Planet to discover whether Mr. Spock still lives (supposedly he died in the last movie). Klingons threaten, as usual. Somewhat slow and humorless, but intriguing. Third in the series of six (so far) Star Trek movies. The laserdisc edition carries the film in widescreen format.
1984 (PG/Family) 105m/C William Shatner, Leonard Nimoy, DeForest Kelley, James Doohan, George Takei, Walter Koenig, Mark Lenard, Robin Curtis, Merritt Butrick, Christopher Lloyd, Judith Anderson, John Larroquette, James B. Sikking, Nichelle Nichols, Cathie Shirriff, Miguel Ferrer, Grace Lee Whitney; **D:** Leonard Nimoy; **M:** James Horner. **VHS, Beta, LV, 8mm $14.95** *PAR*

Star Trek 4: The Voyage Home 🐾🐾🐾

Kirk and the gang go back in time (to the 1980s, conveniently) to save the Earth of the future from destruction. Filled with hilarious moments and exhilarating action; great special effects enhance the timely conservation theme. Watch for the stunning going-back-in-time sequence. Spock is particularly funny as he tries to fit in and learn 80s lingo. Best of the "Trek" series is available in widescreen format on laserdisc and as part of Paramount's "director's series," in which Nimoy discusses various special effects aspects. **Hound Advisory:** Salty language.

1986 (PG/Jr. High-Adult**)** 119m/C William Shatner, DeForest Kelley, Catherine Hicks, James Doohan, Nichelle Nichols, George Takei, Walter Koenig, Mark Lenard, Leonard Nimoy; **D:** Leonard Nimoy; **W:** Nicholas Meyer. **VHS, Beta, LV, 8mm $14.95** PAR

Star Trek 5: The Final Frontier 🐾🐾

A renegade Vulcan kidnaps the Enterprise and takes it on a journey to the mythic center of the universe. Shatner's big-action directorial debut (he also co-wrote the script) is a poor follow-up to the Nimoy-directed fourth entry in the series. Heavy-handed and pretentiously pseudo-theological. Available in widescreen format on laserdisc. **Hound Advisory:** Profanity, roughhousing.

1989 (PG/Primary-Adult**)** 107m/C William Shatner, Leonard Nimoy, DeForest Kelley, James Doohan, Laurence Luckinbill, Walter Koenig, George Takei, Nichelle Nichols, David Warner; **D:** William Shatner; **W:** William Shatner; **M:** Jerry Goldsmith. **VHS, Beta, LV, 8mm $14.95** PAR

Star Trek 6: The Undiscovered Country 🐾🐾🐾

The final chapter in the long running Star Trek series is finally here. The Federation and the Klingon Empire are preparing a much-needed peace summit but Captain Kirk has his doubts about the true intentions of the Federation's longtime enemies. When a Klingon ship is attacked, Kirk and the crew of the Enterprise, who are accused of the misdeed, must try to find the real perpetrator. Has an exciting, climactic ending. As is typical of the series, the film highlights current events-glasnost—in its plotlines. Meyer also directed Star Trek movies 2 ("The Wrath of Khan") and 4 ("The Voyage Home"). **Hound Advisory:** Violence.

1991 (PG/Jr. High-Adult**)** 110m/C William Shatner, Leonard Nimoy, DeForest Kelley, James Doohan, George Takei, Walter Koenig, Nichelle Nichols, Christopher Plummer, Kim Cattrall, Iman, David Warner, Mark Lenard, Grace Lee Whitney, Brock Peters, Kurtwood Smith, Rosana De Soto, John Schuck, Michael Dorn; **D:** Nicholas Meyer; **W:** Nicholas Meyer, Denny Martin; **M:** Cliff Eidelman. **VHS, Beta, CD-I $14.95** PAR

Star Trek: Animated, Vol. 1

Episodes of an Emmy-winning Saturday-morning cartoon revival of the classic "Star Trek" series, utilizing the voices of the original cast, with fair animation, literate scripts, and general quality control that made these respectable additions to Starfleet lore. Volume 1 includes "More Tribbles, More Troubles" and "The Infinite Vulcan." Additional volumes available.

1973 (Family**)** 48m/C **V:** William Shatner, Leonard Nimoy, DeForest Kelley, James Doohan, Nichelle Nichols, George Takei, Walter Koenig, Majel Barrett. **VHS $12.95** PAR, WTA

Star Trek the Next Generation Episode 1-2: Encounter at Farpoint

Gene Roddenberry, the creator of the original "Star Trek" television series, spearheaded this episodic reincarnation for network syndication. This series, set 80 or so years beyond the original, enjoys an entirely new crew and a modernized vessel. Also, the new series places less emphasis on violent solutions to conflicts than the original TV series. In this first installment, entitled "Encounter at Farpoint, Parts 1 and 2," a powerful life force named "Q" threatens the lives of Captain Jean-Luc Picard and his crew as they attempt to figure out what's going on at Farpoint Station. Look for a cameo appearance by DeForest Kelly, "Bones" from the original series, as a very old man waxing nostalgic about the old U.S.S. Enterprise. Excellent production values, including fine special effects. Additional episodes available. Further volumes of episodes are continually being released on video.

1987 (Family**)** 96m/C Patrick Stewart, Michael Dorn, Jonathon Frakes, Gates McFadden, Marina Sirtis, Denise Crosby, Brent Spiner, Wil Wheaton, LeVar Burton; **Cameos:** DeForest Kelley; **W:** Gene Roddenberry. **VHS, LV $19.95** PAR, MOV

Star Wars 🐾🐾🐾🐾

First of Lucas' "Star Wars" trilogy and one of the biggest box-office hits of all time, drawing successfully on both fairy tale and sci-fi traditions. Yarn looks for spins on the old cliches until it all clicks as an epic original: the young hero, captured princess, hot-shot pilot, cute robots, demonic villain, and a wizard-like old Jedi knight. Storyline and characterizations blend together with marvelous f/x to make you care about the rebel forces engaged in a life-or-death struggle with the tyrant leaders of the Galactic Empire. Followed by superior "The Empire Strikes Back" (1980) and "Return of the Jedi" (1983). **Hound Advisory:** Battle scenes, other space-induced violence.

1977 (PG/Family**)** 121m/C Mark Hamill, Carrie Fisher, Harrison Ford, Alec Guinness, Peter Cushing, Kenny Baker, James Earl Jones, David Prowse, Anthony Daniels; **D:** George Lucas; **W:** George Lucas; **M:** John Williams. **Award Nominations:** Academy Awards '77: Best Director (Lucas), Best Original Screenplay, Best Picture, Best Supporting Actor (Guinness); **Awards:** Academy Awards '77: Best Art Direction/Set Decoration, Best Costume Design, Best Film Editing, Best Sound, Best Visual Effects, Best Original Score; Golden Globe Awards '78: Best Score; Los Angeles Film Critics Association Awards '77: Best Film; National Board of Review Awards '77: 10 Best Films of the Year; People's Choice Awards '78: Best Film. **VHS, Beta, LV $19.98** FOX, RDG, HMV

Starbird and Sweet William 🐾🐾

On a solo plane flight, a young Native American crashes in the wilderness. He must fight for survival in the harsh woods with his only friend, a bear cub. Fair family nature adventure, also known as "The Adventures of Starbird."

1973 (G/Family**)** 95m/C A. Martinez, Louise Fitch, Dan Haggerty, Skip Homeier; **D:** Jack B. Hively. **VHS $79.95** VCI

Starchaser: The Legend of Orin 🎬🎬

Animated fantasy about heroic young cyborg Orin, who combats galactic pirates to save the world of the future. Strictly Saturday-morning TV-quality, but inexplicably released to theaters.
1985 (**PG**/*Jr. High-Adult*) 107m/C **D:** Steven Hahn. **VHS, Beta, LV $14.95** *PAR*

Starcom: Galactic Adventures

TV-cartoon adventures of future heroes fighting the antisocial Emperor Dark. In "Fire and Ice," Slim and Crowbar crash on the volcanic moon. A defense satellite malfunctions and turns deadly in "The Long Fall," and in "The Caverns of Mars," Slim's niece and nephew get trapped in an underground city on Mars.
1987 (*Primary-Jr. High*) 66m/C **VHS $24.95** *WTA*

Starman 🎬🎬🎬🎬

Peaceful alien from an advanced civilization lands in Wisconsin. Employing state-of-the-art alien analysis, he decides to hide beneath the guise of a grieving young widow's recently deceased husband. Pleased with that idea, star guy then makes the widow drive him across country with the government in pursuit so he can rendezvous with his spacecraft. On the road together, they get to know each other. Well-acted, carefully directed sci-fi romance with a road flick running through it (don't see too many of those) brings an interesting twist to the "Stranger in a Strange Land" theme. Bridges is engaging as the likeable starman in wonder at what Wisconsin (and the rest of the planet) has to offer, while Allen is lovely and earthy (just the thing for a guy from outer space), creating a one-of-a-kind romance. Available in widescreen format on laserdisc. **Hound Advisory:** Mature themes; sex; violence; profanity.
1984 (**PG**/*Jr. High-Adult*) 115m/C Jeff Bridges, Karen Allen, Charles Martin Smith, Richard Jaeckel; **D:** John Carpenter; **W:** Bruce A. Evans, Raynold Gideon; **M:** Jack Nitzsche. **VHS, Beta, LV $12.95** *COL*

Starship 🎬

Lame British/Australian "Star Wars" ripoff is about underaged human freedom fighters on a planet run by evil robots. Lorca and the Outlaws (pic's original title) have help from one cute little mechanical man in their fight for truth, justice, and the Lucasfilm way. Okay special effects, and that's it. **Hound Advisory:** Violence.
1987 (**PG**/*Jr. High-Adult*) 91m/C John Tarrant, Cassandra Webb, Donough Rees, Deep Roy, Ralph Cotterill; **D:** Roger Christian. **VHS, Beta** *HHE*

Starvengers

Animated adventures of the spacegoing robot Starvengers. Made in Japan-brand cartoonery.
1982 (*Family*) 105m/C **VHS, Beta $19.98** *FUS, WTA, FHE*

State Fair 🎬🎬🎬

The second version of the glossy slice of Americana about a family at the Iowa State Fair, featuring plenty of great songs by Rodgers and Hammerstein. The best of three versions, it was adapted by Hammerstein from the 1933 screen version of Phil Strong's novel. Remade again in 1962. 🎵It Might as Well Be Spring; It's a Grand Night for Singing; That's For Me; Isn't It Kinda Fun?; All I Owe Iowa; Our State Fair.
1945 (*Jr. High-Adult*) 100m/C Charles Winninger, Jeanne Crain, Dana Andrews, Vivian Blaine, Dick Haymes, Fay Bainter, Frank McHugh, Percy Kilbride, Donald Meek, William Marshall, Harry Morgan; **D:** Walter Lang; **W:** Oscar Hammerstein; **M:** Richard Rodgers, Oscar Hammerstein. **Award Nominations:** Academy Awards '45: Best Original Score; **Awards:** Academy Awards '45: Best Song ("It Might as Well Be Spring"). **VHS, Beta $19.98** *FOX*

State Fair 🎬🎬

Third film version of the story of a farm family who travel to their yearly state fair and experience life. The original songs are still there, but otherwise this is a letdown. Texas setting required dropping the song "All I Owe Iowa." 🎵Our State Fair; It's a Grand Night for Singing; That's for Me; It Might as Well Be Spring; Isn't It Kinda Fun?; More Than Just a Friend; It's the Little Things in Texas; Willing and Eager; This Isn't Heaven.
1962 (*Family*) 118m/C Pat Boone, Ann-Margret, Bobby Darin, Tom Ewell, Alice Faye, Pamela Tiffin, Wally Cox; **D:** Jose Ferrer. **VHS, Beta $19.98** *FOX*

Stay Tuned 🎬

Suburban yuppie couple buys a large-screen TV and satellite dish from Hellvision salesman, are sucked into their dish, and wind up starring in hellish TV shows such as "Wayne's Underworld," "Northern Overexposure," "Sadistic Home Videos," and "My Three Sons of Bitches." If they can survive for 24 hours, they'll be able to return to their normal lives. Clever idea for a film is wasted as this one never experiences good reception; viewers may not want to stay tuned to the low comedy and frantic yucks.
1992 (**PG-13**/*Jr. High-Adult*) 90m/C John Ritter, Pam Dawber, Jeffrey Jones, Eugene Levy, David Tom, Heather McComb; **D:** Peter Hyams; **W:** Tom S. Parker; **M:** Bruce Broughton. **VHS, LV $19.98** *WAR*

The Steadfast Tin Soldier

Beautifully illustrated (not animated) version of the classic Hans Christian Andersen fable, read aloud by British actor Irons as part of the "Rabbit Ears" series of videos from Random House.
1986 (*Preschool-Primary*) 30m/C **VHS, Beta $19.95** *KUI, RAN, VEC*

Steel Magnolias 🎬🎬🎬

Julia Roberts plays a young woman stricken with severe diabetes who chooses to live her life to the fullest despite her bad health. Much of the action centers around a Louisiana beauty shop where the women get together to discuss the goings-on of their lives. Screenplay by R. Harling, based on his partially autobiographical play. Sweet, poignant, and often hilarious, yet just as often overwrought. MacLaine is funny as a bitter divorcee; Parton is sexy and fun as the hairdresser. But Field and Roberts go off the deep end and make it all entirely too weepy. **Hound Advisory:** Brief profanity.
1989 (**PG**/*Jr. High-Adult*) 118m/C Sally Field, Dolly Parton, Shirley MacLaine, Daryl Hannah, Olympia Dukakis, Julia Roberts, Tom Skerritt, Sam Shepard, Dylan McDermott, Kevin J. O'Connor, Bil McCutcheon, Ann Wedgeworth, Janine Turner; **D:** Herbert Ross; **W:** Robert Harling; **M:** Georges Delerue. **Award Nominations:** Academy Awards '89: Best Supporting Actress (Wiest); **Awards:**

Golden Globe Awards '90: Best Supporting Actress (Roberts); People's Choice Awards '90: Best Film—Drama. **VHS, Beta, LV, 8mm $19.95** *COL*

Stepmonster ♂

Twelve-year-old Todd tries to convince anyone who'll listen that his dumb father's fiancee can change into a scaly forest beast. Childish and predictable junk, with barely a cool creature costume to recommend it. **Hound Advisory:** Profanity, violence (against monsters, mainly), sex talk.
1992 **(PG-13** / *Jr. High-Adult)* 84m/C Alan Thicke, Robin Riker, Corey Feldman, John Astin, Ami Dolenz, George Gaynes. **VHS $89.98** *NHO*

The Sting ♂♂♂♩

Newman and Redford together again in this sparkling story of a pair of con artists in 1930s Chicago. They set out to fleece a big-time racketeer, pitting brain against brawn and pistol. Very inventive, excellent acting, Scott Joplin's wonderful ragtime music adapted by Marvin Hamlisch. The same directorial and acting team from "Butch Cassidy and the Sundance Kid" triumphs again.
1973 **(PG** / *Jr. High-Adult)* 129m/C Paul Newman, Robert Redford, Robert Shaw, Charles Durning, Eileen Brennan, Harold Gould, Ray Walston; *D:* George Roy Hill; *W:* David S. Ward; *M:* Marvin Hamlisch. **Award Nominations:** Academy Awards '73: Best Actor (Redford), Best Cinematography, Best Sound; **Awards:** Academy Awards '73: Best Adapted Score, Best Art Direction/Set Decoration, Best Costume Design, Best Director (Hill), Best Film Editing, Best Picture, Best Story & Screenplay; Directors Guild of America Awards '73: Best Director (Hill); People's Choice Awards '75: Best Film. **VHS, Beta, LV $14.95** *MCA, BTV*

The Sting 2 ♂♩

Complicated comic plot concludes with the final con game, involving a fixed boxing match where the stakes top a million dollars and the payoff could be murder. Lame sequel to "The Sting." **Hound Advisory:** Violence.
1983 **(PG** / *Family)* 102m/C Jackie Gleason, Mac Davis, Teri Garr, Karl Malden, Oliver Reed; *D:* Jeremy Paul Kagan; *W:* David S. Ward. **VHS, Beta, LV $19.98** *MCA*

Stingiest Man in Town

The cartoon bear gets more than he bargained for in this birthday adventure. Additional volumes available.
1978 *(Family-Family)* 50m/C *V:* Tom Bosley, Walter Matthau, Paul Frees, Theodore Bikel, Robert Morse, Dennis Day. **VHS $12.95** *WAR*

Stingray: Invaders of the Deep

Spinoff of the popular British puppet TV adventure "Thunderbirds," this tale acted by marionettes depicts the fearless (and expressionless) Captain Tempest leading his futuristic submarine, "Stingray," against the aliens invading Marineville. More cool special f/x from Gerry Anderson.
1981 *(Preschool-Primary)* 92m/C *D:* David Elliott, John Kelly, Desmond Saunders. **VHS, Beta, LV** *FHE*

The Stone Boy ♂♂♂♩

Boy accidentally shoots and kills his older brother in a hunting accident near their Montana farm. The family is torn apart by sadness and guilt. Sensitive, unflinching look at him and other family members reacting to the most personal of tragedies, with an excellent cast led by Duvall's crystal-clear perfor-

mance. Script by Gina Berriault; based on her short story. **Hound Advisory:** Violence, mature themes.
1984 **(PG** / *Jr. High-Adult)* 93m/C Glenn Close, Robert Duvall, Jason Presson, Frederic Forrest, Wilford Brimley, Linda Hamilton; *D:* Christopher Cain; *M:* James Horner. **VHS, Beta $59.98** *FOX*

Stone Fox ♂♂

Wyoming, 1905. Following his grandfather's stroke, 12-year-old orphan Willy's only hope for saving the family farm is to win a dogsled race in which undefeated Indian champ Stone Fox is also entered. Good start, tearjerking finale, but terribly draggy in between. Somewhat softened made-for-TV version of the children's book by John Reynolds Gardiner.
1987 *(Family)* 96m/C Buddy Ebsen, Joey Cramer, Belinda J. Montgomery, Gordon Tootoosis; *D:* Harvey Hart. **VHS $14.98** *WOV*

Stop! or My Mom Will Shoot ♂

Getty is an overbearing mother paying a visit to her cop son (Stallone) in Los Angeles. When mom witnesses a crime she has to stay in town longer than intended, which gives her time to meddle in her son's work and romantic lives. If Stallone wants to change his image this so-called comedy isn't the way to do it-because the joke is only on him. Viewers who rent this may find the joke is on them.
1992 **(PG-13** / *Jr. High-Adult)* 87m/C Sylvester Stallone, Estelle Getty, JoBeth Williams, Roger Rees, Martin Ferrero, Gailard Sartain, Dennis Burkley; *D:* Roger Spottiswoode; *W:* William Osborne; *M:* Alan Silvestri. **VHS, Beta, LV $19.98** *MCA*

Stories and Fables, Vol. 1

Series of live-action stories for children. Each volume contains two tales about kings, emperors and warriors, filmed in exotic locales from around the world. Additional volumes available.
1985 *(Family)* 50m/C **VHS, Beta $49.95** *DIS*

Stories from the Black Tradition

A "Children's Circle" tape presenting five Caldecott award-winning classic children's books: "A Story - A Story" by Gail E. Haley, "Mufaro's Beautiful Daughters" by John Steptoe, "Why Mosquitoes Buzz in People's Ears" retold by Verna Aardema, "The Village of Round and Square Houses" by Ann Grifalconi, and "Goggles!" by Ezra Jack Keats.
1992 *(Primary-Jr. High)* 52m/C **VHS $19.95** *CCC, MLT, WKV*

Stories to Remember: Baby's Morningtime

Nineteen animated morning poems for children taken from illustrator Kay Chorao's "The Baby's Good Morning Book," including "Ducks at Dawn," "Getting Out of Bed," "The Year's at the Spring," and others.
1992 *(Preschool)* 25m/C **Performed by:** Judy Collins. **VHS $12.98** *LTY, BMG, FFF*

Stories to Remember: Baby's Nursery Rhymes

A collection of nursery rhymes designed to capture the attention of even the youngest infant.

1991 *(Family)* 26m/C **VHS $14.98** *LTY, BMG, MVD*

Stories to Remember: Baby's Storytime

Animated adaptation of illustrator Kay Chorao's "The Baby's Story Book" provides a retelling of 12 classic tales, including "The Gingerbread Boy," "The Princess and the Pea," "Henny Penny," "The Three Little Pigs," and others.
1992 *(Preschool)* 26m/C *M:* Arlo Guthrie. **VHS $12.98** *LTY, BMG, FFF*

Stories to Remember: Beauty and the Beast

This animated version of the fairy tale was made for PBS's "Long Ago and Far Away" program; other tapes in the series include "Noah's Ark," "Pegasus," "Baby's Morningtime," "Baby's Storytime," and "Baby's Bedtime."
1991 *(Preschool-Primary)* 26m/C **VHS $12.98** *FCT, LTY*

Stories to Remember: Merlin and the Dragons

Well-animated fantasy of medieval wizardry as the mighty Merlin the Magician recounts a childhood tale to young Arthur, the would-be king. Based on the story by Jane Yolen.
1991 *(Family)* 27m/C **VHS $14.95** *FCT, LTY, BMG*

Stories to Remember: Noah's Ark

Animated biblical story taken from Peter Spier's prize-winning picture book.
1992 *(Preschool-Primary)* 27m/C *M:* Stewart Copeland. **VHS $12.98** *LTY, BMG, FFF*

Stories to Remember: Pegasus

Farrow narrates a particularly beautiful animated version of the Greek myth about the winged horse given as a gift from the Olympian gods.
19?? *(Preschool-Primary)* 25m/C **VHS $12.98** *FCT, BMG, LTY*

Stories to Remember: The Wild Swans

Banished princess must save her brothers from her evil stepmother's spell while maintaining her vow of silence. Based on a story by Hans Christian Andersen.
1994 *(Primary-Jr. High)* 36m/C *V:* Sigourney Weaver. **VHS $12.98** *BMG, LTY*

Stormalong

Comic actor Candy reads the tall tale of the New England sea captain in this installment of the "Rabbit Ears" storytelling series.
1992 *(Preschool-Primary)* 30m/C **VHS $9.95** *MVD,*

Storms

Clips from "Fantasia," "Bambi," and "The Old Mill" emphasize the power of storms. Demonstrations show their origins and safety measures for storms are examined.
1990 *(Preschool-Jr. High)* 14m/C **VHS, Beta $285.00** *MTI, DSN*

Stormy, the Thoroughbred

Stormy, the pony not good enough for the game, is sold as a workhorse. Soon, however, he joins a string of polo ponies and proves his worth. A live-action episode of TV's "Wonderful World of Disney."
1990 *(Preschool-Primary)* 46m/C **VHS, Beta $250.00** *MTI, DSN*

The Story Lady 🎞🎞◁

Retired widow's tale-spinning abilities get her a TV slot as hostess on a cable kids' program. She becomes so popular that network execs want to exploit her as a spokesperson for a toy company. Only a young girl can keep The Story Lady from selling out. Rosy, little, acclaimed made-for-TV tale.
1993 *(G/Family)* 93m/C Jessica Tandy, Lisa Jakub, Ed Begley Jr., Charles Durning, Stephanie Zimbalist; *D:* Larry Elikann. **VHS $89.95** *UNT*

The Story of a Cowboy Angel 🎞

Rather than go to jail, a western desperado gets sentenced to work on a ranch belonging to a young widow. But he's still got a bad attitude until a wintery visitation from his deceased partner Murff, who must earn his angel's wings by spreading the holiday spirit.
1981 *(Family)* 90m/C Slim Pickens. **VHS, Beta $69.98** *LIV, VES*

The Story of 15 Boys 🎞🎞◁

After a shipwreck, 15 schoolmates cooperate to survive on a desert island in perilous, pirate-filled waters. Rousing Japanese-animated version of the only Jules Verne tale the great fantasy/adventure author penned expressly for young readers.
1990 *(Family)* 80m/C **VHS $14.99** *JFK, WTA*

The Story of Seabiscuit 🎞🎞◁

The famous racing winner Seabiscuit is featured in a fluffy story of a racetrack romance. Temple is in love with a jockey but wants him to give up racing. Her uncle, who is Seabiscuit's trainer, has other things in mind.
1949 *(Family)* 93m/C Shirley Temple, Barry Fitzgerald, Lon McCallister, Rosemary DeCamp; *D:* David Butler. **VHS $19.98** *MGM, BTV*

The Story of the Dancing Frog

Two very unusual frogs, George and Gertrude, dance around the globe in this cartoon narrated by Plummer.
1989 *(Family)* 30m/C **VHS, Beta $14.95** *FHE*

Stowaway 🎞🎞🎞

After her missionary parents are killed in a Chinese revolution, Shirley stows away on a line bound for San Francisco and plays cupid to a bickering couple who adopt her. 🎵Good Night, My Love; One Never Knows, Does One; You Gotta S-M-I-L-E to Be H-A-P-P-Y; I Wanna Go To the Zoo; That's What I Want For Christmas.
1936 *(Family)* 86m/B Shirley Temple, Robert Young, Alice Faye, Eugene Pallette, Helen Westley, Arthur Treacher, Astrid Allwyn; *D:* William A. Seiter. **VHS, Beta $19.98** *FOX*

Stowaways on the Ark

Clumps from the cartoon series featuring Willie the Wood-worm, who gets himself into trouble by boring holes in the side of Noah's ark.
1989 (*Preschool-Primary*) 90m/C **VHS, Beta $19.99** *CEL, WTA*

Straight Talk 🦴🦴🦴⌐

Shirlee is a down-home gal from Arkansas who heads for Chicago to start life anew. She finds a job as a receptionist at WNDY radio, but is mistaken for the new radio psychologist. Her homespun advice ("Get off the cross. Somebody needs the wood.") becomes hugely popular and soon "Dr." Shirlee is the toast of the town. Parton's advice is the funniest part of this flimsy comedy, but she is helped immensely by Dunne and Orbach. On the other hand, Woods as the love interest/journalist who's suspicious of the good Dr.'s credentials seems a mite underwhelmed by the proceedings. **Hound Advisory:** Profanity.
1992 (*PG/Jr. High-Adult*) 91m/C Dolly Parton, James Woods, Griffin Dunne, Michael Madsen, Deidre O'Connell, John Sayles, Teri Hatcher, Spalding Gray, Jerry Orbach, Philip Bosco, Charles Fleischer, Jay Thomas; *D:* Barnet Kellman; *W:* Craig Bolotin, Patricia Resnick; *M:* Brad Fiedel. **VHS, Beta $19.99** *HPH*

Strange Invaders 🦴🦴🦴

Space folks have taken over a midwestern town in the '50s, assuming the locals' appearance and attire before returning to their ship. Seems one of them married an Earthling - but divorced and moved with her half-breed daughter to New York City. So the hicksters from space visit the Big Apple. Spoof of 50's sci-fi amusingly renders the story of confused alien body snatchers. **Hound Advisory:** Violence.
1983 (*PG/Jr. High-Adult*) 94m/C Paul LeMat, Nancy Allen, Diana Scarwid, Michael Lerner, Louise Fletcher, Wallace Shawn, Fiona Lewis, Kenneth Tobey, June Lockhart, Charles Lane, Dey Young, Mark Goddard; *D:* Michael Laughlin. **VHS, Beta, LV $79.95** *VES*

Strangers in Good Company 🦴🦴🦴

Quiet little film about a bus load of elderly women lost in the Canadian wilderness. They wait for rescue without histrion-ics, using the opportunity instead to get to know each other and nature. Loving metaphor to growing older with non-actors in every role is beautifully made, intelligent, uncom-mon, and worthwhile.
1991 (*PG/Jr. High-Adult*) 101m/C Alice Diabo, Mary Meigs, Cissy Meddings, Beth Webber, Winifred Holden, Constance Garneau, Catherine Roche, Michelle Sweeney; *D:* Cynthia Scott; *W:* Cynthia Scott, David Wilson, Gloria Demers, Sally Bochner; *M:* Marie Bernard. **VHS, Beta $94.95** *TOU*

Strangers on a Train 🦴🦴🦴🦴

Long before there was "Throw Momma from the Train," there was this Hitchcock super-thriller about two passengers who accidentally meet and plan to "trade" murders. Amoral Walker wants the exchange and the money he'll inherit by his father's death; Granger would love to end his stifling marriage and wed Roman, a senator's daughter, but finds the idea ultimately sickening. What happens is pure Hitchcock. Screenplay co-written by murder mystery great Chandler. Patricia Hitchcock, the director's only child, plays Roman's

sister. The concluding "carousel" scene is a masterpiece. From the novel by Patricia Highsmith.
1951 (*Jr. High-Adult*) 101m/B Farley Granger, Robert Walker, Ruth Roman, Leo G. Carroll, Patricia Hitchcock, Marion Lorne; *D:* Alfred Hitchcock; *W:* Raymond Chandler; *M:* Dimitri Tiomkin. **Award Nominations:** Academy Awards '51: Best Black and White Cinematography; **Awards:** National Board of Review Awards '51: 10 Best Films of the Year. **VHS, Beta, LV $19.98** *WAR, MLB*

Strawberry Shortcake and the Baby Without a Name

One of a series of cartoon specials promoting the ever-so-cute natives of Strawberry Land, really a merchandising blitz for "Strawberry Shortcake" greeting cards and toys. In this adventure (or is it just an ad?), the nefarious Purple Pieman, continuous villain of the series, comes home with something completely different: an affectionate monster and a baby without a name. What will Strawberry and the others do? Additional volumes available.
1984 (*Family*) 60m/C **VHS, Beta $29.95** *FHE, WTA*

Street Frogs: Keep on Rappin'

Street Frogs rap up a storm in this animated adventure.
1987 (*Primary*) 40m/C **VHS, Beta $14.98** *LHV, WAR, WTA*

Strega Nonna and Other Stories

Animated story of a man who unleashes a torrent of pasta from the pasta pot of Grandmother Witch that threatens to destroy the town. Also includes "The Foolish Frog," "A Story - a Story," and "Tikki Tikki Tembo." Volume IV of the "Children's Circle" series from Weston Woods.
1978 (*Preschool-Primary*) 35m/C **VHS, Beta $19.95** *CCC,, FCT*

Strictly Ballroom 🦴🦴🦴⌐

Offbeat, cheerfully tacky dance/romance from Down Under amusingly turns every movie cliche it encounters slightly askew. Scott (Mercurio) has been in training for the Pan-Pacific ballroom championships since the age of six. While talented, he also refuses to follow convention and scandalizes the stuffy dance establishment with his new steps. When his longtime partner leaves him, Scott takes up with a love-struck beginner (Morice), with some surprises of her own. Ballet dancer Mercurio (in his film debut) is appropriately arrogant yet vulnerable, while Morice is great as the plain Jane turned steel butterfly. One of a kind with a wonderful supporting cast is a substantial debut for director Luhrmann. **Hound Advisory:** Profanity.
1992 (*PG/Jr. High-Adult*) 94m/C Paul Mercurio, Tara Morice, Bill Hunter, Pat Thomsen, Barry Otto, Gia Carides, Peter Whitford, John Hannan, Sonia Kruger-Tayler, Kris McQuade, Pip Mushin, Leonie Page, Antonio Vargas, Armonia Benedito; *D:* Baz Luhrmann; *W:* Craig Pearce, Baz Luhrmann; *M:* David Hershfelder. **Award Nominations:** Golden Globe Awards '94: Best Film—Musical/Comedy; **Awards:** Australian Film Institute '92: Best Costume Design, Best Director (Luhrmann), Best Film, Best Supporting Actor (Otto), Best Supporting Actress (Thomsen), Best Writing. **VHS, LV $96.03** *MAX, TOU, BTV*

Strike Up the Band ♫♫♪

High school band turns to hot swing music and enters a national radio contest. Rooney and Garland display their usual charm in this high-energy stroll down memory lane. ♫Over the Waves; The Light Cavalry Overture; Walkin Down Broadway; Five Foot Two, Eyes of Blue; After the Ball; Nobody; Strike Up the Band. **1940** *(Family)* 120m/B Judy Garland, Mickey Rooney, Paul Whiteman, William Tracy, June Preisser; **D:** Busby Berkeley. **Award Nominations:** Academy Awards '40: Best Song ("Our Love Affair"), Best Score; **Awards:** Academy Awards '40: Best Sound. **VHS, Beta, LV $19.98** *MGM*

Sub-Mariner: Atlantis Under Attack

Marvel Comics characters in 'toon form star in these episodes. In the title feature Atuma kidnaps Lord Bashy and lures Sub-Mariner to the Forbidden Caverns. The superheroes reunite to fight Dr. Doom in "Dr. Doom's Day." **1966** *(Primary-Jr. High)* 35m/C **VHS $14.95** *WTA*

Suburban Commando ♫♫

Muscular alien superhero (on steroids?) crashes to Earth while on a mission. He does his best to remain inconspicuous, renting a room with the suburban Wilcoxes and getting into goofy scrapes around the neighborhood. Wimpy family man Charlie Wilcox finally gains confidence from the big guy from beyond. Occasionally cute, lowbrow vehicle for wrestler Hogan, aimed at younger fans. **Hound Advisory:** Typical World-Wrestling-Federation roughhousing, though care is taken that a space monster gets the worst of it. Salty language. **1991** *(PG/Jr. High-Adult)* 88m/C Hulk Hogan, Christopher Lloyd, Shelley Duvall, Larry Miller, William Ball, JoAnn Dearing, Jack Elam, Roy Dotrice, Christopher Neame, Tony Longo; **D:** Burt Kennedy. **VHS, LV $14.95** *COL, NLC*

Sudden Terror ♫♫

Murder of an African dignitary is witnessed by a young boy (Lester, of "Oliver!") who has trouble convincing his parents and the police about the incident. Pint-sized suspense, but less than original. Shot on location in Malta. **1970** *(PG/Adult)* 95m/C Mark Lester, Lionel Jeffries, Susan George, Tony Bonner; **D:** John Hough. **VHS, Beta** *FOX*

Sudie & Simpson ♫♫♪

Heart-tugging tale set in a viciously racist town in 1940s Georgia. Sudie, a 12-year-old white girl, forms a forbidden friendship with a gentle, educated black man secretly living in a shack in the woods, even though he could be lynched if they're found out. Superbly acted by Gilbert and Oscar-winner Gossett, but subplots about child molestation (graphically described) and sex education are more like encumbrances than assets. Made for cable TV, and based on the novel by Sara Flanagan Carter. **Hound Advisory:** Mature themes; sex talk; salty language. **1990** *(Jr. High-Adult)* 95m/C Sara Gilbert, Louis Gossett Jr., Frances Fisher, John M. Jackson, Paige Danahy, Ken Strong; **D:** Joan Tewkesbury; **W:** Sara Flanagan Carter, Ken Koser. **VHS $89.95** *WOV*

Sugar Cane Alley ♫♫♫

After the loss of his parents, an 11-year-old West Indian orphan goes to work with his grandmother on an island sugar plantation. She realizes that her boy's only hope to escape grinding poverty is an education. Set in Martinique in the 1930s. Poignant, memorable and too seldom seen. **1983** *(PG/Preschool-Adult)* 106m/C Garry Cadenat, Darling Legitimus, Douta Seck; **D:** Euzhan Palcy; **W:** Euzhan Palcy. **VHS, Beta, LV $29.95** *MED, FCT*

Summer Magic ♫♫

Impecunious recent widow is forced to leave Boston and settle her family in a small town in Maine. Typical, forgettable Disney drama served to showcase Mills early in her career. Remake of "Mother Carey's Chickens." **1963** *(Family)* 116m/C Hayley Mills, Burl Ives, Dorothy McGuire, Deborah Walley, Una Merkel, Eddie Hodges; **D:** James Neilson; **M:** Buddy Baker. **VHS, Beta $69.95** *DIS*

Summer Rental ♫♫

Candy plays a harried air-traffic controller, trying to have a few days to relax with his family in sunny Florida. But a mean rich guy finally goads him and his kids into a machismo-flavored sailboat race. The star could add something hefty to the limpest of plots, and does so here. Watch the first hour for yuks, then rewind. **Hound Advisory:** Salty language, sex talk. Running joke about a woman who proudly asks everyone to inspect her newly augmented breasts. **1985** *(PG/Jr. High-Adult)* 87m/C John Candy, Rip Torn, Richard Crenna, Karen Austin, Kerri Green, John Larroquette, Pierrino Mascarino; **D:** Carl Reiner; **M:** Alan Silvestri. **VHS, Beta, LV, 8mm $14.95** *PAR*

Summer School ♫♫♪

Semi-responsible high-school teacher's vacation plans are ruined when he gets stuck teaching remedial English to a bunch of party-hearty kids in California summer school. But our hero finds life is more than a beach, as he encounters romance, the kids bond, and classroom antics make a direct hit on the funny bone. **Hound Advisory:** Sexual stuff, with an almost-funny/almost alarming subplot about a teen nymphet who constantly offers herself to her teacher (who resists). Drinking, salty language, and one teen pregnancy. **1987** *(PG-13/Jr. High-Adult)* 98m/C Mark Harmon, Kirstie Alley, Nels Van Patten, Courtney Thorne-Smith, Lucy Lee Flippin, Shawnee Smith, Robin Thomas, Dean Cameron; **D:** Carl Reiner; **W:** Jeff Franklin; **M:** Danny Elfman. **VHS, Beta, LV $14.95** *PAR*

Summer Switch

Mary Rodgers authored the famous "Freaky Friday" in which a mother and daughter switched bodies for the day. This ABC Afterschool Special takes its inspiration from an equal-time Rodgers book, in which a boy at summer camp wishes he could trade places with his executive dad. The two find themselves awkwardly in each other's places just before dad's vital business meeting. Two versions on video, one 46 minutes long, the other abridged to a half-hour. **1984** *(Primary-Jr. High)* 46m/C **VHS, Beta** *LCA, NWV*

A Summer to Remember 🐾🐾

Deaf boy (played by Gerlis, himself deaf since birth) forms a friendship with an escaped lab orangutan through sign language. Becomes less-sophisticated simian "Free Willy" when carnival baddies abduct the ape. Parents depicted as morons while music seems to sample "Sesame Street." Made-for-TV monkeyshines whose cleverest touch isn't even in the movie - it's "Harry and the Hendersons," another primate title, as a coming attraction on the tape. **Hound Advisory:** Roughhousing.
1984 (PG/*Family*) 93m/C Tess Harper, James Farentino, Burt Young, Louise Fletcher, Sean Gerlis, Bridgette Anderson; *D:* Robert Lewis; *M:* Charles Fox. **VHS, Beta $14.98** *MCA*

Summerdog 🐾🐾

Harmless but trite tale about a city family vacationing in Maine who adopt a stray mutt. Hobo the dog ends up saving them from numerous perils and even unmasks their evil landlord as a criminal fence.
1978 (G/*Family*) 90m/C James Congdon, Elizabeth Eisenman, Oliver Zabriskie, Tavia Zabriskie; *D:* John Clayton. **VHS, Beta $29.95** *GEM*

Sundance and the Kid 🐾🐾

Two brothers try to collect an inheritance against all odds. Originally known as "Sundance Cassidy and Butch the Kid."
1976 (PG/*Jr. High-Adult*) 84m/C John Wade, Karen Blake; *D:* Arthur Pitt. **VHS, Beta** *NO*

The Sunshine Boys 🐾🐾🐾

Two veteran vaudeville partners, who have shared a love-hate relationship for decades, reunite for a television special. Adapted by Neil Simon from his play. Matthau was a replacement for Jack Benny, who died before the start of filming. Burns, for his first starring role since "Honolulu" in 1939, won an Oscar.
1975 (PG/*Jr. High-Adult*) 111m/C George Burns, Walter Matthau, Richard Benjamin, Lee Meredith, F. Murray Abraham, Carol Arthur, Howard Hesseman; *D:* Herbert Ross; *W:* Neil Simon. **Award Nominations:** Academy Awards '75: Best Actor (Matthau), Best Adapted Screenplay, Best Art Direction/Set Decoration; **Awards:** Academy Awards '75: Best Supporting Actor (Burns); Golden Globe Awards '76: Best Actor—Musical/Comedy (Matthau), Best Film—Musical/Comedy, Best Supporting Actor (Benjamin). **VHS, Beta, LV $14.95** *MGM, BTV*

Sunshine Porcupine

In union with our star the Sun, the Sunshine Porcupine defeats the Ugli-Unks and saves Eggwood from a threatened loss of solar power. Animated production.
1979 (*Preschool-Primary*) 45m/C **VHS, Beta $14.95** *MPI, WTA*

Super Fuzz 🐾◁

Italian-made production (the easygoing Hill is a superstar over there) about a rookie policeman who develops super powers after being accidentally exposed to radiation. Somewhat ineptly, he uses his abilities to combat crime. Somewhat ineptly acted, written, and directed as well. **Hound Advisory:** Roughhousing, salty language.
1981 (PG/*Jr. High-Adult*) 97m/C Terence Hill, Joanne Dru, Ernest Borgnine; *D:* Sergio Corbucci. **VHS, Beta $69.98** *SUE*

Super Mario Bros. 🐾🐾

Fantasy based on the hit Nintendo game series. Two Brooklyn plumbers discover a lost dimension, created when an asteroid struck Earth in dinosaur days. Its princess has been kidnapped and taken to Dinohattan, a fungi-infested underworld ruled by Koopa, a T.Rex evolved to human form. Mario and Luigi fight back, and about 100 elements of the video games show up. Lavish and gaudy mental junk food, harmless enough for kids - unless they happen to be young accountants; the $42 million epic was a big money-loser. Don't hold your breath waiting for the sequel the ending foretells (though there was a cartoon predecessor). **Hound Advisory:** Roughhousing; reptilian snarling; futuristic mayhem.
1993 (PG/*Family*) 104m/C Bob Hoskins, John Leguizamo, Samantha Mathis, Fisher Stevens, Richard Edson, Dana Kaminsky, Dennis Hopper, Fiona Shaw, Mojo Nixon, Lance Henriksen; *D:* Rocky Morton, Annabel Jankel; *W:* Edward Solomon, Parker Bennett, Terry Runte; *M:* Alan Silvestri. **VHS, Beta, LV $96.03** *HPH, BTV, TOU*

Super Mario Bros. Super Show 1

Syndicated TV cartoon series based on the video-game characters Mario and Luigi, plumbers who battle evil King Koopa in a fantasy kingdom. Six cassettes of episode reruns are available.
1989 (PG/*Family*) 30m/C Captain Lou Albano, Danny Wells. **VHS $9.95** *GKK*

Super Seal 🐾◁

Injured seal pup disrupts a family's normal existence after the young daughter adopts him. Marine mush.
1977 (G/*Primary*) 95m/C Foster Brooks, Sterling Holloway, Sarah Brown; *D:* Michael Dugan. **VHS, Beta $39.95** *VCI*

Superdad 🐾

Middle-aged dad is alarmed by his college-bound daughter's choice in boyfriends. Much to the girl's embarrassment, the overprotective parent tries joining her at various teenage activities. Dim Disney family sitcom about the Generation Gap that never bridges the credibility gap, let alone the joke gap.
1973 (G/*Family*) 94m/C Bob Crane, Kurt Russell, Joe Flynn, Barbara Rush, Kathleen Cody, Dick Van Patten; *D:* Vincent McEveety; *M:* Buddy Baker. **VHS, Beta** *DIS*

Supergirl 🐾◁

Unexciting and unsophisticated spinoff of the Christopher Reeve man of steel fests. Based on the comic books about the young cousin to Superman, similarly sent to Earth and in pursuit of a magic paperweight. But a carnival fortuneteller has used it to transform herself as an all-powerful sorceress. Dunaway is a terrifically vile villainess, Slater winsome, but the whole enterprise is dimwitted. **Hound Advisory:** Roughhousing.
1984 (PG/*Jr. High-Adult*) 114m/C Faye Dunaway, Helen Slater, Peter O'Toole, Mia Farrow, Brenda Vaccaro, Marc McClure, Simon Ward, Hart Bochner, Maureen Teefy, David Healy, Matt Frewer; *D:* Jeannot Szwarc; *M:* Jerry Goldsmith. **VHS, Beta, LV $19.95** *LIV*

Superman 1: The Movie 🎬🎬🎬🎬

The DC Comics legend comes alive in this wonderfully entertaining saga of Superman's life, from a baby on the doomed planet Krypton to Metropolis' own Man of Steel. Hackman and Beatty pair marvelously as super criminal Lex Luthor and his bumbling sidekick. Award winning special effects and a script that pays great respect to the Jerry Siegel/Joe Shuster comic-book character yet doesn't take itself too seriously; super-fun. Followed by three increasingly lesser sequels. **Hound Advisory:** Superhero violence.
1978 (PG/*Family*) 144m/C Christopher Reeve, Margot Kidder, Marlon Brando, Gene Hackman, Glenn Ford, Susannah York, Ned Beatty, Valerie Perrine, Jackie Cooper, Marc McClure, Trevor Howard, Sarah Douglas, Terence Stamp, Jack O'Halloran, Phyllis Thaxter; *D:* Richard Donner; *W:* Mario Puzo, Robert Benton, David Newman; *M:* John Williams. **Award Nominations:** Academy Awards '78: Best Film Editing, Best Sound, Best Original Score; **Awards:** Academy Awards '78: Best Visual Effects; National Board of Review Awards '78: 10 Best Films of the Year. VHS, Beta, LV $19.98 *WAR*

Superman 2 🎬🎬🎬

First sequel finds the Man of Steel with his powerful hands full fending off three super-powered villains from his home planet of Krypton (briefly glimpsed in the first film). The romance between reporter Lois Lane and our superhero heats up and the storyline has more pace than the original, making for an enjoyable part II. **Hound Advisory:** Superhero violence, sex talk.
1980 (PG/*Family*) 127m/C Christopher Reeve, Margot Kidder, Gene Hackman, Ned Beatty, Jackie Cooper, Sarah Douglas, Jack O'Halloran, Susannah York, Marc McClure, Terence Stamp, Valerie Perrine, E.G. Marshall; *D:* Richard Lester; *W:* Mario Puzo, David Newman; *M:* John Williams. VHS, Beta, LV $19.98 *WAR*

Superman 3 🎬🎬🎬🎬

Villainous businessman tries to conquer Superman via the expertise of bumbling computer expert Pryor and use of artificial Kryptonite. Superman explores his darker side after undergoing transformation into sleazy superbum. Promising, satirical start is ultimately defeated by uneven story and direction and often less-than-super f/x. Instead of Lois Lane, Clark Kent's long-lost love interest Lana Lang (O'Toole) pops up as the requisite heroine. **Hound Advisory:** Super roughhousing.
1983 (PG/*Jr. High-Adult*) 123m/C Christopher Reeve, Richard Pryor, Annette O'Toole, Jackie Cooper, Margot Kidder, Marc McClure, Annie Ross, Robert Vaughn; *D:* Richard Lester; *W:* David Newman; *M:* John Williams. VHS, Beta, LV $19.98 *WAR*

Superman 4: The Quest for Peace 🎬🎬

In answer to a child's wish, the Man of Steel endeavors to rid the world of all atomic weapons, thereby pitting himself against plutonium entrepreneur Lex Luthor and his super-powered creation, Nuclear Man. Special effects are dimestore quality and it seems that someone walked off with parts of the plot. Reeve deserves credit for remaining true to his classic character through good sequels and bad. **Hound Advisory:** Salty language, superhero roughhousing.

1987 (PG/*Jr. High-Adult*) 90m/C Christopher Reeve, Gene Hackman, Jon Cryer, Marc McClure, Margot Kidder, Mariel Hemingway, Sam Wanamaker; *D:* Sidney J. Furie; *W:* Mark Rosenthal; *M:* John Williams; *V:* Susannah York. VHS, Beta, LV $19.98 *WAR, APD*

Superman & the Mole Men 🎬🎬🎬🎬

The cast of the 1950s TV show made this rarely seen feature as a pilot for the series. Superman faces the danger threatened by the invasion of radioactive mole-men who make their way to the surface world from the bowels of the earth through an oil-well shaft. Simple fun.
1951 (*Family*) 58m/C George Reeves, Phyllis Coates, Phyllis Coates, Jeff Corey; *D:* Lee Sholem. VHS, Beta $19.98 *WAR*

Superman: The Serial, Vol. 1

The live-action Superman was first seen in this 15-chapter serial, tracing the Man of Steel from his origins on Krypton to his fight to save Metropolis from the evil Spider Lady and her ray gun. Columbia Pictures came up with an innovative way to avoid a big f/x budget: whenever Superman soars into action, he turns into a cartoon drawing! **Hound Advisory:** Roughhousing.
1948 (*Family*) 248m/B Kirk Alyn, Noel Neill, Pierre Watkin, Tommy "Butch" Bond, Thomas Carr; *D:* Spencer Gordon Bennet. VHS, Beta $29.95 *WAR*

SuperTed

Cartoon episodes from a popular British TV show about a toy stuffed bear transformed by an alien into a whimsical superhero. SuperTed now battles silly villains like Bulk, Skeleton, and Texas Pete. Lots better done than many toy product 'toons; additional volumes available.
1984 (*Family*) 49m/C VHS, Beta $19.95 *DIS, WTA*

Support Your Local Gunfighter 🎬🎬🎬

Western con man comes to the small town of Purgatory and is thought to be a notorious gunfighter. He decides to go with the mistaken identity and use it to his profitable advantage. A delightful, deliberately cliche-filled western that counts as a worthy follow-up, not a sequel, to "Support Your Local Sheriff" (1969).
1971 (G/*Jr. High-Adult*) 92m/C James Garner, Jack Elam, Suzanne Pleshette, Harry Morgan, Dub Taylor, John Dehner, Joan Blondell, Ellen Corby, Henry Jones; *D:* Burt Kennedy. VHS $19.98 *MGM*

Support Your Local Sheriff 🎬🎬🎬🎬

Amiable, irreverent western spoof with more than its fair share of laughs. When a stranger stumbles into a gold rush town, he winds up becoming sheriff. Garner is perfect as the deadpan sheriff, particularly in the scene where he convinces Dern to remain in jail, in spite of the lack of bars. Neatly subverts every western cliche it encounters, yet keeps respect for formula western. Followed by "Support Your Local Gunfighter."
1969 (G/*Family*) 92m/C James Garner, Joan Hackett, Walter Brennan, Bruce Dern, Jack Elam, Harry Morgan; *D:* Burt Kennedy; *W:* William Bowers. VHS, Beta, LV $19.98 *FOX, MGM*

The Sure Thing 🦴🦴🦴

Ivy League students who don't like each other end up travelling to California together, and of course, falling in love. Charming performances make up for predictability of comedic romance. Can't-miss director (and ex-Meathead) Reiner's second direct hit at the box office. **Hound Advisory:** PG-13 seems overstated; no explicit sex or nudity, mild language.
1985 (PG-13/*Jr. High-Adult*) 94m/C John Cusack, Daphne Zuniga, Anthony Edwards, Boyd Gaines, Lisa Jane Persky, Viveca Lindfors, Nicolette Sheridan, Tim Robbins; **D:** Rob Reiner; **W:** Jonathan Roberts. VHS, Beta, LV, 8mm $14.95 COL, SUE

Surf Ninjas 🦴🦴

Martial-arts action comedy about two young California surfer dudes who are actually long-lost crown princes of the obscure nation of Patu San. The country's bionic bumbler warlord (Nielsen, hilarious but onscreen too briefly) wants the boys to stay lost. Frivolous tale, sort of a Teenage Mutant Ninja Turtle plot without Leonardo and co., has unexpectedly funny dialogue and situations early on, but gimmicky plot inevitably runs into shallow waters. **Hound Advisory:** Violence (largely non-serious), sex talk.
1993 (PG/*Jr. High-Adult*) 87m/C Ernie Reyes Jr., Nick Cowen, Rob Schneider, Leslie Nielsen, Tone Loc, John Karlen, Ernie Reyes Sr.; **D:** Neal Israel; **W:** Dan Gordon; **M:** David Kitay. VHS, LV COL, NLC, IME

Susannah of the Mounties 🦴🦴🦴

Adorable young girl left orphaned after a wagon train massacre is adopted by a Mountie. An Indian squabble gives Shirley a chance to play little peacemaker and teach Scott how to tap dance, too. Could she be any cuter? Available colorized.
1939 (*Family*) 78m/B Shirley Temple, Randolph Scott, Margaret Lockwood, J. Farrell MacDonald, Moroni Olsen, Victor Jory; **D:** William A. Seiter. VHS, Beta $19.98 FOX

Susie, the Little Blue Coupe

A car ready to be junked is suddenly souped-up and revving to hit the road in this lesson of change and adaptation from Walt Disney's animation factory.
1952 (*Preschool-Primary*) 8m/C VHS, Beta $165.00 DSN, MTI

Suspicion 🦴🦴🦴

Hitchcock's suspense thriller about a woman who gradually realizes she is married to a killer and may be next on his list. Excellent production unravels at the end due to RKO's insistence that Grant retain his "attractive" image, forcing the writers to leave his guilt or innocence undetermined. Available colorized.
1941 (*Jr. High-Adult*) 99m/B Cary Grant, Joan Fontaine, Cedric Hardwicke, Nigel Bruce, May Whitty, Leo G. Carroll, Heather Angel; **D:** Alfred Hitchcock. **Award Nominations:** Academy Awards '41: Best Picture; **Awards:** Academy Awards '41: Best Actress (Fontaine). VHS, Beta, LV $19.98 RKO, MED, MLB

Swamp Thing 🦴🦴

Well-regarded comic book was the basis for this superhero/monster tale about a noble scientist accidentally turned into a lonely half-vegetable, half-man, all-cheapo-rubber-suit swamp creature. He fights an evil rival over a secret formula, with a sexy lady agent caught in the middle, occasionally topless. More silly than scary, but deemed worth a sequel, "The Return of Swamp Thing," and a TV series. **Hound Advisory:** Violence, nudity.
1982 (PG/*Primary-Adult*) 91m/C Adrienne Barbeau, Louis Jourdan, Ray Wise; **D:** Wes Craven; **W:** Wes Craven. VHS, Beta, LV $14.95 COL, SUE

The Swarm 🦴

Low-brow insect contest as scientist Caine fends off a swarm of killer bees when they attack metro Houston. The bees are really just black spots painted on the film. And the acting is terrible. "B" movie on bees, but it's still better than "The Bees."
1978 (PG/*Jr. High-Adult*) 116m/C Michael Caine, Katharine Ross, Richard Widmark, Lee Grant, Richard Chamberlain, Olivia de Havilland, Henry Fonda, Fred MacMurray, Patty Duke, Ben Johnson, Jose Ferrer, Slim Pickens, Bradford Dillman, Cameron Mitchell; **D:** Irwin Allen; **W:** Sterling Silliphant; **M:** Jerry Goldsmith, John Williams. VHS, Beta $19.98 WAR

The Sweater

Mail order mixup, a sweater, and a small boy and his passion for hockey all figure in the award-winning title short from Canada. Also includes "The Ride" and "Getting Started."
1982 (*Family*) 30m/C VHS $14.95 FCT, NFB, INC

Sweet 15

Marta Delacruz is approaching her 15th birthday — in Mexican-American culture a celebration that ushers her into adulthood. But plans of a lavish party and a dream date are displaced by more urgent matters when she finds her proud father never attained US citizenship despite his many years in the country. With immigration cops cracking down, Mr. Delacruz considers taking the family back south of the border. Marta tries to come up with a solution on her own, and does some real growing up in the process. Revealing and satisfying tale originally aired as part of PBS-TV's "WonderWorks" series.
1990 (*Family*) 120m/C Karla Montana, Panchito Gomez, Tony Plana, Jenny Gago, Susan Ruttan; **D:** Victoria Hochberg. VHS $29.95 PME, HMV, FCT

Sweet Liberty 🦴🦴

Alda's hometown is overwhelmed by Hollywood chaos during the filming of a movie version of his novel about the American Revolution. Pleasant but predictable. **Hound Advisory:** Mature themes; alcohol use; subtle sex scenes.
1986 (PG/*Jr. High-Adult*) 107m/C Alan Alda, Michael Caine, Michelle Pfeiffer, Bob Hoskins, Lillian Gish; **D:** Alan Alda; **W:** Alan Alda; **M:** Bruce Broughton. VHS, Beta, LV $19.95 MCA

Swing Kids 🦴🦴

In 1939 Hamburg, big band "swing" music is used by a group of teenagers to rebel against conformity demanded by Hitler. Plot concentrates on three boys and the strains that Nazi power and propaganda put on their friendship. Although the premise is historically based, a disturbing wrong-end-of-the-telescope aspect affects the production; effective moments of searing drama and brutality get paired with youth-pandering visits to the dance floor or record den. Hopefully, the targeted young audience already knows that WWII was fought over larger issues than pop music and long hair. Made through Disney's Hollywood Pictures division. **Hound Advisory:** Brutality, profane language, alcohol use, mature themes. One character commits suicide.

1993 (PG-13/*Jr. High-Adult***)** 114m/C Robert Sean Leonard, Christian Bale, Frank Whaley, Barbara Hershey, Tushka Bergen, David Tom, Kenneth Branagh; ***D:*** Thomas Carter; ***W:*** Jonathan Marc Feldman; ***M:*** James Horner. VHS, Beta, LV **$19.99** *HPH*

Swing Shift 🐾🐾◁

When Hawn takes a job at an aircraft plant after husband Harris goes off to war, she learns more than riveting, courtesy of fellow worker Russell. Lahti steals the romantic comedy-drama as her friend and co-worker. In spite of performances, detailed reminiscence of the American home front during WWII never seems to gel. Produced by Hawn. **Hound Advisory:** Profanity, sex.

1984 (PG/*Jr. High-Adult***)** 100m/C Goldie Hawn, Kurt Russell, Ed Harris, Christine Lahti, Holly Hunter, Chris Lemmon, Belinda Carlisle, Fred Ward, Roger Corman, Lisa Pelikan; ***D:*** Jonathan Demme; ***W:*** Ron Nyswaner, Bo Goldman. VHS, Beta, LV **$19.98** *WAR*

The Swiss Family Robinson 🐾🐾🐾

Family seeking to escape Napoleon's war in Europe sets sail for New Guinea, but shipwrecks on a deserted tropical island. There they build an idyllic life, only to be confronted by a band of pirates. Lots of grandiose adventure for family viewing in the Disney tradition, even if some of it is farfetched at times. Filmed on location on the island of Tobago. Based on the novel by Johann Wyss.

1960 (*Family***)** 126m/C John Mills, Dorothy McGuire, James MacArthur, Tommy Kirk, Janet Munro, Sessue Hayakawa; ***D:*** Ken Annakin. VHS, Beta, LV **$19.99** *DIS, IGP*

The Sword & the Rose 🐾🐾◁

Mary Tudor, widowed sister of King Henry VIII, shuns the advances of a power-hungry ignoble noblemen for the love of a valiant commoner, who swashbuckles to the rescue. Don't be surprised if you find none of this in the history books; adventure was the priority in this Disney production filmed in England and adapted from Charles Major's book "When Knighthood Was in Flower."

1953 (*Family***)** 91m/C Richard Todd, Glynis Johns, Michael Gough, Jane Barrett, James Robertson Justice; ***D:*** Ken Annakin. VHS, Beta, LV **$19.99** *DIS, HHE, BTV*

The Sword in the Stone 🐾🐾🐾

The Disney version of the first segment of T.H. White's "The Once and Future King" wherein King Arthur, as a 12-year-old boy, is instructed in the ways of the world by Merlin the Magician and Archimedes the owl. With a heavy emphasis on slapstick gags, it's short of the masterpiece rank - just compare Merlin's performing tableware with the delightful singing and dancing bric-a-brac in "Beauty and the Beast." But kids will be entertained.

1963 (G/*Family***)** 79m/C ***D:*** Wolfgang Reitherman, Wolfgang Reitherman; ***V:*** Ricky Sorenson, Sebastian Cabot, Karl Swenson, Junius Matthews, Alan Napier, Norman Alden, Martha Wentworth, Barbara Jo Allen. VHS, Beta, LV **$24.99** *DIS, KUI, HMV*

Sword of the Valiant 🐾◁

Rattletrap filming of the poem "Sir Gawain And The Green Knight," based on a King Arthur legend of youthful Sir Gawain spending a year to prepare for a challenge by the supernatural, seemingly undefeatable Green Knight (Connery). Terrible f/x.

1983 (PG/*Sr. High-Adult***)** 102m/C Sean Connery, Miles O'Keeffe, Cyrielle Claire, Leigh Lawson, Trevor Howard, Peter Cushing, Wilfrid Brambell, Lila Kedrova, John Rhys-Davies; ***D:*** Stephen Weeks. VHS, Beta **$69.95** *MGM*

Sylvester 🐾🐾

A 16-year-old orphan girl and a cranky stockyard boss team up to train a battered horse named Sylvester for the National Equestrian trials. Nice riding sequences and good performances can't disguise a familiar plot, but kids will enjoy this one. **Hound Advisory:** Salty language, roughhousing.

1985 (PG/*Family***)** 104m/C Melissa Gilbert, Richard Farnsworth, Michael Schoeffling, Constance Towers; ***D:*** Tim Hunter. VHS, Beta, LV **$79.95** *COL*

Sylvia Anderson's The Animates

Thirteen mini-cartoons featuring British comic characters from one half of the Gerry and Sylvia Anderson team who devised "Thunderbirds" and "Captain Scarlet vs. the Mysterons" for British TV.

1978 (*Preschool-Primary***)** 57m/C VHS, Beta *FHE*

Table for Five 🐾🐾◁

Divorced father takes his children on a Mediterranean cruise and while at sea, he learns that his ex-wife has died. The father and his ex-wife's husband struggle over who should raise the children. Sentimental and well-acted tale of an unbrady bunch. **Hound Advisory:** Salty language, sex talk, mature themes.

1983 (PG/*Jr. High-Adult***)** 120m/C Jon Voight, Millie Perkins, Richard Crenna, Robbie Kiger, Roxana Zal, Son Hoang Bui, Marie-Christine Barrault, Kevin Costner; ***D:*** Robert Lieberman; ***W:*** David Seltzer; ***M:*** Miles Goodman. VHS, Beta, LV **$14.98** *FOX*

Tailor of Gloucester

Beatrix Potter's classic tale of sharing is narrated by Streep.

19?? (*Preschool-Primary***)** 30m/C VHS **$15.99** *KUI, COL*

Tailspin Tommy

One of the first movie serials derived from a newspaper comic strip, this otherwise unremarkable Universal production stars the aviator hero performing airborne stunts (recycled scenes from other movies, actually). In 12 chapters. Followup, "Tailspin Tommy and the Great Air Mystery," is also available.

1934 (*Jr. High-Adult***)** ?m/B Maurice Murphy, Noah Beery Jr., Walter Miller, Patricia Farr, Grant Withers, John Davidson, William Desmond, Charles A. Browne; ***D:*** Louis Friedlander. VHS **$24.95** *GPV*

Take Down 🦴🦴

Hermann is charming as a high-school English teacher who reluctantly takes charge as coach of a last-place student wrestling squad because nobody else wants the job. Through hard work and understanding, he turns the team into winners. Innocuous, though predictable on every count.
1979 (PG/*Family*) 96m/C Lorenzo Lamas, Kathleen Lloyd, Maureen McCormick, Edward Herrmann; **D:** Keith Merrill. **VHS, Beta $29.95** *UNI*

Take the Money and Run 🦴🦴🦴

Allen's directing debut; he also co-wrote and starred. "Documentary" follows a timid, would-be bank robber who can't get his career off the ground and keeps landing in jail. Little plot, but who cares? Nonstop one-liners and slapstick.
1969 (PG/*Jr. High-Adult*) 85m/C Woody Allen, Janet Margolin, Marcel Hillaire, Louise Lasser; **D:** Woody Allen; **W:** Woody Allen; **M:** Marvin Hamlisch. **VHS, Beta, LV $19.98** *FOX*

The Tale of Mr. Jeremy Fisher and the Tale of Peter Rabbit

Two more classic tales from Beatrix Potter narrated by Streep.
19?? (*Preschool-Jr. High*) 30m/C **VHS $15.99** *KUI, COL*

The Tale of Peter Rabbit

Another round of Beatrix Potter's rabbit vs. Mr. McGregor. Burnett narrates and sings in this animated special for HBO cable, with songs by Stephen Lawrence and Sheldon Harnick.
1991 (*Preschool-Primary*) 27m/C **V:** Carol Burnett. **VHS $12.98** *FHE, LIV*

The Tale of Peter Rabbit and Benjamin Bunny

Released to commemorate the 100th anniversary of Beatrix Potter's series, this is a faithful translation of her classic story of two mischievous bunnies and their adventurous trip to Mr. MacGregor's garden. Potter's own watercolors are adapted to exceptional animation.
1993 (*Preschool-Primary*) 30m/C **VHS $19.95** *GKK, ING*

The Tale of Samuel Whiskers

Released to commemorate the 100th anniversary of Beatrix Potter's series, this retells her story of cats and rats, with her watercolors faithfully translated to animation. See also "The Tale of Peter Rabbit and Benjamin Bunny."
1993 (*Preschool-Primary*) 30m/C **VHS $19.95** *GKK*

The Tale of the Bunny Picnic

Muppet Bunnies prepare for their annual picnic but Bean, the smallest bunny, is too tiny to help. When he wanders off he finds the farmer's junkyard dog has a nasty surprise for his pals unless Bean can warn them first.
1992 (*Preschool-Primary*) 50m/C **VHS $12.99** *JHV, BTV*

A Tale of Two Chipmunks

Three Chip 'n' Dale Disney cartoons: "Chicken in the Rough," "The Lone Chipmunks" and "Chips Ahoy."
1953 (G/*Family*) 24m/C **VHS, Beta, LV $14.95** *DIS*

A Tale of Two Critters

Young raccoon and a playful bear cub develop a rare friendship growing up in the wilderness.
1977 (G/*Preschool-Primary*) 48m/C **VHS, Beta $250.00** *MTI, DSN*

Talent for the Game 🦴🦴🦴

Minor-league baseball pleasantry about a talent scout who recruits a phenomenal young pitcher from rural Idaho, then sees the innocent kid unfairly pressured by the greedy team owner. Okay, with a fairy-tale ending that aims a little too hard to please. **Hound Advisory:** Ballparkish language.
1991 (PG/*Jr. High-Family*) 91m/C Edward James Olmos, Lorraine Bracco, Jeff Corbett, Jamey Sheridan, Terry Kinney; **D:** Robert M. Young; **W:** David Himmelstein, Tom Donnelly, Larry Ferguson; **M:** David Newman. **VHS, Beta, LV $14.95** *PAR*

Tales of Beatrix Potter 🦴🦴🦴🦴

The Royal Ballet Company of England performs in this adaptation of the adventures of Beatrix Potter's colorful and memorable creatures. Beautifully done.
1971 (G/*Family*) 90m/C **D:** Reginald Mills. **VHS $14.98** *REP, HMV*

Tales of Beatrix Potter

Six stories from Potter's canon, including "Peter Rabbit," "Two Bad Mice," "Miss Moppet," and "Jeremy Fisher," illustrated by Potter's original drawings and narrated by Sydney Walker.
1985 (*Preschool-Primary*) 43m/C **VHS, Beta $24.95** *VES, RDG, HMV*

Tales of Deputy Dawg, Vol. 1

Terrytoons' pessimistic dawg rides again, undoing the bad guys in spite of himself. Additional volumes available.
196? (*Family*) 90m/C **V:** Dayton Allen. **VHS $59.98** *FOX*

The Tales of Hoffman 🦴🦴🦴

The British creators of the sentimental classic "The Red Shoes" followed up with this highly stylized ballet-opera, based on music and stories of Jacques Offenbach. Hoffman is a heartbroken poet who tells residents of an inn of his ill-fated romances, which all have a touch of the supernatural about them. Though innately tragic, the tales' fairy-tale quality that might be your best chance (other than "The Maestro's Company" and the Marx Brothers) to expose youngsters to a night at the opera. Standout: the "Dr. Coppelius" segment, about a doll-like mechanical girl who literally goes to pieces for love. **Hound Advisory:** Alcohol use.
1951 (*College-Adult*) 138m/C Robert Rounseville, Robert Helpmann, Moira Shearer; **D:** Michael Powell, Emeric Pressburger; **M:** Royal Philharmonic Orchestra. **VHS $39.95** *HMV, PME*

Tales of Pluto Series

The inimitable hound stars in a collection of hilarious Disney cartoons. Available on separate tapes, they are "Wonder Dog," "Pluto's Surprise Package," and "Dog Watch."
1990 (*Preschool-Primary*) 8m/C **VHS, Beta $170.00** *MTI, DSN*

The Talking Eggs

Animated version of the popular children's folktale features all African Americans, with narration by Danny Glover. Selina is invited to the home of a mysterious old woman who encourages her to take some eggs, but only the ones who speak to her. They are magical for Selina, but turn into a curse when her brother steals some for himself.
1992 (*Preschool-Primary*) 25m/C **VHS $195.00** *CHF*

The Talking Parcel

British TV cartoon special about a girl who finds a package on the beach. Inside is a talking parrot who sweeps her away to a fantastic land containing mythological and whimsical beasts. Based on the book by Gerald Durrell.
1978 (*Family*) 40m/C **VHS, Beta** *NO*

The Tall Blond Man with One Black Shoe 🎬🎬🎬

A violinist is completely unaware that rival spies mistakenly think he is also a spy, and that he is the center of a plot to booby-trap an overly ambitious agent at the French Secret Service. A sequel followed called "Return of the Tall Blond Man with One Black Shoe" which was followed by a disappointing American remake, "The Man with One Red Shoe." In French with English subtitles or dubbed.
1972 (*PG/Jr. High-Adult*) 90m/C Pierre Richard, Bernard Blier, Jean Rochefort, Mireille Darc, Jean Carmet; **D:** Yves Robert; **W:** Francis Veber; **M:** Vladimir Cosma. **VHS, Beta, 8mm $24.95** *CVC, COL, VYY*

Tall Tales and Legends: Johnny Appleseed

True story of the legendary American who spent his life planting apple trees across the country, with the accent on comedy as Short hilariously communes with nature and talks to animals (missing: the Swedenborgian religious motives that drove the real-life Appleseed).
1986 (*Family*) 60m/C Martin Short, Rob Reiner, Molly Ringwald. **VHS $19.98** *FOX*

Tammy and the Bachelor 🎬🎬🎬

Backwoods Southern girl becomes involved with a romantic pilot and his snobbish family. They don't quite know what to make of her but she wins them over with her down-home philosophy. Features the hit tune, "Tammy." Charming performance by Reynolds.
1957 (*Family*) 89m/C Debbie Reynolds, Leslie Nielsen, Walter Brennan, Fay Wray, Sidney Blackmer, Mildred Natwick, Louise Beavers; **D:** Joseph Pevney, Oscar Brodney. **VHS, Beta $14.98** *MCA*

Tammy and the Doctor 🎬🎬

Dee reprises Debbie Reynolds's backwoods gal ("Tammy and the Bachelor"). Tammy becomes a nurse's aide, attracting the attention of young doctor Fonda, in his film debut.
1963 (*Family*) 88m/C Sandra Dee, Peter Fonda, MacDonald Carey; **D:** Harry Keller; **W:** Oscar Brodney. **VHS, Beta $14.98** *MCA*

Tank 🎬🎬

Retired Army officer Garner's son is thrown into jail on a trumped-up charge by a small town sheriff. Dad comes to the rescue with his restored Sherman tank. Trite and unrealistic portrayal of good versus bad made palatable by Garner's performance. **Hound Advisory:** Violence; mature themes.
1983 (*PG/Jr. High-Adult*) 113m/C James Garner, Shirley Jones, C. Thomas Howell, Mark Herrier, Sandy Ward, Jenilee Harrison, Dorian Harewood, G.D. Spradlin; **D:** Marvin J. Chomsky. **VHS, Beta, LV $19.95** *MCA*

Taps 🎬🎬🎬

Military academy students (age 12 and up) learn their school is to be closed, so they grab the guns and turn the compound into an armed fortress against the outside world. Antiwar morality play about excesses of zeal and patriotism in youthful minds, aspiring to be another "Lord of the Flies." It doesn't quite make it, but still impressive at times. **Hound Advisory:** Profanity, violence, mature themes.
1981 (*PG/Jr. High-Adult*) 126m/C Timothy Hutton, George C. Scott, Ronny Cox, Sean Penn, Tom Cruise; **D:** Harold Becker; **W:** Darryl Ponicsan, Robert Mark Kamen; **M:** Maurice Jarre. **VHS, Beta $19.98** *FOX*

Tarka the Otter

Nicely done nature film from Britain, set in the 1920s. A young otter encounters danger as he pursued his favorite eel meals, and is captured by a well-meaning fellow who wants to turn Tarka into a pet. Based on the book by Henry Williamson.
1978 (*Family*) 91m/C **VHS, Beta $39.95** *TWE*

Tarzan and His Mate 🎬🎬🎬

Second entry in the lavishly produced MGM Tarzan series. Weissmuller and O'Sullivan cohabit in unmarried bliss before the Hays Code moved them to a tree house with twin beds. Many angry elephants, nasty white hunters, and hungry lions. Laserdisc includes the original trailer.
1934 (*Jr. High-Adult*) 93m/B Johnny Weissmuller, Maureen O'Sullivan, Neil Hamilton, Paul Cavanagh; **D:** Jack Conway. **VHS, LV $19.98** *MGM, FCT*

Tarzan Escapes 🎬🎬🎬

Jane is tricked by evil hunters into abandoning her fairy tale life with Tarzan, so the Ape Man sets out to reunite with his one true love. The third entry in MGM's Weissmuller/O'Sullivan series is still among the better Tarzan movies thanks to the leads, but the Hays Office made sure Jane was wearing a lot more clothes this time around.
1936 (*Family*) 95m/B Johnny Weissmuller, Maureen O'Sullivan, John Buckler, Benita Hume, William Henry; **D:** Richard Thorpe. **VHS $19.98** *FOX, FCT*

Tarzan Finds a Son 🎬🎬🎬

Weissmuller and O'Sullivan returned to their roles after three years with the addition of the five-year-old Sheffield as Boy. He's an orphan whose awful relatives hope he stays lost so they can collect an inheritance. Jane and Tarzan fight to adopt the tyke and when the new family are captured by a wicked tribe only an elephant stampede can save them. More of what you expect in a Tarzan adventure.

1939 (*Family*) 90m/B Johnny Weissmuller, Maureen O'Sullivan, Johnny Sheffield, Ian Hunter, Henry Stephenson, Frieda Inescort, Henry Wilcoxon; *D:* Richard Thorpe. **VHS $19.98** *MGM*

Tarzan, the Ape Man 🐾🐾🐾

The definitive Tarzan movie; the first Tarzan talkie; the original of the long series starring Weissmuller. Dubiously faithful to the Edgar Rice Burroughs story, but recent attempts to remake, update or improve it (notably the pretentious 1984 Greystoke) have failed to near the original's entertainment value or even its technical quality. O'Sullivan as Jane and Weissmuller bring style and wit to their classic roles.
1932 (*Family*) 99m/B Johnny Weissmuller, Maureen O'Sullivan, Neil Hamilton; *D:* Woodbridge S. Van Dyke. **VHS, Beta, LV $19.98** *MGM, FCT*

Tarzan's New York Adventure 🐾🐾🐾⬩

O'Sullivan's final appearance as Jane is a so-so adventure with some humorous moments when Tarzan meets the big city. When Boy is kidnapped by an evil circus owner, Tarzan, Jane, and Cheta head out to rescue him. Tarzan shows off his jungle prowess by climbing skyscrapers and diving off the Brooklyn Bridge into the Hudson River. Lincoln, the screen's first Tarzan, has a cameo.
1942 (*Family*) 70m/B Johnny Weissmuller, Maureen O'Sullivan, Johnny Sheffield, Virginia Grey, Charles Bickford, Paul Kelly, Chill Wills, Russell Hicks, Cy Kendall; *Cameos:* Elmo Lincoln; *D:* Richard Thorpe. **VHS $19.98** *MGM*

Tarzan's Secret Treasure 🐾🐾🐾⬩

Tarzan saves an expedition from a savage tribe only to be repaid by having the greedy hunters hold Jane and Boy hostage. They want Tarzan's help in finding a secret cache of gold. But Tarzan doesn't take kindly to threats to his family and teaches those evil-doers a lesson.
1941 (*Family*) 81m/B Johnny Weissmuller, Maureen O'Sullivan, Johnny Sheffield, Reginald Owen, Barry Fitzgerald, Tom Conway, Philip Dorn; *D:* Richard Thorpe. **VHS $19.98** *MGM*

Techno Police 🐾🐾

Animated "Robocop" clone, but without that title's overwhelming live-action gore. Cyborg police officers patrol a futuristic urban landscape.
1987 (*Family*) 77m/C **VHS, Beta $14.99** *JFK, WTA*

Ted E. Bear: The Bear Who Slept Through Christmas

Cartoon holiday TV special. As Christmas approaches, all the bears are getting ready to go to sleep for the winter, except Ted E. Bear, who wants to see the fat guy in the red suit. Additional volumes available.
1983 (*Family*) 60m/C *V:* Tom Smothers, Arte Johnson, Barbara Feldon, Kelly Lange. **VHS, Beta $14.95** *FHE, WTA*

The Teddy Bears' Christmas

Teddy bear Ben goes on a quest to find his owner's little sister Sally a teddy bear of her own to love, just in time for Christmas.
1993 (*Preschool-Primary*) 26m/C **VHS $12.98** *FHE, WTA*

The Teddy Bears' Picnic

Little girl has the chance to find out what teddy bears do when they come to life one day per year in this cute cartoon.
1989 (*Family*) 30m/C **VHS, Beta $14.95** *FHE, WTA*

Teen Alien WOOF!

On Halloween night some kids explore a spooky old house. Aliens are afoot, and the wrapup turns the thing into a subteen version of "Invasion of the Body Snatchers." Generally non-threatening thriller for juvie audiences in which the real horror is the acting and direction. Also known as "The Varrow Mission."
1988 (*PG/Jr. High-Adult*) 88m/C Vern Adix, Michael Dunn. **VHS, Beta $79.95** *PSM*

Teen Witch 🐾

Semi-musical, totally forgettable farce about a demure high school girl who inherits magic powers on her 16th birthday. Benign sorcery gets her good looks, popularity, and the dishiest guy in class. She also plays pranks on grouchy teachers, but nothing extreme - or interesting. Note Sargent, of TV's "Bewitched," in a cameo.
1989 (*PG-13/Jr. High-Adult*) 94m/C Robin Lively, Zelda Rubinstein, Dan Gauthier, Joshua Miller, Dick Sargent; *D:* Dorian Walker. **VHS, Beta $89.95** *MED, VTR*

Teen Wolf 🐾🐾⬩

Nice, average teenager begins to show werewolf tendencies not part of usual adolescent transition - making him popular at high school when he leads the basketball team to victory. The underlying message is to be yourself, regardless of body hair. Lighthearted comedy, carried by the Fox charm, was made before "Back to the Future" but released afterwards to capitalize on his stardom. Inspired a sequel and a TV cartoon series, both also on video. **Hound Advisory:** Salty wolfboy language, sex talk.
1985 (*PG/Family*) 92m/C Michael J. Fox, James Hampton, Scott Paulin, Susan Ursitti; *D:* Rod Daniel; *M:* Miles Goodman. **VHS, Beta, LV, 8mm $14.95** *PAR*

Teen Wolf: All-American Werewolf

TV cartoon spinoff of the feature film. Young Scott Howard and his family seem normal enough by day but when the full moon hits, Scott and his family transform into wacky werewolves.
1986 (*Primary-Jr. High*) 120m/C **VHS, Beta $39.95** *WTA*

Teen Wolf Too 🐾🐾

Sequel to "Teen Wolf," without Michael J. Fox (surprise, surprise). Instead his character's cousin goes to college on a boxing scholarship and develops lycanthropy. More evidence that the sequel is rarely as good as the original. **Hound Advisory:** Sex talk, full-moon roughhousing, salty language, growling.
1987 (*PG/Jr. High-Adult*) 95m/C Jason Bateman, Kim Darby, John Astin, Paul Sand; *D:* Christopher Leitch. **VHS, Beta $14.95** *PAR*

"Teenage Mutant Ninja Turtles" waiting for pizza delivery

Teen Wolf: Wolf of My Dreams

Teen Wolf goes to Hollywood to meet his big screen werewolf idol and has a howl of a time.
1986 *(Primary-Jr. High)* 40m/C **VHS, Beta $9.98** *WTA, FHE*

Teenage Mutant Ninja Turtles 1: The Movie 🦴🦴◁

Live-action hit about the four sewer-dwelling turtles turned into warrior ninja mutants due to radiation, who try to rid NYC of the evil samurai-masked gang chieftain Shredder. Brought to life by Jim Henson's studios, the mighty terrapins Donatello, Leonard, Michelangelo, and Raphael are wonderful creations. Muppet magic and some clever lines glide around minimalist plot. The much-discussed violence is a non-issue; fights with Shredder's minions are bloodless, very funny slapstick gymnastics. History does record, however, some young fans who tried to run away to the sewers after seeing this... **Hound Advisory:** Much roughhousing. Every human kid in the movie belongs to Shredder's gang, a vast, ultra-cool tribe of urban Lost Boys whose criminal lifestyle is initially glamorized, though the message that juvenile delinquency leads to a certain emptiness (with allusions to Pinocchio) eventually is presented persuasively.

1990 (PG/ *Primary-Adult)* 95m/C Judith Hoag, Elias Koteas; *D:* Steven Barron; *W:* Todd W. Langen; *M:* John Du Prez; *V:* Robbie Rist, Corey Feldman, Brian Tochi, Kevin Clash, David McCharen. **VHS, Beta, LV, 8mm $24.99** *FHE, LIV, WTA*

Teenage Mutant Ninja Turtles 2: The Secret of the Ooze 🦴🦴

The teen terrapins search for the toxic waste that turned them into marketable martial-artist kid idols, but their old enemy Shredder has similar notions to breed mutant monsters of his own. Same formula, same comic attitude, same story sloppiness as the first film; between the two flicks there's one good, whole feature waiting to be spliced together. Dedicated to the memory of the late Jim Henson. **Hound Advisory:** Martial-arts roughhousing, again done as slapstick comedy.

1991 (PG/ *Jr. High-Adult)* 88m/C Francois Chau, David Warner, Paige Turco, Ernie Reyes Jr., Vanilla Ice; *D:* Michael Pressman. **VHS, Beta $22.98** *COL, NLC*

Teenage Mutant Ninja Turtles 3 🦴🦴

The Turtles hit 17th-century Japan to rescue loyal friend, reporter April O'Neil, dragged back centuries by a magic scepter. More plot (and budget) than the mutant heroes' previous live-action shell games, but enthusiasm seems to be

lagging. Martial arts remain blood-free gymnastics and swashbuckling, but they're not funny slapstick routines anymore. Better gags come from the parallel plight of several surprised samurai teleported to modern NYC. **Hound Advisory:** Martial roughhousing.
1993 (PG/*Primary-Jr. High*) 95m/C Elias Koteas, Paige Turco, Stuart Wilson, Sab Shimono, Vivian Wu; **D:** Stuart Gillard; **W:** Stuart Gillard; **M:** John Du Prez; **V:** Randi Mayem Singer, Matt Hill, Jim Raposa, David Fraser. **VHS, LV** *NLC, COL, IME*

Teenage Mutant Ninja Turtles: The Epic Begins

Original tale of the hardshelled heroes and their mentor Splinter the Rat, and how the team started their mission to clean up the streets by battling reprobates left and right. Turtle fans will want to compare/contrast this with the first two Mutant Ninja Turtle live-action movies covering much the same ground (but with actually less violence than these cartoons). Additional volumes available.
1987 (*Family*) 72m/C **VHS, Beta, LV $29.95** *FHE, WTA*

The Ten Commandments 🐾🐾🐾

Hollywood's garish Bible epics are mostly a motley bunch. On the short list of over-achievers is this stirring, mammoth-scale retelling of the life story of Moses, who turned his back on a privileged life to lead his enslaved people to freedom from Pharaoh and receive the title tablets. Exceptional cast, with Fraser Heston (son of Charlton) as the baby Moses at the beginning. Parting of Red Sea rivals any modern special effects. Available in widescreen on laserdisc. **Hound Advisory:** Original Sin of such religious epics was that they could depict all the violence and debauchery they wanted as long as Godliness prevailed in the last reel. This is no exception: brutality, mature themes, scary moments as the Ten Plagues ravage Egypt.
1956 (G/*Family*) 219m/C Charlton Heston, Yul Brynner, Anne Baxter, Yvonne De Carlo, Nina Foch, John Derek, H.B. Warner, Henry Wilcoxon, Judith Anderson, John Carradine, Douglass Dumbrille, Cedric Hardwicke, Martha Scott, Vincent Price, Debra Paget; **D:** Cecil B. DeMille; **M:** Elmer Bernstein. **Award Nominations:** Academy Awards '56: Best Art Direction/Set Decoration (Color), Best Color Cinematography, Best Costume Design (Color), Best Film Editing, Best Picture, Best Sound; **Awards:** Academy Awards '56: Best Special Effects. **VHS, Beta, LV $35.00** *PAR, FUS, IGP*

Ten Little Indians 🐾🐾

Ten people are gathered in an isolated inn under mysterious circumstances. One by one they are murdered, each according to a verse from a children's nursery rhyme. Not-so-grand British adaptation of the novel and stage play by Agatha Christie. **Hound Advisory:** Roughhousing.
1975 (PG/*Jr. High-Adult*) 98m/C Herbert Lom, Richard Attenborough, Oliver Reed, Elke Sommer, Charles Aznavour, Stephane Audran, Gert Frobe, Adolfo Celi, Orson Welles; **D:** Peter Collinson. **VHS, Beta, LV $59.98** *NLC*

Ten Who Dared 🐾◁

Fact-based tale of a team of Civil War vets braving the treacherous Colorado River in 1869 in an attempt to chart its course. Poorly paced tale from the Disney frontier-fun assembly line, sorely lacking even in the expected action.

1960 (*Family*) 92m/C Brian Keith, John Beal, James Drury; **D:** William Beaudine. **VHS, Beta $69.95** *DIS*

Tender Mercies 🐾🐾🐾🐾

Divorced, down-and-out country & western singer finds his life redeemed by the love of a young widow and her small son. He sobers up, gets Born Again, and is strong enough to survive when tragedy hits again. Wonderful, life-affirming, grassroots flick of the sort that Hollywood is always accused of never making anymore. Duvall does own warbling. **Hound Advisory:** Alcohol use, mature themes.
1983 (PG/*Jr. High-Adult*) 88m/C Robert Duvall, Tess Harper, Betty Buckley, Ellen Barkin, Wilford Brimley; **D:** Bruce Beresford; **W:** Horton Foote Jr.; **M:** George Dreyfus. **Award Nominations:** Academy Awards '83: Best Director (Beresford), Best Picture, Best Song ("Over You"); **Awards:** Academy Awards '83: Best Actor (Duvall), Best Original Screenplay; Golden Globe Awards '83: Best Actor—Drama (Duvall). **VHS, Beta, LV $14.98** *REP, BTV, HMV*

The Tender Tale of Cinderella Penguin

Five short animated tales retold through clever animation from Canada. In addition to the title story there's "Metamorphoses," "Froggie Went A' Courting," "The Sky Is Blue," and "The Owl and the Raven."
1991 (*Family*) 30m/C **VHS $14.95** *FCT, SMA, NFB*

The Tender Warrior 🐾🐾

Yet another animal adventure with "Grizzly Adams" star Haggerty as a woodsman; the twist is he's a grouchy moonshiner at odds with the nature-loving boy hero in the swamplands of Georgia.
1971 (G/*Family*) 85m/C Dan Haggerty, Charles Lee, Liston Elkins; **D:** Stewart Raffill. **VHS, Beta $59.95** *VCD*

The Tender Years 🐾🐾

Sentimental drama of a minister trying to outlaw dog fighting, spurred on by his son's fondness for a particular dog.
1947 (*Jr. High-Adult*) 81m/B Joe E. Brown, Richard Lyon, Noreen Nash, Charles Drake, Josephine Hutchinson; **D:** Harold Schuster. **VHS, Beta $12.95** *TCF*

Tennessee Tuxedo in Brushing Off a Toothache

The wacky penguin joins his pal Chumly the walrus in episodes from the '60s TV cartoon series.
196? (*Family*) 60m/C **VHS $14.99** *WTA*

Tennis Racquet

Walt Disney's Goofy plays one of the wackiest tennis games ever seen.
1977 (*Preschool-Primary*) 8m/C Goofy. **VHS, Beta $155.00** *DSN,*

The Terminator 🐾🐾🐾

Futuristic cyborg is sent to present-day Earth. His job: kill the woman who will conceive the child destined to become the great liberator and arch-enemy of the Earth's future rulers. The cyborg is also pursued by another futuristic visitor, who falls in love with the intended victim. Cameron's pacing is just right in this exhilarating, explosive thriller which displays

Arnie as one cold-blooded villain who utters a now famous line: "I'll be back." Followed by "Terminator 2: Judgment Day." **Hound Advisory:** Brutality, profanity, brief nudity, sex.

1984 (R/ *Sr. High-Adult)* 108m/C Arnold Schwarzenegger, Michael Biehn, Linda Hamilton, Paul Winfield, Lance Henriksen, Bill Paxton, Rick Rossovich, Dick Miller; *D:* James Cameron; *M:* Brad Fiedel. VHS, Beta, LV *NO*

Terminator 2: Judgment Day 🎬🎬🎬🎬

He said he'd be back and he is, programmed to protect the boy who will be mankind's post-nuke resistance leader. But the T-1000, a shape-changing, ultimate killing machine, is also on the boy's trail. Twice the mayhem, five times the special effects, ten times the budget of the first, but without Arnold it'd be half the movie. The word hasn't been invented to describe the special effects, particularly THE scariest nuclear holocaust scene yet. Worldwide megahit, but the $100 million budget nearly ruined the studio; Arnold accepted his $12 million in the form of a jet. Laserdisc features include pan and scan, widescreen and a "Making of T-2" short. **Hound Advisory:** Brutality, profanity.

1991 (R/ *Sr. High-Adult)* 139m/C Arnold Schwarzenegger, Linda Hamilton, Edward Furlong, Robert Patrick, Earl Boen, Joe Morton; *D:* James Cameron; *M:* Brad Fiedel. **Award Nominations:** Academy Awards '91: Best Cinematography, Best Sound; **Awards:** Academy Awards '91: Best Makeup, Best Sound, Best Sound Effects Editing, Best Visual Effects; MTV Movie Awards '92: Best Actor (Schwarzenegger), Best Actress (Hamilton), Best Film, Breakthrough Performance (Furlong), Most Desirable Female (Hamilton), Best Action Sequence; People's Choice Awards '92: Best Film. VHS, LV, 8mm $14.98 *LIV*

Terms of Endearment 🎬🎬🎬

Weeper follows the changing relationship between a young woman and her mother, over a thirty-year period. By turns comedy and high-level soap opera, this was Brooks' debut as screenwriter and director. Superb supporting cast headed by Nicholson's slyly charming neighbor/astronaut, with stunning performances by Winger and MacLaine as the two women who often know and love each other too well. Adapted from Larry McMurtry's novel. **Hound Advisory:** Profanity; sex.

1983 (PG/ *Jr. High-Adult)* 132m/C Shirley MacLaine, Jack Nicholson, Debra Winger, John Lithgow, Jeff Daniels, Danny DeVito; *D:* James L. Brooks; *W:* James L. Brooks; *M:* Michael Gore. **Award Nominations:** Academy Awards '83: Best Actress (Winger), Best Art Direction/Set Decoration, Best Film Editing, Best Sound, Best Supporting Actor (Lithgow), Best Original Score; **Awards:** Academy Awards '83: Best Actress (MacLaine), Best Adapted Screenplay, Best Director (Brooks), Best Picture, Best Supporting Actor (Nicholson); Golden Globe Awards '84: Best Actress—Drama (MacLaine), Best Film—Drama, Best Screenplay, Best Supporting Actor (Nicholson). VHS, Beta, LV $19.95 *PAR, BTV, HMV*

Terror in the Jungle 🎬

Plane crashes in Peruvian wilds and young boy survivor meets Jivaro Indians who think he's a god thanks to his golden hair. Cheapo jungle adventure, with horrible script - and a misleading video box cover depicting a sexy, scantily clad blonde. We won't get fooled again.

1968 (PG/ *Jr. High-Adult)* 95m/C Jimmy Angle, Robert Burns, Fawn Silver; *D:* Tom De Simone; *M:* Les Baxter. VHS $19.95 *ACA*

Terrytoons Olympics

Collection of Terrytoon characters in Olympic-style events.

1966 *(Preschool-Primary)* 42m/C VHS $5.99 *VTR*

Tess 🎬🎬🎬

Sumptuous adaptation of the Thomas Hardy novel "Tess of the D'Ubervilles." Kinski is wonderful as an innocent farm girl who is seduced by the young aristocrat she works for and then finds marriage to a man of her own class only brings more grief. Polanski's direction is faithful and artful. Visually captivating, but plotted like a Victorian novel at nearly three hours (though essentially faithful to the book, if that matters). **Hound Advisory:** Mature themes.

1980 (PG/ *Jr. High-Adult)* 170m/C Nastassia Kinski, Peter Firth, Leigh Lawson, John Collin; *D:* Roman Polanski; *W:* Roman Polanski. **Award Nominations:** Academy Awards '80: Best Director (Polanski), Best Picture, Best Original Score; **Awards:** Academy Awards '80: Best Art Direction/Set Decoration, Best Cinematography, Best Costume Design; Cesar Awards '80: Best Director (Polanski), Best Film; Golden Globe Awards '81: Best Foreign Film; Los Angeles Film Critics Association Awards '80: Best Director (Polanski); National Board of Review Awards '80: 10 Best Films of the Year. VHS, Beta, LV $14.95 *COL*

Tex 🎬🎬🎬🎬

First and best movie inspired by S.E. Hinton's young-adult novels is a loosely plotted tale of Oklahoma boys trying to raise themselves while dad does the rodeo circuit. Older Mason develops an ulcer vying for a college scholarship while repeatedly bailing young, irresponsible Tex out of trouble. Excellent performances by all. Dillon makes his character understandable and sympathetic, even when blundering through booze, drugs, and pointless classroom pranks. Allegedly the first pic under the Disney banner to use four-letter words, but the Hound heard nothing foul, just credible teen talk. **Hound Advisory:** Mature themes, salty language, sex talk, drug use, violence.

1982 (PG/ *Primary-Adult)* 103m/C Matt Dillon, Jim Metzler, Meg Tilly, Bill McKinney, Frances Lee McCain, Ben Johnson, Emilio Estevez; *D:* Tim Hunter; *M:* Pino Donaggio. VHS, Beta, LV *DIS, OM*

That Darn Cat 🎬🎬

Mediocre Disney comedy about a Siamese cat named D.C. ("Darned Cat," get it?) that provides enough clues for an allergy-afflicted FBI Agent to thwart kidnappers. Some funny slapstick and performances. Based on the book "Undercover Cat" by The Gordons.

1965 (G/ *Family)* 115m/C Hayley Mills, Dean Jones, Dorothy Provine, Neville Brand, Elsa Lanchester, Frank Gorshin, Roddy McDowall; *D:* Robert Stevenson. VHS, Beta $19.99 *DIS*

That Gang of Mine 🎬🎬

"East Side Kids" episode about gang member Mugg's ambition to be a jockey. Good racing scenes.

1940 *(Family)* 62m/B Bobby Jordan, Leo Gorcey, Clarence Muse, Dave O'Brien; *D:* Joseph H. Lewis. VHS, Beta $24.95 *NOS, DVT, HEG*

That Night 🎬🎬🎬

View of romance through the eyes of a young girl, circa 1961. Ten-year-old Alice is the confidant of rebellious 17-year-old neighbor Cheryl who enlists the young girl's aid as a go-between with her wrong side of the tracks boyfriend. Barely released to theaters, this sentimental tale gets a considerable lift from the cast. Based on a novel by Alice McDermott. **Hound Advisory:** Sex, mature themes.

1993 (PG-13/*Jr. High-Adult*) 89m/C C. Thomas Howell, Juliette Lewis, Eliza Dushku, Helen Shaver, John Dossett; **D:** Craig Bolotin; **W:** Craig Bolotin. **VHS, Beta, LV** *WAR*

That Sinking Feeling 🎬🎬🎬

Group of bored Scottish teenagers decide to steal 90 sinks from a plumber's warehouse. After the success of Forsythe's "Gregory's Girl," this earlier effort from the filmmaker's career was released to his great (and needless) reluctance; despite rough edges it's genuinely funny as the boys try to get rid of the sinks and turn a profit.
1979 (PG/*Sr. High-Adult*) 82m/C Robert Buchanan, John Hughes, Billy Greenlees, Alan Love; **D:** Bill Forsyth; **W:** Bill Forsyth. **VHS, Beta, LV** $59.98 *SUE*

That Was Then. . .This Is Now 🎬🎬

Adaptation of S.E. Hinton's teen novel about two guys from the wrong side of the tracks. Bryan gradually matures and turns toward a responsible life, and away from his wild, adoptive brother Mark. Far from a success - the scruffy Sheffer and "Mighty Duck" Estevez seem best suited to each other's roles instead of their respective Gallant and Goofus acts. And there's a silly finale contrived to end the tale on an upbeat note. But it does capture Hinton's moody mileau of young people fending for themselves in a hostile society where parents or other moral guardians are absent or ineffective. **Hound Advisory:** Violence, mature themes, profanity, drug use.
1985 (R/*Sr. High-Adult*) 102m/C Emilio Estevez, Craig Sheffer, Kim Delaney, Jill Schoelen, Barbara Babcock, Frank Howard, Larry B. Scott, Morgan Freeman; **D:** Christopher Cain; **W:** Emilio Estevez. **VHS, Beta, LV** $79.95 *PAR*

That's Dancing!

Anthology features some of film's finest moments in dance from classical ballet to break-dancing.
1985 (G/*Family*) 104m/C Fred Astaire, Ginger Rogers, Ruby Keeler, Cyd Charisse, Gene Kelly, Shirley MacLaine, Liza Minnelli, Sammy Davis Jr., Mikhail Baryshnikov, Ray Bolger, Jennifer Beals, Dean Martin; **D:** Jack Haley Jr.; **M:** Henry Mancini. **VHS, Beta, LV** $19.98 *MGM*

That's Entertainment

A compilation of scenes from the classic MGM musicals beginning with "The Broadway Melody" (1929) and ending with "Gigi" (1958). Great fun, especially for movie buffs.
1974 (G/*Family*) 132m/C Judy Garland, Fred Astaire, Frank Sinatra, Gene Kelly, Esther Williams, Bing Crosby; **D:** Jack Haley Jr.; **M:** Henry Mancini. **VHS, Beta, LV** $19.98 *MGM*

That's Entertainment, Part 2

Cavalcade of great musical and comedy sequences from MGM movies of the past. Also stars Jeanette MacDonald, Nelson Eddy, the Marx Brothers, Laurel and Hardy, Jack Buchanan, Ann Miller, Mickey Rooney, Louis Armstrong, Oscar Levant, Cyd Charisse, Elizabeth Taylor, Maurice Chavalier, Bing Crosby, Jimmy Durante, Clark Gable, and the Barrymores. Not as unified as its predecessor, but priceless nonetheless.
1976 (G/*Family*) 133m/C Fred Astaire, Gene Kelly. **VHS, Beta, LV** $19.98 *MGM*

That's Entertainment, Part 3 🎬🎬⁴⁄

Third volume contains 62 MGM musical numbers from over 100 films, hosted by nine of the original stars, and is based on outtakes and unfinished numbers from studio archives. One new technique used here is a split-screen showing both the actual film with a behind-the-scenes shot that includes cameramen, set designers, and dancers scurrying around. Although it has its moments, TE3 doesn't generate the same reverence for Hollywood's Golden Age that its predecessors managed to do. That 18-year gap between sequels may say something about what the studio execs thought of their film vault's remainders.
1993 (G/*Family*) 113m/C **D:** Bud Friedgen, Michael J. Sheridan; **W:** Bud Friedgen, Michael J. Sheridan; **M:** Marc Shaiman. **VHS, Beta, LV** *MGM*

That's My Hero!

Re-edited episodes of "The Secret Lives of Waldo Kitty," a Saturday-morning kids' show mixing live-action scenes of a daydreaming tabby cat with cartoon depictions of his fantasies, usually takeoffs on popular movie and TV adventures. Tapes of the original show are also available.
1975 (*Family*) 72m/C **VHS, Beta** *SUE, OM*

Their Only Chance 🎬🎬

Nature docu-drama about Steve Hoddy, a man with an amazing talent for communicating with animals, shown as he helps wounded beasts get back to the wilderness.
1978 (G/*Family*) 84m/C Jock Mahoney, Steve Hoddy; **D:** David Siddon. **VHS, Beta** *NO*

They Went That-a-Way & That-a-Way 🎬⁴⁄

Two bumbling deputies go undercover as convicts, then have to plan an escape when they realize nobody's going to let them out of prison. Lackluster family comedy, with a script by Conway.
1978 (PG/*Family*) 96m/C Tim Conway, Richard Kiel; **D:** Edward Montagne; **W:** Tim Conway. **VHS, Beta** $69.98 *SUE*

Thief of Baghdad 🎬🎬🎬⁴⁄

Fresh from "The Jungle Book," Sabu went on to play the nimble-witted young rogue Abu, who enlists the aid of a powerful genie to outwit the treacherous Grand Vizier of Baghdad and help a prince escape from a prison and realize his true love. Magnificent Arabian Nights spectacular, with lush Technicolor photography, epic special effects. Ingram makes the screen's greatest (non-animated) genie. The silent "Thief of Baghdad" (1924), with a superbly swashbuckling Douglas Fairbanks Sr., is also on cassette.
1940 (*Family*) 106m/C Sabu, Conrad Veidt, June Duprez, Rex Ingram, Tim Whelan, Michael Powell; **D:** Ludwig Berger; **M:** Miklos Rozsa. **VHS, Beta, LV** $14.98 *SUE, MLB, FUS*

Thief of Baghdad 🎬🎬

An Arabian Nights fantasy about a thief in love with a Sultan's daughter who has been poisoned. He seeks out the magical

blue rose which is the antidote. Not as lavish as the previous two productions of this title, nor as much fun.
1961 (*Family*) 89m/C Georgia Moll, Steve Reeves; **D:** Arthur Lubin. **VHS, Beta $59.98** *SUE*

The Thief of Baghdad 🎬🎬◁

TV adaptation of the fantasy-adventure has special effects that don't quite make the grade but a cast that often does; McDowall is a delight as the wily thief who helps the rather stuffy prince win the hand of Princess Yasmine.
1978 (*G/Family*) 101m/C Peter Ustinov, Roddy McDowall, Terence Stamp, Frank Finlay, Ian Holm; **D:** Clive Donner. **VHS, Beta $29.95** *GEM*

The Thin Man 🎬🎬🎬◁

Married sleuths Nick and Nora Charles investigate the mysterious disappearance of a wealthy inventor. Charming and sophisticated, this was the model for all husband-and-wife detective teams that followed. Don't miss Asta, their wire-hair terrier. Based on the novel by Dashiell Hammett. Its enormous popularity triggered five sequels, starting with "After the Thin Man."
1934 (*Family*) 90m/B William Powell, Myrna Loy, Maureen O'Sullivan, Cesar Romero, Porter Hall, Nat Pendleton, Minna Gombell, Natalie Moorhead, Edward Ellis; **D:** Woodbridge S. Van Dyke. **VHS, Beta, LV $19.95** *MGM, HMV*

The Thing Called Love 🎬🎬◁

"Singles" takes to Nashville in this unsentimental tale of four twentysomething singles trying to make their mark in the world of country music. The idea for the plot comes from the real-life Bluebird Cafe - the place where all aspiring singers and songwriters want to perform. Phoenix, Mathis, Mulroney, and Bullock do their own singing; look for Oslin as the cafe owner. Phoenix's last completed film role. **Hound Advisory:** Profanity and sex.
1993 (*PG-13/Jr. High-Adult*) 116m/C River Phoenix, Samantha Mathis, Sandra Bullock, Dermot Mulroney, K.T. Oslin, Anthony Clark, Webb Wilder; **Cameos:** Trisha Yearwood; **D:** Peter Bogdanovich; **W:** Allan Moyle, Carol Heikkinen. **VHS, Beta, LV** *PAR*

Think Big 🎬🎬◁

Twin bodybuilders, the Pauls (previously billed as 'The Barbarian Brothers'), are lunkhead truck drivers who pick up a brilliant teenage girl running from bad guys who want her revolutionary energy invention. Funnier than it sounds, with enjoyable goofing by the supporting cast. More than a spot of profanity. **Hound Advisory:** Excessive profanity, slapstick violence, and just a hint of sex.
1990 (*PG-13/Jr. High-Adult*) 86m/C Peter Paul, David Paul, Martin Mull, Ari Meyers, Richard Kiel, David Carradine, Richard Moll, Peter Lupus; **W:** Jim Wynorski, R.J. Robertson. **VHS, Beta, LV $89.98** *LIV, VTR*

Third Man on the Mountain 🎬🎬◁

Thrilling Disney epic about mountain climbing, shot in Switzerland and based on James Ramsey Ullman's "Banner in the Sky" (another title by which the film is known). In 1865 Switzerland young Rudi is determined to ascend the same forbidding peak as his ancestors have. But, after he joins a British expedition, Rudi learns there's more to climbing than he imagined.

1959 (*G/Family*) 106m/C James MacArthur, Michael Rennie, Janet Munro, James Donald, Herbert Lom, Laurence Naismith; **Cameos:** Helen Hayes; **D:** Ken Annakin. **VHS, Beta $69.95** *DIS*

13 Ghosts 🎬🎬◁

Castle, gimmicky mogul who inspired "Matinee," did this fun spook story. Typical American family moves to a castle with a lost treasure and 12 grotesque specters who need just one more victim to make their quota. Naturally it's the family's little boy who's hip to what's going on, thanks to his special ghost-viewing eyeglasses; such 3D-type spectacles were made available to patrons when this played theaters. Allegedly, fearful moviegoers could choose to see or not to see the blurry, ghouls, depending on which lens they used, an effect missing on video. Hamilton, the Wicked Witch from "The Wizard of Oz," has a great role as the housekeeper.
1960 (*Jr. High-Adult*) 88m/C Charles Herbert, Jo Morrow, Martin Milner, Rosemary DeCamp, Donald Woods, Margaret Hamilton; **D:** William Castle. **VHS, Beta $9.95** *GKK*

The 39 Steps 🎬🎬🎬🎬

Classic Hitchcock mistaken-man-caught-in-intrigue thriller, featuring some of his most often copied set pieces and the surest visual flair of his pre-war British period. Man on vacation in London meets a strange woman investigating a spy ring, who tells him a little something about what she knows. Soon she's dead and he's on the run to Scotland. The laserdisc version includes a twenty-minute documentary tracing the director's British period. Remade twice, in 1959 and 1979.
1935 (*Jr. High-Adult*) 81m/B Robert Donat, Madeleine Carroll, Godfrey Tearle, Lucie Mannheim, Peggy Ashcroft, John Laurie, Wylie Watson; **D:** Alfred Hitchcock; **W:** Charles Bennett, Alma Reville; **M:** Louis Levy. **VHS, Beta, LV, 8mm $8.95** *CNG, NOS, SUE*

This Boy's Life 🎬🎬🎬

In the 1950s divorcee Carolyn and her troubled adolescent son Toby settle in the town of Concrete, outside Seattle. She's hitched with Dwight (De Niro), a slick but rough-edged mechanic who proves to be a domestic tyrant for the rebellious boy. Strong performances by all, but keep your eye on DiCaprio (great in his first major role) as the confused and abused Toby, divided between dreams of prep school and the allure of the going-nowhere crowd. Based on the memoirs of Tobias Wolff; director Caton-Jones sensitively illustrates the skewed understanding of masculinity in the 1950s. **Hound Advisory:** Mature themes, domestic violence, profanity, juvenile drinking and smoking.
1993 (*R/Sr. High-Adult*) 115m/C Robert De Niro, Ellen Barkin, Leonardo DiCaprio, Jonah Blechman, Eliza Dushku, Chris Cooper, Carla Gugino, Zachary Ansley, Tracey Ellis, Kathy Kinney, Gerrit Graham; **D:** Michael Caton-Jones; **W:** Robert Getchell; **M:** Carter Burwell. **VHS, Beta, LV $95.99** *WAR, FCT, BTV*

This is My Life 🎬🎬◁

Dottie is torn between her skyrocketing career as a stand-up comic and her two small daughters. Immensely personable Kavner plays the divorced mom who is determined to chuck her cosmetic sales job for show business, but as offers pour in, she finds her girls suffering as a result of her success. Good

performances highlight an otherwise average drama. **Hound Advisory:** Salty language, sex, mature themes.

1992 (PG-13/*Jr. High-Adult*) 105m/C Julie Kavner, Samantha Mathis, Carrie Fisher, Dan Aykroyd, Gaby Hoffman; **D:** Nora Ephron; **W:** Nora Ephron, Delia Ephron. **VHS $19.98** *FXV*

Thoroughbreds Don't Cry 🎬🎬🎵

There's no crying in horse racing. Future "National Velvet" and "Black Stallion" horseman Rooney plays a jockey who rides in a fixed race on the orders of his no-good father. The kid has guilty feelings about it later and tries to redeem himself, but his good intentions backfire. Well-acted equine melodrama, with Garland as the hero's girlfriend adding a few songs.

1937 (*Family*) 80m/B Judy Garland, Mickey Rooney, Sophie Tucker, Sir C. Aubrey Smith, Ronald Sinclair, Forrester Harvey; **D:** Alfred E. Green. **VHS $19.98** *MGM, MVD*

Those Calloways 🎬🎬🎵

Those small-town Calloways attempt to establish a sanctuary for the flocks of wild geese who fly over the woods of Swiftwater, Maine. Okay Disney family fare, with good cast. Based on Paul Annixter's novel "Swiftwater."

1965 (PG/*Family*) 131m/C Brian Keith, Vera Miles, Brandon de Wilde, Walter Brennan, Ed Wynn, John Qualen, Linda Evans; **D:** Norman Tokar; **M:** Max Steiner. **VHS, Beta $69.95** *DIS*

Those Daring Young Men in Their Jaunty Jalopies 🎬🎬

Daring young 1920s drivers in noisy slow cars trek 1500 miles across country to a Monte Carlo finish line and call it a race. Sputtering attempt to conjure up the inspired zaniness of "Those Magnificent Men in Their Flying Machines."

1969 (G/*Family*) 125m/C Tony Curtis, Susan Hampshire, Terry-Thomas, Eric Sykes, Gert Frobe, Peter Cook, Dudley Moore, Jack Hawkins; **D:** Ken Annakin. **VHS $39.95** *PAR, FCT*

Thrashin' 🎬🎵

New-to-L.A. teen must prove his skills to a tough gang on skateboards by entering a treacherous race. For skateboarding fans only, but stunts won't disappoint them. **Hound Advisory:** Salty language, roughhousing.

1986 (PG-13/*Jr. High-Adult*) 93m/C Josh Brolin, Pamela Gidley, Robert Rusler, Chuck McCann; **D:** David Winters; **M:** Barry Goldberg. **VHS, Beta** *NO*

Three Amigos 🎬🎬

Three out-of-work silent screen stars are asked to defend a Mexican town from bandits; they think it's a public appearance stint. Spoof of Three Stooges and Mexican bandito movies that at times falls short, given the enormous amount of comedic talent involved. Generally enjoyable with some very funny scenes. Co-written by former "Saturday Night Live" producer Michaels. Short's first major film appearance.

1986 (PG/*Jr. High-Adult*) 105m/C Chevy Chase, Steve Martin, Martin Short, Joe Mantegna, Patrice Martinez, Jon Lovitz, Alfonso Arau, Randy Newman; **D:** John Landis; **W:** Steve Martin, Randy Newman, Lorne Michaels; **M:** Elmer Bernstein. **VHS, Beta, LV $14.99** *HBO*

The Three Billy Goats Gruff/The Three Little Pigs

Hunter narrates these classic children's stories from the "Rabbit Ears" series.

1991 (*Preschool-Primary*) 30m/C **VHS, LV $15.99** *KUI, NLC*

The Three Caballeros 🎬🎬🎬

Donald Duck stars in this journey through Latin America, where he falls in love with a local chick (so to speak) and tours the country on a flying serape. Full of music, variety, and live-action/animation segments. Stories include "Pablo the Penguin," "Little Gauchito," and adventures with Joe Carioca, who was first introduced in Disney's "Saludos Amigos." Produced initially for political reasons (to cement US relations with its southern neighbors during wartime), today this stands as one of their very best pieces of animation. 🎵The Three Caballeros; Baia.

1945 (*Family*) 71m/C **V:** Sterling Holloway, Aurora Miranda. **VHS, Beta, LV $24.99** *DIS, APD, WTA*

Three Decades of Donald Duck Series

Time-spanning Disney set of three separate Donald Duck tapes: "Donald's Nephews" (1938), "Fire Chief" (1940), and "Up a Tree" (1955).

1990 (*Preschool-Primary*) 8m/C **VHS, Beta $170.00** *MTI, DSN*

Three Fugitives 🎬🎬

Ex-con determined to go straight is taken hostage by a bungling first-time bank robber, who is only attempting the holdup in order to support his withdrawn little girl. All three wind up hunted by the cops, learn to like each other on the lam, etc. Comedy works, pathos is way too maudlin and slow. Like "Three Men and a Baby" and others, this is a calculated Disney/Touchstone remake of a French film; here "Les Fugitifs" done by the same director so you're not missing anything. **Hound Advisory:** Violence, mainly slapstick.

1989 (PG-13/*Jr. High-Adult*) 96m/C Nick Nolte, Martin Short, James Earl Jones, Kenneth McMillan, Sarah Rowland Doroff, Alan Ruck; **D:** Francis Veber; **W:** Francis Veber. **VHS, Beta, LV $19.99** *TOU*

The Three Little Pigs

Walt Disney's "Silly Symphony" retelling of the famous pig tale that teaches the importance of careful planning is one of his very best shorts and took an Academy Award for Best Cartoon, Short Subject.

1933 (*Preschool-Primary*) 13m/C **VHS, Beta $195.00** *DSN, MTI*

The Three Lives of Thomasina 🎬🎬🎬

In turn-of-the-century Scotland, a veterinarian orders his daughter's beloved cat destroyed when the pet is diagnosed with tetanus. After Thomasina's death (with scenes of kitty heaven), a beautiful and mysterious healer from the woods is able to bring the animal back to life, restoring feline (with add-on bonus to standard nine lives) to the little girl mourning

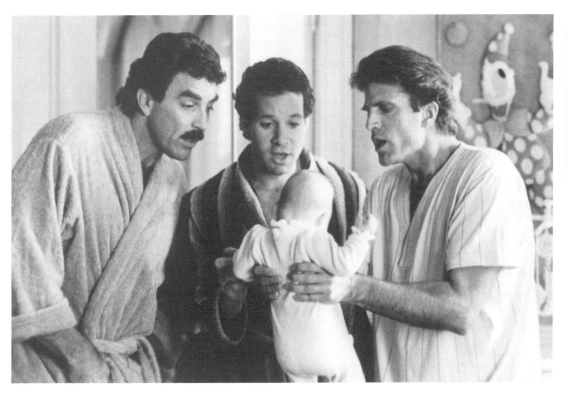

Child care tips in "Three Men and a Baby" (1987)

her previous demise. Lovely Disney fairy tale with good performances by all.
1963 (PG/Family) 95m/C Patrick McGoohan, Susan Hampshire, Karen Dotrice, Matthew Garber; *D:* Don Chaffey. **VHS, Beta $19.99** *DIS, TVC*

Three Men and a Baby 🦴🦴🦴

The lives of three swinging bachelors living in New York are shaken by the sudden arrival of a baby girl - possibly the daughter of one of them. The libertines take turns fathering the tyke under trying circumstances, especially when some crooks come sniffing around. Well-paced, charming and fun, with good acting from all. Remake of the French movie "Three Men and a Cradle," also on video and worth checking out in its own right. **Hound Advisory:** Salty language, sex talk, drug talk.
1987 (PG/Primary-Adult) 102m/C Tom Selleck, Steve Guttenberg, Ted Danson, Margaret Colin, Nancy Travis, Philip Bosco, Celeste Holm, Derek De Lint, Cynthia Harris, Lisa Blair, Michelle Blair; *D:* Leonard Nimoy; *W:* James Orr, Jim Cruickshank; *M:* Marvin Hamlisch. **VHS, Beta, LV, 8mm $19.99** *TOU, BVV*

Three Men and a Cradle 🦴🦴🦴🦴

Remade in the U.S. in 1987 as "Three Men and a Baby," this French film features the same plot about a bachelor trio living together who suddenly find themselves the guardians of a

baby girl. After the initial shock wears off, they fall in love with her and won't let her go. Fans of the American version may like the original even more. In French with English subtitles.
1985 (PG-13/Sr. High-Adult) 100m/C Roland Giraud, Michel Boujenah, Andre Dussollier; *D:* Coline Serreau; *W:* Coline Serreau. **Award Nominations:** Academy Awards '85: Best Foreign Language Film; **Awards:** Cesar Awards '86: Best Film, Best Supporting Actor (Boujenah). **VHS, LV $19.98** *LIV, MGM, INJ*

Three Men and a Little Lady 🦴🦴🦴

In this lesser but still entertaining sequel to "Three Men and a Baby," the mother of the once-abandoned child decides that her daughter needs a legitimate father. Although she would prefer to marry Selleck's character, he doesn't get the message, so the mom chooses a snooty British film director. All comes out well in the end, though. **Hound Advisory:** Salty language, sex talk.
1990 (PG/Sr. High-Adult) 100m/C Tom Selleck, Steve Guttenberg, Ted Danson, Nancy Travis, Robin Weisman, Christopher Cazenove, Fiona Shaw, Sheila Hancock, John Boswall, Jonathan Lynn, Sydney Walsh; *D:* Emile Ardolino; *W:* Charlie Peters, Sara Parriott, Josann McGibbon; *M:* James Newton Howard. **VHS, Beta, LV $19.99** *TOU*

Three Musketeers 🦴🦴

Very loose adaptation of Alexander Dumas, depicting the Musketeers in the form of a trio of American pals in the

Foreign Legion, fighting against nefarious sheik El Shaitan. Wayne is the D'Artagnan equivalent, in the weakest of his serial efforts. In 12 chapters.

1933 *(Family)* 215m/B John Wayne, Raymond Hatton, Lon Chaney Jr. **VHS, Beta $24.95** *NOS, VCN, VDM*

The Three Musketeers 𝄞𝄞◁

Three royal guards who are "all for one and one for all" join forces with rookie D'Artagnan to battle the power-hungry Cardinal Richelieu (portrayed by ace screen villain Price). Colorful edition of the adventure classic by Alexander Dumas, with an all-star cast and grand Hollywood production values. Singer/dancer Kelly seems overaged for the youthful hothead D'Artagnan, but his light-stepping moves suit the swordfights perfectly. **Hound Advisory:** Violence.

1948 *(Family)* 126m/C Lana Turner, Gene Kelly, June Allyson, Gig Young, Angela Lansbury, Van Heflin, Keenan Wynn, Robert Coote, Reginald Owen, Frank Morgan, Vincent Price, Patricia Medina; **D:** George Sidney. **VHS, Beta, LV $19.98** *MGM, CCB*

Three Musketeers 𝄞𝄞

Hanna-Barbera cartoon TV version of the classic Alexander Dumas tale about three of the king's swordsmen and the upstart D'Artagnan pitted against the devious Cardinal Richelieu in France.

1973 *(Family)* 74m/C **VHS, Beta $26.95** *WTA*

Three Musketeers 𝄞𝄞𝄞

Extravagant, funny version of the Dumas classic, more for the young-at-heart than the very young. Three swashbucklers and newcomer D'Artagnan set out to save the honor of the French Queen. To do so they must oppose the evil cardinal who has his eyes on the power behind the throne. Winning combination of slapstick and high adventure throws some sexual bawdiness in for good measure. Followed by "The Four Musketeers" and "The Return of the Musketeers." **Hound Advisory:** Swashbuckling violence, modest sex, alcohol use.

1974 *(PG/Jr. High-Adult)* 105m/C Richard Chamberlain, Oliver Reed, Michael York, Raquel Welch, Frank Finlay, Christopher Lee, Faye Dunaway, Charlton Heston, Geraldine Chaplin, Simon Ward, Jean-Pierre Cassel; **D:** Richard Lester. **VHS, Beta** *COL*

The Three Musketeers 𝄞𝄞◁

Yet another version, this time from Disney, of the classic swashbuckler with Porthos, Athos, Aramis, and the youthful D'Artegnan banding together against the evil Cardinal Richelieu and the tempting Milady DeWinter to save France. Cute stars, a lot of action stunts and swordplay, a few jokes, and cartoon bad guys. Okay for the family crowd. **Hound Advisory:** Swashbuckling MTV violence.

1993 *(PG/Jr. High-Adult)* 105m/C Kiefer Sutherland, Charlie Sheen, Chris O'Donnell, Oliver Platt, Rebecca DeMornay, Tim Curry, Gabrielle Anwar, Julie Delpy, Michael Wincott; **D:** Stephen Herek; **W:** David Loughery; **M:** Michael Kamen. **VHS, LV** *DIS*

The Three Musketeers: All for One and One for All! 𝄞𝄞

Animated adaptation of the legendary Dumas tale about D'Artagnan and his three swashbuckling friends fighting their honor and glory versus the plotters and pretenders against the throne of France.

1977 *(Family)* 85m/C **VHS $14.99** *JFK*

3 Ninjas 𝄞𝄞◁

There's barely an original moment in this lively cross between "Home Alone" and kung-fu pics, about three brothers who are trained as ninjas by their Japanese grandpa. When bad guys try to kidnap the boys, they're in for trouble. Likeable kids, funny action, short running time - all add up to surprisingly enjoyable, no-brainer family fun. **Hound Advisory:** Roughhousing - but with an emphasis on slapstick pratfalls and bumbling villains, no serious violence.

1992 *(PG/Family)* 84m/C Victor Wong, Michael Treanor, Max Elliott Slade, Chad Power, Rand Kingsley, Alan McRae, Margarita Franco, Toru Tanaka, Patrick Laborteaux; **D:** Jon Turteltaub; **W:** Edward Emanuel; **M:** Rick Marvin. **VHS, Beta, LV $19.99** *TOU, PMS*

3 Ninjas Kick Back 𝄞𝄞◁

Sequel to the popular "3 Ninjas." Three brothers help their grandfather protect a ceremonial knife won in a ninja tournament in Japan 50 years earlier. Gramps' ancient adversary in that tournament, now an evil tycoon, wants the sword back and he's willing to enlist the aid of his three American grandchildren, members of garage band Teenage Vomit, to get it. The showdown eventually heads to Japan, where "Kick Back," unlike predecessors, dispenses with the Japan-bashing. High-spirited action fare that kids will enjoy. **Hound Advisory:** Roughhousing; beware tasteless gag about flatulence, fat women, and a garage band called Teenage Vomit.

1994 *(PG/Jr. High-Adult)* 95m/C Victor Wong, Max Elliott Slade, Sean Fox, Evan Bonifant, Sab Shimono, Dustin Nguyen, Jason Schombing, Caroline Junko King, Angelo Tiffe; **D:** Charles Kanganis; **W:** Mark Saltzman; **M:** Rick Marvin. **VHS** *NYR*

Three O'Clock High 𝄞𝄞◁

Nervous, nerdy Jerry stumbles into a 3 p.m. duel with the new bully in high school and tries every trick possible to avoid his fate, but naturally the ordeal turns out to be a growing experience for our student hero. Debuting director Joanou has fun with snazzy camera tricks and a high-school-as-Hell attitude. **Hound Advisory:** Roughhousing, salty language.

1987 *(PG/Primary-Adult)* 97m/C Casey Siemaszko, Anne Ryan, Stacey Glick, Jonathan Wise, Richard Tyson, Jeffrey Tambor, Philip Baker Hall, John P. Ryan; **D:** Phil Joanou; **W:** Richard Christian Matheson, Thomas Szollosi; **M:** Tangerine Dream. **VHS, Beta, LV $79.95** *MCA*

Three Sesame Street Stories

Jim Henson's muppets are set to animation in three tales based on the PBS children's series.

1990 *(Preschool-Primary)* 30m/C **VHS $7.95**

Three Stooges

Long a fave with kids (and adult males), the slapstick Stooges are widely available in their original short subjects. Thirteen one-hour volumes are in this 1930s series; a separate "Other Nyuks" set from Columbia compiles Stooge offerings from the 1940s. Other titles like "The Lost Stooges" and "Medium Rare" concentrate mainly on Stooge cameo appearances and TV guest spots, mainly for hardcore Stoogephiles. Beware of a few tapes out there that are really episodes of a lame Stooges cartoon series, done when the original comedians got too old for roughhousing and head-bopping.
193? *(Family)* 60m/B Moe Howard, Shemp Howard, Larry Fine. **VHS, Beta, LV $9.95** *DVT*

Three Stooges: A Ducking They Will Go

Comedy trio nyuks it up in "Three Little Twirps" (1943), "Ants in the Pantry" (1936), and "A Ducking They Did Go" (1939), where they are conned into selling shares in a phony duck hunting club.
193? *(Family)* 50m/B Moe Howard, Curly Howard, Larry Fine. **VHS $14.95** *COL*

Three Stooges: A Plumbing We Will Go

Early Stooges episodes entitled "Violent is the Word for Curly" (1938), "Punch Drunks" (1934), and "A Plumbing We Will Go" (1940).
1934 *(Family)* 60m/B Moe Howard, Curly Howard, Larry Fine. **VHS $14.95** *COL*

Three Stooges: Cash and Carry

Stooges comedy shorts include "Cash and Carry" (1937), "No Census, No Feeling" (1940), and "Some More of Samoa" (1941).
194? *(Family)* 56m/B Moe Howard, Curly Howard, Larry Fine. **VHS $14.95** *COL*

Three Stooges: If a Body Meets a Body

Stooges madness abounds in "Spook Louder" (1943), "Men in Black" (1934), and "If a Body Meets a Body" (1945).
1934 *(Family)* 53m/B Moe Howard, Curly Howard, Larry Fine. **VHS $14.95** *COL*

Three Stooges: In the Sweet Pie and Pie

Wealthy Tiska, Taska, and Baska Jones need to marry three death row convicts in order to claim their inheritance "In the Sweet Pie and Pie" (1941), but then the Stooges are freed. Also features "Phony Express" (1943), and "Playing the Ponies" (1937).
194? *(Family)* 48m/B Moe Howard, Curly Howard, Larry Fine. **VHS $14.95** *COL*

Three Stooges Meet Hercules 🦴🦴🦴

In probably the best of their few feature films, the Stooges hop aboard a time machine and go from Ithaca, New York to Ithaca, ancient Greece, joining a wimpy scientist and his girlfriend. There the maiden is kidnapped by Hercules (a bad guy!), and the Stooges' brainy nerd friend must get pumped up to fight the muscleman.
1961 *(Family)* 80m/B Moe Howard, Larry Fine, Joe DeRita, Vicki Trickett, Quinn Redeker; *D:* Edward L. Bernds. **VHS, Beta $9.95** *GKK*

Three Stooges: So Long Mr. Chumps

The boys blend violence and buffoonery as only they can in "So Long Mr. Chumps" (1941), which finds Larry, Moe, and Curly searching for an honest man. Also features "Three Loan Wolves" (1946), and "Even as I.O.U." (1942).
194? *(Family)* 50m/B Moe Howard, Curly Howard, Larry Fine. **VHS $14.95** *COL*

Three Stooges: What's the Matador?

The boys go for belly laughs in "Boob in Arms" (1940), "What's the Matador?" (1942), and "Mutts to You" (1938).
194? *(Family)* 60m/B Moe Howard, Curly Howard, Larry Fine. **VHS $14.95** *COL*

The Three Worlds of Gulliver 🦴🦴🦴

Colorful version of the Jonathan Swift classic that fits in more of the book than most adaptations. Here, after his tribulations with the small and small-minded Lilliputians, Gulliver and his fiancee drift to another island - Brobdingnag, inhabited by a superstitious race of giants. Now it's Gulliver's turn to view things from a tiny perspective. Occasional stop-motion f/x by Ray Harryhausen.
1959 *(Family)* 100m/C Kerwin Mathews, Jo Morrow, Basil Sydney, Mary Ellis; *D:* Jack Sher; *W:* Arthur Ross, Jack Sher; *M:* Bernard Herrmann. **VHS, Beta, LV $14.95** *COL, MLB, CCB*

Through the Looking Glass

Animated, contemporary version of the Alice in Wonderland story, with a wild assortment of celebrity voices.
1987 *(Preschool-Primary)* 90m/C *V:* Leif Erickson, Phyllis Diller, Jonathan Winters, Mr. T. **VHS, Beta** *MED*

Throw Momma from the Train 🦴🦴🦴

DeVito plays a man, henpecked by his horrific mother, who tries to persuade his writing professor (Crystal) to exchange murders. DeVito will kill Crystal's ex-wife and Crystal will kill DeVito's mother. Only mama isn't going to be that easy to get rid of. Fast-paced and entertaining black comedy. Ramsey steals the film. Inspired by Hitchcock's "Strangers on a Train." **Hound Advisory:** Salty language.
1987 *(PG-13/Jr. High-Adult)* 88m/C Danny DeVito, Billy Crystal, Anne Ramsey, Kate Mulgrew, Kim Greist, Branford Marsalis, Rob Reiner, Bruce Kirby; *D:* Danny DeVito; *W:* Stu Silver; *M:* David Newman. **VHS, Beta, LV $9.98** *ORI*

Thumbelina

Japanese-made animation of the Hans Christian Andersen tale about a thumb-sized girl. While she searches for her prince's

Tulip Kingdom, numerous friendly animals want her as a bride instead. A few genuinely funny bits make this easier to take, though songs are dreadful, and the picture looks elongated and weird; it seems they transferred a wide-screen cartoon (meant to project through a distorting lens) to video without image correction, so everything's tall and skinny. **1984** (G/Family) 64m/C **D:** Y. Serigawa. **VHS, Beta $19.95** COL, WTA

Thumbelina 𝄢𝄢◁

Bluth's long-in-production adaptation of Hans Christian Andersen's fable about a thumb-sized little girl searching for her handsome, and also miniature, prince. Subplot about Thumbelina being detoured into a concert career ("Rock-A-Doodle" all over again?) is a typical postmodern Bluth touch that seems jarring in its fairy-tale context. Blah songs by Barry Manilow.
1994 (G/Family) 80m/C **D:** Don Bluth, Gary Goldman; **W:** Don Bluth; **M:** William Ross, Barry Manilow, Barry Manilow, Jack Feldman, Bruce Sussman; **V:** Jodi Benson, Gary Imhoff, Charo, Gilbert Gottfried, Carol Channing, John Hurt, Will Ryan, June Foray, Kenneth Mars. **VHS, Beta, LV $24.95** WAR

Thumpkin and the Easter Bunnies

When Johnny's eggs accidentally drop out of his bag, one by one they are retrieved and decorated by the animals who live in the meadow.
1992 (Preschool-Primary) 26m/C **VHS $12.98** FHE

Thundarr the Barbarian, Vol. 1

Outdated (we hope) Saturday-morning cartoon heroics set in a barbaric future world after a comet destroys civilization in 1994 (don't say nobody warned us). In this episode, Thundarr, Princess Ariel, and Ookla the Mot fight sorcery and slavery. Additional volumes available.
1980 (Preschool-Primary) 57m/C **VHS, Beta $19.95** WOV, WTA

Thunderball 𝄢𝄢

Fourth installment in Ian Fleming's James Bond series finds 007 on a mission to thwart SPECTRE, which has threatened to blow up Miami by atomic bomb if 100 million pounds in ransom is not paid. One of the more tedious Bond entries but a big box-office success. Tom Jones sang the title song. Remade as "Never Say Never Again" in 1983 with Connery reprising his role as Bond after a 12-year absence. **Hound Advisory:** Violence, alcohol use, suggested sex.
1965 (PG/Jr. High-Adult) 125m/C Sean Connery, Claudine Auger, Adolfo Celi, Lucianna Paluzzi, Rik von Nutter, Martine Beswick, Molly Peters, Guy Doleman, Bernard Lee, Lois Maxwell, Desmond Llewelyn; **D:** Terence Young; **W:** John Hopkins, Richard Maibaum; **M:** John Barry. **VHS, Beta, LV $19.98** MGM, TLF

Thunderbirds

Popular sci-fi show from the British TV team of Gerry and Sylvia Anderson, this mixes terrific special effects and miniature sets with a cast composed entirely of marionette puppets, manipulated by electronics and invisible wires ("Super Marionation," they liked to call it). Yes, wooden acting triumphs in the sagas of the Tracy family, who run a high-tech interplanetary lifeguard agency called International Rescue and save the day anytime someone is plunging into

the sun or drifting aimlessly in the ocean. Genuine cult item that has inspired spinoffs, feature films, and more than one rock band. Each tape in the series features one full-length adventure.
1966 (Preschool-Primary) 92m/C **VHS, Beta** FHE

Thunderbirds 6 𝄢𝄢

Feature version of Gerry and Sylvia Anderson's hit British puppet TV show (in 'Super Marionation') about International Rescue and their missions on land, sea, and space.
1966 (Preschool-Jr. High) 89m/C **D:** David Lane. **VHS, Beta $49.95** MGM

Thunderbirds 2086

Revival of the famed British puppet spectacle about an elite group of cadets flying around the galaxy for International Rescue to protect the world from danger. Each tape in the series contains two episodes.
1984 (Family) 50m/C **VHS, Beta $39.95** MPI, WTA

Thunderbirds are Go 𝄢𝄢◁

Feature film spinoff of the futuristic British TV series featuring rave electronic marionette faves, the Tracy family and their International Rescue team. Here the crew try to save the disabled Zero X spacecraft. Filled with spectacular gadgets, explosions, and remarkable puppetry.
1966 (Family) 92m/C **D:** Gerry Anderson. **VHS, Beta $19.95** MGM

Thunderbirds: Countdown to Disaster

Those high-flying marionettes return for another rousing adventure.
1981 (Family) 90m/C **VHS, LV $39.98** FHE

Thunderbirds in Outerspace

The team of marionettes must venture into the darkness of space for this mission.
1981 (Family) 90m/C **VHS, LV $39.98** FHE

Thunderbirds to the Rescue

The marionette rescue team responds to calls for help from land, sea, and air.
19?? (Family) 90m/C **VHS $39.98** FHE

Thundercats

Hailing from the planet Thundera (makes sense), these felines possess extraordinary intellectual and physical prowess far beyond those of ordinary kitties. Voyaging to Earth, where mankind is extinct, they use their advanced abilities to fight the villainous Mumma-Ra and start a brand new world. Rankin-Bass animated TV feature launching a "Thundercats" cartoon series for viewers who couldn't get enough of the T-cats and their line of toy action figures.
1985 (Preschool-Primary) 80m/C **VHS, Beta** FHE

Thundercats, Vol. 1: Exodus

Those unforgettable Thundercats rise to the occasion when they encounter sinister mutants. Additional volumes available.
1985 *(Family)* 75m/C **VHS, Beta $24.95** *FHE, WTA*

Thursday's Game ♫♫♫

Two crisis-besieged businessmen meet every Thursday, using poker as a ruse to work on their business and marital problems. Wonderful cast; intelligently written. Made for television. **Hound Advisory:** Mature themes.
1974 *(PG/Jr. High-Adult)* 99m/C Gene Wilder, Ellen Burstyn, Bob Newhart, Cloris Leachman, Nancy Walker, Valerie Harper, Rob Reiner; *D:* James L. Brooks; *W:* James L. Brooks. **VHS, Beta, LV $69.95** *VMK*

The Tiger and the Brahmin

Kingsley, best known for his portrayal in "Gandhi," relates an Indian folktale against brilliant illustrations, from an episode of the acclaimed "Rabbit Ears" series first aired on Showtime cable TV.
1991 *(Family)* 30m/C *M:* Ravi Shankar. **VHS $9.95** *FCT, MLT*

Tiger Bay ♫♫♫

Young Polish sailor, on leave in Cardiff, murders his unfaithful girlfriend. Lonely ten-year-old Gillie sees the crime and takes the murder weapon, thinking it will make her more popular with her peers. Confronted by a police detective, she convincingly lies but eventually the sailor finds Gillie and kidnaps her, hoping to keep her quiet until he can get aboard his ship. A delicate relationship evolves between the child and the killer as she tries to help him escape and the police close in. Marks Hayley Mills' first major role and one of her finest performances.
1959 *(Family)* 107m/B John Mills, Horst Buchholz, Hayley Mills, Yvonne Mitchell; *D:* J. Lee Thompson. **VHS, Beta $19.95** *PAR*

Tiger Town ♫♫◁

Alex is a young Detroit Tigers baseball fan who fixates from afar on the team's oldest player Billy 'The Hawk' Young. Alex decides he's Billy's good luck charm, a la "Angels in the Outfield"; as long as the boy attends the game, the aging athlete will bat his way closer to a pennant victory. But how can Alex slip away from school to help his idol? A simple, unusually somber Disney drama (realistic, almost drab) made for the Magic Kingdom's cable channel.
1983 *(G/Family)* 76m/C Roy Scheider, Justin Henry, Ron McLarty, Bethany Carpenter, Noah Moazezi; *D:* Alan Shapiro. **VHS, Beta $69.95** *DIS*

A Tiger Walks ♫♫◁

Universal Pictures brought a number of newspaper comic strips to film as serials. This one features the title character, a heroic pilot, in battle against the oriental supervillain known as the Dragon, who wants to stop the formation of a worldwide airline. In 13 chapters.
1964 *(Family)* 88m/C Sabu, Pamela Franklin, Brian Keith, Vera Miles, Kevin Corcoran, Peter Brown, Una Merkel, Frank McHugh, Edward Andrews; *D:* Norman Tokar; *M:* Buddy Baker. **VHS, Beta $69.95** *DIS*

Tigersharks: Power of the Shark

Undersea superheroes are challenged by the evil Mantanas and Captain Bizarrly in this animated adventure flotsam.
1987 *(Family)* 40m/C **VHS, Beta $14.95** *LHV, WAR, WTA*

Till the Clouds Roll By ♫♫◁

All-star, high-gloss musical biography of songwriter Jerome Kern, that, in typical Hollywood fashion, bears little resemblance to the composer's life. Filled with wonderful songs from his Broadway hit. ♫Showboat Medley; Till the Clouds Roll By; Howja Like to Spoon with Me?; The Last Time I Saw Paris; They Didn't Believe Me; I Won't Dance; Why Was I Born?; Who?; Sunny.
1946 *(Family)* 137m/C Robert Walker, Van Heflin, Judy Garland, Frank Sinatra, Lucille Bremer, Kathryn Grayson, June Allyson, Dinah Shore, Lena Horne, Virginia O'Brien, Tony Martin; *D:* Richard Whorf. **VHS, Beta, LV $19.98** *CNG, NOS, MGM*

Tilt ♫

Flimsy storyline concerns a 14-year-old runaway girl's adventures with an aspiring rock star. Her pinball expertise eventually leads to a match against pinball champ Durning. Cheap looking, overlong tale came out at just about the time video games nearly wiped pinball off the planet. **Hound Advisory:** Profanity; sex talk; drug talk; pinball.
1978 *(PG/Jr. High-Adult)* 111m/C Charles Durning, Ken Marshall, Brooke Shields, Geoffrey Lewis; *D:* Rudy Durand; *W:* Rudy Durand, Donald Cammell. **VHS** *NO*

Tim Tyler's Luck

Well-remembered relic from when Universal Pictures was in the movie-serial business. This adaptation of Lyman Young's newspaper comic-strip follows Tim's African quest for his missing father. The hero must stay one step ahead of the evil ivory-hunter Spider Webb and his armored jungle tank. Good production values include a musical score Universal used again and again. In twelve chapters. **Hound Advisory:** Violence.
1937 *(Jr. High-Adult)* 235m/B Frankie Thomas Jr., Frances Robinson, Al Shear, Norman Willis, Earl Douglas, Jack Mulhall, Frank Mayo, Pat O'Brien; *D:* Ford Beebe, Wyndham Gittens. **VHS $29.95** *NOS, GPV, FCT*

Time Bandits ♫♫♫

11-year-old boy, neglected by his parents, takes off with a gang of time-travelling dwarfs using God's own map of holes in the Cosmos to commit robberies in the eras of Robin Hood, Napoleon, Agamemnon, and other legends. Epic fantasy-comedy from members of England's Monty Python team won comparisons with "The Wizard of Oz" when it first came out. Time has proven the Bandits to not be at Wizard's level, but it remains a frenetic mix of satire, amazing f/x, and high adventure. Produced by former Beatle George Harrison; the hit-hungry Disney company backed out of a chance to finance the offbeat tale, then had to watch as it became a surprise at the box office. **Hound Advisory:** Violence, including a pitiless fate served up for the young hero's nitwit mom and dad.

1981 (PG/Family) 110m/C John Cleese, Sean Connery, Shelley Duvall, Katherine Helmond, Ian Holm, Michael Palin, Ralph Richardson, Kenny Baker, Peter Vaughan, David Warner; **D:** Terry Gilliam; **W:** Michael Palin, Terry Gilliam. **VHS, Beta, LV $19.95** *PAR*

Time for Table Manners

Winnie the Pooh and friends teach the importance of washing hands before meals, saying please and thank you, cleanliness, and self-respect.
1990 (*Preschool-Primary*) 6m/C **VHS, Beta $140.00** *MTI, DSN*

Time of Tears 𝄞𝄞

Young boy has his first experience of grief when he befriends a nice old man who turns out to be a long-estranged relative, trying to reconcile with the family before he dies. Compassionate but no-frills kiddie tearjerker.
1985 (**PG**/*Jr. High-Adult*) 95m/C **VHS, Beta $19.95** *STE, NWV*

Timefighters in the Land of Fantasy

Cartoon team of time-travelers venture into the worlds of such classic fairy tales as Cinderella and Jack and the Beanstalk.
1984 (*Family*) 94m/C **VHS, Beta $24.95** *PAR, WTA*

Timeless Tales from Hallmark

Collection of animated fairy tales from the Hanna-Barbera crew, sponsored by Hallmark Cards in their initial TV appearances. See individual titles for descriptions; programs include "The Elves and the Shoemaker," "The Emperor's New Clothes," "Puss in Boots," "Rapunzel," "Rumpelstiltskin," "The Steadfast Tin Soldier," "Thumbelina," and "The Ugly Duckling."
1990 (*Family*) 30m/C **VHS, Beta $29.95** *TTC, IME*

Timerider 𝄞𝄞

Motorcyclist riding through the California desert is accidentally thrown back in time to 1877, the result of a scientific experiment gone awry. There he and his machine find no gas stations and lots of surprised cowboys. Not exactly "Back to the Future," but occasionally fun; director Dear went on to do "Harry and the Hendersons." **Hound Advisory:** Violence, sex, salty language.
1983 (**PG**/*Jr. High-Adult*) 93m/C Fred Ward, Belinda Bauer, Peter Coyote, Richard Masur, Ed Lauter, L.Q. Jones, Tracy Walter; **D:** William Dear. **VHS, Beta, LV** *NO*

Timmy's Gift: A Precious Moments Christmas

Holiday cartoon about a young angel who is given the monumental task of delivering a crown to the baby Jesus on the very first Christmas.
1991 (*Family*) 23m/C **VHS, Beta $14.95**

The Tin Soldier

Canadian animated version of Hans Christian Andersen's "The Steadfast Tin Soldier," about a music-box ballerina and a toy soldier united by a pair of matchmaking mice.

1986 (*Family*) 30m/C **VHS $9.99** *VTR, WTA*

Tiny Toon Adventures: How I Spent My Vacation 𝄞𝄞𝄞

How the tiny toons of Acme Acres spend their summer vacation in this animated adventure that spoofs several popular films and amusements. Plucky Duck and Hampton Pig journey to "Happy World Land" (a takeoff on Walt Disney World), Babs and Buster Bunny's water adventure parodies "Deliverance," there's a spoof of "The Little Mermaid," and the Road Runner even makes a cameo appearance. Parents will be equally entertained by the level of humor and the fast-paced action. Based on the Steven Spielberg TV cartoon series, this is the first made-for-home-video animated feature ever released in the United States.
1991 (*Family*) 80m/C **VHS, Beta, LV, 8mm $19.95** *WAR*

Tiny Toon Big Adventures

"Journey to the Center of Acme Acres" has Buster and Babs venturing where no rabbits have gone before. In "A Ditch in Time," a time-travelling Plucky Duck tries to get back to the present in order to complete a homework assignment.
1993 (*Family*) 42m/C **VHS $12.95** *WAR, WTA, BTV*

Tiny Toon Fiendishly Funny Adventures

Cartoon collection from the TV series with spooky themes. "Duck in the Dark" has Plucky's imagination getting the best of him. In "Little Cake of Horrors," Hamton Pig's diet leads to extremes and in "The Night of the Living Pets," overaffectionate pet lover Elmyra goes too far. "Hare-Raising Night" features Babs and Buster tangling with a mad scientist.
1993 (*Family*) 38m/C **VHS $12.95** *WAR, WTA, BTV*

Tiny Toon Island Adventures

Two tropical 'toons: "No Toon Is an Island" has The Acme Acres gang searching for lost treasure and in "Buster and Babs Go Hawaiian," Polynesian pleasures are apparent.
1993 (*Family*) 42m/C **VHS $12.95** *WAR, WTA, BTV*

Tiny Toons in Two-Tone Town

"Two-Tone Town" has Buster and Babs helping two 1930s former cartoon stars get their flagging careers going again. "Fields of Honey" is a toon spoof of the movie "Field of Dreams."
1992 (*Family*) 44m/C **VHS, Beta $12.95** *WAR*

Tiny Toons Music Television

In the TV episodes "TT Music Television" and "Toon TV," VJ's Buster and Babs do their own thing to the songs "Yakity-Yak" and "The Name Game."
1992 (*Family*) 44m/C **VHS, Beta $12.95** *WAR*

Tiny Toons: The Best of Buster and Babs

Two episodes from the cable TV series. In "Promise Her Anything," Buster asks Babs to dance and in "Thirteensome-thing," Babs stars in her own TV show.
1993 *(Family)* 44m/C VHS, Beta $12.95 *WAR*

Tito and Me 🦴🦴🦴

Uproarious all-ages film from Yugoslavia can be savored as both comedy and potent attack on political tyranny. It's 1954, and 10-year-old Zoran (a Spanky McFarland lookalike) is so bombarded by propaganda praising fearless leader Marshall Tito that he adopts Yugoslavia's dictator as his personal hero and imaginary pal. Zoran's classroom essay "Why I Love Marshall Tito" wins him a place in a junior Communist march to Tito's hometown, right alongside the girl of his dreams. But the adult guide is a fanatical taskmaster who bullies slowpoke Zoran during the hike, sparking the disaster that ends the child's Tito-worship. Smart, sharp and perceptive, but never dragged down by its weighty themes - and who could resist that carioca-beat soundtrack? In Serbo-Croatian with English subtitles. **Hound Advisory:** Salty language.
1992 *(College-Adult)* 104m/C Dimitrie Vojnov, Laza Ristovski, Anica Dobra, Predrag Manojlovic, Olivera Markovic; *D:* Goran Markovic; *W:* Goran Markovic. VHS $89.98 *FXL, FCT*

To Catch a Thief 🦴🦴🦴

On the French Riviera, a reformed jewel thief falls for a wealthy American woman, who suspects he's up to his old tricks when a rash of jewel thefts occur. Oscar-winning photography by Robert Burks, a notable fireworks scene, and snappy dialogue. A change of pace for Hitchcock, this charming comedy-thriller proved to be as popular as his other efforts. Kelly met future husband Prince Ranier during shooting in Monaco. Based on the novel by David Dodge.
1955 *(Jr. High-Adult)* 103m/C Cary Grant, Grace Kelly, Jessie Royce Landis, John Williams, Charles Vanel, Brigitte Auber; *D:* Alfred Hitchcock; *W:* John Michael Hayes. **Award Nominations:** Academy Awards '55: Best Art Direction/Set Decoration (Color), Best Costume Design (Color); **Awards:** Academy Awards '55: Best Color Cinematography. VHS, Beta, LV $19.95 *PAR, MLB, HMV*

To Kill a Mockingbird 🦴🦴🦴🦴

Powerful, faithful adaptation of Pulitzer-winning Harper Lee novel by Horton Foote. It's both an evocative portrayal of childhood innocence and a denunciation of bigotry taking place in a small town in Alabama in the 1930s. Peck provides a career performance as Atticus Finch, a morally forthright lawyer (and a widower with two children) who takes on the unpopular defense of a black man accused of raping a white woman. His children, meanwhile, are fascinated with the mysterious but dimwitted Boo Radley, played by Duvall in his debut. Lee based her characterization of "Dill" on Truman Capote, a childhood friend. **Hound Advisory:** Mature themes.
1962 *(Family)* 129m/B Gregory Peck, Brock Peters, Phillip Alford, Mary Badham, Robert Duvall, Rosemary Murphy, William Windom, Alice Ghostley, John Megna, Frank Overton, Paul Fix, Collin Wilcox; *D:* Robert Mulligan; *W:* Horton Foote; *M:* Elmer Bernstein. **Award Nominations:** Academy Awards '62: Best Black and White Cinematography, Best Director (Mulligan), Best Picture, Best Supporting Actress (Badham), Best Original Score; **Awards:** Academy Awards '62: Best Actor (Peck), Best Adapted Screenplay, Best Art Direction/Set Decoration (B & W); Golden Globe Awards '63: Best Actor—Drama (Peck), Best Score. VHS, Beta, LV $14.95 *KUI, MCA, BTV*

To Sir, with Love 🦴🦴◁

Teacher in London's tough East End tosses books in the wastebasket and proceeds to educate his class about life. Skillful and warm performance by Poitier as the idealistic instructor, and the supporting cast also performs nicely, though this sentimental favorite looks a bit corny today. And these 'bad kids' are teacher's pets compared to school youth in, for example, "Lean on Me." Based on the novel by E.R. Braithwaite. LuLu's title song made the hit parade in 1967-68.
1967 *(Family-Family)* 105m/C Sidney Poitier, Lulu, Judy Geeson, Christian Roberts, Suzy Kendall, Faith Brook; *D:* James Clavell; *W:* James Clavell. VHS, Beta $14.95 *COL*

To the Last Man 🦴

An early Scott sagebrush epic, about two feuding families. Temple is seen in a small role. Based on Zane Grey's novel of the same name.
1933 *(Family)* 70m/B Randolph Scott, Esther Ralston, Jack LaRue, Noah Beery Sr., Buster Crabbe, Gail Patrick, Barton MacLane, Fuzzy Knight, John Carradine, Jay Ward, Shirley Temple; *D:* Henry Hathaway. VHS, Beta $9.95 *NOS, DVT, MLB*

Tobor the Great 🦴◁

Silly, overly juvenile vintage sci-fi about a boy, his inventor grandfather, and their pride and joy, Tobor the Robot. Villainous commie spies try to misuse Tobor, only to be thwarted in the end. Apparently aimed at viewers unable to figure out where the name 'Tobor' came from.
1954 *(Family)* 77m/B Charles Drake, Billy Chapin, Karin Booth, Taylor Holmes, Joan Gerber, Steve Geray; *D:* Lee Sholem. VHS, LV $19.98 *REP*

Toby McTeague 🦴🦴

Scenic but mediocre Canadian tale set in a snowy town where impulsive teen Toby and his widowed dad are constantly at odds. When the family's Siberian husky-breeding business is threatened, the only answer is for Toby to try for the cash prize in a regional dogsled race. Git along, doggies. **Hound Advisory:** Salty language. One canine casualty.
1987 *(PG/Jr. High-Adult)* 94m/C Winston Rekert, Wannick Bisson, Timothy Webber; *D:* Jean-Claude Lord. VHS, Beta, LV $14.95 *COL, NLC*

Toby Tyler 🦴🦴🦴

Toby, a turn-of-the-century boy, realizes the perennial dream of running off to join the circus, and teams up with a chimpanzee. Highly enjoyable Disney film still appeals to circus-goers of all ages.
1959 *(G/Family)* 93m/C Kevin Corcoran, Henry Calvin, Gene Sheldon, Bob Sweeney, Mr. Stubbs; *D:* Charles T. Barton. VHS, Beta $69.95 *DIS*

Tom & Jerry Kids: Out of This World Fun

Video repackaging of episodes from Hanna-Barbera's TV Tom & Jerry spinoff. Additional volumes available.
1991 *(Preschool-Primary)* 43m/C **VHS $12.95** *WTA*

Tom & Jerry On Parade

The cat and mouse are featured in "Cruise Cat," "Designs on Jerry," "His Mouse Friday," "Little School Mouse," "Pet Peeve," and "Pushbutton Kitty."
1954 *(Preschool-Jr. High)* 41m/C **VHS $12.95** *WTA*

Tom and Jerry: Starring

The real stuff from Hanna-Barbera's legendary cartoon cat and mouse team, not to be confused with "Tom and Jerry: The Movie."
1988 *(Family)* 60m/C Tom & Jerry. **VHS, Beta $14.95** *MGM, WTA*

Tom and Jerry: The Movie 🦴🦴

Everybody's favorite cartoon cat/mouse duo (who began life in a 1940 MGM short "Puss Gets the Boot") have their own feature. And indeed, it opens with a wild chase that's pure T & J, until the plot turns into a hackneyed takeoff on "The Rescuers," with the battling pair now goody-goodies, saving a little girl heiress from evil relatives (and dig her father, a shameless Indiana Jones clone). Unlike their past work, Tom and Jerry speak and sing, both bad moves. True fans should stick to the original cartoons.
1993 *(G/Family)* 84m/C **D:** Phil Roman; **W:** Dennis Marks; **M:** Henry Mancini, Leslie Bricusse; **V:** Richard Kind, Dana Hill, Charlotte Rae, Henry Gibson, Rip Taylor, Howard Morris, Edmund Gilbert, David Lander. **VHS $24.98** *FHE, WTA*

Tom & Jerry: The Very Best Of Tom & Jerry

Features Tom and Jerry in six favorite episodes.
19?? *(Preschool-Primary)* 44m/C **VHS $12.95** *WTA*

Tom & Jerry's Cartoon Cavalcade

Features six vintage William Hanna-Joseph Barbera 'toons starring Tom and Jerry. Includes "Casanova Cat," "Jerry's Cousin," "Fine Feathered Friend," "Jerry & the Lion," "Mouse for Sale," and "Southbound Duckling."
1954 *(Preschool-Jr. High)* 42m/C **VHS $12.95** *WTA*

Tom & Jerry's Comic Capers

Tom and Jerry star in six more bigscreen cartoon shorts. Includes "Downhearted Duckling," "Fit to Be Tied," "The Flying Sorceress," "Hatch Up Your Troubles," "Polka Dot Puss," and "Puppy Tale."
1955 *(Preschool-Jr. High)* 42m/C **VHS $12.95** *WTA*

Tom & Jerry's Festival of Fun

More fun with that crazy cat and mouse. Includes "Blue Cat Blues," "Little Quacker," "Sufferin' Cats," "Tennis Chumps," "Touche Pussycat," and "The Truce Hurts."

1956 *(Preschool-Jr. High)* 43m/C **VHS $12.95** *WTA*

Tom & Jerry's 50th Birthday Classics

Anniversary compilation of the animated pair's best 'toons, including their 1940 debut "Puss Gets the Boot," as well as "Mouse in the House," "Dog Trouble," "Cat Fishin'," "Yankee Doodle Mouse," "Heavenly Puss" and "Part Time Pal."
19?? *(Family)* 57m/C **VHS, Beta, LV $14.95** *MGM, WTA*

Tom Brown's School Days 🦴🦴🦴 ⏴

Adaptation on the classic book by Thomas Hughes, detailing the rigors of the Victorian British school system on a newcomer lad who suffers tribulations and adversity but ultimately perseveres under the direction of benevolent headmaster Dr. Arnold. British-made, but with a largely, and obviously, American cast that dispels some of the mood.
1940 *(Family)* 86m/B Cedric Hardwicke, Jimmy Lydon, Freddie Bartholomew; **D:** Robert Stevenson. **VHS, Beta $19.95** *NOS, HHT, PSM*

Tom Brown's School Days 🦴🦴🦴

Nineteenth-century English boy Tom enrolls at Rugby School and is beset by bullies, but in the end he comes out a better, stronger young man for the harsh experience. Vivid and powerful recreation of the era and its values. Show it to kids today who complain about not enough arcade video games in the cafeteria.
1951 *(Family)* 93m/B Robert Newton, John Howard Davies, James Hayter; **D:** Gordon Parry. **VHS, Beta $19.95** *VCI*

Tom Chapin: This Pretty Planet

Chapin's concert features songs about the environment, nature, and friends, and offers animation and spectacular nature footage. Songs include "Uh Oh Accident," "Alphabet Soup," "Family Tree," "Good Garbage," and "Sing a Whale Song."
1992 *(Family)* 50m/C **VHS $14.98** *SMV, FFF*

Tom Sawyer 🦴🦴🦴

Readers Digest produced this flavorful account of the boisterous Tom, his superstitious friend Huck, and the choices they face when they accidentally witness a graveyard murder. Comes closer than most adaptations to capturing the flavor of the Mark Twain classic and you couldn't ask for a better cast, headed confidently by Whitaker as Tom and Foster as Becky Thatcher - with Hank just about the scariest Injun Joe ever. One big flaw: an ill-advised notion to turn this into a musical has left the story burdened with several forgettable songs. ♫River Song; Gratification; Tom Sawyer; Freebootin'; Aunt Polly's Soliloquy; If'n I Was God; A Man's Gotta Be What He's Born To Be; How Come?; Hannibal, Mo. **Hound Advisory:** Violence, alcohol use.
1973 *(G/Family)* 104m/C Johnny Whitaker, Jodie Foster, Celeste Holm, Warren Oates, Jeff East; **D:** Don Taylor; **M:** John Williams. **VHS, LV $19.98** *MGM*

Tom eyes Jerry as snack

tom thumb 🎵🎵◁

Fairy grants a childless couple's wish for a son, no matter how small. Tom arrives, thumb-sized but big in spirit, and he saves the village treasury from thieves (one of them, Sellers, pointlessly padded in a grotesque fat suit). Well-remembered children's film hasn't aged well over the years; satire and anachronisms clash with the Brothers Grimm material rather than enhance it. Undeniable highlight is the modish musical numbers, showcasing Tamblyn's dancing alongside the George Pal Puppetoons. An Oscar winner for special effects. **Hound Advisory:** Roughhousing, alcohol use.
1958 (*Family*) 92m/C Russ Tamblyn, Peter Sellers, Terry-Thomas; **D:** George Pal. VHS, Beta, LV **$39.95** *MGM*

Tom Thumb

This program from the "Grimm's Fairytale" series follows the adventures of tiny Mr. Thumb as he escapes from one danger after another.
1978 (*Preschool-Primary*) 10m/C **VHS, Beta** *CHF*

Tomboy & the Champ 🎵◁

Sickly sweet family drama about a music-loving Angus bull and the adoring little girl who sees to it that 'Champy' enters and wins a stockyard blue ribbon. Only too late does the heroine realize this means her dear beast will be turned into steak. The solution to this dilemma is as sentimental and yucky as it gets.
1958 (*Family*) 82m/C Candy Moore, Ben Johnson, Jesse White; **D:** Francis D. Lyon. VHS, Beta **$29.95** *VCI*

Tombstone 🎵🎵🎵

Saga of Wyatt Earp and his band of law-abiding large moustaches beat the longer, slower Kasdan/Costner vehicle to the big screen by several months. And yes, it is violent, with a band of sadistic villains running amuck. Legendary lawman Wyatt (Russell) moves to Tombstone, Arizona, aiming to start a new life with his brothers, but alas, that's not to be. The infamous gunfight at the OK Corral is here, Delany wanders about in period costume as Wyatt's romantic interest, the bad guys, led by Booth, Biehn, and Lange, are really bad, and best of all, Kilmer steals the show in a stand-out performance as the tubercular Doc Holliday, alcoholic, lover, gunslinger, and philosopher. You'll want to compare it with Dennis Quaid's emaciated Doc in Costner's epic. As the moralistic center of the sagebrush fable, Russell spends a lot of time looking troubled by the violence while adding to the body count. A mixed bag of western thrills that suffers some from '90s revisionism. **Hound Advisory:** Violence (numerous shooting incidents, including a variety of ruthless killings); profanity; alcohol use.
1993 (**R**/*Sr. High-Adult*) 130m/C Kurt Russell, Val Kilmer, Michael Biehn, Sam Elliott, Dana Delany, Bill Paxton, Powers Boothe, Stephen Lang, Jason Priestly, Dana Wheeler-Nicholson, Billy Zane, Thomas Haden Church, Joanna Pacula, Michael Rooker, Harry Carey Jr., Billy Bob Thornton, Charlton Heston, Robert Burke, John Corbett, Buck Taylor, Terry O'Quinn, Pedro Armendariz Jr., Chris Mitchum, Jon Tenney; **D:** George P. Cosmatos; **W:** Kevin Jarre; **M:** Bruce Broughton. VHS, LV *HPH*

The Tomi Ungerer Library

Four animated stories from the popular children's author/artist as well as a brief interview with the author about his work.
1993 (*Preschool-Primary*) 35m/C **VHS $14.95** *CCC,*

Tommy 🎵🎵

Peter Townsend's rock opera (as imploded onto the screen in the usual laid-back Russell manner) about the deaf, dumb, and blind boy who becomes a celebrity due to his amazing skill at the pinball machines. Story is told entirely in song, as a parade of rock musicians perform throughout the affair, with varying degrees of success. Despite some good moments, bombastic vision ultimately falls prey to ill-conceived production concepts and miscasting. ♫Underture; Captain Walker Didn't Come Home; It's A Boy; '51 is Going to Be A Good Year; What About the Boy?; The Amazing Journey; Christmas; See Me, Feel Me; Eyesight to the Blind. **Hound Advisory:** Drug use; mature themes.
1975 (**PG**/*Jr. High-Adult*) 108m/C Ann-Margret, Elton John, Oliver Reed, Tina Turner, Roger Daltrey, Eric Clapton, Keith Moon, Pete Townshend, Jack Nicholson, Robert Powell; **D:** Ken Russell; **W:** Ken Russell. **Award Nominations:** Academy Awards '75: Best Actress (Ann-Margret), Best Original Score; **Awards:** Golden Globe Awards '76: Best Actress—Musical/Comedy (Ann-Margret). VHS, Beta, LV **$14.95** *COL, MVD, WME*

Tommy Tricker & the Stamp Traveller 🎵🎵🎵🎵

Canadian postal service asked producer Rock Demers for a movie to promote stamp collecting, and he delivered. Winning fantasy is about children who discover a magic formula that shrinks them down to ride around the globe on stamps. Roaming from Canada to China to Australia, graced with far-out special f/x and great music (by the McGarrigle Sisters), this is one of the very best from Les Productions la Fete. And yes, it did get kids interested in stamp collecting.
1990 (*Family*) 30m/C Lucas Evans, Anthony Rogers, Jill Stanley; **D:** Michael Rubbo. VHS, Beta **$39.95** *FHE*

Tony Draws a Horse 🎵🎵◁

An eight-year-old draws an anatomically correct stallion on the door of his father's office, leading to a rift between the parents on how to handle telling the boy the facts of life. Somewhat sitcommish but engaging picture based on the play by Lesley Storm. **Hound Advisory:** Sex talk.
1951 (*Sr. High-Adult*) 90m/B Cecil Parker, Anne Crawford, Derek Bond, Barbara Murray, Mervyn Johns, Barbara Everest, David Hurst; **D:** John Paddy Carstairs. VHS **$19.95** *NOS*

Too Smart for Strangers with Winnie the Pooh

Winnie the Pooh and Tigger, along with Tyne Daly and Gavin MacLeod present tips on how children can defend themselves against strangers.
1985 (*Primary-Jr. High*) 40m/C **VHS, Beta $29.95** *DIS*

Toot, Whistle, Plunk & Boom

Professor Owl traces the roots of musical instruments and keeps children alert with catchy tunes explaining all of it. An Oscar-winning short subject from Disney.
1953 *(Primary-Jr. High)* 10m/C **VHS, Beta $205.00** *MTI, DSN*

Tooter Turtle in Kink of Swat

Repackaged TV cartoons from yesteryear, in which Tooter, with the help of Wizard the Lizard, travels through time to become the next "Babe Rube." When he fails, he needs the Wizard to bring him home, as always.
1967 *(Preschool-Primary)* 60m/C **VHS $17.95** *WTA*

Tootsie 🦴🦴🦴🦴

Stubborn, unemployed actor disguises himself as a woman to secure a part on a soap opera. As his popularity on television mounts, his love life becomes increasingly soap operatic. Hoffman is delightful, as is the rest of the stellar cast. Debut of Davis; Murray's performance unbilled. Laserdisc version features audio commentary by director Sidney Pollack, behind the scenes footage and photographs, and complete coverage of Tootsie's production. **Hound Advisory:** Sexual situations.
1982 (PG/*Jr. High-Adult*) 110m/C Dustin Hoffman, Jessica Lange, Teri Garr, Dabney Coleman, Bill Murray, Charles Durning, Geena Davis, George Gaynes, Estelle Getty, Christine Ebersole, Sydney Pollack; **D:** Sydney Pollack; **W:** Larry Gelbart, Murray Schisgal, Don McGuire; **M:** Dave Grusin. **Award Nominations:** Academy Awards '82: Best Actor (Hoffman), Best Cinematography, Best Director (Pollack), Best Film Editing, Best Original Screenplay, Best Picture, Best Song ("It Might Be You"), Best Sound, Best Supporting Actress (Garr); **Awards:** Academy Awards '82: Best Supporting Actress (Lange); British Academy Awards '83: Best Actor (Hoffman); Golden Globe Awards '83: Best Actor—Musical/Comedy (Hoffman), Best Film—Musical/Comedy, Best Supporting Actress (Lange). **VHS, Beta, LV $29.95** *COL, VYG, CRC*

Top Cat and the Beverly Hills Cats

Revival of the vintage Top Cat cartoon characters from Hanna-Barbera. Their lives take a twist when an inheritance moves them from alley to Beverly Hills estate.
1984 *(Family)* 92m/C **VHS, Beta $29.95** *TTC, WTA*

Top Gun 🦴🦴⌐

Young Navy pilots compete against one another on the ground and in the air at the elite Fighter Weapons School. Cruise isn't bad as a maverick who comes of age in Ray Bans, but Edwards shines as his buddy. Awesome aerial photography and high-cal beefcake divert from the contrived plot and stock characters. The Navy subsequently noticed an increased interest in fighter pilots. If you're looking for slickness and action, seek no further. Features Berlin's Oscar-winning song "Take My Breath Away." **Hound Advisory:** Mild profanity; suggested sex; violence; alcohol use.
1986 (PG/*Jr. High-Adult*) 109m/C Tom Cruise, Kelly McGillis, Val Kilmer, Tom Skerritt, Anthony Edwards, Meg Ryan, Rick Rossovich, Michael Ironside, Barry Tubb, Whip Hubley, John Stockwell, Tim Robbins, Adrian Pasdar; **D:** Tony Scott; **W:** Jim Cash, Jack Epps Jr.; **M:** Harold Faltermeyer. **Award Nominations:** Academy Awards '86: Best Film Editing, Best Sound; **Awards:** Academy Awards '86: Best Song ("Take My Breath Away"); Golden Globe Awards '87: Best Song ("Take My Breath Away"); People's Choice Awards '87: Best Film. **VHS, Beta, LV, 8mm, CD-I $14.95** *PAR*

Top Rock

Compilation of Hanna-Barbera cartoon characters frolicking to upbeat songs from the 1980's.
1984 *(Preschool-Primary)* 30m/C **VHS, Beta** *TTC*

Topper 🦴🦴🦴⌐

George and Marion Kerby return as ghosts after a fatal car accident, determined to assist their pal Cosmo Topper. Producer Hal Roach's first big-budget effort is a sophisticated comedy led by a charming cast. Great script is complemented by trick photography and special effects. Immensely popular at the box office, inspiring two sequels ("Topper Takes a Trip" and "Topper Returns"), a television series, and a television remake in 1979. Also available colorized.
1937 *(Family)* 97m/B Cary Grant, Roland Young, Constance Bennett, Billie Burke, Eugene Pallette, Hoagy Carmichael; **D:** Norman Z. McLeod. **VHS, Beta $9.95** *MED, CCB, VTR*

Topper Returns 🦴🦴🦴

Cosmo Topper helps ghostly Blondell find the man who mistakenly murdered her. Humorous conclusion to the trilogy preceded by "Topper" and "Topper Takes a Trip." Followed by a television series. Also available colorized.
1941 *(Family)* 87m/B Roland Young, Joan Blondell, Dennis O'Keefe, Carole Landis, Eddie Anderson, H.B. Warner, Billie Burke; **D:** Roy Del Ruth. **VHS, Beta, LV $16.95** *SNC, NOS, CAB*

Topper Takes a Trip 🦴🦴🦴

Cosmo Topper and his wife have a falling out and ghost Marion Kerby helps them get back together. The special effects sequences are especially funny. Followed by "Topper Returns." Also available colorized.
1939 *(Family)* 85m/B Constance Bennett, Roland Young, Billie Burke, Franklin Pangborn, Alan Mowbray; **D:** Norman Z. McLeod. **VHS, Beta $14.95** *MED, VTR*

Torn Curtain 🦴🦴⌐

American scientist poses as a defector to East Germany in order to uncover details of the Soviet missile program. He and his fiancee, who follows him behind the Iron Curtain, attempt to escape to freedom. Derivative and uninvolving.
1966 *(Jr. High-Adult)* 125m/C Paul Newman, Julie Andrews, Lila Kedrova, David Opatoshu; **D:** Alfred Hitchcock; **W:** Brian Moore; **M:** John Addison. **VHS, Beta, LV $19.95** *MCA*

The Tortoise and the Hare

This Academy Award winner for Best Cartoon Production relates the classic story of how the slow but determined reptile bested the overconfident mammal in a race. One of Disney's original "Silly Symphonies."
1935 *(Preschool-Primary)* 8m/C **VHS, Beta $170.00** *DSN, MTI*

Toto le Heros 🦴🦴🦴

Thomas is a bitter old man who as a child fantasized that he was a secret agent named Toto. He harbors deep resentment over not living the life he should have, maintaining he and his rich neighbor were switched at birth in the maternity ward (Thomas even barges into his neighbor's birthday party

demanding that he be given the boy's gifts). Flashbacks and fast forwards show glimpses of life, not necessarily as it was, but how the old man perceives it. Sounds complex but the story is actually clear and fluid thanks to precise, prophetic visuals. The script was conceived initially as a movie about kids; grownup segments were added later, but the childhood scenes retain a rare sense of tot logic, obsession, and vengeance. Belgian production is in French with English subtitles. **Hound Advisory:** Mature themes, violence, sex, nudity.
1991 (PG-13/*Jr. High-Adult*) 90m/C Michel Bouquet, Jo De Backer, Thomas Godet, Mireille Perrier, Sandrine Blancke, Didier Ferney, Hugo Harold Harrisson, Gisela Uhlen, Peter Bohlke; *D:* Jaco Van Dormael; *W:* Jaco Van Dormael. **VHS, Beta** $89.95 *PAR, BTV*

Touched by Love 🐾🐾🐾

True story of a handicapped child who begins to communicate when her teacher suggests she write to her idol, Elvis Presley. Sincere and well-performed family drama; not mere Graceland name-dropping.
1980 (PG/*Jr. High-Adult*) 95m/C Deborah Raffin, Diane Lane, Christina Raines, Clu Gulager, John Amos; *D:* Gus Trikonis; *W:* Hesper Anderson; *M:* John Barry. **VHS, Beta** $59.95 *COL*

Tough Guys 🐾🐾🐾

Two aging ex-cons, who staged America's last train robbery in 1961, try to come to terms with modern life after many years in prison. Amazed and hurt by the treatment of the elderly in the 1980s, frustrated with their inability to find something worthwhile to do, they begin to plan one last heist. Tailor-made for Lancaster and Douglas, who seem to enjoy each other's company but are not always strongly supported by the script. **Hound Advisory:** Mild profanity; sex; violence.
1986 (PG/*Jr. High-Adult*) 103m/C Burt Lancaster, Kirk Douglas, Charles Durning, Eli Wallach, Lyle Alzado, Dana Carvey, Alexis Smith, Darlanne Fluegel, Billy Barty, Monty Ash; *D:* Jeff Kanew; *W:* James Orr, Jim Cruickshank; *M:* James Newton Howard. **VHS, Beta, LV** $19.95 *TOU*

Toughlove 🐾🐾

Gary's parents can't stop the rebellious teen's slide into drugs and delinquency, even though dad's an assistant high school principal himself. After much agony, the adults stop blaming themselves and decide on a 'tough love' approach to the kid, locking him out of the house until he behaves. Well-acted but didactic TV movie that dramatizes, but doesn't unduly glorify or simplify, the philosophy and methods of Toughlove International, a support group for families of problem kids. **Hound Advisory:** Drug use, mature themes.
1985 (*Sr. High-Adult*) 100m/C Lee Remick, Bruce Dern, Piper Laurie, Louise Latham, Dana Elcar, Jason Patric, Eric Schiff, Dedee Pfeiffer; *D:* Glenn Jordan. **VHS, Beta** $39.95 *FRH*

Touring the Firehouse

Jackie the Dalmatian provides the narration for this fun look at a fireman's day, including a look at the control center, how the equipment works, how firemen wash their trucks, putting out a small fire, and rescuing a cat from a tree.
1992 (*Preschool-Primary*) 30m/C **VHS** $14.99 *GKK*

The Toy 🐾🐾

Penniless black janitor is hired by a multimillionaire oil man to be the new "toy" of the rich guy's spoiled nine-year-old son. Naturally Pryor softens the hearts of both these caricatures with heavy-handed lecturing about social inequities and earning friends. Slow and terrible remake of a French comedy "Le Jouet" (not yet on tape stateside). **Hound Advisory:** Profanity, sex talk, brief nudity.
1982 (PG/*Primary-Adult*) 99m/C Richard Pryor, Jackie Gleason, Ned Beatty, Wilfrid Hyde-White; *D:* Richard Donner. **VHS, Beta, LV, 8mm** $9.95 *COL*

Toys 🐾🐾

Critics generally disliked this epic fable - just as many first scorned "The Wizard of Oz," "Fantasia," and "Willy Wonka and the Chocolate Factory." Difference is, those are timeless fantasies; this is a Cold-War era script that didn't get produced until its flower-power themes were long stale. Clownish son of a toy manufacturer tries to keep the playful spirit of the fantastic toy factory alive after it's taken over by his uncle, a crazed general with plans to retool the assembly line and make toy-sized automated weapons. Bizarre, visually captivating film holds one dumbstruck for about an hour, then succumbs to tedium with its hard-sell messages of military folly. Lack of any child characters should be noted, as should some unnecessary sex and profanity. **Hound Advisory:** Salty language, one sex scene. Climactic violence tries to convey war's destruction via toy-on-toy massacres.
1992 (PG-13/*Jr. High-Adult*) 121m/C Robin Williams, Joan Cusack, Michael Gambon, L.L. Cool J., Robin Wright; *Cameos:* Donald O'Connor; *D:* Barry Levinson; *W:* Valerie Curtin, Barry Levinson. **VHS** $19.98 *FXV*

Trader Tom of the China Seas

Heroic island merchant and a shipwrecked beauty get involved in espionage while helping the UN to safeguard the Asian front. A minor effort from the sunset of Republic's movie-serial era; from here on, television took over the weekly adventure format.
1954 (*Family*) 167m/B Harry Lauter, Aline Towne, Lyle Talbot, Fred Graham. **VHS** $29.98 *REP*

Trading Hearts 🐾🐾

Little girl plays matchmaker between an over-the-hill baseball player and her own single mom, an unsuccessful lounge singer. The two lovebirds detest each other immediately, and you can guess the rest. Set in 1957 and scripted by sportswriter Frank Deford. For more single mom meets over-the-hill baseball player romances, see "Rookie of the Year" and "Little Big League." **Hound Advisory:** Salty language, alcohol use.
1987 (PG/*Jr. High-Adult*) 88m/C Beverly D'Angelo, Raul Julia, Jerry Lewis, Parris Buckner, Robert Gwaltney; *D:* Neil Leifer; *W:* Frank Deford. **VHS, Beta, LV** $14.95 *LIV*

Trading Mom 🐾🐾

Mrs. Martin's kids are bummed out because the hardworking single mom seems to have no time for them. A magical neighbor introduces them to the Mommy Market, where they

VIDEOHOUND'S FAMILY VIDEO RETRIEVER

can pick a parent more to their liking, but predictably all the choices — a glamorous aristocrat, a hardy outdoorswoman, a circus performer go badly wrong. All moms are played by Spacek, a neat trick in a picture that never seems as fun as it should be and may remind you of 1994's "North" by Rob Reiner. Based on a British children's novel "The Mummy Market," written by Nancy Brelis — herself the mother of screenwriter/director Tia Brelis.
1994 (PG/*Primary-Adult*) 82m/C Sissy Spacek, Anna Chlumsky, Aaron Michael Metchik, Asher Metchik, Maureen Stapleton; *D:* Tia Brelis; *M:* David Kitay. **VHS, LV** *VMK*

Trail of the Pink Panther WOOF!

The last and by far the least in Sellers' "Pink Panther" series. Inspector Clouseau disappears, and a lady TV reporter looks up his old enemies and associates while trying to find out why. Made after Sellers died; director Edwards did a Frankenstein job of pasting together old, unreleased (and unfunny) Sellers outtakes from other "Pink Panther" features, disguised here as flashbacks. It didn't work, and neither did subsequent "Curse of the Pink Panther" and "Son of the Pink Panther." **Hound Advisory:** Salty language, nudity, sex talk.
1982 (PG/*Jr. High-Adult*) 97m/C Peter Sellers, David Niven, Herbert Lom, Capucine, Burt Kwouk, Robert Wagner, Robert Loggia; *D:* Blake Edwards; *W:* Blake Edwards, Frank Waldman; *M:* Henry Mancini. **VHS, Beta, LV** $14.95 *MGM*

Transformers

Series of single-episode cartoon tapes derived, of course, from the toy product line, demonstrating the shape-changing robot warriors of Cybertron at their transforming best. Additional volumes available.
1986 (*Preschool-Primary*) 30m/C **VHS, Beta** *FHE*

Transformers: The Movie 🦴

Full-length cartoon with the universe-defending robots fighting the powers of evil. Speaking of evil, the Transformers started out as shape-changing toy robots on store shelves, so this waste of film amounts to a big fat commercial. Noted as maverick movie genius Welles' final bow; he provides the voice of a planet.
1986 (G/*Primary*) 85m/C *D:* Nelson Shin; *V:* Orson Welles, Eric Idle, Judd Nelson, Leonard Nimoy, Robert Stack. **VHS, Beta** $19.95 *FHE*

Trap on Cougar Mountain 🦴🦯

Young Erik crusades to save his cougar friend Jason from the snares and bullets of hunters. Another one-man nature effort from writer/actor/producer/director Larsen.
1972 (G/*Family*) 97m/C Erik Larsen, Keith Larsen, Karen Steele; *D:* Keith Larsen. **VHS, Beta, LV** $9.95 *NWV, STE*

Travels of Marco Polo

Animated version of the adventurer's famed journeys.
1972 (*Preschool-Jr. High*) 48m/C **VHS, Beta** *MGM*

Treasure Island 🦴🦴🦴

"Wizard of Oz" director Fleming's adaptation of Robert Louis Stevenson's 18th-century English pirate tale. Neither Coo-

per, as Jim Hawkins, the cabin boy who inspires the treasure hunt, or Beery as one-legged Long John Silver, seem very English, but the spirit of high-seas adventure fun survives. Also available colorized.
1934 (*Family*) 102m/B Wallace Beery, Jackie Cooper, Lionel Barrymore, Lewis Stone, Otto Kruger, Douglass Dumbrille, Chic Sale, Nigel Bruce; *D:* Victor Fleming. **VHS, Beta, LV** $19.98 *MGM, TLF, HMV*

Treasure Island 🦴🦴🦴🦯

Spine-tingling Robert Louis Stevenson tale of pirates and buried treasure, in which young cabin boy Jim Hawkins matches wits with the treacherous Long John Silver. Some editions excise extra violence, and Stevenson's ending is revised, but this gets the rollicking, full Disney treatment. Excellent casting. **Hound Advisory:** Violence.
1950 (PG/*Family*) 96m/C Bobby Driscoll, Robert Newton, Basil Sydney, Walter Fitzgerald, Denis O'Dea, Ralph Truman, Finlay Currie; *D:* Byron Haskin. **VHS, Beta, LV** $19.99 *DIS, IGP*

Treasure Island

Made-for-TV animated musical adaptation of the adventurous story of Long John Silver and young Jim Hawkins (who's accompanied by a tiny mouse friend named Hiccup in this version) of the novel by Robert Louis Stevenson.
1972 (*Family*) 75m/C *V:* Richard Dawson, Davy Jones, Larry Storch. **VHS** $19.98 *WAR*

Treasure Island 🦴🦴

Unexceptional British reheat of familiar pirate tale, with Welles taking pseudonymous screenwriting credit as 'O.W. Jeeves.' He also mutteringly portrays Long John Silver, and for good or ill he's the most interesting thing onscreen.
1972 (G/*Family*) 94m/C Orson Welles, Kim Burfield, Walter Slezak, Lionel Stander; *D:* John Hough; *W:* Orson Welles. **VHS** $79.95 *BTV*

Treasure Island 🦴🦴🦴🦯

Shiver me timbers, lad! Lengthy but excellent made-for-cable-TV version of the classic Robert Louis Stevenson pirate yarn. Innkeeper's boy is left with a treasure map that earns him a visit from the infamous Long John Silver, played with glee by Heston. His son Fraser wrote, produced and directed, while the Chieftains handle the soundtracking with Celtic abandon.
1989 (*Family-Family*) 131m/C Charlton Heston, Christian Bale, Julian Glover, Richard Johnson, Oliver Reed, Christopher Lee, Clive Wood, Nicholas Amer, Michael Halsey; *D:* Fraser Heston; *W:* Fraser Heston. **VHS** $79.98 *TTC*

The Treasure of Matecumbe 🦴🦴

Motley crew of adventurers led by a young boy search for buried pirate treasure in a remote part of the Florida Keys shortly after the Civil War. Mediocre Disney adventure comes across like a "Huckleberry Finn" knockoff; in fact it's based on Robert Lewis Taylor's acclaimed novel "A Journey to Matecumbe." **Hound Advisory:** Violence.
1976 (G/*Family*) 107m/C Billy Attmore, Robert Foxworth, Joan Hackett, Peter Ustinov, Vic Morrow; *D:* Vincent McEveety; *M:* Buddy Baker. **VHS, Beta** $69.95 *DIS*

The Treasure of Swamp Castle 🎥🎥🎥

In medieval times an exiled prince returns to claim his long-lost bride, his ancestral castle, and the treasure hidden within the ruins — not necessarily in that order. This English-dubbed Hungarian feature cartoon isn't the expected action fairy tale but a screwball comedy of errors, as both the villains and the clueless prince try to outwit each other. It's fun for kids and smart enough for grownups. **Hound Advisory:** Alcohol use, brief nudity.
1990 (*Family*) 80m/C **VHS $39.95** *JTC, WTA*

Treasure of the Sierra Madre 🎥🎥🎥🎥

Three prospectors in search of gold in Mexico find suspicion, treachery and greed. Bogart is superbly believable as the paranoid, and ultimately homicidal, Fred C. Dobbs. Huston directed his father and wrote the screenplay, based on a B. Traven story. Watch for a very young Baretta (Blake), still wet behind the ears after the "Our Gang" comedies. Both Hustons won an Oscar, the first and last time a father and son scored together.
1948 (*Family*) 126m/B Humphrey Bogart, Walter Huston, Tim Holt, Bruce (Herman Brix) Bennett, Barton MacLane, Robert (Bobby) Blake, Alfonso Bedoya; *D:* John Huston; *W:* John Huston; *M:* Max Steiner. **Award Nominations:** Academy Awards '48: Best Picture; **Awards:** Academy Awards '48: Best Director (Huston), Best Screenplay, Best Supporting Actor (Huston); National Board of Review Awards '48: 10 Best Films of the Year, Best Actor (Huston). **VHS, Beta, LV $19.98** *MGM, FOX, TLF*

A Tree Grows in Brooklyn 🎥🎥🎥🎥

Sensitive young Irish lass growing up in turn-of-the-century Brooklyn tries to rise above her tenement existence. As the girl dreaming of a better life, Garner is wonderful, earning a special Oscar for her performance. Dunn, as the gentle alcoholic father who makes a slim living as a singing waiter, also stands out amid the generally superior performances. Kazan's impressive directorial debut used a script based on the novel by Betty Smith. **Hound Advisory:** Alcohol use; sex talk.
1945 (*Family*) 128m/B Peggy Ann Garner, James Dunn, Dorothy McGuire, Joan Blondell, Lloyd Nolan, Ted Donaldson, James Gleason, John Alexander, Charles Halton; *D:* Elia Kazan; *M:* Jerry Goldsmith. **Award Nominations:** Academy Awards '45: Best Screenplay; **Awards:** Academy Awards '45: Best Supporting Actor (Dunn); National Board of Review Awards '45: 10 Best Films of the Year. **VHS, Beta, LV $14.98** *KUI, FOX, BTV*

Trenchcoat 🎥🎥

Made-for-TV adaptation of the first of British writer John Christopher's popular young adult sci-fi books. Alien invaders, in the form of towering three-legged machines, control humans through mind implants at the age of 16. Two boys try to escape Tripod captivity and join the resistance.
1983 (*Family*) 95m/C Margot Kidder, Robert Hays; *D:* Michael Tuchner; *W:* Jeffrey Price, Peter S. Seaman; *M:* Charles Fox. **VHS, Beta** *DIS, OM*

The Trial of the Incredible Hulk 🎥🎥

Made-for-TV movie spun off from Ferrigno's "Incredible Hulk" TV series, although it really showcases another Marvel Comics character, Daredevil. A (blind) lawyer by day, Matt Murdock turns into an acrobatic ninja-type to battle gang-sters; meanwhile the Hulk briefly becomes his client in the courtroom. **Hound Advisory:** Violence.
1989 (*Family*) 96m/C Bill Bixby, Lou Ferrigno, Rex Smith, John Rhys-Davies, Marta DuBois, Nancy Everhard, Nicholas Hormann; *D:* Bill Bixby. **VHS $19.95** *STE*

Trick or Treat

Vintage Disney cartoon in which Donald plays the gags on Halloween, only for them to backfire when his nephews and Witch Hazel reverse the tricks.
1952 (*Preschool-Primary*) 8m/C **VHS, Beta $170.00** *MTI, DSN*

The Trip to Bountiful 🎥🎥🎥

An elderly widow, unhappy living in her son's fancy modern home, makes a pilgrimage back to her childhood home in Bountiful, Texas. Based on the Horton Foote play. Fine acting with Oscar-winning performance from Page.
1985 (*PG/Jr. High-Adult*) 102m/C Geraldine Page, Rebecca DeMornay, John Heard, Carlin Glynn, Richard Bradford; *D:* Peter Masterson; *W:* Horton Foote. **Award Nominations:** Academy Awards '85: Best Adapted Screenplay; **Awards:** Academy Awards '85: Best Actress (Page); Independent Spirit Awards '86: Best Actress (Page), Best Screenplay; National Media Owl Awards '87: First Prize. **VHS, Beta, LV, 8mm $14.95** *COL, BTV, SUE*

Troll 🎥🎥

Mischievous troll haunts an urban apartment building, tries to make a little girl a princess, and turn all humans into mythical flora and fauna. The PG-13 rating is much too harsh for this mild fantasy, with charming creatures matched against some awfully embarrassing performances by most of the grownups (exception: "Lassie's" June Lockhart and her daughter Anne as the same sassy witch). The gorier "Troll 2" has nothing in common but the title. **Hound Advisory:** The hairy old troll is meant to be a wicked soul, but he seems cute and mellow. Salty language, monster roughhousing, but nothing really scary.
1985 (*PG-13/Jr. High-Adult*) 86m/C Noah Hathaway, Gary Sandy, Anne Lockhart, Sonny Bono, Shelley Hack, June Lockhart, Michael Moriarty; *D:* John Carl Buechler; *M:* Richard Band. **VHS, Beta, LV $79.98** *LIV, VES*

Troll Classic Book Videos

Group of children's story programs based on fairy tales. Included are "The Bremen Town Musicians," "The Elves and the Shoemaker," "Gingerbread Boy," "The Golden Goose," "Henny Penny," "The House That Jack Built," "Jack and the Beanstalk," "Little Red Riding Hood," "Rumpelstiltskin," "Stone Soup," "Three Little Pigs," "The Twelve Days of Christmas," and "The Ugly Duckling."
1988 (*Preschool-Primary*) 10m/C **VHS $449.25**

Trolls & the Christmas Express

Mischievous trolls threaten to keep Santa Claus from delivering his gifts in this whimsical cartoon originally broadcast on cable TV.
1981 (*Preschool-Jr. High*) 25m/C *V:* Roger Miller, Hans Conried. **VHS, Beta** *PAR, MTI, WTA*

Tron 🦴🦴

Computer programmer is sucked into the memory banks of a giant mainframe, where he exists as a warrior in a virtual-reality civilization running parallel to the outside world. The bewildered hero fights video game-style battles against a rogue artificial intelligence seeking to dominate mankind. The sketchy plot of this much-anticipated Disney sci-fi sounds better than it plays; obviously more attention was paid to incredible computer-graphics f/x than the script. **Hound Advisory:** Violence (clean and bloodless among nonhumans). Sex talk (human).
1982 (PG/*Primary-Adult*) 96m/C Jeff Bridges, Bruce Boxleitner, David Warner, Cindy Morgan, Barnard Hughes, Dan Shor; **D:** Steven Lisberger. VHS, Beta, LV $19.99 DIS

Troop Beverly Hills 🦴🦴◁

To be close to her daughter during a divorce, fashion-conscious, free-spending housewife Phyllis volunteers to lead a scout troop based in their posh neighborhood of Beverly Hills. Result is a lot of wimp-out-of-water gags, as rich girls of Troop Beverly Hills compete in a survival hike. Long's perpetually upbeat personality propels this silly comedy mixing pratfalls and materialism. **Hound Advisory:** Profanity, sex talk, alcohol use.
1989 (PG/*Jr. High-Adult*) 105m/C Shelley Long, Craig T. Nelson, Betty Thomas, Mary Gross, Stephanie Beacham, Audra Lindley, Edd Byrnes, Ami Foster, Jenny Lewis, Kellie Martin; **D:** Jeff Kanew; **W:** Pamela Norris, Margaret Grieco Oberman; **M:** Randy Edelman. VHS, Beta, LV, 8mm $14.95 COL

The Trouble with Angels 🦴🦴◁

Two young girls turn a convent upside down with their endless practical jokes. Eventually they do a bit of growing up when they're unwillingly left at school during the Christmas holiday and spend quality time with habit-clad Russell, who's everything a Mother Superior should be: understanding, wise, and graceful. Wholesome, if overlong, Catholic comedy. Followed by "Where Angels Go, Trouble Follows."
1966 (*Preschool-Primary*) 112m/C Hayley Mills, June Harding, Rosalind Russell, Gypsy Rose Lee, Binnie Barnes; **D:** Ida Lupino; **M:** Jerry Goldsmith. VHS, Beta, LV $14.95 COL

True Grit 🦴🦴🦴

Hard-drinking, one-eyed U.S. Marshal Rooster Cogburn is hired by a 14-year-old girl to find her father's killer. Wayne's rip-snortin' performance makes him the best saddle pal a kid could ever want and won him his only Oscar. Based on the Charles Portis novel. Followed by "Rooster Cogburn." **Hound Advisory:** Violence, including scary moments in a snake pit. Alcohol use.
1969 (G/*Family*) 128m/C John Wayne, Glen Campbell, Kim Darby, Robert Duvall; **D:** Henry Hathaway; **M:** Elmer Bernstein. **Award Nominations:** Academy Awards '69: Best Song ("True Grit"); **Awards:** Academy Awards '69: Best Actor (Wayne); Golden Globe Awards '70: Best Actor—Drama (Wayne); National Board of Review Awards '69: 10 Best Films of the Year. VHS, Beta, LV $14.95 PAR, HHE, TLF

True Lies 🦴🦴◁

Brain candy with a bang offers eye popping special effects and a large dose of unbelievability. Sort of like a big screen "Scarecrow and Mrs. King" as supposed computer salesman Ah-nuld keeps his spy work secret from mousy, neglected wife Curtis, who has a few secrets of her own and inadvertently ends up right in the thick of things. Raunchy and extremely sexist, but not without charm; the stupidity is part of the fun. Perfectly cast sidekick Arnold holds his own as a pig, but Heston is wasted as the head honcho. Tons of special effects culminate in a smashing finish. Very loosely adapted from the 1991 French comedy "La Total." **Hound Advisory:** Violence; profanity; sex talk; Curtis does a strip tease in brief undergarments.
1994 (R/*Sr. High-Adult*) 141m/C Arnold Schwarzenegger, Jamie Lee Curtis, Tom Arnold, Bill Paxton, Tia Carrere, Art Malik, Eliza Dushku, Charlton Heston, Grant Heslov; **D:** James Cameron; **W:** James Cameron. VHS NYR

Truly, Madly, Deeply 🦴🦴🦴

The recent death of her lover drives a young woman into despair and anger, until he turns up at her apartment one day. Tender and well written tale of love and the supernatural, with believable characters and plot-line. Playwright Minghella's directorial debut. **Hound Advisory:** Brief profanity.
1991 (PG/*Sr. High-Adult*) 107m/C Juliet Stevenson, Alan Rickman, Bill Paterson, Michael Maloney, Christopher Rozycki, Keith Bartlett, David Ryall, Stella Maris; **D:** Anthony Minghella; **W:** Anthony Minghella. VHS TOU

The Truth About Mother Goose

An Oscar-nominated Disney short that presents three Mother Goose classics, along with their backgrounds: "Jack Horner," "Mary, Mary Quite Contrary," and "London Bridge."
1957 (*Preschool-Primary*) 15m/C VHS, Beta $200.00 DSN, MTI

Tubby the Tuba

Tubby the Tuba searches for a melody he can call his own, in a cartoon remake of George Pal's Oscar-winning stop-motion short.
1977 (*Family*) 81m/C Pearl Bailey, Jack Gilford, Hermione Gingold. VHS, Beta $9.99 VTR, WTA, LIV

Tuck Everlasting 🦴🦴◁

In the early 1900s, a little girl befriends a backwoods family with an incredible secret — they will never age or die. Brittle, low-budget adaptation of Natalie Babbitt's novel has definite charm and a good moral about mortality, but (like the Tucks themselves), it goes on way too long. **Hound Advisory:** Brief violence
1985 (*Family*) 120m/C Fred A. Keller, James McGuire; **D:** Frederick King Keller. VHS, Beta $14.98 LIV, VES

Tucker: The Man and His Dream 🦴🦴🦴

Portrait of Preston Tucker, entrepreneur and industrial idealist, who in 1946 tried to build the car of the future and was effectively run out of business by the powers-that-were. Ravishing, ultra-nostalgic lullaby to the American Dream. Watch for Jeff's dad, Lloyd, in a bit role. **Hound Advisory:** Salty language.

1988 (PG/*Jr. High-Adult*) 111m/C Jeff Bridges, Martin Landau, Dean Stockwell, Frederic Forrest, Mako, Joan Allen, Christian Slater, Lloyd Bridges, Elias Koteas, Nina Siemaszko, Corin "Corky" Nemec, Marshall Bell, Don Novello, Peter Donat, Dean Goodman, Patti Austin; *D:* Francis Ford Coppola; *W:* Arnold Schulman, David Seidler; *M:* Joe Jackson, Carmine Coppola. **Award Nominations:** Academy Awards '88: Best Art Direction/Set Decoration, Best Costume Design, Best Supporting Actor (Landau); **Awards:** Golden Globe Awards '89: Best Supporting Actor (Landau). **VHS, Beta, LV, 8mm $14.95** *PAR*

Turf Boy 🐾🐾

Desperate for cash, a boy and his uncle try to get an old horse into prime condition for racing. A minor equine melodrama, just the right length for an old-time matinee double-feature.
1942 (*Jr. High-Adult*) 68m/B Robert "Buzzy" Henry, James Seay, Doris Day, William Halligan, Gavin Gordon; *D:* William Beaudine. **VHS $15.95** *NOS, LOO*

Turk 182! 🐾◁

Angry teen brother of a disabled, alcoholic fireman takes on local political bosses to win back the pension the firefighter deserves. The kid's weapon: a public graffiti campaign that plasters the title catch phrase all over town. Boy fights City Hall, audience loses, in this contrived, mostly silly feel-good plot. **Hound Advisory:** Alcohol use, profanity, mature themes, including an attempted suicide.
1985 (PG-13/*Jr. High-Adult*) 96m/C Timothy Hutton, Robert Culp, Robert Urich, Kim Cattrall, Peter Boyle, Darren McGavin, Paul Sorvino; *D:* Bob (Benjamin) Clark. **VHS, Beta $79.98** *FOX*

Turner and Hooch 🐾🐾

Slobbering pooch witnesses his master's murder, and a fussy police detective is partnered with the drooling, ugly mutt and a weak script in his search for the culprit. Hanks is his usual charming self, but even he can't wholly salvage this Touchstone effort. Came out not long after Universal's cop 'n' dog action/comedy "K-9"; take your pick. **Hound Advisory:** Violence, sex talk.
1989 (PG/*Jr. High-Adult*) 99m/C Tom Hanks, Mare Winningham, Craig T. Nelson, Scott Paulin, J.C. Quinn; *D:* Roger Spottiswoode; *W:* Jim Cash, Jack Epps Jr., Michael Blodgett. **VHS, Beta, LV $19.99** *TOU*

Turtle Diary 🐾🐾🐾

"Free Willy" for grownups, though kids may be hooked by the premise and reeled in. Slow-paced but warm portrait of two lonely, bookish adult Londoners brought together in a scheme to secretly release giant turtles from the city aquarium into their rightful home, the sea. The animals' freedom somehow liberates the humans' spirits as well. Based on the Russell Hoban novel. **Hound Advisory:** Salty language, mature themes.
1986 (PG/*Sr. High-Adult*) 90m/C Ben Kingsley, Glenda Jackson, Richard Johnson, Michael Gambon, Rosemary Leach, Jeroen Krabbe, Eleanor Bron; *D:* John Irvin; *W:* Harold Pinter. **VHS, Beta, LV $79.98** *LIV, VES*

Tut and Tuttle 🐾◁

Young dabbler in magic is transported to ancient Egypt, where he uses his wits against the evil Horemheb, who has kidnapped the child Prince Tut. Juvenile TV adventure, an early directorial effort for Ron Howard and broadcast as "Through the Magic Pyramid."
1982 (*Preschool*) 97m/C Christopher Barnes, Eric Greene, Hans Conried, Vic Tayback. **VHS, Beta** *TLF*

TV's Best Adventures of Superman

This first package of episodes from the original television series, which ran from 1951-1957, contains "Superman on Earth," the black & white series pilot about the Man of Steel's childhood on Krypton and Earth, and "All That Glitters," the series final episode, wherein Lois Lane and Jimmy Olsen acquire super powers. Also includes the 1941 animated cartoon "Superman," the first-ever screen appearance of the superhero. Additional episodes available.
1951 (*Family*) 62m/C George Reeves, Phyllis Coates, Noel Neill, Jack Larson, John Hamilton, Robert Shayne. **VHS, Beta $19.98** *WAR, MOV*

'Twas the Night Before Christmas

Santa Claus may not visit Junctionville because of an insulting letter printed in a local newspaper, so Joshua Trundle and Father Mouse look for a way to mend his hurt feelings. A Rankin-Bass cartoon adaptation of the classic Clement Moore poem.
1982 (*Family*) 25m/C *V:* Joel Grey, George Gobel. **VHS, Beta** *MTI, WAR, WTA*

'Twas the Night Before Christmas

Clement Moore's poem is retold through animation.
1991 (*Preschool-Primary*) 27m/C **VHS $14.98** *FHE, FFF*

Twelve Chairs 🐾🐾🐾

Take-off on Russian folktale first filmed in Yugoslavia in 1927. A rich matron admits on her deathbed that she has hidden her jewels in the upholstery of one of twelve chairs that are no longer in her home. A Brooksian treasure hunt ensues.
1970 (PG/*Jr. High-Adult*) 94m/C Mel Brooks, Dom DeLuise, Frank Langella, Ron Moody, Bridget Brice; *D:* Mel Brooks; *W:* Mel Brooks. **VHS, Beta, LV $59.95** *MED*

20,000 Leagues Under the Sea 🐾🐾🐾◁

Stout-hearted seafaring men of the 19th century investigate rumors of a monster sinking ships, discover it's actually a scientific genius named Nemo who's invented the atomic submarine a century early and uses the futuristic craft in a personal war against the surface world. One of Walt Disney's most celebrated and successful live actioners, with first-rate cast and f/x. Based on the novel by Jules Verne; for a non-Disney sequel, see "The Mysterious Island."
1954 (*Family*) 127m/C Kirk Douglas, James Mason, Peter Lorre, Paul Lukas, Robert J. Wilke, Carleton Young; *D:* Richard Fleischer. **Award Nominations:** Academy Awards '54: Best Film Editing; **Awards:** Academy Awards '54: Best Art Direction/Set Decoration (Color), Best Special Effects; National Board of Review Awards '54: 10 Best Films of the Year. **VHS, Beta, LV $19.99** *DIS*

20,000 Leagues Under the Sea 🐾🐾

Straight animated retelling of the Jules Verne classic science fiction novel about two men and a boy held by the obsessed Captain Nemo aboard his fantastic submarine, as envisioned by the Hanna-Barbera studios.
1973 (*Preschool-Primary*) 60m/C **VHS, Beta $19.98** *LIV, PSM, WOV*

20,000 Leagues Under the Sea

A lighthearted twist on the Verne tale happens when a cool kid and his weird friends go sailing to find a radical sea serpent.
1990 *(Preschool-Primary)* 25m/C **VHS $9.99** *VTR*

20,000 Leagues Under the Sea 🦴🦴

Hanna-Barbera cartoon adaptation of the Jules Verne classic can't compare to the Disney version, as Captain Nemo reveals his submarine, the Nautilus, to an astounded world.
1990 *(Family)* 47m/C **VHS $9.99** *STE*

Twice Upon a Time 🦴🦴🦴🦴

George Lucas was executive producer for this one-of-a-kind cartoon fantasy that, shamefully, never got substantial theatrical release. Synonamess Botch, an incompetent villain who manufactures nightmares, sabotages the Cosmic Clock. To the rescue come occupants of Frivoli, the magical land where dreams originate. Heroes include the Chaplinesque mute Mumford and his shape-changing pal Ralph the All-Purpose Animal (voice by Lorenzo Music, who also does Garfield the Cat). Filmed in "lumage," an eye-catching style of cutout/collage animation, with sly dialogue to entertain young and old alike. **Hound Advisory:** The PG rating has no earthly explanation.
1983 (PG/*Primary-Adult*) 75m/C **D:** Charles Swenson, John Korty; **V:** Lorenzo Music, Marshall Efron, Paul Frees, Hamilton Camp. **VHS, Beta, LV $14.95** *WAR, FCT, WTA*

Twilight of the Cockroaches 🦴🦴

Allegorical Japanimation feature, definitely off-limits to small kids despite the cutesy characters — who nonetheless have sex and die violently. Mix of live-action and animation occurs in the messy apartment of a lonely bachelor. The (cartoon) roaches, with their own organized society, falsely think that just because Mr. Saito no longer cleans up after himself, they're safe from insecticide. Then Saito's fastidious new girlfriend moves in, and the bugs face extermination. Effective argument in favor of the cockroach lifestyle. Note, however, the two "innocent" roach kingdoms in peril look like Japan and Germany; it's not hard to interpret this as a defense of the Axis powers from WWII. **Hound Advisory:** Mature themes, violence, sex, alcohol use.
1990 *(Jr. High-Adult)* 105m/C **D:** Hiroaki Yoshida; **V:** Kaoru Kobayashi, Setsuko Karamsumarau. **VHS, LV $34.95** *FCT, STP, LUM*

Twilight Zone: The Movie 🦴🦴🦴

Narrated by Meredith, four short horrific tales are anthologized as a tribute to Rod Sterling and his popular television series. Three of the episodes, "Kick the Can," "It's a Good Life" and "Nightmare at 20,000 Feet," are based on original "Twilight Zone" scripts. Most effective of the four is the Miller-directed "Nightmare," with Lithgow as a terrified airplane passenger who spots a demon riding the wing. Morrow was killed during a helicopter stunt during filming.

1983 (PG/*Family*) 101m/C Dan Aykroyd, Albert Brooks, Vic Morrow, Kathleen Quinlan, John Lithgow, Billy Mumy, Scatman Crothers, Kevin McCarthy, Bill Quinn, Selma Diamond, Abbe Lane, John Larroquette, Jeremy Licht, Patricia Barry, William Schallert, Burgess Meredith, Cherie Currie; **D:** John Landis, Steven Spielberg, George Miller, Joe Dante; **W:** John Landis; **M:** Jerry Goldsmith. **VHS, Beta, LV $19.98** *WAR*

Twist 🦴🦴🦴

Amusing documentary about the dance craze and American pop culture. Hank Ballard and the Midnighters first recorded "The Twist" in 1960 but it was Chubby Checker's cover version and Dick Clark's promotion of the record on "American Bandstand" that really started everyone moving - from kids to grandparents. Includes interviews, newsreel, and tv footage.
1993 (PG/*Jr. High-Adult*) 78m/C **D:** Ron Mann. **VHS, LV $94.98** *COL, IME, MVD*

Two of a Kind 🦴🦴🦴

In his television movie debut, Burns plays an elderly man whose mentally handicapped grandson helps him put the starch back in his shirt. Sensitively produced and performed.
1982 *(Family)* 102m/C George Burns, Robby Benson, Cliff Robertson, Barbara Barrie, Frances Lee McCain, Geri Jewell, Ronny Cox; **D:** Roger Young. **VHS, Beta $49.95** *FOX*

2000 Year Old Man 🦴🦴🦴

Animated version of the classic Mel Brooks/Carl Reiner comedy routine, adapted as a network TV special complete with studio audience laughter and gags about the commercial breaks (nonexistent on tape). Neither detract from the wry hilarity as a 2,000 year old man recounts dating Joan of Arc, Robin Hood's press agent, what women are for, and Shakespeare's lost play "Queen Alexandra and Murray."
1982 (G/*Family*) 25m/C **D:** Leo Salkin; **V:** Carl Reiner, Mel Brooks. **VHS, Beta $19.95** *MED*

2001: A Space Odyssey 🦴🦴🦴🦴

Space voyage to Jupiter turns chaotic when a computer, HAL 9000, takes over. Seen by some as a mirror of man's historical use of machinery and by others as a grim vision of the future, film scores with stunning storyline, special effects and music. A definitive sci-fi viewing experience. Martin Balsam originally recorded the voice of HAL, but was replaced by Raines. From Arthur C. Clarke's novel "The Sentinel." Followed by a sequel "2010: The Year We Make Contact." Laserdisc edition is presented in letterbox format and features a special supplementary section on the making of "2001," a montage of images from the film, production documents, memos and photos. Also included on the disc is a NASA film entitled "Art and Reality," which offers footage from the Voyager I and II flybys of Jupiter.
1968 *(Family)* 139m/C Keir Dullea, Gary Lockwood, William Sylvester, Dan Richter; **D:** Stanley Kubrick; **W:** Arthur C. Clarke, Stanley Kubrick; **V:** Douglas Raines. **Award Nominations:** Academy Awards '68: Best Art Direction/Set Decoration, Best Director (Kubrick), Best Story & Screenplay; **Awards:** Academy Awards '68: Best Visual Effects; National Board of Review Awards '68: 10 Best Films of the Year. **VHS, Beta, LV $19.98** *MGM, VYG, CRC*

2010 : The Year We Make Contact 🎬🎬🎬

Sequel to "2001: A Space Odyssey" continues screen adaptation of Arthur C. Clarke's novel "The Sentinel" 16 years after the sci-fi classic was released. Americans and Russians unite to investigate the abandoned starship Discovery and its decaying orbit around Jupiter, trying to determine why the HAL 9000 computer sabotaged its mission years before, while signs of cosmic change are detected on and around the giant planet. Lacks the original's wallop, but worthy of a view. **Hound Advisory:** Violence.
1984 (PG/*Jr. High-Adult*) 116m/C Roy Scheider, John Lithgow, Helen Mirren, Bob Balaban, Keir Dullea, Madolyn Smith, Mary Jo Deschanel; *D:* Peter Hyams; *W:* Peter Hyams; *M:* David Shire; *V:* Douglas Raines. VHS, Beta, LV $19.95 MGM

Ub Iwerks Cartoonfest

Iwerks was one of Walt Disney's original cohorts and even helped concoct Mickey Mouse. Later Iwerks went on to careers with several animation studios. Five volumes of Iwerks works (mostly adaptations of classic fairy tales), some B&W, some color, are available in this videocassette series.
193? (*Family*) 57m/C VHS, Beta $19.98 CCB, WTA

The Ugly Dachshund 🎬🎬🎬

Jones and Pleshette are married dog lovers breeding dachshunds. Then they take in a great dane puppy, who grows to massive full-size thinking he's a wiener dog because he's been raised with them. Just imagine what happens when such a large dog acts as if he's small and you've got the picture. Though it's a one-joke setup at best, small kids should enjoy this runt from the Disney film litter.
1965 (*Adult*) 93m/C Dean Jones, Suzanne Pleshette, Charlie Ruggles, Kelly Thordsen, Parley Baer; *D:* Norman Tokar. VHS, Beta DIS, OM

The Ugly Duckling

The Hans Christian Andersen story meets Disney animation and the result is 'toon magic in this Academy Award winner that teaches acceptance regardless of looks. It was also the last of the Disney's original cycle of "Silly Symphonies."
1939 (*Preschool-Primary*) 8m/C VHS, Beta $170.00 DSN, MTI

The Ugly Duckling

Paintings illustrate this version of the Hans Christian Andersen classic about the aesthetically challenged immature waterfowl; singer/actress Cher reads the text. Product of the distinguished "Rabbit Ears" video series from Random House.
1986 (*Preschool-Primary*) 30m/C VHS, Beta $19.95 KUI, RAN, VEC

The Ugly Duckling and other Classic Fairytales

Presentation of three classic stories in animated form, from the acclaimed "Children's Circle" series by Weston Woods.
1985 (*Preschool-Primary*) 36m/C VHS, Beta $14.95 CCC,, BTV

Ugly Little Boy

Future scientists time-teleport a child from the Neanderthal age to the present for study. They treat the poor cave-kid like a specimen; only the nurse assigned to him comes to view the boy as human. Strangely unmoving adaptation of one of Isaac Asimov's most famous sci-fi short stories.
1977 (*Preschool*) 26m/C Kate Reid; *D:* Barry Morse, Don Thompson. VHS, Beta LCA

Uncle Buck 🎬🎬🎬

The Russells leave town and reluctantly put kids in the temporary care of good ol' Uncle Buck, a lovable slob who spends much of his time bowling, eating, and trying to make up with his girlfriend. The young children adore Buck, but moody punk teen Tia's disputes with him over her clothes and lifestyle cause real hurt on both sides. John Hughes wrote/directed this uneven comedy with its heart in the right place but seesawing between mean-spirited slapstick and intelligent drama. A hit with audiences thanks to the Candy man, then a short-lived TV series without him. **Hound Advisory:** Salty language, sex talk, alcohol use.
1989 (PG/*Jr. High-Adult*) 100m/C John Candy, Amy Madigan, Jean Kelly, Macaulay Culkin, Jay Underwood, Gaby Hoffman, Laurie Metcalf, Elaine Bromka, Garrett M. Brown; *D:* John Hughes; *W:* John Hughes; *M:* Ira Newborn. VHS, Beta, LV $19.95 MCA

Under Capricorn 🎬🎬🎬

Bergman is an Irish lass who follows her convict husband Cotten out to 1830s Australia where he makes a fortune. She turns to drink, perhaps because of his neglect, and has her position usurped by a housekeeper with designs on her husband. When Bergman's cousin (Wilding) arrives, Cotten may have cause for his violent jealousy. There's a plot twist involving old family skeletons, but this is definitely lesser Hitchcock. Adapted from the Helen Simpson novel. Remade in 1982.
1949 (*Jr. High-Adult*) 117m/C Ingrid Bergman, Joseph Cotten, Michael Wilding, Margaret Leighton, Jack Watling, Cecil Parker, Denis O'Dea; *D:* Alfred Hitchcock. VHS, Beta, LV $14.98 VES

Under the Rainbow WOOF!

"Comic" situations are encountered by a Hollywood talent scout and a secret service agent in a hotel filled with party-animal midget actors hired to portray Munchkins during the filming of "The Wizard of Oz." Nazi dwarf spy adds to prevailing lack of taste in this attempt at humor. Not really for kids. Or adults. **Hound Advisory:** Nudity, sex, alcohol use, profanity.
1981 (PG/*Primary-Adult*) 97m/C Chevy Chase, Carrie Fisher, Eve Arden, Joseph Maher, Robert Donner, Mako, Pat McCormick, Billy Barty, Zelda Rubinstein; *D:* Steve Rash; *W:* Pat McCormick, Martin Smith, Harry Hurwitz. VHS, Beta $19.98 WAR

Undercover Blues 🎬🎬🎬

Comedy-thriller starring Turner and Quaid as married spies Jane and Jeff Blue, on parental leave from the espionage biz, who are on vacation with their 11-month-old daughter in New Orleans. But the holiday is interrupted when they're recruited

Household hints with John Candy in "Uncle Buck"

by their boss to stop an old adversary from selling stolen weapons. The leads play cute together and the baby is adorable but this is strictly routine escapism. Stick with "The Thin Man" instead. **Hound Advisory:** Profanity; violence; sex talk.
1993 (PG-13/*Jr. High-Adult*) 90m/C Kathleen Turner, Dennis Quaid, Fiona Shaw, Stanley Tucci, Larry Miller, Obba Babatunde, Park Overall, Tom Arnold, Saul Rubinek, Michelle Schuelke; *D:* Herbert Ross; *W:* Ian Abrams; *M:* David Newman. **VHS, LV** *MGM*

Underdog: The Tickle Feather Machine

Underdog comes up against Simon Bar Sinister's most fiendish plan. Also includes the comic misadventures of Tennessee Tuxedo and Chumly, Commander McBragg and the Go-Go Gophers.
1966 (*Family*) 60m/C Underdog. **VHS $14.99** *UAV, WTA*

Undergrads 🐾🐾🐾

Bright generational Disney comedy with Carney, estranged from his stick-in-the-mud son, deciding to attend college with his free-thinking grandson. Made for television.
1985 (*Family*) 102m/C Art Carney, Chris Makepeace, Jackie Burroughs, Len Birman; *D:* Steven Hilliard Stern. **VHS, Beta $59.95** *DIS*

Undersea Adventures of Captain Nemo: Vol. 1

Not a "20,000 Leagues Under the Sea" adaptation, but a modern-day cartoon series with Captain Mark Nemo and his crew of the research submarine Nautilus on a series of daring voyages and rescues. Heavy on the ecological themes. Additional volumes available.
1975 (*Primary*) 60m/C **VHS, Beta** *FHE*

The Undersea Adventures of Snelgrove Snail

Group of aquatic puppets sing songs and generally have all kinds of fun together.
1989 (*Primary*) 45m/C **VHS, Beta $14.95** *FHE*

Undersea Kingdom

One of the earlier Republic serials, but not one of the greats. Ray "Crash" Corrigan, usually seen above sea level as a cowboy hero, battles the tyrants in the lost city of Atlantis. In 12 chapters of 13 minutes each; first one runs 20 minutes. Later re-edited down into the feature "Sharad of Atlantis."
1936 (*Family*) 226m/B Ray Corrigan, Lon Chaney Jr.; *D:* B. Reeves Eason. **VHS, LV $29.98** *NOS, SNC, VCN*

Unico in the Island of Magic

Japanese cartoon in which Unico the baby unicorn travels to a mystical land which includes evil beings, magical puppets and all sorts of odd characters. See also "The Fantastic Adventures of Unico."
1977 (*Family*) 92m/C **VHS $19.95** *COL, WTA*

Unicorn Tales 1

Four stories for children, adapted from classic fairy tales, and told in a modern way, with music. Includes "The Magic Pony Ride" (based on the Ugly Duckling), "The Stowaway" (based on Pinocchio), "Carnival Circus" (based on Cinderella), and "The Maltese Unicorn" (based on The Boy Who Cried Wolf). Additional volumes available.
1980 (*Preschool-Primary*) 90m/C **VHS, Beta** *FOX*

Unidentified Flying Oddball 🐾🐾

Astronaut and his identical-twin robot co-pilot find their spaceship turning into a time machine that throws them back into Camelot and at the mercy of Merlin the magician. Farcical fantasy from Disney (with good special effects) doesn't realize full potential of great source material, Mark Twain's classic "A Connecticut Yankee at King Arthur's Court."
1979 (G/*Family*) 92m/C Dennis Dugan, Jim Dale, Ron Moody, Kenneth More, Rodney Bewes; *D:* Russ Mayberry. **VHS, Beta $69.95** *DIS*

Unknown Island 🐾🐾◁

The "Jurassic Park" of 1948, about an expedition to an remote island where dinosaurs still exist, though much screen time goes to a King Kong impersonator. Prehistoric special f/ x all around. **Hound Advisory:** Violence.
1948 (*Jr. High-Adult*) 76m/C Virginia Grey, Philip Reed, Richard Denning, Barton MacLane; *D:* Jack Bernhard. **VHS $19.95** *NOS, MOV, HEG*

Unsinkable Donald Duck with Huey, Dewey & Louie

Three vintage Disney cartoons featuring Donald and his nephews: "Sea Scouts," "Donald's Day Off" and "Lion Around."
1945 (G/*Family*) 25m/C **VHS, Beta, LV $14.95** *DIS*

Untamed Heart 🐾🐾🐾◁

Adam (Slater), the painfully shy busboy with a heart condition, loves Caroline (Tomei), the bubbly waitress, from afar. She doesn't notice him until he saves her from some would-be rapists and their love blooms in the coffee shop where they both work. Tomei and Slater are both strong in the leads and Perez, as Caroline's best buddy Cindy, hurls comic barbs with ease. Charmingly familiar surroundings help set this formulaic romance apart. Filmed on location in Minneapolis. Laserdisc version is in letterbox format. **Hound Advisory:** Profanity.
1993 (PG-13/*Jr. High-Adult*) 102m/C Christian Slater, Marisa Tomei, Rosie Perez, Kyle Secor, Willie Garson; *D:* Harold Ramis; *W:* Tom Sierchio; *M:* Cliff Eidelman. **VHS, Beta, LV $19.98** *MGM*

Up Against the Wall 🐾🐾

Black kid from the Chicago projects attends school in the affluent suburbs, but there too he must resist temptation, crime, and violence. Well-intentioned but didactic cautionary drama, adapted from the book by African-American author/

commentator Dr. Jawanza Kunjufu. **Hound Advisory:** Violence, drug use, mature themes.
1991 (PG-13/*Jr. High-Adult*) 103m/C Marla Gibbs, Stoney Jackson, Catero Colbert, Ron O'Neal, Salli Richardson; *D:* Ron O'Neal. **VHS** $79.98 *BMG*

Up the Down Staircase 🦴🦴🦴

Naive, newly trained New York public school teacher is determined to teach English literature to a group of poor students. In her first year she grapples not only with kids but also a bureaucratic faculty, a fragile romance, triumph and tragedy. Good production and acting in this straightforward adaptation of Bel Kaufman's celebrated scrapbook-style novel. **Hound Advisory:** Mature themes.
1967 (*Adult*) 124m/C Sandy Dennis, Patrick Bedford, Eileen Heckart, Ruth White, Jean Stapleton, Sorrell Booke; *D:* Robert Mulligan. **VHS** *WAR, OM*

Using Simple Machines

Basic concepts of mechanical physics are explored, with demonstrations of simple machines.
1990 (*Primary-Jr. High*) 14m/C **VHS, Beta** $250.00 *MTI, DSN*

Valley Girl 🦴🦴◁

Teen romantic-comedy is not a film for the young ones, despite glowing reviews that might have made you think otherwise. Leather-jacketed rebel Randy falls for Julie, a trendy California high schooler. But her tightknit clique of friends don't approve. Will Julie drop Randy to keep her popularity? Julie has a nice, honest relationship with her (ex-hippie) parents, and Cage is great in his first major role, but John Hughes would later do variations on this theme without the brief but exploitive nudity, drugs and sex titillation. Inspired by the popularity of Frank Zappa's novelty tune "Valley Girl," which is just about the only song not heard on the hit-heavy soundtrack. **Hound Advisory:** Profanity, drug use, sex, nudity, roughhousing.
1983 (R/*Sr. High-Adult*) 95m/C Nicolas Cage, Deborah Foreman, Colleen Camp, Frederic Forrest; *D:* Martha Coolidge. **VHS, Beta, LV** $29.98 *VES*

The Valley of Gwangi 🦴🦴🦴

"Jurassic Park" goes west, as cowboys discover a lost valley of dinosaurs and try to capture a vicious, carnivorous allosaurus for a carnival. The creatures (including an adorable, miniature prehistoric horse) move via the stop-motion model animation by f/x maestro Ray Harryhausen, here at his finest. **Hound Advisory:** Dinosaur roughhousing.
1969 (G/*Family*) 95m/C James Franciscus, Gila Golan, Richard Carlson, Laurence Naismith, Freda Jackson; *D:* James O'Connolly. **VHS, Beta, LV** $19.98 *WAR*

Velveteen Rabbit

Discarded stuffed toy rabbit finds the meaning of love and receives a fabulous gift. Beautifully told Canadian version of the classic Margery Williams fairy tale.
1985 (*Preschool-Primary*) 30m/C **VHS, Beta** $14.95 *FHE, WTA*

Velveteen Rabbit

Classic Margery Williams story of a toy rabbit that wants to be real, presented by the Enchanted Musical Playhouse.
1985 (*Family*) 60m/C Marie Osmond. **VHS** $7.99 *VTR*

The Velveteen Rabbit

Margery Williams' well-known children's story gets a new rendering in this cassette.
1988 (*Preschool-Primary*) 30m/C **VHS** $9.95 *RAN, KUI, VEC*

Vengeance of the Space Pirate

Fully animated space fantasy for kids, from the Japanese creators of the similar "Space Warriors: Battle for Earth Station S/1."
1987 (*Family*) 102m/C **Beta** $14.99 *JFK, WTA*

A Very Merry Cricket

Cartoon in which the adventurous Chester C. Cricket sets out to rescue the real spirit of Christmas from rampant commercialism. Sequel to "The Cricket in Times Square."
1973 (*Family*) 30m/C *D:* Chuck Jones; *V:* Mel Blanc. **VHS, Beta** $14.95 *FHE, WTA*

Vice Versa 🦴🦴🦴

Another oft-rerun '80s comedy plot about a workaholic father and his 11-year-old son who switch bodies, with predictable slapstick results. Reinhold and Savage carry this, appearing to have a great time in spite of secondhand story. **Hound Advisory:** Salty language, sex talk.
1988 (PG/*Jr. High-Adult*) 97m/C Judge Reinhold, Fred Savage, Swoosie Kurtz, David Proval, Corinne Bohrer, Jane Kaczmarek, William Prince, Gloria Gifford; *D:* Brian Gilbert; *W:* Dick Clement, Ian LaFrenais; *M:* David Shire. **VHS, Beta, LV** $14.95 *COL*

Victory 🦴🦴◁

Soccer match between WWII prisoners of war and their captors, a German team, gives the players a chance to escape through the sewer tunnels. But the game's heating up; should the Allied athletes bolt to freedom or stay to beat the Nazis on the field? Not particularly believable as either a sports flick (even with Pele and other soccer stars) or a great escape, but watchable. **Hound Advisory:** Violence, but not as bad as you might expect.
1981 (PG/*Jr. High-Adult*) 116m/C Sylvester Stallone, Michael Caine, Max von Sydow, Pele, Carole Laure, Bobby Moore, Daniel Massey; *D:* John Huston; *W:* Jeff Maguire, Djordje Milicevic; *M:* Bill Conti. **VHS, Beta** $19.98 *FOX, WAR*

A View to a Kill 🦴🦴

This James Bond mission takes him to the United States, where he must stop the evil Max Zorin from destroying California's Silicon Valley. Feeble and unexciting plot with unscary villain. Duran Duran performs the catchy title tune. Moore's last appearance as 007. **Hound Advisory:** Violence, sex, alcohol use.
1985 (PG/*Jr. High-Adult*) 131m/C Roger Moore, Christopher Walken, Tanya Roberts, Grace Jones, Patrick Macnee, Lois Maxwell, Dolph Lundgren, Desmond Llewelyn; *D:* John Glen; *W:* Michael G. Wilson; *M:* John Barry. **VHS, Beta, LV** $19.98 *FOX, TLF*

The Villain 🎬🎬

Labored spoof of westerns that gets its gags from the "Roadrunner" cartoons. Douglas plays Cactus Jack, a bandit who keeps trying to kidnap a fair damsel or wipe out the simple-minded cowboy hero "Handsome Stranger" (early Schwarzenegger) accompanying her. But the pair ride on obliviously as Jack knocks himself off cliffsides, blows himself up, etc. This worked in a 10-minute Chuck Jones 'toon, but here it's slowed to feature length. Kids might be amused. **Hound Advisory:** Roughhousing, cartoon violence.

1979 (PG/*Jr. High-Adult*) 93m/C Kirk Douglas, Ann-Margret, Arnold Schwarzenegger, Paul Lynde, Foster Brooks, Ruth Buzzi, Jack Elam, Strother Martin, Robert Tessier, Mel Tillis; *D:* Hal Needham. **VHS $14.95** *COL*

Vip, My Brother Superman

The Vips are modern-day descendants of superbeings about to become legends in their own times. SuperVip is broad of chest and pure in spirit while his brother MiniVip possesses only limited powers. From the creator of "Allegro Non Troppo" comes this enticing, amusing piece of animation.

1990 (*Family*) 90m/C *D:* Bruno Bozzetto. **VHS $59.95** *EXP, TPV*

Visionaries, Vol. 1: The Age of Magic Begins

Through an inexplicable turn of the planets, Prysmos is left in the dark. The sorcery of the middle ages prevails in this stricken land, and the visionaries, with their feel for the future, must restore the universe to proper balance...oh yes, and Visionaries action figures with real holographs were available at shopping centers everywhere. Additional volumes available.

1987 (*Family*) 30m/C **VHS, Beta $29.95** *WTA*

The Voyage of the Yes 🎬🎬

Two teenagers, one white and one black, in a small sailboat hit rough weather and battle the elements while learning about themselves. Uplifting with noble intentions though regrettably bland made-for-television movie.

1972 (PG/*Jr. High-Adult*) 100m/C Desi Arnaz Jr., Mike Evans, Beverly Garland, Skip Homeier, Della Reese, Scoey Mitchell; *D:* Lee H. Katzin. **VHS** *NO*

Voyage to the Bottom of the Sea 🎬🎬🎬

Crew of an atomic submarine must destroy a deadly radiation belt which has set the polar ice cap ablaze. Fun stuff, with good special effects and photography. Later became a television show.

1961 (*Family*) 106m/C Walter Pidgeon, Joan Fontaine, Barbara Eden, Peter Lorre, Robert Sterling, Michael Ansara, Frankie Avalon; *D:* Irwin Allen; *W:* Irwin Allen, Charles Bennett. **VHS, Beta, LV $14.98** *FOX, FCT*

Voyager from the Unknown

Feature-length compilation from the short-lived TV series "Voyagers." Phineas Boggs is a time-traveller with a mission to fix any details of history that go astray. A little orphan named Jeffrey (who's considerably smarter) gets to accompany the hapless hero.

1983 (*Family*) 91m/C Jon-Erik Hexum, Meeno Peluce, Ed Begley Jr., Faye Grant, Fionnula Flanagan. **VHS, Beta $39.95** *MCA*

Wackiest Wagon Train in the West 🎬

Hapless wagon master is saddled with a dummy assistant as they guide a party of five characters across the West. Based on the short-lived TV sitcom "Dusty's Trail." Produced by the same folks who delivered the series "Gilligan's Island," which this closely resembles.

1977 (G/*Family*) 86m/C Bob Denver, Forrest Tucker, Jeannine Riley. **VHS, Beta $19.95** *MED*

Wacky & Packy

Cartoon series collection about a caveman and his woolly mammoth in the modern world, causing trouble wherever they go.

1975 (*Family*) 70m/C **VHS, Beta $29.95** *PSM, WTA*

The Wacky World of Mother Goose

Rankin-Bass production for small fry, featuring their distinct stop-motion animation previously seen in the likes of "Daydreamer" and "Mad Monster Party." Storybook characters like Tom Thumb, Mother Hubbard, Sleeping Beauty, Jack Horner and even the Three Men in a Tub figure in a conspiracy by Count Warptwist to take the place of Mother Goose.

1967 (*Preschool-Primary*) 81m/C *V:* Margaret Rutherford. **VHS, Beta $14.95** *COL, SUE*

Wagons East 🎬🎬

Pioneers head west and then change their minds. Candy (who died during filming) plays the drunken former wagonmaster hired to get them back home, but he's oddly underused. Script does little in the way of original or inventively recycled humor, making genre parody head east slowly. **Hound Advisory:** Roughhousing, off-color humor

1994 (PG-13/*Jr. High-Adult*) 100mm/C John Candy, Richard Lewis, Ellen Greene, John C. McGinley, Robert Picardo, William Sanderson, Thomas F. Duffy, Russell Means, Rodney Grant, Michael Horse, Gailard Sartain, Lochlynm Munro, Stuart Proud Eagle Grant; *D:* Peter Markle; *W:* Matthew Carlson. **VHS** *NYR*

Waif Goodbye to the Paw Paws

Aunt Pruney dresses up as a waif to trick the Paw Paws, but her plan is nipped in the bud by Dark Paw. He conjures up a terrible lightning storm to teach her a lesson she'll never forget. Ripped from today's headlines, this obscure 'toon comes from Hanna-Barbera.

1990 (*Family*) 30m/C **VHS, Beta $9.95** *TTC, WTA*

Wait Till Your Mother Gets Home 🎬🎬

"Mr. Mom"-like zaniness abounds as a football coach cares for the kids and does chores while his wife takes her first job in 15 years. Almost too darn cute, but well written. Made for TV.

1983 (*Family*) 97m/C Paul Michael Glaser, Dee Wallace Stone, Peggy McKay, David Doyle, Raymond Buktenica, James Gregory, Joey Lawrence, Lynne Moody; **D:** Bill Persky. **VHS, Beta $9.99** *PSM*

Wait Until Spring, Bandini 🐾🐾◁

Flavorful immigrant tale about a transplanted Italian family weathering the winter in 1925 Colorado, as seen through the eyes of a young son. Alternately funny and moving, with one of Dunaway's scenery-chewing performances as a local temptation for the father. Based on the autobiographical novel by John Fante, co-produced by Francis Ford Coppola. **Hound Advisory:** Mature themes, mainly brief marital straying.

1990 (*PG-13/Jr. High-Family*) 104m/C Joe Mantegna, Faye Dunaway, Burt Young, Ornella Muti, Alex Vincent, Renato Vanni, Michael Bacall, Daniel Wilson; **D:** Dominique Deruddere; **M:** Angelo Badalamenti. **VHS $19.98** *WAR*

Waiting for the Light 🐾🐾◁

Lightweight comedy set amid small-town panic during the Cuban missile crisis. Chicago-transplant Garr and her two kids inherit a diner in the Pacific Northwest. Aunt Zena (MacLaine), a magician, arrives and after some unlikely events, is mistaken for an angel by the gullible townspeople. The divine sighting becomes a boost for restaurant business. Professional troupe keeps the less-than-heavenly story flying. **Hound Advisory:** Profanity.

1990 (*PG/Jr. High-Adult*) 94m/C Shirley MacLaine, Teri Garr, Vincent Schiavelli, John Bedford Lloyd; **D:** Christopher Monger; **W:** Christopher Monger. **VHS, LV, 8mm $19.95** *COL*

Walk Like a Man 🐾◁

In a take-off of Tarzan movies, Mandel is a man raised by wolves. Comic problems arise when he is found by his mother and the family attempts to civilize him. Juvenile script wastes fine cast.

1987 (*PG/Jr. High-Adult*) 86m/C Howie Mandel, Christopher Lloyd, Cloris Leachman, Colleen Camp, Amy Steel, George DiCenzo; **D:** Melvin Frank. **VHS, Beta $79.95** *MGM*

Walking on Air

In the near future, paralyzed adolescent Danny realizes that he and his wheelchair-bound friends are prisoners of gravity; in the weightlessness of space they would have full mobility. He campaigns to allow disabled kids into the space program. Uplifting (in more ways than one) "WonderWorks" story, based on an idea by sci-fi author Ray Bradbury, which explains why a "Bradbury Science Museum" figures prominently in the plot.

1987 (*Family*) 60m/C Lynn Redgrave, Jordan Marder, James Treuer, Katheryn Trainor; **D:** Ed Kaplan. **VHS $14.95** *PME, FCT, BTV*

Walking Tall 🐾🐾🐾◁

Tennessee sheriff takes a stand against syndicate-run gambling and his wife is murdered in response. Ultra-violent crime saga wowed the movie going public and spawned several sequels and a TV series. Based on the true story of folk-hero Buford Pusser, admirably rendered by Baker. **Hound Advisory:** Brutality, profanity.

1973 (*R/Sr. High-Adult*) 126m/C Joe Don Baker, Elizabeth Hartman, Noah Beery Jr., Gene Evans, Rosemary Murphy, Felton Perry; **D:** Phil Karlson. **VHS, Beta, LV $29.98** *LIV*

Wally Gator

Count 'em: 17 episodes from the Hanna-Barbera show about the alligator who resides at the zoo.

1984 (*Preschool-Primary*) 80m/C **VHS, Beta $19.95** *TTC, WTA*

A Walt Disney Christmas

Six classic cartoons with a wintry theme are combined for this program: "Pluto's Christmas Tree" (1952), "On Ice," "Donald's Snowball Fight;" two Silly Symphonies from 1932-33: "Santa's Workshop" and "The Night Before Christmas;" and an excerpt from the 1948 feature "Melody Time," entitled "Once Upon a Wintertime."

1982 (*Family*) 46m/C **VHS, Beta $12.99** *DIS, WTA*

Walt Disney Films in French

Exclusive release of well-known Disney films for the French, without English subtitles, recommended for fun language training.

1986 (*G/Family*) 100m/C **VHS, Beta** *INJ*

The Waltons: The Children's Carol 🐾🐾

The winter solstice brings no special joy to Walton's Mountain; WWII has taken many men, with short wave reports indicating the Nazi terror spreading across Europe. But huddled in the glow of Walton's barn, the children rediscover the true meaning of Christmas.

1980 (*Family*) 94m/C Judy Norton-Taylor, Jon Walmsley, Mary McDonough, Eric Scott, Kami Cotler, Joe Conley, Ronnie Clare, Leslie Winston, Peggy Rea; **D:** Lawrence Dobkin. **VHS, Beta $14.98** *LHV*

Waltz King 🐾🐾

Typically hokey Disney biography of the young composer Johann Strauss during his old Viennese heyday. Fine music, pretty German locations.

1963 (*Family*) 94m/C Kerwin Mathews, Senta Berger, Brian Aherne; **D:** Steve Previn. **VHS, Beta $69.95** *DIS*

A Waltz Through the Hills

Two orphans head into the Australian outback and experience many adventures en route to the coast where they can set sail for England and their grandparents. Part of the "Wonderworks" series.

1988 (*Family*) 116m/C Tina Kemp, Andre Jansen, Ernie Dingo, Dan O'Herlihy; **D:** Frank Arnold. **VHS $29.95** *PME, HMV, FCT*

War Games 🐾🐾🐾

Teen computer hacker, thinking that he's sneaking an advance look at a new line of video games, breaks into the US missile-defense system and challenges it to a game of Global Thermonuclear Warfare. The game might just turn out to be

the real thing if the boy can't stop it. Oft-imitated formula of high-tech whiz kids getting into trouble has seldom been better; plot moves like gangbusters, though it slackens toward the end. **Hound Advisory:** Salty language.
1983 (PG/ *Sr. High-Adult)* 110m/C Matthew Broderick, Dabney Coleman, John Wood, Ally Sheedy; **D:** John Badham; **W:** Walter F. Parkes, Lawrence Lasker. **VHS, Beta, LV $19.98** *FOX*

The War of the Worlds 𝄞𝄞𝄞𝄞

H.G. Wells's classic novel of the invasion of Earth by Martians, updated to 1950s California, with spectacular special effects of destruction caused by the Martian war machines. Pretty scary and tense; based more on Orson Welles's radio broadcast than on the book. Still very popular; hit the top 20 in sales when released on video. Classic thriller later made into a TV series. Produced by George Pal (appearing in cameo as a street person), who brought the world much sci-fi, including "The Time Machine," "Destination Moon," and "When Worlds Collide."
1953 *(Family)* 85m/C Gene Barry, Ann Robinson, Les Tremayne, Lewis Martin, Robert Cornthwaite, Sandro Giglio; **D:** Byron Haskin. **Award Nominations:** Academy Awards '53: Best Film Editing, Best Sound; **Awards:** Academy Awards '53: Best Special Effects. **VHS, Beta, LV $14.95** *PAR*

Warriors of the Wind 𝄞𝄞

Re-edited American release of the Japanese animated feature "Nausicaa," about a fantasy world where kingdoms fight their petty wars in the shadow of the dominant life form - enormous, vaguely godlike caterpillar insects. As always, there's one of those prophecies promising that a human messiah will bring peace to people and bugs alike; best to ignore the story and marvel at the creature designs. **Hound Advisory:** Violence.
1985 (PG/ *Jr. High-Adult)* 85m/C **D:** Kazuo Komatsubara. **VHS, Beta $9.95** *NWV, STE, WTA*

Watcher in the Woods 𝄞𝄞

American family rents an English country house, and their children are haunted by blue lights and ghostly visions of a long-missing young girl. Ill-fated early excursion by Disney into PG territory; after a few good scares the story builds to a sloppy, unsatisfying conclusion, hastily re-edited from an original aha!-it-was-aliens cop-out that bombed with preview audiences. Based on a novel by Florence Engel Randall.
1981 (PG/ *Family)* 83m/C Bette Davis, Carroll Baker, David McCallum, Ian Bannen, Lynn-Holly Johnson; **D:** John Hough; **W:** Brian Clemens. **VHS, Beta $14.99** *DIS*

Water Babies 𝄞𝄞

When a chimney sweep's 12-year-old apprentice is wrongly accused of stealing silver, the boy and his dog fall into a pond and eventually rescue some of the characters they find there. Combination of live-action and animated fairytale story set in 19th-century London. Based on the book by Charles Kingsley. Boring, unless you're a young child with equivalent standards.
1979 (G/ *Family)* 93m/C James Mason, Billie Whitelaw, David Tomlinson, Paul Luty, Sammantha Coates; **D:** Lionel Jeffries. **VHS, Beta $29.98** *SUE*

Watership Down 𝄞𝄞𝄞

Wonderfully animated story based on Richard Adams's allegorical novel about a tribe of wild rabbits displaced when their den is fumigated. The survivors find fear and oppression in other bunny societies while searching for a new and better home, in a sometimes lyrical, sometimes harsh narrative that doesn't condescend or yield to childishness. If you want a real downer, check out "The Plague Dogs," from the same team. **Hound Advisory:** Animal violence, mature themes.
1978 (PG/ *Jr. High-Adult)* 92m/C **D:** Martin Rosen; **W:** Martin Rosen; **V:** Ralph Richardson, Zero Mostel, John Hurt, Denholm Elliott, Harry Andrews, Michael Hordern, Joss Ackland. **VHS, Beta, 8mm $14.95** *WAR, TVC, WTA*

The Way We Were 𝄞𝄞𝄞

Big box-office hit follows a love story between opposites from the 1930s to the 1950s. Streisand is a Jewish political radical who meets the handsome WASP Redford at college. They're immediately attracted to one another, but it takes years before they act on it and eventually marry. They move to Hollywood where Redford is a screenwriter and left-wing Streisand becomes involved in the Red scare and the blacklist, much to Redford's dismay. Will their obvious differences drive them apart? Old-fashioned and sweet romance, with much gloss. Hit title song sung by Streisand. Adapted by Arthur Laurents from his novel. **Hound Advisory:** Mature themes.
1973 (PG/ *Jr. High-Adult)* 118m/C Barbra Streisand, Robert Redford, Bradford Dillman, Viveca Lindfors, Herb Edelman, Murray Hamilton, Patrick O'Neal, James Woods, Sally Kirkland; **D:** Sydney Pollack; **W:** Arthur Laurents; **M:** Marvin Hamlisch. **Award Nominations:** Academy Awards '73: Best Actress (Streisand), Best Art Direction/Set Decoration, Best Cinematography; Academy Awards '76: Best Costume Design; **Awards:** Academy Awards '73: Best Song ("The Way We Were"), Best Original Score; Golden Globe Awards '74: Best Song ("The Way We Were"); National Board of Review Awards '73: 10 Best Films of the Year. **VHS, Beta, LV, 8mm $19.95** *COL*

Wayne's World 𝄞𝄞

Surprise-hit comedy based on a "Saturday Night Live" sketch about two rock-loving Illinois teen guys who have their own basement cable-TV show, which they make entertaining by sheer force of their ebullient personalities. Joke is that both Wayne and Garth are played by adult comics, their teenspeak slang and trend-spoofing adventures an affectionate parody of modern youth culture. Good-natured but probably not destined to last; this film's references to early '90s topics already makes it look like a relic. "Wayne's World 2," released a year later, is more of the same, no more and no less. A video compilation of original "Wayne's World" sketches from "Saturday Night Live" is also available. **Hound Advisory:** Salty language.
1992 (PG-13/ *Jr. High-Adult)* 93m/C Mike Myers, Dana Carvey, Rob Lowe, Tia Carrere, Brian Doyle-Murray, Lara Flynn Boyle, Kurt Fuller, Colleen Camp, Donna Dixon, Ed O'Neill; **Cameos:** Alice Cooper, Meatloaf; **D:** Penelope Spheeris; **W:** Mike Myers, Bonnie Turner, Terry Turner; **M:** J. Peter Robinson. **VHS, LV $24.95** *PAR, FCT*

Wayne's World 2 𝄞𝄞

Good-natured rerun of the original has plenty of sophomoric gags, but feels tired. Wayne and Garth are on their own, planning a major concert, Waynestock. "If you book them they will come," Jim Morrison says in a dream. Meanwhile,

Wayne and Garth Party On

Wayne's girlfriend (Carrere) is falling for slimeball record promoter Walken. Offers a few brilliantly funny segments. If you liked the "Bohemian Rhapsody" spot in the original, get ready for the Village People here. Heston has a funny cameo, and Walken and Basinger push the limits without going over the top. Feature film debut for director Surjik. **Hound Advisory:** Sex talk.

1993 (PG-13/*Jr. High-Adult*) 94m/C Mike Myers, Dana Carvey, Tia Carrere, Christopher Walken, Ralph Brown, Kim Basinger, James Hong, Chris Farley, Ed O'Neill, Olivia D'Abo, Kevin Pollak, Drew Barrymore; *Cameos:* Charlton Heston, Rip Taylor, Aerosmith; *D:* Stephen Surjik; *W:* Mike Myers, Bonnie Turner, Terry Turner; *M:* Carter Burwell. **VHS, Beta** *PAR*

We of the Never Never 🦴🦴🦴

The Rescuers may have had to go Down Under but the Wilderness Family were saved the trip by this sincere and well-done drama based on the memoirs of Jeannie Gunn, a pioneer woman in turn-of-the-century Australia. The city-bred heroine marries a rancher and moves from civilized Melbourne to the barren outback of the Northern Territory. There she must fight for her rights as well as for those of the aborigines.

1982 (G/*Jr. High-Adult*) 136m/C Angela Punch McGregor, Arthur Dignam, Tony Barry; *D:* Igor Auzins. **VHS, Beta $59.95** *COL*

We Think the World is Round

Animated adventure about Christopher Columbus's voyage to the new world. Only this time the story is told by his three sailing ships, the Nina, the Pinta, and the Santa Maria. "Look Who's Talking," 1492 style.

1992 (*Preschool-Primary*) 30m/C **VHS $9.98** *TTC, BTV, WTA*

Wee Wendy

Wee Wendy and her people are aliens who land on earth and set up a village on an island in a lake, in this children's animated movie.

1989 (*Family*) 100m/C **VHS, Beta $14.95** *CEL, WTA*

Wee Willie Winkie 🦴🦴🦴

Precocious little girl is taken in by a British regiment in India and manages to resolve conflict between the colonials and the rebels. Although directed by Ford in a departure from his usual rugged western, it's still a sugar-coated treat; if you're a cinematic diabetic, be forewarned. Inspired by the Rudyard Kipling story. **Hound Advisory:** Mild violence.

1937 (PG/*Family*) 99m/B Shirley Temple, Victor McLaglen, Sir C. Aubrey Smith, June Lang, Michael Whalen, Cesar Romero, Constance Collier; *D:* John Ford. **VHS, Beta $19.98** *FOX*

Weekend at Bernie's 🎬🎬◁

Two computer nerds discover embezzlement at their workplace after being invited to their boss's beach house for a weekend party. They find their host murdered. They endeavor to keep up appearances by (you guessed it) dressing and strategically posing the corpse during the party. Kiser as the dead man is memorable, and the two losers gamely keep the silliness flowing. Lots of fun. **Hound Advisory:** Profanity. **1989** (PG-13/*Jr. High-Adult*) 101m/C Andrew McCarthy, Jonathan Silverman, Catherine Mary Stewart, Terry Kiser, Don Calfa, Louis Giambalvo; **D:** Ted Kotcheff; **W:** Robert Klane; **M:** Andy Summers. VHS, VHS, Beta $14.95 *LIV*

Weekend at Bernie's 2 🎬◁

Unlikely but routine sequel to the original's cavorting cadaver slapstick, except now McCarthy and Silverman are frantically hunting for Bernie's (Kiser) cash stash, a quest that takes them and poor dead Bernie to the Caribbean. See Bernie get stuffed in a suitcase, see Bernie hang glide, see Bernie tango, see Bernie attract the opposite sex. Thin script with one-joke premise done to death but fun for those in the mood for the postmortem antics of a comedic stiff. Plenty of well-executed gags involving the well-preserved corpse (particularly one that's been dead for two films now) should lure back fans of the 1989 original. **Hound Advisory:** Salty language. **1993** (PG/*Jr. High-Adult*) 89m/C Andrew McCarthy, Jonathan Silverman, Terry Kiser, Tom Wright, Steve James, Troy Beyer, Barry Bostwick; **D:** Robert Klane; **W:** Robert Klane; **M:** Peter Wolf. VHS, LV *COL*

Weird Science 🎬🎬

Two sex-starved high school computer geeks use their software skills to materialize the ideal woman. Acting as a sort of seductive fairy godmother, she wreaks 'zany' havoc in their lives from the outset. The actors are sometimes appealing, and even with this lame-o plot Hughes can write teen dialogue with the best of them, but many of the jokes are in poor taste, and the gaudy comic tale seems to go on forever. **Hound Advisory:** Much talk of sex and body functions. Roughhousing, nudity. **1985** (PG-13/*Jr. High-Adult*) 94m/C Kelly Le Brock, Anthony Michael Hall, Ilan Mitchell-Smith, Robert Downey Jr., Bill Paxton; **D:** John Hughes; **W:** John Hughes; **M:** Ira Newborn. VHS, Beta, LV $19.95 *MCA*

Welcome Back Wil Cwac Cwac

Ten more short TV cartoons for the very young, with the hapless duckling from Welsh TV. **1990** (*Family*) 43m/C VHS, Beta $14.95 *FHE*

Welcome Home, Roxy Carmichael 🎬🎬

Caustic satire of teen angst and small-town society in a vapid Ohio community eagerly awaiting a visit by Hollywood superstar Carmichael, a local vixen who cleared out years ago. Soulful 15-year-old misfit named Dinky - loathed and mistreated by most everyone - decides she's Roxy's long-lost daughter, but if anything, Ryder's moody performance suggests blood ties to the Addams Family. Offbeat material definitely strikes a nerve or two, but "Roxy's" relentless bitterness and hateful characters soon wear out welcome. **Hound Advisory:** Profanity, sex talk, mature themes. The legendary Roxy is constantly discussed but never clearly seen, except for her bare backside during a nude swim. **1990** (PG-13/*Preschool-Jr. High*) 98m/C Winona Ryder, Jeff Daniels, Laila Robins, Dinah Manoff, Ava Fabian, Robbie Kiger, Sachi Parker; **D:** Jim Abrahams. VHS, Beta, LV, 8mm $14.95 *PAR*

Welcome to Pooh Corner: Vol. 1

Disney's series of made-for-video episodes use Winnie the Pooh's misadventures in the Hundred Acre Wood to instruct children, both directly and by example, using all Pooh's cronies like Tigger, Christopher Robin, and Eeyore. Additional volumes available. **1984** (*Family*) 111m/C VHS, Beta *DIS*

We're Back! A Dinosaur's Story 🎬🎬

Steven Spielberg put this dinosaur cartoon in theaters at the same time as "Jurassic Park," offering an alternative for young viewers easily scared by the PG-13 monster blockbuster. Commendable idea; disappointing movie, as a talking, time-traveling T.Rex and his prehistoric posse visit modern NYC. Kids befriend the gentle giants, but they're captured by an evil carnival owner (right out of "Something Wicked This Way Comes") intent on returning the reptiles to savagery. Overplotted and disorganized, with merely adequate animation (it seems the smarter dinosaurs are, the simpler they look), adapted and inflated from a children's picture-book by Hudson Talbott. **1993** (G/*Family*) 78m/C **D:** Dick Zondag, Ralph Zondag, Phil Nibbelink, Simon Wells; **W:** John Patrick Shanley; **V:** John Goodman, Felicity Kendal, Walter Cronkite, Joey Shea, Jay Leno, Julia Child, Kenneth Mars, Martin Short, Rhea Perlman, Rene LeVant, Blaze Berdahl, Charles Fleischer, Yeardley Smith. VHS $24.98 *MCA*

West Side Story 🎬🎬🎬◁

Gang rivalry and ethnic tension on New York's West Side erupts in a ground-breaking musical. Loosely based on Shakespeare's "Romeo and Juliet," the story follows the Jets and the Sharks as they fight for their turf while Tony and Maria fight for love. Features frenetic and brilliant choreography by co-director Robbins, who also directed the original Broadway show, and a high-caliber score by Bernstein and Sondheim. Wood's voice was dubbed by Marni Nixon and Jimmy Bryant dubbed Beymer's. Laserdisc version includes the complete storyboards, production sketches, re-issue trailer, and an interview with Wise in a letterbox format with digital stereo surround sound. ♫Prologue; Jet Song; Something's Coming; Dance at the Gym; Maria; America; Tonight; One Hand, One Heart; Gee, Officer Krupke. **1961** (*Jr. High-Adult*) 151m/C Natalie Wood, Richard Beymer, Russ Tamblyn, Rita Moreno, George Chakiris, Simon Oakland, Ned Glass; **D:** Robert Wise, Jerome Robbins; **W:** Ernest Lehman; **M:** Leonard Bernstein, Stephen Sondheim. **Award Nominations:** Academy Awards '61: Best Adapted Screenplay; **Awards:** Academy Awards '61: Best Art Direction/Set Decoration (Color), Best Color Cinematography, Best Costume Design (Color), Best Director (Wise), Best Film Editing, Best Picture, Best Sound, Best Supporting Actor (Chakiris), Best Supporting Actress (Moreno), Best Score; Directors Guild of America Awards '61: Best Director (Wise), Best Director (Robbins). VHS, Beta, LV $19.98 *MGM, KUI, FOX*

Westward Ho, the Wagons! 🦴🦴

Promised land lies west, but to get there America's homesteaders have to cross the arduous Oregon Trail, facing starvation, bandits and Indians both hostile and benign. Overly familiar pioneer yarn from Disney, featuring "Davy Crockett" Parker and four Mouseketeers in the cast. Based on the novel by Mary Jane Carr.
1956 *(Family)* 94m/B Fess Parker, Kathleen Crowley, Jeff York, Sebastian Cabot, George Reeves; **D:** William Beaudine. **VHS, Beta $69.95** *DIS*

Whale for the Killing 🦴🦴◁

Eco-minded TV movie, based on the book by "Never Cry Wolf" author Farley Mowat. Naturalist in a Newfoundland fishing community cares for a stranded humpbacked whale, and confronts locals who want to sell the giant sea creature to Russian whalers. Heavy on the sermonizing, but effective.
1981 *(Jr. High-Adult)* 145m/C Richard Widmark, Peter Strauss, Dee Wallace Stone, Bruce McGill, Kathryn Walker; **D:** Richard T. Heffron; **M:** Basil Poledouris. **VHS, Beta $59.98** *FOX*

Whale of a Tale 🦴🦴

Young boy trains a killer whale to do tricks in the big show at a Marineland amusement park, in this obscure ancestor of "Free Willy."
1976 *(G/Family)* 90m/C William Shatner, Marty Allen, Abby Dalton, Andy Devine, Nancy O'Conner; **D:** Ewing Miles Brown. **VHS, Beta $39.95** *VCI, WTA*

What About Bob? 🦴🦴🦴

Neurotic, hypochondriac Bob can barely make a move without his new psychiatrist. When the doctor takes his family to their New England cottage for a vacation, Bob follows, refusing to leave the poor shrink alone. The joke is that the doctor's wife and children find Bob an ideal pal and playmate, just the opposite of dry old dad. Appealing all-ages comedy from veteran Muppeteer Frank Oz. **Hound Advisory:** Alcohol use. Very funny profanity as Bob experiments with the notion that he has Tourette's syndrome (uncontrollable swearing).
1991 *(PG/Jr. High-Adult)* 99m/C Richard Dreyfuss, Bill Murray, Julie Hagerty, Charlie Korsmo, Tom Aldredge, Roger Bowen, Fran Brill, Kathryn Erbe, Doris Belack, Susan Willis; **D:** Frank Oz; **W:** Tom Schulman, Alvin Sargent; **M:** Miles Goodman. **VHS, Beta, LV $19.99** *BVV*

What is Love?

Mr. Rogers hosts a program designed to help kids understand the different aspects of human love and relationships.
1986 *(Primary)* 30m/C Fred Rogers. **VHS, Beta** *NO*

What the Moon Saw 🦴🦴🦴

What a sweet little movie. Steven spends a season with his grandmother in the city. She works at a theater putting on "Sinbad's Last Adventure," a somewhat threadbare children's play. But Steven's mind magnifies the show into a lavish, magical spectacle that helps the boy deal with assorted real-life tribulations. It rambles a bit, but this Australian-made family treat is really worth seeking out.
1990 *(Family)* 86m/C **VHS $39.98** *FHE, BTV*

What's Eating Gilbert Grape 🦴🦴🦴

Offbeat is mildly descriptive. Depp stars as Gilbert Grape, the titular head of a very dysfunctional family living in a big house in a small Iowa town. His Momma (Cates) weighs more than 500 pounds and hasn't left the house in 7 years, he has two squabbling teenage sisters, he's having an affair with an older married woman (Steenburgen), and 17-year-old brother Arnie (DiCaprio) is mentally retarded, requiring constant supervision or he'll climb the water tower. What's a good-hearted grocery clerk to do? Well, when free-spirited Becky (Lewis) is momentarily marooned in town, Gilbert may have found a true soulmate. Performances, especially DiCaprio's, make this a keeper, though scenes between Lewis and Depp tend to stall. Cates came to the attention of filmmakers while on a guest on a TV talk show. Based on the novel by Hedges, who adapted for the screen. **Hound Advisory:** Mature themes; salty language; sexual situations.
1993 *(PG-13/Sr. High-Adult)* 118m/C Johnny Depp, Leonardo DiCaprio, Juliette Lewis, Mary Steenburgen, Darlene Cates, Laura Harrington, Mary Kate Schellhardt, Kevin Tighe, John Reilly, Crispin Glover, Penelope Branning; **D:** Lasse Hallstrom; **W:** Peter Hedges; **M:** Alan Parker, Bjorn Isfalt. **Award Nominations:** Academy Awards '93: Best Supporting Actor (DiCaprio); Golden Globe Awards '94: Best Supporting Actor (DiCaprio); **Awards:** National Board of Review Awards '93: Best Supporting Actor (DiCaprio). **VHS, Beta, LV** *PAR*

What's Love Got to Do With It? 🦴🦴◁

Energetic biopic of powerhouse songstress Tina Turner. Short sequences cover her early life before moving into her abusive relationship with Ike and solo comeback success. Bassett may not look like Tina, but her exceptionally strong performance leaves no question as to who she's supposed to be, even during on-stage Tina sequences. Some credibility is lost when the real Tina is shown in the final concert sequence. Fishburne is a sympathetic but still chilling Ike, rising to the challenge of showing both Ike's initial charm and longtime cruelty. Based on "I, Tina" by Turner and Kurt Loder. **Hound Advisory:** Mature themes; violence; profanity.
1993 *(R/Sr. High-Adult)* 118m/C Angela Bassett, Laurence "Larry" Fishburne, Vanessa Bell Calloway, Jenifer Lewis, Phyllis Stickney, Khandi Alexander, Pamela Tyson, Penny Johnson, Rae'ven Kelly, Robert Miranda, Chi; **D:** Brian Gibson; **W:** Kate Lanier; **M:** Stanley Clarke. **Award Nominations:** Academy Awards '93: Best Actor (Fishburne), Best Actress (Bassett); **Awards:** Golden Globe Awards '94: Best Actress—Musical/Comedy (Bassett). **VHS, LV** *BVV*

What's New Mr. Magoo?, Vol. 1

Four episodes from a 1970s resurrection of the classic Magoo series. Includes "What's Zoo Magoo," "Museum Magoo," "Magoo's Monster Mansion," and "Mountain Man Magoo." Additional volumes available.
1978 *(Preschool-Jr. High)* 42m/C **VHS $12.95** *PAR, FCT, WTA*

What's Under My Bed? and Other Creepy Stories

Four scary (but not too scary) stories for children from part of the "Children's Circle" series from Weston Woods. "What's Under my Bed?" lets children know that even grown-ups get

scared. "The Three Robbers" provides an excellent role model in the form of a brave and bright little girl. "Teeny-tiny and the Witch Woman" is a version of the Grimm Brothers' "Hansel and Gretel." Least scary is "Georgie the Ghost." Excellent production values, from sound to graphics.
1990 *(Family)* 30m/C Rosanna Arquette, Bruce Spence; **D:** Michael Pattinson. VHS **$19.95** *CCC, FCT, WKV*

What's Up, Doc? 🐾🐾🐾

Shy musicologist Ryan travels from Iowa to San Francisco with his fiance Kahn for a convention. He meets the eccentric Streisand at his hotel and becomes involved in a chase to recover four identical flight bags containing top secret documents, a wealthy woman's jewels, the professor's musical rocks, and Streisand's clothing. Bogdanovich's homage to the screwball comedies of the '30s is not quite up to the level of the classics it honors, though still highly entertaining. Kahn's feature film debut.
1972 *(G/Family)* 94m/C Barbra Streisand, Ryan O'Neal, Kenneth Mars, Austin Pendleton, Randy Quaid; **D:** Peter Bogdanovich; **W:** David Newman, Buck Henry. VHS, Beta **$14.95** *WAR*

What's Wrong with Wilma?

"Flintstones" video release that focuses on Fred and Barney as youngsters and their campaign against drugs in the stone age. See also "The Flintstone Kids: Just Say No." Another artifact of the Reagan Years.
1984 *(Preschool-Primary)* 22m/C VHS, Beta *TTC*

When Dinosaurs Ruled the Earth 🐾🐾

This gets a plug in "Jurassic Park"; its title appears on a banner torn down by the T.Rex at the climax. Sort of a follow-up to the Raquel Welch version of "One Million Years B.C." (not on video), it repeats the mix of bikini-clad cavegirls and cool dinosaur f/x. Plot sees a superstitious tribe in a series of natural disasters caused by the sudden formation of Earth's moon. They blame a blonde cutie, who, in the silliest subplot, takes a nap in a giant eggshell and is mistakenly adopted by the loving dinosaur mama. Fast-paced but about as scientifically accurate as "The Flintstones." Dinosaurs are a combination of Jim Danforth's stop-motion work and live lizards filmed in closeup. **Hound Advisory:** Violence; alcohol use.
1970 *(G/Family)* 96m/C Victoria Vetri, Robin Hawdon, Patrick Allen, Drewe Henley, Sean Caffrey, Magda Konopka, Imogen Hassall, Patrick Holt, Jan Rossini; **D:** Val Guest; **W:** Val Guest. VHS, Beta, LV **$19.95** *WAR, FCT, MLB*

When Every Day was the Fourth of July 🐾🐾

Made-for-TV nostalgia piece, clumsily derivative of "To Kill a Mockingbird." In a New England town in the '30s a nine-year-old girl asks her lawyer father to defend a pal, a mute handyman accused of murder. Meanwhile her brothers turn pint-sized sleuths to unmask the real culprit. Well-received enough to inspire a sequel, "The Long Days of Summer," also available on tape. **Hound Advisory:** Violence. Accusations of child-molestation in the courtroom.

1978 *(Jr. High-Adult)* 100m/C Katy Kurtzman, Dean Jones, Louise Sorel, Harris Yulin, Chris Petersen, Geoffrey Lewis, Scott Brady, Henry Wilcoxon, Michael Pataki; **D:** Dan Curtis. VHS, Beta **$49.95** *LIV*

When Magoo Flew

When Mr. Magoo decides to go to the movies, he ends up on an airplane and gets chased by police over a stolen briefcase. Nominated for an Oscar for Best Short Subject.
1954 *(Family)* 7m/C **V:** Jim Backus. VHS, Beta *CHF*

When Mom and Dad Break Up

Introduces the concept of divorce to children ages four to twelve and offers methods of coping.
1989 *(Family)* 32m/C VHS, Beta **$24.95** *PAR*

When the North Wind Blows 🐾🐾

Old trapper on the run from the law befriends a snow tiger in the Alaskan wilderness. Scenic nature adventure from "Wilderness Family" writer/director Raffil.
1974 *(G/Family)* 113m/C Henry Brandon, Herbert Nelson, Dan Haggerty; **D:** Stewart Raffill. VHS, Beta **$54.95** *VCI*

When the Whales Came 🐾🐾

Ineffective conservationist fable about two children in a WWI-era fishing village on a remote British isle. Weak story has Gracie and Daniel befriending a shunned old codger who says the community was cursed for killing narwhal whales long ago. When more narwhals (finally) appear, will grouchy grownups listen this time and spare them? Nice music, interesting locale, but a dull, preachy plot merely inspires whale of a slumber. Scripter Michael Morpurgo adapted his own novel "Why the Whales Came." **Hound Advisory:** Alcohol use.
1989 *(PG/Jr. High-Adult)* 100m/C Paul Scofield, Helen Mirren, David Threlfall, David Suchet, Jeremy Kemp, Max Rennie, Helen Pearce, Barbara Jefford; **D:** Clive Rees; **W:** Michael Morpugo; **M:** Christopher Gunning, Ruth Rennie. VHS, Beta, LV **$14.98** *FOX*

When Wolves Cry 🐾🐾

Ill-conceived French tearjerker with an international cast mixes terminal illness, family drama, and antinuke politics. And, yes, wolves. Estranged dad and young son reunite on a Corsican vacation. Then a radiation leak from stray nuclear warheads gives the lad leukemia just in time for Christmas. Based on a novel by Michel Bataille. Also known as "The Christmas Tree."
1969 *(G/Family)* 108m/C William Holden, Virna Lisi, Brook Fuller, Andre Bourvil; **D:** Terence Young. VHS, Beta **$24.95** *GEM, VCI*

Where Angels Go, Trouble Follows 🐾🐾

Followup to "The Trouble with Angels," with Russell reprising her role as the wise Mother Superior challenged by her mischief loving students. Younger, 'mod' nun Sister George urges her to change with the times and take the convent students on a bus trip to a California peace rally. Very dated and contrived, but still mildly amusing. Note that Wickes also dons a habit in both the "Sister Act" flicks.

1968 (*Family*) 94m/C Rosalind Russell, Stella Stevens, Binnie Barnes, Mary Wickes, Susan St. James, Dolores Sutton, Alice Rawlings; *Cameos:* Milton Berle, Arthur Godfrey, Van Johnson, Robert Taylor; *D:* James Neilson; *W:* Blanche Hanalis. **VHS $14.95** *COL*

Where the Lilies Bloom 🦴🦴🦴

Touching story of four backwoods children left orphans when their father dies. They don't report his death to authorities out of fear the family will be separated into institutions. Stanton is great as the crusty landlord the children gradually accept as a friend. Based on the book by Vera and Bill Cleaver.
1974 (G/*Family*) 96m/C Julie Gholson, Jan Smithers, Matthew Burrill, Helen Harmon, Harry Dean Stanton, Rance Howard, Sudie Bond, Tom Spratley, Helen Bragdon, Alice Beardsley; *D:* William A. Graham. **VHS $14.95** *MGM*

Where the Red Fern Grows 🦴🦴🦴

Young Billy Coleman, dwelling in the Ozarks during the Depression, learns maturity from his love and responsibility for two redbone hounds. Well produced, if sentimental, boy-and-his-dogs family fare works despite a surplus of Andy Williams songs. The ending is guaranteed to bring a tear or two. Based on the novel by Wilson Rawls, who also narrates. **Hound Advisory:** Violence, both in cougar attacks and the sudden, shocking death of a child.
1974 (G/*Family*) 97m/C James Whitmore, Beverly Garland, Jack Ging, Loni Chapman, Stewart Peterson; *D:* Norman Tokar. **VHS, Beta $14.98** *FHE, VES, HHE*

Where the Red Fern Grows: Part 2 🦴🦴◁

Sequel to the popular '70s family movie finds Billy Coleman returning from WWII with an artificial leg and a case of malaise that his dying Grandpa tries to cure by bringing him two additional 'coon dog pups. After more cutesy closeups of puppies than even "Beethoven's 2nd" dared, the story settles down into soap opera and maudlin dialogue. Though the actors give it their best, tale told once frustrates everyone's attempt to do it again. **Hound Advisory:** Roughhousing.
1992 (G/*Family*) 105m/C Wilford Brimley, Doug McKeon, Lisa Whelchel, Chad McQueen; *D:* Jim McCullough. **VHS $14.95** *VCI*

Where the River Runs Black 🦴🦴

In the remote Brazilian jungle a baby results from the (discreet) encounter between a young missionary and a native woman. When both parents get killed, river dolphins become the boy's guardians. Kindly priest eventually finds Lazaro and introduces him to the modern world, where the kid beholds intolerance, corruption - and the man who murdered his mother. Offbeat, but too slow and self-important to evoke the childlike sense of wonder required by this plot. **Hound Advisory:** Violence, very brief distant nudity.
1986 (PG/*Jr. High-Adult*) 96m/C Charles Durning, Peter Horton, Ajay Naidu, Conchata Ferrell, Alessandro Rabelo, Castulo Guerra; *D:* Christopher Cain; *M:* James Horner. **VHS, Beta $79.98** *FOX*

Where the Spirit Lives 🦴🦴◁

Historical drama about Indian children kidnapped by Canadian government agents and forced to live in dreadful boarding schools where they are abused emotionally and physically. New arrival refuses to put up with it and tries to escape. Engrossing and vivid, with a good sense of the era. **Hound Advisory:** Mature themes.
1989 (PG/*Jr. High-Adult*) 97m/C Michelle St. John; *D:* Bruce Pittman. **VHS $79.95** *BTV, HHE, UWA*

Where the Toys Come From

Stop-motion Disney creation in which two Christmas toys, a camera and a pair of binoculars, take a trip around the world in order to find out where they came from.
1984 (*Family*) 58m/C **VHS, Beta $12.99** *DIS*

Where the Wild Things Are

Animated version of the classic Maurice Sendak story of Max, the small boy who reigns over a fantasy kingdom inhabited by weird and delightful monsters.
1976 (*Preschool-Primary*) 8m/C **VHS, Beta $19.95**

Where Time Began 🦴🦴

Antique manuscript details a route to an amazing world far below the Earth's surface. A professor and his friends decide to follow directions and see the wonders for themselves. Cheap, Spanish-made redo of Jules Verne's "Journey to the Center of the Earth," with a good cast but goofy dinosaur f/x.
1977 (G/*Family*) 87m/C Kenneth More, Pep Munne, Jack Taylor; *D:* J.P. Simon. **VHS, Beta $69.98** *SUE*

Where's Spot?

Features Eric Hill's adorable puppy Spot in five stories for the very young: "Where's Spot?," "Spot's First Walk," "Spot's Birthday Party," "Spot Goes Splash," and "Spot Finds a Key." Like the Hill books, the video box features trademark hide-and-seek activities for toddlers. See also "Spot Goes to the Farm."
1993 (*Preschool*) 30m/C **VHS $14.99** *BVV, BTV*

Where's Willie? 🦴🦴

Boy genius Willie exasperates his outdoorsy sheriff father with electronic pranks, until both learn to accept each other. It's a surprise that this cheapie (made in Texas) is about relationships and not an action-comedy. Not so surprising is meanders somewhat dully, and if Willie's so smart why couldn't he fix the muffled audio? Also on video as "Computer Wizard."
1977 (G/*Family*) 91m/C Guy Madison, Henry Darrow, Kate Woodville, Marc Gilpin; *D:* John Florea. **VHS, Beta** *NO*

Whistle Down the Wind 🦴🦴🦴◁

Three motherless children of strict religious upbringing find a murderer hiding in their family's barn and believe him to be Jesus Christ. A well done and hardly grim or dull allegory of childhood innocence based on a novel by Mills's mother, Mary Hayley Bell. Relying heavily on child characters, it portrays childhood well and realistically, with Mills perfect in her role as the eldest child. Forbes's directorial debut uses religious symbolism judiciously; Richard Attenborough's second production.

1962 (*Jr. High-Adult*) 98m/B Hayley Mills, Bernard Lee, Alan Bates; **D:** Bryan Forbes; **M:** Malcolm Arnold. **VHS, Beta $19.98** *SUE, NLC*

White Christmas 🦴🦴🦴

Two ex-army buddies become a popular comedy team and play at a financially unstable Vermont inn at Christmas for charity's sake. Many swell Irving Berlin songs rendered with zest. Paramount's first Vista Vision film. Presented in widescreen on laserdisc. ♫The Best Things Happen While You're Dancing; Love, You Didn't Do Right By Me; Choreography; Count Your Blessings Instead of Sheep; What Can You Do With a General; Mandy; The Minstrel Show; Sisters; Heat Wave.

1954 (*Family*) 120m/C Bing Crosby, Danny Kaye, Rosemary Clooney, Vera-Ellen, Dean Jagger; **D:** Michael Curtiz; **W:** Norman Panama. **VHS, Beta, LV, 8mm, CD-I $14.95** *PAR, FUS*

White Fang 🦴🦴🦴

Spectacular adventure manages to stay true to both the Disney family-movie style and writer Jack London's unsentimental depiction of Gold Rush days. Tenderfoot miner Jack Casey befriends a heroic wolf-dog and they struggle, together and separately, to survive both human and natural dangers in Alaska. Gets gooey just near the end. Beautiful cinematography. **Hound Advisory:** Violence (animals get the worst of it), alcohol use.

1991 (PG/*Jr. High-Adult*) 109m/C Klaus Maria Brandauer, Ethan Hawke, Seymour Cassel, James Remar, Susan Hogan; **D:** Randal Kleiser; **W:** Jeanne Rosenberg, Nick Thiel, David Fallon; **M:** Basil Poledouris. **VHS, LV $19.99** *BVV, DIS, TVC*

White Fang 2: The Myth of the White Wolf 🦴🦴

White boy and his wolf-dog lead starving Native American tribe to caribou during the Alaskan Gold Rush. Simplistic story with obvious heroes and villains, yes, but this is also wholesome (and politically correct) family fare compliments of Disney. Sequel to "White Fang" with Ethan Hawke focuses less on the wolf, a flaw, and more on Bairstow and his love interest Craig, a Haida Indian princess, while exploring Native American mythology and dreams in sequences that tend to stop the action cold. Still, kids will love it, and there are plenty of puppies to achieve required awwww factor. Beautiful scenery filmed on location in Colorado and British Columbia. **Hound Advisory:** Roughhousing.

1994 (PG/*Jr. High-Adult*) 106m/C Scott Bairstow, Alfred Molina, Geoffrey Lewis, Charmaine Craig, Victoria Racimo, Paul Coeur, Anthony Michael Ruivivar, Al Harrington; **Cameos:** Ethan Hawke; **D:** Ken Olin; **W:** David Fallon; **M:** John Debney. **VHS** *NYR*

White Fang and the Hunter 🦴🦴

Adventures of a boy and his dog who survive an attack from wild wolves and then help to solve a murder mystery. Loosely based on the novel by Jack London; no relation to the Disney "White Fang" sagas.

1985 (G/*Family*) 87m/C Pedro Sanchez, Robert Wood; **D:** Alfonso Brescia. **VHS, Beta $19.95** *STE, HHE*

White Mama 🦴🦴🦴

A poor widow (Davis, in a splendid role) takes in a street-wise black kid (Harden) in return for protection from the neighborhood's dangers, and they discover friendship. Poignant drama, capably directed by Cooper, featuring sterling performances all around. Made-for-TV drama at its best.

1980 (*Family*) 96m/C Bette Davis, Ernest Harden, Eileen Heckart, Virginia Capers, Lurene Tuttle, Anne Ramsey; **D:** Jackie Cooper. **VHS, Beta $59.95** *LIV*

The White Seal

Man's presence in the Bering Sea poses a threat to Kitock's safety. The little white seal searches the frigid waters for a new home in this environmentally themed TV cartoon.

1975 (*Preschool-Primary*) 30m/C **V:** Roddy McDowall, June Foray. **VHS, Beta $9.95** *FHE, WTA*

White Water Summer 🦴🦴

Four mismatched teen campers trek into the Sierras, and find themselves struggling through dangerous rapids and rock climbs. Bacon seems miscast as a rugged outdoorsman who shows the tenderfoots how to survive, if they don't kill each other first. Great nature scenery, anyway. **Hound Advisory:** Salty language, roughhousing.

1987 (PG/*Jr. High-Adult*) 90m/C Kevin Bacon, Sean Astin, Jonathan Ward, Matt Adler; **D:** Jeff Bleckner; **M:** Michael Boddicker. **VHS, Beta, LV $29.95** *COL*

Whitewater Sam 🦴

In the 1820s mountain man Sam and his wonder husky Sybar survive one peril after another in the hostile wilds of the Great Northwest. Clumsy, virtually plotless nature adventure with blurry visuals; either writer/producer/director/star Larsen used soft focus a lot or Sybar kept licking the lens. **Hound Advisory:** Violence, in savage cougar, bear and Indian attacks (that Sam seems to survive with barely a scratch).

1978 (G/*Family*) 87m/C Keith Larsen; **D:** Keith Larsen; **W:** Keith Larsen. **VHS, Beta** *MON*

Who Framed Roger Rabbit? 🦴🦴🦴🦴

Technically marvelous, cinematically hilarious, eye-popping combo of cartoon and live-action creates a Hollywood of the 1940s where animated characters are alive and a repressed minority, working in films and dwelling in their own Toontown ghetto. A 'toon-hating detective is hired to trail the sexy wife of comedy star Roger Rabbit and instead uncovers murder, mayhem, and a multi-zillion dollar conspiracy. Special appearances by famous cartoon characters from the past, with one major absentee - legal rights to Popeye and his friends couldn't be secured. Coproduced by Touchstone (Disney) and Amblin (Spielberg). A complete rethinking of the source novel, "Who Censored Roger Rabbit?" by Gary K. Wolf, which dealt not with cartoons but comic-strips. **Hound Advisory:** Reports of nude scenes involving Roger Rabbit's humanoid wife Jessica are wildly exaggerated. There's violence - 95% of it against 'toons, who are virtually

Ethan Hawke in "White Fang" (1991)

indestructible anyway - plus salty language, alcohol use, sex puns that will easily elude toddler viewers.
1988 (PG/*Jr. High-Adult*) 104m/C Bob Hoskins, Christopher Lloyd, Joanna Cassidy, Alan Tilvern, Stubby Kaye; **D:** Robert Zemeckis; **W:** Jeffrey Price, Peter S. Seaman; **M:** Alan Silvestri; **V:** Charles Fleischer, Mae Questel, Kathleen Turner, Amy Irving, Mel Blanc, June Foray, Frank Sinatra. **Award Nominations:** Academy Awards '88: Best Art Direction/Set Decoration, Best Cinematography, Best Sound; **Awards:** Academy Awards '88: Best Film Editing, Best Visual Effects; National Board of Review Awards '88: 10 Best Films of the Year. VHS, Beta, LV $19.99 *TOU, WTA*

Who Has Seen the Wind? 🐾🐾

Two boys grow up in Saskatchewan during the Depression. So-so family viewing drama. Ferrer as a bootlegger steals the otherwise small-paced show. **Hound Advisory:** Alcohol use; salty language.
1977 (*Family*) 102m/C Jose Ferrer, Brian Painchaud, Charmion King, Helen Shaver. VHS, Beta *SUE*

Who Will Be My Friend?

A combination of live action and animation shows how little Molly copes with her first day at school with the help of her toy dinosaur doll.
19?? (*Preschool-Primary*) 25m/C VHS

Who'll Save Our Children? 🐾🐾🐾

Two kids are abandoned on the doorstep of a middle-aged, childless couple, who care for the foundlings for years and are on the point of adopting then when the real parents reappear and sue for custody. Superior, sometimes painful family drama, made for TV. Based on "The Orchard Children" by Rachel Maddox.
1982 (*Jr. High-Adult*) 96m/C Shirley Jones, Len Cariou, Conchata Ferrell, Frances Sternhagen, Cassie Yates, David Hayward; **D:** George Schaefer. VHS, Beta *TLF*

Why Christmas Trees Aren't Perfect

Animated holiday tale of kindness and its reward. Sweetly told until a fairly heavy-handed finale.
1990 (*Family*) 25m/C VHS $14.95 *WTA*

Why Shoot the Teacher? 🐾🐾🐾

Novice teacher takes charge of a proverbial one-room schoolhouse in an isolated prairie town in 1930s Saskatchewan. The chilly reception he gets matches the weather, but eventually he warms up to the hardworking farm kids that comprise his pupils. Don't be put off by the dire title; this is a sweet-spirited comedy-drama with heart, adapted from the novel by Max Braithwaite. **Hound Advisory:** Salty language; mature themes.
1979 (*Family*) 101m/C Bud Cort, Samantha Eggar, Chris Wiggins; **D:** Silvio Narizzano. VHS, Beta $69.98 *SUE*

Widget of the Jungle

Episodes from the cartoon TV series starring the little shape-changing alien Widget, a "world-watcher" fighting on behalf of the environment. Here he goes to Africa to foil some elephant ivory poachers. Also contains an extremely "Free Willy"-ish story entitled "Kona, The Captive Whale."

1990 (*Preschool-Jr. High*) 47m/C VHS, Beta $14.95 *FHE, WTA*

Widget's Great Whale Adventure

The delightful alien's power to talk with animals helps him prevent lawless hunters from capturing immature whales. Also includes another animated story entitled "Gorilla My Dream."
1990 (*Preschool-Jr. High*) 47m/C VHS, Beta $14.95 *FHE, WTA*

Wil Cwac Cwac: Vol. 1

Wil Cwac Cwac is a mischief-prone duckling living in a village of farm animals in this set of ten cute short cartoons from Welsh TV (dubbed over with American voices) for the very young. Also available: "The Further Adventures of Wil Cwac Cwac" and "Welcome Back, Wil Cwac Cwac."
1983 (*Preschool*) 50m/C VHS, Beta $9.95 *FHE*

Wild and Woody

Find out how Woody Woodpecker won the West in this collection of nine Lantz cartoons from the 50s and the 60s.
1965 (*Family*) 51m/C **V:** Grace Stafford. VHS, Beta $14.95 *MCA, WTA*

The Wild Child 🐾🐾🐾🐾

Brilliant film based on the journal of a 19th century physician who attempted to educate and civilize a young feral boy who had been found dwelling like a wild beast by himself in a French forest. Not gimmicky in the least, with director Truffaut as the doctor trying to reach the boy's dormant intellect. Tenderly told, the perfect antidote to the "Problem Child" pictures. In French with English subtitles.
1970 (G/*Sr. High-Adult*) 85m/B **D:** Francois Truffaut; **W:** Jean Gruault; **M:** Antoine Duhamel. VHS $19.99 *MGM, INJ, FCT*

The Wild Country 🐾🐾🐾

Disney fare detailing the trials and tribulations of a Pittsburgh family moving into an inhospitable Wyoming ranch in the 1880s. Ronny Howard acts alongside real life father Rance and brother Clint. Based on the novel "Little Britches" by Ralph Moody. **Hound Advisory:** Violence.
1971 (G/*Family*) 92m/C Steve Forrest, Ron Howard, Clint Howard, Rance Howard; **D:** Robert Totten. VHS, Beta $69.96 *DIS*

Wild Geese Calling

Dan Tolliver rescues a Canada gander, nurses it back to health and, once he realizes he is unable to control it he releases the bird into the wild. A live-action tale from TV's "Wonderful World of Disney."
1990 (*Preschool-Primary*) 33m/C VHS, Beta $250.00 *MTI, DSN*

Wild Hearts Can't Be Broken 🐾🐾🐾

True story of Sonora Webster, a 1930s Georgia teen who runs away from a foster home to a carnival. She becomes a stunt horse rider, specializing in jumping with the animal 40 feet into a pool of water (just when you thought movies had exploited every sporting event ever known). Diving injury threatens her career, but she persists and rides and dives again. Storyline has little tension, but that doesn't detract

from this fresh, well-written Disney film with a feisty heroine and a novel sport.
1991 (G/*Family*) 89m/C Gabrielle Anwar, Cliff Robertson, Dylan Kussman, Michael Schoeffling, Kathleen York, Frank Renzulli; *D:* Steve Miner; *W:* Oley Sassone; *M:* Mason Daring. **VHS, Beta $19.99** *DIS*

Wild Horse Hank 🎭🎭

A young woman risks everything to save a herd of wild mustangs from being slaughtered for use as dog food. Crenna's good; otherwise, it's sentimental family fare. Based on the novel "The Wild Horse Killers" by Mel Ellis.
1979 (*Family*) 94m/C Linda Blair, Richard Crenna, Michael Wincott, Al Waxman; *D:* Eric Till. **VHS, Beta $69.98** *LIV, VES*

Wild Pony 🎭🎭🎭

Compelling frontier family drama with as much to interest adults as kids. Hot-headed young farmer dies after a drunken fight with an innocent rancher. The widow, facing a harsh winter alone with two kids, proposes the only logical move — a marriage of convenience to the guilt-ridden rancher. How these characters interact is unpredictable and the stuff of truly great drama, and no surprise; director Sullivan later went on to steer Canada's successful "Anne of Green Gables" series. **Hound Advisory:** Violence, alcohol use.
1983 (*Family*) 87m/C Marilyn Lightstone, Art Hindle, Josh Byrne; *D:* Kevin Sullivan; *M:* Hagood Hardy. **VHS, Beta $14.98** *FHE, VES, LIV*

The Wild Puffalumps

Animated fantasy adventure about two kids entering a land of weird animals.
1987 (*Preschool-Primary*) 22m/C **VHS, Beta $14.95** *FHE, WTA*

Wild Swans

Danish fairy tale about eleven princes turned into wild swans by an evil queen. Only their sister's hard work and devotion can return them to human form.
1980 (*Primary*) 11m/C **VHS, Beta $19.95** *MTI, WTA*

Wild Swans

Young girl must save her six brothers, who have been turned into swans by an evil witch. Cartoon adaptation of the classic fairy tale.
198? (*Family*) 62m/C **VHS, Beta $14.95** *COL, WKV*

Wildcats 🎭🎭

Naive lady phys. ed instructor is saddled with the job of coaching a completely undisciplined inner-city high-school football team. Formulaic connect-the-dots comedy, shares both the premise and the director of the original "Bad News Bears." Hawn is winning as her character gains confidence both on the field and off - in a custody battle with an ex-husband over her daughters - but it all feels like a long sitcom episode. **Hound Advisory:** Profanity; mature themes; sex talk; brief nudity.
1986 (R/*Sr. High-Adult*) 106m/C Goldie Hawn, James Keach, Swoosie Kurtz, Bruce McGill, M. Emmet Walsh, Woody Harrelson, Wesley Snipes, Tab Thacker; *D:* Michael Ritchie; *M:* James Newton Howard. **VHS, Beta, LV $19.98** *WAR*

Will Vinton's Claymation Comedy of Horrors

Halloween fantasy wherein Wilshire Pig and Sheldon Snail are after the powers of the legendary Frankenswine, so they set out for the Doctor's spooky castle. Very funny TV special showcasing Vinton's brand of stop-motion animation magic and wild humor.
1992 (*Family*) 27m/C **VHS $12.98** *MOV, LIV*

Will Vinton's Claymation Easter

Claymation brings to life the story of the Easter Bunny and Vinton's perennial troublemaker, Wilshire Pig. The pig tries to take the place of the E.B. through a series of underhanded tricks, but justice wins out in the end. Clever and entertaining for all ages.
1992 (*Family*) 27m/C **VHS $12.98** *FHE*

Willie Mays & The Say-Hey Kid

In return for making a great catch and saving the pennant, baseball great Mays (doing his own 'toon voice) must provide a home for Veronica, a lonely orphan. Condensed version of a one-hour Rankin-Bass cartoon done for Saturday-morning TV.
1972 (*Preschool-Primary*) 30m/C **VHS $9.95** *WTA*

Willie, the Operatic Whale

Willie the whale has dreams of singing opera at the Met, including Figaro, Pagliacci, Tristan and Isolde, and Mephistopheles, but a maestro brought out to sea to hear him badly misunderstands. A classic Disney short cartoon with all the voices (not to mention the singing) performed by the legendary Eddy.
1946 (*Family*) 29m/C **VHS, Beta $12.99** *DIS, MTI, DSN*

The Willies WOOF!

Three youngsters attempt to outdo each other with juvenile tales of horror and scariness while camping in the backyard. Pointless, doltish, and terribly acted. Watch closely - if you watch at all - and you'll hear a poke at Astin's role in "The Goonies." **Hound Advisory:** Violence and grossness, including a poodle cooked in a microwave, monsters snatching children, children eating flies.
1990 (PG-13/*Sr. High-Adult*) 120m/C James Karen, Sean Astin, Kathleen Freeman, Jeremy Miller; *D:* Brian Peck. **VHS, LV $19.95** *PSM*

Willow 🎭🎭

Blockbuster fantasy combined the talents of writer/producer George Lucas with director Ron Howard, but results are disappointing. Recycled plotline filches from stories of Moses, Peter Pan, Ulysses and many others as Willow, a friendly dwarf and aspiring wizard, becomes guardian of an infant princess. Every ten minutes or so we're reminded of a prophecy that the baby will successfully end the tyranny of evil queen Bavmorda (thanks, there goes the suspense), and the plot is one chase/fight after another as the Queen's imperial stormtroopers try to seize the tyke. Superb special effects (including a memorable dragon), but only small kids unfamiliar with Myths 101 will be enthralled. **Hound Advisory:** Violence.

1988 (PG/*Jr. High-Adult*) 118m/C Warwick Davis, Val Kilmer, Jean Marsh, Joanne Whalley-Kilmer, Billy Barty, Pat Roach, Ruth Greenfield, Patricia Hayes, Gavan O'Herlihy, Kevin Pollak; *D:* Ron Howard; *W:* Bob Dolman; *M:* James Horner. VHS, Beta, LV, 8mm $14.95 *COL*

Willy McBean & His Magic Machine

Early Arthur Rankin Jr./Jules Bass production done entirely through stop-motion animation, long before "A Nightmare Before Christmas." Inventor Rasputin von Rotten wants to become the greatest man in history, so he goes back in time to upstage Columbus, Merlin the Magician, and others. Boy named Willy races after him, trying to unmask the imposter at every step. Somewhat tedious, and the puppet characters lack personality, but with enough fun touches (like a T.Rex mysteriously wearing sneakers) to keep you watching. Nice ending points out a real-life 'magic machine' - movies. **Hound Advisory:** It would take a greater genius than von Rotten to figure out why the cassette distributor has put a PG on this kiddie fare.

1959 (*Family*) 94m/C *D:* Arthur Rankin Jr. VHS, Beta $39.95 *PSM*

Willy Wonka & the Chocolate Factory 🎵🎵🎵🎵

Charlie, a poor English boy, wins a tour of the most wonderfully strange candy factory in the world, run by mysterious man-child recluse Willy Wonka. He leads Charlie and four other kids on a thrilling tour of the complex, but hidden traps wait for each child who misbehaves. In theaters for only about a week, this box-office disappointment was rescued by TV rebroadcasts (just like "The Wizard of Oz") and has earned its reputation as a top-quality children's film with much to engage the adult intellect as well. Wilder's ever-so-demented Wonka is a delight; listen close to his slightly off-color mutterings. Adapted from "Charlie and the Chocolate Factory" by Roald Dahl (who hated this movie) with a memorable musical score by Anthony Newley and Leslie Bricusse. 🎵Willy Wonka, the Candy Man; Cheer Up, Charlie; I've Got a Golden Ticket; Oompa-Loompa-Doompa-Dee-Doo; Pure Imagination. **Hound Advisory:** Some mildly gruesome imagery if you freeze-frame during Willy Wonka's psychedelic high-speed boat trip.

1971 (G/*Family*) 100m/C Gene Wilder, Jack Albertson, Denise Nickerson, Peter Ostrum, Roy Kinnear, Aubrey Woods, Michael Bollner, Ursula Reit, Leonard Stone, Dodo Denney; *D:* Mel Stuart; *M:* Leslie Bricusse. VHS, Beta, LV $14.95 *WAR, APD, HMV*

Wind 🎵🎵◁

Fairly routine romance on the water/sports drama gains buoyancy via good performances and scenic crashing waves. Sailor Will Parker (Modine) chooses the opportunity to be on the America's Cup team over opportunity of being with girlfriend Grey. Then he has the dubious honor of making a technical error that causes the team to lose. Undaunted, he locates Grey and her new engineer boyfriend (Skarsgard) and convinces them to design the ultimate boat for the next set of races. When ESPN carried extensive coverage of the America's Cup races for the first time in the summer of '92, viewers discovered that a little goes a long way. The same holds true here, though the race footage is stunning. **Hound Advisory:** Salty language.

1992 (PG-13/*Jr. High-Adult*) 123m/C Matthew Modine, Jennifer Grey, Cliff Robertson, Jack Thompson, Stellan Skarsgard, Rebecca Miller, Ned Vaughn; *D:* Carroll Ballard; *W:* Rudy Wurlitzer, Mac Gudgeon; *M:* Basil Poledouris. VHS, LV, 8mm *COL*

The Wind and the Lion 🎵🎵🎵

In turn-of-the-century Morocco, a sheik (Connery) kidnaps a feisty American woman (Bergen) and her children and holds her as a political hostage. President Teddy Roosevelt (Keith) sends in the Marines to free the captives, who are eventually released by their captor. Directed with venue and style by Milius. Highly entertaining, if heavily fictionalized. Based very loosely on a historical incident.

1975 (PG/*Jr. High-Adult*) 120m/C Sean Connery, Candice Bergen, Brian Keith, John Huston, Geoffrey Lewis; *D:* John Milius; *W:* John Milius; *M:* Jerry Goldsmith. VHS, Beta, LV $59.95 *MGM*

The Wind in the Willows

The Children's Theatre Company and School of Minneapolis perform their own unique interpretation of the Kenneth Grahame story.

1983 (*Family*) 75m/C VHS, Beta $39.95 *MCA, WTA*

Wind in the Willows

Series narrates adventures of Mole, Toad, and other famous animated Kenneth Grahame characters.

1988 (*Primary-Jr. High*) 60m/C VHS *NO*

Wind in the Willows, Vol. 1

Delightful and intricate stop-motion animation brings Kenneth Grahame's animal characters Mole, Ratty, Badger, and Toad of Toad Hall to life in this multivolume British series, boasting voices by eminent character actors and a literate script. Additional volumes available.

1983 (*Family*) 60m/C *V:* Ian Carmichael, Beryl Reid. VHS $12.95 *HBO*

The Window 🎵🎵🎵◁

A little boy has a reputation for telling lies, so no one believes him when he says he witnessed a murder — except the killers. Almost unbearably tense, claustrophobic thriller about the helplessness of childhood. Based on "The Boy Who Cried Murder" by Cornell Woolrich. Driscoll was awarded a special miniature Oscar as Outstanding Juvenile for his performance. **Hound Advisory:** Mature themes.

1949 (*Jr. High-Adult*) 73m/B Bobby Driscoll, Barbara Hale, Arthur Kennedy, Ruth Roman; *D:* Ted Tetzlaff. **Award Nominations:** Academy Awards '49: Best Film Editing; **Awards:** Edgar Allan Poe Awards '49: Best Screenplay. VHS, Beta, LV $19.95 *MED*

Wings of Desire 🎵🎵🎵◁

An ethereal, haunting modern fable about one of many angels observing human life in and above the broken existence of

Berlin, and how he begins to long to experience life as humans do. A moving, unequivocable masterpiece, with as many beautiful things to say about spiritual need as about the schizophrenic emptiness of contemporary Germany; Wenders' magnum opus. In German with English subtitles, and with black-and-white sequences. Magnificent cinematography by Henri Alekan. **Hound Advisory:** Mature themes.
1988 (PG-13/*Sr. High-Adult*) 130m/C Bruno Ganz, Peter Falk, Solveig Dommartin, Otto Sander, Curt Bois; *D:* Wim Wenders; *W:* Wim Wenders, Peter Handke. **VHS, Beta, LV $19.98** *ORI, GLV, INJ*

A Winner Never Quits 𝄞𝄞◁

True story based on the life of 1940s baseball player Pete Gray, who lost his right arm in a boyhood accident. He's determined to prove himself on the diamond during WWII. Though teammates consider him a sideshow freak, he becomes an inspiration to fans. Properly wholesome, made-for-TV effort. Cynics can see Woody Allen's "Radio Days" for a hilarious spoof of a Pete Gray-type ballplayer.
1986 (PG/*Jr. High-Adult*) 96m/C Keith Carradine, Mare Winningham, Huckleberry Fox, Dennis Weaver, Dana Delany, G.W. Bailey, Charles Hallahan, Fionnula Flanagan, Jack Kehoe; *D:* Mel Damski; *W:* Burt Prelutsky. **VHS $59.95** *COL*

Winners of the West

A landowner schemes to prevent a railroad from running through his property. The railroad's chief engineer leads the good guys in an attempt to prevent sabotage. A fun serial in thirteen chapters, full of shooting, blown-up bridges, locomotives afire, etc.; and of course, the requisite damsel in distress.
1940 (*Family*) 250m/B Anne Nagel, Dick Foran, James Craig, Harry Woods; *D:* Ray Taylor, Ford Beebe. **VHS $24.95** *GPV, VCN, NOS*

Winnie the Pooh

One of the Disney Video-A-Long books on videocassette, this tape features Winnie telling three favorite stories: "Winnie the Pooh and Tigger, Too," "Winnie the Pooh and the Honey Tree," and "Winnie the Pooh and the Blustery Day."
1985 (*Preschool*) 30m/C **VHS, Beta** *DIS, APD*

Winnie the Pooh

Four original, non-Disney stories starring the A.A. Milne favorite bear and all his friends. Stories include "Kanga and Roo Come to the Forest," "Pooh Invents a New Game and Eeyore Joins In," "Rabbit Has a Busy Day and Learns What Christopher Robin Does in the Morning," and "Christopher Robin and Pooh Discover an Enchanted Place."
1989 (*Preschool-Family*) 60m/C **VHS $14.98** *FOX, FCT*

Winnie the Pooh and a Day for Eeyore 𝄞𝄞𝄞

The fourth in the Disney animated series sees Pooh, Tigger and their friends throw a birthday party for Eeyore, the depressed donkey.
1973 (G/*Family*) 25m/C *V:* Sterling Holloway, Sebastian Cabot. **VHS, Beta, LV $12.99** *DIS, MTI, DSN*

Winnie the Pooh & Friends

Winnie the Pooh and his friends from the Hundred Acre Wood are trying to arrange a birthday party for Eeyore the mule.
1984 (*Family*) 46m/C *V:* Sterling Holloway, Sebastian Cabot, John Fiedler. **VHS, Beta $49.95** *DIS*

Winnie the Pooh and the Blustery Day

Another classic A.A. Milne tale about Pooh, the Hundred Acre Woods and Tigger, this time caught in a galestorm.
1968 (*Family*) 24m/C *D:* Wolfgang Reitherman; *V:* Sterling Holloway, John Fiedler, Paul Winchell, Hal Smith, Ralph Wright. **VHS, Beta $12.99** *DIS, MTI, DSN*

Winnie the Pooh and the Honey Tree

Pooh becomes stuck in Rabbit's hole after attempting to steal some honey from a beehive. The first of Disney's Pooh features.
1965 (*Family*) 25m/C *D:* Wolfgang Reitherman; *V:* Sterling Holloway, Ralph Wright, Hal Smith, Barbara Luddy, Clint Howard, Junius Matthews, Howard Morris, Bruce Reitherman. **VHS, Beta, LV $12.99** *DIS, DSN, MTI*

Winnie the Pooh and Tigger Too

A.A. Milne's classic characters - as animated by Disney - encounter Tigger and his irascible bouncing, find it intolerable, and discover a questionable cure involving circular logic. "The wonderful thing about tiggers is tiggers are wonderful things..."
1974 (G/*Family*) 25m/C *D:* John Lounsbery; *V:* Sterling Holloway, Paul Winchell, Junius Matthews, John Fiedler, Timothy Turner, Dori Whitaker. **VHS, Beta, LV $12.99** *DIS, MTI, DSN*

Winnie the Pooh Discovers the Seasons

Winnie and friends learn some basic science vocabulary and concepts, while exploring animal habitats.
1990 (*Preschool-Primary*) 8m/C **VHS, Beta $170.00** *MTI, DSN*

Winsome Witch

Compilation of Hanna-Barbera's "Winsome Witch" cartoons, in which a good-natured dropout from the Fairy Godmother School freelances as a witch and steps into some amusing retellings of "Snow White" and other tales. Additional volumes available.
1965 (*Family*) 55m/C **VHS, Beta $19.95** *TTC, WTA*

Winter of the Witch

Tame kiddie short, produced by the folks behind Parents Magazine, about what happens when Nicky and her mother discover a witch in the attic. The not-so-wicked witch helps them make magic pancakes that bring joy and simple f/x to all.
1970 (*Primary-Jr. High*) 25m/C Hermione Gingold. **VHS, Beta** *LCA*

Winter Wolf

Excellent entry in the "Legends" series imparts much information in a brief plot about a part-Indian girl caught in the public panic when wolves appear on the outskirts of her ranching community. Nature expert visits and teaches about wolves in fact and lore, and why they need not be feared. **1992** (*Family*) 30m/C **D:** Kathleen Phelan; **W:** Kathleen Phelan. **VHS $14.98** BMG, MIR

The Witch Who Turned Pink

When a green witch turns pink, she and the scandalized inhabitants of her woods desperately seek the means to regain her original shade. Colorful cartoon. **198?** (*Family*) 30m/C **VHS $6.95** KAR, WTA

Witcheroo

Selection of all-new Disney cartoons (excerpted from TV shows) with Halloween themes. "Ghoul of My Dreams" features Darkwing Duck who must come to the rescue of the citizens of St. Canard when an evil spell puts everyone to sleep. In "Good Times, Bat Times," Chip 'n' Dale befriend an apprentice witch with a lovesick bat. Disney also issued two similar spooky collections on tape at the same time, "Boo-Busters" and "Monster Bash." **1993** (*Family*) 44m/C **VHS $12.99** DIS, WTA

The Witches 𝄆𝄆𝄆 ⊲

Nine-year-old Luke, at a seaside resort with his grandmother, discovers that the Royal Society for the Prevention of Cruelty to Children meeting there is really a witch convention to launch the Grand High Witch's scheme to turn all England's children into mice. How can he stop them? Top-notch fantasy from the tart pen of "Willy Wonka" creator Roald Dahl (who, of course, hated this adaptation of his book), blends delightful f/x with a funny, imaginative adventure storyline. The final project of executive producer Jim Henson. **Hound Advisory:** Fantasy violence in the witch-busting finale. Fundamentalists and neo-pagans (both of whom have complained against Roald Dahl's book for different reasons) may or may not care that these bald, purple-eyed movie witches are pure invention, with all the reality of Margaret Hamilton in "The Wizard of Oz." **1990** (PG/*Jr. High-Adult*) 92m/C Anjelica Huston, Mai Zetterling, Jasen Fisher, Rowan Atkinson, Charlie Potter, Bill Paterson, Brenda Blethyn, Jane Horrocks; **D:** Nicolas Roeg; **W:** Allan Scott; **M:** Stanley Myers. **VHS, Beta, LV, 8mm $14.95** WAR, FCT, LHV

Witches' Brew 𝄆𝄆

Three young women try to use their undeveloped skills in witchcraft and black magic to help Garr's husband get a prestigious position at a university, with calamitous results. Oft-funny spoof is silly and oft-predictable. Turner's role is small as an older, experienced witch. **1979** (PG/*Jr. High-Adult*) 98m/C Teri Garr, Richard Benjamin, Lana Turner, Kathryn Leigh Scott; **D:** Richard Shorr, Herbert L. Strock. **VHS, Beta $59.98** SUE

Witch's Night Out

Rankin-Bass cartoon for the Halloween season on TV, in which a broom-riding mama takes a night on the town. She

meets two children who ask to be transformed into their favorite monsters. **1979** (*Preschool-Primary*) 30m/C **V:** Gilda Radner. **VHS, Beta $10.95** FHE,, WTA

With Honors 𝄆𝄆𝄆 ⊲

Pesci is a bum who finds desperate Harvard student Fraser's honors thesis, and, like any quick-witted bum with a yen for literature, holds it for ransom. Desperate to salvage his future gold card, Fraser and his roommates agree to fix Joe's homeless state. Self-involved students learn something about love and life while Madonna drones on the soundtrack. Fraser is believable as the ambitious student about to endure Pesci's enlightenment. Pesci is Pesci, doing his best to overcome numerous script cliches. **Hound Advisory:** Profanity. **1994** (PG-13/*Jr. High-Adult*) 100m/C Joe Pesci, Brendan Fraser, Moira Kelly, Patrick Dempsey, Josh Hamilton, Gore Vidal; **D:** Alek Keshishian; **W:** William Mastrosimone; **M:** Patrick Leonard. **VHS** WAR

With Six You Get Eggroll 𝄆𝄆

Widow with three sons and a widower with a daughter elope and then must deal with the antagonism of their children and even their dogs. Brady Bunch-esque family comedy means well, but doesn't cut it. Hershey's debut. Farr, Christopher, and Tayback have small parts. To date, Day's last big-screen appearance. **1968** (G/*Family*) 95m/C Doris Day, Brian Keith, Pat Carroll, Alice Ghostley, Vic Tayback, Jamie Farr, William Christopher, Barbara Hershey; **D:** Howard Morris. **VHS, Beta $59.98** FOX

The Wiz 𝄆𝄆

Based on the black-oriented Broadway version of the long-time favorite "The Wizard of Oz," with Charlie Smalls' original score augmented by Quincy Jones. Waiflike Ross is Dorothy, a Harlem schoolteacher whisked to a fantasy version of New York City in a search for her identity. Stupendous sets, crazy costumes and memorable makeup effects (by Stan Winston and Albert Whitlock) tend to overwhelm the characterizations that were so crucial to the 1939 Judy Garland classic. One exception: Jackson's sweetly hapless scarecrow. Much of the dialogue and details (like the Wicked Witch's sweatshop) are very specific to the New York urban African American experience - if you don't know the history and geography it's more puzzling than fun. ♫The Feeling That We Have; Can I Go On Not Knowing; Glinda's Theme; He's the Wizard; Soon as I Get Home; You Can't Win; Ease on Down the Road; What Would I Do If I Could Feel?; Slide Some Oil to Me. **1978** (G/*Family*) 133m/C Diana Ross, Michael Jackson, Nipsey Russell, Ted Ross, Mabel King, Thelma Carpenter, Richard Pryor, Lena Horne; **D:** Sidney Lumet; **W:** Joel Schumacher; **M:** Quincy Jones. **VHS, Beta, LV $19.98** MCA, FCT

The Wizard WOOF!

Autistic little Jimmy's been a handful, so mom and stepdad dump him in an institution. To the rescue comes brother Corey, who snatches the boy and races for California, where Jimmy can prove his hidden genius as a game wizard at 'Video Armageddon,' a Nintendo championship at the Universal

Winnie the Pooh and the Blustery Day

Studios theme park. Yechh! There's more, like a sassy little girl who cries rape to get her way, but it adds up to a feature-length promo for that aforementioned game company and amusement park. Nothing kid or adult characters say or do is remotely credible, and dramatic highlight is the debut of ... Super Mario 3. Game Over! **Hound Advisory:** Salty language, roughhousing, alcohol talk.
1989 (**PG**/*Family*) 99m/C Fred Savage, Beau Bridges, Christian Slater, Luke Edwards, Jenny Lewis; *D:* Todd Holland; *W:* David Chisholm. **VHS, Beta, LV** $19.95 *MCA*

The Wizard of Loneliness 🦴🦴◁

Alienated 12-year-old Wendell goes to live with his grandparents during WWII, and slowly uncovers family secrets centering on his pretty young war-widow aunt. Excellent performances boost a moody, distracted, coming-of-age plot with a violent denouement. Based on the novel by John Nichols. **Hound Advisory:** Mature themes, violence, salty language, sex.
1988 (**PG-13**/*Jr. High-Adult*) 110m/C Lukas Haas, Lea Thompson, John Randolph, Lance Guest, Anne Pitoniak, Jeremiah Warner, Dylan Baker; *D:* Jenny Bowen; *W:* Nancy Larson; *M:* Michel Colombier. **VHS, Beta, LV** *NO*

The Wizard of Oz 🦴🦴🦴🦴

We won't dwell on those interpretations of L. Frank Baum tale as metaphor for the political-economic situation at the turn of the century. MGM didn't, and the result was pure entertainment. Farm girl Dorothy rides a tornado from B&W Kansas to a brightly colored world over the rainbow, full of munchkins, flying monkeys, a talking scarecrow, a tin man and a cowardly lion. She must appease the Oz the Great and Powerful and outwit the Wicked Witch if she is ever to go home. Delightful vaudeville performances from Lahr, Bolger, and Hamilton. Director Fleming originally wanted Shirley Temple (see "The Blue Bird") for the role of Dorothy, but settled for the overaged Garland, who made the song "Somewhere Over the Rainbow" her own and earned a special Academy Award. 50th anniversary edition is repackaged with rare clips of Bolger's "Scarecrow Dance" and the cut "Jitterbug" number, and shots of Buddy Ebsen as the Tin Man before he left the production due to an allergy to the makeup. Laserdisc edition has digital sound, commentary by film historian Ronald Haver, test footage, trailers and stills, as well as Jerry Maren's memories as a Munchkin. Yet another special release, "The Ultimate Oz," adds a documentary, a reproduction of the original script, still photos, and liner notes. The sequel-interested should see also Disney's "Return to Oz." ♫Munchkinland; Ding Dong the Witch is Dead; Follow the Yellow Brick Road; If I Only Had a Brain/a Heart/the Nerve; If I Were the King of the Forest; The Merry Old Land of Oz; Threatening Witch; Into the Forest of the Wild Beast; The City Gates are Open. **1939** (*Family*) 101m/C Judy Garland, Margaret Hamilton, Ray Bolger, Jack Haley, Bert Lahr, Frank Morgan, Charley Grapewin, Clara Blandick, Mitchell Lewis, Billie Burke; *D:* Victor Fleming; *W:* Noel Langley; *M:* Herbert Stothart. **Award Nominations:** Academy Awards '39: Best Color Cinematography, Best Interior Decoration, Best Picture, Best Special Effects; **Awards:** Academy Awards '39: Best Song ("Over the Rainbow"), Best Original Score. **VHS, Beta, LV $19.98** *MGM, VYG, APD*

The Wizard of Oz 🐾🐾

All-animated version of the L. Frank Baum classic "The Wizard of Oz," more ideally suited for young children. Featured is the voice of Quinn, who played "Annie" on Broadway. **1982** (*Family*) 78m/C *V:* Lorne Greene, Aileen Quinn. **VHS, Beta $14.95** *PAR, WTA*

The Wizard of Oz: Danger in a Strange Land

Cartoon takeoff on the L. Frank Baum "Oz" characters, produced by Ted Turner's company, not terribly faithful to the original books and stories. Two episodes here: "Time Town" and "The Day the Music Died." Additional volumes available. **1991** (*Family*) 44m/C **VHS, Beta $12.98** *TTC, WTA*

The Wizard of Speed and Time 🐾🐾🐾

Ambitious, self-taught young movie-f/x master is hired by a greedy producer to jazz up a TV show with his gags and gadgets. But he doesn't know the exec is secretly out to stop him at all costs. Jittlov, a true special-effects expert who's done work for Disney, plays himself in this personally financed all-ages comedy. Though brimming with inside jokes and occasional self-pity, this indulgence succeeds. Its zippy, joyful style evokes a Pee Wee Herman-esque vision of Hollywood and a sincere plea for dreamers everywhere to persevere despite the odds (and unions). Constant visual trickery incorporates footage from Jittlov's many stop-motion and complex collage short subjects; be quick with the FREEZE and REWIND buttons to appreciate it all. **Hound Advisory:** Roughhousing and minor double entendres, but nothing that would merit a PG. Maybe it's a conspiracy by the unions. **1988** (*PG/Jr. High-Adult*) 95m/C Mike Jittlov, Richard Kaye, Page Moore, David Conrad, Steve Brodie, John Massari, Frank Laloggia, Philip Michael Thomas, Angelique Pettyjohn, Arnetia Walker, Paulette Breen; *D:* Mike Jittlov; *W:* Mike Jittlov, Richard Kaye, Deven Chierighino; *M:* John Massari. **VHS, LV** *WTA*

Wizards 🐾🐾◁

After doing a series of taboo-breaking adults-only animated features, Bakshi softened - just a little - with this odd mixture of Tolkien satire and political cynicism. In a magic land (evolved after our civilization is nuked), a Skeletor lookalike uses an old projector and rediscovered Nazi propaganda

newsreels to incite his armies and conquer peaceful kingdoms. His good-guy brother, the dwarfish wizard Avatar, reluctantly schleps to the rescue. Not for all tastes, but genuinely thought-provoking. **Hound Advisory:** Violence, salty language, mature themes. **1977** (*PG/Jr. High-Adult*) 81m/C *D:* Ralph Bakshi. **VHS, Beta, LV $19.98** *FOX, WTA*

Wizards of the Lost Kingdom 🐾🐾◁

Boy magician, aided by genial swordmaster Kor the Conqueror, battles a powerful wizard for control of a kingdom. Harmless, brainless fairy tale fare. Poor f/x and halfhearted performances by all but roguish Svenson, whose modern-slang wisecracks strike the right campy note. **Hound Advisory:** Fantasy violence. **1985** (*PG/Jr. High-Adult*) 76m/C Bo Svenson, Vidal Peterson, Thom Christopher; *D:* Hector Olivera. **VHS, Beta $19.95** *MED*

Wizards of the Lost Kingdom 2 🐾

Boy wizard is charged with vanquishing the evil tyrants from three kingdoms. Barely a sequel; no plot continuation or cast from earlier kiddie sword epic. **Hound Advisory:** FAM Violence. **1989** (*PG/Jr. High-Adult*) 80m/C David Carradine, Bobby Jacoby, Lana Clarkson, Mel Welles, Susan Lee Hoffman, Sid Haig; *D:* Charles B. Griffith. **VHS, Beta $79.95** *MED*

The Woman Who Raised a Bear as Her Son

Old woman adopts an orphaned polar bear cub who must learn lessons about how to treat others. **1990** (*Preschool-Primary*) 27m/C **VHS $12.95** *WTA, FHE*

The Wombles

Series for children based on the British TV show about a race of adorable subterranean creatures who live in a London park and care for the environment. **1986** (*Preschool-Primary*) 60m/C **VHS, Beta** *COL*

Wonder Man 🐾🐾◁

Wartime fantasy diversion starring Kaye in dual roles. As nightclub entertainer Buzzy he witnesses a murder and gets killed by gangsters to ensure his silence. But you can't keep Buzzy down; he returns as a ghost, possessing his studious twin brother (Kaye again) to give evidence to police. Heavier on the song-and-dance comedy than the supernatural elements, though the brief, Oscar-winning ghost f/x are good even by modern standards, and Kaye is a delight throughout. Watch for Schafer, Mrs. Howell from "Gilligan's Island." Tape includes the original theatrical trailer. ♫So In Love; Bali Boogie; Ortchi Chornya; Opera Number. **Hound Advisory:** Alcohol use; mild violence. **1945** (*Family*) 98m/C Danny Kaye, Virginia Mayo, Vera-Ellen, Steve Cochran, S.Z. Sakall, Otto Kruger; *D:* H. Bruce Humberstone. **Award Nominations:** Academy Awards '45: Best Song ("So in Love"), Best Sound, Best Original Score; **Awards:** Academy Awards '45: Best Special Effects. **VHS, Beta $19.98** *HBO, SUE*

Inspecting road signs on the Yellow Brick Road in "The Wizard of Oz"

Wonderful Wizard of Oz 🎵🎵

Another version of Frank Baum's classic story, this time part of a Canadian cartoon series (though suspiciously Japanese-looking in design and voices) that's nonetheless faithful to the original "Oz" books. Others in the series: "The Marvelous Land of Oz," "Emerald City of Oz," and "Ozma of Oz." **1987** (*Family*) 93m/C **VHS $59.95** *WTA*

Wonderful World of Puss 'N Boots

Japanese-animated version of the classic fairy tale about the brave, clever cat who helps out his master. **1970** (*Preschool-Primary*) 80m/C **VHS, Beta** *MED, VES*

The Wonderful World of the Brothers Grimm 🎵🎵🎵

Big-budget musical fantasy based very loosely on the lives of those famous fairy-tale mongers, the Grimm brothers. Hokey made in Hollywood romantic and business conflicts come between dreamer Wilhelm and the more pragmatic Jacob. Highlights are adaptations of three Grimm stories, "The Dancing Princesses," "The Cobbler and the Elves" and "The Singing Bone" (featuring a notably fearsome dragon), done using George Pal's stop-motion Puppetoon f/x. Originally a showcase for the new Cinerama widescreen process; both that and the cliches suffer on home video. 🎵The Theme From the Wonderful World of the Brothers Grimm; Gypsy Rhapsody; Christmas Land; Ah-Oom; Above the Stars; Dee-Are-A-Gee-O-En (Dragon). **1962** (*Family*) 134m/C Laurence Harvey, Karl-Heinz Boehm, Claire Bloom, Buddy Hackett, Terry-Thomas, Russ Tamblyn, Yvette Mimieux, Oscar Homolka, Walter Slezak, Beulah Bondi, Martita Hunt, Otto Kruger, Barbara Eden, Jim Backus, Arnold Stang; **D:** Henry Levin, George Pal; **W:** William Roberts. **Award Nominations:** Academy Awards '62: Best Art Direction/Set Decoration (Color), Best Color Cinematography, Best Original Score; **Awards:** Academy Awards '62: Best Costume Design (Color). **VHS, Beta, LV $19.98** *MGM*

The Wonderful World of Wombles

Adventure starring the adorable animated Womble characters from Britain, underground critters on a mission against pollution. See also "Wombling Free" and "The Wombles." **1987** (*Preschool-Primary*) 60m/C **VHS, Beta** *COL*

Wonderland Cove 🎵

The five MacKenzie orphans of Hawaii don't want to be scattered in foster homes, so they create a fictitious guardian uncle on paper. When a social worker gets suspicious, the kids hire a grouchy neighbor to impersonate Uncle. He's played with believable salt by Gulager, who's the best thing about

this TV pilot for the short-lived series "The MacKenzies of Paradise Cove." **Hound Advisory:** alcohol use
1975 (*Family*) 78m/C Clu Gulager, Sean Marshall, Randi Kiger, Lori Walsh; **D:** Jerry Thorpe. **Beta $59.95** *PSM*

Wonders of Aladdin

Feeble Italian-American co-production of the genie-in-the-lamp saga, with song-and-dance man O'Connor decidedly overaged (and a few continents off) as the title Arabian hero, putting the emphasis on slapstick. Tiny kids may love it, adults will yawn.
1961 (*Family*) 93m/C Donald O'Connor, Vittorio De Sica; **D:** Henry Levin, Mario Bava. **VHS, Beta $59.95** *NLC*

Woody Woodpecker & His Friends: Vol. 1

Ten favorite 1940-1955 Walter Lantz "cartunes" were chosen for this tape: "Knock," "Bandmaster," "Ski for Two," "Hot Noon," "The Legend of Rockabye Point," "Wet Blanket Policy," "To Catch a Woodpecker," "Musical Moments from Chopin," "Bats in the Belfry," and "Crazy Mixed-Up Pup." Additional volumes available.
1982 (*Family*) 80m/C **VHS, Beta, LV $9.95** *MCA*

Woody Woodpecker Collector's Edition, Vol. 1

Collection of the hilarious bird's greatest cartoons. "Woody Woodpecker (Cracked Nut)" is the very first Woody appearance. "Banquet Busters" — Woody and Andy Panda crash Mrs. Van Glutton's dinner party. Woody also stars in "Born to Peck" and "The Redwood Sap." Additional volumes available.
1990 (*Family*) 30m/C **VHS, Beta, LV $12.95** *MCA*

Woof!

Charming British TV movie about young Eric, a boy with an uncontrollable tendency to turn into a dog and back again. With the help of school buddy he tackles this little problem with common sense and a quick change of clothes. Based on the book by Allan Ahlberg.
1990 (*Family*) 82m/C **VHS $39.98** *FHE, UND, BTV*

Words by Heart

An African American family in turn of the century Missouri faces issues of discrimination and prejudice. Twelve-year-old Lena wins a speech contest and begins to question their place in the community and their aspirations for a better life. Based on a book by Ouida Sebestyen. Aired by PBS as part of the "Wonderworks" family movie series.
1984 (*Family*) 116m/C Charlotte Rae, Robert Hooks, Alfre Woodard; **D:** Robert Thompson. **VHS $29.95** *PME, FCT, HMV*

The World According to Gumby

Another collection of episodes from the original Gumby series spun off from "Howdy Doody." Segments include "The Big

Eye," "Outcast Marbles," "Tail Tale," "Haunted Hot Dog," and "Indian Challenge."
1956 (*Family*) 30m/C **VHS, Beta $14.95** *WTA*

A World Apart

Blistering drama told from the view of a 13-year-old white girl in South Africa, resentful that her crusading journalist mother tirelessly fights against the racist government but makes no time for her family. Not just a political morality tale, but a look at the personal sacrifices activists must make in their private lives. Heavily lauded, with good reason. The autobiographical script is based on writer Slovo's parents, apartheid fighters Joe Slovo and Ruth First. **Hound Advisory:** Mature themes, profanity, violence.
1988 (**PG**/*Jr. High-Adult*) 114m/C Barbara Hershey, Jodhi May, Linda Mvusi, David Suchet, Jeroen Krabbe, Paul Freeman, Tim Roth; **D:** Chris Menges; **W:** Shawn Slovo; **M:** Hans Zimmer. **VHS, Beta, LV $9.98** *MED*

A World is Born

Evolution of the world from prehistoric times is set to music by Igor Stravinsky, and glorious animation in this excerpt from Walt Disney's 1940 "Fantasia."
1990 (*Preschool-Primary*) 20m/C **VHS, Beta $250.00** *MTI, DSN*

The World of Andy Panda

Collection of nine Andy Panda cartoons done by Lantz in the 1940s, featuring "Apple Andy," "Crow Crazy," and "Meatless Tuesday."
1946 (*Family*) 62m/C **VHS, Beta $14.95** *MCA, WTA*

World of David the Gnome: Kangaroo Adventure

Cartoon adventure series based on the bestselling gnome tomes by Rien Poortvliet and Wil Huygen. In this one the main character, a globetrotting gnome named David, must aid some Australian birds when they are captured by a mean hunter. Additional volumes available.
1987 (*Family*) 45m/C **V:** Tom Bosley. **VHS, Beta $14.95** *FHE, LIV*

World of Hans Christian Andersen

Animated Hans Christian Andersen relates the delightful tales that made him a legend in the storytelling business.
1985 (*Preschool-Primary*) 73m/C **VHS, Beta $19.95** *COL, WTA*

The World of Henry Orient

Charming, eccentric comedy about two 15-year-old girls who, madly in love with an egotistical concert pianist, pursue him all around New York City. Sellers is hilarious, Walker and Spaeth are adorable as his teen groupies; Bosley and Lansbury are great as Walker's indulgent parents. For anyone who has ever been uncontrollably infatuated. Screenplay by the father/daughter team, Nora and Nunnally Johnson, based on Nora Johnson's novel. Music by Elmer Bernstein.
1964 (*Family*) 106m/C Peter Sellers, Tippy Walker, Merrie Spaeth, Tom Bosley, Angela Lansbury, Paula Prentiss; **D:** George Roy Hill; **W:** Nunnally Johnson, Nora Johnson; **M:** Elmer Bernstein. **VHS, Beta, LV $19.98** *MGM, FCT*

A World of Stories with Katharine Hepburn

Venerable actress tells six of her favorite fairy tales. Includes illustrations from the stories.
1993 (*Primary*) 78m/C **VHS $19.95** *WST, KUL*

World of Strawberry Shortcake

The Peculiar Purple Pieman of Porcupine Peak poses pitfalls aplenty for Ms. Shortcake and pals. Pernicious tape peddling pointless playthings to preschoolers.
1980 (*Preschool-Primary*) 60m/C **VHS, Beta $14.95** *FHE, WTA*

The World's Greatest Athlete 𝄞𝄞

Lame Disney comedy about Tarzan-like jungle-man Vincent recruited by unsuccessful American college coach Amos and his bumbling assistant Conway. Fun special effects, weak script add up to mediocre family fare. Cameo by Howard Cosell as - who else? - himself.
1973 (*G/Family*) 89m/C Jan-Michael Vincent, Tim Conway, John Amos, Roscoe Lee Browne, Dayle Haddon; *Cameos:* Howard Cosell; *D:* Robert Scheerer; *M:* Marvin Hamlisch. **VHS, Beta** *DIS, OM*

The Worst Witch 𝄞𝄞𝄞

Well-cast British TV fantasy (with songs) about Miss Cackle's Academy for Witches, where newcomer Mildred can never get her magic straight but winds up a hero anyway. Adapted from the children's book series by Jill Murphy.
1986 (*G/Family*) 70m/C Diana Rigg, Charlotte Rae, Tim Curry, Fairuza Balk; *D:* Robert Young. **VHS, Beta $79.95** *PSM*

Wowser: Wow-Wow Wowser

Helpful dog aids his master by trying out a group of inventions. Additional volumes available.
1989 (*Preschool-Primary*) 110m/C **VHS, Beta $39.95** *CEL, WTA*

Wrinkles: In Need of Cuddles

Another popular toy bites the dust in a Saturday-morning TV adaptation.
1986 (*Preschool*) 48m/C Ami Foster; *D:* Lee Mendelson. **VHS, Beta $14.98** *LIV, WTA*

The Wrong Man 𝄞𝄞𝄞𝄞

Nightclub musician Fonda is falsely accused of a robbery and his life is destroyed. Taken almost entirely from the real-life case of mild-mannered bass player "Manny" Balestrero; probes his anguish at being wrongly accused; and showcases Miles (later to appear in "Psycho") and her character's agony. Harrowing, especially following more lighthearted Hitchcock fare such as "The Trouble with Harry." Part of the "A Night at the Movies" series, this tape simulates a 1956 movie evening with a color Bugs Bunny cartoon, "A Star Is Bored," a newsreel and coming attractions for "Toward the Unknown."
1956 (*Sr. High-Adult*) 126m/B Henry Fonda, Vera Miles, Anthony Quayle, Nehemiah Persoff; *D:* Alfred Hitchcock. **VHS, Beta, LV $19.98** *WAR, MLB*

Wuthering Heights 𝄞𝄞𝄞

The third screening of the classic Emily Bronte romance about two doomed lovers. Fuest's version features excellent photography, and Calder-Marshall's and Dalton's performances are effective, but fail even to approach the intensity and pathos of the 1939 film original (or of the book). Filmed on location in Yorkshire, England.
1970 (*G/Jr. High-Adult*) 105m/C Anna Calder-Marshall, Timothy Dalton, Harry Andrews, Pamela Brown, Judy Cornwell, James Cossins, Rosalie Crutchley, Hilary Dwyer, Hugh Griffith, Ian Ogilvy; *D:* Robert Fuest. **VHS, Beta $14.95** *CNG, KAR, TVC*

X-Men: Deadly Reunions

TV episode of the cartoon series bringing to animated life the wildly popular Marvel Comics superhero troupe. While Rogue and Cyclops do battle with the ever-menacing Magento, Wolverine is confronted by his ancient arch-rival, Sabertooth. Can you tell the players without a scorecard? Additional episodes available.
1993 (*Primary-Jr. High*) 25m/C **VHS $9.95** *PGV*

Xanadu   WOOF!

Dorky star-vehicle remake (of 1947's "Down to Earth") eminently of the disco era, which is now better forgotten. Newton-John is a mystical muse who descends to Earth to help two friends open a roller disco. In the process she proves that as an actor, she's a singer. Kelly attempts to soft shoe some grace into the proceedings, though he seems mystified as anyone as to why he's on the set. Don Bluth adds an animated sequence. ♫I'm Alive; The Fall; Don't Walk Away; All Over the World; Xanadu; Magic; Suddenly; Dancing; Suspended in Time.
1980 (*PG/Jr. High-Adult*) 96m/C Olivia Newton-John, Michael Beck, Gene Kelly, Sandahl Bergman; *D:* Robert Greenwald. **VHS, Beta, LV $14.98** *MCA, MLB*

Xuxa: Funtastic Birthday Party

Xuxa, the superstar Latin-American children's entertainer watches a magic show, sings, and dances with friends.
1994 (*Primary-Jr. High*) 40m/C **VHS $14.98**

Yanco 𝄞𝄞

A young Mexican boy makes visits to an island where he plays his homemade violin. Unfortunately, no one can understand or tolerate his love for music, save for an elderly violinist, who gives him lessons on an instrument known as "Yanco." No dialogue. Not exactly riveting, but sensitively played.
1964 (*Family*) 95m/B Ricardo Ancona, Jesus Medina, Maria Bustamante. **VHS, Beta $19.95** *WFV, DVT, INJ*

Yankee Doodle Cricket

Follow-up to "The Cricket in Times Square" finds animated animals present to compose "Yankee Doodle Dandy," help Thomas Jefferson write The Declaration of Independence, and assist Paul Revere.
1976 (*Primary*) 26m/C **VHS, Beta $14.95** *CHI, FHE, WTA*

Yankee Doodle Dandy 𝄢𝄢𝄢𝄢

Nostalgic view of the Golden Era of show business and the man who made it glitter - George M. Cohan. His early days, triumphs, songs, musicals and romances are brought to life by the inexhaustible Cagney in a rare and wonderful song-and-dance performance. Told in flashback, covering the Irishman's struggling days as a young song writer and performer to his salad days as the toast of Broadway. Cagney, never more charismatic, dances up a storm, reportedly inventing most of the steps on the spot. ♪Give My Regards to Broadway; Yankee Doodle Dandy; You're a Grand Old Flag; Over There; I Was Born in Virginia; Off the Record; You're a Wonderful Girl; Blue Skies, Grey Skies; Oh You Wonderful Girl.
1942 (*Family*) 126m/B James Cagney, Joan Leslie, Walter Huston, Richard Whorf, Irene Manning, Rosemary DeCamp, Jeanne Cagney, S.Z. Sakall, Walter Catlett, Frances Langford, Eddie Foy Jr., George Tobias, Michael Curtiz; **D:** Michael Curtiz; **W:** Robert Buckner. **Award Nominations:** Academy Awards '42: Best Director (Curtiz), Best Picture, Best Story, Best Supporting Actor (Huston); **Awards:** Academy Awards '42: Best Actor (Cagney), Best Sound, Best Score. **VHS, Beta, LV $29.98** *MGM, FOX, FCT*

The Year My Voice Broke 𝄢𝄢𝄢

Danny is an undersized, thoughtful boy in an Australian outback town, deeply infatuated with childhood playmate Freya, an orphan teen now gaining a reputation as the village tramp. While Freya considers Danny her best friend, she keeps their relationship platonic - and gets pregnant by a tougher, older guy. An overflow of melodrama in the second half is the only false note in this bluesy portrait of first love at its most bittersweet. Writer/director Duigan followed un-lucky-in-love Danny's further romantic mishaps in "Flirting." **Hound Advisory:** Sex, implied more than shown. Mature themes, alcohol use.
1987 (**PG-13**/*Sr. High-Adult*) 103m/C Noah Taylor, Leone Carmen, Ben Mendelsohn, Graeme Blundell, Lynette Curran, Malcolm Robertson, Judi Farr; **D:** John Duigan; **W:** John Duigan; **M:** Christine Woodruff. **VHS, Beta, LV $89.95** *LIV*

Year of the Comet 𝄢𝄢

Amusing adventure/romantic comedy throws straightlaced Maggie (Miller) together with carefree Oliver (Daly) in a quest for a rare bottle of wine. Fine wine is Maggie's passion, and snagging this particular bottle will boost her status in the family business. Oliver is a pretzels and beer kind of guy, but his boss wants this bottle and will pay a lot to get it. Wants to be another "Romancing the Stone," but plot and characters are too thin. Nice chemistry between Miller and Daly sort of saves this one despite a disappointing script. Beautiful location shots of Scotland. **Hound Advisory:** Profanity and violence.
1992 (**PG-13**/*Jr. High-Adult*) 135m/C Penelope Ann Miller, Timothy Daly, Louis Jourdan, Art Malik, Ian Richardson, Ian McNeice, Timothy Bentinck, Julia McCarthy, Jacques Mathou; **D:** Peter Yates; **W:** William Goldman; **M:** Hummie Mann. **VHS, LV $19.95** *NLC*

The Year Without a Santa Claus

Hip, funny, stop-motion-animated TV special shows the panic that hits the North Pole when a tired Santa decides to take December 25th off for once. A stylish standout in the

children's Christmas parade from the Rankin-Bass Animagic works. Great musical numbers are fun for adults, too, especially Heatmiser and Coldmiser. Based on the award-winning book by Phyllis McGinley.
1974 (*Family*) 50m/C **V:** Mickey Rooney, Shirley Booth. **VHS, Beta $12.95** *LIV, WTA, TVC*

The Yearling 𝄢𝄢𝄢◁

Tearjerking adaptation of the Marjorie Kinnan Rawlings novel about how a young boy's love for a yearling fawn during the post Civil War era. His father's encouragement and his mother's bitterness play against the story of unqualified love amid poverty and the boy's coming of age. Evocative recreation of wilderness Florida of another era. Jarman was awarded a special Oscar as outstanding child actor. **Hound Advisory:** The title deer distinguishes itself as one of the least heroic animal stars in history, but it still must share Old Yeller's fate.
1946 (*Family*) 128m/C Gregory Peck, Jane Wyman, Claude Jarman Jr., Chill Wills, Henry Travers, Jeff York, Forrest Tucker, June Lockhart, Margaret Wycherly; **D:** Clarence Brown. **Award Nominations:** Academy Awards '46: Best Actor (Peck), Best Actress (Wyman), Best Director (Brown), Best Film Editing, Best Picture; **Awards:** Academy Awards '46: Best Color Cinematography, Best Interior Decoration; Golden Globe Awards '47: Best Actor—Drama (Peck). **VHS, Beta, LV $19.98** *KUI, MGM, TLF*

Yellow Submarine 𝄢𝄢𝄢◁

Acclaimed all-ages animated phantasmagoria based on a plethora of mid-career Beatles songs. The Fab Four fight the music-hating Blue Meanies to save Sgt. Pepper, the Nowhere Man, Strawberry Fields, and Pepperland. The first full-length British animated feature in 14 years features a host of talented cartoonists pulling out all the stops with wild op-art animation and imagery. Speaking voices were NOT provided by the Beatles themselves but rather sound-alikes John Clive (John), Geoff Hughes (Paul), Peter Batten (George), and Paul Angelis (Ringo). The group themselves do appear in a short scene at the end of the film. ♪Yellow Submarine; All You Need is Love; Hey, Bulldog; When I'm Sixty Four; Nowhere Man; Lucy in the Sky With Diamonds; Sgt. Pepper's Lonely Hearts Club Band; A Day in the Life; All Together Now.
1968 (**G**/*Family*) 87m/C **D:** George Duning, Dick Emery; **W:** Erich Segal; **M:** George Martin. **VHS, Beta, LV $19.95** *MVD, MGM, WTA*

Yellowstone Cubs

Disney live-action nature footage allows the viewer to share in the misadventures of Tuffy and Tubby, a pair of cute bears who always manage to find trouble.
1976 (*Preschool-Primary*) 45m/C **VHS, Beta $250.00** *MTI, DSN*

Yentl 𝄢𝄢◁

The famous Barbra adaptation of Isaac Bashevis Singer's story set in 1900s Eastern Europe about a Jewish girl who masquerades as a boy in order to study the Talmud, and who becomes enmeshed in romantic miscues. Lushly photographed, with a repetitive score that nevertheless won an Oscar. Singer was reportedly appalled by the results of Streisand's hyper-controlled project. ♪A Piece of Sky; No

Matter What Happens; This Is One of Those Moments; Tomorrow Night; Where Is It Written; No Wonder; The Way He Makes Me Feel; Papa, Can You Hear Me; Will Someone Ever Look at Me That Way?.
Hound Advisory: Brief nudity.
1983 (PG/*Jr. High-Adult*) 134m/C Barbra Streisand, Mandy Patinkin, Amy Irving, Nehemiah Persoff, Steven Hill, Allan Cordunner, Ruth Goring, David DeKeyser, Bernard Spear; **D:** Barbra Streisand; **M:** Michel Legrand, Alan Bergman, Marilyn Bergman. **Award Nominations:** Academy Awards '83: Best Art Direction/Set Decoration, Best Song ("Papa, Can You Hear Me?", "The Way He Makes Me Feel"), Best Supporting Actress (Irving); **Awards:** Academy Awards '83: Best Original Score; Golden Globe Awards '84: Best Director (Streisand), Best Film—Musical/Comedy. **VHS, Beta, LV $39.98** *MGM, IME*

Yes, Virginia, There is a Santa Claus

Realistic cartoon retelling the true story of little Virginia O'Hanlon, whose belief in Santa Claus inspired that most famous column in the New York Sun newspaper in 1897. Award-winning animation courtesy of the Bill Melendez team otherwise responsible for "Peanuts" in prime time.
1974 (*Preschool-Jr. High*) 30m/C **V:** Jim Backus, Courtney Lemmon, Louis Nye. **VHS, Beta $14.95** *WTA, PAR*

Yogi and the Invasion of the Space Bears

Yogi Bear and Boo Boo are kidnapped by aliens who threaten to clone them thousands of times, posing a threat to picnic baskets throughout Jellystone Park and the rest of the world. Hanna-Barbera made-for-TV cartoon feature.
1991 (*Family*) 90m/C **V:** Daws Butler, Don Messick, Sorrell Booke, Julie Bennett. **VHS, Beta $29.95** *TTC, WTA*

Yogi and the Magical Flight of the Spruce Goose

Yogi and other Hanna-Barbera characters visit Long Beach and Howard Hughes' famous wooden airliner the Spruce Goose. They manage to use the craft in a fantasy voyage to rescue trapped animals. Made-for-TV cartoon feature.
1984 (*Family*) 96m/C **V:** Daws Butler, Don Messick, Paul Winchell, John Stephenson. **VHS, Beta $29.95** *TTC, WTA*

Yogi's First Christmas

Made-for-TV cartoon feature in which Hanna-Barbera characters like Huckleberry Hound, Snagglepuss, Auggie Doggie and others convene at Jellystone Park for Noel with the title bear. Complications arise with the revelation that their lodge is to be bulldozed for a freeway. Can Santa save the day?
1980 (*Family*) 100m/C **D:** Ray Patterson; **V:** Daws Butler, Don Messick, John Stephenson, Janet Waldo, Hal Smith. **VHS, Beta, LV $19.95** *TTC, IME, WTA*

Yogi's Great Escape

Yogi learns that Jellystone Park is to be closed down and the bear population moved to zoos. He, Boo Boo and three cubs go on the run with Ranger Smith in a cross-country pursuit. Made-for-TV cartoon feature.
1984 (*Family*) 96m/C **V:** Daws Butler, Don Messick, Susan Blu, Frank Welker. **VHS, Beta $29.95** *TTC, WTA*

Yogi's Treasure Hunt: Heavens to Planetoid!

Yogi ventures farther and wide in these recyclings from a recent syndicated TV series finding him and other Hanna-Barbera characters aboard the S.S. Jolly Roger, roaming the globe in search of treasure for charitable causes (like the salaries of cut-rate animators?). In these three adventures, the gang explores outer-space, the mountains of Peru, and below the earth's crust. Additional volumes available.
1985 (*Family*) 80m/C **VHS, Beta $29.95** *TTC, WTA*

You Only Live Twice 🎵🎵📢

007 travels to Japan to take on arch-nemesis Blofeld, who has been capturing Russian and American spacecraft in an attempt to start WWIII. Great location photography, but implausible plot defies even Bond standard. Theme sung by Nancy Sinatra. **Hound Advisory:** Violence, alcohol use, suggested sex.
1967 (PG/*Jr. High-Adult*) 125m/C Sean Connery, Mie Hama, Akiko Wakabayashi, Tetsuro Tamba, Karin Dor, Charles Gray, Donald Pleasence, Tsai Chin, Bernard Lee, Lois Maxwell, Desmond Llewelyn; **D:** Lewis Gilbert; **M:** John Barry. **VHS, Beta, LV $19.98** *MGM, TLF*

Young & Free 🎵📢

Following the death of his parents, a young man must learn to face the perils of an unchartered wilderness alone. Ultimately he must choose between returning to civilization, or remain with his beloved wife and life in the wild.
1978 (*Sr. High-Adult*) 87m/C Erik Larsen; **D:** Keith Larsen. **VHS, Beta $59.95** *MON*

A Young Children's Concert with Raffi

Concert starring the famed Canadian children's entertainer.
1985 (*Preschool*) 50m/C **VHS, Beta $19.98** *MLT, A&M*

The Young Detectives on Wheels 🎵🎵📢

Sandra and Mark find stolen emeralds in their backyard, and their father is arrested for the theft. The kids turn to a neighborhood assortment of BMX bike riders and young computer hackers to solve the crime and unmask the true criminals. Fun, if somewhat overlong New Zealand family film. Mystery is foggy in parts, but Sandra makes a nicely untypical and spunky heroine. **Hound Advisory:** Roughhousing.
1987 (*Family*) 107m/C **VHS $39.98** *VMK, FHE, BTV*

Young Eagles

Low-budget vintage serial devoted to the exploits of an adventurous Boy Scout troop. In 12 chapters, lasting 13 minutes each. What Merit Badge will you earn for sitting through the whole thing?
1934 (*Family*) 156m/B Bobby Cox, Jim Vance, Carter Dixon. **VHS, Beta $39.95** *VYY, VCN, MLB*

Young Einstein 🦴🦴

Goofy, irreverent Australian farce starring, directed, co-scripted and co-produced by Serious, depicting Einstein as a young Outback clod who splits beer atoms and invents rock and roll. Mysterious winner of several Aussie awards will likely prove fun for the kids. **Hound Advisory:** Profanity.
1989 (PG/*Jr. High-Adult*) 91m/C Yahoo Serious, Odile Le Clezio, John Howard, Pee Wee Wilson, Su Cruickshank; *D:* Yahoo Serious; *W:* Yahoo Serious. VHS, Beta, LV $19.95 *WAR*

Young Frankenstein 🦴🦴🦴🦴

Young Dr. Frankenstein (Wilder), a brain surgeon, inherits the family castle back in Transylvania. He's skittish about the family business, but upon learning his grandfather's secrets, he becomes obsessed with making his own monster. Once a Frankensteen, always a Frankensteen. Hilarious parody is crowded with numerous classic moments in faithful black and white, including Wilder and monster Boyle singing and dancing to Irving Berlin's "Puttin' on the Ritz," and Hackman's cameo as a blind man who befriends young Franky. **Hound Advisory:** Vulgarity; suggested sex.
1974 (PG/*Jr. High-Adult*) 108m/B Peter Boyle, Gene Wilder, Marty Feldman, Madeline Kahn, Cloris Leachman, Teri Garr, Kenneth Mars, Richard Haydn; *Cameos:* Gene Hackman; *D:* Mel Brooks; *W:* Gene Wilder, Mel Brooks; *M:* John Morris. VHS, Beta, LV $14.98 *FOX, HMV*

Young Guns 🦴🦴🦴◁

Sophomoric Wild Bunch look-alike that ends up resembling a western version of the Bowery Boys with lots of guns, bullets, and bodies. Ensemble of semi-hip young stars provides an MTV portrait of Billy the Kid and his gang as they move from prairie trash to demi-legends. Followed by YGII. **Hound Advisory:** Profanity, violence.
1988 (R/*Sr. High-Adult*) 107m/C Emilio Estevez, Kiefer Sutherland, Lou Diamond Phillips, Charlie Sheen, Casey Siemaszko, Dermot Mulroney, Terence Stamp, Terry O'Quinn, Jack Palance, Brian Keith, Patrick Wayne, Sharon Thomas; *D:* Christopher Cain; *W:* John Fusco; *M:* Anthony Marinelli, Brian Backus. VHS, Beta, LV $14.98 *LIV, VES*

Young Magician 🦴🦴🦴

Polish children's feature, done as part of Rock Demers' "Tales for All" series, about how young Peter develops uncontrollable telekinetic powers (just by reading a book on magic tricks!) with no control over them. Grownups fear the kid, but just when you think it couldn't be more predictable, the story gets truly interesting through Peter's friendship with a boy violinist who teaches that even superhumans need practice and discipline.
1988 (*Family*) 99m/C Rusty Jedwab, Natasza Maraszek, Edward Garson; *D:* Waldemar Dziki. VHS, Beta *FHE*

Young Robin Hood

The Hanna-Barbera folks took advantage of the recently hip Robin Hood legend to issue this feature-length cartoon knockoff. This time "The Prince of Thieves" is 14 years old and, with his band of youthful Merry Men, intends to besiege Nottingham Castle.
1991 (*Family*) 90m/C VHS, Beta $29.95 *TTC, WTA*

Young Sherlock Holmes 🦴🦴

Can't-miss premise does: Holmes and Watson meet as schoolboys in London and join on their first case, a series of bizarre murders committed by an Egyptian cult (who look like Hare Krishnas). You're in trouble when not one, but two onscreen disclaimers declare this is based on NO work by Sir Arthur Conan Doyle; inspiration instead comes from the hi-tech f/x department of Steven Spielberg's production company, with cult-induced hallucinations spawning unreal monsters and a climax ripped off from "Indiana Jones and the Temple of Doom." In there somewhere is a melancholy turn by Rowe as the lonely adolescent Sherlock. **Hound Advisory:** Violence, but not as bad as the PG-13 rating would suggest.
1985 (PG-13/*Sr. High-Adult*) 109m/C Nicholas Rowe, Alan Cox, Sophie Ward, Freddie Jones, Michael Hordern; *D:* Barry Levinson; *W:* Chris Columbus; *M:* Bruce Broughton. VHS, Beta, LV, 8mm $14.95 *PAR*

You're a Good Man, Charlie Brown

Not a cartoon, but a straight, filmed version of Charles Schulz's stage musical (originally a record album, then a Broadway hit), bringing to life his immortal "Peanuts" characters in a series of true-to-the-comic-strip sketches and songs.
1987 (*Preschool-Jr. High*) 60m/C VHS, Beta $14.95 *BAR, KAR, WTA*

You're Not Elected, Charlie Brown!/ A Charlie Brown Christmas

Peanuts doubleheader, including Charlie Brown and Linus running against each other for the office of student body president. "A Charlie Brown Christmas," dating from 1965, is one of the first of the animated "Peanuts" specials, and features Charlie Brown worrying that the holiday has become over-commercialized.
1965 (*Family*) 50m/C *D:* Bill Melendez; *W:* Charles M. Schulz. VHS, Beta $11.95 *SHV, VTR, WTA*

Yours, Mine & Ours 🦴🦴🦴

Bigger, better, big screen version of "The Brady Bunch." It's the story of a lovely lady (Ball) with eight kids who marries a widower (Fonda) who has ten. Imagine the zany shenanigans! Family comedy manages to be both wholesome and funny. Based on a true story.
1968 (*Family*) 114m/C Lucille Ball, Henry Fonda, Van Johnson, Tim Matheson, Tom Bosley, Tracy Nelson; *D:* Melville Shavelson; *W:* Melville Shavelson. VHS, Beta, LV $14.95 *MGM*

Yukon Flight 🦴🦴

A Renfrew of the Mounties adventure. The hero finds illegal gold mining operations and murder in the Yukon.
1940 (*Family*) 57m/B James Newill, Dave O'Brien. VHS, Beta $19.95 *NOS, VCN*

The Zax From Dr. Seuss on the Loose

North-going Zax and a south-going Zax meet face-to-face midway on their journeys; neither is willing to budge to let the other through.

1974 (*Primary*) 5m/C *W:* Theodore (Dr. Seuss) Geisel. **VHS, Beta** *BFA*

Zebra in the Kitchen 𝄞𝄞◁

Critter comedy from "Flipper" creator Tors takes the "Free Willy" concept to its extremes. Little Chris is so upset by the way his pet cougar gets treated in a bleak zoo that he liberates the big cat, and in the process unlocks the whole menagerie. For much of the remaining run time, townsfolk are spooked by stray ostriches, monkeys, elephants, and that zebra (it looks weird because none of the 'terrified' human extras ever make a sound or even a facial expression). It does get boring and repetitive very quickly.
1965 (*Family*) 92m/C Jay North, Martin Milner, Andy Devine, Joyce Meadows, Jim Davis; *D:* Ivan Tors. **VHS $19.98** *MGM, BTV*

Zebrahead 𝄞𝄞𝄞

Zack and Nikki are two high schoolers in love — which would be okay except Zack's white and Nikki's black. Will their romance succumb to the pressures of society, family, and friends? With mature theme, urban violence, sexual situations, and drugs, it won't be everyone's cup of tea. But writer/director Drazan's expressive debut is a small gem featuring one of the last appearances by Sharkey (as Zack's dad) and outstanding performances by the young and largely unknown cast, particularly Rappaport and Wright. Great musical score enriches the action. Filmed on location in Detroit, with plenty of authentic Motown scenery displayed. Developed with assistance by the Sundance Institute. **Hound Advisory:** Violence; profanity; drug use; sexual situations.
1992 (**R**/*Sr. High-Adult*) 102m/C Michael Rappaport, N'Bushe Wright, Ray Sharkey, DeShonn Castle, Ron Johnson, Marsha Florence, Paul Butler, Abdul Hassan Sharif, Dan Ziskie, Candy Ann Brown, Helen Shaver, Luke Reilly, Martin Priest; *D:* Tony Drazan; *W:* Tony Drazan; *M:* Taj Mahal. **VHS, LV, 8mm $29.95** *COL*

Zelly & Me 𝄞𝄞𝄞

Psychological drama about a young orphan living with her possessive grandmother. Granny forces the child to become a participant in her own somewhat twisted version of reality (including an obsession with Joan of Arc) through humiliation and isolation from anyone she cares for. Written by Rathborne, this is well-acted and interesting despite the introspective plot and confusing gaps in the narrative. **Hound Advisory:** Mature themes.
1988 (**PG**/*Sr. High-Adult*) 87m/C Isabella Rossellini, Alexandra Johnes, David Lynch, Glynis Johns, Kaiulani Lee, Joe Morton; *D:* Tina Rathborne; *W:* Tina Rathborne; *M:* Pino Donaggio. **VHS, Beta, LV $79.95** *COL*

Zero to Sixty 𝄞

Newly divorced man finds his car has been repossessed for nonpayment. Seeking out the manager of the finance company, he gets a job as a repo man with a sassy 16-year-old girl as his assistant. Repartee develops, stuff happens, and the movie ends.
1978 (**PG**/*Jr. High-Adult*) 96m/C Darren McGavin, Sylvia Miles, Denise Nickerson, Joan Collins; *D:* Don Weis. **VHS, Beta $69.98** *SUE*

Ziggy's Gift

Ziggy, the lovable cartoon character created by Tom Wilson, stars (but never speaks) in this TV Christmas program. Recruited as a street-corner Santa by what turns out to be a criminal gang, the hapless Ziggy nonetheless spreads holiday kindness and good cheer.
1983 (*Family*) 30m/C *M:* Harry Nilsson. **VHS, Beta $19.95** *LIV, VES, WTA*

Zillion

Five-part cartoon miniseries featuring the White Knights who will battle until the death for their planet called Maris.
1990 (*Primary-Jr. High*) 30m/C **VHS $14.95** *WTA, STP, TPV*

Zombies of the Stratosphere

The heyday of the movie serial was long past when Republic released this 12-chapter revival of their "Rocket Man" character for silly but undeniable fun. He fights not zombies but meanies from Mars, in cahoots with Earth gangsters to hijack our whole planet. Yes, that is Nimoy, later to be Mr. Spock, as a rookie Martian, complete with pointy ears. **Hound Advisory:** Violence.
1952 (*Family*) 152m/B Judd Holdren, Aline Towne, Leonard Nimoy, John Crawford, Ray Boyle; *D:* Fred Brannon. **VHS, Beta, LV $14.98** *REP, VCN, MLB*

The Zoo Gang 𝄞◁

Group of teens want to open a nightclub but meet opposition from a mean rival gang and a stupid youth-comedy script. Vereen's dignity barely survives his thankless role as a vagrant ex-wrestler who helps out. **Hound Advisory:** Roughhousing, salty language, alcohol use.
1985 (**PG-13**/*Primary-Jr. High*) 96m/C Jackie Earle Haley, Tiffany Helm, Ben Vereen, Jason Gedrick, Eric Gurry; *D:* John Watson, Pen Densham; *W:* John Watson, Pen Densham; *M:* Patrick Gleeson. **VHS, Beta $9.99** *NWV, STE*

Zoobilee Zoo, Vol. 1: Land of Rhymes & Other Stories

A special fantasy/educational program for children in which the residents of a magical zoo are portrayed by various dancers and actors. This volume is entitled "Land of Rhymes and Other Stories" and includes "Land of Rhymes," "Singa-long 1," and "Bravo's Puppets." Additional volumes available.
1987 (*Family*) 70m/C Ben Vereen. **VHS, Beta $14.95** *COL*

Zoom the White Dolphin

Sunny but basic cartoon feature about a family on a tropical island who befriend their watery neighbors, a clan of porpoises led by the albino Zoom.
1974 (*Primary-Jr. High*) 94m/C **VHS, Beta** *SUE*

Zorro Rides Again

Fast-moving, fun serial in which Zorro, here placed in 'present-day' (1930s) California, risks his life to outwit enemy agents and make sure the railroad goes through. The first chapter runs 30 minutes, the rest 17. **Hound Advisory:** Roughhousing.

1937 (*Family*) 217m/B John Carroll, Helen Christian, Noah Beery Sr., Duncan Renaldo; *D:* William Witney, John English. **VHS, Beta $27.95** *NOS, VCN, MED*

Zorro, Vol. 1

In addition to the two Disney "Zorro" movies, six feature-length volumes of the TV series are on video starring Madison as the masked avenger of old California. **1958** (*Family*) 75m/B Guy Williams, Gene Sheldon, Britt Lomond, Henry Calvin, Jan Avran, Eugenia Paul, Annette Funicello, Richard Anderson, Jolene Brand. **VHS, Beta** *DIS*

Zorro's Black Whip

Lady crime reporter dons the mask of her slain crime-fighting brother (not Zorro, incidentally; he really has nothing to do with it) to continue the struggle for truth and justice. Makers of this okay 12-episode Republic serial brainstormed for a method of hand-to-hand combat that was 'ladylike,' so they settled for the whip. **Hound Advisory:** Roughhousing. **1944** (*Family*) 182m/B George Lewis, Linda Stirling, Lucien Littlefield, Francis McDonald, Tom London; *D:* Spencer Gordon Bennet; *W:* Wallace Grissell. **VHS, LV $29.98** *NOS, GPV, MED*

Zorro's Fighting Legion

Zorro forms a legion to help the president of Mexico fight a band of outlaws endeavoring to steal gold shipments. A serial in 12 chapters. **Hound Advisory:** Roughhousing. **1939** (*Family*) 215m/B Reed Hadley, Sheila Darcy; *D:* William Witney, John English. **VHS, LV $29.98** *NOS, VCN, VDM*

Indexes

Alternate Titles Index

The **ALTERNATE TITLES INDEX** lists variant titles for movies, including foreign titles. Titles are listed in alphabetical order followed by a cross-reference to the appropriate title as listed in the main video review section.

Abbott and Costello Meet the Ghosts *See* Abbott and Costello Meet Frankenstein (1948)

Ace *See* The Great Santini (1980)

The Adventure of Lyle Swan *See* Timerider (1983)

Adventures at Rugby *See* Tom Brown's School Days (1940)

The Adventures of Chatran *See* The Adventures of Milo & Otis (1989)

The Adventures of Hercules *See* Hercules 2 (1985)

The Adventures of the Great Mouse Detective *See* The Great Mouse Detective (1986)

And Then There Were None *See* Ten Little Indians (1975)

Andy Colby's Incredibly Awesome Adventure *See* Andy and the Airwave Rangers (1989)

An Angel Passed Over Brooklyn *See* The Man Who Wagged His Tail (1957)

Anne of Green Gables: The Sequel *See* Anne of Avonlea (1987)

Arthur the King *See* Merlin and the Sword (1985)

Atomic Rocketship *See* Flash Gordon: Rocketship (1936)

Babes in Toyland *See* March of the Wooden Soldiers (1934)

Bach et Bottine *See* Bach & Broccoli (1987)

Bachelor Knight *See* The Bachelor and the Bobby-Soxer (1947)

Bang Bang *See* Bang Bang Kid (1967)

Banner in the Sky *See* Third Man on the Mountain (1959)

The Bar Sinister *See* It's a Dog's Life (1955)

Batman: The Animated Movie *See* Batman: Mask of the Phantasm (1993)

Batmen of Africa *See* Darkest Africa (1936)

Behind the Iron Mask *See* The Fifth Musketeer (1979)

The Big Heart *See* Miracle on 34th Street (1947)

Blake Edwards' Son of the Pink Panther *See* Son of the Pink Panther (1993)

Blood Thirst *See* Salem's Lot (1979)

Bloomfield *See* The Hero (1971)

Blue Sierra *See* Courage of Lassie (1946)

Bruce Brown's The Endless Summer 2 *See* The Endless Summer 2 (1994)

Buckaroo Banzai *See* The Adventures of Buckaroo Banzai Across the Eighth Dimension (1984)

Cactus Jack *See* The Villain (1979)

California Man *See* Encino Man (1992)

Carquake *See* Cannonball (1976)

The Christmas Tree *See* When Wolves Cry (1969)

Christmas Vacation *See* National Lampoon's Christmas Vacation (1989)

Code 645 *See* G-Men Never Forget (1948)

The Company of Strangers *See* Strangers in Good Company (1991)

Cop Tips Waitress $2 Million *See* It Could Happen to You (1994)

The Courage of Kavik, the Wolf Dog *See* Kavik, the Wolf Dog (1984)

Crazy Jack and the Boy *See* Silence (1973)

The Creature Wasn't Nice *See* Spaceship (1981)

Cria Cuervos *See* Cria (1976)

Crossed Swords *See* The Prince and the Pauper (1978)

Der Himmel Uber Berlin *See* Wings of Desire (1988)

Dick Tracy Meets Karloff *See* Dick Tracy Meets Gruesome (1947)

Dick Tracy's Amazing Adventure *See* Dick Tracy Meets Gruesome (1947)

Disney's Blank Check *See* Blank Check (1993)

Double Trouble *See* No Deposit, No Return (1976)

East of the Bowery *See* Follow the Leader (1944)

Emil Und Die Detektive *See* Emil and the Detective (1964)

Ercole e la Regina de Lidia *See* Hercules Unchained (1959)

Escape from the Dark *See* The Littlest Horse Thieves (1976)

European Vacation See National Lampoon's European Vacation (1985)

Evil Dead 3 See Army of Darkness (1992)

Except For Me and Thee See Friendly Persuasion (1956)

Eyewitness See Sudden Terror (1970)

The Fabulous Baron Munchausen See The Original Fabulous Adventures of Baron Munchausen (1961)

The First Great Train Robbery See The Great Train Robbery (1979)

The Flight of the White Stallions See Miracle of the White Stallions (1963)

Flipper and the Pirates See Flipper's New Adventure (1964)

Flying Aces See The Flying Deuces (1939)

Follow That Bird See Sesame Street Presents: Follow That Bird (1985)

Francis See Francis the Talking Mule (1949)

Friz Freleng's Looney Looney Looney Bugs Bunny Movie See Looney Looney Looney Bugs Bunny Movie (1981)

From the Mixed-Up Files of Mrs. Basil E. Frankweiler See The Hideaways (1973)

Galaxy Express 999 See Galaxy Express (1982)

The Ghost Creeps See Boys of the City (1940)

Gilbert Grape See What's Eating Gilbert Grape (1993)

Girl in Pawn See Little Miss Marker (1934)

Godzilla vs. Hedora See Godzilla vs. the Smog Monster (1972)

Godzilla vs. Mechagodzilla See Godzilla vs. the Cosmic Monster (1974)

Godzilla vs. the Bionic Monster See Godzilla vs. the Cosmic Monster (1974)

Gojira Tai Hedora See Godzilla vs. the Smog Monster (1972)

Gojira Tai Megaro See Godzilla vs. Megalon (1976)

Gojira Tai Meka-Gojira See Godzilla vs. the Cosmic Monster (1974)

Gokiburi See Twilight of the Cockroaches (1990)

Golden Hands of Kurigal See Federal Agents vs. Underworld, Inc. (1949)

Goodbye, Children See Au Revoir Les Enfants (1987)

Great American Bugs Bunny-Road Runner Chase See The Bugs Bunny/Road Runner Movie (1979)

The Great Balloon Adventure See Olly Olly Oxen Free (1978)

The Great Schnozzle See Palooka (1934)

Guardian of the Wilderness See Mountain Man (1977)

Haakon Haakonsen See Shipwrecked (1990)

Handle With Care See Citizens Band (1977)

Hans Christian Andersen's Thumbelina See Thumbelina (1994)

Hard Driver See The Last American Hero (1973)

Hector Servadac's Ark See On the Comet (1968)

Hercules Goes Bananas See Hercules in New York (1970)

Hercules: The Movie See Hercules in New York (1970)

Here Come the Tigers See Manny's Orphans (1978)

Hol Volt, Hol Nem Volt See A Hungarian Fairy Tale (1987)

Hollywood Cowboy See Hearts of the West (1975)

Home Front See Morgan Stewart's Coming Home (1987)

Home is Where the Heart Is See Square Dance (1987)

Hot and Cold See Weekend at Bernie's (1989)

House Without Windows See Seven Alone (1975)

Huggers See Crazy Moon (1987)

Hunchback See The Hunchback of Notre Dame (1982)

I Am a Fugitive from the Chain Gang See I Am a Fugitive from a Chain Gang (1932)

I Was a Teenage Boy See Something Special (1986)

Il Figlio del Capitano Blood See Son of Captain Blood (1962)

Il Ladro Di Bagdad See Thief of Baghdad (1961)

Il Mio Nome e Nessuno See My Name is Nobody (1974)

Il Natale Che Quasi Non Fu See The Christmas That Almost Wasn't (1966)

The Infra Superman See Infra-Man (1976)

It Happened One Summer See State Fair (1945)

Jean de Florette 2 See Manon of the Spring (1987)

Joe Palooka See Palooka (1934)

Johnny Zombie See My Boyfriend's Back (1993)

Just Ask for Diamond See Diamond's Edge (1988)

Kaiju Soshingeki See Destroy All Monsters (1968)

King of the Jungleland See Darkest Africa (1936)

Koneko Monogatari See The Adventures of Milo & Otis (1989)

La Belle et Laete See Beauty and the Beast (1946)

La Gloire de Mon Pere See My Father's Glory (1991)

La Isla Del Tesoro See Treasure Island (1972)

La Planete Sauvage See Fantastic Planet (1973)

La Tatiche de Ercole See Hercules (1958)

La Vie Devant Soi See Madame Rosa (1977)

The Lane Frost Story See 8 Seconds (1994)

Le Chateau de Ma Mere See My Mother's Castle (1991)

Le Grand Blond Avec Une Chassure Noire See The Tall Blond Man with One Black Shoe (1972)

Le Meraviglie Di Aladino See Wonders of Aladdin (1961)

Le Voleur De Bagdad See Thief of Baghdad (1961)

Legend in Leotards See Return of Captain Invincible (1983)

Legend of Cougar Canyon See The Secret of Navajo Cave (1976)

L'Enfant Sauvage See The Wild Child (1970)

Les Jeux Interdits See Forbidden Games (1952)

Les Mille Et Une Nuits See Wonders of Aladdin (1961)

Les Quatre Cents Coups See The 400 Blows (1959)

Les Vacances de Monsieur Hulot See Mr. Hulot's Holiday (1953)

L'Inafferrabile Invincible See Mr. Superinvisible (1973)

Loaded Weapon 1 See National Lampoon's Loaded Weapon 1 (1993)

Louis L'Amour's "The Shadow Riders" See The Shadow Riders (1982)

Macskafogo See Cat City (1987)

Mad Trapper of the Yukon See Challenge To Be Free (1976)

A Man in Mommy's Bed See With Six You Get Eggroll (1968)

Manhattan Project: The Deadly Game See The Manhattan Project (1986)

Manon des Sources See Manon of the Spring (1987)

Mark of the Claw See Dick Tracy's Dilemma (1947)

Mark Twain See The Adventures of Mark Twain (1985)

The Marx Brothers at the Circus See At the Circus (1939)

Mauri See Big Mo (1973)

The Medicine Hat Stallion See Peter Lundy and the Medicine Hat Stallion (1977)

Men in Tights *See* Robin Hood: Men in Tights (1993)

The Mighty Ducks 2 *See* D2: The Mighty Ducks (1994)

The Miracle of Fatima *See* Miracle of Our Lady of Fatima (1952)

Mr. Bug Goes to Town *See* Hoppity Goes to Town (1941)

Mr. Celebrity *See* Turf Boy (1942)

Mr. Invisible *See* Mr. Superinvisible (1973)

Mr. Quilp *See* The Old Curiosity Shop (1975)

Mitt Liv Som Hund *See* My Life as a Dog (1985)

A Modern Hero *See* Knute Rockne: All American (1940)

Monsieur Hulot's Holiday *See* Mr. Hulot's Holiday (1953)

Monte Carlo or Bust *See* Those Daring Young Men in Their Jaunty Jalopies (1969)

My Favourite Year *See* My Favorite Year (1982)

Na Komete *See* On the Comet (1968)

Naked Space *See* Spaceship (1981)

Neil Simon's Brighton Beach Memoirs *See* Brighton Beach Memoirs (1986)

Neil Simon's Lost in Yonkers *See* Lost in Yonkers (1993)

The Neptune Disaster *See* Neptune Factor (1973)

The Newcomers *See* The Wild Country (1971)

Ninja Dragons *See* Magic Kid (1992)

Nuovo Cinema Paradiso *See* Cinema Paradiso (1988)

The Nutcracker *See* George Balanchine's The Nutcracker (1993)

Nyoka and the Lost Secrets of Hippocrates *See* Nyoka and the Tigermen (1942)

One Cup of Coffee *See* Pastime (1991)

Out of Rosenheim *See* Bagdad Cafe (1988)

Perils from Planet Mongo *See* Flash Gordon: Rocketship (1936)

Perils of Nyoka *See* Nyoka and the Tigermen (1942)

Peter Rabbit and Tales of Beatrix Potter *See* Tales of Beatrix Potter (1971)

Phar Lap: Heart of a Nation *See* Phar Lap (1984)

Phoebe *See* Zelly & Me (1988)

Pinocchio Dans le Space *See* Pinocchio in Outer Space (1964)

Pinocchio's Adventure in Outer Space *See* Pinocchio in Outer Space (1964)

Pippi Langstrump Pa de Sju Haven *See* Pippi in the South Seas (1968)

Pony Express *See* Peter Lundy and the Medicine Hat Stallion (1977)

Preppies *See* Making the Grade (1984)

Pride of Kentucky *See* The Story of Seabiscuit (1949)

Ptang, Yang, Kipperbang *See* Kipperbang (1982)

Purple Death from Outer Space *See* Flash Gordon Conquers the Universe (1940)

Queen of Broadway *See* Kid Dynamite (1943)

Quei Temerari Sulle Loro Pazze, Scatenate, Scalcinate Carriole *See* Those Daring Young Men in Their Jaunty Jalopies (1969)

Radio Ranch *See* The Phantom Empire (1935)

Rainbow on the River *See* It Happened in New Orleans (1936)

Raise Ravens *See* Cria (1976)

Rebel with a Cause *See* The Loneliness of the Long Distance Runner (1962)

Retik, the Moon Menace *See* Radar Men from the Moon (1952)

The Revenge of Milady *See* The Four Musketeers (1975)

Ride a Dark Horse *See* Man & Boy (1971)

Rites of Summer *See* White Water Summer (1987)

Rob Roy *See* Rob Roy - The Highland Rogue (1953)

Rookies *See* Buck Privates (1941)

Rookies Come Home *See* Buck Privates Come Home (1947)

Rudyard Kipling's Jungle Book *See* The Jungle Book (1942)

Rue Cases Negres *See* Sugar Cane Alley (1983)

Sabrina Fair *See* Sabrina (1954)

Sakima and the Masked Marvel *See* The Masked Marvel (1943)

Santa Claus Defeats the Aliens *See* Santa Claus Conquers the Martians (1964)

Satan's Satellites *See* Zombies of the Stratosphere (1952)

Scrooge *See* A Christmas Carol (1951)

Season of Dreams *See* Stacking (1987)

Slaves of the Invisible Monster *See* The Invisible Monster (1950)

Slip Slide Adventures *See* Water Babies (1979)

Smokey and the Bandit Ride Again *See* Smokey and the Bandit, Part 2 (1980)

Smorgasbord *See* Cracking Up (1983)

Snow White and the Three Clowns *See* Snow White and the Three Stooges (1961)

Sombra, the Spider Woman *See* The Black Widow (1947)

Space Soldiers *See* Flash Gordon: Rocketship (1936)

Spaceship to the Unknown *See* Flash Gordon: Rocketship (1936)

Spot *See* Dog Pound Shuffle (1975)

Stakeout 2 *See* Another Stakeout (1993)

Stand and Deliver *See* Bowery Blitzkrieg (1941)

Star Child *See* Space Raiders (1983)

Starblazers *See* Space Battleship Yamato (1983)

The Super Inframan *See* Infra-Man (1976)

Superfantagenio *See* Aladdin (1986)

Superman and the Strange People *See* Superman & the Mole Men (1951)

Supersnooper *See* Super Fuzz (1981)

Surf Warriors *See* Surf Ninjas (1993)

That Man Flintstone *See* The Man Called Flintstone (1966)

Thoroughbred *See* Run for the Roses (1978)

Tim Burton's The Nightmare Before Christmas *See* The Nightmare Before Christmas (1993)

Time Flyers *See* The Blue Yonder (1986)

To Elvis, With Love *See* Touched by Love (1980)

Toto the Hero *See* Toto le Heros (1991)

Trois Hommes et un Couffin *See* Three Men and a Cradle (1985)

U-238 and the Witch Doctor *See* Jungle Drums of Africa (1953)

Un Angelo e Sceso a Brooklyn *See* The Man Who Wagged His Tail (1957)

An Underwater Odyssey *See* Neptune Factor (1973)

When Knighthood Was in Flower *See* The Sword & the Rose (1953)

When the Girls Meet the Boys *See* Girl Crazy (1943)

Wilderness Family, Part 2 *See* Further Adventures of the Wilderness Family, Part 2 (1977)

Willy Milly *See* Something Special (1986)

A Window to the Sky *See* The Other Side of the Mountain (1975)

The Worlds of Gulliver *See* The Three Worlds of Gulliver (1959)

A Yankee in King Arthur's Court *See* A Connecticut Yankee in King Arthur's Court (1949)

Intermission!

MPAA Index

The **MPAA INDEX** lists the titles of videos with their respective MPAA Rating, whether it be a G, PG, PG13, or R-rated film. A list of Unrated features is also included following the individual ratings.

G RATED

Across the Great Divide
The Adventures of Mark Twain
The Adventures of Milo & Otis
The Adventures of the Wilderness Family
Against A Crooked Sky
Airport
Aladdin
Alice in Wonderland
All Dogs Go to Heaven
All I Want for Christmas
Almos' a Man
The Amazing Dobermans
Amazing Mr. Blunden
An American Tail
An American Tail: Fievel Goes West
Amy
Andre
The Andromeda Strain
Animal Crackers
The Apple Dumpling Gang
The Apple Dumpling Gang Rides Again
Around the World in 80 Days
Babar: The Movie
Bambi
Bang Bang Kid
The Barefoot Executive
Battle for the Planet of the Apes

Battle of Britain
The Bears & I
Beauty and the Beast
Bedknobs and Broomsticks
Beneath the Planet of the Apes
The Beniker Gang
Benji
Benji the Hunted
Bernard and the Genie
Big Mo
The Billion Dollar Hobo
Black Beauty
Black Beauty
The Black Hole
The Boatniks
Bon Voyage, Charlie Brown
The Boy Friend
Boy of Two Worlds
Brian's Song
Brothers Lionheart
Brothers O'Toole
The Bugs Bunny/Road Runner Movie
Bugs Bunny Superstar
Bugs Bunny's 3rd Movie: 1,001 Rabbit Tales
Bugsy Malone
Cancel My Reservation
Candleshoe
Canine Commando
The Care Bears Movie
The Care Bears Movie 2: A New Generation
The Castaway Cowboy

The Cat from Outer Space
Challenge To Be Free
Challenge to Lassie
Change of Habit
The Charge of the Model T's
Charley and the Angel
Charlie, the Lonesome Cougar
Charlotte's Web
Cheetah
Child of Glass
Chitty Chitty Bang Bang
C.H.O.M.P.S.
Christian the Lion
The Christmas That Almost Wasn't
A Christmas to Remember
Clarence
Comic Book Kids
Computer Wizard
The Computer Wore Tennis Shoes
Courage of Lassie
Daffy Duck's Movie: Fantastic Island
Daffy Duck's Quackbusters
Danny
Darby O'Gill & the Little People
Davy Crockett and the River Pirates
Deathcheaters
Dennis the Menace: Dinosaur Hunter
Destroy All Monsters

Digby, the Biggest Dog in the World
Dr. Syn, Alias the Scarecrow
The Dog Who Stopped the War
Don't Change My World
DuckTales the Movie: Treasure of the Lost Lamp
Duncan's World
Elmer
Escape from the Planet of the Apes
Escape to Witch Mountain
The Ewok Adventure
Ferngully: The Last Rain Forest
Fiddler on the Roof
Finian's Rainbow
Fish Hawk
For the Love of Benji
The Fox and the Hound
Freaky Friday
Funny Girl
Further Adventures of the Wilderness Family, Part 2
George!
George Balanchine's The Nutcracker
The Glacier Fox
The Glenn Miller Story
Godzilla vs. Megalon
Godzilla vs. the Cosmic Monster

Godzilla vs. the Smog Monster
Golden Voyage of Sinbad
The Goodbye Bird
The Great Land of Small
The Great Mouse Detective
The Great Muppet Caper
Greenstone
Gulliver's Travels
Guns of the Magnificent Seven
Gus
Gypsy Colt
Happily Ever After
Hawmps!
Hazel's People
He is My Brother
Head
Heidi
Hell Hounds of Alaska
Hello, Dolly!
The Hellstrom Chronicle
Help!
Herbie Goes Bananas
Herbie Goes to Monte Carlo
Herbie Rides Again
Hercules in New York
Here Comes Droopy
Here Comes Garfield
High Country Calling
Homeward Bound
Homeward Bound: The Incredible Journey

Honey, I Shrunk the Kids
The Horse in the Gray Flannel Suit
Hot Lead & Cold Feet
How the West was Won
Huckleberry Finn
Hugo the Hippo
Ice Station Zebra
The Invisible Boy
The Island at the Top of the World
Jack the Giant Killer
Jason and the Argonauts
Jesus Christ, Superstar
The Jetsons: The Movie
Jiminy Cricket's Christmas
Joe Panther
Jonathan Livingston Seagull
Joni
Kid from Not-So-Big
King of the Grizzlies
Lady and the Tramp
The Land Before Time
The Land of Faraway
Lantern Hill
Lassie, Come Home
The Last Flight of Noah's Ark
The Last Unicorn
The Legend of Black Thunder Mountain
Legend of Boggy Creek
The Legend of Sleepy Hollow
Legend of the Northwest
The Legend of Young Robin Hood
Life & Times of Grizzly Adams
The Lion King
Little Boy Lost
Little Heroes
The Little Mermaid
The Little Mermaid
Little Nemo: Adventures in Slumberland
The Little Prince
The Littlest Horse Thieves
The Living Desert
Living Free
Looking for Miracles
Looney Looney Looney Bugs Bunny Movie
The Love Bug
Lt. Robin Crusoe, U.S.N.
Luggage of the Gods
Magic of Lassie
The Magic Voyage
Man & Boy
A Man for All Seasons

Man from Button Willow
Man from Clover Grove
The Man Who Skied Down Everest
Melody
Menace on the Mountain
Mickey's Christmas Carol
Million Dollar Duck
A Minor Miracle
The Misadventures of Merlin Jones
Miss Annie Rooney
Mr. Superinvisible
Mountain Family Robinson
The Muppet Christmas Carol
The Muppet Movie
Muppets Take Manhattan
The Music Man
My Father's Glory
My Neighbor Totoro
My Side of the Mountain
Neptune Factor
Never a Dull Moment
The New Adventures of Pippi Longstocking
Nikki, the Wild Dog of the North
No Deposit, No Return
No Drums, No Bugles
The North Avenue Irregulars
Now You See Him, Now You Don't
The Odd Couple
Oklahoma!
The Old Curiosity Shop
Old Yeller
Oliver!
On a Clear Day You Can See Forever
Once Upon a Forest
Once Upon a Scoundrel
The One and Only, Genuine, Original Family Band
101 Dalmatians
One Magic Christmas
One of Our Dinosaurs Is Missing
Outside Chance of Maximillian Glick
Paco
Palooka
Pepper and His Wacky Taxi
Peter Pan
Pete's Dragon
Phantom Tollbooth
Pinocchio
Pippi Goes on Board
Pippi in the South Seas

Pippi Longstocking
Pippi on the Run
The Pirates of Penzance
Pistol: The Birth of a Legend
Planet of the Apes
Pony Express Rider
Popi
Prancer
The Princess and the Goblin
The Puppetoon Movie
Race for Your Life, Charlie Brown
Raggedy Ann and Andy: A Musical Adventure
Red Riding Hood
The Rescuers
The Rescuers Down Under
Return from Witch Mountain
The Return of Jafar
Return of the Pink Panther
Return to Boggy Creek
Ride a Wild Pony
Ring of Bright Water
Robinson Crusoe & the Tiger
Rock-a-Doodle
Rover Dangerfield
Rumpelstiltskin
Running Wild
Sarah, Plain and Tall
Scandalous John
Scrooge
Sea Gypsies
The Secret Garden
The Secret of Navajo Cave
Secret of NIMH
Sesame Street Presents: Follow That Bird
Seven Alone
1776
The Seventh Voyage of Sinbad
The Shaggy D.A.
The Shaggy Dog
Shinbone Alley
Silence
The Silver Stallion: King of the Wild Brumbies
Sinbad and the Eye of the Tiger
Skylark
Sleeping Beauty
Sleeping Beauty
Smith!
Smurfs & the Magic Flute
Snoopy, Come Home
Snow Treasure
Snow White and the Seven Dwarfs

Snowball Express
Son of Captain Blood
Sounder
Star Trek: The Motion Picture
Starbird and Sweet William
The Story Lady
Summerdog
Super Seal
Superdad
Support Your Local Gunfighter
Support Your Local Sheriff
The Sword in the Stone
A Tale of Two Chipmunks
A Tale of Two Critters
Tales of Beatrix Potter
The Ten Commandments
The Tender Warrior
That Darn Cat
That's Dancing!
That's Entertainment
That's Entertainment, Part 2
That's Entertainment, Part 3
Their Only Chance
The Thief of Baghdad
Third Man on the Mountain
Those Daring Young Men in Their Jaunty Jalopies
Thumbelina
Tiger Town
Toby Tyler
Tom and Jerry: The Movie
Tom Sawyer
Transformers: The Movie
Trap on Cougar Mountain
Treasure Island
The Treasure of Matecumbe
True Grit
2000 Year Old Man
Unidentified Flying Oddball
Unsinkable Donald Duck with Huey, Dewey & Louie
The Valley of Gwangi
Wackiest Wagon Train in the West
Walt Disney Films in French
Water Babies
We of the Never Never
We're Back! A Dinosaur's Story
Whale of a Tale
What's Up, Doc?

When Dinosaurs Ruled the Earth
When the North Wind Blows
When Wolves Cry
Where the Lilies Bloom
Where the Red Fern Grows
Where the Red Fern Grows: Part 2
Where Time Began
Where's Willie?
White Fang and the Hunter
Whitewater Sam
The Wild Child
The Wild Country
Wild Hearts Can't Be Broken
Willy Wonka & the Chocolate Factory
Winnie the Pooh and a Day for Eeyore
Winnie the Pooh and Tigger Too
With Six You Get Eggroll
The Wiz
The World's Greatest Athlete
The Worst Witch
Wuthering Heights
Yellow Submarine

PG RATED
Adios Amigo
Adventures in Dinosaur City
The Adventures of a Gnome Named Gnorm
The Adventures of Baron Munchausen
The Adventures of Buckaroo Banzai Across the Eighth Dimension
The Adventures of Huck Finn
The Adventures of Sherlock Holmes' Smarter Brother
The Age of Innocence
The Air Up There
Airborne
Airplane!
Airplane 2: The Sequel
Airport '75
Airport '77
Aladdin
Alan & Naomi
All the President's Men
Allan Quartermain and the Lost City of Gold
Allegro Non Troppo
Almost an Angel
Aloha, Bobby and Rose
Aloha Summer
Always

Gumball Rally
Hadley's Rebellion
Hairspray
Hambone & Hillie
Hard Country
Hardly Working
Harley
Harper Valley P.T.A.
Harry & Son
Harry and the
  Hendersons
Harry & Walter Go to
  New York
Heart Like a Wheel
Heartbeeps
The Heartbreak Kid
Heartland
Hearts of the West
Her Alibi
Hercules
Hercules 2
The Hero
A Hero Ain't Nothin'
  But a Sandwich
Hero at Large
High Anxiety
Hocus Pocus
Home Alone
Home Alone 2: Lost in
  New York
Home Movies
Honey, I Blew Up the
  Kid
Honkytonk Man
Hook
Hoosiers
Hot Shot
Hot to Trot!
House of Wax
Housekeeping
Housesitter
Howard the Duck
Howard's End
Huck and the King of
  Hearts
The Hunchback of
  Notre Dame
The Hunt for Red
  October
Hyper-Sapien: People
  from Another Star
I Love Trouble
I Never Sang For My
  Father
I Ought to Be in
  Pictures
I Wanna Hold Your
  Hand
Ice Castles
Ice Pirates
Iceman
Improper Channels
The In Crowd
In Search of a Golden
  Sky
In the Army Now
The Incredible
  Shrinking Woman
The Incredible Two-
  Headed Transplant

Indiana Jones and the
  Last Crusade
Indiana Jones and the
  Temple of Doom
Infra-Man
Innerspace
International Velvet
Into the West
Invaders from Mars
Invasion of the Body
  Snatchers
Iron Will
Irreconcilable
  Differences
Island of Dr. Moreau
It Came from
  Hollywood
It Could Happen to
  You
Jabberwocky
Jane & the Lost City
Jean de Florette
Jeremiah Johnson
The Jewel of the Nile
Jimmy the Kid
Joe Versus the Volcano
Joey
The Journey of Natty
  Gann
Journey to Spirit Island
Journey to the Center
  of the Earth
Junior Bonner
Just Tell Me You Love
  Me
Just the Way You Are
The Karate Kid
The Karate Kid: Part 2
The Karate Kid: Part 3
Kidco
King Kong
King of the Wind
King Ralph
Kipperbang
Kiss Me Goodbye
Knights & Emeralds
Kotch
Kramer vs. Kramer
Krull
Labyrinth
Land That Time Forgot
Lassie
The Last American
  Hero
The Last Starfighter
Lawrence of Arabia
Leader of the Band
A League of Their
  Own
The Learning Tree
Legend
Legend of the Lone
  Ranger
The Legend of Wolf
  Mountain
Leonard Part 6
Liar's Moon
Lies My Father Told
  Me
Life with Mikey

Lightning: The White
  Stallion
The Lion in Winter
Lionheart
Little Big League
Little Big Man
Little Buddha
The Little Girl Who
  Lives Down the Lane
Little Man Tate
Little Miss Marker
Little Miss Millions
Little Monsters
Little Nikita
The Little Rascals
A Little Romance
Live and Let Die
Local Hero
The Long Day Closes
The Lord of the Rings
The Lords of Flatbush
Lost in Yonkers
Love and Death
Love at First Bite
Mac and Me
MacArthur
Madame Rosa
Magic Kid
Maid to Order
The Main Event
Major League 2
Making Contact
Making the Grade
The Man from Snowy
  River
Man of La Mancha
The Man Who Would
  Be King
The Man with One Red
  Shoe
The Man with the
  Golden Gun
Man, Woman & Child
Mannequin
Mannequin 2: On the
  Move
Manny's Orphans
Manon of the Spring
Mario
Marvin & Tige
Masters of the
  Universe
Matilda
Matinee
Maverick
Max Dugan Returns
Meatballs
The Meteor Man
A Midnight Clear
Midnight Madness
The Mighty Ducks
The Miracle
Miss Firecracker
Mr. Mom
Mr. Nanny
Mr. North
Misunderstood
Modern Problems
Mom and Dad Save
  the World

Mommie Dearest
The Money Pit
Monkey Trouble
Monty Python and the
  Holy Grail
Moon-Spinners
Moonraker
More American Graffiti
Movie, Movie
Munchie
Munchies
My American Cousin
My Best Friend Is a
  Vampire
My Bodyguard
My Father the Hero
My Favorite Year
My Girl
My Girl 2
My Grandpa is a
  Vampire
My Heroes Have
  Always Been
  Cowboys
My Mom's a Werewolf
My Mother's Castle
My Name is Nobody
My Science Project
Mystery Mansion
Nate and Hayes
The Natural
The Navigator
Never Cry Wolf
Never Say Never
  Again
The NeverEnding Story
The NeverEnding Story
  2: Next Chapter
Newsies
The Next Karate Kid
Night Crossing
The Night the Lights
  Went Out in Georgia
The Nightmare Before
  Christmas
Norma Rae
North
Nothing in Common
Nukie
Octopussy
Ode to Billy Joe
Off Beat
Oh, God!
Oh, God! Book 2
Oh, God! You Devil
Oh, Heavenly Dog!
Oklahoma Crude
Old Enough
On Golden Pond
On Her Majesty's
  Secret Service
On the Right Track
Once Upon a Crime
Once Upon a Time in
  the West
One Crazy Summer
One on One
Only the Lonely
Oscar

The Other Side of the
  Mountain
The Other Side of the
  Mountain, Part 2
Out of Time
Out on a Limb
The Outlaw Josey
  Wales
The Outsiders
Over the Edge
Over the Top
Overboard
Paint Your Wagon
The Paper Chase
Paper Moon
Papillon
Pastime
The Peanut Butter
  Solution
Pee Wee's Big
  Adventure
The People That Time
  Forgot
Phar Lap
Piece of the Action
The Pink Panther
  Strikes Again
Pirate Movie
Places in the Heart
Plain Clothes
Planet of the Dinosaurs
Play It Again, Sam
Pogo for President: "I
  Go Pogo"
The Polar Bear King
Police Academy 3:
  Back in Training
Police Academy 4:
  Citizens on Patrol
Police Academy 5:
  Assignment Miami
  Beach
Police Academy 6: City
  Under Siege
Poltergeist
Popeye
The Poseidon
  Adventure
Prehysteria
The Prime of Miss Jean
  Brodie
The Prince and the
  Pauper
Princess and the
  Goblin
The Princess Bride
The Private Eyes
Prize Fighter
Problem Child
The Prodigal
Project X
The Projectionist
Promises in the Dark
Purple People Eater
The Purple Rose of
  Cairo
Queen of Hearts
The Quest
Racing with the Moon
Rad

VIDEOHOUND'S FAMILY VIDEO RETRIEVER

Radio Days
Raiders of the Lost Ark
A Rare Breed
Real Genius
The Reivers
The Remains of the
   Day
Remote
The Rescue
Return of Captain
   Invincible
Return of the Jedi
The Return of the
   Musketeers
Return to Oz
Return to Snowy River
Revenge of the Pink
   Panther
Rhinestone
Rich Kids
The Right Stuff
The River
The River Rat
A River Runs Through It
Robin and Marian
Robot Jox
Rock 'n' Roll High
   School
Rocket Gibraltar
The Rocketeer
Rocky
Rocky 2
Rocky 3
Rocky 4
Rocky 5
Romancing the Stone
Romeo and Juliet
Rookie of the Year
Rooster Cogburn
The Rousters
Roxanne
Rudy
Run for the Roses
Running Brave
Russkies
Ryan's Daughter
Salem's Lot
Samantha
Sam's Son
The Sandlot
Santa Claus: The
   Movie
Saturday the 14th
Savannah Smiles
Searching for Bobby
   Fischer
The Secret Garden
Secret Places
A Separate Peace
Seven Minutes in
   Heaven
7 Ninja Kids
The Shadow Riders
Shadowlands
Shag: The Movie
Sheena
Shipwrecked
The Shootist
Short Circuit
Short Circuit 2

Sidekicks
Silence of the North
Silent Movie
The Silver Streak
Simon
Sister Act
Sister Act 2: Back in
   the Habit
Six Pack
Six Weeks
Sixteen Candles
Skateboard
The Skateboard Kid
Ski Patrol
Sleeper
Sleepless in Seattle
Sleuth
Small Change
Smile
Smokey and the Bandit
Smokey and the
   Bandit, Part 2
Smokey and the
   Bandit, Part 3
Something Wicked This
   Way Comes
Somewhere in Time
Somewhere Tomorrow
Son of the Pink
   Panther
Space Raiders
Spaceballs
SpaceCamp
Spaced Invaders
Spaceship
Spies Like Us
Spirit of the Eagle
Splash
The Spy Who Loved
   Me
Stacking
Stand and Deliver
Star Trek 2: The Wrath
   of Khan
Star Trek 3: The
   Search for Spock
Star Trek 4: The
   Voyage Home
Star Trek 5: The Final
   Frontier
Star Trek 6: The
   Undiscovered Country
Star Wars
Starchaser: The Legend
   of Orin
Starman
Starship
Steel Magnolias
The Sting
The Sting 2
The Stone Boy
Straight Talk
Strange Invaders
Strangers in Good
   Company
Strictly Ballroom
Suburban Commando
Sudden Terror
Sugar Cane Alley
Summer Rental

A Summer to
   Remember
Sundance and the Kid
The Sunshine Boys
Super Fuzz
Super Mario Bros.
Super Mario Bros.
   Super Show 1
Supergirl
Superman 1: The
   Movie
Superman 2
Superman 3
Superman 4: The
   Quest for Peace
Surf Ninjas
Swamp Thing
The Swarm
Sweet Liberty
Swing Shift
Sword of the Valiant
Sylvester
Table for Five
Take Down
Take the Money and
   Run
Talent for the Game
The Tall Blond Man
   with One Black Shoe
Tank
Taps
Teen Alien
Teen Wolf
Teen Wolf Too
Teenage Mutant Ninja
   Turtles 1: The Movie
Teenage Mutant Ninja
   Turtles 2: The Secret
   of the Ooze
Teenage Mutant Ninja
   Turtles 3
Ten Little Indians
Tender Mercies
Terms of Endearment
Terror in the Jungle
Tess
Tex
That Sinking Feeling
They Went That-a-Way
   & That-a-Way
Those Calloways
Three Amigos
The Three Lives of
   Thomasina
Three Men and a
   Baby
Three Men and a Little
   Lady
Three Musketeers
The Three Musketeers
3 Ninjas
3 Ninjas Kick Back
Three O'Clock High
Thunderball
Thursday's Game
Tilt
Time Bandits
Time of Tears
Timerider
Toby McTeague

Tommy
Tootsie
Top Gun
Touched by Love
Tough Guys
The Toy
Trading Hearts
Trading Mom
Trail of the Pink
   Panther
Treasure Island
The Trip to Bountiful
Tron
Troop Beverly Hills
Truly, Madly, Deeply
Tucker: The Man and
   His Dream
Turner and Hooch
Turtle Diary
Twelve Chairs
Twice Upon a Time
Twilight Zone: The
   Movie
Twist
2010 : The Year We
   Make Contact
Uncle Buck
Under the Rainbow
Vice Versa
Victory
A View to a Kill
The Villain
The Voyage of the Yes
Waiting for the Light
Walk Like a Man
War Games
Warriors of the Wind
Watcher in the Woods
Watership Down
The Way We Were
Wee Willie Winkie
Weekend at Bernie's 2
What About Bob?
When the Whales
   Came
Where the River Runs
   Black
Where the Spirit Lives
White Fang
White Fang 2: The
   Myth of the White
   Wolf
White Water Summer
Who Framed Roger
   Rabbit?
Willow
The Wind and the Lion
A Winner Never Quits
The Witches
Witches' Brew
The Wizard
The Wizard of Speed
   and Time
Wizards
Wizards of the Lost
   Kingdom
Wizards of the Lost
   Kingdom 2
A World Apart
Xanadu

Yentl
You Only Live Twice
Young Einstein
Young Frankenstein
Zelly & Me
Zero to Sixty

PG13 RATED
Ace Ventura: Pet
   Detective
Across the Tracks
The Addams Family
Addams Family Values
Adventures in
   Babysitting
Adventures in Spying
Airheads
American Anthem
American Boyfriends
American Flyers
Amos and Andrew
Another Stakeout
Arachnophobia
Arena
Aspen Extreme
Back to School
Bad Medicine
Batman
Batman Returns
Beastmaster 2: Through
   the Portal of Time
Bebe's Kids
Beverly Hills Brats
Big Shots
Big Trouble in Little
   China
Black Magic
Blame It on the Night
Blankman
Blue Chips
Book of Love
Bopha!
Breaking the Rules
Brighton Beach
   Memoirs
Buffy the Vampire
   Slayer
The Butcher's Wife
Cabin Boy
Calendar Girl
Can't Buy Me Love
Captain America
Captain Ron
Car 54, Where Are
   You?
Cat's Eye
Chaplin
City Slickers
City Slickers 2: The
   Legend of Curly's
   Gold
Clara's Heart
Class Act
Clean Slate
The Client
Club Paradise
Cocoon
Coupe de Ville
Crazy Moon
Critters

Crocodile Dundee
Crooklyn
Crusoe
Cry-Baby
Dances with Wolves
Dave
A Day in October
Death Becomes Her
Desperately Seeking
 Susan
Dirty Dancing
Diving In
Doc Hollywood
Doin' Time on Planet
 Earth
Dominick & Eugene
Don't Tell Mom the
 Babysitter's Dead
The Double O Kid
The Dove
Dragnet
Dragon: The Bruce Lee
 Story
Dream a Little Dream
Dream Date
The Dream Team
Drop Dead Fred
Dutch
Edward Scissorhands
8 Seconds
Enemy Mine
Erik the Viking
F/X 2: The Deadly Art
 of Illusion
Face the Music
Far and Away
A Far Off Place
Fatal Instinct
Father Hood
Ferris Bueller's Day Off
The Fifth Monkey
Fire in the Sky
First Born
The Flamingo Kid
For Keeps
Forrest Gump
1492: Conquest of
 Paradise
Freaked
The Fugitive
The Gate
Geronimo: An
 American Legend
Ghost
Ghoulies
Gleaming the Cube
The Golden Child
Gorillas in the Mist
Gotcha!
Greedy
Green Card
Gremlins 2: The New
 Batch
Gross Anatomy
Grumpy Old Men
Gung Ho
Heart and Souls
Heartbreak Hotel
The Heavenly Kid
Hero

Hiding Out
Highlander: The
 Gathering
Holy Matrimony
A Home of Our Own
Honeymoon in Vegas
Hope and Glory
Hot Shots! Part Deux
House of Cards
How I Got into
 College
If Looks Could Kill
I'll Do Anything
Immediate Family
Indian Summer
Jack the Bear
Jersey Girl
Johnny Dangerously
Josh and S.A.M.
Jurassic Park
Just One of the Guys
K-9
Kindergarten Cop
King of the Hill
Kuffs
La Bamba
L.A. Story
The Lady in White
Ladybugs
Ladyhawke
Last Action Hero
The Last Prostitute
Lean on Me
Leap of Faith
Legend of Billie Jean
License to Drive
Light of Day
Lightning Jack
Like Father, Like Son
Lisa
Little Shop of Horrors
Little Sister
The Little Thief
The Longshot
Look Who's Talking
Look Who's Talking
 Now
Look Who's Talking,
 Too
Lords of Magick
Lorenzo's Oil
Love Your Mama
Lucas
Mad Max: Beyond
 Thunderdome
Madame Sousatzka
Made in America
Madhouse
Making Mr. Right
Malcolm X
The Man in the Moon
The Man Without a
 Face
The Manhattan Project
Martians Go Home!
Mask
The Mask
Meet the Hollowheads
Memoirs of an Invisible
 Man

Men Don't Leave
Mermaids
Metropolitan
Mrs. Doubtfire
Mr. & Mrs. Bridge
Mr. Baseball
Mr. Destiny
Mr. Wonderful
The Monster Squad
Moonstruck
Morgan Stewart's
 Coming Home
Moving Violations
Much Ado About
 Nothing
Murphy's Romance
My Boyfriend's Back
My Life
My Stepmother Is an
 Alien
Mystery Date
The Naked Gun: From
 the Files of Police
 Squad
Naked Gun 2 1/2: The
 Smell of Fear
Naked Gun 33 1/3:
 The Final Insult
National Lampoon's
 Christmas Vacation
National Lampoon's
 European Vacation
National Lampoon's
 Loaded Weapon 1
The Night Before
Night of the Comet
No Big Deal
No Holds Barred
Norman's Awesome
 Experience
Odd Jobs
Of Mice and Men
Oh, What a Night
Only You
Opportunity Knocks
Oxford Blues
Paradise
Parenthood
P.C.U.
Peggy Sue Got
 Married
The Pelican Brief
A Perfect World
Permanent Record
Philadelphia
Pink Cadillac
The Playboys
Police Academy 2:
 Their First Assignment
Poltergeist 2: The
 Other Side
Poltergeist 3
The Power of One
Prelude to a Kiss
Pretty in Pink
Princes in Exile
Problem Child 2
Quigley Down Under
Radio Flyer
The Real McCoy

Reality Bites
Regarding Henry
Remo Williams: The
 Adventure Begins
Renaissance Man
The Return of Swamp
 Thing
Reunion
Rich in Love
Robin Hood: Men in
 Tights
Robin Hood: Prince of
 Thieves
Robocop 3
Rock 'n' Roll High
 School Forever
Running Mates
Running on Empty
Sarafina!
Satisfaction
Say Anything
School Ties
Scrooged
Secret of the Ice Cave
See You in the
 Morning
The Shadow
Shadow of the Wolf
She-Devil
She's Having a Baby
Shout
Silverado
Sing
Singles
Smooth Talk
Sneakers
So I Married an Axe
 Murderer
Solarbabies
Some Kind of
 Wonderful
Something Special
Sommersby
Son-in-Law
Soul Man
Square Dance
Stay Tuned
Stepmonster
Stop! or My Mom Will
 Shoot
Summer School
The Sure Thing
Swing Kids
Teen Witch
That Night
The Thing Called Love
Think Big
This is My Life
Thrashin'
Three Fugitives
Three Men and a
 Cradle
Throw Momma from
 the Train
Toto le Heros
Toys
Troll
Turk 182!
Undercover Blues
Untamed Heart

Up Against the Wall
Wagons East
Wait Until Spring,
 Bandini
Wayne's World
Wayne's World 2
Weekend at Bernie's
Weird Science
Welcome Home, Roxy
 Carmichael
What's Eating Gilbert
 Grape
The Willies
Wind
Wings of Desire
With Honors
The Wizard of
 Loneliness
The Year My Voice
 Broke
Year of the Comet
Young Sherlock Holmes
The Zoo Gang

R RATED
Above the Rim
Alive
All the Right Moves
Alligator
American Heart
Angelo My Love
Army of Darkness
Backbeat
The Bay Boy
Beverly Hills Cop
Beverly Hills Cop 2
Beverly Hills Cop 3
Boyz N the Hood
The Breakfast Club
A Bronx Tale
Bustin' Loose
Caddyshack
The Commitments
Conan the Barbarian
The Crow
The Crush
Darkman
Dazed and Confused
F/X
Fame
Fast Times at
 Ridgemont High
Flashdance
Flirting
Four Weddings and a
 Funeral
Foxes
The Good Son
Highlander
Highlander 2: The
 Quickening
House
House Party
House Party 2: The
 Pajama Jam
House Party 3
The Howling
The Joy Luck Club
The Last of the
 Mohicans

Little Darlings
Lord of the Flies
The Lost Boys
Major League
M*A*S*H
Menace II Society
The Paper
Poetic Justice
Police Academy
The Program
Rain Man
Rambling Rose
Revenge of the Nerds
Robocop
Robocop 2
Rumble Fish
Secret Admirer
Serial Mom
The Snapper
Speed
Stand By Me
The Terminator
Terminator 2: Judgment
   Day
That Was Then. . .This
   Is Now
This Boy's Life
Tombstone
True Lies
Valley Girl
Walking Tall
What's Love Got to
   Do With It?
Wildcats
Young Guns
Zebrahead

UNRATED
Abbott and Costello
   Cartoon Festival
Abbott and Costello
   Meet Captain Kidd
Abbott and Costello
   Meet Dr. Jekyll and
   Mr. Hyde
Abbott and Costello
   Meet Frankenstein
Abel's Island
The Absent-Minded
   Professor
Adam's Rib
Adventures in
   Dinosaurland
Adventures in Odyssey:
   The Knight Travellers
The Adventures of a
   Two-Minute Werewolf
The Adventures of an
   American Rabbit
The Adventures of
   Babar
Adventures of Black
   Beauty
The Adventures of
   Bullwhip Griffin
Adventures of Buster
   the Bear
Adventures of Captain
   Future

The Adventures of
   Captain Marvel
The Adventures of
   Charlie and Cubby
The Adventures of
   Curious George
The Adventures of
   Frank and Jesse
   James
The Adventures of
   Frontier Fremont
The Adventures of
   Huckleberry Finn
Adventures of Little
   Koala: Laura and the
   Mystery Egg
Adventures of Little
   Lulu and Tubby
Adventures of Mighty
   Mouse, Vol. 1
The Adventures of
   Oliver Twist
The Adventures of
   Peter Cottontail
The Adventures of
   Peter Cottontail and
   His Friends of the
   Green Forest
Adventures of
   Pinocchio
The Adventures of
   Pinocchio
The Adventures of
   Raggedy Ann &
   Andy: Pirate
   Adventure
Adventures of Red
   Ryder
Adventures of Reddy
   the Fox
The Adventures of
   Robin Hood
The Adventures of
   Rocky & Bullwinkle:
   Birth of Bullwinkle
The Adventures of
   Sinbad the Sailor
Adventures of Smilin'
   Jack
The Adventures of
   SuperTed
The Adventures of
   Teddy Ruxpin
The Adventures of the
   Ding-A-Ling Brothers
Adventures of the
   Flying Cadets
The Adventures of the
   Little Koala and
   Friends
The Adventures of the
   Little Prince
Adventures of the Little
   Prince
The Adventures of Tin
   Tin
The Adventures of Tom
   Sawyer
Adventures of Tom
   Sawyer

The Adventures of
   Ultraman
The Adventures of
   Walt Disney's Alice
Aesop and His Friends
Aesop's Fables
Aesop's Fables: The
   Boy Who Cried
   Wolf/The Wolf and
   the Lamb
Aesop's Fables, Vol. 1:
   The Hen with the
   Golden Egg
Africa Screams
Africa Texas Style
African Journey
The African Queen
Ah, Wilderness!
Aladdin and His Magic
   Lamp
Aladdin and the Magic
   Lamp
Aladdin and the
   Wonderful Lamp
Alakazam the Great!
Ali Baba and the Forty
   Thieves
Ali Baba's Revenge
Alice in Wonderland
Alice in Wonderland in
   Paris
Alice's Adventures in
   Wonderland
All New Adventures of
   Tom Sawyer: Mischief
   on the Mississippi
All This and Tex Avery
   Too!
Alligator Pie
Almost Angels
Alvin & the Chipmunks:
   A Chipmunk
   Christmas
Alvin & the Chipmunks:
   Alvin's Christmas
   Carol
Alvin & the Chipmunks:
   Batmunk
Amahl and the Night
   Visitors
Amazing Adventures of
   Joe 90
The Amazing Spider-
   Man
An American Christmas
   Carol
American Folk Heroes
   and Tall Tales
An American in Paris
An American Summer
Anansi
Anchors Aweigh
And Baby Makes Six
And Now Miguel
And the Children Shall
   Lead
Androcles and the Lion
Andy and the Airwave
   Rangers

Andy Hardy Gets
   Spring Fever
Andy Hardy Meets
   Debutante
Andy Hardy's Double
   Life
Andy Hardy's Private
   Secretary
Animal Farm
Animals Are Beautiful
   People
Animalympics: Winter
   Games
Anne of Avonlea
Anne of Green Gables
Annie Oakley
The Ant and the
   Aardvark
Antarctica
Archie, Vol. 1
Ariel's Undersea
   Adventure, Vol. 1:
   Whale of a Tale
Arnold of the Ducks
Around the World in
   80 Days
Asterix: Asterix the
   Gaul
At the Circus
Atom Man vs.
   Superman
Attic In the Blue
Babar and Father
   Christmas
Babar Comes to
   America
Babar: Monkey
   Business
Babar Returns
Babar the Elephant
   Comes to America
Babar the Little
   Elephant
Babar's First Step
Babar's Triumph
Babes in Arms
Babes in Toyland
Babes on Broadway
The Baby-Sitter's Club
Baby, Take a Bow
Bach & Broccoli
The Bachelor and the
   Bobby-Soxer
Back Home
Back to Hannibal: The
   Further Adventures of
   Tom Sawyer and
   Huckleberry Finn
The Bad Seed
The Ballad of Paul
   Bunyan
Ballet Shoes
The Band Wagon
Barnaby and Me
Barney & Friends:
   Barney Rhymes with
   Mother Goose
Barney & Friends:
   Barney's Best
   Manners

Barney & the Backyard
   Gang
Barney in Concert
Barney's Christmas
   Surprise
Baron Munchausen
Battle for Moon
   Station Dallos
Battle of the Bullies
Battling with Buffalo
   Bill
B.C.: A Special
   Christmas
B.C.: The First
   Thanksgiving
Be My Valentine,
   Charlie Brown/Is This
   Goodbye, Charlie
   Brown?
Beach Blanket Bingo
Beach Party
Beauty and the Beast
Bedrock Wedlock
Bedrockin' and Rappin'
Beetle Bailey: Military
   Madness
The Bellboy
The Belle of New York
The Belles of St.
   Trinian's
The Bells of St. Mary's
The Belstone Fox
Ben and Me
Benji at Work
Benji's Very Own
   Christmas Story
The Berenstain Bears'
   Christmas
Berenstain Bears'
   Comic Valentine
Berenstain Bears'
   Easter Surprise
Berenstain Bears Meet
   Big Paw
The Best Christmas
   Pageant Ever
The Best of Betty
   Boop, Vol. 1
The Best of Betty
   Boop, Vol. 2
Best of Bugs Bunny &
   Friends
The Best of Gumby
The Best of Terrytoons
Bethie's Really Silly
   Clubhouse
Betty Boop
Betty Boop Special
   Collector's Edition:
   Volume 1
Beverly Hills Teens
Big Bird in China
Big Bird in Japan
Big Red
The Big Store
Bigfoot and Wildboy
Bikini Beach
Bill
Bill and Coo
Bill: On His Own

Billie
A Billion for Boris
Billy Bunny's Animal Song
Billy Possum
The Birds
The Black Arrow
Black Beauty
The Black Planet
The Black Tulip
The Black Widow
Blackbeard's Ghost
Blackstar
Blake of Scotland Yard
Blood Brothers
The Blue Bird
Blue Fire Lady
Blue Murder at St. Trinian's
The Blue Yonder
Blues Busters
Bluetoes the Christmas Elf
The Bluffers: Fantasy-Filled Adventure Begins
The Bluffers: Mystery of Clandestino's Castle
BMX Bandits
Bob the Quail
Bobby Goldsboro's Easter Egg Mornin'
Bobby Raccoon
Bobobobs: Around the Galaxy in 80 Days
The Bollo Caper
Bongo
Boo-Busters
Born Free
Born to Run
Bowery Blitzkrieg
Bowery Buckaroos
Box of Delights
The Boy God
Boy Takes Girl
The Boy Who Drew Cats
The Boy Who Left Home to Find Out About the Shivers
The Boy Who Loved Trolls
The Boy with the Green Hair
Boyd's Shadow
Boys of the City
Boys Town
Bozo the Clown: Ding Dong Dandy Adventures
Brain 17
The Brave Little Toaster
Bravestarr: The Legend Returns
Breakin' Through
Breaking the Ice
Brer Rabbit and Boss Lion

Brer Rabbit and the Wonderful Tar Baby
Brer Rabbit Tales
The Bridge on the River Kwai
Bridge to Terabithia
Bringing Up Baby
Brother Future
Bubbe's Boarding House: Chanukah at Bubbe's
Buck Privates
Buck Privates Come Home
Buck Rogers Conquers the Universe
Bucky O'Hare: Bye-Bye Berserker Baboon
Bugs Bunny: All American Hero
Bugs Bunny Cartoon Festival
Bugs Bunny: Festival of Fun
The Bulldozer Brigade
Bunnicula: Vampire Rabbit
Burn 'Em Up Barnes
The Bushbaby
Buttons and Rusty Series
Bye, Bye, Birdie
The Cabbage Patch Kid's First Christmas
Caddie Woodlawn
The Caddy
Caldecott Collection
The California Raisins: Meet the Raisins
Camel Boy
Camelot
Cannon Movie Tales: The Emperor's New Clothes
The Canterville Ghost
Cantinflas
Captain America
Captain America 2: Death Too Soon
Captain Blood
Captain Harlock, Vol. 1
Captain January
Captain Kangaroo & His Friends
Captain Kangaroo's Merry Christmas Stories
Captain Planet & the Planeteers: A Hero for Earth
Captain Pugwash
Captain Scarlet vs. The Mysterons
Captains Courageous
The Capture of Grizzly Adams
Care Bears: Family Storybook
Carnival of the Animals

Carousel
Cartoons for Big Kids
Casey at the Bat
Casper's Halloween
The Cat
Cat City
The Cat in the Hat
The Cat in the Hat Comes Back
The Cat in the Hat Gets Grinched
Charade
Charlie and the Great Balloon Chase
The Charlie Brown and Snoopy Show: Vol. 1
A Charlie Brown Christmas
Charmkins
Chatterer the Squirrel
Children's Heroes of the Bible: Story of Jesus
Child's Christmas in Wales
A Child's Garden of Verses
Chip 'n' Dale Animated Antics Series
Chip 'n' Dale Rescue Rangers: Crimebusters
Chipmunk and His Bird Friends
Chips the War Dog
Chocolate Fever
A Christmas Carol
Christmas Cartoons
The Christmas Collection
Christmas Comes to Willow Creek
Christmas Eve on Sesame Street
A Christmas Fantasy
The Christmas Messenger
The Christmas Party
Christmas Stories
A Christmas Story
The Christmas Toy
The Christmas Tree
A Christmas Tree/Puss-In-Boots
Christmas Video Sing-Along
Christopher's Xmas Mission
Christy
The Chronicles of Narnia
Chuck Amuck: The Movie
Cinderella
Cinderfella
Cindy Eller
Cinema Paradiso
Circus Angel
Citizen Kane
City Boy

City Lights
Clarence, the Cross-eyed Lion
Classic Fairy Tales
The Classic Tales Collection
Clifford's Fun with Numbers
Clifford's Singalong Adventure
Clipped Wings
Clowning Around
Clowning Around 2
Clue You In: The Case of the Mad Movie Mustacher
The Clutching Hand
C.L.U.T.Z.
The Cocoanuts
Comeback Kid
A Connecticut Yankee
A Connecticut Yankee in King Arthur's Court
Conspiracy of Love
COPS: Crime Doesn't Pay
Corduroy and Other Bear Stories
The Corn is Green
The Cosmic Eye
The Count of Monte Cristo
Country Girl
Country Music with the Muppets
Country Rock
Courage of Black Beauty
Courage of the North
The Court Jester
The Courtship of Eddie's Father
The Cricket in Times Square
The Crimson Ghost
Curious George
Curley
Curly Top
Daddy Long Legs
The Dancing Frog
Danger Mouse, Vol. 1
Daniel and the Towers
Daredevils of the Red Circle
Darkest Africa
Davey and Goliath
David and Goliath
David and Lisa
David and the Magic Pearl
David Copperfield
David the Gnome
Davy Crockett
A Day at the Races
A Day for Thanks on Walton's Mountain
The Day Jimmy's Boa Ate the Wash and Other Stories
Daydreamer

Dear Brigitte
Death of a Goldfish
Death of the Incredible Hulk
Defenders of the Earth: The Story Begins
Defenders of the Vortex
The Delicate Delinquent
Dennis the Menace in Mayday for Mother
Dennis the Menace: Spies, Robbers and Ghosts
Dennis the Movie Star
A Dentist and a Toothfairy
Denver the Last Dinosaur
Devil Horse
Dial "M" for Murder
Diamonds on Wheels
Dick Deadeye
Dick Tracy
Dick Tracy, Detective
Dick Tracy Meets Gruesome
Dick Tracy Returns
Dick Tracy vs. Crime Inc.
Dick Tracy vs. Cueball
Dick Tracy's Dilemma
Did I Ever Tell You How Lucky You Are?
Dinky: Dinky Finds a Home
Dinky: Much Ado About Nothing
Dinosaurs, Dinosaurs, Dinosaurs
Disney's Adventures in Wonderland
Disney's Darkwing Duck: His Favorite Adventures
Disney's Greatest Lullabies
Disney's Haunted Halloween
Disney's Sing-Along Songs: The Twelve Days of Christmas
Disney's Sing-Along Songs, Vol. 1: Heigh-Ho
Disney's Sing-Along Songs, Vol. 2: Zip-A-Dee-Doo-Dah
Disney's Sing-Along Songs, Vol. 3: You Can Fly!
Disney's Sing-Along Songs, Vol. 4: The Bare Necessities
Disney's Sing-Along Songs, Vol. 5: Fun with Music
Disney's Sing-Along Songs, Vol. 6: Under the Sea

Disney's Sing-Along Songs, Vol. 7: Disneyland Fun
Disney's Sing-Along Songs, Vol. 8: Very Merry Christmas Songs
Disney's Sing-Along Songs, Vol. 9: I Love to Laugh!
Disney's Sing-Along Songs, Vol. 10: Be Our Guest
Disney's Sing-Along Songs, Vol. 11: Friend Like Me
Disney's TaleSpin, Vol. 1: True Baloo
Disney's Wonderful World of Winter
The Disorderly Orderly
Doctor Doolittle
Dr. Seuss' ABC
Dr. Seuss' Butter Battle Book
Dr. Seuss' Caldecotts
Dr. Seuss' Cat in the Hat
Dr. Seuss' Hoober-Bloob Highway
Dr. Seuss' Horton Hears a Who/How the Grinch Stole Christmas
Dr. Seuss: I Am NOT Going to Get Up Today!
Dr. Seuss on the Loose
Dr. Seuss Sleep Book
Dr. Seuss' The Lorax
Dr. Strange
Doctor Who: An Unearthly Child
Doctor Who and the Daleks
Doctor Zhivago
The Dog Days of Arthur Cane
A Dog of Flanders
The Dog Who Dared
Don Cooper: Sing-Along Story Songs
Don Winslow of the Coast Guard
Don Winslow of the Navy
Donny Deinonychus: The Educational Dinosaur, Vol. 1
Don't Eat the Pictures: Sesame Street at the Metropolitan Museum of Art
Don't Wake Your Mom
The Donut Repair Club: On Tour
Dorothy in the Land of Oz
Dot & Keeto
Dot & Santa Claus

Dot & the Kangaroo
Dot & the Koala
Dot & the Smugglers
Dot & the Whale
Doug, Vol. 1: How Did I Get Into This Mess?
The Doughnuts
A Dream for Christmas
Dreaming of Paradise
Duck Soup
DuckTales: Accidental Adventurers
Dumbo
Dusty
East of Eden
East of the Sun, West of the Moon
Easter Bunny is Coming to Town
Easter Egg Mornin'
Easter Parade
Edison Twins
8 Sesame Street Stories
Elephant Boy
The ElmChanted Forest
Emil and the Detective
Emmet Otter's Jug-Band Christmas
The Emperor's New Clothes
The Emperor's New Clothes and Other Folktales
Encyclopedia Brown: Case of the Missing Time Capsule
The Endless Summer
EPIC: Days of the Dinosaurs
The Ernest Green Story
The Errand Boy
Escapade in Florence
Escapade in Japan
Escape of the One-Ton Pet
The Ewoks: Battle for Endor
The Ezra Jack Keats Library
Fabulous Joe
Faeries
A Family Circus Christmas
Family Circus Easter
Family Jewels
Famous Five Get into Trouble
Fangface
Fangface Spooky Spoofs
Fantasia
The Fantastic Adventures of Unico
The Fantastic World of D.C. Collins
Farmer Alfalfa Show & Play Your Hunch
The Farmer's Daughter

Fat Albert & the Cosby Kids, Vol. 1
Father Figure
Father of the Bride
Father's Little Dividend
Fatty Finn
Federal Agents vs. Underworld, Inc.
Felix the Cat: An Hour of Fun
Felix the Cat: The Movie
Ferdy
Fievel's American Tails: A Mouse Known as Zorrowitz/Aunt Sophie's Visit
50 Classic All-Star Cartoons, Vol. 1
50 Classic All-Star Cartoons, Vol. 2
50 Degrees Below Zero
50 Simple Things Kids Can Do to Save the Earth, Parts 1 & 2
The Fig Tree
Fighting Devil Dogs
Fighting Marines
The Fighting Prince of Donegal
Fighting with Kit Carson
Finn McCoul
The Fire in the Stone
Fireman Sam: Hero Next Door
The First Christmas
The First Easter Rabbit
First Men in the Moon
Fisher-Price Grimm's Fairy Tales: Briar Rose
Fisherman's Wharf
Five Lionni Classics
Five Sesame Street Stories
The 5000 Fingers of Dr. T
The Flame Trees of Thika
Flaming Frontiers
The Flash
Flash Gordon Conquers the Universe
Flash Gordon: Rocketship
Flash Gordon: Vol. 1
Flash, the Teenage Otter
Flight of Dragons
Flight of the Grey Wolf
The Flintstone Kids
The Flintstone Kids: "Just Say No"
The Flintstones

The Flintstones: Fred Flintstone Woos Again
The Flintstones: Rappin' n' Rhymin'
Flipper
Flipper's New Adventure
Flipper's Odyssey
Flower Angel
Flower Drum Song
The Flying Deuces
Flying Wild
Follow Me, Boys!
Follow that Bunny!
Follow That Sleigh!
Follow the Fleet
Follow the Leader
Foofur & His Friends
For Better or For Worse: The Bestest Present
For Our Children: The Concert
Forbidden Games
Force on Thunder Mountain
Foreign Correspondent
Four Babar Classics
Four by Dr. Seuss
The 400 Blows
The Fourth King
The Fourth Wish
Fraggle Rock: A Festive Fraggle Holiday
Fraggle Rock, Vol. 1: Meet the Fraggles
Francis Goes to the Races
Francis Joins the WACs
Francis the Talking Mule
Free to Be. . .You and Me
Friendly Persuasion
A Friendship in Vienna
Frog
Frog and Toad are Friends
Frog and Toad Together
Frog Goes to Dinner
The Frog Prince
Frog Prince
Frogs!
Frosty Returns
Frosty the Snowman
Frosty's Winter Wonderland/The Leprechauns' Christmas Gold
Fun & Fancy Free
Funny Face
The Further Adventures of Wil Cwac Cwac
G-Men Never Forget
G-Men vs. the Black Dragon
Gabby Cartoonies
Gaiking

Galaxy High School: Welcome to Galaxy High
Gallavants
Gandy Goose: One Man Navy
The Gang's All Here Series
Garfield
A Garfield Christmas
Garfield Goes Hollywood
Garfield: His 9 Lives
Garfield in Paradise
Garfield on the Town
Garfield's Feline Fantasy
Garfield's Halloween Adventure
Garfield's Thanksgiving
Gateway to the Mind
Gay Purr-ee
The Geisha Boy
General Spanky
Gentle Ben
Gentle Giant
George of the Jungle
Gerald McBoing-Boing
Gerald McBoing Boing, Vol. 1: Favorite Sing-Along Songs
Geronimo
The Get Along Gang, Vol. 1
The Ghost Belonged to Me
Ghost Chasers
The Ghost Goes West
Ghost in the Noonday Sun
The Ghost of Thomas Kempe
Ghost Stories
Ghostbusters: Back to the Past
Ghostwriter, Vol. 1: Ghost Story
G.I. Joe, Vol. 1: A Real American Hero
Giant
Gidget
Gidget Goes Hawaiian
Gidget Goes to Rome
The Gift of Amazing Grace
Gift of the Whales
Gift of Winter
Gigglesnort Hotel, Vol. 1
Gilligan's Planet
A Gingerbread Christmas
The Gingerbread Man and Other Nursery Stories
The Gingham Dog and the Calico Cat
Girl Crazy
The Girl Who Spelled Freedom

The Gnome-Mobile
Go Go Gophers: Up in the Air
Go West
Gobots
Gobots: Battle of the Rock Lords
Going My Way
Going to the Doctor
The Gold Bug
The Gold Rush
Goldie Gold & Action Jack II
Goliath 2
Gone are the Days
Gone with the Wind
Gonzo Presents Muppet Weird Stuff
Goober & the Ghost Chasers
The Good Time Growing Show
Goodbye, Miss 4th of July
Goof Troop: Goin' Fishin'
A Goofy Look at Valentine's Day
Goofy's Field Trip Series
The Goosehill Gang and the Gold Rush Treasure Map
Government Agents vs. the Phantom Legion
Grandizer
The Grass is Always Greener Over the Septic Tank
The Grasshopper and the Ants
Great Bible Stories: Abraham
The Great Cheese Conspiracy
The Great Harbor Rescue
Great Love Experiment
The Great Mike
Great Race
The Great Rupert
Great St. Trinian's Train Robbery
The Greatest Show on Earth
The Greatest Stories Ever Told: The Creation
Green Archer
Green Eggs and Ham from Dr. Seuss on the Loose
The Green Hornet
Gregory's Girl
Grendel, Grendel, Grendel
Greyfriars Bobby
Grimm's Fairy Tales: Beauty and the Beast

Grizzly Adams: The Legend Continues
Gryphon
Gulliver in Lilliput
Gulliver's Travels
Gumby Adventures
Gumby and the Moon Boggles
Gumby, Vol. 1: The Return of Gumby
Gumby's Holiday Special
Gumby's Supporting Cast
Guys and Dolls
Hair Bear Bunch
Halloween is Grinch Night
Hammerman: Nobody's Perfect
Hang Your Hat on the Wind
Hanna-Barbera Storybook Classics
Hans Brinker
Hap Palmer's Follow Along Songs
The Happiest Millionaire
Happy Holidays with Darkwing Duck and Goofy
The Happy Prince
Hard-Boiled Mahoney
The Hare and the Hedgehog
Harold and His Amazing Green Plants
Harold and the Purple Crayon and Other Harold Stories
Hashimoto: Hashimoto San
Hashimoto: Strange Companion
Hatari
Haunted Mansion Mystery
The Haunting of Barney Palmer
Have Picnic Basket, Will Travel
Hawk of the Wilderness
HBTV: Old Time Rock & Roll
He-Man & the Masters of the Universe, Vol. 1
Heathcliff & Cats & Co., Vol. 1
Heathcliff & Marmaduke
Heathcliff: The Movie
Heathcliff's Double & Other Tails
Hector's Bunyip
Heidi
Heidi

Henry Hamilton: Graduate Ghost
Henry's Cat
Hercules
Hercules Unchained
Here Comes Peter Cottontail
Here Comes Santa Claus
Hero High's Supermagic Adventures
Heroes on Hot Wheels, Vol. 1
Hey, Cinderella!
Hey There, It's Yogi Bear
High Noon
High Society
Hillbilly Bears
Hiroshima Maiden
His Girl Friday
The Hobbit
The Hoboken Chicken Emergency
Hobo's Christmas
Hockey Night
Holiday Inn
Hollywood on Parade
Hollywood or Bust
Holt of the Secret Service
Home at Last
Home for Christmas
Home to Stay
Homecoming: A Christmas Story
Homer Price Stories
Hop on Pop
Hoppity Goes to Town
The Horn Blows at Midnight
Horse Feathers
The Horse That Played Center Field
The Horse Without a Head
Horsemasters
Horton Hatches the Egg
Horton Hears a Who!
The Hound that Thought He was a Raccoon
The House of Dies Drear
The House with a Clock in Its Walls
A House Without a Christmas Tree
How Green was My Valley
How the Rhino Got His Skin/How the Camel Got His Hump
How the Whale Got His Throat
How to Be a Perfect Person in Just Three Days

How to Eat Fried Worms
How to Play Baseball
How to Stuff a Wild Bikini
The Howdy Doody Show (Puppet Playhouse)/The Gabby Hayes Show
H.R. Pufnstuf, Vol. 1
Hulk Hogan's Rock 'n' Wrestling
The Human Comedy
The Hunchback of Notre Dame
A Hungarian Fairy Tale
Hurricane Express
I Am a Fugitive from a Chain Gang
I am the Cheese
I Confess
I Live with Me Dad
I Remember Mama
Ida Fanfanny and Three Magical Tales
I'm a Little Teapot
I'm Not Oscar's Friend Anymore...and Other Stories
In Search of the Castaways
Incident at Hawk's Hill
Incredible Agent of Stingray
The Incredible Hulk
The Incredible Hulk Returns
The Incredible Journey
The Incredible Mr. Limpet
The Incredible Rocky Mountain Race
The Incredible Voyage of Stingray
Indian Paint
Inspector Clouseau: Ape Suzette
Inspector Clouseau: Napoleon Blown-Aparte
Inspector Gadget, Vol. 1
Invaders from Mars
The Invisible Monster
Invitation to the Dance
Ira Sleeps Over
Island of the Blue Dolphins
Islands
It Came Upon a Midnight Clear
It Happened at the World's Fair
It Happened in New Orleans
It Happened One Night
It's a Dog's Life
It's a Short Summer, Charlie Brown

It's a Wonderful Life
It's Not Easy Being Green
It's the Great Pumpkin, Charlie Brown (triple feature)
It's the Muppets, Vol. 1: Meet the Muppets
It's the Wolf
Jabberjaw
Jack & the Beanstalk
Jack and the Beanstalk
Jack Frost
Jacob Have I Loved
Jacob Two: Two Meets the Hooded Fang
Jamaica Inn
James Bond, Jr.
James Hound: Give Me Liberty
James Hound: Mr. Winlucky
Jane Eyre
Janosch: Fables from the Magic Forest
Jayce & the Wheeled Warriors, Vol. 1
Jazz Time Tale
Jem, Vol. 1: Truly Outrageous
Jesse James Rides Again
Jesus of Nazareth
A Jetson's Christmas Carol
The Jetsons Meet the Flintstones
Joey Runs Away and Other Stories
Johann's Gift to Christmas
John & Julie
John Henry
John the Fearless
Johnny Appleseed
Johnny Shiloh
Johnny the Giant Killer
Johnny Tremain & the Sons of Liberty
Johnny Woodchuck's Adventures
The Jolson Story
Jonah and the Whale
Josie & the Pussycats in Outer Space
Journey Back to Oz
Journey for Margaret
Journey to the Center of the Earth
Judgment at Nuremberg
The Jungle Book
The Jungle Book
Jungle Book: Mowgli Comes to the Jungle
Jungle Drums of Africa
A Jungle for Joey
Just Around the Corner
Just William's Luck

Justin Morgan Had a Horse
K-9000
The Karate Kat: Aristokratic Kapers
Katy and the Katerpillar Kids
Kavik, the Wolf Dog
Kermit and Piggy Story
Key Largo
Kid Colter
Kid Dynamite
A Kid for Two Farthings
The Kid from Left Field
The Kid Who Loved Christmas
The Kid with the 200 I.Q.
The Kid with the Broken Halo
Kidnapped
The King and I
King Arthur & the Knights of the Round Table, Vol. 1
King Kong
King Kong: Rocket Island
King Kong: Treasure Trap
King of the Rocketmen
Kismet
Kissyfur!: Hugs and Kissyfur
Knute Rockne: All American
Koi and the Kola Nuts
Konrad
Lady Lovelylocks & the Pixietails, Vol. 1
The Lady Vanishes
Lamb Chop's Play Along: Action Songs
Lamb Chop's Sing-Along Play-Along
Land of the Lost
Land of the Lost, Vol. 1
Lassie: Adventures of Neeka
Lassie: The Miracle
Lassie: Well of Love
Lassie's Great Adventure
Lassie's Rescue Rangers
The Last of the Mohicans
Law of the Wild
The Lawrenceville Stories
Lazer Tag Academy: The Movie
The Left-Handed Gun
The Legend of Hiawatha
Legend of Lobo
The Legend of Manxmouse

The Legend of Sleepy Hollow
Legend of the White Horse
The Legend of Zelda: Missing Link
Lend a Paw
Les Miserables
Let the Balloon Go
Let's Go to the Zoo with Captain Kangaroo
Let's Pretend with Barney
Let's Sing Again
Life Begins for Andy Hardy
Life on the Mississippi
Life with Father
The Light in the Forest
The Light Princess
Like Jake and Me
Lili
Lilies of the Field
The Lion, the Witch and the Wardrobe
Little Critter Series: Just Me and My Dad
The Little Crooked Christmas Tree
Little Dog Lost
The Little Drummer Boy
The Little Engine That Could
The Little Fox
Little Hiawatha
The Little House
Little House on the Prairie
Little Lord Fauntleroy
The Little Match Girl
Little Men
Little Miss Broadway
Little Miss Marker
Little Orphan Annie
The Little Prince & Friends
The Little Prince, Vols. 1-5
The Little Princess
Little Rascals Christmas Special
Little Sister Rabbit
Little Toot
Little Tough Guys
The Little Troll Prince
Little Wizards: The Singing Sword
Little Women
Little Women Series
The Littlest Angel
The Littlest Outlaw
The Littlest Rebel
Littlest Warrior
Locke the Superpower
Lollipop Dragon: Magic Lollipop Adventure
Lollipop Dragon: The Great Christmas Race
The Lone Ranger

The Lone Ranger and the Lost City of Gold
The Lone Ranger: Code of the Pioneers
Lone Star Kid
The Lone Wolf
The Loneliest Runner
The Loneliness of the Long Distance Runner
Lord of the Flies
Lost in a Harem
Lost in Dinosaur World
Lost in the Barrens
The Lost Jungle
Lost Legacy: A Girl Called Hatter Fox
Lots of Luck
Love Finds Andy Hardy
Love Happy
Love Laughs at Andy Hardy
Love Leads the Way
Lucky Luke: Ballad of the Daltons
Lucky Luke: Daisy Town
Lumpkin the Pumpkin
Macron 1: Dark Discovery in a New World
Mad Monster Party
Mad Scientist
Madeline
Madeline's Christmas
Magic Pony
Magic Snowman
The Magic Sword
The Magical Princess Gigi
The Maltese Falcon
Man and His World
The Man Called Flintstone
The Man in the Iron Mask
The Man in the Santa Claus Suit
The Man Who Wagged His Tail
Man's Best Friend
Maple Town
Maple Town: Case of the Missing Candy
March of the Wooden Soldiers
Marco Polo, Jr.
Maricela
Mark Twain and Me
Mark Twain's A Connecticut Yankee in King Arthur's Court
Marvelous Land of Oz
Mary Poppins
The Marzipan Pig
The Masked Marvel
Matt the Gooseboy
Maurice Sendak Library
Maurice Sendak's Really Rosie

Max Fleischer's Cartoon Capers, Vol. 1: Playin' Around
Maxie's World: Dancin' & Romancin'
Max's Chocolate Chicken and Other Stories for Young Children
Meet Me in St. Louis
The Member of the Wedding
Men of Boys Town
Merlin and the Sword
A Merry Mirthworm Christmas
Merry Mother Goose
Mickey Mouse Club, Vol. 1
Mickey Mouse: The Early Years Series
Mickey's Birthday Party
Mickey's Crazy Careers
Mickey's Field Trips Series
Mighty Hercules: Champion of the People!
Mighty Hercules: Conqueror of Evil!
The Mighty Hercules: Mightiest Mortal!
Mighty Joe Young
Mighty Mouse
Mighty Mouse in the Great Space Chase
Mighty Orbots: Devil's Asteroid
The Mighty Pawns
Mighty Thor: Enter Hercules
Mike Mulligan and His Steam Shovel
Million Dollar Kid
The Mini-Monsters: Adventures at Camp Mini-Mon
Miracle at Moreaux
Miracle Down Under
Miracle of Our Lady of Fatima
Miracle of the Heart: A Boys Town Story
Miracle of the White Stallions
Miracle on Ice
Miracle on 34th Street
The Miracle Worker
A Mirthworm Masquerade
Mr. & Mrs. Condor
Mr. & Mrs. Quack
Mr. & Mrs. Smith
Mr. Bill Looks Back Featuring Sluggo's Greatest Hits
Mr. Bill's Real-Life Adventures
Mr. Hulot's Holiday

Mr. Magoo: 1001 Arabian Night's Dream
Mr. Magoo: Cyrano De Bergerac/A Midsummer Night's Dream
Mr. Magoo: Don Quixote de la Mancha
Mr. Magoo in Sherwood Forest
Mr. Magoo in the King's Service
Mr. Magoo: King Arthur/The Count of Monte Cristo
Mr. Magoo: Little Snow White
Mr. Magoo: Sherlock Holmes/Dr. Frankenstein
The Mr. Magoo Show, Vol. 1
Mr. Magoo: The Three Musketeers
Mr. Magoo's Christmas Carol
Mr. Magoo's Storybook
Mister Rogers Meets an Astronaut
Mister Rogers: Music and Feelings
Mister Rogers: Musical Stories
Mister Rogers: When Parents Are Away
Mr. Rossi Looks For Happiness
Mr. Rossi's Dreams
Mr. Rossi's Vacation
Mr. Smith Goes to Washington
Mr. Wise Guy
Mr. Wizard's World: Air and Water Wizardry
Monkees, Volume 1
Monkey Business
The Monkey People
Monkeys, Go Home!
Monkey's Uncle
Monster Bash
Moon Pilot
The Moon Stallion
Mooncussers
Moondreamers, Vol. 1
More Adventures of Roger Ramjet
More Dinosaurs
More Song City U.S.A.
More Stories for the Very Young
Mosby's Marauders
Moschops: Adventures in Dinosaurland
Mother Goose Rock 'n' Rhyme
Mountain Man

The Mouse and the
  Motorcycle
Mouse on the
  Mayflower
The Mouse That
  Roared
Mowgli's Brothers
Muppet Babies:
  Explore with Us
Muppet Babies: Let's
  Build
Muppet Babies: Time
  to Play
Muppet Babies Video
  Storybook, Vol. 1
Muppet Musicians of
  Bremen
Muppet Revue
Muppet Treasures
Muppet Video Series
Muppets Moments
Muscle Beach Party
My Dear Uncle
  Sherlock
My Dog, the Thief
My Favorite Brunette
My Friend Flicka
My Friend Walter
My Life as a Dog
My Little Pony
My Little Pony: The
  Movie
My Old Man
My Pet Monster, Vol.
  1
Mysterious Doctor
  Satan
Mysterious Island
Mysterious Tadpole
  and Other Stories
Mystery Island
Nadia
Nancy Drew, Reporter
Napoleon and
  Samantha
National Velvet
Nearly No Christmas
'Neath Brooklyn Bridge
Nestor the Long-Eared
  Christmas Donkey
The New Adventures
  of Winnie the Pooh,
  Vol. 1: Great Honey
  Pot Robbery
New Adventures of
  Zorro, Vol. 1
New Archies: Stealing
  the Show
New Zoo Revue, Vol.
  1
A Night at the Opera
The Night Before
  Christmas
The Night Before
  Christmas and Best-
  Loved Yuletide
  Carols
A Night in Casablanca
The Night They Saved
  Christmas

Nightingale
The Nine Lives of
  Elfego Baca
1994 Winter Olympics
  Highlights Video
No Man's Valley
No Time for Sergeants
Noah's Animals and
  Other Stories
Nobody's Boy
Noel
The Norfin Adventures:
  The Great Egg
  Robbery
Norman the Doorman
  and Other Stories
North by Northwest
Not My Kid
Not Quite Human
Notorious
Nursery Rhymes
Nutcase
Nutcracker Fantasy
The Nutcracker Prince
The Nutty Professor
Nuzzling with the
  Noozles
Nyoka and the
  Tigermen
An Officer and a Duck
Old MacDonald's Farm
  and Other Animal
  Tales
The Old Mill
Old Yeller
The Olden Days Coat
Oliver Twist
Ollie Hopnoodle's
  Haven of Bliss
Olly Olly Oxen Free
The Olympic Champ
On the Comet
On the Edge: The
  Survival of Dana
On the Town
On Vacation with
  Mickey and Friends
Once a Hero
Once Upon a Brothers
  Grimm
Once Upon a Time
One Fish, Two Fish,
  Red Fish, Blue Fish
101 Problems of
  Hercules
One Little Indian
The Original Fabulous
  Adventures of Baron
  Munchausen
Orphan Train
Our Little Girl
Ovide and the Gang
The Owl and the
  Pussycat
Owl Moon and Other
  Stories
Ox Tales
Ozma of Oz
Paddington Bear

Paddington Goes to
  the Movies
Paddy Beaver
Pajama Party
Panda and the Magic
  Serpent
The Paper Bag Princess
Parade
The Paradine Case
The Parent Trap
The Party
Pat and Mike
Paul Bunyan
Peachboy
Pecos Bill
Pee Wee's Playhouse
  Festival of Fun
Penny Serenade
The Perils of Penelope
  Pitstop
The Perils of
  Problemina
Peter and the Magic
  Egg
Peter and the Wolf
Peter Cottontail: How
  He Got His Hop
Peter Cottontail's
  Adventures
Peter Lundy and the
  Medicine Hat Stallion
Peter-No-Tail
Peter Pan
Peter Pan & the
  Pirates: Demise of
  Hook
Peter Pan/Hiawatha
Peter Rabbit and Other
  Tales
The Phantom Creeps
The Phantom Empire
Phantom of the Opera
The Philadelphia Story
The Pickwick Papers
The Pied Piper/
  Cinderella
The Pied Piper of
  Hamelin
The Pigeon that
  Worked a Miracle
The Pigs' Wedding and
  Other Stories
The Pinballs
The Pink Panther
Pink Panther: Fly in the
  Pink
Pink Panther: Pink
  Christmas
Pink Panther: Tickled
  Pink
Pinocchio
Pinocchio and the
  Emperor of the Night
Pinocchio in Outer
  Space
Pinocchio's Christmas
Pippin
Pirates of Dark Water:
  The Saga Begins
P.K. and the Kid

Plastic Man
Play-Along Video: Hey,
  You're as Funny as
  Fozzie Bear
Play-Along Video:
  Mother Goose
  Stories
Play-Along Video:
  Sing-Along, Dance-
  Along, Do-Along
Play-Along Video:
  Wow, You're a
  Cartoonist!
Playbox 1
Playtime
Please Don't Eat the
  Daisies
Pluto
Pluto (limited gold
  edition)
Pluto's Christmas Tree
The Point
Police Academy, the
  Series
Pollyanna
Pontoffel Pock, Where
  Are You?
Poochie
Pooh Learning: Helping
  Others
Pooh Learning: Making
  Friends
Pooh Learning: Sharing
  and Caring
Pooh Playtime: Cowboy
  Pooh
Pooh Playtime:
  Detective Tigger
Pooh Playtime: Pooh
  Party
Pooh's Great School
  Bus Adventure
The Poor Little Rich
  Girl
The Popples
Posse Impossible
Possible Possum:
  Freight Fright
Potato Head Kids, Vol.
  1
Potsworth and the
  Midnight Patrol
Pound Puppies
Precious Pupp
Prehysteria! 2
The Pretty Piggies: The
  Adventure Begins
Primo Baby
The Prince and the
  Great Race
The Prince and the
  Pauper
The Prince of Central
  Park
Prince Valiant
Princess Scargo and
  the Birthday Pumpkin
Professor Iris: Music
  Mania

Pssst! Hammerman's
  After You
Puff and the Incredible
  Mr. Nobody
Puff the Magic Dragon
Puff the Magic Dragon
  in the Land of Living
  Lies
Punky Brewster: Little
  Orphan Punky
The Pure Hell of St.
  Trinian's
Puss in Boots
Puss 'n Boots Travels
  Around the World
Quark the Dragon
  Slayer
Quarterback Princess
The Quiet Man
Rabbit Ears Storybook
  Classics Collection
Raccoons: Let's Dance
Raccoons on Ice
Radar Men from the
  Moon
Radio Patrol
Raft Adventures of
  Huck & Jim
Raggedy Ann and
  Andy
Railway Children
The Railway Dragon
Rainbow Brite: A Horse
  of a Different Color
Rambo: Children for
  Peace
Ramona
Ramona: Goodbye,
  Hello
Rascal
Rascals and Robbers
Reading Rainbow: A
  Chair for My Mother
Reading Rainbow:
  Abiyoyo
Reading Rainbow:
  Alistair in Outer
  Space
Reading Rainbow:
  Alistair's Time
  Machine
Reading Rainbow:
  Animal Cafe
Reading Rainbow:
  Arthur's Eyes
Reading Rainbow: Barn
  Dance!
Reading Rainbow: Bea
  and Mr. Jones
Reading Rainbow:
  Berlioz the Bear
Reading Rainbow: Best
  Friends
Reading Rainbow:
  Bored - Nothing to
  Do!
Reading Rainbow:
  Brush
Reading Rainbow: Bugs

VIDEOHOUND'S FAMILY VIDEO RETRIEVER

Secret Life of Walter Mitty
Secret Lives of Waldo Kitty Volume 1
The Secret of El Zorro
Secret of the Seal
Serendipity the Pink Dragon
Sesame Songs: Dance Along!
Sesame Songs: Elmo's Sing-Along Guessing Game
Sesame Songs: Monster Hits!
Sesame Songs: Rock & Roll!
Sesame Songs: Sing-Along Earth Songs
Sesame Songs: Sing, Hoot & Howl
Sesame Songs: Sing Yourself Silly!
Sesame Songs: We All Sing Together
Sesame Street: Bedtime Stories and Songs
Sesame Street: Best of Ernie and Bert
Sesame Street: Big Bird's Favorite Party Games
Sesame Street: Count It Higher
Sesame Street: Developing Self-Esteem
Sesame Street: I'm Glad I'm Me
Sesame Street: Play-Along Games and Songs
Sesame Street Visits the Firehouse
Seven Brides for Seven Brothers
Seven Faces of Dr. Lao
The Seven Little Foys
Shadow of a Doubt
Shadow of the Eagle
The Shakiest Gun in the West
Shall We Dance
Shalom Sesame
Shamu & You: Exploring the World of Birds
Shamu & You: Exploring the World of Fish
Shamu & You: Exploring the World of Mammals
Shamu & You: Exploring the World of Reptiles
Shane
Shari Lewis & Lamb Chop: In the Land of No Manners

Shari Lewis & Lamb Chop: One Minute Bible Stories, New Testament
Shari Lewis: Don't Wake Your Mom
Shari Lewis: Have I Got a Story for You
Shari Lewis: Kooky Classics
Shari Lewis: One Minute Bedtime Stories
Sharon, Lois & Bram at the Young People's Theatre
Sharon, Lois & Bram: Back by Popular Demand-Live
Sharon, Lois & Bram: Live in Your Living Room
Sharon, Lois & Bram: Sing A to Z
Sharon, Lois & Bram's Elephant Show: Babysitting
Shazam!
Shazzan
She-Ra, Vol. 1
Shelley Duvall's Bedtime Stories
Shelley Duvall's Rock 'n' Rhymeland
Sherlock Hound: Dr. Watson I Presume?
Shining Time Station: Singsongs, Vol. 1
Shining Time Station: 'Tis a Gift Holiday Special
Shirley Temple Baby Berlesques
Shirley Temple Festival
Shirley Temple Storybook Theater
A Shot in the Dark
Sigmund & the Sea Monsters, Vol. 1
The Sign of Zorro
The Silver Fox and Sam Davenport
Silver Stallion
Silverhawks: Sky Shadows
Silverhawks: The Original Story
The Simpsons Christmas Special
Sinbad the Sailor
Since You Went Away
Sing Along with Little Lulu
Sing, Giggle & Grin
Sing, Stretch & Shape Up
Sing Together
Singin' in the Rain
Sir Prancelot
Skeezer

Skills for the New Technology Series
Sleeping Beauty
The Small One
Smart Alecks
Smile for Auntie and Other Stories
Smoke
Smokey the Bear: Founder's Day Folly
Smokey the Bear: Silliest Show on Earth
A Smoky Mountain Christmas
Smuggler's Cove
Smurfs
The Sneetches from Dr. Seuss on the Loose
Sniffles Bells the Cat
Snorks
The Snow Queen
Snow White
Snow White and Rose Red
Snow White and the Three Stooges
The Snowman
Snuffy the Elf Who Saved Christmas
So Dear to My Heart
Someday Me Series
Son of Dinosaurs
Son of Flubber
Son of Kong
Son of Zorro
Song City U.S.A.
The Song of Sacajawea
Songs for Us Series
Songs from Mother Goose
Sorcerer's Apprentice
Sorrowful Jones
The Sound of Music
Sourdough
South Pacific
Space Angel, Vol. 1
Space Battleship Yamato
Space Firebird
Space Warriors: Battle for Earth Station S/1
Spaceketeers
Sparky's Magic Piano
Speaking of Animals, Vol. 1
Special Valentine with Family Circus
Speed Racer
Spellbound
Spider-Woman
Spiderman
Spiderman & His Amazing Friends: Origin of the Spider Friends
Spiderman: The Deadly Dust
Spiderman, Vol. 1: Dr. Doom

Spiral Zone: Ride the Whirlwind
Spiral Zone: Zone of Darkness
Spirit of the Eagle
Spook Busters
Spooks Run Wild
Spot Goes to the Farm
Spy Smasher
Squanto and the First Thanksgiving
Squiddly Diddly
Stage Fright
Stand Up and Cheer
Stanley and the Dinosaurs
Stanley the Ugly Duckling
Star Fairies
Star Street: Adventures of the Star Kids
Star Street: The Happy Birthday Movie
Star Trek: Animated, Vol. 1
Star Trek the Next Generation Episode 1-2: Encounter at Farpoint
Starcom: Galactic Adventures
Starvengers
State Fair
The Steadfast Tin Soldier
Stingiest Man in Town
Stingray: Invaders of the Deep
Stone Fox
Stories and Fables, Vol. 1
Stories from the Black Tradition
Stories to Remember: Baby's Morningtime
Stories to Remember: Baby's Nursery Rhymes
Stories to Remember: Baby's Storytime
Stories to Remember: Beauty and the Beast
Stories to Remember: Merlin and the Dragons
Stories to Remember: Noah's Ark
Stories to Remember: Pegasus
Stories to Remember: The Wild Swans
Stormalong
Storms
Stormy, the Thoroughbred
The Story of a Cowboy Angel
The Story of 15 Boys
The Story of Seabiscuit

The Story of the Dancing Frog
Stowaway
Stowaways on the Ark
Strangers on a Train
Strawberry Shortcake and the Baby Without a Name
Street Frogs: Keep on Rappin'
Strega Nonna and Other Stories
Strike Up the Band
Sub-Mariner: Atlantis Under Attack
Sudie & Simpson
Summer Magic
Summer Switch
Sunshine Porcupine
Superman & the Mole Men
Superman: The Serial, Vol. 1
SuperTed
Susannah of the Mounties
Susie, the Little Blue Coupe
Suspicion
The Sweater
Sweet 15
The Swiss Family Robinson
The Sword & the Rose
Sylvia Anderson's The Animates
Tailor of Gloucester
Tailspin Tommy
The Tale of Mr. Jeremy Fisher and the Tale of Peter Rabbit
The Tale of Peter Rabbit
The Tale of Peter Rabbit and Benjamin Bunny
The Tale of Samuel Whiskers
The Tale of the Bunny Picnic
Tales of Beatrix Potter
Tales of Deputy Dawg, Vol. 1
The Tales of Hoffman
Tales of Pluto Series
The Talking Eggs
The Talking Parcel
Tall Tales and Legends: Johnny Appleseed
Tammy and the Bachelor
Tammy and the Doctor
Tarka the Otter
Tarzan and His Mate
Tarzan Escapes
Tarzan Finds a Son
Tarzan, the Ape Man

VIDEOHOUND'S FAMILY VIDEO RETRIEVER

Winnie the Pooh and
  the Blustery Day
Winnie the Pooh and
  the Honey Tree
Winnie the Pooh
  Discovers the
  Seasons
Winsome Witch
Winter of the Witch
Winter Wolf
The Witch Who Turned
  Pink
Witcheroo
Witch's Night Out
The Wizard of Oz
The Wizard of Oz
The Wizard of Oz:
  Danger in a Strange
  Land
The Woman Who
  Raised a Bear as
  Her Son
The Wombles
Wonder Man
Wonderful Wizard of
  Oz
Wonderful World of
  Puss 'N Boots
The Wonderful World
  of the Brothers
  Grimm
The Wonderful World
  of Wombles
Wonderland Cove
Wonders of Aladdin
Woody Woodpecker &
  His Friends: Vol. 1
Woody Woodpecker
  Collector's Edition,
  Vol. 1
Woof!
Words by Heart
The World According
  to Gumby
A World is Born
The World of Andy
  Panda
World of David the
  Gnome: Kangaroo
  Adventure
World of Hans
  Christian Andersen
The World of Henry
  Orient
A World of Stories
  with Katharine
  Hepburn
World of Strawberry
  Shortcake
Wowser: Wow-Wow
  Wowser
Wrinkles: In Need of
  Cuddles
The Wrong Man
X-Men: Deadly
  Reunions
Xuxa: Funtastic
  Birthday Party
Yanco
Yankee Doodle Cricket

Yankee Doodle Dandy
The Year Without a
  Santa Claus
The Yearling
Yellowstone Cubs
Yes, Virginia, There is
  a Santa Claus
Yogi and the Invasion
  of the Space Bears
Yogi and the Magical
  Flight of the Spruce
  Goose
Yogi's First Christmas
Yogi's Great Escape
Yogi's Treasure Hunt:
  Heavens to
  Planetoid!
Young & Free
A Young Children's
  Concert with Raffi
The Young Detectives
  on Wheels
Young Eagles
Young Magician
Young Robin Hood
You're a Good Man,
  Charlie Brown
You're Not Elected,
  Charlie Brown!/A
  Charlie Brown
  Christmas
Yours, Mine & Ours
Yukon Flight
The Zax From Dr.
  Seuss on the Loose
Zebra in the Kitchen
Ziggy's Gift
Zillion
Zombies of the
  Stratosphere
Zoobilee Zoo, Vol. 1:
  Land of Rhymes &
  Other Stories
Zoom the White
  Dolphin
Zorro Rides Again
Zorro, Vol. 1
Zorro's Black Whip
Zorro's Fighting Legion

Cast/Director Index

The **CAST/DIRECTOR INDEX** lists the video accomplishments of thousands of actors and directors in straight alphabetical format by last name (names are presented in a first name, last name format, but alphabetization begins with the last name). Directors are indicated by a black triangular symbol (dingbat) next to their name. Every cast member credited in the main review section is indexed here, creating an intriguing array of videographies for the famous and not-so-famous.

Lee Aaker
Rin Tin Tin, Hero of the West '55

Caroline Aaron
Edward Scissorhands '90

Paul Aaron▶
The Miracle Worker '79

Bud Abbott
Abbott and Costello Meet Captain Kidd '52
Abbott and Costello Meet Dr. Jekyll and Mr. Hyde '52
Abbott and Costello Meet Frankenstein '48
Africa Screams '49
Buck Privates '41
Buck Privates Come Home '47
Jack & the Beanstalk '52
Lost in a Harem '44

Phillip Abbott
The Fantastic World of D.C. Collins '84
The Invisible Boy '57

Kareem Abdul-Jabbar
The Fish that Saved Pittsburgh '79
Fletch '85
Purple People Eater '88

Hakeem Abdul-Samad
Ernest Goes to Camp '87

Walter Abel
Curley '47
Fabulous Joe '47
Holiday Inn '42

Ian Abercrombie
Army of Darkness '92

Michael Aberne
The Commitments '91

John Abineri
The Moon Stallion '85

F. Murray Abraham
All the President's Men '76
Amadeus '84
Last Action Hero '93
The Sunshine Boys '75

Jim Abrahams▶
Airplane! '80
Big Business '88
Hot Shots! Part Deux '93
Welcome Home, Roxy Carmichael '90

Michele Abrams
Buffy the Vampire Slayer '92

Tony Acierto
Journey to Spirit Island '92

Bettye Ackerman
Prehysteria 2 '94

Leslie Ackerman
Blame It on the Night '84

Joss Ackland
Bill & Ted's Bogus Journey '91
The Hunt for Red October '90
The Mighty Ducks '92
Once Upon a Crime '92

David Ackroyd
A Smoky Mountain Christmas '86

Acquanetta
Grizzly Adams: The Legend Continues '90

Jane Actman
The Last of the Mohicans '85

Eddie Acuff
G-Men Never Forget '48

Beverly Adams
How to Stuff a Wild Bikini '65

Brandon Adams
The Sandlot '93

Brooke Adams
Invasion of the Body Snatchers '78

Don Adams
Back to the Beach '87
Jimmy the Kid '82

Julie Adams
Francis Joins the WACs '54

Marla Adams
Gotcha! '85

Mason Adams
F/X '86
The Kid with the Broken Halo '82
Son-in-Law '93

Maud Adams
Jane & the Lost City '87
The Man with the Golden Gun '74
Octopussy '83

Nick Adams
Mosby's Marauders '66
No Time for Sergeants '58
Rebel Without a Cause '55

Stanley Adams
Lilies of the Field '63

Tom Adams
The Fighting Prince of Donegal '66

George Adamson
Christian the Lion '76

Nancy Addison
Somewhere Tomorrow '85

Georges Adet
Love and Death '75

Vern Adix
Teen Alien '88

Suzanne Adkinson
Racing with the Moon '84

Matt Adler
Diving In '90
Doin' Time on Planet Earth '88
Flight of the Navigator '86
White Water Summer '87

Percy Adlon▶
Bagdad Cafe '88

Edvin Adolphson
Boy of Two Worlds '70

Iris Adrian
Million Dollar Kid '44

Max Adrian
The Boy Friend '71

Frank Adu
Love and Death '75

Ben Affleck
School Ties '92

Janet Agren
Aladdin '86

Jenny Agutter
Amy '81
Darkman '90
The Man in the Iron Mask '77
Railway Children '70
Secret Places '85

Brian Aherne
I Confess '53
Prince Valiant '54
Waltz King '63

Monique Ahrens
A Dog of Flanders '59

Ahui
Robinson Crusoe & the Tiger '72

Kyoko Ai
Destroy All Monsters '68

Charles Aidman
Menace on the Mountain '70

Danny Aiello
Bang the Drum Slowly '73
Moonstruck '87
Old Enough '84
The Purple Rose of Cairo '85
Radio Days '87

Holly Aird
The Flame Trees of Thika '81

Franklin Ajaye
Car Wash '76

Karen Akers
The Purple Rose of Cairo '85

Claude Akins
Battle for the Planet of the Apes '73
Pecos Bill '86

Marc Alaimo
Arena '88

Miguel Alamo
Daniel and the Towers '90s

John Albasiny
Kipperbang '82

Josh Albee
The Adventures of Tom Sawyer '73
The Runaways '75

Anna Maria Alberghetti
Cinderfella '60

Hans Albers
Baron Munchausen '43

Eddie Albert
The Birch Interval '78
Brenda Starr '86

Escape to Witch Mountain
'75
The Heartbreak Kid '72
Miracle of the White
Stallions '63
Oklahoma! '55
Roman Holiday '53

Edward Albert
Butterflies Are Free '72
The Rescue '88

Frank Albertson
Ah, Wilderness! '35
It's a Wonderful Life '46
Room Service '38

Jack Albertson
Charlie and the Great
Balloon Chase '82
Miracle on 34th Street '47
The Poseidon Adventure
'72
Shirley Temple Storybook
Theater '60
Willy Wonka & the
Chocolate Factory '71

Alan Alda
Sweet Liberty '86

Alan Alda▶
Sweet Liberty '86

Rutanya Alda
Mommie Dearest '81
Prancer '89
Racing with the Moon '84

Tom Aldredge
The Adventures of Huck
Finn '93
What About Bob? '91

Adell Aldrich▶
The Kid from Left Field '79

Kay Aldridge
Nyoka and the Tigermen
'42

Miguel Alejandro
Popi '69

Jane Alexander
All the President's Men '76
A Friendship in Vienna '88
The Great White Hope '70
Kramer vs. Kramer '79
Night Crossing '81
Square Dance '87

Jason Alexander
Blankman '94
Brighton Beach Memoirs
'86
Coneheads '93
North '94
The Paper '94

John Alexander
The Horn Blows at
Midnight '45
The Jolson Story '46
A Tree Grows in Brooklyn
'45

Khandi Alexander
Greedy '94
What's Love Got to Do
With It? '93

Max Alexander
Roxanne '87

Spike Alexander
Brain Donors '92

Constantin Alexandrov
Gorillas in the Mist '88

Phillip Alford
To Kill a Mockingbird '62

James Algar▶
The Living Desert '53

Muhammad Ali
The Greatest '77

Jed Allan
Lassie: Adventures of
Neeka '68
Man from Clover Grove
'78

William Alland
Citizen Kane '41

Michael Alldredge
Robot Jox '89

Bill Allen
Rad '86

Corey Allen
Rebel Without a Cause '55

Corey Allen▶
Avalanche '78
The Man in the Santa
Claus Suit '79

Debbie Allen
The Fish that Saved
Pittsburgh '79

Eugene Allen
House Party 2: The Pajama
Jam '91

Gavin Allen
Runaway '89

Irwin Allen▶
The Swarm '78
Voyage to the Bottom of
the Sea '61

Joan Allen
Josh and S.A.M. '93
Peggy Sue Got Married
'86
Searching for Bobby
Fischer '93
Tucker: The Man and His
Dream '88

Judith Allen
Bright Eyes '34

Karen Allen
Animal Behavior '89
King of the Hill '93
Raiders of the Lost Ark '81
The Sandlot '93
Scrooged '88
Starman '84

Marty Allen
Whale of a Tale '76

Mikki Allen
Regarding Henry '91

Nancy Allen
Home Movies '79
I Wanna Hold Your Hand
'78
Poltergeist 3 '88
Robocop '87
Robocop 2 '90
Robocop 3 '91
Strange Invaders '83

Patrick Allen
When Dinosaurs Ruled the
Earth '70

Steve Allen
Alice in Wonderland '85

Woody Allen
Annie Hall '77
Bananas '71
Broadway Danny Rose '84
Love and Death '75
Play It Again, Sam '72
Sleeper '73
Take the Money and Run
'69

Woody Allen▶
Annie Hall '77
Bananas '71
Broadway Danny Rose '84
Love and Death '75
The Purple Rose of Cairo
'85
Radio Days '87
Sleeper '73
Take the Money and Run
'69

Roger Allers▶
The Lion King '94

Kirstie Alley
Look Who's Talking '89
Look Who's Talking Now
'93
Look Who's Talking, Too
'90
Madhouse '90
Star Trek 2: The Wrath of
Khan '82
Summer School '87

Sara Allgood
Challenge to Lassie '49
How Green was My Valley
'41
Jane Eyre '44

Astrid Allwyn
Stowaway '36

June Allyson
Girl Crazy '43
The Glenn Miller Story '54
The Kid with the Broken
Halo '82
Little Women '49
The Three Musketeers '48
Till the Clouds Roll By '46

Maria Conchita Alonso
A Fine Mess '86

Glen Alsworth
Cry from the Mountain '85

Robert Altman▶
M*A*S*H '70
Popeye '80

Tony Alva
Skateboard '77

Trini Alvarado
The Babe '92
Rich Kids '79
Satisfaction '88

Kirk Alyn
Atom Man vs. Superman
'50
Federal Agents vs.
Underworld, Inc. '49
Superman: The Serial, Vol.
1 '48

Lyle Alzado
Ernest Goes to Camp '87
Tough Guys '86

Vittorio Amandola
Queen of Hearts '89

Betty Amann
Nancy Drew, Reporter '39

Rod Amateau▶
The Garbage Pail Kids
Movie '87

Don Ameche
The Boatniks '70
Cocoon '85
Cocoon: The Return '88
Corrina, Corrina '94
Harry and the Hendersons
'87

Amedee
Forbidden Games '52

Nicholas Amer
Treasure Island '89

Leon Ames
The Absent-Minded
Professor '61
The Misadventures of
Merlin Jones '63
Monkey's Uncle '65
Peggy Sue Got Married
'86
Son of Flubber '63

Rosemary Ames
Our Little Girl '35

Trudi Ames
Bye, Bye, Birdie '63

Jon Amiel▶
Queen of Hearts '89
Sommersby '93

Suzy Amis
Fandango '85
Plain Clothes '88
Rich in Love '93
Rocket Gibraltar '88

John Amos
American Flyers '85
Beastmaster '82
Touched by Love '80
The World's Greatest
Athlete '73

Morey Amsterdam
Beach Party '63
Muscle Beach Party '64

Franco Amurri▶
Monkey Trouble '94

Ricardo Ancona
Yanco '64

Luana Anders
Goin' South '78
Irreconcilable Differences
'84

Angry Anderson
Mad Max: Beyond
Thunderdome '85

Bridgette Anderson
Savannah Smiles '82
A Summer to Remember
'84

Carl Anderson
Jesus Christ, Superstar '73

Eddie Anderson
Gone with the Wind '39
Topper Returns '41

Ingrid Anderson
Hercules '83

Jean Anderson
Back Home '90

Judith Anderson
Cinderfella '60
Rebecca '40

**Star Trek 3: The Search
for Spock '84
The Ten Commandments
'56**

Lindsay Anderson
Chariots of Fire '81

Loni Anderson
Munchie '92

Louis Anderson
Ferris Bueller's Day Off '86

Melissa Sue Anderson
Little House on the Prairie
'74
The Loneliest Runner '76
On the Edge: The Survival
of Dana '79

Melody Anderson
Flash Gordon '80

Michael Anderson Jr.
The Great Land of Small
'86
In Search of the
Castaways '62

Michael Anderson Sr.▶
Around the World in 80
Days '56
Doc Savage '75

Miles Anderson
A Far Off Place '93

Mitchell Anderson
Back to Hannibal: The
Further Adventures of
Tom Sawyer and
Huckleberry Finn '90
Goodbye, Miss 4th of July
'88

Richard Anderson
Zorro, Vol. 1 '58

Stephanie Anderson
Calendar Girl '93

Marcel Andre
Beauty and the Beast '46

Andre the Giant
The Princess Bride '87

Ursula Andress
Clash of the Titans '81
Dr. No '62
The Fifth Musketeer '79

Anthony Andrews
The Scarlet Pimpernel '82

Dana Andrews
Airport '75 '75
State Fair '45

Edward Andrews
Sixteen Candles '84
A Tiger Walks '64

Harry Andrews
Death on the Nile '78
Man of La Mancha '72
Wuthering Heights '70

Julie Andrews
Gonzo Presents Muppet
Weird Stuff '85
Little Miss Marker '80
Mary Poppins '64
The Sound of Music '65
Torn Curtain '66

Stanley Andrews
The Adventures of Frank
and Jesse James '48

Heather Angel
Suspicion '41

Jimmy Angle
Terror in the Jungle '68

Christien Anholt
Reunion '88

Evelyn Ankers
Black Beauty '46

Ann-Margret
Bye, Bye, Birdie '63
The Cheap Detective '78
Grumpy Old Men '93
I Ought to Be in Pictures '82
Newsies '92
State Fair '62
Tommy '75
The Villain '79

Ken Annakin▶
Call of the Wild '72
The Fifth Musketeer '79
The New Adventures of Pippi Longstocking '88
Pirate Movie '82
The Swiss Family Robinson '60
The Sword & the Rose '53
Third Man on the Mountain '59
Those Daring Young Men in Their Jaunty Jalopies '69

Jean-Jacques Annaud▶
The Bear '89

Francesca Annis
Flipper's New Adventure '64
Krull '83

Michael Ansara
And Now Miguel '66
The Bears & I '74
The Fantastic World of D.C. Collins '84
Guns of the Magnificent Seven '69
Voyage to the Bottom of the Sea '61

Zachary Ansley
Christmas Comes to Willow Creek '87
Princes in Exile '90
This Boy's Life '93

Susan Anspach
The Devil & Max Devlin '81
Gone are the Days '84
Misunderstood '84
Play It Again, Sam '72

David Anspaugh▶
Hoosiers '86
Rudy '93

Paul Anstad
Snow Treasure '67

Gerald Anthony
Secret of the Ice Cave '89

Lysette Anthony
Face the Music '92
Krull '83
Look Who's Talking Now '93
Oliver Twist '82

Paul Anthony
House Party '90

Susan Anton
The Boy Who Loved Trolls '84
Cannonball Run 2 '84
Making Mr. Right '86

Lou Antonio▶
The Last Prostitute '91

Gabrielle Anwar
For Love or Money '93
If Looks Could Kill '91
The Three Musketeers '93
Wild Hearts Can't Be Broken '91

Kazuya Aoyama
Godzilla vs. the Cosmic Monster '74

Noel Appleby
My Grandpa is a Vampire '92
The Navigator '88

Christina Applegate
Don't Tell Mom the Babysitter's Dead '91

Royce D. Applegate
Gettysburg '93

Michael Apted▶
Coal Miner's Daughter '80
First Born '84
Gorillas in the Mist '88
Kipperbang '82

Amy Aquino
Alan & Naomi '92

Alfonso Arau
Romancing the Stone '84
Scandalous John '71
Three Amigos '86

Allan Arbus
Daniel and the Towers '90s

Jonas Arby
Running on Empty '88

Anne Archer
Cancel My Reservation '72
Family Prayers '91
Hero at Large '80

Eve Arden
At the Circus '39
Grease '78
Grease 2 '82
Under the Rainbow '81

Emile Ardolino▶
Chances Are '89
Dirty Dancing '87
George Balanchine's The Nutcracker '93
Sister Act '92
Three Men and a Little Lady '90

Allison Argo
Cry from the Mountain '85

David Argue
BMX Bandits '83

Alan Arkin
Bad Medicine '85
Coupe de Ville '90
Edward Scissorhands '90
Hearts of the West '75
Improper Channels '82
Indian Summer '93
North '94
Popi '69
Return of Captain Invincible '83
The Rocketeer '91

Simon '80

Robert Arkins
The Commitments '91

Allan Arkush▶
Heartbeeps '81
Rock 'n' Roll High School '79

Pedro Armendariz Jr.
Tombstone '93

Pedro Armendariz Sr.
From Russia with Love '63
The Littlest Outlaw '54

Henry Armetta
Fisherman's Wharf '39
Let's Sing Again '36

Alun Armstrong
Black Beauty '94

Bess Armstrong
Nothing in Common '86
The Skateboard Kid '93

Curtis Armstrong
The Adventures of Huck Finn '93
Bad Medicine '85
Better Off Dead '85
One Crazy Summer '86
Revenge of the Nerds '84

Louis Armstrong
The Glenn Miller Story '54
Hello, Dolly! '69
High Society '56

R.G. Armstrong
Dick Tracy '90
The Great White Hope '70
My Name is Nobody '74
The Shadow Riders '82

Robert Armstrong
King Kong '33
Mighty Joe Young '49
Palooka '34
Son of Kong '33

Robin B. Armstrong▶
Pastime '91

Todd Armstrong
Jason and the Argonauts '63

Desi Arnaz Jr.
The Voyage of the Yes '72

Desi Arnaz Sr.
Escape Artist '82

James Arness
The Farmer's Daughter '47

Jeanetta Arnetta
Ladybugs '92
The Shadow Riders '82

Dorothy Arnold
The Phantom Creeps '39

Edward Arnold
Mr. Smith Goes to Washington '39

Frank Arnold▶
A Waltz Through the Hills '88

Jack Arnold▶
The Mouse That Roared '59

Roseanne (Barr) Arnold
She-Devil '89

Tom Arnold
Hero '92
True Lies '94
Undercover Blues '93

David Arquette
Buffy the Vampire Slayer '92

Lewis Arquette
Book of Love '91

Patricia Arquette
Holy Matrimony '94

Rosanna Arquette
Desperately Seeking Susan '85
Silverado '85

Jeri Arrendondo
Spirit of the Eagle '90

Carol Arthur
The Sunshine Boys '75

Jean Arthur
Mr. Smith Goes to Washington '39
Shane '53

Johnny Arthur
The Masked Marvel '43

Leslie Ash
Curse of the Pink Panther '83

Monty Ash
Tough Guys '86

Dana Ashbrook
Ghost Dad '90

Hal Ashby▶
Being There '79
Bound for Glory '76

Peggy Ashcroft
Madame Sousatzka '88
The 39 Steps '35

Jane Asher
Dreamchild '85
The Prince and the Pauper '62

William Asher▶
Beach Blanket Bingo '65
Beach Party '63
Bikini Beach '64
How to Stuff a Wild Bikini '65
Muscle Beach Party '64

Elizabeth Ashley
Dragnet '87

John Ashley
Beach Blanket Bingo '65
Beach Party '63
Bikini Beach '64
How to Stuff a Wild Bikini '65
Muscle Beach Party '64

Jonathan Ashmore
A Kid for Two Farthings '55

John Ashton
Beverly Hills Cop '84
Beverly Hills Cop 2 '87
Little Big League '94
She's Having a Baby '88
Some Kind of Wonderful '87

Luke Askew
Legend of the White Horse '85

Robin Askwith
Hans Brinker '69

Gregoire Aslan
Golden Voyage of Sinbad '73

Ed Asner
Change of Habit '69
A Friendship in Vienna '88
Gus '76

Armand Assante
Animal Behavior '89
Fatal Instinct '93
1492: Conquest of Paradise '92
Little Darlings '80
The Lords of Flatbush '74

Fred Astaire
The Amazing Dobermans '76
The Band Wagon '53
The Belle of New York '52
Easter Parade '48
Finian's Rainbow '68
Follow the Fleet '36
Funny Face '57
Holiday Inn '42
The Man in the Santa Claus Suit '79
Shall We Dance '37
That's Dancing! '85
That's Entertainment '74
That's Entertainment, Part 2 '76

Shay Astar
Ernest Scared Stupid '91

John Astin
Brothers O'Toole '73
Huck and the King of Hearts '93
National Lampoon's European Vacation '85
Pepper and His Wacky Taxi '72
Stepmonster '92
Teen Wolf Too '87

MacKenzie Astin
The Garbage Pail Kids Movie '87
Iron Will '93

Sean Astin
Encino Man '92
The Goonies '85
Like Father, Like Son '87
Rudy '93
White Water Summer '87
The Willies '90

Mary Astor
Little Women '49
The Maltese Falcon '41
Meet Me in St. Louis '44

Roscoe Ates
Regl'ar Fellers '41

William Atherton
Ghostbusters '84
The Pelican Brief '93
Real Genius '85

Harvey Atkin
Meatballs '79

Christopher Atkins
Pirate Movie '82

Eileen Atkins
Oliver Twist '82

Felicia Atkins
The Errand Boy '61

Tom Atkins
Skeezer '82

Jayne Atkinson
Free Willy '93

Rowan Atkinson
Bernard and the Genie '91
Four Weddings and a
Funeral '93
Hot Shots! Part Deux '93
Never Say Never Again
'83
The Witches '90

Richard Attenborough
David Copperfield '70
Doctor Doolittle '67
Jurassic Park '93
Ten Little Indians '75

Richard Attenborough▶
A Bridge Too Far '77
Chaplin '92
Shadowlands '93

Billy Attmore
The Treasure of
Matecumbe '76

Edith Atwater
It Happened at the
World's Fair '63

Lionel Atwill
Captain America '44
Captain Blood '35

Brigitte Auber
To Catch a Thief '55

Rene Auberjonois
King Kong '76
M*A*S*H '70
My Best Friend Is a
Vampire '88
Police Academy 5:
Assignment Miami Beach
'88
A Smoky Mountain
Christmas '86

Lenore Aubert
Abbott and Costello Meet
Frankenstein '48

James Aubrey
Lord of the Flies '63

Jimmy Aubrey
Courage of the North '35

Danielle Aubry
Bikini Beach '64

Michel Auclair
Beauty and the Beast '46

Stephane Audran
Ten Little Indians '75

Mischa Auer
The Christmas That Almost
Wasn't '66

Patrick Auffay
The 400 Blows '59

Claudine Auger
Secret Places '85
Thunderball '65

Florrie Augger
Bugsy Malone '76

Robert August
The Endless Summer '66
The Endless Summer 2 '94

Jean-Pierre Aumont
The Horse Without a Head
'63
Lili '53

Georges Auric
Beauty and the Beast '46

Karen Austin
Summer Rental '85

Patti Austin
Tucker: The Man and His
Dream '88

Paul Austin
The Manhattan Project '86

Ray Austin▶
Highlander: The Gathering
'93

Daniel Auteuil
Jean de Florette '87
Manon of the Spring '87

Gene Autry
The Phantom Empire '35

Igor Auzins▶
We of the Never Never
'82

Frankie Avalon
Back to the Beach '87
Beach Blanket Bingo '65
Beach Party '63
Bikini Beach '64
Grease '78
How to Stuff a Wild Bikini
'65
Muscle Beach Party '64
Voyage to the Bottom of
the Sea '61

Luis Avalos
Ghost Fever '87

James Avery
Beastmaster 2: Through
the Portal of Time '91

Margaret Avery
The Fish that Saved
Pittsburgh '79

Tex Avery▶
All This and Tex Avery
Tool '92
Bugs Bunny Superstar '75

John G. Avildsen
The Karate Kid: Part 3 '89

John G. Avildsen▶
8 Seconds '94
For Keeps '88
The Karate Kid '84
The Karate Kid: Part 2 '86
The Karate Kid: Part 3 '89
Lean on Me '89
The Power of One '92
Rocky '76
Rocky 5 '90

Rick Aviles
Ghost '90

Jan Avran
Zorro, Vol. 1 '58

Philippe Avron
Circus Angel '65

Hoyt Axton
Christmas Comes to Willow
Creek '87
Gremlins '84
Heart Like a Wheel '83
The Rousters '83

Dan Aykroyd
Chaplin '92
Coneheads '93
Dragnet '87
Driving Miss Daisy '89
Ghostbusters '84
Ghostbusters 2 '89
The Great Outdoors '88
My Girl '91
My Girl 2 '94
My Stepmother Is an Alien
'88
North '94
Sneakers '92
Spies Like Us '85
This is My Life '92
Twilight Zone: The Movie
'83

Danielle Aykroyd
Coneheads '93

Felix Aylmer
Alice in Wonderland '50

Lew Ayres
Battle for the Planet of the
Apes '73
Salem's Lot '79

Annette Azcuy
Bill & Ted's Bogus Journey
'91

Shabana Azmi
Madame Sousatzka '88
Son of the Pink Panther
'93

Charles Aznavour
Ten Little Indians '75

Candice Azzara
Doin' Time on Planet Earth
'88

Obba Babatunde
Philadelphia '93
Undercover Blues '93

Barbara Babcock
Far and Away '92
On the Edge: The Survival
of Dana '79
That Was Then. . .This Is
Now '85

Lauren Bacall
All I Want for Christmas
'91
Key Largo '48
Mr. North '88
The Shootist '76

Michael Bacall
Wait Until Spring, Bandini
'90

Barbara Bach
Give My Regards to Broad
Street '84
The Spy Who Loved Me
'77

Catherine Bach
Cannonball Run 2 '84

Brian Backer
Fast Times at Ridgemont
High '82
Moving Violations '85

Jim Backus
Billie '65
C.H.O.M.P.S. '79
Now You See Him, Now
You Don't '72
Pat and Mike '52
Pete's Dragon '77

The Pied Piper of Hamelin
'57
Rebel Without a Cause '55
The Wonderful World of
the Brothers Grimm '62

Kevin Bacon
The Air Up There '94
Footloose '84
Hero at Large '80
She's Having a Baby '88
White Water Summer '87

Lloyd Bacon▶
Knute Rockne: All American
'40

Hermione Baddeley
The Belles of St. Trinian's
'53
A Christmas Carol '51
Mary Poppins '64

Diedrich Bader
The Beverly Hillbillies '93

John Badham▶
American Flyers '85
Another Stakeout '93
Bingo Long Traveling All-
Stars & Motor Kings '76
Short Circuit '86
War Games '83

Mary Badham
To Kill a Mockingbird '62

Buddy Baer
Jack & the Beanstalk '52

Max Baer Jr.▶
Ode to Billy Joe '76

Meredith Baer
The Chicken Chronicles '77

Parley Baer
The Adventures of
Huckleberry Finn '60
Dave '93
The Ugly Dachshund '65

Carol Bagdasarian
The Aurora Encounter '85
The Charge of the Model
T's '76

Ross Bagley
The Little Rascals '94

Chuck Bail▶
Gumball Rally '76

G.W. Bailey
Mannequin '87
Police Academy 6: City
Under Siege '89
A Winner Never Quits '86

Conrad Bain
Bananas '71
C.H.O.M.P.S. '79

Ron Bain
Experience Preferred. . .
But Not Essential '83

Fay Bainter
Babes on Broadway '41
The Human Comedy '43
Journey for Margaret '42
Secret Life of Walter Mitty
'47
State Fair '45

Jimmy Baio
The Bad News Bears in
Breaking Training '77

Scott Baio
Bugsy Malone '76

Foxes '80

Scott Bairstow
White Fang 2: The Myth
of the White Wolf '94

Richard Bakalayan
The Computer Wore Tennis
Shoes '69

Blanche Baker
French Postcards '79
Sixteen Candles '84

Carroll Baker
Giant '56
How the West was Won
'63
Kindergarten Cop '90
Watcher in the Woods '81

Diane Baker
The Horse in the Gray
Flannel Suit '68
Journey to the Center of
the Earth '59
The Joy Luck Club '93

Dylan Baker
Delirious '91
The Wizard of Loneliness
'88

Jill Baker
Hope and Glory '87

Joby Baker
Gidget '59

Joe Don Baker
Fletch '85
Guns of the Magnificent
Seven '69
Junior Bonner '72
Leonard Part 6 '87
The Natural '84
Reality Bites '94
Walking Tall '73

Kathy Baker
Dad '89
Edward Scissorhands '90
Permanent Record '88
The Right Stuff '83

Kenny Baker
The Elephant Man '80
The Empire Strikes Back
'80
Return of the Jedi '83
Sleeping Beauty '89
Star Wars '77
Time Bandits '81

Kenny L. Baker
Amadeus '84
At the Circus '39
Sleeping Beauty '89

Ray Baker
Camp Nowhere '94

Tom Baker
The Chronicles of Narnia
'89
Golden Voyage of Sinbad
'73

Gary Bakewell
Backbeat '94

**William "Billy"
Bakewell**
Davy Crockett, King of the
Wild Frontier '55
Gone with the Wind '39
Radar Men from the Moon
'52

Brenda Bakke
Hot Shots! Part Deux '93

Ralph Bakshi▶
Fire and Ice '83
The Lord of the Rings '78
Wizards '77

Bob Balaban
Amos and Andrew '93
Close Encounters of the
   Third Kind '77
For Love or Money '93
Girlfriends '78
Greedy '94
2010 : The Year We
   Make Contact '84

Bob Balaban▶
My Boyfriend's Back '93

Belinda Balaski
The Howling '81

Adam Baldwin
Hadley's Rebellion '84
My Bodyguard '80
Radio Flyer '92

Alec Baldwin
Beetlejuice '88
The Hunt for Red October
   '90
Prelude to a Kiss '92
The Shadow '94
She's Having a Baby '88

Daniel Baldwin
Car 54, Where Are You?
   '94

Peter Baldwin▶
The Hoboken Chicken
   Emergency '84
Lots of Luck '85

Stephen Baldwin
8 Seconds '94
The Lawrenceville Stories
   '80s

Christian Bale
Empire of the Sun '87
The Land of Faraway '87
Newsies '92
Swing Kids '93
Treasure Island '89

Ina Balin
The Projectionist '71

Fairuza Balk
Outside Chance of
   Maximillian Glick '88
Return to Oz '85
The Worst Witch '86

Geza Balkay
A Hungarian Fairy Tale '87

Angeline Ball
The Commitments '91

Lucille Ball
Follow the Fleet '36
Room Service '38
Sorrowful Jones '49
Yours, Mine & Ours '68

William Ball
Suburban Commando '91

Carroll Ballard▶
The Black Stallion '79
Never Cry Wolf '83
Wind '92

Jerry Ballew
Cry from the Mountain '85

Martin Balsam
All the President's Men '76
Little Big Man '70

Talia Balsam
Nadia '89
On the Edge: The Survival
   of Dana '79

Allison Balson
Legend of the White Horse
   '85

Gerry Bamman
Home Alone 2: Lost in
   New York '92
Lorenzo's Oil '92

Alexis Banas
The Haunting of Barney
   Palmer '90s

Anne Bancroft
The Elephant Man '80
Honeymoon in Vegas '92
Jesus of Nazareth '77
The Miracle Worker '62
Silent Movie '76

George Bancroft
Little Men '40

Albert Band▶
Prehysteria '93
Prehysteria 2 '94

Charles Band▶
Prehysteria '93

Antonio Banderas
Philadelphia '93

Joy Bang
Play It Again, Sam '72

Jonathan Banks
Beverly Hills Cop '84
Nadia '89

Leslie Banks
Jamaica Inn '39

Ian Bannen
George's Island '91
Ghost Dad '90
Hope and Glory '87
The Prodigal '83
Watcher in the Woods '81

Yoshimitu Banno▶
Godzilla vs. the Smog
   Monster '72

Jack Bannon
Miracle of the Heart: A
   Boys Town Story '86

Christine Baranski
Addams Family Values '93

Olivia Barash
Child of Glass '78

Adrienne Barbeau
Back to School '86
Cannonball Run '81
Charlie and the Great
   Balloon Chase '82
Swamp Thing '82

Joseph Barbera▶
The Jetsons: The Movie '90

Katie Barberi
The Garbage Pail Kids
   Movie '87

George Barbier
Little Miss Broadway '38

Joan Barclay
Blake of Scotland Yard '36
Flying Wild '41

Roy Barcroft
Federal Agents vs.
   Underworld, Inc. '49
G-Men Never Forget '48
Jesse James Rides Again
   '47
Radar Men from the Moon
   '52
Son of Zorro '47

Brigitte Bardot
Dear Brigitte '65

Lynn Bari
Francis Joins the WACs '54

Lex Barker
The Farmer's Daughter '47

Ellen Barkin
The Adventures of
   Buckaroo Banzai Across
   the Eighth Dimension '84
Desert Bloom '86
Eddie and the Cruisers '83
Harry & Son '84
Into the West '92
Tender Mercies '83
This Boy's Life '93

Peter Barkworth
The Littlest Horse Thieves
   '76

Binnie Barnes
The Trouble with Angels
   '66
Where Angels Go, Trouble
   Follows '68

Christopher Barnes
Battle of the Bullies '85
Tut and Tuttle '82

Sandy Baron
Broadway Danny Rose '84

Douglas Barr
Spaced Invaders '90

Jean-Marc Barr
Hope and Glory '87

Leonard Barr
Diamonds are Forever '71

**Marie-Christine
Barrault**
Table for Five '83

Gabriel Barre
Luggage of the Gods '87

Edith Barrett
Jane Eyre '44

Jane Barrett
The Sword & the Rose '53

Barbara Barrie
Breaking Away '79
Child of Glass '78
Two of a Kind '82

Colin Barrie
Melody '71

Robert Barron
Bill & Ted's Excellent
   Adventure '89
Sea Hound '47

Steven Barron▶
Coneheads '93
Electric Dreams '84
Teenage Mutant Ninja
   Turtles 1: The Movie '90

Zelda Barron▶
Secret Places '85
Shag: The Movie '89

Diana Barrows
My Mom's a Werewolf '89

**Donald (Don "Red")
Barry**
Adventures of Red Ryder
   '40
The Shakiest Gun in the
   West '68

Gene Barry
The War of the Worlds
   '53

Neill Barry
Joey '85
Old Enough '84

Patricia Barry
Sammy, the Way-Out Seal
   '62
Twilight Zone: The Movie
   '83

Raymond J. Barry
Cool Runnings '93

Tony Barry
Little Boy Lost '78
The Quest '86
We of the Never Never
   '82

Deborah Barrymore
Lionheart '87

Drew Barrymore
Babes in Toyland '86
Cat's Eye '85
Conspiracy of Love '87
E.T.: The Extra-Terrestrial
   '82
Irreconcilable Differences
   '84
See You in the Morning
   '89
Wayne's World 2 '93

Ethel Barrymore
The Farmer's Daughter '47
The Paradine Case '47

Lionel Barrymore
Ah, Wilderness! '35
Captains Courageous '37
David Copperfield '35
It's a Wonderful Life '46
Key Largo '48
Since You Went Away '44
Treasure Island '34

Paul Bartel
Frankenweenie '84
Rock 'n' Roll High School
   '79

Paul Bartel▶
Cannonball '76
The Longshot '86

Freddie Bartholomew
Captains Courageous '37
David Copperfield '35
Little Lord Fauntleroy '36
Tom Brown's School Days
   '40

Scott Bartle
Hector's Bunyip '86

Bennie Bartlett
Clipped Wings '53

Bonnie Bartlett
Dave '93

Dick Bartlett▶
Ollie Hopnoodle's Haven
   of Bliss '88

Hall Bartlett▶
Jonathan Livingston Seagull
   '73

Keith Bartlett
Truly, Madly, Deeply '91

Robin Bartlett
Baby Boom '87
If Looks Could Kill '91
Lean on Me '89
Regarding Henry '91

Robyn Barto
Blue Skies Again '83

Charles T. Barton▶
Abbott and Costello Meet
   Frankenstein '48
Africa Screams '49
Buck Privates Come Home
   '47
The Shaggy Dog '59
Toby Tyler '59

Billy Barty
The Amazing Dobermans
   '76
Foul Play '78
Legend '86
Masters of the Universe
   '87
Rumpelstiltskin '86
Snow White '89
Tough Guys '86
Under the Rainbow '81
Willow '88

Mikhail Baryshnikov
That's Dancing! '85

Gary Basaraba
One Magic Christmas '85

Dante Basco
Hook '91

Richard Basehart
Being There '79
Hans Brinker '69
Island of Dr. Moreau '77
Mark Twain's A
   Connecticut Yankee in
   King Arthur's Court '78

Count Basie
Cinderfella '60

Toni Basil
Pajama Party '64

Kim Basinger
Batman '89
Hard Country '81
My Stepmother Is an Alien
   '88
The Natural '84
Never Say Never Again
   '83
The Real McCoy '93
Wayne's World 2 '93

Richard Baskin▶
Sing '89

Jules Bass▶
The Ballad of Paul Bunyan
   '72
Daydreamer '66
Flight of Dragons '82
Frosty the Snowman '69
The Hobbit '78
The Last Unicorn '82
Mad Monster Party '68
The Return of the King '80

Santa Claus is Coming to
Town '70

Albert Basserman
Foreign Correspondent '40
The Red Shoes '48
Since You Went Away '44

Angela Bassett
Boyz N the Hood '91
Malcolm X '92
What's Love Got to Do
With It? '93

Michal Bat-Adam▶
Boy Takes Girl '83

Joy Batchelor▶
Animal Farm '55

Jason Bateman
Breaking the Rules '92
Teen Wolf Too '87

Justine Bateman
Satisfaction '88

Kent Bateman
Breaking the Rules '92

Alan Bates
The Go-Between '71
Whistle Down the Wind
'62

Barbara Bates
The Caddy '53

Florence Bates
I Remember Mama '48
Rebecca '40
Secret Life of Walter Mitty
'47
Since You Went Away '44

Kathy Bates
Dick Tracy '90
A Home of Our Own '93
Men Don't Leave '89
North '94
Prelude to a Kiss '92

Timothy Bateson
The Mouse That Roared
'59

Randall Batinkoff
Buffy the Vampire Slayer
'92
Christy '94
For Keeps '88
School Ties '92

Belinda Bauer
Flashdance '83
Robocop 2 '90
Timerider '83

Steven Bauer
Gleaming the Cube '89

Mario Bava▶
Wonders of Aladdin '61

Alan Baxter
Saboteur '42

Anne Baxter
I Confess '53
The Ten Commandments
'56

Warner Baxter
Stand Up and Cheer '34

Gary Bayer
Not My Kid '85

Geoffrey Bayldon
The Bushbaby '70
Madame Sousatzka '88

Stephen Bayly▶
Diamond's Edge '88

Michael Beach
Lean on Me '89

Stephanie Beacham
Troop Beverly Hills '89

John Beal
The Kid Who Loved
Christmas '90
Ten Who Dared '60

Jennifer Beals
Flashdance '83
That's Dancing! '85

Orson Bean
Innerspace '87

Sean Bean
Black Beauty '94

**Matthew "Stymie"
Beard**
Little Rascals Christmas
Special '79

Alice Beardsley
Where the Lilies Bloom '74

Emmanuelle Beart
Date with an Angel '87
Manon of the Spring '87

Clyde Beatty
Africa Screams '49
Darkest Africa '36
The Lost Jungle '34

Ned Beatty
Back to Hannibal: The
Further Adventures of
Tom Sawyer and
Huckleberry Finn '90
Back to School '86
The Big Bus '76
Captain America '89
A Cry in the Wild '90
The Haunting of Barney
Palmer '90s
The Incredible Shrinking
Woman '81
Konrad '85
The Last American Hero
'73
Prelude to a Kiss '92
Promises in the Dark '79
Purple People Eater '88
Rudy '93
The Silver Streak '76
Superman 1: The Movie
'78
Superman 2 '80
The Toy '82

Warren Beatty
Dick Tracy '90

Warren Beatty▶
Dick Tracy '90

William Beaudine▶
Blues Busters '50
Bowery Buckaroos '47
Follow the Leader '44
Ghost Chasers '51
Hard-Boiled Mahoney '47
Spook Busters '46
Ten Who Dared '60
Turf Boy '42
Westward Ho, the
Wagons! '56

Julie Beaulieu
Bridge to Terabithia '85

Gabrielle Beaumont▶
Gone are the Days '84

Louise Beavers
General Spanky '36
Tammy and the Bachelor
'57

John Beck
Audrey Rose '77
The Big Bus '76
Sleeper '73

Julian Beck
Poltergeist 2: The Other
Side '86

Michael Beck
The Golden Seal '83
Xanadu '80

Vincent Beck
Santa Claus Conquers the
Martians '64

Graham Beckel
Hazel's People '75
The Paper Chase '73

Gretchen Becker
Huck and the King of
Hearts '93

Harold Becker▶
Taps '81

Scotty Beckett
Ali Baba and the Forty
Thieves '43
The Jolson Story '46
Stand Up and Cheer '34

Kate Beckinsale
Much Ado About Nothing
'93

Don Beddoe
Buck Privates Come Home
'47
Jack the Giant Killer '62

Bonnie Bedelia
The Boy Who Could Fly
'86
Heart Like a Wheel '83
Salem's Lot '79

Patrick Bedford
Up the Down Staircase '67

Kabir Bedi
Octopussy '83

Alfonso Bedoya
Treasure of the Sierra
Madre '48

Ford Beebe▶
Buck Rogers Conquers the
Universe '39
Don Winslow of the Coast
Guard '43
Don Winslow of the Navy
'43
The Last of the Mohicans
'32
The Phantom Creeps '39
Radio Patrol '37
Shadow of the Eagle '32
Tim Tyler's Luck '37
Winners of the West '40

Greg Beeman▶
License to Drive '88
Mom and Dad Save the
World '92

Holly Beeman
The Legend of Black
Thunder Mountain '79

Steve Beeman
The Legend of Black
Thunder Mountain '79

Tom Beeman▶
The Legend of Black
Thunder Mountain '79

Noah Beery Jr.
The Capture of Grizzly
Adams '82
Fighting with Kit Carson
'33
Million Dollar Kid '44
'Neath Brooklyn Bridge '42
Seven Faces of Dr. Lao '63
Tailspin Tommy '34
Walking Tall '73

Noah Beery Sr.
Adventures of Red Ryder
'40
Devil Horse '32
Fighting with Kit Carson
'33
To the Last Man '33
Zorro Rides Again '37

Wallace Beery
Ah, Wilderness! '35
Treasure Island '34

Ed Begley Jr.
Citizens Band '77
Dark Horse '92
Goin' South '78
Greedy '94
The Legend of Sleepy
Hollow '86
Renaissance Man '94
She-Devil '89
The Story Lady '93
Voyager from the Unknown
'83

Sam Behrens
Alive '93
And You Thought Your
Parents Were Weird! '91

Barbara Bel Geddes
I Remember Mama '48

Doris Belack
Opportunity Knocks '90
What About Bob? '91

Harry Belafonte
Buck and the Preacher '72
Free to Be. . .You and Me
'83
Muppet Revue '85

Louise Belaire
Return to Boggy Creek '77

Leon Belasco
Fisherman's Wharf '39

Christopher Bell
Sarah, Plain and Tall '91
Skylark '93

George Anthony Bell
House Party 2: The Pajama
Jam '91

James Bell
My Friend Flicka '43

Marshall Bell
Tucker: The Man and His
Dream '88

Martin Bell▶
American Heart '92

Rex Bell
Battling with Buffalo Bill
'31

Earl Bellamy▶
Against A Crooked Sky '75
Seven Alone '75

Ralph Bellamy
Cancel My Reservation '72
Disorderlies '87
His Girl Friday '40
Love Leads the Way '84
Oh, God! '77

Kathleen Beller
Promises in the Dark '79

Cynthia Belliveau
The Dream Team '89

Vicki Belmonte
The Grass is Always
Greener Over the Septic
Tank '78

Robert Beltran
Night of the Comet '84

James Belushi
Curly Sue '91
K-9 '89
Little Shop of Horrors '86
The Man with One Red
Shoe '85
Mr. Destiny '90
Once Upon a Crime '92
Only the Lonely '91

John Belushi
Goin' South '78

Richard Belzer
Fame '80

Steven Benally Jr.
The Secret of Navajo
Cave '76

Robert Benchley
Foreign Correspondent '40

Scott Benderer
Great Love Experiment '84

William Bendix
A Connecticut Yankee in
King Arthur's Court '49

Billy Benedict
Bowery Buckaroos '47
Follow the Leader '44
Ghost Chasers '51
Hard-Boiled Mahoney '47
Spook Busters '46

Dirk Benedict
Battlestar Galactica '78

Nick Benedict
Pistol: The Birth of a
Legend '90

Paul Benedict
The Addams Family '91
The Freshman '90

Armonia Benedito
Strictly Ballroom '92

Roberto Benigni
Son of the Pink Panther
'93

Annette Bening
The Great Outdoors '88
Regarding Henry '91

Richard Benjamin
Love at First Bite '79
Saturday the 14th '81
The Sunshine Boys '75
Witches' Brew '79

The Trial of the Incredible
  Hulk '89

Bill Bixby▶
Death of the Incredible
  Hulk '90
The Trial of the Incredible
  Hulk '89

Anna Bjorn
More American Graffiti '79

Craig Black
Flirting '89

Karen Black
Airport '75 '75
The Double O Kid '92
Invaders from Mars '86

Noel Black▶
Conspiracy of Love '87
Quarterback Princess '85

Ryan Black
Geronimo '93

Honor Blackman
Jason and the Argonauts
  '63

Sidney Blackmer
High Society '56
Tammy and the Bachelor
  '57

Gerard Blain
Hatari '62

Vivian Blaine
Guys and Dolls '55
State Fair '45

Janet Blair
The One and Only,
  Genuine, Original Family
  Band '68

Linda Blair
Airport '75 '75
Wild Horse Hank '79

Lisa Blair
Three Men and a Baby
  '87

Michelle Blair
Three Men and a Baby
  '87

Andre B. Blake
Philadelphia '93

Karen Blake
Sundance and the Kid '76

Madge Blake
Singin' in the Rain '52

Marie Blake
Love Finds Andy Hardy '38

Pamela Blake
Kid Dynamite '43
Sea Hound '47

Robert (Bobby) Blake
Andy Hardy's Double Life
  '42
Treasure of the Sierra
  Madre '48

Colin Blakely
Evil Under the Sun '82
Little Lord Fauntleroy '80
The Pink Panther Strikes
  Again '76

Susan Blakely
Hiroshima Maiden '88
The Lords of Flatbush '74

My Mom's a Werewolf '89
Over the Top '86

Jewel Blanch
Against A Crooked Sky '75

Sandrine Blancke
Toto le Heros '91

Clara Blandick
The Wizard of Oz '39

Mark Blankfield
Robin Hood: Men in Tights
  '93

Jonah Blechman
This Boy's Life '93

Jeff Bleckner▶
White Water Summer '87

Tempestt Bledsoe
Dream Date '93

Brian Blessed
Flash Gordon '80
Man of La Mancha '72
Much Ado About Nothing
  '93
Return to Treasure Island,
  Vol. 1 '85
Robin Hood: Prince of
  Thieves '91

Brenda Blethyn
A River Runs Through It '92
The Witches '90

Jason Blicker
African Journey '89
American Boyfriends '89

Bernard Blier
The Tall Blond Man with
  One Black Shoe '72

Dan Blocker
The Errand Boy '61

Dirk Blocker
Bonanza: The Return '93

Joan Blondell
Support Your Local
  Gunfighter '71
Topper Returns '41
A Tree Grows in Brooklyn
  '45

Anne Bloom
Dirt Bike Kid '86

Claire Bloom
Clash of the Titans '81
The Wonderful World of
  the Brothers Grimm '62

Jeffrey Bloom▶
Dog Pound Shuffle '75

John Bloom
The Incredible Two-Headed
  Transplant '71

Verna Bloom
Honkytonk Man '82
The Journey of Natty
  Gann '85

Eric Blore
Shall We Dance '37

Roberts Blossom
Always '89
Citizens Band '77
Doc Hollywood '91
Home Alone '90

Michael Blouin
The Great Land of Small
  '86

Simone Blue
Nadia '89

Mark Blum
Crocodile Dundee '86
Desperately Seeking Susan
  '85

Alan Blumenfeld
Problem Child 2 '91

Graeme Blundell
The Year My Voice Broke
  '87

Don Bluth▶
All Dogs Go to Heaven
  '89
An American Tail '86
The Land Before Time '88
Rock-a-Doodle '92
Secret of NIMH '82
Thumbelina '94

Margaret Blye
Little Darlings '80

Ann Blyth
Kismet '55

David Blyth▶
My Grandpa is a Vampire
  '92

Jeff Blyth▶
Cheetah '89

Robert Blythe
Experience Preferred. . .
  But Not Essential '83

Eric Boardman
Son of Dinosaurs '90

Hart Bochner
Making Mr. Right '86
Mr. Destiny '90
Supergirl '84

Hart Bochner▶
P.C.U. '94

Lloyd Bochner
The Horse in the Gray
  Flannel Suit '68
Naked Gun 2 1/2: The
  Smell of Fear '91
Spiderman '81

Wolfgang Bodison
Little Big League '94

Karl-Heinz Boehm
The Wonderful World of
  the Brothers Grimm '62

Earl Boen
Terminator 2: Judgment
  Day '91

Dirk Bogarde
A Bridge Too Far '77

Humphrey Bogart
The African Queen '51
Casablanca '42
Key Largo '48
The Maltese Falcon '41
Sabrina '54
Treasure of the Sierra
  Madre '48

Paul Bogart▶
Cancel My Reservation '72
A House Without a
  Christmas Tree '72
Oh, God! You Devil '84

Peter Bogdanovich▶
Mask '85
Paper Moon '73
The Thing Called Love '93
What's Up, Doc? '72

Gail Boggs
Ghost '90

Peter Bohlke
Toto le Heros '91

Corinne Bohrer
Vice Versa '88

Curt Bois
Wings of Desire '88

Sarel Bok
A Far Off Place '93

James Bolam
The Loneliness of the Long
  Distance Runner '62

Buddy Boles
Regl'ar Fellers '41

John Boles
Curly Top '35
The Littlest Rebel '35
Stand Up and Cheer '34

Ray Bolger
Babes in Toyland '61
Daydreamer '66
That's Dancing! '85
The Wizard of Oz '39

Michael Bollner
Willy Wonka & the
  Chocolate Factory '71

Joseph Bologna
The Big Bus '76
Coupe de Ville '90
Jersey Girl '92
My Favorite Year '82
Not Quite Human '87

Craig Bolotin▶
That Night '93

Christopher Bolton
City Boy '93

Emily Bolton
Moonraker '79

Fortuna Bonanova
Ali Baba and the Forty
  Thieves '43

Ivan Bonar
MacArthur '77

Derek Bond
Tony Draws a Horse '51

James Bond III
The Fish that Saved
  Pittsburgh '79

Sudie Bond
I am the Cheese '83
Where the Lilies Bloom '74

Tommy "Butch" Bond
Atom Man vs. Superman
  '50
Superman: The Serial, Vol.
  1 '48

Ward Bond
Bringing Up Baby '38
Gone with the Wind '39
Gypsy Colt '54
It Happened One Night
  '34
It's a Wonderful Life '46
The Maltese Falcon '41

The Quiet Man '52

Beulah Bondi
It's a Wonderful Life '46
Mr. Smith Goes to
  Washington '39
Penny Serenade '41
So Dear to My Heart '49
The Wonderful World of
  the Brothers Grimm '62

Peter Bonerz▶
Police Academy 6: City
  Under Siege '89

Helena Bonham Carter
Howard's End '92

Evan Bonifant
3 Ninjas Kick Back '94

Tony Bonner
Quigley Down Under '90
Sudden Terror '70

Maria Bonnerie
The Polar Bear King '94

Sonny Bono
Airplane 2: The Sequel '82
Hairspray '88
Troll '85

Brian Bonsall
Blank Check '93
Father Hood '93

Sorrell Booke
Up the Down Staircase '67

Pat Boone
Journey to the Center of
  the Earth '59
State Fair '62

Richard Boone
Against A Crooked Sky '75
Big Jake '71
The Shootist '76

Charley Boorman
Hope and Glory '87

John Boorman▶
Hope and Glory '87

Katrine Boorman
Hope and Glory '87

Adrian Booth
Captain America '44

Connie Booth
Little Lord Fauntleroy '80
Monty Python and the
  Holy Grail '75

Edwina Booth
The Last of the Mohicans
  '32

Karin Booth
Tobor the Great '54

Powers Boothe
Tombstone '93

Veda Ann Borg
The Bachelor and the
  Bobby-Soxer '47
Guys and Dolls '55

Ernest Borgnine
The Black Hole '79
The Double McGuffin '79
The Greatest '77
Ice Station Zebra '68
Jesus of Nazareth '77
Love Leads the Way '84
Neptune Factor '73

The Poseidon Adventure
'72
The Prince and the Pauper
'78
Super Fuzz '81

Milan Borich
My Grandpa is a Vampire
'92

Robert Boris▶
Oxford Blues '84

Phillip Borsos▶
The Grey Fox '83
One Magic Christmas '85

Philip Bosco
The Dream Team '89
F/X 2: The Deadly Art of
Illusion '91
The Money Pit '86
Straight Talk '92
Three Men and a Baby
'87

Tom Bosley
Bang Bang Kid '67
Gus '76
The World of Henry Orient
'64
Yours, Mine & Ours '68

Barbara Bosson
The Last Starfighter '84

Barry Bostwick
Movie, Movie '78
Weekend at Bernie's 2 '93

John Boswall
Three Men and a Little
Lady '90

Hobart Bosworth
The Last of the Mohicans
'32

Wade Boteler
The Green Hornet '39

Niki Botholo
The Ewoks: Battle for
Endor '85

Joseph Bottoms
The Black Hole '79
The Dove '74

Sam Bottoms
Bronco Billy '80
The Outlaw Josey Wales
'76

Timothy Bottoms
Hambone & Hillie '84
Invaders from Mars '86
The Land of Faraway '87
Love Leads the Way '84
The Other Side of the
Mountain, Part 2 '78
The Paper Chase '73

Michel Boujenah
Three Men and a Cradle
'85

Carol Bouquet
For Your Eyes Only '81

Michel Bouquet
Toto le Heros '91

Andre Bourvil
When Wolves Cry '69

Dennis Boutsikaris
*batteries not included '87
The Dream Team '89

Julie Bovasso
Moonstruck '87

Simmy Bow
The Doberman Gang '72

Eric Bowen
The Gods Must Be Crazy
2 '89

Jenny Bowen▶
Animal Behavior '89
The Wizard of Loneliness
'88

Michael Bowen
Night of the Comet '84

Roger Bowen
M*A*S*H '70
What About Bob? '91

Malick Bowens
Bophal '93

Dallas Bower▶
Alice in Wonderland '50

David Bower
Four Weddings and a
Funeral '93

David Bowie
Labyrinth '86

Judi Bowker
Clash of the Titans '81

Jessica Bowman
Remote '93

Ralph Bowman
Flaming Frontiers '38

Rob Bowman▶
Airborne '93

Bruce Boxleitner
The Babe '92
Kuffs '92
Tron '82

Alan Boyce
Permanent Record '88

Brittany Boyd
Lassie '94

Cameron Boyd
King of the Hill '93

Sarah Boyd
Old Enough '84

William Boyd
Oliver Twist '33

Sally Boyden
Barnaby and Me '77

Charles Boyer
Around the World in 80
Days '56

Sully Boyer
Car Wash '76
The Manhattan Project '86

Brad Boyle
Hoosiers '86

Lara Flynn Boyle
Baby's Day Out '94
Dead Poets Society '89
How I Got into College
'89
Poltergeist 3 '88
Wayne's World '92

Peter Boyle
The Dream Team '89

Ghost in the Noonday Sun
'74
Honeymoon in Vegas '92
Johnny Dangerously '84
The Shadow '94
Turk 182! '85
Young Frankenstein '74

Ray Boyle
Zombies of the
Stratosphere '52

William Boyle
Hawk of the Wilderness
'38

Reizl Bozyk
Crossing Delancey '88

Bruno Bozzetto▶
Allegro Non Troppo '76
Mr. Rossi's Dreams '83
Mr. Rossi's Vacation '83
Vip, My Brother Superman
'90

Lorraine Bracco
The Dream Team '89
Radio Flyer '92
Sing '89
Talent for the Game '91

Eddie Bracken
Home Alone 2: Lost in
New York '92

Jesse Bradford
King of the Hill '93

Lane Bradford
The Invisible Monster '50

Richard Bradford
Goin' South '78
Legend of Billie Jean '85
Little Nikita '88
More American Graffiti '79
Permanent Record '88
The Trip to Bountiful '85

Benjamin C. Bradlee
Born Yesterday '93

Scott Brady
When Every Day was the
Fourth of July '78

**Eric (Hans Gudegast)
Braeden**
Escape from the Planet of
the Apes '71

Sonia Braga
The Last Prostitute '91

Helen Bragdon
Where the Lilies Bloom '74

John Brahm▶
Miracle of Our Lady of
Fatima '52

Wilfrid Brambell
Sword of the Valiant '83

Marco Brambilla
Cool Runnings '93

Kenneth Branagh
Much Ado About Nothing
'93
Swing Kids '93

Kenneth Branagh▶
Much Ado About Nothing
'93

Lillo Brancato
A Bronx Tale '93
Renaissance Man '94

Jolene Brand
Zorro, Vol. 1 '58

Neville Brand
The Adventures of
Huckleberry Finn '60
Cahill: United States
Marshal '73
That Darn Cat '65

Klaus Maria Brandauer
Never Say Never Again
'83
White Fang '91

Jonathan Brandis
Ladybugs '92
The NeverEnding Story 2:
Next Chapter '91
Sidekicks '93

Marlon Brando
The Freshman '90
Guys and Dolls '55
Superman 1: The Movie
'78

Henry Brandon
When the North Wind
Blows '74

Michael Brandon
Promises in the Dark '79

Penelope Branning
What's Eating Gilbert
Grape '93

Fred Brannon▶
The Crimson Ghost '46
Federal Agents vs.
Underworld, Inc. '49
G-Men Never Forget '48
The Invisible Monster '50
Jesse James Rides Again
'47
Jungle Drums of Africa '53
King of the Rocketmen '49
Radar Men from the Moon
'52
Zombies of the
Stratosphere '52

Benjamin Brazier
Heidi '93

Lidia Brazzi
The Christmas That Almost
Wasn't '66

Rossano Brazzi
The Christmas That Almost
Wasn't '66
South Pacific '58

Rossano Brazzi▶
The Christmas That Almost
Wasn't '66

Peter Breck
Benji '74

Bobby Breen
Breaking the Ice '38
Fisherman's Wharf '39
It Happened in New
Orleans '36
Let's Sing Again '36

Patrick Breen
For Love or Money '93

Paulette Breen
The Wizard of Speed and
Time '88

Jana Brejchova
The Original Fabulous
Adventures of Baron
Munchausen '61

Tia Brelis▶
Trading Mom '94

Lucille Bremer
Meet Me in St. Louis '44
Till the Clouds Roll By '46

Eileen Brennan
Babes in Toyland '86
The Cheap Detective '78
Clue '85
My Old Man '79
The New Adventures of
Pippi Longstocking '88
The Sting '73

Walter Brennan
The Gnome-Mobile '67
How the West was Won
'63
The One and Only,
Genuine, Original Family
Band '68
Support Your Local Sheriff
'69
Tammy and the Bachelor
'57
Those Calloways '65

Dori Brenner
Baby Boom '87

Evelyn Brent
Holt of the Secret Service
'42

Romney Brent
The Sign of Zorro '60

Alfonso Brescia▶
White Fang and the
Hunter '85

Bobbie Bresee
Ghoulies '85

Kevin Breslin
On the Edge: The Survival
of Dana '79

Martin Brest
Fast Times at Ridgemont
High '82

Martin Brest▶
Beverly Hills Cop '84
Going in Style '79

Richard Brestoff
Car Wash '76

Griffith Brewer
The Peanut Butter Solution
'85

Juliette Brewer
The Little Rascals '94

Diane Brewster
Courage of Black Beauty
'57
The Invisible Boy '57

Maia Brewton
Adventures in Babysitting
'87
Back to the Future '85

Kevin Breznahan
Alive '93

Jean-Claude Brialy
The 400 Blows '59

Bridget Brice
Twelve Chairs '70

Beth Brickell
Gentle Ben '69

Marshall Brickman▶
The Manhattan Project '86
Simon '80

Paul Brickman▶
Men Don't Leave '89

Beau Bridges
The Fifth Musketeer '79
Greased Lightning '77
Heart Like a Wheel '83
Night Crossing '81
Norma Rae '79
The Other Side of the
  Mountain '75
The Red Pony '49
Sidekicks '93
The Wizard '89

James Bridges▶
The Paper Chase '73

Jeff Bridges
American Heart '92
Bad Company '72
Hearts of the West '75
King Kong '76
Kiss Me Goodbye '82
The Last American Hero
  '73
See You in the Morning
  '89
Starman '84
Tron '82
Tucker: The Man and His
  Dream '88

Lloyd Bridges
Airplane! '80
Airplane 2: The Sequel '82
High Noon '52
Honey, I Blew Up the Kid
  '92
Hot Shots! Part Deux '93
Joe Versus the Volcano '90
Running Wild '73
Tucker: The Man and His
  Dream '88

Julie Briggs
Bowery Buckaroos '47

Fran Brill
Old Enough '84
What About Bob? '91

Patti Brill
Hard-Boiled Mahoney '47

Steven Brill
The Mighty Ducks '92

Nick Brimble
Robin Hood: Prince of
  Thieves '91

Wilford Brimley
Cocoon '85
Cocoon: The Return '88
Country '84
The Electric Horseman '79
The Ewoks: Battle for
  Endor '85
Harry & Son '84
The Natural '84
Remo Williams: The
  Adventure Begins '85
The Stone Boy '84
Tender Mercies '83
Where the Red Fern
  Grows: Part 2 '92

Ritch Brinkley
Cabin Boy '94

Jimmy Briscoe
Spaced Invaders '90

Morgan Brittany
The Prodigal '83

Pamela Britton
Anchors Aweigh '45

Tony Britton
Dr. Syn, Alias the
  Scarecrow '64
Horsemasters '61

Herman Brix
Fighting Devil Dogs '38
Hawk of the Wilderness
  '38

Anders Peter Bro
A Day in October '92

Lily Broberg
Famous Five Get into
  Trouble '87

Anne Brochet
Cyrano de Bergerac '90

Charles Brock
Sourdough '77

Deborah Brock▶
Andy and the Airwave
  Rangers '89
Rock 'n' Roll High School
  Forever '91

Roy Brocksmith
Arachnophobia '90
Big Business '88
Bill & Ted's Bogus Journey
  '91

Matthew Broderick
Ferris Bueller's Day Off '86
The Freshman '90
Ladyhawke '85
Max Dugan Returns '83
Out on a Limb '92
Project X '87
War Games '83

Steve Brodie
The Wizard of Speed and
  Time '88

Adrien Brody
Home at Last '88
King of the Hill '93

James Brolin
City Boy '93
Pee Wee's Big Adventure
  '85

Josh Brolin
The Goonies '85
Thrashin' '86

Valri Bromfield
Mr. Mom '83

Elaine Bromka
Uncle Buck '89

Sheila Bromley
Nancy Drew, Reporter '39

Sydney Bromley
Crystalstone '88
The NeverEnding Story '84

Eleanor Bron
Black Beauty '94
Help! '65
Turtle Diary '86

Charles Bronson
House of Wax '53
Once Upon a Time in the
  West '68
Pat and Mike '52

Claudio Brook
The Bees '78

Faith Brook
To Sir, with Love '67

Jayne Brook
Clean Slate '94
Kindergarten Cop '90

Peter Brook▶
Lord of the Flies '63

Hillary Brooke
Abbott and Costello Meet
  Captain Kidd '52
Africa Screams '49
Jane Eyre '44
The Philadelphia Story '40

Jacqueline Brookes
Naked Gun 2 1/2: The
  Smell of Fear '91

Dorothea Brooking▶
The Moon Stallion '85

Adam Brooks▶
Red Riding Hood '89

Aimee Brooks
Say Anything '89

Albert Brooks
I'll Do Anything '93
Twilight Zone: The Movie
  '83

Avery Brooks
The Ernest Green Story '93

Elisabeth Brooks
The Howling '81

Foster Brooks
Cracking Up '83
Super Seal '77
The Villain '79

Geraldine Brooks
Challenge to Lassie '49

James L. Brooks▶
I'll Do Anything '93
Terms of Endearment '83
Thursday's Game '74

Margaret Brooks
The Bushbaby '70

Mel Brooks
Free to Be. . .You and Me
  '83
High Anxiety '77
Robin Hood: Men in Tights
  '93
Silent Movie '76
Spaceballs '87
Twelve Chairs '70

Mel Brooks▶
High Anxiety '77
Robin Hood: Men in Tights
  '93
Silent Movie '76
Spaceballs '87
Twelve Chairs '70
Young Frankenstein '74

Peter Brooks
Gidget Goes to Rome '63

Phyllis Brooks
Little Miss Broadway '38
Rebecca of Sunnybrook
  Farm '38

Rand Brooks
Gone with the Wind '39

Pierce Brosnan
Mrs. Doubtfire '93

Otto Brower▶
Devil Horse '32
The Phantom Empire '35

Barry Brown
Bad Company '72

Bruce Brown▶
The Endless Summer '66
The Endless Summer 2 '94

Bryan Brown
F/X '86
F/X 2: The Deadly Art of
  Illusion '91
Give My Regards to Broad
  Street '84
Gorillas in the Mist '88

Candy Ann Brown
Zebrahead '92

Clancy Brown
Highlander '86

Clarence Brown▶
Ah, Wilderness! '35
The Human Comedy '43
National Velvet '44
The Yearling '46

David G. Brown
Chasing Dreams '81

Dwier Brown
The Cutting Edge '92
Mom and Dad Save the
  World '92

Ewing Miles Brown▶
Whale of a Tale '76

Garrett M. Brown
Uncle Buck '89

Georg Stanford Brown
House Party 2: The Pajama
  Jam '91
The Kid with the Broken
  Halo '82

**Georg Stanford
Brown▶**
Miracle of the Heart: A
  Boys Town Story '86

Gibran Brown
Marvin & Tige '84

James Brown
Adios Amigo '75
Rin Tin Tin, Hero of the
  West '55

Jim Brown
Ice Station Zebra '68

Joe E. Brown
Around the World in 80
  Days '56
The Tender Years '47

Johnny Mack Brown
Fighting with Kit Carson
  '33
Flaming Frontiers '38

Pamela Brown
Alice in Wonderland '50
Wuthering Heights '70

Peter Brown
The Aurora Encounter '85
A Tiger Walks '64

Ralph Brown
Wayne's World 2 '93

Reb Brown
Captain America 2: Death
  Too Soon '79

Ron Brown
Charlie, the Lonesome
  Cougar '67
The Legend of Black
  Thunder Mountain '79

Ruth Brown
Hairspray '88

Sarah Brown
Super Seal '77

Thomas Wilson Brown
Honey, I Shrunk the Kids
  '89

Tom Brown
Adventures of Smilin' Jack
  '43
Anne of Green Gables '34
Buck Privates Come Home
  '47

Charles A. Browne
Tailspin Tommy '34

Coral Browne
American Dreamer '84
Dreamchild '85

Lucille Browne
Law of the Wild '34

Roscoe Lee Browne
The Cowboys '72
Mark Twain's A
  Connecticut Yankee in
  King Arthur's Court '78
The World's Greatest
  Athlete '73

Ricou Browning
Flipper's New Adventure
  '64

Ricou Browning▶
Salty '73

Brenda Bruce
Back Home '90

Colin Bruce
Crusoe '89

Nigel Bruce
The Blue Bird '40
The Corn is Green '45
Journey for Margaret '42
Lassie, Come Home '43
Rebecca '40
Stand Up and Cheer '34
Suspicion '41
Treasure Island '34

Jane Brucker
Dirty Dancing '87

Eric Bruskotter
Major League 2 '94

Dora Bryan
Great St. Trinian's Train
  Robbery '66

John Bryant
Courage of Black Beauty
  '57

William Bryant
Mountain Family Robinson
  '79

Andrew Bryniarski
Batman Returns '92
The Program '93

Yul Brynner
The King and I '56
The Ten Commandments
  '56

Nicolas Cage
Amos and Andrew '93
Honeymoon in Vegas '92
It Could Happen to You
'94
Moonstruck '87
Peggy Sue Got Married
'86
Racing with the Moon '84
Rumble Fish '83
Valley Girl '83

James Cagney
The Seven Little Foys '55
Yankee Doodle Dandy '42

Jeanne Cagney
Yankee Doodle Dandy '42

William Cagney
Palooka '34

Christopher Cain
Force on Thunder Mountain
'77

Christopher Cain▶
Elmer '76
The Next Karate Kid '94
The Stone Boy '84
That Was Then. . .This Is
Now '85
Where the River Runs
Black '86
Young Guns '88

Michael Caine
Battle of Britain '69
A Bridge Too Far '77
Death Becomes Her '92
Dirty Rotten Scoundrels '88
Educating Rita '83
Harry & Walter Go to
New York '76
The Man Who Would Be
King '75
Mr. Destiny '90
The Muppet Christmas
Carol '92
Sleuth '72
The Swarm '78
Sweet Liberty '86
Victory '81

Shakira Caine
The Man Who Would Be
King '75

Anna Calder-Marshall
Wuthering Heights '70

Zoe Caldwell
Lantern Hill '90
The Purple Rose of Cairo
'85

Jade Calegory
Mac and Me '88

Don Calfa
Weekend at Bernie's '89

Nicole Calfan
The Four Musketeers '75

Louis Calhern
Duck Soup '33
High Society '56
Notorious '46
The Red Pony '49

Monica Calhoun
Bagdad Cafe '88

John Call
Santa Claus Conquers the
Martians '64

Mark Callan▶
Hector's Bunyip '86

Michael Callan
Gidget Goes Hawaiian '61
Mysterious Island '61

Joseph Calleia
The Caddy '53
The Jungle Book '42
The Light in the Forest '58
The Littlest Outlaw '54

Simon Callow
Amadeus '84
Four Weddings and a
Funeral '93
Mr. & Mrs. Bridge '91

Cab Calloway
The Littlest Angel '69

Vanessa Bell Calloway
What's Love Got to Do
With It? '93

Henry Calvin
The Sign of Zorro '60
Toby Tyler '59
Zorro, Vol. 1 '58

John Calvin
Dragonworld '94

Pablito Calvo
The Man Who Wagged
His Tail '57

Dean Cameron
Summer School '87

James Cameron▶
The Terminator '84
Terminator 2: Judgment
Day '91
True Lies '94

Kirk Cameron
The Best of Times '86
Like Father, Like Son '87

Rod Cameron
G-Men vs. the Black
Dragon '43

Trent Cameron
The Kid Who Loved
Christmas '90

Tony Camilieri
Bill & Ted's Excellent
Adventure '89

Colleen Camp
Clue '85
D.A.R.Y.L. '85
Greedy '94
Police Academy 2: Their
First Assignment '85
Police Academy 4: Citizens
on Patrol '87
Smile '75
Smokey and the Bandit,
Part 3 '83
Valley Girl '83
Walk Like a Man '87
Wayne's World '92

Hamilton Camp
Arena '88
Casey at the Bat '85

Joe Camp▶
Benji '74
Benji the Hunted '87
The Double McGuffin '79
For the Love of Benji '77
Hawmps! '76
Oh, Heavenly Dog! '80

Joseph Campanella
Comic Book Kids '82
Magic Kid '92

Bill Campbell
The Rocketeer '91

Bruce Campbell
Army of Darkness '92

Cheryl Campbell
Chariots of Fire '81
Greystoke: The Legend of
Tarzan, Lord of the
Apes '84

Christian Campbell
City Boy '93

Glen Campbell
True Grit '69

Julia Campbell
Opportunity Knocks '90

Naomi Campbell
Cool As Ice '91

Tisha Campbell
House Party '90
House Party 2: The Pajama
Jam '91
House Party 3 '94

Torquil Campbell
The Golden Seal '83

Tony Campisi
A Home of Our Own '93

Giana Maria Canale
Hercules '58

John Candy
Brewster's Millions '85
Cool Runnings '93
Delirious '91
The Great Outdoors '88
Home Alone '90
Little Shop of Horrors '86
Once Upon a Crime '92
Only the Lonely '91
Sesame Street Presents:
Follow That Bird '85
Spaceballs '87
Splash '84
Summer Rental '85
Uncle Buck '89
Wagons East '94

Dyan Cannon
Authorl Authorl '82
Merlin and the Sword '85
Revenge of the Pink
Panther '78

Judy Canova
The Adventures of
Huckleberry Finn '60

Cantinflas
Around the World in 80
Days '56

Yakima Canutt
Gone with the Wind '39

Yakima Canutt▶
The Adventures of Frank
and Jesse James '48
G-Men Never Forget '48

Peter Capaldi
Local Hero '83

Virginia Capers
Ferris Bueller's Day Off '86
The North Avenue
Irregulars '79
White Mama '80

John Capodice
Honeymoon in Vegas '92

Frank Capra
A Bronx Tale '93

Frank Capra▶
It Happened One Night
'34
It's a Wonderful Life '46
Mr. Smith Goes to
Washington '39

Kate Capshaw
Indiana Jones and the
Temple of Doom '84
My Heroes Have Always
Been Cowboys '91
SpaceCamp '86

Capucine
Curse of the Pink Panther
'83
The Pink Panther '64
Trail of the Pink Panther
'82

Irene Cara
Fame '80

Paul Carafotes
Journey to the Center of
the Earth '88

Antony Carbone
Skateboard '77

Pat Cardi
And Now Miguel '66

Tantoo Cardinal
Dances with Wolves '90

Claudia Cardinale
Jesus of Nazareth '77
Once Upon a Time in the
West '68
The Pink Panther '64
Son of the Pink Panther
'93

Rene Cardona Jr.▶
Robinson Crusoe & the
Tiger '72

Nathalie Cardone
The Little Thief '89

Christopher Carey
Captain America 2: Death
Too Soon '79

Harry Carey Jr.
Back to the Future, Part 3
'90
Bandolero! '68
Cahill: United States
Marshal '73
Challenge to White Fang
'86
Mask '85
Tombstone '93

Harry Carey Sr.
Devil Horse '32
The Last of the Mohicans
'32
Mr. Smith Goes to
Washington '39
So Dear to My Heart '49

MacDonald Carey
Shadow of a Doubt '43
Tammy and the Doctor '63

Michele Carey
Scandalous John '71

Ron Carey
High Anxiety '77

Timothy Carey
Beach Blanket Bingo '65

Bikini Beach '64

Timothy Carhart
Beverly Hills Cop 3 '94
Pink Cadillac '89

Gia Carides
Strictly Ballroom '92

Len Cariou
The Lady in White '88
Who'll Save Our Children?
'82

George Carlin
Bill & Ted's Bogus Journey
'91
Bill & Ted's Excellent
Adventure '89
Car Wash '76

Lewis John Carlino▶
The Great Santini '80

Belinda Carlisle
Swing Shift '84

Kitty Carlisle Hart
A Night at the Opera '35
Radio Days '87

Johann Carlo
Nadia '89

Linda Carlson
The Beverly Hillbillies '93

Richard Carlson
The Valley of Gwangi '69

Slim Carlson
Sourdough '77

Steve Carlson
Brothers O'Toole '73

Ing-mari Carlsson
My Life as a Dog '85

Milly Carlucci
Hercules '83

Roger C. Carmel
Hardly Working '81
My Dog, the Thief '69

Leone Carmen
The Year My Voice Broke
'87

Jean Carmet
The Tall Blond Man with
One Black Shoe '72

Hoagy Carmichael
Topper '37

Tullio Carminati
Roman Holiday '53

Michael Carmine
*batteries not included '87

Primo Carnera
Hercules Unchained '59

Art Carney
The Blue Yonder '86
Going in Style '79
Last Action Hero '93
Miracle of the Heart: A
Boys Town Story '86
Movie, Movie '78
The Night They Saved
Christmas '87
Undergrads '85

Cindy Carol
Dear Brigitte '65
Gidget Goes to Rome '63

Michael Ceveris
Rock 'n' Roll High School
Forever '91

Amadee Chabot
Muscle Beach Party '64

Don Chaffey▶
C.H.O.M.P.S. '79
The Fourth Wish '75
Greyfriars Bobby '61
The Horse Without a Head
'63
Jason and the Argonauts
'63
Magic of Lassie '78
Pete's Dragon '77
Ride a Wild Pony '75
The Three Lives of
Thomasina '63

Julian Chagrin
The Christmas Tree '75

George Chakiris
West Side Story '61

Feodor Chaliapin
Moonstruck '87

Nathalie Chalifour
Mario '74

Sarah Chalke
City Boy '93

Richard Chamberlain
Allan Quartermain and the
Lost City of Gold '86
The Count of Monte Cristo
'74
The Four Musketeers '75
The Man in the Iron Mask
'77
The Return of the
Musketeers '89
The Swarm '78
Three Musketeers '74

Wilt Chamberlain
Conan the Destroyer '84

Howland Chamberlin
Francis the Talking Mule
'49

Marge Champion
The Party '68

Irene Champlin
Flash Gordon: Vol. 1 '53

Michael Paul Chan
The Joy Luck Club '93

Norman Chancer
Local Hero '83

Tanis Chandler
Spook Busters '46

Lon Chaney Jr.
Abbott and Costello Meet
Frankenstein '48
High Noon '52
My Favorite Brunette '47
Three Musketeers '33
Undersea Kingdom '36

Stockard Channing
The Big Bus '76
The Cheap Detective '78
The Fish that Saved
Pittsburgh '79
Grease '78
Not My Kid '85

Rosalind Chao
The Joy Luck Club '93

Memoirs of an Invisible
Man '92

Billy Chapin
Tobor the Great '54

Miles Chapin
Bless the Beasts and
Children '71
French Postcards '79

Tom Chapin
Lord of the Flies '63

Charlie Chaplin
City Lights '31
The Gold Rush '25

Charlie Chaplin▶
City Lights '31
The Gold Rush '25

Geraldine Chaplin
The Age of Innocence '93
Chaplin '92
Cria '76
Doctor Zhivago '65
The Four Musketeers '75
The Return of the
Musketeers '89
Three Musketeers '74

Alexander Chapman
Princes in Exile '90

Constance Chapman
My Friend Walter '93

Daniel Chapman
Philadelphia '93

Graham Chapman
And Now for Something
Completely Different '72
Monty Python and the
Holy Grail '75

Loni Chapman
Where the Red Fern
Grows '74

Marguerite Chapman
Spy Smasher '42

Michael Chapman▶
All the Right Moves '83

Dave Chappelle
Robin Hood: Men in Tights
'93

Patricia Charbonneau
Robocop 2 '90

Jon Chardiet
Beat Street '84

Cyd Charisse
The Band Wagon '53
Singin' in the Rain '52
That's Dancing! '85

Josh Charles
Dead Poets Society '89
Don't Tell Mom the
Babysitter's Dead '91

Ian Charleson
Chariots of Fire '81
Greystoke: The Legend of
Tarzan, Lord of the
Apes '84

Robert Charlton▶
No Big Deal '83

Chevy Chase
Benji at Work '93
Caddyshack '80
Cops and Robbersons '94
Fletch '85

Fletch Lives '89
Foul Play '78
Funny Farm '88
Hero '92
Memoirs of an Invisible
Man '92
Modern Problems '81
National Lampoon's
Christmas Vacation '89
National Lampoon's
European Vacation '85
Oh, Heavenly Dog! '80
Sesame Street Presents:
Follow That Bird '85
Spies Like Us '85
Three Amigos '86
Under the Rainbow '81

Duane Chase
The Sound of Music '65

Stephan Chase
The Black Arrow '84

Nathan Lee Chasing
His Horse
Dances with Wolves '90

Francois Chau
Teenage Mutant Ninja
Turtles 2: The Secret of
the Ooze '91

Maury Chaykin
Dances with Wolves '90
George's Island '91
Hero '92
Mr. Destiny '90
Sommersby '93

Jeremiah S. Chechik▶
Benny & Joon '93
National Lampoon's
Christmas Vacation '89

Chubby Checker
Purple People Eater '88

Michael Chekhov
Spellbound '45

Cher
Mask '85
Mermaids '90
Moonstruck '87

Patrice Chereau
The Last of the Mohicans
'92

Virginia Cherrill
City Lights '31

John Cherry▶
Ernest Rides Again '93

John R. Cherry III▶
Dr. Otto & the Riddle of
the Gloom Beam '86
Ernest Goes to Camp '87
Ernest Goes to Jail '90
Ernest Saves Christmas '88
Ernest Scared Stupid '91

Karen Cheryl
Here Comes Santa Claus
'84

George Cheseboro
Holt of the Secret Service
'42

Morris Chestnut
Boyz N the Hood '91
The Ernest Green Story '93

Kevin Timothy
Chevalia
Homeward Bound: The
Incredible Journey '93

Maurice Chevalier
In Search of the
Castaways '62
Monkeys, Go Home! '66

Richard Chevolleau
Indian Summer '93

Chi
What's Love Got to Do
With It? '93

Huang Chien-lung
Infra-Man '76

Lois Chiles
Death on the Nile '78
Moonraker '79

Tsai Chin
The Joy Luck Club '93
You Only Live Twice '67

William Ching
Pat and Mike '52

Kieu Chinh
The Girl Who Spelled
Freedom '86
The Joy Luck Club '93

Jade Chinn
The Girl Who Spelled
Freedom '86

Michael Chinyamurindi
Bophal '93

Erik Chitty
First Men in the Moon '64

Anna Chlumsky
My Girl '91
My Girl 2 '94
Trading Mom '94

Marvin J. Chomsky▶
Tank '83

Mona Chong
On Her Majesty's Secret
Service '69

Rae Dawn Chong
American Flyers '85
Beat Street '84
Soul Man '86

Joyce Chopra▶
Smooth Talk '85

Navin Chowdhry
Madame Sousatzka '88

Joseph Chrest
King of the Hill '93

Keith Christensen
Little Heroes '91

Claudia Christian
Arena '88

Helen Christian
Zorro Rides Again '37

Robert Christian
Bustin' Loose '81

Roger Christian▶
Starship '87

Audrey Christie
Harper Valley P.T.A. '78

Julie Christie
Doctor Zhivago '65
The Go-Between '71

Dennis Christopher
Breaking Away '79
Chariots of Fire '81

Kay Christopher
Dick Tracy's Dilemma '47

Thom Christopher
Wizards of the Lost
Kingdom '85

William Christopher
With Six You Get Eggroll
'68

Art Chudabala
Gleaming the Cube '89

Byron Ross Chudnow▶
The Amazing Dobermans
'76
Daring Dobermans '73
The Doberman Gang '72

Thomas Haden Church
Tombstone '93

Berton Churchill
Dimples '36

Julien Ciamaca
My Father's Glory '91
My Mother's Castle '91

Eduardo Ciannelli
Foreign Correspondent '40
Mysterious Doctor Satan
'40

Charles Cioffi
Newsies '92

Rene Clair▶
The Ghost Goes West '36

Cyrielle Claire
Sword of the Valiant '83

Bob Clampett▶
Bugs Bunny Cartoon
Festival '44
Bugs Bunny Superstar '75
Looney Looney Looney
Bugs Bunny Movie '81
A Salute to Mel Blanc '58

Eric Clapton
Tommy '75

Ronnie Clare
The Waltons: The
Children's Carol '80

Angela Clark
Miracle of Our Lady of
Fatima '52
The Seven Little Foys '55

Anthony Clark
The Thing Called Love '93

Blake Clark
Ladybugs '92

Bob (Benjamin) Clark▶
A Christmas Story '83
Rhinestone '84
Turk 182! '85

Candy Clark
American Graffiti '73
Buffy the Vampire Slayer
'92
Cat's Eye '85
Citizens Band '77
Cool As Ice '91
Hambone & Hillie '84
More American Graffiti '79

Carl Clark
Sourdough '77

Colbert Clark▶
Fighting with Kit Carson
'33

Boon Collins▶
Spirit of the Eagle '90

Eddie Collins
The Blue Bird '40

Joan Collins
Great Adventure '75
Zero to Sixty '78

Lewis D. Collins▶
Adventures of the Flying
Cadets '44

Patrick Collins
Dirt Bike Kid '86

Phil Collins
Hook '91

Ray Collins
The Bachelor and the
Bobby-Soxer '47
Citizen Kane '41
Francis the Talking Mule
'49
The Human Comedy '43

Stephen Collins
All the President's Men '76
Brewster's Millions '85
Star Trek: The Motion
Picture '80

Peter Collinson▶
Earthling '80
Ten Little Indians '75

Ronald Colman
Around the World in 80
Days '56

Jacque Lynn Colton
Heartbreak Hotel '88

Robbie Coltrane
The Adventures of Huck
Finn '93
Oh, What a Night '92

Chris Columbus▶
Adventures in Babysitting
'87
Heartbreak Hotel '88
Home Alone '90
Home Alone 2: Lost in
New York '92
Mrs. Doubtfire '93
Only the Lonely '91

Jack Colvin
The Incredible Hulk '77
The Incredible Hulk Returns
'88

Michael Colyar
Hot Shots! Part Deux '93
House Party 3 '94

Dorothy Comingore
Citizen Kane '41

Betty Compson
Hard-Boiled Mahoney '47

Cristi Conaway
Batman Returns '92

Jeff Conaway
Grease '78
Pete's Dragon '77

David Condon
Clipped Wings '53

Jackie Condon
The Return of Our Gang
'25

Donna Conforti
Santa Claus Conquers the
Martians '64

James Congdon
Summerdog '78

Joe Conley
A Day for Thanks on
Walton's Mountain '82
The Waltons: The
Children's Carol '80

Jimmy Conlin
Dick Tracy's Dilemma '47

Didi Conn
Grease 2 '82

Christopher Connelly
Benji '74
Hawmps! '76
The Incredible Rocky
Mountain Race '77
Liar's Moon '82

Jennifer Connelly
Labyrinth '86
The Rocketeer '91
Seven Minutes in Heaven
'86

Bart Conner
Rad '86

Sean Connery
A Bridge Too Far '77
Darby O'Gill & the Little
People '59
Diamonds are Forever '71
Dr. No '62
From Russia with Love '63
The Great Train Robbery
'79
Highlander '86
Highlander 2: The
Quickening '91
The Hunt for Red October
'90
Indiana Jones and the Last
Crusade '89
The Man Who Would Be
King '75
Never Say Never Again
'83
Robin and Marian '76
Sword of the Valiant '83
Thunderball '65
Time Bandits '81
The Wind and the Lion '75
You Only Live Twice '67

Harry Connick Jr.
Little Man Tate '91

Billy Connolly
The Return of the
Musketeers '89

Kevin Connolly
Alan & Naomi '92
The Beverly Hillbillies '93

Walter Connolly
The Adventures of
Huckleberry Finn '39
It Happened One Night
'34

Kevin Connor▶
At the Earth's Core '76
Land That Time Forgot '75
The People That Time
Forgot '77

Chuck Connors
Airplane 2: The Sequel '82
The Capture of Grizzly
Adams '82
Flipper '63

Old Yeller '57
Pat and Mike '52

Kevin R. Connors
Prehysterial 2 '94

David Conrad
The Wizard of Speed and
Time '88

Hans Conried
Brothers O'Toole '73
Davy Crockett, King of the
Wild Frontier '55
The 5000 Fingers of Dr. T
'53
Oh, God! Book 2 '80
Tut and Tuttle '82

Frances Conroy
The Adventures of Huck
Finn '93
Rocket Gibraltar '88

Ruaidhri Conroy
Into the West '92

Tim Considine
Daring Dobermans '73
The Shaggy Dog '59

Yvonne Constant
Monkeys, Go Home! '66

Michael Constantine
My Life '93
The North Avenue
Irregulars '79
Prancer '89
The Reivers '69

John Conte
Lost in a Harem '44

Therese Conte▶
Chasing Dreams '81

Tom Conti
American Dreamer '84

Chantal Contouri
Goodbye, Miss 4th of July
'88

Frank Converse
Anne of Avonlea '87
Brother Future '91
Home at Last '88

**William Converse-
Roberts**
The Fig Tree '87

Bert Convy
Cannonball Run '81
Hero at Large '80
The Love Bug '68
The Man in the Santa
Claus Suit '79

Jack Conway▶
Tarzan and His Mate '34

James L. Conway▶
The Incredible Rocky
Mountain Race '77
The Last of the Mohicans
'85

Kevin Conway
Gettysburg '93
Rambling Rose '91

Morgan Conway
Dick Tracy, Detective '45
Dick Tracy vs. Cueball '46

Tim Conway
The Apple Dumpling Gang
'75

**The Apple Dumpling Gang
Rides Again '79**
The Billion Dollar Hobo '78
Gus '76
The Longshot '86
The Private Eyes '80
Prize Fighter '79
The Shaggy D.A. '76
They Went That-a-Way &
That-a-Way '78
The World's Greatest
Athlete '73

Tom Conway
Tarzan's Secret Treasure
'41

Jackie Coogan
Escape Artist '82
The Shakiest Gun in the
West '68

Keith Coogan
Adventures in Babysitting
'87
Book of Love '91
Cheetah '89
Don't Tell Mom the
Babysitter's Dead '91
Hiding Out '87

Bart Robinson Cook
George Balanchine's The
Nutcracker '93

Carole Cook
The Incredible Mr. Limpet
'64
Sixteen Candles '84

Elisha Cook Jr.
The Maltese Falcon '41
Salem's Lot '79
Shane '53

Fielder Cook▶
The Hideaways '73
Homecoming: A Christmas
Story '71

Peter Cook
Black Beauty '94
The Princess Bride '87
Those Daring Young Men
in Their Jaunty Jalopies
'69

Sophie Cook
The Chronicles of Narnia
'89

Alan Cooke▶
Nadia '89

Tony Cookson▶
And You Thought Your
Parents Were Weird! '91

Martha Coolidge▶
Lost in Yonkers '93
Plain Clothes '88
Rambling Rose '91
Real Genius '85
Valley Girl '83

Rita Coolidge
Club Med '83

Chris Cooper
This Boy's Life '93

Gary Cooper
Naked Gun 33 1/3: The
Final Insult '94

Gary Cooper
Friendly Persuasion '56
High Noon '52

Gladys Cooper
Rebecca '40
The Secret Garden '49

Jackie Cooper
Superman 1: The Movie
'78
Superman 2 '80
Superman 3 '83
Treasure Island '34

Jackie Cooper▶
The Night They Saved
Christmas '87
White Mama '80

Lawrence Cooper
My Friend Walter '93

Maggie Cooper
And Baby Makes Six '79

Melville Cooper
The Adventures of Robin
Hood '38
Rebecca '40
Shirley Temple Storybook
Theater '60

Robert Coote
The Three Musketeers '48

Joan Copeland
Her Alibi '88

Teri Copley
Brain Donors '92

Francis Ford Coppola▶
Finian's Rainbow '68
The Outsiders '83
Peggy Sue Got Married
'86
Rumble Fish '83
Tucker: The Man and His
Dream '88

Sofia Coppola
Peggy Sue Got Married
'86

Jeff Corbett
Talent for the Game '91

John Corbett
Tombstone '93

Barry Corbin
My Science Project '85
Nothing in Common '86
Permanent Record '88
Six Pack '82

Bruno Corbucci▶
Aladdin '86

Sergio Corbucci▶
Super Fuzz '81

Ellen Corby
A Day for Thanks on
Walton's Mountain '82
Homecoming: A Christmas
Story '71
I Remember Mama '48
It's a Wonderful Life '46
Support Your Local
Gunfighter '71

Donna Corcoran
Gypsy Colt '54

Kevin Corcoran
Johnny Shiloh '63
Mooncussers '62
Old Yeller '57
Pollyanna '60
Savage Sam '63
The Shaggy Dog '59
A Tiger Walks '64

Country Girl '54
Going My Way '44
High Society '56
Holiday Inn '42
My Favorite Brunette '47
That's Entertainment '74
White Christmas '54

Cathy Lee Crosby
Coach '78

Denise Crosby
Curse of the Pink Panther '83
Star Trek the Next Generation Episode 1-2: Encounter at Farpoint '87

Gary Crosby
Justin Morgan Had a Horse '81

Mary Crosby
Ice Pirates '84

Ben Cross
Chariots of Fire '81
The Flame Trees of Thika '81

Rupert Crosse
The Reivers '69

Scatman Crothers
Bronco Billy '80
The Great White Hope '70
The Journey of Natty Gann '85
The Shootist '76
The Silver Streak '76
Twilight Zone: The Movie '83

Lindsay Crouse
All the President's Men '76
Iceman '84
Places in the Heart '84

Ashley Crow
Little Big League '94

Cameron Crowe▶
Say Anything '89
Singles '92

Russell Crowe
The Silver Stallion: King of the Wild Brumbies '94

Ed Crowley
Running on Empty '88

Kathleen Crowley
Westward Ho, the Wagons! '56

Pat Crowley
Hollywood or Bust '56

Patricia Crowley
Menace on the Mountain '70

Su Cruickshank
Young Einstein '89

Tom Cruise
All the Right Moves '83
Far and Away '92
Legend '86
The Outsiders '83
Rain Man '88
Taps '81
Top Gun '86

Rosalie Crutchley
The Hunchback of Notre Dame '82
Wuthering Heights '70

Abigail Cruttenden
Kipperbang '82

Alexis Cruz
Gryphon '88

Carlina Cruz
Maricela '88

Gretchen Cryer
Hiding Out '87

Jon Cryer
Hiding Out '87
Morgan Stewart's Coming Home '87
Pretty in Pink '86
Superman 4: The Quest for Peace '87

Billy Crystal
City Slickers '91
City Slickers 2: The Legend of Curly's Gold '94
The Princess Bride '87
Throw Momma from the Train '87

Lindsay Crystal
City Slickers 2: The Legend of Curly's Gold '94

Eszter Csakanyi
A Hungarian Fairy Tale '87

George Cukor▶
Adam's Rib '50
David Copperfield '35
Little Women '33
Pat and Mike '52
The Philadelphia Story '40

Kieran Culkin
Father of the Bride '91
Home Alone '90
Home Alone 2: Lost in New York '92

Macaulay Culkin
George Balanchine's The Nutcracker '93
Getting Even with Dad '94
The Good Son '93
Home Alone '90
Home Alone 2: Lost in New York '92
My Girl '91
Only the Lonely '91
Rocket Gibraltar '88
See You in the Morning '89
Uncle Buck '89

Quinn Culkin
The Good Son '93

Brett Cullen
Prehysteria '93

Max Cullen
Lightning Jack '94

Mark Cullingham▶
Gryphon '88

John Cullum
Morgan Stewart's Coming Home '87
The Prodigal '83

Robert Culp
The Castaway Cowboy '74
The Pelican Brief '93
Sammy, the Way-Out Seal '62
Turk 182! '85

Alan Cumming
Bernard and the Genie '91

Irving Cummings▶
Curly Top '35
Just Around the Corner '38
Little Miss Broadway '38
The Poor Little Rich Girl '36

Jim Cummings
The Lion King '94

Quinn Cummings
The Goodbye Girl '77

Robert Cummings
Beach Party '63
Dial "M" for Murder '54
Saboteur '42

Eli Cummins
Dakota '88
Harley '90

Peter Cummins
Blue Fire Lady '78

Sean S. Cunningham▶
Manny's Orphans '78

Lynette Curran
The Year My Voice Broke '87

Cherie Currie
Foxes '80
Twilight Zone: The Movie '83

Finlay Currie
The Adventures of Huckleberry Finn '60
Treasure Island '50

Louise Currie
The Adventures of Captain Marvel '41
The Masked Marvel '43
Million Dollar Kid '44

Tim Curry
Annie '82
Clue '85
Home Alone 2: Lost in New York '92
The Hunt for Red October '90
Legend '86
National Lampoon's Loaded Weapon 1 '93
Oliver Twist '82
The Shadow '94
The Three Musketeers '93
The Worst Witch '86

Jane Curtin
Coneheads '93

Alan Curtis
Buck Privates '41

Dan Curtis▶
When Every Day was the Fourth of July '78

Dick Curtis
Government Agents vs. the Phantom Legion '51

Jamie Lee Curtis
The Adventures of Buckaroo Banzai Across the Eighth Dimension '84
Amazing Grace & Chuck '87
Annie Oakley '85
Dominick & Eugene '88
Forever Young '92
My Girl '91
My Girl 2 '94
True Lies '94

Ken Curtis
Pony Express Rider '76
The Quiet Man '52

Liane Curtis
Sixteen Candles '84

Robin Curtis
Star Trek 3: The Search for Spock '84

Tony Curtis
The Bad News Bears Go to Japan '78
The Count of Monte Cristo '74
Francis the Talking Mule '49
Great Race '65
Little Miss Marker '80
Those Daring Young Men in Their Jaunty Jalopies '69

Vondie Curtis-Hall
Crooklyn '94

Michael Curtiz
Yankee Doodle Dandy '42

Michael Curtiz▶
The Adventures of Huckleberry Finn '60
The Adventures of Robin Hood '38
Captain Blood '35
Casablanca '42
Life with Father '47
White Christmas '54
Yankee Doodle Dandy '42

Ann Cusack
A League of Their Own '92

Cyril Cusack
David Copperfield '70
Far and Away '92

Joan Cusack
Addams Family Values '93
Hero '92
Men Don't Leave '89
My Bodyguard '80
Say Anything '89
Sixteen Candles '84
Toys '92

John Cusack
Better Off Dead '85
The Journey of Natty Gann '85
One Crazy Summer '86
Say Anything '89
Sixteen Candles '84
Stand By Me '86
The Sure Thing '85

Niamh Cusack
The Playboys '92

Sinead Cusack
Rocket Gibraltar '88

Susie Cusack
Hero '92

Peter Cushing
At the Earth's Core '76
Doctor Who and the Daleks '65
Star Wars '77
Sword of the Valiant '83

Bob Custer
Law of the Wild '34

Iain Cuthbertson
Gorillas in the Mist '88
Railway Children '70

Michael Cutting▶
The Little Crooked Christmas Tree '93

Charles Cyphers
Major League '89

Howard da Silva
David and Lisa '62
Mommie Dearest '81
1776 '72

Augusta Dabney
Running on Empty '88

Olivia D'Abo
Clean Slate '94
Conan the Destroyer '84
Greedy '94
Wayne's World 2 '93

Morton DaCosta▶
The Music Man '62

Ami Daemion
The Silver Stallion: King of the Wild Brumbies '94

Willem Dafoe
Cry-Baby '90

Jean-Michel Dagory
Clowning Around '92
Clowning Around 2 '93

Arlene Dahl
Journey to the Center of the Earth '59

Elizabeth Daily
Fandango '85
Pee Wee's Big Adventure '85

Masaaki Daimon
Godzilla vs. the Cosmic Monster '74

Badgett Dale
Lord of the Flies '90

Dick Dale
Back to the Beach '87

Esther Dale
Curly Top '35

James Dale
Federal Agents vs. Underworld, Inc. '49

Jim Dale
The Adventures of Huckleberry Finn '85
Digby, the Biggest Dog in the World '73
Hot Lead & Cold Feet '78
Pete's Dragon '77
Unidentified Flying Oddball '79

Virginia Dale
Holiday Inn '42

Marcel Dalio
Casablanca '42
Sabrina '54

John Dall
The Corn is Green '45

Joe Dallesandro
Cry-Baby '90

Abby Dalton
Whale of a Tale '76

Timothy Dalton
Brenda Starr '86
Flash Gordon '80
The Lion in Winter '68

Peter Davison
Black Beauty '94

Pam Dawber
Stay Tuned '92

Anthony M. (Antonio Marghereti) Dawson
Dial "M" for Murder '54
Dr. No '62

Anthony M. (Antonio Margheti) Dawson▶
Mr. Superinvisible '73

Kamala Dawson
Lightning Jack '94

Vicky Dawson
Carbon Copy '81

Doris Day
Please Don't Eat the Daisies '60
Turf Boy '42
With Six You Get Eggroll '68

Josette Day
Beauty and the Beast '46

Laraine Day
Foreign Correspondent '40
Journey for Margaret '42

Patrick Day
The Adventures of Huckleberry Finn '85

Robert Day▶
The Grass is Always Greener Over the Septic Tank '78

Daniel Day-Lewis
The Age of Innocence '93
The Bounty '84
The Last of the Mohicans '92

Lyman Dayton▶
Dream Machine '91

Remo de Angelis
Great Adventure '75

Jo De Backer
Toto le Heros '91

Brenda de Banzie
The Pink Panther '64

Manuel de Blas
Great Adventure '75

Jan De Bont▶
Speed '94

Celia de Burgh
Phar Lap '84

Yvonne De Carlo
The Ten Commandments '56

Olivia de Havilland
The Adventures of Robin Hood '38
Airport '77 '77
Captain Blood '35
The Fifth Musketeer '79
Gone with the Wind '39
The Swarm '78

Katherine De Hetre
Joni '79

Nic de Jager
The Gods Must Be Crazy '84

Ate De Jong▶
Drop Dead Fred '91

Simon de la Brosse
The Little Thief '89

George de la Pena
Brain Donors '92
Kuffs '92

Derek De Lint
Three Men and a Baby '87

Stanislas Carre de Malberg
Au Revoir Les Enfants '87

Pierre De Moro▶
Savannah Smiles '82

Robert De Niro
Bang the Drum Slowly '73
A Bronx Tale '93
This Boy's Life '93

Robert De Niro▶
A Bronx Tale '93

Joe De Santis
And Now Miguel '66

Vittorio De Sica
Wonders of Aladdin '61

Tom De Simone▶
Terror in the Jungle '68

Rosana De Soto
La Bamba '87
Stand and Deliver '88
Star Trek 6: The Undiscovered Country '91

Andre de Toth▶
House of Wax '53

Brandon de Wilde
The Member of the Wedding '52
Shane '53
Those Calloways '65

Fay De Witt
Comic Book Kids '82

Richard Deacon
Billie '65
Blackbeard's Ghost '67
Carousel '56
The Gnome-Mobile '67
The One and Only, Genuine, Original Family Band '68

Lucy Deakins
The Boy Who Could Fly '86
Cheetah '89
The Great Outdoors '88
Little Nikita '88

James Dean
East of Eden '54
Giant '56
Rebel Without a Cause '55

Jeanne Dean
Clipped Wings '53

Jimmy Dean
Diamonds are Forever '71

Loren Dean
1492: Conquest of Paradise '92
Say Anything '89

Ron Dean
Rudy '93

Gina DeAngelis
Radio Days '87

William Dear▶
Angels in the Outfield '94
Harry and the Hendersons '87
If Looks Could Kill '91
Timerider '83

JoAnn Dearing
Suburban Commando '91

John DeBello▶
Attack of the Killer Tomatoes '77

Rosemary DeCamp
The Jungle Book '42
The Story of Seabiscuit '49
13 Ghosts '60
Yankee Doodle Dandy '42

Guy Decomble
The 400 Blows '59

Frances Dee
Gypsy Colt '54
Little Women '33

Ruby Dee
Buck and the Preacher '72
Cop and a Half '93
The Ernest Green Story '93

Sandra Dee
Gidget '59
Tammy and the Doctor '63

Rick Dees
La Bamba '87

Eddie Deezen
I Wanna Hold Your Hand '78
Midnight Madness '80

Don DeFore
A Rare Breed '81

Calvert Deforest
Leader of the Band '87

Philip DeGuere▶
Dr. Strange '78

Wayne Dehart
A Perfect World '93

John Dehner
The Day of the Dolphin '73
The Left-Handed Gun '58
Mountain Man '77
Support Your Local Gunfighter '71

David DeKeyser
Yentl '83

Albert Dekker
East of Eden '54

Fred Dekker▶
The Monster Squad '87
Robocop 3 '91

Pilar Del Rey
And Now Miguel '66

Roy Del Ruth▶
Topper Returns '41

Kim Delaney
Christmas Comes to Willow Creek '87
That Was Then. . .This Is Now '85

Dana Delany
Housesitter '92

Tombstone '93
A Winner Never Quits '86

Dorothy Dell
Little Miss Marker '34

Gabriel Dell
Blues Busters '50
Bowery Buckaroos '47
Escape Artist '82
Follow the Leader '44
Hard-Boiled Mahoney '47
Kid Dynamite '43
Little Tough Guys '38
Million Dollar Kid '44
'Neath Brooklyn Bridge '42
Smart Alecks '42
Spook Busters '46

Victorien Delmare
My Mother's Castle '91

Julie Delpy
The Three Musketeers '93

Claudio Deluca
Small Change '76

Frank Deluca
Small Change '76

Dom DeLuise
The Adventures of Sherlock Holmes' Smarter Brother '78
Cannonball Run '81
Cannonball Run 2 '84
The Cheap Detective '78
Going Bananas '88
Johnny Dangerously '84
Silent Movie '76
Smokey and the Bandit, Part 2 '80
Spaceballs '87
Twelve Chairs '70

Michael DeLuise
Encino Man '92

William Demarest
The Jolson Story '46
Rebecca of Sunnybrook Farm '38
Sorrowful Jones '49

Jack DeMave
The Man Without a Face '93

Tulio Demicheli▶
Son of Captain Blood '62

Cecil B. DeMille▶
The Greatest Show on Earth '52
The Ten Commandments '56

Jonathan Demme▶
Citizens Band '77
Philadelphia '93
Swing Shift '84

Rebecca DeMornay
Pecos Bill '86
The Three Musketeers '93
The Trip to Bountiful '85

Janet Dempsey
Regl'ar Fellers '41

Patrick Dempsey
Can't Buy Me Love '87
Coupe de Ville '90
Face the Music '92
For Better and For Worse '92
With Honors '94

Richard Dempsey
The Chronicles of Narnia '89

Hugh Dempster
A Christmas Carol '51

Jacques Demy
The 400 Blows '59

Michael Denison
Shadowlands '93

Brian Dennehy
Annie Oakley '85
Butch and Sundance: The Early Days '79
Cocoon '85
Cocoon: The Return '88
F/X '86
F/X 2: The Deadly Art of Illusion '91
Foul Play '78
Little Miss Marker '80
Never Cry Wolf '83
Return to Snowy River '88
The River Rat '84
Silverado '85

Barbara Dennek
Playtime '67

Dodo Denney
Willy Wonka & the Chocolate Factory '71

Richard Denning
Black Beauty '46
Unknown Island '48

Sandy Dennis
Up the Down Staircase '67

Reginald Denny
Abbott and Costello Meet Dr. Jekyll and Mr. Hyde '52
My Favorite Brunette '47
Rebecca '40

Pen Densham▶
The Zoo Gang '85

Christa Denton
The Gate '87

Bob Denver
Back to the Beach '87
Wackiest Wagon Train in the West '77

John Denver
Oh, God! '77

Brian DePalma▶
Home Movies '79

Elisabeth Depardieu
Jean de Florette '87

Gerard Depardieu
Cyrano de Bergerac '90
1492: Conquest of Paradise '92
Green Card '90
Jean de Florette '87
My Father the Hero '93

Johnny Depp
Benny & Joon '93
Cry-Baby '90
Edward Scissorhands '90
What's Eating Gilbert Grape '93

John Derek
The Ten Commandments '56

Joe DeRita
Three Stooges Meet
  Hercules '61

Bruce Dern
The 'Burbs '89
The Cowboys '72
The Incredible Two-Headed
  Transplant '71
Smile '75
Support Your Local Sheriff
  '69
Toughlove '85

Laura Dern
Foxes '80
Jurassic Park '93
Mask '85
A Perfect World '93
Rambling Rose '91
Smooth Talk '85

Cleavant Derricks
Off Beat '86

Dominique Deruddere▶
Wait Until Spring, Bandini
  '90

Michael Des Barres
Pink Cadillac '89

Stefan DeSalle
Russkies '87

Anne DeSalvo
My Favorite Year '82

Caleb Deschanel▶
Crusoe '89
Escape Artist '82

Mary Jo Deschanel
The Right Stuff '83
2010 : The Year We
  Make Contact '84

Robert Desiderio
Gross Anatomy '89
Oh, God! You Devil '84

William Desmond
Courage of the North '35
Tailspin Tommy '34

Geory Desmouceaux
Small Change '76

Ivan Desny
Escapade in Florence '62

Tamara DeTreaux
Ghoulies '85

Howard Deutch▶
Getting Even with Dad '94
The Great Outdoors '88
Pretty in Pink '86
Some Kind of Wonderful
  '87

William Devane
The Bad News Bears in
  Breaking Training '77
Chips the War Dog '90
Hadley's Rebellion '84

Andy Devine
The Adventures of
  Huckleberry Finn '60
Ali Baba and the Forty
  Thieves '43
How the West was Won
  '63
Smoke '70
Whale of a Tale '76
Zebra in the Kitchen '65

Danny DeVito
Batman Returns '92

Goin' South '78
Going Ape! '81
Jack the Bear '93
The Jewel of the Nile '85
Johnny Dangerously '84
Renaissance Man '94
Romancing the Stone '84
Terms of Endearment '83
Throw Momma from the
  Train '87

Danny DeVito▶
Throw Momma from the
  Train '87

Francis Devlaeminck
Small Change '76

Laurent Devlaeminck
Small Change '76

Alan Devlin
The Playboys '92

J.G. Devlin
The Miracle '91

Jon DeVries
Sarah, Plain and Tall '91
Skylark '93

Elaine Devry
The Cheyenne Social Club
  '70

Colleen Dewhurst
And Baby Makes Six '79
Anne of Avonlea '87
Anne of Green Gables '85
Annie Hall '77
The Boy Who Could Fly
  '86
The Cowboys '72
Ice Castles '79
Lantern Hill '90

Billy DeWolfe
Billie '65

Susan Dey
Comeback Kid '80
Love Leads the Way '84

Cliff DeYoung
Annie Oakley '85
F/X '86
Flight of the Navigator '86
Secret Admirer '85

Alice Diabo
Strangers in Good
  Company '91

Despo Diamantidou
Love and Death '75

Selma Diamond
Bang the Drum Slowly '73
Twilight Zone: The Movie
  '83

Sully Diaz
Gryphon '88

Leonardo DiCaprio
This Boy's Life '93
What's Eating Gilbert
  Grape '93

George DiCenzo
Back to the Future '85
18 Again! '88
The New Adventures of
  Pippi Longstocking '88
Sing '89
Walk Like a Man '87

Bobby DiCicco
I Wanna Hold Your Hand
  '78

Splash '84

Andy Dick
In the Army Now '94

John Diehl
Madhouse '90
Remote '93

Gene Dietch▶
Alice in Wonderland in
  Paris

Marlene Dietrich
Judgment at Nuremberg
  '61
Stage Fright '50

Arthur Dignam
We of the Never Never
  '82

Matt Dill
The Boy Who Loved Trolls
  '84

Ricky Dillard
Leap of Faith '92

Bradford Dillman
Escape from the Planet of
  the Apes '71
The Swarm '78
The Way We Were '73

Brendan Dillon Jr.
Lords of Magick '88

Kevin Dillon
Immediate Family '89
A Midnight Clear '92
No Big Deal '83
The Rescue '88

Matt Dillon
The Flamingo Kid '84
Liar's Moon '82
Little Darlings '80
Mr. Wonderful '93
My Bodyguard '80
The Outsiders '83
Over the Edge '79
Rumble Fish '83
Singles '92
Tex '82

Melinda Dillon
Bound for Glory '76
Captain America '89
A Christmas Story '83
Close Encounters of the
  Third Kind '77
Harry and the Hendersons
  '87

Victor Dimattia
Dennis the Menace:
  Dinosaur Hunter '87

Richard Dimitri
Johnny Dangerously '84

Dennis Dimster
Olly Olly Oxen Free '78

Alan Dinehart
Baby, Take a Bow '34

Ernie Dingo
Clowning Around '92
Clowning Around 2 '93
Crocodile Dundee 2 '88
A Waltz Through the Hills
  '88

Michael Dinner▶
Hot to Trot! '88
Off Beat '86

Bob Dishy
Brighton Beach Memoirs
  '86
My Boyfriend's Back '93

Divine
Hairspray '88

Carter Dixon
Young Eagles '34

Donna Dixon
Spies Like Us '85
Wayne's World '92

Ivan Dixon
Car Wash '76

MacIntyre Dixon
Funny Farm '88

Pamela Dixon
Magic Kid '92

Edward Dmytryk▶
He is My Brother '75

Lawrence Dobkin▶
The Waltons: The
  Children's Carol '80

Anica Dobra
Tito and Me '92

Kevin Dobson
Orphan Train '79

Peter Dobson
Sing '89

Robert Dogui
Almos' a Man '78

Matt Doherty
The Mighty Ducks '92
So I Married an Axe
  Murderer '93

Shannen Doherty
Girls Just Want to Have
  Fun '85

Michael Dolan
Light of Day '87

Guy Doleman
Thunderball '65

Ami Dolenz
Stepmonster '92

Mickey Dolenz
Head '68
Monkees, Volume 1 '66

Jerzy Domaradzki▶
Legend of the White Horse
  '85

Larry Domasin
Island of the Blue Dolphins
  '64

Arturo Dominici
Hercules '58

Solveig Dommartin
Wings of Desire '88

Troy Donahue
Cry-Baby '90

James Donald
The Bridge on the River
  Kwai '57
Third Man on the
  Mountain '59

Juli Donald
Brain Donors '92

Roger Donaldson▶
The Bounty '84
Nutcase '80

Ted Donaldson
The Red Stallion '47
A Tree Grows in Brooklyn
  '45

Peter Donat
The Babe '92
The Bay Boy '85
School Ties '92
Tucker: The Man and His
  Dream '88

Richard Donat
My American Cousin '85

Robert Donat
The Ghost Goes West '36
The 39 Steps '35

Ludwig Donath
The Jolson Story '46

Vincent J. Donehue▶
Peter Pan '60

Stanley Donen
Movie, Movie '78

Stanley Donen▶
Charade '63
Funny Face '57
The Little Prince '74
Movie, Movie '78
On the Town '49
Seven Brides for Seven
  Brothers '54
Singin' in the Rain '52

Brian Donlevy
The Errand Boy '61
How to Stuff a Wild Bikini
  '65

Jeff Donnell
Gidget Goes to Rome '63

Clive Donner▶
Babes in Toyland '86
Merlin and the Sword '85
Oliver Twist '82
The Scarlet Pimpernel '82
The Thief of Baghdad '78

Richard Donner▶
The Goonies '85
Ladyhawke '85
Maverick '94
Radio Flyer '92
Scrooged '88
Superman 1: The Movie
  '78
The Toy '82

Robert Donner
Lassie: Well of Love '90
Under the Rainbow '81

Vincent D'Onofrio
Adventures in Babysitting
  '87
Mr. Wonderful '93

**Mary Agnes
  Donoghue▶**
Paradise '91

Jack Donohue▶
Babes in Toyland '61

King Donovan
Singin' in the Rain '52

Paul Donovan▶
George's Island '91
Norman's Awesome
  Experience '88

Tate Donovan
Holy Matrimony '94
Not My Kid '85
SpaceCamp '86

Terence Donovan
The Man from Snowy River '82

Alison Doody
Indiana Jones and the Last Crusade '89
Major League 2 '94

James Doohan
Star Trek: The Motion Picture '80
Star Trek 2: The Wrath of Khan '82
Star Trek 3: The Search for Spock '84
Star Trek 4: The Voyage Home '86
Star Trek 5: The Final Frontier '89
Star Trek 6: The Undiscovered Country '91

Paul Dooley
Breaking Away '79
Kiss Me Goodbye '82
My Boyfriend's Back '93
Popeye '80
Rich Kids '79
Sixteen Candles '84

Lucinda Dooling
Miracle on Ice '81

Robert DoQui
A Dream for Christmas '73
Robocop '87

Karin Dor
You Only Live Twice '67

Ann Doran
Mr. Wise Guy '42
Rebel Without a Cause '55

Johnny Doran
The Hideaways '73

Stephen Dorff
Backbeat '94
The Gate '87
The Power of One '92

Jacques Dorfman▶
Shadow of the Wolf '92

Michael Dorn
Star Trek 6: The Undiscovered Country '91
Star Trek the Next Generation Episode 1-2: Encounter at Farpoint '87

Philip Dorn
Tarzan's Secret Treasure '41

Sarah Rowland Doroff
Three Fugitives '89

Diana Dors
Amazing Mr. Blunden '72
Oliver Twist '48

John Dossett
That Night '93

Julian Roy Doster
Menace II Society '93

Karen Dotrice
The Gnome-Mobile '67

The Three Lives of Thomasina '63

Roy Dotrice
Amadeus '84
The Cutting Edge '92
Suburban Commando '91

Doug E. Doug
Class Act '91
Cool Runnings '93

Angela Douglas
Digby, the Biggest Dog in the World '73

Brandon Douglas
Chips the War Dog '90
Journey to Spirit Island '92

Earl Douglas
Tim Tyler's Luck '37

Gordon Douglas▶
Dick Tracy vs. Cueball '46

Illeana Douglas
Alive '93

Kirk Douglas
Greedy '94
Home Movies '79
The Man from Snowy River '82
Tough Guys '86
20,000 Leagues Under the Sea '54
The Villain '79

Melvyn Douglas
Being There '79
Captains Courageous '37
I Never Sang For My Father '70

Michael Douglas
The Jewel of the Nile '85
Napoleon and Samantha '72
Romancing the Stone '84

Sarah Douglas
Beastmaster 2: Through the Portal of Time '91
Conan the Destroyer '84
The People That Time Forgot '77
The Return of Swamp Thing '89
Solarbabies '86
Superman 1: The Movie '78
Superman 2 '80

Brad Dourif
Amos and Andrew '93

Tony Dow
Back to the Beach '87

Ann Dowd
It Could Happen to You '94
Philadelphia '93

Lesley-Anne Down
The Great Train Robbery '79
The Hunchback of Notre Dame '82
The Pink Panther Strikes Again '76

Brian Downey
George's Island '91

Robert Downey Jr.
Back to School '86
Chances Are '89
Chaplin '92

First Born '84
Heart and Souls '93
Weird Science '85

Johnny Downs
Adventures of the Flying Cadets '44
March of the Wooden Soldiers '34

David Doyle
Wait Till Your Mother Gets Home '83

Maria Doyle
The Commitments '91

Brian Doyle-Murray
Cabin Boy '94
Caddyshack '80
Club Paradise '86
Groundhog Day '93
How I Got into College '89
Modern Problems '81
National Lampoon's Christmas Vacation '89
Scrooged '88
Sixteen Candles '84
Wayne's World '92

Tony Doyle
Adventures in Dinosaur City '92

Stan Dragoti▶
Love at First Bite '79
The Man with One Red Shoe '85
Mr. Mom '83

Betsy Drake
Clarence, the Cross-eyed Lion '65

Charles Drake
A Night in Casablanca '46
The Tender Years '47
Tobor the Great '54

Jim Drake▶
Mr. Bill's Real-Life Adventures '86
Police Academy 4: Citizens on Patrol '87

Larry Drake
Darkman '90

Tom Drake
Courage of Lassie '46
The Great Rupert '50
Meet Me in St. Louis '44

Polly Draper
Making Mr. Right '86

Tony Drazan▶
Zebrahead '92

Arthur Dreifuss▶
Regl'ar Fellers '41

Beau Dremann
My Science Project '85

Fran Drescher
Car 54, Where Are You? '94

Richard Dreyfuss
Always '89
American Graffiti '73
Another Stakeout '93
The Apprenticeship of Duddy Kravitz '74
Close Encounters of the Third Kind '77
The Goodbye Girl '77
Lost in Yonkers '93

Stand By Me '86
What About Bob? '91

Moosie Drier
Charlie and the Great Balloon Chase '82
Homeward Bound '80

Brian Drillinger
Brighton Beach Memoirs '86

Bobby Driscoll
So Dear to My Heart '49
Treasure Island '50
The Window '49

Joanne Dru
The Light in the Forest '58
Super Fuzz '81

James Drury
Ten Who Dared '60

Fred Dryer
The Fantastic World of D.C. Collins '84

Charles S. Dubin▶
Cinderella '64

Ja'net DuBois
Piece of the Action '77

Marta DuBois
The Trial of the Incredible Hulk '89

David Duchovny
Beethoven '92
Chaplin '92

Rick Ducommun
Blank Check '93
The 'Burbs '89
Class Act '91
Encino Man '92
Little Monsters '89

John Joseph Duda
Prancer '89

Michael Dudikoff
I Ought to Be in Pictures '82

Lesley Dudley
John & Julie '57

Howard Duff
Kramer vs. Kramer '79
Oh, God! Book 2 '80

Peter Duffell▶
Experience Preferred. . . But Not Essential '83

Nicola Duffett
Howard's End '92

Ciara Duffy
The Snapper '93

Karen Duffy
Blank Check '93

Thomas F. Duffy
Wagons East '94

Dennis Dugan
Can't Buy Me Love '87
The Howling '81
The New Adventures of Pippi Longstocking '88
Parenthood '89
She's Having a Baby '88
Unidentified Flying Oddball '79

Dennis Dugan▶
Brain Donors '92

Problem Child '90

Michael Dugan▶
Super Seal '77

Andrew Duggan
The Bears & I '74
The Incredible Mr. Limpet '64

John Duigan▶
Flirting '89
The Year My Voice Broke '87

Olympia Dukakis
Dad '89
Look Who's Talking '89
Look Who's Talking Now '93
Look Who's Talking, Too '90
Moonstruck '87
Rich Kids '79
Steel Magnolias '89

Bill Duke
Menace II Society '93

Bill Duke▶
Sister Act 2: Back in the Habit '93

Patty Duke
Billie '65
The Miracle Worker '62
The Miracle Worker '79
Prelude to a Kiss '92
Something Special '86
The Swarm '78

Robin Duke
Club Paradise '86

David Dukes
Date with an Angel '87
See You in the Morning '89

Keir Dullea
David and Lisa '62
Oh, What a Night '92
2001: A Space Odyssey '68
2010 : The Year We Make Contact '84

Douglass Dumbrille
A Day at the Races '37
Lost in a Harem '44
Spook Busters '46
The Ten Commandments '56
Treasure Island '34

Margaret Dumont
Animal Crackers '30
At the Circus '39
The Big Store '41
The Cocoanuts '29
A Day at the Races '37
Duck Soup '33
The Horn Blows at Midnight '45
A Night at the Opera '35

Dennis Dun
Big Trouble in Little China '86

Faye Dunaway
The Four Musketeers '75
Little Big Man '70
Mommie Dearest '81
Oklahoma Crude '73
Supergirl '84
Three Musketeers '74
Wait Until Spring, Bandini '90

Searching for Bobby
Fischer '93
What's Love Got to Do
With It? '93

Carrie Fisher
The 'Burbs '89
Drop Dead Fred '91
The Empire Strikes Back
'80
The Man with One Red
Shoe '85
Return of the Jedi '83
Star Wars '77
This is My Life '92
Under the Rainbow '81

Cindy Fisher
Liar's Moon '82

David Fisher▶
Liar's Moon '82

Frances Fisher
Sudie & Simpson '90

Jasen Fisher
The Witches '90

Shug Fisher
Huckleberry Finn '75

Tricia Leigh Fisher
Book of Love '91

Bill Fishman▶
Car 54, Where Are You?
'94

Robert Fiske
Green Archer '40

Louise Fitch
Starbird and Sweet William
'73

Peter Fitz
Au Revoir Les Enfants '87

Barry Fitzgerald
Bringing Up Baby '38
Going My Way '44
How Green was My Valley
'41
The Quiet Man '52
The Story of Seabiscuit '49
Tarzan's Secret Treasure
'41

Ciaran Fitzgerald
Into the West '92

Geraldine Fitzgerald
Arthur '81
Arthur 2: On the Rocks '88
The Last American Hero
'73
Poltergeist 2: The Other
Side '86

Walter Fitzgerald
Treasure Island '50

Colleen Fitzpatrick
Hairspray '88

Kate Fitzpatrick
Return of Captain
Invincible '83

Paul Fix
The Bad Seed '56
To Kill a Mockingbird '62

Jack Fjeldstad
The Polar Bear King '94

Darron Flagg
Bagdad Cafe '88

Fannie Flagg
My Best Friend Is a
Vampire '88

Joe Flaherty
Back to the Future, Part 2
'89
Looking for Miracles '90
One Crazy Summer '86
Sesame Street Presents:
Follow That Bird '85

Lanny Flaherty
Sommersby '93

Paul Flaherty▶
Clifford '92
18 Again! '88

Robert Flaherty▶
Elephant Boy '37

Georges Flament
The 400 Blows '59

Fionnula Flanagan
The Ewok Adventure '84
Voyager from the Unknown
'83
A Winner Never Quits '86

Ian Geer Flanders
Silence '73

Susan Flannery
Gumball Rally '76

James Flavin
King Kong '33

Flea
Back to the Future, Part 2
'89

James Fleet
Four Weddings and a
Funeral '93

Charles Fleischer
Back to the Future, Part 2
'89
Straight Talk '92

Dave Fleischer▶
Betty Boop Special
Collector's Edition:
Volume 1 '35
Gulliver's Travels '39
Hoppity Goes to Town '41

Max Fleischer▶
Betty Boop Special
Collector's Edition:
Volume 1 '35

Richard Fleischer▶
Conan the Destroyer '84
Doctor Doolittle '67
The Prince and the Pauper
'78
20,000 Leagues Under the
Sea '54

Noah Fleiss
Josh and S.A.M. '93

Rhonda Fleming
A Connecticut Yankee in
King Arthur's Court '49
Since You Went Away '44
Spellbound '45

Victor Fleming▶
Captains Courageous '37
Gone with the Wind '39
Treasure Island '34
The Wizard of Oz '39

Gordon Flemyng▶
Doctor Who and the
Daleks '65

Dexter Fletcher
Lionheart '87

Louise Fletcher
The Boy Who Could Fly
'86
The Cheap Detective '78
Invaders from Mars '86
Islands '87
Strange Invaders '83
A Summer to Remember
'84

Sam Flint
Spy Smasher '42

Jay C. Flippen
Oklahoma! '55

Flipper
Flipper's Odyssey '66

Lucy Lee Flippin
Summer School '87

James T. Flocker▶
The Secret of Navajo
Cave '76

John Florea▶
Computer Wizard '77
Where's Willie? '77

Dann Florek
The Flintstones '94

Marsha Florence
Zebrahead '92

Robert Florey▶
The Cocoanuts '29

George Flower
Across the Great Divide
'76
Further Adventures of the
Wilderness Family, Part
2 '77
In Search of a Golden Sky
'84
Mountain Family Robinson
'79

Darlanne Fluegel
Battle Beyond the Stars
'80
Tough Guys '86

Joel Fluellen
A Dream for Christmas '73
The Great White Hope '70

**The Flying Karamazov
Brothers**
The Jewel of the Nile '85

Errol Flynn
The Adventures of Robin
Hood '38
Captain Blood '35
The Prince and the Pauper
'37

Joe Flynn
The Computer Wore Tennis
Shoes '69
Million Dollar Duck '71
My Dog, the Thief '69
Now You See Him, Now
You Don't '72
Superdad '73

Miriam Flynn
18 Again! '88
National Lampoon's
Christmas Vacation '89

Sean Flynn
Son of Captain Blood '62

Spiros Focas
The Jewel of the Nile '85

Nina Foch
An American in Paris '51
Child of Glass '78
Salty '73
The Ten Commandments
'56

Megan Follows
Anne of Avonlea '87
Anne of Green Gables '85
Back to Hannibal: The
Further Adventures of
Tom Sawyer and
Huckleberry Finn '90
Hockey Night '84
The Olden Days Coat '81
Stacking '87

Megan Folson
Heartland '81

Bridget Fonda
Doc Hollywood '91
It Could Happen to You
'94
Jacob Have I Loved '88
Little Buddha '93
Shag: The Movie '89
Singles '92

Henry Fonda
The Cheyenne Social Club
'70
Home to Stay '79
How the West was Won
'63
My Name is Nobody '74
On Golden Pond '81
Once Upon a Time in the
West '68
The Red Pony '76
The Swarm '78
The Wrong Man '56
Yours, Mine & Ours '68

Jane Fonda
The Electric Horseman '79
On Golden Pond '81

Peter Fonda
Cannonball Run '81
Tammy and the Doctor '63

Joan Fontaine
Jane Eyre '44
Rebecca '40
Suspicion '41
Voyage to the Bottom of
the Sea '61

Dick Foran
Winners of the West '40

Bryan Forbes
A Shot in the Dark '64

Bryan Forbes▶
International Velvet '78
Whistle Down the Wind
'62

Faith Ford
North '94

Francis Ford
The Quiet Man '52

Glenn Ford
The Courtship of Eddie's
Father '62
Smith! '69
Superman 1: The Movie
'78

Greg Ford▶
Daffy Duck's Quackbusters
'89

Harrison Ford
American Graffiti '73
The Empire Strikes Back
'80
The Fugitive '93
Indiana Jones and the Last
Crusade '89
Indiana Jones and the
Temple of Doom '84
Raiders of the Lost Ark '81
Regarding Henry '91
Return of the Jedi '83
Star Wars '77

Jack Ford
The Joy Luck Club '93

John Ford▶
How Green was My Valley
'41
How the West was Won
'63
The Quiet Man '52
Wee Willie Winkie '37

Paul Ford
The Music Man '62

Wallace Ford
Shadow of a Doubt '43
Spellbound '45

Whitey Ford
Robotech, Vol. 1: Booby
Trap '85

Deborah Foreman
Valley Girl '83

Tailinh Forest Flower
Geronimo '93

Carol Forman
The Black Widow '47
Federal Agents vs.
Underworld, Inc. '49

Milos Forman▶
Amadeus '84

Frederic Forrest
The Adventures of
Huckleberry Finn '85
Lassie '94
Stacking '87
The Stone Boy '84
Tucker: The Man and His
Dream '88
Valley Girl '83

Steve Forrest
The Last of the Mohicans
'85
Mommie Dearest '81
Spies Like Us '85
The Wild Country '71

William Forrest
The Masked Marvel '43

Robert Forster
Alligator '80
Avalanche '78
The Black Hole '79
Once a Hero '88

Bill Forsyth▶
Comfort and Joy '84
Gregory's Girl '80
Housekeeping '87
Local Hero '83
That Sinking Feeling '79

Bruce Forsyth
Bedknobs and Broomsticks
'71

Rosemary Forsyth
A Friendship in Vienna '88

John Forsythe
Scrooged '88

William Forsythe
Dick Tracy '90

Nick Apollo Forte
Broadway Danny Rose '84

Bob Fosse
The Little Prince '74

Brigitte Fossey
Forbidden Games '52

Ami Foster
Troop Beverly Hills '89

Frances Foster
Crooklyn '94

Gloria Foster
The House of Dies Drear '88
Leonard Part 6 '87
Man & Boy '71

Jodie Foster
Bugsy Malone '76
Candleshoe '78
Foxes '80
Freaky Friday '76
The Little Girl Who Lives Down the Lane '76
Little Man Tate '91
Maverick '94
Napoleon and Samantha '72
One Little Indian '73
Sommersby '93
Tom Sawyer '73

Jodie Foster▶
Little Man Tate '91

Julia Foster
The Loneliness of the Long Distance Runner '62

Lewis R. Foster▶
The Sign of Zorro '60

Meg Foster
The Legend of Sleepy Hollow '79
Masters of the Universe '87

Norman Foster▶
Davy Crockett and the River Pirates '56
Davy Crockett, King of the Wild Frontier '55
Indian Paint '64
The Nine Lives of Elfego Baca '58
The Sign of Zorro '60

Phil Foster
Bang the Drum Slowly '73

Preston Foster
I Am a Fugitive from a Chain Gang '32
My Friend Flicka '43

Frederique Fouche
Clowning Around 2 '93

Douglas Fowley
Mr. Wise Guy '42
Singin' in the Rain '52

Bernard Fox
The Private Eyes '80

Edward Fox
Battle of Britain '69
The Bounty '84
A Bridge Too Far '77
The Go-Between '71

Never Say Never Again '83

Huckleberry Fox
The Blue Yonder '86
Konrad '85
Misunderstood '84
A Winner Never Quits '86

James Fox
Greystoke: The Legend of Tarzan, Lord of the Apes '84
The Remains of the Day '93

Matthew Fox
My Boyfriend's Back '93

Michael J. Fox
Back to the Future '85
Back to the Future, Part 2 '89
Back to the Future, Part 3 '90
Doc Hollywood '91
For Love or Money '93
Greedy '94
Life with Mikey '93
Light of Day '87
Midnight Madness '80
Teen Wolf '85

Peter Fox
A Minor Miracle '83

Sean Fox
3 Ninjas Kick Back '94

Sonny Fox
The Christmas That Almost Wasn't '66

Wallace Fox▶
Bowery Blitzkrieg '41
The Great Mike '44
Kid Dynamite '43
Million Dollar Kid '44
'Neath Brooklyn Bridge '42
Smart Alecks '42

Robert Foxworth
The Treasure of Matecumbe '76

Eddie Foy Jr.
Gidget Goes Hawaiian '61
Yankee Doodle Dandy '42

Tracy Fraim
Dream Machine '91

William A. Fraker▶
Legend of the Lone Ranger '81

Jonathon Frakes
Star Trek the Next Generation Episode 1-2: Encounter at Farpoint '87

Anthony (Tony) Franciosa
Ghost in the Noonday Sun '74

Anne Francis
Funny Girl '68

Kay Francis
The Cocoanuts '29
Little Men '40

Pietro Francisci▶
Hercules '58
Hercules Unchained '59

James Franciscus
The Amazing Dobermans '76

Beneath the Planet of the Apes '70
Jonathan Livingston Seagull '73
Snow Treasure '67
The Valley of Gwangi '69

Don Francks
Finian's Rainbow '68

Margarita Franco
3 Ninjas '92

Charles Frank
The Right Stuff '83

Joanna Frank
Say Anything '89

Melvin Frank▶
The Court Jester '56
Walk Like a Man '87

William Frankfather
Born Yesterday '93
Defense Play '88

Diane Franklin
Better Off Dead '85

Don Franklin
Fast Forward '84

John Franklin
The Addams Family '91

Pamela Franklin
David Copperfield '70
Flipper's New Adventure '64
The Horse Without a Head '63
The Prime of Miss Jean Brodie '69
A Tiger Walks '64

Richard Franklin▶
Cloak & Dagger '84
F/X 2: The Deadly Art of Illusion '91

Arthur Franz
Invaders from Mars '53
The Member of the Wedding '52

Eduard Franz
Francis the Talking Mule '49

Brendan Fraser
Airheads '94
Encino Man '92
School Ties '92
With Honors '94

John Fraser
Horsemasters '61

Moyra Fraser
The Boy Friend '71

Stuart Fratkin
Prehysteria '93
Remote '93

James Frawley▶
The Big Bus '76
The Muppet Movie '79

William Frawley
The Adventures of Huckleberry Finn '39
Miracle on 34th Street '47

Rupert Frazer
Back Home '90
Empire of the Sun '87

Stephen Frears▶
Hero '92

The Snapper '93

Lynne Frederick
Amazing Mr. Blunden '72

Al Freeman Jr.
Finian's Rainbow '68
Malcolm X '92

J.E. Freeman
It Could Happen to You '94

Joan Freeman▶
Satisfaction '88

Kathleen Freeman
The Disorderly Orderly '64
The Errand Boy '61
Innerspace '87
Naked Gun 33 1/3: The Final Insult '94
The Nutty Professor '63
The Willies '90

Mona Freeman
Black Beauty '46

Morgan Freeman
Driving Miss Daisy '89
Harry & Son '84
Lean on Me '89
The Power of One '92
Robin Hood: Prince of Thieves '91
That Was Then. . .This Is Now '85

Morgan Freeman▶
Bopha! '93

Paul Freeman
Raiders of the Lost Ark '81
A World Apart '88

Friz Freleng▶
Best of Bugs Bunny & Friends '40
Bugs Bunny Cartoon Festival '44
Bugs Bunny Superstar '75
Bugs Bunny's 3rd Movie: 1,001 Rabbit Tales '82
Daffy Duck's Movie: Fantastic Island '83
Looney Looney Looney Bugs Bunny Movie '81
A Salute to Mel Blanc '58

David French
Bingo '91

Harold French▶
Rob Roy - The Highland Rogue '53

Leigh French
Aloha, Bobby and Rose '74

Susan French
House '86

Victor French
Little House on the Prairie '74

Matt Frewer
Honey, I Shrunk the Kids '89
Supergirl '84

Leonard Frey
Fiddler on the Roof '71

Brenda Fricker
Angels in the Outfield '94
Home Alone 2: Lost in New York '92

So I Married an Axe Murderer '93

Richard Friedenberg▶
The Adventures of Frontier Fremont '75
Life & Times of Grizzly Adams '74

Bud Friedgen▶
That's Entertainment, Part 3 '93

William Friedkin▶
Blue Chips '94

Louis Friedlander▶
Tailspin Tommy '34

Colin Friels
Darkman '90

Rachel Friend
The Quest '86

Gert Frobe
Chitty Chitty Bang Bang '68
Ten Little Indians '75
Those Daring Young Men in Their Jaunty Jalopies '69

Toby Froud
Labyrinth '86

E. Max Frye▶
Amos and Andrew '93

Sean Frye
E.T.: The Extra-Terrestrial '82

Virgil Frye
Secret of the Ice Cave '89

Leo Fuchs
Avalon '90

Robert Fuest▶
Wuthering Heights '70

John Fujioka
Conspiracy of Love '87

Jun Fukuda▶
Godzilla vs. Megalon '76
Godzilla vs. the Cosmic Monster '74

Lucio Fulci▶
Challenge to White Fang '86

Full Force
House Party '90

Brook Fuller
When Wolves Cry '69

Kurt Fuller
Bingo '91
Calendar Girl '93
No Holds Barred '89
Wayne's World '92

Penny Fuller
The Beverly Hillbillies '93

Rikki Fulton
Comfort and Joy '84

Annette Funicello
Babes in Toyland '61
Back to the Beach '87
Beach Blanket Bingo '65
Beach Party '63
Bikini Beach '64
Head '68
Horsemasters '61

How to Stuff a Wild Bikini
'65
Lots of Luck '85
The Misadventures of
Merlin Jones '63
Monkey's Uncle '65
Muscle Beach Party '64
Pajama Party '64
The Shaggy Dog '59
Zorro, Vol. 1 '58

Sidney J. Furie▶
Ladybugs '92
Superman 4: The Quest for
Peace '87

Edward Furlong
American Heart '92
A Home of Our Own '93
Terminator 2: Judgment
Day '91

Chris Furrh
Lord of the Flies '90

Joseph Furst
Diamonds are Forever '71

Stephen Furst
The Dream Team '89
Magic Kid '92
Midnight Madness '80

George Furth
Butch Cassidy and the
Sundance Kid '69

Marianne Gaba
How to Stuff a Wild Bikini
'65

Christopher Gable
The Boy Friend '71

Clark Gable
Gone with the Wind '39
It Happened One Night
'34

June Gable
Brenda Starr '86

Zsa Zsa Gabor
Lili '53

Radu Gabrea▶
Secret of the Ice Cave '89

Mike Gabriel▶
The Rescuers Down Under
'90

Holly Gagnier
Girls Just Want to Have
Fun '85

Jenny Gago
Sweet 15 '90

Boyd Gaines
The Sure Thing '85

M.C. Gainey
Leap of Faith '92

Courtney Gains
Back to the Future '85
The 'Burbs '89
Can't Buy Me Love '87

Charlotte Gainsbourg
The Little Thief '89

Johnny Galecki
National Lampoon's
Christmas Vacation '89

Bronagh Gallagher
The Commitments '91

Peter Gallagher
Dreamchild '85

Camillo Gallardo
Singles '92

Rosina Galli
Fisherman's Wharf '39

Zach Galligan
Gremlins '84
Gremlins 2: The New
Batch '90
The Lawrenceville Stories
'80s

Mason Gamble
Dennis the Menace '93

Michael Gambon
Clean Slate '94
Toys '92
Turtle Diary '86

Tom Gamen
Lord of the Flies '63

Robin Gammell
Project X '87

James Gammon
The Adventures of Huck
Finn '93
Cabin Boy '94
Coupe de Ville '90
Major League '89
Major League 2 '94

Richard Gant
The Freshman '90

Bruno Ganz
Wings of Desire '88

Matthew Garber
The Gnome-Mobile '67
The Three Lives of
Thomasina '63

Victor Garber
Life with Mikey '93
Sleepless in Seattle '93

Andy Garcia
Blue Skies Again '83
Hero '92
Stand and Deliver '88

Priscilla Garcia
Once Upon a Scoundrel
'73

Vincent Gardenia
Bang the Drum Slowly '73
The Front Page '74
Greased Lightning '77
Home Movies '79
The Last Flight of Noah's
Ark '80
Little Shop of Horrors '86
Moonstruck '87

Reginald Gardiner
The Flying Deuces '39
The Horn Blows at
Midnight '45

John David Garfield
Golden Voyage of Sinbad
'73
The Other Side of the
Mountain '75

William Gargan
The Canterville Ghost '44
Miss Annie Rooney '42

Beverly Garland
The Voyage of the Yes '72
Where the Red Fern
Grows '74

Boots Garland
Pistol: The Birth of a
Legend '90

Judy Garland
Andy Hardy Meets
Debutante '40
Babes in Arms '39
Babes on Broadway '41
Easter Parade '48
Girl Crazy '43
Judgment at Nuremberg
'61
Life Begins for Andy Hardy
'41
Love Finds Andy Hardy '38
Meet Me in St. Louis '44
Strike Up the Band '40
That's Entertainment '74
Thoroughbreds Don't Cry
'37
Till the Clouds Roll By '46
The Wizard of Oz '39

Lee Garlington
My Life '93

Constance Garneau
Strangers in Good
Company '91

James Garner
The Castaway Cowboy '74
Fire in the Sky '93
Maverick '94
Murphy's Romance '85
One Little Indian '73
Support Your Local
Gunfighter '71
Support Your Local Sheriff
'69
Tank '83

Peggy Ann Garner
The Cat '66
Jane Eyre '44
A Tree Grows in Brooklyn
'45

Gale Garnett
Mr. & Mrs. Bridge '91

Tay Garnett▶
Challenge To Be Free '76
A Connecticut Yankee in
King Arthur's Court '49

Janeane Garofalo
Reality Bites '94

Teri Garr
The Black Stallion '79
The Black Stallion Returns
'83
Close Encounters of the
Third Kind '77
Escape Artist '82
First Born '84
Head '68
Mr. Mom '83
Mom and Dad Save the
World '92
Oh, God! '77
Once Upon a Brothers
Grimm '77
Pajama Party '64
The Sting 2 '83
Tootsie '82
Waiting for the Light '90
Witches' Brew '79
Young Frankenstein '74

Donna Garrat
Diamonds are Forever '71

Betty Garrett
On the Town '49

Leif Garrett
The Outsiders '83
Peter Lundy and the
Medicine Hat Stallion '77
Skateboard '77

Patsy Garrett
Benji '74
Dennis the Menace:
Dinosaur Hunter '87
For the Love of Benji '77

Barbara Garrick
Sleepless in Seattle '93

Rian Garrick
Mooncussers '62

Greer Garson
The Happiest Millionaire
'67

Willie Garson
Untamed Heart '93

Christopher Gartin
No Big Deal '83

John W. Gates
Legend of Boggy Creek
'75

Larry Gates
Funny Lady '75

Nils Gaup▶
Shipwrecked '90

Dan Gauthier
Son-in-Law '93
Teen Witch '89

Matt Gauthier
Lords of Magick '88

Jack Gautier
Playtime '67

Roberto Gavaldon▶
The Littlest Outlaw '54

Cassandra Gaviola
Conan the Barbarian '82

Lisa Gaye
The Sign of Zorro '60

Crystal Gayle
Country Music with the
Muppets '85

Jackie Gayle
Pepper and His Wacky
Taxi '72
Plain Clothes '88

Mitch Gaylord
American Anthem '86

George Gaynes
Dead Men Don't Wear
Plaid '82
It Came Upon a Midnight
Clear '84
Police Academy '84
Police Academy 2: Their
First Assignment '85
Police Academy 3: Back in
Training '86
Police Academy 4: Citizens
on Patrol '87
Police Academy 5:
Assignment Miami Beach
'88
Police Academy 6: City
Under Siege '89
Stepmonster '92
Tootsie '82

Mitzi Gaynor
South Pacific '58

Eunice Gayson
Dr. No '62
From Russia with Love '63

Gyula Gazdag▶
A Hungarian Fairy Tale '87

Ben Gazzara
Neptune Factor '73

Cynthia Geary
8 Seconds '94

Jason Gedrick
The Heavenly Kid '85
Stacking '87
The Zoo Gang '85

Prunella Gee
Never Say Never Again
'83

Ellen Geer
Silence '73

Will Geer
Bandolero! '68
The Billion Dollar Hobo '78
Jeremiah Johnson '72
Napoleon and Samantha
'72
The Reivers '69
Silence '73

Judy Geeson
To Sir, with Love '67

Martha Gehman
F/X '86
Father of the Bride '91
The Flamingo Kid '84

Grant Gelt
Avalon '90

Chief Dan George
The Bears & I '74
Cancel My Reservation '72
Little Big Man '70
The Outlaw Josey Wales
'76

Gladys George
The Maltese Falcon '41

Susan George
Lightning: The White
Stallion '86
Sudden Terror '70

Marita Geraghty
Groundhog Day '93

Gil Gerard
Buck Rogers in the 25th
Century '79

Steve Geray
Tobor the Great '54

Joan Gerber
Tobor the Great '54

George Gerdes
Iron Will '93

Richard Gere
Sommersby '93

Sean Gerlis
A Summer to Remember
'84

Nane Germon
Beauty and the Beast '46

Clyde Geronimi▶
Alice in Wonderland '51
101 Dalmatians '61
Sleeping Beauty '59

Daniel Gerroll
Big Business '88
Drop Dead Fred '91
A Far Off Place '93

Alex Gerry
The Bellboy '60

Gina Gershon
Pretty in Pink '86

Jami Gertz
Jersey Girl '92
The Lost Boys '87
Sixteen Candles '84
Solarbabies '86

Nicolas Gessner▶
The Little Girl Who Lives
Down the Lane '76

Balthazar Getty
December '91
Lord of the Flies '90
My Heroes Have Always
Been Cowboys '91

Estelle Getty
Mannequin '87
Mask '85
Stop! or My Mom Will
Shoot '92
Tootsie '82

John Getz
Curly Sue '91
Don't Tell Mom the
Babysitter's Dead '91

Julie Gholson
Where the Lilies Bloom '74

Alice Ghostley
To Kill a Mockingbird '62
With Six You Get Eggroll
'68

Louis Giambalvo
Weekend at Bernie's '89

Giancarlo Giannini
American Dreamer '84
Once Upon a Crime '92

Cynthia Gibb
Short Circuit 2 '88

Marla Gibbs
The Meteor Man '93
Up Against the Wall '91

Susan Gibney
And You Thought Your
Parents Were Weird! '91

Brian Gibson▶
Poltergeist 2: The Other
Side '86
What's Love Got to Do
With It? '93

Colin Gibson
John & Julie '57

Eleanor Gibson
The Haunting of Barney
Palmer '90s

Henry Gibson
Brenda Starr '86
The Incredible Shrinking
Woman '81
Innerspace '87

Mel Gibson
The Bounty '84
Forever Young '92
Mad Max: Beyond
Thunderdome '85
The Man Without a Face
'93

Maverick '94
The River '84

Mel Gibson▶
The Man Without a Face
'93

Mimi Gibson
Courage of Black Beauty
'57

Thomas Gibson
Far and Away '92

Virginia Gibson
Seven Brides for Seven
Brothers '54

Pamela Gidley
Permanent Record '88
Thrashin' '86

John Gielgud
Arthur '81
Arthur 2: On the Rocks '88
Chariots of Fire '81
The Elephant Man '80
The Hunchback of Notre
Dame '82
The Power of One '92

Stefan Gierasch
Dave '93

Gloria Gifford
Vice Versa '88

Sandro Giglio
The War of the Worlds
'53

Billy Gilbert
Breaking the Ice '38
His Girl Friday '40
Mr. Wise Guy '42

Brian Gilbert▶
Vice Versa '88

Helen Gilbert
Andy Hardy Gets Spring
Fever '39

Lewis Gilbert▶
Educating Rita '83
Moonraker '79
The Spy Who Loved Me
'77
You Only Live Twice '67

Lou Gilbert
The Great White Hope '70

Marcus Gilbert
Army of Darkness '92

Melissa Gilbert
Little House on the Prairie
'74
The Miracle Worker '79
Sylvester '85

Sara Gilbert
The Mouse and the
Motorcycle '80s
Sudie & Simpson '90

Connie Gilchrist
The Misadventures of
Merlin Jones '63

Jack Gilford
Arthur 2: On the Rocks '88
Cocoon '85
Cocoon: The Return '88
Daydreamer '66
Harry & Walter Go to
New York '76

Stuart Gillard▶
Teenage Mutant Ninja
Turtles 3 '93

Dana Gillespie
The People That Time
Forgot '77

Anita Gillette
Moonstruck '87

Terry Gilliam
And Now for Something
Completely Different '72
Monty Python and the
Holy Grail '75

Terry Gilliam▶
The Adventures of Baron
Munchausen '89
Jabberwocky '77
Monty Python and the
Holy Grail '75
Time Bandits '81

Sidney Gilliat
The Lady Vanishes '38

Sidney Gilliat▶
Great St. Trinian's Train
Robbery '66

Isabel Gillies
Metropolitan '90

Richard Gilliland
A Day for Thanks on
Walton's Mountain '82

Anne Gillis
'Neath Brooklyn Bridge '42

Larry Gilman
Cool Runnings '93

Jack Gilpin
Funny Farm '88

Marc Gilpin
Computer Wizard '77
Where's Willie? '77

Jack Ging
Mosby's Marauders '66
Where the Red Fern
Grows '74

Hermione Gingold
How to Be a Perfect
Person in Just Three
Days '84
The Music Man '62

Robert Ginty
Madhouse '90

Christian Gion▶
Here Comes Santa Claus
'84

Rocky Giordani
Cop and a Half '93

Bob Giraldi▶
Club Med '83
Hiding Out '87

Joseph Girard
Hurricane Express '32

Hippolyte Girardot
Manon of the Spring '87

Roland Giraud
Three Men and a Cradle
'85

Annabeth Gish
Coupe de Ville '90
Desert Bloom '86
Hiding Out '87

Shag: The Movie '89

Lillian Gish
The Adventures of
Huckleberry Finn '85
Follow Me, Boys! '66
Hambone & Hillie '84
Sweet Liberty '86

Sheila Gish
Highlander '86

Robert Gist
Jack the Giant Killer '62

Wyndham Gittens▶
Tim Tyler's Luck '37

Robin Givens
Blankman '94

Anton Glanzelius
My Life as a Dog '85

Darel Glaser
Bless the Beasts and
Children '71

Michael Glaser
Butterflies Are Free '72

Paul Michael Glaser
Wait Till Your Mother Gets
Home '83

Paul Michael Glaser▶
The Air Up There '94
The Cutting Edge '92

Ned Glass
West Side Story '61

Isabel Glasser
Forever Young '92

Matthew Glave
Baby's Day Out '94

Jackie Gleason
Nothing in Common '86
Smokey and the Bandit '77
Smokey and the Bandit,
Part 2 '80
Smokey and the Bandit,
Part 3 '83
The Sting 2 '83
The Toy '82

James Gleason
A Tree Grows in Brooklyn
'45

Joanna Gleason
F/X 2: The Deadly Art of
Illusion '91

Paul Gleason
The Breakfast Club '85
The Ewoks: Battle for
Endor '85
Morgan Stewart's Coming
Home '87
She's Having a Baby '88

Nicholas Gledhill
Careful, He Might Hear
You '84

John Glen▶
For Your Eyes Only '81
Octopussy '83
A View to a Kill '85

Charles Glenn
Philadelphia '93

Roy Glenn
Jungle Drums of Africa '53

Scott Glenn
The Hunt for Red October
'90
Miss Firecracker '89
More American Graffiti '79
My Heroes Have Always
Been Cowboys '91
The Right Stuff '83
The River '84
Silverado '85

Stacey Glick
Brighton Beach Memoirs
'86
Three O'Clock High '87

Bruce Glover
Diamonds are Forever '71

Crispin Glover
Back to the Future '85
Back to the Future, Part 2
'89
Racing with the Moon '84
What's Eating Gilbert
Grape '93

Danny Glover
And the Children Shall
Lead '85
Angels in the Outfield '94
Bophal '93
Iceman '84
Places in the Heart '84
Silverado '85

John Glover
Annie Hall '77
Gremlins 2: The New
Batch '90
Meet the Hollowheads '89
Rocket Gibraltar '88
Scrooged '88
Something Special '86

Julian Glover
The Empire Strikes Back
'80
For Your Eyes Only '81
Indiana Jones and the Last
Crusade '89
The Secret Garden '87
Treasure Island '89

Carlin Glynn
Sixteen Candles '84
The Trip to Bountiful '85

George Gobel
The Fantastic World of
D.C. Collins '84

Justin Gocke
My Grandpa is a Vampire
'92

Gary Goddard▶
Masters of the Universe
'87

Mark Goddard
Strange Invaders '83

Thomas Godet
Toto le Heros '91

Alexander Godunov
The Money Pit '86
North '94

Angela Goethals
Heartbreak Hotel '88
Home Alone '90

Peter Michael Goetz
Father of the Bride '91
My Girl '91

Gila Golan
The Valley of Gwangi '69

Menahem Golan▶
Over the Top '86

Jack Gold
Little Lord Fauntleroy '80

Willis Goldbeck▶
Love Laughs at Andy
  Hardy '46

Adam Goldberg
Dazed and Confused '93

**Gary David
  Goldberg▶**
Dad '89

Whoopi Goldberg
Clara's Heart '88
Corrina, Corrina '94
Ghost '90
Made in America '93
Sarafinal '92
Sister Act '92
Sister Act 2: Back in the
  Habit '93

Jeff Goldblum
The Adventures of
  Buckaroo Banzai Across
  the Eighth Dimension '84
Annie Hall '77
Invasion of the Body
  Snatchers '78
Jurassic Park '93
The Legend of Sleepy
  Hollow '79
The Right Stuff '83
Silverado '85

Annie Golden
Baby Boom '87
Desperately Seeking Susan
  '85

Norman D. Golden II
Cop and a Half '93

Ricky Paull Goldin
Hyper-Sapien: People from
  Another Star '86

Gary Goldman▶
Thumbelina '94

Philippe Goldman
Small Change '76

Allan Goldstein
The Lawrenceville Stories
  '80s

Allan Goldstein▶
The House of Dies Drear
  '88
Outside Chance of
  Maximillian Glick '88

Bob(cat) Goldthwait
Hot to Trot! '88
One Crazy Summer '86
Police Academy 3: Back in
  Training '86
Police Academy 4: Citizens
  on Patrol '87
Scrooged '88

Tony Goldwyn
Ghost '90
Kuffs '92
The Pelican Brief '93

Richard Golfier
Small Change '76

Valeria Golino
Clean Slate '94
Hot Shots! Part Deux '93
Rain Man '88

Arlene Golonka
The Hoboken Chicken
  Emergency '84

Minna Gombell
The Thin Man '34

Panchito Gomez
Paco '75
Sweet 15 '90

Thomas Gomez
Sorrowful Jones '49

Caroline Goodall
Hook '91
The Moon Stallion '85
The Silver Stallion: King of
  the Wild Brumbies '94

Cuba Gooding Jr.
Boyz N the Hood '91
Lightning Jack '94

Saul Goodkind▶
Buck Rogers Conquers the
  Universe '39
The Phantom Creeps '39

Dean Goodman
Tucker: The Man and His
  Dream '88

Dody Goodman
Cool As Ice '91
Splash '84

John Goodman
Always '89
Arachnophobia '90
The Babe '92
Born Yesterday '93
The Flintstones '94
King Ralph '91
Matinee '92
Revenge of the Nerds '84

Bill Goodwin
The Jolson Story '46

Laura Jane Goodwin
Crystalstone '88

Michael Goodwin
Date with an Angel '87

**Allen (Gooritz)
  Garfield**
Beverly Hills Cop 2 '87
Desert Bloom '86
Family Prayers '91
Irreconcilable Differences
  '84
Paco '75
Skateboard '77

Ray Goosens▶
Pinocchio in Outer Space
  '64

Bernard Gorcey
Blues Busters '50
Bowery Buckaroos '47
Clipped Wings '53
Ghost Chasers '51
Hard-Boiled Mahoney '47
Spook Busters '46

David Gorcey
Blues Busters '50
Bowery Buckaroos '47
Flying Wild '41
Ghost Chasers '51
Hard-Boiled Mahoney '47
Mr. Wise Guy '42
Spook Busters '46

Elizabeth Gorcey
Kidco '83

Leo Gorcey
Blues Busters '50
Bowery Blitzkrieg '41
Bowery Buckaroos '47
Boys of the City '40
Clipped Wings '53
Flying Wild '41
Follow the Leader '44
Ghost Chasers '51
Hard-Boiled Mahoney '47
Kid Dynamite '43
Little Tough Guys '38
Million Dollar Kid '44
Mr. Wise Guy '42
'Neath Brooklyn Bridge '42
Smart Alecks '42
Spook Busters '46
Spooks Run Wild '41
That Gang of Mine '40

Bert I. Gordon▶
The Magic Sword '62

Eve Gordon
Avalon '90
Paradise '91

Gale Gordon
The 'Burbs '89

Gavin Gordon
Turf Boy '42

Hayes Gordon
Return of Captain
  Invincible '83

Keith Gordon
Back to School '86
Home Movies '79
Legend of Billie Jean '85

Keith Gordon▶
A Midnight Clear '92

Mary Gordon
Follow the Leader '44
Million Dollar Kid '44

Ruth Gordon
Any Which Way You Can
  '80
The Big Bus '76
Jimmy the Kid '82
My Bodyguard '80
The Prince of Central Park
  '77

Steve Gordon▶
Arthur '81

Stuart Gordon▶
Robot Jox '89

Joseph Gordon-Levitt
Angels in the Outfield '94
Holy Matrimony '94

Galyn Gorg
Robocop 2 '90

Marius Goring
The Red Shoes '48

Ruth Goring
Yentl '83

Buddy Gorman
Ghost Chasers '51

Robert Gorman
Mr. Nanny '93

Eydie Gorme
Alice in Wonderland '85

Felim Gormley
The Commitments '91

Frank Gorshin
The Meteor Man '93

That Darn Cat '65

Rene Goscinny▶
Lucky Luke: Ballad of the
  Daltons '78
Lucky Luke: Daisy Town '71

Louis Gossett Jr.
The Bushbaby '70
Enemy Mine '85
Goodbye, Miss 4th of July
  '88
Sudie & Simpson '90

Roland Got
G-Men vs. the Black
  Dragon '43

Will Gotay
Stand and Deliver '88

Walter Gotell
The African Queen '51
For Your Eyes Only '81
From Russia with Love '63
Moonraker '79
The Spy Who Loved Me
  '77

Staffan Gotestam
Brothers Lionheart '85

Michael Gothard
For Your Eyes Only '81

Gilbert Gottfried
Bad Medicine '85
Problem Child '90
Problem Child 2 '91

Lisa Gottlieb▶
Just One of the Guys '85

Michael Gottlieb▶
Mannequin '87
Mr. Nanny '93

Thomas Gottschalk
Sister Act 2: Back in the
  Habit '93

Michael Gough
The Age of Innocence '93
Batman '89
Batman Returns '92
The Go-Between '71
Oxford Blues '84
Rob Roy - The Highland
  Rogue '53
The Sword & the Rose '53

Elliott Gould
A Bridge Too Far '77
Casey at the Bat '85
The Devil & Max Devlin
  '81
Frog '89
Frogs! '90s
Harry & Walter Go to
  New York '76
The Last Flight of Noah's
  Ark '80
M*A*S*H '70
Matilda '78

Harold Gould
Love and Death '75
The Sting '73

Jason Gould
Say Anything '89

Robert Goulet
Naked Gun 2 1/2: The
  Smell of Fear '91
Scrooged '88

Andre Gower
The Monster Squad '87

Harry Goz
Bill '81
Bill: On His Own '83
Mommie Dearest '81

Betty Grable
Follow the Fleet '36

Nickolas Grace
Diamond's Edge '88

Elizabeth Gracen
Death of the Incredible
  Hulk '90

Sally Gracie
Opportunity Knocks '90

David Graf
Police Academy 2: Their
  First Assignment '85
Police Academy 3: Back in
  Training '86
Police Academy 4: Citizens
  on Patrol '87
Police Academy 5:
  Assignment Miami Beach
  '88
Police Academy 6: City
  Under Siege '89

Ilene Graff
Ladybugs '92

Todd Graff
Dominick & Eugene '88
Opportunity Knocks '90

Aimee Graham
Amos and Andrew '93

Billy Graham
The Prodigal '83

Fred Graham
Trader Tom of the China
  Seas '54

Gary Graham
Robot Jox '89

Gerrit Graham
Cannonball '76
Home Movies '79
The Man with One Red
  Shoe '85
Martians Go Home! '90
Spaceship '81
This Boy's Life '93

Heather Graham
Shout '91

Therese Graham
Country '84

William A. Graham
Just William's Luck '47

William A. Graham▶
Change of Habit '69
Orphan Train '79
Where the Lilies Bloom '74

Gloria Grahame
It's a Wonderful Life '46
Oklahoma! '55

Hepburn Grahame
Crusoe '89

Margot Grahame
Fabulous Joe '47

**Vladimir
  Grammatikov▶**
The Land of Faraway '87

Farley Granger
Strangers on a Train '51

Marc Granger
Amazing Mr. Blunden '72

Beth Grant
Rain Man '88
Speed '94

Cary Grant
The Bachelor and the
Bobby-Soxer '47
Bringing Up Baby '38
Charade '63
His Girl Friday '40
Monkey Business '52
North by Northwest '59
Notorious '46
Penny Serenade '41
The Philadelphia Story '40
Suspicion '41
To Catch a Thief '55
Topper '37

David Marshall Grant
American Flyers '85
Forever Young '92

Faye Grant
Voyager from the Unknown
'83

Hugh Grant
Four Weddings and a
Funeral '93
The Remains of the Day
'93

Kathryn Grant
The Seventh Voyage of
Sinbad '58

Lee Grant
Airport '77 '77
A Billion for Boris '90
Little Miss Marker '80
The Swarm '78

Leon Grant
Beat Street '84

Polly Grant
My Friend Walter '93

Richard E. Grant
The Age of Innocence '93
L.A. Story '91

Rodney Grant
Dances with Wolves '90
Geronimo: An American
Legend '93
Wagons East '94

Schuyler Grant
Anne of Avonlea '87
Anne of Green Gables '85

**Stuart Proud Eagle
Grant**
Wagons East '94

Bonita Granville
The Lone Ranger '56
Love Laughs at Andy
Hardy '46
Nancy Drew, Reporter '39

Charley Grapewin
Ah, Wilderness! '35
Captains Courageous '37
The Wizard of Oz '39

Alex Grasshof▶
Pepper and His Wacky
Taxi '72

Karen Grassle
The Best Christmas
Pageant Ever '86
Little House on the Prairie
'74

Ernest Graves
Hercules in New York '70

Karron Graves
The Fig Tree '87

Peter Graves
Airplane! '80
Airplane 2: The Sequel '82
Savannah Smiles '82

Charles Gray
Diamonds are Forever '71
You Only Live Twice '67

Coleen Gray
Cry from the Mountain '85

David Barry Gray
Cops and Robbersons '94

Dolores Gray
Kismet '55

Erin Gray
Buck Rogers in the 25th
Century '79
Six Pack '82

John Gray▶
Billy Galvin '86

Linda Gray
Bonanza: The Return '93
The Grass is Always
Greener Over the Septic
Tank '78

Marc Gray
Flirting '89

Spalding Gray
Clara's Heart '88
King of the Hill '93
The Paper '94
Straight Talk '92

Kathryn Grayson
Anchors Aweigh '45
Andy Hardy's Private
Secretary '41
Till the Clouds Roll By '46

Joe V. Greco
Only the Lonely '91

Adolph Green
My Favorite Year '82
Simon '80

Alfred E. Green▶
The Jolson Story '46
Thoroughbreds Don't Cry
'37

Brian Austin Green
An American Summer '90

Carlotta Green
Hercules 2 '85

Kerri Green
The Goonies '85
Lucas '86
Summer Rental '85

Mitzie Green
Little Orphan Annie '32

Nigel Green
Africa Texas Style '67
Jason and the Argonauts
'63
Mysterious Island '61

Seth Green
Airborne '93
My Stepmother Is an Alien
'88
Radio Days '87
Something Special '86

Walon Green▶
The Hellstrom Chronicle '71

**Richard Alan
Greenberg▶**
Little Monsters '89

David Greene▶
The Count of Monte Cristo
'74
Hard Country '81

Ellen Greene
Little Shop of Horrors '86
Wagons East '94

Eric Greene
Tut and Tuttle '82

Graham Greene
Dances with Wolves '90
Huck and the King of
Hearts '93
Lost in the Barrens '91
Maverick '94
North '94

James Greene
The Moon Stallion '85

Lorne Greene
Battlestar Galactica '78
The Errand Boy '61
Shirley Temple Storybook
Theater '60

Michael Greene
The Night Before '88

Peter Greene
The Mask '94

Richard Greene
The Little Princess '39

Shecky Greene
Splash '84

Ruth Greenfield
Willow '88

Billy Greenlees
That Sinking Feeling '79

Sydney Greenstreet
Casablanca '42
The Maltese Falcon '41

Robert Greenwald▶
Xanadu '80

David Greenwalt▶
Secret Admirer '85

Charlotte Greenwood
Oklahoma! '55

Joan Greenwood
Mysterious Island '61

Jane Greer
Billie '65
Dick Tracy, Detective '45
Immediate Family '89
Sinbad the Sailor '47

Leighton Greer
Skeezer '82

Bradley Gregg
Madhouse '90

Andre Gregory
Author! Author! '82

James Gregory
Beneath the Planet of the
Apes '70
Wait Till Your Mother Gets
Home '83

Mary Gregory
Lassie: Well of Love '90

John Gregson
Hans Brinker '69

Richard Greig
Animal Crackers '30

Kim Greist
Homeward Bound: The
Incredible Journey '93
Throw Momma from the
Train '87

Joyce Grenfell
The Belles of St. Trinian's
'53
Blue Murder at St.
Trinian's '56
The Pure Hell of St.
Trinian's '61

Googy Gress
Babes in Toyland '86

Jennifer Grey
American Flyers '85
Dirty Dancing '87
Ferris Bueller's Day Off '86
Wind '92

Joel Grey
Remo Williams: The
Adventure Begins '85

Shirley Grey
Hurricane Express '32

Virginia Grey
The Big Store '41
Tarzan's New York
Adventure '42
Unknown Island '48

Michael Greyeyes
Geronimo '93

Richard Grieco
If Looks Could Kill '91

David Alan Grier
Blankman '94
In the Army Now '94

Pam Grier
Bill & Ted's Bogus Journey
'91
Greased Lightning '77
Something Wicked This
Way Comes '83

Jonathan Gries
Real Genius '85

Tom Gries▶
The Greatest '77

Joe Grifasi
Bad Medicine '85
Benny & Joon '93
Chances Are '89
F/X '86

Jennifer Griffin
A Perfect World '93

Lorie Griffin
Aloha Summer '88

Tony Griffin
Robin Hood: Men in Tights
'93

Andy Griffith
Hearts of the West '75
No Time for Sergeants '58

Charles B. Griffith▶
Eat My Dust '76

**Wizards of the Lost
Kingdom 2 '89**

Eva Griffith
Ride a Wild Pony '75

Geraldine Griffith
Experience Preferred. . .
But Not Essential '83

Hugh Griffith
Oliver! '68
Wuthering Heights '70

James Griffith
The Legend of Sleepy
Hollow '79

Melanie Griffith
Born Yesterday '93
One on One '77
Paradise '91
Smile '75

Thomas Ian Griffith
The Karate Kid: Part 3 '89

Mark Griffiths▶
A Cry in the Wild '90

Richard Griffiths
Naked Gun 2 1/2: The
Smell of Fear '91

Frank Grimes
Crystalstone '88

Gary Grimes
Cahill: United States
Marshal '73
Culpepper Cattle Co. '72

Scott Grimes
Critters '86
Frog '89
Frogs! '90s
It Came Upon a Midnight
Clear '84

Tammy Grimes
Mr. North '88
No Big Deal '83

Alan Grint
The Secret Garden '87

Charles Grodin
Beethoven '92
Beethoven's 2nd '93
Clifford '92
Dave '93
The Grass is Always
Greener Over the Septic
Tank '78
The Great Muppet Caper
'81
Heart and Souls '93
The Heartbreak Kid '72
The Incredible Shrinking
Woman '81
King Kong '76
So I Married an Axe
Murderer '93

Clare Grogan
Gregory's Girl '80

C.P. Grogan
Comfort and Joy '84

David Groh
A Hero Ain't Nothin' But a
Sandwich '78
Hot Shot '86

Sam Groom
Run for the Roses '78

Arye Gross
Boris and Natasha: The
Movie '92

Coupe de Ville '90
A Midnight Clear '92
Soul Man '86

Edan Gross
And You Thought Your
Parents Were Weird! '91

Mary Gross
Baby Boom '87
Big Business '88
Club Paradise '86
Troop Beverly Hills '89

Michael Gross
Alan & Naomi '92
Big Business '88
Cool As Ice '91

Paul Gross
Aspen Extreme '93

Yoram Gross▶
Camel Boy '84
EPIC: Days of the
Dinosaurs '87

David Grossman
Frog '89

Charles Grosvenor▶
Once Upon a Forest '93

Richard Grove
Army of Darkness '92

Robert Grubb
Mad Max: Beyond
Thunderdome '85

Gary Grubbs
The Ernest Green Story '93

Christopher Guard
Return to Treasure Island,
Vol. 1 '85

Dominic Guard
The Go-Between '71

Harry Guardino
The Adventures of Bullwhip
Griffin '66
Any Which Way You Can
'80
Matilda '78

Castulo Guerra
Where the River Runs
Black '86

Johnny Guerro
The Secret of Navajo
Cave '76

Christopher Guest
Girlfriends '78
Heartbeeps '81
Little Shop of Horrors '86
The Princess Bride '87

Lance Guest
I Ought to Be in Pictures
'82
Just the Way You Are '84
The Last Starfighter '84
The Wizard of Loneliness
'88

Nicholas Guest
National Lampoon's
Christmas Vacation '89

Val Guest▶
Just William's Luck '47
When Dinosaurs Ruled the
Earth '70

Georges Guetary
An American in Paris '51

Cary Guffey
Close Encounters of the
Third Kind '77

Carla Gugino
Son-in-Law '93
This Boy's Life '93

Adam Guier
Pistol: The Birth of a
Legend '90

Paul Guilfoyle
Billy Galvin '86

Robert Guillaume
The Kid from Left Field '79
The Kid with the 200 I.Q.
'83
The Kid with the Broken
Halo '82
Lean on Me '89
The Meteor Man '93

John Guillermin▶
Death on the Nile '78
King Kong '76
Sheena '84

Alec Guinness
The Bridge on the River
Kwai '57
Doctor Zhivago '65
The Empire Strikes Back
'80
Lawrence of Arabia '62
Little Lord Fauntleroy '80
Oliver Twist '48
Scrooge '70
Star Wars '77

Tom Guiry
Lassie '94
The Sandlot '93

Clu Gulager
And Now Miguel '66
My Heroes Have Always
Been Cowboys '91
Touched by Love '80
Wonderful Cove '75

Dorothy Gulliver
Shadow of the Eagle '32

David Gulpilil
Crocodile Dundee '86

Moses Gunn
The Great White Hope '70
The House of Dies Drear
'88
The NeverEnding Story '84

Bob Gunton
Father Hood '93

Kamlesh Gupta
Crystalstone '88

Alizia Gur
From Russia with Love '63

Eric Gurry
Something Special '86
The Zoo Gang '85

Louis Guss
Moonstruck '87

Steve Guttenberg
Bad Medicine '85
The Chicken Chronicles '77
Cocoon '85
Cocoon: The Return '88
Miracle on Ice '81
Pecos Bill '86
Police Academy '84
Police Academy 2: Their
First Assignment '85

Police Academy 3: Back in
Training '86
Police Academy 4: Citizens
on Patrol '87
Short Circuit '86
Three Men and a Baby
'87
Three Men and a Little
Lady '90

Lucy Gutteridge
The Secret Garden '87

Ronald Guttman
Josh and S.A.M. '93

Jasmine Guy
Runaway '89

Joe Guzaldo
Bingo '91

Luis Guzman
Mr. Wonderful '93

Robert Gwaltney
Trading Hearts '87

Edmund Gwenn
Challenge to Lassie '49
Foreign Correspondent '40
It's a Dog's Life '55
Lassie, Come Home '43
Life with Father '47
Miracle on 34th Street '47

David Gwillim
The Island at the Top of
the World '74

Jack Gwillim
The Bushbaby '70

Michael Gwynn
Jason and the Argonauts
'63

Fred Gwynne
The Boy Who Could Fly
'86
The Littlest Angel '69
Off Beat '86
Simon '80

Peter Gwynne
The Dove '74

Lukas Haas
Alan & Naomi '92
The Lady in White '88
Leap of Faith '92
Rambling Rose '91
See You in the Morning
'89
Solarbabies '86
The Wizard of Loneliness
'88

Shelley Hack
Annie Hall '77
Troll '85

Buddy Hackett
Muscle Beach Party '64
The Music Man '62
Scrooged '88
The Wonderful World of
the Brothers Grimm '62

Joan Hackett
Escape Artist '82
Support Your Local Sheriff
'69
The Treasure of
Matecumbe '76

Gene Hackman
A Bridge Too Far '77
Downhill Racer '69

Geronimo: An American
Legend '93
Hoosiers '86
I Never Sang For My
Father '70
Misunderstood '84
The Poseidon Adventure
'72
Superman 1: The Movie
'78
Superman 2 '80
Superman 4: The Quest for
Peace '87

Julie Ann Haddock
The Great Santini '80

Dayle Haddon
The World's Greatest
Athlete '73

Ron Haddrick
Quigley Down Under '90

Sara Haden
Andy Hardy Gets Spring
Fever '39
Andy Hardy Meets
Debutante '40
Andy Hardy's Double Life
'42
Andy Hardy's Private
Secretary '41
The Great Rupert '50
Love Laughs at Andy
Hardy '46
The Poor Little Rich Girl
'36

Reed Hadley
Zorro's Fighting Legion '39

Molly Hagan
Some Kind of Wonderful
'87

Dennis Hage
Hadley's Rebellion '84

Jean Hagen
Adam's Rib '50
The Shaggy Dog '59
Singin' in the Rain '52

Julie Hagerty
Airplane! '80
Airplane 2: The Sequel '82
Bad Medicine '85
What About Bob? '91

Merle Haggard
Huckleberry Finn '75

Piers Haggard▶
Back Home '90
The Fiendish Plot of Dr. Fu
Manchu '80
Return to Treasure Island,
Vol. 1 '85

Dan Haggerty
The Adventures of Frontier
Fremont '75
Blood Brothers '77
The Capture of Grizzly
Adams '82
Life & Times of Grizzly
Adams '74
Spirit of the Eagle '90
Starbird and Sweet William
'73
The Tender Warrior '71
When the North Wind
Blows '74

Michael Hagiwara
Prehysteria! 2 '94

Larry Hagman
The Big Bus '76

Steven Hahn▶
Starchaser: The Legend of
Orin '85

Charles Haid
The Rescue '88

Charles Haid▶
Iron Will '93

David Haig
The Moon Stallion '85

Sid Haig
Wizards of the Lost
Kingdom 2 '89

Louisa Haigh
Shipwrecked '90

Corey Haim
The Double O Kid '92
Dream a Little Dream '89
Dream Machine '91
Fast Getaway '91
First Born '84
License to Drive '88
The Lost Boys '87
Lucas '86
Murphy's Romance '85
Oh, What a Night '92
Secret Admirer '85

Donald Haines
Flying Wild '41

John Halas▶
Animal Farm '55

Don Haldane▶
Nikki, the Wild Dog of the
North '61

Alan Hale
The Adventures of Robin
Hood '38
It Happened One Night
'34
The Man in the Iron Mask
'39
The Prince and the Pauper
'37

Alan Hale Jr.
The Fifth Musketeer '79
Hambone & Hillie '84
Johnny Dangerously '84
The North Avenue
Irregulars '79

Barbara Hale
The Boy with the Green
Hair '48
Flight of the Grey Wolf
'76
The Window '49

Georgina Hale
The Boy Friend '71
The Gold Rush '25

Jonathan Hale
Bringing Up Baby '38

Jerry Haleva
Hot Shots! Part Deux '93

Brian Haley
Baby's Day Out '94

Jack Haley
The Poor Little Rich Girl
'36
Rebecca of Sunnybrook
Farm '38
The Wizard of Oz '39

Jack Haley Jr.▶
That's Dancing! '85
That's Entertainment '74

Cast/Director Index

Valerie Harper
Thursday's Game '74

Rebecca Harrell
Prancer '89

Woody Harrelson
Doc Hollywood '91
Wildcats '86

Al Harrington
White Fang 2: The Myth of the White Wolf '94

Laura Harrington
What's Eating Gilbert Grape '93

Barbara Harris
Dirty Rotten Scoundrels '88
Freaky Friday '76
Movie, Movie '78
The North Avenue Irregulars '79
Peggy Sue Got Married '86

Brad Harris
Hercules '83

Cassandra Harris
For Your Eyes Only '81

Cynthia Harris
Three Men and a Baby '87

Ed Harris
Places in the Heart '84
The Right Stuff '83
Swing Shift '84

Harry Harris▶
Alice in Wonderland '85
A Day for Thanks on Walton's Mountain '82
The Runaways '75

Julie Harris
East of Eden '54
Gorillas in the Mist '88
Housesitter '92
The Member of the Wedding '52

Julius W. Harris
Live and Let Die '73

Mel Harris
K-9 '89

Neil Patrick Harris
Clara's Heart '88
Purple People Eater '88

Richard Harris
Camelot '67
Gulliver's Travels '77
The Hero '71
King of the Wind '93
Robin and Marian '76

Richard Harris▶
The Hero '71

Robin Harris
House Party '90

Rosemary Harris
Crossing Delancey '88

Zelda Harris
Crooklyn '94

Cathryn Harrison
Blue Fire Lady '78

George Harrison
Help! '65

Jenilee Harrison
Tank '83

John Kent Harrison▶
City Boy '93

Kathleen Harrison
A Christmas Carol '51

Linda Harrison
Beneath the Planet of the Apes '70
Cocoon '85
Planet of the Apes '68

Lottie Harrison
Lost in a Harem '44

Rex Harrison
Doctor Doolittle '67
The Fifth Musketeer '79
The Prince and the Pauper '78

Hugo Harold Harrisson
Toto le Heros '91

Deborah Harry
Hairspray '88
Satisfaction '88

Christopher Hart
The Addams Family '91
Addams Family Values '93

Harvey Hart▶
The Prince of Central Park '77
Stone Fox '87

Ian Hart
Backbeat '94

Linda Hart
A Perfect World '93

Roxanne Hart
Highlander '86
Oh, God! You Devil '84
Old Enough '84

Susan Hart
Pajama Party '64

Jennifer Harte
Prehysterial 2 '94

Linda Hartley
The Fire in the Stone '85

Mariette Hartley
Encino Man '92
Improper Channels '82

David Hartman
The Island at the Top of the World '74

Elizabeth Hartman
Walking Tall '73

Lisa Hartman
Just Tell Me You Love Me '80

Phil Hartman
Coneheads '93
Greedy '94
How I Got into College '89

William Hartnell
The Mouse That Roared '59

Rainbow Harvest
Old Enough '84

Anthony Harvey▶
The Lion in Winter '68

Don Harvey
American Heart '92

Forrester Harvey
Thoroughbreds Don't Cry '37

Laurence Harvey
The Wonderful World of the Brothers Grimm '62

Patrick Hasburgh▶
Aspen Extreme '93

Byron Haskin▶
Treasure Island '50
The War of the Worlds '53

Imogen Hassall
When Dinosaurs Ruled the Earth '70

Marilyn Hassett
The Other Side of the Mountain '75
The Other Side of the Mountain, Part 2 '78

Signe Hasso
Journey for Margaret '42

Bob Hastings
Harper Valley P.T.A. '78

Masami Hata▶
Little Nemo: Adventures in Slumberland '92

Masanori Hata▶
The Adventures of Milo & Otis '89

Richard Hatch
Battlestar Galactica '78

Teri Hatcher
Straight Talk '92

Hurd Hatfield
Her Alibi '88

Henry Hathaway▶
How the West was Won '63
Prince Valiant '54
To the Last Man '33
True Grit '69

Kellen Hathaway
Dennis the Menace '93

Noah Hathaway
The NeverEnding Story '84
Troll '85

Bob Hathcock▶
DuckTales the Movie: Treasure of the Lost Lamp '90

Raymond Hatton
Three Musketeers '33

Tom Hatton
Spies Like Us '85

Rutger Hauer
Buffy the Vampire Slayer '92
Ladyhawke '85

Cole Hauser
School Ties '92

Fay Hauser
Jimmy the Kid '82
Marvin & Tige '84

Wings Hauser
Beastmaster 2: Through the Portal of Time '91

Nigel Havers
Chariots of Fire '81
Empire of the Sun '87
The Little Princess '87

Robin Hawdon
When Dinosaurs Ruled the Earth '70

Ethan Hawke
Alive '93
Dad '89
Dead Poets Society '89
Explorers '85
A Midnight Clear '92
Mystery Date '91
Reality Bites '94
Rich in Love '93
White Fang '91

Ian Hawkes
Queen of Hearts '89

Jack Hawkins
The Bridge on the River Kwai '57
Lawrence of Arabia '62
Those Daring Young Men in Their Jaunty Jalopies '69

Ronnie Hawkins
Club Med '83

Howard Hawks▶
Bringing Up Baby '38
Hatari '62
His Girl Friday '40
Monkey Business '52

Goldie Hawn
Butterflies Are Free '72
Death Becomes Her '92
Foul Play '78
Housesitter '92
The One and Only, Genuine, Original Family Band '68
Overboard '87
Swing Shift '84
Wildcats '86

Sessue Hayakawa
The Bridge on the River Kwai '57
The Geisha Boy '58
The Swiss Family Robinson '60

Yutaka Hayashi
Godzilla vs. Megalon '76

Sterling Hayden
Prince Valiant '54

Richard Haydn
Clarence, the Cross-eyed Lion '65
Please Don't Eat the Daisies '60
The Sound of Music '65
Young Frankenstein '74

Allan Hayes
Sam's Son '84

Allison Hayes
Francis Joins the WACs '54

Helen Hayes
Airport '70
Candleshoe '78
Herbie Rides Again '74
One of Our Dinosaurs Is Missing '75

Isaac Hayes
It Could Happen to You '94

Robin Hood: Men in Tights '93

Patricia Hayes
The NeverEnding Story '84
Willow '88

Peter Lind Hayes
The 5000 Fingers of Dr. T '53

David Hayman
Hope and Glory '87

Dick Haymes
State Fair '45

Jim Haynie
Men Don't Leave '89

Robert Hays
Airplane! '80
Airplane 2: The Sequel '82
Cat's Eye '85
Homeward Bound: The Incredible Journey '93
Trenchcoat '83

Dennis Haysbert
Major League '89
Major League 2 '94
Mr. Baseball '92

James Hayter
Tom Brown's School Days '51

David Hayward
Who'll Save Our Children? '82

Louis Hayward
The Man in the Iron Mask '39

Chris Haywood
The Navigator '88
Quigley Down Under '90

James Hazeldine
My Friend Walter '93

Jane Hazlegrove
Heidi '93

Glenne Headly
Dick Tracy '90
Dirty Rotten Scoundrels '88
Fandango '85
Getting Even with Dad '94
Making Mr. Right '86
The Purple Rose of Cairo '85

Anthony Heald
The Client '94

David Healy
Supergirl '84

Katherine Healy
Six Weeks '82

Mary Healy
The 5000 Fingers of Dr. T '53

John Heard
Big '88
Home Alone '90
Home Alone 2: Lost in New York '92
The Pelican Brief '93
Radio Flyer '92
Rambling Rose '91
The Trip to Bountiful '85

Ann Hearn
Lorenzo's Oil '92

George Hearn
See You in the Morning
'89
Sneakers '92

Patty Hearst
Cry-Baby '90

Joey Heatherton
Cry-Baby '90

Patricia Heaton
Beethoven '92
Memoirs of an Invisible
Man '92

Anne Heche
The Adventures of Huck
Finn '93

Eileen Heckart
The Bad Seed '56
Butterflies Are Free '72
Up the Down Staircase '67
White Mama '80

Amy Heckerling▶
Fast Times at Ridgemont
High '82
Johnny Dangerously '84
Look Who's Talking '89
Look Who's Talking, Too
'90
National Lampoon's
European Vacation '85

Dan Hedaya
The Addams Family '91
The Adventures of
Buckaroo Banzai Across
the Eighth Dimension '84
Benny & Joon '93
For Love or Money '93
Joe Versus the Volcano '90
Mr. Wonderful '93
The Prince of Central Park
'77
Rookie of the Year '93
A Smoky Mountain
Christmas '86

David Hedison
Live and Let Die '73

Jack Hedley
For Your Eyes Only '81

Trine Hedman▶
Famous Five Get into
Trouble '87

Tippi Hedren
The Birds '63

Kyle T. Heffner
Flashdance '83

Richard T. Heffron▶
Whale for the Killing '81

Van Heflin
Airport '70
Shane '53
The Three Musketeers '48
Till the Clouds Roll By '46

O.P. Heggie
Anne of Green Gables '34

Robert Hegyes
Just Tell Me You Love Me
'80

Peter Hehir
I Live with Me Dad '86

Katherine Heigl
King of the Hill '93
My Father the Hero '93

Stuart Heisler▶
The Lone Ranger '56

Carol Heiss
Snow White and the Three
Stooges '61

Marg Helgenberger
Always '89

Richard Hell
Desperately Seeking Susan
'85

Olle Hellbrom▶
Brothers Lionheart '85
Pippi Goes on Board '71
Pippi in the South Seas '68
Pippi Longstocking '68

Randee Heller
Fast Break '79
The Karate Kid '84

Gerome Hellman▶
Promises in the Dark '79

Levon Helm
Coal Miner's Daughter '80
The Right Stuff '83
Smooth Talk '85

Tiffany Helm
The Zoo Gang '85

Katherine Helmond
The Lady in White '88
Overboard '87
Scout's Honor '80
Time Bandits '81

Tom Helmore
Flipper's New Adventure
'64

Robert Helpmann
The Red Shoes '48
The Tales of Hoffman '51

David Hemblen
Short Circuit 2 '88

Mark Hembrow
Return to Snowy River '88

Mariel Hemingway
Delirious '91
Superman 4: The Quest for
Peace '87

David Hemmings
Camelot '67
Man, Woman & Child '83
The Old Curiosity Shop '75

David Hemmings▶
Dark Horse '92

Anouska Hempel
On Her Majesty's Secret
Service '69

Sherman Hemsley
Ghost Fever '87
Love at First Bite '79
Mr. Nanny '93

Bill Henderson
City Slickers '91
Clue '85

Tony Hendra
Life with Mikey '93

Gloria Hendry
Live and Let Die '73

Drewe Henley
When Dinosaurs Ruled the
Earth '70

Marilu Henner
Cannonball Run 2 '84
Johnny Dangerously '84
L.A. Story '91

Paul Henreid
Casablanca '42

Lance Henriksen
The Right Stuff '83
Super Mario Bros. '93
The Terminator '84

Buck Henry
Grumpy Old Men '93

Charlotte Henry
Bowery Blitzkrieg '41
March of the Wooden
Soldiers '34

Justin Henry
Kramer vs. Kramer '79
Sixteen Candles '84
Tiger Town '83

Lenny Henry
Bernard and the Genie '91

Mike Henry
Adios Amigo '75
Smokey and the Bandit '77
Smokey and the Bandit,
Part 2 '80
Smokey and the Bandit,
Part 3 '83

Robert "Buzzy" Henry
The Great Mike '44
Turf Boy '42

William Henry
Tarzan Escapes '36

Pamela Hensley
Buck Rogers in the 25th
Century '79
Doc Savage '75

Brian Henson▶
The Muppet Christmas
Carol '92

Jim Henson
Country Music with the
Muppets '85
Muppets Moments '85

Jim Henson▶
The Dark Crystal '82
The Great Muppet Caper
'81
Labyrinth '86
Muppets Moments '85

Audrey Hepburn
Always '89
Charade '63
Funny Face '57
Robin and Marian '76
Roman Holiday '53
Sabrina '54

Dee Hepburn
Gregory's Girl '80

Katharine Hepburn
Adam's Rib '50
The African Queen '51
Bringing Up Baby '38
The Lion in Winter '68
Little Women '33
Olly Olly Oxen Free '78
On Golden Pond '81
Pat and Mike '52
The Philadelphia Story '40
Rooster Cogburn '75

Charles Herbert
13 Ghosts '60

Louis Herbert
Forbidden Games '52

Percy Herbert
Mysterious Island '61

Stephen Herek▶
Bill & Ted's Excellent
Adventure '89
Critters '86
Don't Tell Mom the
Babysitter's Dead '91
The Mighty Ducks '92
The Three Musketeers '93

Al Herman▶
Renfrew of the Royal
Mounted '37

Jimmy Herman
Dances with Wolves '90
Geronimo '93

Tibor Hernadi▶
Felix the Cat: The Movie
'91

Sammy Hernandez
Cop and a Half '93

Mark Herrier
Tank '83

Edward Herrmann
Big Business '88
Born Yesterday '93
The Day of the Dolphin '73
The Great Waldo Pepper
'75
The Lawrenceville Stories
'80s
The Lost Boys '87
The Man with One Red
Shoe '85
My Boyfriend's Back '93
The North Avenue
Irregulars '79
Overboard '87
The Paper Chase '73
The Purple Rose of Cairo
'85
Take Down '79

Barbara Hershey
Hoosiers '86
The Natural '84
The Right Stuff '83
Swing Kids '93
With Six You Get Eggroll
'68
A World Apart '88

Jean Hersholt
Heidi '37

Marshall Herskovitz▶
Jack the Bear '93

Jason Hervey
Back to School '86
Back to the Future '85

Grant Heslov
True Lies '94

Howard Hesseman
The Big Bus '76
Clue '85
Flight of the Navigator '86
Little Miss Millions '93
Police Academy 2: Their
First Assignment '85
The Sunshine Boys '75

Gordon Hessler▶
Golden Voyage of Sinbad
'73

Charlton Heston
Airport '75 '75
Almost an Angel '90
Beneath the Planet of the
Apes '70
Call of the Wild '72
The Four Musketeers '75
The Greatest Show on
Earth '52
Planet of the Apes '68
The Prince and the Pauper
'78
The Ten Commandments
'56
Three Musketeers '74
Tombstone '93
Treasure Island '89
True Lies '94

Fraser Heston▶
Treasure Island '89

Allan Hewitt
The Computer Wore Tennis
Shoes '69

Love Hewitt
Little Miss Millions '93

Paul Hewitt
A Perfect World '93

Pete Hewitt▶
Bill & Ted's Bogus Journey
'91

Jon-Erik Hexum
Voyager from the Unknown
'83

John Heyl
A Separate Peace '73

Barton Heyman
Billy Galvin '86

Winston Hibler▶
Charlie, the Lonesome
Cougar '67

William Hickey
Da '88
Hobo's Christmas '87
National Lampoon's
Christmas Vacation '89
One Crazy Summer '86
Pink Cadillac '89

Darryl Hickman
Johnny Shiloh '63
Men of Boys Town '41

Dwayne Hickman
How to Stuff a Wild Bikini
'65
My Dog, the Thief '69

Catherine Hicks
Like Father, Like Son '87
Peggy Sue Got Married
'86
Star Trek 4: The Voyage
Home '86

Leonard Hicks
Santa Claus Conquers the
Martians '64

Russell Hicks
Tarzan's New York
Adventure '42

Taral Hicks
A Bronx Tale '93

Anthony Higgins
For Love or Money '93
Raiders of the Lost Ark '81

Colin Higgins▶
Foul Play '78

Joe Higgins
Flipper's New Adventure '64

Michael Higgins
Crusoe '89
School Ties '92

Arthur Hill
The Andromeda Strain '71
A Bridge Too Far '77
Love Leads the Way '84
One Magic Christmas '85

Benny Hill
Chitty Chitty Bang Bang '68

Bernard Hill
The Bounty '84

Dana Hill
Cross Creek '83
National Lampoon's European Vacation '85

George Roy Hill▶
Butch Cassidy and the Sundance Kid '69
Funny Farm '88
The Great Waldo Pepper '75
A Little Romance '79
The Sting '73
The World of Henry Orient '64

James Hill
Christian the Lion '76

James Hill▶
The Belstone Fox '73
Black Beauty '71
Born Free '66

Lauryn Hill
King of the Hill '93
Sister Act 2: Back in the Habit '93

Leslie Hill
Flirting '89

Ralston Hill
1776 '72

Robert F. Hill▶
Blake of Scotland Yard '36

Steven Hill
Running on Empty '88
Yentl '83

Terence Hill
My Name is Nobody '74
Super Fuzz '81

Walter Hill▶
Brewster's Millions '85
Geronimo: An American Legend '93

Marcel Hillaire
Take the Money and Run '69

Arthur Hiller▶
Author! Author! '82
The Babe '92
Man of La Mancha '72
Miracle of the White Stallions '63
Popi '69
The Silver Streak '76

Bernard Hiller
Avalon '90

Wendy Hiller
Anne of Avonlea '87
David Copperfield '70
The Elephant Man '80
A Man for All Seasons '66

John Hillerman
Audrey Rose '77
Paper Moon '73

Beverly Hills
Knights & Emeralds '87

Lawrence Hilton-Jacobs
Cooley High '75

Art Hindle
Invasion of the Body Snatchers '78
Wild Pony '83

Samuel S. Hinds
It's a Wonderful Life '46

Gregory Hines
Renaissance Man '94

Pat Hingle
Baby Boom '87
Batman '89
Batman Returns '92
Brewster's Millions '85
Hazel's People '75
Lightning Jack '94
Norma Rae '79
Running Brave '83
Running Wild '73

Akihiko Hirata
Godzilla vs. the Cosmic Monster '74

Bettina Hirsch▶
Munchies '87

Judd Hirsch
Running on Empty '88

Alfred Hitchcock▶
The Birds '63
Dial "M" for Murder '54
Foreign Correspondent '40
I Confess '53
Jamaica Inn '39
The Lady Vanishes '38
Mr. & Mrs. Smith '41
North by Northwest '59
Notorious '46
The Paradine Case '47
Rear Window '54
Rebecca '40
Saboteur '42
Shadow of a Doubt '43
Spellbound '45
Stage Fright '50
Strangers on a Train '51
Suspicion '41
The 39 Steps '35
To Catch a Thief '55
Torn Curtain '66
Under Capricorn '49
The Wrong Man '56

Patricia Hitchcock
Strangers on a Train '51

Jack B. Hively▶
The Adventures of Huckleberry Finn '78
Lassie: Adventures of Neeka '68
Starbird and Sweet William '73

Judith Hoag
Teenage Mutant Ninja Turtles 1: The Movie '90

Rose Hobart
The Farmer's Daughter '47

Halliwell Hobbes
Journey for Margaret '42

Lyndall Hobbs▶
Back to the Beach '87

Mara Hobel
Mommie Dearest '81

Victoria Hochberg▶
Jacob Have I Loved '88
Sweet 15 '90

Steve Hoddy
Their Only Chance '78

Patricia Hodge
Diamond's Edge '88

Eddie Hodges
The Adventures of Huckleberry Finn '60
Summer Magic '63

Mike Hodges▶
Flash Gordon '80

Ralph Hodges
Sea Hound '47

Thomas E. Hodges
Lucas '86

Tobias Hoesl
The Polar Bear King '94

John Hofeus
Return to Boggy Creek '77

Basil Hoffman
The Double O Kid '92

Dustin Hoffman
All the President's Men '76
Dick Tracy '90
Hero '92
Hook '91
Kramer vs. Kramer '79
Little Big Man '70
Papillon '73
Rain Man '88
Tootsie '82

Gaby Hoffman
Field of Dreams '89
The Man Without a Face '93
Sleepless in Seattle '93
This is My Life '92
Uncle Buck '89

Hermann Hoffman▶
The Invisible Boy '57
It's a Dog's Life '55

Philip S. Hoffman
Leap of Faith '92

Robert Hoffman
Joe Panther '76

Shawn Hoffman
Adventures in Dinosaur City '92

Susan Lee Hoffman
Wizards of the Lost Kingdom 2 '89

Hulk Hogan
Mr. Nanny '93
No Holds Barred '89
Suburban Commando '91

Michael Hogan
The Peanut Butter Solution '85

Pat Hogan
Davy Crockett, King of the Wild Frontier '55
Indian Paint '64

Paul Hogan
Almost an Angel '90
Crocodile Dundee '86
Crocodile Dundee 2 '88
Lightning Jack '94

Robert Hogan
Gone are the Days '84

Susan Hogan
White Fang '91

Hal Holbrook
All the President's Men '76
Fletch Lives '89
The Great White Hope '70

Sarah Holcomb
Caddyshack '80

Fay Holden
Andy Hardy Gets Spring Fever '39
Andy Hardy Meets Debutante '40
Andy Hardy's Double Life '42
Andy Hardy's Private Secretary '41
Life Begins for Andy Hardy '41
Love Finds Andy Hardy '38
Love Laughs at Andy Hardy '46

Mark Holden
Blue Fire Lady '78

William Holden
The Bridge on the River Kwai '57
Country Girl '54
Earthling '80
Sabrina '54
When Wolves Cry '69

Winifred Holden
Strangers in Good Company '91

Geoffrey Holder
Doctor Doolittle '67
Live and Let Die '73

Judd Holdren
Zombies of the Stratosphere '52

Ronald Holgate
1776 '72

Agnieszka Holland▶
The Secret Garden '93

Nicholas Holland
Dusty '85

Steve Holland
Flash Gordon: Vol. 1 '53

Steve Holland▶
Better Off Dead '85
How I Got into College '89
One Crazy Summer '86

Todd Holland▶
The Wizard '89

Steve Hollar
Hoosiers '86

David Holliday
Sleeping Beauty '89

Judy Holliday
Adam's Rib '50

Polly Holliday
Gremlins '84
Konrad '85
Lots of Luck '85

Earl Holliman
Giant '56
Smoke '70

Tommy Hollis
Malcolm X '92

Sterling Holloway
The Adventures of Huckleberry Finn '60
Super Seal '77

W.E. Holloway
Elephant Boy '37

Lauren Holly
Dragon: The Bruce Lee Story '93

Celeste Holm
Cinderella '64
High Society '56
Three Men and a Baby '87
Tom Sawyer '73

Ian Holm
Chariots of Fire '81
Dreamchild '85
Greystoke: The Legend of Tarzan, Lord of the Apes '84
The Man in the Iron Mask '77
The Thief of Baghdad '78
Time Bandits '81

Brittany Ashton Holmes
The Little Rascals '94

Fred Holmes▶
Dakota '88
Harley '90

Luree Holmes
How to Stuff a Wild Bikini '65
Pajama Party '64

Phillips Holmes
General Spanky '36

Taylor Holmes
Tobor the Great '54

Hans Holt
Almost Angels '62

Jack Holt
Holt of the Secret Service '42
The Littlest Rebel '35

Patrick Holt
When Dinosaurs Ruled the Earth '70

Tim Holt
Treasure of the Sierra Madre '48

Mark Holton
Pee Wee's Big Adventure '85

Skip Homeier
Johnny Shiloh '63
Starbird and Sweet William '73
The Voyage of the Yes '72

Oscar Homolka
I Remember Mama '48
Mooncussers '62
The Wonderful World of
   the Brothers Grimm '62

Inoshiro Honda▶
Destroy All Monsters '68

James Hong
Big Trouble in Little China
   '86
The Golden Child '86
Wayne's World 2 '93

Darla Hood
Little Rascals Christmas
   Special '79

Harry Hook▶
Lord of the Flies '90

Jan Hooks
Batman Returns '92
Coneheads '93
Pee Wee's Big Adventure
   '85

Kevin Hooks
Innerspace '87
Sounder '72

Robert Hooks
Words by Heart '84

Kaitlyn Hooper
Addams Family Values '93

Kristen Hooper
Addams Family Values '93

Tobe Hooper▶
Invaders from Mars '86
Poltergeist '82
Salem's Lot '79

Peter Hooten
Dr. Strange '78

Hoover the Dog
Little Heroes '91

Bob Hope
Cancel My Reservation '72
My Favorite Brunette '47
The Seven Little Foys '55
Sorrowful Jones '49

Anthony Hopkins
Audrey Rose '77
The Bounty '84
A Bridge Too Far '77
Chaplin '92
The Elephant Man '80
Howard's End '92
The Hunchback of Notre
   Dame '82
International Velvet '78
The Lion in Winter '68
The Remains of the Day
   '93
Shadowlands '93

Bo Hopkins
American Graffiti '73
Culpepper Cattle Co. '72
The Legend of Wolf
   Mountain '92
More American Graffiti '79
A Smoky Mountain
   Christmas '86

Telma Hopkins
The Kid with the Broken
   Halo '82

Dennis Hopper
Giant '56
Hoosiers '86
My Science Project '85

Rebel Without a Cause '55
Rumble Fish '83
Speed '94
Super Mario Bros. '93

William Hopper
Rebel Without a Cause '55

John Hora
Innerspace '87

Gerard Horan
Much Ado About Nothing
   '93

Michael Hordern
A Christmas Carol '51
Dr. Syn, Alias the
   Scarecrow '64
The Old Curiosity Shop '75
Oliver Twist '82
The Secret Garden '87
Young Sherlock Holmes '85

Gen Horiuchi
George Balanchine's The
   Nutcracker '93

Nicholas Hormann
The Trial of the Incredible
   Hulk '89

Jeffrey Hornaday▶
Shout '91

Geoffrey Horne
The Bridge on the River
   Kwai '57

James W. Horne▶
Green Archer '40
Holt of the Secret Service
   '42

Lena Horne
Till the Clouds Roll By '46
The Wiz '78

Jane Horrocks
The Witches '90

Michael Horse
House of Cards '92
Legend of the Lone Ranger
   '81
Wagons East '94

Edward Everett Horton
Shall We Dance '37

Peter Horton
Where the River Runs
   Black '86

Emil Horvath Jr.
On the Comet '68

Tushka Hose
Hector's Bunyip '86

Bob Hoskins
Hook '91
Mermaids '90
Super Mario Bros. '93
Sweet Liberty '86
Who Framed Roger
   Rabbit? '88

Farina Hoskins
The Return of Our Gang
   '25

Jannie Hoskins
The Return of Our Gang
   '25

Joan Hotchkis
Ode to Billy Joe '76

John Hough▶
The Black Arrow '84

Escape to Witch Mountain '75
Return from Witch
   Mountain '78
Sudden Terror '70
Treasure Island '72
Watcher in the Woods '81

Katherine Houghton
Mr. North '88

John Houseman
The Cheap Detective '78
My Bodyguard '80
The Naked Gun: From the
   Files of Police Squad '88
The Paper Chase '73

Donald Houston
The Bushbaby '70
The Prince and the Pauper
   '62

George Houston
Let's Sing Again '36

Renee Houston
The Belles of St. Trinian's
   '53

Arliss Howard
Men Don't Leave '89
Plain Clothes '88
The Prodigal '83

Barbara Howard
Running Mates '86

Clint Howard
Cocoon '85
Eat My Dust '76
Far and Away '92
Gentle Ben '69
Gentle Giant '67
Gung Ho '85
Huckleberry Finn '75
Rock 'n' Roll High School
   '79
Salty '73
The Wild Country '71

Curly Howard
Snow White and the Three
   Stooges '61
Three Stooges: A Ducking
   They Will Go '30s
Three Stooges: A Plumbing
   We Will Go '34
Three Stooges: Cash and
   Carry '40s
Three Stooges: If a Body
   Meets a Body '34
Three Stooges: In the
   Sweet Pie and Pie '40s
Three Stooges: So Long
   Mr. Chumps '40s
Three Stooges: What's the
   Matador? '40s

David Howard▶
The Lost Jungle '34

Elston Howard
Robotech, Vol. 1: Booby
   Trap '85

Frank Howard
That Was Then. . .This Is
   Now '85

Jean Howard
Huckleberry Finn '75

John Howard
The Philadelphia Story '40
Young Einstein '89

Ken Howard
1776 '72

Leslie Howard
Gone with the Wind '39

Moe Howard
Snow White and the Three
   Stooges '61
Three Stooges '30s
Three Stooges: A Ducking
   They Will Go '30s
Three Stooges: A Plumbing
   We Will Go '34
Three Stooges: Cash and
   Carry '40s
Three Stooges: If a Body
   Meets a Body '34
Three Stooges: In the
   Sweet Pie and Pie '40s
Three Stooges Meet
   Hercules '61
Three Stooges: So Long
   Mr. Chumps '40s
Three Stooges: What's the
   Matador? '40s

Rance Howard
Eat My Dust '76
Far and Away '92
Gentle Ben '69
Huckleberry Finn '75
Where the Lilies Bloom '74
The Wild Country '71

Ron Howard
American Graffiti '73
The Courtship of Eddie's
   Father '62
Eat My Dust '76
Huckleberry Finn '75
More American Graffiti '79
The Music Man '62
The Shootist '76
Smoke '70
The Wild Country '71

Ron Howard▶
Cocoon '85
Far and Away '92
Gung Ho '85
The Paper '94
Parenthood '89
Splash '84
Willow '88

Shemp Howard
Africa Screams '49
Buck Privates '41
Three Stooges '30s

Trevor Howard
Battle of Britain '69
The Count of Monte Cristo
   '74
Ryan's Daughter '70
Superman 1: The Movie
   '78
Sword of the Valiant '83

Clark Howat
Billy Jack '71

C. Thomas Howell
Breaking the Rules '92
E.T.: The Extra-Terrestrial
   '82
Gettysburg '93
The Outsiders '83
The Return of the
   Musketeers '89
Secret Admirer '85
Soul Man '86
Tank '83
That Night '93

Peter Howell
Shadowlands '93

Frankie Howerd
Great St. Trinian's Train
   Robbery '66

Sally Ann Howes
Chitty Chitty Bang Bang
   '68

Olin Howland
Nancy Drew, Reporter '39

John Howley▶
Happily Ever After '93

Wang Hsieh
Infra-Man '76

Li Hsiu-hsien
Infra-Man '76

Hua-Shan▶
Infra-Man '76

Faith Hubley▶
The Cosmic Eye '71

Season Hubley
Caddie Woodlawn '88

Whip Hubley
Russkies '87
Top Gun '86

Cooper Huckabee
Joni '79

Walter Hudd
Elephant Boy '37
The Prince and the Pauper
   '62

David Huddleston
Life with Mikey '93
Santa Claus: The Movie
   '85

Reginald Hudlin▶
House Party '90

Ernie Hudson
Airheads '94
The Crow '93
Ghostbusters '84
Ghostbusters 2 '89
In the Army Now '94

Hugh Hudson▶
Chariots of Fire '81
Greystoke: The Legend of
   Tarzan, Lord of the
   Apes '84

Rochelle Hudson
Curly Top '35
Rebel Without a Cause '55

Rock Hudson
Avalanche '78
Giant '56
Ice Station Zebra '68

Toni Hudson
Just One of the Guys '85

David Huffman
Ice Castles '79

Billy Hufsey
Magic Kid '92

Daniel Hugh-Kelly
The Good Son '93

Albert Hughes▶
Menace II Society '93

Allen Hughes▶
Menace II Society '93

Andrew Hughes
Destroy All Monsters '68

Barnard Hughes
The Adventures of
   Huckleberry Finn '85
Da '88

Doc Hollywood '91
Hobo's Christmas '87
Homeward Bound '80
The Lost Boys '87
Oh, God! '77
Sister Act 2: Back in the
 Habit '93
Tron '82

Carol Hughes
Flash Gordon Conquers
 the Universe '40
Renfrew of the Royal
 Mounted '37
Silver Stallion '41

Catherine Hughes
Radio Patrol '37

Finola Hughes
Aspen Extreme '93

Helen Hughes
The Peanut Butter Solution
 '85

John Hughes
That Sinking Feeling '79

John Hughes▶
The Breakfast Club '85
Curly Sue '91
Ferris Bueller's Day Off '86
She's Having a Baby '88
Sixteen Candles '84
Uncle Buck '89
Weird Science '85

Ken Hughes▶
Chitty Chitty Bang Bang
 '68

Kristen Hughes
Jane & the Lost City '87

Lloyd Hughes
Blake of Scotland Yard '36

Megan Hughes
Adventures in Dinosaur
 City '92

Miko Hughes
Cops and Robbersons '94
Jack the Bear '93

Terry Hughes▶
The Butcher's Wife '91

Tresa Hughes
Skylark '93

Wendy Hughes
Careful, He Might Hear
 You '84

Tom Hulce
Amadeus '84
Dominick & Eugene '88
Parenthood '89

Dianne Hull
Aloha, Bobby and Rose
 '74
The New Adventures of
 Pippi Longstocking '88

Henry Hull
Boys Town '38

Warren Hull
Bowery Blitzkrieg '41

**H. Bruce
Humberstone▶**
Wonder Man '45

Benita Hume
It Happened in New
 Orleans '36
Tarzan Escapes '36

Dylan Hundley
Metropolitan '90

Jackson Hunsicker▶
Frog Prince '88

Bonnie Hunt
Beethoven '92
Beethoven's 2nd '93
Dave '93
Rain Man '88

David Hunt
Date with an Angel '87

Helen Hunt
Bill: On His Own '83
Frog Prince '88
Girls Just Want to Have
 Fun '85
Only You '92
Peggy Sue Got Married
 '86
Project X '87
Quarterback Princess '85

Jimmy Hunt
Invaders from Mars '53

Linda Hunt
If Looks Could Kill '91
Kindergarten Cop '90
Popeye '80
She-Devil '89
Silverado '85

Martita Hunt
The Wonderful World of
 the Brothers Grimm '62

Peter Hunt▶
The Adventures of
 Huckleberry Finn '85
Gulliver's Travels '77
Hyper-Sapien: People from
 Another Star '86
It Came Upon a Midnight
 Clear '84
On Her Majesty's Secret
 Service '69
1776 '72
Skeezer '82

Bill Hunter
Return of Captain
 Invincible '83
Strictly Ballroom '92

Holly Hunter
Always '89
Animal Behavior '89
Miss Firecracker '89
Swing Shift '84

Ian Hunter
The Adventures of Robin
 Hood '38
Andy Hardy's Private
 Secretary '41
The Little Princess '39
Tarzan Finds a Son '39

Kaki Hunter
Just the Way You Are '84

Kim Hunter
Beneath the Planet of the
 Apes '70
Escape from the Planet of
 the Apes '71
Planet of the Apes '68

Tab Hunter
Grease 2 '82
The Kid from Left Field '79

Tim Hunter▶
Sylvester '85
Tex '82

G.P. Huntley Jr.
Journey for Margaret '42

Howard Huntsberry
La Bamba '87

David Hurst
Tony Draws a Horse '51

Paul Hurst
Gone with the Wind '39

Rick Hurst
Going Ape! '81

John Hurt
The Elephant Man '80
King Ralph '91
A Man for All Seasons '66
Night Crossing '81
Spaceballs '87

Mary Beth Hurt
The Age of Innocence '93
D.A.R.Y.L. '85
My Boyfriend's Back '93

William Hurt
Mr. Wonderful '93

William T. Hurtz▶
Little Nemo: Adventures in
 Slumberland '92

Harry Hurwitz▶
The Projectionist '71

Frantisek Husak
A Hungarian Fairy Tale '87

Waris Hussein▶
And Baby Makes Six '79
Doctor Who: An Unearthly
 Child '63
Melody '71

Olivia Hussey
Death on the Nile '78
Romeo and Juliet '68

Ruth Hussey
The Philadelphia Story '40

Anjelica Huston
The Addams Family '91
Addams Family Values '93
Ice Pirates '84
Mr. North '88
The Witches '90

Danny Huston▶
Mr. North '88

Jimmy Huston▶
My Best Friend Is a
 Vampire '88

John Huston
Battle for the Planet of the
 Apes '73
A Minor Miracle '83
The Wind and the Lion '75

John Huston▶
The African Queen '51
Annie '82
Key Largo '48
The Maltese Falcon '41
The Man Who Would Be
 King '75
Treasure of the Sierra
 Madre '48
Victory '81

Walter Huston
Treasure of the Sierra
 Madre '48
Yankee Doodle Dandy '42

Josephine Hutchinson
The Adventures of
 Huckleberry Finn '60
North by Northwest '59
The Tender Years '47

Ken Hutchison
Ladyhawke '85

Betty Hutton
The Greatest Show on
 Earth '52

Lauren Hutton
My Father the Hero '93

Marion Hutton
Love Happy '50

Robert Hutton
Cinderfella '60

Timothy Hutton
And Baby Makes Six '79
Father Figure '80
Iceman '84
Taps '81
Turk 182! '85

Willard Huyck▶
French Postcards '79
Howard the Duck '86

Nessa Hyams▶
Leader of the Band '87

Peter Hyams▶
Stay Tuned '92
2010 : The Year We
 Make Contact '84

Tracy Hyde
Melody '71

Alex Hyde-White
Indiana Jones and the Last
 Crusade '89

Wilfrid Hyde-White
In Search of the
 Castaways '62
Oh, God! Book 2 '80
Scout's Honor '80
The Toy '82

Martha Hyer
Bikini Beach '64
The Delicate Delinquent '56
First Men in the Moon '64
Sabrina '54

Frances Hyland
Home to Stay '79

Warren Hymer
Mr. Wise Guy '42

Mike Hynson
The Endless Summer '66

Joyce Hyser
Just One of the Guys '85

Masato Ibu
Empire of the Sun '87

Ice Cube
Boyz N the Hood '91

Kurt Ida
The Adventures of
 Huckleberry Finn '78

Eric Idle
The Adventures of Baron
 Munchausen '89
And Now for Something
 Completely Different '72
Jabberwocky '77
Mom and Dad Save the
 World '92

Monty Python and the
 Holy Grail '75

Cinnamon Idles
Kidco '83
Sixteen Candles '84

Jean Image▶
Aladdin and His Magic
 Lamp '69

Iman
House Party 2: The Pajama
 Jam '91
L.A. Story '91
Star Trek 6: The
 Undiscovered Country
 '91

Frieda Inescort
Tarzan Finds a Son '39

Sarah Inglis
Battle of the Bullies '85

Rex Ingram
The Adventures of
 Huckleberry Finn '39
Thief of Baghdad '40

Frank Inn
Benji the Hunted '87

Neil Innes
Monty Python and the
 Holy Grail '75

Harold Innocent
Robin Hood: Prince of
 Thieves '91

John Ireland
Kavik, the Wolf Dog '84

Kathy Ireland
Mr. Destiny '90
Mom and Dad Save the
 World '92
National Lampoon's
 Loaded Weapon 1 '93

Michael Ironside
Father Hood '93
Highlander 2: The
 Quickening '91
Top Gun '86

John Irvin▶
Turtle Diary '86

Kathleen Irvine
Greenstone '85

Kevin Irvine▶
Greenstone '85

Amy Irving
Crossing Delancey '88
Rumpelstiltskin '86
Yentl '83

David Irving▶
Cannon Movie Tales: The
 Emperor's New Clothes
 '89
Rumpelstiltskin '86
Sleeping Beauty '89

George Irving
Captain January '36

Bill Irwin
Popeye '80

Chris Isaak
Little Buddha '93

Robert Iscove▶
The Lawrenceville Stories
 '80s

Mervyn Johns
A Christmas Carol '51
Tony Draws a Horse '51

A.J. Johnson
House Party '90

Alan Johnson▶
Solarbabies '86

Anne-Marie Johnson
Dream Date '93
Robot Jox '89

Arte Johnson
The Charge of the Model
T's '76
Love at First Bite '79
Munchie '92

Ben Johnson
Angels in the Outfield '94
Bonanza: The Return '93
Junior Bonner '72
Mighty Joe Young '49
My Heroes Have Always
Been Cowboys '91
Radio Flyer '92
The Shadow Riders '82
Shane '53
The Swarm '78
Tex '82
Tomboy & the Champ '58

Brad Johnson
Always '89

Candy Johnson
Beach Party '63
Bikini Beach '64
Muscle Beach Party '64
Pajama Party '64

Celia Johnson
The Prime of Miss Jean
Brodie '69

Don Johnson
Born Yesterday '93
Paradise '91

Georgann Johnson
Murphy's Romance '85

Kearo Johnson
Love Your Mama '89

Kenneth Johnson▶
The Incredible Hulk '77
Short Circuit 2 '88

Kyle Johnson
The Learning Tree '69

Lamont Johnson▶
The Last American Hero
'73
One on One '77

Lynn-Holly Johnson
For Your Eyes Only '81
Ice Castles '79
Watcher in the Woods '81

Michelle Johnson
Death Becomes Her '92
Far and Away '92
Gung Ho '85

Noble Johnson
King Kong '33

Patrick Read Johnson▶
Baby's Day Out '94
Spaced Invaders '90

Penny Johnson
What's Love Got to Do
With It? '93

Richard Johnson
Diving In '90
Treasure Island '89
Turtle Diary '86

Rita Johnson
My Friend Flicka '43

Ron Johnson
Zebrahead '92

Sunny Johnson
Flashdance '83

Tor Johnson
Carousel '56

Van Johnson
The Human Comedy '43
The Pied Piper of Hamelin
'57
The Purple Rose of Cairo
'85
Yours, Mine & Ours '68

Joe Johnston▶
Honey, I Shrunk the Kids
'89
The Rocketeer '91

John Dennis Johnston
Pink Cadillac '89

I. Stanford Jolley
The Crimson Ghost '46
King of the Rocketmen '49

Allan Jones
A Day at the Races '37
A Night at the Opera '35

Amy Holden Jones▶
Maid to Order '87

Barry Jones
Prince Valiant '54

Ben Jones
Don't Change My World
'83

Carolyn Jones
House of Wax '53
How the West was Won
'63

Christopher Jones
Ryan's Daughter '70

Chuck Jones
Chuck Amuck: The Movie
'91
Innerspace '87

Chuck Jones▶
Best of Bugs Bunny &
Friends '40
Bugs Bunny Cartoon
Festival '44
The Bugs Bunny/Road
Runner Movie '79
Bugs Bunny's 3rd Movie:
1,001 Rabbit Tales '82
A Christmas Carol '84
Looney Looney Looney
Bugs Bunny Movie '81
Phantom Tollbooth '69
A Salute to Chuck Jones
'60
A Salute to Mel Blanc '58
A Very Merry Cricket '73

Davy Jones
Head '68
Monkees, Volume 1 '66

Dean Jones
Beethoven '92
Blackbeard's Ghost '67

Herbie Goes to Monte
Carlo '77
The Horse in the Gray
Flannel Suit '68
The Love Bug '68
Million Dollar Duck '71
Mr. Superinvisible '73
Monkeys, Go Home! '66
Once Upon a Brothers
Grimm '77
The Shaggy D.A. '76
Snowball Express '72
That Darn Cat '65
The Ugly Dachshund '65
When Every Day was the
Fourth of July '78

Dick Jones
Nancy Drew, Reporter '39

Doug Jones
Hocus Pocus '93

Duane Jones
Beat Street '84

Ed "Too Tall" Jones
The Double McGuffin '79

Eddie Jones
Sneakers '92

Freddie Jones
The Elephant Man '80
Erik the Viking '89
Krull '83
Young Sherlock Holmes '85

Gordon Jones
The Green Hornet '39

Grace Jones
Conan the Destroyer '84
A View to a Kill '85

Henry Jones
Arachnophobia '90
The Bad Seed '56
Butch Cassidy and the
Sundance Kid '69
Napoleon and Samantha
'72
Support Your Local
Gunfighter '71

James Earl Jones
Allan Quartermain and the
Lost City of Gold '86
Bingo Long Traveling All-
Stars & Motor Kings '76
Clean Slate '94
Conan the Barbarian '82
Field of Dreams '89
The Great White Hope '70
The Greatest '77
The Hunt for Red October
'90
Lone Star Kid '88
The Meteor Man '93
Piece of the Action '77
Return of the Jedi '83
The Sandlot '93
Sneakers '92
Sommersby '93
Soul Man '86
Star Wars '77
Three Fugitives '89

Janet Jones
American Anthem '86
The Flamingo Kid '84
Police Academy 5:
Assignment Miami Beach
'88

Jeffrey Jones
Amadeus '84
Beetlejuice '88
Ferris Bueller's Day Off '86

Howard the Duck '86
The Hunt for Red October
'90
Mom and Dad Save the
World '92
Out on a Limb '92
Stay Tuned '92

Jennifer Jones
Dick Tracy '37
Since You Went Away '44

Lisa Jones
Life & Times of Grizzly
Adams '74

L.Q. Jones
Grizzly Adams: The Legend
Continues '90
Lightning Jack '94
Timerider '83

Marcia Mae Jones
The Little Princess '39

Nicholas Jones
Black Beauty '94

Richard T. Jones
Renaissance Man '94

Sam Jones
Flash Gordon '80
Jane & the Lost City '87

Shirley Jones
Carousel '56
The Cheyenne Social Club
'70
The Courtship of Eddie's
Father '62
The Music Man '62
Oklahoma! '55
Tank '83
Who'll Save Our Children?
'82

Simon Jones
Club Paradise '86
Green Card '90

Terry Jones
And Now for Something
Completely Different '72
Erik the Viking '89
Jabberwocky '77
Monty Python and the
Holy Grail '75

Terry Jones▶
Erik the Viking '89
Monty Python and the
Holy Grail '75

Tommy Lee Jones
The Client '94
Coal Miner's Daughter '80
The Fugitive '93
House of Cards '92
Nate and Hayes '83
The River Rat '84

Samson Jorah
Never Cry Wolf '83

Bobby Jordan
Bowery Blitzkrieg '41
Bowery Buckaroos '47
Boys of the City '40
Flying Wild '41
Hard-Boiled Mahoney '47
Kid Dynamite '43
'Neath Brooklyn Bridge '42
Spook Busters '46
Spooks Run Wild '41
That Gang of Mine '40

Glenn Jordan▶
Sarah, Plain and Tall '91
Toughlove '85

Leslie Jordan
Ski Patrol '89

Neil Jordan▶
The Miracle '91

Richard Jordan
Gettysburg '93
The Hunt for Red October
'90
Rooster Cogburn '75
Shout '91
Solarbabies '86

William Jordan
The Buddy Holly Story '78
I Wanna Hold Your Hand
'78

Victor Jory
Gone with the Wind '39
Green Archer '40
The Miracle Worker '62
Papillon '73
Susannah of the Mounties
'39

Larry Joshua
A Midnight Clear '92

Allyn Joslyn
The Horn Blows at
Midnight '45

Louis Jourdan
The Count of Monte Cristo
'74
The Man in the Iron Mask
'77
Octopussy '83
The Paradine Case '47
The Return of Swamp
Thing '89
Swamp Thing '82
Year of the Comet '92

Milla Jovovich
Chaplin '92
Kuffs '92

Robert Joy
Big Shots '87
Desperately Seeking Susan
'85
The Lawrenceville Stories
'80s
Miracle at Moreaux '86

Edward Judd
First Men in the Moon '64

Raul Julia
The Addams Family '91
Addams Family Values '93
Escape Artist '82
Gumball Rally '76
Trading Hearts '87

Gordon Jump
Making the Grade '84

Katy Jurado
High Noon '52
Once Upon a Scoundrel
'73

Nathan Juran▶
First Men in the Moon '64
Jack the Giant Killer '62
The Seventh Voyage of
Sinbad '58

Peter Jurasik
Problem Child '90

Curt Jurgens
Battle of Britain '69
Miracle of the White
Stallions '63

Cecil Kellaway
Francis Goes to the Races '51

Tina Kellegher
The Snapper '93

Harry Keller▶
Tammy and the Doctor '63

Barbara Kellerman
The Chronicles of Narnia '89

Sally Kellerman
Back to School '86
The Big Bus '76
Boris and Natasha: The Movie '92
Foxes '80
A Little Romance '79
M*A*S*H '70
Moving Violations '85
Secret of the Ice Cave '89

Susan Kellerman
Oh, Heavenly Dog! '80

Barry Kelley
Francis Goes to the Races '51
Jack the Giant Killer '62

Brett Kelley
Sommersby '93

DeForest Kelley
Star Trek: The Motion Picture '80
Star Trek 2: The Wrath of Khan '82
Star Trek 3: The Search for Spock '84
Star Trek 4: The Voyage Home '86
Star Trek 5: The Final Frontier '89
Star Trek 6: The Undiscovered Country '91

Sheila Kelley
Singles '92

Barnet Kellman▶
Straight Talk '92

David Kellogg▶
Cool As Ice '91

John Kellogg
Jacob Have I Loved '88

Brian Kelly
Flipper's New Adventure '64
Flipper's Odyssey '66

Craig Kelly
Silence '73

David Kelly
Into the West '92

David Patrick Kelly
Crooklyn '94
The Crow '93
Malcolm X '92

Gene Kelly
An American in Paris '51
Anchors Aweigh '45
Invitation to the Dance '56
On the Town '49
Singin' in the Rain '52
That's Dancing! '85
That's Entertainment '74
That's Entertainment, Part 2 '76
The Three Musketeers '48

Xanadu '80

Gene Kelly▶
The Cheyenne Social Club '70
Hello, Dolly! '69
Invitation to the Dance '56
On the Town '49
Singin' in the Rain '52

Grace Kelly
Country Girl '54
Dial "M" for Murder '54
High Noon '52
High Society '56
Rear Window '54
To Catch a Thief '55

Jean Kelly
Uncle Buck '89

Moira Kelly
Chaplin '92
The Cutting Edge '92
With Honors '94

Nancy Kelly
The Bad Seed '56

Patsy Kelly
Freaky Friday '76
The North Avenue Irregulars '79
Please Don't Eat the Daisies '60

Paul Kelly
Tarzan's New York Adventure '42

Paula Kelly
The Andromeda Strain '71

Rae'ven Kelly
What's Love Got to Do With It? '93

Ron Kelly▶
King of the Grizzlies '69

Pert Kelton
The Music Man '62

Richard Kelton
Silence '73

Violet Kemble-Cooper
Gone with the Wind '39

Warren Kemmerling
Eat My Dust '76

Jeremy Kemp
The Belstone Fox '73
When the Whales Came '89

Martin Kemp
Aspen Extreme '93

Tina Kemp
A Waltz Through the Hills '88

Will Kempe
Metropolitan '90

Rachel Kempson
Little Lord Fauntleroy '80

Cy Kendall
The Green Hornet '39
Tarzan's New York Adventure '42

David Kendall▶
Luggage of the Gods '87

Suzy Kendall
To Sir, with Love '67

Alexa Kenin
Honkytonk Man '82
Pretty in Pink '86

Arthur Kennedy
Lawrence of Arabia '62
The Window '49

Burt Kennedy▶
Suburban Commando '91
Support Your Local Gunfighter '71
Support Your Local Sheriff '69

Douglas Kennedy
The Lone Ranger and the Lost City of Gold '58

Edgar Kennedy
Duck Soup '33
Little Orphan Annie '32

George Kennedy
Airport '70
Airport '75 '75
Airport '77 '77
Bandolero! '68
Cahill: United States Marshal '73
Charade '63
Death on the Nile '78
The Double McGuffin '79
Guns of the Magnificent Seven '69
Island of the Blue Dolphins '64
The Naked Gun: From the Files of Police Squad '88
Naked Gun 2 1/2: The Smell of Fear '91
Naked Gun 33 1/3: The Final Insult '94
A Rare Breed '81

Graham Kennedy
Return of Captain Invincible '83

Ken Kennedy▶
Grizzly Adams: The Legend Continues '90

Mimi Kennedy
Death Becomes Her '92
Immediate Family '89

Patsy Kensit
Monty Python and the Holy Grail '75

Barbara Kent
Oliver Twist '33

Robert Kent
Dimples '36
The Phantom Creeps '39

Gwen Kenyon
The Great Mike '44

Jessie Keosian
Green Card '90

Joanna Kerns
An American Summer '90

Sondra Kerns
Magic Kid '92

Bill Kerr
Dusty '85
Miracle Down Under '87
Pirate Movie '82

Bruce Kerr
The Man from Snowy River '82

Deborah Kerr
The King and I '56

John Kerr
South Pacific '58

Irvin Kershner▶
The Empire Strikes Back '80
Never Say Never Again '83
Robocop 2 '90

Brian Kerwin
Murphy's Romance '85

Lance Kerwin
Enemy Mine '85
The Loneliest Runner '76
Salem's Lot '79

Maureen Kerwin
Reunion '88

Alek Keshishian▶
With Honors '94

Michael Keusch▶
Huck and the King of Hearts '93

Evelyn Keyes
Gone with the Wind '39
The Jolson Story '46

Irwin Keyes
The Flintstones '94

Persis Khambatta
Star Trek: The Motion Picture '80

Leleti Khumalo
Sarafina! '92

Guy Kibbee
Babes in Arms '39
Captain Blood '35
Captain January '36
The Horn Blows at Midnight '45
Little Lord Fauntleroy '36
Miss Annie Rooney '42
Mr. Smith Goes to Washington '39

Chris Kidd
Cry from the Mountain '85

Michael Kidd
Smile '75

Myrna Kidd
Cry from the Mountain '85

Margot Kidder
The Great Waldo Pepper '75
Superman 1: The Movie '78
Superman 2 '80
Superman 3 '83
Superman 4: The Quest for Peace '87
Trenchcoat '83

Nicole Kidman
BMX Bandits '83
Far and Away '92
Flirting '89
My Life '93
The Prince and the Great Race '83

Richard Kiel
Moonraker '79
The Silver Streak '76
The Spy Who Loved Me '77

They Went That-a-Way & That-a-Way '78
Think Big '90

Udo Kier
For Love or Money '93

Randi Kiger
Wonderland Cove '75

Robbie Kiger
Table for Five '83
Welcome Home, Roxy Carmichael '90

Percy Kilbride
State Fair '45

Terence Kilburn
A Christmas Carol '38
National Velvet '44

Richard Kiley
The Adventures of Huckleberry Finn '85
The Canterville Ghost '91
The Little Prince '74

Jean-Claude Killy
Club Med '83

Peter Kilman
Olly Olly Oxen Free '78

Val Kilmer
Real Genius '85
The Real McCoy '93
Tombstone '93
Top Gun '86
Willow '88

Valentine Kim
Harley '90

Sharron Kimberly
The Party '68

Bruce Kimmel
Spaceship '81

Bruce Kimmel▶
Spaceship '81

Kenneth Kimmins
My Best Friend Is a Vampire '88

Alan King
Author! Author! '82
Cat's Eye '85

Allan Winton King▶
Silence of the North '81

Caroline Junko King
3 Ninjas Kick Back '94

Charmion King
Anne of Green Gables '85
Who Has Seen the Wind? '77

Henry King▶
Carousel '56

Mabel King
The Wiz '78

Manuel King
Darkest Africa '36

Perry King
The Lords of Flatbush '74

Regina King
Poetic Justice '93

Rick King▶
Hot Shot '86

Walter Woolf King
A Night at the Opera '35

Sonia Kruger-Tayler
Strictly Ballroom '92

David Krumholtz
Addams Family Values '93
Life with Mikey '93

Gene Krupa
The Glenn Miller Story '54

Jack Kruschen
Dear Brigitte '65
Mountain Man '77

Eve Kryll
Making Contact '86

Akira Kubo
Destroy All Monsters '68

Stanley Kubrick▶
2001: A Space Odyssey '68

Buzz Kulik▶
Brian's Song '71

Koreyoshi Kurahara▶
Antarctica '84

Ron Kurowski
Spaceship '81

Alwyn Kurts
Earthling '80

Swoosie Kurtz
Reality Bites '94
Vice Versa '88
Wildcats '86

Katy Kurtzman
Child of Glass '78
When Every Day was the Fourth of July '78

Shishir Kurup
Coneheads '93

Clyde Kusatsu
Dr. Strange '78
Made in America '93

Dylan Kussman
Dead Poets Society '89
Wild Hearts Can't Be Broken '91

Nancy Kwan
Dragon: The Bruce Lee Story '93
Flower Drum Song '61
Lt. Robin Crusoe, U.S.N. '66

Ken Kwapis▶
The Beniker Gang '83
Sesame Street Presents: Follow That Bird '85

Burt Kwouk
Empire of the Sun '87
The Pink Panther Strikes Again '76
Revenge of the Pink Panther '78
Son of the Pink Panther '93
Trail of the Pink Panther '82

La Chanze
Leap of Faith '92

Alison La Placa
Fletch '85
Madhouse '90

Rosemary La Planche
Federal Agents vs. Underworld, Inc. '49

Steven La Rocque▶
Samantha '92

Patti LaBelle
Sing '89

Patrick Laborteaux
3 Ninjas '92

Catherine Lacey
The Lady Vanishes '38

Margaret Lacey
Diamonds are Forever '71

Ronald Lacey
Making the Grade '84
Raiders of the Lost Ark '81

Harry Lachman▶
Baby, Take a Bow '34

Andre Lacombe
The Bear '89

Denis Lacroix
Running Brave '83

Jerry Lacy
Play It Again, Sam '72

Alan Ladd
Citizen Kane '41
My Favorite Brunette '47
Shane '53

Cheryl Ladd
Lisa '90

David Ladd
A Dog of Flanders '59

Diane Ladd
Father Hood '93
National Lampoon's Christmas Vacation '89
Plain Clothes '88
Rambling Rose '91
Something Wicked This Way Comes '83

Pat Laffan
The Snapper '93

Art LaFleur
Forever Young '92
Jack the Bear '93
The Sandlot '93

Caroline Lagerfelt
Home at Last '88

Bert Lahr
Just Around the Corner '38
The Wizard of Oz '39

Christine Lahti
Gross Anatomy '89
Housekeeping '87
Miss Firecracker '89
Running on Empty '88
Stacking '87
Swing Shift '84

Harvey Laidman▶
The Boy Who Loved Trolls '84

Ricki Lake
Cabin Boy '94
Cry-Baby '90
Hairspray '88
Serial Mom '94

Frank Laloggia
The Wizard of Speed and Time '88

Frank Laloggia▶
The Lady in White '88

Rene Laloux▶
Fantastic Planet '73

Jean LaMarre
Malcolm X '92

Fernando Lamas
The Cheap Detective '78

Lorenzo Lamas
Take Down '79

Christopher Lambert
Greystoke: The Legend of Tarzan, Lord of the Apes '84
Highlander '86
Highlander 2: The Quickening '91
Highlander: The Gathering '93

Jack Lambert
Dick Tracy's Dilemma '47

Mark Lamberti▶
Cartoons for Big Kids '89

Charles Lamont▶
Abbott and Costello Meet Captain Kidd '52
Abbott and Costello Meet Dr. Jekyll and Mr. Hyde '52
Ring of Bright Water '69

Albert Lamorisse▶
Circus Angel '65
The Red Balloon '56

Pascal Lamorisse
The Red Balloon '56

Dorothy Lamour
The Greatest Show on Earth '52
My Favorite Brunette '47
Pajama Party '64

Zohra Lampert
Alan & Naomi '92

Burt Lancaster
Airport '70
Field of Dreams '89
Island of Dr. Moreau '77
Judgment at Nuremberg '61
Local Hero '83
Rocket Gibraltar '88
Tough Guys '86

James Lancaster
Gettysburg '93

Elsa Lanchester
Blackbeard's Ghost '67
David Copperfield '35
Die Laughing '80
The Ghost Goes West '36
Lassie, Come Home '43
My Dog, the Thief '69
Pajama Party '64
The Secret Garden '49
That Darn Cat '65

Micheline Lanctot
The Apprenticeship of Duddy Kravitz '74

Geoffrey Land
Against A Crooked Sky '75

David Landau
Horse Feathers '32

Martin Landau
North by Northwest '59
Tucker: The Man and His Dream '88

Dinsdale Landen
Digby, the Biggest Dog in the World '73

David Lander
The Man with One Red Shoe '85

Michael Landes
An American Summer '90

Steve Landesburg
Leader of the Band '87

Carole Landis
Daredevils of the Red Circle '38
Topper Returns '41

Jessie Royce Landis
Gidget Goes to Rome '63
North by Northwest '59
To Catch a Thief '55

John Landis▶
Beverly Hills Cop 3 '94
Oscar '91
Spies Like Us '85
Three Amigos '86
Twilight Zone: The Movie '83

Monte Landis
The Mouse That Roared '59

Hal Landon Jr.
Bill & Ted's Bogus Journey '91

Michael Landon
The Errand Boy '61
Little House on the Prairie '74
The Loneliest Runner '76
Sam's Son '84

Michael Landon▶
Little House on the Prairie '74
The Loneliest Runner '76
Sam's Son '84

Michael Landon Jr.
Bonanza: The Return '93

Paul Landres▶
Flipper's Odyssey '66

Karen Landry
Heartbreak Hotel '88

Abbe Lane
Twilight Zone: The Movie '83

Charles Lane
Billie '65
Mr. Smith Goes to Washington '39
Murphy's Romance '85
Strange Invaders '83

Diane Lane
Chaplin '92
Indian Summer '93
A Little Romance '79
The Outsiders '83
Rumble Fish '83
Six Pack '82
Touched by Love '80

Lola Lane
Burn 'Em Up Barnes '34

Nathan Lane
Life with Mikey '93

Priscilla Lane
Saboteur '42

Eric Laneuville▶
The Ernest Green Story '93
The Mighty Pawns '87

Sidney Lanfield▶
Sorrowful Jones '49

Doreen Lang
Almost an Angel '90

June Lang
Captain January '36
Wee Willie Winkie '37

Richard Lang▶
Christmas Comes to Willow Creek '87

Stephen Lang
Gettysburg '93
Project X '87
Tombstone '93

Walter Lang▶
The Blue Bird '40
The King and I '56
The Little Princess '39
Snow White and the Three Stooges '61
State Fair '45

Sue Ane Langdon
The Cheyenne Social Club '70

Hope Lange
I am the Cheese '83
The Love Bug '68
The Prodigal '83

Jessica Lange
Country '84
King Kong '76
Men Don't Leave '89
Tootsie '82

Frank Langella
Dave '93
1492: Conquest of Paradise '92
Masters of the Universe '87
Twelve Chairs '70

Frances Langford
Yankee Doodle Dandy '42

Margaret Langrick
American Boyfriends '89
Harry and the Hendersons '87
My American Cousin '85

Victor Lanoux
National Lampoon's European Vacation '85

Angela Lansbury
Bedknobs and Broomsticks '71
The Court Jester '56
Death on the Nile '78
National Velvet '44
The Pirates of Penzance '83
The Three Musketeers '48
The World of Henry Orient '64

Joi Lansing
Easter Parade '48
Singin' in the Rain '52

Robert Lansing
Life on the Mississippi '80

William Lanteau
On Golden Pond '81

Anthony M. Lanza▶
The Incredible Two-Headed Transplant '71

Anthony LaPaglia
Black Magic '92
The Client '94
So I Married an Axe Murderer '93

James Lapine▶
Life with Mikey '93

Bryan Larkin
She-Devil '89

Mary Laroche
Gidget '59

John Larroquette
Madhouse '90
Star Trek 3: The Search for Spock '84
Summer Rental '85
Twilight Zone: The Movie '83

Erik Larsen
Trap on Cougar Mountain '72
Young & Free '78

Ham Larsen
Further Adventures of the Wilderness Family, Part 2 '77
Mountain Family Robinson '79

Keith Larsen
Trap on Cougar Mountain '72
Whitewater Sam '78

Keith Larsen▶
Trap on Cougar Mountain '72
Whitewater Sam '78
Young & Free '78

Lars Oluf Larsen
A Day in October '92

Darrell Larson
Hero '92

Eric Larson▶
Sleeping Beauty '59

Anna-Lotta Larsson
The Polar Bear King '94

Jack LaRue
Captains Courageous '37
Follow the Leader '44
To the Last Man '33

Tommy Lasorda
Ladybugs '92

Louise Lasser
Bananas '71
Sing '89
Take the Money and Run '69

Sydney Lassick
The Billion Dollar Hobo '78
Cool As Ice '91

Lassie
Lassie: Adventures of Neeka '68

Lyle Latelle
Dick Tracy, Detective '45
Dick Tracy Meets Gruesome '47
Dick Tracy's Dilemma '47

Louise Latham
Paradise '91
Toughlove '85

Stan Lathan▶
Beat Street '84

Matt Lattanzi
Catch Me. . .If You Can '89
Diving In '90
Roxanne '87

Jack Laufer
Lost in Yonkers '93

John Laughlin
Footloose '84

Michael Laughlin▶
Strange Invaders '83

Tom Laughlin
Billy Jack '71
South Pacific '58

Tom Laughlin▶
Billy Jack '71

Charles Laughton
Abbott and Costello Meet Captain Kidd '52
The Canterville Ghost '44
Jamaica Inn '39
The Paradine Case '47

Frank Launder▶
The Belles of St. Trinian's '53
Blue Murder at St. Trinian's '56
Great St. Trinian's Train Robbery '66
The Pure Hell of St. Trinian's '61

Cyndi Lauper
Life with Mikey '93

Matthew Laurance
Eddie and the Cruisers '83

Carole Laure
Victory '81

Stan Laurel
The Flying Deuces '39
March of the Wooden Soldiers '34

Tammy Lauren
The Last Flight of Noah's Ark '80

Veronica Lauren
Homeward Bound: The Incredible Journey '93

Michael Laurence
Conspiracy of Love '87

Paula Laurence
For Love or Money '93

John Laurie
The 39 Steps '35

Piper Laurie
Dream a Little Dream '89
Francis Goes to the Races '51
Return to Oz '85
Rich in Love '93
Toughlove '85

Ed Lauter
The Chicken Chronicles '77
Girls Just Want to Have Fun '85
Goodbye, Miss 4th of July '88

King Kong '76
The Rocketeer '91
School Ties '92
Timerider '83

Harry Lauter
Trader Tom of the China Seas '54

Linda Lavin
Maricela '88
See You in the Morning '89

John Phillip Law
Golden Voyage of Sinbad '73

Phyllida Law
Much Ado About Nothing '93

Peter Lawford
The Canterville Ghost '44
Easter Parade '48
Little Women '49

Barbara Lawrence
Oklahoma! '55

Joey Lawrence
Wait Till Your Mother Gets Home '83

Marc Lawrence
Goin' Coconuts '78
The Man with the Golden Gun '74
'Neath Brooklyn Bridge '42

Martin Lawrence
House Party '90
House Party 2: The Pajama Jam '91

Rosina Lawrence
General Spanky '36

Steve Lawrence
Alice in Wonderland '85

Denis Lawson
Local Hero '83
Return of the Jedi '83

Leigh Lawson
Madame Sousatzka '88
Sword of the Valiant '83
Tess '80

Priscilla Lawson
Flash Gordon: Rocketship '36

Richard Lawson
Poltergeist '82

Frank Lawton
David Copperfield '35

Paul Lazar
Philadelphia '93

Eusebio Lazaro
The Return of the Musketeers '89

George Lazenby
On Her Majesty's Secret Service '69

Kelly Le Brock
Weird Science '85

Odile Le Clezio
Young Einstein '89

John Le Mesurier
The Adventures of Sherlock Holmes' Smarter Brother '78

Jabberwocky '77

Britt Leach
Baby Boom '87

Rosemary Leach
Ghost in the Noonday Sun '74
Turtle Diary '86

Wilford Leach▶
The Pirates of Penzance '83

Cloris Leachman
The Beverly Hillbillies '93
Butch Cassidy and the Sundance Kid '69
Charley and the Angel '73
Herbie Goes Bananas '80
High Anxiety '77
The North Avenue Irregulars '79
Prancer '89
Thursday's Game '74
Walk Like a Man '87
Young Frankenstein '74

Cynthia Leake
Fire and Ice '83

David Lean▶
The Bridge on the River Kwai '57
Doctor Zhivago '65
Lawrence of Arabia '62
Oliver Twist '48
Ryan's Daughter '70

Michael Learned
Dragon: The Bruce Lee Story '93

Rex Lease
The Clutching Hand '36

Jean-Pierre Leaud
The 400 Blows '59

Brian Leckner
Bonanza: The Return '93

Jacqueline Lecomte
Playtime '67

Bryan Leder
Metropolitan '90

Anna Lee
How Green was My Valley '41
Jack the Giant Killer '62
The Sound of Music '65

Bernard Lee
Diamonds are Forever '71
Dr. No '62
From Russia with Love '63
Live and Let Die '73
The Man with the Golden Gun '74
Moonraker '79
On Her Majesty's Secret Service '69
The Spy Who Loved Me '77
Thunderball '65
Whistle Down the Wind '62
You Only Live Twice '67

Billy Lee
Regl'ar Fellers '41

Brandon Lee
The Crow '93

Charles Lee
The Tender Warrior '71

Christopher Lee
Airport '77 '77
The Boy Who Left Home to Find Out About the Shivers '81
Captain America 2: Death Too Soon '79
The Four Musketeers '75
Gremlins 2: The New Batch '90
The Land of Faraway '87
The Man with the Golden Gun '74
Return from Witch Mountain '78
Return of Captain Invincible '83
The Return of the Musketeers '89
Three Musketeers '74
Treasure Island '89

Florence Lee
City Lights '31

Gypsy Rose Lee
The Trouble with Angels '66

Jason Scott Lee
Back to the Future, Part 2 '89
Dragon: The Bruce Lee Story '93

Jerry Lee
K-9 '89

Jesse Lee
Matinee '92

Joanna Lee
Making the Grade '84
Sam's Son '84

Joie Lee
Crooklyn '94

Kaiulani Lee
Zelly & Me '88

Karen Lee
Eye on the Sparrow '91

Lila Lee
Stand Up and Cheer '34

Mary Lee
Nancy Drew, Reporter '39

Michele Lee
The Love Bug '68

Sheryl Lee
Backbeat '94
Jersey Girl '92

Sondra Lee
Peter Pan '60

Spike Lee
Crooklyn '94
Malcolm X '92

Spike Lee▶
Crooklyn '94
Malcolm X '92

Stephen Lee
Prehysteria '93

Phil Leeds
Ghost '90

Darling Legitimus
Sugar Cane Alley '83

James LeGros
Singles '92

John Leguizamo
Regarding Henry '91
Super Mario Bros. '93

Michael Lehmann▶
Airheads '94

Paul Leiber
Bill: On His Own '83

Ron Leibman
Norma Rae '79
Phar Lap '84
Rhinestone '84

Arnold Leibovit▶
The Puppetoon Movie '87

Neil Leifer▶
Trading Hearts '87

Barbara Leigh
Junior Bonner '72

Janet Leigh
Bye, Bye, Birdie '63
Little Women '49
Prince Valiant '54

Jennifer Jason Leigh
Fast Times at Ridgemont
High '82

Vivien Leigh
Gone with the Wind '39

Margaret Leighton
The Go-Between '71
Under Capricorn '49

Leila
From Russia with Love '63

Christopher Leitch▶
Courage Mountain '89
Teen Wolf Too '87

Donovan Leitch
Dark Horse '92
The In Crowd '88

Paul LeMat
Aloha, Bobby and Rose
'74
American Graffiti '73
Citizens Band '77
Jimmy the Kid '82
More American Graffiti '79
The Night They Saved
Christmas '87
P.K. and the Kid '85
Strange Invaders '83

Harvey Lembeck
Beach Blanket Bingo '65
Beach Party '63
Bikini Beach '64
How to Stuff a Wild Bikini
'65
Pajama Party '64

Michael Lembeck
On the Right Track '81

Ole Lemmeke
A Day in October '92

Chris Lemmon
Dad '89
Swing Shift '84

Jack Lemmon
Airport '77 '77
Dad '89
The Front Page '74
Great Race '65
Grumpy Old Men '93
The Odd Couple '68

Jack Lemmon▶
Kotch '71

Rusty Lemorande▶
Journey to the Center of
the Earth '88

Mark Lenard
Star Trek 3: The Search
for Spock '84
Star Trek 4: The Voyage
Home '86
Star Trek 6: The
Undiscovered Country
'91

John Lennon
Help! '65

Terry Lennon▶
Daffy Duck's Quackbusters
'89

Jay Leno
Collision Course '89

Lotte Lenya
From Russia with Love '63

Kay Lenz
House '86

Rick Lenz
Scandalous John '71

Malcolm Leo▶
It Came from Hollywood
'82

Leon
Above the Rim '94
Cool Runnings '93

Annie Leon
Hope and Glory '87

Valerie Leon
Never Say Never Again
'83
The Spy Who Loved Me
'77

Robert Sean Leonard
The Age of Innocence '93
Dead Poets Society '89
Mr. & Mrs. Bridge '91
Much Ado About Nothing
'93
My Best Friend Is a
Vampire '88
Swing Kids '93

Sheldon Leonard
Guys and Dolls '55
It's a Wonderful Life '46
Sinbad the Sailor '47

Mario Leonardi
Cinema Paradiso '88

Sergio Leone▶
Once Upon a Time in the
West '68

Al Leong
Bill & Ted's Excellent
Adventure '89

Chauncey Leopardi
Huck and the King of
Hearts '93
The Sandlot '93

Ken Lerner
Fast Getaway '91

Michael Lerner
Amos and Andrew '93
Blank Check '93
Newsies '92
Strange Invaders '83

Mervyn LeRoy▶
The Bad Seed '56

I Am a Fugitive from a
Chain Gang '32
Little Women '49
No Time for Sergeants '58

**Brad "The Animal"
Lesley**
Little Big League '94

Lorna Lesley
Little Boy Lost '78

Joan Leslie
Yankee Doodle Dandy '42

Michael Lessac▶
House of Cards '92

Len Lesser
How to Stuff a Wild Bikini
'65

Ben Lessy
Pajama Party '64

Betty Lester
House Party 3 '94

Buddy Lester
Cracking Up '83

Jeff Lester
Once a Hero '88

Mark Lester
Black Beauty '71
Melody '71
Oliver! '68
The Prince and the Pauper
'78
Sudden Terror '70

Richard Lester▶
Butch and Sundance: The
Early Days '79
The Four Musketeers '75
Help! '65
The Return of the
Musketeers '89
Robin and Marian '76
Superman 2 '80
Superman 3 '83
Three Musketeers '74

Dennis Letts
The Last Prostitute '91

Martin Lev
Bugsy Malone '76

Brian Levant▶
Beethoven '92
The Flintstones '94
Problem Child 2 '91

Oscar Levant
An American in Paris '51
The Band Wagon '53

Calvin Levels
Adventures in Babysitting
'87

William A. Levey▶
Lightning: The White
Stallion '86

Henry Levin▶
Journey to the Center of
the Earth '59
Run for the Roses '78
Scout's Honor '80
The Wonderful World of
the Brothers Grimm '62
Wonders of Aladdin '61

Peter Levin▶
Comeback Kid '80

Barry Levinson▶
Avalon '90

The Natural '84
Rain Man '88
Toys '92
Young Sherlock Holmes '85

Abe Levitow▶
Gay Purr-ee '62

Steve Levitt
The Incredible Hulk Returns
'88

Eugene Levy
Club Paradise '86
Splash '84
Stay Tuned '92

Eugene Levy▶
Once Upon a Crime '92

Margaret LeWars
Dr. No '62

Al Lewis
Car 54, Where Are You?
'94
My Grandpa is a Vampire
'92

Alun Lewis
Experience Preferred. . .
But Not Essential '83

Brittney Lewis
Dream Machine '91

Charlotte Lewis
The Golden Child '86

Diana Lewis
Andy Hardy Meets
Debutante '40
Go West '40

Elbert Lewis
Square Dance '87

Fiona Lewis
Innerspace '87
Strange Invaders '83

Gary Lewis
Hardly Working '81

Geoffrey Lewis
Bronco Billy '80
Catch Me. . .If You Can
'89
Culpepper Cattle Co. '72
The Great Waldo Pepper
'75
The Man Without a Face
'93
Maverick '94
Night of the Comet '84
Pink Cadillac '89
Smile '75
Tilt '78
When Every Day was the
Fourth of July '78
White Fang 2: The Myth
of the White Wolf '94
The Wind and the Lion '75

George Lewis
Indian Paint '64
The Sign of Zorro '60
Zorro's Black Whip '44

Gilbert Lewis
The Kid Who Loved
Christmas '90

Greg Lewis
Prehysterial 2 '94

Jenifer Lewis
Corrina, Corrina '94
Renaissance Man '94

What's Love Got to Do
With It? '93

Jenny Lewis
A Friendship in Vienna '88
Troop Beverly Hills '89
The Wizard '89

Jerry Lewis
The Bellboy '60
The Caddy '53
Cinderfella '60
Cracking Up '83
The Delicate Delinquent '56
The Disorderly Orderly '64
The Errand Boy '61
Family Jewels '65
The Geisha Boy '58
Hardly Working '81
Hollywood or Bust '56
The Nutty Professor '63
Trading Hearts '87

Jerry Lewis▶
The Bellboy '60
Cracking Up '83
The Errand Boy '61
Family Jewels '65
Hardly Working '81
The Nutty Professor '63

Joseph H. Lewis▶
Boys of the City '40
That Gang of Mine '40

Juliette Lewis
Meet the Hollowheads '89
My Stepmother Is an Alien
'88
National Lampoon's
Christmas Vacation '89
That Night '93
What's Eating Gilbert
Grape '93

Matthew Lewis
The Legend of Wolf
Mountain '92

Mitchell Lewis
The Wizard of Oz '39

Phill Lewis
Brother Future '91
City Slickers '91

Rawle Lewis
Cool Runnings '93

Richard Lewis
Once Upon a Crime '92
Robin Hood: Men in Tights
'93
Wagons East '94

Robert Lewis▶
A Summer to Remember
'84

John Ley
BMX Bandits '83

Richard Libertini
Animal Behavior '89
Fletch '85
Fletch Lives '89
Popeye '80

Jeremy Licht
Father Figure '80
Twilight Zone: The Movie
'83

G. Gordon Liddy
Adventures in Spying '92

Anki Liden
My Life as a Dog '85

Isabel Lorca
Lightning: The White
  Stallion '86
She's Having a Baby '88

Jack Lord
Dr. No '62

Jean-Claude Lord▶
Toby McTeague '87

Justine Lord
Skeezer '82

Traci Lords
Cry-Baby '90
Serial Mom '94

Donna Loren
Bikini Beach '64
Muscle Beach Party '64
Pajama Party '64

Sophia Loren
Man of La Mancha '72

Teala Loring
Hard-Boiled Mahoney '47

Marion Lorne
Strangers on a Train '51

Peter Lorre
Casablanca '42
The Maltese Falcon '41
My Favorite Brunette '47
20,000 Leagues Under the
  Sea '54
Voyage to the Bottom of
  the Sea '61

Joan Lorring
The Corn is Green '45

Joseph Losey▶
The Boy with the Green
  Hair '48
The Go-Between '71

Louanne
Oh, God! Book 2 '80

Lori Loughlin
Back to the Beach '87
The Night Before '88
Rad '86
Secret Admirer '85

Julia Louis-Dreyfus
Jack the Bear '93
National Lampoon's
  Christmas Vacation '89
North '94

Anita Louise
The Little Princess '39

John Lounsbery▶
The Rescuers '77
Winnie the Pooh and
  Tigger Too '74

Alan Love
That Sinking Feeling '79

June Love
Courage of the North '35

Montagu Love
The Adventures of Robin
  Hood '38
The Prince and the Pauper
  '37

Mother Love
Mr. Nanny '93

Frank Lovejoy
House of Wax '53

Jon Lovitz
Big '88
City Slickers 2: The Legend
  of Curly's Gold '94
A League of Their Own
  '92
Mr. Destiny '90
Mom and Dad Save the
  World '92
My Stepmother Is an Alien
  '88
National Lampoon's
  Loaded Weapon 1 '93
North '94
Three Amigos '86

Harrison Lowe
Geronimo '93

Rob Lowe
The Outsiders '83
Oxford Blues '84
Square Dance '87
Wayne's World '92

Carey Lowell
Club Paradise '86
Sleepless in Seattle '93

Curt Lowens
A Midnight Clear '92

Andrew Lowery
My Boyfriend's Back '93
School Ties '92

Dick Lowry▶
Smokey and the Bandit,
  Part 3 '83

Judith Lowry
The Effect of Gamma Rays
  on Man-in-the-Moon
  Marigolds '73

T.J. Lowther
A Perfect World '93

Myrna Loy
Airport '75 '75
The Bachelor and the
  Bobby-Soxer '47
A Connecticut Yankee '31
The Red Pony '49
The Thin Man '34

Lisa Lu
The Joy Luck Club '93

Arthur Lubin▶
Ali Baba and the Forty
  Thieves '43
Buck Privates '41
Escapade in Japan '57
Francis Goes to the Races
  '51
Francis Joins the WACs '54
Francis the Talking Mule
  '49
The Incredible Mr. Limpet
  '64
Thief of Baghdad '61

George Lucas▶
American Graffiti '73
Star Wars '77

Lisa Lucas
Hadley's Rebellion '84
A House Without a
  Christmas Tree '72

George Luce
Danny '79

Laurence Luckinbill
Star Trek 5: The Final
  Frontier '89

Kathryn Ludlow
Courage Mountain '89

Pamela Ludwig
Over the Edge '79

Lorna Luft
Grease 2 '82

Bela Lugosi
Abbott and Costello Meet
  Frankenstein '48
The Phantom Creeps '39
Spooks Run Wild '41

Baz Luhrmann▶
Strictly Ballroom '92

Paul Lukas
The Lady Vanishes '38
Little Women '33
20,000 Leagues Under the
  Sea '54

Keye Luke
Bowery Blitzkrieg '41
The Green Hornet '39
Gremlins '84

Lulu
To Sir, with Love '67

Carl Lumbly
Brother Future '91

Sidney Lumet
Running on Empty '88

Sidney Lumet▶
Running on Empty '88
The Wiz '78

Joanna Lumley
Curse of the Pink Panther
  '83
On Her Majesty's Secret
  Service '69

Barbara Luna
Spiderman '81

Art Lund
The Last American Hero
  '73

Deanna Lund
Hardly Working '81

Natalie Lund
The Legend of Wolf
  Mountain '92

Nicole Lund
The Legend of Wolf
  Mountain '92

Dolph Lundgren
Masters of the Universe
  '87
Rocky 4 '85
A View to a Kill '85

William Lundigan
Andy Hardy's Double Life
  '42

Jessica Lundy
Madhouse '90

Cherie Lunghi
Oliver Twist '82

Min Luong
Gleaming the Cube '89

Ida Lupino
Junior Bonner '72

Ida Lupino▶
The Trouble with Angels
  '66

Patti LuPone
Driving Miss Daisy '89
Family Prayers '91

Peter Lupus
Muscle Beach Party '64
Think Big '90

Hamilton Luske
Bongo '47

Hamilton Luske▶
Lady and the Tramp '55
101 Dalmatians '61
Peter Pan '53

Jaques Lussier
Norman's Awesome
  Experience '88

Paul Luty
Water Babies '79

Bob Lydiard
The Paper Chase '73

Jimmy Lydon
Life with Father '47
Little Men '40
Tom Brown's School Days
  '40

Dorothy Lyman
Ollie Hopnoodle's Haven
  of Bliss '88

Jeffery Lynas
Lies My Father Told Me
  '75

David Lynch
Zelly & Me '88

David Lynch▶
The Elephant Man '80

John Lynch
The Secret Garden '93

Kate Lynch
Meatballs '79

Kelly Lynch
Curly Sue '91
For Better and For Worse
  '92

Richard Lynch
Little Nikita '88

Paul Lynde
Beach Blanket Bingo '65
Bye, Bye, Birdie '63
Son of Flubber '63
The Villain '79

Adrian Lyne▶
Foxes '80

Carol Lynley
The Light in the Forest '58
The Poseidon Adventure
  '72

Barbara Lynn
Godzilla vs. the Cosmic
  Monster '74

Jonathan Lynn
Three Men and a Little
  Lady '90

Jonathan Lynn▶
Clue '85
Greedy '94

Francis D. Lyon▶
Tomboy & the Champ '58

Richard Lyon
The Tender Years '47

Bruce Lyons
The Navigator '88

Byron Mabe
The Doberman Gang '72

Kate Maberly
The Secret Garden '93

Zachary Mabry
The Little Rascals '94

Bernie Mac
Above the Rim '94
House Party 3 '94

James MacArthur
Kidnapped '60
The Light in the Forest '58
Mosby's Marauders '66
The Swiss Family Robinson
  '60
Third Man on the
  Mountain '59

Marc Macaulay
Cop and a Half '93

Donald MacBride
Buck Privates Come Home
  '47
Room Service '38

Ralph Macchio
The Karate Kid '84
The Karate Kid: Part 2 '86
The Karate Kid: Part 3 '89
The Outsiders '83

Simon MacCorkindale
Death on the Nile '78

J. Farrell MacDonald
Susannah of the Mounties
  '39

Ray Macdonald
Babes on Broadway '41

Alistair MacDougall
Bonanza: The Return '93

Andie MacDowell
Four Weddings and a
  Funeral '93
Green Card '90
Greystoke: The Legend of
  Tarzan, Lord of the
  Apes '84
Groundhog Day '93

Paul Mace
The Lords of Flatbush '74

Sterling Macer
Dragon: The Bruce Lee
  Story '93

Hamilton MacFadden▶
Stand Up and Cheer '34

Tara MacGowan
Secret Places '85

Jack MacGowran
The Quiet Man '52

Stephen Macht
A Friendship in Vienna '88
The Monster Squad '87

Helen Mack
His Girl Friday '40
Son of Kong '33

Fulton Mackay
Local Hero '83

Matthew Mackay
The Peanut Butter Solution
  '85

The Naked Gun: From the
Files of Police Squad '88
Regarding Henry '91
Shirley Temple Storybook
Theater '60

Silvia Marco
The Man Who Wagged
His Tail '57

Andrea Marcovicci
Jack the Bear '93

Richard Marcus
Enemy Mine '85

Jordan Marder
Walking on Air '87

Janet Margolin
Annie Hall '77
David and Lisa '62
Take the Money and Run
'69

Stuart Margolin
The Big Bus '76
A Fine Mess '86

Miriam Margolyes
The Age of Innocence '93
The Butcher's Wife '91

David Margulies
Family Prayers '91
Ghostbusters 2 '89
Out on a Limb '92
Running on Empty '88

Edwin L. Marin▶
A Christmas Carol '38
Miss Annie Rooney '42

Jacques Marin
The Island at the Top of
the World '74

Dan Marino
Ace Ventura: Pet Detective
'93

Stella Maris
Truly, Madly, Deeply '91

Monte Markham
Defense Play '88
Guns of the Magnificent
Seven '69

Monte Markham▶
Defense Play '88

Fletcher Markle▶
The Incredible Journey '63

Peter Markle▶
Wagons East '94

Goran Markovic▶
Tito and Me '92

Olivera Markovic
Tito and Me '92

John Marley
The Greatest '77

Hugh Marlowe
Monkey Business '52

Kelli Maroney
Fast Times at Ridgemont
High '82
Night of the Comet '84

Richard Marquand▶
Return of the Jedi '83

Andre Marquis
Paco '75

Kenneth Mars
The Apple Dumpling Gang
Rides Again '79
Butch Cassidy and the
Sundance Kid '69
Fletch '85
For Keeps '88
Goin' Coconuts '78
Radio Days '87
Son of Dinosaurs '90
What's Up, Doc? '72
Young Frankenstein '74

Maurice Marsac
Clarence, the Cross-eyed
Lion '65

Branford Marsalis
Throw Momma from the
Train '87

Carol Marsh
Alice in Wonderland '50
A Christmas Carol '51

David Marsh▶
Lords of Magick '88

Garry Marsh
Just William's Luck '47

Jean Marsh
Horsemasters '61
Return to Oz '85
Willow '88

Joan Marsh
Follow the Leader '44

Mae Marsh
How Green was My Valley
'41
The Quiet Man '52

Bryan Marshall
Return to Snowy River '88

E.G. Marshall
The Littlest Angel '69
National Lampoon's
Christmas Vacation '89
Shirley Temple Storybook
Theater '60
Superman 2 '80

Frank Marshall▶
Alive '93
Arachnophobia '90

Garry Marshall
A League of Their Own
'92

Garry Marshall▶
The Flamingo Kid '84
Nothing in Common '86
Overboard '87

George Marshall▶
How the West was Won
'63

Herbert Marshall
Foreign Correspondent '40
The Secret Garden '49

Joshua Marshall
Flirting '89

Ken Marshall
Krull '83
Tilt '78

Penny Marshall▶
Big '88
A League of Their Own
'92
Renaissance Man '94

Sean Marshall
Pete's Dragon '77

Wonderland Cove '75

William Marshall
Blacula '72
State Fair '45

Zena Marshall
Dr. No '62

K.C. Martel
E.T.: The Extra-Terrestrial
'82

Gillian Martell
Oliver Twist '85

Lisa Repo Martell
American Boyfriends '89

Andrea Martin
All I Want for Christmas
'91
Boris and Natasha: The
Movie '92
Club Paradise '86

Barney Martin
Arthur 2: On the Rocks '88

Bill Martin
Rocket Gibraltar '88

Christopher Martin
Class Act '91
House Party '90
House Party 2: The Pajama
Jam '91
House Party 3 '94

Dean Martin
Airport '70
Bandolero! '68
The Caddy '53
Cannonball Run '81
Cannonball Run 2 '84
Hollywood or Bust '56
That's Dancing! '85

Dewey Martin
Savage Sam '63
Seven Alone '75

Dick Martin
Carbon Copy '81

Duane Martin
Above the Rim '94

George Martin
Crossing Delancey '88

Helen Martin
Doc Hollywood '91
A Hero Ain't Nothin' But a
Sandwich '78
House Party 2: The Pajama
Jam '91

Kellie Martin
Christy '94
Matinee '92
Troop Beverly Hills '89

Lewis Martin
The War of the Worlds
'53

Marion Martin
The Great Mike '44
The Man in the Iron Mask
'39

Mary Martin
Peter Pan '60

Millicent Martin
Horsemasters '61

Pamela Sue Martin
A Cry in the Wild '90

Ricci Martin
Just Tell Me You Love Me
'80

Steve Martin
Dead Men Don't Wear
Plaid '82
Dirty Rotten Scoundrels '88
Father of the Bride '91
Housesitter '92
L.A. Story '91
Leap of Faith '92
Little Shop of Horrors '86
Parenthood '89
Roxanne '87
Three Amigos '86

Strother Martin
Butch Cassidy and the
Sundance Kid '69
Rooster Cogburn '75
The Villain '79

Tony Martin
The Big Store '41
Till the Clouds Roll By '46

Margo Martindale
Lorenzo's Oil '92

Elsa Martinelli
Hatari '62
Once Upon a Crime '92

A. Martinez
The Cowboys '72
Joe Panther '76
Once Upon a Scoundrel
'73
She-Devil '89
Starbird and Sweet William
'73

Claudio Martinez
Daring Dobermans '73

James Martinez
Leader of the Band '87

Patrice Martinez
Three Amigos '86

Leslie Martinson▶
The Fantastic World of
D.C. Collins '84
The Kid with the 200 I.Q.
'83
The Kid with the Broken
Halo '82

Andrew Marton▶
Africa Texas Style '67
Clarence, the Cross-eyed
Lion '65
Gypsy Colt '54

Lee Marvin
Paint Your Wagon '69

Chico Marx
Animal Crackers '30
At the Circus '39
The Big Store '41
The Cocoanuts '29
A Day at the Races '37
Duck Soup '33
Go West '40
Horse Feathers '32
Love Happy '50
Monkey Business '31
A Night at the Opera '35
A Night in Casablanca '46
Room Service '38

Groucho Marx
Animal Crackers '30
At the Circus '39
The Big Store '41
The Cocoanuts '29
A Day at the Races '37

Duck Soup '33
Go West '40
Horse Feathers '32
Love Happy '50
Monkey Business '31
A Night at the Opera '35
A Night in Casablanca '46
Room Service '38

Harpo Marx
Animal Crackers '30
At the Circus '39
The Big Store '41
The Cocoanuts '29
A Day at the Races '37
Duck Soup '33
Go West '40
Horse Feathers '32
Love Happy '50
Monkey Business '31
A Night at the Opera '35
A Night in Casablanca '46
Room Service '38

Zeppo Marx
Animal Crackers '30
The Cocoanuts '29
Duck Soup '33
Horse Feathers '32
Monkey Business '31

Ron Masak
Harper Valley P.T.A. '78
Man from Clover Grove
'78

Pierrino Mascarino
Summer Rental '85

Nelson Mashita
Darkman '90

Hilary Mason
Robot Jox '89

James Mason
Evil Under the Sun '82
Jesus of Nazareth '77
Journey to the Center of
the Earth '59
North by Northwest '59
Prince Valiant '54
Salem's Lot '79
20,000 Leagues Under the
Sea '54
Water Babies '79

Lawrence Mason
The Crow '93

Leroy Mason
Silver Stallion '41

Marsha Mason
Audrey Rose '77
The Cheap Detective '78
Drop Dead Fred '91
The Goodbye Girl '77
Max Dugan Returns '83
Promises in the Dark '79

Tom Mason
Men Don't Leave '89

John Massari
The Wizard of Speed and
Time '88

Michael Massee
The Crow '93

Daniel Massey
Victory '81

Dick Massey
The Commitments '91

Ilona Massey
Love Happy '50

Jim McCullough▶
The Aurora Encounter '85
The Charge of the Model
    T's '76
Where the Red Fern
    Grows: Part 2 '92

Bil McCurcheon
Steel Magnolias '89

Bill McCutcheon
Mr. Destiny '90

Hattie McDaniel
Gone with the Wind '39
Since You Went Away '44

James McDaniel
Malcolm X '92

Dylan McDermott
Jersey Girl '92
Steel Magnolias '89

Shane McDermott
Airborne '93

Conor McDermottroe
Quigley Down Under '90

Ruth McDevitt
Change of Habit '69
The Shakiest Gun in the
    West '68

Christopher McDonald
Chances Are '89
Fatal Instinct '93
Grumpy Old Men '93
Monkey Trouble '94

Francis McDonald
Zorro's Black Whip '44

Garry McDonald
Pirate Movie '82

Marie McDonald
The Geisha Boy '58

Mary McDonnell
Blue Chips '94
Dances with Wolves '90
Sneakers '92

Mary McDonough
A Day for Thanks on
    Walton's Mountain '82
The Waltons: The
    Children's Carol '80

Frances McDormand
The Butcher's Wife '91
Darkman '90

Roddy McDowall
The Adventures of Bullwhip
    Griffin '66
Battle for the Planet of the
    Apes '73
Bedknobs and Broomsticks
    '71
The Cat from Outer Space
    '78
Conquest of the Planet of
    the Apes '72
Doin' Time on Planet Earth
    '88
Escape from the Planet of
    the Apes '71
Evil Under the Sun '82
Funny Lady '75
How Green was My Valley
    '41
Lassie, Come Home '43
My Friend Flicka '43
Overboard '87
Planet of the Apes '68
The Poseidon Adventure
    '72

That Darn Cat '65
The Thief of Baghdad '78

Malcolm McDowell
Bophal '93
Cross Creek '83
Merlin and the Sword '85

Ian McElhinney
The Playboys '92

John McEnery
Black Beauty '94
Land That Time Forgot '75

Peter McEnery
The Fighting Prince of
    Donegal '66
Moon-Spinners '64

Jamie McEnnan
Munchie '92

Reba McEntire
North '94

Bernard McEveety
One Little Indian '73

Bernard McEveety▶
The Bears & I '74
Napoleon and Samantha
    '72
One Little Indian '73

Vincent McEveety▶
Amy '81
The Apple Dumpling Gang
    Rides Again '79
The Castaway Cowboy '74
Charley and the Angel '73
Gus '76
Herbie Goes Bananas '80
Herbie Goes to Monte
    Carlo '77
Million Dollar Duck '71
Smoke '70
Superdad '73
The Treasure of
    Matecumbe '76

Geraldine McEwan
Robin Hood: Prince of
    Thieves '91

Gates McFadden
Star Trek the Next
    Generation Episode 1-2:
    Encounter at Farpoint '87

**George "Spanky"
McFarland**
The Aurora Encounter '85
General Spanky '36

Hamish McFarlane
The Navigator '88

Darren McGavin
Airport '77 '77
Captain America '89
A Christmas Story '83
The Delicate Delinquent '56
The Natural '84
No Deposit, No Return '76
Turk 182! '85
Zero to Sixty '78

Cindy McGee
Fast Forward '84

Vonetta McGee
Blacula '72
Brother Future '91

Johnny Rae McGhee
Project X '87

Bruce McGill
Citizens Band '77

Whale for the Killing '81
Wildcats '86

Kelly McGillis
The Babe '92
North '94
Top Gun '86

John C. McGinley
Car 54, Where Are You?
    '94
Highlander 2: The
    Quickening '91
A Midnight Clear '92
Wagons East '94

Ted McGinley
Revenge of the Nerds '84

Scott McGinnis
Making the Grade '84
Odd Jobs '85

John McGiver
The Adventures of Tom
    Sawyer '73

Patrick McGoohan
Baby. . .Secret of the Lost
    Legend '85
Dr. Syn, Alias the
    Scarecrow '64
Ice Station Zebra '68
The Man in the Iron Mask
    '77
The Silver Streak '76
The Three Lives of
    Thomasina '63

Barry McGovern
Joe Versus the Volcano '90

Elizabeth McGovern
King of the Hill '93
Racing with the Moon '84
She's Having a Baby '88

J.P. McGowan▶
Hurricane Express '32

Stuart E. McGowan▶
The Billion Dollar Hobo '78

Michael McGrady
The Babe '92

Walter McGrail
The Green Hornet '39

Derek McGrath
Freaked '93

Joseph McGrath▶
Digby, the Biggest Dog in
    the World '73

Michael McGreevey
Sammy, the Way-Out Seal
    '62

**Angela Punch
McGregor**
We of the Never Never
    '82

Biff McGuire
Child of Glass '78

Don McGuire▶
The Delicate Delinquent '56

Dorothy McGuire
Friendly Persuasion '56
Old Yeller '57
The Runaways '75
Summer Magic '63
The Swiss Family Robinson
    '60
A Tree Grows in Brooklyn
    '45

Kim McGuire
Cry-Baby '90

Michael McGuire
Home to Stay '79

Stephen McHattie
Beverly Hills Cop 3 '94
Geronimo: An American
    Legend '93

Doug McHenry▶
House Party 2: The Pajama
    Jam '91

Frank McHugh
Going My Way '44
Mighty Joe Young '49
State Fair '45
A Tiger Walks '64

John McIntire
Cloak & Dagger '84
Francis the Talking Mule
    '49
Herbie Rides Again '74
Honkytonk Man '82
The Light in the Forest '58
Rooster Cogburn '75

Tim McIntire
Aloha, Bobby and Rose
    '74
Gumball Rally '76

Marvin J. McIntyre
Fandango '85

Peggy McKay
Wait Till Your Mother Gets
    Home '83

Michael McKean
Airheads '94
Book of Love '91
Clue '85
Coneheads '93
Daniel and the Towers '90s
D.A.R.Y.L. '85
Light of Day '87
Memoirs of an Invisible
    Man '92
Short Circuit 2 '88

Donna McKechnie
Breakin' Through '84

Lafe McKee
Law of the Wild '34

Lonette McKee
Brewster's Millions '85
Malcolm X '92

Ian McKellan
The Scarlet Pimpernel '82
The Shadow '94

Danica McKellar
Sidekicks '93

Siobhan McKenna
Doctor Zhivago '65

Virginia McKenna
Born Free '66
Christian the Lion '76
Ring of Bright Water '69

Dallas McKennon
Mystery Mansion '83

Kevin McKenzie
Olly Olly Oxen Free '78

Doug McKeon
Night Crossing '81
On Golden Pond '81
Where the Red Fern
    Grows: Part 2 '92

Charles McKeown
The Adventures of Baron
    Munchausen '89

Leo McKern
The Adventures of Sherlock
    Holmes' Smarter Brother
    '78
Candleshoe '78
Help! '65
The Horse Without a Head
    '63
Ladyhawke '85
The Mouse That Roared
    '59
Ryan's Daughter '70

Robert McKimson▶
Best of Bugs Bunny &
    Friends '40
Bugs Bunny's 3rd Movie:
    1,001 Rabbit Tales '82

Bill McKinney
Bronco Billy '80
Cannonball '76
City Slickers 2: The Legend
    of Curly's Gold '94
Heart Like a Wheel '83
The Outlaw Josey Wales
    '76
The Shootist '76
Tex '82

Ray McKinnon
A Perfect World '93

Duncan McLachlan▶
The Double O Kid '92

Andrew V. McLaglen
Since You Went Away '44

Andrew V. McLaglen▶
Bandolero! '68
Cahill: United States
    Marshal '73
Monkeys, Go Home! '66
The Shadow Riders '82

Victor McLaglen
Prince Valiant '54
The Quiet Man '52
Wee Willie Winkie '37

Ron McLarty
Tiger Town '83

Norman Z. McLeod▶
Horse Feathers '32
Little Men '40
Monkey Business '31
Secret Life of Walter Mitty
    '47
Topper '37
Topper Takes a Trip '39

Allyn Ann McLerie
And Baby Makes Six '79

Tom McLoughlin▶
Date with an Angel '87

Marshall McLuhan
Annie Hall '77

Ed McMahon
The Kid from Left Field '79

Horace McMahon
The Delicate Delinquent '56

Michael McManus
Mr. Bill's Real-Life
    Adventures '86

Sharon McManus
Anchors Aweigh '45

Kenneth McMillan
Blue Skies Again '83
Cat's Eye '85
Heartbeeps '81
Salem's Lot '79
Three Fugitives '89

Andrew Ian McMillian
Kavik, the Wolf Dog '84

Sam McMurray
Getting Even with Dad '94
L.A. Story '91

Mercedes McNab
Addams Family Values '93

Barbara McNair
Change of Habit '69

Billy McNamara
Dream a Little Dream '89

Brian McNamara
Arachnophobia '90
Mystery Date '91
Short Circuit '86

Ian McNaughton▶
And Now for Something
   Completely Different '72

Howard McNear
The Errand Boy '61

Ian McNeice
Year of the Comet '92

Kristy McNichol
Just the Way You Are '84
Little Darlings '80
My Old Man '79
The Night the Lights Went
   Out in Georgia '81
Pirate Movie '82

Sandy McPeak
Eye on the Sparrow '91
Ode to Billy Joe '76

Kris McQuade
Strictly Ballroom '92

Armelia McQueen
Ghost '90

Butterfly McQueen
The Adventures of
   Huckleberry Finn '85
Gone with the Wind '39

Chad McQueen
The Karate Kid '84
Skateboard '77
Where the Red Fern
   Grows: Part 2 '92

Steve McQueen
Junior Bonner '72
Papillon '73
The Reivers '69

George McQuilkin▶
Caddie Woodlawn '88

Alan McRae
3 Ninjas '92

Elizabeth McRae
The Incredible Mr. Limpet
   '64

Frank McRae
*batteries not included '87
Last Action Hero '93
Lightning Jack '94

Gerald McRaney
Hobo's Christmas '87
The NeverEnding Story '84

Ian McShane
The Fifth Musketeer '79

Micheal McShane
Robin Hood: Prince of
   Thieves '91

John McTiernan▶
The Hunt for Red October
   '90
Last Action Hero '93

Caroline McWilliams
Mermaids '90

Courtland Mead
Dragonworld '94
The Little Rascals '94

Jayne Meadows
City Slickers '91

Joyce Meadows
Zebra in the Kitchen '65

Stephen Meadows
A Cry in the Wild '90

Karen Meagher
Experience Preferred. . .
   But Not Essential '83

Colm Meaney
The Commitments '91
Far and Away '92
Into the West '92
The Last of the Mohicans
   '92
The Snapper '93

Angela Means
House Party 3 '94

Russell Means
The Last of the Mohicans
   '92
Wagons East '94

Anne Meara
Fame '80
The Longshot '86

DeAnn Mears
The Loneliest Runner '76

Meatloaf
Leap of Faith '92

Peter Medak▶
Breakin' Through '84
Ghost in the Noonday Sun
   '74

Cissy Meddings
Strangers in Good
   Company '91

Kay Medford
Funny Girl '68

Jesus Medina
Yanco '64

Patricia Medina
Francis the Talking Mule
   '49
Snow White and the Three
   Stooges '61
The Three Musketeers '48

Cary Medoway▶
The Heavenly Kid '85

Donald Meek
Fabulous Joe '47
Little Miss Broadway '38
State Fair '45

George Meeker
The Invisible Monster '50

Ralph Meeker
Gentle Giant '67

Armand Meffre
Here Comes Santa Claus
   '84

John Megna
To Kill a Mockingbird '62

Shane Meier
Andre '94

Mary Meigs
Strangers in Good
   Company '91

John Meillon
Crocodile Dundee '86
Crocodile Dundee 2 '88
The Fourth Wish '75
Ride a Wild Pony '75

Gus Meins▶
March of the Wooden
   Soldiers '34

Isabelle Mejias
The Bay Boy '85

Andre Melancon▶
The Dog Who Stopped the
   War '84

Wendel Meldrum
City Boy '93

Bill Melendez▶
Bon Voyage, Charlie
   Brown '80
The Charlie Brown and
   Snoopy Show: Vol. 1 '83
A Charlie Brown Christmas
   '65
Dick Deadeye '76
Snoopy, Come Home '72
You're Not Elected, Charlie
   Brown!/A Charlie Brown
   Christmas '65

John Melendez
Airheads '94

Frank Melton
Stand Up and Cheer '34

Ben Mendelsohn
Quigley Down Under '90
The Year My Voice Broke
   '87

David Mendenhall
Going Bananas '88
Over the Top '86
Secret of the Ice Cave '89
Space Raiders '83

Ramon Menendez▶
Stand and Deliver '88

Chris Menges▶
A World Apart '88

Asha Menina
House of Cards '92

Adolphe Menjou
Little Miss Marker '34
Pollyanna '60

Heather Menzies
The Sound of Music '65

**William Cameron
Menzies▶**
Invaders from Mars '53

Christian Meoli
Alive '93

Marian Mercer
Out on a Limb '92

Chantal Mercier
Small Change '76

Michele Mercier
Call of the Wild '72

Paul Mercurio
Strictly Ballroom '92

Burgess Meredith
Clash of the Titans '81
Foul Play '78
Grumpy Old Men '93
Rocky '76
Rocky 2 '79
Rocky 3 '82
Rocky 5 '90
Santa Claus: The Movie
   '85
Twilight Zone: The Movie
   '83

Iris Meredith
Green Archer '40

Judi Meredith
Jack the Giant Killer '62

Lee Meredith
The Sunshine Boys '75

Joseph Merhi▶
Magic Kid '92

Eda Reiss Merin
Don't Tell Mom the
   Babysitter's Dead '91

Lee Meriwether
Brothers O'Toole '73

Una Merkel
The Parent Trap '61
Summer Magic '63
A Tiger Walks '64

Joanna Merlin
Fame '80

Ethel Merman
Airplane! '80

Dina Merrill
The Courtship of Eddie's
   Father '62
The Greatest '77
Running Wild '73

Gary Merrill
Huckleberry Finn '74
Mysterious Island '61

Keith Merrill▶
Take Down '79

Jane Merrow
The Lion in Winter '68

Susan Merson
Lost in Yonkers '93

William Mervyn
Railway Children '70

Laurie Metcalf
Desperately Seeking Susan
   '85
Making Mr. Right '86
Uncle Buck '89

Mark Metcalf
Mr. North '88
One Crazy Summer '86

Aaron Michael Metchik
Trading Mom '94

Asher Metchik
Trading Mom '94

Art Metrano
Going Apel '81
The Heartbreak Kid '72
Police Academy 2: Their
   First Assignment '85
Police Academy 3: Back in
   Training '86

Nancy Mette
Meet the Hollowheads '89

Alan Metter▶
Back to School '86
Girls Just Want to Have
   Fun '85

Jim Metzler
Hot to Trot! '88
Tex '82

Emile Meyer
Shane '53

Nicholas Meyer▶
Star Trek 2: The Wrath of
   Khan '82
Star Trek 6: The
   Undiscovered Country
   '91

Ari Meyers
Dark Horse '92
Think Big '90

Michelle Meyrink
One Magic Christmas '85
Permanent Record '88
Real Genius '85
Revenge of the Nerds '84

Eric Meza▶
House Party 3 '94

Richard Michaels▶
Blue Skies Again '83
Homeward Bound '80

Karli Michaelson
The Kid with the 200 I.Q.
   '83

Dave Michener▶
The Great Mouse Detective
   '86

Frank Middlemass
Oliver Twist '85

Charles Middleton
Dick Tracy Returns '38
Duck Soup '33
Flash Gordon Conquers
   the Universe '40
Flash Gordon: Rocketship
   '36
Spook Busters '46

Robert Middleton
The Court Jester '56

Bette Midler
Big Business '88
Hocus Pocus '93

Toshiro Mifune
Shadow of the Wolf '92

Lita Milan
The Left-Handed Gun '58

Alyssa Milano
Little Sister '92
Old Enough '84

Peter Miles
The Red Pony '49

Sarah Miles
Hope and Glory '87
Ryan's Daughter '70

Sylvia Miles
Crossing Delancey '88
Evil Under the Sun '82
No Big Deal '83
She-Devil '89
Sleeping Beauty '89
Sleeping Beauty '89
Zero to Sixty '78

Vera Miles
The Castaway Cowboy '74
Follow Me, Boys! '66
Gentle Giant '67
One Little Indian '73
Run for the Roses '78
Those Calloways '65
A Tiger Walks '64
The Wrong Man '56

Lewis Milestone▶
The Red Pony '49

Penelope Milford
The Golden Seal '83

John Milius▶
Conan the Barbarian '82
The Wind and the Lion '75

Ray Milland
Dial "M" for Murder '54
Escape to Witch Mountain '75

Gavin Millar▶
Dreamchild '85
My Friend Walter '93

Stuart Millar▶
Rooster Cogburn '75

Ann Miller
Easter Parade '48
On the Town '49
Room Service '38

Aubree Miller
The Ewok Adventure '84
The Ewoks: Battle for Endor '85

Barry Miller
Fame '80
Peggy Sue Got Married '86

Cheryl Miller
Clarence, the Cross-eyed Lion '65
Man from Clover Grove '78
Mountain Man '77

Claude Miller▶
The Little Thief '89

David Miller▶
Love Happy '50

Dennis Miller
Madhouse '90
The Quest '86

Denny Miller
Buck and the Preacher '72
The Party '68

Dick Miller
Explorers '85
Gremlins '84
Heart Like a Wheel '83
The Howling '81
Innerspace '87
Matinee '92
Project X '87
Rock 'n' Roll High School '79
The Terminator '84

Garry Miller
Amazing Mr. Blunden '72

George Miller▶
Andre '94
Goodbye, Miss 4th of July '88
The Man from Snowy River '82
The NeverEnding Story 2: Next Chapter '91

George Miller▶
Lorenzo's Oil '92
Mad Max: Beyond Thunderdome '85
Miracle Down Under '87
Twilight Zone: The Movie '83

Harvey Miller▶
Bad Medicine '85

Jason Miller
Light of Day '87
Rudy '93

Jeremy Miller
The Willies '90

Joshua Miller
And You Thought Your Parents Were Weird! '91
Teen Witch '89

Larry Miller
Corrina, Corrina '94
Suburban Commando '91
Undercover Blues '93

Mark Miller
Savannah Smiles '82

Penelope Ann Miller
Adventures in Babysitting '87
Big Top Pee Wee '88
Chaplin '92
The Freshman '90
Kindergarten Cop '90
The Shadow '94
Year of the Comet '92

Randall Miller▶
Class Act '91

Rebecca Miller
Wind '92

Robert Ellis Miller▶
Brenda Starr '86

Sidney Miller
Boys Town '38
Men of Boys Town '41

Walter Miller
Shadow of the Eagle '32
Tailspin Tommy '34

Warren Miller
Philadelphia '93

Spike Milligan
Digby, the Biggest Dog in the World '73
Ghost in the Noonday Sun '74

Hayley Mills
Back Home '90
The Flame Trees of Thika '81
In Search of the Castaways '62
Moon-Spinners '64
The Parent Trap '61
Pollyanna '60
Summer Magic '63
That Darn Cat '65

Tiger Bay '59
The Trouble with Angels '66
Whistle Down the Wind '62

John Mills
Africa Texas Style '67
Dr. Strange '78
Oklahoma Crude '73
Ryan's Daughter '70
The Swiss Family Robinson '60
Tiger Bay '59

Juliet Mills
Barnaby and Me '77
Jonathan Livingston Seagull '73

Reginald Mills▶
Tales of Beatrix Potter '71

Samantha Mills
Prehysteria '93

Martin Milner
Life with Father '47
13 Ghosts '60
Zebra in the Kitchen '65

Sandra Milo
Bang Bang Kid '67

F.A. Milovich
The Legend of Black Thunder Mountain '79

Josh Milrad
Beastmaster '82

Ernest Milton
Alice in Wonderland '50

John Omirah Miluwi
Gorillas in the Mist '88

Yvette Mimieux
The Black Hole '79
Monkeys, Go Home! '66
Neptune Factor '73
The Wonderful World of the Brothers Grimm '62

Sal Mineo
Escape from the Planet of the Apes '71
Giant '56
Rebel Without a Cause '55

Jan Miner
Mermaids '90

Steve Miner▶
Forever Young '92
House '86
My Father the Hero '93
Soul Man '86
Wild Hearts Can't Be Broken '91

Anthony Minghella▶
Mr. Wonderful '93
Truly, Madly, Deeply '91

Rob Minkoff▶
Honey, I Shrunk the Kids '89
The Lion King '94

Liza Minnelli
Arthur '81
Arthur 2: On the Rocks '88
Muppets Moments '85
Silent Movie '76
That's Dancing! '85

Vincente Minnelli▶
An American in Paris '51
The Band Wagon '53

The Courtship of Eddie's Father '62
Father of the Bride '50
Father's Little Dividend '51
Kismet '55
Meet Me in St. Louis '44
On a Clear Day You Can See Forever '70

Kristin Minter
Cool As Ice '91

Fabrizio Mioni
Hercules '58

Evan Mirand
My Best Friend Is a Vampire '88

Mark Miranda
Lassie: Adventures of Neeka '68

Robert Miranda
Chips the War Dog '90
Lost in Yonkers '93
Sister Act '92
What's Love Got to Do With It? '93

Helen Mirren
The Fiendish Plot of Dr. Fu Manchu '80
2010 : The Year We Make Contact '84
When the Whales Came '89

Mr. Stubbs
Toby Tyler '59

Mr. T
Freaked '93
Rocky 3 '82

Stacy Mistysyn
Princes in Exile '90

Cameron Mitchell
Buck and the Preacher '72
Carousel '56
Escapade in Japan '57
My Favorite Year '82
The Swarm '78

David Mitchell▶
Club Med '83

John Cameron Mitchell
Book of Love '91

Millard Mitchell
Singin' in the Rain '52

Red Mitchell
8 Seconds '94

Scoey Mitchell
The Voyage of the Yes '72

Thomas Mitchell
Gone with the Wind '39
High Noon '52
It's a Wonderful Life '46
Mr. Smith Goes to Washington '39
Shirley Temple Storybook Theater '60

Warren Mitchell
Knights & Emeralds '87

Yvonne Mitchell
Tiger Bay '59

Ilan Mitchell-Smith
How to Be a Perfect Person in Just Three Days '84
Journey to the Center of the Earth '88

Weird Science '85

Chris Mitchum
Big Jake '71
Tombstone '93

Robert Mitchum
The Human Comedy '43
Matilda '78
Mr. North '88
The Red Pony '49
Ryan's Daughter '70
Scrooged '88

Hayao Miyazaki▶
My Neighbor Totoro '93

Isaac Mizrahi
For Love or Money '93

Moshe Mizrahi▶
Madame Rosa '77

Noah Moazezi
Tiger Town '83

Mary Ann Mobley
My Dog, the Thief '69

Roger Mobley
Emil and the Detective '64
Jack the Giant Killer '62

Richard Moder▶
Lassie: Adventures of Neeka '68

Matthew Modine
Gross Anatomy '89
Wind '92

Donald Moffatt
The Best of Times '86
Housesitter '92
Promises in the Dark '79
Regarding Henry '91
The Right Stuff '83

D.W. Moffett
Lisa '90

Zakes Mokae
Dad '89
Gross Anatomy '89

Jerry Molen
Rain Man '88

Alfred Molina
Ladyhawke '85
Maverick '94
Raiders of the Lost Ark '81
White Fang 2: The Myth of the White Wolf '94

Angela Molina
1492: Conquest of Paradise '92

Edouard Molinaro▶
Just the Way You Are '84

Georgia Moll
Thief of Baghdad '61

Richard Moll
Dream Date '93
The Flintstones '94
Hard Country '81
Highlander: The Gathering '93
House '86
Sidekicks '93
Think Big '90

Clifford Mollison
A Christmas Carol '51

Christopher Monger▶
Waiting for the Light '90

Lawrence Monoson
Mask '85

Marilyn Monroe
Love Happy '50
Monkey Business '52

Phil Monroe▶
The Bugs Bunny/Road
Runner Movie '79

Edward Montagne▶
They Went That-a-Way &
That-a-Way '78

Lee Montague
Madame Sousatzka '88

Monte Montague
Radio Patrol '37

Carlos Montalban
Bananas '71

Ricardo Montalban
Cannonball Run 2 '84
Conquest of the Planet of
the Apes '72
Escape from the Planet of
the Apes '71
Joe Panther '76
The Naked Gun: From the
Files of Police Squad '88
Star Trek 2: The Wrath of
Khan '82

Karla Montana
Sweet 15 '90

Yves Montand
Jean de Florette '87
Manon of the Spring '87
On a Clear Day You Can
See Forever '70

Lisa Montell
The Nine Lives of Elfego
Baca '58

Maria Montez
Ali Baba and the Forty
Thieves '43

**Belinda J.
Montgomery**
Stone Fox '87

Douglass Montgomery
Little Women '33

Julia Montgomery
Revenge of the Nerds '84

Lee Montgomery
Girls Just Want to Have
Fun '85

Robert Montgomery
Mr. & Mrs. Smith '41

Lynne Moody
Wait Till Your Mother Gets
Home '83

Ron Moody
David Copperfield '70
Dog Pound Shuffle '75
Oliver! '68
Twelve Chairs '70
Unidentified Flying Oddball
'79

Keith Moon
Tommy '75

Archie Moore
The Adventures of
Huckleberry Finn '60

Bobby Moore
Victory '81

Candy Moore
Tomboy & the Champ '58

Clayton Moore
The Adventures of Frank
and Jesse James '48
The Crimson Ghost '46
G-Men Never Forget '48
Jesse James Rides Again
'47
Jungle Drums of Africa '53
The Lone Ranger '56
The Lone Ranger and the
Lost City of Gold '58
The Lone Ranger: Code of
the Pioneers '55
Nyoka and the Tigermen
'42
Radar Men from the Moon
'52

Constance Moore
Buck Rogers Conquers the
Universe '39

Deborah Maria Moore
Chaplin '92

Demi Moore
The Butcher's Wife '91
Ghost '90
One Crazy Summer '86

Dennis Moore
Spooks Run Wild '41

Dickie Moore
Miss Annie Rooney '42
Oliver Twist '33

Dudley Moore
Arthur '81
Arthur 2: On the Rocks '88
Foul Play '78
Like Father, Like Son '87
Santa Claus: The Movie
'85
Six Weeks '82
Those Daring Young Men
in Their Jaunty Jalopies
'69

Erin O'Brien Moore
Our Little Girl '35

Joanna Moore
Never a Dull Moment '68
Scout's Honor '80
Son of Flubber '63

Juanita Moore
A Dream for Christmas '73

Julianne Moore
Benny & Joon '93
The Fugitive '93

Mary Tyler Moore
Change of Habit '69
Six Weeks '82

Page Moore
The Wizard of Speed and
Time '88

Robert Moore▶
The Cheap Detective '78

Roger Moore
Cannonball Run '81
For Your Eyes Only '81
Live and Let Die '73
The Man with the Golden
Gun '74
Moonraker '79
Octopussy '83
The Spy Who Loved Me
'77
A View to a Kill '85

Terry Moore
Beverly Hills Brats '89
The Great Rupert '50
Mighty Joe Young '49
Since You Went Away '44

Tom Moore▶
Return to Boggy Creek '77

Agnes Moorehead
Citizen Kane '41
How the West was Won
'63
Jane Eyre '44
Pollyanna '60
Shirley Temple Storybook
Theater '60
Since You Went Away '44

Natalie Moorhead
The Thin Man '34

Philippe Mora▶
Return of Captain
Invincible '83

Esai Morales
Great Love Experiment '84
In the Army Now '94
La Bamba '87

Santos Morales
Hot to Trot! '88

Dolores Moran
The Horn Blows at
Midnight '45

Jackie Moran
Buck Rogers Conquers the
Universe '39

Polly Moran
Adam's Rib '50

Rick Moranis
Brewster's Millions '85
Club Paradise '86
The Flintstones '94
Ghostbusters '84
Ghostbusters 2 '89
Hockey Night '84
Honey, I Blew Up the Kid
'92
Honey, I Shrunk the Kids
'89
Little Shop of Horrors '86
Parenthood '89
Spaceballs '87

Tony Mordente▶
Just Tell Me You Love Me
'80

Kenneth More
Battle of Britain '69
Scrooge '70
Unidentified Flying Oddball
'79
Where Time Began '77

Jeanne Moreau
The 400 Blows '59

Marsha Moreau
Miracle at Moreaux '86

Nathaniel Moreau
George's Island '91

Andre Morell
The Bridge on the River
Kwai '57

Rita Moreno
The King and I '56
Popi '69
Singin' in the Rain '52
West Side Story '61

Audrey Morgan
Love Your Mama '89

Cindy Morgan
Tron '82

Frank Morgan
Courage of Lassie '46
Dimples '36
The Human Comedy '43
The Three Musketeers '48
The Wizard of Oz '39

Harry Morgan
The Apple Dumpling Gang
'75
The Apple Dumpling Gang
Rides Again '79
The Barefoot Executive '71
The Cat from Outer Space
'78
Charley and the Angel '73
Dragnet '87
The Glenn Miller Story '54
Scandalous John '71
Scout's Honor '80
The Shootist '76
Snowball Express '72
State Fair '45
Support Your Local
Gunfighter '71
Support Your Local Sheriff
'69

Henry Morgan
High Noon '52
How the West was Won
'63

Ralph Morgan
Dick Tracy vs. Crime Inc.
'41
General Spanky '36

Janusz Morgenstern▶
Legend of the White Horse
'85

Cathy Moriarty
Another Stakeout '93
Kindergarten Cop '90
Matinee '92

Michael Moriarty
Bang the Drum Slowly '73
Secret of the Ice Cave '89
Troll '85

Tara Morice
Strictly Ballroom '92

**Philippe Morier-
Genoud**
Au Revoir Les Enfants '87
Cyrano de Bergerac '90

Noriyuki "Pat" Morita
Babes in Toyland '86
Cancel My Reservation '72
Collision Course '89
Honeymoon in Vegas '92
The Karate Kid '84
The Karate Kid: Part 2 '86
The Karate Kid: Part 3 '89
The Next Karate Kid '94
North '94

Karen Morley
The Littlest Rebel '35

Robert Morley
The African Queen '51
Alice in Wonderland '85
Oh, Heavenly Dog! '80

Joshua Morrell
Making Contact '86

Adrian Morris
Radio Patrol '37

Anita Morris
18 Again! '88
Little Miss Millions '93
Martians Go Home! '90
A Smoky Mountain
Christmas '86

Chester Morris
The Great White Hope '70

Colleen Morris
Prehysteria '93

David Burton Morris▶
Jersey Girl '92

Garrett Morris
Cooley High '75

Haviland Morris
Sixteen Candles '84

Howard Morris
High Anxiety '77
The Nutty Professor '63
Splash '84

Howard Morris▶
Goin' Coconuts '78
With Six You Get Eggroll
'68

Jane Morris
Nothing in Common '86

Judy Morris
Phar Lap '84

Ernie Morrison
The Return of Our Gang
'25

Kenny Morrison
The NeverEnding Story 2:
Next Chapter '91

Sammy Morrison
Flying Wild '41
Follow the Leader '44
'Neath Brooklyn Bridge '42
Spooks Run Wild '41

Tom Morrison
Rocky 5 '90

Bruce Morrow
Dirty Dancing '87

Jo Morrow
13 Ghosts '60
The Three Worlds of
Gulliver '60

Vic Morrow
The Adventures of Tom
Sawyer '73
The Bad News Bears '76
The Treasure of
Matecumbe '76
Twilight Zone: The Movie
'83

Barry Morse▶
Ugly Little Boy '77

David Morse
The Good Son '93

Hollingsworth Morse▶
Justin Morgan Had a
Horse '81

Natalie Morse
The Little Match Girl '87

Robert Morse
The Boatniks '70
Cannon Movie Tales: The
Emperor's New Clothes
'89

Jane Mortifee
My American Cousin '85

Joe Morton
Forever Young '92
Of Mice and Men '92
Speed '94
Terminator 2: Judgment Day '91
Zelly & Me '88

Rocky Morton▶
Super Mario Bros. '93

Jonas Moscartolo
Ernest Scared Stupid '91

Gastone Moschin
Mr. Superinvisible '73

David Moscow
Big '88
Newsies '92

David Moses
Daring Dobermans '73

Gilbert Moses▶
The Fish that Saved Pittsburgh '79
Runaway '89

Rick Moses
Avalanche '78

Roger E. Mosley
The Greatest '77

Donny Most
Huckleberry Finn '75

Josh Mostel
Animal Behavior '89
City Slickers '91
City Slickers 2: The Legend of Curly's Gold '94
Jesus Christ, Superstar '73
Little Man Tate '91
The Money Pit '86
Radio Days '87

Zero Mostel
Muppet Treasures '85
Muppets Moments '85
Once Upon a Scoundrel '73

Collin Mothupi
Cheetah '89

John Moulder-Brown
Rumpelstiltskin '86

Alan Mowbray
It Happened in New Orleans '36
The King and I '56
Topper Takes a Trip '39

Armin Mueller-Stahl
Avalon '90
Holy Matrimony '94
The Power of One '92

Nino Muhlach
The Boy God '86

Geraldine Muir
Hope and Glory '87

Russell Mulcahy▶
Highlander '86
Highlander 2: The Quickening '91
The Real McCoy '93
The Shadow '94

Kate Mulgrew
Camp Nowhere '94
Remo Williams: The Adventure Begins '85

Throw Momma from the Train '87

Jack Mulhall
Burn 'Em Up Barnes '34
The Clutching Hand '36
Mr. Wise Guy '42
Radio Patrol '37
Tim Tyler's Luck '37

Chris Mulkey
Heartbreak Hotel '88
K-9000 '89

Martin Mull
Clue '85
Lots of Luck '85
Mr. Mom '83
My Bodyguard '80
Pecos Bill '86
Ski Patrol '89
Think Big '90

Jack Mullaney
George! '70

Richard Mulligan
Babes in Toyland '86
The Big Bus '76
A Fine Mess '86
The Heavenly Kid '85
The Hideaways '73
Little Big Man '70

Robert Mulligan▶
Clara's Heart '88
Kiss Me Goodbye '82
The Man in the Moon '91
To Kill a Mockingbird '62
Up the Down Staircase '67

Dermot Mulroney
Samantha '92
The Thing Called Love '93
Young Guns '88

Billy Mumy
Bless the Beasts and Children '71
Dear Brigitte '65
Sammy, the Way-Out Seal '62
Twilight Zone: The Movie '83

Trond Munch
Shipwrecked '90

Herbert Mundin
The Adventures of Robin Hood '38

Paul Muni
I Am a Fugitive from a Chain Gang '32

Pep Munne
Where Time Began '77

Caroline Munro
At the Earth's Core '76
Golden Voyage of Sinbad '73
The Spy Who Loved Me '77

Janet Munro
Darby O'Gill & the Little People '59
Horsemasters '61
The Swiss Family Robinson '60
Third Man on the Mountain '59

Lochlynm Munro
Wagons East '94

Jules Munshin
Easter Parade '48

Ona Munson
Gone with the Wind '39

Jim Henson's Muppets
The Great Muppet Caper '81
The Muppet Movie '79
Muppets Take Manhattan '84
Sesame Street Presents: Follow That Bird '85

Jimmy T. Murakami▶
Battle Beyond the Stars '80

Walter Murch▶
Return to Oz '85

Jack Murdock
Rain Man '88

Eddie Murphy
Beverly Hills Cop '84
Beverly Hills Cop 2 '87
Beverly Hills Cop 3 '94
The Golden Child '86

George Murphy
Little Miss Broadway '38

Johnny Murphy
The Commitments '91

Maurice Murphy
Tailspin Tommy '34

Maurice Murphy▶
Fatty Finn '84

Michael Murphy
Batman Returns '92
Clean Slate '94
Cloak & Dagger '84

Rosemary Murphy
To Kill a Mockingbird '62
Walking Tall '73

Timothy Patrick Murphy
Doin' Time on Planet Earth '88
Sam's Son '84

Barbara Murray
Tony Draws a Horse '51

Bill Murray
Caddyshack '80
Ghostbusters '84
Ghostbusters 2 '89
Groundhog Day '93
Little Shop of Horrors '86
Meatballs '79
Scrooged '88
Tootsie '82
What About Bob? '91

Chic Murray
Gregory's Girl '80

Don Murray
Conquest of the Planet of the Apes '72
I am the Cheese '83
Justin Morgan Had a Horse '81
Peggy Sue Got Married '86
Quarterback Princess '85

Joel Murray
One Crazy Summer '86

John Murray
Moving Violations '85

Ken Murray
Follow Me, Boys! '66

Stephen Murray
Alice in Wonderland '50

Tom Murray
The Gold Rush '25

Christina Murrull
The Kid with the 200 I.Q. '83

Clarence Muse
The Black Stallion '79
A Dream for Christmas '73
That Gang of Mine '40

Pip Mushin
Strictly Ballroom '92

John Musker▶
Aladdin '92
The Great Mouse Detective '86
The Little Mermaid '89

Ornella Muti
Flash Gordon '80
Once Upon a Crime '92
Oscar '91
Wait Until Spring, Bandini '90

Floyd Mutrux▶
Aloha, Bobby and Rose '74

Linda Mvusi
A World Apart '88

Harry Myers
City Lights '31

Mike Myers
So I Married an Axe Murderer '93
Wayne's World '92
Wayne's World 2 '93

Alan Myerson▶
Police Academy 5: Assignment Miami Beach '88

Jim Nabors
Cannonball Run 2 '84

Michael Nader
The Flash '90

Eiros Nadies
The Gods Must Be Crazy 2 '89

Anne Nagel
Don Winslow of the Navy '43
The Green Hornet '39
Winners of the West '40

Austin Nagler
Ernest Scared Stupid '91

Ivan Nagy▶
Captain America 2: Death Too Soon '79

Ajay Naidu
Where the River Runs Black '86

Jimmy Nail
Crusoe '89

J. Carroll Naish
Captain Blood '35

Laurence Naismith
Amazing Mr. Blunden '72
The Bushbaby '70
Diamonds are Forever '71
Greyfriars Bobby '61

Jason and the Argonauts '63
The Prince and the Pauper '62
Third Man on the Mountain '59
The Valley of Gwangi '69

Kathy Najimy
Hocus Pocus '93
Sister Act '92
Sister Act 2: Back in the Habit '93

Roger Nakagawa
Escapade in Japan '57

Takeya Nakamura▶
The Little Drummer Boy '68

Reggie Nalder
Salem's Lot '79

Jack Nance
Ghoulies '85

Agnes Nano
Cinema Paradiso '88

Alan Napier
Challenge to Lassie '49

Charles Napier
Citizens Band '77
Ernest Goes to Jail '90
In Search of a Golden Sky '84
The Incredible Hulk Returns '88

Eve Napier
Crazy Moon '87

Marshall Napier
The Navigator '88

Tom Nardini
Africa Texas Style '67

Kathrine Narducci
A Bronx Tale '93

Silvio Narizzano▶
Why Shoot the Teacher? '79

Mary Nash
The Philadelphia Story '40

Noreen Nash
The Red Stallion '47
The Tender Years '47

Stephen Nathan
1776 '72

Masako Natsume
Antarctica '84

Mildred Natwick
The Court Jester '56
A House Without a Christmas Tree '72
Kiss Me Goodbye '82
The Quiet Man '52
Tammy and the Bachelor '57

Melinda Naud
A Day for Thanks on Walton's Mountain '82

David Naughton
Midnight Madness '80

James Naughton
Cat's Eye '85
The Paper Chase '73

Erastheo J. Navda▶
The Boy God '86**

Derek Nimmo
One of Our Dinosaurs Is
Missing '75

Leonard Nimoy
Invasion of the Body
Snatchers '78
Star Trek: The Motion
Picture '80
Star Trek 2: The Wrath of
Khan '82
Star Trek 3: The Search
for Spock '84
Star Trek 4: The Voyage
Home '86
Star Trek 5: The Final
Frontier '89
Star Trek 6: The
Undiscovered Country
'91
Zombies of the
Stratosphere '52

Leonard Nimoy▶
Holy Matrimony '94
Star Trek 3: The Search
for Spock '84
Star Trek 4: The Voyage
Home '86
Three Men and a Baby
'87

Yvette Nipar
Ski Patrol '89

David Niven
Around the World in 80
Days '56
Candleshoe '78
Curse of the Pink Panther
'83
Death on the Nile '78
No Deposit, No Return '76
The Pink Panther '64
Please Don't Eat the
Daisies '60
Trail of the Pink Panther
'82

Cynthia Nixon
Amadeus '84
The Manhattan Project '86

John P. Nixon
Legend of Boggy Creek
'75

Marni Nixon
The Sound of Music '65

Mojo Nixon
Rock 'n' Roll High School
Forever '91
Super Mario Bros. '93

Waweru Njenga
Morgan Stewart's Coming
Home '87

Felix Nobis
Flirting '89

James Noble
Chances Are '89

Trisha Noble
The Private Eyes '80

Philippe Noiret
Cinema Paradiso '88
The Return of the
Musketeers '89

Jeanette Nolan
Cloak & Dagger '84

Kathleen Nolan
Amy '81

Lloyd Nolan
Airport '70
Ice Station Zebra '68
It Came Upon a Midnight
Clear '84
A Tree Grows in Brooklyn
'45

Nick Nolte
Blue Chips '94
I Love Trouble '94
I'll Do Anything '93
Lorenzo's Oil '92
Three Fugitives '89

John Ford Noonan
Adventures in Babysitting
'87

Tommy Noonan
Adam's Rib '50
Last Action Hero '93
The Man with One Red
Shoe '85
The Monster Squad '87
Robocop 2 '90

Tommy Norden
Flipper's Odyssey '66

Jeffrey Nordling
Holy Matrimony '94

Lee Norman
Buck Privates '41

Zack Norman
Romancing the Stone '84

Aaron Norris▶
Sidekicks '93

Christopher Norris
Eat My Dust '76

Chuck Norris
Sidekicks '93

Kimberly Norris
Geronimo '93

Alan North
Billy Galvin '86
Highlander '86
Lean on Me '89

Heather North
The Barefoot Executive '71

Jay North
Scout's Honor '80
Zebra in the Kitchen '65

Sheree North
The Shootist '76

Alex Norton
Comfort and Joy '84
Gregory's Girl '80

B.W.L. Norton▶
Baby . . .Secret of the Lost
Legend '85
More American Graffiti '79

Dee Dee Norton
Dakota '88

Jim Norton
Memoirs of an Invisible
Man '92

Randy Norton
Fire and Ice '83

Judy Norton-Taylor
A Day for Thanks on
Walton's Mountain '82
The Waltons: The
Children's Carol '80

Jack Noseworthy
Alive '93

Max Nosseck▶
Black Beauty '46

Christopher Noth
Baby Boom '87

Michael Nouri
Flashdance '83

Don Novello
Tucker: The Man and His
Dream '88

Jay Novello
Miracle of Our Lady of
Fatima '52

Danny Nucci
Book of Love '91

Elliott Nugent▶
My Favorite Brunette '47

Bill Nunn
Regarding Henry '91
Sister Act '92

France Nuyen
The Joy Luck Club '93
South Pacific '58

Nlxau
The Gods Must Be Crazy
'84
The Gods Must Be Crazy
2 '89

Carroll Nye
Gone with the Wind '39

Louis Nye
The Charge of the Model
T's '76
Harper Valley P.T.A. '78

Jack Oakie
Little Men '40

Simon Oakland
On a Clear Day You Can
See Forever '70
West Side Story '61

Wheeler Oakman
The Lost Jungle '34

Warren Oates
And Baby Makes Six '79
My Old Man '79
Tom Sawyer '73

Philip Ober
Escapade in Japan '57
North by Northwest '59

Hugh O'Brian
Africa Texas Style '67
Doin' Time on Planet Earth
'88
The Shootist '76

Austin O'Brien
Last Action Hero '93
My Girl 2 '94
Prehysteria '93

Clay O'Brien
One Little Indian '73

Dave O'Brien
Spooks Run Wild '41
That Gang of Mine '40
Yukon Flight '40

Edmond O'Brien
Moon Pilot '62

Joan O'Brien
It Happened at the
World's Fair '63

Margaret O'Brien
Amy '81
The Canterville Ghost '44
Jane Eyre '44
Journey for Margaret '42
Little Women '49
Meet Me in St. Louis '44
The Secret Garden '49

Pat O'Brien
Airborne '93
The Boy with the Green
Hair '48
Knute Rockne: All American
'40
Scout's Honor '80
Tim Tyler's Luck '37

Virginia O'Brien
The Big Store '41
Till the Clouds Roll By '46

Colm O'Byrne
The Snapper '93

Ric Ocasek
Hairspray '88

P.J. Ochlan
Little Man Tate '91

Arthur O'Connell
Citizen Kane '41
Gidget '59
Huckleberry Finn '74
Monkey's Uncle '65
Seven Faces of Dr. Lao '63

Deidre O'Connell
Pastime '91
Straight Talk '92

Jerry O'Connell
Calendar Girl '93
Ollie Hopnoodle's Haven
of Bliss '88
Stand By Me '86

Pat O'Connell
The Endless Summer 2 '94

Nancy O'Conner
Whale of a Tale '76

James O'Connolly▶
The Valley of Gwangi '69

Brian O'Connor
Song City U.S.A. '89

Derrick O'Connor
Hope and Glory '87

Donald O'Connor
Francis Goes to the Races
'51
Francis Joins the WACs '54
Francis the Talking Mule
'49
Singin' in the Rain '52
Wonders of Aladdin '61

Glynnis O'Connor
Conspiracy of Love '87
Johnny Dangerously '84
Night Crossing '81
Ode to Billy Joe '76

Kevin J. O'Connor
Hero '92
Peggy Sue Got Married
'86
Steel Magnolias '89

Tim O'Connor
Naked Gun 2 1/2: The
Smell of Fear '91

Una O'Connor
The Adventures of Robin
Hood '38
The Canterville Ghost '44
David Copperfield '35

Hugh O'Conor
Da '88

Denis O'Dea
Treasure Island '50
Under Capricorn '49

David Odell▶
Martians Go Home! '90

Sias Odendal▶
Nukie '93

Chris O'Donnell
Men Don't Leave '89
School Ties '92
The Three Musketeers '93

Rosie O'Donnell
Another Stakeout '93
Car 54, Where Are You?
'94
The Flintstones '94
A League of Their Own
'92
Sleepless in Seattle '93

Sammy Ogg
Miracle of Our Lady of
Fatima '52

George Ogilvie▶
Mad Max: Beyond
Thunderdome '85

Ian Ogilvy
Death Becomes Her '92
Wuthering Heights '70

Keiko Oginome
Antarctica '84

Soon-Teck Oh
A Home of Our Own '93
Legend of the White Horse
'85
The Man with the Golden
Gun '74

Jack O'Halloran
King Kong '76
Superman 1: The Movie
'78
Superman 2 '80

Natsuko Ohama
Speed '94

Catherine O'Hara
Beetlejuice '88
Dick Tracy '90
Home Alone '90
Home Alone 2: Lost in
New York '92
The Paper '94

Maureen O'Hara
Big Jake '71
How Green was My Valley
'41
Jamaica Inn '39
Miracle on 34th Street '47
Only the Lonely '91
The Parent Trap '61
The Quiet Man '52
The Red Pony '76
Sinbad the Sailor '47

Dan O'Herlihy
The Last Starfighter '84

Suzze Pai
Big Trouble in Little China '86

Janis Paige
Hero '92
Please Don't Eat the Daisies '60

Robert Paige
The Red Stallion '47

Didier Pain
My Father's Glory '91
My Mother's Castle '91

Brian Painchaud
Who Has Seen the Wind? '77

Nestor Paiva
The Nine Lives of Elfego Baca '58

Alan J. Pakula▶
All the President's Men '76
The Pelican Brief '93
See You in the Morning '89

George Pal▶
Seven Faces of Dr. Lao '63
tom thumb '58
The Wonderful World of the Brothers Grimm '62

Laszlo Pal▶
Journey to Spirit Island '92

Holly Palance
The Best of Times '86

Jack Palance
Bagdad Cafe '88
Batman '89
City Slickers '91
City Slickers 2: The Legend of Curly's Gold '94
Cops and Robbersons '94
Great Adventure '75
Oklahoma Crude '73
Shane '53
Young Guns '88

Euzhan Palcy▶
Sugar Cane Alley '83

Michael Palin
And Now for Something Completely Different '72
Jabberwocky '77
Monty Python and the Holy Grail '75
Time Bandits '81

Eugene Pallette
The Adventures of Robin Hood '38
The Ghost Goes West '36
Mr. Smith Goes to Washington '39
Stowaway '36
Topper '37

Lilli Palmer
Miracle of the White Stallions '63

Chazz Palminteri
A Bronx Tale '93

Alan Palo
Prehysterial 2 '94

Carlos Palomino
Geronimo: An American Legend '93

Gwyneth Paltrow
Hook '91

Lucianna Paluzzi
Muscle Beach Party '64
Thunderball '65

Norman Panama▶
Barnaby and Me '77
The Court Jester '56

Franklin Pangborn
Just Around the Corner '38
Topper Takes a Trip '39

Stuart Pankin
Arachnophobia '90
Dirt Bike Kid '86
Mannequin 2: On the Move '91

Joe Pantoliano
Baby's Day Out '94
Calendar Girl '93
Eddie and the Cruisers '83
Empire of the Sun '87
The Fugitive '93
The Goonies '85
The In Crowd '88
La Bamba '87

John Paragon
Frog Prince '88

Kiri Paramore
Flirting '89

Michael Pare
Eddie and the Cruisers '83

Mila Parely
Beauty and the Beast '46

Woodrow Parfrey
Oklahoma Crude '73

Jerry Paris▶
Never a Dull Moment '68
Police Academy 2: Their First Assignment '85
Police Academy 3: Back in Training '86

Virginia Paris
Stand and Deliver '88

MacDonald Parke
The Mouse That Roared '59

Alan Parker▶
Bugsy Malone '76
The Commitments '91
Fame '80

Cecil Parker
The Court Jester '56
The Lady Vanishes '38
The Pure Hell of St. Trinian's '61
Tony Draws a Horse '51
Under Capricorn '49

Cecilia Parker
Ah, Wilderness! '35
Andy Hardy Gets Spring Fever '39
Andy Hardy Meets Debutante '40
Andy Hardy's Double Life '42
The Lost Jungle '34
Love Finds Andy Hardy '38

Corey Parker
How I Got into College '89

Eleanor Parker
Hans Brinker '69
The Sound of Music '65

Fess Parker
Davy Crockett and the River Pirates '56
Davy Crockett, King of the Wild Frontier '55
The Light in the Forest '58
Old Yeller '57
Westward Ho, the Wagons! '56

Jarrett Parker
Lords of Magick '88

Jean Parker
The Flying Deuces '39
The Ghost Goes West '36
Little Women '33

Mary-Louise Parker
The Client '94
Mr. Wonderful '93

Monica Parker
Improper Channels '82

Noelle Parker
Ernest Saves Christmas '88

Sachi Parker
Peggy Sue Got Married '86
Welcome Home, Roxy Carmichael '90

Sage Parker
Dirt Bike Kid '86

Sarah Jessica Parker
First Born '84
Flight of the Navigator '86
Footloose '84
Girls Just Want to Have Fun '85
Hocus Pocus '93
Honeymoon in Vegas '92
L.A. Story '91
Somewhere Tomorrow '85

Suzy Parker
Funny Face '57

Wes Parker
Cry from the Mountain '85

Bert Parks
The Freshman '90

Gordon Parks▶
The Learning Tree '69

Larry Parks
The Jolson Story '46

Michael Parks
Hard Country '81
Savannah Smiles '82

Tom Parks
Ladybugs '92

Trina Parks
Diamonds are Forever '71

Helen Parrish
Little Tough Guys '38

Julie Parrish
The Doberman Gang '72

Gordon Parry▶
Tom Brown's School Days '51

Estelle Parsons
Dick Tracy '90
I Never Sang For My Father '70

Fern Parsons
Hoosiers '86

Karyn Parsons
Class Act '91

Nancy Parsons
Ladybugs '92

Dolly Parton
Rhinestone '84
A Smoky Mountain Christmas '86
Steel Magnolias '89
Straight Talk '92

Natalie Pascaud
Mr. Hulot's Holiday '53

Adrian Pasdar
Top Gun '86

Robert Pastorelli
Dances with Wolves '90
Sister Act 2: Back in the Habit '93

Franca Pasut▶
Flashdance '83

Michael Pataki
American Anthem '86
On the Edge: The Survival of Dana '79
Rocky 4 '85
When Every Day was the Fourth of July '78

Michael Pate
Return of Captain Invincible '83

Bill Paterson
The Adventures of Baron Munchausen '89
Chaplin '92
Comfort and Joy '84
Truly, Madly, Deeply '91
The Witches '90

Mandy Patinkin
Dick Tracy '90
French Postcards '79
The Princess Bride '87
Yentl '83

Angela Paton
Groundhog Day '93

Laurie Paton
Norman's Awesome Experience '88

Jason Patric
Geronimo: An American Legend '93
The Lost Boys '87
Solarbabies '86
Toughlove '85

Dennis Patrick
The Air Up There '94

Gail Patrick
To the Last Man '33

Lee Patrick
Fisherman's Wharf '39
The Maltese Falcon '41
Seven Faces of Dr. Lao '63

Nigel Patrick
Battle of Britain '69

Robert Patrick
Fire in the Sky '93
Terminator 2: Judgment Day '91

Luanna Patten
Follow Me, Boys! '66
Johnny Tremain & the Sons of Liberty '58
So Dear to My Heart '49

Neva Patterson
David and Lisa '62
The Runaways '75

Ray Patterson▶
Yogi's First Christmas '80

Sarah Patterson
Snow White '89

Scott Patterson
Little Big League '94

Will Patton
The Client '94

Adrian Paul
Highlander: The Gathering '93

Alexandra Paul
American Flyers '85
Just the Way You Are '84

Byron Paul▶
Lt. Robin Crusoe, U.S.N. '66

David Paul
Think Big '90

Don Michael Paul
Aloha Summer '88

Eugenia Paul
Zorro, Vol. 1 '58

Peter Paul
Think Big '90

Scott Paulin
Captain America '89
The Right Stuff '83
Teen Wolf '85
Turner and Hooch '89

Pat Paulsen
Harper Valley P.T.A. '78

Lennox Pawle
David Copperfield '35

Bill Paxton
Indian Summer '93
The Terminator '84
Tombstone '93
True Lies '94
Weird Science '85

Gilles Payant
Big Red '62

David Paymer
City Slickers '91
City Slickers 2: The Legend of Curly's Gold '94
Heart and Souls '93
Searching for Bobby Fischer '93

John Payne
Miracle on 34th Street '47

Amanda Pays
The Flash '90
Oxford Blues '84

E.J. Peaker
Hello, Dolly! '69

Alice Pearce
The Belle of New York '52
Dear Brigitte '65

Helen Pearce
When the Whales Came '89

Richard Pearce▶
Country '84
Heartland '81
Leap of Faith '92

Sierra Pecheur
Bronco Billy '80

Bob Peck
Jurassic Park '93

Brian Peck▶
The Willies '90

Cecilia Peck
My Best Friend Is a
Vampire '88

Gregory Peck
Amazing Grace & Chuck
'87
How the West was Won
'63
MacArthur '77
The Paradine Case '47
Roman Holiday '53
Spellbound '45
To Kill a Mockingbird '62
The Yearling '46

Tony Peck
Brenda Starr '86

Sam Peckinpah▶
Junior Bonner '72

Larry Peerce▶
The Other Side of the
Mountain '75
The Other Side of the
Mountain, Part 2 '78
A Separate Peace '73

Antonio Pelaez▶
Crystalstone '88

Pele
Hot Shot '86
Victory '81

Lisa Pelikan
Ghoulies '85
Swing Shift '84

Clara Peller
Moving Violations '85

Meeno Peluce
Scout's Honor '80
Voyager from the Unknown
'83

Elizabeth Pena
*batteries not included '87
La Bamba '87

Austin Pendleton
The Front Page '74
Mr. & Mrs. Bridge '91
Mr. Nanny '93
My Boyfriend's Back '93
Short Circuit '86
Simon '80
What's Up, Doc? '72

Nat Pendleton
At the Circus '39
Buck Privates Come Home
'47
Horse Feathers '32
The Thin Man '34

Susan Penhaligon
Land That Time Forgot '75

Arthur Penn▶
The Left-Handed Gun '58
Little Big Man '70
The Miracle Worker '62

Christopher Penn
All the Right Moves '83
Beethoven's 2nd '93
Footloose '84
Josh and S.A.M. '93

Rumble Fish '83

Sean Penn
Fast Times at Ridgemont
High '82
Racing with the Moon '84
Taps '81

Jon Maynard Pennell
The Program '93

Sydney Penny
Hyper-Sapien: People from
Another Star '86

George Peppard
Battle Beyond the Stars
'80
How the West was Won
'63

Conchita Perez
Cria '76

Rosie Perez
It Could Happen to You
'94
Untamed Heart '93

Vincent Perez
Cyrano de Bergerac '90

Joey Perillo
Philadelphia '93

Anthony Perkins
The Black Hole '79
Friendly Persuasion '56

Elizabeth Perkins
Avalon '90
Big '88
The Flintstones '94
Indian Summer '93

Millie Perkins
Pistol: The Birth of a
Legend '90
Table for Five '83

Max Perlich
Born Yesterday '93
The Butcher's Wife '91
Ferris Bueller's Day Off '86
Maverick '94

Rhea Perlman
Class Act '91

Ron Perlman
The Adventures of Huck
Finn '93
Ice Pirates '84

Mireille Perrier
Toto le Heros '91

Jacques Perrin
Cinema Paradiso '88

Valerie Perrine
The Electric Horseman '79
The Last American Hero
'73
Maid to Order '87
Superman 1: The Movie
'78
Superman 2 '80

Felton Perry
Robocop '87
Robocop 2 '90
Robocop 3 '91
Walking Tall '73

Frank Perry▶
David and Lisa '62
Mommie Dearest '81

Gil Perry
Sourdough '77

Jeffery Perry
The Chronicles of Narnia
'89

Luke Perry
Buffy the Vampire Slayer
'92
8 Seconds '94

Roger Perry
The Cat '66

Bill Persky▶
Wait Till Your Mother Gets
Home '83

Lisa Jane Persky
Coneheads '93
The Great Santini '80
Peggy Sue Got Married
'86
The Sure Thing '85

Nehemiah Persoff
Shirley Temple Storybook
Theater '60
The Wrong Man '56
Yentl '83

Theo Pertsindis
The Fire in the Stone '85

Joe Pesci
Home Alone '90
Home Alone 2: Lost in
New York '92
With Honors '94

**Xavier Normann
Petemann**
Mario '74

Bernadette Peters
Annie '82
Heartbeeps '81
Pink Cadillac '89
Silent Movie '76

Brock Peters
The Adventures of
Huckleberry Finn '78
Star Trek 6: The
Undiscovered Country
'91
To Kill a Mockingbird '62

Elizabeth Peters
She-Devil '89

Molly Peters
Thunderball '65

Susan Peters
Andy Hardy's Double Life
'42

Chris Petersen
When Every Day was the
Fourth of July '78

Pat Petersen
Cold River '81

William L. Petersen
Amazing Grace & Chuck
'87

Wolfgang Petersen▶
Enemy Mine '85
The NeverEnding Story '84

Amanda Peterson
Can't Buy Me Love '87
Explorers '85

Cassandra Peterson
Pee Wee's Big Adventure
'85

Clifford Peterson
Charlie, the Lonesome
Cougar '67

Stewart Peterson
Against A Crooked Sky '75
Pony Express Rider '76
Seven Alone '75
Where the Red Fern
Grows '74

Vidal Peterson
Wizards of the Lost
Kingdom '85

Ian Petrella
A Christmas Story '83

Dan Petrie Jr.▶
In the Army Now '94

Daniel Petrie▶
The Bay Boy '85
Cocoon: The Return '88
Lassie '94
Mark Twain and Me '91
Neptune Factor '73
Rocket Gibraltar '88
Six Pack '82
Square Dance '87

Donald Petrie▶
Grumpy Old Men '93
Opportunity Knocks '90

Doris Petrie
The Olden Days Coat '81

Christopher Pettiet
The Goodbye Bird '93

Lori Petty
Free Willy '93
In the Army Now '94
A League of Their Own
'92

Angelique Pettyjohn
The Wizard of Speed and
Time '79

Joseph Pevney▶
Tammy and the Bachelor
'57

Dedee Pfeiffer
Toughlove '85

Michelle Pfeiffer
The Age of Innocence '93
Batman Returns '92
Grease 2 '82
Ladyhawke '85
Sweet Liberty '86

JoAnn Pflug
M*A*S*H '70

Kathleen Phelan▶
Winter Wolf '92

Shawn Phelan
Breaking the Rules '92

Buster Phelps
Little Orphan Annie '32

John Philbin
Martians Go Home! '90

Robert Philip
Adios Amigo '75

Lee Philips▶
On the Right Track '81

Mary Philips
Prince Valiant '54

Britta Phillips
Satisfaction '88

Chynna Phillips
Goodbye, Miss 4th of July
'88
Say Anything '89

Ethan Phillips
Green Card '90
Lean on Me '89

Julianne Phillips
Fletch Lives '89

Leslie Phillips
Empire of the Sun '87

Lou Diamond Phillips
Dakota '88
Harley '90
La Bamba '87
Shadow of the Wolf '92
Stand and Deliver '88
Young Guns '88

MacKenzie Phillips
American Graffiti '73
More American Graffiti '79

Michelle Phillips
American Anthem '86

Sian Phillips
The Age of Innocence '93
Clash of the Titans '81
The Ewoks: Battle for
Endor '85
Heidi '93

Max Phipps
Nate and Hayes '83
Return of Captain
Invincible '83

**Leaf (Joaquin Rafael)
Phoenix**
Parenthood '89
Russkies '87
SpaceCamp '86

River Phoenix
Explorers '85
Indiana Jones and the Last
Crusade '89
Little Nikita '88
Running on Empty '88
Sneakers '92
Stand By Me '86
The Thing Called Love '93

Robert Picardo
Back to School '86
Explorers '85
The Howling '81
Innerspace '87
Matinee '92
Wagons East '94

Irving Pichel
Dick Tracy '37
General Spanky '36
Oliver Twist '33

Irving Pichel▶
The Great Rupert '50

John Pickard
Government Agents vs. the
Phantom Legion '51

Nicholas Pickard
The Land of Faraway '87

Slim Pickens
The Apple Dumpling Gang
'75
Charlie and the Great
Balloon Chase '82
The Cowboys '72
Hawmps! '76
The Howling '81
Never a Dull Moment '68

Pony Express Rider '76
The Story of a Cowboy
  Angel '81
The Swarm '78

Josh Picker
Flirting '89

Cindy Pickett
Ferris Bueller's Day Off '86
The Goodbye Bird '93
Hot to Trot! '88
Son-in-Law '93

Vivian Pickles
Candleshoe '78

Ronald Pickup
My Friend Walter '93

Molly Picon
Cannonball Run '81
Fiddler on the Roof '71

Walter Pidgeon
Big Red '62
Cinderella '64
Funny Girl '68
How Green was My Valley
  '41
Neptune Factor '73
Voyage to the Bottom of
  the Sea '61

Charles B. Pierce▶
Legend of Boggy Creek
  '75

David Pierce
Little Man Tate '91

Wendell Pierce
It Could Happen to You
  '94

Sarah Pierse
The Navigator '88

Frank Pietrangolare
A Bronx Tale '93

Tim Pigott-Smith
The Hunchback of Notre
  Dame '82
The Remains of the Day
  '93

Lorraine Pilkington
The Miracle '91

Jeffrey Pillars
Ernest Rides Again '93

Bronson Pinchot
Beverly Hills Cop '84
Beverly Hills Cop 3 '94
The Flamingo Kid '84

Larry Pine
Plain Clothes '88

Tonya Pinkins
Above the Rim '94

Leah K. Pinsent
The Bay Boy '85

Danny Pintauro
The Beniker Gang '83

Nino Pipitone
G-Men vs. the Black
  Dragon '43

Danuel Pipoly
Lord of the Flies '90

Joe Piscopo
Huck and the King of
  Hearts '93
Johnny Dangerously '84

Sidekicks '93

Marie-France Pisier
French Postcards '79

Anne Pitoniak
House of Cards '92
Old Enough '84
The Wizard of Loneliness
  '88

Arthur Pitt▶
Sundance and the Kid '76

Brad Pitt
Across the Tracks '89
A River Runs Through It '92

Bruce Pittman▶
The Olden Days Coat '81
Where the Spirit Lives '89

ZaSu Pitts
Francis Joins the WACs '54
Francis the Talking Mule
  '49
Life with Father '47

Jeremy Piven
Car 54, Where Are You?
  '94
P.C.U. '94
Singles '92

Mary Kay Place
Captain Ron '92
Explorers '85
The Girl Who Spelled
  Freedom '86
Modern Problems '81
Samantha '92
Smooth Talk '85

Michele Placido
Big Business '88

Tony Plana
Sweet 15 '90

Scott Plank
The In Crowd '88
Pastime '91

Dana Plato
Return to Boggy Creek '77

Edward Platt
North by Northwest '59
Rebel Without a Cause '55

Oliver Platt
Beethoven '92
Benny & Joon '93
The Three Musketeers '93

Alice Playten
Legend '86

Donald Pleasence
The Black Arrow '84
The Count of Monte Cristo
  '74
Escape to Witch Mountain
  '75
Hearts of the West '75
Horsemasters '61
Oh, God! '77
You Only Live Twice '67

John Pleshette
The Kid with the Broken
  Halo '82

Suzanne Pleshette
The Adventures of Bullwhip
  Griffin '66
The Birds '63
Blackbeard's Ghost '67
The Geisha Boy '58
Oh, God! Book 2 '80

The Shaggy D.A. '76
Support Your Local
  Gunfighter '71
The Ugly Dachshund '65

George Plimpton
Little Man Tate '91

Martha Plimpton
The Goonies '85
Josh and S.A.M. '93
Parenthood '89
The River Rat '84
Running on Empty '88
Samantha '92

Joan Plowright
Avalon '90
Dennis the Menace '93

Amanda Plummer
Gryphon '88
Joe Versus the Volcano '90
So I Married an Axe
  Murderer '93

Christopher Plummer
Battle of Britain '69
Dragnet '87
International Velvet '78
The Man Who Would Be
  King '75
Return of the Pink Panther
  '74
Somewhere in Time '80
The Sound of Music '65
Star Trek 6: The
  Undiscovered Country
  '91

Glenn Plummer
Menace II Society '93
Pastime '91
Speed '94

Alison Podbrey
The Peanut Butter Solution
  '85

Judith Pogany
A Hungarian Fairy Tale '87

Ken Pogue
Crazy Moon '87
The Grey Fox '83
Miracle at Moreaux '86

Eric Pohlmann
The Belles of St. Trinian's
  '53

Priscilla Pointer
Rumpelstiltskin '86

Sidney Poitier
Buck and the Preacher '72
Lilies of the Field '63
Little Nikita '88
Piece of the Action '77
Sneakers '92
To Sir, with Love '67

Sidney Poitier▶
Buck and the Preacher '72
Fast Forward '84
Ghost Dad '90
Piece of the Action '77

Roman Polanski▶
Tess '80

Jon Polito
Blankman '94
The Crow '93
The Freshman '90
Highlander '86

Oscar Polk
Gone with the Wind '39

Ben Pollack
The Glenn Miller Story '54

Jeff Pollack▶
Above the Rim '94

Sydney Pollack
Death Becomes Her '92
Tootsie '82

Sydney Pollack▶
The Electric Horseman '79
Jeremiah Johnson '72
Tootsie '82
The Way We Were '73

Cheryl Pollak
My Best Friend Is a
  Vampire '88

Kevin Pollak
Avalon '90
Clean Slate '94
Grumpy Old Men '93
Indian Summer '93
L.A. Story '91
Wayne's World 2 '93
Willow '88

Tracy Pollan
Great Love Experiment '84

Michael J. Pollard
Dick Tracy '90
Roxanne '87
Scrooged '88

Snub Pollard
The Errand Boy '61

Sarah Polley
The Adventures of Baron
  Munchausen '89
Lantern Hill '90

Eileen Pollock
Far and Away '92

Teri Polo
Aspen Extreme '93
Mystery Date '91

Max Pomeranc
Searching for Bobby
  Fischer '93

Paulina Porizkova
Her Alibi '88

Alison Porter
Curly Sue '91

Don Porter
Buck Privates Come Home
  '47

Eric Porter
The Belstone Fox '73
Little Lord Fauntleroy '80
Oliver Twist '85

Eric Porter▶
Marco Polo, Jr. '72

Richard Portnow
Kindergarten Cop '90
Meet the Hollowheads '89
Say Anything '89
Sister Act '92

Ted Post▶
Beneath the Planet of the
  Apes '70

Tiffanie Poston
Adventures in Dinosaur
  City '92

Tom Poston
Carbon Copy '81

Pam Potillo
And the Children Shall
  Lead '85

Charlie Potter
The Witches '90

H.C. Potter▶
The Farmer's Daughter '47

Annie Potts
Breaking the Rules '92
Ghostbusters '84
Ghostbusters 2 '89
It Came Upon a Midnight
  Clear '84
Pretty in Pink '86

Nell Potts
The Effect of Gamma Rays
  on Man-in-the-Moon
  Marigolds '73

Georges Poujouly
Forbidden Games '52

CCH Pounder
Bagdad Cafe '88
Benny & Joon '93
The Ernest Green Story '93
Robocop 3 '91

Phyllis Povah
Pat and Mike '52

Brittney Powell
Airborne '93
Dragonworld '94

Jane Powell
Seven Brides for Seven
  Brothers '54

Lee Powell
Fighting Devil Dogs '38

Michael Powell
Thief of Baghdad '40

Michael Powell▶
The Red Shoes '48
The Tales of Hoffman '51

Robert Powell
The Hunchback of Notre
  Dame '82
Jesus of Nazareth '77
Tommy '75

William Powell
Life with Father '47
The Thin Man '34

Chad Power
3 Ninjas '92

Taryn Power
The Count of Monte Cristo
  '74
Sinbad and the Eye of the
  Tiger '77

Tyrone Power Jr.
Cocoon '85
Shag: The Movie '89

Alexandra Powers
Mask '85

Leslie Ann Powers
Hairspray '88

Stefanie Powers
The Boatniks '70
Herbie Rides Again '74

Sally Prager
The Hideaways '73

Stanley Prager▶
Bang Bang Kid '67

William Ragsdale
Mannequin 2: On the
Move '91

Umberto Raho
Aladdin '86

Steve Railsback
Calendar Girl '93
The Golden Seal '83
Nukie '93

Ivan Raimi
Army of Darkness '92

Sam Raimi
Indian Summer '93

Sam Raimi▶
Army of Darkness '92
Darkman '90

Theodore Raimi
Army of Darkness '92

Christina Raines
Touched by Love '80

Ford Rainey
Mountain Man '77

Claude Rains
The Adventures of Robin
Hood '38
Casablanca '42
Lawrence of Arabia '62
Mr. Smith Goes to
Washington '39
Notorious '46
The Pied Piper of Hamelin
'57
The Prince and the Pauper
'37

Tommy Rall
Seven Brides for Seven
Brothers '54

Jessie Ralph
The Blue Bird '40
Little Lord Fauntleroy '36

Sheryl Lee Ralph
Sister Act 2: Back in the
Habit '93

Esther Ralston
To the Last Man '33

Henry Ramer
Hockey Night '84

Carlos Ramirez
Anchors Aweigh '45

Frank Ramirez
Smith! '69

Harold Ramis
Baby Boom '87
Ghostbusters '84
Ghostbusters 2 '89

Harold Ramis▶
Caddyshack '80
Club Paradise '86
Groundhog Day '93
Untamed Heart '93

**Anne Elizabeth
Ramsay**
A League of Their Own
'92

Bruce Ramsay
Alive '93

Remak Ramsay
Mr. & Mrs. Bridge '91

Anne Ramsey
Goin' South '78
The Goonies '85
Meet the Hollowheads '89
Throw Momma from the
Train '87
White Mama '80

Marion Ramsey
Police Academy 3: Back in
Training '86
Police Academy 5:
Assignment Miami Beach
'88
Police Academy 6: City
Under Siege '89

Nick Ramus
Geronimo '93
Journey to Spirit Island '92

Ethan Randall
All I Want for Christmas
'91
Dutch '91
A Far Off Place '93

Lexi Randall
Heidi '93
Sarah, Plain and Tall '91
Skylark '93

Tony Randall
The Adventures of
Huckleberry Finn '60
Fatal Instinct '93
The Littlest Angel '69
Seven Faces of Dr. Lao '63

Theresa Randle
Beverly Hills Cop 3 '94
Malcolm X '92

Jane Randolph
Abbott and Costello Meet
Frankenstein '48

John Randolph
King Kong '76
National Lampoon's
Christmas Vacation '89
The Runaways '75
The Wizard of Loneliness
'88

Arthur Rankin Jr.▶
The Ballad of Paul Bunyan
'72
Flight of Dragons '82
Frosty the Snowman '69
The Hobbit '78
The Return of the King '80
Santa Claus is Coming to
Town '70

Anthony Rapp
Adventures in Babysitting
'87
Dazed and Confused '93
School Ties '92

Michael Rappaport
Zebrahead '92

Jean-Paul Rappeneau▶
Cyrano de Bergerac '90

Irving Rapper▶
The Corn is Green '45

David Rasche
Bingo '91
Delirious '91

Steve Rash▶
The Buddy Holly Story '78
Can't Buy Me Love '87
Son-in-Law '93
Under the Rainbow '81

Sharif Rashed
Crooklyn '94

Thalmus Rasulala
Adios Amigo '75
Blacula '72
Mom and Dad Save the
World '92

Basil Rathbone
The Adventures of Robin
Hood '38
Captain Blood '35
The Court Jester '56
David Copperfield '35
The Magic Sword '62

Tina Rathborne▶
Zelly & Me '88

Elden Ratliff
The Mighty Ducks '92

Tzvi Ratner-Stauber
Family Prayers '91

Devin Ratray
Home Alone '90
Home Alone 2: Lost in
New York '92

Heather Rattray
Across the Great Divide
'76
Further Adventures of the
Wilderness Family, Part
2 '77
Mountain Family Robinson
'79
Sea Gypsies '78

John Ratzenberger
The Empire Strikes Back
'80

Alice Rawlings
Where Angels Go, Trouble
Follows '68

John Rawlins▶
Dick Tracy Meets
Gruesome '47
Dick Tracy's Dilemma '47

Herbert Rawlinson
Blake of Scotland Yard '36
Smart Alecks '42

Aldo Ray
Pat and Mike '52
Seven Alone '75

James Ray
She's Having a Baby '88

Nicholas Ray▶
Rebel Without a Cause '55

Martha Raye
Pippin '81

Ernest Rayford
Love Your Mama '89

Bill Raymond
The Crow '93

Devon Raymond
Singles '92

Gary Raymond
Jason and the Argonauts
'63

Gene Raymond
Mr. & Mrs. Smith '41

Paula Raymond
Adam's Rib '50

Spiro Razatos▶
Fast Getaway '91

Peggy Rea
Made in America '93
The Waltons: The
Children's Carol '80

Ronald Reagan
Knute Rockne: All American
'40

James Rebhorn
8 Seconds '94
I Love Trouble '94
Lorenzo's Oil '92
Skylark '93

Francis Reddy
Mario '74

Helen Reddy
Airport '75 '75
Pete's Dragon '77

Quinn Redeker
Three Stooges Meet
Hercules '61

Robert Redford
All the President's Men '76
A Bridge Too Far '77
Butch Cassidy and the
Sundance Kid '69
Downhill Racer '69
The Electric Horseman '79
The Great Waldo Pepper
'75
Jeremiah Johnson '72
The Natural '84
Sneakers '92
The Sting '73
The Way We Were '73

Robert Redford▶
A River Runs Through It '92

Corin Redgrave
Four Weddings and a
Funeral '93

Jemma Redgrave
Howard's End '92

Lynn Redgrave
The Big Bus '76
Morgan Stewart's Coming
Home '87
Walking on Air '87

Michael Redgrave
Battle of Britain '69
The Go-Between '71
Heidi '67
The Lady Vanishes '38
The Loneliness of the Long
Distance Runner '62

Vanessa Redgrave
Camelot '67
Howard's End '92
A Man for All Seasons '66

Carol Reed▶
Oliver! '68

Christopher Reed
Rudy '93

Donna Reed
The Caddy '53
The Human Comedy '43
It's a Wonderful Life '46

Jerry Reed
Smokey and the Bandit '77
Smokey and the Bandit,
Part 2 '80
Smokey and the Bandit,
Part 3 '83

Oliver Reed
The Adventures of Baron
Munchausen '89
The Black Arrow '84
Condorman '81
The Four Musketeers '75
Oliver! '68
The Prince and the Pauper
'78
The Return of the
Musketeers '89
The Sting 2 '83
Ten Little Indians '75
Three Musketeers '74
Tommy '75
Treasure Island '89

Pamela Reed
The Best of Times '86
Kindergarten Cop '90
The Right Stuff '83

Philip Reed
Unknown Island '48

Robert Reed
The Love Bug '68

Tracy Reed
Piece of the Action '77

Walter Reed
Government Agents vs. the
Phantom Legion '51

Clive Rees▶
When the Whales Came
'89

Donough Rees
Starship '87

Roger Rees
If Looks Could Kill '91
Robin Hood: Men in Tights
'93
Stop! or My Mom Will
Shoot '92

Della Reese
The Kid Who Loved
Christmas '90
The Voyage of the Yes '72

Christopher Reeve
The Remains of the Day
'93
Somewhere in Time '80
Superman 1: The Movie
'78
Superman 2 '80
Superman 3 '83
Superman 4: The Quest for
Peace '87

George Reeves
Gone with the Wind '39
Superman & the Mole Men
'51
Westward Ho, the
Wagons! '56

Keanu Reeves
Babes in Toyland '86
Bill & Ted's Bogus Journey
'91
Bill & Ted's Excellent
Adventure '89
Little Buddha '93
Much Ado About Nothing
'93
The Night Before '88
Parenthood '89
Permanent Record '88
Speed '94

Lisa Reeves
The Chicken Chronicles '77

Warner Richmond
The Lost Jungle '34

Dan Richter
2001: A Space Odyssey
'68

Deborah Richter
Square Dance '87

Jason James Richter
Cops and Robbersons '94
Free Willy '93

W.D. Richter▶
The Adventures of
Buckaroo Banzai Across
the Eighth Dimension '84

Don Rickles
Beach Blanket Bingo '65
Bikini Beach '64
Muscle Beach Party '64

Alan Rickman
Quigley Down Under '90
Robin Hood: Prince of
Thieves '91
Truly, Madly, Deeply '91

Tom Rickman▶
The River Rat '84

Robert Ridgely
Philadelphia '93

Vicki Ridler
George's Island '91

Peter Riegert
Crossing Delancey '88
Local Hero '83
The Mask '94
Oscar '91

Richard Riehle
Hero '92
Holy Matrimony '94
Lightning Jack '94
Of Mice and Men '92

Charles Riesner▶
The Big Store '41
Lost in a Harem '44

Dean Riesner▶
Bill and Coo '47

Diana Rigg
Evil Under the Sun '82
The Great Muppet Caper
'81
On Her Majesty's Secret
Service '69
Snow White '89
The Worst Witch '86

Robin Riker
Alligator '80
Stepmonster '92

Elaine Riley
Clipped Wings '53

Jeannine Riley
Wackiest Wagon Train in
the West '77

John Riley
Greenstone '85

Shane Rimmer
Crusoe '89
Dreamchild '85
The People That Time
Forgot '77

Taro Rin▶
Galaxy Express '82

Molly Ringwald
The Breakfast Club '85
Face the Music '92
For Keeps '88
P.K. and the Kid '85
Pretty in Pink '86
Sixteen Candles '84
Tall Tales and Legends:
Johnny Appleseed '86

Leon Rippy
Kuffs '92

Robbie Rist
He is My Brother '75

Laza Ristovski
Tito and Me '92

Cyril Ritchard
Hans Brinker '69
Peter Pan '60

Clint Ritchie
Against A Crooked Sky '75

Michael Ritchie▶
The Bad News Bears '76
Cops and Robbersons '94
Downhill Racer '69
Fletch '85
Fletch Lives '89
The Golden Child '86
Smile '75
Wildcats '86

Martin Ritt
Conrack '74

Martin Ritt▶
Casey's Shadow '78
Conrack '74
Cross Creek '83
The Great White Hope '70
Murphy's Romance '85
Norma Rae '79
Sounder '72

John Ritter
The Barefoot Executive '71
Comeback Kid '80
Hero at Large '80
North '94
Problem Child '90
Problem Child 2 '91
Scandalous John '71
A Smoky Mountain
Christmas '86
Stay Tuned '92

Thelma Ritter
How the West was Won
'63
Miracle on 34th Street '47
Rear Window '54

Harry Ritz
Silent Movie '76

Carlos Rivas
The King and I '56

Chita Rivera
Once Upon a Brothers
Grimm '77
Pippin '81

Joan Rivers
Spaceballs '87

Pat Roach
Willow '88

Jason Robards Sr.
Fighting Marines '36

Jason Robards Jr.
The Adventures of Huck
Finn '93
All the President's Men '76

A Christmas to Remember
'78
Dream a Little Dream '89
Heidi '93
A House Without a
Christmas Tree '72
Legend of the Lone Ranger
'81
Little Big League '94
Mark Twain and Me '91
Max Dugan Returns '83
Once Upon a Time in the
West '68
The Paper '94
Parenthood '89
Philadelphia '93
Reunion '88
Something Wicked This
Way Comes '83
Square Dance '87

Sam Robards
Fandango '85

David Robb
The Flame Trees of Thika
'81

Gale Robbins
The Belle of New York '52

Jerome Robbins▶
West Side Story '61

Matthew Robbins▶
*batteries not included '87
Bingo '91
Dragonslayer '81
Legend of Billie Jean '85

Oliver Robbins
Poltergeist '82
Poltergeist 2: The Other
Side '86

Tim Robbins
Erik the Viking '89
Howard the Duck '86
Miss Firecracker '89
The Sure Thing '85
Top Gun '86

Yves Robert▶
My Father's Glory '91
My Mother's Castle '91
The Tall Blond Man with
One Black Shoe '72

Bill Roberts
Bongo '47

Christian Roberts
To Sir, with Love '67

Doris Roberts
The Fig Tree '87
National Lampoon's
Christmas Vacation '89

Ian Roberts
The Power of One '92

Julia Roberts
Hook '91
I Love Trouble '94
The Pelican Brief '93
Satisfaction '88
Steel Magnolias '89

Ken Roberts
The Great Land of Small
'86

Michael D. Roberts
Ice Pirates '84
Rain Man '88

Pernell Roberts
The Errand Boy '61
Magic of Lassie '78

Paco '75
Shirley Temple Storybook
Theater '60

Rachel Roberts
The Belstone Fox '73
Foul Play '78

Tanya Roberts
Beastmaster '82
Sheena '84
A View to a Kill '85

Ted Jan Roberts
Magic Kid '92

Tony Roberts
Annie Hall '77
18 Again! '88
Million Dollar Duck '71
Play It Again, Sam '72
Radio Days '87

Cliff Robertson
Gidget '59
Two of a Kind '82
Wild Hearts Can't Be
Broken '91
Wind '92

Jenny Robertson
Jacob Have I Loved '88

John S. Robertson▶
Little Orphan Annie '32
Our Little Girl '35

Malcolm Robertson
The Year My Voice Broke
'87

Kim Robillard
Rain Man '88

Barry Robins
Bless the Beasts and
Children '71

Laila Robins
Welcome Home, Roxy
Carmichael '90

Andre Robinson
Love Your Mama '89

**Andrew (Andy)
Robinson**
Mask '85
Not My Kid '85

**Angela Louise
Robinson**
Pink Cadillac '89

Ann Robinson
The War of the Worlds
'53

Bill Robinson
Just Around the Corner '38
The Littlest Rebel '35
Rebecca of Sunnybrook
Farm '38

Charles Robinson
Daring Dobermans '73

Chris Robinson
Amy '81
Savannah Smiles '82

Edward G. Robinson
Key Largo '48
Never a Dull Moment '68

Frances Robinson
Tim Tyler's Luck '37

Joe Robinson
Diamonds are Forever '71

Phil Alden Robinson▶
Field of Dreams '89
Sneakers '92

Tiffany Gail Robinson
Pink Cadillac '89

Rafael H. Robledo
Darkman '90

May Robson
Bringing Up Baby '38
It Happened in New
Orleans '36
Little Orphan Annie '32

Wayne Robson
The Grey Fox '83

Alex Rocco
Boris and Natasha: The
Movie '92
Dream a Little Dream '89
Gotcha! '85
The Grass is Always
Greener Over the Septic
Tank '78
Herbie Goes Bananas '80
The Lady in White '88
P.K. and the Kid '85

Marc Rocco▶
Dream a Little Dream '89

Eric Rochant▶
The Fifth Monkey '90

Catherine Roche
Strangers in Good
Company '91

Eugene Roche
Foul Play '78
Oh, God! You Devil '84

Sean Roche▶
Chasing Dreams '81

Suzzy Roche
Crossing Delancey '88

Jean Rochefort
The Tall Blond Man with
One Black Shoe '72

Chris Rock
Coneheads '93

Charles Rocket
Dances with Wolves '90
Delirious '91
Hocus Pocus '93
How I Got into College
'89

Robert Rockwell
Lassie: Adventures of
Neeka '68

Marcia Rodd
Citizens Band '77

Anton Rodgers
Dirty Rotten Scoundrels '88

**Marie Antoinette
Rodgers**
Journey to Spirit Island '92

Alex Rodine
Son of Dinosaurs '90

Marco Rodriguez
The Crow '93

Paul Rodriguez
Made in America '93

Ben Rodska
Oliver Twist '85

Last Action Hero '93
Leader of the Band '87
Lost in Yonkers '93
Radio Days '87

Charlie Ruggles
Breaking the Ice '38
Bringing Up Baby '38
Follow Me, Boys! '66
The Parent Trap '61
Son of Flubber '63
The Ugly Dachshund '65

Derya Ruggles
Remote '93

Vyto Ruginis
Clean Slate '94

Barbara Ruick
Carousel '56

Anthony Michael Ruivivar
White Fang 2: The Myth of the White Wolf '94

Janice Rule
American Flyers '85

Sig Rumann
A Day at the Races '37
The Errand Boy '61
A Night at the Opera '35
A Night in Casablanca '46

Kicki Rundgren
My Life as a Dog '85

Joseph Runningfox
Geronimo '93

Jennifer Runyon
18 Again! '88
The In Crowd '88

Ying Ruocheng
Little Buddha '93

Barbara Rush
Superdad '73

Deborah Rush
The Purple Rose of Cairo '85

Jared Rushton
Big '88
A Cry in the Wild '90
Honey, I Shrunk the Kids '89
The Lady in White '88

Robert Rusler
Shag: The Movie '89
Thrashin' '86

William Russ
Aspen Extreme '93
Pastime '91
The Right Stuff '83

Brian Russell
Charlie, the Lonesome Cougar '67

Bryan Russell
Emil and the Detective '64

Chuck Russell▶
The Mask '94

John Russell
The Blue Bird '40

Ken Russell▶
The Boy Friend '71
Tommy '75

Keri Russell
Honey, I Blew Up the Kid '92

Kurt Russell
The Barefoot Executive '71
The Best of Times '86
Big Trouble in Little China '86
Captain Ron '92
Charley and the Angel '73
The Computer Wore Tennis Shoes '69
Follow Me, Boys! '66
The Horse in the Gray Flannel Suit '68
It Happened at the World's Fair '63
Mosby's Marauders '66
Now You See Him, Now You Don't '72
The One and Only, Genuine, Original Family Band '68
Overboard '87
Superdad '73
Swing Shift '84
Tombstone '93

Nipsey Russell
Car 54, Where Are You? '94
The Wiz '78

Rosalind Russell
His Girl Friday '40
The Trouble with Angels '66
Where Angels Go, Trouble Follows '68

James Russo
Beverly Hills Cop '84
Fast Times at Ridgemont High '82

Rene Russo
Major League '89
Mr. Destiny '90

Jon Rust▶
Smurfs & the Magic Flute '81

Angelo Rutherford
Gentle Ben '69

Ann Rutherford
Andy Hardy Gets Spring Fever '39
Andy Hardy Meets Debutante '40
Andy Hardy's Double Life '42
A Christmas Carol '38
Fighting Marines '36
Gone with the Wind '39
Life Begins for Andy Hardy '41
Love Finds Andy Hardy '38
Secret Life of Walter Mitty '47

Allison Rutledge-Parisi
Metropolitan '90

Susan Ruttan
Chances Are '89
Sweet 15 '90

Basil Ruysdael
Davy Crockett, King of the Wild Frontier '55

David Ryall
Truly, Madly, Deeply '91

Anne Ryan
Three O'Clock High '87

Eileen Ryan
Benny & Joon '93

Fran Ryan
Chances Are '89

John P. Ryan
The Right Stuff '83
Three O'Clock High '87

Meg Ryan
Innerspace '87
Joe Versus the Volcano '90
Prelude to a Kiss '92
Sleepless in Seattle '93
Top Gun '86

Mitchell Ryan
Hot Shots! Part Deux '93
Peter Lundy and the Medicine Hat Stallion '77

Peggy Ryan
Miss Annie Rooney '42

Remi Ryan
Robocop 3 '91

Robert Ryan
The Boy with the Green Hair '48

Bobby Rydell
Bye, Bye, Birdie '63

Christopher Rydell
Gotcha! '85
How I Got into College '89

Mark Rydell▶
The Cowboys '72
Harry & Walter Go to New York '76
On Golden Pond '81
The Reivers '69
The River '84

Winona Ryder
The Age of Innocence '93
Beetlejuice '88
Edward Scissorhands '90
Lucas '86
Mermaids '90
Reality Bites '94
Square Dance '87
Welcome Home, Roxy Carmichael '90

Sabu
Elephant Boy '37
The Jungle Book '42
Thief of Baghdad '40
A Tiger Walks '64

William Sadler
Bill & Ted's Bogus Journey '91
Freaked '93
Project X '87

Elizabeth Sagal
Flashdance '83

Marianne Sagebrecht
Bagdad Cafe '88

Kenji Sahara
Destroy All Monsters '68

Eva Marie Saint
Cancel My Reservation '72
A Christmas to Remember '78
Love Leads the Way '84
North by Northwest '59
Nothing in Common '86

Michael St. Gerard
Hairspray '88

Susan St. James
Carbon Copy '81
Love at First Bite '79
Where Angels Go, Trouble Follows '68

Jill St. John
Diamonds are Forever '71

Michelle St. John
Geronimo '93
Where the Spirit Lives '89

S.Z. Sakall
Casablanca '42
Wonder Man '45
Yankee Doodle Dandy '42

Amy Sakasitz
Dennis the Menace '93
A Home of Our Own '93

Harold Sakata
Goin' Coconuts '78

Gene Saks▶
Brighton Beach Memoirs '86
The Odd Couple '68

Chloe Salaman
Dragonslayer '81

Theresa Saldana
I Wanna Hold Your Hand '78
The Night Before '88

Chic Sale
Treasure Island '34

Kario Salem
1492: Conquest of Paradise '92

Pamela Salem
Never Say Never Again '83

Meredith Salenger
Dream a Little Dream '89
The Journey of Natty Gann '85

Sam Saletta
The Little Rascals '94

Diane Salinger
The Butcher's Wife '91
Pee Wee's Big Adventure '85

Matt Salinger
Captain America '89

Benjamin Salisbury
Captain Ron '92

Leo Salkin▶
2000 Year Old Man '82

Albert Salmi
Dragonslayer '81
Menace on the Mountain '70

Mikael Salomon▶
A Far Off Place '93

Jennifer Salt
Play It Again, Sam '72

Emma Samms
Delirious '91

Chris Samples
King of the Hill '93

Robert Sampson
The Grass is Always Greener Over the Septic Tank '78

Robot Jox '89

Will Sampson
Fish Hawk '79
Poltergeist 2: The Other Side '86

Andy Samuels
The Return of Our Gang '25

Haydon Samuels
I Live with Me Dad '86

Laura San Giacomo
Quigley Down Under '90

Pedro Sanchez
White Fang and the Hunter '85

Paul Sand
The Legend of Sleepy Hollow '79
Once Upon a Brothers Grimm '77
Teen Wolf Too '87

Walter Sande
Don Winslow of the Navy '43

Otto Sander
Wings of Desire '88

George Sanders
Foreign Correspondent '40
In Search of the Castaways '62
Rebecca '40
A Shot in the Dark '64

Jay O. Sanders
Angels in the Outfield '94
Mr. Destiny '90
My Boyfriend's Back '93

William Sanderson
Wagons East '94

Adam Sandler
Airheads '94
Coneheads '93

Mark Sandrich▶
Follow the Fleet '36
Holiday Inn '42
Shall We Dance '37

Julian Sands
Arachnophobia '90
Oxford Blues '84

Sonny Sands
The Bellboy '60

Tommy Sands
Babes in Toyland '61

Gary Sandy
Troll '85

Erskine Sanford
Citizen Kane '41

Isabel Sanford
Love at First Bite '79

Saundra Santiago
Beat Street '84

Joseph Santley▶
The Cocoanuts '29

Reni Santoni
Dead Men Don't Wear Plaid '82
Guns of the Magnificent Seven '69

Ade Sapara
Crusoe '89

Mia Sara
Ferris Bueller's Day Off '86
Legend '86

Chris Sarandon
Collision Course '89
Goodbye, Miss 4th of July '88
The Princess Bride '87

Susan Sarandon
The Client '94
The Front Page '74
The Great Waldo Pepper '75
Lorenzo's Oil '92

Leilani Sarelle Ferrer
Shag: The Movie '89

Dick Sargent
Billie '65
Teen Witch '89

Joseph Sargent▶
MacArthur '77
Skylark '93

Michael Sarrazin
Gumball Rally '76

Gailard Sartain
Ernest Goes to Camp '87
Ernest Goes to Jail '90
Getting Even with Dad '94
Hard Country '81
Leader of the Band '87
The Real McCoy '93
Stop! or My Mom Will Shoot '92
Wagons East '94

Katsuhiko Sasakai
Godzilla vs. Megalon '76

Ron Satlof▶
Spiderman: The Deadly Dust '78

Paul Satterfield
Arena '88

Alfred Sauchelli Jr.
A Bronx Tale '93

Mary Jane Saunders
Sorrowful Jones '49

Terry Saunders
The King and I '56

Carlos Saura▶
Cria '76

Ben Savage
Big Girls Don't Cry. . .They Get Even '92
Little Monsters '89

Fred Savage
The Boy Who Could Fly '86
Little Monsters '89
The Princess Bride '87
Vice Versa '88
The Wizard '89

John Savage
Bad Company '72

Dany Saval
Moon Pilot '62

Telly Savalas
Alice in Wonderland '85
Cannonball Run 2 '84
On Her Majesty's Secret Service '69

John Savident
Brain Donors '92

Toni Sawyer
My Life '93

John Saxon
Battle Beyond the Stars '80
The Bees '78
Beverly Hills Cop 3 '94
The Electric Horseman '79
My Mom's a Werewolf '89

John Sayles
Matinee '92
Straight Talk '92

Syd Saylor
The Lost Jungle '34

Siluck Saysanasy
The Peanut Butter Solution '85

Raphael Sbarge
Back to Hannibal: The Further Adventures of Tom Sawyer and Huckleberry Finn '90
My Science Project '85

Prunella Scales
Howard's End '92
My Friend Walter '93

Alan Scarfe
The Bay Boy '85

Diana Scarwid
Brenda Starr '86
Mommie Dearest '81
Rumble Fish '83
Strange Invaders '83

Wendy Schaal
Innerspace '87

Armand Schaefer▶
Fighting with Kit Carson '33
Hurricane Express '32
Law of the Wild '34
The Lost Jungle '34

George Schaefer▶
Lost Legacy: A Girl Called Hatter Fox '77
Once Upon a Scoundrel '73
Who'll Save Our Children? '82

Francis Schaeffer▶
Baby on Board '92

Franklin J. Schaffner▶
Lionheart '87
Papillon '73
Planet of the Apes '68

William Schallert
The Computer Wore Tennis Shoes '69
House Party 2: The Pajama Jam '91
Innerspace '87
Twilight Zone: The Movie '83

Jerry Schatzberg▶
Misunderstood '84
Reunion '88

Robert Scheerer▶
Hans Brinker '69
The World's Greatest Athlete '73

Roy Scheider
Tiger Town '83
2010 : The Year We Make Contact '84

Andrew Scheinman▶
Little Big League '94

Catherine Schell
Gulliver's Travels '77
On Her Majesty's Secret Service '69
Return of the Pink Panther '74

Maximilian Schell
The Black Hole '79
A Far Off Place '93
The Freshman '90
Heidi '67
Judgment at Nuremberg '61

Ronnie Schell
Gus '76

August Schellenberg
Free Willy '93
Geronimo '93
Iron Will '93

Mary Kate Schellhardt
What's Eating Gilbert Grape '93

Robert Schenkkan
The Manhattan Project '86

Fred Schepisi▶
Barbarosa '82
Iceman '84
Mr. Baseball '92
Roxanne '87

Vincent Schiavelli
The Adventures of Buckaroo Banzai Across the Eighth Dimension '84
Amadeus '84
Batman Returns '92
Better Off Dead '85
Fast Times at Ridgemont High '82
Ghost '90
Waiting for the Light '90

Paul Schibli▶
The Nutcracker Prince '91

Eric Schiff
Toughlove '85

Joseph Schildkraut
The Man in the Iron Mask '39

Gus Schilling
Citizen Kane '41

Vivian Schilling
The Legend of Wolf Mountain '92

Thomas Schlamme▶
Miss Firecracker '89
So I Married an Axe Murderer '93

Charlie Schlatter
18 Again! '88
Heartbreak Hotel '88

John Schlesinger▶
Madame Sousatzka '88

Dan Schneider
Better Off Dead '85

John Schneider
Christmas Comes to Willow Creek '87

Paul Schneider▶
Something Special '86

Rob Schneider
The Beverly Hillbillies '93
Home Alone 2: Lost in New York '92
Surf Ninjas '93

Romy Schneider
The Hero '71

Ernest B. Schoedsack▶
King Kong '33
Mighty Joe Young '49
Son of Kong '33

Michael Schoeffling
Mermaids '90
Sixteen Candles '84
Sylvester '85
Wild Hearts Can't Be Broken '91

Jill Schoelen
Adventures in Spying '92
Babes in Toyland '86
That Was Then. . .This Is Now '85

Reiner Schoene
Return to Treasure Island, Vol. 1 '85

Ingeborg Schoener
Mr. Superinvisible '73

Jason Schombing
3 Ninjas Kick Back '94

Inge Schoner
George! '70

Dale Schott▶
The Care Bears Movie 2: A New Generation '86

Paul Schrader▶
Light of Day '87

Bitty Schram
A League of Their Own '92

Rick Schroder
Across the Tracks '89
Earthling '80
The Last Flight of Noah's Ark '80
Little Lord Fauntleroy '80

Frank C. Schroeder▶
Pistol: The Birth of a Legend '91

John Schuck
Butch and Sundance: The Early Days '79
Holy Matrimony '94
M*A*S*H '70
My Mom's a Werewolf '89
The New Adventures of Pippi Longstocking '88
Star Trek 6: The Undiscovered Country '91

Michelle Schuelke
Undercover Blues '93

Rebecca Schull
My Life '93

Emily Schulman
Caddie Woodlawn '88

Carl Schultz▶
Blue Fin '78
Careful, He Might Hear You '84

Michael A. Schultz▶
Car Wash '76
Carbon Copy '81

Cooley High '75
Disorderlies '87
Greased Lightning '77

Joel Schumacher▶
The Client '94
The Incredible Shrinking Woman '81
The Lost Boys '87

Hans Schumm
Spy Smasher '42

Reinhold Schunzel
Notorious '46

Harold Schuster▶
Courage of Black Beauty '57
My Friend Flicka '43
So Dear to My Heart '49
The Tender Years '47

Ivyann Schwan
Problem Child 2 '91

Scott Schwartz
Kidco '83

Arnold Schwarzenegger
Conan the Barbarian '82
Conan the Destroyer '84
Hercules in New York '70
Kindergarten Cop '90
Last Action Hero '93
The Terminator '84
Terminator 2: Judgment Day '91
True Lies '94
The Villain '79

Eric Schweig
The Last of the Mohicans '92

Annabella Sciorra
Mr. Wonderful '93

Dean Scofield
Prehysteria 2 '94

Paul Scofield
A Man for All Seasons '66
When the Whales Came '89

Peter Scolari
Camp Nowhere '94
Mr. Bill's Real-Life Adventures '86

Martin Scorsese▶
The Age of Innocence '93

Nicolette Scorsese
Aspen Extreme '93

Amber Scott
Hook '91

Barry Scott
Ernest Goes to Jail '90

Campbell Scott
Singles '92

Carey Scott
Diving In '90
Making the Grade '84

Connie Scott
Flipper '63

Cynthia Scott▶
Strangers in Good Company '91

Debralee Scott
Just Tell Me You Love Me '80

Police Academy '84

Donovan Scott
Savannah Smiles '82
Sheena '84

Eric Scott
A Day for Thanks on
  Walton's Mountain '82
The Waltons: The
  Children's Carol '80

George C. Scott
The Day of the Dolphin
  '73
Movie, Movie '78
Oklahoma Crude '73
Oliver Twist '82
The Prince and the Pauper
  '78
Taps '81

Jonathan Scott
The Chronicles of Narnia
  '89

Kathryn Leigh Scott
Witches' Brew '79

Larry B. Scott
A Hero Ain't Nothin' But a
  Sandwich '78
Revenge of the Nerds '84
SpaceCamp '86
That Was Then. . .This Is
  Now '85

Martha Scott
Father Figure '80
The Ten Commandments
  '56

Oz Scott▶
Bustin' Loose '81

Randolph Scott
Follow the Fleet '36
Rebecca of Sunnybrook
  Farm '38
Susannah of the Mounties
  '39
To the Last Man '33

Ridley Scott▶
1492: Conquest of
  Paradise '92
Legend '86

Kristin Scott Thomas
Four Weddings and a
  Funeral '93

Tony Scott▶
Beverly Hills Cop 2 '87
Top Gun '86

Susan Seaforth Hayes
Billie '65
Dream Machine '91

Jenny Seagrove
Local Hero '83
Nate and Hayes '83

Douglas Seale
Ernest Saves Christmas '88
Mr. Destiny '90

Ann Sears
The Bridge on the River
  Kwai '57

George Seaton▶
Airport '70
Country Girl '54
Miracle on 34th Street '47

James Seay
Turf Boy '42

Jean Seberg
Airport '70
The Mouse That Roared
  '59
Paint Your Wagon '69

Douta Seck
Sugar Cane Alley '83

Kyle Secor
City Slickers '91
Untamed Heart '93

Kyra Sedgwick
Cindy Eller '91
Heart and Souls '93
Mr. & Mrs. Bridge '91
Singles '92

Robert Sedgwick
Morgan Stewart's Coming
  Home '87

George Segal
Carbon Copy '81
Look Who's Talking '89
Look Who's Talking Now
  '93
Not My Kid '85

Peter Segal▶
Naked Gun 33 1/3: The
  Final Insult '94

Pamela Segall
Say Anything '89
Something Special '86

Arthur Seidelman
The Kid Who Loved
  Christmas '90

Arthur Seidelman▶
A Friendship in Vienna '88
Hercules in New York '70

Susan Seidelman▶
Desperately Seeking Susan
  '85
Making Mr. Right '86
She-Devil '89

William A. Seiter▶
Dimples '36
Room Service '38
Stowaway '36
Susannah of the Mounties
  '39

George B. Seitz▶
Andy Hardy Meets
  Debutante '40
Andy Hardy's Double Life
  '42
Andy Hardy's Private
  Secretary '41
Life Begins for Andy Hardy
  '41
Love Finds Andy Hardy '38

Lesley Selander▶
The Lone Ranger and the
  Lost City of Gold '58
The Red Stallion '47

David Selby
Rich Kids '79

Sarah Selby
Huckleberry Finn '75

Henry Selick▶
The Nightmare Before
  Christmas '93

Connie Sellecca
Captain America 2: Death
  Too Soon '79

Tom Selleck
Her Alibi '88
Mr. Baseball '92
Quigley Down Under '90
The Shadow Riders '82
Three Men and a Baby
  '87
Three Men and a Little
  Lady '90

Peter Sellers
Being There '79
The Fiendish Plot of Dr. Fu
  Manchu '80
Ghost in the Noonday Sun
  '74
The Mouse That Roared
  '59
The Party '68
The Pink Panther '64
The Pink Panther Strikes
  Again '76
Return of the Pink Panther
  '74
Revenge of the Pink
  Panther '78
A Shot in the Dark '64
tom thumb '58
Trail of the Pink Panther
  '82
The World of Henry Orient
  '64

David Seltzer▶
Lucas '86

Arna Selznick▶
The Care Bears Movie '84

Ralph Senesky▶
A Dream for Christmas '73

Y. Serigawa▶
Thumbelina '84

Yahoo Serious
Young Einstein '89

Yahoo Serious▶
Young Einstein '89

Pepe Serna
The Adventures of
  Buckaroo Banzai Across
  the Eighth Dimension '84
Fandango '85

Nestor Serrano
Brenda Starr '86

Coline Serreau▶
Three Men and a Cradle
  '85

Brian Setzer
La Bamba '87

Joan Severance
No Holds Barred '89

William Severn
Journey for Margaret '42

Dan Seymour
Hard-Boiled Mahoney '47
A Night in Casablanca '46

Jane Seymour
Battlestar Galactica '78
Benji at Work '93
Heidi '93
Live and Let Die '73
Oh, Heavenly Dog! '80
The Scarlet Pimpernel '82
Sinbad and the Eye of the
  Tiger '77
Somewhere in Time '80

Ralph Seymour
Rain Man '88

Sha-Na-Na
Grease '78

Glenn Shadix
Bingo '91

Tom Shadyac▶
Ace Ventura: Pet Detective
  '93

Matt Shakman
Meet the Hollowheads '89

Tupac Shakur
Above the Rim '94
Poetic Justice '93

Tony Shalhoub
Honeymoon in Vegas '92

Daniel Shalikar
Honey, I Blew Up the Kid
  '92

Joshua Shalikar
Honey, I Blew Up the Kid
  '92

Chuck Shamata
Princes in Exile '90

Jeremy Shamos
Kid Colter '85

Jim Shane
Chasing Dreams '81

Amelia Shankley
Dreamchild '85
The Little Princess '87

Don Shanks
Blood Brothers '77
The Last of the Mohicans
  '85
The Legend of Wolf
  Mountain '92
Life & Times of Grizzly
  Adams '74
Mountain Man '77
Spirit of the Eagle '90

John Patrick Shanley▶
Joe Versus the Volcano '90

Frank Shannon
Flash Gordon Conquers
  the Universe '40
Flash Gordon: Rocketship
  '36

Harry Shannon
Citizen Kane '41

Alan Shapiro▶
The Crush '93
Tiger Town '83

Ken Shapiro▶
Modern Problems '81

Paul Shapiro▶
Hockey Night '84
Miracle at Moreaux '86

Abdul Hassan Sharif
Zebrahead '92

Omar Sharif
Doctor Zhivago '65
Funny Girl '68
Funny Lady '75
Lawrence of Arabia '62
Oh, Heavenly Dog! '80

David Shark
The Legend of Wolf
  Mountain '92

Ray Sharkey
Cop and a Half '93

Zebrahead '92

Albert Sharpe
Darby O'Gill & the Little
  People '59

David Sharpe
Silver Stallion '41

Ben Sharpsteen▶
Dumbo '41
Pinocchio '40

William Shatner
Airplane 2: The Sequel '82
Bill & Ted's Bogus Journey
  '91
Judgment at Nuremberg
  '61
National Lampoon's
  Loaded Weapon 1 '93
Star Trek: The Motion
  Picture '80
Star Trek 2: The Wrath of
  Khan '82
Star Trek 3: The Search
  for Spock '84
Star Trek 4: The Voyage
  Home '86
Star Trek 5: The Final
  Frontier '89
Star Trek 6: The
  Undiscovered Country
  '91
Whale of a Tale '76

William Shatner▶
Star Trek 5: The Final
  Frontier '89

Shari Shattuck
Arena '88

Mickey Shaughnessy
The Adventures of
  Huckleberry Finn '60
My Dog, the Thief '69

Melville Shavelson▶
The Seven Little Foys '55
Yours, Mine & Ours '68

Helen Shaver
That Night '93
Who Has Seen the Wind?
  '77
Zebrahead '92

Bobbi Shaw
Beach Blanket Bingo '65
How to Stuff a Wild Bikini
  '65
Pajama Party '64

Fiona Shaw
Super Mario Bros. '93
Three Men and a Little
  Lady '90
Undercover Blues '93

Martin Shaw
Golden Voyage of Sinbad
  '73

Montague Shaw
Holt of the Secret Service
  '42

Oscar Shaw
The Cocoanuts '29

Robert Shaw
Battle of Britain '69
From Russia with Love '63
A Man for All Seasons '66
Robin and Marian '76
The Sting '73

Phil Silvers
The Boatniks '70
The Cheap Detective '78
The Chicken Chronicles '77

Alicia Silverstone
The Crush '93

Alastair Sim
The Belles of St. Trinian's '53
Blue Murder at St. Trinian's '56
A Christmas Carol '51
The Littlest Horse Thieves '76
Stage Fright '50

Michael Simkins
Heidi '93

Beverly Simmons
Buck Privates Come Home '47

Jean Simmons
Androcles and the Lion '52
Guys and Dolls '55
Heidi '67

Pat Simmons
My Science Project '85

Peter Simmons
Renaissance Man '94

Francis Simon▶
The Chicken Chronicles '77

J.P. Simon▶
Where Time Began '77

Paul Simon
Annie Hall '77

Robert Simon
The Nine Lives of Elfego Baca '58

Robert F. Simon
Spiderman: The Deadly Dust '78

Freddie Simpson
A League of Their Own '92

O.J. Simpson
Hambone & Hillie '84
The Naked Gun: From the Files of Police Squad '88
Naked Gun 2 1/2: The Smell of Fear '91
Naked Gun 33 1/3: The Final Insult '94

Raeanin Simpson
Little Heroes '91

Joan Sims
One of Our Dinosaurs Is Missing '75

Frank Sinatra
Anchors Aweigh '45
Cannonball Run 2 '84
Guys and Dolls '55
High Society '56
On the Town '49
That's Entertainment '74
Till the Clouds Roll By '46

Frank Sinatra Jr.
Pepper and His Wacky Taxi '72

Sinbad
Coneheads '93

Gordon John Sinclair
Erik the Viking '89

Gregory's Girl '80

Madge Sinclair
Almos' a Man '78
Conrack '74

Ronald Sinclair
Thoroughbreds Don't Cry '37

Donald Sinden
The Island at the Top of the World '74

Lori Singer
Footloose '84
The Man with One Red Shoe '85

Marc Singer
Beastmaster '82
Beastmaster 2: Through the Portal of Time '91

John Singleton▶
Boyz N the Hood '91
Poetic Justice '93

Gary Sinise
Forrest Gump '94
Jack the Bear '93
A Midnight Clear '92
Of Mice and Men '92

Gary Sinise▶
Of Mice and Men '92

Marina Sirtis
Star Trek the Next Generation Episode 1-2: Encounter at Farpoint '87

Kathleen Sisk
The Girl Who Spelled Freedom '86

Meadow Sisto
Captain Ron '92

Pedzisai Sithole
African Journey '89

Frank Sivero
Cop and a Half '93

Eva Six
Beach Party '63

Tom Sizemore
Heart and Souls '93

Calvin Skaggs▶
The Fig Tree '87

Lilia Skala
Flashdance '83
Heartland '81
Lilies of the Field '63

Stellan Skarsgard
Wind '92

Tom Skerritt
Ice Castles '79
Maid to Order '87
M*A*S*H '70
Poltergeist 3 '88
A River Runs Through It '92
Silence of the North '81
SpaceCamp '86
Steel Magnolias '89
Top Gun '86

Anita Skinner
Girlfriends '78

Jerzy Skolimowski
Big Shots '87

Sel Skolnick
Manny's Orphans '78

Ione Skye
Samantha '92
Say Anything '89

Tristine Skyler
Kidco '83

Demian Slade
Better Off Dead '85

Mark Slade
Salty '73

Max Elliott Slade
3 Ninjas '92
3 Ninjas Kick Back '94

Jeremy Slate
Dream Machine '91

Christian Slater
Gleaming the Cube '89
Kuffs '92
Legend of Billie Jean '85
Robin Hood: Prince of Thieves '91
Tucker: The Man and His Dream '88
Untamed Heart '93
The Wizard '89

Helen Slater
City Slickers '91
Lassie '94
Legend of Billie Jean '85
Supergirl '84

Leo Slezak
Baron Munchausen '43

Walter Slezak
Black Beauty '71
Emil and the Detective '64
Sinbad the Sailor '47
Treasure Island '72
The Wonderful World of the Brothers Grimm '62

Everett Sloane
Citizen Kane '41
The Disorderly Orderly '64

Georgia Slowe
The Black Arrow '84

Errol Slue
Baby on Board '92

Jean Smart
Homeward Bound: The Incredible Journey '93
Project X '87

Stian Smestad
Shipwrecked '90

Jack Smight▶
Airport '75 '75
Airport '77 '77
Fast Break '79

Yakov Smirnoff
The Adventures of Buckaroo Banzai Across the Eighth Dimension '84

Alexis Smith
The Age of Innocence '93
Casey's Shadow '78
The Horn Blows at Midnight '45
The Little Girl Who Lives Down the Lane '76
Tough Guys '86

Anna Deavere Smith
Dave '93
Philadelphia '93

Bill Smith
Spirit of the Eagle '90

Bruce Smith▶
Bebe's Kids '92

Bubba Smith
Police Academy '84
Police Academy 2: Their First Assignment '85
Police Academy 3: Back in Training '86
Police Academy 4: Citizens on Patrol '87
Police Academy 5: Assignment Miami Beach '88
Police Academy 6: City Under Siege '89

Sir C. Aubrey Smith
Little Lord Fauntleroy '36
Rebecca '40
Thoroughbreds Don't Cry '37
Wee Willie Winkie '37

Charles Martin Smith
American Graffiti '73
The Buddy Holly Story '78
Culpepper Cattle Co. '72
Herbie Goes Bananas '80
More American Graffiti '79
Never Cry Wolf '83
No Deposit, No Return '76
Starman '84

Charles Martin Smith▶
Boris and Natasha: The Movie '92

Cliff Smith▶
Radio Patrol '37

Cotter Smith
K-9 '89
The Last Prostitute '91

Cynthia Smith
Benji '74
For the Love of Benji '77

Dean Smith
Seven Alone '75

Jaclyn Smith
The Night They Saved Christmas '87

Kurtwood Smith
The Crush '93
Dead Poets Society '89
Robocop '87
Star Trek 6: The Undiscovered Country '91

Lane Smith
The Mighty Ducks '92
Son-in-Law '93

Lewis Smith
The Adventures of Buckaroo Banzai Across the Eighth Dimension '84
The Heavenly Kid '85

Lois Smith
Green Card '90
Holy Matrimony '94
Skylark '93

Madeleine Smith
Live and Let Die '73

Madolyn Smith
Funny Farm '88
2010 : The Year We Make Contact '84

Dame Maggie Smith
Clash of the Titans '81
Death on the Nile '78

Evil Under the Sun '82
Hook '91
The Prime of Miss Jean Brodie '69
The Secret Garden '93
Sister Act '92
Sister Act 2: Back in the Habit '93

Mel Smith
Brain Donors '92
The Princess Bride '87

Paul Smith
The Fire in the Stone '85
Maverick '94
Popeye '80

Putter Smith
Diamonds are Forever '71

Queenie Smith
The Great Rupert '50

Rex Smith
The Pirates of Penzance '83
The Trial of the Incredible Hulk '89

Robin Smith
Bophal '93

Shawn Smith
The River Rat '84

Shawnee Smith
Summer School '87

Shelley Smith
The Fantastic World of D.C. Collins '84

Will Smith
Made in America '93

William Smith
Conan the Barbarian '82

Willie E. Smith
Legend of Boggy Creek '75

Yeardley Smith
City Slickers '91
Legend of Billie Jean '85

Alan Smithee▶
Ghost Fever '87
Morgan Stewart's Coming Home '87

Jan Smithers
Where the Lilies Bloom '74

Wesley Snipes
Major League '89
Wildcats '86

Carrie Snodgress
Across the Tracks '89
8 Seconds '94
Nadia '89

Suzanne Snyder
The Night Before '88

Barry Sobel
Doc Hollywood '91
Martians Go Home! '90

Steven Soderberg▶
King of the Hill '93

Lars Soderdahl
Brothers Lionheart '85

Iain Softley▶
Backbeat '94

Marilyn Sokol
The Goodbye Girl '77

The Prince and the Pauper
'37
Tarzan Finds a Son '39

Ilse Steppat
On Her Majesty's Secret
Service '69

Philip Sterling
Death of the Incredible
Hulk '90

Robert Sterling
Voyage to the Bottom of
the Sea '61

William Sterling▶
Alice's Adventures in
Wonderland '72

Daniel Stern
Breaking Away '79
City Slickers '91
City Slickers 2: The Legend
of Curly's Gold '94
Coupe de Ville '90
Frankenweenie '84
Home Alone '90
Home Alone 2: Lost in
New York '92
Little Monsters '89
Rookie of the Year '93

Daniel Stern▶
Rookie of the Year '93

Steven Hilliard Stern▶
The Devil & Max Devlin
'81
Miracle on Ice '81
Not Quite Human '87
Undergrads '85

Tom Stern▶
Freaked '93

Frances Sternhagen
Doc Hollywood '91
See You in the Morning
'89
Who'll Save Our Children?
'82

Jimmy Sternman
Boy of Two Worlds '70

Jean-Francois Stevenin
Small Change '76

Andrew Stevens
Miracle on Ice '81
Munchie '92

Art Stevens▶
The Fox and the Hound
'81

Becca Stevens
Boyd's Shadow '92

Bill Stevens
Boyd's Shadow '92

Carolyn Stevens
Boyd's Shadow '92

Connie Stevens
Back to the Beach '87
The Littlest Angel '69

Craig Stevens
Abbott and Costello Meet
Dr. Jekyll and Mr. Hyde
'52
Blues Busters '50
Since You Went Away '44

Fisher Stevens
The Flamingo Kid '84
My Science Project '85
Mystery Date '91

Short Circuit '86
Short Circuit 2 '88
Super Mario Bros. '93

George Stevens▶
Giant '56
I Remember Mama '48
Penny Serenade '41
Shane '53

John Stevens▶
Boyd's Shadow '92

Katie Stevens
Boyd's Shadow '92

Rise Stevens
Going My Way '44

Scooter Stevens
Better Off Dead '85

Stella Stevens
The Courtship of Eddie's
Father '62
The Longshot '86
The Nutty Professor '63
Where Angels Go, Trouble
Follows '68

William Stevens
Boyd's Shadow '92

Adam Stevenson
Back Home '90

Juliet Stevenson
Truly, Madly, Deeply '91

McLean Stevenson
The Cat from Outer Space
'78

Parker Stevenson
Caddie Woodlawn '88
A Separate Peace '73

Robert Stevenson
One of Our Dinosaurs Is
Missing '75

Robert Stevenson▶
The Absent-Minded
Professor '61
Bedknobs and Broomsticks
'71
Blackbeard's Ghost '67
Darby O'Gill & the Little
People '59
The Gnome-Mobile '67
Herbie Rides Again '74
In Search of the
Castaways '62
The Island at the Top of
the World '74
Jane Eyre '44
Johnny Tremain & the Sons
of Liberty '58
Kidnapped '60
The Love Bug '68
Mary Poppins '64
The Misadventures of
Merlin Jones '63
Monkey's Uncle '65
My Dog, the Thief '69
Old Yeller '57
One of Our Dinosaurs Is
Missing '75
The Shaggy D.A. '76
Son of Flubber '63
That Darn Cat '65
Tom Brown's School Days
'40

Amy Stewart
Mark Twain and Me '91

**Catherine Mary
Stewart**
The Last Starfighter '84

Night of the Comet '84
Weekend at Bernie's '89

James Stewart
Airport '77 '77
Bandolero! '68
The Cheyenne Social Club
'70
Dear Brigitte '65
The Glenn Miller Story '54
The Greatest Show on
Earth '52
How the West was Won
'63
It's a Wonderful Life '46
Magic of Lassie '78
Mr. Smith Goes to
Washington '39
The Philadelphia Story '40
Rear Window '54
The Shootist '76

**Kate McGregor
Stewart**
Father of the Bride '91

Mel Stewart
The Kid with the 200 I.Q.
'83

Patrick Stewart
L.A. Story '91
Star Trek the Next
Generation Episode 1-2:
Encounter at Farpoint '87

Paul Stewart
Citizen Kane '41

Peggy Stewart
Son of Zorro '47

Roy Stewart
Live and Let Die '73

Dorothy Stickney
I Never Sang For My
Father '70

Phyllis Stickney
What's Love Got to Do
With It? '93

David Ogden Stiers
Better Off Dead '85
Doc Hollywood '91
Iron Will '93
The Man with One Red
Shoe '85
Oh, God! '77

Hugo Stiglitz
Robinson Crusoe & the
Tiger '72

Ryan Stiles
Hot Shots! Part Deux '93

Victor Stiles
Santa Claus Conquers the
Martians '64

Ben Stiller
Empire of the Sun '87
Reality Bites '94

Ben Stiller▶
Reality Bites '94

Jerry Stiller
Hairspray '88

Whit Stillman▶
Metropolitan '90

Sara Stimson
Little Miss Marker '80

Sting
The Adventures of Baron
Munchausen '89

Linda Stirling
The Crimson Ghost '46
Jesse James Rides Again
'47
Zorro's Black Whip '44

Alexander Stitt▶
Grendel, Grendel, Grendel
'82

Nigel Stock
The Lion in Winter '68

Amy Stock-Poynton
Bill & Ted's Bogus Journey
'91
Bill & Ted's Excellent
Adventure '89

Dean Stockwell
Anchors Aweigh '45
Beverly Hills Cop 2 '87
Bonanza: The Return '93
The Boy with the Green
Hair '48
Legend of Billie Jean '85
The Secret Garden '49
Tucker: The Man and His
Dream '88

Guy Stockwell
And Now Miguel '66

John Stockwell
My Science Project '85
Quarterback Princess '85
Top Gun '86

Mink Stole
Cry-Baby '90
Serial Mom '94

Shirley Stoler
Malcolm X '92

Josiane Stoleru
Cyrano de Bergerac '90

Brad Stoll
Lost in Yonkers '93

Ben Stoloff▶
Palooka '34

Eric Stoltz
Fast Times at Ridgemont
High '82
The Grass is Always
Greener Over the Septic
Tank '78
Lionheart '87
Mask '85
Say Anything '89
Some Kind of Wonderful
'87

Mark Stolzenberg
Luggage of the Gods '87

Bobby Stone
Flying Wild '41

Christopher Stone
The Howling '81

Harold J. Stone
The Invisible Boy '57

Leonard Stone
Willy Wonka & the
Chocolate Factory '71

Lewis Stone
Andy Hardy Gets Spring
Fever '39
Andy Hardy Meets
Debutante '40
Andy Hardy's Double Life
'42

Andy Hardy's Private
Secretary '41
David Copperfield '35
Life Begins for Andy Hardy
'41
Love Finds Andy Hardy '38
Love Laughs at Andy
Hardy '46
Treasure Island '34

Sharon Stone
Allan Quartermain and the
Lost City of Gold '86
Irreconcilable Differences
'84
Police Academy 4: Citizens
on Patrol '87

Larry Storch
The Adventures of
Huckleberry Finn '78
The Incredible Rocky
Mountain Race '77

Adam Storke
Death Becomes Her '92

Gale Storm
Smart Alecks '42

Kjell Stormoen
Shipwrecked '90

Mark Story▶
Odd Jobs '85

Madeleine Stowe
Another Stakeout '93
The Last of the Mohicans
'92

Michael Stoyanov
Freaked '93

Beatrice Straight
Poltergeist '82

Glenn Strange
Abbott and Costello Meet
Frankenstein '48

Lee Strasberg
Going in Style '79

Marcia Strassman
And You Thought Your
Parents Were Weird! '91
Another Stakeout '93
Fast Getaway '91
Honey, I Blew Up the Kid
'92
Honey, I Shrunk the Kids
'89

David Strathairn
Big Girls Don't Cry. .
.They Get Even '92
Dominick & Eugene '88
Iceman '84
A League of Their Own
'92
Lost in Yonkers '93
Sneakers '92

Charles Stratton
Munchies '87

Peter Strauss
Whale for the Killing '81

Robert Strauss
Family Jewels '65

Meryl Streep
Death Becomes Her '92
Kramer vs. Kramer '79
She-Devil '89

Barbra Streisand
Funny Girl '68

Parade '74
Playtime '67

Jacques Tati▶
Mr. Hulot's Holiday '53
Parade '74
Playtime '67

John Tatoulis▶
The Silver Stallion: King of
the Wild Brumbies '94

Roy Tatum
Don't Change My World
'83

Norman Taurog▶
Boys Town '38
The Caddy '53
Girl Crazy '43
It Happened at the
World's Fair '63
Men of Boys Town '41

Vic Tayback
The Cheap Detective '78
Tut and Tuttle '82
With Six You Get Eggroll
'68

Benedict Taylor
The Black Arrow '84

Buck Taylor
And Now Miguel '66
Pony Express Rider '76
Tombstone '93

Clarice Taylor
Sommersby '93

Delores Taylor
Billy Jack '71

Don Taylor
Father of the Bride '50
Father's Little Dividend '51

Don Taylor▶
Escape from the Planet of
the Apes '71
Island of Dr. Moreau '77
Tom Sawyer '73

Dub Taylor
Back to the Future, Part 3
'90
My Heroes Have Always
Been Cowboys '91
Pony Express Rider '76
Support Your Local
Gunfighter '71

Elizabeth Taylor
Courage of Lassie '46
Father of the Bride '50
Father's Little Dividend '51
The Flintstones '94
Giant '56
Jane Eyre '44
Lassie, Come Home '43
Life with Father '47
Little Women '49
National Velvet '44

Holland Taylor
Cop and a Half '93
The Jewel of the Nile '85
She's Having a Baby '88

Jack Taylor
Where Time Began '77

Lili Taylor
Rudy '93
Say Anything '89

Mark L. Taylor
Arachnophobia '90

Meshach Taylor
Class Act '91
Explorers '85
Mannequin '87
Mannequin 2: On the
Move '91

Noah Taylor
Flirting '89
The Year My Voice Broke
'87

Ray Taylor▶
Adventures of Smilin' Jack
'43
Adventures of the Flying
Cadets '44
Don Winslow of the Coast
Guard '43
Don Winslow of the Navy
'43
Flaming Frontiers '38
Winners of the West '40

Regina Taylor
Lean on Me '89

Renee Taylor
Delirious '91
The Errand Boy '61

Robert Taylor
Miracle of the White
Stallions '63

Rod Taylor
The Birds '63
Giant '56

Susan Taylor
A River Runs Through It '92

Vaughn Taylor
Francis Goes to the Races
'51

Leigh Taylor-Young
Secret Admirer '85

Jun Tazaki
Destroy All Monsters '68

Ludmila Tcherina
The Red Shoes '48

Lewis Teague
Alligator '80

Lewis Teague▶
Alligator '80
Cat's Eye '85
The Jewel of the Nile '85

Marshall Teague
The Shadow Riders '82

Conway Tearle
Hurricane Express '32

Godfrey Tearle
The 39 Steps '35

Travis Tedford
The Little Rascals '94

Maureen Teefy
Fame '80
Supergirl '84

Shirley Temple
Baby, Take a Bow '34
The Bachelor and the
Bobby-Soxer '47
The Blue Bird '40
Bright Eyes '34
Captain January '36
Curly Top '35
Dimples '36
Heidi '37
Just Around the Corner '38
Little Miss Broadway '38

Little Miss Marker '34
The Little Princess '39
The Littlest Rebel '35
Miss Annie Rooney '42
Our Little Girl '35
The Poor Little Rich Girl
'36
Rebecca of Sunnybrook
Farm '38
Shirley Temple Baby
Berlesques '33
Shirley Temple Festival '33
Shirley Temple Storybook
Theater '60
Since You Went Away '44
Stand Up and Cheer '34
The Story of Seabiscuit '49
Stowaway '36
Susannah of the Mounties
'39
To the Last Man '33
Wee Willie Winkie '37

Victoria Tennant
L.A. Story '91
Little Lord Fauntleroy '80

Jon Tenney
Lassie '94
Tombstone '93

Bela Ternovsky▶
Cat City '87

Hal Terrance
Kid Colter '85

Denine Terry
No Drums, No Bugles '71

Don Terry
Don Winslow of the Coast
Guard '43
Don Winslow of the Navy
'43

John Terry
Iron Will '93
Of Mice and Men '92

Nigel Terry
The Lion in Winter '68

Terry-Thomas
Blue Murder at St.
Trinian's '56
Those Daring Young Men
in Their Jaunty Jalopies
'69
tom thumb '58
The Wonderful World of
the Brothers Grimm '62

Robert Tessier
The Last of the Mohicans
'85
The Villain '79

Ted Tetzlaff▶
The Window '49

Lauren Tewes
Magic Kid '92

Joan Tewkesbury▶
Sudie & Simpson '90

Peter Tewkesbury▶
Emil and the Detective '64

Tab Thacker
Wildcats '86

Benj Thall
Homeward Bound: The
Incredible Journey '93

Byron Thames
Blame It on the Night '84

Seven Minutes in Heaven
'86

Torin Thatcher
Jack the Giant Killer '62
The Seventh Voyage of
Sinbad '58

Leon Thau▶
Save the Lady '82

John Thaw
Chaplin '92

Phyllis Thaxter
Superman 1: The Movie
'78

Brother Theodore
The 'Burbs '89

Ernest Thesiger
A Christmas Carol '51

David Thewlis
Black Beauty '94

Alan Thicke
Club Med '83
Not Quite Human '87
Stepmonster '92

Tiffany-Amber Thiessen
Son-in-Law '93

Lynne Thigpen
Lean on Me '89
The Paper '94

Betty Thomas
Troop Beverly Hills '89

**Billie "Buckwheat"
Thomas**
General Spanky '36

Dave Thomas
Boris and Natasha: The
Movie '92
Coneheads '93
Sesame Street Presents:
Follow That Bird '85

Frankie Thomas Jr.
Boys Town '38
Nancy Drew, Reporter '39
Tim Tyler's Luck '37

Henry Thomas
Cloak & Dagger '84
E.T.: The Extra-Terrestrial
'82
Fire in the Sky '93
Misunderstood '84
The Quest '86

Jay Thomas
Straight Talk '92

Philip Michael Thomas
The Wizard of Speed and
Time '88

Richard Thomas
Andy and the Airwave
Rangers '89
Battle Beyond the Stars
'80
Homecoming: A Christmas
Story '71

Robin Thomas
Summer School '87

Scott Thomas
Guns of the Magnificent
Seven '69

Sharon Thomas
Young Guns '88

Tim Thomerson
The Legend of Sleepy
Hollow '86
Rhinestone '84

Andrea Thompson
Doin' Time on Planet Earth
'88

Brett Thompson▶
Adventures in Dinosaur
City '92

Caroline Thompson▶
Black Beauty '94

Don Thompson▶
Ugly Little Boy '77

Elizabeth Thompson
Metropolitan '90

Emma Thompson
Howard's End '92
Much Ado About Nothing
'93
The Remains of the Day
'93

Ernest Thompson
Malcolm X '92

Fred Dalton Thompson
Baby's Day Out '94
Born Yesterday '93
Curly Sue '91
The Hunt for Red October
'90

Hal Thompson
Animal Crackers '30

J. Lee Thompson▶
Battle for the Planet of the
Apes '73
Conquest of the Planet of
the Apes '72
Huckleberry Finn '74
Tiger Bay '59

Jack Thompson
Earthling '80
A Far Off Place '93
The Man from Snowy River
'82
Wind '92

Kay Thompson
Funny Face '57

Kenan Thompson
D2: The Mighty Ducks '94

Kevin Thompson
Spaced Invaders '90

Lea Thompson
All the Right Moves '83
Back to the Future '85
Back to the Future, Part 2
'89
Back to the Future, Part 3
'90
The Beverly Hillbillies '93
Dennis the Menace '93
Howard the Duck '86
Some Kind of Wonderful
'87
SpaceCamp '86
The Wizard of Loneliness
'88

Marshall Thompson
The Caddy '53
Clarence, the Cross-eyed
Lion '65
George! '70

Rex Thompson
The King and I '56

National Velvet '44
Stowaway '36

Michael Treanor
3 Ninjas '92

Mary Treen
Clipped Wings '53
It's a Wonderful Life '46

Les Tremayne
The War of the Worlds
'53

Brian Trenchard-Smith▶
BMX Bandits '83
Deathcheaters '76
The Quest '86

John Trent▶
The Bushbaby '70

James Treuer
Walking on Air '87

Noel Trevarthen
Dusty '85

Claire Trevor
Baby, Take a Bow '34
Key Largo '48
Kiss Me Goodbye '82

Vicki Trickett
Three Stooges Meet
Hercules '61

Leopoldo Trieste
Cinema Paradiso '88

Sarah Trigger
Bill & Ted's Bogus Journey
'91
Paradise '91
P.C.U. '94
Sleepless in Seattle '93

Gus Trikonis▶
Touched by Love '80

Louis Tripp
The Gate '87

Paul Tripp
The Christmas That Almost
Wasn't '66

Kate Trotter
Clarence '91

Gary Trousdale▶
Beauty and the Beast '91

Jim True
Singles '92

Ernest Truex
His Girl Friday '40

Francois Truffaut
Close Encounters of the
Third Kind '77
The 400 Blows '59

Francois Truffaut▶
The 400 Blows '59
Small Change '76
The Wild Child '70

Ralph Truman
Treasure Island '50

Natalie Trundy
Battle for the Planet of the
Apes '73
Beneath the Planet of the
Apes '70
Conquest of the Planet of
the Apes '72
Escape from the Planet of
the Apes '71

Huckleberry Finn '74

Tom Tryon
Moon Pilot '62

Millie Tsiginoff
Angelo My Love '83

**Steve "Patalay"
Tsiginoff**
Angelo My Love '83

Irene Tsu
How to Stuff a Wild Bikini
'65

Yoshio Tsuchiya
Destroy All Monsters '68

Le Tuan
Gleaming the Cube '89

Barry Tubb
Mask '85
Top Gun '86

Stanley Tucci
Beethoven '92
It Could Happen to You
'94
The Pelican Brief '93
Prelude to a Kiss '92
Undercover Blues '93

Michael Tuchner▶
The Hunchback of Notre
Dame '82
Not My Kid '85
The Old Curiosity Shop '75
Trenchcoat '83

Christopher Tucker
House Party 3 '94

Forrest Tucker
The Adventures of
Huckleberry Finn '78
Cancel My Reservation '72
The Incredible Rocky
Mountain Race '77
A Rare Breed '81
Wackiest Wagon Train in
the West '77
The Yearling '46

Michael Tucker
D2: The Mighty Ducks '94
For Love or Money '93
The Purple Rose of Cairo
'85
Radio Days '87

Sophie Tucker
Thoroughbreds Don't Cry
'37

Tanya Tucker
Hard Country '81

Paul Tulley
Kid from Not-So-Big '78

Tommy Tune
The Boy Friend '71
Hello, Dolly! '69

Sandy Tung▶
Across the Tracks '89

Robin Tunney
Encino Man '92

Paige Turco
Teenage Mutant Ninja
Turtles 2: The Secret of
the Ooze '91
Teenage Mutant Ninja
Turtles 3 '93

Glynn Turman
Cooley High '75

A Hero Ain't Nothin' But a
Sandwich '78

Debbie Turner
The Sound of Music '65

George Turner
Son of Zorro '47

Janine Turner
Steel Magnolias '89

Jim Turner
Kid Colter '85

Kathleen Turner
House of Cards '92
The Jewel of the Nile '85
Peggy Sue Got Married
'86
Romancing the Stone '84
Serial Mom '94
Undercover Blues '93

Lana Turner
Love Finds Andy Hardy '38
The Three Musketeers '48
Witches' Brew '79

Tina Turner
Mad Max: Beyond
Thunderdome '85
Tommy '75

Tyrin Turner
Menace II Society '93

Ben Turpin
Law of the Wild '34

Jon Turteltaub▶
Cool Runnings '93
3 Ninjas '92

Aida Turturro
Jersey Girl '92

John Turturro
Brain Donors '92
Desperately Seeking Susan
'85
Gung Ho '85
Off Beat '86

Rita Tushingham
Doctor Zhivago '65

Lurene Tuttle
White Mama '80

Twiggy
The Boy Friend '71
Club Paradise '86
The Little Match Girl '87
Madame Sousatzka '88

Jeff Tyler
The Adventures of Tom
Sawyer '73

Tom Tyler
The Adventures of Captain
Marvel '41
Battling with Buffalo Bill
'31

Susan Tyrrell
Big Top Pee Wee '88
Cry-Baby '90
Liar's Moon '82

Cicely Tyson
Bustin' Loose '81
A Hero Ain't Nothin' But a
Sandwich '78
The Kid Who Loved
Christmas '90
Sounder '72

Pamela Tyson
What's Love Got to Do
With It? '93

Richard Tyson
The Babe '92
Kindergarten Cop '90
Three O'Clock High '87

Bob Uecker
Major League '89
Major League 2 '94

Gisela Uhlen
Toto le Heros '91

Tracey Ullman
Give My Regards to Broad
Street '84
I'll Do Anything '93
Robin Hood: Men in Tights
'93

Liv Ullmann
The Bay Boy '85
A Bridge Too Far '77

Martin Umbach
The NeverEnding Story 2:
Next Chapter '91

Miyoshi Umeki
Flower Drum Song '61

Jay Underwood
The Boy Who Could Fly
'86
Desert Bloom '86
Not Quite Human '87
Uncle Buck '89

Ron Underwood▶
City Slickers '91
Heart and Souls '93

Robert Urich
Ice Pirates '84
Turk 182! '85

Susan Ursitti
Defense Play '88
Teen Wolf '85

Peter Ustinov
Blackbeard's Ghost '67
Death on the Nile '78
Evil Under the Sun '82
Lorenzo's Oil '92
The Man Who Wagged
His Tail '57
One of Our Dinosaurs Is
Missing '75
The Thief of Baghdad '78
The Treasure of
Matecumbe '76

Jamie Uys
The Gods Must Be Crazy
'84

Jamie Uys▶
The Gods Must Be Crazy
'84
The Gods Must Be Crazy
2 '89

Brenda Vaccaro
Airport '77 '77
Supergirl '84

Tracy Vaccaro
A Rare Breed '81

Dan Vadis
Bronco Billy '80

Marc Vahanian
The Prince of Central Park
'77

Ladislao Vajda▶
The Man Who Wagged
His Tail '57

Luis Valdez▶
La Bamba '87

Karen Valentine
Hot Lead & Cold Feet '78
The North Avenue
Irregulars '79
Skeezer '82

Tonino Valerii▶
My Name is Nobody '74

Rudy Vallee
The Bachelor and the
Bobby-Soxer '47
I Remember Mama '48

Alida Valli
The Paradine Case '47

Tomas Van Bromssen
My Life as a Dog '85

Lee Van Cleef
Gypsy Colt '54
High Noon '52

Nadine Van Der Velde
Critters '86
Munchies '87

Richard Van Der Wyk
Skateboard '77

Trish Van Devere
The Day of the Dolphin
'73
Movie, Movie '78

Mamie Van Doren
Francis Joins the WACs '54

Jaco Van Dormael▶
Toto le Heros '91

Dick Van Dyke
Bye, Bye, Birdie '63
Chitty Chitty Bang Bang
'68
Dick Tracy '90
Lt. Robin Crusoe, U.S.N.
'66
Mary Poppins '64
Never a Dull Moment '68

Jerry Van Dyke
The Courtship of Eddie's
Father '62

**Woodbridge S. Van
Dyke▶**
Andy Hardy Gets Spring
Fever '39
Journey for Margaret '42
Tarzan, the Ape Man '32
The Thin Man '34

Jo Van Fleet
East of Eden '54

Buddy Van Horn▶
Any Which Way You Can
'80
Pink Cadillac '89

Dick Van Patten
Freaky Friday '76
Gus '76
High Anxiety '77
The Hoboken Chicken
Emergency '84
The New Adventures of
Pippi Longstocking '88
Robin Hood: Men in Tights
'93
Spaceballs '87

Nancy Walker
Girl Crazy '43
Thursday's Game '74

Robert Walker
Since You Went Away '44
Strangers on a Train '51
Till the Clouds Roll By '46

Robert Walker Jr.
Hambone & Hillie '84

Sarah Walker
Housekeeping '87

Sydney Walker
Prelude to a Kiss '92

Tippy Walker
The World of Henry Orient '64

Max Wall
Jabberwocky '77

George Wallace
Radar Men from the Moon '52

Jack Wallace
The Bear '89

Linda Wallace
Charlie, the Lonesome Cougar '67

Marcia Wallace
My Mom's a Werewolf '89

Richard Wallace▶
Sinbad the Sailor '47

Dee Wallace Stone
Critters '86
E.T.: The Extra-Terrestrial '82
The Howling '81
Huck and the King of Hearts '93
Jimmy the Kid '82
Legend of the White Horse '85
Miracle Down Under '87
Secret Admirer '85
Skeezer '82
Wait Till Your Mother Gets Home '83
Whale for the Killing '81

Sue Wallace
Experience Preferred. . . But Not Essential '83

Tommy Lee Wallace▶
Aloha Summer '88

Eli Wallach
Girlfriends '78
How the West was Won '63
Moon-Spinners '64
Movie, Movie '78
Sam's Son '84
Shirley Temple Storybook Theater '60
Tough Guys '86

Roberta Wallach
The Effect of Gamma Rays on Man-in-the-Moon Marigolds '73

Philip Waller
The Mouse and the Motorcycle '80s

Deborah Walley
Beach Blanket Bingo '65
Benji '74
Gidget Goes Hawaiian '61

Summer Magic '63

Shani Wallis
Oliver! '68

Jon Walmsley
A Day for Thanks on Walton's Mountain '82
The Waltons: The Children's Carol '80

Gwynyth Walsh
The Crush '93

J.T. Walsh
Blue Chips '94
The Client '94
Dad '89

Kay Walsh
Greyfriars Bobby '61
Oliver Twist '48
Stage Fright '50

Lori Walsh
Wonderland Cove '75

M. Emmet Walsh
Back to School '86
The Best of Times '86
Camp Nowhere '94
Catch Me. . .If You Can '89
Critters '86
Fletch '85
Harry and the Hendersons '87
Wildcats '86

Raoul Walsh▶
The Horn Blows at Midnight '45

Robert Walsh
Cry-Baby '90

Sydney Walsh
Three Men and a Little Lady '90

Ray Walston
Fast Times at Ridgemont High '82
Johnny Dangerously '84
The Kid with the Broken Halo '82
Of Mice and Men '92
Popeye '80
The Silver Streak '76
Ski Patrol '89
South Pacific '58
The Sting '73

Jessica Walter
Dr. Strange '78
The Flamingo Kid '84
Going Apel '81
Miracle on Ice '81
P.C.U. '94

Rita Walter
Cry from the Mountain '85

Tracey Walter
Philadelphia '93

Tracy Walter
Batman '89
City Slickers '91
Timerider '83

Anrae Walterhouse
The Grass is Always Greener Over the Septic Tank '78

Charles Walters▶
The Belle of New York '52
Easter Parade '48
High Society '56

Lili '53
Please Don't Eat the Daisies '60

James Walters
Shout '91

Julie Walters
Educating Rita '83

Thorley Walters
The Adventures of Sherlock Holmes' Smarter Brother '78
Blue Murder at St. Trinian's '56
The People That Time Forgot '77
The Pure Hell of St. Trinian's '61

Romy Walthall
Camp Nowhere '94

Fred Walton▶
Hadley's Rebellion '84

Lisa Waltz
Brighton Beach Memoirs '86

Sam Wanamaker
Baby Boom '87
Irreconcilable Differences '84
Superman 4: The Quest for Peace '87

Sam Wanamaker▶
Sinbad and the Eye of the Tiger '77

Wayne Wang▶
The Joy Luck Club '93

David S. Ward▶
King Ralph '91
Major League '89
Major League 2 '94
The Program '93

Fred Ward
Big Business '88
Naked Gun 33 1/3: The Final Insult '94
Remo Williams: The Adventure Begins '85
The Right Stuff '83
Secret Admirer '85
Swing Shift '84
Timerider '83

Greg Ward
Kid Colter '85

Jay Ward
To the Last Man '33

John Ward
Holt of the Secret Service '42

Jonathan Ward
Mac and Me '88
White Water Summer '87

Megan Ward
Encino Man '92
Freaked '93
P.C.U. '94

Rachel Ward
Black Magic '92
Dead Men Don't Wear Plaid '82

Roger Ward
Quigley Down Under '90

Sandy Ward
Tank '83

Sela Ward
The Fugitive '93
Nothing in Common '86

Simon Ward
The Four Musketeers '75
Supergirl '84
Three Musketeers '74

Sophie Ward
Young Sherlock Holmes '85

Vincent Ward▶
The Navigator '88

Anthony Warde
The Black Widow '47

Jack Warden
The Apprenticeship of Duddy Kravitz '74
Being There '79
Brian's Song '71
Carbon Copy '81
Death on the Nile '78
Problem Child '90
Problem Child 2 '91

Clyde Ware▶
No Drums, No Bugles '71

Herta Ware
Cocoon '85
Dakota '88

Emily Warfield
Bonanza: The Return '93
Calendar Girl '93
The Man in the Moon '91

Marsha Warfield
Mask '85

Jordan Warkol
The Little Rascals '94

Billy Warlock
Hot Shot '86

David Warner
Mr. North '88
My Best Friend Is a Vampire '88
The Old Curiosity Shop '75
Star Trek 5: The Final Frontier '89
Star Trek 6: The Undiscovered Country '91
Teenage Mutant Ninja Turtles 2: The Secret of the Ooze '91
Time Bandits '81
Tron '82

H.B. Warner
It's a Wonderful Life '46
Mr. Smith Goes to Washington '39
The Ten Commandments '56
Topper Returns '41

Jack Warner
A Christmas Carol '51

Jeremiah Warner
The Wizard of Loneliness '88

Julie Warner
Doc Hollywood '91
Indian Summer '93

Steven Warner
The Little Prince '74

Fran Warren
Abbott and Costello Meet Captain Kidd '52

Jennifer Warren
Ice Castles '79

Lesley Ann Warren
Cinderella '64
Clue '85
The Happiest Millionaire '67
Harry & Walter Go to New York '76
The One and Only, Genuine, Original Family Band '68

Michael Warren
The Kid Who Loved Christmas '90

Ruth Warrick
Citizen Kane '41

Beverly Washburn
Old Yeller '57

Denzel Washington
Carbon Copy '81
Malcolm X '92
Much Ado About Nothing '93
The Pelican Brief '93
Philadelphia '93

Isaiah Washington
Crooklyn '94

Tse-March Washington
Crooklyn '94

Ted Wass
Curse of the Pink Panther '83
The Longshot '86
Oh, God! You Devil '84
Sheena '84

Craig Wasson
Malcolm X '92

Gedde Watanabe
Gung Ho '85
Sixteen Candles '84

Hiroshi Watanabe▶
The Magical Princess Gigi '89

Willard Waterman
Hollywood or Bust '56

Ethel Waters
The Member of the Wedding '52

Harry Waters Jr.
Back to the Future '85
Back to the Future, Part 2 '89

John Waters
Miracle Down Under '87

John Waters▶
Cry-Baby '90
Hairspray '88
Serial Mom '94

James Waterson
Dead Poets Society '89

Sam Waterston
The Boy Who Loved Trolls '84
Lantern Hill '90
The Man in the Moon '91
Serial Mom '94

Ian Watkin
Nutcase '83

Ken Wheat▶
The Ewoks: Battle for Endor '85

Wil Wheaton
December '91
The Last Prostitute '91
The Last Starfighter '84
Stand By Me '86
Star Trek the Next Generation Episode 1-2: Encounter at Farpoint '87

Dana Wheeler-Nicholson
Fletch '85
Tombstone '93

Tim Whelan
Thief of Baghdad '40

Wendy Whelan
George Balanchine's The Nutcracker '93

Lisa Whelchel
The Double McGuffin '79
Where the Red Fern Grows: Part 2 '92

Barbara Whinnery
Hot to Trot! '88

Shonda Whipple
Magic Kid '92

Forest Whitaker
Fast Times at Ridgemont High '82

Johnny Whitaker
The Littlest Angel '69
Napoleon and Samantha '72
Tom Sawyer '73

Jesse White
Bless the Beasts and Children '71
Francis Goes to the Races '51
Matinee '92
Pajama Party '64
Tomboy & the Champ '58

John S. White
The Legend of Sleepy Hollow '79

Ruth White
Up the Down Staircase '67

Sammy White
Pat and Mike '52

Paxton Whitehead
The Adventures of Huck Finn '93
Baby Boom '87
Back to School '86
Boris and Natasha: The Movie '92
Chips the War Dog '90
My Boyfriend's Back '93

Billie Whitelaw
The Secret Garden '87
Water Babies '79

Paul Whiteman
Strike Up the Band '40

John Whitesell▶
Calendar Girl '93

Ray Whiteside
Davy Crockett, King of the Wild Frontier '55

Bradley Whitford
The Client '94

My Life '93
A Perfect World '93
Philadelphia '93

Peter Whitford
Strictly Ballroom '92

Leonard Whiting
Romeo and Juliet '68

Margaret Whiting
Sinbad and the Eye of the Tiger '77

Stuart Whitman
Run for the Roses '78

James Whitmore
Guns of the Magnificent Seven '69
Oklahoma! '55
Planet of the Apes '68
Where the Red Fern Grows '74

Grace Lee Whitney
Star Trek 3: The Search for Spock '84
Star Trek 6: The Undiscovered Country '91

Susan Whitney
Miracle of Our Lady of Fatima '52

Margaret Whitton
The Best of Times '86
Big Girls Don't Cry. . .They Get Even '92
Little Monsters '89
Major League '89
Major League 2 '94
The Man Without a Face '93

May Whitty
The Lady Vanishes '38
Lassie, Come Home '43
Suspicion '41

James Whitworth
Planet of the Dinosaurs '80

Richard Whorf
Yankee Doodle Dandy '42

Richard Whorf▶
Till the Clouds Roll By '46

Mary Wickes
The Canterville Ghost '91
Sister Act '92
Sister Act 2: Back in the Habit '93
Where Angels Go, Trouble Follows '68

Sidney Wicks
Coach '78

Richard Widmark
How the West was Won '63
Judgment at Nuremberg '61
The Swarm '78
Whale for the Killing '81

Jane Wiedlin
Clue '85

David Wieland
Flirting '89

Robert Wiemer▶
Somewhere Tomorrow '85

Alex Wiesendanger
Little Buddha '93

Kai Wiesinger
Backbeat '94

Dianne Wiest
Cops and Robbersons '94
Edward Scissorhands '90
Footloose '84
Little Man Tate '91
The Lost Boys '87
Parenthood '89
The Purple Rose of Cairo '85
Radio Days '87

Chris Wiggins
The Bay Boy '85
Kavik, the Wolf Dog '84
King of the Grizzlies '69
Mark Twain and Me '91
Why Shoot the Teacher? '79

Wiley Wiggins
Dazed and Confused '93

Robert Wightman
A Day for Thanks on Walton's Mountain '82

James Wilby
Dreamchild '85
Howard's End '92

Collin Wilcox
To Kill a Mockingbird '62

Fred M. Wilcox▶
Courage of Lassie '46
Lassie, Come Home '43
The Secret Garden '49

Robert Wilcox
Mysterious Doctor Satan '40

Sophie Wilcox
The Chronicles of Narnia '89

Henry Wilcoxon
A Connecticut Yankee in King Arthur's Court '49
Pony Express Rider '76
Tarzan Finds a Son '39
The Ten Commandments '56
When Every Day was the Fourth of July '78

Christopher Wild
Knights & Emeralds '87

Jack Wild
Melody '71
Oliver! '68
Robin Hood: Prince of Thieves '91

Cornel Wilde
The Fifth Musketeer '79
The Greatest Show on Earth '52

Billy Wilder▶
The Front Page '74
Sabrina '54

Gene Wilder
The Adventures of Sherlock Holmes' Smarter Brother '78
The Little Prince '74
The Silver Streak '76
Thursday's Game '74
Willy Wonka & the Chocolate Factory '71
Young Frankenstein '74

Gene Wilder▶
The Adventures of Sherlock Holmes' Smarter Brother '78

Webb Wilder
The Thing Called Love '93

Michael Wilding
Stage Fright '50
Under Capricorn '49

John Wildman
American Boyfriends '89
My American Cousin '85

Kathleen Wilhoite
Getting Even with Dad '94
Lorenzo's Oil '92

Robert J. Wilke
High Noon '52
20,000 Leagues Under the Sea '54

Fred Willard
Lots of Luck '85
Moving Violations '85
Roxanne '87
Salem's Lot '79

Warren William
The Man in the Iron Mask '39

Adam Williams
North by Northwest '59

Anson Williams▶
Dream Date '93

Barbara Williams
Oh, What a Night '92

Bill Williams
Flight of the Grey Wolf '76

Billy Dee Williams
Batman '89
Bingo Long Traveling All-Stars & Motor Kings '76
Brian's Song '71
The Empire Strikes Back '80
Marvin & Tige '84
Return of the Jedi '83

Carlton Williams
Crooklyn '94

Cindy Williams
American Graffiti '73
Bingo '91
More American Graffiti '79
Spaceship '81

Clarence Williams III
The House of Dies Drear '88
My Heroes Have Always Been Cowboys '91

Dick Anthony Williams
Edward Scissorhands '90

Esther Williams
Andy Hardy's Double Life '42
That's Entertainment '74

Guinn Williams
Mr. Wise Guy '42

Guy Williams
The Prince and the Pauper '62
The Secret of El Zorro '57
The Sign of Zorro '60
Zorro, Vol. 1 '58

Jacqueline Williams
Love Your Mama '89

JoBeth Williams
American Dreamer '84
Desert Bloom '86
Dutch '91
Kramer vs. Kramer '79
Poltergeist '82
Poltergeist 2: The Other Side '86
Stop! or My Mom Will Shoot '92

John Williams
Dear Brigitte '65
Dial "M" for Murder '54
Sabrina '54
To Catch a Thief '55

Kimberly Williams
Father of the Bride '91
Indian Summer '93

Michael Williams
Educating Rita '83

Paul Williams
Battle for the Planet of the Apes '73
The Cheap Detective '78
Frog '89
Frogs! '90s
Muppet Revue '85
The Night They Saved Christmas '87
Smokey and the Bandit '77
Smokey and the Bandit, Part 2 '80
Smokey and the Bandit, Part 3 '83

Paul Williams▶
The Black Planet '82

Rhys Williams
The Corn is Green '45
How Green was My Valley '41

Richard Williams▶
Raggedy Ann and Andy: A Musical Adventure '77

Robin Williams
The Best of Times '86
Club Paradise '86
Dead Poets Society '89
Hook '91
Mrs. Doubtfire '93
Popeye '80
Toys '92

Samm-Art Williams
The Adventures of Huckleberry Finn '85

Scot Williams
Backbeat '94

Treat Williams
Smooth Talk '85

Vanessa Williams
The Kid Who Loved Christmas '90

Clayton Williamson
Clowning Around '92
Clowning Around 2 '93

Fred Williamson
Adios Amigo '75
M*A*S*H '70

Fred Williamson▶
Adios Amigo '75

Nicol Williamson
The Cheap Detective '78**

Return to Oz '85

Mykelti Willimson
Forrest Gump '94

Noble Willingham
City Slickers '91
City Slickers 2: The Legend
  of Curly's Gold '94
Pastime '91

Bruce Willis
Death Becomes Her '92
North '94

Katherine Willis
Little Heroes '91

Norman Willis
Tim Tyler's Luck '37

Susan Willis
What About Bob? '91

Chill Wills
Francis Joins the WACs '54
Giant '56
Tarzan's New York
  Adventure '42
The Yearling '46

Maury Wills
The Sandlot '93

Douglas Wilmer
The Adventures of Sherlock
  Holmes' Smarter Brother
  '78
Golden Voyage of Sinbad
  '73

Brigitte Wilson
Last Action Hero '93

Chandra Wilson
Philadelphia '93

Daniel Wilson
Wait Until Spring, Bandini
  '90

**Don "The Dragon"
  Wilson**
Magic Kid '92

Dooley Wilson
Casablanca '42

Earl Wilson
Beach Blanket Bingo '65

Elizabeth Wilson
The Addams Family '91
Conspiracy of Love '87
Regarding Henry '91
Skylark '93

Flip Wilson
Cancel My Reservation '72
The Fish that Saved
  Pittsburgh '79

Hugh Wilson▶
Police Academy '84

Jim Wilson
Charlie, the Lonesome
  Cougar '67

John D. Wilson▶
Shinbone Alley '70

Lois Wilson
Bright Eyes '34

Mara Wilson
Mrs. Doubtfire '93

Marie Wilson
Fabulous Joe '47
March of the Wooden
  Soldiers '34

Mary Louise Wilson
The Adventures of Huck
  Finn '93
Green Card '90

Michael Wilson
Nutcase '83

Paul Wilson
My Best Friend Is a
  Vampire '88

Pee Wee Wilson
Young Einstein '89

Rita Wilson
Sleepless in Seattle '93

Sandy Wilson▶
American Boyfriends '89
My American Cousin '85

Scott Wilson
The Right Stuff '83

Stuart Wilson
The Age of Innocence '93
Teenage Mutant Ninja
  Turtles 3 '93

Teddy Wilson
The Mighty Pawns '87

Thomas F. Wilson
Back to the Future '85
Back to the Future, Part 2
  '89
Back to the Future, Part 3
  '90

Tom Wilson
Camp Nowhere '94

Trey Wilson
Miss Firecracker '89

Simon Wincer▶
D.A.R.Y.L. '85
Free Willy '93
The Girl Who Spelled
  Freedom '86
Lightning Jack '94
Phar Lap '84
Quigley Down Under '90

Michael Wincott
The Crow '93
1492: Conquest of
  Paradise '92
Robin Hood: Prince of
  Thieves '91
The Three Musketeers '93
Wild Horse Hank '79

William Windom
Back to Hannibal: The
  Further Adventures of
  Tom Sawyer and
  Huckleberry Finn '90
Dennis the Menace:
  Dinosaur Hunter '87
Escape from the Planet of
  the Apes '71
She's Having a Baby '88
Sommersby '93
To Kill a Mockingbird '62

Marie Windsor
Cahill: United States
  Marshal '73
Salem's Lot '79
Smart Alecks '42

Bretaigne Windust▶
The Pied Piper of Hamelin
  '57

Harry Winer▶
SpaceCamp '86

Paul Winfield
Back to Hannibal: The
  Further Adventures of
  Tom Sawyer and
  Huckleberry Finn '90
Big Shots '87
Carbon Copy '81
Conrack '74
Dennis the Menace '93
The Greatest '77
A Hero Ain't Nothin' But a
  Sandwich '78
Huckleberry Finn '74
The Mighty Pawns '87
Sounder '72
Star Trek 2: The Wrath of
  Khan '82
The Terminator '84

Debra Winger
French Postcards '79
Leap of Faith '92
Shadowlands '93
Terms of Endearment '83

Henry Winkler
An American Christmas
  Carol '79
The Lords of Flatbush '74

Henry Winkler▶
Cop and a Half '93
A Smoky Mountain
  Christmas '86

Charles Winninger
Babes in Arms '39
State Fair '45

Mare Winningham
Eye on the Sparrow '91
Turner and Hooch '89
A Winner Never Quits '86

George Winslow
Monkey Business '52

Michael Winslow
Police Academy '84
Police Academy 2: Their
  First Assignment '85
Police Academy 3: Back in
  Training '86
Police Academy 4: Citizens
  on Patrol '87
Police Academy 5:
  Assignment Miami Beach
  '88
Police Academy 6: City
  Under Siege '89
Spaceballs '87

Dennis Winston
The Adventures of Baron
  Munchausen '89

Hattie Winston
Clara's Heart '88

Leslie Winston
The Waltons: The
  Children's Carol '80

Alex Winter
Bill & Ted's Bogus Journey
  '91
Bill & Ted's Excellent
  Adventure '89
Freaked '93

Alex Winter▶
Freaked '93

Vincent Winter
Almost Angels '62
The Horse Without a Head
  '63

David Winters▶
Thrashin' '86

Deborah Winters
Kotch '71

Jonathan Winters
The Fish that Saved
  Pittsburgh '79
The Flintstones '94
The Longshot '86
The Shadow '94

Shelley Winters
Pete's Dragon '77
The Poseidon Adventure
  '72
Purple People Eater '88

Estelle Winwood
Darby O'Gill & the Little
  People '59
The Magic Sword '62

Billy Wirth
The Lost Boys '87

Jonathan Wise
Three O'Clock High '87

Kirk Wise▶
Beauty and the Beast '91

Ray Wise
The Journey of Natty
  Gann '85
Robocop '87
Swamp Thing '82

Robert Wise▶
The Andromeda Strain '71
Audrey Rose '77
The Sound of Music '65
Star Trek: The Motion
  Picture '80
West Side Story '61

Carol Wiseman▶
The Little Princess '87

Joseph Wiseman
Dr. No '62

Googie Withers
The Lady Vanishes '38

Grant Withers
Fighting Marines '36
Let's Sing Again '36
Radio Patrol '37
Tailspin Tommy '34

Jane Withers
Bright Eyes '34
Giant '56

Cora Witherspoon
Just Around the Corner '38

Reese Witherspoon
A Far Off Place '93
Jack the Bear '93
The Man in the Moon '91

William Witney▶
The Adventures of Captain
  Marvel '41
Adventures of Red Ryder
  '40
The Crimson Ghost '46
Daredevils of the Red
  Circle '38
Dick Tracy Returns '38
Dick Tracy vs. Crime Inc.
  '41
Fighting Devil Dogs '38
G-Men vs. the Black
  Dragon '43
Hawk of the Wilderness
  '38
Mysterious Doctor Satan
  '40

Nyoka and the Tigermen
  '42
Spy Smasher '42
Zorro Rides Again '37
Zorro's Fighting Legion '39

Kathryn Witt
Philadelphia '93

Meg Wittner
Born Yesterday '93

Damian Woetzel
George Balanchine's The
  Nutcracker '93

Fred Wolf▶
Little Rascals Christmas
  Special '79
The Point '71

Hillary Wolf
Big Girls Don't Cry. .
  .They Get Even '92
Home Alone 2: Lost in
  New York '92

Kelly Wolf
A Day in October '92
Great Love Experiment '84

Wolfman Jack
American Graffiti '73

Stevie Wonder
Bikini Beach '64
Muscle Beach Party '64

B.D. Wong
Father of the Bride '91
The Freshman '90
Jurassic Park '93
Mystery Date '91

Russell Wong
The Joy Luck Club '93

Victor Wong
Big Trouble in Little China
  '86
The Golden Child '86
The Joy Luck Club '93
3 Ninjas '92
3 Ninjas Kick Back '94

Clive Wood
Treasure Island '89

Elijah Wood
The Adventures of Huck
  Finn '93
Avalon '90
Forever Young '92
The Good Son '93
North '94
Paradise '91
Radio Flyer '92

G. Wood
M*A*S*H '70

John Wood
Ladyhawke '85
The Purple Rose of Cairo
  '85
Shadowlands '93
War Games '83

Lana Wood
Captain America 2: Death
  Too Soon '79
Diamonds are Forever '71
Justin Morgan Had a
  Horse '81

Natalie Wood
Great Race '65
Miracle on 34th Street '47
Rebel Without a Cause '55
West Side Story '61

Peggy Wood
The Sound of Music '65

Robert Wood
White Fang and the
Hunter '85

Sam Wood▶
A Day at the Races '37
A Night at the Opera '35

Alfre Woodard
Blue Chips '94
Bopha! '93
Crooklyn '94
Cross Creek '83
Heart and Souls '93
Miss Firecracker '89
Rich in Love '93
Scrooged '88
Words by Heart '84

Largo Woodruff
Bill '81
Bill: On His Own '83

Aubrey Woods
Willy Wonka & the
Chocolate Factory '71

Donald Woods
13 Ghosts '60

Harry Woods
Monkey Business '31
Winners of the West '40

James Woods
Cat's Eye '85
Chaplin '92
Immediate Family '89
Straight Talk '92
The Way We Were '73

Kevin Jamal Woods
The Little Rascals '94

Kate Woodville
Computer Wizard '77
Where's Willie? '77

John Woodvine
Dragonworld '94

Edward Woodward
Merlin and the Sword '85

Joanne Woodward
A Christmas to Remember
'78
The Effect of Gamma Rays
on Man-in-the-Moon
Marigolds '73
Harry & Son '84
Mr. & Mrs. Bridge '91
Philadelphia '93

Morgan Woodward
Girls Just Want to Have
Fun '85
Running Wild '73

Susan Wooldridge
Hope and Glory '87

Sheb Wooley
High Noon '52
Hoosiers '86

Monty Woolley
Since You Went Away '44

Tom Wopat
Christmas Comes to Willow
Creek '87

Jimmy Workman
The Addams Family '91
Addams Family Values '93

Mary Woronov
Night of the Comet '84
Rock 'n' Roll High School
'79
Rock 'n' Roll High School
Forever '91

Constance Worth
G-Men vs. the Black
Dragon '43

Irene Worth
Lost in Yonkers '93

Adam Worton
Baby's Day Out '94

Jacob Worton
Baby's Day Out '94

Fay Wray
King Kong '33
Tammy and the Bachelor
'57

Amy Wright
Breaking Away '79
Crossing Delancey '88
Girlfriends '78
Miss Firecracker '89
Off Beat '86

Mack V. Wright▶
Sea Hound '47

Max Wright
Konrad '85

N'Bushe Wright
Zebrahead '92

Robin Wright
Forrest Gump '94
The Playboys '92
The Princess Bride '87
Toys '92

Steven Wright
Desperately Seeking Susan
'85

Teresa Wright
Bill: On His Own '83
Escapade in Japan '57
The Fig Tree '87
Shadow of a Doubt '43
Somewhere in Time '80

Thomas J. Wright▶
Highlander: The Gathering
'93
No Holds Barred '89

Tom Wright
Weekend at Bernie's 2 '93

Whittni Wright
I'll Do Anything '93

Donald Wrye▶
Ice Castles '79

Vivian Wu
The Joy Luck Club '93
Teenage Mutant Ninja
Turtles 3 '93

Robert Wuhl
Batman '89
Flashdance '83

Kari Wuhrer
Beastmaster 2: Through
the Portal of Time '91

Jane Wyatt
The Adventures of Tom
Sawyer '73

Margaret Wycherly
The Yearling '46

Link Wyler
Grizzly Adams: The Legend
Continues '90

William Wyler▶
Friendly Persuasion '56
Funny Girl '68
Roman Holiday '53

Jane Wyman
Pollyanna '60
Stage Fright '50
The Yearling '46

John Wyman
For Your Eyes Only '81

George Wyner
The Bad News Bears Go
to Japan '78
Spaceballs '87

Ed Wynn
The Absent-Minded
Professor '61
Babes in Toyland '61
Cinderfella '60
Dear Brigitte '65
The Gnome-Mobile '67
Mary Poppins '64
Those Calloways '65

Keenan Wynn
The Absent-Minded
Professor '61
The Belle of New York '52
Bikini Beach '64
Cancel My Reservation '72
The Capture of Grizzly
Adams '82
Coach '78
Finian's Rainbow '68
Great Race '65
He is My Brother '75
Herbie Rides Again '74
Hyper-Sapien: People from
Another Star '86
Once Upon a Time in the
West '68
The Shaggy D.A. '76
Since You Went Away '44
Smith! '69
Snowball Express '72
Son of Flubber '63
The Three Musketeers '48

Greg Wynne
Mystery Mansion '83

Jim Wynorski▶
Munchie '92
The Return of Swamp
Thing '89

Amanda Wyss
Better Off Dead '85
Fast Times at Ridgemont
High '82

Yossi Yadin
Lies My Father Told Me
'75

Jeff Yagher
Shag: The Movie '89

So Yamamura
Gung Ho '85

Akira Yamauchi
Godzilla vs. the Smog
Monster '72

Jean Yarborough▶
Jack & the Beanstalk '52

Celeste Yarnall
Born Yesterday '93

Lorene Yarnell
Spaceballs '87

Trever Yarrish
Spirit of the Eagle '90

Amy Yasbeck
The Mask '94
Problem Child '90
Problem Child 2 '91
Robin Hood: Men in Tights
'93

Cassie Yates
Father Figure '80
Who'll Save Our Children?
'82

Marjorie Yates
The Long Day Closes '92

Peter Yates▶
Breaking Away '79
Krull '83
Year of the Comet '92

Biff Yeager
Girls Just Want to Have
Fun '85

John Yesno
King of the Grizzlies '69

Don Yesso
Hero '92

Malik Yoba
Cool Runnings '93

Erica Yohn
Corrina, Corrina '94

Jeff York
Davy Crockett and the
River Pirates '56
Old Yeller '57
Savage Sam '63
Westward Ho, the
Wagons! '56
The Yearling '46

Kathleen York
Wild Hearts Can't Be
Broken '91

Marty York
The Sandlot '93

Michael York
The Four Musketeers '75
Island of Dr. Moreau '77
The Return of the
Musketeers '89
Romeo and Juliet '68
Three Musketeers '74

Susannah York
Battle of Britain '69
Diamond's Edge '88
The Land of Faraway '87
A Man for All Seasons '66
Superman 1: The Movie
'78
Superman 2 '80

Bud Yorkin▶
Arthur 2: On the Rocks '88

Hiroaki Yoshida▶
Twilight of the
Cockroaches '90

Alan Young
Androcles and the Lion '52
Beverly Hills Cop 3 '94

Burt Young
Back to School '86
Beverly Hills Brats '89
Diving In '90

**Harry & Walter Go to
New York '76
Rocky '76
Rocky 2 '79
Rocky 3 '82
Rocky 4 '85
Rocky 5 '90
A Summer to Remember
'84
Wait Until Spring, Bandini
'90

Carleton Young
20,000 Leagues Under the
Sea '54

Chris Young
Book of Love '91
December '91
The Great Outdoors '88
P.C.U. '94

Dey Young
Rock 'n' Roll High School
'79
Strange Invaders '83

Gig Young
The Three Musketeers '48

Harold Young▶
Little Tough Guys '38

Loretta Young
The Farmer's Daughter '47

Ric Young
Dragon: The Bruce Lee
Story '93

Robert Young
The Canterville Ghost '44
Conspiracy of Love '87
Journey for Margaret '42
Stowaway '36

Robert Young▶
The Worst Witch '86

Robert M. Young▶
Dominick & Eugene '88
Rich Kids '79
Talent for the Game '91

Roger Young▶
Geronimo '93
Two of a Kind '82

Roland Young
David Copperfield '35
The Philadelphia Story '40
Topper '37
Topper Returns '41
Topper Takes a Trip '39

Sean Young
Ace Ventura: Pet Detective
'93
Baby. . .Secret of the Lost
Legend '85
Fatal Instinct '93
Once Upon a Crime '92

Terence Young▶
Dr. No '62
From Russia with Love '63
Thunderball '65
When Wolves Cry '69

Barrie Youngfellow
It Came Upon a Midnight
Clear '84

Gail Youngs
Hockey Night '84

Jim Youngs
Hot Shot '86

Category Index

The **CATEGORY INDEX** contains 300 genre, sub-genre, thematic, or significant scene classifications, ranging from the very general (such as drama) to the fairly particular (such as genies). While we've done our best to provide serious subject references, we've also had a bit of fun in the making of the various lists. No one list is inclusive; we're continually reclassifying, adding, and subtracting. We've tried to select categories that would be of interest to children and parents, and in some cases these lists represent only a beginning. *VideoHound* invites readers to join in this sometimes fascinating pastime by sending in new titles for existing categories, as well as suggestions on new categories. With your suggestion, please list at least five movies that could be classified under the new category.

Adapted from a Cartoon
Ace Ventura: Pet Detective
The Addams Family
Addams Family Values▶
The Adventures of Captain Marvel
Adventures of Red Ryder
Adventures of Smilin' Jack
Annie
Baby's Day Out
Batman▶
Batman Returns
The Belles of St. Trinian's▶
Brenda Starr
Captain America
The Crow
Dennis the Menace
Dennis the Menace: Dinosaur Hunter
Dick Tracy
Dick Tracy▶
Dick Tracy vs. Cueball
Dick Tracy's Dilemma
Dr. Strange
Fatty Finn
The Flash
Flash Gordon
The Flintstones
Great St. Trinian's Train Robbery
Howard the Duck
The Incredible Hulk
Little Nemo: Adventures in Slumberland
Little Orphan Annie
The Mask▶
The Pink Panther▶
Prince Valiant
The Pure Hell of St. Trinian's
Regl'ar Fellers
The Return of Swamp Thing
Superman 1: The Movie▶
Superman 2▶
Superman 3
Superman 4: The Quest for Peace

Teenage Mutant Ninja Turtles 1: The Movie
Teenage Mutant Ninja Turtles 2: The Secret of the Ooze
Teenage Mutant Ninja Turtles 3
Tom and Jerry: The Movie

Adapted from the Radio
Renfrew of the Royal Mounted
The Shadow
The War of the Worlds▶

Adapted from TV
The Addams Family
Addams Family Values▶
Batman: Mask of the Phantasm
The Beverly Hillbillies
Bonanza: The Return
Boris and Natasha: The Movie
Car 54, Where Are You?
Coneheads
Cooley High▶
Dennis the Menace
Dragnet
The Flintstones
The Fugitive▶
The Jetsons: The Movie
Lassie
The Left-Handed Gun▶
Maverick
The Naked Gun: From the Files of Police Squad▶
Naked Gun 2 1/2: The Smell of Fear
Naked Gun 33 1/3: The Final Insult
1994 Winter Olympics Highlights Video
Star Trek: The Motion Picture
Star Trek 2: The Wrath of Khan▶

Star Trek 3: The Search for Spock
Star Trek 4: The Voyage Home▶
Star Trek 5: The Final Frontier
Star Trek 6: The Undiscovered Country
Thunderbirds are Go
Wackiest Wagon Train in the West
Wayne's World
Wayne's World 2

Adolescence
see Growing Pains; High School Hijinks; Summer Camp; Teen Tribulations

Africa
see also Apartheid
Africa Screams
African Journey
The African Queen▶
The Air Up There
Allan Quartermain and the Lost City of Gold
Animals Are Beautiful People
Bophal▶
The Bushbaby
Cheetah
Darkest Africa
A Far Off Place
The Flame Trees of Thika▶
The Gods Must Be Crazy▶
The Gods Must Be Crazy 2▶
Hatari!
In the Army Now
The Jewel of the Nile
Jungle Drums of Africa
King Kong▶
Koi and the Kola Nuts
Mighty Joe Young
Really Wild Animals: Swinging Safari
Sarafina!▶
A World Apart▶

African America
Above the Rim
Almos' a Man
Anansi
Bebe's Kids
Bingo Long Traveling All-Stars & Motor Kings▶
Bophal▶
Boyz N the Hood▶
Crooklyn▶
A Dream for Christmas▶
The Ernest Green Story
The Great White Hope
A Hero Ain't Nothin' But a Sandwich▶
House Party▶
House Party 2: The Pajama Jam
House Party 3
Jazz Time Tale
Love Your Mama
Malcolm X▶
Menace II Society▶
The Meteor Man
Piece of the Action
Poetic Justice
Reading Rainbow: Mrs. Katz and Tush
Sarafina!▶
Sounder▶
Stories from the Black Tradition
The Talking Eggs
Words by Heart
Zebrahead▶

AIDS
For Our Children: The Concert
Forrest Gump▶
Philadelphia▶

Airborne
Adventures of Smilin' Jack
Adventures of the Flying Cadets
Airplane!▶
Airplane 2: The Sequel
Airport▶

Airport '75
Airport '77
Alive
Always
Battle of Britain
The Buddy Holly Story▶
Dumbo▶
The Flying Deuces▶
The Great Waldo Pepper▶
Hero▶
The Island at the Top of the World
It Happened at the World's Fair
La Bamba▶
Look Who's Talking Now
The Man with the Golden Gun
Moon Pilot
Reading Rainbow: Bored - Nothing to Do!
The Right Stuff▶
Shadow of the Eagle
Thunderbirds: Countdown to Disaster
Thunderbirds to the Rescue
Top Gun

Airplanes
see Airborne

Aliens— Nasty
see also Aliens—Nice
The Adventures of Buckaroo Banzai Across the Eighth Dimension▶
Battle Beyond the Stars
Battlestar Galactica
Captain Scarlet vs. The Mysterons
Critters
Destroy All Monsters
Doctor Who: An Unearthly Child
Doctor Who and the Daleks
The Empire Strikes Back▶
Godzilla vs. the Cosmic Monster
Gremlins▶

Gremlins 2: The New Batch▶
Invaders from Mars
Invasion of the Body Snatchers▶
Mom and Dad Save the World
Munchies
Radar Men from the Moon
Return of the Jedi▶
Revenge of the Mysterons from Mars
Space Angel, Vol. 1
Star Trek: The Motion Picture
Star Trek 3: The Search for Spock
Star Wars▶
Strange Invaders▶
Super Mario Bros.
Superman 1: The Movie▶
Teen Alien
The War of the Worlds▶
Zombies of the Stratosphere

Aliens—Nice

***see also** Aliens— Nasty*
The Aurora Encounter
*batteries not included
The Cat from Outer Space
Close Encounters of the Third Kind▶
Cocoon▶
Cocoon: The Return
Coneheads
The Cosmic Eye▶
Dr. Seuss' Hoober-Bloob Highway
Doin' Time on Planet Earth
The Empire Strikes Back▶
Enemy Mine
Escape to Witch Mountain▶
E.T.: The Extra-Terrestrial▶
The Ewok Adventure
The Ewoks: Battle for Endor
Fire in the Sky
Flight of the Navigator▶
Gremlins▶
Gremlins 2: The New Batch▶
Howard the Duck
Hyper-Sapien: People from Another Star
Labyrinth▶
The Last Starfighter
Mac and Me
Martians Go Home!
Munchie
My Stepmother Is an Alien
Nukie
Pajama Party
Purple People Eater
Return of the Jedi▶
Simon
Spaced Invaders
Star Trek 3: The Search for Spock
Star Trek 4: The Voyage Home▶
Star Wars▶
Starman▶
Suburban Commando
Super Mario Bros.
Supergirl
Superman 1: The Movie▶
Superman 2▶
Superman 3
Superman 4: The Quest for Peace
Teenage Mutant Ninja Turtles 2: The Secret of the Ooze
Wee Wendy

Widget of the Jungle

Amazing Adventures

***see also** Disaster Strikes!; Funny Adventures; Martial Arts; Swashbucklers*
Across the Great Divide
The Adventures of Captain Marvel
The Adventures of Frank and Jesse James
The Adventures of Frontier Fremont
The Adventures of Huck Finn
The Adventures of Huckleberry Finn
The Adventures of Huckleberry Finn▶
The Adventures of Milo & Otis▶
Adventures of Red Ryder
The Adventures of Robin Hood▶
Adventures of Smilin' Jack
The Adventures of SuperTed
The Adventures of the Wilderness Family
The Adventures of Tom Sawyer
The Adventures of Ultraman
Aladdin and the Wonderful Lamp
Ali Baba and the Forty Thieves
Allan Quartermain and the Lost City of Gold
Aloha, Bobby and Rose
The Amazing Spider-Man
Antarctica
Around the World in 80 Days▶
Asterix: Asterix the Gaul
Atom Man vs. Superman
Barney & the Backyard Gang
Batman▶
Batman Returns
The Belstone Fox
Benji the Hunted
The Black Arrow
The Black Stallion▶
The Black Stallion Returns
The Black Widow
Blood Brothers
Blue Fin
BMX Bandits
The Bounty▶
Boy of Two Worlds
Brothers Lionheart
The Bulldozer Brigade
Burn 'Em Up Barnes
The Bushbaby
Call of the Wild
Camel Boy
Candleshoe
Cannonball
Captain America
Captain America 2: Death Too Soon
Captain Blood▶
Captain Harlock, Vol. 1
Captain Planet & the Planeteers: A Hero for Earth
The Cat
Catch Me. . .If You Can
Challenge To Be Free
Challenge to White Fang
Charlie and the Great Balloon Chase
Charlie, the Lonesome Cougar
Cheetah

Child of Glass
Clarence, the Cross-eyed Lion
Cloak & Dagger
Conan the Barbarian▶
Conan the Destroyer
Cool As Ice
The Count of Monte Cristo
Courage Mountain
Courage of Black Beauty
The Crimson Ghost
Crusoe▶
A Cry in the Wild▶
Crystalstone
Danger Mouse, Vol. 1
Daredevils of the Red Circle
Daring Dobermans
Darkest Africa
Davy Crockett and the River Pirates
Davy Crockett, King of the Wild Frontier▶
The Day of the Dolphin
Death of the Incredible Hulk
Diamonds are Forever▶
Dick Deadeye
Dick Tracy▶
Dick Tracy, Detective
Dick Tracy Meets Gruesome
Dick Tracy Returns
Dick Tracy vs. Crime Inc.
Dick Tracy vs. Cueball
Dick Tracy's Dilemma
The Doberman Gang
Doc Savage
Dr. No▶
Dr. Syn, Alias the Scarecrow
Don Winslow of the Coast Guard
Don Winslow of the Navy
Don't Change My World
The Dove
Duncan's World
Edison Twins
Elephant Boy▶
Emil and the Detective
Escapade in Japan
Escape to Witch Mountain▶
F/X 2: The Deadly Art of Illusion
Famous Five Get into Trouble
A Far Off Place
Federal Agents vs. Underworld, Inc.
Fighting Devil Dogs
Fighting Marines
The Fighting Prince of Donegal
The Fire in the Stone
Fish Hawk
The Flash
Flight of Dragons
Flight of the Grey Wolf
Flipper
Flipper's New Adventure
Flipper's Odyssey
For Your Eyes Only▶
From Russia with Love▶
The Fugitive▶
Further Adventures of the Wilderness Family, Part 2
G-Men Never Forget
G-Men vs. the Black Dragon
Gentle Giant
The Ghost of Thomas Kempe
Goin' Coconuts
The Gold Bug

Golden Voyage of Sinbad
The Goonies
Government Agents vs. the Phantom Legion
Great Adventure
The Great Train Robbery▶
The Great Waldo Pepper▶
The Green Hornet
Greenstone
Greystoke: The Legend of Tarzan, Lord of the Apes
Harley
Hatari▶
Hawk of the Wilderness
Hell Hounds of Alaska
Hercules
Hercules 2
Hercules in New York
Hercules Unchained
High Country Calling
Highlander▶
Highlander: The Gathering
Holt of the Secret Service
Homeward Bound: The Incredible Journey▶
Huck and the King of Hearts
The Hunt for Red October▶
Hurricane Express
Ice Station Zebra
If Looks Could Kill
In Search of a Golden Sky
In Search of the Castaways▶
The Incredible Hulk
The Incredible Hulk Returns
The Incredible Journey▶
Indiana Jones and the Last Crusade▶
Indiana Jones and the Temple of Doom▶
Invaders from Mars
The Invisible Monster
Iron Will
The Island at the Top of the World
Island of the Blue Dolphins
Islands
Jack the Giant Killer
Jacob Two: Two Meets the Hooded Fang
Jamaica Inn
Johnny Shiloh
The Journey of Natty Gann▶
Journey to the Center of the Earth
The Jungle Book
Jungle Drums of Africa
Jurassic Park▶
K-9000
The Karate Kid▶
The Karate Kid: Part 2
The Karate Kid: Part 3
Kavik, the Wolf Dog
Kid Colter
Kidnapped
King Kong▶
King Kong
King of the Rocketmen
Lassie: Adventures of Neeka
Lassie, Come Home▶
Lassie: Well of Love
The Last Flight of Noah's Ark
The Last of the Mohicans
Law of the Wild
Legend of Billie Jean
Legend of Lobo
Legend of the Northwest
The Legend of Wolf Mountain

Life & Times of Grizzly Adams
Life on the Mississippi
The Light in the Forest
The Littlest Horse Thieves
Littlest Warrior
Live and Let Die
Lords of Magick
Mad Max: Beyond Thunderdome
The Magic Sword
The Man in the Iron Mask▶
The Man Who Would Be King▶
Mario
The Masked Marvel
Menace on the Mountain
Merlin and the Sword
Moon-Spinners
Mooncussers
Moonraker
Mountain Family Robinson
My Pet Monster, Vol. 1
Mystery Island
Napoleon and Samantha▶
Nate and Hayes
The Navigator▶
Neptune Factor
Never Say Never Again
New Adventures of Zorro, Vol. 1
Night Crossing
Nikki, the Wild Dog of the North▶
No Holds Barred
Nukie
Nyoka and the Tigermen
Octopussy
An Officer and a Duck
On Her Majesty's Secret Service▶
Once a Hero
101 Problems of Hercules
Paco
Papillon▶
Pink Cadillac
Plastic Man
The Polar Bear King
Prince Valiant
The Quest
Radio Patrol
Raft Adventures of Huck & Jim
Raiders of the Lost Ark▶
Rascals and Robbers
The Real McCoy
The Rescue
The Return of Roger Ramjet
Return to Treasure Island, Vol. 1
Revenge of Roger Ramjet
Robin Hood: Prince of Thieves
Robinson Crusoe & the Tiger
Robocop▶
Robocop 2
Robocop 3
The Rocketeer▶
The Rousters
Run, Rebecca, Run
Salty
Savage Sam
Sea Gypsies
Sea Hound
Sea Prince and the Fire Child
The Secret of El Zorro
Secret of the Ice Cave
Sesame Street Presents: Follow That Bird▶
Seven Alone
The Seventh Voyage of Sinbad▶

The Shadow
Shadow of the Eagle
Shadow of the Wolf
Shazam!
Sheena
Shipwrecked
Sidekicks
The Sign of Zorro
The Silver Stallion: King of
the Wild Brumbies
Sinbad and the Eye of the
Tiger▶
Sinbad the Sailor▶
Six Pack
The Skateboard Kid
Smuggler's Cove
Son of Captain Blood
Son of Kong
Son of Zorro
Sourdough
Space Raiders
SpaceCamp
Speed▶
Speed Racer
Spider-Woman
Spiderman
Spiderman: The Deadly
Dust
Spiderman, Vol. 1: Dr.
Doom
Spirit of the Eagle
Spy Smasher▶
The Spy Who Loved Me
Starbird and Sweet William
Starchaser: The Legend of
Orin
The Sting▶
Stingray: Invaders of the
Deep
The Story of 15 Boys
Summerdog
Super Mario Bros.
Supergirl
Superman 1: The Movie▶
Superman 2▶
Superman 3
Superman 4: The Quest for
Peace
Superman & the Mole Men
Swamp Thing
The Swiss Family
Robinson▶
The Sword & the Rose
Tailspin Tommy
A Tale of Two Critters
Tank
Taps
Tarka the Otter
Tarzan and His Mate▶
Tarzan Finds a Son▶
Tarzan, the Ape Man▶
Tarzan's New York
Adventure
Tarzan's Secret Treasure
Techno Police
Ten Who Dared
The Tender Warrior
The Terminator▶
Terminator 2: Judgment
Day▶
Terror in the Jungle
Third Man on the
Mountain
Those Calloways
Thrashin'
Three Musketeers
The Three Musketeers
Three Musketeers
The Three Musketeers
The Three Musketeers: All
for One and One for
All!
Thunderball
Thunderbirds 6
Thunderbirds 2086

Thunderbirds: Countdown
to Disaster
Thunderbirds in Outerspace
Thunderbirds to the Rescue
A Tiger Walks
Tigersharks: Power of the
Shark
Tilt
Tim Tyler's Luck
Toby McTeague
Tom Sawyer▶
Top Gun
Trader Tom of the China
Seas
Trap on Cougar Mountain
Treasure Island
Treasure Island
The Treasure of
Matecumbe
Treasure of the Sierra
Madre▶
The Trial of the Incredible
Hulk
Tut and Tuttle
20,000 Leagues Under the
Sea▶
20,000 Leagues Under the
Sea
Unknown Island
A View to a Kill
The Voyage of the Yes
A Waltz Through the Hills
When the North Wind
Blows
Where the River Runs
Black
Where the Spirit Lives
White Fang▶
White Fang 2: The Myth
of the White Wolf
White Fang and the
Hunter
White Water Summer
Whitewater Sam
Willow
Wonderful World of Puss
'N Boots
Wonderland Cove
World of Hans Christian
Andersen
You Only Live Twice
Young & Free
Young Eagles

Amazing Animals
see also Birds; Cats;
Dinos; King of Beasts
(Dogs); Scary Beasties
The Adventures of Babar
Africa Texas Style
Andre
Animal Farm▶
Animals Are Beautiful
People
Animalympics: Winter
Games
Babar's First Step
Bambi▶
The Barefoot Executive
The Bear▶
The Bears & I
Beastmaster
Beastmaster 2: Through
the Portal of Time
The Belstone Fox
Bless the Beasts and
Children
Bongo
Born Free▶
Bringing Up Baby▶
Bugs Bunny Superstar
Call of the Wild
Charlie, the Lonesome
Cougar
Cheetah

Chip 'n' Dale Rescue
Rangers: Crimebusters
Christian the Lion
The Chronicles of Narnia▶
Clarence, the Cross-eyed
Lion
Courage of the North
A Cry in the Wild▶
Darkest Africa
The Day of the Dolphin
Doctor Doolittle
Dumbo▶
The Electric Horseman
Elephant Boy▶
The Fifth Monkey
Flash, the Teenage Otter
Flight of the Grey Wolf
Flipper
The Fox and the Hound▶
Francis Goes to the Races
Francis Joins the WACs
Francis the Talking Mule▶
Free Willy
Gentle Ben
Gentle Giant
Gift of the Whales
The Glacier Fox
Going Ape!
Going Bananas
The Golden Seal
Gorillas in the Mist▶
The Great Cheese
Conspiracy
The Great Harbor Rescue
The Great Rupert▶
Grizzly Adams: The Legend
Continues
Gus
Harry and the Hendersons
Hatari▶
Hawmps!
High Country Calling
The Hound that Thought
He was a Raccoon
Incident at Hawk's Hill
Island of the Blue Dolphins
Johann's Gift to Christmas
The Jungle Book▶
Jungle Drums of Africa
A Jungle for Joey
King of the Grizzlies
Lassie, Come Home▶
Lassie: The Miracle
Legend of Lobo
Leonard Part 6
The Lion King▶
Living Free
The Marzipan Pig
Matilda
The Misadventures of
Merlin Jones
Monkeys, Go Home!
Monkey's Uncle
Mountain Family Robinson
Mountain Man
Mowgli's Brothers
Napoleon and Samantha▶
Never Cry Wolf▶
Nikki, the Wild Dog of the
North▶
Old MacDonald's Farm
and Other Animal Tales
Once Upon a Forest
Ovide and the Gang
Pippi Longstocking
Planet of the Apes▶
The Polar Bear King
The Pretty Piggies: The
Adventure Begins
Project X▶
Rascal
Reading Rainbow: Perfect
the Pig/Ty's One-Man
Band
Really Wild Animals:
Swinging Safari

Really Wild Animals:
Wonders Down Under
Reddy the Fox
The Rescuers▶
The Rescuers Down Under
Rikki-Tikki-Tavi
Ring of Bright Water▶
Rock-a-Doodle
The Runaways
Sammy, the Way-Out Seal
Seabert: Good Guys Wear
White
Secret of NIMH▶
Sesame Songs: Sing, Hoot
& Howl
Shamu & You: Exploring
the World of Mammals
The Silver Fox and Sam
Davenport
The Silver Streak▶
Speaking of Animals,
Vol. 1
A Summer to Remember
Super Seal
A Tale of Two Critters
Tarka the Otter
The Tender Warrior
Their Only Chance
Those Calloways
The Three Little Pigs
Thumpkin and the Easter
Bunnies
A Tiger Walks
Tomboy & the Champ
The Tortoise and the Hare
Trap on Cougar Mountain
Walk Like a Man
Watership Down▶
Whale of a Tale
When the North Wind
Blows
When the Whales Came
The White Seal
Wind in the Willows,
Vol. 1
Winter Wolf
The Yearling▶
Yogi and the Invasion of
the Space Bears
Yogi and the Magical
Flight of the Spruce
Goose
Yogi's Great Escape
Zebra in the Kitchen

American Indians
see Native America

Amnesia
Clean Slate
Overboard
Regarding Henry▶
Spellbound▶

Amusement Parks
see also Circuses &
Carnivals
Bebe's Kids
Beverly Hills Cop 3
My Life
Strangers on a Train▶

Andy Hardy
Andy Hardy Gets Spring
Fever
Andy Hardy Meets
Debutante
Andy Hardy's Double Life
Andy Hardy's Private
Secretary
Life Begins for Andy
Hardy▶
Love Finds Andy Hardy▶
Love Laughs at Andy
Hardy

Angels
see also Heaven Sent
Always
Angels in the Outfield
Clarence
Date with an Angel
Field of Dreams▶
Heart and Souls
The Heavenly Kid
The Horn Blows at
Midnight▶
It Came Upon a Midnight
Clear
It's a Wonderful Life▶
The Kid with the Broken
Halo
The Littlest Angel
One Magic Christmas
Waiting for the Light
Wings of Desire▶

Animals
see Amazing Animals;
Birds; Cats; Horses; King
of Beasts (Dogs)

Apartheid
see also Africa; Civil
Rights
Bophal▶
The Power of One
Sarafina!▶
A World Apart▶

Asia
see also China
Flower Drum Song
Little Buddha
The Man with the Golden
Gun

At the Movies
Cinema Paradiso▶
Last Action Hero
The Long Day Closes▶
Matinee
The Projectionist▶
The Purple Rose of Cairo▶

Australia
see Down Under

Baby Talk
see also Parenthood
Addams Family Values▶
And Baby Makes Six
Baby Boom
Baby's Day Out
Enemy Mine
Eye on the Sparrow
Father's Little Dividend▶
For Keeps
Funny Girl▶
Immediate Family
In Search of a Golden Sky
Little Man Tate▶
Look Who's Talking▶
Look Who's Talking, Too
My Life
Parenthood▶
Penny Serenade▶
Problem Child 2
Rumpelstiltskin
She's Having a Baby
The Snapper▶
Table for Five
The Tender Years
The Terminator▶
Three Men and a Baby▶
Three Men and a Cradle▶

Babysitters
see also Baby Talk;
Parenthood
Addams Family Values▶

Adventures in Babysitting
Bebe's Kids
Look Who's Talking▶
Mr. Nanny
Uncle Buck

Ballet
see also Gotta Dance!
Brain Donors
George Balanchine's The
    Nutcracker
The Red Shoes▶
Shall We Dance▶
Tales of Beatrix Potter▶
The Tales of Hoffman

Ballooning
Around the World in 80
    Days▶
Around the World in 80
    Days
Charlie and the Great
    Balloon Chase
Mysterious Island▶
Night Crossing
Olly Olly Oxen Free
The Red Balloon▶

Baseball
Amazing Grace & Chuck
Angels in the Outfield
The Babe
The Bad News Bears▶
The Bad News Bears Go
    to Japan
The Bad News Bears in
    Breaking Training
Bang the Drum Slowly▶
Big Mo
Bingo Long Traveling All-
    Stars & Motor Kings▶
Blue Skies Again
Brewster's Millions
Casey at the Bat
Chasing Dreams
Comeback Kid
Field of Dreams▶
How to Play Baseball
The Kid from Left Field
A League of Their Own▶
Little Big League
Major League
Major League 2
Mr. Baseball
Mr. Destiny
The Natural▶
Pastime▶
Rookie of the Year
The Sandlot▶
Talent for the Game
Tiger Town
Trading Hearts
Wait Until Spring, Bandini
A Winner Never Quits

Basketball
Above the Rim
The Absent-Minded
    Professor▶
The Air Up There
Blue Chips
Coach
Fast Break
The Fish that Saved
    Pittsburgh
Hoosiers▶
One on One
Pistol: The Birth of a
    Legend
Reading Rainbow: Dinosaur
    Bob and His Adventures
    with the Family Lazardo
Teen Wolf

Beach Blanket Bingo
see also Surfing
Back to the Beach
Beach Blanket Bingo▶
Beach Party
Bikini Beach
How to Stuff a Wild Bikini
Muscle Beach Party
Pajama Party
Shag: The Movie▶

Bedtime Stories
*see also Fairy Tales;
    Storytelling*
Abel's Island
Adventures in Dinosaurland
Adventures of Buster the
    Bear
The Adventures of Curious
    George
The Adventures of Mark
    Twain▶
The Adventures of Oliver
    Twist
The Adventures of Peter
    Cottontail
The Adventures of Peter
    Cottontail and His
    Friends of the Green
    Forest
Adventures of Reddy the
    Fox
The Adventures of the
    Little Prince
Adventures of the Little
    Prince
The Adventures of Tin Tin
Aesop and His Friends
Aesop's Fables
Aesop's Fables: The Boy
    Who Cried Wolf/The
    Wolf and Lamb
Aesop's Fables, Vol. 1:
    The Hen with the
    Golden Egg
Alice in Wonderland in
    Paris
All New Adventures of
    Tom Sawyer: Mischief on
    the Mississippi
Anansi
Animal Farm▶
Around the World in 80
    Days
Babar and Father
    Christmas
Babar Comes to America
Babar: Monkey Business
Babar Returns
Babar the Elephant Comes
    to America
Babar the Little Elephant
Babar: The Movie
Babar's First Step
Babar's Triumph
The Baby-Sitter's Club
Berenstain Bears' Comic
    Valentine
Berenstain Bears' Easter
    Surprise
Berenstain Bears Meet Big
    Paw
Billy Possum
The Black Tulip
Bob the Quail
The Bollo Caper
The Boy Who Drew Cats
Brer Rabbit Tales
Bunnicula: Vampire Rabbit
Chatterer the Squirrel
Classic Fairy Tales
The Classic Tales
    Collection
A Connecticut Yankee in
    King Arthur's Court

The Cricket in Times
    Square
The Dancing Frog
Davey and Goliath
David and Goliath
David the Gnome
Davy Crockett
The Day Jimmy's Boa Ate
    the Wash and Other
    Stories
Dick Deadeye
Dorothy in the Land of Oz
The Ezra Jack Keats
    Library
Faeries
Flight of Dragons
Frog and Toad are Friends
The Grasshopper and the
    Ants
Great Bible Stories:
    Abraham
Gulliver's Travels
Hanna-Barbera Storybook
    Classics
Harold and the Purple
    Crayon and Other
    Harold Stories
The Hobbit▶
How to Eat Fried Worms
The Hunchback of Notre
    Dame
Jack & the Beanstalk
Jack and the Beanstalk
Joey Runs Away and
    Other Stories
Jonah and the Whale
Journey Back to Oz
Jungle Book: Mowgli
    Comes to the Jungle
Kidnapped
King Arthur & the Knights
    of the Round Table,
    Vol. 1
Koi and the Kola Nuts
The Last Unicorn
The Legend of Hiawatha
The Legend of Manxmouse
Les Miserables
The Lion, the Witch and
    the Wardrobe▶
The Little Engine That
    Could
The Little House
The Little Match Girl
The Little Prince
Little Sister Rabbit
Little Women▶
Little Women
Little Women Series
The Lord of the Rings
Madeline
Marvelous Land of Oz
Maurice Sendak Library
Maurice Sendak's Really
    Rosie
Max's Chocolate Chicken
    and Other Stories for
    Young Children
Mike Mulligan and His
    Steam Shovel
More Stories for the Very
    Young
Mowgli's Brothers
Nursery Rhymes
Paddington Bear
Paddington Goes to the
    Movies
The Paper Bag Princess
Peachboy
Peter and the Wolf
Peter Pan▶
Phantom of the Opera
Phantom Tollbooth▶
The Pickwick Papers
The Pigs' Wedding and
    Other Stories

The Prince and the
    Pauper▶
The Prince and the Pauper
Princess and the Goblin
The Princess and the
    Goblin
Reading Rainbow: A Chair
    for My Mother
Reading Rainbow: Abiyoyo
Reading Rainbow: Alistair
    in Outer Space
Reading Rainbow: Alistair's
    Time Machine
Reading Rainbow: Animal
    Cafe
Reading Rainbow: Arthur's
    Eyes
Reading Rainbow: Barn
    Dance!
Reading Rainbow: Bea and
    Mr. Jones
Reading Rainbow: Berlioz
    the Bear
Reading Rainbow: Best
    Friends
Reading Rainbow: Bored -
    Nothing to Do!
Reading Rainbow: Brush
Reading Rainbow: Bugs
Reading Rainbow: Chickens
    Aren't the Only Ones
Reading Rainbow: Come a
    Tide
Reading Rainbow: Desert
    Giant: The World of the
    Saguaro Cactus
Reading Rainbow: Digging
    Up Dinosaurs
Reading Rainbow: Dinosaur
    Bob and His Adventures
    with the Family Lazardo
Reading Rainbow: Dive to
    the Coral Reef/The
    Magic School Bus Inside
    the Earth
Reading Rainbow: Duncan
    and Delores
Reading Rainbow: Feelings
Reading Rainbow: Florence
    and Eric Take the Cake
Reading Rainbow: Fox on
    the Job
Reading Rainbow:
    Galimoto
Reading Rainbow: Germs
    Make Me Sick!
Reading Rainbow: Gregory
    the Terrible Eater/Gila
    Monsters Meet You at
    the Airport
Reading Rainbow: Hot-Air
    Henry
Reading Rainbow:
    Humphrey the Lost
    Whale: A True Story
Reading Rainbow:
    Imogene's Antlers
Reading Rainbow: Jack,
    the Seal and the Sea
Reading Rainbow: Kate
    Shelley and the Midnight
    Express
Reading Rainbow: Keep
    the Lights Burning, Abbie
Reading Rainbow: Knots
    on a Counting Rope
Reading Rainbow: Liang
    and the Magic
    Paintbrush
Reading Rainbow: Little
    Nino's Pizzeria
Reading Rainbow: Louis the
    Fish
Reading Rainbow: Ludlow
    Laughs

Reading Rainbow: Mama
    Don't Allow
Reading Rainbow:
    Meanwhile Back at the
    Ranch
Reading Rainbow: Miss
    Nelson is Back
Reading Rainbow: Mrs.
    Katz and Tush
Reading Rainbow: Mufaro's
    Beautiful Daughters
Reading Rainbow:
    Mummies Made in Egypt/
    Bringing the Rain to
    Kapiti Plain
Reading Rainbow: My Little
    Island
Reading Rainbow: OPT: An
    Illusionary Tale/A Three
    Hat Day
Reading Rainbow: Ox-Cart
    Man
Reading Rainbow: Paul
    Bunyan
Reading Rainbow: Perfect
    the Pig/Ty's One-Man
    Band
Reading Rainbow:
    Raccoons and Ripe Corn
Reading Rainbow:
    Rechenka's Eggs
Reading Rainbow:
    Rumplestiltskin/Snowy
    Day: Stories and Poems
Reading Rainbow: Sam the
    Sea Cow
Reading Rainbow:
    Seashore Surprises
Reading Rainbow: Silent
    Lotus
Reading Rainbow: Simon's
    Book
Reading Rainbow: Sophie
    and Lou
Reading Rainbow: Space
    Case
Reading Rainbow: Sports
    Pages
Reading Rainbow: Stay
    Away from the Junkyard!
Reading Rainbow: Sunken
    Treasure
Reading Rainbow: Tar
    Beach
Reading Rainbow: The
    Bicycle Man/The
    Adventures of Taxi Dog
Reading Rainbow: The
    Bionic Bunny Show
Reading Rainbow: The Day
    Jimmy's Boa Ate the
    Wash
Reading Rainbow: The Gift
    of the Sacred Dog
Reading Rainbow: The
    Lady with the Ship on
    Her Head
Reading Rainbow: The
    Legend of the Indian
    Paintbrush/The Lifecycle
    of the Honeybee
Reading Rainbow: The Milk
    Makers
Reading Rainbow: The
    Paper Crane
Reading Rainbow: The
    Patchwork Quilt
Reading Rainbow: The
    Piggy in the Puddle
Reading Rainbow: The
    Purple Coat
Reading Rainbow: The
    Robbery at the Diamond
    Dog Diner
Reading Rainbow: The
    Runaway Duck

Reading Rainbow: The Wall
Reading Rainbow: Three by the Sea
Reading Rainbow: Three Days on a River in a Red Canoe
Reading Rainbow: Through Moon and Stars and Night Skies
Reading Rainbow: Tight Times
Reading Rainbow: Tooth-Gnasher Superflash
Reading Rainbow: Tortoise & the Hare/Hill of Fire
Reading Rainbow: Watch the Stars Come Out
Return to Oz
Richard Scarry's Best ABC Video Ever!
Richard Scarry's Best Busy People Video Ever
Rikki-Tikki-Tavi
Rip Van Winkle
Robinson Crusoe
Shari Lewis & Lamb Chop: One Minute Bible Stories, New Testament
Shari Lewis: Don't Wake Your Mom
Shirley Temple Storybook Theater
Stories and Fables, Vol. 1
Stories to Remember: Baby's Morningtime
Stories to Remember: Baby's Nursery Rhymes
Stories to Remember: Baby's Storytime
Stories to Remember: Beauty and the Beast
Stories to Remember: Noah's Ark
Stories to Remember: Pegasus
Stories to Remember: The Wild Swans
The Tender Tale of Cinderella Penguin
Tommy Tricker & the Stamp Traveller
The Tortoise and the Hare
The Truth About Mother Goose
20,000 Leagues Under the Sea
Velveteen Rabbit
The Velveteen Rabbit
The Willies
Wind in the Willows, Vol. 1
The Wizard of Oz
The Wizard of Oz: Danger in a Strange Land
Wonderful Wizard of Oz
World of Hans Christian Andersen
A World of Stories with Katharine Hepburn

Bereavement
The Addams Family
Always
Audrey Rose
Babar's First Step
Beetlejuice▶
Bill & Ted's Bogus Journey
Black Magic
Breaking the Rules
The Canterville Ghost
Carousel▶
Chances Are▶
A Christmas Carol▶
A Christmas Carol
The Crow

Da
Death of a Goldfish
The Devil & Max Devlin
Earthling
The Fig Tree
Four Weddings and a Funeral▶
Ghost▶
Heart and Souls
The Heavenly Kid
Hocus Pocus
Homeward Bound
Into the West▶
It Came Upon a Midnight Clear
It's a Wonderful Life▶
The Kid with the Broken Halo
Kiss Me Goodbye
The Lady in White▶
Mannequin
My Girl
My Girl 2
My Life
Oh, Heavenly Dog!
Only the Lonely
The Peanut Butter Solution▶
Poltergeist▶
Poltergeist 2: The Other Side
Poltergeist 3
Promises in the Dark
Scrooge
Scrooged▶
Sleepless in Seattle▶
Somewhere Tomorrow
Stand By Me▶
Star Trek 3: The Search for Spock
Terms of Endearment▶
13 Ghosts
Topper▶
Topper Returns▶
Topper Takes a Trip▶
Truly, Madly, Deeply▶
Weekend at Bernie's
Weekend at Bernie's 2
What's Eating Gilbert Grape▶
Where the Lilies Bloom▶

Best Friends
Abbott and Costello Meet Frankenstein▶
Adios Amigo
The Adventures of Huck Finn
The Adventures of Huckleberry Finn
The Adventures of Milo & Otis▶
Backbeat▶
Bad Company▶
The Bear▶
Big Mo
Big Shots
Bill & Ted's Bogus Journey
Black Beauty
The Boy Who Could Fly
Breaking the Rules
Butch Cassidy and the Sundance Kid▶
The Caddy
Calendar Girl
The Cat
City Slickers▶
City Slickers 2: The Legend of Curly's Gold
Class Act
Courage of Black Beauty
December
Driving Miss Daisy▶
Drop Dead Fred
Elmer
Enemy Mine

F/X 2: The Deadly Art of Illusion
The Flintstones
Free Willy
Grumpy Old Men▶
Gumby and the Moon Boggles
Hollywood or Bust
Huck and the King of Hearts
Indian Summer
K-9000
The Karate Kid▶
The Karate Kid: Part 2
The Karate Kid: Part 3
Little Rascals Christmas Special
The Littlest Outlaw
Looking for Miracles
The Lords of Flatbush
Lost in the Barrens
Madeline
The Man Who Would Be King▶
My Girl
The Odd Couple▶
One Crazy Summer
Papillon▶
P.K. and the Kid
Racing with the Moon▶
The Red Balloon▶
The Reivers▶
The Return of the Musketeers
Revenge of the Nerds
Russkies
The Sandlot▶
Shag: The Movie▶
Spies Like Us
Stand By Me▶
Star Trek 4: The Voyage Home▶
Starbird and Sweet William
The Sunshine Boys▶
Ten Who Dared
That Sinking Feeling▶
Three Amigos
Three Men and a Baby▶
Three Men and a Cradle▶
Three Musketeers
The Three Musketeers
Three Musketeers
Three Musketeers▶
The Three Musketeers
Thursday's Game▶
Tombstone▶
Top Gun
Tough Guys
Wayne's World
Wayne's World 2
Where the River Runs Black
Where the Toys Come From
White Christmas▶
White Mama▶
Winnie the Pooh & Friends

The Big Sting
see also Heists
Adios Amigo
Barnaby and Me
Blue Murder at St. Trinian's▶
Candleshoe
Curly Sue
Dirty Rotten Scoundrels▶
F/X▶
F/X 2: The Deadly Art of Illusion
Federal Agents vs. Underworld, Inc.
Green Card
Harry & Walter Go to New York
Housesitter

Kid from Not-So-Big
Leap of Faith
Maverick
Never Say Never Again
Opportunity Knocks
Paper Moon▶
Piece of the Action
Popi▶
The Sting▶
The Sting 2
Support Your Local Gunfighter▶
Tootsie▶

Bigfoot
Harry and the Hendersons
Legend of Boggy Creek
Return to Boggy Creek

Biking
American Flyers
BMX Bandits
Breaking Away▶
Pee Wee's Big Adventure▶
Rad

Biography
see Biopics

Biopics
see also Musician Biopics; Nashville Narratives
Amadeus▶
American Graffiti▶
Annie Oakley
Au Revoir Les Enfants▶
The Babe
Backbeat▶
Big Mo
Bound for Glory▶
The Buddy Holly Story▶
Chaplin▶
Chariots of Fire▶
Coal Miner's Daughter▶
Conrack▶
Cross Creek
Davy Crockett
Dragon: The Bruce Lee Story
Dreamchild▶
8 Seconds
The Elephant Man▶
1492: Conquest of Paradise
Funny Girl▶
Funny Lady
Geronimo▶
The Glenn Miller Story▶
Gorillas in the Mist▶
Greased Lightning
The Great White Hope
The Greatest
Heart Like a Wheel▶
I Am a Fugitive from a Chain Gang▶
Jesus Christ, Superstar▶
The Jolson Story▶
Joni
Knute Rockne: All American▶
La Bamba▶
Lawrence of Arabia▶
The Learning Tree
The Left-Handed Gun▶
The Loneliest Runner▶
MacArthur
Malcolm X▶
The Miracle Worker▶
Mommie Dearest
My Father's Glory▶
Nadia
Pistol: The Birth of a Legend
Ring of Bright Water▶
The Seven Little Foys▶
The Ten Commandments▶

This Boy's Life▶
Till the Clouds Roll By
Wait Until Spring, Bandini
Waltz King
What's Love Got to Do With It?
Wild Hearts Can't Be Broken▶
A Winner Never Quits
The Wonderful World of the Brothers Grimm
Yankee Doodle Dandy▶

Birds
Bill and Coo
The Birds▶
Chipmunk and His Bird Friends
The Goodbye Bird
High Anxiety
Howard the Duck
Million Dollar Duck
Mr. & Mrs. Condor
The Pigeon that Worked a Miracle
Sesame Street Presents: Follow That Bird
Shamu & You: Exploring the World of Birds
Spirit of the Eagle
The Talking Parcel
Unsinkable Donald Duck with Huey, Dewey & Louie
Wild Geese Calling
Woody Woodpecker Collector's Edition, Vol. 1

Blindness
see also Physical Problems
Amy▶
Butterflies Are Free▶
City Lights▶
Elmer
Eye on the Sparrow
Ice Castles
Love Leads the Way
The Miracle Worker▶
Places in the Heart▶

Boating
see High Seas Adventure

Books
see also Bedtime Stories; Storytelling
Cross Creek
Crossing Delancey▶
The Joy Luck Club▶
The NeverEnding Story
The Paper Chase▶

Books to Film: Louisa May Alcott
Little Men
Little Women▶
Little Women
Little Women Series

Books to Film: J.M. Barrie
Hook
Peter Pan▶
Peter Pan▶
Peter Pan & the Pirates: Demise of Hook

Books to Film: Frances Hodgson Burnett
Little Lord Fauntleroy▶
The Little Princess▶
The Secret Garden▶

Category Index

Books to Film: Rudyard Kipling
Captains Courageous▶
The Jungle Book
The Man Who Would Be King▶
Wee Willie Winkie▶

Books to Film: Astrid Lindgren
The Land of Faraway
The New Adventures of Pippi Longstocking
Pippi Goes on Board
Pippi in the South Seas
Pippi Longstocking
Pippi on the Run

Books to Film: Jack London
Call of the Wild
Great Adventure
White Fang▶
White Fang and the Hunter

Books to Film: L.M. Montgomery
Anne of Avonlea▶
Anne of Green Gables▶
Lantern Hill

Books to Film: Mark Twain
The Adventures of Huck Finn
The Adventures of Huckleberry Finn
The Adventures of Huckleberry Finn▶
The Adventures of Tom Sawyer
A Connecticut Yankee▶
A Connecticut Yankee in King Arthur's Court
Huck and the King of Hearts
Huckleberry Finn
Mark Twain's A Connecticut Yankee in King Arthur's Court
The Prince and the Pauper▶
The Prince and the Pauper
Tom Sawyer▶
Unidentified Flying Oddball

Bowling
Grease 2
Mr. Wonderful

Boxing
Any Which Way You Can
Arena
Bowery Blitzkrieg
Far and Away
The Great White Hope
The Greatest
Kid Dynamite
The Main Event
Matilda
Movie, Movie
Palooka
The Power of One
Prize Fighter
The Quiet Man▶
Rocky▶
Rocky 2
Rocky 3
Rocky 4
Rocky 5
The Sting 2
Teen Wolf Too

Boy Meets Girl
Adam's Rib▶
The Adventures of Robin Hood▶
The African Queen▶
The Age of Innocence▶
Almost an Angel
Always
American Dreamer
And You Thought Your Parents Were Weird!
Animal Behavior
Anne of Avonlea▶
Annie Hall▶
Arthur▶
Arthur 2: On the Rocks
Aspen Extreme
Baby Boom
Baby. . .Secret of the Lost Legend
Back to the Beach
Barnaby and Me
Beauty and the Beast▶
Benny & Joon
Born Yesterday
Boy Takes Girl
Bringing Up Baby▶
The Butcher's Wife
Can't Buy Me Love
Casablanca▶
The Castaway Cowboy
Chances Are▶
Comeback Kid
Cool Change
Crazy Moon
Crocodile Dundee▶
Crossing Delancey▶
Curly Sue
The Cutting Edge
Date with an Angel
Dear Brigitte
Desperately Seeking Susan▶
Dirty Rotten Scoundrels▶
Doc Hollywood
Doctor Zhivago▶
Dream Date
8 Seconds
Electric Dreams
Face the Music
Far and Away
The Farmer's Daughter▶
For Love or Money
Four Weddings and a Funeral▶
French Postcards
Ghost▶
Gidget
Gidget Goes Hawaiian
Gidget Goes to Rome
The Go-Between▶
Gone with the Wind▶
The Goodbye Girl▶
Green Card
Groundhog Day▶
Her Alibi
Herbie Goes to Monte Carlo
His Girl Friday▶
Honeymoon in Vegas
Housesitter
I Love Trouble
I Never Sang For My Father▶
Ice Castles
The Incredible Mr. Limpet
Innerspace
Irreconcilable Differences
It Could Happen to You▶
It Happened One Night▶
Jane Eyre▶
Jersey Girl
The Jewel of the Nile
Joe Versus the Volcano
Just the Way You Are
The King and I▶

King Ralph
Kipperbang
Kiss Me Goodbye
Kramer vs. Kramer▶
L.A. Story▶
The Last of the Mohicans▶
The Last Prostitute
The Lion in Winter▶
A Little Romance▶
Little Sister
Look Who's Talking▶
Look Who's Talking, Too
Lost in Yonkers
Love Laughs at Andy Hardy
Lt. Robin Crusoe, U.S.N.
Made in America
The Main Event
Making Mr. Right
The Man in the Moon▶
Mannequin
Maverick
Melody
The Misadventures of Merlin Jones
Mr. Wonderful
Moon Pilot
Moonstruck▶
Much Ado About Nothing▶
Murphy's Romance▶
My Girl 2
My Stepmother Is an Alien
Mystery Date
Nothing in Common
Off Beat
Only the Lonely
Only You
Overboard
Oxford Blues
Pat and Mike▶
Peggy Sue Got Married
Places in the Heart▶
Play It Again, Sam▶
The Playboys▶
Poetic Justice
Prelude to a Kiss
The Purple Rose of Cairo▶
The Quiet Man▶
Racing with the Moon▶
Reality Bites▶
Rich in Love
Roman Holiday▶
Romancing the Stone▶
Romeo and Juliet▶
Rooster Cogburn
Roxanne▶
Ryan's Daughter
Sabrina▶
Sarah, Plain and Tall▶
Secret Admirer
See You in the Morning
Seven Minutes in Heaven
She-Devil
She's Having a Baby
Short Circuit
Singles▶
Sixteen Candles▶
Sleepless in Seattle▶
Somewhere Tomorrow
Sommersby
Straight Talk
Strictly Ballroom▶
Tammy and the Bachelor
Tammy and the Doctor
Tarzan Escapes▶
Tender Mercies▶
That Night
The Thing Called Love
Tony Draws a Horse
Untamed Heart
Valley Girl
Waiting for the Light
The Way We Were▶
Wild Hearts Can't Be Broken▶
Wind

The Wind and the Lion▶
Wings of Desire▶
With Six You Get Eggroll
Wuthering Heights
Year of the Comet

Buses
The Big Bus
Forrest Gump▶
The Fugitive▶
A League of Their Own▶
Speed▶
The Trip to Bountiful▶
Where Angels Go, Trouble Follows

Business Gone Beserk
C.H.O.M.P.S.
The Flintstones
For Love or Money
Freaked
Gremlins 2: The New Batch▶
Gung Ho
Herbie Rides Again
His Girl Friday▶
I Love Trouble
Journey to Spirit Island▶
Major League
Naked Gun 2 1/2: The Smell of Fear
The Night They Saved Christmas
The Paper▶
Robocop 3
Scrooged
Tucker: The Man and His Dream▶
Weekend at Bernie's
Weekend at Bernie's 2

Canada
see also Cold Spots; Hockey
American Boyfriends
Anne of Avonlea▶
Anne of Green Gables▶
The Apprenticeship of Duddy Kravitz▶
Bach & Broccoli▶
The Bay Boy
Big Red
A Cry in the Wild▶
Dog Pound Shuffle
The Dog Who Stopped the War▶
The Incredible Journey▶
Lassie's Great Adventure
My American Cousin▶
Renfrew of the Royal Mounted
Strangers in Good Company▶
Who Has Seen the Wind?
Yukon Flight

Cars
see Cool Cars; Fast Cars

Cartoon Classics
see also Mickey Mouse & Friends
Adventures of Little Lulu and Tubby
Adventures of Mighty Mouse, Vol. 1
The Adventures of Rocky & Bullwinkle: Birth of Bullwinkle
Allegro Non Troppo▶
Amazing Adventures of Joe 90
Archie, Vol. 1
The Best of Gumby
Bozo the Clown: Ding Dong Dandy Adventures

Casper's Halloween
Dinky: Dinky Finds a Home
Dinky: Much Ado About Nothing
Fat Albert & the Cosby Kids, Vol. 1
Felix the Cat: An Hour of Fun
Felix the Cat: The Movie
50 Classic All-Star Cartoons, Vol. 1
50 Classic All-Star Cartoons, Vol. 2
The Flintstones
The Flintstones: Fred Flintstone Woos Again
The Flintstones: Rappin' n' Rhymin'
Gandy Goose: One Man Navy
George of the Jungle
Gumby Adventures
Gumby and the Moon Boggles
Gumby, Vol. 1: The Return of Gumby
Gumby's Holiday Special
Gumby's Supporting Cast
Hey There, It's Yogi Bear
Inspector Clouseau: Ape Suzette
Inspector Clouseau: Napoleon Blown-Aparte
The Jetsons Meet the Flintstones
The Jetsons: The Movie
Josie & the Pussycats in Outer Space
King Kong: Rocket Island
King Kong: Treasure Trap
Little Nemo: Adventures in Slumberland
The Lone Ranger
The Man Called Flintstone
Max Fleischer's Cartoon Capers, Vol. 1: Playin' Around
Mighty Hercules: Champion of the People!
Mighty Hercules: Conqueror of Evil!
The Mighty Hercules: Mightiest Mortal!
Mighty Mouse
Mighty Mouse in the Great Space Chase
Mighty Thor: Enter Hercules
Mr. Magoo: 1001 Arabian Night's Dream
Mr. Magoo: Cyrano De Bergerac/A Midsummer Night's Dream
Mr. Magoo: Don Quixote de la Mancha
Mr. Magoo in Sherwood Forest
Mr. Magoo in the King's Service
Mr. Magoo: King Arthur/The Count of Monte Cristo
Mr. Magoo: Little Snow White
Mr. Magoo: Sherlock Holmes/Dr. Frankenstein
The Mr. Magoo Show, Vol. 1
Mr. Magoo: The Three Musketeers
Mr. Magoo's Storybook▶
New Archies: Stealing the Show
The Pink Panther▶
The Pink Panther

Pink Panther: Fly in the Pink
Pink Panther: Tickled Pink
Pogo for President: ''I Go Pogo''
Precious Pupp
Schoolhouse Rock: Grammar Rock
Schoolhouse Rock: History Rock
Schoolhouse Rock: Science Rock
Scooby-Doo
Speed Racer
Thunderbirds
Thunderbirds 6
Thunderbirds: Countdown to Disaster
Thunderbirds to the Rescue
Underdog: The Tickle Feather Machine
Winnie the Pooh
Winnie the Pooh and a Day for Eeyore▶
Winnie the Pooh & Friends
Winnie the Pooh and Tigger Too

Cartoon Tunes
Aladdin▶
All Dogs Go to Heaven
An American Tail▶
An American Tail: Fievel Goes West▶
Beauty and the Beast▶
Charlotte's Web▶
Cinderella▶
Gay Purr-ee
Jack & the Beanstalk
The Jungle Book▶
Lady and the Tramp▶
The Lion King▶
Little Critter Series: Just Me and My Dad
The Little Mermaid▶
The Magic Voyage
Pinocchio▶
Rock-a-Doodle
Shinbone Alley
Sleeping Beauty▶
Snow White and the Seven Dwarfs▶
Thumbelina
Treasure Island
Tubby the Tuba
Water Babies
Yellow Submarine▶
You're a Good Man, Charlie Brown

Cartoonmercials
Abbott and Costello Cartoon Festival
The Adventures of Teddy Ruxpin
Blackstar
The Cabbage Patch Kid's First Christmas
The California Raisins: Meet the Raisins
Care Bears: Family Storybook
The Care Bears Movie
The Care Bears Movie 2: A New Generation
Charmkins
G.I. Joe, Vol. 1: A Real American Hero
Gobots
Gobots: Battle of the Rock Lords
He-Man & the Masters of the Universe, Vol. 1
Heroes on Hot Wheels, Vol. 1

Lady Lovelylocks & the Pixietails, Vol. 1
Lazer Tag Academy: The Movie
The Legend of Zelda: Missing Link
Maple Town
Maple Town: Case of the Missing Candy
My Little Pony: The Movie
Potato Head Kids, Vol. 1
Pound Puppies
Rainbow Brite: A Horse of a Different Color
The Real Ghostbusters
Rubik, the Amazing Cube, Vol. 1
Strawberry Shortcake and the Baby Without a Name
Super Mario Bros. Super Show 1
Transformers
Transformers: The Movie
World of Strawberry Shortcake

Cats
The Adventures of Milo & Otis▶
Batman Returns
Bunnicula: Vampire Rabbit
The Cat
Cat City
The Cat from Outer Space
Cat's Eye
Felix the Cat: An Hour of Fun
Felix the Cat: The Movie
A Garfield Christmas
Garfield: His 9 Lives
Garfield in Paradise
Garfield's Feline Fantasy
Garfield's Halloween Adventure
Garfield's Thanksgiving
Gay Purr-ee
Heathcliff & Marmaduke
Here Comes Garfield
Homeward Bound: The Incredible Journey▶
The Incredible Journey▶
Puss in Boots
Secret Lives of Waldo Kitty Volume 1
That Darn Cat
That's My Hero!
The Three Lives of Thomasina▶
Tom and Jerry: Starring
Tom and Jerry: The Movie
Tom & Jerry's 50th Birthday Classics
Top Cat and the Beverly Hills Cats

Cave People
Encino Man
The Flintstones
When Dinosaurs Ruled the Earth

Charlie Brown & the Peanuts
Be My Valentine, Charlie Brown/Is This Goodbye, Charlie Brown?
Bon Voyage, Charlie Brown
The Charlie Brown and Snoopy Show: Vol. 1
A Charlie Brown Christmas
It's a Short Summer, Charlie Brown

It's the Great Pumpkin, Charlie Brown (triple feature)
Race for Your Life, Charlie Brown
Snoopy, Come Home▶
You're a Good Man, Charlie Brown
You're Not Elected, Charlie Brown!/A Charlie Brown Christmas

Chases
American Graffiti▶
At the Circus
Baby on Board
Beverly Hills Cop
Beverly Hills Cop 3
Buck Privates Come Home▶
Butch Cassidy and the Sundance Kid▶
Charlie and the Great Balloon Chase
Diamonds are Forever▶
Dick Tracy▶
Dr. No▶
Eat My Dust
E.T.: The Extra-Terrestrial▶
For Your Eyes Only▶
Foul Play▶
From Russia with Love▶
The Fugitive▶
The Golden Child
Honeymoon in Vegas
The Hunt for Red October▶
Indiana Jones and the Temple of Doom▶
The Jewel of the Nile
Jurassic Park▶
License to Drive
Live and Let Die
The Man from Snowy River
The Man with the Golden Gun
Memoirs of an Invisible Man
Monkey Trouble▶
North by Northwest▶
Octopussy
On Her Majesty's Secret Service▶
Pee Wee's Big Adventure▶
The Pelican Brief
A Perfect World
Planet of the Apes▶
Raiders of the Lost Ark▶
Return of the Jedi▶
Romancing the Stone▶
Smokey and the Bandit
Smokey and the Bandit, Part 2
Smokey and the Bandit, Part 3
The Spy Who Loved Me
Star Wars▶
The Sting▶
The Terminator▶
Thunderball
Tom and Jerry: The Movie
Tom & Jerry: The Very Best Of Tom & Jerry
Tom & Jerry's 50th Birthday Classics
Top Gun
True Lies
What's Up, Doc?▶
Who Framed Roger Rabbit?▶
Year of the Comet
You Only Live Twice

Child Abuse
Father Hood
Mommie Dearest

Radio Flyer
This Boy's Life▶
Too Smart for Strangers with Winnie the Pooh
Where the Spirit Lives

Childhood Visions
see also Home Alone
All I Want for Christmas
American Heart▶
And Now Miguel
Angels in the Outfield
Au Revoir Les Enfants▶
The Beniker Gang
Big▶
The Black Stallion▶
Blankman
Born to Run
Boyd's Shadow
Camp Nowhere
Captain January
Careful, He Might Hear You▶
Casey's Shadow
The Cat
A Christmas Story▶
Cinema Paradiso▶
Cria▶
Crooklyn▶
David Copperfield▶
Desert Bloom▶
Empire of the Sun▶
E.T.: The Extra-Terrestrial▶
The Flame Trees of Thika▶
Flight of the Grey Wolf
Forbidden Games▶
The Golden Seal
Heidi
Heidi
Heidi▶
Home Alone▶
Home for Christmas
Hook
Hope and Glory▶
Into the West▶
Invaders from Mars
Ira Sleeps Over
Josh and S.A.M.
Journey for Margaret▶
The Kid from Left Field
The Kid with the Broken Halo
King of the Hill▶
The Lady in White▶
Lassie's Great Adventure
Last Action Hero
Lies My Father Told Me▶
Little Buddha
Little Man Tate▶
Little Monsters
The Little Princess▶
The Little Rascals
The Littlest Horse Thieves
Look Who's Talking▶
Look Who's Talking, Too
Lord of the Flies▶
Lord of the Flies
Lost in Yonkers
Magic of Lassie
Magic Snowman
Mommie Dearest
Mosby's Marauders
My Friend Flicka▶
My Life as a Dog▶
My Mother's Castle▶
National Velvet▶
Nobody's Boy
Oliver!▶
Pollyanna▶
Poltergeist▶
Poltergeist 2: The Other Side
The Poor Little Rich Girl
Radio Flyer
Railway Children▶
Real Genius▶

The Red Balloon▶
The Red Pony▶
Return from Witch Mountain
Rock-a-Doodle
Savage Sam
Searching for Bobby Fischer▶
The Secret Garden▶
Sidekicks
Small Change▶
Sudden Terror
Sudie & Simpson
Taps
Tito and Me▶
To Kill a Mockingbird▶
Toto le Heros▶
Treasure Island▶
Turf Boy
Wait Until Spring, Bandini
What the Moon Saw▶
Where's Willie?
Whistle Down the Wind▶
White Fang▶
The Wild Country
The Wizard of Loneliness
A World Apart▶
The Yearling▶

China
see also Asia
Adventures of Smilin' Jack
Big Bird in China
Empire of the Sun▶
The Joy Luck Club▶

Christmas
see also Holidays
All I Want for Christmas
Alvin & the Chipmunks: A Chipmunk Christmas
Alvin & the Chipmunks: Alvin's Christmas Carol
Amahl and the Night Visitors
An American Christmas Carol
Babar and Father Christmas
Babes in Toyland
Barney's Christmas Surprise
B.C.: A Special Christmas
Benji's Very Own Christmas Story
The Berenstain Bears' Christmas
Bernard and the Genie
The Best Christmas Pageant Ever
Bluetoes the Christmas Elf
The Cabbage Patch Kid's First Christmas
Captain Kangaroo's Merry Christmas Stories
A Charlie Brown Christmas
Child's Christmas in Wales
A Christmas Carol▶
A Christmas Carol
Christmas Cartoons
The Christmas Collection
Christmas Comes to Willow Creek
Christmas Eve on Sesame Street
A Christmas Fantasy
The Christmas Messenger
The Christmas Party
Christmas Stories
A Christmas Story
A Christmas Story▶
The Christmas That Almost Wasn't
A Christmas to Remember
The Christmas Toy
The Christmas Tree

A Christmas Tree/Puss-In-Boots
Christmas Video Sing-Along
Christopher's Xmas Mission
Disney's Sing-Along Songs: The Twelve Days of Christmas
Disney's Sing-Along Songs, Vol. 8: Very Merry Christmas Songs
Dot & Santa Claus
Ernest Saves Christmas
A Family Circus Christmas
The First Christmas
Follow That Sleigh!
For Better or For Worse: The Bestest Present
The Fourth King
Frosty Returns
Frosty the Snowman
Frosty's Winter Wonderland/The Leprechauns' Christmas Gold
A Garfield Christmas
George Balanchine's The Nutcracker
A Gingerbread Christmas
Gremlins▶
Gumby's Holiday Special
Happy Holidays with Darkwing Duck and Goofy
Here Comes Santa Claus
Hobo's Christmas
Holiday Inn
Home Alone▶
Home Alone 2: Lost in New York
Home for Christmas
Homecoming: A Christmas Story▶
A House Without a Christmas Tree
It Came Upon a Midnight Clear
It's a Wonderful Life▶
Jack Frost
A Jetson's Christmas Carol
Jiminy Cricket's Christmas
Johann's Gift to Christmas
The Kid Who Loved Christmas
The Lion in Winter▶
The Little Crooked Christmas Tree
The Little Drummer Boy
The Little Match Girl
Little Rascals Christmas Special
The Little Troll Prince
Lollipop Dragon: The Great Christmas Race
Madeline's Christmas
Magic Snowman
The Man in the Santa Claus Suit
March of the Wooden Soldiers▶
A Merry Mirthworm Christmas
Mickey's Christmas Carol▶
Miracle Down Under
Miracle on 34th Street▶
Mr. Magoo's Christmas Carol▶
The Muppet Christmas Carol▶
National Lampoon's Christmas Vacation
Nearly No Christmas
Nestor the Long-Eared Christmas Donkey
The Night Before Christmas

The Night Before Christmas and Best-Loved Yuletide Carols
The Night They Saved Christmas
The Nightmare Before Christmas▶
Noel
The Nutcracker Prince
One Magic Christmas
Pink Panther: Pink Christmas
Pinocchio's Christmas
Pluto's Christmas Tree
Prancer
Raggedy Ann and Andy
Railway Children▶
The Real Story of Oh Christmas Tree
Rudolph the Red-Nosed Reindeer▶
Santa & the 3 Bears
Santa & the Tooth Fairies
Santa Claus Conquers the Martians
Santa Claus is Coming to Town▶
Santa Claus: The Movie
Santabear's First Christmas
Santabear's High Flying Adventure
Santa's First Christmas
Scrooge
Scrooged
Shining Time Station: 'Tis a Gift Holiday Special
The Simpsons Christmas Special
The Small One
A Smoky Mountain Christmas
Snuffy the Elf Who Saved Christmas
Stingiest Man in Town
Ted E. Bear: The Bear Who Slept Through Christmas
The Teddy Bears' Christmas
Timmy's Gift: A Precious Moments Christmas
Tommy Tricker & the Stamp Traveller▶
Trolls & the Christmas Express
'Twas the Night Before Christmas
A Very Merry Cricket
A Walt Disney Christmas
Walt Disney Films in French
The Waltons: The Children's Carol
Where the Toys Come From
White Christmas▶
Why Christmas Trees Aren't Perfect
The Year Without a Santa Claus
Yes, Virginia, There is a Santa Claus
Yogi's First Christmas
You're Not Elected, Charlie Brown/A Charlie Brown Christmas
Ziggy's Gift

Circuses & Carnivals
see also Amusement Parks; Clowning Around
At the Circus
Big Top Pee Wee
Bongo
Bozo the Clown: Ding Dong Dandy Adventures
Carousel▶

Clowning Around
Clowning Around 2
The Court Jester▶
Dumbo▶
Freaked
The Greatest Show on Earth▶
Lili
Parade▶
The Rousters
Seven Faces of Dr. Lao▶
So Dear to My Heart▶
Something Wicked This Way Comes
State Fair
Toby Tyler▶
Wild Hearts Can't Be Broken▶

Civil Rights
see also Apartheid; Slavery
And the Children Shall Lead
Driving Miss Daisy▶
The Ernest Green Story
Hawmps!
We of the Never Never▶

Civil War
see also Southern Belles; Southern Sagas
Bad Company▶
Friendly Persuasion▶
General Spanky
Gettysburg▶
Gone with the Wind▶
Henry Hamilton: Graduate Ghost
How the West was Won▶
It Happened in New Orleans
Johnny Shiloh
Little Women▶
The Littlest Rebel
Menace on the Mountain
Mosby's Marauders
Mysterious Island▶
No Drums, No Bugles
The Shadow Riders

Classics
Adam's Rib▶
The Adventures of Robin Hood▶
The African Queen▶
Airplane!▶
Alice in Wonderland▶
American Graffiti▶
An American in Paris▶
Anchors Aweigh▶
Animal Crackers▶
Annie Hall▶
At the Circus
Bambi▶
Beauty and the Beast▶
Black Beauty▶
Bowery Blitzkrieg
Boys Town▶
The Bridge on the River Kwai▶
Butch Cassidy and the Sundance Kid▶
Caddyshack▶
Casablanca▶
Challenge to Lassie
A Christmas Carol▶
Cinderella▶
Citizen Kane▶
City Lights▶
Curly Top
Dial "M" for Murder▶
Dimples
Duck Soup▶
Dumbo▶
East of Eden▶
Easter Parade▶

E.T.: The Extra-Terrestrial▶
Fantasia▶
Father of the Bride▶
Forbidden Games▶
Foreign Correspondent▶
The 400 Blows▶
Giant▶
Going My Way▶
The Gold Rush▶
Gone with the Wind▶
Grease
High Noon▶
His Girl Friday▶
Horse Feathers▶
How Green was My Valley▶
I Am a Fugitive from a Chain Gang▶
I Remember Mama▶
Invaders from Mars
Invasion of the Body Snatchers▶
It Happened One Night▶
It's a Wonderful Life▶
Judgment at Nuremberg▶
Key Largo▶
The King and I▶
King Kong▶
Lady and the Tramp▶
The Lady Vanishes▶
Lassie, Come Home▶
Lawrence of Arabia▶
Little Women▶
The Maltese Falcon▶
The Man Who Would Be King▶
M*A*S*H▶
Mickey's Crazy Careers
Mighty Joe Young
Miracle on 34th Street▶
Mr. Hulot's Holiday▶
Mr. Smith Goes to Washington▶
Monkey Business▶
Moonstruck▶
The Muppet Movie▶
Mysterious Island▶
National Velvet▶
A Night at the Opera▶
A Night in Casablanca
North by Northwest▶
Old Yeller▶
Oliver Twist▶
Once Upon a Time in the West▶
101 Dalmatians▶
The Philadelphia Story▶
Pinocchio▶
Planet of the Apes▶
The Quiet Man▶
Rebel Without a Cause▶
The Red Pony▶
The Red Shoes▶
Shadow of a Doubt▶
Shane▶
Singin' in the Rain▶
Sleeping Beauty▶
The Sound of Music▶
Star Wars▶
Strangers on a Train▶
Suspicion▶
Tarzan, the Ape Man▶
The Ten Commandments▶
Thief of Baghdad▶
The Thin Man▶
The Three Musketeers
To Kill a Mockingbird▶
Topper▶
Treasure of the Sierra Madre▶
The War of the Worlds▶
West Side Story▶
White Christmas▶
The Wizard of Oz▶
Yankee Doodle Dandy▶
The Yearling▶

Clowning Around
see also Circuses & Carnivals
Clowning Around
Clowning Around 2
The Court Jester▶
Poltergeist▶

Cold Spots
Antarctica
Challenge To Be Free
Christmas Comes to Willow Creek
Cool Runnings
Doctor Zhivago▶
Ice Station Zebra
Kavik, the Wolf Dog
Never Cry Wolf▶
Shadow of the Wolf
White Fang 2: The Myth of the White Wolf

College Capers
see also Elementary School Escapades; High School Hijinks; Teacher, Teacher
Adventures in Spying
Animal Behavior
Back to School
Blue Chips
Catch Me. . .If You Can
The Computer Wore Tennis Shoes
Ernest Rides Again
Escapade in Florence
The Freshman
Girl Crazy▶
Gotcha!
Gross Anatomy
Horse Feathers▶
House Party 2: The Pajama Jam
How I Got into College
The Kid with the 200 I.Q.
Little Sister
Making the Grade
Midnight Madness
The Misadventures of Merlin Jones
Monkey's Uncle
Odd Jobs
The Paper Chase▶
P.C.U.
The Program
Revenge of the Nerds
Rudy
Soul Man
The Sure Thing▶
Teen Wolf Too
Undergrads▶
Witches' Brew
With Honors

Comedy with an Edge
see also Laugh Riots
The Addams Family
Addams Family Values▶
Battle of the Bullies
Death Becomes Her
Freaked
I Ought to Be in Pictures
Serial Mom▶
She-Devil
So I Married an Axe Murderer
Throw Momma from the Train▶
Toto le Heros▶

Coming to America
Avalon▶
Buck Privates Come Home▶
Far and Away
Green Card

Maricela
Monkey Business▶
Wait Until Spring, Bandini

Computers
see also Robots;
Technological Nightmares
The Computer Wore Tennis
    Shoes
The Double O Kid
Electric Dreams
Skills for the New
    Technology Series
Superman 3
War Games▶

Cool Cars
see also Fast Cars
American Graffiti▶
Back to the Future▶
Car Wash
Chitty Chitty Bang Bang
Coupe de Ville
Dream Machine
Ferris Bueller's Day Off▶
Gung Ho
Herbie Rides Again
License to Drive
The Love Bug
Moving Violations
Pepper and His Wacky
    Taxi
Reading Rainbow: Tooth-
    Gnasher Superflash
Susie, the Little Blue Coupe
Tucker: The Man and His
    Dream▶
Zero to Sixty

Courtroom Capers
see also Lawyers
Adam's Rib▶
The Client
Ernest Goes to Jail
Judgment at Nuremberg▶
The Paradine Case
Philadelphia▶
To Kill a Mockingbird▶
When Every Day was the
    Fourth of July

Cowboys & Indians
Adios Amigo
Adventures of Red Ryder
Against A Crooked Sky
The Apple Dumpling Gang
The Apple Dumpling Gang
    Rides Again
Bad Company▶
Bandolero!
Bang Bang Kid
Barbarosa▶
Battling with Buffalo Bill
Big Jake
Bonanza: The Return
Bowery Buckaroos
Bravestarr: The Legend
    Returns
Bronco Billy
Brothers O'Toole
Buck and the Preacher
Butch and Sundance: The
    Early Days
Butch Cassidy and the
    Sundance Kid▶
Cahill: United States
    Marshal
The Cheyenne Social Club
City Slickers▶
City Slickers 2: The Legend
    of Curly's Gold
Courage of the North
The Cowboys▶
Culpepper Cattle Co.
Devil Horse
The Electric Horseman

Fievel's American Tails: A
    Mouse Known as
    Zorrowitz/Aunt Sophie's
    Visit
Fighting with Kit Carson
Flaming Frontiers
Geronimo: An American
    Legend
Go West
Goin' South▶
Guns of the Magnificent
    Seven
Hearts of the West▶
High Noon▶
How the West was Won▶
Hurricane Express
The Incredible Rocky
    Mountain Race
Indian Paint
Jeremiah Johnson▶
Jesse James Rides Again
Junior Bonner▶
King of the Grizzlies
The Last of the Mohicans
The Left-Handed Gun▶
Legend of the Lone Ranger
Lightning Jack
Little Big Man▶
The Lone Ranger
The Lone Ranger and the
    Lost City of Gold
The Lone Ranger: Code of
    the Pioneers
Lucky Luke: Ballad of the
    Daltons
Lucky Luke: Daisy Town
Man & Boy
Man from Button Willow
The Man from Snowy River
Maverick
Mosby's Marauders
My Heroes Have Always
    Been Cowboys
My Name is Nobody
The Nine Lives of Elfego
    Baca
Once Upon a Time in the
    West▶
One Little Indian
The Outlaw Josey Wales▶
Peter Lundy and the
    Medicine Hat Stallion
The Phantom Empire
Pony Express Rider▶
Quigley Down Under
Renfrew of the Royal
    Mounted
Return to Snowy River
Rin Tin Tin, Hero of the
    West
Rooster Cogburn
Running Wild
Scandalous John
The Shadow Riders
The Shakiest Gun in the
    West
Shane▶
The Shootist▶
Silver Stallion
Silverado▶
Sundance and the Kid
Support Your Local
    Gunfighter▶
Support Your Local
    Sheriff▶
Tales of Deputy Dawg,
    Vol. 1
To the Last Man
Tombstone▶
True Grit▶
The Villain
Wackiest Wagon Train in
    the West
Wagons East
Westward Ho, the
    Wagons!

The Wild Country
Winners of the West
Young Guns
Yukon Flight
Zorro Rides Again
Zorro, Vol. 1
Zorro's Black Whip
Zorro's Fighting Legion

Crime Doesn't Pay
see also It's the Mob; On
the Run; Stupid Crime
All Dogs Go to Heaven
Almost an Angel
Batman▶
Batman Returns
The Bay Boy
Beverly Hills Cop
Beverly Hills Cop 2
Beverly Hills Cop 3
Boys Town▶
Bugsy Malone
The Cat
Charade▶
Crocodile Dundee 2
The Crow
Dead Men Don't Wear
    Plaid
Diamonds on Wheels
Dick Tracy
Dick Tracy▶
Dick Tracy, Detective
Dick Tracy Returns
Dick Tracy vs. Crime Inc.
Dick Tracy vs. Cueball
Dick Tracy's Dilemma
The Doberman Gang
The Dream Team
Emil and the Detective
Escapade in Florence
Fast Getaway
The Fire in the Stone
Flipper's New Adventure
Flying Wild
Follow the Leader
The Goonies
The Grey Fox▶
Johnny Dangerously
The Meteor Man
Moonraker
The Naked Gun: From the
    Files of Police Squad▶
'Neath Brooklyn Bridge
Never a Dull Moment
No Deposit, No Return
The North Avenue
    Irregulars
Oliver!▶
Oliver Twist
Oliver Twist▶
A Perfect World
The Real McCoy
Rear Window▶
Return of Captain
    Invincible
Savannah Smiles
The Shadow
Shadow of a Doubt▶
Shadow of the Eagle
Stage Fright▶
Superman 3
Take the Money and Run▶
Ten Little Indians
That Darn Cat
That Was Then. . .This Is
    Now
Three Fugitives
Tiger Bay▶
Tim Tyler's Luck
Trenchcoat
Walking Tall
Weekend at Bernie's

Dads
see also Moms;
Parenthood
Father of the Bride▶
Getting Even with Dad
Ghost Dad
Life with Father▶
Mom and Dad Save the
    World
My Father the Hero
National Lampoon's
    Christmas Vacation
National Lampoon's
    European Vacation
Parenthood▶
Sleepless in Seattle▶
So I Married an Axe
    Murderer
Superdad
Three Men and a Baby▶
Three Men and a Cradle▶
Three Men and a Little
    Lady
Wait Till Your Mother Gets
    Home

Deafness
see also Physical Problems
Amy▶
Crazy Moon
The Miracle Worker▶
Reading Rainbow: Silent
    Lotus
A Summer to Remember

Death
see Bereavement

Demons & Wizards
Army of Darkness▶
Conan the Barbarian▶
Conan the Destroyer
Ernest Scared Stupid
Fire and Ice
The Hobbit▶
Krull
Ladyhawke▶
The Return of the King
Stories to Remember:
    Merlin and the Dragons
Supergirl
The Sword in the Stone▶
Troll
Warriors of the Wind
Willow
Wizards of the Lost
    Kingdom
Wizards of the Lost
    Kingdom 2

Detectives
see also Policemen; Silly
Detectives
Ace Ventura: Pet Detective
The Adventures of Sherlock
    Holmes' Smarter
    Brother▶
Another Stakeout
The Big Store
The Cheap Detective▶
Clean Slate
Clue You In: The Case of
    the Mad Movie
    Mustacher
Curse of the Pink Panther
Dead Men Don't Wear
    Plaid
Death on the Nile
Dick Tracy
Dick Tracy, Detective
Dick Tracy Meets
    Gruesome
Dick Tracy Returns
Dick Tracy vs. Crime Inc.
Dick Tracy vs. Cueball
Dick Tracy's Dilemma

Dragnet
Emil and the Detective
Encyclopedia Brown: Case
    of the Missing Time
    Capsule
Evil Under the Sun
The Great Mouse Detective
Hard-Boiled Mahoney
Inspector Clouseau: Ape
    Suzette
Inspector Clouseau:
    Napoleon Blown-Aparte
K-9
Little Miss Millions
Love Happy
The Maltese Falcon▶
My Favorite Brunette
Mystery Island
The Naked Gun: From the
    Files of Police Squad▶
Naked Gun 33 1/3: The
    Final Insult
Nancy Drew, Reporter
The Pink Panther▶
The Pink Panther Strikes
    Again▶
The Private Eyes
Return of the Pink Panther
Revenge of the Pink
    Panther
A Shot in the Dark▶
The Thin Man▶
Trail of the Pink Panther
Who Framed Roger
    Rabbit?▶
The Young Detectives on
    Wheels
Young Sherlock Holmes

Dinos
see also Scary Beasties
Adventures in Dinosaur
    City
Adventures in Dinosaurland
At the Earth's Core
Baby. . .Secret of the Lost
    Legend
Barney & Friends: Barney
    Rhymes with Mother
    Goose
Barney & Friends: Barney's
    Best Manners
Clifford
Dennis the Menace:
    Dinosaur Hunter
Denver the Last Dinosaur
Dinosaurs, Dinosaurs,
    Dinosaurs
Donny Deinonychus: The
    Educational Dinosaur,
    Vol. 1
EPIC: Days of the
    Dinosaurs
Jurassic Park▶
The Land Before Time▶
Land of the Lost
Land of the Lost, Vol. 1
Land That Time Forgot
Let's Pretend with Barney
Lost in Dinosaur World
More Dinosaurs
My Science Project
One of Our Dinosaurs Is
    Missing
The People That Time
    Forgot
Planet of the Dinosaurs
Prehysteria
Prehysteria 2
Reading Rainbow: Digging
    Up Dinosaurs
Son of Dinosaurs
Super Mario Bros.
Unknown Island
The Valley of Gwangi▶

We're Back! A Dinosaur's
Story
When Dinosaurs Ruled the
Earth

Disaster Strikes!
*see also Amazing
Adventures; Nuclear War*
Airport▶
Airport '75
Airport '77
Alive
Avalanche
The Big Bus
The Poseidon Adventure

Disney Animated
Movies
Aladdin▶
Alice in Wonderland▶
Bambi▶
Beauty and the Beast▶
The Brave Little Toaster
Cinderella▶
DuckTales the Movie:
Treasure of the Lost
Lamp
Dumbo▶
Fantasia▶
The Fox and the Hound▶
The Great Mouse Detective
The Jungle Book▶
Lady and the Tramp▶
The Lion King▶
The Little Mermaid▶
The Nightmare Before
Christmas▶
101 Dalmatians▶
Peter Pan▶
Pinocchio▶
The Rescuers▶
The Rescuers Down Under
The Return of Jafar▶
Sleeping Beauty▶
Snow White and the Seven
Dwarfs▶
The Sword in the Stone▶
The Three Caballeros▶

Disney Family Movies
The Absent-Minded
Professor▶
The Adventures of Bullwhip
Griffin
The Adventures of Huck
Finn
The Air Up There
Almost Angels
Amy▶
Angels in the Outfield
The Apple Dumpling Gang
The Apple Dumpling Gang
Rides Again
Babes in Toyland
The Barefoot Executive
The Bears & I
Bedknobs and Broomsticks
Benji the Hunted
Big Red
The Black Arrow
The Black Hole
Blackbeard's Ghost
Blank Check
The Blue Yonder
Born to Run
Breakin' Through
Candleshoe
The Castaway Cowboy
The Cat from Outer Space
Charley and the Angel
Charlie, the Lonesome
Cougar
Cheetah
Child of Glass
The Computer Wore Tennis
Shoes

Condorman
Darby O'Gill & the Little
People▶
Davy Crockett and the
River Pirates▶
Davy Crockett, King of the
Wild Frontier▶
The Devil & Max Devlin
Diamonds on Wheels
Dr. Syn, Alias the
Scarecrow
Emil and the Detective
Escapade in Florence
Escape to Witch
Mountain▶
A Far Off Place
The Fighting Prince of
Donegal
Flight of the Grey Wolf
Flight of the Navigator▶
Freaky Friday
Fun & Fancy Free
The Girl Who Spelled
Freedom
The Gnome-Mobile
Gone are the Days
Greyfriars Bobby▶
Gus
Herbie Goes Bananas
Herbie Goes to Monte
Carlo
Herbie Rides Again
Homeward Bound: The
Incredible Journey
Honey, I Blew Up the Kid
Honey, I Shrunk the Kids
The Horse in the Gray
Flannel Suit
The Horse Without a Head
Horsemasters
Hot Lead & Cold Feet
In Search of the
Castaways▶
The Incredible Journey▶
Iron Will
The Island at the Top of
the World
Johnny Shiloh
Johnny Tremain & the Sons
of Liberty
The Journey of Natty
Gann▶
Justin Morgan Had a
Horse
King of the Grizzlies
The Last Flight of Noah's
Ark
The Light in the Forest
The Littlest Horse Thieves
The Littlest Outlaw
Lots of Luck
The Love Bug
Love Leads the Way
Lt. Robin Crusoe, U.S.N.
Mary Poppins▶
Menace on the Mountain
Mickey's Christmas Carol▶
Million Dollar Duck
Miracle Down Under
Miracle of the White
Stallions
The Misadventures of
Merlin Jones
Monkeys, Go Home!
Monkey's Uncle
Moon Pilot
Moon-Spinners
Mooncussers
Mosby's Marauders
My Dog, the Thief
Napoleon and Samantha▶
Never a Dull Moment
Newsies
Night Crossing
Nikki, the Wild Dog of the
North▶

The Nine Lives of Elfego
Baca
No Deposit, No Return
The North Avenue
Irregulars
Now You See Him, Now
You Don't
Old Yeller▶
The One and Only,
Genuine, Original Family
Band
One Little Indian
One Magic Christmas
One of Our Dinosaurs Is
Missing
The Parent Trap
Pete's Dragon
Pollyanna▶
Return from Witch
Mountain
Return to Oz
Ride a Wild Pony
Rob Roy - The Highland
Rogue
The Rocketeer▶
Sammy, the Way-Out Seal
Savage Sam
Scandalous John
The Secret of El Zorro
The Shaggy D.A.
The Shaggy Dog
The Sign of Zorro
Smith!
Smoke
Snowball Express
So Dear to My Heart▶
Son of Flubber
Summer Magic
Superdad
The Swiss Family
Robinson▶
The Sword & the Rose
Ten Who Dared
That Darn Cat
Third Man on the
Mountain
Those Calloways
The Three Lives of
Thomasina▶
3 Ninjas
3 Ninjas Kick Back
A Tiger Walks
Toby Tyler▶
Treasure Island▶
The Treasure of
Matecumbe
20,000 Leagues Under the
Sea▶
The Ugly Dachshund
Undergrads▶
Unidentified Flying Oddball
Waltz King
Watcher in the Woods
Westward Ho, the
Wagons!
White Fang▶
White Fang 2: The Myth
of the White Wolf
The Wild Country
Wild Hearts Can't Be
Broken▶
The World's Greatest
Athlete

Divorce
see also Marriage
All I Want for Christmas
Clara's Heart
Conspiracy of Love
E.T.: The Extra-Terrestrial▶
Face the Music
Father Figure
High Society
Irreconcilable Differences
Kramer vs. Kramer▶
Mrs. Doubtfire▶

Mr. Wonderful
Nothing in Common
The Odd Couple▶
Peggy Sue Got Married
Play It Again, Sam▶
Rich Kids
See You in the Morning
Table for Five
When Mom and Dad
Break Up

Dr. Seuss
The Cat in the Hat
The Cat in the Hat Comes
Back
The Cat in the Hat Gets
Grinched
Did I Ever Tell You How
Lucky You Are?
Dr. Seuss' ABC
Dr. Seuss' Butter Battle
Book
Dr. Seuss' Cat in the Hat
Dr. Seuss' Hoober-Bloob
Highway
Dr. Seuss' Horton Hears a
Who/How the Grinch
Stole Christmas
Dr. Seuss: I Am NOT
Going to Get Up Today!
Dr. Seuss on the Loose
Dr. Seuss Sleep Book
Dr. Seuss' The Lorax
The 5000 Fingers of Dr.
T▶
Halloween is Grinch Night
Hop on Pop
Horton Hatches the Egg
Horton Hears a Who!
One Fish, Two Fish, Red
Fish, Blue Fish
The Zax From Dr. Seuss
on the Loose

Doctors & Nurses
see also AIDS; Hospitals
Bad Medicine
Death Becomes Her
Doc Hollywood
Doctor Dolittle
The Elephant Man▶
Gross Anatomy
M*A*S*H▶
Mr. North
Promises in the Dark
Skeezer

Documentaries
Animals Are Beautiful
People
Chuck Amuck: The Movie
Don't Eat the Pictures:
Sesame Street at the
Metropolitan Museum of
Art
The Endless Summer▶
The Endless Summer 2
The Glacier Fox
The Hellstrom Chronicle▶
Kidco
The Living Desert▶
The Man Who Skied Down
Everest
Their Only Chance
Twist

Dogs
see King of Beasts (Dogs)

Down Under
Born to Run
Cool Change
Dusty
Little Boy Lost
The Man from Snowy River
Miracle Down Under

Phar Lap
The Prince and the Great
Race
The Quest
Quigley Down Under
Really Wild Animals:
Wonders Down Under
The Rescuers Down Under
Return to Snowy River
Ride a Wild Pony
Run, Rebecca, Run
The Silver Stallion: King of
the Wild Brumbies
Strictly Ballroom▶
Under Capricorn
A Waltz Through the Hills
We of the Never Never▶

Drama
*see also Historical
Happenings; Tearjerkers*
Above the Rim
Across the Tracks
Adventures of the Flying
Cadets
Africa Texas Style
African Journey
Airborne
Alan & Naomi
All the President's Men▶
All the Right Moves
Amazing Grace & Chuck
American Anthem
An American Christmas
Carol
American Flyers
American Heart▶
An American Summer
Amy▶
And Now Miguel
Andre
Angelo My Love▶
Anne of Green Gables▶
Au Revoir Les Enfants▶
The Babe
Bach & Broccoli▶
Back Home
Backbeat▶
Ballet Shoes
The Bay Boy
The Bear▶
The Bears & I
The Beniker Gang
The Best Christmas
Pageant Ever
Big Mo
Big Red
Bill▶
Bill: On His Own▶
Billy Galvin
Billy Jack
The Birch Interval▶
Black Beauty
Black Beauty▶
Blake of Scotland Yard
Bless the Beasts and
Children
Blue Chips
Blue Fire Lady
Bophal▶
Born Free▶
Born to Run
Bound for Glory▶
The Boy Who Could Fly
The Boy with the Green
Hair
Boys Town▶
Boyz N the Hood▶
Brenda Starr
The Bridge on the River
Kwai▶
A Bronx Tale▶
Brother Future
Captains Courageous▶
The Capture of Grizzly
Adams

VIDEOHOUND'S FAMILY VIDEO RETRIEVER

Further Adventures of the
   Wilderness Family,
   Part 2
Getting Even with Dad
The Gift of Amazing Grace
The Good Son
Goodbye, Miss 4th of July
The Grass is Always
   Greener Over the Septic
   Tank
The Great Outdoors
The Great Santini▶
Greedy
Greenstone
Gypsy Colt
Harry & Son
Harry and the Hendersons
The Haunting of Barney
   Palmer
Heidi
Heidi
Heidi▶
Henry Hamilton: Graduate
   Ghost
Hero▶
Hobo's Christmas
Holy Matrimony
Home at Last
A Home of Our Own
Home to Stay▶
Homecoming: A Christmas
   Story▶
Homeward Bound
Homeward Bound: The
   Incredible Journey▶
Honey, I Blew Up the Kid
Honey, I Shrunk the Kids
Hope and Glory▶
The Horse in the Gray
   Flannel Suit
Hot Lead & Cold Feet
House of Cards
A House Without a
   Christmas Tree
Housekeeping▶
How Green was My
   Valley▶
How the West was Won▶
Huck and the King of
   Hearts
I Live with Me Dad
I Never Sang For My
   Father▶
I Ought to Be in Pictures
I'll Do Anything
Immediate Family
In Search of a Golden Sky
In Search of the
   Castaways▶
Indiana Jones and the Last
   Crusade▶
Into the West▶
It's a Wonderful Life▶
Jack the Bear
Jacob Have I Loved
Joey
Josh and S.A.M.
The Joy Luck Club▶
The Kid Who Loved
   Christmas
King of the Hill▶
Kotch▶
Kramer vs. Kramer▶
Kuffs
La Bamba▶
Labyrinth▶
Lantern Hill
The Last Unicorn
The Legend of Black
   Thunder Mountain
Liar's Moon
Lies My Father Told Me▶
Life with Father▶
Light of Day
Like Jake and Me
The Lion in Winter▶

The Lion King▶
Little Buddha
Little Critter Series: Just
   Me and My Dad
Little House on the
   Prairie▶
Little Sister Rabbit
Little Women▶
The Long Day Closes▶
Look Who's Talking Now
Looking for Miracles
Lorenzo's Oil▶
The Lost Boys
Lost in Yonkers
Lots of Luck
Love Finds Andy Hardy▶
Love Laughs at Andy
   Hardy
Love Your Mama
Made in America
Magic Kid
Man & Boy
The Man in the Iron
   Mask▶
The Man in the Moon▶
The Man in the Santa
   Claus Suit
Man, Woman & Child
Mask▶
Maverick
Meet Me in St. Louis▶
Meet the Hollowheads
The Member of the
   Wedding
Menace on the Mountain
Miracle Down Under
Miracle on 34th Street▶
Mrs. Doubtfire▶
Mr. & Mrs. Bridge▶
Misunderstood
Monkey Trouble▶
Moonstruck▶
Mowgli's Brothers
My Father the Hero
My Father's Glory▶
My Friend Walter
My Girl 2
My Grandpa is a Vampire
My Heroes Have Always
   Been Cowboys
My Life
My Mother's Castle▶
My Old Man
National Lampoon's
   Christmas Vacation
National Lampoon's
   European Vacation
Nearly No Christmas
Night Crossing
North
Not My Kid
Not Quite Human
Nothing in Common
The Old Mill
Old Yeller▶
Ollie Hopnoodle's Haven
   of Bliss
Olly Olly Oxen Free
On Golden Pond▶
The One and Only,
   Genuine, Original Family
   Band
Only the Lonely
Our Little Girl
Out on a Limb
Outside Chance of
   Maximillian Glick▶
Over the Top
Overboard
Paco
Paradise▶
The Parent Trap
Parenthood▶
Peggy Sue Got Married
Penny Serenade▶
Phar Lap

Philadelphia▶
Places in the Heart▶
Please Don't Eat the
   Daisies
Pollyanna▶
Popi▶
Prehysteria
The Prodigal
Queen of Hearts▶
The Quiet Man▶
Radio Flyer
Railway Children▶
Rain Man▶
A Rare Breed
The Real McCoy
Rebecca of Sunnybrook
   Farm
The Red Pony▶
Regarding Henry▶
Rich in Love
The River Rat
A River Runs Through It▶
Rocket Gibraltar▶
Romeo and Juliet▶
Rumble Fish▶
Running Mates
Running on Empty▶
Samantha
Searching for Bobby
   Fischer▶
The Secret Garden▶
See You in the Morning
Sesame Songs: Monster
   Hits!
Seven Alone
Seven Faces of Dr. Lao▶
Shadow of a Doubt▶
The Shadow Riders
Silence
The Silver Stallion: King of
   the Wild Brumbies
Since You Went Away▶
Sixteen Candles▶
Skylark
Smoke
The Snapper▶
Son-in-Law
Son of Flubber
The Sound of Music▶
State Fair▶
State Fair
Stepmonster
The Stone Boy▶
Stop! or My Mom Will
   Shoot
Sugar Cane Alley▶
Summer Magic
The Swiss Family
   Robinson▶
Sylvester
Tank
Terms of Endearment▶
Tex▶
That Was Then. . .This Is
   Now
This Boy's Life▶
This is My Life
The Three Lives of
   Thomasina▶
Three Men and a Cradle▶
3 Ninjas
3 Ninjas Kick Back
Tito and Me▶
Toby McTeague
Toughlove
Toys
Trading Mom
Treasure of the Sierra
   Madre▶
The Trip to Bountiful▶
The Ugly Dachshund
Uncle Buck
Undergrads▶
Wait Till Your Mother Gets
   Home

The Waltons: The
   Children's Carol
What About Bob?▶
What's Eating Gilbert
   Grape▶
When Mom and Dad
   Break Up
When Wolves Cry
Where the Lilies Bloom▶
The Wild Country
Wild Pony▶
Wild Swans
Winnie the Pooh & Friends
With Six You Get Eggroll
The Wizard
The Wizard of Loneliness
A World Apart▶
The Young Detectives on
   Wheels
Yours, Mine & Ours▶

Fantasy
see also Folk Tales
Adventures in Dinosaur
   City
The Adventures of a
   Gnome Named Gnorm
The Adventures of Babar
The Adventures of Baron
   Munchausen▶
Adventures of Black Beauty
The Adventures of Mark
   Twain▶
The Adventures of Sinbad
   the Sailor
The Adventures of the
   Little Prince
Adventures of the Little
   Prince
Aladdin
Aladdin and His Magic
   Lamp
Alice in Wonderland
Alice's Adventures in
   Wonderland
Alligator Pie
Amazing Mr. Blunden
Babar: Monkey Business
Babar the Elephant Comes
   to America
Babar's Triumph
Baby. . .Secret of the Lost
   Legend
Baron Munchausen▶
Batman▶
Batman Returns
*batteries not included
Battle for Moon Station
   Dallos
Beastmaster
Beastmaster 2: Through
   the Portal of Time
Benji's Very Own Christmas
   Story
Bernard and the Genie
Big▶
Big Top Pee Wee
Big Trouble in Little China
Bigfoot and Wildboy
Bill and Coo
Bill & Ted's Excellent
   Adventure
The Blue Bird▶
Box of Delights
The Boy God
The Boy Who Could Fly
The Boy Who Loved Trolls
Bridge to Terabithia
Brothers Lionheart
Caldecott Collection
The Canterville Ghost
Charley and the Angel
Child's Christmas in Wales
The Christmas Party

The Christmas That Almost
   Wasn't
The Chronicles of Narnia▶
Circus Angel▶
Clarence
Clash of the Titans
Cocoon▶
Cocoon: The Return
Conan the Barbarian▶
Conan the Destroyer
A Connecticut Yankee▶
Corduroy and Other Bear
   Stories
The Crow
Daddy Long Legs
Darby O'Gill & the Little
   People▶
The Dark Crystal
Daydreamer▶
The Devil & Max Devlin
Digby, the Biggest Dog in
   the World
Disney's Adventures in
   Wonderland
Disney's TaleSpin, Vol. 1:
   True Baloo
Dr. Seuss' ABC
Dr. Seuss' Hoober-Bloob
   Highway
Dr. Seuss on the Loose
Dr. Seuss' The Lorax
Dragonslayer▶
Dragonworld▶
Dream a Little Dream
Dreamchild▶
DuckTales: Accidental
   Adventurers
Edward Scissorhands▶
The ElmChanted Forest
EPIC: Days of the
   Dinosaurs
E.T.: The Extra-Terrestrial▶
The Ewok Adventure
The Ewoks: Battle for
   Endor
Explorers
Field of Dreams▶
Fire and Ice
Flight of Dragons
Flight of the Navigator▶
Flower Angel
Francis Goes to the Races
Francis Joins the WACs
Francis the Talking Mule▶
Frog Prince
Frogs!
George's Island
Ghostbusters: Back to the
   Past
The Gnome-Mobile
Golden Voyage of Sinbad
The Great Cheese
   Conspiracy
The Great Land of Small
Green Eggs and Ham from
   Dr. Seuss on the Loose
Greenstone
Grendel, Grendel, Grendel
Grimm's Fairy Tales:
   Beauty and the Beast
Gryphon
Gulliver in Lilliput▶
Gulliver's Travels
He-Man & the Masters of
   the Universe, Vol. 1
Heartbreak Hotel
Hector's Bunyip
Henry Hamilton: Graduate
   Ghost
Herbie Rides Again
Hercules
Hey There, It's Yogi Bear
Highlander 2: The
   Quickening
The Hobbit▶
Hook

Hoppity Goes to Town
The Horse That Played Center Field
H.R. Pufnstuf, Vol. 1
A Hungarian Fairy Tale
Hyper-Sapien: People from Another Star
The Incredible Mr. Limpet
Indiana Jones and the Last Crusade▶
It's a Wonderful Life▶
Jack Frost
Jack the Giant Killer
Jason and the Argonauts▶
Jonathan Livingston Seagull
Journey to the Center of the Earth▶
The Jungle Book
A Kid for Two Farthings
King Kong▶
King Kong
Kiss Me Goodbye
Kissyfur!: Hugs and Kissyfur
Krull
L.A. Story▶
Ladyhawke▶
The Land of Faraway
Land of the Lost
The Last Unicorn
Legend
Legend of the White Horse
The Light Princess
Like Father, Like Son
The Lion, the Witch and the Wardrobe▶
The Little Mermaid
Little Monsters
Little Nemo: Adventures in Slumberland
Locke the Superpower
The Lord of the Rings
Lords of Magick
The Magical Princess Gigi
Making Contact
The Man in the Santa Claus Suit
The Man Who Wagged His Tail
Mannequin 2: On the Move
Maple Town: Case of the Missing Candy
Marco Polo, Jr.
Mario
Marvelous Land of Oz
Masters of the Universe
Maurice Sendak Library
Maurice Sendak's Really Rosie
Merlin and the Sword
Mighty Joe Young
Million Dollar Duck
Mr. Destiny
Mr. Magoo's Storybook▶
The Moon Stallion
Munchie
My Friend Walter
My Neighbor Totoro
My Pet Monster, Vol. 1
My Science Project
My Stepmother Is an Alien
Mystery Island
The Navigator▶
The NeverEnding Story
The NeverEnding Story 2: Next Chapter
The New Adventures of Winnie the Pooh, Vol. 1: Great Honey Pot Robbery
The Nightmare Before Christmas▶
The Olden Days Coat
Once a Hero
Once Upon a Time

One Magic Christmas
The Original Fabulous Adventures of Baron Munchausen▶
Out of Time
Ozma of Oz
Panda and the Magic Serpent
The Peanut Butter Solution▶
Peter-No-Tail
Peter Pan▶
Peter Pan & the Pirates: Demise of Hook
Pete's Dragon
Phantom Tollbooth▶
Pinocchio's Christmas
The Point▶
The Polar Bear King
Prancer
Prehysteria
Prehysterial 2
Prelude to a Kiss
Puff and the Incredible Mr. Nobody
Puff the Magic Dragon in the Land of Living Lies
The Puppetoon Movie
Raccoons on Ice
Radio Flyer
The Railway Dragon
Rainbow Brite: A Horse of a Different Color
Reading Rainbow: Perfect the Pig/Ty's One-Man Band
The Red Balloon▶
The Reluctant Dragon
The Rescuers Down Under
Return from Witch Mountain
The Return of Jafar▶
The Return of the King
Return to Oz
Robotman and Friends
Rookie of the Year
Rose-Petal Place
Rosie's Walk
Rumpelstiltskin
Rupert
Rupert and the Runaway Dragon
Samson and Sally: The Song of the Whales▶
Santa Claus Conquers the Martians
Santa Claus: The Movie
Santabear's First Christmas
Santabear's High Flying Adventure
Seabert: Good Guys Wear White
Secret of NIMH▶
Serendipity the Pink Dragon
Seven Faces of Dr. Lao▶
The Seventh Voyage of Sinbad▶
The Shaggy Dog
Sherlock Hound: Dr. Watson I Presume?
Shirley Temple Storybook Theater
Sigmund & the Sea Monsters, Vol. 1
Sinbad and the Eye of the Tiger▶
The Sneetches from Dr. Seuss on the Loose
Solarbabies
Something Wicked This Way Comes
Somewhere in Time
Son of Flubber
Son of Kong
Space Firebird

Space Raiders
Space Warriors: Battle for Earth Station S/1
Splash▶
Stand Up and Cheer
Stories to Remember: Merlin and the Dragons
The Story of a Cowboy Angel
Stowaways on the Ark
Super Mario Bros.
Supergirl
Superman 1: The Movie▶
Superman 2▶
Superman 3
Superman 4: The Quest for Peace
Superman & the Mole Men
Superman: The Serial, Vol. 1
The Sword in the Stone▶
Sword of the Valiant
Tales of Beatrix Potter▶
The Talking Parcel
Ted E. Bear: The Bear Who Slept Through Christmas
Teenage Mutant Ninja Turtles 1: The Movie
Teenage Mutant Ninja Turtles: The Epic Begins
Thief of Baghdad▶
Thief of Baghdad
The Thief of Baghdad
The Three Worlds of Gulliver
Through the Looking Glass
Thunderbirds in Outerspace
Thundercats, Vol. 1: Exodus
Time Bandits▶
Timefighters in the Land of Fantasy
Tobor the Great
tom thumb
Tommy Tricker & the Stamp Traveller▶
Trading Mom
Transformers: The Movie
20,000 Leagues Under the Sea▶
20,000 Leagues Under the Sea
The Undersea Adventures of Snelgrove Snail
Undersea Kingdom
Unico in the Island of Magic
Unidentified Flying Oddball
The Valley of Gwangi▶
The Velveteen Rabbit
Vengeance of the Space Pirate
Vice Versa▶
Visionaries, Vol. 1: The Age of Magic Begins
Walking on Air
Warriors of the Wind
Watership Down▶
Welcome to Pooh Corner: Vol. 1
Where the Wild Things Are
Willow
Willy McBean & His Magic Machine
Wind in the Willows
Wind in the Willows, Vol. 1
Wings of Desire▶
Winnie the Pooh and the Blustery Day
Winnie the Pooh and the Honey Tree
Winter of the Witch
The Wizard of Oz

The Wizard of Oz: Danger in a Strange Land
The Wizard of Speed and Time▶
Wizards
Wizards of the Lost Kingdom
Wizards of the Lost Kingdom 2
The Wonderful World of the Brothers Grimm
Woofl▶
World of David the Gnome: Kangaroo Adventure
The Worst Witch
Young Magician▶
The Zax From Dr. Seuss on the Loose

Farming
see **On the Farm**

Fast Cars
see also ***Cool Cars***
Burn 'Em Up Barnes
Cannonball
Cannonball Run
Cannonball Run 2
Catch Me. . .If You Can
Eat My Dust
Greased Lightning
Great Race
Gumball Rally
Heart Like a Wheel▶
The Heavenly Kid
Herbie Goes Bananas
Herbie Goes to Monte Carlo
Heroes on Hot Wheels, Vol. 1
The Last American Hero▶
The Perils of Penelope Pitstop
Rebel Without a Cause▶
Six Pack
Smokey and the Bandit
Those Daring Young Men in Their Jaunty Jalopies

Fifties
see ***Nifty '50s***

Film Noir
Key Largo▶
The Maltese Falcon▶
The Window▶
The Wrong Man▶

Film Stars
see also ***Price of Fame***
Calendar Girl
Chaplin▶
Dear Brigitte
Hurricane Express
My Favorite Year▶
Play It Again, Sam▶
The Purple Rose of Cairo▶
That's Entertainment
That's Entertainment, Part 2
That's Entertainment, Part 3

Firemen
see also ***Policemen***
Always
Club Paradise
Mighty Joe Young
Roxanne▶
Sesame Street Visits the Firehouse
Touring the Firehouse
Turk 182!

Flight
see ***Airborne***

Flying Saucer
see ***Aliens— Nasty;
Aliens—Nice***

Folk Tales
see also ***Fairy Tales***
Adventures of Tom Sawyer
Ali Baba and the Forty Thieves
American Folk Heroes and Tall Tales
Anansi
The Ballad of Paul Bunyan
Brer Rabbit and Boss Lion
Clash of the Titans
Darby O'Gill & the Little People▶
East of the Sun, West of the Moon
Erik the Viking
Field of Dreams▶
Finn McCoul
Force on Thunder Mountain
Golden Voyage of Sinbad
Grendel, Grendel, Grendel
Hercules
Hercules 2
Hercules Unchained
Into the West▶
Invitation to the Dance
Jason and the Argonauts▶
John Henry
Johnny Appleseed
King Arthur & the Knights of the Round Table, Vol. 1
Koi and the Kola Nuts
The Legend of Sleepy Hollow
Matt the Gooseboy
Merlin and the Sword
Mighty Hercules: Champion of the People!
Mighty Hercules: Conqueror of Evil!
The Mighty Hercules: Mightiest Mortal!
The Monkey People
Monty Python and the Holy Grail▶
The Owl and the Pussycat
Paul Bunyan
Pecos Bill
Princess Scargo and the Birthday Pumpkin
Rip Van Winkle
Room for Heroes
The Secret of Navajo Cave
Serendipity the Pink Dragon
Stories and Fables, Vol. 1
Stormalong
The Talking Eggs
Tall Tales and Legends: Johnny Appleseed
The Wonderful World of the Brothers Grimm

Football
Ace Ventura: Pet Detective
All the Right Moves
The Best of Times
Brian's Song▶
Gus
Horse Feathers▶
Knute Rockne: All American▶
The Program
Quarterback Princess
Rudy
School Ties▶
Wildcats

France

An American in Paris▶
Charade▶
Dirty Rotten Scoundrels▶
French Postcards
Inspector Clouseau: Ape
  Suzette
Inspector Clouseau:
  Napoleon Blown-Aparte
Madeline
The Man in the Iron
  Mask▶
Monkeys, Go Home!
My Father's Glory▶
The Scarlet Pimpernel▶
To Catch a Thief▶

Friendship
  see Best Friends

Funny Adventures
  *see also Amazing
  Adventures; Laugh Riots*
The Absent-Minded
  Professor▶
Adventures in Babysitting
Adventures in Spying
The Adventures of Bullwhip
  Griffin
The Amazing Dobermans
Andy and the Airwave
  Rangers
Another Stakeout
Baby on Board
Back to the Future▶
Back to the Future, Part 2
Back to the Future, Part 3
Bagdad Cafe▶
Beverly Hills Cop
Beverly Hills Cop 2
Beverly Hills Cop 3
Bingo
Boris and Natasha: The
  Movie
Brothers O'Toole
Cannonball Run
Cannonball Run 2
Club Med
Collision Course
Crocodile Dundee
Crocodile Dundee 2
Dirt Bike Kid
Dog Pound Shuffle
The Double O Kid
Fast Getaway
The Fifth Musketeer
Forever Young
Foul Play▶
Ghostbusters▶
Ghostbusters 2
The Golden Child
Hambone & Hillie
Ice Pirates
Jane & the Lost City
The Jewel of the Nile
Just Tell Me You Love Me
Kindergarten Cop
Kuffs
Last Action Hero
Leonard Part 6
Magic Kid
The Man with One Red
  Shoe
Memoirs of an Invisible
  Man
Midnight Madness
Mr. Nanny
Mr. Superinvisible
Mom and Dad Save the
  World
Monkey's Uncle
My Dog, the Thief
My Science Project
No Deposit, No Return
Pippi Goes on Board
Pippi in the South Seas

Pippi Longstocking
Pippi on the Run
Prehysteria
The Reivers▶
The Return of the
  Musketeers
Romancing the Stone▶
Russkies
The Silver Streak▶
Ski Patrol
Smokey and the Bandit
Smokey and the Bandit,
  Part 2
Smokey and the Bandit,
  Part 3
Stepmonster
The Sting 2
Stop! or My Mom Will
  Shoot
Suburban Commando
Super Fuzz
Surf Ninjas
The Tall Blond Man with
  One Black Shoe
Teenage Mutant Ninja
  Turtles 1: The Movie
Teenage Mutant Ninja
  Turtles 2: The Secret of
  the Ooze
Teenage Mutant Ninja
  Turtles 3
That Sinking Feeling▶
Think Big
Those Daring Young Men
  in Their Jaunty Jalopies
Three Amigos
Three Fugitives
Three Musketeers▶
3 Ninjas
3 Ninjas Kick Back
Tough Guys
Trenchcoat
True Lies
Under the Rainbow
Year of the Comet

Gangs
  *see also Crime Doesn't
  Pay; It's the Mob*
All Dogs Go to Heaven
Blues Busters
Bowery Blitzkrieg
Boyz N the Hood▶
Broadway Danny Rose▶
Clipped Wings
Diamonds on Wheels
Dick Tracy vs. Cueball
The Doberman Gang
The Dog Who Stopped the
  War▶
Emil and the Detective
Ghost Chasers
Gone are the Days
The Great Mike
Hard-Boiled Mahoney
Harley
Johnny Dangerously
Just William's Luck
Key Largo▶
The Longshot
Menace II Society▶
The Meteor Man
Million Dollar Kid
Mystery Date
'Neath Brooklyn Bridge
Never a Dull Moment
The Outsiders
Paco
Prize Fighter
Rumble Fish▶
Smart Alecks
Spook Busters
West Side Story▶
Wonder Man

Garfield

Garfield
A Garfield Christmas
Garfield Goes Hollywood
Garfield: His 9 Lives
Garfield in Paradise
Garfield on the Town
Garfield's Feline Fantasy
Garfield's Halloween
  Adventure
Garfield's Thanksgiving
Here Comes Garfield

Genies

Aladdin▶
Aladdin and the Magic
  Lamp
Ali Baba's Revenge
Bernard and the Genie
Mr. Magoo: 1001 Arabian
  Night's Dream
Shazzan
Thief of Baghdad▶
The Thief of Baghdad
Wonders of Aladdin

Ghosts, Ghouls, &
Goblins
  *see also Demons &
  Wizards*
Amazing Mr. Blunden
Beetlejuice▶
The Canterville Ghost
Casper's Halloween
The Gate
Ghost▶
Ghost Dad
The Ghost Goes West▶
Ghost Stories
Ghostbusters▶
Ghostbusters 2
The Haunting of Barney
  Palmer
Heart and Souls
The House of Dies Drear
My Friend Walter
Poltergeist▶
Poltergeist 2: The Other
  Side
Poltergeist 3
The Princess and the
  Goblin
Somewhere Tomorrow
13 Ghosts
Topper▶
Topper Returns▶
Topper Takes a Trip▶
Watcher in the Woods

Giants
  see also Monsters, General
Godzilla vs. Megalon
The Princess Bride
Quark the Dragon Slayer
The Spy Who Loved Me

Gifted Children

And You Thought Your
  Parents Were Weird!
Dear Brigitte
Escape to Witch
  Mountain▶
Little Man Tate▶
On the Right Track
Real Genius▶
Rookie of the Year
Searching for Bobby
  Fischer▶

Go Fish

Captains Courageous▶
The Day of the Dolphin
Forrest Gump▶
Free Willy
Grumpy Old Men▶
On Golden Pond▶

A River Runs Through It▶
Whale for the Killing

Godzilla & Friends

Destroy All Monsters
Godzilla vs. Megalon
Godzilla vs. the Cosmic
  Monster
Godzilla vs. the Smog
  Monster

Going Native

The Bounty▶
Dances with Wolves▶
Lord of the Flies▶
Lord of the Flies
Robinson Crusoe
The Swiss Family
  Robinson▶

Golf

The Caddy
Caddyshack▶

Gory Stories
  *see also Oooh...That's
  Scary!*
Army of Darkness▶
Destroy All Monsters
Ghoulies
Robocop 2
Walking Tall

Gotta Dance!
  *see also Ballet; Gotta
  Sing!*
An American in Paris▶
Anchors Aweigh▶
Babes in Arms
The Band Wagon▶
Beat Street
The Belle of New York
Breakin' Through
Captain January
Dirty Dancing▶
Fame▶
Fast Forward
Flashdance
Flower Drum Song
Follow the Fleet▶
Footloose
Girls Just Want to Have
  Fun
Grease
Grease 2
The In Crowd
Invitation to the Dance
Reading Rainbow: Sophie
  and Lou
Sesame Songs: Dance
  Along!
Seven Brides for Seven
  Brothers▶
Shag: The Movie▶
Shall We Dance?
Singin' in the Rain▶
Strictly Ballroom▶
Swing Kids
That's Dancing!
That's Entertainment, Part 2
That's Entertainment, Part 3
Twist
Yankee Doodle Dandy▶

Gotta Sing!
  *see also Cartoon Tunes;
  Gotta Dance!*
Almost Angels
An American in Paris▶
Anchors Aweigh▶
Andy Hardy Meets
  Debutante
Annie
Babes in Arms
Babes in Toyland
Babes on Broadway

The Band Wagon▶
Beach Blanket Bingo▶
Beach Party
Beat Street
Bedknobs and Broomsticks
The Belle of New York
Bikini Beach
Blame It on the Night
The Boy Friend▶
Breakin' Through
Breaking the Ice
The Buddy Holly Story▶
Bugsy Malone
Bye, Bye, Birdie▶
Camelot
Car Wash
Carousel▶
Chitty Chitty Bang Bang
Cinderella
Coal Miner's Daughter▶
The Cocoanuts
Comic Book Kids
A Connecticut Yankee in
  King Arthur's Court
The Court Jester▶
Cry-Baby▶
Curly Top
Dimples
Disorderlies
Doctor Doolittle
Easter Parade▶
Eddie and the Cruisers
Fame▶
Fast Forward
Fiddler on the Roof▶
Finian's Rainbow
Fisherman's Wharf
The 5000 Fingers of Dr.
  T▶
Flashdance
Flower Drum Song
Follow the Fleet▶
Footloose
Funny Face▶
Funny Girl▶
Funny Lady
George Balanchine's The
  Nutcracker
Girl Crazy▶
The Glenn Miller Story▶
Going My Way▶
Grease
Grease 2
Guys and Dolls▶
Hairspray▶
Hans Brinker
The Happiest Millionaire
Head▶
Hello, Dolly!
Help!▶
High Society
Holiday Inn
How to Stuff a Wild Bikini
Huckleberry Finn
The In Crowd
Invitation to the Dance
It Happened at the
  World's Fair
Jesus Christ, Superstar▶
The Jolson Story▶
Just Around the Corner
The King and I▶
Kismet
La Bamba▶
Labyrinth▶
Let's Sing Again
Life Begins for Andy
  Hardy▶
Light of Day
Lili▶
Little Miss Broadway
The Little Prince
Little Shop of Horrors▶
The Littlest Angel
The Littlest Rebel

Man of La Mancha
March of the Wooden
 Soldiers▶
Mary Poppins▶
Meet Me in St. Louis▶
The Muppet Christmas
 Carol▶
The Muppet Movie▶
Muppets Take Manhattan▶
Muscle Beach Party
The Music Man▶
The New Adventures of
 Pippi Longstocking
Newsies
Oklahoma!▶
The Old Curiosity Shop
Oliver!▶
On a Clear Day You Can
 See Forever
Once Upon a Brothers
 Grimm
The One and Only,
 Genuine, Original Family
 Band
Paint Your Wagon
Pajama Party
Peter Pan▶
Pippin▶
Pirate Movie
The Poor Little Rich Girl
Popeye
Rebecca of Sunnybrook
 Farm
The Red Shoes▶
Rock 'n' Roll High School▶
Rock 'n' Roll High School
 Forever
Rumpelstiltskin
Sarafina!▶
Satisfaction
Scrooge
Seven Brides for Seven
 Brothers▶
The Seven Little Foys▶
1776▶
Shall We Dance▶
Shout
Sing
Singin' in the Rain▶
Sleeping Beauty
Song City U.S.A.
The Sound of Music▶
South Pacific▶
State Fair▶
State Fair
Stowaway▶
Strike Up the Band
That's Dancing!
That's Entertainment
That's Entertainment, Part 2
That's Entertainment, Part 3
Till the Clouds Roll By
Tommy
Waltz King
West Side Story▶
What's Love Got to Do
 With It?
White Christmas▶
Willy Wonka & the
 Chocolate Factory▶
The Wiz
The Wizard of Oz▶
Wonder Man
Xanadu
Yankee Doodle Dandy▶
Yentl

Grand Hotel
Dirty Dancing▶
For Love or Money
Holiday Inn
A Night in Casablanca
Room Service
Snowball Express

Great Britain
see also Ireland; Scotland
Amazing Mr. Blunden
Back Home
Camelot
The Corn is Green▶
Diamonds on Wheels
Four Weddings and a
 Funeral▶
The Great Muppet Caper▶
How Green was My
 Valley▶
Jack and the Beanstalk
King Ralph
The Lion in Winter▶
The Long Day Closes▶
A Man for All Seasons▶
The Secret Garden▶
Shadowlands▶
That Sinking Feeling▶
Year of the Comet

Great Death Scenes
Buffy the Vampire Slayer
Butch Cassidy and the
 Sundance Kid▶
Gettysburg▶
Highlander▶
Highlander: The Gathering
Jurassic Park▶
Monty Python and the
 Holy Grail▶
Shadowlands▶
The Wizard of Oz▶

Great Depression
see also Homeless
Bound for Glory▶
Charley and the Angel
A Christmas to Remember
Fatty Finn
Homecoming: A Christmas
 Story▶
Honkytonk Man
It Happened One Night▶
The Journey of Natty
 Gann▶
Just Around the Corner
King of the Hill▶
Of Mice and Men▶
Paper Moon▶
Places in the Heart▶
Rambling Rose▶
Sounder▶
Who Has Seen the Wind?
Why Shoot the Teacher?▶
Wild Hearts Can't Be
 Broken▶

Great Escapes
*see also POW/MIA; War,
General*
Butch Cassidy and the
 Sundance Kid▶
A Day in October
Escape Artist▶
Escape to Witch
 Mountain▶
The Great Train Robbery▶
Ladyhawke▶
Mysterious Island▶
Night Crossing▶
North by Northwest▶
Papillon▶
A Perfect World
Raiders of the Lost Ark▶
Romancing the Stone▶
The Sound of Music▶
To Catch a Thief▶
Torn Curtain
Victory
Zebra in the Kitchen

Growing Older
*batteries not included
The Best of Times

The Cheyenne Social Club
Citizen Kane▶
City Slickers▶
Cocoon▶
Cocoon: The Return
Dad
Dream a Little Dream
Driving Miss Daisy▶
Going in Style▶
Greedy
Grumpy Old Men▶
Home to Stay▶
Ira Sleeps Over
Kotch▶
Lightning Jack
Miss Firecracker▶
My Heroes Have Always
 Been Cowboys
On Golden Pond▶
Pastime▶
Rocket Gibraltar▶
The Shootist▶
Strangers in Good
 Company▶
The Sunshine Boys▶
Toto le Heros▶
Tough Guys
Two of a Kind

Growing Pains
see also Teen Tribulations
Across the Great Divide
Ah, Wilderness!▶
Alan & Naomi
All the Right Moves
Aloha Summer
American Boyfriends
American Graffiti▶
An American Summer
Angelo My Love▶
Anne of Green Gables▶
The Apprenticeship of
 Duddy Kravitz▶
Au Revoir Les Enfants▶
Big▶
The Birch Interval▶
Blue Fin
Breaking Away▶
Brighton Beach Memoirs
A Bronx Tale▶
Calendar Girl
Can't Buy Me Love
The Chicken Chronicles
City Boy
Clowning Around 2
Courage Mountain
Crazy Moon
Cria▶
A Cry in the Wild▶
Culpepper Cattle Co.
Dakota
Dead Poets Society▶
December
Desert Bloom▶
Dirty Dancing▶
Edward Scissorhands▶
Experience Preferred. . .
 But Not Essential
Family Prayers
Fandango
Fast Times at Ridgemont
 High▶
The Fire in the Stone
The Flamingo Kid▶
The 400 Blows▶
Foxes
A Friendship in Vienna
Frogs!
Gidget
Goodbye, Miss 4th of July
The Great Outdoors
The Great Santini▶
Gregory's Girl▶
Hairspray▶
A Hero Ain't Nothin' But a
 Sandwich▶

Holy Matrimony
Huck and the King of
 Hearts
The Human Comedy▶
If Looks Could Kill
Indian Paint
Jacob Have I Loved
Joey
The Journey of Natty
 Gann▶
The Karate Kid▶
The Karate Kid: Part 2
The Karate Kid: Part 3
King of the Hill▶
Kipperbang
Labyrinth▶
The Last Prostitute
The Lawrenceville Stories
The Learning Tree
The Legend of Young
 Robin Hood
The Lion King▶
A Little Romance▶
Little Women▶
The Long Day Closes▶
The Lords of Flatbush
Lost Legacy: A Girl Called
 Hatter Fox
Lucas▶
Maid to Order
The Man from Snowy River
The Man in the Moon▶
The Man Without a Face
Matinee
The Member of the
 Wedding
Metropolitan▶
A Midnight Clear▶
More American Graffiti
Mosby's Marauders
My American Cousin▶
My Bodyguard▶
My Girl
My Girl 2
My Life as a Dog▶
No Time for Sergeants▶
Ode to Billy Joe
Oh, What a Night
Old Enough
One on One
The Outsiders
Over the Edge▶
The Paper Chase▶
P.C.U.
Peter Lundy and the
 Medicine Hat Stallion
The Power of One
The Prodigal
Racing with the Moon▶
Rambling Rose▶
The Reivers▶
Reunion▶
A River Runs Through It▶
Rumble Fish▶
The Sandlot▶
Sarafina!▶
A Separate Peace
Seven Minutes in Heaven
Shipwrecked
Shout
Smooth Talk▶
Some Kind of Wonderful
Sounder▶
SpaceCamp
Square Dance
Stacking
Star Wars▶
Sweet 15
Swing Kids
The Sword in the Stone▶
Teenage Mutant Ninja
 Turtles 2: The Secret of
 the Ooze
Tex▶
That Night

That Was Then. . .This Is
 Now
This Boy's Life▶
Toby Tyler▶
Tomboy & the Champ
Top Gun
A Tree Grows in
 Brooklyn▶
What's Eating Gilbert
 Grape▶
Where the Red Fern
 Grows: Part 2
Who Has Seen the Wind?
Why Shoot the Teacher?▶
The Wild Child▶
With Honors
The Year My Voice Broke▶
The Yearling▶
Young Sherlock Holmes

Gymnastics
American Anthem
Nadia

Hallmark Hall of Fame
Sarah, Plain and Tall▶
The Secret Garden▶
Skylark

Heaven Sent
see also Angels
All Dogs Go to Heaven
Almost an Angel
Always
Carousel▶
Chances Are▶
Charley and the Angel
Clarence
Date with an Angel
Field of Dreams▶
Ghost▶
Ghost Dad
The Heavenly Kid
The Horn Blows at
 Midnight▶
It Came Upon a Midnight
 Clear
It's a Wonderful Life▶
Kiss Me Goodbye
The Littlest Angel
Mr. Destiny
Oh, God!▶
Oh, God! Book 2
Oh, God! You Devil
One Magic Christmas
The Three Lives of
 Thomasina
Truly, Madly, Deeply▶
Xanadu

Heists
see also The Big Sting
The Apple Dumpling Gang
The Boatniks
Butch and Sundance: The
 Early Days
Daring Dobermans
Getting Even with Dad
Going in Style▶
The Great Train Robbery▶
Holy Matrimony
The Horse Without a Head
Lightning Jack
My Dog, the Thief
The Pink Panther▶
The Real McCoy
Sneakers
To Catch a Thief▶
Tough Guys

High School Hijinks
*see also College Capers;
Elementary School
Escapades; Teacher,
Teacher; Teen Tribulations*
Buffy the Vampire Slayer

The Chicken Chronicles
Class Act
Coach
Coneheads
Cooley High▶
Cry-Baby▶
Dazed and Confused▶
The Ernest Green Story
Fast Times at Ridgemont High▶
Ferris Bueller's Day Off▶
Grease 2
Great Love Experiment
Great St. Trinian's Train Robbery
Hadley's Rebellion
Hiding Out
Hoosiers▶
The Lawrenceville Stories
My Bodyguard▶
On the Edge: The Survival of Dana
Peggy Sue Got Married
Rock 'n' Roll High School▶
Rock 'n' Roll High School Forever
School Ties▶
Sidekicks
Sister Act 2: Back in the Habit
Some Kind of Wonderful
Summer School
Three O'Clock High
Tom Brown's School Days▶

High Seas Adventure
see also Go Fish; Scuba Diving; Submarines
The Adventures of Huckleberry Finn
The Adventures of Sinbad the Sailor
The African Queen▶
The Boatniks
The Bounty▶
Cabin Boy
Captain Ron
Captains Courageous▶
Cry from the Mountain
Don Winslow of the Coast Guard
The Dove
He is My Brother
The Hunt for Red October▶
The Incredible Mr. Limpet
The Jewel of the Nile
Live and Let Die
Monkey Business▶
Oxford Blues
The Poseidon Adventure
Romancing the Stone▶
Save the Lady
Sea Gypsies
Sinbad the Sailor▶
Wind
Wonderland Cove

Historical Happenings
see also Medieval Romps; Period Piece
The Adventures of Tom Sawyer
Amadeus▶
Battle of Britain
The Blue Yonder
A Bridge Too Far
A Connecticut Yankee▶
Dances with Wolves▶
David Copperfield▶
David Copperfield
Doctor Zhivago▶
1492: Conquest of Paradise
Geronimo: An American Legend

Gettysburg▶
The Hunchback of Notre Dame▶
Jesus of Nazareth▶
Johnny Tremain & the Sons of Liberty
Justin Morgan Had a Horse
The Last of the Mohicans▶
The Lion in Winter▶
Lionheart
Little House on the Prairie▶
A Man for All Seasons▶
Mountain Man
Orphan Train▶
The Power of One
The Right Stuff▶
Rob Roy - The Highland Rogue
Robin and Marian
The Scarlet Pimpernel▶
The Ten Commandments▶
Ten Who Dared
Who Has Seen the Wind?

Hockey
see also Skating
The Cutting Edge
D2: The Mighty Ducks
Hockey Night
The Mighty Ducks
Miracle on Ice
Raccoons on Ice

Holidays
see also Christmas
B.C.: The First Thanksgiving
Bobby Goldsboro's Easter Egg Mornin'
Bubbe's Boarding House: Chanukah at Bubbe's
Casper's Halloween
A Day for Thanks on Walton's Mountain
Disney's Haunted Halloween
Disney's Wonderful World of Winter
Easter Bunny is Coming to Town
Easter Egg Mornin'
Easter Parade▶
Family Circus Easter
The First Easter Rabbit
Follow that Bunny!
Frosty Returns
Groundhog Day▶
Gumby's Holiday Special
Happy Holidays with Darkwing Duck and Goofy
Here Comes Peter Cottontail
The Hoboken Chicken Emergency
Hocus Pocus
The Legend of Sleepy Hollow
Lumpkin the Pumpkin
Mouse on the Mayflower
Reading Rainbow: Mrs. Katz and Tush
Spaced Invaders
Special Valentine with Family Circus
Squanto and the First Thanksgiving
Thumpkin and the Easter Bunnies
Trick or Treat
Will Vinton's Claymation Comedy of Horrors
Will Vinton's Claymation Easter
Witch's Night Out

Home Alone
see also Childhood Visions
Adventures in Babysitting
And You Thought Your Parents Were Weird!
The Apple Dumpling Gang
Baby's Day Out
Blank Check
Bless the Beasts and Children
Camp Nowhere
Cloak & Dagger
Courage Mountain
Dirt Bike Kid
Don't Tell Mom the Babysitter's Dead
Explorers
Famous Five Get into Trouble
A Far Off Place
Gleaming the Cube
The Goonies
He is My Brother
Home Alone▶
Home Alone 2: Lost in New York
Honey, I Shrunk the Kids
Hook
The Horse Without a Head
Invaders from Mars
Just William's Luck
Legend of Billie Jean
The Littlest Horse Thieves
Lord of the Flies▶
Lord of the Flies
Mr. Wise Guy
Monkey Trouble▶
The Monster Squad
The Rescue
Shipwrecked
Snow Treasure
3 Ninjas
3 Ninjas Kick Back
A Waltz Through the Hills
The Window▶
Young Sherlock Holmes

Homeless
see also Great Depression
The Billion Dollar Hobo
City Lights▶
Curly Sue
Home for Christmas
Into the West▶
Little Dog Lost
Sounder▶
Summer Magic
With Honors

Horses
Black Beauty
Black Beauty▶
The Black Stallion▶
The Black Stallion Returns
Blue Fire Lady
Born to Run
Casey's Shadow
City Slickers 2: The Legend of Curly's Gold
Courage of Black Beauty
Courage of the North
Danny
Dark Horse
Devil Horse
The Electric Horseman
The Flying Deuces▶
The Great Mike
Gypsy Colt
The Horse in the Gray Flannel Suit
Horsemasters
Hot to Trot!
Indian Paint
International Velvet
Into the West▶

Justin Morgan Had a Horse
King of the Wind
Legend of the White Horse
The Littlest Horse Thieves
The Littlest Outlaw
The Man from Snowy River
Miracle of the White Stallions
My Friend Flicka▶
Primo Baby
The Prince and the Great Race
The Quiet Man▶
A Rare Breed
The Red Pony
Return to Snowy River
Ride a Wild Pony
Run, Appaloosa, Run
Running Wild
Silver Stallion
The Silver Stallion: King of the Wild Brumbies
Stormy, the Thoroughbred
Wild Hearts Can't Be Broken▶
Wild Horse Hank
Wild Pony▶

Hospitals
see also Doctors & Nurses
The Adventures of Curious George
Disorderlies
The Disorderly Orderly
Gross Anatomy

Hunting
see also Go Fish
The Bear▶
The Belstone Fox
Caddyshack▶
The Silver Fox and Sam Davenport
Those Calloways

In Concert
Barney in Concert
For Our Children: The Concert
Sharon, Lois & Bram at the Young People's Theatre
Sharon, Lois & Bram: Back by Popular Demand-Live
Sharon, Lois & Bram: Live in Your Living Room
Sharon, Lois & Bram: Sing A to Z
Tom Chapin: This Pretty Planet

Inventors
see also Mad Scientists; Scientists
Chitty Chitty Bang Bang
C.H.O.M.P.S.
Honey, I Blew Up the Kid
Honey, I Shrunk the Kids
Not Quite Human
Reading Rainbow: Alistair's Time Machine
The Saga of Windwagon Smith
Where's Willie?
Wowser: Wow-Wow Wowser

Ireland
see also Great Britain
The Commitments▶
Darby O'Gill & the Little People▶
Far and Away
The Fighting Prince of Donegal

Into the West▶
The Playboys▶
The Quiet Man▶
Ryan's Daughter
The Snapper▶

Islands in the Sea
Aloha Summer
Cabin Boy
Captain Ron
The Castaway Cowboy
Club Paradise
Crusoe
Fighting Marines
Hawk of the Wilderness
Island of Dr. Moreau
Island of the Blue Dolphins
Joe Versus the Volcano
Jurassic Park▶
The Last Flight of Noah's Ark
Lt. Robin Crusoe, U.S.N.
My Father the Hero
Mysterious Island▶
Pippi in the South Seas
Robinson Crusoe
South Pacific▶

Italy
Cinema Paradiso▶
Escapade in Florence
A Rare Breed

It's the Mob
see also Crime Doesn't Pay; Gangs; Stupid Crime
Another Stakeout
Baby on Board
Blank Check
A Bronx Tale▶
Bugsy Malone
Car 54, Where Are You?
The Client
Comfort and Joy▶
Cops and Robbersons
Dick Tracy▶
Ernest Goes to Jail
The Freshman
Hiding Out
Magic Kid
Making the Grade
Odd Jobs
7 Ninja Kids

It's True!
see also Biopics
Alive
All the President's Men▶
Andre
Au Revoir Les Enfants▶
Backbeat▶
Big Mo
Bill▶
Bill: On His Own▶
Camel Boy
Chariots of Fire▶
Christian the Lion
Conrack▶
Cool Runnings
David and Lisa▶
The Dove
The Elephant Man▶
Empire of the Sun▶
The Ernest Green Story
Eye on the Sparrow
Fire in the Sky
Geronimo▶
The Girl Who Spelled Freedom▶
Goodbye, Miss 4th of July
The Great Train Robbery▶
The Grey Fox▶
Heart Like a Wheel▶
Heartland▶
A Home of Our Own

I Am a Fugitive from a
　Chain Gang▶
Iron Will
Island of the Blue Dolphins
Jesus Christ, Superstar▶
Joni
Justin Morgan Had a
　Horse
Kidco
King of the Wind
Knute Rockne: All
　American▶
The Last American Hero▶
Lean on Me▶
Legend of Boggy Creek
Life & Times of Grizzly
　Adams
Little Boy Lost
Little Heroes
Lone Star Kid
Lorenzo's Oil▶
Love Leads the Way
Mark Twain and Me
Mask▶
Miracle of Our Lady of
　Fatima
The Miracle Worker▶
Mountain Man
Night Crossing
Norma Rae▶
The Other Side of the
　Mountain
Phar Lap
Quarterback Princess
Ring of Bright Water▶
Rudy
Running Brave
Sea Gypsies
Searching for Bobby
　Fischer▶
Shadowlands▶
Silence of the North
Skeezer
The Sound of Music▶
Squanto and the First
　Thanksgiving
Stand and Deliver▶
Ten Who Dared
Till the Clouds Roll By
Touched by Love
Walking Tall
What's Love Got to Do
　With It?
The Wild Child▶
Wild Hearts Can't Be
　Broken▶
A Winner Never Quits
A World Apart▶
The Wrong Man▶
Yours, Mine & Ours▶

James Bond
Diamonds Are Forever▶
Dr. No▶
For Your Eyes Only▶
From Russia with Love▶
Live and Let Die
The Man with the Golden
　Gun
Moonraker
Never Say Never Again
Octopussy
On Her Majesty's Secret
　Service▶
The Spy Who Loved Me
Thunderball
A View to a Kill
You Only Live Twice

Japan
see also *Asia*
Big Bird in Japan
Escapade in Japan
Hiroshima Maiden
Mr. Baseball
Peachboy

3 Ninjas Kick Back
You Only Live Twice

Journalism
see *Newsroom Notes*

Judaism
The Apprenticeship of
　Duddy Kravitz▶
Au Revoir Les Enfants▶
Crossing Delancey▶
Fiddler on the Roof▶
A Friendship in Vienna
Funny Girl▶
Lies My Father Told Me▶
Miracle at Moreaux
Outside Chance of
　Maximillian Glick▶
Radio Days▶
Reading Rainbow: Mrs.
　Katz and Tush
School Ties▶
Yentl

Jungle Stories
see also *Treasure Hunt*
Africa Screams
Baby. . .Secret of the Lost
　Legend
Elephant Boy▶
George of the Jungle
Greystoke: The Legend of
　Tarzan, Lord of the
　Apes
Jane & the Lost City
The Jungle Book
The Jungle Book▶
Jungle Book: Mowgli
　Comes to the Jungle
Jungle Drums of Africa
Land of the Lost
The Lion King▶
The Lost Jungle
Mowgli's Brothers
Rikki-Tikki-Tavi
Romancing the Stone▶
Sheena
Son of Kong
Tarzan and His Mate▶
Tarzan Escapes▶
Tarzan Finds a Son▶
Tarzan, the Ape Man▶
Tarzan's Secret Treasure
Terror in the Jungle
Where the River Runs
　Black
Widget of the Jungle
The World's Greatest
　Athlete

Kidnapped!
see also *Missing Persons*
Ace Ventura: Pet Detective
Against A Crooked Sky
Baby's Day Out
Beach Blanket Bingo▶
Beethoven's 2nd
Benji▶
Beverly Hills Brats
Fire in the Sky
Kid Colter
The Light in the Forest
Mr. Nanny
The Nightmare Before
　Christmas▶
No Deposit, No Return
A Perfect World
The Real McCoy
Son of the Pink Panther
Tarzan's New York
　Adventure
3 Ninjas

A Kid's Best Friend
Andre
Black Beauty▶

Flipper
Free Willy
Iron Will
Lassie
Lassie, Come Home▶
Lassie: The Miracle
Monkey Trouble▶

Kindness of Strangers
Forrest Gump▶
Lilies of the Field▶
Mr. North

King of Beasts (Dogs)
The Adventures of Milo &
　Otis▶
All Dogs Go to Heaven
The Amazing Dobermans
Antarctica
Barney's Christmas Surprise
Beethoven
Beethoven's 2nd
Benji▶
Benji the Hunted
Benji's Very Own Christmas
　Story
Big Red
Bingo
Bunnicula: Vampire Rabbit
Call of the Wild
Canine Commando
Challenge To Be Free
Challenge to Lassie
Challenge to White Fang
The Charlie Brown and
　Snoopy Show: Vol. 1
Chips the War Dog
C.H.O.M.P.S.
Clean Slate
Courage of Lassie
Courage of the North
Daring Dobermans
Digby, the Biggest Dog in
　the World
The Doberman Gang
A Dog of Flanders
Dog Pound Shuffle
The Dog Who Dared
The Dog Who Stopped the
　War▶
Dusty
Elmer
Fabulous Joe
Famous Five Get into
　Trouble
For the Love of Benji▶
The Fox and the Hound▶
Frankenweenie
George!
Goober & the Ghost
　Chasers
Great Adventure
Greyfriars Bobby▶
Hambone & Hillie
Heathcliff & Marmaduke
Here Comes Droopy
Homeward Bound: The
　Incredible Journey▶
The Incredible Journey▶
Iron Will
It's a Dog's Life
K-9
K-9000
Kavik, the Wolf Dog
Lady and the Tramp▶
Lassie
Lassie: Adventures of
　Neeka
Lassie, Come Home▶
Lassie: The Miracle
Lassie: Well of Love
Lassie's Great Adventure
Lassie's Rescue Rangers
Legend of the Northwest
Little Dog Lost
Little Heroes

The Lone Wolf
Look Who's Talking Now
Love Leads the Way
Magic of Lassie
The Man Who Wagged
　His Tail
Man's Best Friend
Mr. Superinvisible
My Dog, the Thief
Nikki, the Wild Dog of the
　North▶
Oh, Heavenly Dog!
Old Yeller▶
Old Yeller
101 Dalmatians▶
Potsworth and the
　Midnight Patrol
Pound Puppies
Precious Pupp
The Return of Our Gang
Rin Tin Tin, Hero of the
　West
Rin Tin Tin: The Paris
　Conspiracy
Rover Dangerfield
The Sandlot▶
Savage Sam
Scooby-Doo
Scruffy
The Shaggy D.A.
The Shaggy Dog
Silver Stallion
Skeezer
Smoke
Summerdog
The Tender Years
The Thin Man▶
Toby McTeague
Tom and Jerry: The Movie
Turner and Hooch
The Ugly Dachshund
Where the Red Fern
　Grows▶
Where the Red Fern
　Grows: Part 2
White Fang 2: The Myth
　of the White Wolf
White Fang and the
　Hunter
Whitewater Sam
The Wizard of Oz▶
Woof!▶
Wowser: Wow-Wow
　Wowser

Kings
see *Royalty*

Korean War
MacArthur
M*A*S*H▶

Kung Fu
see *Martial Arts*

Labor Unions
see also *Miners*
Gung Ho
Newsies
Norma Rae▶

Lassie
Challenge to Lassie
Courage of Lassie
Lassie: Adventures of
　Neeka
Lassie, Come Home▶
Lassie: The Miracle
Lassie: Well of Love
Lassie's Great Adventure
Lassie's Rescue Rangers
Magic of Lassie

Laugh Riots
see also *Boy Meets Girl;*
Comedy with an Edge;
Funny Adventures; Silly
Spoofs; Sports Comedies
Abbott and Costello Meet
　Captain Kidd
Abbott and Costello Meet
　Dr. Jekyll and Mr. Hyde
Abbott and Costello Meet
　Frankenstein▶
Ace Ventura: Pet Detective
The Adventures of a
　Gnome Named Gnorm
The Adventures of a Two-
　Minute Werewolf
The Adventures of
　Buckaroo Banzai Across
　the Eighth Dimension▶
Africa Screams
Ah, Wilderness!▶
The Air Up There
Airheads
All I Want for Christmas
Aloha Summer
American Boyfriends
American Graffiti▶
Amos and Andrew
And Baby Makes Six
Androcles and the Lion
Andy Hardy Gets Spring
　Fever
Andy Hardy's Double Life
Andy Hardy's Private
　Secretary
Animal Crackers▶
Any Which Way You Can
The Apprenticeship of
　Duddy Kravitz▶
At the Circus
Author! Author!▶
Avalon▶
Baby, Take a Bow
Baby's Day Out
The Bachelor and the
　Bobby-Soxer▶
Back to School
The Bad News Bears▶
The Bad News Bears Go
　to Japan
The Bad News Bears in
　Breaking Training
The Ballad of Paul Bunyan
The Barefoot Executive
B.C.: A Special Christmas
Beethoven
Beethoven's 2nd
Beetle Bailey: Military
　Madness
The Bellboy
The Belles of St. Trinian's▶
The Bells of St. Mary's▶
Benji▶
Better Off Dead
The Beverly Hillbillies
Beverly Hills Brats
Big▶
Big Business
Big Girls Don't Cry. . .
　.They Get Even
Big Shots
The Big Store
Big Top Pee Wee
Billie
The Billion Dollar Hobo
A Billion for Boris
Blank Check
Blankman
Blue Murder at St.
　Trinian's▶
Blues Busters
The Boatniks
Book of Love
Boys of the City
Brain Donors
The Breakfast Club▶

Category Index

Police Academy 5: Assignment Miami Beach
Police Academy 6: City Under Siege
Police Academy, the Series
Pollyanna▶
Popi▶
Pretty in Pink
The Prime of Miss Jean Brodie▶
The Private Eyes
Prize Fighter
Problem Child
Problem Child 2
The Projectionist▶
The Pure Hell of St. Trinian's
Purple People Eater
Quarterback Princess
Queen of Hearts
Race for Your Life, Charlie Brown
Radio Days▶
Ramona
Ramona: Goodbye, Hello
Real Genius▶
Regl'ar Fellers
Remote
Renaissance Man
The Return of Our Gang
Return of the Pink Panther
Revenge of the Nerds
Revenge of the Pink Panther
Rhinestone
Robin Hood: Men in Tights
Rocket Gibraltar▶
Rookie of the Year
Room Service
Samantha
Sammy, the Way-Out Seal
The Sandlot▶
Santa Claus Conquers the Martians
Say Anything▶
Secret Life of Walter Mitty▶
Shag: The Movie▶
The Shaggy D.A.
The Shaggy Dog
Shirley Temple Baby Berlesques
Short Circuit 2
A Shot in the Dark▶
Simon
Sister Act
Sister Act 2: Back in the Habit
Six Weeks
Small Change▶
Smart Alecks
The Snapper▶
Snoopy, Come Home▶
Snow White and the Three Stooges
Snowball Express
Some Kind of Wonderful
Something Special
Son-in-Law
Son of Flubber
Son of the Pink Panther
Sorrowful Jones
Soul Man
Spaceballs
Spaced Invaders
Speaking of Animals, Vol. 1
Spies Like Us
Splash▶
Spook Busters
The Story of Seabiscuit
Summer Rental
Summer School
The Sunshine Boys▶
Super Seal
Superdad

The Sure Thing▶
Sweet Liberty
Swing Shift
Take Down
Take the Money and Run▶
Teen Witch
Teen Wolf
Teen Wolf Too
That Darn Cat
That Gang of Mine
That's Entertainment, Part 2
They Went That-a-Way & That-a-Way
This is My Life
Three Men and a Baby▶
Three Men and a Cradle▶
Three Men and a Little Lady
Three O'Clock High
Three Stooges
Three Stooges: A Ducking They Will Go
Three Stooges: A Plumbing We Will Go
Three Stooges: Cash and Carry
Three Stooges: If a Body Meets a Body
Three Stooges: In the Sweet Pie and Pie
Three Stooges Meet Hercules
Three Stooges: So Long Mr. Chumps
Three Stooges: What's the Matador?
Thursday's Game▶
Tito and Me▶
Toby Tyler▶
Tom Brown's School Days
Tom Brown's School Days▶
Tony Draws a Horse
Tootsie▶
Topper▶
Topper Returns▶
Topper Takes a Trip▶
The Toy
Toys
Trading Hearts
Trail of the Pink Panther
Troop Beverly Hills
The Trouble with Angels
Truly, Madly, Deeply▶
Turk 182!
Turner and Hooch
Twelve Chairs▶
2000 Year Old Man▶
The Ugly Dachshund
Uncle Buck
Undercover Blues
Undergrads▶
Unidentified Flying Oddball
Up the Down Staircase▶
Vice Versa▶
Wait Until Spring, Bandini
Walk Like a Man
Walt Disney Films in French
Wayne's World
Wayne's World 2
Weekend at Bernie's
Weekend at Bernie's 2
Weird Science
Welcome Home, Roxy Carmichael
What About Bob?▶
What's Up, Doc?▶
Where Angels Go, Trouble Follows
Where's Willie?
Who Framed Roger Rabbit?▶
Witches' Brew
With Honors
The Wizard
Wonders of Aladdin

Woody Woodpecker Collector's Edition, Vol. 1
Woofl▶
The World of Henry Orient▶
The Year My Voice Broke▶
Young Einstein
Zebra in the Kitchen
Zero to Sixty

Lawyers
see also Courtroom Capers
Adam's Rib▶
Brain Donors
The Client
Legend of Billie Jean
North
The Paper Chase▶
The Pelican Brief
Philadelphia▶
Regarding Henry▶
To Kill a Mockingbird▶

Life in the 'Burbs
Adventures in Spying
Amos and Andrew
The 'Burbs
Coneheads
Dennis the Menace
Don't Tell Mom the Babysitter's Dead
Edward Scissorhands▶
The Grass is Always Greener Over the Septic Tank
Hocus Pocus
House▶
Madhouse
The Money Pit
Opportunity Knocks
Over the Edge▶
Please Don't Eat the Daisies
Serial Mom▶
The Simpsons Christmas Special
When Every Day was the Fourth of July

Live Action/Animation Combos
Alice in Wonderland
Anchors Aweigh▶
Bedknobs and Broomsticks
Daydreamer▶
Fun & Fancy Free
The Incredible Mr. Limpet
Mary Poppins▶
So Dear to My Heart▶
The Three Caballeros▶
Who Framed Roger Rabbit?▶
Xanadu

Loneliness
see Only the Lonely

Lost Worlds
At the Earth's Core
Jane & the Lost City
Journey to the Center of the Earth▶
Land That Time Forgot
Mysterious Island▶
The People That Time Forgot
When Dinosaurs Ruled the Earth
Where Time Began

Macho Men
see also Amazing Adventures
The Adventures of Captain Marvel

Atom Man vs. Superman
A Bridge Too Far
Buck Rogers in the 25th Century
Cannonball Run
Cannonball Run 2
Captain America
Conan the Barbarian▶
Diamonds are Forever▶
Dick Tracy▶
Dick Tracy, Detective
Dick Tracy Meets Gruesome
Dick Tracy Returns
Dick Tracy vs. Crime Inc.
Dick Tracy vs. Cueball
Dick Tracy's Dilemma
Dr. No▶
For Your Eyes Only▶
G.I. Joe, Vol. 1: A Real American Hero
Giant▶
Gone with the Wind▶
The Green Hornet
Greystoke: The Legend of Tarzan, Lord of the Apes
Hercules
Hercules 2
Hercules in New York
Hot Shots! Part Deux
Infra-Man
Kindergarten Cop
Last Action Hero
Legend of the Lone Ranger
The Man with the Golden Gun
The Masked Marvel
Never Say Never Again
No Holds Barred
Rocky▶
Rocky 2
Rocky 3
Rocky 4
Rocky 5
The Seventh Voyage of Sinbad▶
The Shadow
Speed▶
Suburban Commando
Superman 1: The Movie▶
Superman 2▶
Superman 3
Superman 4: The Quest for Peace
Superman & the Mole Men
Tarzan, the Ape Man▶
Thunderball

Mad Scientists
see also Inventors; Scientists
Brenda Starr
Captain America
Dr. No▶
The Double O Kid
Freaked
The Incredible Two-Headed Transplant
Island of Dr. Moreau
Jurassic Park▶
The Pink Panther Strikes Again▶

Made for Television
see TV Movies; TV Series

Mafia
see It's the Mob

Magic
see also Genies; Magic Carpet Rides
Aladdin and His Magic Lamp
Bedknobs and Broomsticks

The Butcher's Wife
Escape to Witch Mountain▶
Gryphon
The Man in the Santa Claus Suit
Sorcerer's Apprentice
Teen Witch
Tut and Tuttle
Xuxa: Funtastic Birthday Party

Magic Carpet Rides
Aladdin▶
Golden Voyage of Sinbad
The Seventh Voyage of Sinbad▶
Sinbad and the Eye of the Tiger▶
Sinbad the Sailor▶
Thief of Baghdad▶
Thief of Baghdad
The Thief of Baghdad

Marriage
see also Divorce; Wedding Bells
The Age of Innocence▶
Bill Cosby, Himself
Country Girl▶
Dial "M" for Murder▶
Father of the Bride▶
For Keeps
Giant▶
The Heartbreak Kid▶
High Society
Holy Matrimony
Liar's Moon
Mr. & Mrs. Smith▶
Mr. Mom▶
Mr. Wonderful
The Money Pit
Moonstruck▶
On Golden Pond▶
On Her Majesty's Secret Service▶
Paint Your Wagon
Paradise▶
Peggy Sue Got Married
The Philadelphia Story▶
Prelude to a Kiss
Rebecca▶
Rocky 2
Shadowlands▶
She-Devil
She's Having a Baby
Son-in-Law
Suspicion▶
Thursday's Game▶
True Lies
Under Capricorn
Undercover Blues
Yours, Mine & Ours▶

Martial Arts
Aloha Summer
Big Trouble in Little China
Dragon: The Bruce Lee Story
The Karate Kid▶
The Karate Kid: Part 2
The Karate Kid: Part 3
Magic Kid
The Next Karate Kid
Remo Williams: The Adventure Begins
7 Ninja Kids
Sidekicks
Surf Ninjas
Teenage Mutant Ninja Turtles: The Epic Begins
3 Ninjas
3 Ninjas Kick Back

Tiger Bay▶
To Catch a Thief▶
Torn Curtain
Twice Upon a Time▶
Under Capricorn
The Window▶
The Wrong Man▶
The Young Detectives on Wheels
Young Sherlock Holmes

Nashville Narratives
see also *Musician Biopics; Southern Belles; Southern Sagas*
Coal Miner's Daughter▶
Honkytonk Man
The Night the Lights Went Out in Georgia
Rhinestone
A Smoky Mountain Christmas
Tender Mercies▶
The Thing Called Love

Nasty Nazis
see also *Judaism; World War II*
Bedknobs and Broomsticks
Casablanca▶
Clipped Wings
A Day in October
Foreign Correspondent▶
A Friendship in Vienna
The Incredible Mr. Limpet
Indiana Jones and the Last Crusade▶
Indiana Jones and the Temple of Doom▶
Judgment at Nuremberg▶
Madame Rosa▶
Miracle at Moreaux
A Night in Casablanca
Notorious▶
Raiders of the Lost Ark▶
The Rocketeer▶
Snow Treasure
The Sound of Music▶
Swing Kids
Wizards

Native America
The Bears & I
Billy Jack
Dances with Wolves▶
Fish Hawk
Geronimo▶
Geronimo: An American Legend
Island of the Blue Dolphins
Joe Panther
Journey to Spirit Island▶
The Last of the Mohicans
The Last of the Mohicans▶
The Legend of Hiawatha
The Legend of Wolf Mountain
The Light in the Forest
Little Big Man▶
Lost Legacy: A Girl Called Hatter Fox
Poltergeist 2: The Other Side
Princess Scargo and the Birthday Pumpkin
Reading Rainbow: Knots on a Counting Rope
Reading Rainbow: The Gift of the Sacred Dog
Run, Appaloosa, Run
Running Brave
Savage Sam
The Secret of Navajo Cave
Smith!
The Song of Sacajawea

Squanto and the First Thanksgiving
Terror in the Jungle
The Villain
Where the Spirit Lives
White Fang 2: The Myth of the White Wolf
Winter Wolf

Newspapers
see *Newsroom Notes*

Newsroom Notes
see also *Shutterbugs; TV Tales*
All the President's Men▶
The Beniker Gang
Blankman
Brenda Starr
Citizen Kane▶
Delirious
Father Hood
Fletch
Fletch Lives
Foreign Correspondent▶
The Great Muppet Caper▶
Hero▶
His Girl Friday▶
I Love Trouble
Journey for Margaret▶
Just One of the Guys
Kid from Not-So-Big
Newsies
The Paper▶
The Pelican Brief
The Philadelphia Story▶
Roman Holiday▶
Straight Talk
Three O'Clock High
A World Apart▶

Nifty '50s
Back to the Future▶
Back to the Future, Part 2
Book of Love
The Buddy Holly Story▶
Bye, Bye, Birdie▶
Cry-Baby▶
Dead Poets Society▶
Dirty Dancing▶
Father of the Bride▶
Grease
Grease 2
Housekeeping▶
La Bamba▶
The Long Day Closes▶
The Lords of Flatbush
The Man in the Moon▶
Matinee
My Favorite Year▶
Oh, What a Night
Peggy Sue Got Married
The Playboys▶
School Ties▶
Shag: The Movie▶
Shout
Stacking
Strange Invaders▶
Superdad
This Boy's Life▶
Trading Hearts
The War of the Worlds▶
The Way We Were▶

Nuclear War
see also *Disaster Strikes!*
Amazing Grace & Chuck
The Crimson Ghost
Desert Bloom▶
Dr. Seuss' Butter Battle Book
Hiroshima Maiden
The Manhattan Project
Modern Problems
The Spy Who Loved Me

Superman 4: The Quest for Peace
True Lies
Voyage to the Bottom of the Sea▶
War Games▶

Nuns & Priests
The Bells of St. Mary's▶
Change of Habit
For Better and For Worse
Going My Way▶
I Confess
Lilies of the Field▶
Sister Act
Sister Act 2: Back in the Habit
The Sound of Music▶
The Trouble with Angels
Where Angels Go, Trouble Follows

Oceans
see *Go Fish; Scuba Diving; Submarines*

The Olympics
see also *Sports Dramas*
Animalympics: Winter Games
Chariots of Fire▶
Cool Runnings
International Velvet
Miracle on Ice
1994 Winter Olympics Highlights Video
The Olympic Champ
Running Brave
Terrytoons Olympics

On the Farm
Boy Takes Girl
The Castaway Cowboy
Country▶
Doc Hollywood
Giant▶
Jean de Florette▶
Places in the Heart▶
The River
Rock-a-Doodle
The Silver Fox and Sam Davenport
Skylark
Son-in-Law
Sounder▶
Stacking
The Stone Boy▶
Tomboy & the Champ

On the Run
Butch and Sundance: The Early Days
Butch Cassidy and the Sundance Kid▶
Father Hood
The Fugitive▶
A Perfect World

Only the Lonely
Citizen Kane▶
Cyrano de Bergerac▶
Desperately Seeking Susan▶
Doin' Time on Planet Earth
Escapade in Japan
E.T.: The Extra-Terrestrial▶
Hell Hounds of Alaska
Men Don't Leave▶
Only the Lonely
Only You
The Prime of Miss Jean Brodie▶
The Prince of Central Park▶
Sleepless in Seattle▶
Turtle Diary▶

Zelly & Me▶

Oooh...That's Scary!
see also *Gory Stories; Mad Scientists; Monsters, General; Scary Beasties; Scary Bugs; Scary Plants; Vampires; Werewolves*
Alligator▶
Arachnophobia
Army of Darkness▶
Attack of the Killer Tomatoes
Beetlejuice▶
The Birds▶
Black Magic
Blacula
Cat's Eye
Critters
The Crow▶
Ghoulies
Gremlins▶
Gremlins 2: The New Batch▶
House▶
House of Wax▶
The House with a Clock in Its Walls
The Incredible Two-Headed Transplant
Island of Dr. Moreau
It Came from Hollywood
Legend of Boggy Creek
Little Shop of Horrors▶
The Lost Boys
The Mask▶
Matinee
The Monster Squad
Munchies
My Boyfriend's Back
My Grandpa is a Vampire
My Mom's a Werewolf
Return to Boggy Creek
Salem's Lot▶
Saturday the 14th
Spooks Run Wild
The Swarm
Troll
Twilight Zone: The Movie
Watcher in the Woods
The Willies

Opera
see also *Gotta Sing!*
Amahl and the Night Visitors
A Night at the Opera▶

Orphans
see also *Only the Lonely*
Across the Great Divide
The Adventures of Oliver Twist
Aladdin▶
Anne of Green Gables▶
Annie
Babes on Broadway
The Beniker Gang
Big Red
Born Free▶
The Boy with the Green Hair
City Boy
Crystalstone
D.A.R.Y.L.
David Copperfield▶
David Copperfield
Dick Tracy▶
Earthling
Escape to Witch Mountain▶
A Far Off Place
Free Willy
Hector's Bunyip
Home at Last
Immediate Family

Jane Eyre▶
The Kid Who Loved Christmas
The Land Before Time▶
Little Orphan Annie
The Little Princess▶
Mad Max: Beyond Thunderdome
Man, Woman & Child
Manny's Orphans
Mighty Joe Young
Napoleon and Samantha▶
Oliver!▶
Oliver Twist▶
Oliver Twist▶
Oliver Twist
On the Right Track
Orphan Train▶
Paper Moon▶
Penny Serenade▶
Pollyanna▶
The Poor Little Rich Girl
The Prince of Central Park▶
Problem Child
Samantha
Scout's Honor
Snow White and the Seven Dwarfs
Sugar Cane Alley▶
Superman 1: The Movie▶
Susannah of the Mounties
Tarzan Finds a Son▶
Where the River Runs Black
Who'll Save Our Children?▶
Wild Hearts Can't Be Broken▶
The Woman Who Raised a Bear as Her Son
Young & Free

Our Gang
General Spanky
The Little Rascals
Little Rascals Christmas Special
The Return of Our Gang

Over the Airwaves
see also *TV Tales*
Airheads
Citizens Band▶
Comfort and Joy▶
Radio Days▶
Rebecca of Sunnybrook Farm
Sleepless in Seattle▶
Straight Talk
Strike Up the Band

Overlooked Gems
Cross Creek
Crossing Delancey▶
Dazed and Confused▶
Housekeeping▶
The Joy Luck Club▶
Local Hero▶
Metropolitan▶
Miss Firecracker▶
Searching for Bobby Fischer▶
Shag: The Movie▶
Strictly Ballroom▶

Parades
see also *Circuses & Carnivals*
Easter Parade▶
Ferris Bueller's Day Off▶
Miracle on 34th Street▶

Rags to Riches
see also Price of Fame;
Wrong Side of the Tracks
Aladdin▶
Annie
The Beverly Hillbillies
Blank Check
Brewster's Millions
The Buddy Holly Story▶
Citizen Kane▶
Coal Miner's Daughter▶
The Great Rupert▶
Hero▶
It Could Happen to You▶
A Kid for Two Farthings
The Last American Hero▶
Lili▶
Little Lord Fauntleroy▶
Lots of Luck
The Prince and the
Pauper▶
The Prince and the Pauper
Rocky▶
Straight Talk

Raiders of the Lost
Ark
Indiana Jones and the Last
Crusade▶
Indiana Jones and the
Temple of Doom▶
Raiders of the Lost Ark▶

Rebel With a Cause
see also Rebel Without a
Cause
The Adventures of Robin
Hood▶
Billy Jack
Boyz N the Hood▶
Dead Poets Society▶
A Dream for Christmas▶
East of Eden
Gorillas in the Mist▶
The Last American Hero▶
Lawrence of Arabia▶
Legend of Billie Jean
Legend of the Lone Ranger
Little Tough Guys
The Loneliness of the Long
Distance Runner▶
The Manhattan Project
Mr. Smith Goes to
Washington▶
Mountain Man
Norma Rae▶
Project X▶
Robin Hood: Prince of
Thieves
Save the Lady
The Scarlet Pimpernel▶
War Games▶

Rebel Without a
Cause
see also Rebel With a
Cause
Across the Tracks
Cool As Ice
The Electric Horseman
Ferris Bueller's Day Off▶
On the Edge: The Survival
of Dana
Over the Edge▶
Rebel Without a Cause▶
Rocky 4
That Was Then. . .This Is
Now
Top Gun
West Side Story▶

Red Scare
Night Crossing
Tito and Me▶
Tobor the Great

Repressed Men
The Age of Innocence▶
The Remains of the Day▶
Shadowlands▶

Rescue Missions
see also Rescue Missions
Involving Time Travel
Daredevils of the Red
Circle
Dragonworld▶
Ernest Scared Stupid
The Ewok Adventure
Free Willy
The Rescue

Rescue Missions
Involving Time Travel
see also Rescue Missions
Back to the Future▶
Back to the Future, Part 2
Back to the Future, Part 3
Bill & Ted's Excellent
Adventure
The Navigator▶
Star Trek 4: The Voyage
Home▶
Superman 1: The Movie▶
The Terminator▶
Terminator 2: Judgment
Day▶

Revolutionary War
Johnny Tremain & the Sons
of Liberty
1776▶
Sweet Liberty

The Right Choice
The Adventures of Charlie
and Cubby
The Adventures of Teddy
Ruxpin
The Adventures of the
Ding-A-Ling Brothers
Blue Chips
The Boy with the Green
Hair
Dr. Seuss' Butter Battle
Book
The Elephant Man▶
Fat Albert & the Cosby
Kids, Vol. 1
The Ghost Belonged to Me
Hang Your Hat on the
Wind
It Could Happen to You▶
Judgment at Nuremberg▶
Mr. Smith Goes to
Washington▶
The Shootist▶
Soul Man
The Toy
Welcome Back Wil Cwac
Cwac
With Honors

Robots
see also Technological
Nightmares
And You Thought Your
Parents Were Weird!
Bill & Ted's Bogus Journey
Doctor Who: An Unearthly
Child
Doctor Who and the
Daleks
The Empire Strikes Back▶
The Invisible Boy
K-9000
Not Quite Human
Return of the Jedi▶
Robocop▶
Robocop 2
Robocop 3

Robot Jox
Short Circuit
Star Wars▶
The Terminator▶
Terminator 2: Judgment
Day▶
Tobor the Great
Transformers

Rodeos
see also Cowboys &
Indians
8 Seconds
Junior Bonner▶
My Heroes Have Always
Been Cowboys

Romance
see Boy Meets Girl

Royalty
see also Historical
Happenings; Medieval
Romps; Period Piece
Aladdin▶
Ali Baba and the Forty
Thieves
The Court Jester▶
Dr. Syn, Alias the
Scarecrow
The Fifth Musketeer
The Fighting Prince of
Donegal
The King and I▶
King Ralph
The Lion in Winter▶
Lost in a Harem
A Man for All Seasons▶
The Man in the Iron
Mask▶
The Man Who Would Be
King▶
Mannequin 2: On the
Move
Mom and Dad Save the
World
Once Upon a Time
The Polar Bear King
The Prince and the
Pauper▶
The Prince and the Pauper
The Return of the
Musketeers
Return to Oz
Roman Holiday▶
Snow White and the Seven
Dwarfs▶
Surf Ninjas
The Sword & the Rose
Three Musketeers▶
Willow

Running
Across the Tracks
Billie
Forrest Gump▶
The Loneliest Runner▶
The Loneliness of the Long
Distance Runner▶
Running Brave
Sam's Son

Savants
see also Mental
Retardation
Being There▶
Doctor Doolittle
Forrest Gump▶
Rain Man▶
Tony Draws a Horse

Scary Beasties
Alligator▶
Battle for the Planet of the
Apes

Beneath the Planet of the
Apes
Bunnicula: Vampire Rabbit
Conquest of the Planet of
the Apes
Dragonslayer▶
Godzilla vs. Megalon
Godzilla vs. the Cosmic
Monster
Jabberwocky
Jurassic Park▶
King Kong▶
King Kong
Mighty Joe Young
Monty Python and the
Holy Grail▶
Mysterious Island▶
Planet of the Apes▶
Return to Boggy Creek
Son of Kong

Scary Bugs
Arachnophobia
The Bees
The Swarm

Scary Plants
Attack of the Killer
Tomatoes
Invasion of the Body
Snatchers▶
Little Shop of Horrors▶

Sci Fi
see also Fantasy
The Adventures of
Ultraman
Arena
At the Earth's Core
Atom Man vs. Superman
Attack of the Killer
Tomatoes
The Aurora Encounter
*batteries not included
Battle Beyond the Stars
Battle for Moon Station
Dallos
Battle for the Planet of the
Apes
Battlestar Galactica
The Bees
Beneath the Planet of the
Apes
The Black Hole
The Black Planet
Blake of Scotland Yard
Brain 17
Buck Rogers Conquers the
Universe
Buck Rogers in the 25th
Century
Captain Harlock, Vol. 1
Captain Scarlet vs. The
Mysterons
Close Encounters of the
Third Kind▶
Cocoon▶
Conquest of the Planet of
the Apes
Darkman▶
D.A.R.Y.L.
Destroy All Monsters
Doc Savage
Doctor Who: An Unearthly
Child
Doctor Who and the
Daleks
Doin' Time on Planet Earth
The Empire Strikes Back▶
Enemy Mine
Escape from the Planet of
the Apes▶
E.T.: The Extra-Terrestrial▶
Explorers
Fantastic Planet▶
Fire in the Sky

First Men in the Moon
Flash Gordon
Flash Gordon Conquers
the Universe
Flash Gordon: Rocketship
Flash Gordon: Vol. 1
Force on Thunder Mountain
Galaxy Express
Gobots: Battle of the Rock
Lords
Godzilla vs. Megalon
Godzilla vs. the Cosmic
Monster
Godzilla vs. the Smog
Monster
Grandizer
Heartbeeps
Highlander 2: The
Quickening
Howard the Duck
Hyper-Sapien: People from
Another Star
Iceman▶
Incredible Agent of
Stingray
Infra-Man
Innerspace
Invaders from Mars
Invasion of the Body
Snatchers▶
The Invisible Boy
Journey to the Center of
the Earth▶
Journey to the Center of
the Earth
Krull
Land That Time Forgot
The Last Starfighter
Locke the Superpower
Macron 1: Dark Discovery
in a New World
Making Mr. Right
Meet the Hollowheads
Mighty Orbots: Devil's
Asteroid
Moon Pilot
Mysterious Island▶
Norman's Awesome
Experience
The Olden Days Coat
On the Comet▶
The Original Fabulous
Adventures of Baron
Munchausen▶
The People That Time
Forgot
The Phantom Empire
Pirates of Dark Water: The
Saga Begins
Planet of the Apes▶
Planet of the Dinosaurs
Purple People Eater
Puss in Boots
Radar Men from the Moon
Return from Witch
Mountain
The Return of Swamp
Thing
Return of the Jedi▶
Robot Jox
Robotech: The Macross
Saga, Vol. 1
Robotech, Vol. 1: Booby
Trap
Saber Rider and the Star
Sheriffs: All That Glitters
Silverhawks: Sky Shadows
Silverhawks: The Original
Story
Sleeper▶
Solarbabies
Space Angel, Vol. 1
Space Battleship Yamato
Space Firebird
Space Raiders

Space Warriors: Battle for
 Earth Station S/1
Spaceballs
SpaceCamp
Spaced Invaders
Spaceketeers
Spaceship
Spiral Zone: Zone of
 Darkness
Star Trek: The Motion
 Picture
Star Trek 2: The Wrath of
 Khan▶
Star Trek 3: The Search
 for Spock
Star Trek 4: The Voyage
 Home▶
Star Trek 5: The Final
 Frontier
Star Trek 6: The
 Undiscovered Country
Star Trek: Animated, Vol. 1
Star Trek the Next
 Generation Episode 1-2:
 Encounter at Farpoint
Star Wars▶
Starchaser: The Legend of
 Orin
Starman▶
Starship
Starvengers
Superman: The Serial,
 Vol. 1
Teen Alien
Terminator 2: Judgment
 Day▶
The Three Worlds of
 Gulliver
Thunderbirds are Go
Thunderbirds in Outerspace
Timefighters in the Land of
 Fantasy
Timerider
Tobor the Great
The Trial of the Incredible
 Hulk
Tron
2001: A Space Odyssey▶
2010 : The Year We
 Make Contact▶
Ugly Little Boy
Undersea Kingdom
The Valley of Gwangi▶
Vengeance of the Space
 Pirate
Voyage to the Bottom of
 the Sea▶
Voyager from the Unknown
The War of the Worlds▶
Weird Science
When Dinosaurs Ruled the
 Earth
Where Time Began
Zombies of the
 Stratosphere

Scientists

see also *Inventors; Mad
 Scientists*
The Andromeda Strain
Beach Party
Darkman▶
The Day of the Dolphin
Dead Men Don't Wear
 Plaid
Die Laughing
Doctor Doolittle
The Incredible Hulk Returns
Jurassic Park▶
Mad Scientist
Mr. Superinvisible
Mr. Wizard's World: Air
 and Water Wizardry
Monkey Business▶
Monkey's Uncle
My Science Project

My Stepmother Is an Alien
Neptune Factor
Project X▶
Real Genius▶
Return of Captain
 Invincible
Schoolhouse Rock: Science
 Rock
Simon
Son of Flubber
Swamp Thing
Unknown Island
Using Simple Machines
Where Time Began

Scotland

see also *Great Britain*
Challenge to Lassie
Comfort and Joy▶
Gregory's Girl▶
Greystoke: The Legend of
 Tarzan, Lord of the
 Apes
Local Hero▶
The Prime of Miss Jean
 Brodie▶
Ring of Bright Water▶
Rob Roy - The Highland
 Rogue
The Three Lives of
 Thomasina▶
Year of the Comet

Scuba Diving

Flipper
Flipper's New Adventure
Neptune Factor
Never Say Never Again
Thunderball

Serial Adventures

The Adventures of Captain
 Marvel
The Adventures of Frank
 and Jesse James
Adventures of Red Ryder
Adventures of Smilin' Jack
Adventures of the Flying
 Cadets
Atom Man vs. Superman
Battling with Buffalo Bill
The Black Widow
Blake of Scotland Yard
Bugs Bunny Superstar
Burn 'Em Up Barnes
Captain America
The Clutching Hand
The Crimson Ghost
Daredevils of the Red
 Circle
Darkest Africa
Devil Horse
Dick Tracy
Dick Tracy Returns
Dick Tracy vs. Crime Inc.
Don Winslow of the Coast
 Guard
Don Winslow of the Navy
Federal Agents vs.
 Underworld, Inc.
Fighting Devil Dogs
Fighting Marines
Fighting with Kit Carson
Flaming Frontiers
Flash Gordon Conquers
 the Universe
Flash Gordon: Vol. 1
G-Men Never Forget
G-Men vs. the Black
 Dragon
Government Agents vs. the
 Phantom Legion
Green Archer
The Green Hornet
Hawk of the Wilderness
Holt of the Secret Service

Hurricane Express
The Invisible Monster
Jesse James Rides Again
Jungle Drums of Africa
King of the Rocketmen
The Last of the Mohicans
Law of the Wild
The Lone Ranger
The Lost Jungle
The Masked Marvel
Mysterious Doctor Satan
Nyoka and the Tigermen
The Phantom Creeps
The Phantom Empire
Radar Men from the Moon
Radio Patrol
Sea Hound
Shadow of the Eagle
Son of Zorro
Spy Smasher▶
Superman: The Serial,
 Vol. 1
Tailspin Tommy
Three Musketeers
Tim Tyler's Luck
Trader Tom of the China
 Seas
Transformers
Undersea Kingdom
Winners of the West
Young Eagles
Zombies of the
 Stratosphere
Zorro Rides Again
Zorro's Black Whip
Zorro's Fighting Legion

Sesame Street

Big Bird in Japan
Sesame Songs: Elmo's
 Sing-Along Guessing
 Game
Sesame Songs: Monster
 Hits!
Sesame Songs: Rock &
 Roll!
Sesame Songs: Sing-Along
 Earth Songs
Sesame Songs: Sing, Hoot
 & Howl
Sesame Songs: Sing
 Yourself Silly!
Sesame Songs: We All
 Sing Together
Sesame Street: Bedtime
 Stories and Songs
Sesame Street: Count It
 Higher
Sesame Street: Play-Along
 Games and Songs
Three Sesame Street
 Stories

Shutterbugs

see also *Newsroom Notes*
Adventures in Spying
Backbeat▶
Don't Change My World
Funny Face▶
Gift of the Whales
Return to Boggy Creek

Silence is Golden

The Adventures of Walt
 Disney's Alice
City Lights▶
The Gold Rush▶
Silent Movie

Silly Detectives

see also *Detectives*
Ace Ventura: Pet Detective
The Adventures of Sherlock
 Holmes' Smarter
 Brother▶
Clean Slate

Clue
Curse of the Pink Panther
Dead Men Don't Wear
 Plaid
Dragnet
Fatal Instinct
The Naked Gun: From the
 Files of Police Squad▶
Naked Gun 2 1/2: The
 Smell of Fear
Naked Gun 33 1/3: The
 Final Insult
The Pink Panther▶
The Pink Panther Strikes
 Again▶
Return of the Pink Panther
Revenge of the Pink
 Panther
A Shot in the Dark▶
Trail of the Pink Panther

Silly Spoofs

see also *Laugh Riots*
The Adventures of Sherlock
 Holmes' Smarter
 Brother▶
Airplane!▶
Airplane 2: The Sequel
Animal Farm▶
Bad Medicine
Bananas▶
Being There▶
The Big Bus
Big Trouble in Little China
Bill & Ted's Bogus Journey
Bill & Ted's Excellent
 Adventure
Bugsy Malone
The 'Burbs
The Cheap Detective▶
Christopher's Xmas Mission
Dead Men Don't Wear
 Plaid
Dragnet
Erik the Viking
Fatal Instinct
Frankenweenie
The Freshman
Hairspray▶
High Anxiety
Home Movies
Hot Shots! Part Deux
How I Got into College
I'll Do Anything
The Incredible Shrinking
 Woman
Jabberwocky
Johnny Dangerously
Last Action Hero
Love and Death▶
Mad Monster Party
The Meteor Man
Monty Python and the
 Holy Grail▶
The Mouse That Roared▶
Movie, Movie
My Best Friend Is a
 Vampire
The Naked Gun: From the
 Files of Police Squad▶
Naked Gun 2 1/2: The
 Smell of Fear
Naked Gun 33 1/3: The
 Final Insult
National Lampoon's
 Loaded Weapon 1
The Nutty Professor▶
Oscar
P.C.U.
The Princess Bride▶
Return of Captain
 Invincible
Robin Hood: Men in Tights
Saturday the 14th
Scrooged
Serial Mom▶

Silent Movie
Sleeper▶
Smile▶
Spaceballs
Spaceship
Stay Tuned
Strange Invaders▶
Support Your Local
 Gunfighter▶
Support Your Local
 Sheriff▶
Surf Ninjas
Three Amigos
The Villain
Who Framed Roger
 Rabbit?▶
Young Frankenstein▶

Sing-Alongs

Barney & Friends: Barney
 Rhymes with Mother
 Goose
Barney & Friends: Barney's
 Best Manners
Barney & the Backyard
 Gang
Barney in Concert
Bedrockin' and Rappin'
Bethie's Really Silly
 Clubhouse
Big Bird in Japan
Billy Bunny's Animal Song
Clifford's Singalong
 Adventure
Country Rock
Disney's Greatest Lullabies
Disney's Sing-Along Songs:
 The Twelve Days of
 Christmas
Disney's Sing-Along Songs,
 Vol. 1: Heigh-Ho
Disney's Sing-Along Songs,
 Vol. 2: Zip-A-Dee-Doo-
 Dah
Disney's Sing-Along Songs,
 Vol. 3: You Can Fly!
Disney's Sing-Along Songs,
 Vol. 4: The Bare
 Necessities
Disney's Sing-Along Songs,
 Vol. 5: Fun with Music
Disney's Sing-Along Songs,
 Vol. 6: Under the Sea
Disney's Sing-Along Songs,
 Vol. 7: Disneyland Fun
Disney's Sing-Along Songs,
 Vol. 8: Very Merry
 Christmas Songs
Disney's Sing-Along Songs,
 Vol. 9: I Love to Laugh!
Disney's Sing-Along Songs,
 Vol. 10: Be Our Guest
Disney's Sing-Along Songs,
 Vol. 11: Friend Like Me
Don Cooper: Sing-Along
 Story Songs
The Donut Repair Club: On
 Tour
The Flintstones: Rappin' n'
 Rhymin'
Gerald McBoing Boing,
 Vol. 1: Favorite Sing-
 Along Songs
Hap Palmer's Follow Along
 Songs
HBTV: Old Time Rock &
 Roll
It's Not Easy Being Green
Lamb Chop's Play Along:
 Action Songs
Lamb Chop's Sing-Along
 Play-Along
Mister Rogers: Music and
 Feelings
Mister Rogers: Musical
 Stories

More Song City U.S.A.
The Night Before Christmas and Best-Loved Yuletide Carols
Puff the Magic Dragon
Raggedy Ann and Andy: A Musical Adventure
Schoolhouse Rock: Grammar Rock
Schoolhouse Rock: History Rock
Schoolhouse Rock: Science Rock
Sesame Songs: Elmo's Sing-Along Guessing Game
Sesame Songs: Monster Hits!
Sesame Songs: Rock & Roll!
Sesame Songs: Sing-Along Earth Songs
Sesame Songs: Sing, Hoot & Howl
Sesame Songs: Sing Yourself Silly!
Sesame Songs: We All Sing Together
Sesame Street: Bedtime Stories and Songs
Sesame Street: Count It Higher
Sesame Street: Play-Along Games and Songs
Sharon, Lois & Bram at the Young People's Theatre
Sharon, Lois & Bram: Back by Popular Demand-Live
Sharon, Lois & Bram: Live in Your Living Room
Sharon, Lois & Bram: Sing A to Z
Sharon, Lois & Bram's Elephant Show: Babysitting
Shining Time Station: Singsongs, Vol. 1
Shining Time Station: 'Tis a Gift Holiday Special
Sing Together
Songs for Us Series
Songs from Mother Goose
Tom Chapin: This Pretty Planet

Sixties Sagas
Hair Bear Bunch
Head▶
More American Graffiti
Where Angels Go, Trouble Follows
Yellow Submarine▶

Skateboarding
Gleaming the Cube
Skateboard

Skating
see also *Hockey*
Airborne
Breaking the Ice
The Cutting Edge
Hans Brinker
Ice Castles
Xanadu

Skiing
Aspen Extreme
Avalanche
Better Off Dead
Club Med
Downhill Racer
For Your Eyes Only▶
The Man Who Skied Down Everest

On Her Majesty's Secret Service▶
The Other Side of the Mountain
The Other Side of the Mountain, Part 2
Ski Patrol
Snowball Express

Slavery
see also *Civil Rights*
The Adventures of Huckleberry Finn▶
Brother Future
Buck and the Preacher
The House of Dies Drear

Soccer
Gregory's Girl▶
The Hero
Hot Shot
Ladybugs
Victory

Southern Belles
see also *Nashville Narratives; Southern Sagas*
Driving Miss Daisy▶
Gone with the Wind▶
Miss Firecracker▶
Rich in Love
Steel Magnolias▶
The Trip to Bountiful▶

Southern Sagas
see also *Nashville Narratives; Southern Belles*
Boyd's Shadow
Brer Rabbit and the Wonderful Tar Baby
Driving Miss Daisy▶
Fletch Lives
Forrest Gump▶
Gettysburg▶
Gone with the Wind▶
The Great Santini▶
Miss Firecracker▶
Norma Rae▶
Paradise▶
Rambling Rose▶
Rich in Love
Running Mates
Shag: The Movie▶
Sounder▶
Tammy and the Bachelor
Tammy and the Doctor
Tank
To Kill a Mockingbird▶
The Trip to Bountiful▶
Walking Tall
Where the Lilies Bloom▶

Special F/X Extravaganzas
Alice in Wonderland
Batman▶
Beetlejuice▶
Big Trouble in Little China
The Black Hole
The Ewok Adventure
Innerspace
Jurassic Park▶
The Mask▶
Poltergeist▶
Return of the Jedi▶
The Shadow
Star Trek 2: The Wrath of Khan▶
Star Trek 4: The Voyage Home▶
Star Wars▶
Superman 2▶
The Terminator▶

Terminator 2: Judgment Day▶
2001: A Space Odyssey▶
2010 : The Year We Make Contact▶
Who Framed Roger Rabbit?▶

Sports
see *Baseball; Basketball; Biking; Boxing; Fast Cars; Football; Golf; Hockey; The Olympics; Scuba Diving; Skating; Skiing; Soccer; Sports Comedies; Sports Dramas; Surfing; Tennis*

Sports Comedies
The Air Up There
Angels in the Outfield
The Bad News Bears
The Bad News Bears Go to Japan
The Bad News Bears in Breaking Training
The Best of Times
Billie
Bingo Long Traveling All-Stars & Motor Kings▶
Blue Skies Again
Bowery Blitzkrieg
Comeback Kid
Cool Runnings
D2: The Mighty Ducks
Fast Break
The Fish that Saved Pittsburgh
Ladybugs
A League of Their Own▶
Little Big League
The Longshot
Major League
Major League 2
The Mighty Ducks
Mr. Baseball
Pat and Mike▶
Prize Fighter
Rookie of the Year
The Sandlot▶
Trading Hearts
Wildcats
The World's Greatest Athlete

Sports Dramas
Above the Rim
Airborne
All the Right Moves
American Anthem
American Flyers
The Babe
Bang the Drum Slowly▶
Big Mo
Blue Chips
Breaking Away▶
Brian's Song▶
Chariots of Fire▶
Chasing Dreams
Coach
The Cutting Edge
Diving In
Downhill Racer
8 Seconds
Field of Dreams▶
Heart Like a Wheel▶
The Hero
Hockey Night
Hoosiers▶
Hot Shot
Ice Castles
International Velvet
Knute Rockne: All American▶
The Last American Hero▶
The Loneliest Runner▶

Miracle on Ice
Nadia
The Natural▶
One on One
Over the Top
Pastime▶
Pistol: The Birth of a Legend
The Program
Rocky▶
Rocky 2
Rocky 3
Rocky 4
Rocky 5
Rudy
Running Brave
Talent for the Game
Tiger Town
Victory
Wind
A Winner Never Quits

Spy Stories
Adventures in Spying
Boris and Natasha: The Movie
Casablanca▶
The Charge of the Model T's
Clipped Wings
Cloak & Dagger
Condorman
A Day in October
The Day of the Dolphin
Deathcheaters
Defense Play
Diamonds are Forever▶
Dr. No▶
The Double O Kid
Duck Soup▶
The Fantastic World of D.C. Collins
For Your Eyes Only▶
Foreign Correspondent▶
From Russia with Love▶
Gotcha!
Holt of the Secret Service
The Hunt for Red October▶
Ice Station Zebra
If Looks Could Kill
Jungle Drums of Africa
Live and Let Die
The Man with One Red Shoe
The Man with the Golden Gun
Mr. Superinvisible
Moonraker
My Favorite Brunette
Never Say Never Again
A Night in Casablanca
North by Northwest▶
Notorious▶
Octopussy
On Her Majesty's Secret Service▶
One of Our Dinosaurs Is Missing
Saboteur▶
Sneakers
Spy Smasher▶
The Spy Who Loved Me
The Tall Blond Man with One Black Shoe▶
The 39 Steps▶
Thunderball
Torn Curtain
Trenchcoat
True Lies
Under the Rainbow
Undercover Blues
A View to a Kill
You Only Live Twice

Star Wars
The Empire Strikes Back▶
The Ewok Adventure
The Ewoks: Battle for Endor
Return of the Jedi▶
Star Wars▶

Stepparents
see also *Family Ties; Parenthood*
Big Girls Don't Cry. . .They Get Even
Cinderella▶
Lassie
Out on a Limb
This Boy's Life▶

Storytelling
see also *Bedtime Stories*
The Gingham Dog and the Calico Cat
The Princess Bride▶
The Story Lady

Struggling Musicians
see also *Music*
Backbeat▶
Eddie and the Cruisers
Light of Day
Oh, God! You Devil
Rhinestone
Satisfaction
Singles▶
Tender Mercies▶

Stupid Crime
see also *Crime Doesn't Pay; It's the Mob*
Airheads
Amos and Andrew
The Apple Dumpling Gang
The Apple Dumpling Gang Rides Again
Baby on Board
Baby's Day Out
Cop and a Half
Dr. Otto & the Riddle of the Gloom Beam
Ernest Goes to Jail
A Fine Mess
Her Alibi
Herbie Goes Bananas
Home Alone▶
Home Alone 2: Lost in New York
Once Upon a Crime
Oscar
Out on a Limb
Sister Act
Stop! or My Mom Will Shoot

Submarines
For Your Eyes Only▶
The Hunt for Red October▶
Mysterious Island▶
The Spy Who Loved Me
20,000 Leagues Under the Sea▶
Voyage to the Bottom of the Sea▶
You Only Live Twice

Subways
see also *Trains*
Adventures in Babysitting
The Fugitive▶
Highlander 2: The Quickening
Speed▶

Summer Camp
Addams Family Values▶
Camp Nowhere

Diving In
Doin' Time on Planet Earth
Don't Tell Mom the
    Babysitter's Dead
Dream Date
Dream Machine
Dutch
East of Eden▶
The Effect of Gamma Rays
    on Man-in-the-Moon
    Marigolds▶
Encino Man
The Ernest Green Story
Escape Artist▶
E.T.: The Extra-Terrestrial▶
Fame▶
Fast Times at Ridgemont
    High▶
Ferris Bueller's Day Off▶
The Flamingo Kid▶
Flirting▶
Footloose
For Keeps
Foxes
A Friendship in Vienna
Girls Just Want to Have
    Fun
Gleaming the Cube
The Goodbye Bird
Goodbye, Miss 4th of July
Grease
Grease 2
Hadley's Rebellion
Hairspray▶
Harley
The Heavenly Kid
A Home of Our Own
Hoosiers▶
How I Got into College
How to Stuff a Wild Bikini
I am the Cheese
I Wanna Hold Your Hand▶
If Looks Could Kill
The In Crowd
Kid Dynamite
Knights & Emeralds
La Bamba▶
Lantern Hill
Life Begins for Andy
    Hardy▶
Lisa
Little Darlings
A Little Romance▶
The Little Thief
The Loneliest Runner▶
The Loneliness of the Long
    Distance Runner▶
Looking for Miracles
The Lost Boys
Love Laughs at Andy
    Hardy
Lucas▶
Making the Grade
The Man in the Moon▶
The Manhattan Project
Meatballs
The Member of the
    Wedding
Mermaids▶
Metropolitan▶
The Miracle
Miss Annie Rooney
Monkey Business▶
Morgan Stewart's Coming
    Home
Muscle Beach Party
My American Cousin▶
My Best Friend Is a
    Vampire
My Boyfriend's Back
My Father the Hero
My Girl 2
My Science Project
Mystery Date

New Archies: Stealing the
    Show
The Night Before
No Big Deal
Not My Kid
On the Edge: The Survival
    of Dana
One Crazy Summer
Outside Chance of
    Maximillian Glick▶
The Outsiders
Over the Edge▶
Pajama Party
Parenthood▶
Peggy Sue Got Married
Pippin▶
Pretty in Pink
The Prime of Miss Jean
    Brodie▶
Primo Baby
Princes in Exile
Quarterback Princess
Racing with the Moon▶
Rad
Rambling Rose▶
Rebel Without a Cause▶
Rock 'n' Roll High School
    Forever
Romeo and Juliet▶
Running Mates
Say Anything▶
Secret Admirer
Seven Minutes in Heaven
Shag: The Movie▶
Shout
Sing
Sixteen Candles▶
Skateboard
Solarbabies
Some Kind of Wonderful
Something Special
Stand and Deliver▶
Starchaser: The Legend of
    Orin
Summer School
Swing Kids
Teen Wolf
Teenage Mutant Ninja
    Turtles 2: The Secret of
    the Ooze
Tex▶
That Night
That Was Then. . .This Is
    Now
This Boy's Life▶
Thrashin'
Three O'Clock High
Tom Brown's School Days▶
Toughlove
Treasure Island
Troop Beverly Hills
The Trouble with Angels
Uncle Buck
Up Against the Wall
Valley Girl
The Voyage of the Yes
Weird Science
Welcome Home, Roxy
    Carmichael
Where Angels Go, Trouble
    Follows
Wild Pony▶
The Year My Voice Broke▶
Young Guns
Zebrahead▶
The Zoo Gang

Tennis
Tennis Racquet

That's Showbiz
The Boy Friend▶
Bugs Bunny Superstar
Chaplin▶
Delirious
Dog Pound Shuffle

The Errand Boy
F/X▶
F/X 2: The Deadly Art of
    Illusion
Face the Music
Fame▶
Funny Girl▶
Funny Lady
Help!▶
I'll Do Anything
Last Action Hero
Life with Mikey
Matinee
Mommie Dearest
The Muppet Movie▶
Muppets Take Manhattan▶
My Favorite Year▶
The Party▶
Pastime▶
The Purple Rose of Cairo▶
Sam's Son
Silent Movie
Sweet Liberty
Tootsie▶
Under the Rainbow
What's Love Got to Do
    With It?
Who Framed Roger
    Rabbit?▶
The Wizard of Speed and
    Time▶

3 Stooges
Snow White and the Three
    Stooges
Three Stooges
Three Stooges: A Ducking
    They Will Go
Three Stooges: A Plumbing
    We Will Go
Three Stooges: Cash and
    Carry
Three Stooges: If a Body
    Meets a Body
Three Stooges: In the
    Sweet Pie and Pie
Three Stooges Meet
    Hercules
Three Stooges: So Long
    Mr. Chumps
Three Stooges: What's the
    Matador?

Time Travel
see also Rescue Missions
Involving Time Travel
Adventures in Dinosaur
    City
Amazing Mr. Blunden
Army of Darkness▶
Back to the Future▶
Back to the Future, Part 2
Back to the Future, Part 3
Beastmaster 2: Through
    the Portal of Time
Bill & Ted's Bogus Journey
Bill & Ted's Excellent
    Adventure
The Blue Yonder
Brother Future
Buck Rogers in the 25th
    Century
Doctor Who: An Unearthly
    Child
Doctor Who and the
    Daleks
Escape from the Planet of
    the Apes▶
Groundhog Day▶
Hercules in New York
Highlander 2: The
    Quickening
The Jetsons Meet the
    Flintstones
Land of the Lost, Vol. 1
Lords of Magick

Mannequin 2: On the
    Move
The Navigator▶
Peggy Sue Got Married
Teenage Mutant Ninja
    Turtles 3
Terminator 2: Judgment
    Day▶
Three Stooges Meet
    Hercules
Time Bandits▶
Timefighters in the Land of
    Fantasy
Unidentified Flying Oddball
Voyager from the Unknown

Tom & Jerry
Tom & Jerry Kids: Out of
    This World Fun
Tom & Jerry On Parade
Tom and Jerry: Starring
Tom and Jerry: The Movie
Tom & Jerry: The Very
    Best Of Tom & Jerry
Tom & Jerry's Cartoon
    Cavalcade
Tom & Jerry's Comic
    Capers
Tom & Jerry's Festival of
    Fun
Tom & Jerry's 50th
    Birthday Classics

Toys
Babes in Toyland
Not Quite Human
The Toy
Toys
Where the Toys Come
    From

Trading Places
Big▶
Cinderfella
Class Act
Condorman
Dave▶
Desperately Seeking
    Susan▶
Doctor Doolittle
Dream a Little Dream
18 Again!
Freaky Friday
Greystoke: The Legend of
    Tarzan, Lord of the
    Apes
Heart Like a Wheel▶
Hiding Out
The Incredible Mr. Limpet
Just One of the Guys
The Lady Vanishes▶
Ladybugs
Like Father, Like Son
Maid to Order
The Man Who Wagged
    His Tail
Monkey Business▶
Overboard
The Prince and the
    Pauper▶
The Prince and the Pauper
Roman Holiday▶
The Scarlet Pimpernel▶
The Shaggy D.A.
The Shaggy Dog
The Shakiest Gun in the
    West
Something Special
Soul Man
Tootsie▶
Vice Versa▶
Wait Till Your Mother Gets
    Home
Wonder Man
Yentl

Trains
see also Subways
From Russia with Love▶
The Fugitive▶
The Great Harbor Rescue
The Great Train Robbery▶
The Grey Fox▶
Hot Lead & Cold Feet
The Lady Vanishes▶
The Little Engine That
    Could
Once Upon a Time in the
    West▶
Reading Rainbow: Kate
    Shelley and the Midnight
    Express
Shining Time Station:
    Singsongs, Vol. 1
Shining Time Station: 'Tis a
    Gift Holiday Special
The Silver Streak▶
Strangers on a Train▶
Throw Momma from the
    Train▶
Tough Guys

Treasure Hunt
City Slickers 2: The Legend
    of Curly's Gold
Ernest Rides Again
The Gold Bug
Greedy
The Jewel of the Nile▶
Romancing the Stone▶
Secret of the Ice Cave
Tarzan's Secret Treasure
Treasure Island
Treasure Island
The Treasure of
    Matecumbe
Treasure of the Sierra
    Madre▶

Trees
Lassie: Adventures of
    Neeka
The Little Crooked
    Christmas Tree
Reddy the Fox
The Wizard of Oz▶

TV Movies
The Adventures of a Two-
    Minute Werewolf
The Adventures of
    Huckleberry Finn
The Adventures of
    Huckleberry Finn▶
The Adventures of Tom
    Sawyer
African Journey
An American Christmas
    Carol
And Baby Makes Six
And the Children Shall
    Lead
Anne of Avonlea▶
Anne of Green Gables▶
Annie Oakley
Babes in Toyland
Back Home
Back to Hannibal: The
    Further Adventures of
    Tom Sawyer and
    Huckleberry Finn
Battle of the Bullies
The Beniker Gang
Bill▶
Bill: On His Own▶
The Black Arrow
Black Magic
Bon Voyage, Charlie
    Brown
The Boy Who Left Home
    to Find Out About the
    Shivers

Category Index

Westerns
see *Cowboys & Indians*

Winnie the Pooh
The New Adventures of
Winnie the Pooh, Vol. 1:
Great Honey Pot
Robbery
Pooh Learning: Helping
Others
Pooh Learning: Making
Friends
Pooh Learning: Sharing
and Caring
Pooh Playtime: Cowboy
Pooh
Pooh Playtime: Detective
Tigger
Pooh Playtime: Pooh Party
Winnie the Pooh and the
Blustery Day
Winnie the Pooh and the
Honey Tree

Witches' Brew
see also *Demons &
Wizards*
Black Magic
Dr. Strange
Hocus Pocus
Lost Legacy: A Girl Called
Hatter Fox
Lumpkin the Pumpkin
My Little Pony: The Movie
The Polar Bear King
Return to Oz
Sabrina, the Teenaged
Witch
The Witch Who Turned
Pink
The Witches▶
Witches' Brew
Witch's Night Out
The Wizard of Oz▶
The Worst Witch

Wonderworks Movies
African Journey
And the Children Shall
Lead
Anne of Avonlea▶
Anne of Green Gables▶
The Boy Who Loved Trolls
Bridge to Terabithia
Brother Future
The Canterville Ghost
The Chronicles of Narnia▶
City Boy
Clowning Around
Clowning Around 2
Daniel and the Towers
The Fig Tree
Frog▶
Frogs!
Gryphon
The Haunting of Barney
Palmer
Hector's Bunyip
Hiroshima Maiden
The Hoboken Chicken
Emergency
Home at Last
The House of Dies Drear
How to Be a Perfect
Person in Just Three
Days
Jacob Have I Loved
Konrad▶
Lantern Hill
The Little Princess▶
Lone Star Kid
Looking for Miracles
Maricela
The Mighty Pawns
Miracle at Moreaux
My Friend Walter

Runaway
Sweet 15
Walking on Air
A Waltz Through the Hills
Words by Heart

World War I
The African Queen▶
The Charge of the Model
T's
Courage Mountain
Land That Time Forgot
Lawrence of Arabia▶
Miracle of Our Lady of
Fatima
When the Whales Came

World War II
see also *Postwar; POW/
MIA*
Adventures of Smilin' Jack
Alan & Naomi
Au Revoir Les Enfants▶
Back Home
Battle of Britain
Bedknobs and Broomsticks
The Bridge on the River
Kwai▶
A Bridge Too Far
Canine Commando
The Canterville Ghost
Casablanca▶
Chips the War Dog
A Day in October
December
Empire of the Sun▶
Forbidden Games▶
Foreign Correspondent▶
A Friendship in Vienna
G-Men vs. the Black
Dragon
Hiroshima Maiden
Hope and Glory▶
The Human Comedy▶
The Incredible Mr. Limpet
Journey for Margaret▶
Judgment at Nuremberg▶
A League of Their Own▶
The Little Thief
MacArthur
A Midnight Clear▶
Miracle at Moreaux
Miracle of the White
Stallions
An Officer and a Duck
Racing with the Moon▶
Reunion▶
Saboteur▶
Since You Went Away▶
Snow Treasure
The Sound of Music▶
South Pacific▶
Swing Shift
Victory
The Wizard of Loneliness

Wrestling
Hadley's Rebellion
No Holds Barred
Take Down

Wrong Side of the
Tracks
see also *Rags to Riches*
Breaking Away▶
Captains Courageous▶
Carbon Copy
Careful, He Might Hear
You▶
Cool As Ice
Cry-Baby▶
Dirty Dancing▶
Far and Away
The Flamingo Kid▶
Grease
It Happened One Night▶

Jersey Girl
King Ralph
Liar's Moon
The Man from Snowy River
Off Beat
Pretty in Pink
Return to Snowy River
Rocky▶
Rumble Fish▶
Some Kind of Wonderful
That Night
A Tree Grows in
Brooklyn▶
Valley Girl

Distributor Index

A&M—A & M Video

AAI—Arts America, Inc.

ACA—Academy Entertainment

ADL—Anti-Defamation League of B'nai B'rith

AFR—Afro-Am Distributing Company

AHV—Active Home Video

AIM—AIMS Media

AMB—Ambrose Video Publishing, Inc.

AOV—Admit One Video

APD—Applause Productions, Inc.

AUD—Audio-Forum

AVE—A*Vision

BAR—Barr Films

BFA—Phoenix/BFA Films

BFS—Video Collectibles

BFV—Best Film & Video Corporation

BMG—BMG

BMV—Bennett Marine Video

BPG—Bridgestone Multimedia

BTV—Baker & Taylor Video

BVV—Buena Vista Home Video

CAB—Cable Films & Video

CAF—Cabin Fever Entertainment

CAN—Cannon Video

CCB—Critics' Choice Video, Inc.

CCC—Children's Circle

CEL—Celebrity Home Entertainment

CFV—Carousel Film & Video

CHF—Churchill Media

CHI—Center for Humanities, Inc.

CNG—Congress Entertainment, Ltd.

COL—Columbia Tristar Home Video

CRC—Criterion Collection

CSM—Coliseum Video

CVC—Connoisseur Video Collection

DIS—Walt Disney Home Video

DSN—Disney Educational Productions

DVT—Discount Video Tapes, Inc.

ECU—EcuFilm

EVD—European Video Distributor

EXP—Expanded Entertainment

FCT—Facets Multimedia, Inc.

FFF—Fast Forward

FHE—Family Home Entertainment

FHS—Films for the Humanities & Sciences

FLI—Films Inc. Video

FMT—Format International

FOC—Focus on Animals

FOX—CBS/Fox Video

FRG—Fright Video

FRH—Fries Home Video

FUS—Fusion Video

FXL—Fox/Lorber Home Video

FXV—FoxVideo

GBV—Western Publishing Co., Inc.

GEM—Video Gems

GHV—Genesis Home Video

GKK—Goodtimes Entertainment

GLV—German Language Video Center

GPV—Grapevine Video

GVV—Glenn Video Vistas, Ltd.

HBO—HBO Home Video

HEG—Horizon Entertainment

HHE—Hollywood Home Entertainment

HHT—Hollywood Home Theatre

HMD—Hemdale Home Video

HMV—Home Vision Cinema

HPH—Hollywood Pictures Home Video

HSE—High/Scope Educational Research Foundation

HTV—Hen's Tooth Video

IGP—Ignatius Press

IHF—International Historic Films, Inc. (IHF)

IME—Image Entertainment

IMP—Imperial Entertainment Corporation

INC—Increase/ SilverMine Video

ING—Ingram Entertainment

INJ—Ingram International Films

INT—Interama, Inc.

JCF—Judaica Captioned Film Center, Inc.

JEF—JEF Films, Inc.

JFK—Just for Kids Home Video

JHV—Jim Henson Video

JTC—J2 Communications

KAR—Karol Video

KEP—Keep the Faith Inc.

KUI—Knowledge Unlimited, Inc.

KUL—Kultur Video

LCA—Learning Corporation of America

LGV—Lyons Group

LHV—Lorimar Home Video

LIV—Live Home Video

LME—Lucerne Media

LOO—Loonic Video

LSV—LSVideo, Inc.

LTY—Lightyear Entertainment

LUM—Lumivision Corporation

MAS—Mastervision, Inc.

MAX—Miramax Pictures Home Video

MCA—MCA/Universal Home Video

MCG—Management Company Entertainment Group (MCEG), Inc.

MGM—MGM/UA Home Entertainment

MIR—Miramar Productions

MLB—Mike LeBell's Video

MLT—Music for Little People

MNC—Monarch Home Video

MON—Monterey Home Video

MOV—Movies Unlimited

MPI—MPI Home Video

MRV—Moore Video

MTI—Coronet/MTI Film & Video

MTT—MTI Teleprograms, Inc.

MTX—MNTEX Entertainment, Inc.

MVC—Moviecraft, Inc.

MVD—Music Video Distributors

NFB—National Film Board of Canada

NHO—New Horizons Home Video

NLC—New Line Home Video

NOS—Nostalgia Family Video

NWV—New World Entertainment

NYR—Not Yet Released

ORI—Orion Home Video

PAR—Paramount Home Video

PBC—Princeton Book Company Publishers

PBS—PBS Video

PGV—Polygram Video (PV)

PIC—Picture Start

PME—Public Media Video

PMH—PM Entertainment Group, Inc.

PMS—Professional Media Service Corp.

PPI—PPI Entertainment Group

PRS—Proscenium Entertainment

PSM—Prism Entertainment

PSS—Price Stern Sloan, Inc.

PTB—Proud To Be...A Black Video Collection

PYR—Pyramid Film & Video

RAN—Random House Home Video

RDG—Reader's Digest Home Video

REP—Republic Pictures Home Video

RHI—Rhino Home Video

RHU—Random House Media

RHV—Regency Home Video

RIN—Rincon Children's Entertainment/BMG Kidz

RKO—RKO Pictures

RXM—Rex Miller

SAL—Salenger Films, Inc.

SCH—Schoolmasters Video

SGE—SGE Home Video

SHV—Snoopy's Home Video Library

SIG—Signals

SIM—Simitar Entertainment

SMA—Smarty Pants Video

SMV—Sony Music Video Enterprises

SNC—Sinister Cinema

SPW—Sparrow Distribution

STE—Starmaker Entertainment, Inc.

STP—Streamline Pictures

SUE—Sultan Entertainment

SUP—Super Source

SVE—Society for Visual Education, Inc. (SVE)

SVI—Strand/VCI Entertainment

SWC—Simon Wiesenthal Center

TCF—20th Century Fox Film Corporation

TIM—Timeless Video Inc.

TLF—Time-Life Video and Television

TMG—The Maier Group

TOU—Touchstone Home Video

TPI—Thomson Productions, Inc.

TPV—Tapeworm Video Distributors

TRI—Triboro Entertainment Group

TTC—Turner Home Entertainment Company

TVC—The Video Catalog

TWE—Trans-World Entertainment

UAV—UAV Corporation

UND—Uni Distribution

UNI—Unicorn Video, Inc.

UNT—Unity Productions

UWA—University of Washington Educational Media Collection

VAI—Video Artists International, Inc.

VAN—Vantage Communications, Inc.

VBL—Video Bible Library, Inc.

VCD—Video City Productions

VCI—Video Communications, Inc. (VCI)

VCN—Video Connection

VDC—Vidcrest

VDM—Video Dimensions

VEC—Valencia Entertainment Corporation

VES—Vestron Video

VGD—Vanguard Video

VHE—VCII Home Entertainment, Inc.

VMK—Vidmark Entertainment

VPJ—The Video Project

VRS—Video Resources

VTR—Video Treasures

VYG—Voyager Company

VYY—Video Yesteryear

WAR—Warner Home Video, Inc.

WEA—Warner/Elektra/Atlantic (WEA) Corporation

WFV—Western Film & Video, Inc.

WKV—Wood Knapp & Company, Inc.

WME—Warren Miller Entertainment

WNE—WNET/Thirteen Non-Broadcast

WOM—Wombat Film and Video

WOV—Worldvision Home Video, Inc.

WSH—Wishing Well Distributing

WST—White Star

WTA—Whole Toon Catalogue

XVC—Xenon

Distributor Guide

The **DISTRIBUTOR GUIDE** alphabetically lists the full address and phone, toll-free, and fax numbers of 200 distributors. Each video in the main section has at least one and as many as three distributor codes located at the bottom of the review. Those reviews with the code **OM** are on moratorium (distributed at one time, though not currently). Since a title enjoying such status was once distributed, it may well linger on your local video store shelf. When the distributor is not known, the code **NO** appears in the review. For new releases to the theater that have not yet made it to video (but likely will in the coming year), the code **NYR** (not yet released) appears.

A & M VIDEO *(A&M)*
1416 N. LaBrea Ave.
Hollywood, CA 90028
213-469-2411

**ACADEMY
ENTERTAINMENT** *(ACA)*
9250 Wilshire Blvd.,
Ste. 400
Beverly Hills, CA
90212
800-972-0001

**ACTIVE HOME
VIDEO** *(AHV)*
12121 Wilshire Blvd.,
No. 401
Los Angeles, CA
90025
310-447-6131
800-824-6109
Fax: 310-207-0411

**ADMIT ONE
VIDEO** *(AOV)*
PO Box 66, Sta. O
Toronto, ON, Canada
M4A 2M8
416-463-5714

**AFRO-AM
DISTRIBUTING
COMPANY** *(AFR)*
407 E. 25th St., Ste.
600
Chicago, IL 60616
312-791-1611
Fax: 312-791-0921

AIMS MEDIA *(AIM)*
9710 DeSoto Ave.
Chatsworth, CA
91311-4409
818-773-4300
800-367-2467
Fax: 818-341-6700

**AMBROSE VIDEO
PUBLISHING,
INC.** *(AMB)*
1290 Avenue of the
Americas, Ste. 2245
New York, NY 10104
212-265-7272
800-526-4663
Fax: 212-265-8088

**ANTI-DEFAMATION
LEAGUE OF B'NAI
B'RITH** *(ADL)*
Audio-Visual Dept.
823 United Nations
Plaza
New York, NY 10017
212-490-2525
Fax: 212-867-0779

**APPLAUSE
PRODUCTIONS,
INC.** *(APD)*
85 Longview Rd.
Port Washington, NY
11050
516-883-2825
Fax: 516-883-7460

**ARTS AMERICA,
INC.** *(AAI)*
9 Benedict Pl.
Greenwich, CT 06830-
5321
203-869-4693
Fax: 203-661-1174

AUDIO-FORUM *(AUD)*
96 Broad St.
Guilford, CT 06437
203-453-9794
800-243-1234
Fax: 203-453-9774

A*VISION *(AVE)*
A Time Warner
Company
75 Rockefeller Plaza

New York, NY 10019
212-275-2900
Fax: 212-765-0899

**BAKER & TAYLOR
VIDEO** *(BTV)*
501 S. Gladiolus
Momence, IL 60954
800-775-2300
Fax: 800-775-3500

BARR FILMS *(BAR)*
12801 Schabarum
Irwindale, CA 91706
818-338-7828
800-234-7878
Fax: 818-814-2672

**BENNETT MARINE
VIDEO** *(BMV)*
730 Washington St.
Marina del Rey, CA
90292
213-821-3329
800-262-8862
Fax: 213-306-3162

**BEST FILM & VIDEO
CORPORATION** *(BFV)*
108 New South Rd.
Hicksville, NY 11801-
5223
516-931-6969

BMG *(BMG)*
6363 Sunset Blvd., 6th
Fl.
Hollywood, CA 90028-
7318
213-468-4067

**BRIDGESTONE
MULTIMEDIA** *(BPG)*
1979 Palomar Oaks
Way
Carlsbad, CA 92009
619-431-9888
800-523-0988
Fax: 619-431-0489

**BUENA VISTA HOME
VIDEO** *(BVV)*
500 S. Buena Vista St.
Burbank, CA 91521
818-562-3560
Fax: 818-567-6464

**CABIN FEVER
ENTERTAINMENT** *(CAF)*
100 W. Putnam Ave.
Greenwich, CT 06830
203-863-5200
Fax: 203-863-5258

**CABLE FILMS &
VIDEO** *(CAB)*
Country Club Sta.
PO Box 7171
Kansas City, MO
64113
913-362-2804
Fax: 913-341-7365

**CANNON
VIDEO** *(CAN)*
8200 Wilshire Blvd.,
3rd Fl.
Beverly Hills, CA
90211
213-966-5600
Fax: 213-653-5485

**CAROUSEL FILM &
VIDEO** *(CFV)*
260 5th Ave., Rm. 405
New York, NY 10001
212-683-1660
Fax: 212-683-1662

**CBS/FOX
VIDEO** *(FOX)*
1330 Avenue of the
Americas, 5th Fl.
New York, NY 10019
212-373-4800
800-800-2369
Fax: 212-373-4802

**CELEBRITY HOME
ENTERTAINMENT** *(CEL)*
22025 Ventura Blvd.
PO Box 4112
Woodland Hills, CA
91365-4112
818-595-0666
Fax: 818-716-0168

**CENTER FOR
HUMANITIES,
INC.** *(CHI)*
Communications Park
Box 1000
Mount Kisco, NY
10549
914-666-4100
800-431-1242
Fax: 914-666-5319

**CHILDREN'S
CIRCLE** *(CCC)*
389 Newtown Tpke.
Weston, CT 06883
203-222-0002
800-KIDS-VID
Fax: 203-226-3818

**CHURCHILL
MEDIA** *(CHF)*
12210 Nebraska Ave.
Los Angeles, CA
90025
310-207-6600
800-334-7830
Fax: 310-207-1330

**COLISEUM
VIDEO** *(CSM)*
430 W. 54th St.
New York, NY 10019
212-489-8130
800-288-8130
Fax: 212-582-5690

**COLUMBIA TRISTAR
HOME VIDEO** *(COL)*
3400 Riverside Dr.

Burbank, CA 91505-4627
818-972-8193
Fax: 818-972-0937

CONGRESS ENTERTAINMENT, LTD. *(CNG)*
Learn Plaza, Ste. 6
PO Box 845
Tannersville, PA 18372-0845
717-620-9001
800-847-8273
Fax: 717-620-9278

CONNOISSEUR VIDEO COLLECTION *(CVC)*
1543 7th St., Ste. 202
Santa Monica, CA 90401-2636
310-393-9000
Fax: 310-458-8881

CORONET/MTI FILM & VIDEO *(MTI)*
108 Wilmot Rd.
Deerfield, IL 60015
708-940-1260
800-777-8100
Fax: 708-940-3640

CRITERION COLLECTION *(CRC)*
c/o The Voyager Company
1 Bridge St.
Irvington, NY 10533-1543

CRITICS' CHOICE VIDEO, INC. *(CCB)*
PO Box 549
Elk Grove Village, IL 60009
800-367-7765
Fax: 800-544-9852

DISCOUNT VIDEO TAPES, INC. *(DVT)*
PO Box 7122
Burbank, CA 91510
818-843-3366
Fax: 818-843-3821

DISNEY EDUCATIONAL PRODUCTIONS *(DSN)*
500 S. Buena Vista St.
Burbank, CA 91521
800-621-2131

ECUFILM *(ECU)*
810 Twelfth Ave., S.
Nashville, TN 37203
615-242-6277
800-251-4091

EUROPEAN VIDEO DISTRIBUTOR *(EVD)*
2321 W. Olive Ave., Ste. A
Burbank, CA 91506
818-848-5902
800-423-6752
Fax: 818-848-1965

EXPANDED ENTERTAINMENT *(EXP)*
28024 Dorothy Dr.

Agoura Hills, CA 91301-2635
818-991-2884
800-996-TOON
Fax: 818-991-3773

FACETS MULTIMEDIA, INC. *(FCT)*
1517 W. Fullerton Ave.
Chicago, IL 60614
312-281-9075

FAMILY HOME ENTERTAINMENT *(FHE)*
c/o Live Home Video
15400 Sherman Way
PO Box 10124
Van Nuys, CA 91410-0124
818-499-5827

FAST FORWARD *(FFF)*
3420 Ocean Park Blvd., Ste. 3075
Santa Monica, CA 90405
310-396-4434
Fax: 310-396-2292

FILMS FOR THE HUMANITIES & SCIENCES *(FHS)*
PO Box 2053
Princeton, NJ 08543-2053
609-275-1400
800-257-5126
Fax: 609-275-3767

FILMS INC. VIDEO *(FLI)*
5547 N. Ravenswood Ave.
Chicago, IL 60640-1199
312-878-2600
800-323-4222

FOCUS ON ANIMALS *(FOC)*
PO Box 150
Trumbull, CT 06611
203-377-1116

FORMAT INTERNATIONAL *(FMT)*
3921 N. Meridian St.
Indianapolis, IN 46208-4011
317-924-5163

FOX/LORBER HOME VIDEO *(FXL)*
419 Park Ave., S., 20th Fl.
New York, NY 10019
212-532-3392
800-229-9994
Fax: 212-685-2625

FOXVIDEO *(FXV)*
2121 Avenue of the Stars, 25th Fl.
Los Angeles, CA 90067
310-203-3900
800-800-2FOX
Fax: 310-774-5811

FRIES HOME VIDEO *(FRH)*
6922 Hollywood Blvd., 12th Fl.

Hollywood, CA 90028
213-466-2266
Fax: 213-466-2126

FRIGHT VIDEO *(FRG)*
PO Box 179
Billerica, MA 01821
508-663-2510

FUSION VIDEO *(FUS)*
100 Fusion Way
Country Club Hills, IL 60478
708-799-2073
800-338-7710
Fax: 708-799-8375

GENESIS HOME VIDEO *(GHV)*
15820 Arminta St.
Van Nuys, CA 91406
818-787-0660
800-344-1060

GERMAN LANGUAGE VIDEO CENTER *(GLV)*
7625 Pendleton Pike
Indianapolis, IN 46226-5298
317-547-1257
800-252-1957
Fax: 317-547-1263

GLENN VIDEO VISTAS, LTD. *(GVV)*
6924 Canby Ave., Ste. 103
Reseda, CA 91335
818-881-8110
Fax: 818-981-5506

GOODTIMES ENTERTAINMENT *(GKK)*
16 E. 40th St., 8th Fl.
New York, NY 10016-0113
212-951-3000
Fax: 212-481-9067

GRAPEVINE VIDEO *(GPV)*
PO Box 46161
Phoenix, AZ 85063
602-973-3661
Fax: 602-973-0060

HBO HOME VIDEO *(HBO)*
1100 6th Ave.
New York, NY 10036
212-512-7400

HEMDALE HOME VIDEO *(HMD)*
7966 Beverly Blvd.
Los Angeles, CA 90048
213-966-3758
Fax: 213-651-3107

HEN'S TOOTH VIDEO *(HTV)*
2805 E. State Blvd.
Fort Wayne, IN 46805
219-471-4332
Fax: 219-471-4449

HIGH/SCOPE EDUCATIONAL RESEARCH FOUNDATION *(HSE)*
600 N. River St.

Ypsilanti, MI 48198-2898
313-485-2000
800-40-PRESS
Fax: 313-485-0704

HOLLYWOOD HOME ENTERTAINMENT *(HHE)*
6165 Crooked Creek Rd., Ste. B
Norcross, GA 30092-3105

HOLLYWOOD HOME THEATRE *(HHT)*
1540 N. Highland Ave., Ste. 110
Hollywood, CA 90028
213-466-0127

HOLLYWOOD PICTURES HOME VIDEO *(HPH)*
Fairmont Bldg. 526
500 S. Buena Vista St.
Burbank, CA 91505-9842

HOME VISION CINEMA *(HMV)*
5547 N. Ravenswood Ave.
Chicago, IL 60640-1199
312-878-2600
800-826-3456
Fax: 312-878-8648

HORIZON ENTERTAINMENT *(HEG)*
45030 Trevor Ave.
Lancaster, CA 93534
805-940-1040
800-323-2061
Fax: 805-940-8511

IGNATIUS PRESS *(IGP)*
15 Oakland Ave.
Harrison, NY 10528-9974
914-835-4216
Fax: 914-835-8406

IMAGE ENTERTAINMENT *(IME)*
9333 Oso Ave.
Chatsworth, CA 91311
818-407-9100

IMPERIAL ENTERTAINMENT CORPORATION *(IMP)*
4640 Lankershim Blvd., 4th Fl.
North Hollywood, CA 91602
818-762-0005

INCREASE/SILVERMINE VIDEO *(INC)*
6860 Canby Ave., Ste. 118
Reseda, CA 91335
818-342-2880
800-233-2880
Fax: 818-342-4029

INGRAM ENTERTAINMENT *(ING)*
1123 Heil Quaker Blvd.

La Vergne, TN 37086
615-793-5000
800-759-5000
Fax: 615-793-3875

INGRAM INTERNATIONAL FILMS *(INJ)*
10990 E. 55th Ave.
Denver, CO 80239
303-373-4583
800-356-3577

INTERAMA, INC. *(INT)*
301 W. 53rd St., Ste. 19E
New York, NY 10019
212-977-4830
Fax: 212-581-6582

INTERNATIONAL HISTORIC FILMS, INC. (IHF) *(IHF)*
PO Box 29035
Chicago, IL 60629
312-927-2900
Fax: 312-927-9211

J2 COMMUNICATIONS *(JTC)*
10850 Wilshire Blvd., Ste. 1000
Los Angeles, CA 90024
310-474-5252
800-521-8273
Fax: 310-474-1219

JEF FILMS, INC. *(JEF)*
Film House
143 Hickory Hill Circle
Osterville, MA 02655-1322
508-428-7198

JIM HENSON VIDEO *(JHV)*
500 S. Buena Vista St.
Burbank, CA 91521
818-562-3883
Fax: 818-567-6466

JUDAICA CAPTIONED FILM CENTER, INC. *(JCF)*
PO Box 21439
Baltimore, MD 21208-0439
410-655-6767

JUST FOR KIDS HOME VIDEO *(JFK)*
6320 Canoga Ave., Penthouse Ste.
PO Box 4112
Woodland Hills, CA 91365-4112
818-715-1980
800-445-8210
Fax: 818-716-0168

KAROL VIDEO *(KAR)*
PO Box 7600
Wilkes Barre, PA 18773
717-822-8899

KEEP THE FAITH INC. *(KEP)*
PO Box 1069
141 Main

Clifton, NJ 07014-
1065
201-471-7494
800-221-1564
Fax: 201-471-7584

**KNOWLEDGE
UNLIMITED,
INC.** *(KUI)*
Box 52
Madison, WI 53701-
0052
608-836-6660
800-356-2303
Fax: 608-831-1570

KULTUR VIDEO *(KUL)*
121 Hwy. No. 36
West Long Branch, NJ
07764
908-229-2343
800-458-5887
Fax: 908-229-0066

**LEARNING
CORPORATION OF
AMERICA** *(LCA)*
c/o Coronet/MTI
108 Wilmot Rd.
Deerfield, IL 60015
708-940-1260
800-621-2131
Fax: 708-940-3600

**LIGHTYEAR
ENTERTAINMENT** *(LTY)*
350 5th Ave., Ste.
5101
New York, NY 10118
212-563-4610
800-229-7867
Fax: 212-563-1932

**LIVE HOME
VIDEO** *(LIV)*
15400 Sherman Way
PO Box 10124
Van Nuys, CA 91410-
0124
818-988-5060

LOONIC VIDEO *(LOO)*
2022 Taraval St., Ste.
6427
San Francisco, CA
94116
510-526-5681

**LORIMAR HOME
VIDEO** *(LHV)*
15838 N. 62nd St.,
Ste. 100
Scottsdale, AZ 85254
800-345-1441

LSVIDEO, INC. *(LSV)*
PO Box 415
Carmel, IN 46032

**LUCERNE
MEDIA** *(LME)*
37 Ground Pine Rd.
Morris Plains, NJ
07950
201-538-1401
800-341-2293
Fax: 201-538-0855

**LUMIVISION
CORPORATION** *(LUM)*
1490 Lafayette St.,
Ste. 407

Denver, CO 80218
303-860-0400
800-776-5864
Fax: 303-860-0425

LYONS GROUP *(LGV)*
2435 N. Center
Expressway, Ste.
1600
Richardson, TX 75083-
3884
214-390-6000
800-418-2371
Fax: 214-390-6066

**THE MAIER
GROUP** *(TMG)*
235 E. 95th St.
New York, NY 10128
212-534-4100
Fax: 212-410-2145

**MANAGEMENT
COMPANY
ENTERTAINMENT
GROUP (MCEG),
INC.** *(MCG)*
1888 Century Park, E.,
Ste. 1777
Los Angeles, CA
90067-1721
310-282-0871
Fax: 310-315-7850

**MASTERVISION,
INC.** *(MAS)*
969 Park Ave.
New York, NY 10028
212-879-0448
Fax: 212-744-3560

**MCA/UNIVERSAL
HOME
VIDEO** *(MCA)*
70 Universal City Plaza
Universal City, CA
91608-9955
818-777-6419
Fax: 818-733-0226

**MGM/UA HOME
ENTERTAINMENT** *(MGM)*
10000 W. Washington
Blvd.
Culver City, CA 90232
310-280-6212

**MIKE LEBELL'S
VIDEO** *(MLB)*
75 Freemont Pl.
Los Angeles, CA
90005
213-938-3333
Fax: 213-938-3334

**MIRAMAR
PRODUCTIONS** *(MIR)*
200 2nd Ave., W.
Seattle, WA 98119
206-284-4700
800-245-6472
Fax: 206-286-4433

**MIRAMAX PICTURES
HOME
VIDEO** *(MAX)*
500 S. Buena Vista St.
Burbank, CA 91521

**MNTEX
ENTERTAINMENT,
INC.** *(MTX)*

PO Box 667
Prior Lake, MN 55372-
0667
612-440-6028
Fax: 612-447-8173

**MONARCH HOME
VIDEO** *(MNC)*
1123 Heil Quaker
Blvd.
La Vergne, TN 37086-
7006
615-793-5000
800-759-5000
Fax: 615-793-3875

**MONTEREY HOME
VIDEO** *(MON)*
28038 Dorothy Dr.,
Ste. 1
Agoura Hills, CA
91301
818-597-0047
800-424-2593
Fax: 818-597-0105

MOORE VIDEO *(MRV)*
PO Box 5703
Richmond, VA 23220
804-745-9785
Fax: 804-745-9785

**MOVIECRAFT,
INC.** *(MVC)*
PO Box 438
Orland Park, IL 60462
708-460-9082
Fax: 708-460-9099

**MOVIES
UNLIMITED** *(MOV)*
6736 Castor Ave.
Philadelphia, PA 19149
215-722-8298
800-523-0823

**MPI HOME
VIDEO** *(MPI)*
15825 Rob Roy Dr.
Oak Forest, IL 60452
708-687-7881
Fax: 708-687-3797

**MTI TELEPROGRAMS,
INC.** *(MTT)*
108 Wilmot Rd.
Deerfield, IL 60015-
9990
708-940-1260
800-621-2131

**MUSIC FOR LITTLE
PEOPLE** *(MLT)*
Box 1460
Redway, CA 95560
707-923-3991
800-727-2233
Fax: 707-923-3241

**MUSIC VIDEO
DISTRIBUTORS** *(MVD)*
O'Neill Industrial
Center
1210 Standbridge St.
Norristown, PA 19403
215-272-7771
800-888-0486
Fax: 215-272-6074

**NATIONAL FILM
BOARD OF
CANADA** *(NFB)*
1251 Avenue of the
Americas, 16th Fl.

New York, NY 10020-
1173
212-596-1770
800-542-2164

**NEW HORIZONS
HOME VIDEO** *(NHO)*
2951 Flowers Rd., S.,
Ste. 237
Atlanta, GA 30341
404-458-3488
800-854-3323
Fax: 404-458-2679

**NEW LINE HOME
VIDEO** *(NLC)*
116 N. Robertson
Blvd.
Los Angeles, CA
90048
310-967-6670
Fax: 310-854-0602

**NEW WORLD
ENTERTAINMENT** *(NWV)*
1440 S. Sepulveda
Blvd.
Los Angeles, CA
90025
310-444-8100

**NOSTALGIA FAMILY
VIDEO** *(NOS)*
PO Box 606
Baker City, OR 97814
503-523-9034

**NOT YET
RELEASED** *(NYR)*
United States

**ORION HOME
VIDEO** *(ORI)*
1888 Century Park E.
Los Angeles, CA
90067
310-282-0550

**PARAMOUNT HOME
VIDEO** *(PAR)*
Bluhdorn Bldg, 1st Fl.
5555 Melrose Ave.
Los Angeles, CA
90038
213-956-8090
Fax: 213-956-1100

PBS VIDEO *(PBS)*
1320 Braddock Pl.
Alexandria, VA 22314-
1698
703-739-5380
800-344-3337
Fax: 703-739-5269

**PHOENIX/BFA
FILMS** *(BFA)*
PO Box 1850
New York, NY 10156-
1850
212-684-5910
800-221-1274

PICTURE START *(PIC)*
1727 W. Catalpa
Chicago, IL 60640
312-769-2489
800-528-TAPE
Fax: 312-769-4467

**PM ENTERTAINMENT
GROUP, INC.** *(PMH)*
9450 Chivers Ave.

Sun Valley, CA 91352
818-504-6332
800-934-2111
Fax: 818-504-6380

**POLYGRAM VIDEO
(PV)** *(PGV)*
825 8th Ave.
New York, NY 10019
212-333-8000
800-825-7781
Fax: 212-603-7960

**PPI ENTERTAINMENT
GROUP** *(PPI)*
88 Saint Frances St.
Newark, NJ 07105
201-344-4214
Fax: 201-344-0465

**PRICE STERN SLOAN,
INC.** *(PSS)*
11150 Olympic Blvd.,
6th Fl.
Los Angeles, CA
90064-1823
310-477-6100
800-421-0892
Fax: 310-445-3933

**PRINCETON BOOK
COMPANY
PUBLISHERS** *(PBC)*
PO Box 57
Pennington, NJ 08534
609-737-8177
800-326-7149
Fax: 609-737-1869

**PRISM
ENTERTAINMENT** *(PSM)*
1888 Century Park, E.,
Ste. 1000
Los Angeles, CA
90067
310-277-3270
Fax: 310-203-8036

**PROFESSIONAL MEDIA
SERVICE
CORP.** *(PMS)*
19122 S. Vermont Ave.
Gardena, CA 90248
310-532-9024
800-223-7672
Fax: 800-253-8853

**PROSCENIUM
ENTERTAINMENT** *(PRS)*
PO Box 909
Hightstown, NJ 08520
609-448-9124
800-222-6260
Fax: 609-448-9499

PROUD TO BE**A
BLACK VIDEO
COLLECTION** *(PTB)*
1235-E East Blvd., Ste.
209
Charlotte, NC 28203
704-523-2227

**PUBLIC MEDIA
VIDEO** *(PME)*
5547 N. Ravenswood
Ave.
Chicago, IL 60640-
1199
312-878-2600
800-826-3456
Fax: 312-878-8406

PYRAMID FILM & VIDEO *(PYR)*
Box 1048
2801 Colorado Ave.
Santa Monica, CA 90406
310-828-7577
800-421-2304
Fax: 310-453-9083

RANDOM HOUSE HOME VIDEO *(RAN)*
225 Park Ave., S.
New York, NY 10003
212-254-1600
800-733-3000
Fax: 212-848-2436

RANDOM HOUSE MEDIA *(RHU)*
400 Hahn Rd.
Westminster, MD 21157
410-848-1900
800-492-0782
Fax: 410-857-1948

READER'S DIGEST HOME VIDEO *(RDG)*
Reader's Digest Rd.
Pleasantville, NY 10570
800-776-6868

REGENCY HOME VIDEO *(RHV)*
9911 W. Pico Blvd.
Los Angeles, CA 90035
310-552-2431
Fax: 310-552-9039

REPUBLIC PICTURES HOME VIDEO *(REP)*
12636 Beatrice St.
Los Angeles, CA 90066-0930
310-306-4040

REX MILLER *(RXM)*
Rte. 1, Box 457-D
East Prairie, MO 63845
314-649-5048

RHINO HOME VIDEO *(RHI)*
10635 Santa Monica Blvd., 2nd Fl.
Los Angeles, CA 90025-4900
310-828-1980
800-843-3670
Fax: 310-453-5529

RINCON CHILDREN'S ENTERTAINMENT/ BMG KIDZ *(RIN)*
1525 Crossroads of the World
Hollywood, CA 90028

RKO PICTURES *(RKO)*
1801 Avenue of the Stars, Ste. 448
Los Angeles, CA 90067
310-277-0707

SALENGER FILMS, INC. *(SAL)*
1635 12th St.

Santa Monica, CA 90404-9988
310-450-1300
800-775-5025
Fax: 310-450-1010

SCHOOLMASTERS VIDEO *(SCH)*
745 State Circle
PO Box 1941
Ann Arbor, MI 48106
313-761-5175
800-521-2832
Fax: 313-761-8711

SGE HOME VIDEO *(SGE)*
Div. of Shapiro Glickenhaus Entertainment
12001 Ventura Pl., 4th Fl.
Studio City, CA 91604
818-766-8500
Fax: 818-766-7873

SIGNALS *(SIG)*
PO Box 64428
St. Paul, MN 55164-0428
800-669-5225
Fax: 612-659-4320

SIMITAR ENTERTAINMENT *(SIM)*
3850 Annapolis Ln., Ste. 140
Plymouth, MN 55447
612-559-6660
800-486-TAPE
Fax: 612-559-0210

SIMON WIESENTHAL CENTER *(SWC)*
9760 W. Pico Blvd.
Los Angeles, CA 90035-4792
310-553-9036
Fax: 310-553-8007

SINISTER CINEMA *(SNC)*
PO Box 4369
Medford, OR 97501-0168
503-773-6860

SMARTY PANTS VIDEO *(SMA)*
15104 Detroit Ave., Ste. 2
Lakewood, OH 44107-3916
216-221-5300
Fax: 216-221-5348

SNOOPY'S HOME VIDEO LIBRARY *(SHV)*
c/o Media Home Entertainment
510 W. 6th St., Ste. 1032
Los Angeles, CA 90014-1311
213-236-1336

SOCIETY FOR VISUAL EDUCATION, INC. (SVE) *(SVE)*
55 E. Monroe, 34th Fl.

Chicago, IL 60603-5803
312-849-9100
800-829-1900
Fax: 312-849-9101

SONY MUSIC VIDEO ENTERPRISES *(SMV)*
550 Madison Ave.
New York, NY 10022
212-833-7095
Fax: 212-833-8620

SPARROW DISTRIBUTION *(SPW)*
101 Winners Circle
Brentwood, TN 37027
615-371-6800
800-877-4443
Fax: 615-371-6909

STARMAKER ENTERTAINMENT, INC. *(STE)*
151 Industrial Way, E.
Eatontown, NJ 07724
908-389-1020
800-233-3738
Fax: 908-389-1021

STRAND/VCI ENTERTAINMENT *(SVI)*
3350 Ocean Park Blvd., Ste. 205
Santa Monica, CA 90405
310-396-7011
Fax: 310-392-2472

STREAMLINE PICTURES *(STP)*
PO Box 691418
W. Hollywood, CA 90069
310-998-0070
Fax: 310-998-1145

SULTAN ENTERTAINMENT *(SUE)*
335 N. Maple Dr., Ste. 351
Beverly Hills, CA 90210-3899
310-285-6000

SUPER SOURCE *(SUP)*
PO Box 410777
San Francisco, CA 94141
415-777-1964
800-331-6304
Fax: 415-777-0187

TAPEWORM VIDEO DISTRIBUTORS *(TPV)*
12420 Montague St., Ste. B
Arleta, CA 91331
818-896-8899
800-367-8437
Fax: 818-896-3855

THOMSON PRODUCTIONS, INC. *(TPI)*
PO Box 1225
Orem, UT 84059
801-226-0155
800-228-8491

TIME-LIFE VIDEO AND TELEVISION *(TLF)*
1450 E. Parham Rd.

Richmond, VA 23280
804-266-6330
800-621-7026

TIMELESS VIDEO INC. *(TIM)*
10010 Canoga Ave., Ste. B2
Chatsworth, CA 91311
818-773-0284
Fax: 818-773-0176

TOUCHSTONE HOME VIDEO *(TOU)*
500 S. Buena Vista St.
Burbank, CA 91521
818-562-3883

TRANS-WORLD ENTERTAINMENT *(TWE)*
8899 Beverly Blvd., 8th Fl.
Los Angeles, CA 90048-2412
213-969-2800

TRIBORO ENTERTAINMENT GROUP *(TRI)*
12 W. 27th St., 15th Fl.
New York, NY 10001
212-686-6116
Fax: 212-686-6178

TURNER HOME ENTERTAINMENT COMPANY *(TTC)*
1 CNN Center
N. Tower, 12th Fl.
Atlanta, GA 30348
404-827-2000

20TH CENTURY FOX FILM CORPORATION *(TCF)*
PO Box 900
Beverly Hills, CA 90213
310-277-2211

UAV CORPORATION *(UAV)*
PO Box 7647
Charlotte, NC 28241
704-548-7300
Fax: 704-548-3335

UNI DISTRIBUTION *(UND)*
60 Universal City Plaza
Universal City, CA 91608
818-777-4400
Fax: 818-766-5740

UNICORN VIDEO, INC. *(UNI)*
9811 Independence Ave.
Chatsworth, CA 91311
818-407-1333
800-528-4336
Fax: 818-407-8246

UNITY PRODUCTIONS *(UNT)*
PO Box 31
Aberdeen, SD 57401-0031

UNIVERSITY OF WASHINGTON EDUCATIONAL MEDIA COLLECTION *(UWA)*
Kane Hall, DG-10
Seattle, WA 98195
206-543-9909
Fax: 206-685-7892

VALENCIA ENTERTAINMENT CORPORATION *(VEC)*
45030 Trevor Ave.
Lancaster, CA 93534-2648
805-940-1040
800-323-2601
Fax: 805-940-8511

VANGUARD VIDEO *(VGD)*
436 Creamery Way, Ste. D
Exton, PA 19341
800-323-7432

VANTAGE COMMUNICATIONS, INC. *(VAN)*
PO Box 546-G
Nyack, NY 10960
914-268-0715
800-872-0068
Fax: 914-268-3429

VCII HOME ENTERTAINMENT, INC. *(VHE)*
13418 Wyandotte St.
North Hollywood, CA 91605
818-764-1777
800-350-1931
Fax: 818-764-0231

VESTRON VIDEO *(VES)*
c/o Live Home Video
15400 Sherman Way
PO Box 10124
Van Nuys, CA 91410-0124
818-988-5060

VIDCREST *(VDC)*
PO Box 69642
Los Angeles, CA 90069
213-650-7310
Fax: 213-654-4810

VIDEO ARTISTS INTERNATIONAL, INC. *(VAI)*
158 Linwood Plaza, Ste. 301
Fort Lee, NJ 07024
201-944-0099
800-477-7146
Fax: 201-947-8850

VIDEO BIBLE LIBRARY, INC. *(VBL)*
Box 17515
Portland, OR 97217
503-892-7707
Fax: 503-254-8318

THE VIDEO CATALOG *(TVC)*
PO Box 64428

Saint Paul, MN 55164-0428
612-659-4312
800-733-6656
Fax: 612-659-4320

VIDEO CITY PRODUCTIONS *(VCD)*
4266 Broadway
Oakland, CA 94611
510-428-0202
800-847-8400
Fax: 510-654-7802

VIDEO COLLECTIBLES *(BFS)*
350 Newkirk Rd.
Richmond Hill, ON, Canada L4C 3G7
905-884-1433
800-387-5758

VIDEO COMMUNICATIONS, INC. (VCI) *(VCI)*
6535 E. Skelley Dr.
Tulsa, OK 74145
918-622-6460
800-331-4077
Fax: 918-665-6256

VIDEO CONNECTION *(VCN)*
3123 W. Sylvania Ave.
Toledo, OH 43613
419-472-7727
800-365-0449

VIDEO DIMENSIONS *(VDM)*
322 8th Ave., 4th Fl.
New York, NY 10011
212-929-6135

VIDEO GEMS *(GEM)*
12228 Venice Blvd., No. 504
Los Angeles, CA 90066

THE VIDEO PROJECT *(VPJ)*
5332 College Ave., Ste. 101
Oakland, CA 94618
510-655-9050
800-4-PLANET
Fax: 510-655-9115

VIDEO RESOURCES *(VRS)*
220 W. 71st St.
New York, NY 10023
212-724-7055
Fax: 212-595-0189

VIDEO TREASURES *(VTR)*
500 Kirts Blvd.
Troy, MI 48084
810-362-9660
800-786-8777
Fax: 810-362-4454

VIDEO YESTERYEAR *(VYY)*
Box C
Sandy Hook, CT 06482
203-426-2574
800-243-0987
Fax: 203-797-0819

VIDMARK ENTERTAINMENT *(VMK)*
2644 30th St.
Santa Monica, CA 90405-3009
310-314-2000

VOYAGER COMPANY *(VYG)*
1 Bridge St.
Irvington, NY 10533-1543

WALT DISNEY HOME VIDEO *(DIS)*
500 S. Buena Vista St.
Burbank, CA 91521
818-562-3560

WARNER/ELEKTRA/ ATLANTIC (WEA) CORPORATION *(WEA)*
9451 LBJ Fwy., Ste. 107
Dallas, TX 75243
214-234-6200

WARNER HOME VIDEO, INC. *(WAR)*
4000 Warner Blvd.
Burbank, CA 91522
818-954-6000

WARREN MILLER ENTERTAINMENT *(WME)*
505 Pier Ave.
Hermosa Beach, CA 90254
310-376-2494

WESTERN FILM & VIDEO, INC. *(WFV)*
30941 Agoura Rd., Ste. 302
Westlake Village, CA 91361
818-889-7350

WESTERN PUBLISHING CO., INC. *(GBV)*
1220 Mound Ave.
Racine, WI 53404
414-633-2431

WHITE STAR *(WST)*
121 Hwy. 36
West Long Branch, NJ 07764
908-229-2343
800-458-5887
Fax: 908-229-0066

WHOLE TOON CATALOGUE *(WTA)*
PO Box 369
Issaquah, WA 98027-0369
206-391-8747
Fax: 206-391-9064

WISHING WELL DISTRIBUTING *(WSH)*
PO Box 1008
Silver Lake, WI 53170
414-889-8501
800-888-9355
Fax: 414-889-8591

WNET/THIRTEEN NON-BROADCAST *(WNE)*
356 W. 58th St.

New York, NY 10019
212-560-3045

WOMBAT FILM AND VIDEO *(WOM)*
1560 Sherman Ave., Ste. 100
Evanston, IL 60201
708-328-6700
800-323-9084
Fax: 708-328-6706

WOOD KNAPP & COMPANY, INC. *(WKV)*
Knapp Press
5900 Wilshire Blvd.
Los Angeles, CA 90036
213-965-3500
800-521-2666
Fax: 213-930-2742

WORLDVISION HOME VIDEO, INC. *(WOV)*
1700 Broadwaay
New York, NY 10019-5905
212-261-2700

XENON *(XVC)*
211 Arizona Ave.
Santa Monica, CA 90401
800-468-1913

VideoHound's **Family Album**
(Video Notes)

VideoHound's **Family Album**
(Video Notes)

VideoHound's **Family Album**
(Video Notes)

VideoHound's **Family Album**
(Video Notes)

VideoHound's **Family Album**
(Video Notes)

VideoHound's **Family Album**
(Video Notes)

VideoHound's **Family Album**
(Video Notes)

VideoHound's **Family Album**
(Video Notes)

VideoHound's **Family Album**

(Video Notes)

VideoHound's **Family Album**
(Video Notes)

VideoHound's **Family Album**
(Video Notes)

VideoHound's **Family Album**
(Video Notes)